정재현 토익

실전 모의고사

1000제

LC+RC

정재현 토익
실전 모의고사 1000제 LC+RC

지은이 정재현어학연구소
펴낸이 임상진
펴낸곳 (주)넥서스

초판 1쇄 발행 2021년 7월 9일
초판 6쇄 발행 2024년 8월 5일

출판신고 1992년 4월 3일 제311-2002-2호
10880 경기도 파주시 지목로 5
Tel (02)330-5500 Fax (02)330-5555

ISBN 979-11-6683-102-7 13740

www.nexusbook.com

내 인생 첫 토익 실전서

정재현 토익

문제집 + 해설집

실전 모의고사

1000제

LC+RC

정재현어학연구소 지음

넥서스

머리말

여러분이 만약 이번 토익 시험에 어떤 문제가 나올지 미리 알 수 있다면, 그리고 시험을 치르면서 함정이 눈에 보이고 지문에서 단서가 어디에 있는지 쉽게 찾을 수 있다면 어떨 것 같나요? 시험장에서 문제가 술술 풀리면 정말 재미있겠죠?

저는 20년째 토익과 연애 중으로, 토익 문제 풀이와 연구가 정말 재미있습니다. 왜냐하면 저와 정재현어학연구소의 연구원들은 오랜 시간 토익을 치르며 분석하여, 토익을 꿰뚫을 수 있는 데이터를 가지고 있기 때문입니다. 특정 유형이 1년에 몇 회 출제되는지, 특정 어휘가 정답으로 몇 회 출제되었는지 등이 정리된 DB를 보면 다음 시험에 어떤 문제가 나올지 짐작이 가능합니다. 그래서 기출문제 그대로 수록한 실전서가 아니라 적중률 높은 문제로 구성된 실전서를 만들고 싶다는 생각을 오래전부터 해 왔습니다. 학생들이 시험장에서 만날 가능성이 가장 높은 유형의 문제를 이 교재에서 푼 후, 실제 시험장에서 재미있게 문제를 풀 수 있게 되기를 바랐습니다. 그 바람을 담아 <정재현 토익 실전 모의고사 1000제 LC+RC> 교재를 만들었습니다. 드디어 여러분께 보여 드릴 수 있게 되어 무척 기쁩니다.

<정재현 토익 실전 모의고사 1000제 LC+RC>는 정재현어학연구소의 DB를 분석하여 "빈출" 위주로 선별된 문제와 어휘로 구성되어 있습니다. 5세트 내에 동일한 문제 유형을 배제하고 빈출 유형을 모두 넣어 10세트 이상을 공부한 효과를 낼 수 있습니다. 문제의 정답 보기는 물론 오답 보기조차 빈출도를 기준으로 선정하여 토익 필수 어휘를 학습할 수 있도록 했습니다. Part 5 어휘 문제는 오답 보기를 모아 추가 문제를 만들어 온라인으로 제공하고 있습니다. 적중률은 물론 난이도 역시 실제 토익과 똑같이 맞추어 LC와 RC를 한 번에 해결하면서, 쉽고 빠르게 목표 점수를 만들어 준다는 점이 이 교재의 가장 큰 장점입니다.

적중률 높은 문제 개발을 위해서 방대한 DB를 정리하고 분석한 정재현어학연구소 연구원분들과 좋은 교재를 만들기 위해 함께 고민해 주시고, 배려해 주시고, 정성을 다해 주신 넥서스 출판사에 진심으로 감사드립니다.

마지막으로 <정재현 토익 실전 모의고사 1000제 LC+RC>를 선택해 주신 여러분이 '토익'이라는 도전을 기쁘게 마무리할 수 있기를 소망합니다.

여러분을 온 마음으로 응원합니다.

여러분의 토익 선생님, 정재현 드림

CONTENTS

● 머리말   4

● 구성과 특징   6

● 토익 핵심 정보   8

● 학습 스케줄   10

● 토익 점수 환산표   11

Actual Test **1**   14

Actual Test **2**   58

Actual Test **3**   100

Actual Test **4**   142

Actual Test **5**   184

● OMR Sheets   227

⊕ 별책 부록   정답+스크립트+해석+해설

구성과 특징

토익
최신 경향을 반영한
실전 모의고사 5회

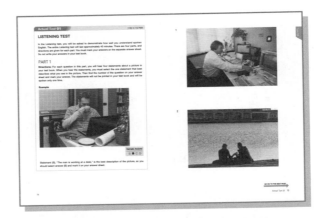

토익 최신 출제 경향을 반영한 모의고사로 실전을 완벽 대비할 수 있습니다. LC와 RC를 한 권으로 구성한 실전 5회분으로 정기 토익 시험을 대비해서 실제 시험 환경과 같이 최종 마무리를 할 수 있습니다.

저자의 노하우가 담긴
쉽고 자세한
정답 및 해설

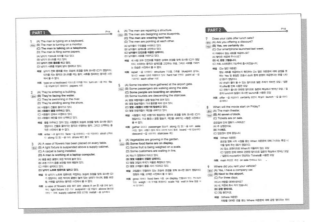

해설집을 따로 구매할 필요 없이 한 권에 담아 정답 및 해설을 확인하며 바로 복습할 수 있습니다. 정답 키워드가 되는 부분을 표시하여 쉽게 정답을 찾고 이해할 수 있도록 구성하였습니다.

혼공족들을 위한
6종 무료 부가자료

1 실전용·복습용·고사장 버전 MP3

실전용, 복습용 MP3 외에 실제 고사장 소음이 들어간
버전까지 제공하므로 실제 시험 환경과 가장 유사하게
대비할 수 있습니다.

2 추가 어휘 문제집

기출 어휘와 토익이 좋아하는 덩어리 표현을 함께 틈틈이 암기해
보세요. www.nexusbook.com

3 모바일 단어장

본 도서에 수록된 어휘 중에서 중요한 어휘를 언제
어디서든 복습할 수 있도록 모바일 단어장을 제공합니다.

4 온라인 받아쓰기

Listening 받아쓰기 프로그램을 통해 청취력뿐만 아니라
영어 실력을 향상시킬 수 있습니다.

5 어휘 리스트 & 테스트

본문에 수록된 어휘 중에서도 특히 중요한 빈출 어휘 리스트와
이를 학습할 수 있는 테스트지를 온라인으로 제공합니다.
www.nexusbook.com

6 청취력 향상용 MP3

호주, 영국식 발음을 대비하여 추가로 연습할 수 있는 MP3를
제공합니다.
www.nexusbook.com

쉽고 빠른
MP3 이용법

1 넥서스북 홈페이지에서 도서 검색 후 3종
MP3 다운로드 www.nexusbook.com

2 구글 플레이, 앱스토어에서 "콜롬북스"
어플 설치 후 도서명으로 검색 후 3종
MP3 다운로드

3 QR코드를 스캔한 후 모바일 페이지에서
바로 듣기

MP3 바로 듣기
정답 자동 채점
모바일 단어장
받아쓰기 테스트

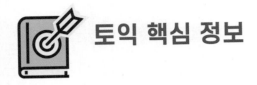

토익 핵심 정보

2016년 5월 29일 정기 시험부터 현재의 영어 사용 환경을 반영한 신(新)토익이 시행되었습니다. 전체 문항 수와 시험 시간은 동일하지만 각 파트별로 문항 수는 변화가 있으며 그동안 출제되지 않았던 그래프와 문자 메시지, 채팅, 삼중 지문 등 새로운 지문 유형과 문제가 출제됩니다.

🔍 신토익 시험의 구성

구성	Part	Part별 내용	문항 수	시간	배점
Listening Comprehension	1	사진 묘사	6	45분	495점
	2	질의 응답	25		
	3	짧은 대화	39		
	4	설명문	30		
Reading Comprehension	5	단문 공란 채우기	30	75분	495점
	6	장문 공란 채우기	16		
	7	단일 지문	29		
		이중 지문	10		
		삼중 지문	15		
Total	7 Parts		200문제	120분	990점

🔍 신토익 이후 달라진 부분

Part 1 문항 10개에서 6개로 감소

Part 2 문항 30개에서 25개로 감소

Part 3 문항 30개에서 39개로 증가, 〈3인 대화〉, 〈5턴 이상의 대화〉, 〈의도 파악, 시각 정보 연계 문제〉 추가

Part 4 문항 30개로 기존과 동일, 〈의도 파악 문제〉, 〈시각 정보 연계 문제〉 추가

Part 5 문항 40개에서 30개로 감소

Part 6 문항 12개에서 16개로 증가, 〈알맞은 문장 고르기〉 추가

Part 7 문항 48개에서 54개로 증가, 〈문자 메시지·온라인 채팅 지문〉, 〈의도 파악, 문장 삽입 문제〉, 〈삼중 지문〉 추가

🔍 신토익 핵심 정보

Part 3	화자의 의도 파악 문제	2~3문항	대화문에서 화자가 한 말의 의도를 묻는 유형
	시각 정보 연계 문제	2~3문항	대화문과 시각 정보(도표, 그래픽 등) 간 연관 관계를 파악하는 유형
	3인 대화	대화 지문 1~2개	일부 대화문에서 세 명 이상의 화자가 등장함
	5턴 이상의 대화		주고받는 대화가 5턴 이상으로 늘어난 대화 유형
Part 4	화자의 의도 파악 문제	2~3문항	담화문에서 화자가 한 말의 의도를 묻는 유형
	시각 정보 연계 문제	2~3문항	담화문과 시각 정보(도표, 그래픽 등) 간 연관 관계를 파악하는 유형
Part 6	알맞은 문장 고르기	4문항 (지문당 1문항)	• 지문의 흐름상 빈칸에 들어갈 알맞은 문장 고르기 • 선택지가 모두 문장으로 제시되며 문맥 파악이 필수
Part 7	문장 삽입 문제	2문항 (지문당 1문항)	주어진 문장을 삽입할 수 있는 적절한 위치 고르기
	문자 메시지 · 온라인 채팅	각각 지문 1개	2명이 대화하는 문자 메시지, 다수가 참여하는 온라인 채팅
	의도 파악 문제	2문항 (지문당 1문항)	• 화자가 한 말의 의도를 묻는 문제 • 문자 메시지, 온라인 채팅 지문에서 출제
	삼중 지문	지문 3개	세 개의 연계 지문에 대한 이해도를 묻는 문제

학습 스케줄

테스트가 끝난 후 각 테스트별로 점검해 보세요.
테스트별로 맞힌 개수를 확인하며 실력이 향상됨을 체크해 보세요.

정답 확인 전

	테스트 날짜	시험 소요 시간	체감 난이도
Actual Test 01			상 중 하
Actual Test 02			상 중 하
Actual Test 03			상 중 하
Actual Test 04			상 중 하
Actual Test 05			상 중 하

정답 확인 후

	맞힌 개수	환산 점수	총점
Actual Test 01	LC: RC:		점
Actual Test 02	LC: RC:		점
Actual Test 03	LC: RC:		점
Actual Test 04	LC: RC:		점
Actual Test 05	LC: RC:		점

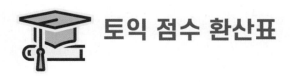

토익 점수 환산표

정답 수	Listening Comprehension	정답 수	Reading Comprehension
96-100	475-495	96-100	460-495
91-95	435-495	91-95	425-490
86-90	405-475	86-90	395-465
81-85	370-450	81-85	370-440
76-80	345-420	76-80	335-415
71-75	320-390	71-75	310-390
66-70	290-360	66-70	280-365
61-65	265-335	61-65	250-335
56-60	235-310	56-60	220-305
51-55	210-280	51-55	195-270
46-50	180-255	46-50	165-240
41-45	155-230	41-45	140-215
36-40	125-205	36-40	115-180
31-35	105-175	31-35	95-145
26-30	85-145	26-30	75-120
21-25	60-115	21-25	60-95
16-20	30-90	16-20	45-75
11-15	5-70	11-15	30-55
6-10	5-60	6-10	10-40
1-5	5-50	1-5	5-30
0	5-35	0	5-15

Actual Test

01

시작 시간   :

종료 시간   :

LISTENING TEST

In the Listening test, you will be asked to demonstrate how well you understand spoken English. The entire Listening test will last approximately 45 minutes. There are four parts, and directions are given for each part. You must mark your answers on the separate answer sheet. Do not write your answers in your test book.

PART 1

Directions: For each question in this part, you will hear four statements about a picture in your test book. When you hear the statements, you must select the one statement that best describes what you see in the picture. Then find the number of the question on your answer sheet and mark your answer. The statements will not be printed in your test book and will be spoken only one time.

Example

Statement (B), "The man is working at a desk," is the best description of the picture, so you should select answer (B) and mark it on your answer sheet.

1

2

GO ON TO THE NEXT PAGE →

3

4

5

6

GO ON TO THE NEXT PAGE

PART 2

Directions: You will hear a question or statement and three responses spoken in English. They will not be printed in your test book and will be spoken only one time. Select the best response to the question or statement and mark the letter (A), (B), or (C) on your answer sheet.

7   Mark your answer on your answer sheet.

8   Mark your answer on your answer sheet.

9   Mark your answer on your answer sheet.

10   Mark your answer on your answer sheet.

11   Mark your answer on your answer sheet.

12   Mark your answer on your answer sheet.

13   Mark your answer on your answer sheet.

14   Mark your answer on your answer sheet.

15   Mark your answer on your answer sheet.

16   Mark your answer on your answer sheet.

17   Mark your answer on your answer sheet.

18   Mark your answer on your answer sheet.

19   Mark your answer on your answer sheet.

20   Mark your answer on your answer sheet.

21   Mark your answer on your answer sheet.

22   Mark your answer on your answer sheet.

23   Mark your answer on your answer sheet.

24   Mark your answer on your answer sheet.

25   Mark your answer on your answer sheet.

26   Mark your answer on your answer sheet.

27   Mark your answer on your answer sheet.

28   Mark your answer on your answer sheet.

29   Mark your answer on your answer sheet.

30   Mark your answer on your answer sheet.

31   Mark your answer on your answer sheet.

PART 3

Directions: You will hear some conversations between two or more people. You will be asked to answer three questions about what the speakers say in each conversation. Select the best response to each question and mark the letter (A), (B), (C), or (D) on your answer sheet. The conversations will not be printed in your test book and will be spoken only one time.

32 What kind of company is the man calling?

(A) A software developer
(B) A clothing company
(C) A catering firm
(D) An electronics store

33 What problem are the speakers talking about?

(A) An incorrect product price
(B) A wrong e-mail address
(C) A delayed delivery
(D) A misplaced document

34 What information does the woman ask for?

(A) An order number
(B) The model of a product
(C) A delivery location
(D) The quantity of items

35 What problem does the man have?

(A) He has misplaced a document.
(B) He cannot access a Web site.
(C) He has not completed some work.
(D) He went to the wrong location.

36 What does the woman remind the man to do?

(A) Attend a training session
(B) Arrange a business trip
(C) Submit a form
(D) Speak with his supervisor

37 What will the woman most likely do next?

(A) Make an announcement
(B) Reschedule a meeting
(C) Provide a temporary password
(D) Update a company Web site

38 What is the woman's occupation?

(A) Fitness trainer
(B) Art instructor
(C) Tour guide
(D) Professional chef

39 What does the woman enjoy about her job?

(A) Meeting people
(B) Using modern technology
(C) Improving her skills
(D) Building a reputation

40 What is the woman asked to do?

(A) Complete a survey
(B) Attend a conference
(C) Work additional days
(D) Plan a fundraiser

41 What does the man want to replace?

(A) Event programs
(B) Audio guides
(C) Display lights
(D) Gallery furniture

42 What does the woman ask the man about?

(A) Setting up exhibits
(B) Creating advertisements
(C) Comparing prices
(D) Organizing transportation

43 What does the woman mean when she says, "I'm not using mine right now"?

(A) She forgot to bring her phone with her.
(B) Her phone has run out of battery.
(C) She is too busy to check some information.
(D) She can lend her phone to the man.

GO ON TO THE NEXT PAGE

44 What kind of device will be demonstrated to investors?

(A) A smartphone
(B) A set of headphones
(C) A laptop computer
(D) A video camera

45 Why has a meeting time been changed?

(A) Some equipment is not set up yet.
(B) A room has been double-booked.
(C) There is heavy traffic in the area.
(D) The visitors are not available this morning.

46 What will the man most likely do next?

(A) Hang up a sign
(B) Call the investors
(C) Drive to the airport
(D) Purchase some food

---

47 Where do the speakers work?

(A) At a recruitment company
(B) At a department store
(C) At an accounting firm
(D) At a real estate agency

48 What does the man advise the woman to do first?

(A) Attend a meeting
(B) Review some preferences
(C) Order office supplies
(D) Clean a workspace

49 What does the man imply when he says, "My office is just across the hall"?

(A) He would like to move to a different room.
(B) He has changed a training location.
(C) He would prefer not to be disturbed.
(D) He will be free to give assistance.

50 Where is the conversation taking place?

(A) At a board meeting
(B) At an professional conference
(C) At a store's grand opening
(D) At a group interview session

51 What does the woman ask about?

(A) Submitting a complaint
(B) Getting a partial refund
(C) Changing her seat
(D) Printing some documents

52 What does the man remind the woman to do?

(A) Keep her receipt
(B) Use the main entrance
(C) Complete a survey
(D) Wear an ID badge

---

53 What problem does the woman mention?

(A) A product was damaged.
(B) An employee is absent.
(C) A delivery arrived late.
(D) A shipment was labeled incorrectly.

54 Why does the woman call Charles?

(A) To inquire about transportation
(B) To arrange compensation
(C) To request a customer's contact details
(D) To complain about a service

55 What information does Charles request?

(A) The name of a customer
(B) The destination of a delivery
(C) The amount of a payment
(D) The cost of some merchandise

56 Where most likely do the speakers work?

(A) At a shipping firm
(B) At a supermarket
(C) At a manufacturing plant
(D) At a catering company

57 What are the speakers trying to do?

(A) Reduce expenses
(B) Develop new products
(C) Attract more clients
(D) Hire employees

58 What does the woman recommend doing?

(A) Placing an advertisement
(B) Contacting a supplier
(C) Relocating a business
(D) Cleaning up a room

59 What are the men responsible for at the park?

(A) Leading hikes
(B) Selling souvenirs
(C) Giving lectures
(D) Feeding animals

60 What has probably helped to increase attendance at the park?

(A) A change in operating hours
(B) An extensive advertising campaign
(C) A drop in admission fees
(D) A new transportation service

61 What does the woman say will happen on Saturday?

(A) Visitors will be given free admission.
(B) A new employee will start work.
(C) Some equipment will arrive.
(D) The budget will be reviewed.

STARR STEAKHOUSE

Add an extra side dish to any steak you order!

Mashed potatoes	(Add $3.00)
Grilled Mushrooms	(Add $4.00)
Garden Salad	(Add $2.00)
French Fries	(Add $2.00)

62 What type of event will the man attend this evening?

(A) A birthday party
(B) A sports game
(C) A business conference
(D) An outdoor concert

63 Look at the graphic. Which side dish does the man decide to add?

(A) Mashed potatoes
(B) Grilled Mushrooms
(C) Garden Salad
(D) French Fries

64 What does the woman suggest that the man do?

(A) Sample a dessert
(B) Use a credit card
(C) Order a drink
(D) Take his food out

GO ON TO THE NEXT PAGE

Camptime Supplies Customer Receipt	
Date: May 17	
Sleeping Bag	$85
Two-Person Tent	$125
Backpack	$110
Hiking Boots	$60
Total	$380

65 What problem with an item does the woman mention?

(A) It is too small.
(B) It has a tear.
(C) It is the wrong color.
(D) Its zipper is broken.

66 Look at the graphic. Which item is being discussed?

(A) A sleeping bag
(B) A tent
(C) A backpack
(D) Some hiking boots

67 What does the man offer to do for the woman?

(A) Give her a catalog
(B) Recommend some campsites
(C) Place a rush order
(D) Show her some merchandise

Destination	Departure Time	Status
Manchester	12:10 P.M.	Delayed 1 hour
Liverpool	12:25 P.M.	Delayed 30 minutes
Leeds	12:30 P.M.	Delayed 40 minutes
Sheffield	12:45 P.M.	Delayed 25 minutes

68 Look at the graphic. What is the status of the man's train?

(A) Delayed 1 hour
(B) Delayed 30 minutes
(C) Delayed 40 minutes
(D) Delayed 25 minutes

69 What kind of business do the speakers probably work for?

(A) An architectural firm
(B) A pharmaceutical company
(C) A real estate agency
(D) A car manufacturer

70 What does the woman say she will do?

(A) Meet the man at the station
(B) Reassign a task
(C) Postpone a meeting
(D) Set up a meeting room

PART 4

Directions: You will hear some talks given by a single speaker. You will be asked to answer three questions about what the speaker says in each talk. Select the best response to each question and mark the letter (A), (B), (C), or (D) on your answer sheet. The talks will not be printed in your test book and will be spoken only one time.

71 What type of business is being advertised?

(A) A landscaping company
(B) A financial consultancy
(C) A home cleaning service
(D) An interior design firm

72 What does the speaker say clients like about the business?

(A) Its convenient location
(B) Its experienced staff members
(C) Its money-back guarantee
(D) Its eco-friendly approach

73 What will the listeners receive if they book the company's services online?

(A) A discount coupon
(B) A product catalog
(C) A complimentary product
(D) A free consultation

74 Why will some representatives visit the listeners' branch?

(A) To meet a new employee
(B) To receive corporate training
(C) To attend an awards ceremony
(D) To demonstrate some equipment

75 What does the speaker need volunteers for?

(A) Designing a brochure
(B) Giving building tours
(C) Planning a menu
(D) Transporting the visitors

76 According to the speaker, what should be included in an e-mail?

(A) A recent photo
(B) A preferred time
(C) A list of supplies
(D) A supervisor's name

77 Who most likely is the speaker?

(A) A delivery driver
(B) An event planner
(C) An accountant
(D) A carpenter

78 What information does the speaker require?

(A) A product code
(B) An address
(C) An item description
(D) A telephone number

79 What does the speaker imply when he says, "We will consider this when calculating your invoice"?

(A) A bank transfer has been declined.
(B) A payment is overdue.
(C) A parking fine has been received.
(D) A discount will be applied.

80 What is the speaker calling about?

(A) Exhibition tickets
(B) Shipping options
(C) Lighting installations
(D) Catering services

81 What did the speaker recently see?

(A) A promotional flyer
(B) A Web advertisement
(C) A product presentation
(D) A magazine article

82 What does the speaker suggest doing?

(A) Extending a project deadline
(B) Comparing some prices
(C) Returning the call quickly
(D) Arranging a meeting

GO ON TO THE NEXT PAGE

83 What is the broadcast mainly about?

(A) Community events
(B) Traffic
(C) Weather
(D) Financial news

84 What does the speaker advise listeners to do?

(A) Remain in their homes
(B) Use public transport
(C) Purchase additional supplies
(D) Avoid congested areas

85 What does the speaker say will happen at 9 A.M.?

(A) Some commercials will be played.
(B) A traffic update will be heard.
(C) A safety announcement will be made.
(D) A guest will be interviewed.

86 Where do the listeners work?

(A) At a fitness center
(B) At a hair salon
(C) At a dental clinic
(D) At a financial institution

87 What is scheduled to happen tomorrow morning?

(A) A delivery will arrive.
(B) A training session will be held.
(C) A new employee will start.
(D) An anniversary will be celebrated.

88 Why does the speaker want someone to stay late?

(A) To unload a truck
(B) To meet some investors
(C) To prepare some gifts
(D) To review some documents

89 What is the topic of the workshop?

(A) Customer support
(B) Online advertising
(C) Product design
(D) Financial management

90 What kind of assignment are the listeners asked to complete?

(A) A knowledge test
(B) A customer survey
(C) A team presentation
(D) A business proposal

91 Why does the speaker say, "The conference room upstairs is free"?

(A) To recommend a way to save costs
(B) To suggest a different location
(C) To make a change to a schedule
(D) To offer the listeners refreshments

92 Where does the speaker most likely work?

(A) At a factory
(B) At a restaurant
(C) At a pharmacy
(D) At a laboratory

93 What does the speaker imply when he says, "The lab equipment is on the workbench"?

(A) An experiment will go ahead on schedule.
(B) A delivery has recently been made.
(C) A new policy has been ignored.
(D) A room has been cleaned as requested.

94 What is the speaker worried about?

(A) Unsafe conditions
(B) Inaccurate data
(C) Absent staff
(D) Increased expenses

Negotiation Workshop	
February 5	Identifying Strengths and Weaknesses
February 12	Problem-Solving Techniques
February 19	Creating Value
February 26	Cross-Cultural Negotiations

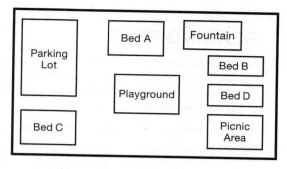

95 Look at the graphic. When is the talk taking place?

(A) February 5
(B) February 12
(C) February 19
(D) February 26

96 What will happen in an hour?

(A) The speaker will distribute some paperwork.
(B) The speaker will assign people to groups.
(C) The listeners will watch a video.
(D) The listeners will take a break.

97 What are the listeners reminded to do?

(A) Sign a consent form
(B) Pick up a brochure
(C) Complete a survey
(D) Recommend the class to others

98 Who is the speaker?

(A) A local politician
(B) A company representative
(C) A volunteer coordinator
(D) A schoolteacher

99 Look at the graphic. Which plot will be left empty for now?

(A) Bed A
(B) Bed B
(C) Bed C
(D) Bed D

100 What does the speaker say she will do at two o'clock?

(A) Pass out some snacks
(B) Speak to a journalist
(C) Take some photographs
(D) Bring some more flowers

This is the end of the Listening test. Turn to Part 5 in your test book.

GO ON TO THE NEXT PAGE

READING TEST

In the Reading test, you will read a variety of texts and answer several different types of reading comprehension questions. The entire Reading test will last 75 minutes. There are three parts, and directions are given for each part. You are encouraged to answer as many questions as possible within the time allowed.

You must mark your answers on the separate answer sheet. Do not write your answers in your test book.

PART 5

Directions: A word or phrase is missing in each of the sentences below. Four answer choices are given below each sentence. Select the best answer to complete the sentence. Then mark the letter (A), (B), (C), or (D) on your answer sheet.

101 All customers who use their TR Maxwell cards must pay ------- bills by the twenty-seventh of each month.

(A) they
(B) their
(C) themselves
(D) them

102 Several employees have been asking questions about the training course they will be taking -------.

(A) soon
(B) lately
(C) ever
(D) very

103 The water fountains in the garden are scheduled for ------- on a regular basis.

(A) clean
(B) cleaner
(C) cleaning
(D) cleaned

104 Diners are asked to place their orders ------- they are seated to ensure the fastest service possible.

(A) during
(B) prior to
(C) upon
(D) before

105 To make up for the mistake, Weber International offered to ship the items at no ------- charge.

(A) adding
(B) addition
(C) additionally
(D) additional

106 ------- the last managerial meeting, the issue of transfers to foreign facilities was raised again.

(A) Into
(B) During
(C) Above
(D) Between

107 Tenants should use the side entrance this week ------- the renovation of the main lobby.

(A) avoid
(B) avoided
(C) to avoid
(D) are avoiding

108 Mr. Jackson has made the customer satisfaction campaign a top ------- for the salesforce.

(A) rate
(B) priority
(C) excellence
(D) credit

109 Andrew Sullivan requested a ------- after his successful negotiation with Monroe Tire Company.

(A) promoted
(B) promoting
(C) promotion
(D) promotes

110 Most customers who received the brochures noted that the information is ------- to the products.

(A) pure
(B) capable
(C) defective
(D) relevant

111 The award will be given to the person who performs the task most -------.

(A) efficient
(B) efficiency
(C) efficiencies
(D) efficiently

112 None of the elevators can be accessed from 1 A.M. to 5 A.M. ------- the scheduled maintenance.

(A) as of
(B) as for
(C) due to
(D) since

113 The training course is intended for ------- staff members who want to improve their communication skills.

(A) each
(B) all
(C) every
(D) entirely

114 The company's vice president plans to ------- innovative changes in the company's business strategies.

(A) agree
(B) enclose
(C) participate
(D) announce

115 A meeting will be held to determine ------- the candidate is fully qualified for the managerial position.

(A) regarding
(B) whether
(C) such as
(D) because

116 The crowd in the theater loudly applauded the actors ------- their excellent performance.

(A) as
(B) of
(C) for
(D) at

117 Dr. Hamel states that ------- is essential to learning a new skill that can be used in the workplace.

(A) persists
(B) persisted
(C) persistence
(D) persistently

118 Ms. Bellamy's duties include conducting ------- inspections of the factory three times a week.

(A) aware
(B) absent
(C) confident
(D) routine

119 Mr. Rogers was able to arrive ------- than those who took the direct route to the convention center.

(A) quick
(B) more quickly
(C) quickly
(D) most quickly

120 By sending the shipment on Monday, Lagos Technology will ------- that it arrives before the deadline.

(A) reserve
(B) acquire
(C) ensure
(D) correct

GO ON TO THE NEXT PAGE

121 Social media site E-Villa has been ------ to user criticism after accidentally leaking some private data.

(A) response
(B) responded
(C) responsive
(D) responsively

122 Due to the growing demand, Miller, Inc. will increase the number of employees ------- over the next two years.

(A) nearly
(B) previously
(C) gradually
(D) necessarily

123 Carson Footwear offers four ------- types of shoes, all of which are popular with customers.

(A) distinct
(B) distinctly
(C) distinction
(D) distinctively

124 This article may not be reproduced elsewhere ------- the publisher's written consent.

(A) instead
(B) without
(C) unless
(D) along

125 A slight improvement in the working conditions ------- more individuals to work overtime hours.

(A) encourage
(B) to encourage
(C) would encourage
(D) is encouraged

126 Passengers heading to Detroit may get off the airplane ------- it will be on the ground for forty minutes.

(A) despite
(B) even though
(C) in order to
(D) however

127 There will be a special ceremony at headquarters held ------- for those who won awards this year.

(A) slightly
(B) mutually
(C) precisely
(D) exclusively

128 We will offer Jens Holbrook the position ------- Bruce Cramer responds positively before tomorrow.

(A) because
(B) except
(C) unless
(D) against

129 Several restaurants in the city ------- serving ethnic food to diners in the past few months.

(A) begins
(B) will have begun
(C) have begun
(D) will begin

130 The Hudson Convention Center is a popular site for events due to its ------- to major hotels downtown.

(A) direction
(B) proximity
(C) competence
(D) majority

PART 6

Directions: Read the texts that follow. A word, phrase, or sentence is missing in parts of each text. Four answer choices for each question are given below the text. Select the best answer to complete the text. Then mark the letter (A), (B), (C), or (D) on your answer sheet.

Questions 131-134 refer to the following e-mail.

To: Ashley Lomax <alomax@lomaxinc.com>
From: Victor Walton <victorwalton@dtwholesale.net>
Date: August 7
Subject: Please read

Dear Ms. Lomax,

It was wonderful to be part of the ------- at the Annual Conference of Entrepreneurs. I learned so
        131.

much from your presentation on connecting with clients. -------, I've already begun implementing
                                     132.

some of your strategies at my business. I believe that my staff could benefit greatly from your

insights. Do you have room in your schedule for a private speaking event at one of our weekly

meetings? -------. Please find attached a file ------- my company's vision as well as our sales
        133.   **134.**

goals.

Warmest regards,

Victor Walton

---

131 (A) system
    (B) audience
    (C) process
    (D) celebration

132 (A) On the other hand
    (B) As usual
    (C) In fact
    (D) On the contrary

133 (A) We may move to a different building if we keep growing.
    (B) In a weak economy, consumers tend to spend less.
    (C) The tickets for next year's conference are already on sale.
    (D) Our entire sales staff of twelve people will be in attendance.

134 (A) having outlined
    (B) outlined it
    (C) that outlines
    (D) is outlining

GO ON TO THE NEXT PAGE ▶

Doubleday Café
98 Walker Avenue
Aberdeen, MD

Dear Customer,

We at the Doubleday Café have been providing our customers with quality coffee, tea, pastries, and snacks for more than two decades. In fact, we have been open for business longer than just about any other eatery in the city. We therefore regret that we will be closing ------- December 29
135.
of this year. We have been searching for a new owner since Mr. Kennedy made his decision to retire. -------, nobody has offered to purchase the store yet. From now until our final day, all items
136.
for sale will be discounted by 30%. -------. We appreciate your -------, and we hope to see you to
137. **138.**
say goodbye sometime soon.

135 (A) public
(B) effective
(C) actual
(D) uncertain

136 (A) Therefore
(B) Consequently
(C) Likewise
(D) However

137 (A) Some new baked goods have just arrived.
(B) We hope to see you again in the coming year.
(C) This is Mr. Kennedy's way of thanking everyone.
(D) You'll love the taste of our freshly brewed coffee.

138 (A) supporting
(B) supporter
(C) support
(D) supportive

Hiring Process

Tejeda Technology uses the assistance of an outside recruitment firm to ensure that we find

qualified ------- for our open positions. We are also willing to consider applications from people
      139.

with impressive experience and education. Current employees are ------- to apply for any open
                                                                140.

position. -------. Nevertheless, the primary focus will be on finding the person most suitable for
      141.

the role. This is because the HR team must protect the company's overall ------- when making
                                                                      142.

hiring decisions.

139 (A) tenants
    (B) candidates
    (C) consumers
    (D) clients

140 (A) eligible
    (B) prominent
    (C) possible
    (D) voluntary

141 (A) We are delighted to welcome newly hired
       staff members.
    (B) Moreover, several of the interns were
       offered permanent positions.
    (C) Past performance in the company will be
       taken into consideration.
    (D) In fact, the workplace environment
       consistently receives high ratings.

142 (A) profiting
    (B) profitability
    (C) profitable
    (D) profited

GO ON TO THE NEXT PAGE

Questions 143-146 refer to the following article.

August 21 – Local orchards in Greenbrier Valley expect to harvest more apples than normal this year. This ------- is based on two factors. First, farmers planted more trees several years ago, and
143.
they are now beginning to bear fruit. Next, the weather has been unusually pleasant this summer.

Combined, more than 120,000 metric tons of apples should be harvested this year. -------.
144.

The orchards in the valley grow their apples primarily ------- export to European and Asian
145.
countries. Ron Gant, a local apple -------, said "I never expected to harvest this number of
146.
apples. Hopefully, this will become a trend in the years to come."

143 (A) decision
(B) forecast
(C) expense
(D) effort

144 (A) Apples taste delicious and have a lot of
nutritional value.
(B) Such a figure was considered impossible
just two years ago.
(C) Still, apples are one of the area's leading
agricultural products.
(D) Several farms in the valley have been
purchased by this company.

145 (A) in
(B) onto
(C) for
(D) under

146 (A) farmer
(B) farms
(C) farm
(D) farming

PART 7

Directions: In this part you will read a selection of texts, such as magazine and newspaper articles, e-mails, and instant messages. Each text or set of texts is followed by several questions. Select the best answer for each question and mark the letter (A), (B), (C), or (D) on your answer sheet.

Questions 147-148 refer to the following job advertisement.

ANAHEIM

Anaheim, serving our customers at 23 branches across the country, is currently recruiting shop managers, sales staff, and repair crew members in preparation for our grand opening at Linden International Airport on September 1. Managers must have a minimum of two years of experience and must submit a letter of recommendation from a current or former employer. Repair crew members should be capable of repairing the types of bags and suitcases we sell, and this must be confirmed by a letter of reference. For sales staff, a recommendation letter is preferred but not required. Interested parties should complete the preliminary application online by August 12 at www.anaheim-inc.com.

147 What type of business is Anaheim?

(A) A computer repair shop
(B) A delivery service
(C) A luggage company
(D) An airplane designer

148 What is indicated about the open positions at Anaheim?

(A) Some require a professional reference.
(B) Most will begin on August 12.
(C) They provide opportunities for promotion.
(D) They have competitive financial compensation.

GO ON TO THE NEXT PAGE

Questions 149-150 refer to the following e-mail.

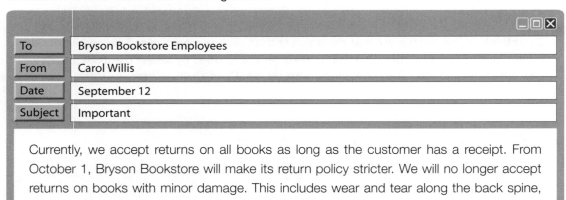

To	Bryson Bookstore Employees
From	Carol Willis
Date	September 12
Subject	Important

Currently, we accept returns on all books as long as the customer has a receipt. From October 1, Bryson Bookstore will make its return policy stricter. We will no longer accept returns on books with minor damage. This includes wear and tear along the back spine, folded pages, and water damage.

Information about this change will be printed on every receipt. We'll also hang up signs to inform customers. Should a customer complain about a return, please advise the person to talk to the manager on duty.

149 Why did Ms. Willis write the e-mail?

(A) To announce a policy change
(B) To show appreciation to the staff
(C) To report a customer trend
(D) To recommend a new book

150 According to the e-mail, what should customers with complaints do?

(A) Fill out a form
(B) Speak to a manager
(C) Call a helpline
(D) Go to the information desk

Questions 151-152 refer to the following text-message chain.

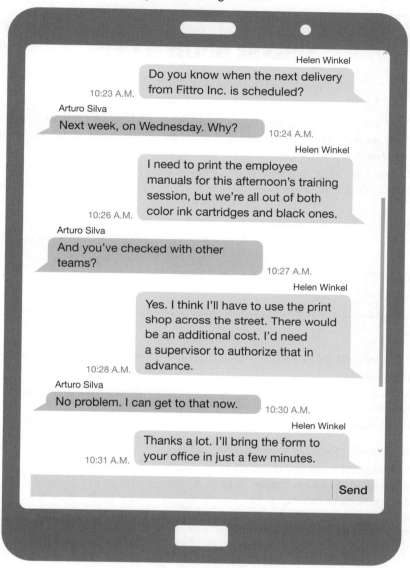

Helen Winkel

Do you know when the next delivery from Fittro Inc. is scheduled?
10:23 A.M.

Arturo Silva

Next week, on Wednesday. Why?
10:24 A.M.

Helen Winkel

I need to print the employee manuals for this afternoon's training session, but we're all out of both color ink cartridges and black ones.
10:26 A.M.

Arturo Silva

And you've checked with other teams?
10:27 A.M.

Helen Winkel

Yes. I think I'll have to use the print shop across the street. There would be an additional cost. I'd need a supervisor to authorize that in advance.
10:28 A.M.

Arturo Silva

No problem. I can get to that now.
10:30 A.M.

Helen Winkel

Thanks a lot. I'll bring the form to your office in just a few minutes.
10:31 A.M.

Send

151 What problem does Ms. Winkel tell Mr. Silva about?

(A) Some office supplies have run out.
(B) An employee manual contains an error.
(C) Some equipment has broken down.
(D) A training session has been canceled.

152 At 10:30 A.M., what does Mr. Silva commit to doing when he writes, "I can get to that now"?

(A) Contacting a print shop
(B) Visiting a store
(C) Proofreading a document
(D) Approving an expense

GO ON TO THE NEXT PAGE

ABILENE HOUSEWARES

– Your Home, Your Style –

After many years of serving the Pacific Northwest, Abilene Housewares is closing its doors. This is your chance to get amazing deals as we get rid of all of our stock at this closeout event.

From August 1 to 7, get up to 75% off curtains, rugs, throw pillows, and more. These great discounts apply to all brands, and the event will be held at all twenty-three of our stores.

We will not be reordering merchandise, so shopping early is recommended to avoid disappointment. Please note that all sales are final on goods purchased during this event.

We hope to see you soon at Abilene Housewares.

153 What is the advertisement about?

(A) A grand opening
(B) A product launch
(C) A clearance sale
(D) A store relocation

154 What is suggested in the advertisement?

(A) Refreshments will be served at the event.
(B) Curtains can be ordered in custom sizes.
(C) Abilene Housewares has multiple locations.
(D) Customers can meet a new manager.

155 What is indicated about items purchased between August 1 and 7?

(A) They have free delivery.
(B) They are all 75% off.
(C) They cannot be returned.
(D) They have an extended warranty.

Questions 156-157 refer to the following e-mail.

E-Mail Message

To: hbaek@metairiellc.com
From: thielev@sbmcon.org
Date: October 10
Subject: Small Business Marketing Conference

Dear Ms. Baek,

We appreciate your attendance at last year's Small Business Marketing Conference. Our records show that you have not yet registered for this year's event, which you can still do for the advance-registration price of $125 on or before October 15. After that day, the fee will be $190 both online and at the door.

Registration for this event gives you access to:

• General seating at all lectures
• A networking cocktail party on November 3
• A signed copy of entrepreneur Jorrin Vente's book, released on November 4

Excluded from the registration fee:

• Small-group consultation session on November 5 (A shuttle will take participants from the convention center to the session. Upon receipt of the extra payment, a special admission badge will be sent along with your main conference badge.)

We hope you will join us for another great conference!

Warmest regards,

Vince Thiele

---

156 Why did Mr. Thiele send the e-mail to Ms. Baek?

(A) To apologize for a lack of information
(B) To inform her about a change of venue
(C) To remind her about an approaching deadline
(D) To request an overdue payment

157 What is indicated about the November 5 event?

(A) It will feature a famous entrepreneur.
(B) It will take place at the convention center.
(C) It is the most popular session.
(D) It is accessed with a different pass.

GO ON TO THE NEXT PAGE

Questions 158-160 refer to the following e-mail.

To	Marty Foster
From	Phyllis Kaminski
Date	Tuesday, May 17
Subject	RE: Amber Valley Hotel Booking

Dear Mr. Foster,

Our records show that you will be checking in to Amber Valley Hotel this Friday, May 20, and checking out on Wednesday, May 24. —[1]—. We hope that you will enjoy your stay with us.

To assist with your plans, I want to make you aware that the city is holding its annual Founders Day Parade on Saturday, May 21. It will begin at Quincy Park and follow a route along Preston Street, ending at City Hall. The parade is free to everyone, and it's an entertaining experience, but on that day, many businesses along Preston Street will be closed, including the city's famous Glassworks Art Museum. —[2]—.

The vehicle entrance for our hotel is on Everton Road, so it will not be affected by the parade. —[3]—. However, because we are located right by the start of the parade, there will be a lot of people setting up from early in the morning. —[4]—.

Warmest regards,

Phyllis Kaminski
Customer Service Agent, Amber Valley Hotel

---

158 What is the purpose of the e-mail?

(A) To recommend learning about a museum
(B) To inform Mr. Foster about a community event
(C) To respond to an inquiry about a check-in policy
(D) To offer assistance in purchasing tickets

159 What is implied about the Amber Valley Hotel?

(A) It has more than one entrance for vehicles.
(B) It is overbooked for May 21.
(C) It opened a new branch on Preston Street.
(D) It is located near Quincy Park.

160 In which of the positions marked [1], [2], [3], and [4] does the following sentence best belong?

"You'll be in town for several days, though, so there will still be time for a visit."

(A) [1]
(B) [2]
(C) [3]
(D) [4]

Questions 161-163 refer to the following e-mail.

To: Undisclosed Recipients
From: Maxtronics Enterprises Customer Care Department
Date: April 18
Subject: Trax 2.0

Dear Valued Customers,

Here at Maxtronics, we're excited about the newest version of Trax, the budget – tracking smartphone app that your business purchased earlier this year. Below you can find just a few of the things to look forward to in version 2.0.

Corporate Discount Scheme (CDS)
Customers will soon be able to get discounts at restaurants, hotels, office supply stores, and more through our Corporate Discount Scheme (CDS). CDS goes live on May 1, and you will be sent a form by mail to sign up for this program sometime next week.

Enhanced Security
In addition to 5 – digit PIN access, you can add an extra level of security with fingerprint recognition technology. This ensures that your company's spending data will not be susceptible to theft if the phone is lost.

Round–the–Clock Assistance
If you have trouble associating new employees to the departmental budget, or accessing archived data, simply contact our chat service. Our friendly and experienced agents can help you to resolve any issues you may have.

At Maxtronics, we strive to bring the best to our customers at all times, and we will continue our commitment to improving our products.

Sincerely,

Laurent Pichette

---

161 Why was the e-mail sent?

(A) To correct some operating instructions
(B) To thank loyal customers for their patronage
(C) To provide information about a phone application
(D) To request feedback on a product

162 What is being mailed to customers of Maxtronics?

(A) A discount coupon
(B) A registration form
(C) A product catalog
(D) A security code

163 The word "associating" in paragraph 4, line 2, is closest in meaning to

(A) recruiting
(B) connecting
(C) containing
(D) socializing

GO ON TO THE NEXT PAGE

Questions 164-167 refer to the following e-mail.

To	Ranjit Dalavi <r_dalavi@loftis.net>
From	Neftalem Luwam <luwam.n@worldhealthep.org>
Date	February 3
Subject	Quarterly Seminar

Dear Mr. Dalavi,

The World Health Equality Foundation (WHEF) invites you to attend our quarterly seminar on February 26 at the Los Angeles Convention Center. This seminar will be presented in two parts, and it is entitled "Forming Alliances to Enhance Water Purification Processes in Developing Countries." —[1]—. Industry experts, who, like you, are studying the effects of unsafe drinking water on health, will share their insights on possible solutions that can be implemented by charities in collaboration with local government officials. By creating partnerships that focus on a common goal, progress can be made. —[2]—.

Our distinguished speaker will be Elena Lentz of the Global Health Association. —[3]—. She is highly respected in the field and has won international awards for her work.

If you are interested in the lecture, you can purchase tickets through the WHEF Web site. —[4]—. Digital files with information to complement the lecture will be posted on our Web site on February 20.

Sincerely,

Neftalem Luwam
WHEF Educational Coordinator

164 What will the seminar be about?

(A) New advances in bottling equipment
(B) Grant opportunities for repairing water infrastructure
(C) Improving water quality through partnerships
(D) Methods for identifying water-related illnesses

165 Who most likely is Mr. Dalavi?

(A) An industry award winner
(B) A medical researcher
(C) A donor to a charity
(D) A specialist in government laws

166 What is scheduled to happen on February 20?

(A) A study will be published by Ms. Lentz.
(B) Tickets will be mailed to some customers.
(C) Supplemental materials will become available.
(D) A registration period will end.

167 In which of the positions marked [1], [2], [3], and [4] does the following sentence best belong?

"Alternatively, you can contact the convention center directly."

(A) [1]
(B) [2]
(C) [3]
(D) [4]

GO ON TO THE NEXT PAGE

Questions 168-171 refer to the following text-message chain.

Akinobu Iguchi

Hi, Tiziano and Connie. Could either of you fill out the bank's international transfer report next Tuesday? I can't do all of my regular tasks because I'm leading the orientation for new staff.
2:11 P.M.

Tiziano Saltarelli

I haven't done that in quite a while. Could you remind me how long it takes?
2:14 P.M.

Akinobu Iguchi

About an hour, but the service isn't available until three o'clock.
2:15 P.M.

Connie Tilton

I should have all of my work done by mid-afternoon on Tuesday, so I can handle it, Akinobu.
2:16 P.M.

Tiziano Saltarelli

I'm afraid I'm leaving for a doctor's appointment at 2:30 that day.
2:18 P.M.

Akinobu Iguchi

No problem. I get it. Connie, thanks for volunteering!
2:21 P.M.

Connie Tilton

I'm happy to help. Can I just download the form I need from the company Web site?
2:22 P.M.

Akinobu Iguchi

Mr. Sidorov has the forms, but I'll get a copy for you. See you at the meeting on Friday, Connie. I'll have it for you then.
2:23 P.M.

Send

168 Why did Mr. Iguchi send the text messages to her coworkers?

(A) To give them some advice
(B) To request more employee manuals
(C) To ask for help with his job duties
(D) To ask them to exchange contact information

169 What is implied about Ms. Tilton?

(A) She will leave work early for a medical appointment.
(B) She is scheduled to meet with Mr. Iguchi later in the week.
(C) She ordinarily handles international bank transfers.
(D) She is planning to give a presentation at a staff orientation.

170 At 2:21 P.M., what does Mr. Iguchi most likely mean when he writes, "I get it"?

(A) He understands Mr. Saltarelli's situation.
(B) He thinks Ms. Tilton has more experience.
(C) He is concerned about Mr. Saltarelli's condition.
(D) He is expecting a delivery of an item.

171 What is suggested about Mr. Sidorov?

(A) He will upload some information to a Web site.
(B) He is one of the company's newest employees.
(C) He assigned some tasks at the last minute.
(D) He is responsible for providing a form.

GO ON TO THE NEXT PAGE

NOTICE TO ALL OGDEN ENTERPRISES STAFF

In an effort to reduce our impact on the environment, the Ogden Enterprises management team asks that all employees follow our new Environmental Responsibility Initiative.

We will expand our recycling program to include all types of plastic, not just beverage bottles. The bins are located in the staff lounge.

Our purchasing department will switch to recycled paper, refillable ink cartridges, and chemical-free whiteboard markers.

In addition to encouraging employees to do double-sided printing, we will also cut down on paper waste by posting all daily briefings on our company intranet, rather than printing them out.

Please remember to reduce your energy consumption when working at the office.

- Keep the Dyco-360 heating system set at 65° F at all times, and only use a space heater if absolutely necessary.
- Change the power management settings on your personal desktop computer so that it goes into Standby Mode after a certain period of inactivity.
- Make sure to turn off the lights, ceiling fan, and presentation equipment (projector, sound system, and microphone) when leaving the meeting room.
- To improve efficiency, the Dyco-360 equipment will be checked daily. All other office equipment will be checked once a quarter.

Thank you for your cooperation.

172 What is the purpose of the notice?

(A) To outline some government regulations
(B) To ask employees for their opinions
(C) To review details of an initiative
(D) To recruit volunteers for an event

173 What is indicated as one way that the company will reduce waste?

(A) Purchasing supplies locally
(B) Changing a product's packaging
(C) Reusing dishes in a staff lounge
(D) Sharing information online

174 How often will personal computers be inspected?

(A) Daily
(B) Weekly
(C) Every other month
(D) Quarterly

175 What is NOT suggested as equipment in the meeting room?

(A) A laptop
(B) A projector
(C) A ceiling fan
(D) A microphone

GO ON TO THE NEXT PAGE

Questions 176-180 refer to the following e-mail and ticket.

To	Katrin Gerstein <k_gerstein@ackermanninc.de>
From	Jonas Drescher <jonasdrescher@besondere.de>
Date	January 3
Subject	Journey to Frankfurt

Dear Ms. Gerstein,

Besondere Rail is running a promotion throughout the month of January. We want more people to try our first-class section, so we are offering customers the chance to change from a standard ticket to a first-class ticket for just €30. In addition, customers who take advantage of this offer will also receive a free Besondere-branded tote bag. It is made from high-quality canvas with leather straps and has our logo printed on the front. When it's empty, it can be compressed into a compact size, making it easy to fit in your handbag or jacket pocket.

There are first-class seats still available on your current journey.

F561	Depart Hamburg	5 Jan., 7:38 A.M.	Arrive Frankfurt	2:09 P.M.	1 change

You could also switch to a slightly later train that would not require a change of trains.

F563	Depart Hamburg	5 Jan., 8:28 A.M.	Arrive Frankfurt	2:41 P.M.	0 change

Please note that this special offer is not available online. If you would like to change your ticket, please arrive early at the station and stop by the ticketing office. Should you have questions about baggage restrictions, please call our helpline at 0333-555-2121.

Thank you for being a Besondere Rail customer.

Warmest regards,

Jonas Drescher
Customer Service Agent

CUSTOMER: Katrin Gerstein   **CONFIRMATION NUMBER**: 189765328
TRAIN: F563   **FROM**: Hamburg   **SECTION**: A (First-class)
DATE: 5 Jan.   **TO**: Frankfurt   **SEAT**: 15C

Please place small bags on overhead shelf or under your seat to leave room for larger bags in the storage area. The departure platform will be announced approximately fifteen minutes prior to boarding. Please watch the digital screens for boarding information.

176 Why did Mr. Drescher write to Ms. Gerstein?

    (A) To remind her to finalize a payment

    (B) To explain a train company's baggage policy

    (C) To encourage her to get an upgrade

    (D) To inform her of a schedule delay

177 What is mentioned about the tote bag?

    (A) It is made entirely of leather.

    (B) It will be printed with the customer's name.

    (C) It has several interior pockets.

    (D) It can fit into small spaces.

178 What most likely is true about Ms. Gerstein?

    (A) She called a helpline.

    (B) She purchased her original ticket online.

    (C) She visited a ticketing office.

    (D) She signed up for a loyalty program.

179 What does the ticket indicate about Ms. Gerstein's train journey?

    (A) Its passengers will need a passport.

    (B) Its platform has not been selected yet.

    (C) It does not have room for excess baggage.

    (D) It will depart in the early afternoon.

180 When will Ms. Gerstein arrive in Frankfurt?

    (A) At 7:38 A.M.

    (B) At 8:28 A.M.

    (C) At 2:09 P.M.

    (D) At 2:41 P.M.

GO ON TO THE NEXT PAGE

Questions 181-185 refer to the following e-mail and receipt.

To: orders@starcroftcl.com
From: gallagherspence@regalantiques.net
Date: March 16
Subject: Order #97823

To Whom It May Concern:

I am writing regarding my recent order with Starcroft Cleaning. I placed an order on the morning of March 11, and I was pleasantly surprised that it arrived the next day. While the service was excellent, I cannot say the same for the products themselves. The cleaning cloths got a hole in them after the first use. The foaming bathroom cleaner's bottle says that it cannot be used on marble, even though that's not what the Web site said, so I didn't even try it. In addition, the wax colors were very different from what was shown on the box. Unfortunately, I threw away the box for the Rustic Pine color, but I still have the box for the Dark Oak color.

I would like to return items A–D for a refund. Please let me know the process for mailing back the items. When my friend suggested that I use your business, I was pleased to find a new supplier. However, I don't expect to carry on using your service in the future.

Sincerely,

Spencer Gallagher

Starcroft Cleaning

www.starcroftcl.com

– Cleaning Supplies for Domestic and Commercial Use –

Customer Receipt   Order Date: March 11   Order #: 97823

	Item Description	Quantity / Price per Item	Line Total
A	30-oz. Self-Foaming Bathroom Cleaner	2 / $3.79	$7.58
B	15-oz. Wax Polish (Dark Oak)	1 / $12.99	$12.99
C	15-oz. Wax Polish (Rustic Pine)	1 / $12.99	$12.99
D	22-oz. Carpet Stain Remover	2 / $5.79	$11.58
E	3-Pack Durable Cleaning Cloths	1 / $4.99	$4.99
Starcroft Cleaning now offers automated shipments on the first of every month for items you use on a recurring basis so you won't have to keep reordering. To find out how to set up this service, visit our Web site.	Subtotal	$50.13
	Coupon Code WAX5	-$1.30
	Standard Delivery	$2.50
	TOTAL	$51.33

NOTE: Returns must be made within 30 days and must be returned in the original packaging.

181 What is suggested about Mr. Gallagher's items?

(A) They had an expired product.
(B) They contained the wrong brand.
(C) They arrived on March 12.
(D) They included three types of wax.

182 What does Mr. Gallagher indicate in his e-mail?

(A) He had trouble contacting a customer call center.
(B) He will bring some items back to a store in person.
(C) He received a recommendation for the business.
(D) He plans to write a review on the company's Web site.

183 In the e-mail, the phrase "carry on" in paragraph 2, line 3, is closest in meaning to

(A) support
(B) create
(C) transport
(D) continue

184 Which product will Mr. Gallagher most likely have to keep?

(A) The self-foaming bathroom cleaner
(B) The Dark Oak wax polish
(C) The Rustic Pine wax polish
(D) The carpet stain remover

185 What is available to Starcroft Cleaning customers?

(A) Free product samples
(B) Regular monthly shipments
(C) Loyalty point earnings
(D) Guaranteed overnight delivery

GO ON TO THE NEXT PAGE

Questions 186-190 refer to the following article, Web page, and e-mail.

LONDON (1 August)—Leadership expert Craig Lennon, who has built up his consulting business from one to three branches in just five years, will visit audiences across the U.K. in his latest speaking tour.

The tour begins with back-to-back London-based lectures on 3 and 4 August at the Canterbury Auditorium. Then Lennon will speak at the Goodwin Plaza in Bristol on 5 August. The following day, on 6 August, the speaking tour will stop at the Ashford University Hall in Edinburgh. After that, Lennon will give a lecture at the Fox Avenue Community Center in Sheffield on 7 August. The final stop on the tour will be at the Victoria Opera House in Manchester on 8 August.

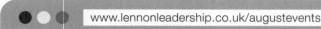

www.lennonleadership.co.uk/augustevents

| HOME | CRAIG'S STORY | **AUGUST EVENTS** | TESTIMONIALS | CONTACT |

Craig Lennon's Finalized Event Schedule for August

Event City	Date	Lecture Topic	Start Time	Tickets
London	3 Aug.	Promoting Diversity in the Workplace	7:00 P.M.	Purchase
London	4 Aug.	Facing Challenges in Communication	7:30 P.M.	Purchase
Bristol	5 Aug.	Staff Motivation and How to Maintain It	7:00 P.M.	Purchase
Edinburgh	6 Aug.	Assessing Employee Performance	7:00 P.M.	Purchase
Sheffield	7 Aug.	Keeping Transitions Free from Stress	8:00 P.M.	Purchase
Manchester	8 Aug.	Facing Challenges in Communication	7:30 P.M.	Purchase

Click on the "Purchase" button to be redirected to the individual venue's box office page.

To	Merlene Tebo <mtebo@miracle-consulting.co.uk>
From	Satya Anagal <s.anagal@lennonleadership.co.uk>
Date	12 August
Subject	Craig Lennon

Dear Ms. Tebo,

Thank you for inviting Mr. Lennon to speak at your company's annual professional development workshop. While he is highly interested in this opportunity, it conflicts with another private event that he already has scheduled.

We're pleased that you enjoyed his recent talk in Sheffield, and we hope you will attend future events. If you have alternative dates for your company workshop, please do not hesitate to share them with me, and I will check with Mr. Lennon about those.

Warmest regards,

Satya Anagal
Lennon Leadership

186 What is indicated about Mr. Lennon?

(A) His business has grown to three locations.
(B) His lectures are free to university students.
(C) He goes on a speaking tour once a year.
(D) He was born and raised in London.

187 Where can audience members learn about motivating employees?

(A) At the Goodwin Plaza
(B) At the Ashford University Hall
(C) At the Fox Avenue Community Center
(D) At the Victoria Opera House

188 Why did Ms. Anagal send the e-mail?

(A) To confirm a ticket price
(B) To apologize for an error
(C) To decline an offer
(D) To promote a new service

189 On what date did Ms. Tebo attend one of Mr. Lennon's events?

(A) August 5
(B) August 6
(C) August 7
(D) August 8

190 Who most likely is Ms. Anagal?

(A) A company founder
(B) A local journalist
(C) An office assistant
(D) A venue owner

GO ON TO THE NEXT PAGE

ADMINISTRATIVE ASSISTANT NEEDED

Uptown Realty has been proud to serve our customers in Somerville, Charlestown, and our newly established office in Everett. For nearly twenty years, we've provided expertise for those buying or selling residential properties. We are currently seeking a part-time administrative assistant in Charlestown. Job responsibilities include answering phone calls, filing paperwork, preparing brochure layouts for open houses, and updating our database. The job is 20 hours per week and must include weekday mornings and afternoons as well as some weekends. Interested parties should submit a résumé by mail to Ashley Mead, 3144 Goodwin Lane, Charlestown, MA 02129 no later than September 30. The manager of the Sales and Outreach Department will conduct interviews beginning October 7.

September 23
Ms. Ashley Mead, 3144 Goodwin Lane, Charlestown, MA 02129

Dear Ms. Mead,

I am writing to express my interest in the administrative assistant position at your Charlestown branch.

I am currently attending morning classes part-time in Everett, but I can easily get to Charlestown for afternoon or weekend work. As you will see from the enclosed résumé, I have a high level of computer proficiency, and I have experience working in an office setting. In addition, I am local to the area, so I am quite familiar with the various residential neighborhoods.

References from past employers or from my current professors can be provided upon request.

Thank you for your consideration.

Warmest regards,

Helen Talbot
Helen Talbot

```
                    ┌─────────────────────────────┐
                    │      E-Mail Message          │
┌───────────────────┴─────────────────────────────┴──────────────┐
│                                                                 │
│  To:       Helen Talbot <htalbot@jolex5.com>                    │
│  From:     Ashley Mead <ashley.mead@uptownrealty.net>           │
│  Date:     October 14                                           │
│  Subject:  Uptown Realty position                               │
├─────────────────────────────────────────────────────────────┬──┤
│                                                             │▲│ │
│  Dear Ms. Talbot,                                           └─┘ │
│                                                                 │
│  We appreciate your interest in working for Uptown Realty. Mr. Hodge was very │
│  impressed with the positive attitude and strong people skills you showed during your │
│  interview with him. You are definitely the strongest candidate, so we are willing to work │
│  around your class schedule and offer you this position.        │
│                                                                 │
│  Attached you will find our standard employment contract. Please review it sometime this │
│  week and let me know whether or not you are happy to go forward under these terms. │
│  If so, I will mail a paper copy for you to sign and return, and your start date would be │
│  October 23.                                                    │
│                                                                 │
│  I look forward to hearing from you.                            │
│                                                                 │
│  Sincerely,                                                     │
│                                                                 │
│  Ashley Mead                                                 ┌─┐│
│                                                              │▼││
└──────────────────────────────────────────────────────────────┴─┘
```

191 What is mentioned about Uptown Realty?

(A) It expects to have more open positions soon.
(B) It will hold a twentieth-anniversary event.
(C) It has recently opened another branch.
(D) It is only open for 20 hours per week.

192 What is one duty for the position indicated in the advertisement?

(A) Developing designs for promotional materials
(B) Responding to written correspondence
(C) Making changes to a Web site
(D) Ordering supplies on behalf of employees

193 What is indicated about Ms. Talbot?

(A) She missed the application deadline.
(B) She lacks the availability requested by the company.
(C) She plans to move to Charlestown.
(D) She is working to get a real estate license.

194 What is implied about Mr. Hodge?

(A) He has recently transferred to the Charlestown branch.
(B) He will call Ms. Talbot on October 23.
(C) He works as an Uptown Realty department head.
(D) He was hired by Ms. Mead.

195 What does Ms. Mead ask Ms. Talbot to do?

(A) Visit the office to attend a training session
(B) E-mail her salary expectations to Mr. Hodge
(C) Provide proof of her educational background
(D) Confirm that she is satisfied with the contract terms

GO ON TO THE NEXT PAGE

Clanton Home Goods

Clanton Espresso Machine Warranty [models K70, K71, K72, K73]

Clanton Home Goods provides an automatic one-year warranty on all of its goods, with an option for a three-year extended warranty at the time of purchase. Defective appliances will be repaired or replaced if they meet the eligibility criteria.

The warranty covers all issues stemming from manufacturing or assembly defects. Customers should note that repairs must be performed by a certified Clanton-branded repair shop. The use of other repair services will invalidate all future warranty claims after that point. Should you need to make a standard warranty claim, please download and print a claim form from our Web site, fill it out, and send the form and the product to the following address: Clanton Home Goods, 9200 Oliver Road, Fort Worth, TX 76102.

www.clantonhg.com/news

| HOME | PRODUCT CATALOG | REVIEWS | CLANTON NEWS | CONTACT |

Customers who purchased the Clanton K72 Espresso Machine in the past two years should be aware that we have identified flaws in the steam wand and temperature-control dial. Without a substantial break between uses, the communication between these two parts may fail, resulting in a lower maximum temperate for frothing milk.

Our research team redesigned these two elements, so the newer version of K72 is not affected. To check whether they have a newer version, customers should look for a small spiral marking on the wand.

In order to get the necessary parts replaced, customers may return their devices by mail to the manufacturer using the address provided on the packaging. Alternatively, the machines can be taken to a Clanton Service Center. In this case, you should first contact us with your zip code for information about how to get to the nearest site.

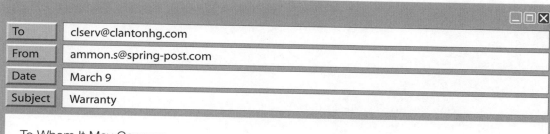

To	clserv@clantonhg.com
From	ammon.s@spring-post.com
Date	March 9
Subject	Warranty

To Whom It May Concern:

I have a Clanton K72 Espresso Machine that I purchased two years ago along with an extended warranty. Recently, I have been experiencing the temperature-control issue you described on your Web site.

I can provide the original receipt and box if necessary, and my zip code is 68103. This is the first issue I've had with this machine, so I want to handle it properly.

Many thanks,

Shawna Ammon

196 What is indicated on the warranty card?

(A) Unauthorized repairs will void the warranty.
(B) Customers can ask for a claim form by mail.
(C) Extended warranties will no longer be offered.
(D) The company may cover shipping costs for returns.

197 What is true about Clanton Home Goods?

(A) It only sells kitchen appliances.
(B) It releases new espresso machines every two years.
(C) It corrected an error in a machine's components.
(D) It recalled items due to safety concerns.

198 What is mentioned about the changed part for the Clanton K72 Espresso Machine?

(A) It takes up less space.
(B) It is marked with a symbol.
(C) It can be removed for cleaning.
(D) It is made from recycled materials.

199 What is implied about Ms. Ammon's espresso machine?

(A) It did not have the correct user manual.
(B) It was purchased from a Web site.
(C) It is no longer being produced.
(D) It is still eligible for a warranty claim.

200 Why most likely did Ms. Ammon email Clanton Home Goods?

(A) She would like to receive a new box.
(B) She would like the company's latest catalog.
(C) She would like to change her delivery address.
(D) She would like directions to a service center.

GO ON TO THE NEXT PAGE

Actual Test

02

시작 시간   :

종료 시간   :

LISTENING TEST

In the Listening test, you will be asked to demonstrate how well you understand spoken English. The entire Listening test will last approximately 45 minutes. There are four parts, and directions are given for each part. You must mark your answers on the separate answer sheet. Do not write your answers in your test book.

PART 1

Directions: For each question in this part, you will hear four statements about a picture in your test book. When you hear the statements, you must select the one statement that best describes what you see in the picture. Then find the number of the question on your answer sheet and mark your answer. The statements will not be printed in your test book and will be spoken only one time.

Example

Sample Answer

Ⓐ ● Ⓒ Ⓓ

Statement (B), "The man is working at a desk," is the best description of the picture, so you should select answer (B) and mark it on your answer sheet.

1

2

GO ON TO THE NEXT PAGE ➤

3

4

5

6

GO ON TO THE NEXT PAGE ▶

PART 2

Directions: You will hear a question or statement and three responses spoken in English. They will not be printed in your test book and will be spoken only one time. Select the best response to the question or statement and mark the letter (A), (B), or (C) on your answer sheet.

7 Mark your answer on your answer sheet.

8 Mark your answer on your answer sheet.

9 Mark your answer on your answer sheet.

10 Mark your answer on your answer sheet.

11 Mark your answer on your answer sheet.

12 Mark your answer on your answer sheet.

13 Mark your answer on your answer sheet.

14 Mark your answer on your answer sheet.

15 Mark your answer on your answer sheet.

16 Mark your answer on your answer sheet.

17 Mark your answer on your answer sheet.

18 Mark your answer on your answer sheet.

19 Mark your answer on your answer sheet.

20 Mark your answer on your answer sheet.

21 Mark your answer on your answer sheet.

22 Mark your answer on your answer sheet.

23 Mark your answer on your answer sheet.

24 Mark your answer on your answer sheet.

25 Mark your answer on your answer sheet.

26 Mark your answer on your answer sheet.

27 Mark your answer on your answer sheet.

28 Mark your answer on your answer sheet.

29 Mark your answer on your answer sheet.

30 Mark your answer on your answer sheet.

31 Mark your answer on your answer sheet.

PART 3

Directions: You will hear some conversations between two or more people. You will be asked to answer three questions about what the speakers say in each conversation. Select the best response to each question and mark the letter (A), (B), (C), or (D) on your answer sheet. The conversations will not be printed in your test book and will be spoken only one time.

32 Where most likely does the woman work?

(A) At a real estate agency
(B) At a repair shop
(C) At an accounting office
(D) At a landscaping company

33 What problem does the man mention?

(A) A computer is not working.
(B) A delivery did not arrive.
(C) A component is missing.
(D) A machine is leaking.

34 What is the man asked to provide?

(A) The name of a customer
(B) A receipt code
(C) A street address
(D) A phone number

35 Where is the conversation most likely taking place?

(A) At a fitness facility
(B) At a bank
(C) At a post office
(D) At a theater

36 What information does the man ask for?

(A) The woman's name
(B) The woman's credit card number
(C) The woman's e-mail address
(D) The woman's phone number

37 What will the woman most likely do next?

(A) Take a swim
(B) Make a payment
(C) Order some food
(D) Attend a consultation

38 What did the woman do yesterday?

(A) She went on a hiking trip.
(B) She requested repairs.
(C) She ordered some clothing.
(D) She bought an item.

39 Why is the woman calling?

(A) To complain about an employee
(B) To report a problem with a purchase
(C) To ask about store opening times
(D) To check the status of a payment

40 What information does the man ask for?

(A) A product name
(B) An order number
(C) A delivery address
(D) A credit card number

41 Where most likely are the speakers?

(A) In a hair salon
(B) In a hospital
(C) In a clothing store
(D) In a fitness center

42 What does Dave ask for?

(A) A discount
(B) A weekend appointment
(C) A complimentary service
(D) An application form

43 What does the woman say she will do?

(A) Make a phone call
(B) Change a business policy
(C) Send a text message
(D) Schedule a delivery

GO ON TO THE NEXT PAGE

44 What has the company recently done?

(A) Launched a new service
(B) Renovated a building
(C) Moved to a new location
(D) Implemented a work policy

45 Why does the woman want to hire additional staff?

(A) Consumer demand has increased.
(B) A work deadline is approaching.
(C) More space is available.
(D) Some employees have left.

46 What does the man recommend doing?

(A) Posting an advertisement
(B) Updating a Web site
(C) Running a training seminar
(D) Attending a job fair

47 What part of the commercial does the man say he is proud of?

(A) The introduction
(B) The script
(C) The acting
(D) The song

48 Why does the man say, "Sheila said next week would be fine"?

(A) To correct a misunderstanding about a task
(B) To explain why a document has not been submitted
(C) To apologize for missing a meeting
(D) To complain about a colleague's performance

49 What does the woman plan to send to Sheila?

(A) A staff list
(B) A schedule
(C) An expense report
(D) A billboard design

50 What kind of business do the speakers work for?

(A) A research laboratory
(B) A library
(C) A real estate agency
(D) A leisure park

51 What is the main topic of the conversation?

(A) The results of a recent golf tournament
(B) The recruitment policy of a company
(C) The latest findings of a project
(D) The venue for an employee retreat

52 Why is the man feeling worried?

(A) He needs to hire more staff urgently.
(B) He must submit a project before a deadline.
(C) He wants to choose an ideal destination.
(D) He has been working long hours recently.

53 What problem does the man mention?

(A) A show received poor reviews.
(B) A network is closing down.
(C) An employee is retiring.
(D) A show is losing viewers.

54 What does the man imply when he says, "That's our most important slot"?

(A) He recommends a new TV show.
(B) He is pleased about a show's success.
(C) He is concerned about the woman's idea.
(D) He will give the woman an assignment.

55 What does the woman say she will do?

(A) Organize a meeting
(B) Cancel a TV show
(C) Hire a new director
(D) Stay late at work

56 Where do the speakers most likely work?

(A) At a movie theater
(B) At a furniture shop
(C) At a post office
(D) At a bookstore

57 What will happen at the business next month?

(A) Rooms will be painted.
(B) Products will be moved.
(C) Lighting will be replaced.
(D) Software will be updated.

58 What does the man agree to do?

(A) Order products
(B) Work late
(C) Train staff
(D) Attend a meeting

---

59 Who most likely is the man?

(A) A comic collector
(B) An exhibition organizer
(C) A building designer
(D) A magazine writer

60 According to the woman, what was the woman's main problem?

(A) Finding a location
(B) Attracting investors
(C) Creating exhibits
(D) Hiring qualified staff

61 What will the museum do by the end of the year?

(A) Open a second branch
(B) Enlarge a building
(C) Unveil a new collection
(D) Host a convention

> ✂ **Sherpa Indian Restaurant** ✂
>
> 75 varieties of curry
>
> 50 types of side dish
>
> 25 traditional beverages
>
> 10 delicious desserts

62 Where does the man most likely work?

(A) In a restaurant
(B) At city hall
(C) In a museum
(D) In a copy shop

63 Look at the graphic. What aspect of the restaurant is the man impressed by?

(A) The number of curries
(B) The number of side dishes
(C) The number of traditional beverages
(D) The number of desserts

64 What will the woman have to pay more for?

(A) A larger size
(B) An express service
(C) A colored option
(D) An electronic copy

GO ON TO THE NEXT PAGE

Customer Complaints

	September	October	November	December

65 What is the man preparing for?

    (A) A product launch
    (B) A client visit
    (C) A career fair
    (D) A board meeting

66 Look at the graphic. When did the woman begin her employment at the company?

    (A) In September
    (B) In October
    (C) In November
    (D) In December

67 What task does the man ask for assistance with?

    (A) Preparing handouts
    (B) Contacting customers
    (C) Organizing a room
    (D) Printing schedules

Title:	*Spring Tulips*
Artist:	Lydia Sandoval
Medium:	Oil Paints
Size:	8"x10"
Price:	$250

68 What does the woman remind the man to do?

    (A) Order some refreshments
    (B) Place an advertisement
    (C) Design an invitation
    (D) Pick up an artist

69 What does the man recommend?

    (A) Contacting a colleague
    (B) Decorating a room
    (C) Preparing more seating
    (D) Rescheduling a delivery

70 Look at the graphic. Which part of the label should be changed?

    (A) Title
    (B) Medium
    (C) Size
    (D) Price

PART 4

Directions: You will hear some talks given by a single speaker. You will be asked to answer three questions about what the speaker says in each talk. Select the best response to each question and mark the letter (A), (B), (C), or (D) on your answer sheet. The talks will not be printed in your test book and will be spoken only one time.

71 What is scheduled to take place this weekend?

(A) A local election
(B) A community parade
(C) A music festival
(D) A sports tournament

72 Where most likely does the speaker work?

(A) At a newspaper agency
(B) At a supermarket
(C) At a car rental company
(D) At a jewelry store

73 What does the speaker recommend doing?

(A) Leaving for work early
(B) Wearing warm clothing
(C) Using public transportation
(D) Bringing a packed lunch

---

74 According to the broadcast, why was last year's concert canceled?

(A) Due to a permit problem
(B) Due to inclement weather
(C) Due to a schedule conflict
(D) Due to a lack of interest

75 Why do organizers say the concert will be the best ever?

(A) Ticket prices will be reduced.
(B) It will be broadcast live on the radio.
(C) It will include a wider variety of food.
(D) Famous musicians will be performing.

76 Who is Andrew Carlson?

(A) An event organizer
(B) A movie director
(C) A musician
(D) A city mayor

77 Where does the speaker work?

(A) In a factory
(B) In a call center
(C) In a bank
(D) In a medical clinic

78 What does the speaker want to purchase?

(A) Company vehicles
(B) Staff uniforms
(C) Electronic devices
(D) Office furniture

79 Why does the speaker say, "Employee comfort is a high priority, right"?

(A) To praise the current work conditions
(B) To encourage the listener to approve a request
(C) To suggest providing a bonus to new workers
(D) To invite the listener to visit a workplace

---

80 What is the announcement mainly about?

(A) A security upgrade
(B) A piece of equipment
(C) A policy change
(D) A deadline extension

81 What benefit does the speaker mention?

(A) Results will be more precise.
(B) Employees will be safer.
(C) Productivity will increase.
(D) Company sales will improve.

82 According to the speaker, what are the listeners required to do?

(A) Read a report
(B) Exchange their IDs
(C) Wear a uniform
(D) Take a test

GO ON TO THE NEXT PAGE

83 Where does the introduction take place?

(A) At a group interview
(B) At a lecture series
(C) At an orientation session
(D) At a press conference

84 What topic will Ms. Brown discuss?

(A) Reducing energy consumption
(B) Improving working relationships
(C) Learning a foreign language
(D) Managing time wisely

85 What are the listeners reminded to do before they leave?

(A) Make a donation
(B) Join a mailing list
(C) Complete a survey form
(D) Leave a business card

86 What is the speaker calling about?

(A) A cruise
(B) A hotel suite
(C) A train ticket
(D) A flight

87 What does the speaker say she has done?

(A) She has upgraded a seat.
(B) She has refunded a payment.
(C) She has amended a contract.
(D) She has canceled a reservation.

88 What does the speaker request the listener do as soon as possible?

(A) E-mail some information
(B) Sign a contract
(C) Transfer some funds
(D) Complete a form

89 What is the purpose of the message?

(A) To make an appointment
(B) To thank a colleague
(C) To advertise a new product
(D) To describe a design plan

90 What does the speaker most likely mean when he says, "I'm about halfway to the clinic"?

(A) He will meet Jacqueline soon.
(B) He may be late for a meeting.
(C) He got a ride from a coworker.
(D) He cannot do a task himself.

91 What is scheduled to happen tomorrow?

(A) A business trip will begin.
(B) A new employee will join a team.
(C) Some equipment will be repaired.
(D) Some uniforms will be delivered.

92 What type of sport will the listeners watch?

(A) Football
(B) Baseball
(C) Basketball
(D) Tennis

93 What does the speaker imply when he says, "Let's give them another five minutes"?

(A) He will wait a little longer for group members.
(B) He will give a short presentation to the listeners.
(C) A building is opening later than expected.
(D) A special guest has been delayed.

94 What does the speaker ask the listeners to do?

(A) Stay in the group
(B) Keep their voices down
(C) Refrain from eating
(D) Obtain a security pass

4-Day Weekend Special Menu

Friday: Grilled Salmon with Herbs
Saturday: Pan Roasted Pork
Sunday: Fresh Crab Salad
Monday: Cream and Mushroom Spaghetti

Destination	Flight Number	Status
Los Angeles	L201	2 hour delay
Tallahassee	T304	45 minute delay
Chicago	C492	Canceled
San Antonio	S420	2 hour delay

95 Who are the listeners?

(A) Health inspectors
(B) Restaurant servers
(C) Delivery drivers
(D) Repair technicians

96 Look at the graphic. Which dish will not be available?

(A) Grilled Salmon with Herbs
(B) Pan Roasted Pork
(C) Fresh Crab Salad
(D) Cream and Mushroom Spaghetti

97 According to the speaker, what should the listeners do after two o'clock today?

(A) Unload some supplies
(B) Pick up a paycheck
(C) Check a notice board
(D) Print a new menu

98 What does the speaker say is responsible for flight delays?

(A) Technical problems
(B) Bad weather
(C) A security issue
(D) A computer system failure

99 Look at the graphic. Which flight should passengers board in order to travel to Chicago?

(A) L201
(B) T304
(C) C492
(D) S420

100 What does the speaker say begins next week?

(A) A reward program
(B) A renovation project
(C) A staff training course
(D) A new flight route

This is the end of the Listening test. Turn to Part 5 in your test book.

GO ON TO THE NEXT PAGE

READING TEST

In the Reading test, you will read a variety of texts and answer several different types of reading comprehension questions. The entire Reading test will last 75 minutes. There are three parts, and directions are given for each part. You are encouraged to answer as many questions as possible within the time allowed.

You must mark your answers on the separate answer sheet. Do not write your answers in your test book.

PART 5

Directions: A word or phrase is missing in each of the sentences below. Four answer choices are given below each sentence. Select the best answer to complete the sentence. Then mark the letter (A), (B), (C), or (D) on your answer sheet.

101 To become a member of our organization, ------- fill out an application form and turn it in.

(A) simple
(B) simpler
(C) simply
(D) simplify

102 Artist Richard Truman signs each of his paintings so that viewers can easily recognize which ones are -------.

(A) he
(B) his
(C) him
(D) himself

103 Visitors are ------- to present a form of picture ID at the main gate to gain access to the facility.

(A) required
(B) applied
(C) expired
(D) respected

104 Reginald Foods is not ------- for any problems incurred by eating food marked as beyond its expiration date.

(A) responsible
(B) responsibleness
(C) responsibly
(D) responsibility

105 According to the company's Web site, all items purchased will be shipped ------- two business days.

(A) among
(B) within
(C) from
(D) behind

106 The demand for locally produced food products ------- at least 50 percent in the next three years.

(A) to grow
(B) will have grown
(C) will grow
(D) has grown

107 At the work site, we will provide volunteers with nails, hammers, safety gear, and other -------.

(A) supplies
(B) qualities
(C) facilities
(D) treatments

108 Joseph Harrison, an ------- for the senior engineer position, will speak with the human resources director tomorrow.

(A) applied
(B) applicant
(C) applying
(D) application

109 Thanks to the upgrades implemented by the IT team, the intranet is ------- operational.

(A) closely
(B) shortly
(C) currently
(D) quickly

110 Ms. Walsh's suggestions for changes to the assembly process are proving ------- helpful.

(A) increase
(B) to increase
(C) increased
(D) increasingly

111 The Broadway Hotel offers ------- transportation to and from the airport by means of its shuttle bus.

(A) whole
(B) skilled
(C) reliable
(D) vacant

112 The company will place greater emphasis on ------- training for new recruits this year.

(A) extend
(B) extends
(C) extensive
(D) extensively

113 ------- her business trip, Ms. Atkins will talk about what she discussed with the foreign buyers.

(A) Then
(B) After
(C) Since
(D) When

114 In order to become a certified engineer, a person must possess a large amount of mechanical -------.

(A) impression
(B) approval
(C) importance
(D) expertise

115 Armo Hall, which can only accommodate up to 80 people, is not considered ------- for major events.

(A) significant
(B) complete
(C) intentional
(D) appropriate

116 Genevieve Textiles ------- in handling exotic materials, especially silk, from locations throughout Asia.

(A) identifies
(B) specializes
(C) measures
(D) considers

117 The firm intends to maintain the confidentiality of its records by ------- its security software regularly.

(A) update
(B) updated
(C) updating
(D) updates

118 Bonuses will be paid to employees next month ------- the firm has recorded a huge profit this quarter.

(A) therefore
(B) whether
(C) as a result
(D) because

119 Individuals ------- wish to donate books to the event should contact Marcy Wayne by this Friday.

(A) whose
(B) which
(C) who
(D) whoever

120 Drivers are expected to pay all their fuel expenses, ------- reimbursement will be provided later.

(A) likewise
(B) but
(C) rather than
(D) as soon as

GO ON TO THE NEXT PAGE

121 ------- Mr. Longfellow makes a decision, a press release will be distributed regarding the future course of the company.

(A) Once
(B) Still
(C) Owing to
(D) Already

122 This morning, Ms. Lake had to attend a number of meetings, ------- in the main conference room.

(A) roughly
(B) relatively
(C) primarily
(D) gradually

123 As assistant director, Mr. Kimber is asked to report his progress ------- to Anita Walker, the company's vice president.

(A) directing
(B) directs
(C) direction
(D) directly

124 The attendees discussed every item on the agenda ------- the possibility of opening a new branch.

(A) unlike
(B) except
(C) despite
(D) opposite

125 Many applicants ------- about the position of branch manager at Prime Bank before Mr. Ventura accepted it.

(A) inquire
(B) inquiring
(C) had inquired
(D) will have inquired

126 Few customers visit our retail store in Weston as it is a ------- small town without popular attractions.

(A) normally
(B) relatively
(C) closely
(D) exactly

127 When ------- for a class at the Hobart Institute, payment must be made immediately to guarantee a seat.

(A) register
(B) registers
(C) registering
(D) registration

128 At Mr. Hamilton's retirement party, many colleagues ------- their appreciation for his outstanding contribution.

(A) thanked
(B) expressed
(C) appeared
(D) commented

129 Plans for the book signing event are ------- since the amount of funding has not yet been determined.

(A) steady
(B) immense
(C) unwanted
(D) tentative

130 Please get in touch with someone in Accounting to obtain ------- for any purchases over $150.

(A) approve
(B) approved
(C) approving
(D) approval

PART 6

Directions: Read the texts that follow. A word, phrase, or sentence is missing in parts of each text. Four answer choices for each question are given below the text. Select the best answer to complete the text. Then mark the letter (A), (B), (C), or (D) on your answer sheet.

Questions 131-134 refer to the following e-mail.

To: <undisclosed_recipients>
From: tworthy@dentondiner.com
Subject: New Policy
Date: August 21

To All Staff Members,

We will be implementing a new policy ------- coffee refills for diners. As of now, serving staff will
     131.
no longer fill up empty or half-empty cups on tables. You should wait for a customer to ask you

to pour a new cup of coffee. This should ------- the amount of coffee we brew on a daily basis.
     132.
-------, we should save a significant amount of money by purchasing fewer coffee beans. We will
133.
post a notice of our policy by the front door. -------. Please let us know how customers respond
     134.
during the next few days.

Regards,

Tina Worthy
Manager, Denton Diner

---

131 (A) regarded
(B) regarding
(C) regardless
(D) regards

132 (A) remove
(B) exchange
(C) double
(D) minimize

133 (A) On the other hand
(B) As a result
(C) However
(D) Despite this

134 (A) The staff meeting provided some more details.
(B) During this time, prices will be expected to rise.
(C) You should also inform diners of this change.
(D) Please let me know which shifts you prefer to work.

GO ON TO THE NEXT PAGE

Questions 135-138 refer to the following Web page.

---

http://www.hamptongamersclub.org

The Hampton Gamers Club (HGC) organizes monthly gaming sessions as well as special events

------- increase interest in gaming in the local community. The events often feature realistic role-
135.

playing games. Many of ------- are watched by a large number of people who want to see how
136.

role-playing games are played. In addition, the HGC hosts a gaming tournament each May. This

year's contest will require gamers to play Dungeons and Wizards. -------. Harold Moss was last
137.

year's -------. The character he played managed to defeat all the others in a seven-hour-long
138.

game.

---

135 (A) so
(B) even if
(C) in order to
(D) so that

136 (A) each
(B) theirs
(C) another
(D) these

137 (A) There are not many seats left for viewers.
(B) Gamers from around the country will be there.
(C) Next year, the tournament will be played in August.
(D) It was widely considered a major success.

138 (A) judge
(B) winner
(C) expert
(D) consultant

Date: July 24
To: All Staff
From: Eric Mudd
Re: Resignation

Good morning, everyone.

I would like to inform you that I just handed in my letter of resignation to CEO Summers as I have

decided to move to Miami, ------- I will be working with another company. My ------- day here will
            139.   **140.**

be this coming Friday, July 28.

Ever since I started working here, I have had the pleasure to work with some of the best people

in the business. During the past five years, we have acquired numerous new clients. In the

process, we ------- one of the top companies in the textile business. It's been an honor to have
            141.

worked here with everyone. -------.
                           142.

I hope that you all continue to work hard, and I wish you continued success in the future.

Sincerely,

Eric Mudd

139 (A) there
    (B) that
    (C) beside
    (D) where

140 (A) latest
    (B) next
    (C) last
    (D) closest

141 (A) will build
    (B) built
    (C) must build
    (D) build

142 (A) My supervisor must sign a few
        documents.
    (B) I enjoy taking on additional
        responsibilities.
    (C) I'm really going to miss all of you after I
        leave.
    (D) A replacement for her will start next
        Monday.

GO ON TO THE NEXT PAGE

October 13

Ms. Linda Marbut

54 Appleton Street
Jacksonville, FL

Dear Ms. Marbut,

This letter is in ------- to the inquiry you made on October 6. You noted that you have been a
                   143.
customer at Laredo Clothes for more than five years but had not known about our membership

club until two weeks ago. You wanted to know if you qualified for membership. All you need to

do is prove you have made two purchases from us and our records show that you have shopped

at our online store several times. -------, you are eligible to join the club. You ------- by visiting our
                                 144.   **145.**
Web site at www.laredoclothes.com/members. -------. Once your application is accepted, you
                                           146.
will become a member of the club and gain several benefits.

Regards,

Chet Rogers

Customr Service Representative
Laredo Clothes

143 (A) respond
(B) responds
(C) response
(D) responded

144 (A) Meanwhile
(B) Therefore
(C) Nevertheless
(D) Otherwise

145 (A) may apply
(B) were applying
(C) applying
(D) would have applied

146 (A) Your purchase of these items qualifies
you for a discount.
(B) Click the "register" button and follow the
directions to do it.
(C) According to our records, your card has
already been mailed to you.
(D) Unfortunately, we have decided that we
need to close the stores.

PART 7

Directions: In this part you will read a selection of texts, such as magazine and newspaper articles, e-mails, and instant messages. Each text or set of texts is followed by several questions. Select the best answer for each question and mark the letter (A), (B), (C), or (D) on your answer sheet.

Questions 147-148 refer to the following invitation.

Grand Opening of Sierra Gym
738 Euclid Avenue
Saturday, January 8

Check out our facility to see if it's right for you.

Pick up a free day pass for a future visit.

Tours and Refreshments: 10 A.M. to 5 P.M.

Participate in a free yoga class*: 11 A.M. or 3 P.M.

*Contact Mary Dawkins directly to inquire about her recommendations for workout gear and ability level.

147 What is the purpose of the January 8 event?
(A) To launch a government health program
(B) To show a business's new renovations
(C) To recruit workers for a business
(D) To introduce a new fitness center

148 Who most likely is Mary Dawkins?
(A) An inspector
(B) A salesperson
(C) An instructor
(D) A realtor

GO ON TO THE NEXT PAGE

Questions 149-150 refer to the following text-message chain.

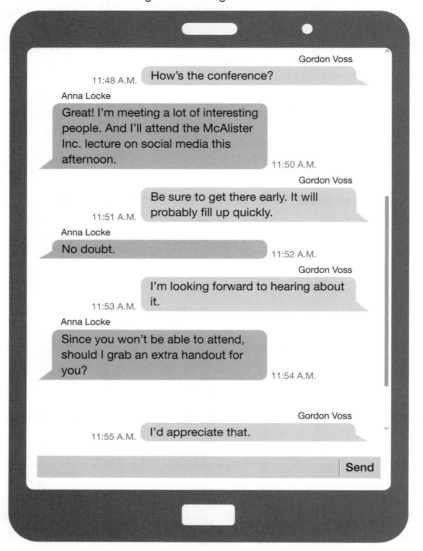

Gordon Voss
11:48 A.M. How's the conference?

Anna Locke
Great! I'm meeting a lot of interesting people. And I'll attend the McAlister Inc. lecture on social media this afternoon.
11:50 A.M.

Gordon Voss
Be sure to get there early. It will probably fill up quickly.
11:51 A.M.

Anna Locke
No doubt.
11:52 A.M.

Gordon Voss
I'm looking forward to hearing about it.
11:53 A.M.

Anna Locke
Since you won't be able to attend, should I grab an extra handout for you?
11:54 A.M.

Gordon Voss
11:55 A.M. I'd appreciate that.

Send

149 At 11:52 A.M., what does Ms. Locke suggest when she writes, "No doubt"?

(A) She plans to meet Mr. Voss in the afternoon.
(B) She wants to get a job at McAlister Inc.
(C) She agrees that a session is likely to be popular.
(D) She is sure she will attend a conference next month.

150 What is suggested about Mr. Voss?

(A) He will miss the talk from McAlister Inc.
(B) He is an expert in social media.
(C) He lost some important conference documents.
(D) He is busy preparing for a talk.

Questions 151-152 refer to the following e-mail.

To: Joelle Burnette
From: Lawrence Holcomb
Date: August 21
Subject: To do

Hi, Joelle,

I would like you to update the details of my meeting with Remsen Enterprises. Originally, one of their representatives was going to visit our office. However, that is no longer possible, so I will travel to New York to visit their office instead. The meeting has also been postponed by one day, so it will now take place on September 6.

Could you please arrange tickets for a flight that arrives in New York no later than 10 A.M. on September 6? For the return flight, I would prefer a morning departure on September 7. Thanks for your help.

Lawrence

151 What is the purpose of the e-mail?
(A) To ask for a deadline extension
(B) To introduce a company
(C) To revise a meeting plan
(D) To confirm some contract terms

152 What is Ms. Burnette asked to do?
(A) Book some airline tickets
(B) Contact Remsen Enterprises
(C) Request a refund from an airline
(D) Recommend a hotel in New York

GET YOUR FAST PASS TODAY!

Are you tired of sitting in your vehicle while you wait in the long lines to pay tolls throughout Sampson County? Purchase a Fast Pass and use the designated lane without stopping. Our cameras will record your location and charge you the correct toll, and we'll send you a bill at the end of each month. In addition to saving time, you can save money. Present your Fast Pass at the Central Parking Lot (CPL) in Avondale and get a ten percent discount on parking when you enter. The lot is conveniently located within walking distance of the city's main bus terminal. To get your Fast Pass, visit www.sampsonfastpass.com. The pass will be mailed to you within three business days of registration.

153 Who would most likely be interested in this advertisement?

(A) Tour guide applicants
(B) Former Avondale residents
(C) Professional photographers
(D) Drivers in Sampson County

154 What is implied about CPL?

(A) It sends a monthly bill.
(B) It has several locations.
(C) It is close to a bus station.
(D) It allows parking for three days.

Farrington Co.

394 Echo Boulevard, Raleigh, NC 27616
www.farringtonco.com · 984-555-6472

Never underestimate a first impression! Your outdoor space is one of the first things a customer will notice when visiting your site. Let Farrington Co. help it to look its best with our expert services.

• Trimming trees and branches to ensure a tidy appearance
• Regular lawn maintenance year-round or seasonally, as needed
• Planting and upkeep of flowerbeds
• Removal of branches, twigs, and stones

Each site is unique. To find out the approximate cost of services at your particular property, please schedule a consultation with one of our crew members. We will visit your site in person to find out more about your needs. This is available at no cost to you, and there is no obligation to use the service.

With Farrington Co., you can trust that our experts will always treat your property with respect and care. In addition, we give back to the community, as through our partnership with Raleigh Job Center, we train low-income individuals living here in Raleigh in order to give them technical skills. This can help them to financially support their family.

To find out more about our story, and to read customer testimonials, visit our Web site.

---

155 What type of business is Farrington Co.?

(A) A transportation service
(B) A landscaping company
(C) An architectural firm
(D) A real estate agency

156 How can customers get an estimate for the service?

(A) By sending in an application
(B) By e-mailing a business owner
(C) By completing an online form
(D) By booking a free consultation

157 What is mentioned about Farrington Co.?

(A) It has the industry's highest safety rating.
(B) It uses environmentally friendly products.
(C) It provides job training to local residents.
(D) It makes donations to worthwhile charities.

GO ON TO THE NEXT PAGE

```
                        E-Mail Message
```

To: Michelle Ebert <m.ebert@blevins.net>
From: Jerry Prescott <j.prescott@blevins.net>
Date: July 28
Subject: Update

Dear Ms. Ebert,

I've just received a call from Daniel Sutter of Veltri Manufacturing, and he is unable to visit you at your office tomorrow. Unfortunately, he had to go out of town unexpectedly to deal with a problem at one of his company's manufacturing facilities. Instead, he'll meet you on August 12 at 2 P.M. I know you're presenting a lecture at the Cambridge Center the day before, but you said you'd be back to work as usual after that. Mr. Sutter's time slot for tomorrow will be replaced with a product demonstration.

JULY 29

Time	Activity	Personnel/Guests
9:30 A.M.	Training	Junior staff
1:00 P.M.	In-person Meeting	Daniel Sutter, Veltri Manufacturing
2:30 P.M.	Video Conference	Nina Sherman, Sherman Consulting
7:00 P.M.	Dinner at Rio's	Freida Hilliard

I will update your plan above and leave a printed copy for you. If you have any questions, just let me know.

Sincerely,

Jerry

158 What is the purpose of the e-mail?
  (A) To remind Ms. Ebert of an approaching deadline
  (B) To inform Ms. Ebert of a schedule change
  (C) To provide research on a manufacturing firm
  (D) To apologize for an earlier error

159 What will Ms. Ebert do on August 11?
  (A) Give a talk
  (B) Take a trip overseas
  (C) Visit Mr. Sutter's office
  (D) Launch a new product

160 When will Ms. Ebert watch a demonstration?
  (A) At 9:30 A.M.
  (B) At 1:00 P.M.
  (C) At 2:30 P.M.
  (D) At 7:00 P.M.

Questions 161-163 refer to the following article.

(BARCELONA, August 2)—German appliance manufacturer Holtzmann announced in a press conference yesterday that it has selected Longview for its new plant. —[1]—

"Because it is so close to major roadways, the site is ideal for our purposes," said Heike Becker, a spokesperson for the company. "We care deeply about the environment, and decreasing the travel distances for our raw materials and finished goods is one way to minimize our impact on air pollution." —[2]—

The Frankfurt-based manufacturer is experiencing incredible growth, building its fourth factory just last year in Montreal, Canada. Company officials are already looking for an opportunity to sell their goods in Asia at some point in the near future. —[3]— Locations being considered for retail stores are Shanghai and Wuhan. —[4]—

161 What benefit of the new site does Ms. Becker mention?

(A) Its affordable wages for employees
(B) Its proximity to transportation infrastructure
(C) Its use of environmentally friendly equipment
(D) Its system of tax incentives

162 According to the article, what does Holtzmann want to do soon?

(A) Release a new product
(B) Grow its customer base in Canada
(C) Enter the Asian market
(D) Launch an online retail store

163 In which of the positions marked [1], [2], [3], and [4] does the following sentence best belong?

"The others are sites in Chengdu and Tianjin."

(A) [1]
(B) [2]
(C) [3]
(D) [4]

GO ON TO THE NEXT PAGE

Questions 164-167 refer to the following memo.

To: All Bassell Employees
From: Kimberly Foster, Operations Director
Date: March 3
Re: Changes ahead

Customers know they can depend on Bassell air conditioners due to our company's high standard of performance. However, despite our excellent reputation, we have been experiencing a steady drop in sales. As discussed in previous meetings, more and more businesses in our area are starting to sell air conditioners. We are reluctant to lower our prices because that would make it difficult to cover the products' costs. We've also tried increasing our advertising, but it hasn't made much of a difference so far.

To deal with our current sales issue, we plan to adjust our strategy regarding what we offer to customers. Beginning next month, customers who purchase one of our air conditioners will be eligible for a complimentary visit from one of our technicians once a year for the first three years. The technician will check for any performance issues that need attention. We hope this will help to set us apart from other businesses.

164 What is indicated about Bassell?

(A) It operates in several countries.
(B) It recently opened a new branch.
(C) It is known for its high quality.
(D) It has hired more technicians.

165 Why is Bassell changing a business strategy?

(A) Raw material costs have increased.
(B) A supplier has gone out of business.
(C) It is facing heavy competition.
(D) Customers have made complaints.

166 The word "cover" in paragraph 1, line 5, is closest in meaning to

(A) achieve
(B) drop out
(C) disguise
(D) pay for

167 What will customers receive in the future?

(A) A yearly catalog
(B) Free annual inspections
(C) Replacement components
(D) Complimentary delivery

April 8

Keenan Cole
438 Goodwin Avenue
Sanford, FL 32771

Dear Mr. Cole,

I would like to invite you to be a volunteer for the 12th Annual Sanford Marathon. —[1]—. The race will take place on Sunday, June 13, starting and ending at Quincy Park. We depend on volunteers for the success of this event, as a lot of people are needed for various duties. —[2]—.

We need about five volunteers to operate the registration table, helping athletes to get checked in for the race. There are also volunteers positioned throughout the course to show runners where to make the necessary turns. Other volunteers will set up stands throughout the course, passing out water, energy drinks, and bananas. —[3]—.

My co-coordinator, Brandon Mengel, remembers you from last year and said that you worked really hard during the event. —[4]—. It is particularly useful to have people on the volunteer team who are familiar with how the marathon operates. If you are able to participate, please let us know no later than April 25. You can do so by e-mailing events@sanford.gov. We hope to hear from you soon.

Thank you,

Diana Holmes

168 What is NOT mentioned as a duty done by volunteers?

(A) Directing athletes on the course
(B) Setting up refreshments stands
(C) Assisting athletes in signing in
(D) Awarding prizes to winners

169 What is indicated about Mr. Cole?

(A) He worked with Mr. Mengel at a previous event.
(B) He applied for a job as a co-coordinator.
(C) He has been training for a marathon.
(D) He recently moved to the city of Sanford.

170 What is Mr. Cole asked to do?

(A) E-mail his preference for volunteer duties
(B) Complete a feedback questionnaire
(C) Update his personal contact details
(D) Confirm his attendance by the deadline

171 In which of the positions marked [1], [2], [3], and [4] does the following sentence best belong?

"Your assistance would be a great help to him."

(A) [1]
(B) [2]
(C) [3]
(D) [4]

GO ON TO THE NEXT PAGE

Anthony Barnett — X

Anthony Barnett [9:03 A.M.]	The people investing in our new building project will be here in about an hour. I'm getting everything ready in Meeting Room 2.
Keith Cervantes [9:04 A.M.]	I thought you had reserved Meeting Room 1 because it's larger.
Anthony Barnett [9:05 A.M.]	Originally I did, but a pipe in the ceiling broke last night and water was leaking everywhere. We have it cleaned up, but the ceiling is stained and the plaster is cracked in a few places. Meeting Room 2 is large enough for our purposes.
Shanna Palazzi [9:06 A.M.]	According to the schedule, the finance team has reserved it for today.
Anthony Barnett [9:07 A.M.]	Don't worry. I've already asked them to reschedule their meeting since we can't reschedule ours. But I'm having trouble lowering the video screen from the ceiling. Keith, you always seem to know the trick to make it work.
Keith Cervantes [9:08 A.M.]	I'm on the way.
Anthony Barnett [9:09 A.M.]	The refreshments are ready at the bakery across the street. I don't have time to stop by the bakery myself because I'm still setting up this room.
Shanna Palazzi [9:10 A.M.]	I can do it. I'll bring the food there around 9:45. Do I just tell the bakery our company name?
Anthony Barnett [9:12 A.M.]	You'll need the order confirmation number, which is RC7394. Thanks a lot!
Shanna Palazzi [9:13 A.M.]	My pleasure. If you need anything else, just let me know.

Send

172 What is Mr. Barnett doing today?

(A) Introducing samples to product testers
(B) Providing training to his coworkers
(C) Meeting some new employees
(D) Preparing for a visit from investors

173 What problem with Meeting Room 1 is mentioned?

(A) It does not have the right equipment.
(B) It is not large enough for the group.
(C) It sustained some damage.
(D) It was double-booked with another team.

174 At 9:08 A.M., what does Mr. Cervantes probably mean when he says, "I'm on the way"?

(A) He will finish some paperwork.
(B) He is willing to help Mr. Barnett.
(C) He can stop to pick up some items.
(D) He is visiting a client's headquarters.

175 What will happen at approximately 9:45 A.M.?

(A) Mr. Barrett will call a bakery.
(B) Ms. Palazzi will take items to Meeting Room 2.
(C) Meeting Room 1 will be inspected.
(D) Ms. Palazzi will be sent a confirmation number.

GO ON TO THE NEXT PAGE

Questions 176-180 refer to the following business card and e-mail.

Pendrell Financial Services

Lydia Gallagher
Senior Financial Analyst

Robinson Building, Suite 4	E-mail: lydiagal@pendrellfinancial.com
876 Nicola Avenue	Office Phone: 604-555-8078, extension 24
Vancouver, Canada	Cell Phone: 778-555-6641
V5K 1A6	Web Site: www.pendrellfinancial.com

To: Lydia Gallagher <lydiagal@pendrellfinancial.com>
From: Daniel Ramsey <d_ramsey@lindaleco.com>
Date: February 16
Subject: Documents

Dear Ms. Gallagher,

It was a pleasure meeting you at the workshop in Ottawa. I learned so much from your teaching. I really appreciate your telling me about the job opening at your firm. I would love the opportunity to work for such a highly respected company. As requested, I'm sending my résumé and cover letter for your reference. I've also attached a copy of my Certified Financial Planner certificate, which is valid for four more years.

You will see that I graduated from the University of Toronto with a bachelor's degree in economics and later a master's degree in business management. I served as an intern at Wakefield Bank. This gave me the opportunity to learn a great deal about the financial consulting field. Following that, I worked for five years at L.S. Consulting. There I met numerous people who helped me to build my extensive network of business professionals. I'll be moving from Montreal to your city next month. So, I would love to meet with you in person then to discuss this matter further.

Warmest regards,

Daniel Ramsey

176 What is the purpose of the e-mail?

(A) To register for an event
(B) To follow up on a request
(C) To inquire about a test result
(D) To announce a job opportunity

177 What is true about Ms. Gallagher?

(A) She used to work at L.S. Consulting.
(B) She has known Mr. Ramsey for four years.
(C) She taught a workshop in Ottawa.
(D) She met Mr. Ramsey through a colleague.

178 What is Mr. Ramsey interested in doing?

(A) Giving feedback about an internship program
(B) Launching a new financial conference
(C) Registering for an upcoming event
(D) Joining the Pendrell Financial Services staff

179 What is NOT indicated about Mr. Ramsey?

(A) He has a lot of business contacts.
(B) He currently holds two degrees.
(C) He is certified in his field.
(D) He has run his own business.

180 Where does Mr. Ramsey want to meet Ms. Gallagher next month?

(A) In Ottawa
(B) In Montreal
(C) In Vancouver
(D) In Toronto

Questions 181-185 refer to the following e-mail and text message.

To	Kenneth Russell <russellk@billericamail.com>
From	Mendoza Hotel <bookings@mendozahotel.com>
Date	June 3
Subject	Reservation Confirmation #57823

Thank you for booking a room at Mendoza Hotel. Please find confirmation of your booking details below.

Name: Kenneth Russell   **Branch**: Boston   **Room Type**: Single
Check-In Date: June 27   **Check-Out Date**: June 30   **Assigned Room**: 306

Airport Shuttle
Incoming Shuttle: 2 P.M.   **Outgoing Shuttle**: none (renting car)

Should you miss your preferred shuttle time above, simply take the next shuttle. As a member of the Mendoza Loyalty Club, you are eligible for a free one-way shuttle trip. Our regular shuttle fees are listed below:

	Standard Shuttle (9 A.M.–9 P.M.)	Early Shuttle (Before 9 A.M.)	Late Shuttle (After 9 P.M.)	Private Van (Anytime)
One-Way	$5.00	$6.00	$7.50	$25.00
Round Trip	$7.50	$10.00	$12.50	$45.00

We understand that some of our guests request specific rooms due to the view, floor, or distance from shared amenities. If we are unable to provide you with the exact room designated in this reservation confirmation, we will give you a voucher for a free breakfast buffet. This can be picked up at the front desk upon check-in.

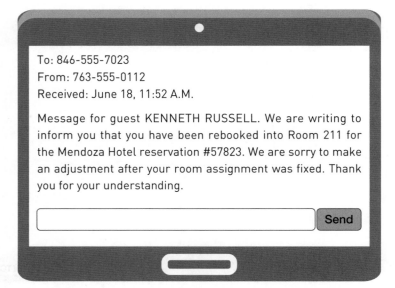

To: 846-555-7023
From: 763-555-0112
Received: June 18, 11:52 A.M.

Message for guest KENNETH RUSSELL. We are writing to inform you that you have been rebooked into Room 211 for the Mendoza Hotel reservation #57823. We are sorry to make an adjustment after your room assignment was fixed. Thank you for your understanding.

Send

181 What is indicated about Mr. Russell?

(A) He will stay for four nights.
(B) He is originally from Boston.
(C) He enrolled in a loyalty program.
(D) He will share the room with someone.

182 How much will Mr. Russell be charged for the shuttle service?

(A) $0.00
(B) $5.00
(C) $6.00
(D) $7.50

183 Why did Mendoza Hotel send the text message to Mr. Russell?

(A) To request the final payment
(B) To promote a new service
(C) To offer a room upgrade
(D) To inform him of a room change

184 What will Mr. Russell be given by the front desk staff?

(A) A meal voucher
(B) A parking pass
(C) A neighborhood map
(D) A partial refund

185 In the text message, the word "fixed" in paragraph 1, line 4, is closest in meaning to

(A) repaired
(B) concentrated
(C) finalized
(D) fastened

GO ON TO THE NEXT PAGE

Questions 186-190 refer to the following article, e-mail, and Web site.

The Rennex Building has recently been completed in the Dallas city center, and in just a short time it has become a recognizable landmark on Ivan Street. The building's unique shape brings a modern look to the downtown area, and it will eventually be home to 40 different offices. Most of the spaces have been rented out already, mainly by financial firms, but there are still a few spots left.

The building's giant windows are well insulated, meaning that less electricity for heating and cooling will be needed compared to other buildings of its size. This is good for the environment, a quality that was important to the building's architect, Timothy Blair. Inside, visitors will be amazed by the cheerful colors selected by interior designer Gabrielle Halstead. In addition to private use on the upper floors, there are two coffee shops and a seafood restaurant on the ground floor for the public.

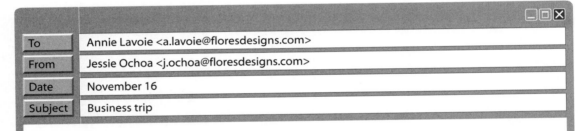

To	Annie Lavoie <a.lavoie@floresdesigns.com>
From	Jessie Ochoa <j.ochoa@floresdesigns.com>
Date	November 16
Subject	Business trip

Dear Annie,

During your business trip to Dallas, you'll be staying at the Arlington Hotel downtown. When you arrive at the airport, there will be a car waiting for you at Morgan Rentals. You can return the rental car to the same place before you fly home. We were hoping that both Timothy Blair and Gabrielle Halstead could attend the meeting. However, only Ms. Halstead will be there. I hope you learn a lot from her project.

Cheers,

Jessie

http://www.morganrentals.com/about

Morgan Rentals is now open for business! We had a successful opening ceremony in April to celebrate the beginning of a great car rental in Dallas. Our fleet of brand-new cars will help you to drive in comfort. Each one is equipped with heated seats, a backup camera, GPS, and an excellent sound system. You can easily extend your booking with our app or on our Web site. And, for each day you rent with us, you can earn airline miles from one of our partners — Center Air, Pensacola Airlines, or Stollings Airlines.

186 Why was the article written?

(A) To report a financial issue
(B) To profile an office building
(C) To announce a city festival
(D) To review downtown coffee shops

187 According to the article, how will a project help the environment?

(A) By installing solar panels
(B) By using recycled materials
(C) By collecting rainwater
(D) By consuming less electricity

188 Who will attend a meeting with Ms. Lavoie in Dallas?

(A) An architect
(B) A city official
(C) An interior designer
(D) A hotel manager

189 What is true about Ms. Lavoie?

(A) She requested a hotel closer to the meeting site.
(B) She will use a car from a newly opened business.
(C) She must pay an extra fee to have a GPS in her vehicle.
(D) She will stay at a hotel on Ivan Street.

190 What is indicated about the rental company on the Web page?

(A) It has partnerships with airlines.
(B) It provides discounts to large groups.
(C) It maintains an impressive safety record.
(D) It has branches throughout Dallas.

GO ON TO THE NEXT PAGE

Charmax – Charcoal air freshener by Spence Inc.

Most air fresheners are made from a mixture of chemicals. Charmax uses 100% activated charcoal to ensure safe and effective results with the following features:

1. Effective – Charmax doesn't cover up the unpleasant odors in your home; it absorbs them into the charcoal, eliminating them from the air. You'll notice a difference within just a few days.

2. Fragrance-free – With Charmax, you won't have to deal with the harsh, artificial odors of most air fresheners. Instead, you can enjoy fresh, pure air.

3. Natural – Charmax contains no chemicals, so it's a non-toxic alternative to other air fresheners on the market.

4. Convenient – Charmax's container is designed to be hung up or sit horizontally, so you can place it anywhere in your home.

5. Long-lasting – With proper care, one bag of Charmax can work continuously for up to one year.

Stock up and save! Buy 10 or more Charmax bags and get 10% off your order.

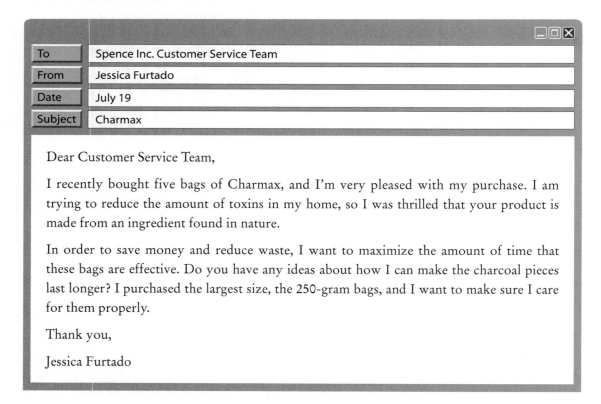

To	Spence Inc. Customer Service Team
From	Jessica Furtado
Date	July 19
Subject	Charmax

Dear Customer Service Team,

I recently bought five bags of Charmax, and I'm very pleased with my purchase. I am trying to reduce the amount of toxins in my home, so I was thrilled that your product is made from an ingredient found in nature.

In order to save money and reduce waste, I want to maximize the amount of time that these bags are effective. Do you have any ideas about how I can make the charcoal pieces last longer? I purchased the largest size, the 250-gram bags, and I want to make sure I care for them properly.

Thank you,

Jessica Furtado

Tips for Using Charmax by Spence Inc.

Extend the life of Charmax by placing the bag in the sun once a month to remove moisture.

Size	Monthly Time Needed in the Sun
50 g	45 minutes
75 g	1 hour
150 g	2 hours
250 g	3 hours

When Charmax reaches the end of its odor-absorbing life, it still hasn't reached the end of its usefulness. You can open the bag, crush the chunks into smaller pieces, and mix the charcoal into the soil of your outdoor flowerbeds.

191 What is true about Charmax?

(A) It comes in a variety of scents.
(B) It is Spence Inc.'s best-selling product.
(C) It comes with a 100% money-back guarantee.
(D) It is eligible for a bulk discount.

192 What is the purpose of the e-mail?

(A) To recommend a change
(B) To ask for some suggestions
(C) To report a problem with a purchase
(D) To place an order for more items

193 What feature of Charmax was Ms. Furtado impressed with?

(A) Feature 1
(B) Feature 2
(C) Feature 3
(D) Feature 4

194 How long should Ms. Furtado leave her Charmax in the sun each month?

(A) For 45 minutes
(B) For 1 hour
(C) For 2 hours
(D) For 3 hours

195 What disposal method for Charmax is recommended by Spence Inc.?

(A) Returning it to the company
(B) Bringing it to a recycling center
(C) Using it in the garden
(D) Adding it to household trash

GO ON TO THE NEXT PAGE

```
E-Mail Message
```

To: All Employees <parksstafflist@parks.najeracity.gov>
From: Ricky Baird <r.baird@najeracity.gov>
Date: April 13
Subject: Please read

With the population expansion of our town, more people are using the city's parks, so it is more essential than ever to keep on top of things.

I would like to share some information with you regarding the Parks Department responsibilities for May. Wesley Donovan has decided to leave our team to pursue a career in running his own landscaping firm. We wish him the best of luck in this endeavor, but it does leave us with a labor shortage as we come into our busy season.

I was able to hire a seasonal worker, Kenton Perry, to handle Mr. Donovan's garden-planting duties, but I still need someone else on short notice to take over the other tasks. If you know of anyone who may be interested, and who can start on May 1, please pass along my contact details.

Thank you!

Ricky

PARK MAINTENANCE TASK	EMPLOYEE	WORKING DAYS
Sports facilities and playground equipment	Yonas Kujawa	Monday, Tuesday, Wednesday, Thursday, Friday
Hedge- and tree-trimming	Linda Harbin	Tuesday, Wednesday, Friday
Mowing and watering	Not Assigned	Tuesday, Friday, Saturday
Garden planting and weeding	Kenton Perry	Monday, Thursday
Electrical repairs and maintenance	Hector Mendoza	Thursday
Parking lot maintenance	Arnold Santana	Monday, Thursday, Saturday

To: Ricky Baird <r.baird@najeracity.gov>
From: Jun Geng <gengjun@tatumpc.com>
Date: April 14
Subject: Parks Department opening

Dear Mr. Baird,

I heard from one of your employees, Hector Mendoza, that you are currently seeking a new staff member for your team. I am interested in applying for the job opening. My former employer, Lou Houchin of LH Inc., can provide you with a testimonial about my job skills and work ethic. You may also wish to speak to Rita Pavone, the director of the community center, where I volunteer on the weekends. I am available to start on the desired date of May 1, or sooner if needed.

I hope to hear from you soon.

Sincerely,

Jun Geng

---

196 What is the purpose of the first e-mail?

(A) To introduce new gardening equipment
(B) To announce a park expansion
(C) To discuss changes in work assignment
(D) To explain a new overtime policy

197 What does Mr. Donovan plan to do?

(A) Recommend a colleague
(B) Train new employees
(C) Move out of town
(D) Start a business

198 What is implied about the seasonal worker that Mr. Baird hired?

(A) He recently received certification.
(B) He will work two days a week.
(C) He may assist Mr. Kujawa with some duties.
(D) He submitted a reference letter from LH Inc.

199 Who first gave Mr. Geng the information about the open position?

(A) Mr. Baird
(B) Mr. Houchin
(C) Mr. Mendoza
(D) Ms. Pavone

200 Which task does Mr. Geng want to take over?

(A) Hedge- and tree-trimming
(B) Mowing and watering
(C) Garden planting and weeding
(D) Parking lot maintenance

GO ON TO THE NEXT PAGE

Actual Test

03

시작 시간	:	
종료 시간	:	

LISTENING TEST

In the Listening test, you will be asked to demonstrate how well you understand spoken English. The entire Listening test will last approximately 45 minutes. There are four parts, and directions are given for each part. You must mark your answers on the separate answer sheet. Do not write your answers in your test book.

PART 1

Directions: For each question in this part, you will hear four statements about a picture in your test book. When you hear the statements, you must select the one statement that best describes what you see in the picture. Then find the number of the question on your answer sheet and mark your answer. The statements will not be printed in your test book and will be spoken only one time.

Example

Sample Answer

Statement (B), "The man is working at a desk," is the best description of the picture, so you should select answer (B) and mark it on your answer sheet.

1

2

GO ON TO THE NEXT PAGE ➤

3

4

5

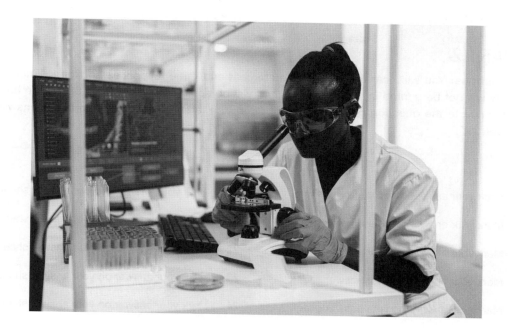

6

GO ON TO THE NEXT PAGE ➤

PART 2

Directions: You will hear a question or statement and three responses spoken in English. They will not be printed in your test book and will be spoken only one time. Select the best response to the question or statement and mark the letter (A), (B), or (C) on your answer sheet.

7	Mark your answer on your answer sheet.	**20**	Mark your answer on your answer sheet.
8	Mark your answer on your answer sheet.	**21**	Mark your answer on your answer sheet.
9	Mark your answer on your answer sheet.	**22**	Mark your answer on your answer sheet.
10	Mark your answer on your answer sheet.	**23**	Mark your answer on your answer sheet.
11	Mark your answer on your answer sheet.	**24**	Mark your answer on your answer sheet.
12	Mark your answer on your answer sheet.	**25**	Mark your answer on your answer sheet.
13	Mark your answer on your answer sheet.	**26**	Mark your answer on your answer sheet.
14	Mark your answer on your answer sheet.	**27**	Mark your answer on your answer sheet.
15	Mark your answer on your answer sheet.	**28**	Mark your answer on your answer sheet.
16	Mark your answer on your answer sheet.	**29**	Mark your answer on your answer sheet.
17	Mark your answer on your answer sheet.	**30**	Mark your answer on your answer sheet.
18	Mark your answer on your answer sheet.	**31**	Mark your answer on your answer sheet.
19	Mark your answer on your answer sheet.		

PART 3

Directions: You will hear some conversations between two or more people. You will be asked to answer three questions about what the speakers say in each conversation. Select the best response to each question and mark the letter (A), (B), (C), or (D) on your answer sheet. The conversations will not be printed in your test book and will be spoken only one time.

32 Which department does the man most likely work in?

(A) Accounting
(B) Human resources
(C) Technical Support
(D) Research and Development

33 According to the man, what are customers doing differently?

(A) They are buying more items online.
(B) They are buying cheaper items.
(C) They are shopping at later times.
(D) They are taking out fewer payment plans.

34 What action do the speakers agree to take?

(A) Developing a new range of products
(B) Starting an advertising campaign
(C) Opening several new stores
(D) Redesigning a Web site

35 What service does the woman offer?

(A) Interior design
(B) Garden landscaping
(C) House cleaning
(D) Property sales

36 Why does the man apologize?

(A) He has another appointment.
(B) His home has no electricity.
(C) He misplaced some materials.
(D) His water has been shut off.

37 What does the woman say she will do?

(A) Inspect a building
(B) Unload a vehicle
(C) Put on special clothing
(D) Purchase supplies

38 Where most likely is the man?

(A) In a supermarket
(B) In a library
(C) In a restaurant
(D) In a university

39 What does the woman imply when she says, "I was just leaving"?

(A) She does not have time to discuss an issue.
(B) She will give the man her table.
(C) She wants the man to accompany her.
(D) She is dissatisfied with a service.

40 What does the woman recommend that the man do?

(A) Purchase a membership
(B) Take a day off work
(C) Buy tickets for an event
(D) Sign up for a class

41 What is the man's job?

(A) A travel agent
(B) A resort employee
(C) A fashion designer
(D) A store clerk

42 What are the speakers mainly discussing?

(A) Store locations
(B) Restaurant reviews
(C) Building plans
(D) Travel itineraries

43 What does the woman request?

(A) A discount coupon
(B) A flight schedule
(C) A city map
(D) A taxi

GO ON TO THE NEXT PAGE

44 Why does the woman congratulate the man?

(A) He won an important contract.
(B) He was given a job promotion.
(C) He recently received an award.
(D) He had some images published.

45 What does the woman want the man to do?

(A) Share a recommendation
(B) Work at the gift shop
(C) Make a donation
(D) Renew a subscription

46 What does the man plan to do tomorrow?

(A) Take a trip
(B) Sign a contract
(C) Send some information
(D) Update a Web site

47 What industry do the speakers work in?

(A) Clothing
(B) Appliances
(C) Computers
(D) Furniture

48 What will Ms. Rourke do tomorrow morning?

(A) Tour a production plant
(B) Return to her company
(C) Meet with shareholders
(D) Attend a product launch

49 What is mentioned about some products?

(A) They are affordably priced.
(B) They are very durable.
(C) They use less power.
(D) They have won awards.

50 What type of business is being discussed?

(A) A cleaning service
(B) A landscaping firm
(C) A Web design company
(D) A hardware store

51 Why does the woman say she is concerned?

(A) A project is behind schedule.
(B) A budget is limited.
(C) An item is sold out.
(D) An area is too small.

52 What does the man say he will do?

(A) Contact a coworker
(B) Prepare a cost estimate
(C) Visit a work site
(D) Change a schedule

53 Who most likely are the women?

(A) Designers
(B) Musicians
(C) Caterers
(D) Photographers

54 What does the man want to know about?

(A) A furniture setup
(B) A delivery schedule
(C) A series of fees
(D) A cancellation period

55 What will the man most likely do next?

(A) Select some colors
(B) Wait for a manager
(C) Sign a contract
(D) Look at some photographs

56 Why does the man say, "Georgina, you're familiar with the Kruger account"?

(A) To make a complaint
(B) To place an order
(C) To thank the woman for her efforts
(D) To request some information

57 What did the man do earlier?

(A) Proofread a proposal
(B) Checked a spreadsheet
(C) Made a phone call
(D) Visited a branch

58 What will the man most likely do next?

(A) Perform some calculations
(B) Read a document
(C) E-mail a colleague
(D) Produce a presentation

59 What will happen at ten o'clock?

(A) An item will be delivered.
(B) A team meeting will be held.
(C) An interview will be conducted.
(D) A client will visit.

60 What problem does the man mention?

(A) He cannot access a room.
(B) He needs help setting up equipment.
(C) His schedule contained an error.
(D) His parking pass has expired.

61 What does the woman suggest doing?

(A) Hiring an assistant
(B) Replacing an ID card
(C) Postponing an event
(D) Reading a user manual

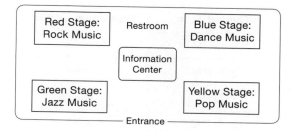

62 What problem does the man mention?

(A) A performance was canceled.
(B) The festival will end soon.
(C) A festival ticket is missing.
(D) The information center is closed.

63 Look at the graphic. Which stage of the music festival will the man go to?

(A) Red Stage
(B) Blue Stage
(C) Green Stage
(D) Yellow Stage

64 Why does the woman say it is a perfect time to arrive at the festival?

(A) The site is less crowded now.
(B) The weather has improved.
(C) The tickets have been discounted.
(D) The main performance has just begun.

GO ON TO THE NEXT PAGE

Guided Tour	Remaining Tickets
1:00 P.M.	Sold Out
2:30 P.M.	4 tickets
4:00 P.M.	2 tickets
5:30 P.M.	8 tickets

NO DUMPING!

Monday-Thursday: 6 P.M. to 9 A.M.
Friday: 9 A.M. to 4 P.M.
Saturday: 5 P.M. to 8 A.M.
Sunday: 9 A.M. to 8 P.M.

65 What are the speakers interested in visiting?

(A) A science museum
(B) A sports venue
(C) A historic home
(D) A television studio

66 What do the speakers have to do?

(A) Bring a room key
(B) Make a dinner reservation
(C) Attend a speech
(D) Check a shuttle time

67 Look at the graphic. When do the speakers want to go on a tour?

(A) 1:00 P.M.
(B) 2:30 P.M.
(C) 4:00 P.M.
(D) 5:30 P.M.

68 Why did the man decide to dump the appliances himself?

(A) To avoid a fee
(B) To save time
(C) To help a colleague
(D) To thank a client

69 Look at the graphic. What day is it?

(A) Thursday
(B) Friday
(C) Saturday
(D) Sunday

70 According to the man, what do the speakers still need to do?

(A) Order materials
(B) Pick up tools
(C) Replace some flooring
(D) Install a device

PART 4

Directions: You will hear some talks given by a single speaker. You will be asked to answer three questions about what the speaker says in each talk. Select the best response to each question and mark the letter (A), (B), (C), or (D) on your answer sheet. The talks will not be printed in your test book and will be spoken only one time.

71 Where most likely are the listeners?

(A) At an airport
(B) At a taxi stand
(C) At a bus stop
(D) At a train station

72 What has caused a delay?

(A) Severe weather
(B) A late arrival
(C) A computer error
(D) An employee absence

73 What are the listeners asked to prepare?

(A) A government ID
(B) A luggage tag
(C) A sales receipt
(D) A boarding pass

74 What is the topic of the broadcast?

(A) A highway project
(B) A shopping center
(C) A sport stadium
(D) A manufacturing facility

75 According to the broadcast, what benefit do city officials expect?

(A) Tax revenues will increase.
(B) Pollution will be reduced.
(C) New jobs will be created.
(D) Residents will be healthier.

76 What will be broadcast next?

(A) A traffic update
(B) A weather report
(C) An advertisement
(D) A debate

77 Where most likely does the speaker work?

(A) At a factory
(B) At a library
(C) At a health club
(D) At a supermarket

78 What can the listeners receive for a limited time?

(A) A drink
(B) A membership card
(C) A t-shirt
(D) A catalog

79 What will happen at 6 P.M.?

(A) A discount sale
(B) A prize draw
(C) Web site maintenance
(D) An orientation class

80 What kind of business does the speaker work for?

(A) A delivery company
(B) A cell phone provider
(C) A supermarket
(D) A vacation resort

81 Why is the speaker calling?

(A) To hire some staff members
(B) To purchase some ingredients
(C) To confirm business hours
(D) To return an order

82 Why does the speaker request a phone call?

(A) To negotiate a price
(B) To reply to a complaint
(C) To confirm a delivery date
(D) To inquire about a business location

GO ON TO THE NEXT PAGE

83 What does the speaker imply when she says, "You should have no problem starting work at nine"?

(A) A team is well-trained.
(B) A system has been installed.
(C) A manual has clear instructions.
(D) A meeting will be short.

84 What happened at the business last week?

(A) Sales were much lower than usual.
(B) A new service for customers was launched.
(C) Financial information was analyzed.
(D) Some orders were not filled on time.

85 What will the listeners have an opportunity to practice?

(A) Discussing decorating options
(B) Reading a profit report
(C) Packaging baked goods
(D) Placing a rush order

86 What kind of goods does the speaker's company sell?

(A) Clothing
(B) Vitamins
(C) Electronics
(D) Cosmetics

87 According to the speaker, what have customers requested?

(A) Faster delivery times
(B) Less expensive products
(C) A variety of sizes
(D) Environmentally friendly packaging

88 What will be sent to the listeners later today?

(A) A sample contract
(B) An updated catalog
(C) A list of duties
(D) A logo design

89 According to the speaker, what will take place on Saturday?

(A) A grand opening event
(B) A staff orientation
(C) A client presentation
(D) A company outing

90 What does the speaker mean when he says, "I am not taking much with me"?

(A) He is happy to carry some items.
(B) He thinks a task will not take long.
(C) He would appreciate some assistance.
(D) He believes a price will be low.

91 What does the speaker ask the listener to do?

(A) Send a document
(B) Return the call
(C) Make an announcement
(D) Update a schedule

92 What is the broadcast mainly about?

(A) Financial management
(B) Party planning ideas
(C) Fashion
(D) Interior design tips

93 Why does the speaker say the listeners might be surprised?

(A) A new product has been launched.
(B) A common belief is wrong.
(C) A mistake was made on a previous show.
(D) A special guest will join the broadcast.

94 Why does the speaker say, "We'll be discussing that next week"?

(A) To invite listeners to call the station
(B) To signal the end of an interview
(C) To promote a future broadcast
(D) To demonstrate a specific product

Cheddar Cheese Sauce
Preparation time: 15 minutes

Ingredients:

500 milliliters of milk
4 tablespoons of plain flour
50 grams of butter
100 grams of grated cheese

Directions:

1. Mix ingredients over medium heat
2. Allow to cool before serving

July 25	July 26	July 27	July 28
☀	☀	☁	☂
Sunny	Sunny	Cloudy	Rain

95 Where is the talk most likely taking place?

(A) At a publishing firm
(B) At a restaurant
(C) At a culinary school
(D) At a television station

96 What problem does the speaker address?

(A) A business is becoming less profitable.
(B) A product will no longer be available.
(C) Several complaints have been received.
(D) Employees failed to follow a procedure correctly.

97 Look at the graphic. Which information will most likely be changed?

(A) 15 minutes
(B) 4 tablespoons
(C) 50 grams
(D) 100 grams

98 What kind of event is the speaker discussing?

(A) A singing contest
(B) A dance performance
(C) An art exhibition
(D) A film festival

99 What does the speaker say is available on a Web site?

(A) A parking pass
(B) A seating chart
(C) A list of venues
(D) An enrollment form

100 Look at the graphic. When is the event being held?

(A) July 25
(B) July 26
(C) July 27
(D) July 28

This is the end of the Listening test. Turn to Part 5 in your test book.

GO ON TO THE NEXT PAGE ▶

READING TEST

In the Reading test, you will read a variety of texts and answer several different types of reading comprehension questions. The entire Reading test will last 75 minutes. There are three parts, and directions are given for each part. You are encouraged to answer as many questions as possible within the time allowed.

You must mark your answers on the separate answer sheet. Do not write your answers in your test book.

PART 5

Directions: A word or phrase is missing in each of the sentences below. Four answer choices are given below each sentence. Select the best answer to complete the sentence. Then mark the letter (A), (B), (C), or (D) on your answer sheet.

101 During the off-season at Longford Beach, Ms. Covello runs her small café by -------.

(A) she
(B) her
(C) herself
(D) hers

102 The Pointsman Museum of Modern Art in Baltimore ------- more than 500,000 visitors annually.

(A) observes
(B) attracts
(C) features
(D) advances

103 The producer's assistant will answer any scheduling ------- regarding next month's rehearsals.

(A) inquire
(B) inquiries
(C) inquirer
(D) inquiringly

104 Roland Electronics will reveal ------- information about its next line of refrigerators at the Tech Valley Expo.

(A) loyal
(B) spacious
(C) detailed
(D) experienced

105 As the sales team failed to reach its goal, it will ------- the number of new hires for next year.

(A) reducing
(B) reduces
(C) be reducing
(D) be reduced

106 ------- negative reviews, the Vesper 7 mobile phone has become one of the top-selling products this year.

(A) Although
(B) Despite
(C) Unless
(D) Even if

107 Poor character development was a major ------- among critics for the latest movie *Pablo's Secrets*.

(A) complain
(B) complaint
(C) complaining
(D) complained

108 According to the company's Web site, its bathroom tiles are available in a ------- of styles.

(A) phase
(B) distribution
(C) connection
(D) variety

109 The agreement between CPA Manufacturing and Holster Industries has undergone ------- revisions.

(A) multiply
(B) multiplied
(C) multiple
(D) multiplying

110 Please update your profile with any new information ------- we may keep our directory current.

(A) even if
(B) so that
(C) yet
(D) while

111 To leave the office building quickly during the lunch break, ------- the stairs instead of the elevator.

(A) used
(B) uses
(C) use
(D) using

112 Crowds at Helsinki Airport will soon be more manageable as the construction of a second terminal is ------- complete.

(A) highly
(B) usually
(C) recently
(D) nearly

113 When you order a storage unit from our Web site, it will be fully assembled ------- delivery.

(A) wherever
(B) prior to
(C) previous
(D) in addition

114 Nelson Tennis Club keeps its membership fees ------- for anyone interested in learning the sport.

(A) necessary
(B) adverse
(C) potential
(D) affordable

115 Among Forge Coffee's numerous competitors, ------- present a more significant challenge than Great Lakes Café.

(A) little
(B) few
(C) both
(D) other

116 The apartment is located ------- Turner Station, which is only two stops away from the downtown area.

(A) to
(B) near
(C) next
(D) between

117 International orders shipped with Q-Mart's express service should arrive in ------- three to five days.

(A) finally
(B) rapidly
(C) briefly
(D) approximately

118 The floor plans and measurements of the shopping mall have been made available for your -------.

(A) indication
(B) subject
(C) reference
(D) presence

119 Ms. Romanov made a ------- offer on the lakeside condominium, but the sellers went with another buyer.

(A) competed
(B) competitive
(C) competition
(D) competitively

120 The holiday parade will start at 10 A.M. on Saturday morning, ------- the weather remains nice.

(A) unless
(B) as if
(C) according to
(D) as long as

GO ON TO THE NEXT PAGE

121 Triumph Software is rumored to unveil a ------- new operating system later this week.

(A) completes
(B) completing
(C) completely
(D) completion

122 Factory workers assigned to the cooling and ventilation division will ------- the company's new line of air conditioners.

(A) allow
(B) assemble
(C) argue
(D) cooperate

123 The new director of the engineering department is Dr. Bryan Evenson, ------- research on AI systems has won numerous awards.

(A) our
(B) each
(C) who
(D) whose

124 Mr. Kantze edits the business contents of *The Daily State*, ------- Ms. Dupree oversees the articles covering entertainment topics.

(A) in spite of
(B) what
(C) while
(D) then

125 Hancock Accounting provides last-minute services for clients who are too ------- to file their income taxes.

(A) busy
(B) busiest
(C) busier
(D) busyness

126 Staff members who have already earned certification in first aid are ------- from tomorrow's training session.

(A) ready
(B) exempt
(C) complimentary
(D) apparent

127 Ladder Burger's decision to change its French fry recipe caused a dramatic ------- in overall sales.

(A) funding
(B) market
(C) impact
(D) decline

128 Our new environmental policy has been ------- successful as office waste has been reduced by 50%.

(A) markedly
(B) diligently
(C) jointly
(D) affordably

129 In the event of heavy rain, all the outdoor performances ------- until further notice.

(A) should postpone
(B) postponing
(C) will be postponed
(D) have postponed

130 After Ms. Kollstad selects a submission for publication, it is ------- to the lead editor for approval.

(A) kept
(B) located
(C) eliminated
(D) forwarded

PART 6

Directions: Read the texts that follow. A word, phrase, or sentence is missing in parts of each text. Four answer choices for each question are given below the text. Select the best answer to complete the text. Then mark the letter (A), (B), (C), or (D) on your answer sheet.

Questions 131-134 refer to the following e-mail.

To: cmorrisey@westburypost.com
From: service@movie-web1.com
Date: September 6
Subject: RE: Please help

I am writing to you because you ------- an issue with logging on to your video streaming service.
        131.
Your current package only allows you to sign in on one device at a time, so the system is working

correctly. It will ------- other sign-in attempts if another device is using the account. ------- you
     132.   **133.**

experience this issue, make sure you have logged out of the account on other devices and try

again. -------.
    134.

Sincerely,

The MovieWeb Team

131 (A) reporting
    (B) will report
    (C) reported
    (D) report

132 (A) share
    (B) depart
    (C) guarantee
    (D) reject

133 (A) Though
    (B) What
    (C) Whenever
    (D) Already

134 (A) Your password must contain one capital
        letter and one symbol.
    (B) We are adding new titles to our movie
        library daily.
    (C) The amount you overpaid will be
        refunded within a few days.
    (D) If this advice does not resolve the issue,
        please let us know.

Are you looking for a way to give your home a modern and classy look? Heartland Furnishings

is the solution! -------. These are available in numerous popular colors. So, you can find the right
        135.

------- for any color scheme.
   136.

------- Heartland Furnishings, we understand that it can be difficult to imagine how a new item
   137.

will fit into your overall décor. That's ------- we allow customers to return products within 30 days
        138.

if they no longer want them. For clear instructions on how to make a return, visit www.heartland-

furnishings.com.

135 (A) We sell rugs, curtains, and other household accessories in a wide range of styles.
(B) Each employee has extensive experience in the interior design industry.
(C) Our delivery crew can drop off your order at your home or office any weekday.
(D) Be sure to sign up for our membership program to earn loyalty points.

136 (A) place
(B) additions
(C) item
(D) parts

137 (A) As
(B) To
(C) On
(D) At

138 (A) when
(B) why
(C) what
(D) how

Questions 139-142 refer to the following article.

City manager Don Reynolds announced that work will commence on Grossman Park next week.

One of the first things to be done is to establish new lanes for cyclists. In the past, they ------- to
139.

share trails with walkers, but will have their own bicycle paths soon. Also, three new restrooms

will be built in the park. They will be located ------- near areas that receive high traffic from
140.

park visitors. Mr. Reynolds said, "We want to make the park safer, cleaner, and more fun for all

residents. -------, we would like much more people to come here. We encourage everyone to
141.

spend lots of time outdoors." -------.
142.

139 (A) force
    (B) will force
    (C) had forced
    (D) were forced

140 (A) strategy
    (B) strategic
    (C) strategized
    (D) strategically

141 (A) Instead
    (B) In addition
    (C) In contrast
    (D) For instance

142 (A) It has been the largest park in the
        downtown area.
    (B) Mr. Reynolds is concerned about the
        maintenance issue.
    (C) He expects the work to be finished no
        later than June 1.
    (D) There are more than ten parks located
        throughout the city.

GO ON TO THE NEXT PAGE

To: susan.logan@thehomeshop.com
From: r_dexter@dgcookware.com
Date: March 20
Subject: DG Cookware

Dear Ms. Logan,

DG Cookware is committed to ------- top-quality cooking pots, and our products would
143.
make an excellent addition to your shop's inventory. We offer a variety of sizes, and all of our

cookware is made of iron. As this ------- is very durable, the pots last for a long time and can
144.
withstand high heat. Based on the other products you currently have in stock, I believe that your

customers would ------- be interested in our line. I recommend starting out with about fifty pots
145.
as a test run. -------. Please let me know when would be a good time to call you to discuss this
146.
opportunity further.

Warmest regards,

Rafael Dexter

Senior Salesperson, DG Cookware

143 (A) provide
(B) providing
(C) provides
(D) provisions

144 (A) material
(B) entry
(C) baggage
(D) facility

145 (A) quite
(B) once
(C) indeed
(D) enough

146 (A) If you do, please fill out the refund
request form in full.
(B) However, you can certainly place a larger
initial order if you prefer.
(C) Clearly, the skill of the cook should be
taken into account.
(D) We have been in business for the past
three decades.

PART 7

Directions: In this part you will read a selection of texts, such as magazine and newspaper articles, e-mails, and instant messages. Each text or set of texts is followed by several questions. Select the best answer for each question and mark the letter (A), (B), (C), or (D) on your answer sheet.

Questions 147-148 refer to the following information.

Seaside Coffee Shop

739 Kenwood Street
438-555-8791
www.seasidecoffeeshop.com

"The best brew in town!"

Opening Hours
Monday–Friday: 7 A.M.–9 P.M.
Saturday: 8 A.M.–10 P.M.
Sunday: 10 A.M.–8 P.M.

Private Meeting Room Availability
Monday–Friday: 9 A.M.–8 P.M.
Saturday: 10 A.M.–9 P.M.
Sunday: 10 A.M.–6 P.M.

Call in advance to have your order ready.
Buy six or more beverages to get an automatic 15% off!

---

147 According to the information, how can customers be eligible for a discount?

(A) By bringing in their own to-go cup
(B) By purchasing more than five drinks
(C) By downloading a coupon from a Web site
(D) By completing a questionnaire

148 When can customers use the private meeting room?

(A) On Tuesday at 7 A.M.
(B) On Wednesday at 8 A.M.
(C) On Friday at 7 P.M.
(D) On Sunday at 7 P.M.

GO ON TO THE NEXT PAGE

Cedar Golf Resort
58 Calvin Street
Bella Vista, CA 96073

Craig Ward
2786 South Street
Bella Vista, CA 96073

Dear Mr. Ward,

We have received your letter regarding the incident that occurred on July 15. We were very sorry to find out that your car was hit by a golf ball while it was parked in our parking lot, causing a dent in the hood.

Our resort does its best to ensure that members only play in the designated areas in order to avoid such problems. However, as stated in our membership agreement and posted throughout the parking lot, visitors park in the lot at their own risk. Therefore, Cedar Golf Resort takes no responsibility in this matter and is not liable for repair costs according to our in-house rules.

However, we regret that you had a negative experience at our resort and would like to make a gesture of goodwill. Please accept the enclosed gift certificate with our compliments. It can be used at the clubhouse for meals and beverages. We hope that you will continue to make Cedar Golf Resort your primary site for golfing. If I can assist you in any other way, please do not hesitate to contact me again.

Sincerely,

Jason Kirby

Jason Kirby

149 Why did Mr. Kirby send the letter?

(A) To promote a new service
(B) To request a payment
(C) To clarify a policy
(D) To prompt a membership renewal

150 What problem is mentioned in the letter?

(A) Mr. Ward missed his golf lesson.
(B) Mr. Ward parked in a prohibited area.
(C) Mr. Ward's membership has expired.
(D) Mr. Ward's car was damaged.

151 What has been sent with Mr. Kirby's letter?

(A) A parking pass
(B) A partial refund
(C) A gift certificate
(D) A membership contract

Emerald Spa Job Openings

Emerald Spa has been one of the area's top spas for the past 15 years. We offer a variety of relaxation and beauty treatments as well as an on-site vegan café. Due to the growing demand for our services, we are currently seeking two full-time massage therapists. The therapists' responsibilities include evaluating the client's needs, manipulating the client's soft tissue and muscles, and advising the client on at-home stretching techniques. Applications will be accepted until September 1. Interviews will be held between September 4 and 8 with the general manager. Out-of-town applicants must make arrangements to visit the spa, as phone interviews are not accepted.

152 What is true about Emerald Spa?

(A) It is the only spa in the area.
(B) It has operated for more than a decade.
(C) It has recently added a dining establishment.
(D) It is moving to a larger facility.

153 What is indicated about interviews?

(A) They will be completed by September 1.
(B) They will run for approximately two weeks.
(C) They will be led by the HR team.
(D) They must be conducted in person.

GO ON TO THE NEXT PAGE

Questions 154-155 refer to the following online chat discussion.

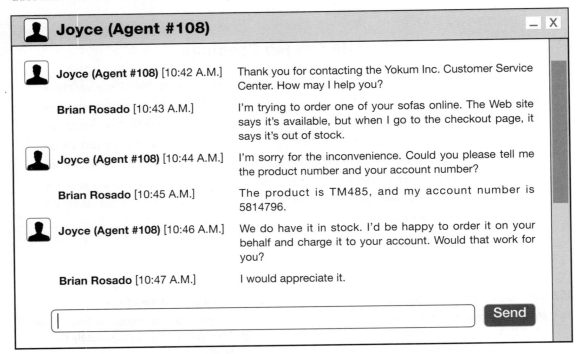

Joyce (Agent #108)   — X

Joyce (Agent #108) [10:42 A.M.]   Thank you for contacting the Yokum Inc. Customer Service Center. How may I help you?

Brian Rosado [10:43 A.M.]   I'm trying to order one of your sofas online. The Web site says it's available, but when I go to the checkout page, it says it's out of stock.

Joyce (Agent #108) [10:44 A.M.]   I'm sorry for the inconvenience. Could you please tell me the product number and your account number?

Brian Rosado [10:45 A.M.]   The product is TM485, and my account number is 5814796.

Joyce (Agent #108) [10:46 A.M.]   We do have it in stock. I'd be happy to order it on your behalf and charge it to your account. Would that work for you?

Brian Rosado [10:47 A.M.]   I would appreciate it.

Send

154 What kind of business most likely is Yokum Inc.?

(A) A cosmetics company
(B) A furniture store
(C) A clothing company
(D) An electronics store

155 At 10:47 A.M., what does Mr. Rosado mean when he writes, "I would appreciate it"?

(A) He needs assistance in restarting his computer.
(B) He is grateful that an item can be returned.
(C) He accepts the proposed solution to an issue.
(D) He would like the agent to cancel an order.

A day of discovery!

The Cullingworth Historical Society (CHS) is a nonprofit organization dedicated to teaching others about historically significant places in our area. On the first and third Saturday of the summer months (June – August), we offer a guided tour of Cullingworth Castle, Fort Tempsford, and the Bramwell Tin Mine.

The excursion begins at 9 A.M. and ends at approximately 4 P.M. Lunch is included in the fee. Each guide takes an intensive 3-month course to learn all about sites and their background, and most of our guides have degrees in related fields as well. You can arrange for a private group or sign up with a general group. Please note that some parts of the tour include stairs or stony walkways that are not level or flat. Everyone must have the physical capacity to navigate these safely.

We offer a full refund when a tour is canceled due to extreme weather. If you signed up but aren't sure whether or not your tour has been canceled, please check our Web site at www.cullingworthhs.org, where we provide such information. Call 672-555-1306 to make your booking today!

156 What is the advertisement about?

(A) A series of history-based lectures
(B) A discount on membership to a group
(C) An opportunity to see historical sites
(D) A class on local history

157 What are the group members expected to do?

(A) Attend a safety training session
(B) Bring along a packed lunch
(C) Meet group members in advance
(D) Walk on uneven surfaces

158 What is true about CHS?

(A) It announces cancellations online.
(B) It is currently seeking more employees.
(C) It has branches across the country.
(D) It opened about three months ago.

GO ON TO THE NEXT PAGE

Questions 159-160 refer to the following e-mail.

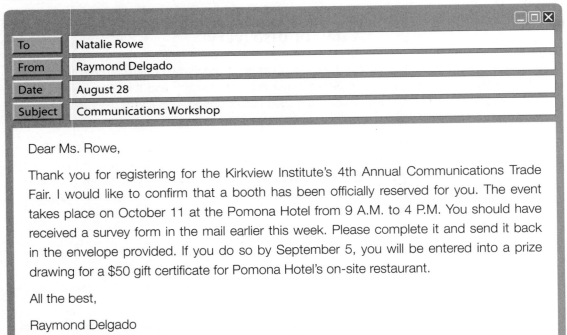

To: Natalie Rowe
From: Raymond Delgado
Date: August 28
Subject: Communications Workshop

Dear Ms. Rowe,

Thank you for registering for the Kirkview Institute's 4th Annual Communications Trade Fair. I would like to confirm that a booth has been officially reserved for you. The event takes place on October 11 at the Pomona Hotel from 9 A.M. to 4 P.M. You should have received a survey form in the mail earlier this week. Please complete it and send it back in the envelope provided. If you do so by September 5, you will be entered into a prize drawing for a $50 gift certificate for Pomona Hotel's on-site restaurant.

All the best,

Raymond Delgado

---

159 Why did Mr. Delgado send the e-mail?
(A) To inform a participant of changes to a schedule
(B) To invite Ms. Rowe to give a talk at an event
(C) To make travel arrangements for an upcoming trade fair
(D) To acknowledge the success of a registration process

160 What does Mr. Delgado ask Ms. Rowe to do?
(A) Contact a hotel
(B) Return a document
(C) Send a payment
(D) Update an address

Questions 161-163 refer to the following advertisement.

Find your new home at Mariposa Apartments!

2705 Boone Avenue, Baltimore, MD 21212

Mariposa Apartments is a newly built apartment complex within walking distance to Caldwell Park and other neighborhood amenities. —[1]—. Each unit comes with a state-of-the-art dishwasher, refrigerator, and microwave. Tenants also have their own assigned parking spot in our underground lot, which is monitored 24 hours a day. There are assigned lockers in the basement where tenants can keep bulky items such as bicycles or boxes.

Mariposa Apartments was created with affordability in mind. The building is mostly made up of one-bedroom apartments. —[2]—. All tenants can enjoy a peaceful environment with beautiful landscaping and a small picnic area. Photos of the grounds as well as individual apartment units are available at www.mariposaapt.com/gallery. —[3]—.

All rentals are being handled by Jill Lampley of our property management team. Ms. Lampley is happy to show you around the site anytime, so call 555-4817 to book a viewing. Don't miss your chance to live in a beautiful building in a popular neighborhood. —[4]—. Make the move to Mariposa Apartments!

161 What is NOT mentioned as an amenity of Mariposa Apartments?

(A) Modern appliances
(B) Secure parking
(C) A fitness center
(D) Additional storage

162 According to the advertisement, why should interested parties contact Ms. Lampley?

(A) To arrange a tour
(B) To request some photos
(C) To submit an application
(D) To renew a contract

163 In which of the positions marked [1], [2], [3], and [4] does the following sentence best belong?

"Larger units are available but are expected to be rented out quickly."

(A) [1]
(B) [2]
(C) [3]
(D) [4]

The National Hospitality Association (NHA), with support from the Glencairn Foundation, is hosting a series of workshops from Wednesday, April 10, to Saturday, April 13. This event is an excellent way for people overseeing luxury accommodations to learn about how to attract more guests to their site.

All workshops will take place at Viewmount Conference Center in Montreal. Participants will be assigned to small groups and work together on several tasks throughout the event. On the final day, groups will give a presentation on their project and receive feedback from the audience.

Our instructors include Jane Lewis from the University of Toronto; Bethany Landis, the head of Ottawa-based Landis Travel; and Reynaldo Fontaine, who launched the popular chain Cabana Inn from his hometown of Calgary. Mr. Fontaine has also written the best-seller *Chain Reaction*, and he will be signing copies on the first day of the event.

To register for this exciting event, visit www.nationalhospitality.ca.

164 For whom is the notice probably intended?

(A) Business professors
(B) Travel agents
(C) Hotel managers
(D) Investment bankers

165 Where will a workshop be held?

(A) In Calgary
(B) In Montreal
(C) In Ottawa
(D) In Toronto

166 What can participants do on the last day of the event?

(A) Watch an award ceremony
(B) Present their projects
(C) Meet the NHA president
(D) Tour a university

167 When will Mr. Fontaine sign books?

(A) April 10
(B) April 11
(C) April 12
(D) April 13

Questions 168-171 refer to the following online chat discussion.

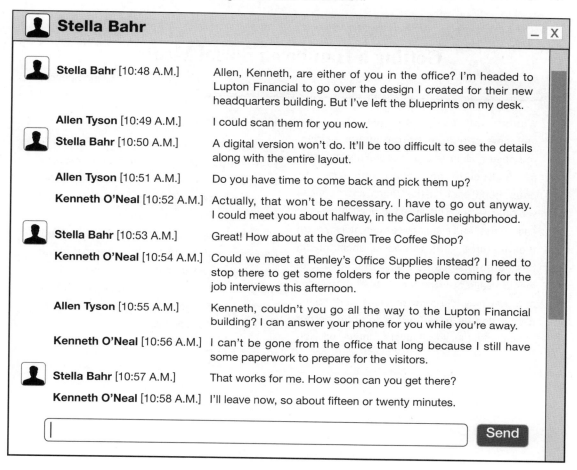

Stella Bahr [10:48 A.M.]   Allen, Kenneth, are either of you in the office? I'm headed to Lupton Financial to go over the design I created for their new headquarters building. But I've left the blueprints on my desk.

Allen Tyson [10:49 A.M.]   I could scan them for you now.

Stella Bahr [10:50 A.M.]   A digital version won't do. It'll be too difficult to see the details along with the entire layout.

Allen Tyson [10:51 A.M.]   Do you have time to come back and pick them up?

Kenneth O'Neal [10:52 A.M.]   Actually, that won't be necessary. I have to go out anyway. I could meet you about halfway, in the Carlisle neighborhood.

Stella Bahr [10:53 A.M.]   Great! How about at the Green Tree Coffee Shop?

Kenneth O'Neal [10:54 A.M.]   Could we meet at Renley's Office Supplies instead? I need to stop there to get some folders for the people coming for the job interviews this afternoon.

Allen Tyson [10:55 A.M.]   Kenneth, couldn't you go all the way to the Lupton Financial building? I can answer your phone for you while you're away.

Kenneth O'Neal [10:56 A.M.]   I can't be gone from the office that long because I still have some paperwork to prepare for the visitors.

Stella Bahr [10:57 A.M.]   That works for me. How soon can you get there?

Kenneth O'Neal [10:58 A.M.]   I'll leave now, so about fifteen or twenty minutes.

Send

168 Who most likely is Ms. Bahr?

(A) A financial consultant
(B) A city official
(C) An architect
(D) A lawyer

169 At 10:50 A.M., what does Ms. Bahr most likely mean when she writes, "A digital version won't do"?

(A) She is concerned that her computer won't work.
(B) She would like to present the original blueprints.
(C) She does not know how to use some software.
(D) She thinks a presentation is too boring.

170 Where do Ms. Bahr and Mr. O'Neal agree to meet?

(A) At Lupton Financial's office
(B) At a coffee shop
(C) At Ms. Bahr's office
(D) At an office supply store

171 What is Mr. O'Neal preparing for?

(A) A survey of some customers
(B) An inspection from an advisor
(C) A meeting with a new client
(D) A visit from some job candidates

GO ON TO THE NEXT PAGE

Getting a Handle on Social Media

by Gloria Spencer

Whether your business is just a few team members or a large staff in multiple cities, you need a clear and purposeful social media policy. Social media can be an excellent promotional tool for the goods and services you offer. —[1]—. The sites and applications are easy to use, and even novices can quickly learn their features. —[2]—. However, social media has its downsides as well. Personal social media usage at work can distract employees and they may idle away precious work hours. It can also be harmful if a company is not careful about its social media content, possibly causing offense.

The solution? Create a policy that protects your company while still giving employees the freedom to express themselves. —[3]—. For employees operating corporate social media accounts, the policy should make clear what should and should not be shared. Users should be particularly careful about exposing the private data of a company. —[4]—. Once the policy is established, review it with staff members once in a while so that they remember the guidelines.

172 Who most likely are the intended readers of this article?

(A) Business owners
(B) Web site developers
(C) Financial experts
(D) Job recruiters

173 What is NOT mentioned about social media in the article?

(A) It can waste time.
(B) It is user-friendly.
(C) It can promote services.
(D) It is free for users.

174 According to the article, what should be done periodically?

(A) Researching popular social media sites
(B) Reminding employees about a policy
(C) Updating company-owned computer equipment
(D) Checking the level of Internet usage

175 In which of the positions marked [1], [2], [3], and [4] does the following sentence best belong?

"For example, sensitive information such as images of prototypes should not be posted online."

(A) [1]
(B) [2]
(C) [3]
(D) [4]

GO ON TO THE NEXT PAGE

Questions 176-180 refer to the following advertisement and e-mail.

NEW ITEMS!   NEW ITEMS!   NEW ITEMS!

Ellsworth Cosmetics

Greenville Mall #A239 (next to JD Department Store)

Be the first of your friends to try the new spring line from Ellsworth Cosmetics. All of our products are made from non-toxic ingredients because we value the health of our customers and of the environment.

Shimmer (Item 624): This scented oil enhances your skin tone and gives you a healthy glow.
Revive (Item 625): This floral-scented face cream provides all-day moisture and a smooth finish.
Nourish (Item 626): This daily face wash dissolves makeup and grime, leaving your skin feeling clean and soft.
Pamper (Item 627): This lip gloss gives you a touch of color while also moisturizing your lips and providing sun protection.

Great products await you online and in our store. And if you spend more than $50 in any single transaction, you'll get a free Ellsworth makeup bag packed with samples.

E-Mail Message

To: help@ellworthcosm.com
From: carlanavarre@wesley-media.com
Date: April 2
Subject: Product issue

Dear Customer Service Team,

On March 29, I placed an order for your new face cream online (order #24671). When it was delivered this morning, I saw that the tube had a hole in it and that the cream was leaking everywhere. I have attached a photo of the issue. Please mail another tube of the cream to me, since this one is not usable. I would really appreciate it if I could receive it by April 5, as I plan to take a vacation on April 6, and I'd like to take this product with me.

Thank you,

Carla Navarre

176 In the advertisement, the word "value" in paragraph 1, line 2, is closest in meaning to

(A) comply with
(B) pay for
(C) care about
(D) participate in

177 How can customers get a free gift?

(A) By signing up for a newsletter
(B) By writing a product review
(C) By recommending the business to others
(D) By spending a certain amount

178 When did Ms. Navarre notice the damaged packaging?

(A) On March 29
(B) On April 2
(C) On April 5
(D) On April 6

179 Which item did Ms. Navarre purchase?

(A) Shimmer
(B) Revive
(C) Nourish
(D) Pamper

180 What does Ms. Navarre ask the customer service team to do?

(A) Send a replacement item
(B) Issue a full refund
(C) Explain a return process
(D) Provide usage instructions

GO ON TO THE NEXT PAGE

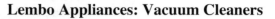

Lembo Appliances: Vacuum Cleaners

Lembo Appliances offers a range of vacuums to suit a variety of needs. Our award-winning upright and stick designs continue to be best-sellers. Check out all of our models below.

14F Handheld Vacuum

This compact vacuum is perfect for cleaning up small messes quickly as well as getting into tight spaces. It is bagless, meaning you can easily remove and empty the collection chamber.

360C Canister Vacuum

Our most versatile model, this vacuum has a long hose to help you get to hard-to-reach areas. Throughout the month of October, customers can get a free promotional pack of accessories for this model (Retail Value: $19.99). E-mail promopack@lemboapp.com with your name, mailing address, and receipt number.

750R Stick Vacuum

We recommend installing the wall-mounted docking station in an accessible place to make it easy to keep this cordless vacuum fully charged and to grab it for a quick cleanup.

2000A Upright Vacuum

A powerful motor gives this vacuum excellent suction to help you tackle even the toughest jobs. It's perfect for both everyday use and deep cleaning.

You can find Lembo vacuums at our trusted partners below:

Electronics World
381 Oakway Street
Baltimore, MD 21237

Tech Time
863 Hillview Avenue
Philadelphia, PA 19106

Accessories Express
6001 Edington Avenue
New York, NY 10036

R-Max
457 Rainbow Boulevard
Washington, D.C. 20032

To:	promopack@lemboapp.com
From:	jwendel@karlata.com
Date:	October 14
Subject:	October offer

Dear Lembo Appliances,

I recently purchased one of your vacuums at the store down the street from my apartment. I was happy to discover on your Web site that I am eligible for some free accessories. I would like to receive them at the following address: Janice Wendel, 865 Pearcy Street, Unit 103, Philadelphia, PA 19106. My receipt number is 645801258.

Thank you,

Janice Wendel

181 What is true about Lembo Appliances?

(A) It has four manufacturing facilities.
(B) It has been recognized for its designs.
(C) It provides discounts on bulk purchases.
(D) It will launch a new vacuum soon.

182 What is implied about the docking station?

(A) It can be attached to a wall.
(B) It must be purchased separately.
(C) It works with all vacuum models.
(D) It comes in various sizes.

183 What is the purpose of the e-mail?

(A) To inquire about a warranty
(B) To report some damage to a device
(C) To order an additional battery
(D) To request some vacuum parts

184 Where most likely did Ms. Wendel purchase a vacuum?

(A) Electronics World
(B) Accessories Express
(C) Tech Time
(D) R-Max

185 What style of vacuum did Ms. Wendel purchase?

(A) 14F Handheld
(B) 360C Canister
(C) 750R Stick
(D) 2000A Upright

GO ON TO THE NEXT PAGE

Questions 186-190 refer to the following e-mails and log sheet.

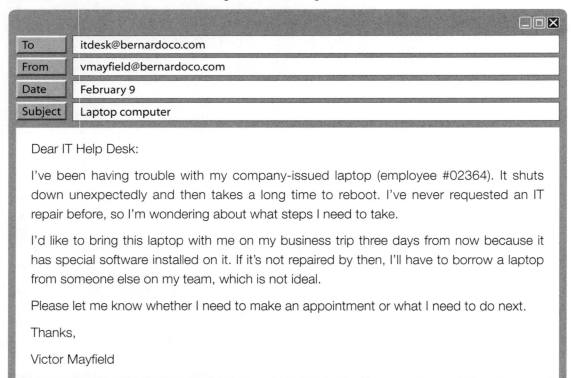

To	itdesk@bernardoco.com
From	vmayfield@bernardoco.com
Date	February 9
Subject	Laptop computer

Dear IT Help Desk:

I've been having trouble with my company-issued laptop (employee #02364). It shuts down unexpectedly and then takes a long time to reboot. I've never requested an IT repair before, so I'm wondering about what steps I need to take.

I'd like to bring this laptop with me on my business trip three days from now because it has special software installed on it. If it's not repaired by then, I'll have to borrow a laptop from someone else on my team, which is not ideal.

Please let me know whether I need to make an appointment or what I need to do next.

Thanks,

Victor Mayfield

IT Help Desk Activity Log: February 10
Technician: Jason Baird

Employee Number	Department	Description	Estimated Working Time
01258	Human Resources	Replacement of laptop screen	25 minutes
01976	Design	Software installation on desktop computer	20 minutes
02364	Marketing	Analysis of malfunctioning laptop	35 minutes
01807	Accounting	Printer setup	10 minutes

To	vmayfield@bernardoco.com
From	jbaird@bernardoco.com
Date	February 10
Subject	Help Desk Update

Dear Mr. Mayfield,

After checking your IT issue, I have found that the problem is due to a broken fan. This is causing the device to overheat. I've placed an order for a replacement component, and it will arrive in four days. As a rough estimate, it will take about an hour to complete the repair once I have the necessary part. Please note that all repair costs will be covered by the office's general budget, rather than your department budget, because the device is more than three years old. I'll be in touch as soon as I'm ready to make the repair.

Jason

186 Why did Mr. Mayfield send the first e-mail?

(A) To change an appointment time
(B) To inquire about a process
(C) To complain about a charge
(D) To order new equipment

187 What is suggested about Mr. Mayfield?

(A) He does not know how to reboot a computer.
(B) He will borrow some equipment from a coworker.
(C) He has placed a rush order for a part.
(D) He has an outdated copy of some software.

188 About how long did Mr. Baird work on Mr. Mayfield's equipment?

(A) 10 minutes
(B) 20 minutes
(C) 25 minutes
(D) 35 minutes

189 In the second e-mail, the word "rough" in paragraph 1, line 3, is closest in meaning to

(A) approximate
(B) unpleasant
(C) difficult
(D) immediate

190 What is mentioned in Mr. Baird's e-mail?

(A) Mr. Baird has worked for the company for three years.
(B) Another IT technician will handle some repairs.
(C) The replacement component has been discontinued.
(D) Mr. Mayfield's department will not incur a fee.

GO ON TO THE NEXT PAGE

RODRIGUEZ DRAINPIPE CARE

~ Residential and Commercial Drainpipe Cleaning ~

Get $25 off a full drainpipe-cleaning service in March! Rodriguez Drainpipe Care has been serving the Shreveport community for nearly two decades. As we're between peak periods, we are looking to bring in more customers. So, it's a great opportunity to save big on your drainpipe cleaning. You don't want to put off this important task. Blocked drainpipes can cause damage to your exterior walls or allow water to leak into your home.

Our regular rates are $225 for a two-story home and $180 for a one-story home. Businesses should contact our office for a quote.

To book your appointment, contact our Bookings Department at 555-7988.

Rodriguez Drainpipe Care

Invoice #8524

Customer: *Gabriella Jones*   Address: *263 Waldeck Avenue*

Property Type: *one-story home*   Contact Number: *555-0361*

Service: *Drainpipe cleaning*   Work Completed: *March 12*

Crew Leader: *Robert Brann*   Total Charge: $180.00 + 6% tax = $190.80

Payments accepted by credit card over the phone. Please settle the payment within two weeks of the completed work. Thank you!

Rodriguez Drainpipe Care
974 Carriage Lane
Shreveport, LA 71106

March 14

Gabriella Jones
263 Waldeck Avenue
Shreveport, LA 71106

Dear Ms. Jones,

Thank you for contacting us this morning about the problem with your bill. Please disregard the first one that was issued and use the newly issued one, which I have enclosed. This was our company's first time running a month-long promotion, so it hasn't gone quite as smoothly as we had hoped. I apologize for any confusion or inconvenience this may have caused.

I'm pleased that you were satisfied with the service and that the team was respectful throughout the procedure. We recommend getting your drainpipes cleaned every six months, so we hope to hear from you in the future.

Warmest regards,

Dean Rendall
Dean Rendall
Bookings Manager, Rodriguez Drainpipe Care

191 According to the advertisement, why is Rodrigues Drainpipe Care offering a discount?

(A) To generate more business during a slow period
(B) To celebrate an achievement
(C) To show appreciation to loyal customers
(D) To introduce a newly offered service

192 What most likely did Mr. Brann do on March 12?

(A) Ordered some equipment
(B) Repaired an exterior wall
(C) Processed a payment
(D) Oversaw a team

193 What is indicated about the bill?

(A) The payment deadline was changed.
(B) The tax should not have been applied.
(C) The wrong price was charged.
(D) The service included a larger area.

194 Why did Mr. Rendell write the letter?

(A) To recommend a service
(B) To acknowledge a mistake
(C) To request some feedback
(D) To schedule a task

195 What is implied about Mr. Rendell?

(A) He has advised the staff to be more professional.
(B) He will send a refund to Ms. Jones.
(C) Customers can contact him at 555-7988.
(D) Rodriguez Drainpipe Care recently hired him.

GO ON TO THE NEXT PAGE

Odell Business Institute

Savvy Solutions
Online Professional Development Class
February 24, 10 A.M.–Noon

Reaching new customers is all about connections. Public relations employees will particularly benefit from this course, which explains how to get the most out of social media platforms. Instructor Elliot Osborne from Mateo Media will provide you with information on developing an eye-catching page, maximizing your social media presence, and creating greater customer engagement. Even if you're already operating corporate social media accounts, you'll find new tips to help you take your business to the next level.

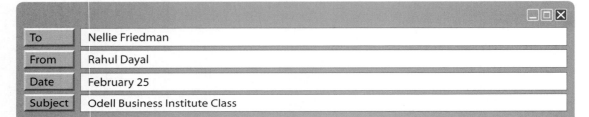

To	Nellie Friedman
From	Rahul Dayal
Date	February 25
Subject	Odell Business Institute Class

Thanks again for approving my request to take some professional development classes through Odell Business Institute. My first class was the one about social media, which was held yesterday. Unfortunately, I'm not sure that it was worth my time. The instructor is an expert in the field, yet he only gave broad advice with nothing specific. Most of it was just common sense to anyone who has been using social media personally for any length of time. Also, the only products he talked about were those made by Mateo Media, although I know there are a lot of other options out there.

I'm going to try one more of the institute's online classes, the upcoming one on how to manage risk. If that one does not meet my standards, then I think we may have to look into other options for business classes. I'll let you know.

Rahul

Odell Business Institute: Online Classes for March

DATE & TIMES	CLASS TITLE	INSTRUCTOR	Fee
March 2, 1–4 P.M.	Writing Business E-mails	Donna Ramsey	£25
March 9, 2–5 P.M.	Negotiation Strategies	Lionel Newton	£25
March 16, 1–4 P.M.	Risk Management	Robert Stennis	£25
March 23, 9–11 A.M.	Hiring the Right Team	Donna Ramsey	£25

To sign up for any of the above classes, please e-mail info@odellbusiness.com. Registration closes three days before the class date.

196 According to the brochure, who would be the ideal participant for the Savvy Solutions class?

(A) A graphic designer
(B) A computer technician
(C) A public relations manager
(D) A financial advisor

197 What is one reason that Mr. Dayal was disappointed with the class?

(A) The information was too general.
(B) There was not enough time for questions.
(C) The instructor was not knowledgeable.
(D) The concepts were difficult to follow.

198 What does Mr. Dayal imply about Mr. Osborne?

(A) He was uncomfortable teaching the students.
(B) He limited his product suggestions to Mateo Media.
(C) He recommended another class to Mr. Dayal.
(D) He has founded his own company.

199 When does Mr. Dayal plan to attend another class?

(A) March 2
(B) March 9
(C) March 16
(D) March 23

200 What do all March online classes have in common?

(A) They require registration one week in advance.
(B) They take place in the afternoon.
(C) They have the same instructor.
(D) They are the same price.

GO ON TO THE NEXT PAGE

Actual Test

04

🕐 시작 시간   :

종료 시간   :

LISTENING TEST

In the Listening test, you will be asked to demonstrate how well you understand spoken English. The entire Listening test will last approximately 45 minutes. There are four parts, and directions are given for each part. You must mark your answers on the separate answer sheet. Do not write your answers in your test book.

PART 1

Directions: For each question in this part, you will hear four statements about a picture in your test book. When you hear the statements, you must select the one statement that best describes what you see in the picture. Then find the number of the question on your answer sheet and mark your answer. The statements will not be printed in your test book and will be spoken only one time.

Example

Sample Answer

Ⓐ ● Ⓒ Ⓓ

Statement (B), "The man is working at a desk," is the best description of the picture, so you should select answer (B) and mark it on your answer sheet.

1

2

GO ON TO THE NEXT PAGE ➤

3

4

5

6

GO ON TO THE NEXT PAGE ➤

PART 2

Directions: You will hear a question or statement and three responses spoken in English. They will not be printed in your test book and will be spoken only one time. Select the best response to the question or statement and mark the letter (A), (B), or (C) on your answer sheet.

7   Mark your answer on your answer sheet.

8   Mark your answer on your answer sheet.

9   Mark your answer on your answer sheet.

10   Mark your answer on your answer sheet.

11   Mark your answer on your answer sheet.

12   Mark your answer on your answer sheet.

13   Mark your answer on your answer sheet.

14   Mark your answer on your answer sheet.

15   Mark your answer on your answer sheet.

16   Mark your answer on your answer sheet.

17   Mark your answer on your answer sheet.

18   Mark your answer on your answer sheet.

19   Mark your answer on your answer sheet.

20   Mark your answer on your answer sheet.

21   Mark your answer on your answer sheet.

22   Mark your answer on your answer sheet.

23   Mark your answer on your answer sheet.

24   Mark your answer on your answer sheet.

25   Mark your answer on your answer sheet.

26   Mark your answer on your answer sheet.

27   Mark your answer on your answer sheet.

28   Mark your answer on your answer sheet.

29   Mark your answer on your answer sheet.

30   Mark your answer on your answer sheet.

31   Mark your answer on your answer sheet.

PART 3

Directions: You will hear some conversations between two or more people. You will be asked to answer three questions about what the speakers say in each conversation. Select the best response to each question and mark the letter (A), (B), (C), or (D) on your answer sheet. The conversations will not be printed in your test book and will be spoken only one time.

32 What kind of business do the speakers probably work at?

(A) A recruitment agency
(B) A mobile phone store
(C) An Internet provider
(D) A clothing manufacturer

33 What do the speakers agree is an important skill?

(A) Being on time for work
(B) Creating attractive displays
(C) Being friendly to customers
(D) Working in a team

34 What does the man provide to the woman?

(A) Some meal vouchers
(B) Some work assignments
(C) An e-mail address
(D) A job reference

35 What has recently happened in the man's neighborhood?

(A) A competition was held.
(B) A park was opened.
(C) A road was repaired.
(D) A cleanup project was completed.

36 Why does the man say he likes the change?

(A) He can win a prize.
(B) He can meet new people.
(C) He can save money.
(D) He can get exercise easily.

37 What does the woman suggest doing?

(A) Contacting a city official
(B) Printing out a map
(C) Checking a Web site
(D) Joining a mailing list

38 Where does the conversation take place?

(A) At an airport
(B) At a hotel
(C) At a bus terminal
(D) At a cinema

39 Why is the woman not able to help the man?

(A) A vehicle has broken down.
(B) A special offer has ended.
(C) Some products have sold out.
(D) Some tickets are unavailable.

40 What will the man probably do next?

(A) Reserve a room
(B) Call a taxi company
(C) Purchase a ticket
(D) Speak to the woman's manager

41 Where most likely do the speakers work?

(A) At a financial institution
(B) At a warehouse
(C) At a bookstore
(D) At a factory

42 What is the man concerned about?

(A) Lack of selection
(B) Poor quality
(C) A high price
(D) A slow delivery

43 What does the woman plan to do?

(A) Conduct some research
(B) Write a report
(C) Adjust a budget
(D) Open a business

GO ON TO THE NEXT PAGE

44 Where most likely are the speakers?

(A) At a gym
(B) At an advertising agency
(C) At a sports stadium
(D) At a shoe store

45 What is Thomas Valeny known for?

(A) Designing a product
(B) Winning a race
(C) Hosting a television show
(D) Founding a business

46 What extra benefit does a product come with?

(A) An extended warranty
(B) Express shipping
(C) A lower price
(D) Upgraded service

47 What is the man responsible for?

(A) Recruiting new staff
(B) Remodeling a room
(C) Planning an orientation
(D) Responding to customers

48 Why does the man say, "we have more participants this month"?

(A) To thank the woman for her contribution
(B) To express satisfaction with a result
(C) To request assistance with a task
(D) To disapprove of a suggestion

49 What does the woman say she will do?

(A) Cancel an appointment
(B) Contact a colleague
(C) Make an announcement
(D) Have a room cleaned

50 Who most likely is the woman?

(A) A restaurant server
(B) An office supervisor
(C) A food critic
(D) A catering manager

51 What does the man say he will do?

(A) Receive a refund
(B) Cancel an event
(C) Wait for an item
(D) Increase an order

52 What will the man provide to the woman?

(A) An order number
(B) A business address
(C) A preferred delivery time
(D) A credit card number

53 What are the speakers discussing?

(A) The dates of a business trip
(B) Reservation procedures
(C) A software upgrade
(D) Bathroom renovations

54 What does Dennis recommend that the woman do?

(A) Place an online order
(B) View items in person
(C) Join a mailing list
(D) Read customer reviews

55 What does the woman ask Dennis to do?

(A) Take some measurements
(B) Update an address
(C) Confirm a price
(D) Suggest a brand

56 What type of business is the woman calling from?

(A) A catering company
(B) A clothing supplier
(C) A recruitment agency
(D) An electronics store

57 What does the man imply when he says, "We actually have more new hires"?

(A) He is pleased with his company's efforts.
(B) He can meet an important deadline.
(C) He is confirming receipt of a job application.
(D) He would like to change an order.

58 What does the man ask the woman to do?

(A) Attend an interview
(B) Compare some prices
(C) Send a revised invoice
(D) Speak to her colleagues

---

59 What is the conversation mainly about?

(A) Designing a building
(B) Creating an advertisement
(C) Repairing a machine
(D) Recruiting new employees

60 What does the man say he will do this afternoon?

(A) Submit a file
(B) Give a speech
(C) Test a product
(D) Visit a client

61 What does the woman ask about?

(A) A product sample
(B) A cost estimate
(C) A phone number
(D) A work timeframe

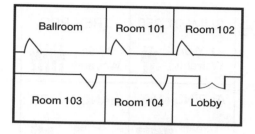

62 What is the man's profession?

(A) A florist
(B) A hotel clerk
(C) A delivery driver
(D) An interior designer

63 According to the man, what has caused a problem?

(A) A form was incomplete.
(B) The customers have changed their minds.
(C) There is heavy traffic in the area.
(D) A payment has not been received yet.

64 Look at the graphic. Where will the man most likely go next?

(A) Room 101
(B) Room 102
(C) Room 103
(D) Room 104

GO ON TO THE NEXT PAGE

SUMMIT 250	TREK PRO
1-Year Warranty	3-Year Warranty
ALPINE MAX	RANGER 600
1-Year Warranty	3-Year Warranty

2-Day Domestic Shipping Rates		
Region 1	West	$5.50
Region 2	Midwest	$7.50
Region 3	South	$9.50
Region 4	Northeast	$11.50

65 Where does the man work?

(A) At a department store
(B) At a university
(C) At a city park
(D) At a library

66 Look at the graphic. Which tent will the man most likely buy?

(A) Summit 250
(B) Trek Pro
(C) Alpine Max
(D) Ranger 600

67 What does the woman say she will do?

(A) Extend the length of a warranty
(B) Add the man to a mailing list
(C) Provide the man with a discount
(D) Demonstrate how to use a product

68 What most likely is the man's job?

(A) Customer service agent
(B) Delivery driver
(C) IT technician
(D) Product developer

69 Look at the graphic. How much will the woman's shipping costs be?

(A) $5.50
(B) $7.50
(C) $9.50
(D) $11.50

70 What will the woman probably do next?

(A) Review a product
(B) Select a size
(C) Request a catalog
(D) Set up an account

PART 4

Directions: You will hear some talks given by a single speaker. You will be asked to answer three questions about what the speaker says in each talk. Select the best response to each question and mark the letter (A), (B), (C), or (D) on your answer sheet. The talks will not be printed in your test book and will be spoken only one time.

71 What type of business does the speaker work for?

(A) At a camping store
(B) At a bookshop
(C) At a hardware store
(D) At a clothing shop

72 What is the purpose of the message?

(A) To schedule a training session
(B) To explain a customer complaint
(C) To agree to a customer event
(D) To order some merchandise

73 What does the speaker plan to do tomorrow?

(A) Change a work schedule
(B) Request some funding
(C) Run an advertisement
(D) Order some supplies

74 What is the report mainly about?

(A) A sports competition
(B) A local election
(C) Weather patterns
(D) Traffic conditions

75 What does the speaker encourage the listeners to do?

(A) Listen to an interview
(B) Download an application
(C) Take an alternative route
(D) Call the radio station

76 According to the speaker, what will happen on Saturday?

(A) A bridge will reopen.
(B) A local law will change.
(C) A new radio show will be broadcast.
(D) An annual festival will be held.

77 What kind of event is being announced?

(A) A music festival
(B) A painting competition
(C) A theater performance
(D) A book club meeting

78 According to the speaker, why should the listeners visit a Web site?

(A) To submit an entry
(B) To read some reviews
(C) To download a brochure
(D) To cast a vote

79 What will be given to people who volunteer on July 10?

(A) An event T-shirt
(B) A front-row seat
(C) A complimentary ticket
(D) A free meal

80 Where does the speaker probably work?

(A) At an office
(B) At a clothing store
(C) At a city park
(D) At a gym

81 According to the speaker, what will be offered to the listeners?

(A) Free parking
(B) Refreshments
(C) Corporate discounts
(D) Company cars

82 Why does the speaker say, "There are boxes at the front desk"?

(A) To ask that the front desk be cleaned
(B) To give the location of clothing
(C) To announce that a business is being relocated
(D) To point out that a delivery has not been sent yet

GO ON TO THE NEXT PAGE

83 According to the advertisement, what is unique about the June issue?

(A) It will announce the winner of an award.
(B) It will focus on start-up companies.
(C) It will provide coupons for services.
(D) It will review new technology.

84 Who is Jessie Ewing?

(A) A computer programmer
(B) A financial expert
(C) A corporate CEO
(D) A magazine editor

85 What can customers get if they sign up for a subscription this month?

(A) A best-selling book
(B) A tote bag
(C) A desktop clock
(D) A wireless speaker

86 What event is the listener attending soon?

(A) A charity banquet
(B) An awards ceremony
(C) A grand opening
(D) A fashion show

87 Why does the speaker say, "I know a place in northwest LA"?

(A) To confirm that some details are correct
(B) To suggest an alternative restaurant
(C) To recommend a place to stay
(D) To show his knowledge of a city

88 What requires the CEO's authorization?

(A) Discussing a company issue
(B) Reserving a hotel room
(C) Upgrading a flight ticket
(D) Using a company vehicle

89 What is the topic of the meeting?

(A) Staffing needs
(B) Event locations
(C) Course fees
(D) Lesson plans

90 What does the speaker imply when he says, "Teaching four classes is a lot"?

(A) He would like to apply for a teaching role.
(B) He would like to take some time off from work.
(C) He is impressed with the teachers' efforts.
(D) He disagrees with a colleague's opinion.

91 What will the speaker most likely do this weekend?

(A) Place an advertisement
(B) Review some résumés
(C) Sign a contract
(D) Print some handouts

92 What does the speaker's company manufacture?

(A) Medical equipment
(B) Delivery containers
(C) Work uniforms
(D) Office supplies

93 What does the speaker say will happen on January 10?

(A) A new CEO will take over.
(B) A business will expand overseas.
(C) A corporate merger will be finalized.
(D) A negotiation will take place.

94 What is the listener asked to do?

(A) Train new employees
(B) Check some sales figures
(C) Translate a document
(D) Sign a contract

7:00	Welcome refreshments
7:30	Comedy show
8:30	Banquet
9:15	After–dinner speeches
10:00	Musical entertainment

KL Electronics		
Model	Pages per Minute	Customer Rating
Lexel	23	9.8
Supra	15	9.6
Indicon	26	8.4
Bolt	18	7.7

95 Where is the speech taking place?

(A) At a training seminar
(B) At a retirement celebration
(C) At a charity fundraiser
(D) At a board meeting

96 What was given to the listeners this morning?

(A) A collection envelope
(B) A set of directions
(C) A product specification
(D) A cruise brochure

97 Look at the graphic. What activity will the listeners enjoy next?

(A) Comedy show
(B) Banquet
(C) After-dinner speeches
(D) Musical entertainment

98 What will the speaker's team do next month?

(A) Attend an industry conference
(B) Move to a new building
(C) Oversee a product launch
(D) Undergo a performance evaluation

99 Why does the speaker ask the listener about KL Electronics?

(A) She sent the speaker some reviews.
(B) She used to work there.
(C) She has purchased items from it.
(D) She shared a coupon for its goods.

100 Look at the graphic. Which model is the speaker thinking about buying?

(A) Lexel
(B) Supra
(C) Indicon
(D) Bolt

This is the end of the Listening test. Turn to Part 5 in your test book.

GO ON TO THE NEXT PAGE

READING TEST

In the Reading test, you will read a variety of texts and answer several different types of reading comprehension questions. The entire Reading test will last 75 minutes. There are three parts, and directions are given for each part. You are encouraged to answer as many questions as possible within the time allowed.

You must mark your answers on the separate answer sheet. Do not write your answers in your test book.

PART 5

Directions: A word or phrase is missing in each of the sentences below. Four answer choices are given below each sentence. Select the best answer to complete the sentence. Then mark the letter (A), (B), (C), or (D) on your answer sheet.

101 Although Ms. Scimia complained about the restaurant's service, she ------- left a positive review on its Web page.

(A) ever
(B) same
(C) too
(D) still

102 Ms. Richardson has announced that ------- will be ordering supplies for the entire office tomorrow.

(A) her
(B) she
(C) hers
(D) herself

103 Ms. Haught in Human Resources helps staff members to ------- transportation for their business trips.

(A) conduct
(B) arrive
(C) arrange
(D) proceed

104 Liz Rinehart's first novel was ------- regarded by critics but did not sell well in bookstores.

(A) high
(B) higher
(C) highest
(D) highly

105 Participants in the study will be ------- with a personalized schedule and directions to the testing site.

(A) alerted
(B) granted
(C) provided
(D) requested

106 Volunteers working for Brisbane Travel Service can give ------- to any visitors who are unfamiliar with the city.

(A) assists
(B) assistance
(C) assisted
(D) assistant

107 ------- the managing director is away on business, the weekly departmental meeting will be postponed.

(A) Also
(B) Regardless of
(C) Why
(D) Since

108 The recent cloudy weather is making it ------- to create electricity from the rooftop solar panels.

(A) difficultly
(B) difficult
(C) difficulty
(D) difficulties

109 The trainers at Galaxy Fitness will teach gym members the most ------- ways to lose weight.

(A) total
(B) effective
(C) enclosed
(D) reluctant

110 To demonstrate its support of education, Olvan Office Supplies offers ------- to teachers and school administrators.

(A) discount
(B) discounted
(C) discounts
(D) discountable

111 The HR Department has requested that managers complete all employee evaluations ------- the end of the week.

(A) by
(B) on
(C) in
(D) as

112 Local organizations in Beverly County have ------- raised over $5,000 for this year's Winter Festival.

(A) succeeding
(B) succeeded
(C) successful
(D) successfully

113 Honeycomb Cable gives a $200 voucher to customers ------- they refer a friend to its service.

(A) seldom
(B) if
(C) while
(D) afterward

114 If the project manager agrees to the ------- version of the draft, construction costs will increase by over 25%.

(A) suggest
(B) suggesting
(C) suggested
(D) suggests

115 Nature enthusiasts ------- stay at Forest Creek Bed, which is conveniently located right outside a national park.

(A) nearly
(B) originally
(C) moderately
(D) frequently

116 The upcoming company retreat will hopefully encourage employees to work ------- over the next quarter.

(A) productive
(B) productivity
(C) productively
(D) productiveness

117 Vert Innovations stopped developing its new smart glasses due to the low ------- for wearable technology.

(A) access
(B) population
(C) demand
(D) payment

118 The documentary will last 90 minutes, and the ------- time will be used for a question-and-answer session.

(A) remain
(B) remained
(C) remaining
(D) remainders

119 At the end of each day, Kraft Bakery distributes its unsold bread ------- several charity organizations.

(A) beside
(B) among
(C) across
(D) concerning

120 American Total Burger has been expanding ------- into Asia by altering its menu to match regional tastes.

(A) strategy
(B) strategic
(C) strategist
(D) strategically

GO ON TO THE NEXT PAGE

121 Woodcracker Furnishings offers a diverse ------- of handcrafted furniture and accessories at reasonable prices.

(A) position
(B) selection
(C) preference
(D) experience

122 Casper Web Security is ------- to protecting your company's network from cyber threats and viruses.

(A) dedication
(B) dedicating
(C) dedicatedly
(D) dedicated

123 Mr. Hart received the promotion on the ------- of his contributions to the Stillwater Bank project.

(A) strength
(B) time
(C) people
(D) money

124 It is ------- that BNC Financial will require additional office space if it continues to grow.

(A) adequate
(B) apparent
(C) exceptional
(D) profitable

125 New recruits are required to write a 15-page report ------- attending the week-long training workshop.

(A) in addition to
(B) on behalf of
(C) in accordance with
(D) as a result of

126 ------- the most talented public speakers worry about presenting at large corporate conventions.

(A) Alike
(B) Even
(C) Such
(D) As

127 Employees who have taken the ------- on previous projects will receive the most consideration for the promotion.

(A) initiative
(B) requirement
(C) advice
(D) restriction

128 Those who lived abroad during the majority of the year qualify for an ------- deadline when filing their taxes.

(A) extend
(B) extends
(C) extensive
(D) extended

129 ------- the extent of the damage from the storm, Long Beach Resort will likely remain closed for the rest of the season.

(A) Just
(B) Provided
(C) Given
(D) Like

130 Stephanie Crane ------- the first draft of her novel by the time she meets with her editor next week.

(A) will have finished
(B) is finishing
(C) finished
(D) finishes

PART 6

Directions: Read the texts that follow. A word, phrase, or sentence is missing in parts of each text. Four answer choices for each question are given below the text. Select the best answer to complete the text. Then mark the letter (A), (B), (C), or (D) on your answer sheet.

Questions 131-134 refer to the following article.

DUBLIN (September 3) – McDaniel's, one of Ireland's top companies in the ------- industry,
                                                                                  131.
announced that it is lowering its prices. This decision ------- by a reduction in the costs of
                                                          132.
the materials needed to make its appliances. The company just updated its Web site and

encourages shoppers to look through all of its products, ------- note not only of their prices but
                                                          133.
also of their features. The company has also announced it will be holding several sales in the

coming months. -------. This should guarantee that shoppers are aware of when they can get
                134.
even more savings.

131 (A) clothing
    (B) manufacturing
    (C) finance
    (D) publishing

132 (A) is prompted
    (B) is being prompted
    (C) was prompted
    (D) will be prompted

133 (A) take
    (B) takes
    (C) took
    (D) taking

134 (A) McDaniel's is hoping to open more stores
       in the next few months.
    (B) Its online calendar shows the precise
       dates of these events.
    (C) Customers have been speaking
       positively about McDaniel's lately.
    (D) The most recent campaign resulted in
       record revenues for the company.

GO ON TO THE NEXT PAGE

To: Wendy Robertson <w.robertson@newtonspring.com>
From: Wolf Den Gym <mark@wolfdengym.com>
Date: April 1
Subject: Gym membership

Dear Ms. Robertson,

You have requested a change in status when your membership is renewed at the end of this month. From May 1, your monthly fee ------- by $19.99, reflecting a change from Premium
135.
status to Standard status. You can continue to attend unlimited onsite classes ------- the end
136.
of this month. You will have one final session in which you can work out with assistance from a professional trainer. If you would like ------- your status back to Premium at any time, just speak
137.
to a Wolf Den Gym employee or reply to this e-mail. I have attached a brochure explaining the various benefits for each membership tier. -------.
138.

Sincerely,

Mark Williams

---

135 (A) must have decreased
(B) has decreased
(C) will decrease
(D) to be decreasing

136 (A) until
(B) earlier
(C) in
(D) since

137 (A) changes
(B) changing
(C) having changed
(D) to change

138 (A) We use any surplus funds to purchase or upgrade equipment.
(B) Lockers can be rented on a monthly basis for a small fee.
(C) Should you have any questions about them, please feel free to contact me.
(D) Instead, the weekly class schedule will be available for download.

Questions 139-142 refer to the following article.

May 3—With events held throughout the country, VC Foods ------- a new line of sports drinks
139.
yesterday. The beverages, called Power Plus, provide an energy boost with caffeine along with
essential minerals to replace those lost while exercising. ------- part of developing the product,
140.
VC Foods got feedback from its target consumers, young athletes. -------. The company is
141.
running ads on social media, on television, ------- in magazines to highlight the drinks' unique
142.
features. The coordinated campaign is sure to fuel sales for Power Plus in the coming months.

139 (A) sampled
   (B) followed
   (C) hired
   (D) launched

140 (A) As
   (B) From
   (C) On
   (D) Off

141 (A) The list of flavors has not been revealed
     yet.
   (B) This helped the company to better
     understand the market.
   (C) More people are working out at home
     rather than at the gym.
   (D) It will be the final round of the sports
     competition.

142 (A) also
   (B) either
   (C) and
   (D) than

GO ON TO THE NEXT PAGE

Arlene Madera
Florence Consulting, Office #314
441 Blackwell Street
Miami, FL 33146

Dear Ms. Madera,

I am writing ------- Terrance Friedman, who has applied for a financial advisor position at your
    143.
firm. As a manager at Cerullo Investments, I have been Mr. Friedman's immediate supervisor for

the past three years. During that time, he worked hard to provide expert advice related to his

clients' specific needs. -------. Moreover, his reputation for excellent service helped us to grow
    144.
our client base significantly. He was always professional and prompt in carrying out his -------,
    145.
and everyone on the team enjoyed working with him. There is ------- doubt that he would make
    146.
an excellent addition to any team.

Warmest regards,

James Lee
Cerullo Investments

143 (A) in case of
(B) in exchange for
(C) on behalf of
(D) except for

144 (A) He was able to increase your investment
portfolio by over twenty percent.
(B) He also participated in professional
development to improve his knowledge.
(C) He graduated from a prestigious
university known for its finance program.
(D) He will relocate to a new city next month
due to family obligations.

145 (A) productions
(B) perspectives
(C) performances
(D) responsibilities

146 (A) no
(B) few
(C) other
(D) a little

PART 7

Directions: In this part you will read a selection of texts, such as magazine and newspaper articles, e-mails, and instant messages. Each text or set of texts is followed by several questions. Select the best answer for each question and mark the letter (A), (B), (C), or (D) on your answer sheet.

Questions 147-148 refer to the following receipt.

Receipt No.: 83389-47893

(This receipt is for your reference only. You do not need to bring it as proof of payment on the day of the event.)

$10 attendance fee received by Regent Bookstore

Charged to credit card ending in xxxx-8865

Credit Card Holder's Name: Melanie Arnott

Details: Claire Pell will read excerpts from her novel Sideways Glances on Sunday, July 5, 2 P.M.

REMEMBER: If you have already purchased Sideways Glances, you may bring it along with you and have it signed by Ms. Pell at the end of the event. Copies may also be purchased in the store for $16.95.

147 What does Ms. Arnott intend to do on July 5?

(A) Pay the credit card company
(B) Attend a public reading
(C) Purchase a new novel
(D) Call the bookstore

148 What is Ms. Arnott advised to bring with her?

(A) A bank card
(B) A valid ID
(C) A copy of a book
(D) A payment receipt

GO ON TO THE NEXT PAGE

Camping Express

Starting August 1, we will allow free in-store pickup for items ordered from the Camping Express Web site. To take advantage of this option, simply choose "In-store Pickup" on the delivery page of your online order and select your preferred location. You will receive an e-mail when your item is ready. Simply go to the store's customer service counter and provide the confirmation code to one of the staff members there. You will also have to put your signature on a release form showing that you picked up the item.

149 What will occur on August 1?

(A) A store will celebrate an anniversary.
(B) A clearance sale will begin.
(C) A change in services will go into effect.
(D) A new camping brand will be available.

150 What is NOT indicated as a step in picking up an item?

(A) Signing a form at the store
(B) Visiting a customer service counter
(C) Presenting a confirmation code
(D) Sending an e-mail to Camping Express

Questions 151-152 refer to the following e-mail.

To: Marcella Escobar <marcella.e@nuzompost.com>
From: Lance Ayala <l_ayala@brentwoodbi.com>
Date: March 8
Subject: Brentwood Business Institute Workshop

Dear Ms. Escobar,

On behalf of Brentwood Business Institute's planning team for the upcoming business workshop, I'd like to thank you for your registration. We hope that you will learn a great deal during the workshop. You will receive a welcome packet in the mail. Please bring all of the packet's materials to the Yuma Conference Center when you come. The workshop begins at 9 A.M., and parking is available on-site. If you need to make copies or scans of documents, or print anything while attending the workshop, you can show your workshop ID to the staff, and they will allow you to use the business center on the first floor. We look forward to seeing you soon.

Lance Ayala

151 Who most likely sent the e-mail?

(A) An event planner
(B) A building owner
(C) A job recruiter
(D) A courier

152 Why should an ID badge be presented?

(A) To get a refund on parking
(B) To claim a reserved seat
(C) To access some office equipment
(D) To enter a stage area

GO ON TO THE NEXT PAGE

As a thank-you for investing in Hubbell Tech,
you are cordially invited to our Annual Appreciation Banquet

Friday, December 8

at Cervantes Hall
163 Geneva Street
Salt Lake City, UT 84116

6:00 P.M.   Doors open, Cocktails served
7:00 P.M.   Speech by President Bailey Kendell
7:30 P.M.   Buffet dinner, Live music

Please feel free to have your spouse or a friend accompany you.

To RSVP, call event planner Marla Souza at 555-9762. For information about parking, directions to the site, etc., please contact the event venue directly by calling Theo Duncan at 555-1133.

153 Why will an event be held on December 8?
(A) To express gratitude to investors
(B) To celebrate a company's anniversary
(C) To present some employee awards
(D) To announce a new service

154 What does the invitation encourage invitees to do?
(A) Make a donation
(B) Meet an event organizer
(C) Submit a nomination
(D) Bring a guest

155 What is implied about Mr. Duncan?
(A) He will give a speech after Mr. Kendell.
(B) He will play music at the event.
(C) He has selected the food for the event.
(D) He is a Cervantes Hall employee.

Questions 156-158 refer to the following information.

⭐ Candlelight Resort ⭐

Bristol, England
Room Information

At Candlelight Resort, guests can expect the best amenities and the highest standard of cleanliness in their rooms. We offer a strong Wi-fi signal at no additional cost. Each room is equipped with a large flat-screen television, balcony with stunning views, and a whirlpool bathtub. In addition, room service meals can be ordered from our Evergreen Restaurant.

Our housekeeping staff will clean your room thoroughly every day. They are also ready around the clock to provide you with additional services. Just dial *8 from your in-room phone if you need to have a spill cleaned up or if you require additional items for your room such as soap, shampoo, or extra towels. Our staff is highly trained to meet your needs regarding comfort and service.

Should you have any questions or complaints about your room, please do not hesitate to contact the front desk, which can be done by dialing *0 from your in-room phone. We wish you a pleasant stay, and we will do everything we can to make that happen. Thank you for choosing Candlelight Resort.

---

156 For whom was this information most likely written?

(A) Evergreen Restaurant employees
(B) Bristol city officials
(C) Candlelight Resort guests
(D) New housekeeping staff members

157 What is mentioned about the housekeeping department?

(A) It has a limited number of towels.
(B) It will recruit more workers.
(C) It has recently changed a policy.
(D) It can be contacted anytime.

158 The word "meet" in paragraph 2, line 4 is closest in meaning to

(A) assemble
(B) encounter
(C) fulfill
(D) introduce

GO ON TO THE NEXT PAGE

Questions 159-160 refer to the following text-message chain.

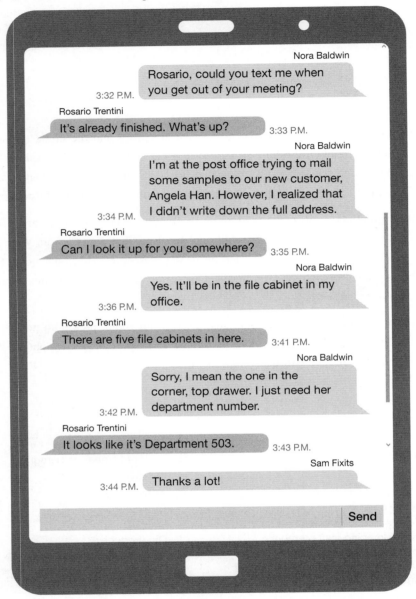

> **Nora Baldwin**
> Rosario, could you text me when you get out of your meeting?
> 3:32 P.M.

> **Rosario Trentini**
> It's already finished. What's up?
> 3:33 P.M.

> **Nora Baldwin**
> I'm at the post office trying to mail some samples to our new customer, Angela Han. However, I realized that I didn't write down the full address.
> 3:34 P.M.

> **Rosario Trentini**
> Can I look it up for you somewhere?
> 3:35 P.M.

> **Nora Baldwin**
> Yes. It'll be in the file cabinet in my office.
> 3:36 P.M.

> **Rosario Trentini**
> There are five file cabinets in here.
> 3:41 P.M.

> **Nora Baldwin**
> Sorry, I mean the one in the corner, top drawer. I just need her department number.
> 3:42 P.M.

> **Rosario Trentini**
> It looks like it's Department 503.
> 3:43 P.M.

> **Sam Fixits**
> Thanks a lot!
> 3:44 P.M.

Send

---

159 What problem does Ms. Baldwin mention?

(A) She cannot find the post office.
(B) She forgot some important samples.
(C) She is missing some address information.
(D) She will be late for a client meeting.

160 At 3:41 P.M., what does Mr. Trentini suggest when he writes, "There are five file cabinets in here"?

(A) He needs more detailed guidance.
(B) He wants to change a project's deadline.
(C) He cannot lift some items by himself.
(D) He does not need to place an order.

To	Benjamin Castillo
From	Blackwell Footwear
Date	September 29
Subject	Haven Hiking Boots

Dear Mr. Castillo,

Thank you for contacting us about your Haven hiking boots from Blackwell Footwear. —[1]—. In answer to your question, the boots should not be placed in the washing machine. —[2]—. If they need to be cleaned, first, remove surface dirt with a brush or soft cloth. Then, take out the insole and wash the boots by hand in warm, soapy water.

After being washed, your boots may partially lose their waterproof coating. Blackwell Footwear has a waterproofing spray that would be perfect in this situation. —[3]—. This can be used on both leather and canvas. In addition, we want all of our customers to enjoy comfortable and safe hiking. Therefore, Blackwell Footwear invites all customers to alternate between two different pairs of boots. —[4]—. This will ensure each pair has sufficient time to air out between uses.

Teresa Kerr

Customer Service Agent, Blackwell Footwear

161 Why did Ms. Kerr send the e-mail?

(A) To apologize for an error
(B) To invite Mr. Castillo to an interview
(C) To announce a store opening
(D) To respond to an inquiry

162 What is Mr. Castillo asked to do?

(A) Read some tips before using the boots
(B) Write a review of their hiking boots
(C) Avoid getting the boots wet
(D) Use more than one pair of boots

163 In which of the positions marked [1], [2], [3], and [4] does the following sentence best belong?

"Please send me your preferred mailing address to receive a sample."

(A) [1]
(B) [2]
(C) [3]
(D) [4]

Questions 164-167 refer to the following article.

FLYNN CITY (April 25)—For the past twenty-five years, Sesame Bakery—located on the ground floor of the Dyson Building in the Wilmington neighborhood—has been serving up freshly baked goods made by hand on site. Owner Carolyn Pulido has built a reputation for not only delicious food but also a welcoming atmosphere. However, she understands that not all customers have time to stop into the shop for a free sample and a chat. That's why she is pleased to be introducing a new delivery option for customers. From May 21, customers can place orders over the phone and have them delivered to their home or business. The delivery fee will be based on the number of items in the order, with very large order incurring no delivery costs at all.

Pulido decided to make the change due to the growing popularity of her goods. She often received comments from customers about how difficult it was to get to the bakery due to the lack of a bus stop or subway station nearby. "I don't make it to Wilmington very often because it's somewhat remote. But when I lived here, I visited Sesame Bakery almost daily. I'm thrilled that I'll now be able to easily get Carolyn's delicious baked goods again," said Rafael Calloway, 46.

"I'm excited about reaching more individuals and businesses," Pulido said. "At first, I was concerned that I wouldn't be able to find reliable drivers with enough experience, but I've recruited a great team and we're all looking forward to this next chapter."

164 What is the main topic of the article?

(A) A neighborhood's popularity
(B) A building expansion
(C) A business's new service
(D) A bakery's relocation

165 What is suggested about the Dyson Building?

(A) Its rental fees have increased.
(B) Its tenants are mainly small businesses.
(C) It is known for its great views.
(D) It is far from public transportation.

166 Who most likely is Rafael Calloway?

(A) A former Wilmington resident
(B) Ms. Pulido's business partner
(C) The owner of the Dyson Building
(D) A local food critic

167 According to the article, what was Ms. Pulido worried about?

(A) Keeping prices down
(B) Facing heavy competition
(C) Finding qualified employees
(D) Creating unique recipes

```
E-Mail Message
```

To: Alvarez Inc. Staff
From: Toni Carlson
Date: March 5
Subject: Dorchester Public Library

Dear Staff,

Modeling its program after a similar one in Taylorsville, the Dorchester Public Library is planning a lecture series here in Dorchester. It will be focused on science and business and will begin in June. —[1]—. The event coordinator, Pauline Fierro, is looking for experts in the field who would be willing to conduct a group session. Workers from our laboratory could teach people about how we develop our medications and run trials. —[2]—.

Ideally, we would cover three lectures. This would be a great way to support the program as well as make local residents more familiar with the Alvarez brand. I think it would be best for different teams to handle each lecture. Not all of the roles include public speaking, as there will be a need for doing the planning as well as preparing the presentation slides and other materials. —[3]—.

Please e-mail me by March 15 to express your interest. Be sure to let me know the best time for you to meet with other group members. —[4]—. If you have further questions, please don't hesitate to ask.

Best,

Toni

168 Why did Ms. Carlson send the e-mail?

(A) To encourage the staff to get library cards
(B) To invite employees to lead some sessions
(C) To gather donations for a fundraiser
(D) To extend an invitation to an industry conference

169 What is suggested about Alvarez Inc.?

(A) It is a pharmaceutical company.
(B) It needs to train some of its employees.
(C) It plans to invest in a company expansion.
(D) It is located in Taylorsville.

170 What benefit of the event does Ms. Carlson mention?

(A) Increasing annual revenue
(B) Learning new technologies
(C) Cutting operating costs
(D) Improving brand recognition

171 In which of the positions marked [1],[2],[3], and [4] does the following sentence best belong?

"This will make it easier for me to assign people to groups."

(A) [1]
(B) [2]
(C) [3]
(D) [4]

GO ON TO THE NEXT PAGE

Questions 172-175 refer to the following online chat discussion.

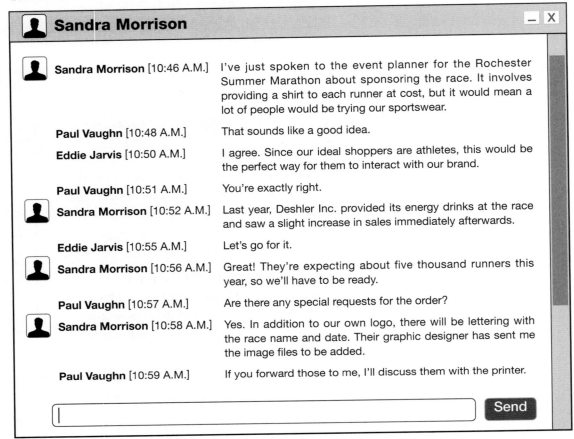

Sandra Morrison — X

Sandra Morrison [10:46 A.M.] I've just spoken to the event planner for the Rochester Summer Marathon about sponsoring the race. It involves providing a shirt to each runner at cost, but it would mean a lot of people would be trying our sportswear.

Paul Vaughn [10:48 A.M.] That sounds like a good idea.

Eddie Jarvis [10:50 A.M.] I agree. Since our ideal shoppers are athletes, this would be the perfect way for them to interact with our brand.

Paul Vaughn [10:51 A.M.] You're exactly right.

Sandra Morrison [10:52 A.M.] Last year, Deshler Inc. provided its energy drinks at the race and saw a slight increase in sales immediately afterwards.

Eddie Jarvis [10:55 A.M.] Let's go for it.

Sandra Morrison [10:56 A.M.] Great! They're expecting about five thousand runners this year, so we'll have to be ready.

Paul Vaughn [10:57 A.M.] Are there any special requests for the order?

Sandra Morrison [10:58 A.M.] Yes. In addition to our own logo, there will be lettering with the race name and date. Their graphic designer has sent me the image files to be added.

Paul Vaughn [10:59 A.M.] If you forward those to me, I'll discuss them with the printer.

Send

172 What does Ms. Morrison tell the other writers about?

(A) A community parade
(B) A promotional opportunity
(C) Some survey results
(D) Some inspection requirements

173 At 10:51 A.M., what does Mr. Vaughn mean when he writes, "You're exactly right"?

(A) A project can be completed in a short time.
(B) Attendance at an event is expected to be high.
(C) A brand has become more popular recently.
(D) Some target customers can be reached.

174 What most likely is Deshler Inc.?

(A) A clothing designer
(B) A fitness center
(C) A marketing firm
(D) A beverage manufacturer

175 What is Ms. Morrison asked to do?

(A) Send some files
(B) Call a designer
(C) Visit a printer
(D) Approve a budget

GO ON TO THE NEXT PAGE

Questions 176-180 refer to the following Web page and e-mail.

http://www.rinehartappliances.com/homeservice

| CATALOG | STORE FINDER | **HOME SERVICE** | CONTACT | EMPLOYMENT |

Rinehart Appliances Home Service

We'll get you up and running within 48 hours of purchase — guaranteed!

When you buy an appliance from Rinehart Appliances, our delivery personnel will make sure it gets to your home promptly. Although all of our goods are of high quality and are extremely durable, our crews are instructed to treat each appliance as if it were fragile. This prevents damage while in transit.

Please check out the rates for our Home Service below.

Number of Items	Delivery Only	Delivery and Installation	Delivery, Installation, and Removal of Old Appliance(s)
1	$15.00	$35.00	$60.00
2	$20.00	$50.00	$90.00
3	$25.00	$55.00	$100.00

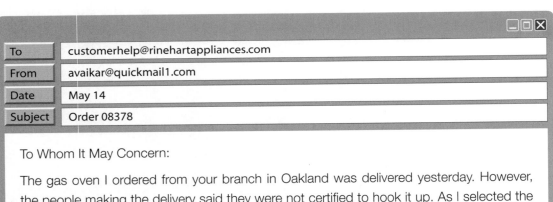

To	customerhelp@rinehartappliances.com
From	avaikar@quickmail1.com
Date	May 14
Subject	Order 08378

To Whom It May Concern:

The gas oven I ordered from your branch in Oakland was delivered yesterday. However, the people making the delivery said they were not certified to hook it up. As I selected the option for delivery and installation, this service should have been included. I hope you are able to send someone by Friday morning. It absolutely needs to be done by then. I have visitors coming to my home on Friday, and I plan to do some cooking for them. If you cannot accommodate my request, I'll have to call a local plumbing business that deals with gas, and I would expect you to cover this charge.

Sincerely,

Amrit Vaikar

176 What is suggested about Rinehart Appliances in the Web page?

(A) It can dispose of customers' old items.
(B) It manufactures a number of fragile items.
(C) It provides free delivery for bulk purchases.
(D) It has recently added new appliances to its line.

177 In the Web page, the word "treat" in paragraph 1, line 3, is closest in meaning to

(A) cure
(B) behave
(C) handle
(D) judge

178 Why did Mr. Vaikar send the e-mail?

(A) To ask for a replacement manual
(B) To report an installation issue
(C) To schedule a delivery date
(D) To place a new order

179 How much did Mr. Vaikar pay for the Home Service?

(A) $15.00
(B) $25.00
(C) $35.00
(D) $50.00

180 According to the e-mail, why might Mr. Vaikar contact a local business?

(A) He hopes to get a better warranty on an item.
(B) He thinks he can purchase a newer model.
(C) He plans to take advantage of a special offer.
(D) He wants to use an appliance for some guests.

GO ON TO THE NEXT PAGE

To: Vasquez Telecommunications <contact@vasqueztelecom.com>
From: Heather Soderberg <h.soderberg@aaragoninc.com>
Date: October 5
Subject: Internet

To Whom It May Concern:

I was surprised by the amount I was charged for my September Internet bill. When I moved to a new home about four months ago, I upgraded to the Premium package. My first few bills were all $60 each. However, my most recent bill was $90. That's $30 more than I was expecting. Through the Premium package, I have unlimited downloads, so even with heavy usage, the bill should be the same. I would appreciate it if you would check my account to find out what has caused the problem.

Thank you,

Heather Soderberg
Account #01489833

To	Heather Soderberg <h.soderberg@aaragoninc.com>
From	Vasquez Customer Service <brucep@vasqueztelecom.com>
Date	October 5
Subject	RE: Internet
Attachment	Vasquez_Pass.pdf

Dear Ms. Soderberg,

We are sorry that you had an issue with your bill. Our team has looked into the details of your account, and we can confirm that you were indeed overcharged on the September bill. I have just issued you a refund in the amount overcharged. This was returned to the account from which your direct debit payment came. By way of apology, I would also like to give you a free one-month Vasquez Pass. You can use the code on the attached document to stream a wide variety of popular films. This service usually costs $12.99 per month.

At Vasquez Telecommunications, we are always looking for ways to improve our services. Would you please take a moment to visit our Web site and complete a brief survey? It can be found on the "Get in Touch" tab on our homepage. We appreciate your understanding in the matter, and we hope that you will continue to be a Vasquez Telecommunications customer.

Warmest regards,

Bruce Powell
Customer Service Team Member
Vasquez Telecommunications

181 Why was the first e-mail written?

(A) To report a broken Internet connection
(B) To confirm an account upgrade
(C) To announce a change of address
(D) To request an account review

182 What is indicated about Ms. Soderberg?

(A) Her computer has been running slowly.
(B) Her bill should not be affected by usage.
(C) She paid to have an Internet line repaired.
(D) She used to work for Vasquez Telecommunications.

183 How much was sent to Ms. Soderberg's account on October 5?

(A) $10
(B) $30
(C) $60
(D) $90

184 What can Ms. Soderberg do with the code provided by Mr. Powell?

(A) Request a replacement
(B) Get a credit on her bill
(C) Watch some movies
(D) Sign into a news site

185 What is Ms. Soderberg asked to do?

(A) Send proof of her payment
(B) Use a debit card in the future
(C) Complete a questionnaire online
(D) Provide more details about her account

GO ON TO THE NEXT PAGE

Hattiesburg Tribune

April 18 — The grounds at Whitwell Park are about to get more colorful. The city has announced plans to turn the northwest section of the park, near the outdoor stage, into a giant flower garden to enhance the park's appearance. The work will begin in early May and will be completed by early June, just before the city's annual Hattiesburg Music Festival, which is held at Whitwell Park.

City officials are looking for volunteers to assist with the digging, adding frames, and planting. About fifty volunteers are needed, and they will work alongside Parks and Recreation workers. To sign up, contact the head of the Parks and Recreation Department, Dorian Pipkin, at 555-8471. If the project does not get enough volunteers, a local landscaping firm will be hired to complete the work.

The changes at Whitwell Park are just one of many project plans proposed since Ann Malley assumed the role of mayor. She wants to encourage residents to get involved in more outdoor activities, so she is investing in local outdoors sites.

To	Wade Atwood <wade@toplandscaping.com>
From	Dorian Pipkin <d.pipkin@hattiesburg.gov>
Date	June 16
Subject	Payment

Dear Mr. Atwood,

I've received your invoice from Top Landscaping for the work your team did at Whitwell Park. The new flower garden looks great, and I think it will be a special attraction for both locals and out-of-town visitors. Our finance team has issued the payment by bank transfer, so it should be with you shortly.

Sincerely,

Dorian Pipkin

Mississippi > Hattiesburg > Community Events

Hattiesburg Music Festival

I attended last year's Hattiesburg Music Festival as well as the most recent one. Both times I had a lot of fun. The bands were wonderful to watch, and the sound system was arranged so that there was a good listening experience in most of the areas of the park. I was particularly amazed by the food court because this year, the festival organizers required vendors to use real dishes instead of disposable ones. It was a great way to make sure much less waste was created. I hope they continue this policy in the coming years. — Ms. D. Sigler, Ellisville, Mississippi

Posted July 2

186 Why was the article written?

(A) To introduce a festival coordinator
(B) To praise the winner of a music contest
(C) To announce upgrades to a park
(D) To give advice about gardening

187 In the article, the word "assumed" in paragraph 3, line 1, is closest in meaning to

(A) predicted
(B) brought up
(C) supposed
(D) took over

188 What is suggested by Mr. Pipkin's e-mail?

(A) A contract will be extended.
(B) An invoice has been corrected.
(C) A project did not get enough volunteers.
(D) A payment has not been approved yet.

189 What is most likely true about Ms. Sigler?

(A) She visited Whitwell Park in June.
(B) She had trouble hearing some performances.
(C) She wants to volunteer for a project.
(D) She is a professional musician.

190 What impressed Ms. Sigler about the festival?

(A) Its variety of food options
(B) Its convenient location
(C) Its outstanding performers from around the world
(D) Its environmentally friendly policy

GO ON TO THE NEXT PAGE

To: Sean Ramirez <sramirez@mercerrealtyco.com>

From: Constance Ashby <constance@elitepartyplanning.net>

Date: September 16

Subject: RE: Inquiry

Dear Mr. Ramirez,

Thank you for contacting me about the upcoming retirement party that you are planning for your coworker. Based on what you told me, I have some recommendations for venues. The quote is attached, and these prices reflect the discount you'll receive by using Elite Party Planning's services. You mentioned that you wanted the option of seaside views, so I've included that in the list as well.

I am happy to make a booking for your preferred date once you have made a selection.

All the best,

Constance

Venue Summary

Prepared by Constance Ashby for Sean Ramirez of Mercer Realty Co.

Event Type: *Retirement Party* Guest List: *To be determined*
Preferred Date: *October 20* Start Time: *7 P.M.*

Venue	Capacity	Rental Fee	Features
The Conaway	100	$1,000	Valet parking free for all guests
Ridge Plaza	50	$500	On-site overnight accommodations available separately
Dovetail Hotel	150	$2,400	Floor-to-ceiling windows with view of coast
GL Conference Center	250	$1,200	Two-minute walk from Uptown Station
Bell Hotel	200	$850	Modern sound system recently installed

Rental fees include setup of tables, chairs, etc. Standard tablecloths are available at each site. Additional decorations must be purchased or rented separately.

To	Constance Ashby <constance@elitepartyplanning.net>
From	Sean Ramirez <sramirez@mercerrealtyco.com>
Date	September 17
Subject	Venue

Dear Ms. Ashby,

Thanks for getting back to me so quickly. None of our guests will need overnight accommodations. However, almost all of them plan to drive to the event, so I'd like to go with the venue that offers valet parking.

Also, I'm wondering if you can recommend a catering business that can handle the event. I would like to find one right away to ensure that there is plenty of time to plan the menu. With our budget, I think a buffet would be the most suitable option, but I'm open to hearing your opinion.

Sincerely,

Sean

191 Why did Ms. Ashby contact Mr. Ramirez?

(A) To ask him to select a new date
(B) To recommend some options for an event
(C) To congratulate him on his retirement
(D) To send him an updated guest list

192 Which venue has a feature that was originally requested by Mr. Ramirez?

(A) The Conaway
(B) Ridge Plaza
(C) Dovetail Hotel
(D) GL Conference Center

193 What is indicated about Bell Hotel?

(A) It is near public transportation.
(B) It has the lowest fee.
(C) It can hold the most people.
(D) It has upgraded some equipment.

194 How much will Mr. Ramirez most likely pay for the rental?

(A) $500
(B) $850
(C) $1,000
(D) $1,200

195 What does Mr. Ramirez plan to do next?

(A) Select a caterer
(B) Purchase some decorations
(C) Print some invitations
(D) Hire a musical group

GO ON TO THE NEXT PAGE

Rose Plaza

For elegance, modernity, and premium customer service, look no further than Rose Plaza. Located in the popular Beaumont neighborhood, Rose Plaza is the perfect place for your next event. Business conferences are particularly popular here because attendees can easily visit the city's best-known sites — such as Willow Beach, just a ten-minute bus ride away — during breaks.

We have a variety of rooms to choose from. The Vesta Room seats up to 40 people, and the Helix Room seats 50-80 people. For seminars, conferences, weddings, and other large gatherings, we recommend one of our two ballrooms. The Titan Room can accommodate 80-150 people, and the Regal Room can accommodate 150-300 people. All rooms feature presentation equipment and a modern sound system, and Wi-fi is available throughout the building.

Our staff is ready to assist you with setup and decorations. We accommodate last-minute reservations whenever possible. To make a reservation, or to find out more, call us at 861-555-3640.

To: Helen Gibson <h.gibson@larkinconsulting.com>
From: Arturo Cahill <a.cahill@larkinconsulting.com>
Date: October 28
Subject: Year-end banquet

Hi, Helen,

I checked out Rose Plaza this morning. You were right that this would be the perfect place for Larkin Consulting's year-end banquet. The room size we need is available on the evenings of December 1, December 6, December 14, and December 17. This last open date comes with complimentary coffee and tea because it's a weekday. We should note that the venue is having its parking lot repaved sometime in December, so there may or may not be space for cars at the venue itself.

I'll talk to Ms. Ellis to see if she approves of using the Rose Plaza. Once that's settled, we can start on the invitations.

Arturo

To	Helen Gibson <h.gibson@larkinconsulting.com>
From	Arturo Cahill <a.cahill@larkinconsulting.com>
Date	October 29
Subject	Venue approved

Hi, Helen,

Ms. Ellis approved using Rose Plaza, and we've decided to go with the day on which we can get free beverages. It'll be one less thing to plan. Can you meet sometime this week to talk about the invitations? We'll need to send them out to all one hundred of our guests. In the meantime, I'll start preparing the guest list.

Arturo

196 What is indicated about Rose Plaza?

(A) It requires a deposit for reservations.
(B) It overlooks Willow Beach.
(C) It is the largest meeting venue in Beaumont.
(D) It can accept bookings on short notice.

197 What is suggested about Ms. Gibson?

(A) She needs to approve the budget.
(B) She recommended using Rose Plaza.
(C) She will receive an award at the banquet.
(D) She must make the final decision.

198 Where will the Larkin Consulting event most likely take place?

(A) In the Vesta Room
(B) In the Helix Room
(C) In the Titan Room
(D) In the Regal Room

199 What potential problem does Mr. Cahill mention?

(A) Issues with selecting a menu
(B) Difficulties with on-site parking
(C) Errors in event invitations
(D) Trouble reserving a large room

200 When will Larkin Consulting most likely hold its event?

(A) December 1
(B) December 6
(C) December 14
(D) December 17

GO ON TO THE NEXT PAGE

Actual Test

05

시작 시간 　　　　:

종료 시간 　　　　:

LISTENING TEST

In the Listening test, you will be asked to demonstrate how well you understand spoken English. The entire Listening test will last approximately 45 minutes. There are four parts, and directions are given for each part. You must mark your answers on the separate answer sheet. Do not write your answers in your test book.

PART 1

Directions: For each question in this part, you will hear four statements about a picture in your test book. When you hear the statements, you must select the one statement that best describes what you see in the picture. Then find the number of the question on your answer sheet and mark your answer. The statements will not be printed in your test book and will be spoken only one time.

Example

Sample Answer

Ⓐ ● Ⓒ Ⓓ

Statement (B), "The man is working at a desk," is the best description of the picture, so you should select answer (B) and mark it on your answer sheet.

1

2

GO ON TO THE NEXT PAGE

3

4

5

6

GO ON TO THE NEXT PAGE

PART 2

Directions: You will hear a question or statement and three responses spoken in English. They will not be printed in your test book and will be spoken only one time. Select the best response to the question or statement and mark the letter (A), (B), or (C) on your answer sheet.

7   Mark your answer on your answer sheet.

8   Mark your answer on your answer sheet.

9   Mark your answer on your answer sheet.

10   Mark your answer on your answer sheet.

11   Mark your answer on your answer sheet.

12   Mark your answer on your answer sheet.

13   Mark your answer on your answer sheet.

14   Mark your answer on your answer sheet.

15   Mark your answer on your answer sheet.

16   Mark your answer on your answer sheet.

17   Mark your answer on your answer sheet.

18   Mark your answer on your answer sheet.

19   Mark your answer on your answer sheet.

20   Mark your answer on your answer sheet.

21   Mark your answer on your answer sheet.

22   Mark your answer on your answer sheet.

23   Mark your answer on your answer sheet.

24   Mark your answer on your answer sheet.

25   Mark your answer on your answer sheet.

26   Mark your answer on your answer sheet.

27   Mark your answer on your answer sheet.

28   Mark your answer on your answer sheet.

29   Mark your answer on your answer sheet.

30   Mark your answer on your answer sheet.

31   Mark your answer on your answer sheet.

PART 3

Directions: You will hear some conversations between two or more people. You will be asked to answer three questions about what the speakers say in each conversation. Select the best response to each question and mark the letter (A), (B), (C), or (D) on your answer sheet. The conversations will not be printed in your test book and will be spoken only one time.

32 Who most likely is the woman?

(A) A scientist
(B) An author
(C) A filmmaker
(D) A factory manager

33 What did the company receive an environmental award for?

(A) Using solar power
(B) Reducing waste
(C) Designing a product
(D) Recycling materials

34 What does the man say the woman will have to do?

(A) Sign a document
(B) Attend a training class
(C) Obtain a security pass
(D) Wear safety gear

35 Where most likely do the speakers work?

(A) At a construction firm
(B) At a recruitment firm
(C) At a finance company
(D) At a printing company

36 How is the business trying to attract more customers?

(A) By adding a delivery option
(B) By reducing its prices
(C) By offering a new service
(D) By extending its business hours

37 What does the woman say she will do?

(A) Hire more employees
(B) Check some details
(C) Meet with a client
(D) Order more supplies

38 What is the topic of the seminar?

(A) Marketing
(B) Customer service
(C) Accounting
(D) Online sales

39 What does the woman say she wants to do?

(A) Enroll at a university
(B) Move to a different company
(C) Attract new employees
(D) Gain a promotion

40 What will the woman most likely do next?

(A) Check a seating chart
(B) Show her ID card
(C) Read a pamphlet
(D) Add a signature

41 In what field do the women most likely work?

(A) Law
(B) Technology
(C) Medicine
(D) Education

42 Why did Ms. Wheeler call the man?

(A) To thank him for his help
(B) To conduct a job interview
(C) To ask for a résumé
(D) To make a job offer

43 What will the man receive in the mail?

(A) A business card
(B) A signed contract
(C) A parking pass
(D) A work schedule

GO ON TO THE NEXT PAGE

44 What are the speakers mainly talking about?

(A) A monthly department meeting
(B) A visit from investors
(C) An overseas job opportunity
(D) A successful business merger

45 What does the woman imply when she says, "I'm interviewing job candidates all morning"?

(A) She is confident a position will be filled.
(B) She is surprised by the number of applications.
(C) She would like the man to assist her.
(D) She is unable to attend a presentation.

46 What does the man remind the woman to do?

(A) Join a business lunch
(B) Contact a supervisor
(C) Bring business cards
(D) Make a reservation

47 Where is the conversation taking place?

(A) At a bookstore
(B) At a clothing store
(C) At a bakery
(D) At a computer shop

48 What does the man want to do?

(A) Return an item
(B) Place a custom order
(C) Watch a demonstration
(D) Apply for a job

49 What will the woman most likely do next?

(A) Speak to a manager
(B) Write down an address
(C) Print out a form
(D) Save a file

50 Where does the woman work?

(A) At a travel agency
(B) At a grocery store
(C) At a restaurant
(D) At a bus company

51 What does the woman offer to contact the man about?

(A) Changes to business hours
(B) Promotional offers
(C) Investment opportunities
(D) Available jobs

52 Why does the woman say, "There's a subway station opposite our new location"?

(A) To complain about local transportation
(B) To suggest that the man take a subway
(C) To correct the directions given to the man
(D) To recommend meeting at the station

53 What type of business does the woman most likely work for?

(A) A restaurant
(B) A newspaper company
(C) A travel agency
(D) A vacation resort

54 Why is the man disappointed?

(A) Some prices have been increased.
(B) He wanted to travel in first class.
(C) He might need to reschedule an appointment.
(D) He needs to travel to a different destination.

55 What will the speakers do tonight?

(A) Meet for dinner
(B) Cancel a reservation
(C) E-mail each other
(D) Speak on the phone

56 What problem does the woman mention?

(A) She is missing some parts from an order.
(B) She was overcharged for an item.
(C) A delivery did not arrive on time.
(D) A machine is not working properly.

57 According to the man, what is the woman eligible to receive?

(A) A refund
(B) Free repairs
(C) A catalog
(D) Some coupons

58 What does the man ask the woman for?

(A) An e-mail address
(B) A purchase date
(C) A credit card number
(D) Driving directions

59 Who most likely are the speakers?

(A) Event organizers
(B) Landscape gardeners
(C) Interior designers
(D) Software developers

60 What will the woman request from Atlas Corporation?

(A) A project budget
(B) A deadline extension
(C) A business location
(D) A color preference

61 What does the woman say she will do later?

(A) Compare some prices
(B) Contact a client
(C) Submit a report
(D) Purchase materials

Wisteria Theater Rules

1. No outside food or beverages.
2. Cameras are not allowed.
3. Turn cell phones off.
4. Keep your ticket stub.

---

62 What does the man thank the woman for?

(A) Hiring a performer
(B) Designing an advertisement
(C) Decorating an area
(D) Inspecting a building

63 What did the woman have trouble doing?

(A) Finding a print shop
(B) Balancing a budget
(C) Tracking sales records
(D) Returning some tools

64 Look at the graphic. Which rule does the man remind the woman about?

(A) Rule 1
(B) Rule 2
(C) Rule 3
(D) Rule 4

GO ON TO THE NEXT PAGE ▶

Plan	Price
Silver	$19.95
Gold	$24.95
Gold Plus	$27.95
Platinum	$32.95

65 What does the man ask the woman for?

(A) A repair service
(B) An invoice
(C) A refund
(D) A brochure

66 Look at the graphic. Which cable subscription does the man currently have?

(A) Silver
(B) Gold
(C) Gold Plus
(D) Platinum

67 What does the woman encourage the man to do?

(A) Complete a form
(B) Transfer some funds
(C) Speak to a manager
(D) Provide an account number

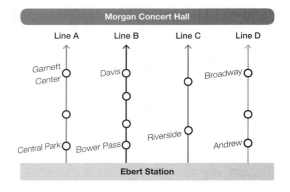

68 Where most likely are the speakers?

(A) At a train station
(B) At a hotel
(C) At a concert hall
(D) At a travel agency

69 Look at the graphic. Which line does the woman suggest taking?

(A) Line A
(B) Line B
(C) Line C
(D) Line D

70 What will the man do today?

(A) Have a job interview
(B) Watch a performance
(C) Meet a new client
(D) Give a presentation

PART 4

Directions: You will hear some talks given by a single speaker. You will be asked to answer three questions about what the speaker says in each talk. Select the best response to each question and mark the letter (A), (B), (C), or (D) on your answer sheet. The talks will not be printed in your test book and will be spoken only one time.

71 What kind of work is being discussed?

(A) Event catering
(B) Furniture restoration
(C) Electronics installation
(D) Overseas shipping

72 According to the speaker, what task should be carried out first?

(A) A tour of a building
(B) Product assembly
(C) Staff recruitment
(D) An item evaluation

73 Why does the speaker say a meeting will be postponed?

(A) A renovation project will start.
(B) A training session will be held.
(C) A public holiday will be observed.
(D) A product delivery will be received.

74 What is the speaker mainly discussing?

(A) An advertising campaign
(B) Contest judges
(C) A product recipe
(D) An IT system

75 What will the bakery offer all attendees?

(A) Cookery lessons
(B) Branded T-shirts
(C) Free parking permits
(D) Refreshments

76 What does the speaker remind the listeners to do?

(A) Distribute some forms
(B) Present a valid ticket
(C) Enter a contest
(D) Arrive on time

77 Who most likely are the listeners?

(A) Tour guides
(B) Product testers
(C) Software developers
(D) Factory workers

78 What will Sam Pearson do?

(A) Write down suggestions
(B) Review the employment contracts
(C) Explain some safety rules
(D) Distribute some uniforms

79 What will happen at eleven o'clock?

(A) The speaker will collect some surveys.
(B) The speaker will respond to questions.
(C) The listeners will watch a video.
(D) The listeners will be assigned to groups.

80 What news does the speaker share with the listeners?

(A) The company will hire more workers.
(B) The company can pay some bonuses.
(C) The company will receive an award.
(D) The company has reached a goal.

81 Where most likely do the listeners work?

(A) At a clothing shop
(B) At a magazine publisher
(C) At a financial institution
(D) At a shipping company

82 What does the speaker mean when she says, "we'll have a technician visit today"?

(A) She is trying to resolve a problem.
(B) She needs to end the meeting early.
(C) She found an error in the schedule.
(D) She needs help from the listeners.

GO ON TO THE NEXT PAGE

83 What does the speaker say is unique about the stadium?

(A) It will have a water collection system.
(B) It will include a roof that can open up.
(C) It will have underground parking spaces.
(D) It will include solar panels.

84 What will happen next week?

(A) A new coach will be hired.
(B) A baseball game will be played.
(C) A celebrity will visit the site.
(D) A contest will be held.

85 According to the speaker, how can listeners participate in an activity?

(A) By contacting a city council member
(B) By completing an online form
(C) By visiting the stadium in person
(D) By sending an e-mail

86 What problem is the speaker discussing?

(A) An increase in unemployment
(B) A decline in tourism
(C) A failed business merger
(D) A budget reduction

87 What recently happened in Abbotsford?

(A) A marketing campaign began.
(B) A hotel was opened.
(C) A concert was held.
(D) A building was demolished.

88 What are the listeners asked to look at?

(A) A guest list
(B) A cost analysis
(C) A blueprint
(D) A street map

89 What is the topic of this week's podcast?

(A) Electric vehicles
(B) Home appliances
(C) Business software
(D) Online advertising

90 Who is the guest on this week's podcast?

(A) A Web designer
(B) A scientist
(C) A CEO
(D) A sales representative

91 Why does the speaker say, "This show is always looking for talented people"?

(A) To give information about an upcoming episode
(B) To introduce today's special guest
(C) To thank listeners for their contributions
(D) To encourage listeners to apply for a job

92 Where are the listeners?

(A) At a beach resort
(B) At a botanical garden
(C) At a business institute
(D) At a historical home

93 What does the speaker suggest when she says, "All of our tables are full"?

(A) People were interested in a workshop.
(B) Some more furniture will be brought in.
(C) The listeners can join a waiting list.
(D) An event will start later than expected.

94 What does the speaker request that the listeners do?

(A) Leave food and drinks outside
(B) Write down their questions
(C) Put away their electronic devices
(D) Pay close attention to a video

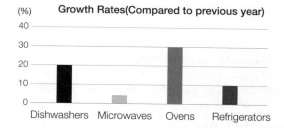

(%) Growth Rates(Compared to previous year)

Dishwashers Microwaves Ovens Refrigerators

9:00 A.M.	Ms. Mary Kelley
10:45 A.M.	Mr. Brian Steltzer
12:30 P.M.	Break for lunch
1:30 P.M.	Mr. Fred Arnott
3:15 P.M.	Ms. Anna Hendry

95 Who is the talk most likely intended for?

(A) Market researchers
(B) Sales personnel
(C) Store managers
(D) Product testers

96 Look at the graphic. What kind of appliances will be redesigned?

(A) Dishwashers
(B) Microwaves
(C) Ovens
(D) Refrigerators

97 What does the company plan to do next month?

(A) Upgrade an online store
(B) Hire more experienced workers
(C) Open a new retail branch
(D) Increase an advertising budget

98 What is the main topic of the seminar series?

(A) Architecture
(B) Human resources
(C) Graphic design
(D) Market research

99 Look at the graphic. When will the listener's seminar begin?

(A) 9:00 A.M.
(B) 10:45 A.M.
(C) 1:30 P.M.
(D) 3:15 P.M.

100 How can seminar speakers receive a gift certificate?

(A) By submitting a form
(B) By attending a meal
(C) By giving another talk
(D) By joining a discussion session

This is the end of the Listening test. Turn to Part 5 in your test book.

GO ON TO THE NEXT PAGE

READING TEST

In the Reading test, you will read a variety of texts and answer several different types of reading comprehension questions. The entire Reading test will last 75 minutes. There are three parts, and directions are given for each part. You are encouraged to answer as many questions as possible within the time allowed.

You must mark your answers on the separate answer sheet. Do not write your answers in your test book.

PART 5

Directions: A word or phrase is missing in each of the sentences below. Four answer choices are given below each sentence. Select the best answer to complete the sentence. Then mark the letter (A), (B), (C), or (D) on your answer sheet.

101 Keynote speaker Daniel Owen will address the attendees who arrived ------- countries throughout Asia.

(A) with
(B) of
(C) from
(D) as to

102 Most of the flowers that are found in the apartment complex ------- well even in rainy weather.

(A) operate
(B) choose
(C) grow
(D) explore

103 The results of the study have ------- guaranteed that the company will exceed its annual revenue target.

(A) yet
(B) already
(C) well
(D) soon

104 Ms. Graham has been placed in charge of the ------- of the community center on Central Street.

(A) opens
(B) openness
(C) opener
(D) opening

105 Ms. Curran will ------- shareholder requests for more information before the next board meeting.

(A) advise
(B) inform
(C) address
(D) install

106 Mr. Taylor will only recruit ------- applicants for the three open positions on his engineering team.

(A) qualified
(B) qualification
(C) qualifies
(D) qualify

107 Most of the subscribers are eagerly awaiting the arrival of the June ------- of the magazine.

(A) purchase
(B) charge
(C) issue
(D) admission

108 Please ------- the receptionist that someone from Berlin Dynamic will be arriving in thirty minutes.

(A) speak
(B) notify
(C) accept
(D) deliver

109 The Golden Meadows neighborhood has changed ------- in the past few years with the population growth.

(A) drama
(B) dramas
(C) dramatic
(D) dramatically

110 The lecture will be about marketing with ------- on convincing young adults to purchase products.

(A) emphasize
(B) emphatic
(C) emphasis
(D) emphasized

111 Ms. Marino's presentation was so ------- that we have invited her to speak at next year's conference.

(A) pleased
(B) informative
(C) unable
(D) helping

112 Anyone checking in at the reception desk must ------- some form of photo identification.

(A) present
(B) inspect
(C) assign
(D) place

113 Managers should speak with each employee in person and try to find solutions to any problems -------.

(A) they
(B) them
(C) their own
(D) themselves

114 We are constantly monitoring the offices to make sure that all the documents are kept -------.

(A) secures
(B) securing
(C) security
(D) secure

115 The Wellborn Academy is ------- closed because everyone on the staff is taking a one-week vacation.

(A) promptly
(B) temporarily
(C) extremely
(D) especially

116 The Rockwell Theater has received numerous inquiries from residents ------- in tickets for an upcoming performance.

(A) interest
(B) interesting
(C) interested
(D) interests

117 Refreshments for those who are at the quarterly meeting will be provided ------- Mr. Compton's talk.

(A) somewhat
(B) following
(C) whenever
(D) depending

118 Shoppers visit Armand Electronics for the ------- priced appliances and excellent customer service.

(A) reason
(B) reasoned
(C) reasonable
(D) reasonably

119 Kappa Textiles has developed a ------- for providing quality wool and silk products for the past decade.

(A) courtesy
(B) destination
(C) reputation
(D) consequence

120 An alarm will sound when workers ------- to enter a restricted part of the production facility.

(A) attempting
(B) attempt
(C) had attempted
(D) will attempt

GO ON TO THE NEXT PAGE

121 Please be aware that when scheduling client ------, you need to allocate a sufficient amount of time.

(A) locations
(B) circumstances
(C) appointments
(D) achievements

122 It is ------ that inspectors be given full access to the laboratory even if they visit on short notice.

(A) particular
(B) immediate
(C) substantial
(D) critical

123 After publishing her newest novel, Samantha Boothe plans to go on a book-signing tour ------ the country.

(A) aboard
(B) ahead of
(C) throughout
(D) besides

124 The terms of the contract indicate ------ it can be cancelled at any time if both parties agree.

(A) what
(B) or
(C) unless
(D) that

125 Mr. Taylor is well-known for his punctuality at meetings ------ his close attention to detail.

(A) as well as
(B) moreover
(C) accordingly
(D) in order that

126 Raptor Company is widely recognized as the ------ manufacturer of chemical products in Australia.

(A) led
(B) leads
(C) leader
(D) leading

127 The board members voted ------ in favor of the proposed merger with their domestic competitor.

(A) typically
(B) extremely
(C) unanimously
(D) fondly

128 As soon as Mr. Dumbarton arrived at the conference center, the CEO's annual speech ------.

(A) were begun
(B) has begun
(C) will begin
(D) began

129 ------ of the researchers takes utmost care to conduct the experiment in a proper manner.

(A) Almost
(B) All
(C) Each
(D) Everybody

130 Only certain individuals at the firm are granted access to the ------ documents stored in its warehouse.

(A) considerate
(B) perishable
(C) surrounding
(D) confidential

PART 6

Directions: Read the texts that follow. A word, phrase, or sentence is missing in parts of each text. Four answer choices for each question are given below the text. Select the best answer to complete the text. Then mark the letter (A), (B), (C), or (D) on your answer sheet.

Questions 131-134 refer to the following article.

ROSEMEAD (April 11)—The editor of *The Rosemead Tribune* has confirmed that Cynthia Exley has been hired as a full-time contributor. Ms. Exley will work on a newly added Fine Dining section that will appear regularly in the paper. It will include ------- of local restaurants
131.
and interviews with chefs. Ms. Exley has written articles for several popular food magazines
------- the years. With so much experience, she is perfect for this role. "I am actively involved
132.
in the local business community, so I can inform readers about lesser-known restaurants that may interest them," said Ms. Exley. "I am also pursuing ------- food-related interests." -------.
133. **134.**
Scheduled for May 20 at the Rosemead Community Center, the session will teach participants how to prepare healthy dishes.

131 (A) upgrades
(B) receipts
(C) reviews
(D) renovations

132 (A) about
(B) over
(C) between
(D) toward

133 (A) another
(B) each other
(C) one
(D) other

134 (A) Consequently, Ms. Exley reported on a few of her food allergies.
(B) Indeed, Ms. Exley explained, she will teach a cooking workshop next month.
(C) Otherwise, Ms. Exley will visit several dining establishments within a week.
(D) Furthermore, Ms. Exley is thinking about opening her own restaurant.

GO ON TO THE NEXT PAGE

NOTICE TO LANCASTER RESIDENTS

Several streets in Lancaster's Rowe Valley neighborhood are scheduled to undergo roadwork beginning June 2 and lasting for approximately two months. During the project, Department of Transportation workers ------- the roadway. -------, the crew plans to seal cracks, fix the drainage
                135.   **136.**
system, and resurface some sections.

------- traveling in the Rowe Valley neighborhood, check the city's Web site to see which
137.
streets are currently closed. Drivers are also reminded to watch for signs indicating that parking is temporarily suspended. -------. For further information, visit www.lancaster.gov/
                         138.
rowevalleyroadwork.

---

135 (A) to upgrade
(B) have upgraded
(C) were upgrading
(D) will upgrade

136 (A) Even so
(B) Nonetheless
(C) Specifically
(D) Otherwise

137 (A) Since
(B) During
(C) Before
(D) Around

138 (A) Driving lanes are separated by yellow lines.
(B) The speed limit may be reduced next year.
(C) Cars in no-parking zones will be towed.
(D) City residents can vote for their favorite one.

Questions 139-142 refer to the following notice.

NOTICE TO CUSTOMERS

Beginning on April 2, Venice Restaurant will start work on the planned ------- of its building. The
                                                                                139.
project aims to add an additional 1,200 square feet to the dining area. This would change the

seating capacity to 135, nearly doubling the ------- 70 seats. The new section will have the same
                                              140.
style and materials as the rest of the restaurant. The contractor in charge of the project expects it

to ------- in early September. -------. For a schedule of planned closures, follow the restaurant on
   141.   142.
social media or visit its Web site at www.venicerestaurant.net.

139 (A) expand
    (B) expansion
    (C) expansive
    (D) expanded

140 (A) final
    (B) following
    (C) current
    (D) now

141 (A) release
    (B) perform
    (C) maintain
    (D) conclude

142 (A) During the summer, our menu features a
        fish special each week.
    (B) Meanwhile, servers have the option of
        getting a new uniform.
    (C) More people are cooking at home rather
        than going out to eat.
    (D) In the interim, the business will remain
        open to diners most days.

GO ON TO THE NEXT PAGE

To: William Farley <w.farley@meadowinc.com>
From: Glenda O'Neal <g.oneal@meadowinc.com>
Date: October 25
Subject: Office Relocation

Dear Mr. Farley,

In preparation for our office relocation, I have contacted Ace Movers. I told their receptionist that

we would like to move on November 18, and -------, their team is not available on that date. This
143.
was the only company whose services were within our price range.

However, if you increase the budget, I ------- other companies to check their availability. I'll do my
144.
best to find out about their various on-site packing services as well. -------.
145.

If you think it is necessary, I don't mind checking the companies' -------. This way, we will know
146.
what will happen if something is lost or broken.

Please let me know what you would like to do,
Glenda

---

143 (A) easily
(B) apparently
(C) solely
(D) considerably

144 (A) contact
(B) have been contacting
(C) am contacting
(D) can contact

145 (A) I am concerned that this item is too
heavy to move on my own.
(B) Then, I will guide you in choosing a
company that meets our needs.
(C) The labels should be printed in a large
size to be easily read.
(D) For instance, the staff will enjoy having
more space at the new site.

146 (A) budgets
(B) nominations
(C) guarantees
(D) estimates

PART 7

Directions: In this part you will read a selection of texts, such as magazine and newspaper articles, e-mails, and instant messages. Each text or set of texts is followed by several questions. Select the best answer for each question and mark the letter (A), (B), (C), or (D) on your answer sheet.

Questions 147-148 refer to the following notice.

Paradise Garden Supplies

Top supplies for your gardening needs!

The tips below will help you to make sure your new roses thrive after being planted in your garden.

1. Choose a spot that will get 6–8 hours of sunlight daily.
2. Dig a hole deep enough so that the roots can be covered by at least 2–3 inches of soil. The plants' pots are compostable, so they can be set directly into the hole without taking the plant out first.
3. Water the plants thoroughly and regularly so that the soil does not dry out.
4. Using a pair of scissors or garden shears, trim off dead or broken stems and branches. This will help to promote growth.

147 What is mentioned about the containers for plants?

(A) They can be put into the recycling bin.
(B) They do not need to be removed.
(C) They should be returned to the company.
(D) They are usually two to three inches wide.

148 What is NOT indicated as advice for planting the roses?

(A) Cutting off broken parts
(B) Using a sunny location
(C) Replacing the soil regularly
(D) Keeping the soil moist

GO ON TO THE NEXT PAGE ▶

Whitaker Bath and Tile

Pine Valley's reliable tile specialist for over 30 years

Your home is a major investment, and it's never too late to make upgrades. A bathroom renovation can help you to add value to your home as well as make it more comfortable and stylish.

Throughout the month of February, we're offering 15% off all materials and 10% off all labor costs for a bathroom renovation. Call 555-8463 to book this service and take advantage of this fantastic deal. Included in the promotion is a free consultation from a bathroom designer, who will help you choose the tile colors, layout, and bathroom fixtures that work for you.

We have hundreds of tiles in our collection, so you're sure to find what you need. Visit our Web site at www.whitakerbath.com to view a gallery of photos from our previous projects. We look forward to serving you!

149 What is suggested about Whitaker Bath and Tile?

(A) It is an established company.
(B) It is adding more services.
(C) It is under new management.
(D) It has the lowest prices.

150 What can customers receive with the special offer?

(A) Some waterproofing treatment
(B) Free design services
(C) A bottle of tile cleaner
(D) An extended warranty

Questions 151-152 refer to the following information.

Almeida Inc. is proud to create useful software for home and office use, and we want to make sure all of our customers can get started with using the software as quickly as possible.

Each program comes with detailed instructions to help you to install the software. However, we understand that some customers may need additional help. If this is the case for you, we recommend visiting our Web site at www.almeidainc.com and looking up the instructional video that corresponds to the software you purchased and your computer type. Alternatively, you can also speak to a technician twenty-four hours a day, seven days a week on our helpline at 1-800-555-0688. Should you have any comments or complaints, you can e-mail us at service@almeidainc.com, and you will receive a response within three business days.

151 Why was the information mainly written?
  (A) To outline the differences between programs
  (B) To recommend downloading a software update
  (C) To explain how to get help with installation
  (D) To request feedback on past purchases

152 What is indicated about Almeida Inc.?
  (A) Its products are not recommended for certain computers.
  (B) Its customer support is available at all times.
  (C) It plans to open more retail branches.
  (D) It can assist customers through video chat.

GO ON TO THE NEXT PAGE

Midvale Plumbing
Certified · Experienced · Comprehensive

– Repairing leaks and cracks in pipes

– Installing dishwashers, washing machines, and water heaters

– Clearing clogged drains

– Installing showers, sinks, and toilets

– Testing gas lines for safety compliance

If you're looking for exceptional work at a reasonable cost, then Midvale Plumbing is the right choice for you. Call us at 555-7113 to get a quote or book an appointment. We are happy to provide customer testimonials to any customers who ask for them.

153 What is suggested about Midvale Plumbing?

(A) It offers services every day.

(B) It has affordable prices.

(C) It is seeking certified plumbers.

(D) It provides quotes by e-mail.

154 What is NOT indicated as a task performed by Midvale Plumbing?

(A) Setting up home appliances

(B) Checking the safety of gas lines

(C) Replacing cracked sinks

(D) Fixing damaged pipes

155 According to the advertisement, what can be provided upon request?

(A) Drawings of the proposed work

(B) Copies of certification documents

(C) A list of the necessary materials needed

(D) Recommendations from former customers

http://www.roxburytheater.com

ROXBURY THEATER TOUR

A behind-the-scenes look at the area's largest working theater!

Roxbury Theater, which dates back to the early 1900s, offers tours year-round. Tours cost $11.50 per person and last for approximately ninety minutes. Your tour guide will tell you all about how the theater has changed over time, and you'll get to see some of the most interesting parts of the theater, such as the costume room, backstage area, and private seating areas. Tours are conducted in English, but fact sheets are available in Spanish, German, and Chinese. There's always something exciting happening at Roxbury Theater, so tour start times vary depending on the show schedule. Some tour participants may even get to watch rehearsals for upcoming shows.

We're proud of our contribution to the local theater community, especially in the past five years since Ethel Saxton bought the theater in an effort to revive the performing arts. At the end of the tour, participants are welcome to visit the theater's gift shop. There is also an option to attend a lecture from a theater expert. This activity costs $8 on top of the tour fee.

Test 05

156 What is true about the Roxbury Theater Tour?

(A) It allows participants to meet performers in person.
(B) It lasts for longer than two hours.
(C) It will be canceled if the group size is too small.
(D) It provides information in a variety of languages.

157 Who most likely is Ms. Saxton?

(A) A theater owner
(B) A tour guide
(C) A famous actress
(D) An entertainment critic

158 According to the Web page, what can theater visitors do for an extra charge?

(A) Join a membership program
(B) View performers practicing
(C) Watch a talk
(D) Visit a backstage area

GO ON TO THE NEXT PAGE

Questions 159-160 refer to the following text-message chain.

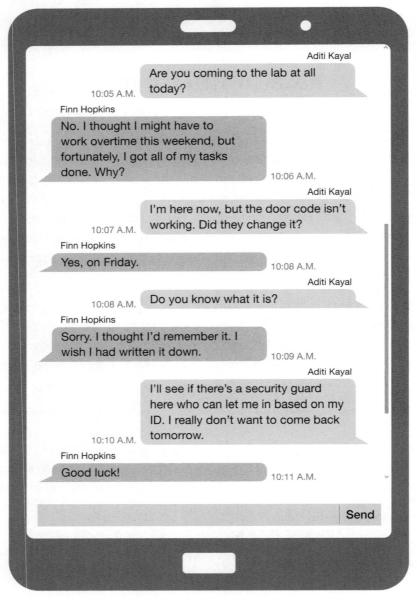

Aditi Kayal

Are you coming to the lab at all today?
10:05 A.M.

Finn Hopkins

No. I thought I might have to work overtime this weekend, but fortunately, I got all of my tasks done. Why?
10:06 A.M.

Aditi Kayal

I'm here now, but the door code isn't working. Did they change it?
10:07 A.M.

Finn Hopkins

Yes, on Friday.
10:08 A.M.

Aditi Kayal

Do you know what it is?
10:08 A.M.

Finn Hopkins

Sorry. I thought I'd remember it. I wish I had written it down.
10:09 A.M.

Aditi Kayal

I'll see if there's a security guard here who can let me in based on my ID. I really don't want to come back tomorrow.
10:10 A.M.

Finn Hopkins

Good luck!
10:11 A.M.

Send

159 At 10:09 A.M., what does Mr. Hopkins imply when he writes, "I wish I had written it down"?

(A) He does not remember a code.
(B) He has forgotten about a policy.
(C) He cannot find a phone number.
(D) He needs proof of an error.

160 What does Ms. Kayal decide to do?

(A) Update her employee ID
(B) Wait for Mr. Hopkins to arrive
(C) Come back the following day
(D) Ask another person for help

Milwaukee Tribune Business Corner

September 8—Splitworks, a flexible workspace located in downtown Milwaukee, has been sold by founder Simon Landry to entrepreneur Shana Durant. —[1]—. Mr. Landry, who was self-employed at the time, started the business because he was tired of working in noisy coffee shops. In addition to using a quiet office environment, members also have access to office equipment such as copy machines and printers, and they can have their business mail sent to the Splitworks address. Ms. Durant is excited about taking over the business. —[2]—. "As the dynamics of our local economy shift, more and more people are becoming self-employed, either full-time or part-time. I'm ready to take this great business idea to the next level. —[3]—." Splitworks occupies the third and fourth floor of the Logan Building, but Ms. Durant is negotiating with the building owner to add the second floor as well, as the current tenant will be leaving soon. Membership to Splitworks is reasonably priced. —[4]—. Then members simply pay $4 per hour or $15 per day every time they use the site.

161 Why was the article written?

(A) To explain a trend in downtown businesses

(B) To report a company's change in ownership

(C) To announce the opening of a new coffee shop

(D) To describe the benefits of self-employment

162 According to the article, what does Ms. Durant hope to do?

(A) Expand an office area

(B) Upgrade some equipment

(C) Move to a new location

(D) Attract more investors

163 In which of the positions marked [1], [2], [3], and [4] does the following sentence best belong?

"The company charges an initial sign-up fee of $100."

(A) [1]

(B) [2]

(C) [3]

(D) [4]

GO ON TO THE NEXT PAGE

To: All Q-Valley Foods Employees
From: Joshua Diaz
Re: Plans for new cereal

Dear Q-Valley Foods Staff,

As you know, our company is planning to launch a new chocolate rice puff cereal for children, and we need a mascot for the product. My department reached out to employees and received a lot of fantastic ideas. The marketing team is thankful to those of you who shared your creative ideas. We had over 50 entries in total. Among these, we've narrowed it down to the three options below:

Suggested Name	Description	Submitted By
Choco	A funny monkey	Katherine Rossetti
Charles Chocolate	A cute teddy bear	Janet Dorsett
Max Breakfast	A cool dog	Raymond Frazier

Among these three, we'd like your help in choosing the final one. Please visit the Q-Valley employee Web site and click the Contest tab. There you can see some sample drawings of what each mascot would look like, and you can vote for your favorite one. Voting will be open until this Friday, September 9.

At our next monthly staff meeting, on September 15, we will announce the winner, and the person who submitted the winning idea will be given a cash prize. Since the cereal will hit the market on October 20, we'll begin airing commercials with the new mascot from October 13. We'll show them to staff members at the October meeting.

If you have any difficulty with using the tab on the Web site, please contact the IT department directly.

Thanks!

Joshua Diaz

164 What will employees assist Mr. Diaz's department in doing?

(A) Completing a survey
(B) Filming a commercial
(C) Drawing a character
(D) Selecting a winner

165 The word "entries" in paragraph 1, line 4, is closest in meaning to

(A) struggles
(B) trends
(C) submissions
(D) entrances

166 What will happen at the next monthly staff meeting?

(A) A vote will be taken.
(B) A prize will be awarded.
(C) New employees will be introduced.
(D) Some samples will be distributed.

167 When does Q-Valley plan to start running new advertisements?

(A) On September 9
(B) On September 15
(C) On October 13
(D) On October 20

GO ON TO THE NEXT PAGE

It takes great courage to start a business. It is perhaps an even greater challenge to change the direction of a successful business. That's exactly what chef Sue Rodding did when she converted her successful fine dining establishment *The Golden Oyster* into a casual diner serving Asian street food called *Street Eats*. "I was so inspired by my travels and my love for the region. I just knew it was something I had to do," Sue says. —[1]—.

Industry expert Peter Landon feels making such a drastic change is inherently risky. "You are basically starting over. Your previous reputation doesn't count for much and you have to build a new brand up from the ground again," says Mr. Landon. "Loyal customers may dislike the changes and stop visiting your premises." Nevertheless, Ms. Rodding is fully committed to her vision, devising succulent menu items with bold new flavor combination alongside assistant chef Trey Barnett. —[2]—. Sue even went as far as to hire interior designer Peter Bairstow, who recently received the Albrighton prize for outstanding work in his field. Restaurant patrons have commented on how Peter's vibrant design features have created the feeling of being in a bustling Asian city. —[3]—.

So two months after opening, is Ms. Rodding happy with the changes? "Absolutely," she says. "Business is thriving, and we've managed to attract a much younger crowd that may have been put off by the formal setting of *The Golden Oyster*." As for the future, Sue has no plans to stop now, and hopes to open new branches of *Street Eats* in Chicago and New York. —[4]—. With the passion and drive Sue clearly possesses, there is no reason why her vision would not be a nationwide success.

168 What is the purpose of this article?

(A) To advertise a job vacancy
(B) To publicize a special opening event
(C) To offer discounted tour packages
(D) To highlight the reinvention of a business

169 What warning does Peter Landon offer?

(A) Building rental costs may rise sharply.
(B) Existing customers may not be happy.
(C) Opening a business in multiple locations is difficult.
(D) Ingredients may be difficult to source.

170 What is indicated about Mr. Bairstow?

(A) He won an award for his work.
(B) He has been a long-term customer of the restaurant.
(C) He owns property in New York.
(D) He helped create new menu items.

171 In which of the positions marked [1], [2], [3], and [4] does the following sentence best belong?

"It is thought that the use of neon lighting contributes to creating an authentic urban vibe."

(A) [1]
(B) [2]
(C) [3]
(D) [4]

GO ON TO THE NEXT PAGE

Questions 172–175 refer to the following online chat discussion.

👤 Denise Powell   — X

👤 Denise Powell [9:08 A.M.]	Hi, Rishu and Kaua. I just wanted to let you know that Worley Plaza is booked for September 15, so we can't hold the retirement dinner there. I've gone ahead and made a reservation at Cruz Hall instead.
Rishu Parekh [9:09 A.M.]	I'm glad that's settled.
Kaua Sousa [9:10 A.M.]	Worley Plaza is definitely a more convenient location, but Cruz Hall is just as nice, and it's substantially cheaper.
Rishu Parekh [9:11 A.M.]	Exactly! We're much better off.
👤 Denise Powell [9:12 A.M.]	We need to start thinking about the catering options next. I've got some brochures if you want to stop by and see them. But please note that I have to visit a client after lunch, so you'll want to do that before noon.
Kaua Sousa [9:13 A.M.]	I'll definitely give those a look. I have some ideas in mind.
👤 Denise Powell [9:13 A.M.]	We should also finalize our plans regarding decorations. What colors are we using for the theme?
Rishu Parekh [9:14 A.M.]	We decided on green and black. There will be lights, streamers, and balloons. I can purchase those online.
👤 Denise Powell [9:15 A.M.]	Thanks, Rishu.
Kaua Sousa [9:15 A.M.]	Rishu, could you wait a few days to do that? I'd like to check to see what we have in the storage room first. There may be things that we can reuse.
Rishu Parekh [9:16 A.M.]	No problem.

Send

172 Why did Ms. Powell start an online chat with the other writers?

(A) To invite them on a tour of a facility
(B) To suggest a time to finish planning
(C) To notify them of a venue selection
(D) To confirm the number of guests for an event

173 At 9:11 A.M., what does Ms. Parekh most likely mean when she writes, "We're much better off"?

(A) She is pleased with a final decision.
(B) She expects good attendance at an event.
(C) She would prefer to make an in-person visit.
(D) She thinks that the caterer will do a good job.

174 What does Ms. Powell most likely intend to do before lunch?

(A) Sample some menu items
(B) Work in her office
(C) Attend a client meeting
(D) E-mail some details

175 What does Mr. Sousa want Ms. Parekh to do?

(A) Label some items in a storage area
(B) Delay purchasing some decorations
(C) Consider some different color options
(D) Announce the theme to coworkers

GO ON TO THE NEXT PAGE

Hidden Gem

by Melanie Hyde

June 18—In the next segment of my travels across Canada, I visited the province of Nova Scotia. I was expecting to encounter only businesses related to the fishing industry, including numerous seafood restaurants. However, I was pleasantly surprised by the diverse culinary options available in Dartmouth. The town itself is less than 10 kilometers from Halifax, the capital of the province of Nova Scotia, and connected via public transportation, and I found a delightful Italian bistro there called Paradiso, which is on Windmill Road. All diners will love the charming atmosphere of the restaurant, which is enhanced by the wooden tables and chairs that were handmade using the maple trees grown in the area. In addition, the menu has been created by world-renowned chef Raimondo Sagese. The portions were very large, and everything I ordered was delicious. If you find yourself in Dartmouth, be sure to put this place on your list.

To follow my summer adventures, with exclusive photos in my Web gallery, visit www. melaniestravels.ca.

To	Gabriel Dale <g.dale@hammond-inc.com>
From	Eva Herbert <e.herbert@hammond-inc.com>
Date	June 29
Subject	Annual trade show

Dear Mr. Dale,

Thank you for explaining our company's reimbursement procedures regarding my business trip for the trade show. I also understand that I will have to pay out of pocket for any meals that exceed the daily budget maximum that you mentioned. I don't think this will happen on most days, but I might treat myself to a great meal at Paradiso. It's in a town only 10 kilometers from the trade show, which takes place in the province's capital. I'm also wondering if I can choose my preferred car rental agency for this trip. I know the company usually uses Ace Cars because it is known for having the lowest prices. However, Roadwaze has much newer vehicles, and it is currently offering fifteen percent off all rentals, which puts it at a similar price point to Ace Cars. Please let me know.

Eva

176 What is a purpose of the article?

(A) To promote a transportation service
(B) To give a restaurant recommendation
(C) To describe a hotel
(D) To provide a travel agency review

177 What is mentioned about the furniture?

(A) It is very comfortable to use.
(B) It has been imported from overseas.
(C) It is made from locally sourced materials.
(D) It features a unique regional style.

178 Who most likely is Mr. Dale?

(A) A trade show presenter
(B) A tour guide
(C) A famous chef
(D) An accountant

179 What is implied about the trade show?

(A) It offers meals to attendees.
(B) It will take place in Halifax.
(C) It is being held for the first time.
(D) It provides free entry for groups.

180 What does Ms. Herbert mention about Roadwaze?

(A) It needs to upgrade its vehicles.
(B) It is currently having a sale.
(C) It is frequently used by the staff.
(D) It has a high safety rating.

GO ON TO THE NEXT PAGE

Questions 181-185 refer to the following advertisement and form.

Tetrick Corporate Development Center (TCDC)
www.tetrickcdc.com

In a competitive business world, education is the right tool to give you an edge. For the past decade, TCDC has helped thousands of people with their professional development through our fun and informative classes on business strategies and corporate activities. We approach these events in a student-centered way, which means our expert instructors will make sure you're getting the support you need. Check out our educational events in June below.

Event ID	Title	Instructor	Date	Time
J082	Evidence-Based Management	Lynn Yang	June 8	2 P.M.–5 P.M.
J146	Driving Social Change	James Ulrich	June 14	9 A.M.–12 P.M.
J158	Tools for the Digital Age	Lynn Yang	June 20	10 A.M.–1 P.M.
J273	Building Your Professional Network	Vineet Pandey	June 29	3 P.M.–6 P.M.

All classes are held at the TCDC Center, which is located at 943 Grandview Drive, Rockford, IL 61101. The building has free on-site parking. The cost of each session is $85, which can be paid through our secure portal online or by sending a check to our business office.

Tetrick Corporate Development Center (TCDC)

Student Registration Form: June Sessions

Inquiries or Comments: 779-555-6681

Name: *Cleo Rossi*

E-mail Address: *rossicleo@irvine-mail.com*   Phone Number: *779-555-0489*

Preferred Form of Contact: [✓] E-mail   [ ] Phone

Company: *Barnes Financial Consulting*

Desired Event(s): *J158*

How did you find out about TCDC? *Recommendation from a colleague*

Payment Type: [✓] Credit Card (You will be brought to the payment page after clicking "Submit".)

[ ] Check (The mailing address will appear after clicking "Submit".)

Would you like to join our mailing list to find out more about upcoming events?

[ ] Yes   [✓] No

Note: Registration is available on a first-come, first-served basis. Should your requested session be full, you will be added to a waiting list. If at least twenty people do not enroll in a session, it will be canceled.

Submit

---

181 What does TCDC do?

(A) Provides marketing services
(B) Recruits workers for jobs
(C) Trains people in business topics
(D) Hosts corporate retreats

182 In the advertisement, the word "approach" in paragraph 1, line 3, is closest in meaning to

(A) deal with
(B) access
(C) request
(D) arrive

183 What is mentioned about the June events?

(A) Some of them may require previous experience.
(B) They will all take place in the afternoon.
(C) Two of them will be taught by James Ulrich.
(D) They need a minimum number of people to register.

184 When does Ms. Rossi plan to attend an event?

(A) On June 8
(B) On June 14
(C) On June 20
(D) On June 29

185 What is suggested about Ms. Rossi?

(A) She works in the finance industry.
(B) She is in a managerial position.
(C) She plans to attend more sessions.
(D) She learned about TCDC through an ad.

GO ON TO THE NEXT PAGE

To Hector McGowan <h.mcgowan@leoindustries.com>

From Natalia Fanucci <n.fanucci@leoindustries.com>

Date September 2

Subject Arrangements

Hector,

I heard that you'll be in charge of making arrangements for the operations director from Sarona Manufacturing when he visits our branch on September 23. I had that same job when he visited last quarter, so I wanted to share what I learned. He is very sensitive to air travel. So, although most clients are happy to have a business dinner on the day they arrive—I know you did this for the Diaz International representatives—I think he would be more comfortable having the evening free and eating in his room. It would be best to keep that in mind when booking the hotel.

I hope this helps,

Natalia

Vanetta Hotel

Atlanta

Enjoy the luxury and comfort of Vanetta Hotel, located just a five-minute drive from Hartsfield–Jackson Atlanta International Airport. The following amenities are available during your stay:

- A king-sized bed and flat-screen TV in each room
- A strong Wi-Fi connection in all parts of the hotel
- Round-the-clock room service from our four-star restaurant
- Free daily passes to Titan Gym (down the street from our hotel)
- Ten percent off parties booking for ten or more people

Call 555-6053 to make your booking or to get more information.

Vanetta Hotel

—Your comfort is our mission! —

September 23

Dear Mr. Ayers,

On behalf of Leo Industries, I would like to welcome you to Atlanta. I hope you had a pleasant flight. Please enjoy a quiet evening and then have a leisurely morning meal tomorrow before heading to our office. We've arranged for HM Transportation to pick you up. So, just call them about 15 minutes before you're ready to leave. Their card is attached to this note. If you need anything, my mobile number is 678-555-0622.

I look forward to seeing you tomorrow!

Hector McGowan

---

186 Why did Ms. Fanucci send the e-mail?

(A) To change the deadline of an assignment
(B) To give advice about preparing for a visit
(C) To recommend a colleague for a job
(D) To report changes to a travel plan

187 Why would Ms. Fanucci most likely think the Vanetta Hotel is a good choice?

(A) It has an on-site business center.
(B) It has a large bed in each room.
(C) It can prepare food for in-room consumption.
(D) It was recommended by Mr. McGowan.

188 Based on the advertisement, what is NOT true about the Vanetta Hotel?

(A) It has Internet throughout.
(B) It is near the airport.
(C) It has an on-site exercise area.
(D) It offers discounts for groups.

189 For what business does Mr. Ayers work?

(A) Diaz International
(B) HM Transportation
(C) Sarona Manufacturing
(D) Vanetta Hotel

190 When most likely will Mr. Ayers go to Mr. McGowan's office?

(A) After lunch on September 23
(B) After dinner on September 23
(C) After breakfast on September 24
(D) After dinner on September 24

GO ON TO THE NEXT PAGE

The Artist Market

5th Anniversary Celebration

Saturday, May 16, 9 A.M. to 6 P.M.

Enjoy free refreshments and meet our talented artists.

Enter our drawing for a chance to win one of three original paintings.

Our Shops:

Cloud Mania: metal sculptures with a sci-fi theme

Gina's World: landscape paintings in watercolor

Earth to Earth: clay vases, bowls, and cups

Sunshine Palace: handmade jewelry and gifts

E-Mail Message

To: Alan Beck <a_beck@eugeneproperties.com>
From: Linda Lee <linda@lindaleecreations.com>
Date: June 4
Subject: The Artist Market

Dear Mr. Beck,

It is my understanding that the pottery shop at The Artist Market will be closing next month, and I would like to find out if the space is available for another vendor. I'm wondering about the monthly fee, what kind of storage is available, and the exact size. I have been operating from a small pottery studio for the past three years, but I'm looking for a site with better foot traffic. I've also added another artist as a business partner, whose pieces were featured in an exhibition at the Fontaine Gallery just last month. Please contact me at 555-9643 at your earliest convenience to discuss this further.

Sincerely,

Linda Lee

Artists Gain Attention after Relocation

August 28

By Adrian Hamilton

Linda Lee and her new partner, Nora Coleman, have recently moved their business to The Artist Market. The shop, Linda Lee Creations, features handmade pottery items that are crafted with expertise and love. I have been slowly adding to my collection with visits to the original studio in the center of the Providence neighborhood. I'm pleased that more people will be able to access Ms. Lee's work, and now Ms. Coleman's, at the more convenient location. Though the studio is no longer a two-minute walk from my home, I'll still be a regular shopper. Everyone should check this business out.

191 What is true about the May 16 event?

(A) There is a fee for admission.
(B) Some participants will win a prize.
(C) It will raise money for a local charity.
(D) Some musicians will give a performance.

192 Which business is leaving The Artist Market in July?

(A) Cloud Mania
(B) Gina's World
(C) Earth to Earth
(D) Sunshine Palace

193 What is the purpose of the e-mail?

(A) To promote a line of products
(B) To ask for directions to a shop
(C) To request a donation to a charity
(D) To get details about a rental space

194 What is suggested by Mr. Hamilton?

(A) He has trained formally as an artist.
(B) He lives in the Providence neighborhood.
(C) He conducted an interview with Ms. Lee.
(D) He wants to purchase Ms. Lee's studio.

195 What is indicated about Ms. Coleman?

(A) She recently displayed her work publicly.
(B) She plans to teach some art classes.
(C) She attended art school with Ms. Lee.
(D) She has won an award for her creations.

GO ON TO THE NEXT PAGE

Frisco Offers Up Treats for Health-Conscious Consumers

KENWOOD (4 April)—After years of developing her own recipes for baked goods as a hobby, Alice Nevin's new café, Frisco, will be open for business from April 6. The coffee shop features classic coffee drinks, cakes, and pastries with a twist—all of the items are sugar-free. Ms. Nevin uses fruit and natural sweeteners such as honey to make her creations.

Ms. Nevin wasn't always in the baking business. She studied economics at Valley University and then got a job at Leona Financial right after graduating. She always loved baking as a hobby. However, when her brother's doctor told him to eat less sugar due to health issues, Ms. Nevin began to create delicious sugar-free alternatives for him. She thought that many people might have similar conditions, so she was inspired to make her treats publicly available. "Many people are cutting down on their sugar consumption these days," said Ms. Nevin. "I hope everyone will give us a chance so they can see that natural flavors can be delicious."

Frisco is located at 103 Nash Street. It will operate daily from 7:30 A.M. to 8:30 P.M.

— Frisco Invites You —

Try a wide range of sugar-free pastries and tour our new coffee shop!

Friday, April 13, 9 P.M.–11 P.M.

We'll also have both caffeinated and non-caffeinated

drinks available, along with prizes for visitors.

This invitation is required for entry, so please bring it with you.

To   Alice Nevin <a.nevin@friscocshop.com>

From   Peter Orton <peterorton@hoffmaninc.com>

Date   April 5

Subject   April 13 event

Dear Alice,

I was delighted to receive your invitation in the mail for the upcoming event at your coffee shop. Thanks for thinking of me! I'm really looking forward to the event. It'll be great to catch up with you, see the site, and—of course—taste your delicious creations. I remember that when we worked together right after we graduated you were already passionate about healthy eating. I can't wait to hear more about how you are doing these days.

Cheers,

Peter

196 Why was the article written?

(A) To review coffee shops in the area
(B) To promote a business's opening
(C) To announce changes to a menu
(D) To give tips on how to cut out sugar

197 What gave Ms. Nevin the idea for her coffee shop?

(A) A community baking contest
(B) A talk with one of her university professors
(C) Health problems of a relative
(D) An international vacation

198 What is indicated about the April 13 event?

(A) Musical entertainment will be provided.
(B) There will be a fee to enter.
(C) Its invitees can bring a guest.
(D) It takes place after business hours.

199 Why did Mr. Orton send the e-mail?

(A) To ask Ms. Nevin for a recipe
(B) To correct an article
(C) To accept an invitation
(D) To confirm his dietary preferences

200 What is suggested about Mr. Orton?

(A) He used to work at Leona Financial.
(B) He can supply goods to Ms. Nevin.
(C) He is unable to eat sugar.
(D) He wants to start his own business.

GO ON TO THE NEXT PAGE

ANSWER SHEET

Actual Test 1

좌석번호
Ⓐ Ⓑ Ⓒ Ⓓ Ⓔ
① ② ③ ④ ⑤ ⑥ ⑦

수험번호		성명	한글
			한자
			영자

응시일자 :   년   월   일

확 인

LISTENING (Part I~IV)

각 문항 1~100번: ANSWER A B C D

NO.	NO.	NO.	NO.	NO.
1	21	41	61	81
2	22	42	62	82
3	23	43	63	83
4	24	44	64	84
5	25	45	65	85
6	26	46	66	86
7	27	47	67	87
8	28	48	68	88
9	29	49	69	89
10	30	50	70	90
11	31	51	71	91
12	32	52	72	92
13	33	53	73	93
14	34	54	74	94
15	35	55	75	95
16	36	56	76	96
17	37	57	77	97
18	38	58	78	98
19	39	59	79	99
20	40	60	80	100

(각 문항 ANSWER Ⓐ Ⓑ Ⓒ Ⓓ)

READING (Part V~VII)

각 문항 101~200번: ANSWER A B C D

NO.	NO.	NO.	NO.	NO.
101	121	141	161	181
102	122	142	162	182
103	123	143	163	183
104	124	144	164	184
105	125	145	165	185
106	126	146	166	186
107	127	147	167	187
108	128	148	168	188
109	129	149	169	189
110	130	150	170	190
111	131	151	171	191
112	132	152	172	192
113	133	153	173	193
114	134	154	174	194
115	135	155	175	195
116	136	156	176	196
117	137	157	177	197
118	138	158	178	198
119	139	159	179	199
120	140	160	180	200

(각 문항 ANSWER Ⓐ Ⓑ Ⓒ Ⓓ)

1. 사용 필기구 : 컴퓨터용 연필(연필을 제외한 사인펜, 볼펜 등은 사용 절대 불가)

2. 잘못된 필기구 사용과 〈보기〉의 올바른 표기 이외의 잘못된 표기로 한 경우에는 당 위원회의 OMR기기가 판독한 결과에 따르며 그 결과는 본인 책임입니다. 1개의 정답만 골라 아래의 올바른 표기대로 정확히 표기하여야 합니다.

〈보기〉 올바른 표기 : ●   잘못된 표기 : Ⓧ Ⓥ ⦶

3. 답안지는 컴퓨터로 처리되므로 훼손하시면 안 되며, 상단의 타이밍마크(▐▐▐▐)부분을 찢거나, 낙서 등을 하면 본인에게 불이익이 발생할 수 있습니다.

4. 감독관의 확인이 없거나 시험 종료 후에 답안 작성을 계속할 경우 시험 무효 처리됩니다.

*서약 내용을 읽으시고 확인란에 반드시 서명하십시오.

서 약

본인은 TOEIC 시험 문제의 일부 또는 전부를 유출하거나 어떠한 형태로든 타인에게 누설 공개하지 않을 것이며 인터넷 또는 인쇄물 등을 이용해 유포하거나 참고 자료로 활용하지 않을 것입니다. 또한 TOEIC 시험 부정 행위 처리 규정을 준수할 것을 서약합니다.

ANSWER SHEET

Actual Test 2

응시일자 :   년   월   일

수험번호

성명 한글
성명 한자
성명 영자

좌석번호
Ⓐ Ⓑ Ⓒ Ⓓ Ⓔ
① ② ③ ④ ⑤ ⑥ ⑦

LISTENING (Part I~IV)

NO.	ANSWER	NO.	ANSWER	NO.	ANSWER	NO.	ANSWER	NO.	ANSWER
	A B C D		A B C D		A B C D		A B C D		A B C D
1	Ⓐ Ⓑ Ⓒ Ⓓ	21	Ⓐ Ⓑ Ⓒ Ⓓ	41	Ⓐ Ⓑ Ⓒ Ⓓ	61	Ⓐ Ⓑ Ⓒ Ⓓ	81	Ⓐ Ⓑ Ⓒ Ⓓ
2	Ⓐ Ⓑ Ⓒ Ⓓ	22	Ⓐ Ⓑ Ⓒ Ⓓ	42	Ⓐ Ⓑ Ⓒ Ⓓ	62	Ⓐ Ⓑ Ⓒ Ⓓ	82	Ⓐ Ⓑ Ⓒ Ⓓ
3	Ⓐ Ⓑ Ⓒ Ⓓ	23	Ⓐ Ⓑ Ⓒ Ⓓ	43	Ⓐ Ⓑ Ⓒ Ⓓ	63	Ⓐ Ⓑ Ⓒ Ⓓ	83	Ⓐ Ⓑ Ⓒ Ⓓ
4	Ⓐ Ⓑ Ⓒ Ⓓ	24	Ⓐ Ⓑ Ⓒ Ⓓ	44	Ⓐ Ⓑ Ⓒ Ⓓ	64	Ⓐ Ⓑ Ⓒ Ⓓ	84	Ⓐ Ⓑ Ⓒ Ⓓ
5	Ⓐ Ⓑ Ⓒ Ⓓ	25	Ⓐ Ⓑ Ⓒ Ⓓ	45	Ⓐ Ⓑ Ⓒ Ⓓ	65	Ⓐ Ⓑ Ⓒ Ⓓ	85	Ⓐ Ⓑ Ⓒ Ⓓ
6	Ⓐ Ⓑ Ⓒ Ⓓ	26	Ⓐ Ⓑ Ⓒ Ⓓ	46	Ⓐ Ⓑ Ⓒ Ⓓ	66	Ⓐ Ⓑ Ⓒ Ⓓ	86	Ⓐ Ⓑ Ⓒ Ⓓ
7	Ⓐ Ⓑ Ⓒ Ⓓ	27	Ⓐ Ⓑ Ⓒ Ⓓ	47	Ⓐ Ⓑ Ⓒ Ⓓ	67	Ⓐ Ⓑ Ⓒ Ⓓ	87	Ⓐ Ⓑ Ⓒ Ⓓ
8	Ⓐ Ⓑ Ⓒ Ⓓ	28	Ⓐ Ⓑ Ⓒ Ⓓ	48	Ⓐ Ⓑ Ⓒ Ⓓ	68	Ⓐ Ⓑ Ⓒ Ⓓ	88	Ⓐ Ⓑ Ⓒ Ⓓ
9	Ⓐ Ⓑ Ⓒ Ⓓ	29	Ⓐ Ⓑ Ⓒ Ⓓ	49	Ⓐ Ⓑ Ⓒ Ⓓ	69	Ⓐ Ⓑ Ⓒ Ⓓ	89	Ⓐ Ⓑ Ⓒ Ⓓ
10	Ⓐ Ⓑ Ⓒ Ⓓ	30	Ⓐ Ⓑ Ⓒ Ⓓ	50	Ⓐ Ⓑ Ⓒ Ⓓ	70	Ⓐ Ⓑ Ⓒ Ⓓ	90	Ⓐ Ⓑ Ⓒ Ⓓ
11	Ⓐ Ⓑ Ⓒ Ⓓ	31	Ⓐ Ⓑ Ⓒ Ⓓ	51	Ⓐ Ⓑ Ⓒ Ⓓ	71	Ⓐ Ⓑ Ⓒ Ⓓ	91	Ⓐ Ⓑ Ⓒ Ⓓ
12	Ⓐ Ⓑ Ⓒ Ⓓ	32	Ⓐ Ⓑ Ⓒ Ⓓ	52	Ⓐ Ⓑ Ⓒ Ⓓ	72	Ⓐ Ⓑ Ⓒ Ⓓ	92	Ⓐ Ⓑ Ⓒ Ⓓ
13	Ⓐ Ⓑ Ⓒ Ⓓ	33	Ⓐ Ⓑ Ⓒ Ⓓ	53	Ⓐ Ⓑ Ⓒ Ⓓ	73	Ⓐ Ⓑ Ⓒ Ⓓ	93	Ⓐ Ⓑ Ⓒ Ⓓ
14	Ⓐ Ⓑ Ⓒ Ⓓ	34	Ⓐ Ⓑ Ⓒ Ⓓ	54	Ⓐ Ⓑ Ⓒ Ⓓ	74	Ⓐ Ⓑ Ⓒ Ⓓ	94	Ⓐ Ⓑ Ⓒ Ⓓ
15	Ⓐ Ⓑ Ⓒ Ⓓ	35	Ⓐ Ⓑ Ⓒ Ⓓ	55	Ⓐ Ⓑ Ⓒ Ⓓ	75	Ⓐ Ⓑ Ⓒ Ⓓ	95	Ⓐ Ⓑ Ⓒ Ⓓ
16	Ⓐ Ⓑ Ⓒ Ⓓ	36	Ⓐ Ⓑ Ⓒ Ⓓ	56	Ⓐ Ⓑ Ⓒ Ⓓ	76	Ⓐ Ⓑ Ⓒ Ⓓ	96	Ⓐ Ⓑ Ⓒ Ⓓ
17	Ⓐ Ⓑ Ⓒ Ⓓ	37	Ⓐ Ⓑ Ⓒ Ⓓ	57	Ⓐ Ⓑ Ⓒ Ⓓ	77	Ⓐ Ⓑ Ⓒ Ⓓ	97	Ⓐ Ⓑ Ⓒ Ⓓ
18	Ⓐ Ⓑ Ⓒ Ⓓ	38	Ⓐ Ⓑ Ⓒ Ⓓ	58	Ⓐ Ⓑ Ⓒ Ⓓ	78	Ⓐ Ⓑ Ⓒ Ⓓ	98	Ⓐ Ⓑ Ⓒ Ⓓ
19	Ⓐ Ⓑ Ⓒ Ⓓ	39	Ⓐ Ⓑ Ⓒ Ⓓ	59	Ⓐ Ⓑ Ⓒ Ⓓ	79	Ⓐ Ⓑ Ⓒ Ⓓ	99	Ⓐ Ⓑ Ⓒ Ⓓ
20	Ⓐ Ⓑ Ⓒ Ⓓ	40	Ⓐ Ⓑ Ⓒ Ⓓ	60	Ⓐ Ⓑ Ⓒ Ⓓ	80	Ⓐ Ⓑ Ⓒ Ⓓ	100	Ⓐ Ⓑ Ⓒ Ⓓ

READING (Part V~VII)

NO.	ANSWER	NO.	ANSWER	NO.	ANSWER	NO.	ANSWER	NO.	ANSWER
	A B C D		A B C D		A B C D		A B C D		A B C D
101	Ⓐ Ⓑ Ⓒ Ⓓ	121	Ⓐ Ⓑ Ⓒ Ⓓ	141	Ⓐ Ⓑ Ⓒ Ⓓ	161	Ⓐ Ⓑ Ⓒ Ⓓ	181	Ⓐ Ⓑ Ⓒ Ⓓ
102	Ⓐ Ⓑ Ⓒ Ⓓ	122	Ⓐ Ⓑ Ⓒ Ⓓ	142	Ⓐ Ⓑ Ⓒ Ⓓ	162	Ⓐ Ⓑ Ⓒ Ⓓ	182	Ⓐ Ⓑ Ⓒ Ⓓ
103	Ⓐ Ⓑ Ⓒ Ⓓ	123	Ⓐ Ⓑ Ⓒ Ⓓ	143	Ⓐ Ⓑ Ⓒ Ⓓ	163	Ⓐ Ⓑ Ⓒ Ⓓ	183	Ⓐ Ⓑ Ⓒ Ⓓ
104	Ⓐ Ⓑ Ⓒ Ⓓ	124	Ⓐ Ⓑ Ⓒ Ⓓ	144	Ⓐ Ⓑ Ⓒ Ⓓ	164	Ⓐ Ⓑ Ⓒ Ⓓ	184	Ⓐ Ⓑ Ⓒ Ⓓ
105	Ⓐ Ⓑ Ⓒ Ⓓ	125	Ⓐ Ⓑ Ⓒ Ⓓ	145	Ⓐ Ⓑ Ⓒ Ⓓ	165	Ⓐ Ⓑ Ⓒ Ⓓ	185	Ⓐ Ⓑ Ⓒ Ⓓ
106	Ⓐ Ⓑ Ⓒ Ⓓ	126	Ⓐ Ⓑ Ⓒ Ⓓ	146	Ⓐ Ⓑ Ⓒ Ⓓ	166	Ⓐ Ⓑ Ⓒ Ⓓ	186	Ⓐ Ⓑ Ⓒ Ⓓ
107	Ⓐ Ⓑ Ⓒ Ⓓ	127	Ⓐ Ⓑ Ⓒ Ⓓ	147	Ⓐ Ⓑ Ⓒ Ⓓ	167	Ⓐ Ⓑ Ⓒ Ⓓ	187	Ⓐ Ⓑ Ⓒ Ⓓ
108	Ⓐ Ⓑ Ⓒ Ⓓ	128	Ⓐ Ⓑ Ⓒ Ⓓ	148	Ⓐ Ⓑ Ⓒ Ⓓ	168	Ⓐ Ⓑ Ⓒ Ⓓ	188	Ⓐ Ⓑ Ⓒ Ⓓ
109	Ⓐ Ⓑ Ⓒ Ⓓ	129	Ⓐ Ⓑ Ⓒ Ⓓ	149	Ⓐ Ⓑ Ⓒ Ⓓ	169	Ⓐ Ⓑ Ⓒ Ⓓ	189	Ⓐ Ⓑ Ⓒ Ⓓ
110	Ⓐ Ⓑ Ⓒ Ⓓ	130	Ⓐ Ⓑ Ⓒ Ⓓ	150	Ⓐ Ⓑ Ⓒ Ⓓ	170	Ⓐ Ⓑ Ⓒ Ⓓ	190	Ⓐ Ⓑ Ⓒ Ⓓ
111	Ⓐ Ⓑ Ⓒ Ⓓ	131	Ⓐ Ⓑ Ⓒ Ⓓ	151	Ⓐ Ⓑ Ⓒ Ⓓ	171	Ⓐ Ⓑ Ⓒ Ⓓ	191	Ⓐ Ⓑ Ⓒ Ⓓ
112	Ⓐ Ⓑ Ⓒ Ⓓ	132	Ⓐ Ⓑ Ⓒ Ⓓ	152	Ⓐ Ⓑ Ⓒ Ⓓ	172	Ⓐ Ⓑ Ⓒ Ⓓ	192	Ⓐ Ⓑ Ⓒ Ⓓ
113	Ⓐ Ⓑ Ⓒ Ⓓ	133	Ⓐ Ⓑ Ⓒ Ⓓ	153	Ⓐ Ⓑ Ⓒ Ⓓ	173	Ⓐ Ⓑ Ⓒ Ⓓ	193	Ⓐ Ⓑ Ⓒ Ⓓ
114	Ⓐ Ⓑ Ⓒ Ⓓ	134	Ⓐ Ⓑ Ⓒ Ⓓ	154	Ⓐ Ⓑ Ⓒ Ⓓ	174	Ⓐ Ⓑ Ⓒ Ⓓ	194	Ⓐ Ⓑ Ⓒ Ⓓ
115	Ⓐ Ⓑ Ⓒ Ⓓ	135	Ⓐ Ⓑ Ⓒ Ⓓ	155	Ⓐ Ⓑ Ⓒ Ⓓ	175	Ⓐ Ⓑ Ⓒ Ⓓ	195	Ⓐ Ⓑ Ⓒ Ⓓ
116	Ⓐ Ⓑ Ⓒ Ⓓ	136	Ⓐ Ⓑ Ⓒ Ⓓ	156	Ⓐ Ⓑ Ⓒ Ⓓ	176	Ⓐ Ⓑ Ⓒ Ⓓ	196	Ⓐ Ⓑ Ⓒ Ⓓ
117	Ⓐ Ⓑ Ⓒ Ⓓ	137	Ⓐ Ⓑ Ⓒ Ⓓ	157	Ⓐ Ⓑ Ⓒ Ⓓ	177	Ⓐ Ⓑ Ⓒ Ⓓ	197	Ⓐ Ⓑ Ⓒ Ⓓ
118	Ⓐ Ⓑ Ⓒ Ⓓ	138	Ⓐ Ⓑ Ⓒ Ⓓ	158	Ⓐ Ⓑ Ⓒ Ⓓ	178	Ⓐ Ⓑ Ⓒ Ⓓ	198	Ⓐ Ⓑ Ⓒ Ⓓ
119	Ⓐ Ⓑ Ⓒ Ⓓ	139	Ⓐ Ⓑ Ⓒ Ⓓ	159	Ⓐ Ⓑ Ⓒ Ⓓ	179	Ⓐ Ⓑ Ⓒ Ⓓ	199	Ⓐ Ⓑ Ⓒ Ⓓ
120	Ⓐ Ⓑ Ⓒ Ⓓ	140	Ⓐ Ⓑ Ⓒ Ⓓ	160	Ⓐ Ⓑ Ⓒ Ⓓ	180	Ⓐ Ⓑ Ⓒ Ⓓ	200	Ⓐ Ⓑ Ⓒ Ⓓ

서 약

확 인

Actual Test 3

ANSWER SHEET

수험번호

응시일자 : 년 월 일

성 명	한글
	한자
	영자

좌석번호

Ⓐ Ⓑ Ⓒ Ⓓ Ⓔ
① ② ③ ④ ⑤ ⑥ ⑦

LISTENING (Part I~IV)

NO.	ANSWER	NO.	ANSWER	NO.	ANSWER	NO.	ANSWER	NO.	ANSWER
	A B C D		A B C D		A B C D		A B C D		A B C D
1	Ⓐ Ⓑ Ⓒ Ⓓ	21	Ⓐ Ⓑ Ⓒ Ⓓ	41	Ⓐ Ⓑ Ⓒ Ⓓ	61	Ⓐ Ⓑ Ⓒ Ⓓ	81	Ⓐ Ⓑ Ⓒ Ⓓ
2	Ⓐ Ⓑ Ⓒ Ⓓ	22	Ⓐ Ⓑ Ⓒ Ⓓ	42	Ⓐ Ⓑ Ⓒ Ⓓ	62	Ⓐ Ⓑ Ⓒ Ⓓ	82	Ⓐ Ⓑ Ⓒ Ⓓ
3	Ⓐ Ⓑ Ⓒ Ⓓ	23	Ⓐ Ⓑ Ⓒ Ⓓ	43	Ⓐ Ⓑ Ⓒ Ⓓ	63	Ⓐ Ⓑ Ⓒ Ⓓ	83	Ⓐ Ⓑ Ⓒ Ⓓ
4	Ⓐ Ⓑ Ⓒ Ⓓ	24	Ⓐ Ⓑ Ⓒ Ⓓ	44	Ⓐ Ⓑ Ⓒ Ⓓ	64	Ⓐ Ⓑ Ⓒ Ⓓ	84	Ⓐ Ⓑ Ⓒ Ⓓ
5	Ⓐ Ⓑ Ⓒ Ⓓ	25	Ⓐ Ⓑ Ⓒ Ⓓ	45	Ⓐ Ⓑ Ⓒ Ⓓ	65	Ⓐ Ⓑ Ⓒ Ⓓ	85	Ⓐ Ⓑ Ⓒ Ⓓ
6	Ⓐ Ⓑ Ⓒ Ⓓ	26	Ⓐ Ⓑ Ⓒ Ⓓ	46	Ⓐ Ⓑ Ⓒ Ⓓ	66	Ⓐ Ⓑ Ⓒ Ⓓ	86	Ⓐ Ⓑ Ⓒ Ⓓ
7	Ⓐ Ⓑ Ⓒ Ⓓ	27	Ⓐ Ⓑ Ⓒ Ⓓ	47	Ⓐ Ⓑ Ⓒ Ⓓ	67	Ⓐ Ⓑ Ⓒ Ⓓ	87	Ⓐ Ⓑ Ⓒ Ⓓ
8	Ⓐ Ⓑ Ⓒ Ⓓ	28	Ⓐ Ⓑ Ⓒ Ⓓ	48	Ⓐ Ⓑ Ⓒ Ⓓ	68	Ⓐ Ⓑ Ⓒ Ⓓ	88	Ⓐ Ⓑ Ⓒ Ⓓ
9	Ⓐ Ⓑ Ⓒ Ⓓ	29	Ⓐ Ⓑ Ⓒ Ⓓ	49	Ⓐ Ⓑ Ⓒ Ⓓ	69	Ⓐ Ⓑ Ⓒ Ⓓ	89	Ⓐ Ⓑ Ⓒ Ⓓ
10	Ⓐ Ⓑ Ⓒ Ⓓ	30	Ⓐ Ⓑ Ⓒ Ⓓ	50	Ⓐ Ⓑ Ⓒ Ⓓ	70	Ⓐ Ⓑ Ⓒ Ⓓ	90	Ⓐ Ⓑ Ⓒ Ⓓ
11	Ⓐ Ⓑ Ⓒ Ⓓ	31	Ⓐ Ⓑ Ⓒ Ⓓ	51	Ⓐ Ⓑ Ⓒ Ⓓ	71	Ⓐ Ⓑ Ⓒ Ⓓ	91	Ⓐ Ⓑ Ⓒ Ⓓ
12	Ⓐ Ⓑ Ⓒ Ⓓ	32	Ⓐ Ⓑ Ⓒ Ⓓ	52	Ⓐ Ⓑ Ⓒ Ⓓ	72	Ⓐ Ⓑ Ⓒ Ⓓ	92	Ⓐ Ⓑ Ⓒ Ⓓ
13	Ⓐ Ⓑ Ⓒ Ⓓ	33	Ⓐ Ⓑ Ⓒ Ⓓ	53	Ⓐ Ⓑ Ⓒ Ⓓ	73	Ⓐ Ⓑ Ⓒ Ⓓ	93	Ⓐ Ⓑ Ⓒ Ⓓ
14	Ⓐ Ⓑ Ⓒ Ⓓ	34	Ⓐ Ⓑ Ⓒ Ⓓ	54	Ⓐ Ⓑ Ⓒ Ⓓ	74	Ⓐ Ⓑ Ⓒ Ⓓ	94	Ⓐ Ⓑ Ⓒ Ⓓ
15	Ⓐ Ⓑ Ⓒ Ⓓ	35	Ⓐ Ⓑ Ⓒ Ⓓ	55	Ⓐ Ⓑ Ⓒ Ⓓ	75	Ⓐ Ⓑ Ⓒ Ⓓ	95	Ⓐ Ⓑ Ⓒ Ⓓ
16	Ⓐ Ⓑ Ⓒ Ⓓ	36	Ⓐ Ⓑ Ⓒ Ⓓ	56	Ⓐ Ⓑ Ⓒ Ⓓ	76	Ⓐ Ⓑ Ⓒ Ⓓ	96	Ⓐ Ⓑ Ⓒ Ⓓ
17	Ⓐ Ⓑ Ⓒ Ⓓ	37	Ⓐ Ⓑ Ⓒ Ⓓ	57	Ⓐ Ⓑ Ⓒ Ⓓ	77	Ⓐ Ⓑ Ⓒ Ⓓ	97	Ⓐ Ⓑ Ⓒ Ⓓ
18	Ⓐ Ⓑ Ⓒ Ⓓ	38	Ⓐ Ⓑ Ⓒ Ⓓ	58	Ⓐ Ⓑ Ⓒ Ⓓ	78	Ⓐ Ⓑ Ⓒ Ⓓ	98	Ⓐ Ⓑ Ⓒ Ⓓ
19	Ⓐ Ⓑ Ⓒ Ⓓ	39	Ⓐ Ⓑ Ⓒ Ⓓ	59	Ⓐ Ⓑ Ⓒ Ⓓ	79	Ⓐ Ⓑ Ⓒ Ⓓ	99	Ⓐ Ⓑ Ⓒ Ⓓ
20	Ⓐ Ⓑ Ⓒ Ⓓ	40	Ⓐ Ⓑ Ⓒ Ⓓ	60	Ⓐ Ⓑ Ⓒ Ⓓ	80	Ⓐ Ⓑ Ⓒ Ⓓ	100	Ⓐ Ⓑ Ⓒ Ⓓ

READING (Part V~VII)

NO.	ANSWER	NO.	ANSWER	NO.	ANSWER	NO.	ANSWER	NO.	ANSWER
	A B C D		A B C D		A B C D		A B C D		A B C D
101	Ⓐ Ⓑ Ⓒ Ⓓ	121	Ⓐ Ⓑ Ⓒ Ⓓ	141	Ⓐ Ⓑ Ⓒ Ⓓ	161	Ⓐ Ⓑ Ⓒ Ⓓ	181	Ⓐ Ⓑ Ⓒ Ⓓ
102	Ⓐ Ⓑ Ⓒ Ⓓ	122	Ⓐ Ⓑ Ⓒ Ⓓ	142	Ⓐ Ⓑ Ⓒ Ⓓ	162	Ⓐ Ⓑ Ⓒ Ⓓ	182	Ⓐ Ⓑ Ⓒ Ⓓ
103	Ⓐ Ⓑ Ⓒ Ⓓ	123	Ⓐ Ⓑ Ⓒ Ⓓ	143	Ⓐ Ⓑ Ⓒ Ⓓ	163	Ⓐ Ⓑ Ⓒ Ⓓ	183	Ⓐ Ⓑ Ⓒ Ⓓ
104	Ⓐ Ⓑ Ⓒ Ⓓ	124	Ⓐ Ⓑ Ⓒ Ⓓ	144	Ⓐ Ⓑ Ⓒ Ⓓ	164	Ⓐ Ⓑ Ⓒ Ⓓ	184	Ⓐ Ⓑ Ⓒ Ⓓ
105	Ⓐ Ⓑ Ⓒ Ⓓ	125	Ⓐ Ⓑ Ⓒ Ⓓ	145	Ⓐ Ⓑ Ⓒ Ⓓ	165	Ⓐ Ⓑ Ⓒ Ⓓ	185	Ⓐ Ⓑ Ⓒ Ⓓ
106	Ⓐ Ⓑ Ⓒ Ⓓ	126	Ⓐ Ⓑ Ⓒ Ⓓ	146	Ⓐ Ⓑ Ⓒ Ⓓ	166	Ⓐ Ⓑ Ⓒ Ⓓ	186	Ⓐ Ⓑ Ⓒ Ⓓ
107	Ⓐ Ⓑ Ⓒ Ⓓ	127	Ⓐ Ⓑ Ⓒ Ⓓ	147	Ⓐ Ⓑ Ⓒ Ⓓ	167	Ⓐ Ⓑ Ⓒ Ⓓ	187	Ⓐ Ⓑ Ⓒ Ⓓ
108	Ⓐ Ⓑ Ⓒ Ⓓ	128	Ⓐ Ⓑ Ⓒ Ⓓ	148	Ⓐ Ⓑ Ⓒ Ⓓ	168	Ⓐ Ⓑ Ⓒ Ⓓ	188	Ⓐ Ⓑ Ⓒ Ⓓ
109	Ⓐ Ⓑ Ⓒ Ⓓ	129	Ⓐ Ⓑ Ⓒ Ⓓ	149	Ⓐ Ⓑ Ⓒ Ⓓ	169	Ⓐ Ⓑ Ⓒ Ⓓ	189	Ⓐ Ⓑ Ⓒ Ⓓ
110	Ⓐ Ⓑ Ⓒ Ⓓ	130	Ⓐ Ⓑ Ⓒ Ⓓ	150	Ⓐ Ⓑ Ⓒ Ⓓ	170	Ⓐ Ⓑ Ⓒ Ⓓ	190	Ⓐ Ⓑ Ⓒ Ⓓ
111	Ⓐ Ⓑ Ⓒ Ⓓ	131	Ⓐ Ⓑ Ⓒ Ⓓ	151	Ⓐ Ⓑ Ⓒ Ⓓ	171	Ⓐ Ⓑ Ⓒ Ⓓ	191	Ⓐ Ⓑ Ⓒ Ⓓ
112	Ⓐ Ⓑ Ⓒ Ⓓ	132	Ⓐ Ⓑ Ⓒ Ⓓ	152	Ⓐ Ⓑ Ⓒ Ⓓ	172	Ⓐ Ⓑ Ⓒ Ⓓ	192	Ⓐ Ⓑ Ⓒ Ⓓ
113	Ⓐ Ⓑ Ⓒ Ⓓ	133	Ⓐ Ⓑ Ⓒ Ⓓ	153	Ⓐ Ⓑ Ⓒ Ⓓ	173	Ⓐ Ⓑ Ⓒ Ⓓ	193	Ⓐ Ⓑ Ⓒ Ⓓ
114	Ⓐ Ⓑ Ⓒ Ⓓ	134	Ⓐ Ⓑ Ⓒ Ⓓ	154	Ⓐ Ⓑ Ⓒ Ⓓ	174	Ⓐ Ⓑ Ⓒ Ⓓ	194	Ⓐ Ⓑ Ⓒ Ⓓ
115	Ⓐ Ⓑ Ⓒ Ⓓ	135	Ⓐ Ⓑ Ⓒ Ⓓ	155	Ⓐ Ⓑ Ⓒ Ⓓ	175	Ⓐ Ⓑ Ⓒ Ⓓ	195	Ⓐ Ⓑ Ⓒ Ⓓ
116	Ⓐ Ⓑ Ⓒ Ⓓ	136	Ⓐ Ⓑ Ⓒ Ⓓ	156	Ⓐ Ⓑ Ⓒ Ⓓ	176	Ⓐ Ⓑ Ⓒ Ⓓ	196	Ⓐ Ⓑ Ⓒ Ⓓ
117	Ⓐ Ⓑ Ⓒ Ⓓ	137	Ⓐ Ⓑ Ⓒ Ⓓ	157	Ⓐ Ⓑ Ⓒ Ⓓ	177	Ⓐ Ⓑ Ⓒ Ⓓ	197	Ⓐ Ⓑ Ⓒ Ⓓ
118	Ⓐ Ⓑ Ⓒ Ⓓ	138	Ⓐ Ⓑ Ⓒ Ⓓ	158	Ⓐ Ⓑ Ⓒ Ⓓ	178	Ⓐ Ⓑ Ⓒ Ⓓ	198	Ⓐ Ⓑ Ⓒ Ⓓ
119	Ⓐ Ⓑ Ⓒ Ⓓ	139	Ⓐ Ⓑ Ⓒ Ⓓ	159	Ⓐ Ⓑ Ⓒ Ⓓ	179	Ⓐ Ⓑ Ⓒ Ⓓ	199	Ⓐ Ⓑ Ⓒ Ⓓ
120	Ⓐ Ⓑ Ⓒ Ⓓ	140	Ⓐ Ⓑ Ⓒ Ⓓ	160	Ⓐ Ⓑ Ⓒ Ⓓ	180	Ⓐ Ⓑ Ⓒ Ⓓ	200	Ⓐ Ⓑ Ⓒ Ⓓ

ANSWER SHEET

Actual Test 4

성명	한글
	한자
	영자

좌석번호	
	Ⓐ Ⓑ Ⓒ Ⓓ Ⓔ
	① ② ③ ④ ⑤ ⑥ ⑦

LISTENING (Part I~IV)

NO.	ANSWER	NO.	ANSWER	NO.	ANSWER	NO.	ANSWER	NO.	ANSWER
	A B C D		A B C D		A B C D		A B C D		A B C D
1	Ⓐ Ⓑ Ⓒ	21	Ⓐ Ⓑ Ⓒ Ⓓ	41	Ⓐ Ⓑ Ⓒ Ⓓ	61	Ⓐ Ⓑ Ⓒ Ⓓ	81	Ⓐ Ⓑ Ⓒ Ⓓ
2	Ⓐ Ⓑ Ⓒ	22	Ⓐ Ⓑ Ⓒ Ⓓ	42	Ⓐ Ⓑ Ⓒ Ⓓ	62	Ⓐ Ⓑ Ⓒ Ⓓ	82	Ⓐ Ⓑ Ⓒ Ⓓ
3	Ⓐ Ⓑ Ⓒ	23	Ⓐ Ⓑ Ⓒ Ⓓ	43	Ⓐ Ⓑ Ⓒ Ⓓ	63	Ⓐ Ⓑ Ⓒ Ⓓ	83	Ⓐ Ⓑ Ⓒ Ⓓ
4	Ⓐ Ⓑ Ⓒ	24	Ⓐ Ⓑ Ⓒ Ⓓ	44	Ⓐ Ⓑ Ⓒ Ⓓ	64	Ⓐ Ⓑ Ⓒ Ⓓ	84	Ⓐ Ⓑ Ⓒ Ⓓ
5	Ⓐ Ⓑ Ⓒ	25	Ⓐ Ⓑ Ⓒ Ⓓ	45	Ⓐ Ⓑ Ⓒ Ⓓ	65	Ⓐ Ⓑ Ⓒ Ⓓ	85	Ⓐ Ⓑ Ⓒ Ⓓ
6	Ⓐ Ⓑ Ⓒ Ⓓ	26	Ⓐ Ⓑ Ⓒ Ⓓ	46	Ⓐ Ⓑ Ⓒ Ⓓ	66	Ⓐ Ⓑ Ⓒ Ⓓ	86	Ⓐ Ⓑ Ⓒ Ⓓ
7	Ⓐ Ⓑ Ⓒ Ⓓ	27	Ⓐ Ⓑ Ⓒ Ⓓ	47	Ⓐ Ⓑ Ⓒ Ⓓ	67	Ⓐ Ⓑ Ⓒ Ⓓ	87	Ⓐ Ⓑ Ⓒ Ⓓ
8	Ⓐ Ⓑ Ⓒ Ⓓ	28	Ⓐ Ⓑ Ⓒ Ⓓ	48	Ⓐ Ⓑ Ⓒ Ⓓ	68	Ⓐ Ⓑ Ⓒ Ⓓ	88	Ⓐ Ⓑ Ⓒ Ⓓ
9	Ⓐ Ⓑ Ⓒ Ⓓ	29	Ⓐ Ⓑ Ⓒ Ⓓ	49	Ⓐ Ⓑ Ⓒ Ⓓ	69	Ⓐ Ⓑ Ⓒ Ⓓ	89	Ⓐ Ⓑ Ⓒ Ⓓ
10	Ⓐ Ⓑ Ⓒ Ⓓ	30	Ⓐ Ⓑ Ⓒ Ⓓ	50	Ⓐ Ⓑ Ⓒ Ⓓ	70	Ⓐ Ⓑ Ⓒ Ⓓ	90	Ⓐ Ⓑ Ⓒ Ⓓ
11	Ⓐ Ⓑ Ⓒ Ⓓ	31	Ⓐ Ⓑ Ⓒ Ⓓ	51	Ⓐ Ⓑ Ⓒ Ⓓ	71	Ⓐ Ⓑ Ⓒ Ⓓ	91	Ⓐ Ⓑ Ⓒ Ⓓ
12	Ⓐ Ⓑ Ⓒ Ⓓ	32	Ⓐ Ⓑ Ⓒ Ⓓ	52	Ⓐ Ⓑ Ⓒ Ⓓ	72	Ⓐ Ⓑ Ⓒ Ⓓ	92	Ⓐ Ⓑ Ⓒ Ⓓ
13	Ⓐ Ⓑ Ⓒ Ⓓ	33	Ⓐ Ⓑ Ⓒ Ⓓ	53	Ⓐ Ⓑ Ⓒ Ⓓ	73	Ⓐ Ⓑ Ⓒ Ⓓ	93	Ⓐ Ⓑ Ⓒ Ⓓ
14	Ⓐ Ⓑ Ⓒ Ⓓ	34	Ⓐ Ⓑ Ⓒ Ⓓ	54	Ⓐ Ⓑ Ⓒ Ⓓ	74	Ⓐ Ⓑ Ⓒ Ⓓ	94	Ⓐ Ⓑ Ⓒ Ⓓ
15	Ⓐ Ⓑ Ⓒ Ⓓ	35	Ⓐ Ⓑ Ⓒ Ⓓ	55	Ⓐ Ⓑ Ⓒ Ⓓ	75	Ⓐ Ⓑ Ⓒ Ⓓ	95	Ⓐ Ⓑ Ⓒ Ⓓ
16	Ⓐ Ⓑ Ⓒ Ⓓ	36	Ⓐ Ⓑ Ⓒ Ⓓ	56	Ⓐ Ⓑ Ⓒ Ⓓ	76	Ⓐ Ⓑ Ⓒ Ⓓ	96	Ⓐ Ⓑ Ⓒ Ⓓ
17	Ⓐ Ⓑ Ⓒ Ⓓ	37	Ⓐ Ⓑ Ⓒ Ⓓ	57	Ⓐ Ⓑ Ⓒ Ⓓ	77	Ⓐ Ⓑ Ⓒ Ⓓ	97	Ⓐ Ⓑ Ⓒ Ⓓ
18	Ⓐ Ⓑ Ⓒ Ⓓ	38	Ⓐ Ⓑ Ⓒ Ⓓ	58	Ⓐ Ⓑ Ⓒ Ⓓ	78	Ⓐ Ⓑ Ⓒ Ⓓ	98	Ⓐ Ⓑ Ⓒ Ⓓ
19	Ⓐ Ⓑ Ⓒ Ⓓ	39	Ⓐ Ⓑ Ⓒ Ⓓ	59	Ⓐ Ⓑ Ⓒ Ⓓ	79	Ⓐ Ⓑ Ⓒ Ⓓ	99	Ⓐ Ⓑ Ⓒ Ⓓ
20	Ⓐ Ⓑ Ⓒ Ⓓ	40	Ⓐ Ⓑ Ⓒ Ⓓ	60	Ⓐ Ⓑ Ⓒ Ⓓ	80	Ⓐ Ⓑ Ⓒ Ⓓ	100	Ⓐ Ⓑ Ⓒ Ⓓ

READING (Part V~VII)

NO.	ANSWER	NO.	ANSWER	NO.	ANSWER	NO.	ANSWER
	A B C D		A B C D		A B C D		A B C D
101	Ⓐ Ⓑ Ⓒ Ⓓ	121	Ⓐ Ⓑ Ⓒ Ⓓ	141	Ⓐ Ⓑ Ⓒ Ⓓ	161	Ⓐ Ⓑ Ⓒ Ⓓ
102	Ⓐ Ⓑ Ⓒ Ⓓ	122	Ⓐ Ⓑ Ⓒ Ⓓ	142	Ⓐ Ⓑ Ⓒ Ⓓ	162	Ⓐ Ⓑ Ⓒ Ⓓ
103	Ⓐ Ⓑ Ⓒ Ⓓ	123	Ⓐ Ⓑ Ⓒ Ⓓ	143	Ⓐ Ⓑ Ⓒ Ⓓ	163	Ⓐ Ⓑ Ⓒ Ⓓ
104	Ⓐ Ⓑ Ⓒ Ⓓ	124	Ⓐ Ⓑ Ⓒ Ⓓ	144	Ⓐ Ⓑ Ⓒ Ⓓ	164	Ⓐ Ⓑ Ⓒ Ⓓ
105	Ⓐ Ⓑ Ⓒ Ⓓ	125	Ⓐ Ⓑ Ⓒ Ⓓ	145	Ⓐ Ⓑ Ⓒ Ⓓ	165	Ⓐ Ⓑ Ⓒ Ⓓ
106	Ⓐ Ⓑ Ⓒ Ⓓ	126	Ⓐ Ⓑ Ⓒ Ⓓ	146	Ⓐ Ⓑ Ⓒ Ⓓ	166	Ⓐ Ⓑ Ⓒ Ⓓ
107	Ⓐ Ⓑ Ⓒ Ⓓ	127	Ⓐ Ⓑ Ⓒ Ⓓ	147	Ⓐ Ⓑ Ⓒ Ⓓ	167	Ⓐ Ⓑ Ⓒ Ⓓ
108	Ⓐ Ⓑ Ⓒ Ⓓ	128	Ⓐ Ⓑ Ⓒ Ⓓ	148	Ⓐ Ⓑ Ⓒ Ⓓ	168	Ⓐ Ⓑ Ⓒ Ⓓ
109	Ⓐ Ⓑ Ⓒ Ⓓ	129	Ⓐ Ⓑ Ⓒ Ⓓ	149	Ⓐ Ⓑ Ⓒ Ⓓ	169	Ⓐ Ⓑ Ⓒ Ⓓ
110	Ⓐ Ⓑ Ⓒ Ⓓ	130	Ⓐ Ⓑ Ⓒ Ⓓ	150	Ⓐ Ⓑ Ⓒ Ⓓ	170	Ⓐ Ⓑ Ⓒ Ⓓ
111	Ⓐ Ⓑ Ⓒ Ⓓ	131	Ⓐ Ⓑ Ⓒ Ⓓ	151	Ⓐ Ⓑ Ⓒ Ⓓ	171	Ⓐ Ⓑ Ⓒ Ⓓ
112	Ⓐ Ⓑ Ⓒ Ⓓ	132	Ⓐ Ⓑ Ⓒ Ⓓ	152	Ⓐ Ⓑ Ⓒ Ⓓ	172	Ⓐ Ⓑ Ⓒ Ⓓ
113	Ⓐ Ⓑ Ⓒ Ⓓ	133	Ⓐ Ⓑ Ⓒ Ⓓ	153	Ⓐ Ⓑ Ⓒ Ⓓ	173	Ⓐ Ⓑ Ⓒ Ⓓ
114	Ⓐ Ⓑ Ⓒ Ⓓ	134	Ⓐ Ⓑ Ⓒ Ⓓ	154	Ⓐ Ⓑ Ⓒ Ⓓ	174	Ⓐ Ⓑ Ⓒ Ⓓ
115	Ⓐ Ⓑ Ⓒ Ⓓ	135	Ⓐ Ⓑ Ⓒ Ⓓ	155	Ⓐ Ⓑ Ⓒ Ⓓ	175	Ⓐ Ⓑ Ⓒ Ⓓ
116	Ⓐ Ⓑ Ⓒ Ⓓ	136	Ⓐ Ⓑ Ⓒ Ⓓ	156	Ⓐ Ⓑ Ⓒ Ⓓ	176	Ⓐ Ⓑ Ⓒ Ⓓ
117	Ⓐ Ⓑ Ⓒ Ⓓ	137	Ⓐ Ⓑ Ⓒ Ⓓ	157	Ⓐ Ⓑ Ⓒ Ⓓ	177	Ⓐ Ⓑ Ⓒ Ⓓ
118	Ⓐ Ⓑ Ⓒ Ⓓ	138	Ⓐ Ⓑ Ⓒ Ⓓ	158	Ⓐ Ⓑ Ⓒ Ⓓ	178	Ⓐ Ⓑ Ⓒ Ⓓ
119	Ⓐ Ⓑ Ⓒ Ⓓ	139	Ⓐ Ⓑ Ⓒ Ⓓ	159	Ⓐ Ⓑ Ⓒ Ⓓ	179	Ⓐ Ⓑ Ⓒ Ⓓ
120	Ⓐ Ⓑ Ⓒ Ⓓ	140	Ⓐ Ⓑ Ⓒ Ⓓ	160	Ⓐ Ⓑ Ⓒ Ⓓ	180	Ⓐ Ⓑ Ⓒ Ⓓ

NO.	ANSWER
	A B C D
181	Ⓐ Ⓑ Ⓒ Ⓓ
182	Ⓐ Ⓑ Ⓒ Ⓓ
183	Ⓐ Ⓑ Ⓒ Ⓓ
184	Ⓐ Ⓑ Ⓒ Ⓓ
185	Ⓐ Ⓑ Ⓒ Ⓓ
186	Ⓐ Ⓑ Ⓒ Ⓓ
187	Ⓐ Ⓑ Ⓒ Ⓓ
188	Ⓐ Ⓑ Ⓒ Ⓓ
189	Ⓐ Ⓑ Ⓒ Ⓓ
190	Ⓐ Ⓑ Ⓒ Ⓓ
191	Ⓐ Ⓑ Ⓒ Ⓓ
192	Ⓐ Ⓑ Ⓒ Ⓓ
193	Ⓐ Ⓑ Ⓒ Ⓓ
194	Ⓐ Ⓑ Ⓒ Ⓓ
195	Ⓐ Ⓑ Ⓒ Ⓓ
196	Ⓐ Ⓑ Ⓒ Ⓓ
197	Ⓐ Ⓑ Ⓒ Ⓓ
198	Ⓐ Ⓑ Ⓒ Ⓓ
199	Ⓐ Ⓑ Ⓒ Ⓓ
200	Ⓐ Ⓑ Ⓒ Ⓓ

Actual Test 5

ANSWER SHEET

수험번호

응시일자 : 　　년　　월　　일

좌석번호
Ⓐ Ⓑ Ⓒ Ⓓ Ⓔ
① ② ③ ④ ⑤ ⑥ ⑦

성명	한글
	한자
	영자

확인

LISTENING (Part I~IV)

NO.	ANSWER	NO.	ANSWER	NO.	ANSWER	NO.	ANSWER	NO.	ANSWER
	A B C D		A B C D		A B C D		A B C D		A B C D
1	Ⓐ Ⓑ Ⓒ Ⓓ	21	Ⓐ Ⓑ Ⓒ Ⓓ	41	Ⓐ Ⓑ Ⓒ Ⓓ	61	Ⓐ Ⓑ Ⓒ Ⓓ	81	Ⓐ Ⓑ Ⓒ Ⓓ
2	Ⓐ Ⓑ Ⓒ Ⓓ	22	Ⓐ Ⓑ Ⓒ Ⓓ	42	Ⓐ Ⓑ Ⓒ Ⓓ	62	Ⓐ Ⓑ Ⓒ Ⓓ	82	Ⓐ Ⓑ Ⓒ Ⓓ
3	Ⓐ Ⓑ Ⓒ Ⓓ	23	Ⓐ Ⓑ Ⓒ Ⓓ	43	Ⓐ Ⓑ Ⓒ Ⓓ	63	Ⓐ Ⓑ Ⓒ Ⓓ	83	Ⓐ Ⓑ Ⓒ Ⓓ
4	Ⓐ Ⓑ Ⓒ Ⓓ	24	Ⓐ Ⓑ Ⓒ Ⓓ	44	Ⓐ Ⓑ Ⓒ Ⓓ	64	Ⓐ Ⓑ Ⓒ Ⓓ	84	Ⓐ Ⓑ Ⓒ Ⓓ
5	Ⓐ Ⓑ Ⓒ Ⓓ	25	Ⓐ Ⓑ Ⓒ Ⓓ	45	Ⓐ Ⓑ Ⓒ Ⓓ	65	Ⓐ Ⓑ Ⓒ Ⓓ	85	Ⓐ Ⓑ Ⓒ Ⓓ
6	Ⓐ Ⓑ Ⓒ Ⓓ	26	Ⓐ Ⓑ Ⓒ Ⓓ	46	Ⓐ Ⓑ Ⓒ Ⓓ	66	Ⓐ Ⓑ Ⓒ Ⓓ	86	Ⓐ Ⓑ Ⓒ Ⓓ
7	Ⓐ Ⓑ Ⓒ Ⓓ	27	Ⓐ Ⓑ Ⓒ Ⓓ	47	Ⓐ Ⓑ Ⓒ Ⓓ	67	Ⓐ Ⓑ Ⓒ Ⓓ	87	Ⓐ Ⓑ Ⓒ Ⓓ
8	Ⓐ Ⓑ Ⓒ Ⓓ	28	Ⓐ Ⓑ Ⓒ Ⓓ	48	Ⓐ Ⓑ Ⓒ Ⓓ	68	Ⓐ Ⓑ Ⓒ Ⓓ	88	Ⓐ Ⓑ Ⓒ Ⓓ
9	Ⓐ Ⓑ Ⓒ Ⓓ	29	Ⓐ Ⓑ Ⓒ Ⓓ	49	Ⓐ Ⓑ Ⓒ Ⓓ	69	Ⓐ Ⓑ Ⓒ Ⓓ	89	Ⓐ Ⓑ Ⓒ Ⓓ
10	Ⓐ Ⓑ Ⓒ Ⓓ	30	Ⓐ Ⓑ Ⓒ Ⓓ	50	Ⓐ Ⓑ Ⓒ Ⓓ	70	Ⓐ Ⓑ Ⓒ Ⓓ	90	Ⓐ Ⓑ Ⓒ Ⓓ
11	Ⓐ Ⓑ Ⓒ Ⓓ	31	Ⓐ Ⓑ Ⓒ Ⓓ	51	Ⓐ Ⓑ Ⓒ Ⓓ	71	Ⓐ Ⓑ Ⓒ Ⓓ	91	Ⓐ Ⓑ Ⓒ Ⓓ
12	Ⓐ Ⓑ Ⓒ Ⓓ	32	Ⓐ Ⓑ Ⓒ Ⓓ	52	Ⓐ Ⓑ Ⓒ Ⓓ	72	Ⓐ Ⓑ Ⓒ Ⓓ	92	Ⓐ Ⓑ Ⓒ Ⓓ
13	Ⓐ Ⓑ Ⓒ Ⓓ	33	Ⓐ Ⓑ Ⓒ Ⓓ	53	Ⓐ Ⓑ Ⓒ Ⓓ	73	Ⓐ Ⓑ Ⓒ Ⓓ	93	Ⓐ Ⓑ Ⓒ Ⓓ
14	Ⓐ Ⓑ Ⓒ Ⓓ	34	Ⓐ Ⓑ Ⓒ Ⓓ	54	Ⓐ Ⓑ Ⓒ Ⓓ	74	Ⓐ Ⓑ Ⓒ Ⓓ	94	Ⓐ Ⓑ Ⓒ Ⓓ
15	Ⓐ Ⓑ Ⓒ Ⓓ	35	Ⓐ Ⓑ Ⓒ Ⓓ	55	Ⓐ Ⓑ Ⓒ Ⓓ	75	Ⓐ Ⓑ Ⓒ Ⓓ	95	Ⓐ Ⓑ Ⓒ Ⓓ
16	Ⓐ Ⓑ Ⓒ Ⓓ	36	Ⓐ Ⓑ Ⓒ Ⓓ	56	Ⓐ Ⓑ Ⓒ Ⓓ	76	Ⓐ Ⓑ Ⓒ Ⓓ	96	Ⓐ Ⓑ Ⓒ Ⓓ
17	Ⓐ Ⓑ Ⓒ Ⓓ	37	Ⓐ Ⓑ Ⓒ Ⓓ	57	Ⓐ Ⓑ Ⓒ Ⓓ	77	Ⓐ Ⓑ Ⓒ Ⓓ	97	Ⓐ Ⓑ Ⓒ Ⓓ
18	Ⓐ Ⓑ Ⓒ Ⓓ	38	Ⓐ Ⓑ Ⓒ Ⓓ	58	Ⓐ Ⓑ Ⓒ Ⓓ	78	Ⓐ Ⓑ Ⓒ Ⓓ	98	Ⓐ Ⓑ Ⓒ Ⓓ
19	Ⓐ Ⓑ Ⓒ Ⓓ	39	Ⓐ Ⓑ Ⓒ Ⓓ	59	Ⓐ Ⓑ Ⓒ Ⓓ	79	Ⓐ Ⓑ Ⓒ Ⓓ	99	Ⓐ Ⓑ Ⓒ Ⓓ
20	Ⓐ Ⓑ Ⓒ Ⓓ	40	Ⓐ Ⓑ Ⓒ Ⓓ	60	Ⓐ Ⓑ Ⓒ Ⓓ	80	Ⓐ Ⓑ Ⓒ Ⓓ	100	Ⓐ Ⓑ Ⓒ Ⓓ

READING (Part V~VII)

NO.	ANSWER	NO.	ANSWER	NO.	ANSWER	NO.	ANSWER	NO.	ANSWER
	A B C D		A B C D		A B C D		A B C D		A B C D
101	Ⓐ Ⓑ Ⓒ Ⓓ	121	Ⓐ Ⓑ Ⓒ Ⓓ	141	Ⓐ Ⓑ Ⓒ Ⓓ	161	Ⓐ Ⓑ Ⓒ Ⓓ	181	Ⓐ Ⓑ Ⓒ Ⓓ
102	Ⓐ Ⓑ Ⓒ Ⓓ	122	Ⓐ Ⓑ Ⓒ Ⓓ	142	Ⓐ Ⓑ Ⓒ Ⓓ	162	Ⓐ Ⓑ Ⓒ Ⓓ	182	Ⓐ Ⓑ Ⓒ Ⓓ
103	Ⓐ Ⓑ Ⓒ Ⓓ	123	Ⓐ Ⓑ Ⓒ Ⓓ	143	Ⓐ Ⓑ Ⓒ Ⓓ	163	Ⓐ Ⓑ Ⓒ Ⓓ	183	Ⓐ Ⓑ Ⓒ Ⓓ
104	Ⓐ Ⓑ Ⓒ Ⓓ	124	Ⓐ Ⓑ Ⓒ Ⓓ	144	Ⓐ Ⓑ Ⓒ Ⓓ	164	Ⓐ Ⓑ Ⓒ Ⓓ	184	Ⓐ Ⓑ Ⓒ Ⓓ
105	Ⓐ Ⓑ Ⓒ Ⓓ	125	Ⓐ Ⓑ Ⓒ Ⓓ	145	Ⓐ Ⓑ Ⓒ Ⓓ	165	Ⓐ Ⓑ Ⓒ Ⓓ	185	Ⓐ Ⓑ Ⓒ Ⓓ
106	Ⓐ Ⓑ Ⓒ Ⓓ	126	Ⓐ Ⓑ Ⓒ Ⓓ	146	Ⓐ Ⓑ Ⓒ Ⓓ	166	Ⓐ Ⓑ Ⓒ Ⓓ	186	Ⓐ Ⓑ Ⓒ Ⓓ
107	Ⓐ Ⓑ Ⓒ Ⓓ	127	Ⓐ Ⓑ Ⓒ Ⓓ	147	Ⓐ Ⓑ Ⓒ Ⓓ	167	Ⓐ Ⓑ Ⓒ Ⓓ	187	Ⓐ Ⓑ Ⓒ Ⓓ
108	Ⓐ Ⓑ Ⓒ Ⓓ	128	Ⓐ Ⓑ Ⓒ Ⓓ	148	Ⓐ Ⓑ Ⓒ Ⓓ	168	Ⓐ Ⓑ Ⓒ Ⓓ	188	Ⓐ Ⓑ Ⓒ Ⓓ
109	Ⓐ Ⓑ Ⓒ Ⓓ	129	Ⓐ Ⓑ Ⓒ Ⓓ	149	Ⓐ Ⓑ Ⓒ Ⓓ	169	Ⓐ Ⓑ Ⓒ Ⓓ	189	Ⓐ Ⓑ Ⓒ Ⓓ
110	Ⓐ Ⓑ Ⓒ Ⓓ	130	Ⓐ Ⓑ Ⓒ Ⓓ	150	Ⓐ Ⓑ Ⓒ Ⓓ	170	Ⓐ Ⓑ Ⓒ Ⓓ	190	Ⓐ Ⓑ Ⓒ Ⓓ
111	Ⓐ Ⓑ Ⓒ Ⓓ	131	Ⓐ Ⓑ Ⓒ Ⓓ	151	Ⓐ Ⓑ Ⓒ Ⓓ	171	Ⓐ Ⓑ Ⓒ Ⓓ	191	Ⓐ Ⓑ Ⓒ Ⓓ
112	Ⓐ Ⓑ Ⓒ Ⓓ	132	Ⓐ Ⓑ Ⓒ Ⓓ	152	Ⓐ Ⓑ Ⓒ Ⓓ	172	Ⓐ Ⓑ Ⓒ Ⓓ	192	Ⓐ Ⓑ Ⓒ Ⓓ
113	Ⓐ Ⓑ Ⓒ Ⓓ	133	Ⓐ Ⓑ Ⓒ Ⓓ	153	Ⓐ Ⓑ Ⓒ Ⓓ	173	Ⓐ Ⓑ Ⓒ Ⓓ	193	Ⓐ Ⓑ Ⓒ Ⓓ
114	Ⓐ Ⓑ Ⓒ Ⓓ	134	Ⓐ Ⓑ Ⓒ Ⓓ	154	Ⓐ Ⓑ Ⓒ Ⓓ	174	Ⓐ Ⓑ Ⓒ Ⓓ	194	Ⓐ Ⓑ Ⓒ Ⓓ
115	Ⓐ Ⓑ Ⓒ Ⓓ	135	Ⓐ Ⓑ Ⓒ Ⓓ	155	Ⓐ Ⓑ Ⓒ Ⓓ	175	Ⓐ Ⓑ Ⓒ Ⓓ	195	Ⓐ Ⓑ Ⓒ Ⓓ
116	Ⓐ Ⓑ Ⓒ Ⓓ	136	Ⓐ Ⓑ Ⓒ Ⓓ	156	Ⓐ Ⓑ Ⓒ Ⓓ	176	Ⓐ Ⓑ Ⓒ Ⓓ	196	Ⓐ Ⓑ Ⓒ Ⓓ
117	Ⓐ Ⓑ Ⓒ Ⓓ	137	Ⓐ Ⓑ Ⓒ Ⓓ	157	Ⓐ Ⓑ Ⓒ Ⓓ	177	Ⓐ Ⓑ Ⓒ Ⓓ	197	Ⓐ Ⓑ Ⓒ Ⓓ
118	Ⓐ Ⓑ Ⓒ Ⓓ	138	Ⓐ Ⓑ Ⓒ Ⓓ	158	Ⓐ Ⓑ Ⓒ Ⓓ	178	Ⓐ Ⓑ Ⓒ Ⓓ	198	Ⓐ Ⓑ Ⓒ Ⓓ
119	Ⓐ Ⓑ Ⓒ Ⓓ	139	Ⓐ Ⓑ Ⓒ Ⓓ	159	Ⓐ Ⓑ Ⓒ Ⓓ	179	Ⓐ Ⓑ Ⓒ Ⓓ	199	Ⓐ Ⓑ Ⓒ Ⓓ
120	Ⓐ Ⓑ Ⓒ Ⓓ	140	Ⓐ Ⓑ Ⓒ Ⓓ	160	Ⓐ Ⓑ Ⓒ Ⓓ	180	Ⓐ Ⓑ Ⓒ Ⓓ	200	Ⓐ Ⓑ Ⓒ Ⓓ

LC+RC

정재현어학연구소 지음

내 인생 첫 토익 실전서
정재헌 토익 특강
실전 모의고사 1000제

스크립트+정답 및 해설

혼공족들을 위한 6종 부가자료 무료 제공

www.nexusbook.com

| 37가지 버전 MP3 | 추가어휘 문제집 | 모바일 단어장 | 온라인 받아쓰기 | 어휘 리스트 & 테스트 | 청킹리된 한상용 추가 MP3 |

MP3 바로듣기
정답 자동 채점
모바일 단어장
받아쓰기 테스트

내 인생 첫 토익 실전서

정재현 토익

LC+RC

실전 모의고사

1000제

정재현어학연구소 지음

MP3 바로 듣기
정답 자동 채점
모바일 단어장
받아쓰기 테스트

혼공족들을 위한 6종 부가자료 무료 제공
www.nexusbook.com

3가지 버전
MP3

추가 어휘
문제집

모바일
단어장

온라인
받아쓰기

어휘 리스트
& 테스트

청취력 향상용
추가 MP3

스크립트+정답 및 해설

내 인생 첫 토익 실전서

정재현 토익

LC+RC

실전 모의고사

1000제

정재현어학연구소 지음

혼공족들을 위한 6종 부가자료 무료 제공
www.nexusbook.com

MP3 바로 듣기
정답 자동 채점
모바일 단어장
받아쓰기 테스트

 3가지 버전 MP3

 추가 어휘 문제집

 모바일 단어장

 온라인 받아쓰기

 어휘 리스트 & 테스트

 청취력 향상용 추가 MP3

스크립트+정답 및 해설

Actual Test

01

PART 1

| 1 (C) | 2 (B) | 3 (D) | 4 (C) | 5 (C) | 6 (B) |

PART 2

7 (B)	8 (B)	9 (B)	10 (C)	11 (A)	12 (B)	13 (B)	14 (C)	15 (A)	16 (C)
17 (A)	18 (A)	19 (C)	20 (B)	21 (C)	22 (C)	23 (A)	24 (A)	25 (C)	26 (B)
27 (A)	28 (C)	29 (B)	30 (C)	31 (B)					

PART 3

32 (B)	33 (B)	34 (D)	35 (B)	36 (A)	37 (C)	38 (B)	39 (A)	40 (C)	41 (B)
42 (C)	43 (D)	44 (B)	45 (C)	46 (D)	47 (D)	48 (B)	49 (D)	50 (B)	51 (D)
52 (A)	53 (C)	54 (B)	55 (C)	56 (D)	57 (A)	58 (B)	59 (C)	60 (D)	61 (C)
62 (B)	63 (D)	64 (C)	65 (B)	66 (C)	67 (D)	68 (D)	69 (D)	70 (B)	

PART 4

71 (C)	72 (C)	73 (C)	74 (C)	75 (B)	76 (D)	77 (A)	78 (B)	79 (D)	80 (C)
81 (B)	82 (C)	83 (C)	84 (A)	85 (D)	86 (C)	87 (D)	88 (C)	89 (B)	90 (C)
91 (B)	92 (D)	93 (C)	94 (A)	95 (B)	96 (C)	97 (B)	98 (C)	99 (A)	100 (B)

PART 5

101 (B)	102 (A)	103 (C)	104 (D)	105 (D)	106 (B)	107 (C)	108 (B)	109 (C)	110 (D)
111 (D)	112 (C)	113 (B)	114 (D)	115 (B)	116 (C)	117 (C)	118 (D)	119 (B)	120 (C)
121 (C)	122 (C)	123 (A)	124 (B)	125 (C)	126 (B)	127 (D)	128 (C)	129 (C)	130 (B)

PART 6

| 131 (B) | 132 (C) | 133 (D) | 134 (C) | 135 (B) | 136 (D) | 137 (C) | 138 (C) | 139 (B) | 140 (A) |
| 141 (C) | 142 (B) | 143 (B) | 144 (B) | 145 (C) | 146 (A) | | | | |

PART 7

147 (C)	148 (A)	149 (A)	150 (B)	151 (A)	152 (D)	153 (C)	154 (C)	155 (C)	156 (C)
157 (D)	158 (B)	159 (D)	160 (B)	161 (C)	162 (B)	163 (B)	164 (C)	165 (B)	166 (C)
167 (D)	168 (C)	169 (B)	170 (A)	171 (D)	172 (C)	173 (D)	174 (D)	175 (A)	176 (C)
177 (D)	178 (C)	179 (B)	180 (D)	181 (C)	182 (C)	183 (D)	184 (C)	185 (B)	186 (A)
187 (A)	188 (C)	189 (C)	190 (C)	191 (C)	192 (A)	193 (B)	194 (C)	195 (D)	196 (A)
197 (C)	198 (B)	199 (D)	200 (D)						

1
캐W (A) The man is typing on a keyboard.
(B) The man is turning on a monitor.
(C) The man is talking on a telephone.
(D) The man is filing some papers.

(A) 남자가 키보드로 타자를 치고 있다.
(B) 남자가 모니터를 켜고 있다.
(C) 남자가 전화 통화를 하고 있다.
(D) 남자가 서류를 파일에 담아 정리하고 있다.

해설　남자가 전화 통화를 하는 모습에 초점을 맞춰 묘사한 (C)가 정답이다. 타자를 치는 동작과 모니터를 켜는 동작, 서류를 정리하는 동작은 사진에서 볼 수 없다.

어휘　type on a keyboard 키보드로 타자를 치다　turn on ~을 켜다　file ~을 파일에 담아 정리하다　papers 서류

2
호M (A) They're entering a building.
(B) They're facing the water.
(C) They're swimming in the river.
(D) They're strolling along the shore.

(A) 사람들이 건물로 들어가고 있다.
(B) 사람들이 물을 마주하고 있다.
(C) 사람들이 강에서 수영하고 있다.
(D) 사람들이 해안을 따라 산책하고 있다.

해설　물을 마주보고 앉아 있는 사람들의 모습에 초점을 맞춰 묘사한 (B)가 정답이다. 건물로 들어가는 동작과 수영하는 동작, 그리고 산책하는 동작은 사진에서 볼 수 없다.

어휘　enter ~로 들어가다　face ~을 마주하다, ~와 직면하다　stroll 산책하다　along (길 등) ~을 따라　shore 해안, 물가

3
영W (A) A vase of flowers has been placed on every table.
(B) A light fixture is suspended above a supply cabinet.
(C) A carpet is being installed.
(D) A man is working at a laptop computer.

(A) 꽃을 꽃은 꽃병이 모든 탁자에 놓여 있다.
(B) 조명 기구가 용품 보관함 위에 매달려 있다.
(C) 카펫이 설치되고 있다.
(D) 남자가 노트북 컴퓨터로 일하고 있다.

해설　한 남자가 노트북 컴퓨터로 작업하는 모습에 초점을 맞춰 묘사한 (D)가 정답이다. 모든 탁자에 꽃병이 놓여 있는 상태가 아니며, 용품 보관함, 카펫을 설치하는 동작은 사진에서 볼 수 없다.

어휘　a vase of flowers 꽃을 꽃은 꽃병　place A on B A를 B에 놓다, 두다　light fixture 조명 기구　suspend ~을 매달다　above (분리된 위치) ~ 위에　supply cabinet 용품 보관함　install ~을 설치하다

4
미M (A) The men are repairing a structure.
(B) The men are designing some blueprints.
(C) The men are wearing hard hats.
(D) The men are pointing at each other.

(A) 남자들이 구조물을 수리하고 있다.
(B) 남자들이 설계도를 고안하고 있다.
(C) 남자들이 안전모를 착용한 상태이다.
(D) 남자들이 서로를 가리키고 있다.

해설　세 사람 모두 안전모를 착용한 상태에 초점을 맞춰 묘사한 (C)가 정답이다. 수리하는 동작과 설계도를 고안하는 모습, 그리고 서로를 가리키는 모습은 사진에서 볼 수 없다.

어휘　repair ~을 수리하다　structure 구조물, 건축물　blueprint 설계도, 청사진　wear (상태) 착용하고 있다　hard hat 안전모　point at ~을 가리키다　each other 서로

5
캐W (A) Some travelers have gathered at the airport gate.
(B) Some passengers are walking along the aisle.
(C) Some people are boarding an airplane.
(D) Some tourists are descending the staircase.

(A) 몇몇 여행객들이 공항 탑승구에 모여 있다.
(B) 몇몇 탑승객들이 기내 통로를 따라 걷고 있다.
(C) 몇몇 사람들이 비행기에 탑승하고 있다.
(D) 몇몇 관광객들이 계단을 내려가고 있다.

해설　사람들이 작은 비행기에 탑승하는 동작에 초점을 맞춰 묘사한 (C)가 정답이다. 기내 통로나 공항 탑승구, 계단을 내려가는 사람은 사진에서 볼 수 없다.

어휘　gather 모이다　passenger 탑승객　along (길 등) ~을 따라　aisle (극장·열차·비행기 등의 좌석 사이에 있는) 통로　board ~에 탑승하다　descend ~을 내려가다　staircase 계단

6
호M (A) Vegetables are growing in the garden.
(B) Some food items are on display.
(C) Some fruit is being weighed on a scale.
(D) Some customers are waiting in line.

(A) 채소가 정원에서 자라고 있다.
(B) 몇몇 식품들이 진열된 상태이다.
(C) 몇몇 과일의 무게가 저울로 측정되고 있다.
(D) 몇몇 고객들이 줄을 서서 기다리고 있다.

해설　과일들이 진열되어 있는 모습에 초점을 맞춰 묘사한 (B)가 정답이다. 정원과 저울, 고객은 사진에서 볼 수 없다.

어휘　grow 자라다　food item 식품　on display 진열되어 있는, 전시되어 있는　weigh ~의 무게를 측정하다　scale 저울　wait in line 줄을 서서 대기하다

7 Does your café offer lunch sets?
영W (A) Are you offering a discount?
미M **(B) Yes, we certainly do.**
(C) Our smartphone launched last week.

이 카페에서 점심 세트를 제공하나요?
(A) 할인은 제공해 주시나요?
(B) 네, 분명 그렇습니다.
(C) 저희 스마트폰이 지난주에 출시되었습니다.

해설　〈Do 일반 의문문〉
점심 세트를 제공하는지 확인하는 Do 일반 의문문에 대해 긍정을 뜻하는 Yes 및 동일한 조동사 do와 함께 분명히 제공한다는 뜻을 나타낸 (B)가 정답이다.
(A) 손님이 물어 볼 수 있는 말이므로 질문 주체가 뒤바뀐 오답 / 질문의 offer를 반복 사용한 오답
(C) 전화기 출시와 관련된 말이므로 질문의 핵심에서 벗어난 오답 / 질문의 lunch와 발음이 유사한 launch를 사용한 오답

어휘　offer ~을 제공하다　certainly 분명히, 확실히　launch ~을 출시하다, 공개하다

8 When will the movie start on Friday?
호M (A) The main theater.
캐W **(B) At seven o'clock.**
(C) Tickets are on sale.

금요일에 언제 영화가 시작하죠?
(A) 주 상영관이요.
(B) 7시에요.
(C) 입장권이 판매 중입니다.

해설　〈When 의문문〉
금요일 영화 시작 시점을 묻는 When 의문문에 대해 7시라는 특정 시각을 알려 주는 (B)가 정답이다.
(A) 장소 표현이므로 When과 어울리지 않는 오답
(C) 입장권 판매 여부와 관련된 말이므로 질문의 핵심에서 벗어난 오답 / 질문의 movie에서 연상되는 Tickets를 사용한 오답

어휘　main 주요한, 주된　on sale 판매되고 있는

9 Where did you rent your vehicle?
영W (A) Yes, I have a company car.
미M **(B) Next to the airport.**
(C) For three days.

어디서 차량을 대여하셨어요?
(A) 네, 저한테 회사 차가 있습니다.
(B) 공항 옆에서요.
(C) 3일 동안이요.

해설　〈Where 의문문〉
차량을 대여한 곳을 묻는 Where 의문문에 대해 공항 옆이라는 위치

를 알려 주는 (B)가 정답이다.
(A) 의문사 의문문에 맞지 않는 Yes로 답변하는 오답
(C) 기간 표현이므로 Where와 어울리지 않는 오답

어휘 rent ~을 대여하다, 임대하다 vehicle 차량 next to ~ 옆에

10 Why was the meeting canceled?
캐W (A) OK, I'll let him know.
호M (B) In the conference room.
(C) Because Ms. Ruiz is busy.

회의가 왜 취소된 건가요?
(A) 네, 제가 그에게 알릴게요.
(B) 대회의실에서요.
(C) 루이즈 씨가 바빠서요.

해설 〈Why 의문문〉
회의가 취소된 이유를 묻는 Why 의문문에 대해 Why와 짝을 이루는 Because와 함께 루이즈 씨가 바쁘다는 점을 언급한 (C)가 정답이다.
(A) Yes와 마찬가지로 의문사 의문문에 맞지 않는 OK로 답변하는 오답
(B) 장소 표현이므로 Why와 어울리지 않는 오답

어휘 cancel ~을 취소하다 let A know A에게 알리다

11 Is this cleaner to be used on wood or metal?
미M (A) It's for wood surfaces only.
영W (B) I'll build it to be strong.
(C) In aisle 3 at the supermarket.

이 세제가 목재에 사용되는 건가요, 아니면 금속용인가요?
(A) 목재 표면 전용입니다.
(B) 튼튼하게 유지되도록 짓겠습니다.
(C) 슈퍼마켓 3번 통로에요.

해설 〈선택 의문문〉
세제가 목재용인지 금속용인지 묻는 선택 의문문에 대해 목재 전용임을 알리는 (A)가 정답이다.
(B) 세제의 용도와 관련 없는 말이므로 질문의 핵심에서 벗어난 오답
(C) 위치 표현으로서 세제의 용도와 관련 없는 말이므로 질문의 핵심에서 벗어난 오답

어휘 cleaner 세척제, 세제, 청소기 surface 표면 aisle 통로, 복도

12 Where did you get that leather briefcase?
캐W (A) No, I rarely use them.
호M (B) I received it as a gift.
(C) Just 300 dollars.

그 가죽 서류 가방은 어디서 난 거예요?
(A) 아니요, 저는 그것들을 좀처럼 사용하지 않아요.
(B) 선물로 받았습니다.
(C) 300달러밖에 하지 않아요.

해설 〈Where 의문문〉
가죽 서류 가방은 어디서 났는지 묻는 Where 의문문에 대해 leather briefcase를 it으로 지칭해 선물로 받았음을 나타낸 (B)가 정답이다.
(A) 의문사 의문문에 맞지 않는 No로 답변하는 오답
(C) 비용 표현이므로 Where와 어울리지 않는 오답

어휘 leather 가죽 briefcase 서류 가방 rarely 좀처럼 ~ 않다 receive ~을 받다

13 How many employees have registered for the training?
영W (A) Usually twice per month.
미M (B) About 7 so far.
(C) The train departing at 12:30.

얼마나 많은 직원들이 교육 시간에 등록했죠?
(A) 보통 한 달에 두 번이요.
(B) 지금까지 약 7명이요.
(C) 12시 30분에 출발하는 열차요.

해설 〈How many 의문문〉
얼마나 많은 직원들이 교육 시간에 등록했는지 묻는 How many 의문문에 대해 대략적인 인원수를 밝히는 (B)가 정답이다.
(A) How often과 어울리는 빈도를 나타내는 말이므로 오답
(C) 기차 출발 시간을 말하고 있으므로 질문의 핵심에서 벗어난 오답 / 질문의 training과 발음이 유사한 train을 사용한 오답

어휘 register for ~에 등록하다 training 교육 usually 보통, 일반적으로 about 약, 대략 so far 지금까지 depart 출발하다, 떠나다

14 Tickets for the dance performance are almost sold out.
호M (A) Eighteen dollars per adult.
캐W (B) We certainly could.
(C) I know, people are really interested in it.

댄스 공연 입장권이 거의 매진됐어요.
(A) 성인 1인당 18달러입니다.
(B) 우리는 분명 그럴 수 있을 거예요.
(C) 그러니까요, 사람들이 정말 관심이 많아요.

해설 〈평서문〉
댄스 공연 입장권이 거의 매진된 사실을 말하는 평서문에 대해 동의를 나타내는 I know와 함께 매진된 이유를 언급하는 (C)가 정답이다.
(A) 가격 정보에 해당되므로 입장권 매진 사실과 관련 없는 오답 / Tickets에서 연상되는 Eighteen dollars를 사용한 오답
(B) 할 수 있을 것이라는 생각을 나타낸 말이므로 입장권 매진 사실과 관련 없는 오답

어휘 sold out 매진된, 품절된 per ~당, ~마다 adult 성인 certainly 분명히, 확실히 be interested in ~에 관심이 있다

15 Which offices are still available for rent?
미M (A) The realtor has a list.
영W (B) I live in a two-bedroom house.
(C) A popular neighborhood.

어느 사무실들이 여전히 임대 가능한가요?
(A) 부동산 중개업자가 목록을 갖고 있어요.
(B) 저는 침실 2개짜리 집에 살고 있어요.
(C) 인기 있는 지역이요.

해설 〈Which 의문문〉
어느 사무실들이 여전히 임대 가능한지 묻는 Which 의문문에 대해 부동산 중개업자가 목록을 갖고 있다는 말로 그 사람에게 물어 봐야 한다는 뜻을 나타낸 (A)가 정답이다.
(B) 답변자 자신이 살고 있는 집의 특징을 나타낸 말이므로 질문의 핵심에서 벗어난 오답
(C) 한 지역의 인기 정도를 나타낸 말이므로 질문의 핵심에서 벗어난 오답

어휘 available 이용 가능한 rent 임대, 대여 realtor 부동산 중개업자 popular 인기 있는 neighborhood 지역, 인근

16 You purchase snacks from the vending machine, right?
캐W (A) That's a shame.
호M (B) She is a newspaper vendor.
(C) Yes, when I've skipped lunch.

자판기에서 간식을 구입하시죠, 맞나요?
(A) 안되셨네요.
(B) 그녀는 신문 판매상이에요.
(C) 네, 점심을 건너뛰었을 때요.

해설 〈부가 의문문〉
자판기에서 간식을 구입하지 않는지 확인하는 부가 의문문에 대해 긍정을 뜻하는 Yes와 함께 자판기에서 간식을 구입하는 조건을 덧붙인 (C)가 정답이다.
(A) 안타까움을 나타내는 말이므로 질문의 핵심에서 벗어난 오답
(B) 답변자 자신의 자판기 이용 여부가 아니라 누군지 알 수 없는 She에 대해 말하고 있으므로 오답

어휘 purchase ~을 구입하다 vending machine 자판기 That's a shame 안됐네요, 아쉽네요, 유감이네요 vendor 판매상, 판매업체 skip ~을 건너뛰다

17 You have Ms. Carlyle's contact information, don't you?
영W (A) Yes, I know her phone number.
미M (B) By signing the contract.
(C) No, she's a lawyer.

칼라일 씨의 연락처를 갖고 계시죠, 그렇지 않나요? (= 갖고 계시죠?)
(A) 네, 그분 전화번호를 알고 있어요.
(B) 계약서에 서명하는 것으로요.
(C) 아니요, 그분은 변호사입니다.

해설 〈부가 의문문〉
칼라일 씨의 연락처를 갖고 있지 않은지 확인하는 부가 의문문에 대해 긍정을 뜻하는 Yes와 함께 전화번호를 알고 있다는 사실을 밝힌 (A)가 정답이다.

(B) 계약서 서명이라는 방법을 말하고 있으므로 질문의 핵심에서 벗어난 오답 / 질문의 contact와 발음이 유사한 contract를 사용한 오답
(C) 직업을 나타낸 말이므로 질문의 핵심에서 벗어난 오답

어휘 contact information 연락처 by (방법) ~하는 것으로, ~함으로써 sign ~에 서명하다 contract 계약(서) lawyer 변호사

18 Why is the lecture ending early?
영W (A) James will know.
호M (B) The new photocopier.
(C) No, I'm leaving at 7 o'clock.

강연이 왜 일찍 끝나는 건가요?
(A) 제임스 씨가 알고 있을 거예요.
(B) 새 복사기요.
(C) 아니요, 저는 7시에 나갈 거예요.

해설 〈Why 의문문〉
강연이 일찍 끝나는 이유를 묻는 Why 의문문에 대해 제임스 씨가 알고 있다는 말로 그 사람에게 물어 보라는 뜻을 나타낸 (A)가 정답이다.
(B) 복사기의 상태와 관련된 말이므로 질문의 핵심에서 벗어난 오답
(C) 의문사 의문문에 맞지 않는 No로 답변하는 오답

어휘 lecture 강연 photocopier 복사기 leave 나가다. 떠나다. 출발하다

19 Who will replace the program director when she retires?
미M (A) Follow the directions, please.
캐W (B) Due to his impressive experience.
(C) Laura Silva, her current assistant.

프로그램 관리부장님께서 은퇴하시면 누가 후임이 되죠?
(A) 지시 사항을 따라 주세요.
(B) 그의 인상적인 경력 때문에요.
(C) 현재 차장이신 로라 실바 씨요.

해설 〈Who 의문문〉
누가 후임 프로그램 관리부장이 되는지 묻는 Who 의문문에 대해 특정 인물의 이름과 직책을 밝히는 (C)가 정답이다.
(A) 지시 사항을 따르도록 당부하는 말이므로 질문의 핵심에서 벗어난 오답 / 질문의 director와 발음이 유사한 directions를 사용한 오답
(B) 이유를 나타내는 Due to로 답변하고 있으므로 Who와 어울리지 않는 오답

어휘 replace ~의 후임이 되다. ~을 대체하다 director 부장. 관리 책임자. 이사 retire 은퇴하다 follow ~을 따르다. 준수하다 directions 지시. 안내. 설명 due to ~ 때문에 impressive 인상적인 current 현재의

20 Haven't you heard any news about the corporate merger?
영W (A) Stacey works for a large company.
호M (B) Not yet, but we'll have to look at the website.
(C) International manufacturing.

기업 합병과 관련해서 아무런 뉴스도 듣지 못하셨어요? (= 들으셨어요?)
(A) 스테이시 씨는 대기업에서 일해요.
(B) 아직이요, 하지만 웹 사이트를 살펴봐야 할 거예요.
(C) 해외 제조요.

해설 〈부정 의문문〉
기업 합병과 관련된 소식을 듣지 못했는지 확인하는 부정 의문문에 대해 부정을 나타내는 Not yet과 함께 소식을 확인할 방법을 언급하는 (B)가 정답이다.
(A) 스테이시의 근무지를 알리는 말이므로 질문의 핵심에서 벗어난 오답 / 질문의 corporate에서 연상되는 company를 사용한 오답
(C) 합병 여부가 아닌 특정 분야를 나타내는 말이므로 질문의 핵심에서 벗어난 오답

어휘 corporate 기업의 merger 합병 work for ~에서 일하다 Not yet (앞서 언급된 말에 대해) 아직 아니다 will have to do ~해야 할 것이다 manufacturing 제조

21 Who can access the laboratory?
캐W (A) She hasn't responded to our calls.
미M (B) Keep your passport accessible.
(C) Only those with keys.

누가 실험실에 출입할 수 있죠?
(A) 그분이 우리 요청에 답변하지 않았어요.
(B) 여권을 바로 제시할 수 있게 해 두세요.
(C) 열쇠가 있는 사람들만요.

해설 〈Who 의문문〉
누가 실험실에 출입할 수 있는지 묻는 Who 의문문에 대해 열쇠가 있는 사람들이라는 말로 일종의 자격을 언급하는 (C)가 정답이다.
(A) 누군지 알 수 없는 She에 대해 말하고 있으므로 실험실 출입 자격과 관련 없는 오답
(B) 여권과 관련된 말이므로 질문의 핵심에서 벗어난 오답 / 질문의 access와 발음이 유사한 accessible을 사용한 오답

어휘 access ~에 접근하다. ~을 이용하다 respond to ~에 답변하다. 대응하다 call 요청, 요구, 전화 (통화) keep A + 형용사 A를 ~한 상태로 유지하다 accessible 접근 가능한. 이용 가능한 those (수식어구와 함께) ~하는 사람들

22 Has the location of the negotiation meeting been
호M changed?
영W (A) Representatives of our company.
(B) I agreed with most of the terms.
(C) Yes, it'll now be at the Royal Plaza.

협상 회의 장소가 변경되었나요?
(A) 우리 회사 대표자들이요.
(B) 저는 대부분의 조건에 동의했습니다.
(C) 네, 현재 로열 플라자에서 열릴 겁니다.

해설 〈Have 일반 의문문〉
협상 회의 장소가 변경되었는지 확인하는 Have 일반 의문문에 대해 긍정을 나타내는 Yes와 함께 특정 장소를 언급하는 (C)가 정답이다.
(A) 회의 참가자에 해당되는 말이므로 질문의 핵심에서 벗어난 오답
(B) 답변자 자신이 동의한 사실을 나타내는 말이므로 질문의 핵심에서 벗어난 오답 / 질문의 negotiation에서 연상되는 agreed를 사용한 오답

어휘 location 장소, 위치, 지점 negotiation 협상, 협의 representative n. 대표자, 직원 agree with ~에 동의하다 term 조건, 조항, 기간, 용어

23 Can I return or exchange sale items?
캐W (A) I'm afraid neither is possible.
미M (B) He is out sick today.
(C) I put them in the stockroom.

세일 제품을 반품하거나 교환할 수 있나요?
(A) 유감이지만 둘 모두 가능하지 않습니다.
(B) 그가 오늘 아파서 결근한 상태예요.
(C) 제가 그것들을 물품 보관실에 넣어 놨어요.

해설 〈선택 의문문〉
세일 제품을 반품하거나 교환할 수 있는지 확인하는 선택 의문문에 대해 두 가지 모두를 부정하는 neither와 함께 불가능하다는 뜻을 나타낸 (A)가 정답이다.
(B) 누군지 알 수 없는 He의 결근을 알리는 말이므로 질문의 핵심에서 벗어난 오답
(C) 물품 보관 장소를 나타낸 말이므로 질문의 핵심에서 벗어난 오답 / 질문의 sale items에서 연상되는 stockroom을 사용한 오답

어휘 return ~을 반품하다, 반납하다 exchange ~을 교환하다 I'm afraid (that) (부정적인 일을 말할 때) 유감이지만 ~이다. ~인 것 같다 neither 둘 모두 아니다 out sick 아파서 결근한 put A in B A를 B에 넣다. 두다

24 What job title would you like listed on your business card?
영W (A) I've been promoted to senior analyst.
호M (B) Yes, she's a good listener.
(C) No, I've run out of them.

명함에 어떤 직위를 기재해 놓고 싶으신가요?
(A) 제가 수석 분석가로 승진되었습니다.
(B) 네, 그녀는 얘기를 잘 들어 줍니다.
(C) 아니요, 저는 그것들을 다 썼어요.

해설 〈What 의문문〉
명함에 표기하고 싶은 직위가 무엇인지 묻는 What 의문문에 대해 승진되어 새로 얻은 직위를 언급하는 (A)가 정답이다.
(B) 의문사 의문문에 맞지 않는 Yes로 답변하는 오답
(C) 의문사 의문문에 맞지 않는 No로 답변하는 오답

어휘 job title 직위 would like A p.p. A가 ~되기를 원하다 list ~을 기재하다, 목록에 올리다 promote ~을 승진시키다 analyst 분석가 run out of ~을 다 쓰다. ~가 다 떨어지다

25 When will you send the manuscript?
미M (A) Of course, I'd be happy to.
캐W (B) Yes, it was very creative.
(C) I'm in the proofreading stages.

원고를 언제 보내실 거예요?
(A) 물론이죠. 기꺼이 그렇게 하겠습니다.
(B) 네, 아주 창의적이었어요.
(C) 교정 단계에 있습니다.

해설 〈When 의문문〉

원고를 보내는 시점을 묻는 When 의문문에 대해 교정 단계에 있다는 말로 아직 보낼 시점을 알 수 없음을 나타낸 (C)가 정답이다.

(A) Yes와 마찬가지로 의문사 의문문에 맞지 않는 Of course로 답변하는 오답

(B) 의문사 의문문에 맞지 않는 Yes로 답변하는 오답

어휘 manuscript 원고 be happy to do 기꺼이 ~하다, ~해서 기쁘다 creative 창의적인 proofreading (문서 등의) 교정 stage 단계

---

26 Have you organized the office supplies downstairs?

영W (A) You need some more plastic folders.

호M **(B) Matthew handles the storage area.**

(C) Yes, the stairs will get new carpet.

아래층의 사무용품을 정리하셨나요?

(A) 당신은 플라스틱 폴더가 좀 더 필요합니다.

(B) 매튜 씨가 보관 구역을 처리합니다.

(C) 네, 계단에 새 카펫이 생길 거에요.

해설 〈Have 일반 의문문〉

사무용품을 정리했는지 확인하는 Have 일반 의문문에 대해 매튜 씨가 보관 구역을 처리한다는 말로 정리 작업을 하지 않았다는 뜻을 나타낸 (B)가 정답이다.

(A) 정리 여부가 아닌 필요 물품을 나타낸 말이므로 질문의 핵심에서 벗어난 오답 / 질문의 office supplies에서 연상되는 plastic folders를 사용한 오답

(C) 긍정을 나타내는 Yes 뒤에 이어지는 말이 정리 작업과 관련 없는 말이므로 오답

어휘 organize ~을 정리하다, 조직하다, 주최하다 supplies 용품, 물품 downstairs 아래층에서, 아래층으로 handle ~을 처리하다, 다루다 storage 보관, 저장 stairs 계단

---

27 How do I submit a request for reimbursement?

미M **(A) Donna can assist you.**

캐W (B) I'll meet a client for lunch.

(C) They took a business trip.

비용 환급 요청서를 어떻게 제출하나요?

(A) 도나 씨가 도와드릴 수 있어요.

(B) 제가 고객과 만나서 점심 식사를 할 겁니다.

(C) 그분들은 출장을 갔어요.

해설 〈How 의문문〉

비용 환급 요청서 제출 방법을 묻는 How 의문문에 대해 그 일을 도와줄 사람을 알려 주는 (A)가 정답이다.

(B) 고객과 만나서 할 일을 말하고 있으므로 질문의 핵심에서 벗어난 오답

(C) 누군지 알 수 없는 They가 출장 간 사실을 말하고 있으므로 질문의 핵심에서 벗어난 오답

어휘 submit ~을 제출하다 request 요청(서) reimbursement 비용 환급 assist ~을 돕다 take a business trip 출장을 떠나다

---

28 We need to prepare for this radio interview.

영W (A) Who made the music playlist?

호M (B) Did you have any difficulty?

(C) Okay, I can start on it now.

우리는 이 라디오 인터뷰를 준비해야 합니다.

(A) 누가 음악 선곡표를 만들었죠?

(B) 어떤 어려움이라도 있었나요?

(C) 좋아요, 제가 지금 시작할 수 있어요.

해설 〈평서문〉

라디오 인터뷰를 준비해야 한다고 알리는 평서문에 대해 동의를 나타내는 Okay와 함께 그 일을 it으로 지칭해 지금 시작할 수 있다는 뜻을 나타낸 (C)가 정답이다.

(A) 음악 선곡표를 만든 사람을 묻고 있으므로 라디오 인터뷰 준비와 관련 없는 오답 / 질문의 radio에서 연상되는 music playlist를 사용한 오답

(B) 과거에 어려움이 있었는지 묻는 말이므로 앞으로 해야 할 일을 말하는 평서문과 시점이 맞지 않는 오답

어휘 prepare for ~을 준비하다, ~에 대비하다 playlist 선곡표, 재생 목록 difficulty 어려움, 문제 start on ~에 대한 일을 시작하다

---

29 Do you enjoy working at the community center?

캐W (A) In the middle of the city.

미M **(B) Well, I really like meeting local residents.**

(C) No, it opened yesterday.

지역 문화 센터에서 일하는 게 즐거우신가요?

(A) 도시 한가운데에 있어요.

(B) 음, 지역 주민들을 만나는 게 정말 좋아요.

(C) 아니요, 어제 개장했어요.

해설 〈Do 일반 의문문〉

지역 문화 센터에서 일하는 게 즐거운지 확인하는 Do 일반 의문문에 대해 지역 주민들을 만나는 게 좋다는 말로 즐겁다는 뜻을 나타낸 (B)가 정답이다.

(A) 위치 표현이므로 일의 즐거움을 묻는 질문의 핵심에서 벗어난 오답

(C) 부정을 뜻하는 No 뒤에 이어지는 말이 개장 시점을 알리고 있으므로 질문의 핵심에서 벗어난 오답

어휘 enjoy -ing ~하는 게 즐겁다, ~하는 것을 즐기다 community center 지역 문화 센터 in the middle of ~ 한가운데에, ~하는 중간에 local 지역의, 현지의 resident 주민

---

30 Ms. Delmont e-mailed to postpone tomorrow's meeting.

호M (A) Please be sure to send me the invoice.

영W (B) Around three in the afternoon.

(C) She's probably going out of town.

델몬트 씨가 내일 회의를 연기하는 이메일을 보냈어요.

(A) 꼭 저에게 거래 내역서를 보내 주시기 바랍니다.

(B) 오후 3시쯤이요.

(C) 아마 (그날) 다른 지역에 가실 겁니다.

해설 〈평서문〉

델몬트 씨가 내일 회의를 연기하는 이메일을 보낸 사실을 알리는 평서문에 대해 Ms. Delmont를 She로 지칭해 회의를 연기한 이유를 추측하는 (C)가 정답이다.

(A) 거래 내역서를 보내도록 요청하는 말이므로 핵심에서 벗어난 오답 / 평서문에 제시된 e-mailed에서 연상되는 send를 사용한 오답

(B) When 의문문에 어울리는 시점 표현이므로 회의가 연기된 사실에 대한 반응으로 어울리지 않는 오답

어휘 postpone ~을 연기하다, 미루다 be sure to do 꼭 ~하다, ~하는 것을 확실히 하다 invoice 거래 내역서, 송장 around ~쯤, 약, 대략 go out of town 다른 지역으로 가다

---

31 Are you thinking about joining the book club this Friday?

미M (A) She's an asset to the group, right?

캐W **(B) Actually, I was there last month.**

(C) A new romantic novel.

이번 주 금요일에 독서 동호회에 가입하실 생각이세요?

(A) 그분은 그룹의 자산이잖아요, 맞죠?

(B) 사실, 지난달에 거기 갔었어요.

(C) 신작 낭만 소설이요.

해설 〈Be 일반 의문문〉

이번 주 금요일에 독서 동호회에 가입할 생각인지 확인하는 Be 일반 의문문에 대해 이미 지난달에 갔다는 말로 이번 주 금요일에 가입할 필요가 없다는 뜻을 나타낸 (B)가 정답이다.

(A) 누군지 알 수 없는 She의 중요성을 말하고 있으므로 질문의 핵심에서 벗어난 오답

(C) 소설 장르를 말하는 답변이므로 질문의 핵심에서 벗어난 오답

어휘 join ~에 가입하다, 합류하다 asset to ~의 자산 actually 사실, 실은

Questions 32-34 refer to the following conversation. 캐W 미M

W ㉜ Thanks for calling the Unique Clothing Company, your best source for custom-designed T-shirts, sweatshirts and hoodies. What can I do for you?

M Hi, I just ordered some T-shirts from your online store for my company's team-building workshop, but ㉝ I made a mistake when typing my e-mail address on the order form. So, I haven't received any invoice or receipt.

W I can correct your e-mail address right away. ㉞ Could you let me know how many items you requested in your order?

여 최고의 맞춤 제작 티셔츠와 운동복, 그리고 후드티를 제공해 드리는 유니크 의류 회사에 전화 주셔서 감사합니다. 무엇을 도와드릴까요?

남 안녕하세요. 저희 회사의 팀워크 향상 워크숍을 위해 귀사의 온라인 매장에서 몇몇 티셔츠를 막 주문했는데, 주문서에 제 이메일 주소를 입력하다가 실수를 했습니다. 그래서 어떤 거래 내역서나 영수증도 받지 못했어요.

여 즉시 이메일 주소를 바로잡아 드릴 수 있습니다. 주문 사항으로 얼마나 많은 제품을 요청하셨는지 알려 주시겠어요?

어휘 source 공급원, 원천, 근원 custom-designed 맞춤 제작의 order v. ~을 주문하다 n. 주문(품) make a mistake 실수하다 form 양식, 서식 receive ~을 받다 invoice 거래 내역서 receipt 영수증 correct ~을 바로잡다, 고치다 right away 즉시, 당장 let A know A에게 알리다 request ~을 요청하다

32 What kind of company is the man calling?
(A) A software developer
(B) A clothing company
(C) A catering firm
(D) An electronics store

남자는 어떤 종류의 회사에 전화하는가?
(A) 소프트웨어 개발업체
(B) 의류 회사
(C) 출장 요리 제공업체
(D) 전자제품 매장

해설 〈기타 세부 사항을 묻는 문제〉
대화를 시작하면서 여자가 Thanks for calling the Unique Clothing Company라는 말로 유니크 의류 회사에 전화한 것에 대해 감사의 인사를 하고 있으므로 (B)가 정답이다.

어휘 developer 개발업체, 개발자 catering 출장 요리 제공(업) firm 회사, 업체 electronics 전자제품

33 What problem are the speakers talking about?
(A) An incorrect product price
(B) A wrong e-mail address
(C) A delayed delivery
(D) A misplaced document

화자들은 어떤 문제와 관련해 이야기하고 있는가?
(A) 부정확한 제품 가격
(B) 잘못된 이메일 주소
(C) 지연된 배송
(D) 분실된 문서

해설 〈문제점을 묻는 문제〉
남자가 대화 중반부에 주문서에 자신의 이메일 주소를 입력하다가 실수를 했다고(I made a mistake when typing my e-mail address) 알린 뒤로, 그 조치 방법과 관련해 이야기하고 있으므로 (B)가 정답이다.

어휘 incorrect 부정확한 delayed 지연된, 지체된 misplaced 분실된

34 What information does the woman ask for?
(A) An order number
(B) The model of a product
(C) A delivery location
(D) The quantity of items

여자는 무슨 정보를 요청하는가?
(A) 주문 번호
(B) 제품의 모델명
(C) 배송 장소
(D) 제품 수량

해설 〈요청 사항을 묻는 문제〉
대화 맨 마지막에 여자가 주문 사항으로 얼마나 많은 제품을 요청했는지 알려 달라고(Could you let me know how many items you requested in your order?) 요청하고 있으므로 제품 수량을 뜻하는 (D)가 정답이다.

어휘 ask for ~을 요청하다 quantity 수량

Questions 35-37 refer to the following conversation. 호M 영W

M Excuse me, Ms. Bronson. ㉟ I've been trying to log in to our company's Web page, but it isn't working.

W Ah, that's because we recently installed new security features. These changes were outlined at the training workshop you missed yesterday, but you'll be assigned new log-in details soon. ㊱ Don't forget to come to the next training class tomorrow, by the way.

M Sure, no problem. So, is there any way for me to get onto our homepage today?

W Yes, just check your e-mail inbox in a few minutes. ㊲ I'll send you a password that you will be able to use only for today.

남 실례합니다, 브론슨 씨. 제가 우리 회사 웹 페이지에 계속 로그인하려고 하는데, 작동하지 않고 있어요.

여 아, 그게 우리가 최근에 새 보안 기능들을 설치했기 때문이에요. 어제 놓치신 교육 워크숍에서 이러한 변경 사항들이 간략히 설명되었지만, 곧 새로운 로그인 상세 정보를 받으시게 될 거예요. 그건 그렇고, 내일 있을 다음 교육 시간에 잊지 말고 오세요.

남 그럼요, 문제없어요. 그럼, 제가 오늘 우리 홈페이지에 접속할 수 있는 방법이라도 있나요?

여 네, 몇 분 후에 이메일 수신함을 확인해 보세요. 오늘 하루에 한해서 사용하실 수 있는 비밀번호를 보내 드리겠습니다.

어휘 try to do ~하려 하다, ~하려 노력하다 work (기계 등이) 작동하다, 기능하다 recently 최근에 install 설치하다 feature 기능, 특징 outline ~을 간략히 설명하다 training 교육 miss ~을 놓치다, ~에 빠지다 assign A B A에게 B를 배정하다, 할당하다 details 상세 정보, 세부 사항 forget to do ~하는 것을 잊다 by the way (화제 전환을 위해) 그건 그렇고, 그런데 way for A to do A가 ~하는 방법 get onto ~에 들어가다, 올라서다 in 시간 ~ 후에 be able to do ~할 수 있다

35 What problem does the man have?
(A) He has misplaced a document.
(B) He cannot access a Web site.
(C) He has not completed some work.
(D) He went to the wrong location.

남자에게 무슨 문제가 있는가?
(A) 문서를 잃어버렸다.
(B) 웹 사이트에 접속할 수 없다.
(C) 일부 작업을 완료하지 못했다.
(D) 엉뚱한 장소로 갔다.

해설 〈문제점을 묻는 문제〉
대화를 시작하면서 남자가 회사 웹 페이지에 계속 로그인하려고 하는데 작동하지 않고 있다는(I've been trying to log-in to our company's Web page, but it isn't working) 문제점을 언급하

고 있으므로 (B)가 정답이다.

어휘 misplace ~을 분실하다, ~을 둔 곳을 잊다 access ~에 접근하다, ~을 이용하다 complete ~을 완료하다

36 What does the woman remind the man to do?
(A) Attend a training session
(B) Arrange a business trip
(C) Submit a form
(D) Speak with his supervisor
여자는 남자에게 무엇을 하도록 상기시키는가?
(A) 교육 시간에 참석하는 일
(B) 출장을 준비하는 일
(C) 양식을 제출하는 일
(D) 상사와 이야기하는 일

해설 〈상기시키는 것을 묻는 문제〉
대화 중반부에 여자가 내일 있을 다음 교육 시간에 잊지 말고 오라고 (Don't forget to come to the next training class tomorrow, by the way) 상기시키고 있으므로 (A)가 정답이다.

어휘 attend ~에 참석하다 training 교육 session (특정 활동을 위한) 시간 arrange ~을 준비하다, 조치하다 submit ~을 제출하다 form 양식, 서식 supervisor 상사, 책임자, 부서장

37 What will the woman most likely do next?
(A) Make an announcement
(B) Reschedule a meeting
(C) Provide a temporary password
(D) Update a company Web site
여자는 곧이어 무엇을 할 것 같은가?
(A) 공지를 하는 일
(B) 회의 일정을 재조정하는 일
(C) 임시 비밀번호를 제공하는 일
(D) 회사 웹 사이트를 업데이트하는 일

해설 〈곧이어 할 일을 묻는 문제〉
대화 마지막 부분에 여자가 오늘 하루만 사용할 수 있는 비밀번호를 보내겠다고(I'll send you a password that you will be able to use only for today) 알리고 있다. 이는 임시로 사용 가능한 비밀번호를 제공하겠다는 뜻이므로 (C)가 정답이다.

어휘 announcement 공지, 발표 reschedule ~의 일정을 재조정하다 provide ~을 제공하다 temporary 임시의, 일시적인

Questions 38-40 refer to the following conversation. 미M 캐W

M Rhonda, you've just completed ㊳ your first term teaching the art class at our institute. What did you think of it?
W I'm pleased with how it went. ㊴ This job is perfect for me because I get to meet other members of the community. I love it!
M I'm glad to hear that. You know, we've had a lot of positive feedback from your students. So, for next term, ㊵ we'd like you to work on Tuesdays and Thursdays. This would be in addition to your usual schedule. Are you available?
W Yes. That sounds great to me.

남 론다 씨, 우리 기관에서 미술 강좌를 가르치시면서 첫 번째 학기를 막 끝내셨는데요. 어떠셨어요?
여 그동안 진행된 것에 대해 만족해요. 지역 사회의 다른 사람들을 만나게 되니까 이 일이 저한텐 아주 잘 맞아요. 정말 마음에 듭니다!
남 그렇게 말씀하시는 걸 들으니 기쁘네요. 사실, 가르치신 학생들에게서 긍정적인 의견을 많이 받았어요. 그래서, 다음 학기에는, 매주 화요일과 목요일에 일해 주셨으면 합니다. 이건 평소의 일정에 추가되는 수업이 될 겁니다. 시간 괜찮으세요?
여 네, 저는 아주 좋은 것 같아요.

어휘 complete ~을 끝내다, 완료하다 term 학기 institute 기관, 단체, 협회 be pleased with ~에 만족하다, 기쁘다 get to do ~하게 되다 community 지역 사회, 지역 공동체 positive 긍정적인 feedback 의견 would like A to do A에게 ~하기를 원하다 in addition to ~에 더해, 덧붙여 usual 평소의, 보통의 available (사람이) 시간이 나는

38 What is the woman's occupation?
(A) Fitness trainer
(B) Art instructor
(C) Tour guide
(D) Professional chef
여자의 직업은 무엇인가?
(A) 피트니스 트레이너
(B) 미술 강사
(C) 투어 가이드
(D) 전문 요리사

해설 〈직업을 묻는 문제〉
대화 시작 부분에 남자가 여자를 지칭하는 your와 함께 미술 강좌를 가르치는 일(teaching art class)을 언급하고 있으므로 (B)가 정답이다.

어휘 occupation 직업 instructor 강사

---

39 What does the woman enjoy about her job?
(A) Meeting people
(B) Using modern technology
(C) Improving her skills
(D) Building a reputation
여자는 자신의 일과 관련해 무엇을 즐거워하는가?
(A) 사람들을 만나는 것
(B) 현대 기술을 활용하는 것
(C) 자신의 능력을 향상시키는 것
(D) 명성을 쌓아 나가는 것

해설 〈기타 세부 사항을 묻는 문제〉
대화 중반부에 여자가 다른 사람들을 만나기 때문에 잘 맞는 일이라는 말과 함께 아주 마음에 든다고(This job is perfect for me because I get to meet other members of the community. I love it!) 알리고 있으므로 (A)가 정답이다.

어휘 improve ~을 개선하다, 향상시키다 reputation 명성, 평판

40 What is the woman asked to do?
(A) Complete a survey
(B) Attend a conference
(C) Work additional days
(D) Plan a fundraiser
여자는 무엇을 하도록 요청받는가?
(A) 설문지를 작성 완료하는 일
(B) 컨퍼런스에 참석하는 일
(C) 추가 요일에 근무하는 일
(D) 모금 행사를 계획하는 일

해설 〈요청 사항을 묻는 문제〉
대화 후반부에 남자가 매주 화요일과 목요일에 일해 달라는 말과 함께 평소의 일정에 추가되는 것이라고(we'd like you to work on Tuesdays and Thursdays. This would be in addition to your usual schedule) 알리고 있으므로 (C)가 정답이다.

어휘 complete ~을 완료하다 survey 설문 조사(지) attend ~에 참석하다 additional 추가적인 fundraiser 모금 행사

M   Ms. Colter, I have a suggestion about our gallery's upcoming exhibition. ㊶ At our previous exhibitions, the audio guides we provided to visitors had very poor sound quality, so I'd like to get rid of them and purchase new ones.

W   That's a great idea. ㊷ Are you planning to compare the prices for different brands? We need to try to stick to our spending budget.

M   Yes, but ㊸ I'll need to borrow someone's phone to do some research. My battery has run out.

W   I'm not using mine right now.

M   Great, I'll let you know what I find out.

남   콜터 씨, 우리 미술관에서 곧 있을 전시회와 관련된 의견이 있어요. 이전의 우리 전시회에서 방문객들에게 제공했던 오디오 가이드가 음질이 아주 형편없었기 때문에 그것들을 없애고 새로운 것을 구입했으면 합니다.

여   아주 좋은 생각이에요. 서로 다른 브랜드들의 가격을 비교해 보실 계획이신가요? 우리 지출 예산을 지키도록 노력해야 하거든요.

남   네, 하지만 조사를 좀 할 수 있도록 누군가의 전화기를 빌려야 할 거예요. 제 배터리가 다 떨어졌거든요.

여   제가 지금은 제 것을 사용하지 않습니다.

남   잘됐네요, 제가 파악하는 것을 알려 드릴게요.

어휘   suggestion 의견, 제안   upcoming 곧 있을, 다가오는   exhibition 전시(회)   previous 이전의   provide ~을 제공하다   poor 형편없는, 저조한, 좋지 못한   sound quality 음질   would like to do ~하고 싶다, ~하고자 하다   get rid of ~을 없애다, 제거하다   purchase ~을 구입하다   plan to do ~할 계획이다   compare ~을 비교하다   try to do ~하려 노력하다   stick to ~을 지키다, 고수하다   spending 지출, 소비   budget 예산   borrow ~을 빌리다   do research 조사하다   run out 다 떨어지다, 다 쓰다   let A know A에게 알리다   find out ~을 파악하다, 알아내다

41   What does the man want to replace?
(A) Event programs
(B) Audio guides
(C) Display lights
(D) Gallery furniture
남자는 무엇을 교체하고 싶어 하는가?
(A) 행사 프로그램
(B) 오디오 가이드
(C) 전시용 조명
(D) 미술관 가구

해설   〈기타 세부 사항을 묻는 문제〉
대화를 시작하면서 남자가 이전의 전시회에서 오디오 가이드의 음질이 좋지 않았던 사실과 함께 그것들을 없애고 새로 구입하고 싶다고 (the audio guides we provided to visitors had very poor

sound quality, so I'd like to get rid of them and purchase new ones) 알리고 있으므로 (B)가 정답이다.

어휘   replace ~을 교체하다   display 전시(품), 진열(품)

42   What does the woman ask the man about?
(A) Setting up exhibits
(B) Creating advertisements
(C) Comparing prices
(D) Organizing transportation
여자는 남자에게 무엇에 관해 묻는가?
(A) 전시물을 설치하는 일
(B) 광고를 만들어내는 일
(C) 가격을 비교하는 일
(D) 교통편을 마련하는 일

해설   〈문의 사항을 묻는 문제〉
대화 중반부에 여자가 다른 브랜드들의 가격을 비교해 볼 계획인지 (Are you planning to compare the prices for different brands?) 묻고 있으므로 (C)가 정답이다.

43   What does the woman mean when she says, "I'm not using mine right now"?
(A) She forgot to bring her phone with her.
(B) Her phone has run out of battery.
(C) She is too busy to check some information.
(D) She can lend her phone to the man.
여자가 "I'm not using mine right now"라고 말할 때 무엇을 의미하는가?
(A) 자신의 전화기를 챙겨 오는 것을 잊었다.
(B) 자신의 전화기 배터리가 다 떨어졌다.
(C) 일부 정보를 확인하기엔 너무 바쁘다.
(D) 남자에게 자신의 전화기를 빌려줄 수 있다.

해설   〈의도 파악 문제〉
대화 후반부에 남자가 조사를 위해 누군가의 전화기를 빌려야 한다는 말과 함께 자신의 배터리가 다 떨어졌다고(I'll need to borrow someone's phone to do some research. My battery has run out) 말하자, 여자가 '제 것을 지금 사용하지 않아요'라고 알리는 흐름이다. 이는 자신의 전화기를 사용하도록 빌려주겠다는 뜻이므로 (D)가 정답이다.

어휘   forget to do ~하는 것을 잊다   run out of ~가 다 떨어지다, ~을 다 쓰다   too A to do ~하기엔 너무 A한   lend A to B A를 B에게 빌려주다

M   Hi, Helen. I brought in some extra pairs of ㊹ the headphones we'll be using in the demonstration this morning with the investors.

W   That's great, but did you hear ㊺ that we've moved the meeting from 10 A.M. to 11 A.M.? Their flight arrived on time, but there is severe traffic congestion between here and the airport.

M   Then they might feel like a little break and a snack when they get here.

W   That's true. ㊻ How about buying some doughnuts?

M   ㊻ OK, I'll go do that now.

남   안녕하세요, 헬렌 씨. 우리가 오늘 아침에 투자자들과 함께 하는 시연회에서 사용할 추가 헤드폰을 몇 개 가져왔습니다.

여   잘됐네요, 하지만 우리가 그 회의를 오전 10시에서 오전 11시로 옮겼다는 얘기를 들으셨나요? 그분들 항공편이 제때 도착하긴 했는데, 이곳과 공항 사이에 극심한 교통 체증이 있어요.

남   그럼, 여기 도착하시면 약간의 휴식을 취하면서 간식을 드시고 싶으실 수도 있겠네요.

여   맞아요, 도넛을 좀 사 오는 건 어때요?

남   좋아요, 지금 바로 그렇게 하겠습니다.

어휘   bring in ~을 가져오다, 챙겨 오다   extra 추가의, 별도의   demonstration 시연회   investor 투자자   arrive 도착하다   on time 제때, 제시간에   severe 극심한, 심각한   traffic congestion 교통 체증   between A and B A와 B 사이에   feel like ~하고 싶다   break 휴식   snack 간식   get here 이곳에 도착하다, 여기로 오다   How about -ing ~하는 게 어때요?

44   What kind of device will be demonstrated to investors?
(A) A smartphone
(B) A set of headphones
(C) A laptop computer
(D) A video camera
어떤 종류의 기기가 투자자들에게 시연될 것인가?
(A) 스마트폰
(B) 헤드폰
(C) 노트북 컴퓨터
(D) 비디오 카메라

해설   〈기타 세부 사항을 묻는 문제〉
대화 초반부에 남자가 시연회에서 헤드폰을 사용한다고(the headphones we'll be using in the demonstration) 언급하고 있으므로 (B)가 정답이다.

어휘   demonstrate ~을 시연하다, 시범을 보이다   investor 투자자

45 Why has a meeting time been changed?
(A) Some equipment is not set up yet.
(B) A room has been double-booked.
(C) There is heavy traffic in the area.
(D) The visitors are not available this morning.

회의 시간이 왜 변경되었는가?
(A) 일부 장비가 아직 설치되지 않은 상태이다.
(B) 방 하나가 이중으로 예약되었다.
(C) 그 지역에 교통량이 극심하다.
(D) 방문객들이 오늘 아침에 시간이 나지 않는다.

해설 〈기타 세부 사항을 묻는 문제〉
대화 중반부에 여자가 회의 시간이 11시로 변경된 사실과 함께, 투자자들이 공항에서 오는 길에 극심한 교통 체증이 발생했다고(that we've moved the meeting from 10 A.M. to 11 A.M.? ~ there is severe traffic congestion between here and the airport) 알리고 있으므로 (C)가 정답이다.

어휘 equipment 장비 set up ~을 설치하다, 설정하다, 준비하다 double-booked 이중 예약된 traffic 교통(량), 차량들 available (사람이) 시간이 나는

46 What will the man most likely do next?
(A) Hang up a sign
(B) Call the investors
(C) Drive to the airport
(D) Purchase some food

남자는 곧이어 무엇을 할 것 같은가?
(A) 표지판을 하나 걸어 두는 일
(B) 투자자들에게 전화하는 일
(C) 공항으로 운전해서 가는 일
(D) 음식을 좀 구입하는 일

해설 〈곧이어 할 일을 묻는 문제〉
대화 후반부에 여자가 도넛 구입을 제안하는(How about buying some doughnuts?) 것에 대해 남자가 바로 그렇게 하겠다고(OK, I'll go do that now) 답변하고 있으므로 (D)가 정답이다.

어휘 hang up ~을 내걸다, 부착하다 investor 투자자 purchase ~을 구입하다

Questions 47-49 refer to the following conversation. 호M 영W

M So, that wraps up your tutorial on recording a client's interactions with ㊼ our real estate agency. There's a lot to learn here, but I feel like you're already starting to understand everything.
W Yes, I think I understand it all. You've been a great help so far.
M Well, how about taking the call I'm expecting from a client in 15 minutes? They're calling to arrange a viewing of 238 Main Street. Oh, but before they call, ㊽ I'd recommend that you familiarize yourself with the client's personal information and preferences. You'll find that beneficial.
W ㊾ OK, I'll go over it.
M ㊾ Good. And if anything's unclear, my office is just across the hall.

남 자, 이것으로 고객과 우리 부동산 중개업체 사이의 대화 내용을 녹음하는 것에 관한 지침 설명을 마무리하겠습니다. 여기에 배울 것이 많이 있기는 하지만, 이미 모든 것을 이해하기 시작한 것 같습니다.
여 네, 전부 이해하고 있는 것 같아요. 지금까지 아주 큰 도움이 되었습니다.
남 그럼. 제가 15분 후에 한 고객사에서 올 것으로 기다리고 있는 전화를 받아 보시는 건 어떠세요? 그쪽 사람들이 메인 스트리트 238번지를 둘러보는 시간을 마련하기 위해 전화합니다. 아, 그런데 그쪽에서 전화하기 전에, 그 고객사의 개인 정보 및 선호 사항을 숙지해 두도록 권해 드리고 싶습니다. 유익하다고 생각하실 겁니다.
여 좋아요. 살펴보겠습니다.
남 좋습니다. 그리고 어떤 것이든 명확하지 않으면, 제 사무실이 복도 바로 맞은편에 있습니다.

어휘 wrap up ~을 마무리하다 tutorial 지침 interactions with ~와의 대화, 소통, 교류 real estate agency 부동산 중개업체 start to do ~하기 시작하다 so far 지금까지 how about -ing? ~하는 건 어때요? expect (오기로 되어 있는 것)을 기다리다 in + 시간 ~ 후에 arrange ~을 마련하다 viewing 둘러보기 recommend that ~하도록 권하다 familiarize oneself with ~을 숙지하다, ~에 익숙해지도록 하다 preference 선호(하는 것) find A + 형용사 A를 ~하다고 생각하다 beneficial 유익한, 이득이 되는 unclear 명확하지 않은 just across ~ 바로 맞은편에

47 Where do the speakers work?
(A) At a recruitment company
(B) At a department store
(C) At an accounting firm
(D) At a real estate agency

화자들은 어디에서 근무하는가?
(A) 인력 채용 전문회사에서
(B) 백화점에서
(C) 회계 법인에서
(D) 부동산 중개업체에서

해설 〈대화 장소를 묻는 문제〉
대화 초반부에 남자가 소속 업체를 our real estate agency라고 언급하고 있으므로 (D)가 정답이다.

어휘 take place (일, 행사 등이) 발생되다, 개최되다 recruitment 채용, 모집 accounting firm 회계 법인 real estate agency 부동산 중개업체

48 What does the man advise the woman to do first?
(A) Attend a meeting
(B) Review some preferences
(C) Order office supplies
(D) Clean a workspace

남자는 여자에게 무엇을 먼저 하도록 권하는가?
(A) 회의에 참석하는 일
(B) 몇몇 선호 사항을 살펴보는 일
(C) 사무용품을 주문하는 일
(D) 업무 공간을 청소하는 일

해설 〈제안 사항을 묻는 문제〉
대화 중반부에 남자가 고객사의 개인 정보 및 선호 사항을 숙지해 두도록 권한다고(I'd recommend that you familiarize yourself with the client's personal information and preferences) 알리고 있으므로 선호 사항을 살펴보는 일을 언급한 (B)가 정답이다.

어휘 attend ~에 참석하다 review ~을 검토하다, 살펴보다 preference 선호(하는 것) order ~을 주문하다 supplies 용품, 물품

49 What does the man imply when he says, "My office is just across the hall"?
(A) He would like to move to a different room.
(B) He has changed a training location.
(C) He would prefer not to be disturbed.
(D) He will be free to give assistance.

남자가 "My office is just across the hall"라고 말할 때 무엇을 의도하는가?
(A) 다른 방으로 옮기고 싶어 한다.
(B) 교육 장소를 변경했다.
(C) 방해받고 싶어 하지 않는다.
(D) 언제든 도움을 제공할 것이다.

해설 〈의도 파악 문제〉
대화 후반부에 여자가 남자의 요청 사항과 관련해 검토해 보겠다고(OK, I'll go over it) 말하자, 남자가 '명확하지 않은 부분이 있으면 (And if anything's unclear)'이라는 조건과 함께 '제 사무실이 복도 맞은편에 있습니다'라고 알리는 상황이다. 이는 명확하지 않은 부분과 관련해 언제든 찾아오면 돕겠다는 뜻이므로 (D)가 정답이다.

어휘 would like to do ~하고 싶어 하다 training 교육, 훈련 location 장소, 지점, 위치 would prefer (not) to do ~하고 싶어 하다(하고 싶어 하지 않다) disturb ~을 방해하다 be free to do 언제든 ~하다 assistance 도움, 지원

Questions 50-52 refer to the following conversation. 미M 캐W

M Hi, ma'am. ⑤⓪ Welcome to the Annual Association of Architects Conference. Is there anything I can help you with?

W Yes, I'm actually a presenter. I'm giving a talk this afternoon. ⑤① Could you tell me where I can print some more handouts? In the morning's first session, I saw that most of the seats were full, so I think I'll need more than the ones I brought.

M There's a print shop across the street. And ⑤② be sure to hold onto your receipt because you can get reimbursed from the event planners.

남 안녕하세요, 고객님. 연례 건축가 협회 컨퍼런스에 오신 것을 환영합니다. 제가 도와드릴 일이라도 있을까요?

여 네, 실은 제가 발표자입니다. 오후에 연설을 할 거예요. 어디서 유인물을 좀 더 출력할 수 있는지 알려 주시겠어요? 오전에 있었던 첫 번째 시간에 대부분의 좌석이 꽉 찬 것을 봤기 때문에 제가 가져온 것보다 더 많이 필요할 것 같아요.

남 길 건너편에 인쇄소가 한 곳 있습니다. 그리고 행사 주최 측으로부터 비용을 환급받으실 수 있으니 꼭 영수증을 챙겨 놓으시기 바랍니다.

어휘 annual 연례적인, 해마다의 help A with B B에 대해 A를 돕다 actually 실은, 사실은 give a talk 연설하다 handout 유인물 session (특정 활동을 위한) 시간 full 꽉 찬, 가득 찬 across ~ 건너편에 be sure to do 꼭 ~하다, ~하는 것을 확실히 하다 hold onto ~을 계속 보유하다, 꼭 잡다 receipt 영수증 get reimbursed 비용을 환급받다 event planners 행사 주최 측

50 Where is the conversation taking place?
(A) At a board meeting
(B) At an professional conference
(C) At a store's grand opening
(D) At a group interview session

대화가 어디에서 진행되고 있는가?
(A) 이사회 회의에서
(B) 전문 컨퍼런스에서
(C) 한 매장의 개장식에서
(D) 단체 면접 장소에서

해설 〈대화 장소를 묻는 문제〉
대화를 시작하면서 남자가 연례 건축가 협회 컨퍼런스에 온 것을 환영한다고(Welcome to the Annual Association of Architects Conference) 인사하는 것으로 장소를 밝히고 있으므로 (B)가 정답이다.

어휘 take place (일, 행사 등이) 발생되다, 개최되다 board 이사회, 이사진 session (특정 활동을 위한) 시간

51 What does the woman ask about?
(A) Submitting a complaint
(B) Getting a partial refund
(C) Changing her seat
(D) Printing some documents

여자는 무엇에 관해 묻는가?
(A) 불만 사항을 제출하는 일
(B) 부분 환불을 받는 일
(C) 좌석을 변경하는 일
(D) 일부 문서를 출력하는 일

해설 〈문의 사항을 묻는 문제〉
대화 중반부에 여자가 어디서 유인물을 좀 더 출력할 수 있는지 알려 달라고(Could you tell me where I can print some more handouts?) 요청하고 있으므로 (D)가 정답이다.

어휘 submit ~을 제출하다 complaint 불만, 불평 partial 부분적인 refund 환불

52 What does the man remind the woman to do?
(A) Keep her receipt
(B) Use the main entrance
(C) Complete a survey
(D) Wear an ID badge

남자는 여자에게 무엇을 하도록 상기시키는가?
(A) 영수증을 보관하는 일
(B) 정문을 이용하는 일
(C) 설문지를 작성 완료하는 일
(D) 출입증을 착용하는 일

해설 〈상기시키는 것을 묻는 문제〉
대화 후반부에 남자가 영수증을 꼭 챙겨 두라고(be sure to hold onto your receipt) 당부하고 있으므로 (A)가 정답이다.

어휘 receipt 영수증 complete ~을 완료하다 survey 설문 조사(지) ID badge 출입증, 신분증

Questions 53-55 refer to the following conversation with three speakers. 영W 호M 미M

W ⑤③ One of our delivery drivers just called and said that he reached his destination late. The delivery truck was stuck in traffic for hours, and the customer, Ms. Blake, wants to cancel her future orders with us.

M1 Oh, that's bad news. ⑤④ We should call Charles in Customer Support to see if he could give her a partial refund to apologize for the inconvenience. That way she might reconsider canceling her other orders.

W Okay, hold on while I give him a call. Hello, Charles. Would you mind getting in touch with our customer, Ms. Blake, and issuing a partial refund? The sooner, the better, if you don't mind.

M2 No problem. ⑤⑤ How much do you want me to send to her?

여 우리 배송 기사님들 중 한 분이 방금 전화해서 배송지에 늦게 도착하셨다고 말씀하셨어요. 배송 트럭이 몇 시간 동안 교통 체증에 갇혀 있었는데, 고객이신 블레이크 씨께서 앞으로 우리에게 주문하는 걸 취소하고 싶어 하세요.

남1 아, 좋지 않은 소식이네요. 그분께 불편함에 대한 사과의 의미로 부분 환불이라도 제공해 드릴 수 있는지 알아 볼 수 있게 고객 지원부의 찰스 씨에게 전화해 봐야 합니다. 그렇게 하면, 다른 주문 사항들을 취소하는 걸 재고해 보실 지도 몰라요.

여 좋아요, 제가 전화해 보는 동안 잠깐만 기다려 주세요. 안녕하세요, 찰스 씨. 우리 고객이신 블레이크 씨에게 전화하셔서 부분 환불을 해 드릴 수 있으신가요? 괜찮으시다면, 빠를수록 좋아요.

남2 좋습니다. 제가 그분께 얼마를 보내 드리면 되죠?

어휘 reach ~에 도달하다, 이르다 destination 목적지, 도착지 be stuck in traffic 교통 체증에 갇히다 cancel ~을 취소하다 order 주문(품) see if ~인지 알아 보다 partial 부분적인, 일부의 refund 환불 apologize for ~에 대해 사과하다 inconvenience 불편함 that way 그렇게 하면, 그런 식으로 reconsider ~을 재고하다 hold on 잠깐 기다리다 while ~하는 동안 give A a call A에게 전화하다 Would you mind -ing? ~해 주시겠어요? get in touch with ~에게 연락하다 issue ~을 지급하다, 발급하다 The sooner, the better 빠를수록 좋다 if you don't mind 괜찮다면 want A to do A에게 ~하기를 원하다

53 What problem does the woman mention?
(A) A product was damaged.
(B) An employee is absent.
(C) A delivery arrived late.
(D) A shipment was labeled incorrectly.

여자는 무슨 문제를 언급하는가?
(A) 제품이 손상되었다.

(B) 직원이 결근했다.
(C) 배송이 늦게 도착했다.
(D) 배송품에 라벨 표기가 잘못되었다.

해설 〈문제점을 묻는 문제〉
대화를 시작하면서 여자가 배송 기사 한 명이 배송지에 늦게 도착했다고 연락한 사실을(One of our delivery drivers just called and said that he reached his destination late) 언급하고 있으므로 (C)가 정답이다.

어휘 damaged 손상된, 피해를 입은 absent 결근한, 부재중인 arrive 도착하다 label v. ~에 라벨로 표기하다 incorrectly 잘못되어, 부정확하게

54 Why does the woman call Charles?
(A) To inquire about transportation
(B) To arrange compensation
(C) To request a customer's contact details
(D) To complain about a service

여자는 왜 찰스에게 전화를 거는가?
(A) 교통편에 관해 문의하기 위해
(B) 비용 보상을 준비하기 위해
(C) 고객의 연락 정보를 요청하기 위해
(D) 서비스에 대해 불평하기 위해

해설 〈목적을 묻는 문제〉
찰스 씨의 이름이 언급되는 중반부에, 남자가 고객에게 부분 환불이라도 제공해 드릴 수 있는지 알아 볼 수 있게 고객 지원부의 찰스 씨에게 전화해야 한다고(We should call Charles in Customer Support to see if he could give her a partial refund ~) 알리고 있다. 이는 비용 환불을 준비하기 위한 조치이므로 (B)가 정답이다.

어휘 inquire about ~에 관해 문의하다 transportation 교통(편) arrange ~을 준비하다, 조치하다 compensation 보상 contact details 연락 정보 complain about ~에 대해 불평하다

55 What information does Charles request?
(A) The name of a customer
(B) The destination of a delivery
(C) The amount of a payment
(D) The cost of some merchandise

찰스 씨는 어떤 정보를 요청하는가?
(A) 고객의 이름
(B) 배송 목적지
(C) 지급 비용 액수
(D) 일부 상품의 비용

해설 〈요청 사항을 묻는 문제〉
대화 맨 마지막에 여자의 전화를 받은 남자가 부분 환불과 관련해 얼마를 보내게 되는지(How much do you want me to send to her?) 묻고 있다. 이는 환불 액수를 묻는 것이므로 (C)가 정답이다.

어휘 destination 목적지, 도착지 amount 액수, 금액 merchandise 상품

Questions 56-58 refer to the following conversation. 호M 캐W

M Wendy, ㉗ I've been trying to come up with ways to spend less money here at ㊱ our catering firm.
W Well, we've already started to purchase low-cost ingredients, and we don't waste any food. ㉗ Do you have any ideas to reduce our expenses?
M I saw a documentary recently, and it said that not only are paper boxes more eco-friendly than plastic ones, but they're much cheaper as well.
W That could save us a few dollars for sure, as long as they're still high quality. ㊳ Let's talk to our packaging supplier and see if they have any paper boxes.

남 웬디 씨, 제가 이곳 우리 출장 요리 회사에서 돈을 덜 소비하는 방법을 계속 생각해 내려 하고 있어요.
여 음, 이미 저가 재료를 구입하기 시작했기에 어떤 식품도 낭비하지 않고 있어요. 우리 지출 비용을 줄일 아이디어라도 있으세요?
남 제가 최근에 본 다큐멘터리가 있는데, 종이 상자가 플라스틱 상자보다 더 환경 친화적일 뿐만 아니라 훨씬 더 저렴하기도 하다고 나오더라고요.
여 그렇게 하는 게 분명 몇 달러라도 절약할 수 있을 거예요, 여전히 고품질이기만 하면요. 우리 포장재 공급 업체에 얘기해서 어떤 종이 상자든 있는지 알아 봐요.

어휘 try to do ~하려 하다 come up with (아이디어, 해결책 등) ~을 생각해 내다, 제시하다 way to do ~하는 방법 catering firm 출장 요리 업체 purchase ~을 구입하다 ingredient (음식) 재료, 성분 waste ~을 낭비하다 reduce ~을 줄이다, 감소시키다 expense 지출 비용 recently 최근에 not only A but (also) B A뿐만 아니라 B도 eco-friendly 환경 친화적인 much (비교급 수식) 훨씬 as well ~도, 또한 save A B A에게 B를 절약하게 하다 as long as ~하기만 하면, ~하는 한 packaging 포장(재) supplier 공급 업체 see if ~인지 알아 보다

56 Where most likely do the speakers work?
(A) At a shipping firm
(B) At a supermarket
(C) At a manufacturing plant
(D) At a catering company

화자들은 어디에서 일하고 있을 것 같은가?
(A) 배송 업체에서
(B) 슈퍼마켓에서
(C) 제조 공장에서
(D) 출장 요리 전문 회사에서

해설 〈근무지를 묻는 문제〉
대화 초반부에 남자가 소속 회사를 our로 지칭해 our catering firm이라고 언급하고 있으므로 (D)가 정답이다.

---

57 What are the speakers trying to do?
(A) Reduce expenses
(B) Develop new products
(C) Attract more clients
(D) Hire employees

화자들은 무엇을 하려고 하는가?
(A) 지출 비용을 줄이는 일
(B) 신제품을 개발하는 일
(C) 더 많은 고객을 끌어들이는 일
(D) 직원을 고용하는 일

해설 〈주제를 묻는 문제〉
대화 시작 부분에 남자가 돈을 덜 소비하는 방법을 생각하고 있다고(I've been trying to come up with ways to spend less money) 알리고 있고, 곧이어 여자도 지출 비용을 줄일 아이디어가 있는지(Do you have any ideas to reduce our expenses?) 물으면서 그 방법을 이야기하는 것으로 대화가 진행되고 있다. 따라서 (A)가 정답이다.

어휘 reduce ~을 줄이다, 감소시키다 expense 지출 비용, 경비 develop ~을 개발하다 attract ~을 끌어들이다 hire ~을 고용하다

58 What does the woman recommend doing?
(A) Placing an advertisement
(B) Contacting a supplier
(C) Relocating a business
(D) Cleaning up a room

여자는 무엇을 하도록 권하는가?
(A) 광고를 내는 일
(B) 공급 업체에 연락하는 일
(C) 업체를 이전하는 일
(D) 방을 청소하는 일

해설 〈제안 사항을 묻는 문제〉
대화 맨 마지막에 여자가 포장재 공급 업체에 얘기해서 어떤 종이 상자든 있는지 알아 보자고(Let's talk to our packaging supplier and see if they have any paper boxes) 제안하고 있으므로 (B)가 정답이다.

어휘 place an advertisement 광고를 내다 contact ~에게 연락하다 supplier 공급 업체 relocate ~을 이전하다

M1 It seems that a lot more people are visiting the park these days. ⑤⑨ Every time I've given a lecture on the park's wildlife, the auditorium has been nearly full.

M2 Yes, ⑤⑨ that's been happening to me as well. ⑥⓪ I think it's because of the new shuttle bus.

M1 You're probably right. It's much easier for visitors to get to and from the park now.

W Exactly. And thanks to bringing in more admission fees, we could finally purchase some of the items that employees have been requesting. For example, ⑥① we've ordered some cordless microphones.

M2 Oh, when are we getting those?

W ⑥① They'll arrive by courier on Saturday.

남1 요즘 훨씬 더 많은 사람들이 공원을 방문하고 있는 것 같아요. 제가 공원의 야생동물에 관해 강연할 때마다 강당이 거의 꽉 찼거든요.

남2 네, 저한테도 그런 일이 계속 생기고 있어요. 새로 생긴 셔틀 버스 때문인 것 같아요.

남1 아마 그 말씀이 맞을 거예요. 지금은 방문객들이 공원을 오가는 게 훨씬 더 쉽거든요.

여 맞아요. 그리고 더 많은 입장료를 거둬들이는 덕분에, 마침내 직원들이 계속 요청해 온 몇몇 물품들을 구입할 수 있을 거예요. 예를 들면, 몇몇 무선 마이크를 주문했어요.

남2 아, 언제 받게 되죠?

여 토요일에 택배회사를 통해 도착할 거예요.

어휘 It seems that ~인 것 같다 a lot (비교급 수식) 훨씬(= much) give a lecture 강연하다 auditorium 강당 nearly 거의 full 꽉 찬, 가득 찬 as well ~도, 또한 get to and from ~을 오가다 thanks to ~ 덕분에 bring in ~을 거둬들이다, 가져오다 admission fee 입장료 purchase ~을 구입하다 request ~을 요청하다 order ~을 주문하다 cordless 무선의 arrive 도착하다 courier 택배회사

59 What are the men responsible for at the park?
(A) Leading hikes
(B) Selling souvenirs
(C) Giving lectures
(D) Feeding animals

남자들은 공원에서 무슨 일을 책임지고 있는가?
(A) 하이킹을 진행하는 일
(B) 기념품을 판매하는 일
(C) 강연을 하는 일
(D) 동물들에게 먹이를 주는 일

해설 〈기타 세부 사항을 묻는 문제〉
대화 초반부에 한 남자가 자신이 강연을 하는 사람임을(Every time I've given a lecture) 언급한 것에 이어 다른 남자가 자신도 같은 상황을 겪고 있다고(that's been happening to me as well) 말하고 있으므로 (C)가 정답이다.

어휘 be responsible for ~에 대한 책임이 있다, ~을 맡고 있다 lead ~을 진행하다, 이끌다 souvenir 기념품 feed ~에게 먹이를 주다

60 What has probably helped to increase attendance at the park?
(A) A change in operating hours
(B) An extensive advertising campaign
(C) A drop in admission fees
(D) A new transportation service

무엇이 공원 방문객 숫자를 늘리는 데 도움이 되었을 것 같은가?
(A) 운영 시간의 변경
(B) 대대적인 광고 캠페인
(C) 입장료의 인하
(D) 새 교통 서비스

해설 〈기타 세부 사항을 묻는 문제〉
대화 초반부에 한 남자가 더 많은 사람들이 공원을 방문하는 것 같다고 언급한 것에 대해 다른 남자가 셔틀 버스가 그 이유인 것 같다(I think it's because of the new shuttle bus) 생각을 밝히고 있으므로 (D)가 정답이다.

어휘 attendance 참가(자의 수) operating hours 운영 시간 extensive 대대적인, 광범위한 advertising 광고 (활동) drop in ~의 감소 admission fee 입장료 transportation 교통(편)

61 What does the woman say will happen on Saturday?
(A) Visitors will be given free admission.
(B) A new employee will start work.
(C) Some equipment will arrive.
(D) The budget will be reviewed.

여자는 토요일에 무슨 일이 있을 것이라고 말하는가?
(A) 방문객들이 무료 입장 서비스를 받을 것이다.
(B) 한 신입사원이 일을 시작할 것이다.
(C) 일부 장비가 도착할 것이다.
(D) 예산이 검토될 것이다.

해설 〈특정 시점의 일을 묻는 문제〉
여자가 대화 후반부에 무선 마이크를 주문한(we've ordered some cordless microphones) 사실과 그것이 토요일에 도착한다는 (They'll arrive by courier on Saturday) 사실을 함께 알리고 있으므로 장비가 도착한다는 의미를 지닌 (C)가 정답이다.

어휘 free 무료의 equipment 장비 arrive 도착하다 budget 예산 review ~을 검토하다, 살펴보다

M Hi. I'd like to order now. I'm in a bit of a hurry, as I've got courtside ⑥② tickets for the basketball championship game tonight. I'll take the T-bone steak, please.

W Oh, I'm sorry if I kept you waiting. OK, one T-bone steak. Would you like to add an extra side dish for a small additional cost?

M Well, I'm not a big fan of salad, so ⑥③ I'll skip the Garden Salad. Let's see, I'll add this one at the bottom. Is it really only an extra 2 dollars?

W Yes, and it's a pretty big portion. ⑥④ You should try something from our cocktail menu, too. Just let me know which one you want.

Starr Steakhouse	
Add an extra side dish to any steak you order!	
Mashed potatoes	(Add $3.00)
Grilled Mushrooms	(Add $4.00)
Garden Salad	(Add $2.00)
⑥③ French Fries	(Add $2.00)

남 안녕하세요. 지금 주문하고 싶습니다. 제가 조금 급한 상황인데, 오늘 밤 농구 챔피언 결정전 코트사이드 입장권을 갖고 있거든요. 티본 스테이크로 하겠습니다.

여 아, 계속 기다리시게 해서 죄송합니다. 네, 티본 스테이크 하나 주문하셨습니다. 소액의 추가 금액만 내시면 별도의 곁들임 요리를 추가하실 수 있는데 하시겠어요?

남 음, 제가 샐러드를 그렇게 좋아하는 편이 아니라서, 가든 샐러드는 건너뛰겠습니다. 어디 보자, 하단에 있는 이걸로 하겠습니다. 정말 2달러만 내면 되는 건가요?

여 네, 그리고 1인분 양이 꽤 많습니다. 저희 칵테일 메뉴에서도 뭔가 하나 드셔 보세요. 어느 것을 원하시는지 알려 주시기만 하면 됩니다.

스타 스테이크하우스	
주문하시는 스테이크에 별도의 곁들임 요리를 추가해 보세요!	
으깬 감자	(추가 금액 3.00달러)
그릴에 구운 버섯	(추가 금액 4.00달러)
가든 샐러드	(추가 금액 2.00달러)
감자튀김	(추가 금액 2.00달러)

어휘 would like to do ~하고 싶다, ~하고자 하다 order 주문하다 in a hurry 급한 a bit of 조금, 약간 courtside 코트사이드(경기장 코트 경계선 옆쪽의 관람 구역) take (주문 등) ~로 하다 keep A -ing A를 계속 ~하게 하다 add ~을 추가하다 extra 별도의, 추가의 side dish 곁들임 요리

additional 추가의 skip ~을 건너뛰다 bottom 하단, 아래 portion 1인분 try ~을 한 번 먹어 보다, 한 번 해 보다 let A know A에게 알리다

62 What type of event will the man attend this evening?
(A) A birthday party
(B) A sports game
(C) A business conference
(D) An outdoor concert

남자는 오늘 저녁에 어떤 종류의 행사에 참석할 것인가?
(A) 생일 파티
(B) 스포츠 경기
(C) 비즈니스 컨퍼런스
(D) 야외 콘서트

해설 〈특정 시점의 일을 묻는 문제〉
대화 시작 부분에 남자가 오늘 밤에 있을 농구 챔피언 결정전 입장권을 갖고 있다고(tickets for the basketball championship game tonight) 알리고 있으므로 (B)가 정답이다.

어휘 attend ~에 참석하다

63 Look at the graphic. Which side dish does the man decide to add?
(A) Mashed potatoes
(B) Grilled Mushrooms
(C) Garden Salad
(D) French Fries

시각 자료를 보시오. 남자는 어떤 곁들임 요리를 추가하기로 결정하는가?
(A) 으깬 감자
(B) 그릴에 구운 버섯
(C) 가든 샐러드
(D) 감자튀김

해설 〈2열 도표 문제〉
대화 중반부에 남자가 가든 샐러드는 건너뛰고 하단에 있는 것으로 하겠다고 알리면서 2달러만 내면 되는지(I'll skip the Garden Salad. Let's see, I'll add this one at the bottom. Is it really only an extra 2 dollars?) 묻고 있다. 메뉴 그림에서 가든 샐러드 밑에 있는 음식이 French Fries이므로 (D)가 정답이다.

어휘 decide to do ~하기로 결정하다 add ~을 추가하다

64 What does the woman suggest that the man do?
(A) Sample a dessert
(B) Use a credit card
(C) Order a drink
(D) Take his food out

여자는 남자에게 무엇을 하도록 권하는가?
(A) 디저트를 시식하는 일
(B) 신용카드를 이용하는 일
(C) 음료를 주문하는 일
(D) 음식을 포장해 가는 일

해설 〈제안 사항을 묻는 문제〉
대화 맨 마지막에 여자가 칵테일 메뉴에서도 뭔가 하나 먹어 보도록 (You should try something from our cocktail menu, too) 권하고 있으며, 이는 음료를 주문하라는 말이므로 (C)가 정답이다.

어휘 sample v. ~을 시식하다, 시음하다 take A out A를 포장해 가다

Questions 65-67 refer to the following conversation and receipt.
영W 미M

W Hello. I bought some items here yesterday, but I need to return one of them.
M All right. Was there anything wrong with it?
W Actually, yes. When I unpacked it last night, I noticed that ⑥⑤ it has a large tear along the side.
M I'm very sorry for the inconvenience. ⑥⑥ You can receive the full amount that you paid for it, um, one hundred ten dollars.
W Thank you very much.
M ⑥⑦ This item is actually sold out now, but I can show you some other ones if you'd like.
W No, thanks. I'd prefer to just get the refund.

Camptime Supplies Customer Receipt	
Date: May 17	
Sleeping Bag	$85
Two-Person Tent	$125
⑥⑥ Backpack	$110
Hiking Boots	$60
Total	$380

여 안녕하세요. 제가 어제 여기서 몇몇 제품을 구입했는데, 그중 하나를 반품해야 합니다.
남 알겠습니다. 뭔가 잘못된 부분이라도 있었나요?
여 실은, 있었어요. 어젯밤에 꺼내 보니까, 측면을 따라 크게 찢어진 부분이 있다는 걸 알았어요.
남 불편함을 드려 대단히 죄송합니다. 지불하신 금액인, 음, 110달러에 대해 전액 돌려받으실 수 있습니다.
여 대단히 감사합니다.
남 이 제품이 사실은 지금 품절된 상태인데, 괜찮으시면 몇 가지 다른 것을 보여 드릴 수 있습니다.
여 아니요, 괜찮아요. 그냥 환불받고 싶어요.

캠프타임 서플라이즈 고객용 영수증	
날짜: 5월 17일	
침낭	85달러
2인용 텐트	125달러
배낭	110달러
등산화	60달러
총액	380달러

어휘 return ~을 반품하다, 반납하다 wrong with ~가 잘못된 unpack (제품, 짐 등) ~을 꺼내다, 풀다 notice that ~임을 알게 되다, 알아차리다 tear 찢어진 부분 along (위치, 이동 등) ~을 따라 inconvenience 불편함 receive ~을 받다 pay for ~에 대한 비용을 지불하다 actually 사실, 실은 sold out 품절된, 매진된 if you'd like 괜찮으시면 would prefer to do ~하고 싶다 refund 환불 receipt 영수증

65 What problem with an item does the woman mention?
(A) It is too small.
(B) It has a tear.
(C) It is the wrong color.
(D) Its zipper is broken.

여자는 제품의 어떤 문제점을 언급하는가?
(A) 너무 작다.
(B) 찢어진 부분이 있다.
(C) 다른 색상이다.
(D) 지퍼가 고장 나 있다.

해설 〈문제점을 묻는 문제〉
대화 중반부에 여자가 제품을 꺼내 본 후 알게 된 사실로 측면에 찢어진 부분이 있다고(it has a large tear along the side) 알리고 있으므로 (B)가 정답이다.

어휘 broken 고장 난, 망가진, 깨진

66 Look at the graphic. Which item is being discussed?
(A) A sleeping bag
(B) A tent
(C) A backpack
(D) Some hiking boots

시각 자료를 보시오. 어느 제품이 이야기되고 있는가?
(A) 침낭
(B) 텐트
(C) 배낭
(D) 등산화

해설 〈2열 도표 문제〉
대화 중반부에 남자가 지불 금액인 110달러를 전액 돌려받을 수 있다고(You can receive the full amount that you paid for it, um, one hundred ten dollars) 알리고 있고, 영수증에서 $110에 해당되는 항목이 Backpack이므로 (C)가 정답이다.

어휘 discuss ~에 대해 이야기하다, ~을 논의하다

67 What does the man offer to do for the woman?
(A) Give her a catalog
(B) Recommend some campsites
(C) Place a rush order
(D) Show her some merchandise

남자는 여자에게 무엇을 하겠다고 제안하는가?
(A) 카탈로그를 하나 제공하는 일
(B) 몇몇 캠프장을 추천해 주는 일

(C) 긴급히 주문하는 일
(D) 일부 상품을 보여 주는 일

해설 〈하겠다는 것이 무엇인지를 묻는 문제〉
대화 후반부에 남자가 특정 제품이 품절된 상태임을 언급하면서 다른 것들을 보여 줄 수 있다고(This item is actually sold out now, but I can show you some other ones) 알리고 있으므로 (D)가 정답이다.

어휘 offer to do ~하겠다고 제안하다 place an order 주문하다 rush 긴급한 merchandise 상품

Questions 68-70 refer to the following conversation and departure board. 호M 캐W

M Hi, Jodie. I'm afraid I won't be back to the office as planned. ⑥ **There's a problem with my train to Sheffield.**
W That's too bad. You know we've got that meeting today with Ms. Reeves, the owner of Reeves Rentals. She's updating her fleet, and she's thinking about placing a bulk order for ⑥ **the hybrid cars that we make.**
M You shouldn't wait for me. There might be further delays to my journey.
W That's a good point. Then ⑦ **I'm going to have Susan give the sales pitch instead of you.** That way, we can start on time.

Destination	Departure Time	Status
Manchester	12:10 P.M.	Delayed 1 hour
Liverpool	12:25 P.M.	Delayed 30 minutes
Leeds	12:30 P.M.	Delayed 40 minutes
⑥ Sheffield	12:45 P.M.	Delayed 25 minutes

남 안녕하세요, 조디 씨. 제가 계획대로 사무실로 돌아가지 못할 것 같습니다. 셰필드로 가는 제 열차에 문제가 생겼습니다.
여 너무 아쉽게 됐네요. 아시다시피 우리가 오늘 리브스 렌탈즈의 리브스 사장님과 잡아 둔 회의가 있잖아요. 그분께서 전체 차량을 업데이트하고 있기 때문에 우리가 제조하는 하이브리드 자동차를 대량 주문하는 것에 대해 생각하고 계시거든요.
남 저를 기다리지 않으셔도 됩니다. 저의 여정이 더 지연될 수도 있어요.
여 좋은 지적입니다. 그럼, 당신 대신 수잔 씨에게 구매 교섭을 해 보도록 부탁드릴게요. 그렇게 하면, 제때 시작할 수 있어요.

목적지	출발 시각	현황
맨체스터	오후 12:10	1시간 지연
리버풀	오후 12:25	30분 지연
리즈	오후 12:30	40분 지연
셰필드	오후 12:45	25분 지연

어휘 I'm afraid (that) (부정적인 일을 말할 때) ~인 것 같다, ~해서 유감이다 as planned 계획대로 fleet (한 단체에서 보유한) 전체 차량, 전체 선박 place a bulk order 대량으로 주문하다 further 추가의, 더 이상의 delay n. 지연, 지체 v. ~을 지연시키다, 지체시키다 journey (긴) 이동, 여정 That's a good point 좋은 지적입니다 then 그럼, 그렇다면 have A do A에게 ~하게 하다 sales pitch 구매 교섭, 판매 권유 instead of ~ 대신 that way 그렇게 하면, 그런 방법으로 on time 제때 status 현황, 상태

68 Look at the graphic. What is the status of the man's train?
(A) Delayed 1 hour
(B) Delayed 30 minutes
(C) Delayed 40 minutes
(D) Delayed 25 minutes
시각 자료를 보시오. 남자의 열차 현황은 어떠한가?
(A) 1시간 지연
(B) 40분 지연
(C) 30분 지연
(D) 25분 지연

해설 〈3열 이상 도표 문제〉
대화 초반부에 남자가 셰필드로 가는 자신의 열차에 문제가 있다고(There's a problem with my train to Sheffield) 알리고 있으며, 도표에서 맨 아래에 쓰여 있는 셰필드행 열차의 현황이 Delayed 25 minutes이므로 (D)가 정답이다.

69 What kind of business do the speakers probably work for?
(A) An architectural firm
(B) A pharmaceutical company
(C) A real estate agency
(D) A car manufacturer
화자들은 어떤 종류의 업체에서 일하고 있을 것 같은가?
(A) 건축 회사
(B) 제약 회사
(C) 부동산 중개업체
(D) 자동차 제조사

해설 〈근무지를 묻는 문제〉
대화 중반부에 여자가 소속 회사를 we로 지칭해 the hybrid cars that we make라는 말로 자동차 제조사에 근무하고 있음을 밝히고 있으므로 (D)가 정답이다.

70 What does the woman say she will do?
(A) Meet the man at the station
(B) Reassign a task
(C) Postpone a meeting
(D) Set up a meeting room
여자는 무엇을 할 것이라고 말하는가?
(A) 역에서 남자를 만나는 일
(B) 업무를 재배정하는 일
(C) 회의를 연기하는 일

(D) 회의실을 마련하는 일

해설 〈미래에 할 일을 묻는 문제〉
대화 맨 마지막 부분에 여자가 남자 대신 수잔 씨에게 구매와 관련된 일을 부탁하겠다고(I'm going to have Susan give the sales pitch instead of you) 알리고 있다. 이는 업무를 다른 사람에게 배정하는 것에 해당되므로 (B)가 정답이다.

어휘 reassign ~을 재배정하다, 재할당하다 postpone ~을 연기하다, 미루다 set up ~을 마련하다, 설치하다, 설정하다

PART 4

P23

Questions 71-73 refer to the following advertisement. 호M

⑦ Is it hard to keep your house tidy when you have a busy work schedule? ⑦ Sparkle Home Cleaning Service can solve all your problems. We service all types of houses and apartments. ⑦ Our clients love that we promise to issue a refund if you are not satisfied with our service. Get your home looking spotless again! Contact Sparkle today! ⑦ If you book our services through our Web site, we'll give you a free sample of Sparkle detergent when we arrive at your location.

업무 일정으로 바쁘실 때 자택을 말끔하게 유지하기가 어려우신가요? 저희 스파클 홈 클리닝 서비스가 모든 문제를 해결해 드릴 수 있습니다. 저희는 모든 종류의 주택 및 아파트에 서비스를 제공해 드립니다. 저희는 고객들께서 저희 서비스에 만족하지 못하실 때 환불해 드릴 것을 약속하는데, 고객들은 이 점을 아주 마음에 들어 하십니다. 다시 한 번 여러분의 자택을 티끌 하나 없어 보이도록 만들어 보세요! 오늘 저희 스파클 사에 연락 주시기 바랍니다! 저희 웹 사이트를 통해 서비스를 예약하시면, 저희가 여러분 자택에 도착할 때 무료 스파클 세척제 샘플을 제공해 드립니다.

어휘 keep A + 형용사 A를 ~하게 유지하다 tidy 말끔한 solve ~을 해결하다 service v. ~에게 서비스를 제공하다 promise to do ~하겠다고 약속하다 issue a refund 환불을 제공하다 be satisfied with ~에 만족하다 get A -ing A를 ~하게 만들다 look + 형용사 ~하게 보이다 spotless 티끌 하나 없는 book v. ~을 예약하다 through ~을 통해 free 무료의 detergent 세척제 arrive 도착하다 location 장소, 지점, 위치

71 What type of business is being advertised?
(A) A landscaping company
(B) A financial consultancy
(C) A home cleaning service
(D) An interior design firm
어떤 종류의 업체가 광고되고 있는가?
(A) 조경 회사

(B) 재무 컨설팅 업체
(C) 주택 청소 서비스 업체
(D) 실내 디자인 회사

해설 〈주제를 묻는 문제〉
담화 시작 부분에 집을 말끔하게 유지하는 것을 어려움을 언급하면서 (Is it hard to keep your house tidy ~) 스파클 홈 클리닝 서비스가 해결해 줄 수 있다고(Sparkle Home Cleaning Service can solve all your problems) 알리고 있다. 따라서 청소 서비스 업체가 광고되고 있음을 알 수 있으므로 (C)가 정답이다.

어휘 advertise ~을 광고하다 landscaping 조경 (작업) financial 재무의, 금융의 consultancy 컨설팅 업체 firm 회사, 업체

72 What does the speaker say clients like about the business?
(A) Its convenient location
(B) Its experienced staff members
(C) Its money-back guarantee
(D) Its eco-friendly approach

화자의 말에 따르면, 고객들이 해당 업체와 관련해 무엇을 마음에 들어 하는가?
(A) 편리한 위치
(B) 경험 많은 직원들
(C) 비용 환불 보장 서비스
(D) 환경 친화적인 접근 방식

해설 〈기타 세부 사항을 묻는 문제〉
담화 중반부에 서비스에 만족하지 못하면 환불을 제공하겠다고 약속하는 것에 대해 고객들이 마음에 들어 한다고(Our clients love that we promise to issue a refund ~) 알리고 있으므로 (C)가 정답이다.

어휘 convenient 편리한 location 위치, 지점 experienced 경험 많은, 숙련된 money-back 비용 환불 guarantee 보장 (서비스) eco-friendly 환경 친화적인 approach 접근(법)

73 What will the listeners receive if they book the company's services online?
(A) A discount coupon
(B) A product catalog
(C) A complimentary product
(D) A free consultation

청자들이 온라인으로 해당 회사의 서비스를 예약하면 무엇을 받는가?
(A) 할인 쿠폰
(B) 제품 카탈로그
(C) 무료 제품
(D) 무료 상담 서비스

해설 〈기타 세부 사항을 묻는 문제〉
담화 맨 마지막에 웹 사이트를 통해 서비스를 예약하면 무료 스파클 세척제 샘플을 제공한다고(If you book our services through our Web site, we'll give you a free sample of Sparkle detergent) 알리고 있다. 이는 무료 제품을 제공한다는 뜻이므로 (C)

가 정답이다.

어휘 receive ~을 받다 book ~을 예약하다 complimentary 무료의(= free) consultation 상담

Questions 74-76 refer to the following excerpt from a meeting.
캐W

Next up, don't forget that **74** representatives from the Stratford branch will be visiting our branch on September 19. They'll participate in the company's sales awards banquet. The ceremony doesn't start until 7 P.M., but the representatives will arrive before 5 P.M. **75** I'd like to have them take a tour of the building. I need about three or four volunteers to help guide them. If you'd like to help out, **76** please e-mail me sometime today. And you must include the name of your supervisor, so I can make sure your work duties will not be interrupted. Thanks.

다음 순서로, Stratford 지사의 직원들께서 9월 19일에 우리 지사를 방문하실 예정이라는 점을 잊지 마시기 바랍니다. 이 분들께서 우리 회사의 영업상 시상식 연회에 참가하실 것입니다. 시상식이 오후 7시나 되어야 시작하지만, 이 직원들께서는 오후 5시 전에 도착합니다. 저는 이 분들께 건물을 견학시켜 드리고자 합니다. 안내를 도와주실 수 있는 약 서너 명의 자원 봉사자가 필요합니다. 도와주시고자 하는 경우, 오늘 중으로 저에게 이메일을 보내 주시기 바랍니다. 그리고 반드시 소속 부서장님의 성함을 포함해 주셔야 여러분의 직무가 지장받지 않도록 보장해 드릴 수 있습니다. 감사합니다.

어휘 forget that ~임을 잊다 representative 직원 branch 지사, 지점 participate in ~에 참가하다 sales 영업, 판매(량) banquet 연회 ceremony 식, 의식 not A until B B나 되어야 A하다 arrive 도착하다 have A do A에게 ~하게 하다 take a tour of ~을 견학하다 about 약, 대략 volunteer 자원 봉사자 help do ~하는 것을 돕다 would like to do ~하고자 하다, ~하고 싶다 help out 돕다 include ~을 포함하다 supervisor 부서장, 책임자, 상사 so (that) (결과) 그래야, 그래서 (목적) ~할 수 있도록 make sure (that) ~하도록 보장하다, 반드시 ~하도록 하다 interrupt ~에 지장을 주다, ~을 방해하다

74 Why will some representatives visit the listeners' branch?
(A) To meet a new employee
(B) To receive corporate training
(C) To attend an awards ceremony
(D) To demonstrate some equipment

왜 몇몇 직원들이 청자들의 지점을 방문하는가?
(A) 신입 사원을 만나기 위해
(B) 회사 교육을 받기 위해
(C) 시상식에 참석하기 위해
(D) 일부 장비를 시연하기 위해

해설 〈목적을 묻는 문제〉
담화 초반부에 다른 지사 소속 직원들이 방문한다는 사실과 함께 그

사람들이 영업상 시상식 연회에 참석한다고(representatives from the Stratford branch will be visiting ~ They'll participate in the company's sales awards banquet) 알리고 있으므로 (C)가 정답이다.

어휘 receive ~을 받다 corporate 회사의, 기업의 training 교육, 훈련 attend ~에 참석하다 demonstrate ~을 시연하다, 시범 보이다 equipment 장비

75 What does the speaker need volunteers for?
(A) Designing a brochure
(B) Giving building tours
(C) Planning a menu
(D) Transporting the visitors

화자는 무엇에 대해 자원 봉사자가 필요한가?
(A) 안내 책자를 디자인하는 일
(B) 건물을 견학시켜 주는 일
(C) 메뉴를 계획하는 일
(D) 방문객들을 운송하는 일

해설 〈기타 세부 사항을 묻는 문제〉
담화 중반부에 건물 견학을 시켜 주는 일을 언급하면서 견학 중의 안내를 맡을 자원 봉사자가 필요하다고(I'd like to have them take a tour of the building. I need about three or four volunteers to help guide them) 알리고 있으므로 (B)가 정답이다.

어휘 brochure 안내 책자, 소책자 plan ~을 계획하다 transport ~을 운송하다, 수송하다

76 According to the speaker, what should be included in an e-mail?
(A) A recent photo
(B) A preferred time
(C) A list of supplies
(D) A supervisor's name

화자의 말에 따르면, 이메일에 무엇이 포함되어야 하는가?
(A) 최근의 사진
(B) 선호하는 시간대
(C) 용품 목록
(D) 부서장 이름

해설 〈기타 세부 사항을 묻는 문제〉
담화 후반부에 자신에게 이메일을 보내라는 말과 함께 소속 부서장 이름을 반드시 포함해야 한다고(please e-mail me sometime today. And you must include the name of your supervisor) 알리고 있으므로 (D)가 정답이다.

어휘 include ~을 포함하다 recent 최근의 preferred 선호하는 supplies 용품, 물품 supervisor 부서장, 책임자, 감독

Good afternoon. My name is Chris Packham, and I'm from Timber Furniture Delivery. ⑰ I'm in a truck full of display units for your trade fair. I think I've taken a wrong turn as I can't find the conference center anywhere. ⑱ Could you please send the exact address to me by text message? ⑲ I think I'm going to be a little late, and I know you paid extra for express delivery. We will consider this when calculating your invoice. I will await your message so that I can complete the delivery.

안녕하세요. 제 이름은 크리스 패컴이며, 팀버 퍼니처 딜리버리 소속 직원입니다. 제가 지금 귀하의 무역 박람회 행사에 필요한 진열 물품을 가득 실은 트럭에 있습니다. 어디에서도 컨퍼런스 센터를 찾을 수 없는 것을 보니 제가 방향을 잘못 바꾼 것 같습니다. 저에게 문자 메시지로 정확한 주소를 보내 주시겠습니까? 제가 조금 늦을 것 같은데, 빠른 배송을 위해 추가 비용을 지불하신 사실을 알고 있습니다. 귀하의 거래 내역서를 계산할 때 이를 고려해 드리겠습니다. 제가 배송을 완료할 수 있도록 메시지 기다리고 있습니다.

어휘 full of ~로 가득한, 꽉 찬 display 진열(품), 전시(품) unit (물품, 상품의) 한 개 trade fair 무역 박람회 take a wrong turn 방향을 잘못 바꾸다 anywhere 어디에서도, 어디든지 exact 정확한 text message 문자 메시지 a little 조금, 약간 pay extra for ~에 대해 추가 비용을 지불하다 express delivery 빠른 배송 consider ~을 고려하다 calculate ~을 계산하다 invoice 거래 내역서, 송장 await ~을 기다리다 so that (목적) ~할 수 있도록, (결과) 그래야, 그래서 complete ~을 완료하다

77 Who most likely is the speaker?
(A) A delivery driver
(B) An event planner
(C) An accountant
(D) A carpenter
화자는 누구일 것 같은가?
(A) 배송 기사
(B) 행사 기획자
(C) 회계 담당자
(D) 목수

해설 〈직업을 묻는 문제〉
담화 시작 부분에 화자가 자신을 소개하면서 상대방의 무역 박람회 행사에 필요한 진열 물품을 가득 실은 트럭에 (I'm in a truck full of display units for your trade fair) 있다고 알리고 있다. 이는 배송 기사가 배송 도중에 할 수 있는 말에 해당되므로 (A)가 정답이다.

78 What information does the speaker require?
(A) A product code
(B) An address
(C) An item description
(D) A telephone number

화자는 어떤 정보를 요청하는가?
(A) 제품 코드
(B) 주소
(C) 제품 설명
(D) 전화번호

해설 〈요청 사항을 묻는 문제〉
담화 중반부에 화자가 문자 메시지로 정확한 주소를 보내 달라고 (Could you please send the exact address to me by text message?) 요청하고 있으므로 (B)가 정답이다.

어휘 description 설명, 묘사

79 What does the speaker imply when he says, "We will consider this when calculating your invoice"?
(A) A bank transfer has been declined.
(B) A payment is overdue.
(C) A parking fine has been received.
(D) A discount will be applied.
화자가 "We will consider this when calculating your invoice"라고 말할 때 무엇을 암시하는가?
(A) 은행 계좌 이체가 거절되었다.
(B) 비용 지불 기한이 지났다.
(C) 주차 위반 벌금이 납부되었다.
(D) 할인이 적용될 것이다.

해설 〈의도 파악 문제〉
화자가 담화 후반부에 조금 늦을 것 같다는 말과 함께 빠른 배송을 위해 추가 비용을 지불한 사실을(I think I'm going to be a little late, and I know you paid extra for express delivery) 언급한 뒤로 '거래 내역서를 계산할 때 이를 고려하겠다'고 알리는 흐름이다. 이는 늦게 도착하는 것을 감안해 미리 지불한 비용에 대한 혜택, 즉 할인을 제공해 줄 수 있다는 뜻을 나타내는 말이므로 (D)가 정답이다.

어휘 bank transfer 은행 계좌 이체 decline ~을 거절하다 overdue 기한이 지난, 이미 했어야 할 fine n. 벌금 receive ~을 받다 apply ~을 적용하다

Hello, Wesley. This is Peggy from Dynamic Interiors. ⑳ I'm calling to discuss the lighting you plan to install as part of the remodeling work at your art gallery. You said you wanted powerful white LED lights for some of your exhibition spaces. Well, ㉑ I just noticed an ad on the Henson Hardware Web site for a sale on those types of lights. It seems like a good deal. I'd like you to go and check out the merchandise on the Web site and let me know if you'd like me to buy it. I was planning to finish the work at your gallery in the next couple of days, so ㉒ I recommend that you call me back about it at your earliest convenience.

안녕하세요, 웨슬리 씨. 저는 다이내믹 인테리어 사의 페기입니다. 귀하의 미술관에서 리모델링 작업의 일환으로 설치하실 계획인 조명 문제를 이야기하기 위해 전화 드렸습니다. 귀하께서는 몇몇 전시 공간에 강력한 백색 LED 조명을 원하신다고 말씀하셨습니다. 저, 그런 종류의 조명에 대해 세일 행사를 하는 헨슨 하드웨어 웹 사이트 광고를 막 알게 되었습니다. 좋은 구매 조건인 것 같습니다. 이 웹 사이트에 가셔서 해당 상품을 확인해 보신 다음, 제가 구입하기를 원하시는지 알려 주셨으면 합니다. 앞으로 며칠 후에 귀하의 미술관 공사 작업을 마무리할 계획이었기 때문에 가급적 빨리 이 부분과 관련해 다시 전화 주시기를 권해 드립니다.

어휘 discuss ~을 이야기하다, 논의하다 plan to do n. ~하려는 계획 v. ~할 계획이다 install ~을 설치하다 as part of ~의 일환으로, 일부로 exhibition 전시(회) notice ~을 알게 되다, 알아차리다 ad 광고 It seems like ~인 것 같다 deal 구매 조건, 거래, 계약 would like A to do A에게 ~하기를 원하다 check out ~을 확인해 보다 merchandise 상품 let A know if A에게 ~인지 알리다 in + 시간 ~ 후에 recommend that ~하도록 권하다 at your earliest convenience 가급적 빨리

80 What is the speaker calling about?
(A) Exhibition tickets
(B) Shipping options
(C) Lighting installations
(D) Catering services
화자는 무엇과 관련해 전화하는가?
(A) 전시회 입장권
(B) 배송 방식 선택
(C) 조명 설치 작업
(D) 출장 요리 서비스

해설 〈주제를 묻는 문제〉
담화 초반부에 상대방이 설치한 계획인 조명 문제를 이야기하려고 전화했다고(I'm calling to discuss the lighting you plan to install ~) 알리고 있으므로 (C)가 정답이다.

어휘 exhibition 전시(회) installation 설치 (작업) catering 출장 요리 제공(업)

81 What did the speaker recently see?
(A) A promotional flyer
(B) A Web advertisement
(C) A product presentation
(D) A magazine article

화자는 최근에 무엇을 보았는가?
(A) 홍보용 전단
(B) 웹 광고
(C) 제품 발표회
(D) 잡지 기사

해설 〈기타 세부 사항을 묻는 문제〉
담화 중반부에 한 웹 사이트에서 제품 세일 광고를 봤다고(I just noticed an ad on the Henson Hardware Web site for a sale on those types of lights) 말하고 있으므로 (B)가 정답이다.

어휘 promotional 홍보의 flyer 전단 advertisement 광고 presentation 발표(회)

82 What does the speaker suggest doing?
(A) Extending a project deadline
(B) Comparing some prices
(C) Returning the call quickly
(D) Arranging a meeting

화자는 무엇을 하도록 권하는가?
(A) 프로젝트 마감시한을 연장하는 일
(B) 몇몇 가격을 비교해 보는 일
(C) 빨리 답신 전화하는 일
(D) 회의를 잡는 일

해설 〈제안 사항을 묻는 문제〉
담화 맨 마지막 부분에 가급적 빨리 다시 전화해 달라고 권하는 (I recommend that you call me back about it at your earliest convenience) 말이 제시되고 있으므로 (C)가 정답이다.

어휘 extend ~을 연장하다 deadline 마감시한 compare ~을 비교하다 return a call 답신 전화하다 arrange ~을 마련하다, 조치하다

Questions 83-85 refer to the following broadcast. 캐W

83 You are listening to the weather report with Helen Conway. Huge storms are expected to sweep through the Eastern states beginning in the early afternoon. As these are expected to bring high winds, **84** residents are advised not to leave the house after 2 P.M. Conditions are expected to be much calmer tomorrow morning. Now, it's time for our political news show. **85** State senator Gareth Eading will be joining us here in the studio at 9 A.M. to answer my questions about new traffic laws.

여러분은 지금 헬렌 콘웨이가 전해 드리는 일기 예보를 청취하고 계십니다. 엄청난 폭풍우가 이른 오후에 시작되어 동부 지역의 여러 주를 휩쓸고 지나갈 것으로 예상됩니다. 강한 바람을 동반할 것으로 예상되고 있으므로, 주민들께서는 오후 2시 이후에는 집 밖으로 나가시지 않도록 권해 드립니다. 기상 상태가 내일 오전에 훨씬 더 차분해질 것으로 예상됩니다. 이제, 정치 소식을 전해 드릴 차례입니다. 가레스 이딩 주 상원의원께서 오전 9시부터 이곳 저희 스튜디오에 함께 자리해 새로운 교통법과 관련된 제 질문에 답변해 주실 예정입니다.

어휘 huge 엄청난, 거대한 be expected to do ~할 것으로 예상되다 sweep through ~을 휩쓸고 지나가다 state (행정 구역) 주 resident 주민 be advised (not) to do ~하도록(하지 않도록) 권장되다 leave ~에서 나가다, 떠나다 condition 상태, 상황, 조건 calm 차분한, 잔잔한 senator 상원의원 join ~와 함께 하다, ~에 합류하다 traffic 교통, 차량들

83 What is the broadcast mainly about?
(A) Community events
(B) Traffic
(C) Weather
(D) Financial news

방송은 주로 무엇에 관한 것인가?
(A) 지역 사회 행사
(B) 교통
(C) 날씨
(D) 금융 소식

해설 〈주제를 묻는 문제〉
담화를 시작하면서 일기 예보를 청취하고 있다는 말로(You are listening to the weather report with Helen Conway) 방송 주제를 언급하면서 앞으로의 기상 상태 및 대처 방법을 알리고 있으므로 (C)가 정답이다.

84 What does the speaker advise listeners to do?
(A) Remain in their homes
(B) Use public transport
(C) Purchase additional supplies
(D) Avoid congested areas

화자는 청자들에게 무엇을 하도록 권하는가?
(A) 집에 머물러 있는 것
(B) 대중교통을 이용하는 것
(C) 추가 용품을 구입하는 것
(D) 혼잡 구역을 피하는 것

해설 〈제안 사항을 묻는 문제〉
담화 중반부에 주민들에게 오후 2시 이후로 집 밖으로 나가지 말라고 (residents are advised not to leave the house after 2 P.M.) 당부하고 있으므로 (A)가 정답이다.

어휘 remain 남아 있다 public transport 대중교통 purchase ~을 구입하다 additional 추가적인 supplies 용품, 물품 avoid ~을 피하다 congested 혼잡한

85 What does the speaker say will happen at 9 A.M.?
(A) Some commercials will be played.
(B) A traffic update will be heard.
(C) A safety announcement will be made.
(D) A guest will be interviewed.

화자는 오전 9시에 무슨 일이 있을 것이라고 말하는가?
(A) 몇몇 광고가 방송될 것이다.
(B) 교통 소식이 전해질 것이다.
(C) 안전 공지가 이뤄질 것이다.
(D) 초대 손님이 인터뷰에 응할 것이다.

해설 〈특정 시점의 일을 묻는 문제〉
담화 맨 마지막에 가레스 이딩 주 상원의원이 스튜디오에 나와서 새로운 교통법과 관련된 화자의 질문에 답변할 것이라고(State senator Gareth Eading will be joining us here in the studio from at 9 A.M. to answer my questions) 알리고 있다. 이는 초대 손님을 인터뷰한다는 뜻이므로 (D)가 정답이다.

어휘 commercial 광고 방송 traffic 교통, 차량들 announcement 공지, 발표

Questions 86-88 refer to the following announcement. 캐W

May I have your attention, please? Before we open up ⑥ our dental clinic today, I wanted to make a quick announcement. As I'm sure you all know, ⑧ tomorrow morning we are holding a small party in honor of our ten-year anniversary. We'll be serving refreshments, and we've invited all of our patients to stop by. Attendees will receive a small gift, ⑧ but the gifts aren't ready yet. I'm wondering if someone could stay after closing time to help do the wrapping. Please raise your hand if you're available. I would really appreciate it.

잠시 주목해 주시겠습니까? 오늘 우리 치과를 열기에 앞서, 간단한 공지 사항을 한 가지 전해 드리고자 합니다. 분명 여러분 모두 아시겠지만, 내일 아침에 우리는 10주년을 기념하는 작은 파티를 개최합니다. 다과를 제공해 드릴 예정이며, 우리 환자 분들 모두 잠시 들르시도록 요청 드렸습니다. 참석하시는 분들께서 작은 선물을 받으시게 되는데, 그 선물이 아직 준비되지 않았습니다. 누군가 업무 종료 후에 남아 포장하는 일을 도와주실 수 있는지 궁금합니다. 시간이 되시면 손을 들어 주시기 바랍니다. 이에 대해 정말 감사하게 생각할 것입니다.

어휘 attention 주목, 관심, 주의 dental clinic 치과 make an announcement 공지하다, 발표하다 hold ~을 개최하다, 열다 in honor of ~을 기념하여, ~을 기리기 위해 anniversary 기념일 serve (음식 등) ~을 제공하다, 내오다 refreshments 다과, 간식 invite A to do A에게 ~하도록 요청하다 patient 환자 stop by 들르다 attendee 참석자 receive ~을 받다 wonder if ~인지 궁금하다 closing time 업무 종료 시간, 영업 종료 시간 help do ~하는 것을 돕다 wrapping 포장 raise ~을 들어 올리다 available (사람이) 시간이 나는 appreciate ~에 대해 감사하다

86 Where do the listeners work?
(A) At a fitness center
(B) At a hair salon
(C) At a dental clinic
(D) At a financial institution
청자들은 어디에서 일하는가?
(A) 피트니스 센터에서
(B) 미용실에서
(C) 치과에서
(D) 금융 기관에서
해설 〈근무지를 묻는 문제〉
담화 초반부에 화자가 our dental clinic이라는 말로 청자들과 함께 근무하는 곳을 밝히고 있으므로 (C)가 정답이다.
어휘 institution 기관, 단체, 협회

87 What is scheduled to happen tomorrow morning?
(A) A delivery will arrive.
(B) A training session will be held.
(C) A new employee will start.
(D) An anniversary will be celebrated.
내일 아침에 무슨 일이 있을 예정인가?
(A) 배송 물품이 도착할 것이다.
(B) 교육 시간이 개최될 것이다.
(C) 신입 사원이 근무를 시작할 것이다.
(D) 기념일을 축하할 것이다.
해설 〈특정 시점의 일을 묻는 문제〉
화자가 담화 중반부에 내일 아침이라는 시점을 언급하면서 10주년을 기념하는 작은 파티를 개최한다고(tomorrow morning we are holding a small party in honor of our ten-year anniversary) 알리고 있으므로 (D)가 정답이다.
어휘 arrive 도착하다 training 교육, 훈련 session (특정 활동을 위한) 시간 hold ~을 개최하다, 열다 anniversary (해마다 돌아오는) 기념일 celebrate ~을 축하하다, 기념하다

88 Why does the speaker want someone to stay late?
(A) To unload a truck
(B) To meet some investors
(C) To prepare some gifts
(D) To review some documents
화자는 왜 누군가 늦게까지 남아 있기를 원하는가?
(A) 트럭에서 물건을 내리기 위해
(B) 몇몇 투자자들을 만나기 위해
(C) 몇몇 선물을 준비하기 위해
(D) 몇몇 문서를 검토하기 위해
해설 〈기타 세부 사항을 묻는 문제〉
담화 후반부에 선물이 준비되지 않은(but the gifts aren't ready yet) 사실과 함께 누군가 업무 종료 후에 남아 포장하는 일을 도와줄 수 있는지 궁금해하고 있다(I'm wondering if someone could stay after closing time to help do the wrapping). 이는 선물 준비를 도와 달라는 뜻이므로 (C)가 정답이다.
어휘 unload ~에서 짐을 내리다 investor 투자자 prepare ~을 준비하다 review ~을 검토하다, 살펴보다

Questions 89-91 refer to the following excerpt from a workshop. 영W

You are all experienced in marketing our products and services here at Orion Telecom, and you know how important it is to reach new customers through the Internet. ⑧ This afternoon I'm going to share some advanced online advertising tips with you. After a two-hour lecture, I'll split you into teams and ask each team to create a Web advertising campaign for a specific Orion service or product. ⑨ Together you'll design a campaign and then present it to the rest of us at the end of the day. Now, ⑨ we don't have much space here in the training room for group work, so... Hmm...Well... the conference room upstairs is free.

여러분 모두가 이곳 오리온 텔레콤에서 우리 제품과 서비스를 마케팅하는 데 경험이 많으시기 때문에 인터넷을 통해 신규 고객에게 다가가는 것이 얼마나 중요한 일인지 아실 겁니다. 오늘 오후에, 제가 몇몇 고급 온라인 광고 팁을 여러분께 공유해 드리겠습니다. 두 시간 동안의 강연 후에는, 여러분을 여러 팀으로 나눠 각 팀에게 우리 오리온의 특정 서비스 또는 제품에 대한 웹 광고 캠페인을 만들어 보도록 요청할 것입니다. 서로 힘을 합쳐서, 캠페인을 고안한 다음, 오늘 하루 일과가 끝날 때 나머지 사람들에게 발표하게 됩니다. 자, 이곳 교육 장소에 그룹 활동을 위한 공간이 많지 않기 때문에 흠... 저.. 위층에 있는 대회의실이 이용 가능합니다.

어휘 experienced 경험이 많은, 숙련된 market ~을 마케팅하다 reach ~에게 다가가다 through ~을 통해 share A with B A를 B와 공유하다 advance 고급의, 발전된, 진보한 advertising 광고 (활동) split A into B A를 B로 나누다 ask A to do A에게 ~하도록 요청하다 create ~을 만들어내다 specific 특정한, 구체적인 design ~을 고안하다 present A to B A를 B에게 발표하다, 제시하다 the rest of ~의 나머지 training 교육 upstairs 위층에 있는 free 이용 가능한

89 What is the topic of the workshop?
(A) Customer support
(B) Online advertising
(C) Product design
(D) Financial management
워크숍 주제는 무엇인가?
(A) 고객 지원
(B) 온라인 광고
(C) 제품 디자인
(D) 재무 관리
해설 〈주제를 묻는 문제〉
담화 초반부에 오늘 오후에 고급 온라인 광고 팁을 공유하겠다는 말로 (This afternoon I'm going to share some advanced online advertising tips with you) 워크숍 주제를 언급하고 있으므로 (B)

가 정답이다.

어휘 advertising 광고 (활동) financial 재무의, 금융의

90 What kind of assignment are the listeners asked to complete?
(A) A knowledge test
(B) A customer survey
(C) A team presentation
(D) A business proposal

청자들은 어떤 종류의 과제를 완료하도록 요청받는가?
(A) 지식 테스트
(B) 고객 설문 조사
(C) 팀 발표
(D) 사업 제안서

해설 〈요청 사항을 묻는 문제〉
담화 중반부에 서로 힘을 합쳐서 캠페인을 고안해 내고 다른 사람에게 발표해야 한다고(Together you'll design a campaign and then present it to the rest of us at the end of the day) 알리고 있다. 이는 팀 발표를 뜻하는 것이므로 (C)가 정답이다.

어휘 survey 설문 조사(지) presentation 발표(회) proposal 제안(서)

91 Why does the speaker say, "The conference room upstairs is free"?
(A) To recommend a way to save costs
(B) To suggest a different location
(C) To make a change to a schedule
(D) To offer the listeners refreshments

화자는 왜 "The conference room upstairs is free"라고 말하는가?
(A) 비용을 절약할 방법을 추천하기 위해
(B) 다른 장소를 제안하기 위해
(C) 일정을 변경하기 위해
(D) 청자들에게 다과를 제공하기 위해

해설 〈의도 파악 문제〉
담화 후반부에 화자가 그룹 활동을 할 공간이 많지 않다고(we don't have much space here in the training room for group work ~) 알리면서 '위층에 있는 대회의실이 이용 가능하다'고 언급하는 상황이다. 이는 다른 곳으로 이동하도록 제안하는 말이므로 (B)가 정답이다.

어휘 way to do ~하는 방법 suggest ~을 제안하다, 권하다 location 장소, 지점, 위치 make a change to ~을 변경하다 offer A B A에게 B를 제공하다 refreshments 다과, 간식

Questions 92-94 refer to the following telephone message. 미M

Good morning, this is Terry, ⑨ **one of the lab technicians.** As you're the facility supervisor, there's something you should be aware of. You circulated a memo last week to inform all staff about important changes. Specifically, you discussed ways to keep the laboratory clean and safe, and ⑨ announced a new policy that requires all equipment to be stored in the appropriate cupboards at the end of each work day. Well, I just arrived in Research Lab 3, and the lab equipment is on the workbench. Perhaps you need to remind staff about the policy. Otherwise, ⑨ our labs won't be as safe as they should be, which concerns me.

안녕하세요, 저는 실험실 기사 중 한 명인 테리입니다. 시설 관리 책임자이시기 때문에 알아 두셔야 하는 일이 있습니다. 지난주에 전 직원에게 중요한 변화를 알리기 위해 회람을 돌리셨습니다. 특히, 실험실을 깨끗하고 안전하게 유지할 방법을 이야기하시면서 모든 장비가 매일 업무 종료 시에 해당 진열장에 보관되어야 한다는 내용의 새로운 방침을 공지하셨습니다. 제가 방금 3 연구 실험실에 도착했는데, 실험실 장비가 작업대에 놓여 있습니다. 아마 직원들에게 이 방침을 상기시켜야 할 것 같습니다. 그렇지 않으면, 우리 실험실들이 마땅히 유지되어야 하는 수준으로 안전해지지 못할 것이며, 이는 저를 우려하게 만드는 부분입니다.

어휘 lab 실험실 facility 시설(물) supervisor 책임자, 부서장, 감독 be aware of ~을 알고 있다 circulate (직원이나 회원 등을 대상으로) ~을 돌리다, 전하다 inform A about B A에게 B를 알리다 specifically 특히, 구체적으로 discuss ~을 이야기하다, 논의하다 way to do ~하는 방법 keep A + 형용사 A를 ~한 상태로 유지하다 announce ~을 공지하다, 발표하다 policy 방침, 정책 require A to do A에게 ~하도록 요구하다, 요청하다 equipment 장비 store v. ~을 보관하다, 저장하다 appropriate 해당되는, 적절한 arrive 도착하다 workbench 작업대 remind A about B A에게 B를 상기시키다, 다시 한 번 알리다 otherwise 그렇지 않으면, 그 외에는 as A as B B만큼 A한 concern ~을 우려시키다, 걱정시키다

92 Where does the speaker most likely work?
(A) At a factory
(B) At a restaurant
(C) At a pharmacy
(D) At a laboratory

화자는 어디에서 일할 것 같은가?
(A) 공장에서
(B) 레스토랑에서
(C) 약국에서
(D) 실험실에서

해설 〈근무지를 묻는 문제〉
담화 시작 부분에 화자가 자신을 실험실 기사라고(one of the lab technicians) 언급하는 부분을 통해 실험실에서 일하는 사람임을 알 수 있으므로 (D)가 정답이다.

93 What does the speaker imply when he says, "The lab equipment is on the workbench"?
(A) An experiment will go ahead on schedule.
(B) A delivery has recently been made.
(C) A new policy has been ignored.
(D) A room has been cleaned as requested.

화자가 "The lab equipment is on the workbench"라고 말할 때 무엇을 의도하는가?
(A) 실험이 예정대로 진행될 것이다.
(B) 배송이 최근에 이뤄졌다.
(C) 새로운 방침이 무시되었다.
(D) 방이 요청대로 청소되었다.

해설 〈의도 파악 문제〉
담화 중반부에 모든 장비가 매일 업무 종료 시에 해당 진열장에 보관되어야 한다는 내용의 새로운 방침을 공지했다고(announced a new policy that requires all equipment to be stored in the appropriate cupboards at the end of each work day) 언급한 뒤로, '실험실 장비가 작업대에 놓여 있다'고 알리는 상황이다. 이는 방침을 준수하지 않은 사람이 있다는 뜻이므로 (C)가 정답이다.

어휘 experiment 실험 go ahead 진행되다 on schedule 예정대로, 일정대로 recently 최근에 policy 정책, 방침 ignore ~을 무시하다 as requested 요청대로

94 What is the speaker worried about?
(A) Unsafe conditions
(B) Inaccurate data
(C) Absent staff
(D) Increased expenses

화자는 무엇에 대해 걱정하는가?
(A) 안전하지 못한 환경
(B) 부정확한 데이터
(C) 결근한 직원
(D) 늘어난 지출 비용

해설 〈기타 세부 사항을 묻는 문제〉
담화 맨 마지막에 실험실들이 제대로 안전해지지 않을 것이라고 언급하면서 그것이 자신을 우려하게 만든다고(our labs won't be as safe as they should be, which concerns me) 알리고 있다. 이는 안전하지 못한 실험실 환경을 말하는 것이므로 (A)가 정답이다.

어휘 unsafe 안전하지 않은 condition 환경, 상태, 조건 absent 결근한, 자리에 없는 increased 늘어난, 증가된 expense 지출 비용, 경비

Questions 95-97 refer to the following talk and schedule. 호M

In today's session of the workshop, you'll continue to build on your skills to help you get the best results. ⑨⑤ You'll learn what to do when you run into problems. I'll teach you a few different techniques for solving a variety of issues. ⑨⑥ After the one-hour lecture, you'll watch a brief video of these techniques in action. Also, there are lots of other classes coming up at our institute, so ⑨⑦ please remember to grab a brochure before you leave today.

Negotiation Workshop	
February 5	Identifying Strengths and Weaknesses
⑨⑤ February 12	Problem-Solving Techniques
February 19	Creating Value
February 26	Cross-Cultural Negotiations

오늘 워크숍 시간에는 계속 이어서 여러분께서 최고의 결과물을 얻는 데 도움이 되는 능력을 한층 더 발전시키게 될 것입니다. 여러분께서 문제점과 마주치게 될 때 무엇을 해야 하는지 배우게 될 텐데요, 제가 다양한 문제를 해결하는 몇 가지 서로 다른 기술들을 가르쳐 드릴 겁니다. 한 시간 길이의 강연 후에는, 이러한 기술들이 실제로 적용되는 것을 보여주는 간단한 동영상을 시청하시게 됩니다. 또한, 저희 기관에서 앞으로 열리는 다른 강좌들도 많이 있으므로, 오늘 돌아가시기 전에 안내 책자를 챙겨 가시는 것도 기억해 두시기 바랍니다.

협상 워크숍	
2월 5일	강점과 약점 식별
2월 12일	문제 해결 기술
2월 19일	가치 창조
2월 26일	다른 문화 간의 협상

어휘 session (특정 활동을 위한) 시간 continue to do 계속 ~하다 build on ~을 한층 더 발전시키다, 키워 나가다 help A do A가 ~하는 데 도움을 주다 result 결과(물) what to do 무엇을 해야 하는지, ~하는 것 run into ~와 마주치다, 우연히 만나다 solve ~을 해결하다 a variety of 다양한 issue 문제, 사안 brief 간단한, 짧은 in action 실제 적용되는, 실행되는, 활동 중인 come up 다가오다, 곧 발생되다 institute 기관, 협회 brochure 안내 책자, 소책자 leave 나가다, 떠나다, 출발하다 negotiation 협상 identify ~을 식별하다, 확인하다 strength 강점, 장점 weakness 약점, 단점 create ~을 창조하다, 만들어내다 value 가치, 값어치 cross-cultural 다른 문화 간의, 다문화의

95 Look at the graphic. When is the talk taking place?
(A) February 5
(B) February 12
(C) February 19
(D) February 26

시각 자료를 보시오. 언제 담화가 진행되고 있는가?
(A) 2월 5일
(B) 2월 12일
(C) 2월 19일
(D) 2월 26일

해설 〈2열 도표 문제〉
담화 초반부에 문제점과 마주칠 때 다양한 해결 방법을 가르쳐 주겠다고(You'll learn what to do when you run into problems. I'll teach you a few different techniques for solving a variety of issues) 알리고 있다. 도표에서 문제 해결 기술(Problem-Solving Techniques)이 표기된 날짜가 February 12이므로 (B)가 정답이다.

96 What will happen in an hour?
(A) The speaker will distribute some paperwork.
(B) The speaker will assign people to groups.
(C) The listeners will watch a video.
(D) The listeners will take a break.

한 시간 후에 무슨 일이 있을 것인가?
(A) 화자가 일부 문서를 배부할 것이다.
(B) 화자가 사람들을 여러 조로 배치할 것이다.
(C) 청자들이 동영상을 시청할 것이다.
(D) 청자들이 휴식 시간을 가질 것이다.

해설 〈특정 시점의 일을 묻는 문제〉
담화 중반부에 한 시간 길이의 강연을 먼저 듣고 간단한 동영상을 시청한다는 말로(After the one-hour lecture, you'll watch a brief video) 진행 순서를 알리고 있으므로 (C)가 정답이다.

어휘 distribute ~을 배부하다, 나눠 주다 paperwork 문서 (작업) assign ~을 배치하다, 배정하다 take a break 휴식하다, 쉬다

97 What are the listeners reminded to do?
(A) Sign a consent form
(B) Pick up a brochure
(C) Complete a survey
(D) Recommend the class to others

청자들에게 무엇을 하도록 상기시키는가?
(A) 동의서에 서명하는 일
(B) 안내 책자를 가져가는 일
(C) 설문지를 작성 완료하는 일
(D) 해당 강좌를 다른 이들에게 추천하는 일

해설 〈상기시키는 것을 묻는 문제〉
담화 맨 마지막에 다른 강좌들도 확인해 볼 수 있는 안내 책자를 챙겨 가도록(please remember to grab a brochure) 당부하고 있으므로 (B)가 정답이다.

어휘 consent form 동의서 pick up ~을 가져가다, 가져오다 brochure 안내 책자, 소책자 complete ~을 완료하다 survey 설문 조사(지)

Questions 98-100 refer to the following excerpt from a meeting and layout. 캐W

Thanks for helping with the preparations of the flowerbeds here at Brumley Park. ⑨⑧ I'm Nancy, and I'm in charge of coordinating the volunteers working at this site. You can see on the layout that there are four flowerbeds in the area. ⑨⑨ We'll leave one of the beds empty for now, the one between the fountain and the parking lot. That will be planted later by students from Sycamore Elementary School. I'll be working alongside you all day, except for ⑩⑩ at two o'clock, when I need to talk to a reporter from the local newspaper who is writing an article about the park.

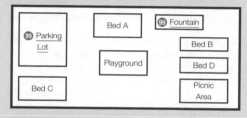

이곳 브림리 공원의 화단 준비 작업에 도움을 주시는 것에 대해 감사드립니다. 저는 낸시이며, 이곳에서 자원 봉사자 업무를 조정하는 일을 맡고 있습니다. 구역 내에 네 곳의 화단이 있다는 것을 배치도에서 보실 수 있을 겁니다. 저희가 당분간은 화단 중 한 곳, 즉 분수대와 주차장 사이에 있는 곳을 비워 놓게 될 것입니다. 이곳은 나중에 시커모어 초등학교 학생들에 의해 꽃이 심어질 것입니다. 제가 2시를 제외하고 여러분과 함께 하루 종일 작업할 예정인데, 그 시간엔 공원에 관한 기사를 작성하실 지역 신문사 기자 한 분과 이야기를 나눠야 합니다.

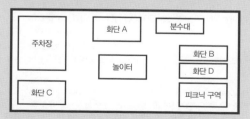

어휘 help with ~을 돕다 preparation 준비 flowerbed 화단 in charge of ~을 맡고 있는, 책임지고 있는 coordinate ~을 조정하다 volunteer 자원 봉사자 layout 배치(도), 구획, 구성 leave A + 형용사 A를 ~한 상태로 두다, 만들다 for now 당분간은, 현재로서는 between A and B A와 B 사이에 fountain 분수대 parking lot 주차장 plant (식물을) ~에 심다 alongside ~와 함께 except for ~을 제외하고 local 지역의, 현지의 article (신문 등의) 기사

98 Who is the speaker?
(A) A local politician
(B) A company representative
(C) A volunteer coordinator
(D) A schoolteacher

화자는 누구인가?
(A) 지역 정치인
(B) 회사 대표
(C) 자원 봉사 진행 담당자
(D) 학교 교사

해설 〈직업을 묻는 문제〉
화자가 담화를 시작하면서 자신의 이름과 함께 자원 봉사자 업무를 조정하는 일을 맡고 있다고(I'm Nancy, and I'm in charge of coordinating the volunteers) 소개하고 있으므로 (C)가 정답이다.

어휘 local 지역의, 현지의 politician 정치인 representative 대표 coordinator 진행 담당자, 편성 책임자

99 Look at the graphic. Which plot will be left empty for now?
(A) Bed A
(B) Bed B
(C) Bed C
(D) Bed D

시각 자료를 보시오. 어느 구획이 당분간 비워진 채로 있을 것인가?
(A) 화단 A
(B) 화단 B
(C) 화단 C
(D) 화단 D

해설 〈배치도 문제〉
담화 중반부에 분수대와 주차장 사이에 있는 화단을 비운 상태로 둘 것이라고(We'll leave one of the beds empty for now, the one between the fountain and the parking lot) 알리고 있다. 배치도에서 오른쪽 상단의 분수대(Fountain)와 왼쪽 상단의 주차장 (Parking Lot) 사이에 위치한 화단이 Bed A이므로 (A)가 정답이다.

100 What does the speaker say she will do at two o'clock?
(A) Pass out some snacks
(B) Speak to a journalist
(C) Take some photographs
(D) Bring some more flowers

화자는 2시에 무엇을 할 것이라고 말하는가?
(A) 몇몇 간식을 나눠 주는 일
(B) 한 기자와 이야기하는 일
(C) 몇몇 사진을 촬영하는 일
(D) 좀 더 많은 꽃을 가져오는 일

해설 〈특정 시점의 일을 묻는 문제〉
담화 맨 마지막에 2시라는 시점을 언급하면서 그때 지역 신문사 기자

와 이야기를 나눈다고(at two o'clock, when I need to talk to a reporter from the local newspaper) 알리고 있으므로 (B)가 정답이다.

어휘 pass out ~을 나눠 주다 take a photograph 사진을 촬영하다

PART 5 P26

101 **해석** TR 맥스웰 카드를 사용하고 계시는 모든 고객께서는 반드시 매월 27일까지 청구서 비용을 지불하셔야 합니다.

해설 〈소유격 대명사〉
동사 pay와 명사 목적어 bills 사이에 위치한 빈칸은 명사를 수식할 소유격 대명사 자리이므로 (B) their가 정답이다.

어휘 customer 고객 bill 청구서, 고지서 by (기한) ~까지

102 **해석** 여러 직원들은 자신들이 곧 수강하게 될 교육 과정에 관해 질문을 해 오고 있다.

해설 〈부사 어휘〉
빈칸 앞에 미래 시제로 쓰인 동사 will be taking과 어울리는 부사가 필요하므로 '곧, 머지않아' 등으로 가까운 미래를 나타낼 때 사용하는 (A) soon이 정답이다. (B) lately는 현재완료 시제와 어울리는 부사이므로 오답이다.

어휘 several 여럿의, 몇몇의 training 교육 take a course 수강하다 lately 최근에

103 **해석** 정원에 있는 분수대는 정기적으로 세척 일정이 잡혀 있다.

해설 〈① 명사 자리(전치사 뒤) ② 사람 명사 VS. 사물 명사〉
전치사 for 뒤에 위치한 빈칸은 전치사의 목적어 역할을 할 명사 자리인데, 분수대에 예정되어 있는 일을 나타내는 명사가 쓰여야 알맞으므로 '세척, 청소'를 의미하는 명사 (C) cleaning이 정답이다. 또 다른 명사 (B) cleaner는 '세제, 청소기' 등을 뜻하므로 문장의 의미에 어울리지 않는다.

어휘 water fountain 분수대 scheduled 예정된 on a regular basis 정기적으로 cleaner 세제, 청소기 cleaning 세척, 청소

104 **해석** 최대한 가장 빠른 서비스를 보장하기 위해 식당 손님들은 착석하기 전에 주문을 하도록 요청받는다.

해설 〈전치사 VS. 접속사〉
빈칸 앞뒤로 주어와 동사가 포함된 절이 하나씩 위치한 구조이므로 빈칸은 이 절들을 연결할 접속사 자리이다. 따라서 유일한 접속사로 제시된 (D) before가 정답이다. 나머지 단어들은 모두 전치사이므로 오답이다.

어휘 diner 식사[식당] 손님 be asked to do ~하도록 요청받다 place an order 주문하다 be seated 착석하다, 자리에 앉다 ensure ~을 보장하다 during ~ 중에, ~ 동안 prior to ~에 앞서, ~ 전에 upon ~하자마자

105 **해석** 실수를 만회하기 위해 웨버 인터내셔널 사는 추가 요금 없이 제품을 배송하겠다고 제안했다.

해설 〈형용사 자리(명사 앞)〉
형용사 no와 명사 charge 사이에 위치한 빈칸은 명사를 수식할 또 다른 형용사가 쓰여야 하는 자리이므로 형용사인 (D) additional이 정답이다. 복합 명사의 경우도 생각해 볼 수 있지만, 명사 (B) addition은 charge와 복합 명사를 구성하기에 의미상 적합하지 않으므로 오답이다.

어휘 make up for ~을 만회하다, 보충하다 offer to do ~하겠다고 제안하다 ship ~을 배송하다, 선적하다 at no additional charge 추가 요금 없이 add ~을 추가하다 addition 추가(되는 것) additionally 추가적으로

106 **해석** 지난번 관리자 회의 중에, 외국의 시설로 이전하는 문제가 또 다시 제기되었다.

해설 〈전치사 어휘〉
빈칸 뒤에 위치한 명사구 '지난번 관리자 회의'는 지속 시간의 의미를 갖는 명사구이므로 이러한 명사(구)와 어울리는 전치사로 '~ 중에, ~ 동안'을 뜻하는 (B) During이 정답이다.

어휘 managerial 관리의, 관리직의 raise an issue 문제를 제기하다 transfer 이전, 이동 facility 시설(물) into (이동) ~ 안으로, (변화) ~로, ~한 상태로 during ~ 중에, ~ 동안 above (위치) ~보다 위에, ~보다 높이, (수량, 정도, 능력 등) ~을 넘어, ~보다 뛰어나 between (A and B) (A와 B) 사이에

107 **해석** 세입자들께서는 이번 주에 중앙 로비 개조 공사를 피할 수 있도록 옆문을 이용하셔야 합니다.

해설 〈부정사(부사적 용법)〉
빈칸 앞에 이미 문장의 동사 should use가 있으므로 또 다른 동사 avoid는 준동사의 형태로 쓰여야 한다. 따라서 '~하기 위해'라는 의미로 목적을 나타내는 to부정사의 형태인 (C) to avoid가 정답이다.

어휘 tenant 세입자, 입주자 renovation 개조, 보수 avoid ~을 피하다

108 **해석** 잭슨 씨는 영업사원들에게 고객 만족 캠페인을 최우선 사항으로 삼았다.

해설 〈명사 어휘〉
빈칸에 쓰일 명사는 make의 목적어 the customer satisfaction campaign와 동격에 해당되는 목적격 보어 보이며, 바로 앞에 위치한 형용사 top의 수식을 받기에 적합한 것이어야 한다. 따라서 '고객 만족 캠페인 = 최우선 사항'이라는 동격 관계를 형성할 수 있는 (B) priority가 정답이다.

어휘 make A B A를 B로 만들다 satisfaction 만족 sales 영업, 판매, 매출 force 직원들, 인력 rate 요금, 속도, 비율, 등급 top priority 최우선 사항 excellence 훌륭함, 우수함 credit 신용(도), 입금(액), 칭찬, 인정

109 해석 앤드류 설리반은 먼로 타이어 회사와의 성공적인 협상 후에 승진을 요청했다.

해설 〈명사 자리(관사 뒤)〉
부정 관사 a 뒤에 위치한 빈칸은 명사 자리이므로 명사인 (C) promotion이 정답이다.

어휘 request ~을 요청하다　after ~ 후에　successful 성공적인　negotiation 협상, 협의　promote ~을 승진시키다, 홍보하다　promotion 승진, 홍보

110 해석 안내 책자를 받은 대부분의 고객들은 정보가 그 제품들과 관련되어 있다는 점에 주목했다.

해설 〈형용사 어휘〉
빈칸 뒤에 위치한 전치사 to와 어울릴 수 있는 형용사가 필요하므로 to와 함께 '~와 관련된'이라는 의미를 구성하는 (D) relevant가 정답이다.

어휘 receive ~을 받다　brochure 안내 책자, 소책자　note that ~라는 점에 주목하다, ~임을 특별히 언급하다　pure 순수한, 깨끗한, 순진한　capable 할 수 있는　defective 결함 있는　relevant (to) (~와) 관련된

111 해석 그 상은 가장 효율적으로 업무를 수행하는 사람에게 주어질 것이다.

해설 〈부사 자리(완전한 문장 구조 뒤)〉
관계대명사 who가 이끄는 절에 동사 performs와 목적어 the task가 있는 완전한 문장 구조를 이루고 있으므로 빈칸은 목적어 뒤에서 동사를 수식할 부사가 쓰여야 알맞은 구조가 된다. 따라서 부사인 (D) efficiently가 정답이다.

어휘 perform ~을 수행하다, 실시하다　task 업무, 일　efficient 효율적인　efficiency 효율(성)　efficiently 효율적으로

112 해석 예정된 유지 보수 작업으로 인해 어떤 엘리베이터도 오전 1시부터 오전 5시까지 이용하실 수 없습니다.

해설 〈전치사 어휘〉
빈칸 뒤에 위치한 명사구는 '예정된 유지 보수 작업'을 의미하는데, 이 작업은 엘리베이터를 이용할 수 없는 이유에 해당되므로 '~로 인해, ~ 때문에'라는 뜻으로 이유를 나타내는 전치사 (C) due to가 정답이다. (D) since는 전치사인 경우 '~ 이후로'라는 의미이므로 오답이다.

어휘 access ~을 이용하다, ~에 접근하다　scheduled 예정된　maintenance 유지 보수, 시설 관리　as of (날짜 등과 함께) ~부로, ~부터　as for ~에 관해서라면, ~의 경우　due to ~로 인해, ~ 때문에　since ~ 이후로[이래로]

113 해석 그 교육 과정은 의사소통 능력을 개선하고자 하는 모든 직원들을 대상으로 한다.

해설 〈수량 형용사〉
빈칸 뒤에 위치한 명사구 staff members를 수식할 형용사가 빈칸에 필요한데, staff members가 복수형이므로 복수 명사 앞에 사용할 수 있는 (B) all이 정답이다. (A) each와 (C) every는 단수 명사를 수식하며, (D) entirely는 부사이다.

114 해석 회사의 부사장은 회사의 사업 전략에 있어 혁신적인 변화를 발표할 계획이다.

해설 〈동사 어휘〉
우선, 빈칸 뒤에 위치한 명사구 innovative changes를 목적어로 취할 타동사가 필요하므로 타동사인 (B) enclose와 (D) announce 중에서 하나를 골라야 한다. 이 둘 중에서, '혁신적인 변화를 발표할 계획이다'와 같은 의미가 자연스러우므로 '~을 발표하다'를 뜻하는 (D) announce가 정답이다. (A) agree와 (C) participate은 목적어를 가질 수 없는 자동사이다.

어휘 vice president 부사장　plan to do ~할 계획이다　innovative 혁신적인　strategy 전략　agree 동의하다, 합의하다　enclose ~을 동봉하다　participate 참가하다　announce ~을 발표하다, 공지하다

115 해석 그 후보자가 해당 관리자 직책에 대해 충분히 자격을 갖추고 있는지 결정하기 위해 회의가 개최될 것이다.

해설 〈명사절 접속사〉
to부정사로 쓰인 타동사 determine 뒤로 빈칸이 있고, 그 뒤로 주어와 동사가 포함된 절이 위치한 상태이다. 따라서 빈칸 이하의 절이 determine의 목적어 역할을 할 명사절이 되어야 알맞으므로 명사절 접속사인 (B) whether가 정답이다. (A) regarding과 (C) such as는 전치사이며, (D) because는 부사절 접속사이다.

어휘 hold ~을 개최하다　determine ~을 결정하다　candidate 후보자, 지원자　fully 충분히, 완전히, 전적으로　be qualified for ~에 대한 자격을 갖추고 있다, ~에 적격이다　managerial 관리의, 관리직의　position 직책, 일자리　regarding ~에 관해　whether ~인지 (아닌지)　such as ~와 같은

116 해석 영화관 내의 관객들은 훌륭한 연기에 대해 배우들에게 큰 소리로 박수를 쳐 주었다.

해설 〈전치사 어휘〉
빈칸 뒤에 위치한 명사구 '훌륭한 연기'는 관객들이 크게 박수 쳐 준 이유 또는 대상에 해당된다. 따라서 동사 applaud와 어울려 '~에 대해, ~로' 등의 의미로 이유 혹은 대가를 나타낼 때 사용하는 전치사 (C) for가 정답이다.

어휘 crowd 사람들, 무리, 군중　loudly 큰 소리로　applaud ~에게 박수치다　performance 연기, 공연, 연주

117 해석 하멜 박사는 끈기가 직장에서 활용될 수 있는 새로운 기술을 배우는 데 있어 필수라고 말한다.

해설 〈명사 자리(주어)〉
주절의 동사 states의 목적어 역할을 하는 that절에서 that과 is 사이에 위치한 빈칸은 이 that절의 주어 역할을 할 명사 자리이므로 명사인 (C) persistence가 정답이다.

어휘 state that ~라고 말하다　be essential to ~에 필수이다　persist 끈질기게 계속하다, 고집하다　persistence 끈기, 집요함, 지속(성)　persistently 끈질기게, 고집스럽게

118 해석 벨라미 씨의 직무는 일주일에 세 번씩 공장에 대한 일상적인 점검을 수행하는 것을 포함하고 있다.

해설 〈형용사 어휘〉
빈칸에 쓰일 형용사는 바로 뒤에 위치한 명사 inspections를 수식해 점검 작업의 특성을 나타낼 수 있는 것이어야 하므로 '일상적인 점검'이라는 의미를 구성하는 (D) routine이 정답이다.

어휘 duty 직무, 임무　include ~을 포함하다　conduct ~을 수행하다, 실시하다　inspection 점검　aware 알고 있는, 인식하고 있는　absent 부재중인, 결근한　confident 자신감 있는, 확신하는　routine 일상적인

119 해석 로저스 씨는 컨벤션 센터로 가는 최단 경로를 택한 사람들보다 더 빨리 도착할 수 있었다.

해설 〈비교급〉
빈칸 뒤에 위치한 than은 비교급 형용사 또는 부사와 함께 쓰이므로 비교급 부사인 (B) more quickly가 정답이다.

어휘 be able to do ~할 수 있다　arrive 도착하다　those who ~하는 사람들　direct route 가장 빠른 경로, 직통 노선　quick 빠른, 신속한　quickly 빨리, 신속히

120 해석 월요일에 배송 물품을 보냄으로써, 라고스 테크놀로지는 그것이 마감 시한 전에 도착하는 것을 확실히 할 것이다.

해설 〈동사 어휘〉
빈칸 바로 뒤에 that절이 위치해 있으므로 that절을 목적어로 취할 수 있는 동사가 빈칸에 쓰여야 한다. 따라서 that절과 함께 '반드시 ~하도록 하다, ~하는 것을 보장하다' 등의 의미를 나타낼 때 사용하는 (C) ensure가 정답이다.

어휘 by (방법) ~함으로써, ~해서　shipment 배송(품)　ensure that 반드시 ~하도록 하다, ~하는 것을 보장하다　arrive 도착하다　deadline 마감 시한　reserve ~을 예약하다, 따로 남겨 두다　acquire ~을 얻다, 획득하다　correct ~을 정정하다, 바로잡다

121 해석 소셜 미디어 사이트 E-빌라는 실수로 일부 개인 데이터를 유출시킨 뒤로 이용자들의 비난에 신속하게 대응해 왔다.

해설 〈형용사 자리(be동사 뒤)〉
현재완료 시제로 쓰인 be동사 has been 뒤는 주격 보어 자리이므로 형용사 (C) responsive가 정답이다. 명사 (A) response가 쓰이려면 주어와 동격이 되어야 하는데 주어인 Social media site E-Villa와 동격 관계가 아니므로 오답이다. 또한 동사 respond는 자동사로서 수동태 형태로 사용할 수 없으므로 (B) responded는 오답이다.

어휘 criticism 비난, 비평　accidentally 실수로, 뜻하지 않게　leak ~을 유출시키다, 누설하다　response 대응, 반응, 답변　respond 대응하다, 반응하다, 답변하다　responsive 즉각 대응하는, 반응하는　responsively 대응하여, 반응하여

122 해석 증가하는 수요로 인해, 밀러 주식회사는 향후 2년 동안에 걸쳐 직원 숫자를 점차적으로 늘릴 것이다.

해설 〈부사 어휘〉

빈칸에 쓰일 부사는 동사 increase를 수식해 직원 숫자를 늘리는 방식을 나타내야 한다. 또한, 빈칸 뒤 over가 이끄는 기간 전치사구와 의미가 어울리는 '점차적으로'를 뜻하는 (C) gradually가 정답이다.

어휘 due to ~로 인해   growing 증가하는, 늘어나는   demand 수요   increase ~을 늘리다. 증가시키다   the number of ~의 숫자, 수   over ~ 동안에 걸쳐   nearly 거의   previously 이전에, 과거에   gradually 점차적으로   necessarily 필수적으로, 반드시

123 해석 카슨 풋웨어는 네 가지의 완전히 다른 종류의 신발을 제공하는데, 모두 고객들에게 인기가 있다.

해설 〈형용사 자리(형용사와 명사 사이)〉
숫자 표현인 형용사 four와 명사 types 사이에 위치한 빈칸은 four와 함께 명사를 수식할 형용사 자리이므로 형용사인 (A) distinct가 정답이다.

어휘 offer ~을 제공하다   be popular with ~에게 인기가 있다   distinct 완전히 다른, 뚜렷한, 별개의   distinctly 뚜렷하게, 분명히   distinction (뚜렷한) 차이, 뛰어남   distinctively 특징적으로, 구별하여

124 해석 이 기사는 출판사의 서면 동의 없이는 다른 곳에서 재사용할 수 없습니다.

해설 〈전치사 어휘〉
빈칸 뒤에 위치한 명사구 the publisher's written consent를 목적어로 취할 전치사가 빈칸에 필요하므로 전치사인 (B) without과 (D) along 중에서 의미가 적절한 것을 골라야 한다. '서면 동의 없이 복제될 수 없다'와 같은 의미가 적합하므로 '~ 없이, ~하지 않고' 등을 뜻하는 (B) without이 정답이다. (A) instead는 부사이며, (C) unless는 접속사이다.

어휘 article (잡지 등의) 기사   reproduce ~을 복제하다. 다시 만들어 내다   publisher 출판사, 출판인   written consent 서면 동의   instead 대신에   without ~ 없이, ~하지 않고   unless ~가 아니라면, ~하지 않는다면   along (거리, 해안 등)을 따라

125 해석 업무 환경의 약간의 개선은 더 많은 사람들에게 초과 근무를 장려하게 될 것이다.

해설 〈① 수일치 ② 능동태/수동태〉
빈칸 앞에는 주어와 in 전치사구가, 빈칸 뒤에는 명사구와 to부정사구가 있으므로 빈칸이 문장의 동사 자리임을 알 수 있다. 따라서 동사의 형태가 아닌 (B) to encourage는 우선 오답 처리해야 하며, 빈칸 뒤에 목적어가 위치한 구조에 맞지 않는 수동태 (D) is encouraged도 오답이다. 남은 동사 중에서 (A) encourage는 3인칭 단수 주어 A slight improvement와 수 일치가 맞지 않으므로 조동사가 포함되어 있어 수 일치에 상관없이 사용 가능한 (C) would encourage가 정답이다.

어휘 slight 약간의, 조금의   improvement 개선, 향상   working conditions 업무 환경   encourage A to do A에게 ~하도록 장려하다, 권장하다   individual 사람, 개인   work overtime hours 초과 근무하다

126 해석 디트로이트로 향하는 승객들께서는 비록 비행기가 지상에 40분 동안 있지만 비행기에서 내리실 수 있습니다.

해설 〈전치사 VS. 접속사〉
빈칸 앞뒤에 주어와 동사가 포함된 절이 하나씩 위치해 있으므로 빈칸은 두 개의 절을 연결할 접속사 자리임을 알 수 있다. 따라서 접속사인 (B) even though와 (D) however 중에 의미가 알맞은 것을 골라야 하는데, '비록 비행기가 지상에 40분 동안만 머물겠지만 비행기에서 내릴 수 있다'와 같은 의미가 되어야 적절하다. 따라서 '비록 ~이기는 하지만'을 뜻하는 (B) even though가 정답이다. (A) despite은 전치사이다.

어휘 passenger 승객   head to ~로 향하다. 가다   get off ~에서 내리다   despite ~에도 불구하고   even though 비록 ~이기는 하지만   in order to do ~하기 위해   however ad. 하지만, 그러나 conj. 아무리 ~라 할지라도

127 해석 오직 올해에 상을 받은 사람들만을 위해 개최되는 특별 행사가 본사에 서 있을 것이다.

해설 〈부사 어휘〉
빈칸에 쓰일 부사는 행사에서 축하하고자 하는 대상자들을 나타내는 for 전치사구와 어울려 그 의미를 강조하는 역할을 해야 알맞으므로 '오직, 오로지'라는 의미로 쓰이는 (D) exclusively가 정답이다.

어휘 ceremony 행사, 식, 의식   headquarters 본사   hold ~을 개최하다   those who ~하는 사람들   win an award 상을 받다   slightly 약간, 조금   mutually 서로, 상호간에   precisely 정확하게   exclusively 오직 (~만), 독점적으로

128 해석 우리는 브루스 크레이머 씨가 내일이 되기 전에 긍정적으로 답변하지 않는다면 젠스 홀브록 씨에게 그 직책을 제안할 것이다.

해설 〈전치사 VS. 접속사〉
빈칸 앞뒤로 주어와 동사가 각각 포함된 절이 하나씩 쓰여 있으므로 빈칸은 두 절을 연결할 접속사 자리임을 알 수 있다. 따라서 접속사인 (A) because와 (C) unless 중에서 하나를 골라야 하는데, '브루스 크레이머 씨가 긍정적으로 답변하지 않는다면 젠스 홀브록 씨에게 직책을 제안할 것이다'와 같은 의미가 되어야 자연스러우므로 '~하지 않는다면' 등의 뜻으로 부정 조건을 나타내는 접속사 (C) unless가 정답이다. (B) except와 (D) against는 전치사이다.

어휘 offer A B A에게 B를 제안하다   position 직책, 일자리   respond 답변하다, 응답하다   positively 긍정적으로   except ~을 제외하고, ~ 외에는   unless ~하지 않는다면, ~가 아니라면   against ~에 반대하여, ~에 맞서, ~에 기대어

129 해석 도시 내 여러 레스토랑들이 지난 몇 달 동안 식당 손님들에게 민족 전통 음식을 제공하기 시작했다.

해설 〈시제(현재완료)〉
각 보기가 모두 동사의 형태이고 시제만 다르므로 시제 관련 단서를 찾아 어울리는 동사를 골라야 한다. 문장 끝부분에 위치한 기간 표현인 in the past few months와 어울리는 시제는 현재완료 시제이므로 (C) have begun이 정답이다.

어휘 several 여럿의, 몇몇의   serve (음식 등) ~을 제공하다, 내오다   ethnic 민속적인, 민족의   diner 식사 손님

130 해석 허드슨 컨벤션 센터는 시내에 있는 주요 호텔에 대한 접근성으로 인해 행사용으로 인기 있는 장소이다.

해설 〈명사 어휘〉
빈칸에 쓰일 명사는 바로 뒤에 위치한 전치사 to와 어울려 컨벤션 센터와 주요 호텔들 사이의 위치 관계를 나타낼 수 있는 것이어야 하므로 to와 함께 '~에 대한 접근성, 근접함'라는 의미를 구성하는 (B) proximity가 정답이다.

어휘 popular 인기 있는   site 장소, 부지, 현장   due to ~로 인해   direction 방향, 지휘, 감독   proximity 접근(성), 근접   competence 능력, 권한   majority 대다수, 대부분

PART 6

[131-134] 이메일

수신: 애슐리 로맥스 〈alomax@lomaxinc.com〉
발신: 빅터 월튼 〈victorwalton@dtwholesale.net〉
날짜: 8월 7일
제목: 읽어 보시기 바랍니다.

로맥스 씨께,

연례 기업가 컨퍼런스 행사에서 **131** 청중의 일부가 될 수 있어 기뻤습니다. 저는 귀하의 발표를 통해 고객들과 관계를 맺는 일에 관해 아주 많은 것을 배웠습니다. **132** 실제로, 저는 이미 저희 회사에 귀하의 전략 몇 가지를 시행하기 시작했습니다. 저희 직원들이 귀하의 통찰력으로부터 대단히 큰 도움을 받을 수 있을 것으로 생각합니다. 귀하의 일정에 저희 주간 회의 중 하나에 참석해 개별 연설 행사를 진행하실 여유가 있으신지요? **133** 12명으로 구성된 저희 영업사원 전체가 참석할 것입니다. 저희 회사의 영업 목표뿐 아니라 비전을 **134** 간략히 설명해 드리는 파일을 첨부해 드렸으니 확인해 보시기 바랍니다.

안녕히 계십시오.

빅터 월튼

어휘 annual 연례적인, 해마다의   entrepreneur 기업가   presentation 발표(회)   connect with ~와 관계를 맺다, 연결되다   implement ~을 시행하다   strategy 전략   benefit from ~로부터 이득을 얻다   insight 통찰력   room (관사 없이) 여유, 여지, 공간   private 개별적인, 개인의, 사적인   attached 첨부된   as well as ~뿐만 아니라 …도   sales 영업, 판매, 매출

131 해설 〈명사 어휘(문맥)〉
보기가 모두 명사이므로 의미가 알맞은 것을 찾아야 한다. 다음 문장에 상대방의 발표를 통해 많은 것을 배웠다는 말이 쓰여 있으므로 글쓴이가 참가자였음을 알 수 있다. 따라서 참가자 신분을 나타내는 명사로서 '청중, 관객' 등을 의미하는 (B) audience가 정답이다.

어휘 audience 청중, 관객, 시청자들 process 과정 celebration 기념 행사, 축하 행사

132 해설 〈접속부사〉
문장 시작 부분에 콤마와 함께 빈칸이 제시되는 경우는 접속부사 문제이므로 빈칸 앞뒤 문장의 의미 흐름부터 파악해야 한다. 빈칸 앞 문장에는 상대방의 발표를 통해 많은 것을 배웠다는 말이, 다음 문장에는 이미 상대방이 가르쳐 준 전략을 시행하기 시작했다는 말이 쓰여 있다. 따라서 구체적인 실제 사례를 말하는 흐름이므로 '실제로, 사실' 등의 의미로 구체적인 정보를 추가할 때 사용하는 (C) In fact가 정답이다.

어휘 on the other hand 반면에, 다른 한편으로는 as usual 평소와 마찬가지로, 늘 그렇듯이 in fact 실제로, 사실 on the contrary 대조적으로

133 (A) 저희가 계속 성장한다면 다른 건물로 옮길 수도 있습니다.
(B) 불안정한 경제 상황 하에서, 소비자들은 덜 소비하는 경향이 있습니다.
(C) 내년에 열릴 컨퍼런스 행사 입장권이 이미 판매 중입니다.
(D) 12명으로 구성된 저희 영업사원 전체가 참석할 것입니다.

해설 〈빈칸에 알맞은 문장 넣기〉
앞 문장에 회사로 와서 개별적인 연설을 할 시간이 있는지 묻는 말이 쓰여 있으며, 이 연설 행사와 관련된 정보로서 참석 인원의 규모를 알리는 (D)가 정답이다. 나머지 문장들은 이 연설 행사의 개최와 관련 없는 내용을 담고 있으므로 오답이다.

어휘 keep -ing 계속 ~하다 grow 성장하다, 자라다 economy 경제 consumer 소비자 tend to do ~하는 경향이 있다 on sale 판매 중인 entire 전체의 in attendance 참석한

134 해설 〈주격 관계대명사〉
우선, 빈칸 앞에 명령문을 이끄는 동사 find가 이미 쓰여 있으므로 보기에 제시된 또 다른 동사 outline이 동사의 형태로 쓰일 수 없다. 따라서 빈칸 이하 부분은 a file을 뒤에서 수식하는 수식어구가 되어야 하므로 주격 관계대명사 that이 이끄는 절에 동사 outline를 사용하여 뒤의 명사구를 목적어로 취하는 형태인 (C) that outlines가 정답이다.

어휘 outline ~을 간략히 설명하다

[135-138] 편지

더블데이 카페
워커 애비뉴 98번지
애버딘, MD

고객 여러분께,

저희 더블데이 카페는 고객 여러분께 20년 넘게 고급 커피와 차, 패스트리, 그리고 스낵을 제공해 왔습니다. 실제로, 저희는 우리 도시 내의 거의 다른 어떤 식당보다 더 오래 영업을 지속해 오고 있습니다. 따라서 저희는 올해 **135** 12월 29일 부로 폐업할 예정이라는 사실을 유감스럽게 생각합니다. 저희는 케네디 씨께서 은퇴 결정을 내리신 이후로 새 주인을 계속 찾아왔습니다. **136** 하지만, 아직 아무도 매장을 매입할 제안을 하지 않았습니다. 지금부터 마지막 날까지, 판매되는 모든 제품은 30퍼센트 할인될 것입니다. **137** 이는 케네디 씨께서 모든 분들께 감사드리는 방법입니다. 저희는 여러분의 **138** 성원에 감사드리며, 조만간 작별 인사를 드리기 위해 뵐 수 있기를 바랍니다.

어휘 provide A with B A에게 B를 제공하다 quality a. 고급의, 양질의 more than ~가 넘는 decade 10년 in fact 실제로, 사실 just about 거의, 대략 eatery 식당, 음식점 therefore 따라서, 그러므로 regret that ~임을 유감으로 생각하다 search for ~을 찾다 owner 소유주 since ~한 이후로 make one's decision to do ~하겠다는 결정을 내리다 retire 은퇴하다, 퇴직하다 offer to do ~하도록 제안하다 purchase ~을 매입하다, 구입하다 for sale 판매되는, 판매 중인 by (차이) ~만큼, ~ 정도 appreciate ~에 대해 감사하다

135 해설 〈형용사 어휘〉
빈칸 바로 앞에 문을 닫을 예정이라는 말이 쓰여 있으므로 빈칸 뒤에 위치한 날짜는 그 시점임을 알 수 있다. 따라서 날짜 등과 함께 '~부로, ~부터'라는 의미로 효력이 발휘되는 시점을 나타낼 때 사용하는 (B) effective가 정답이다.

어휘 public 공공의, 일반 대중의 effective (날짜 등과 함께) ~부로, ~부터 actual 실제의, 사실상의 uncertain 불확실한

136 해설 〈접속부사〉
빈칸 앞 문장에는 새로운 주인을 계속 찾았다는 말이, 빈칸 뒤에는 매장을 매입하려는 사람이 없었다는 말이 쓰여 있다. 따라서, 빈칸 앞뒤의 내용은 서로 대조적인 흐름임을 알 수 있다. 따라서 '하지만, 그러나' 등의 의미로 대조 또는 반대를 나타낼 때 사용하는 (D) However가 정답이다.

어휘 therefore 따라서, 그러므로 consequently 그 결과, 그래서 likewise 마찬가지로 however 하지만, 그러나

137 (A) 몇몇 새 제과 제품이 방금 도착했습니다.
(B) 저희는 내년에 여러분을 다시 뵐 수 있기를 바랍니다.
(C) 이는 케네디 씨께서 모든 분들께 감사드리는 방법입니다.
(D) 갓 끓여낸 저희 커피 맛이 아주 마음에 드실 것입니다.

해설 〈빈칸에 알맞은 문장 넣기〉
빈칸 앞 문장에는 문을 닫는 마지막 날까지 제품을 30퍼센트 할인 판매한다는 말이 쓰여 있다. 따라서 이와 같은 조치를 This로 지칭하면서

앞서 카페 주인으로 언급된 케네디 씨가 고객에게 감사하는 방법이라고 말한 (C)가 정답이다. 나머지 문장들은 모두 앞 문장과 흐름상 어울리지 않는 내용을 담고 있다.

어휘 baked goods 제과 제품 arrive 도착하다 one's way of -ing ~하는 방법 freshly brewed (커피 등) 갓 끓여낸

138 해설 〈① 명사 자리(소유격 뒤) ② 사람 명사 VS. 사물 명사〉
빈칸은 소유격 대명사 your의 수식을 받음과 동시에 동사 appreciate의 목적어 역할을 할 명사 자리이다. 명사 보기인 (B) supporter와 (C) support 중에 의미상 적합한 것은 '후원'이므로 (C) support가 정답이다.

어휘 support v. ~을 지원하다, 후원하다 n. 지원, 후원, 성원 supporter 지지자, 후원자 supportive 지원하는, 도와주는

[139-142] 정보

고용 과정

저희 테헤다 테크놀로지 사는 공석에 대해 자질이 있는 **139** 지원자를 찾는 것을 확실히 하기 위해 외부 채용 전문 업체의 도움을 받고 있습니다. 저희는 또한 인상적인 경력과 학력을 지닌 분들께서 제출하시는 지원서도 기꺼이 고려해 볼 것입니다. 현재 재직 중인 직원들도 어떤 공석이든 지원할 **140** 자격이 있습니다. **141** 회사 내에서 과거에 보여 준 업무 능력이 고려될 것입니다. 그렇지만, 주된 초점은 해당 역할에 가장 적합한 사람을 찾는 데 있을 것입니다. 그 이유는 인사팀이 고용 결정을 내릴 때는 반드시 회사의 전반적인 **142** 수익성을 지켜야 하기 때문입니다.

어휘 hiring 고용 process 과정 use the assistance of ~의 도움을 받다 recruitment firm 채용 전문 업체 ensure that 반드시 ~하도록 하다, ~임을 보장하다 qualified 적격인, 자격이 있는 open position 공석 be willing to do 기꺼이 ~하다, ~할 의향이 있다 consider ~을 고려하다 application 지원(서), 신청(서) impressive 인상적인 current 현재의 apply for ~에 지원하다, ~을 신청하다 nevertheless 그럼에도 불구하고 primary 주된, 주요한 focus 초점 suitable for ~에 적합한, 어울리는 HR team 인사팀 protect ~을 지키다, 보호하다 overall 전반적인 make a decision 결정을 내리다

139 해설 〈명사 어휘〉
보기가 모두 명사이므로 의미가 알맞은 것을 찾아야 한다. 빈칸은 바로 앞에 위치한 동사 find의 목적어로서 해당 업체가 공석(open positions)을 충원하기 위해 찾는 대상을 나타내야 한다. 즉 공석에 대한 지원자 또는 후보자를 찾는 것이므로 '지원자, 후보자'를 의미하는 (B) candidates가 정답이다.

어휘 tenant 세입자 candidate 지원자, 후보자 consumer 소비자 client 고객, 의뢰인

140 해설 〈형용사 어휘(부정사와 어울리는 어휘)〉
빈칸 앞뒤 부분의 내용으로 볼 때, 현재 재직 중인 직원들도 공석에 지원할 수 있다는 의미가 되어야 자연스럽다. 따라서, 빈칸 뒤의 to부정사와 어울려 '~할 자격이 있는'을 뜻하는 (A) eligible이 정답이다. (C)

possible의 경우 사람 주어로 쓰지 않는 것이 원칙이며, 가주어 It으로 시작되는 문장의 be동사 뒤에 위치하는 보어로 쓰인다.

어휘 eligible 자격이 있는, 할 수 있는 prominent 중요한, 유명한, 두드러진 possible 가능한 voluntary 자발적인

141 (A) 저희는 새롭게 고용된 직원들을 맞이하게 되어 기쁩니다.
(B) 더욱이, 여러 인턴 직원들이 정규직을 제안받았습니다.
(C) 회사 내에서 과거에 보여 준 업무 능력이 고려될 것입니다.
(D) 실제로, 업무 환경이 지속적으로 높은 평가를 받고 있습니다.

해설 〈빈칸에 알맞은 문장 넣기〉
앞 문장에 현재 재직 중인 직원들도 지원할 수 있다는 내용이 있으므로 직원들이 지원할 경우 활용 가능한 평가 방법에 해당하는 (C)가 보기 중 가장 적합하다. 나머지 문장들은 빈칸 앞에서 각각 언급된 현재 재직 중인 직원들의 지원 가능성 및 가장 우선시되는 고용 기준을 말하는 흐름과 맞지 않는 내용을 담고 있으므로 오답이다.

어휘 be delighted to do ~해서 기쁘다 moreover 더욱이, 게다가 several 여럿, 몇몇 offer A B A에게 B를 제안하다, 제공하다 permanent position 정규직 (일자리) performance 업무 능력, 성과, 실적 take A into consideration A를 고려하다 in fact 실제로, 사실 workplace environment 업무 환경 consistently 지속적으로 receive ~을 받다 ratings 평가, 등급, 점수

142 **해설** 〈명사 자리(소유격 뒤)〉
빈칸은 바로 앞에 위치한 소유격 company's와 형용사 overall의 수식을 동시에 받을 명사 자리이므로 명사인 (B) profitability가 정답이다.

어휘 profit n. 수익 v. 이익을 얻다, ~에게 이익이 되다 profitability 수익성 profitable 수익성 있는

[143-146] 기사

8월 21일 - 그린브리어 밸리 내 지역 과수원들이 올해 평소보다 더 많은 사과를 수확할 것으로 예상하고 있다. 이 **143** 예측은 두 가지 요소를 바탕으로 한 것이다. 첫째, 농부들이 수년 전에 더 많은 나무를 심었으며, 이 나무들이 이제 결실을 맺기 시작하고 있다는 것이다. 다음으로는, 올 여름에는 날씨가 평소와 달리 쾌청했다. 모두 합쳐, 12만 톤이 넘는 사과가 올해 수확될 것이다. **144** 이와 같은 수치는 불과 2년 전만 해도 불가능한 것으로 여겨졌다.

이 계곡 내의 과수원들은 주로 유럽 및 아시아 국가로의 **145** 수출용으로 사과를 재배하고 있다. 지역 사과 **146** 농부 론 그랜트 씨는 "저는 이와 같은 양의 사과를 수확할 것이라고 전혀 예상하지 못했습니다. 바라는 것은, 이와 같은 상황이 앞으로도 계속 하나의 추세가 되는 것입니다."라고 밝혔다.

어휘 local 지역의, 현지의 orchard 과수원 expect to do ~할 것으로 예상되다 harvest ~을 수확하다 than normal 평소보다 be based on ~을 바탕으로 하다, 기반으로 하다 factor 요소 plant ~을 심다 several 여럿의, 몇몇의 bear fruit 결실을 맺다 unusually 평소와 달리, 대단히 pleasant 쾌적한, 기분 좋은 combined 모두 합쳐, 통합해 more than ~가 넘는 metric ton 미터톤(1,000킬로그램) grow ~을 재배하다, 기르다 primarily 주로 export n. 수출(품) hopefully 바라건대, 희망하여 trend 추세, 동향

143 **해설** 〈명사 어휘(문맥)〉
빈칸 앞에 위치한 This는 바로 앞 문장에서 말한 것을 가리키는데, 앞 문장에 사과 수확량과 관련된 예상(expect)이 쓰여 있으므로 이를 나타낼 명사로 '예측, 예상'을 의미하는 (B) forecast가 정답이다.

어휘 decision 결정 forecast 예측, 예상 expense 지출 (비용) effort 노력

144 (A) 사과들은 맛이 좋으며, 아주 많은 영양 가치를 지니고 있다.
(B) 이와 같은 수치는 불과 2년 전만 해도 불가능한 것으로 여겨졌다.
(C) 여전히, 사과가 이 지역의 손꼽히는 농산물들 중의 하나이다.
(D) 계곡 내의 여러 농장이 이 회사에 매입되어 왔다.

해설 〈빈칸에 알맞은 문장 넣기〉
빈칸 바로 앞 문장에 총 사과 수확량을 말하는 수치가 쓰여 있다. 따라서 이와 같은 수치를 Such a figure로 지칭해 과거의 상황과 비교하는 의미를 담은 (B)가 정답이다. 나머지 문장들은 이러한 수확량과 관련 없는 내용을 담고 있어 흐름상 맞지 않는다.

어휘 taste 형용사 ~한 맛이 나다 nutritional 영양적인 value 가치 figure 수치, 숫자 consider A 형용사 A를 ~한 것으로 여기다 leading 손꼽히는, 선도적인, 앞서 가는 agricultural product 농산물 purchase ~을 매입하다, 구입하다

145 **해설** 〈전치사 어휘〉
빈칸 뒤의 export는 명사로 쓰일 때 '수출(품)'을 의미하므로 이 문장에서 말하는 사과 재배의 목적인 것으로 판단할 수 있다. 따라서 ' ~을 위해, ~의 용도로' 등의 의미로 목적, 용도를 나타낼 때 사용하는 (C) for가 정답이다.

어휘 onto ~ 위로

146 **해설** 〈① 명사 자리(동격) ② 사람 명사 VS. 사물 명사〉
빈칸은 주어 Ron Grant와 동사 said 사이에 콤마와 함께 삽입된 구에 속해 있는데, 이 구는 주어 Ron Grant에 대한 동격에 해당되는 명사구이다. 따라서 apple과 함께 복합 명사를 구성할 사람 명사가 빈칸에 쓰여야 하므로 '농부'를 의미하는 사람 명사 (A) farmer가 정답이다.

어휘 farming 농업, 농사

[147-148] 구인 광고

애너하임

전국 각지에 위치한 지점 23곳에서 고객들께 서비스를 제공해 드리는 저희 애너하임은 9월 1일에 있을 린덴 국제공항 지점 개장식 준비로 현재 매장 매니저들과 영업사원들, 그리고 수리 담당 직원들을 모집하고 있습니다. 매니저들은 최소 2년의 경력을 지니고 있어야 하며, 현 직장 또는 이전의 고용주로부터 받은 **148** 추천서 한 장을 반드시 제출해야 합니다. 수리 담당 직원들은 **147** 저희가 판매하는 여러 종류의 가방과 여행 가방을 수리할 수 있는 능력을 지니고 있어야 하며, **148** 이는 반드시 추천서를 통해 확인되어야 합니다. **148** 영업사원들의 경우, 추천서가 선호되기는 하지만, 필수는 아닙니다. 관심 있는 분들께서는 8월 12일까지 www.anaheim-inc.com에서 온라인으로 예비 지원서를 작성해야 합니다.

어휘 branch 지점, 지사 currently 현재 recruit ~을 모집하다 repair n. 수리 v. ~을 수리하다 in preparation for ~에 대한 준비로 submit ~을 제출하다 a letter of recommendation 추천서(= a letter of reference) former 이전의, 전직 ~의 employer 고용주 be capable of -ing ~할 수 있다 confirm ~을 확인해 주다 preferred 선호되는, 우대되는 required 필수인, 필요한 party 사람, 당사자 complete ~을 작성 완료하다 preliminary 예비의, 사전의 application 지원(서), 신청(서) by (기한) ~까지

147 애너하임은 어떤 종류의 업체인가?
(A) 컴퓨터 수리 매장
(B) 배송 서비스 업체
(C) 가방 판매 업체
(D) 항공기 설계 업체

해설 〈주제 및 목적〉
본문 중반부에 여러 가지 가방 제품을 판매하는 곳이라고(~ the types of bags and suitcases we sell ~) 알리는 부분이 있으므로 (C)가 정답이다.

어휘 repair 수리 luggage 가방, 수하물

148 애너하임의 공석과 관련해 무엇이 언급되는가?
(A) 일부는 경력상의 추천서를 필요로 한다.
(B) 대부분 8월 12일에 시작될 것이다.
(C) 승진 기회를 제공한다.
(D) 경쟁력 있는 금전적 보상이 있다.

해설 〈진위 확인 (전체 진위 유형)〉
지문 중반부 이후로 제시되는 자격 요건과 관련해, 매니저들과 수리 담당 직원들은 반드시 추천서를 제출해야 한다는 사실을(~ must submit a letter of recommendation ~ must be confirmed by a letter of reference), 영업사원들은 추천서 제출이 의무가 아니라는 것을(For sales staff, a recommendation letter ~ but

not required) 밝히고 있으므로 추천서 제출이 일부에만 적용된다고 언급한 (A)가 정답이다.

어휘 require ~을 필요로 하다 reference 추천(서) provide ~을 제공하다 opportunity 기회 promotion 승진, 진급 competitive 경쟁력 있는 financial 금전적인, 재무의 compensation 보상

[149-150] 이메일

> 수신: 브라이슨 서점 직원
> 발신: 캐롤 월리스
> 날짜: 9월 12일
> 제목: 중요 사항
>
> 현재, 우리는 고객이 영수증을 소지하고 있는 한 모든 도서에 대해 반품을 받고 있습니다. ⑭⑨ 10월 1일부터, 우리 브라이슨 서점은 반품 정책을 더욱 엄격하게 만들 것입니다. 우리는 경미한 손상이 있는 도서에 대해 더 이상 반품을 받지 않을 것입니다. 여기에는 책등을 따라 발생된 마모와 접힌 페이지들, 그리고 물에 의한 손상이 포함됩니다.
>
> 이 변경 사항과 관련된 정보가 모든 영수증에 인쇄됩니다. 우리는 또한 고객들께 알리기 위해 표지판도 걸어 놓을 것입니다. ⑮⓪ 만일 고객이 반품과 관련해 불만을 제기할 경우, 근무 중인 매니저와 이야기하도록 권해 드리기 바랍니다.

어휘 currently 현재 accept ~을 받아들이다, 수용하다 return 반품, 반환 as long as ~하는 한, ~하기만 하면 receipt 영수증 make A 형용사 A를 ~하게 만들다 policy 정책, 방침 strict 엄격한 no longer 더 이상 ~ 않다 minor 경미한, 사소한 damage 손상, 피해 include ~을 포함하다 wear and tear 마모 along (길게 생긴 부분이나 길 등) ~을 따라 back spine 책등(책꽂이에 꽂았을 때 책 제목 등이 보이는 옆면) folded 접힌 hang up ~을 걸어 놓다 sign 표지(판) complain about ~에 대해 불만을 제기하다 advise A to do A에게 ~하도록 권하다, 조언하다 on duty 근무 중인

149 월리스 씨는 왜 이메일을 썼는가?
(A) 정책 변경을 알리기 위해
(B) 직원들에게 감사의 뜻을 전하기 위해
(C) 고객 동향을 알리기 위해
(D) 새로운 책을 추천하기 위해

해설 〈주제 및 목적〉
첫 단락에 10월 1일부터 반품 정책을 더욱 엄격하게 만들 것이라고 (Bryson Bookstore will make its return policy stricter) 알린 후, 그 변경 사항을 설명하는 내용으로 지문이 구성되어 있다. 이는 정책 변경을 알리는 것에 해당되므로 (A)가 정답이다.

어휘 announce ~을 알리다, 발표하다 policy 정책, 방침 appreciation 감사(의 뜻) trend 동향, 추세

150 이메일에 따르면, 불만이 있는 고객들은 무엇을 해야 하는가?
(A) 양식 작성하기
(B) 매니저와 이야기하기
(C) 상담 서비스에 전화하기
(D) 안내 데스크로 찾아 가기

해설 〈세부사항〉
고객 불만과 관련된 정보가 제시된 두 번째 단락에, 고객이 반품과 관련해 불만을 제기할 경우에 근무 중인 매니저와 이야기하도록 (Should a customer complain about a return, please advise the person to talk to the manager ~) 알리고 있으므로 (B)가 정답이다.

어휘 fill out ~을 작성하다 form 양식, 서식 helpline (전화) 상담 서비스

[151-152] 문자 메시지 대화

> **[오전 10:23] 헬렌 윈켈**
> 피트로 주식회사에서 오는 다음 배송 일정이 언제 잡혀 있는지 아시나요?
>
> **[오전 10:24] 아르투로 실바**
> 다음 주 수요일이요. 왜 그러시죠?
>
> **[오전 10:26] 헬렌 윈켈**
> 오늘 오후에 있을 교육 시간에 필요한 직무 설명서를 출력해야 하는데. ⑮① 컬러 잉크 카트리지와 흑백 카트리지 둘 다 떨어졌어요.
>
> **[오전 10:27] 아르투로 실바**
> 그럼 다른 팀에도 확인해 보셨나요?
>
> **[오전 10:28] 헬렌 윈켈**
> 네. 길 건너편에 있는 프린트 매장을 이용해야 할 것 같아요. 추가 비용이 들어갈 겁니다. ⑮② 상사 한 분이 미리 이것을 승인해 주셔야 할 것 같습니다.
>
> **[오전 10:30] 아르투로 실바**
> 좋습니다. 지금 처리해 드릴 수 있어요.
>
> **[오전 10:31] 헬렌 윈켈**
> 정말 감사합니다. 잠시 후에 사무실로 양식을 가져오겠습니다.

어휘 delivery 배송(품) schedule ~의 일정을 잡다 employee manual 직무 설명서 training 교육 session (특정 활동을 위한) 시간 be out of ~가 다 떨어지다, ~을 다 쓰다 both A and B A와 B 둘 모두 additional 추가의 need A to do A가 ~하기를 원하다 supervisor 상사, 부서장, 책임자 authorize ~을 승인하다 in advance 미리, 사전에 get to ~을 시작하다, ~에 착수하다 form 양식, 서식 in + 시간 ~ 후에

151 윈켈 씨가 실바 씨에게 무슨 문제점에 관해 말하는가?
(A) 일부 사무용품이 다 떨어졌다.
(B) 직무 설명서에 오류가 포함되어 있다.
(C) 일부 장비가 고장 났다.
(D) 교육 시간이 취소되었다.

해설 〈세부사항〉
윈켈 씨가 10시 26분에 작성한 메시지에 컬러 잉크 카트리지와 흑백 카트리지 둘 모두 다 떨어졌다는(~ we're all out of both color ink cartridges

---

and black ones) 문제점이 언급되어 있으므로 (A)가 정답이다.

어휘 supplies 용품, 물품 run out 다 떨어지다, 다 쓰다 employee manual 직무 설명서 contain ~을 포함하다, 담고 있다 equipment 장비 break down 고장 나다 session (특정 활동을 위한) 시간 cancel ~을 취소하다

152 오전 10시 30분에, 실바 씨가 "I can get to that now"라고 썼을 때 무엇을 하겠다고 약속하는가?
(A) 프린트 매장에 연락하기
(B) 매장 방문하기
(C) 문서 교정 보기
(D) 비용 승인하기

해설 〈의도 파악〉
제시된 문장은 앞서 언급된 일을 that으로 지칭해 그 일을 지금 바로 해 주겠다고 알리는 의미를 나타낸다. 이는 바로 앞 문장에서 윈켈 씨가 추가 비용이 든다고 말하면서 상사의 승인이 필요하다고(~ an additional cost. I'd need a supervisor to authorize that ~) 말한 것에 대한 답변이므로 비용을 승인해 주겠다는 뜻에 해당된다. 따라서 (D)가 정답이다.

어휘 contact ~에 연락하다 proofread (문서 등) ~을 교정 보다 approve ~을 승인하다 expense (지출) 비용

[153-155] 광고

> **아빌렌 가정용품**
> — 여러분의 주택, 여러분의 스타일 —
>
> 태평양 연안 북서부 지역에 오랫동안 서비스를 제공해 온 끝에, 저희 아빌렌 가정용품이 ⑮③ 문을 닫습니다. 저희가 ⑮③ 이 정리 세일 행사에서 모든 재고품을 처분하는 관계로, 이번이 놀라운 특가품을 구입하실 수 있는 기회입니다.
>
> ⑮⑤ 8월 1일부터 7일까지, 커튼과 양탄자, 소형 쿠션을 비롯한 그 외의 많은 제품에 대해 최대 75퍼센트까지 할인받으십시오. 이 엄청난 할인은 모든 브랜드에 적용되며, 이번 행사는 ⑮④ 저희 매장 23곳에서 모두 열립니다.
>
> 저희가 상품을 다시 주문하지 않을 예정이므로, 실망하지 않으시도록 조기에 쇼핑하시는 것이 권장됩니다. ⑮⑤ 이번 행사 중에 구입하시는 모든 상품에 대해 교환 및 환불은 불가능하다는 점에 유의하십시오.
>
> 곧 저희 아빌렌 가정용품에서 뵐 수 있기를 바랍니다.

어휘 serve ~에 서비스를 제공하다 amazing 놀라운 deal 거래 상품, 거래 조건 get rid of ~을 없애다, 제거하다 stock 재고(품) closeout 정리 세일 up to 최대 ~까지 throw pillow 소형 쿠션 apply to ~에 적용되다 hold (행사 등) ~을 열다, 개최하다 reorder ~을 다시 주문하다 merchandise 상품(= goods) avoid ~을 피하다 disappointment 실망 note that ~라는 점에 유의하다, 주목하다 all sales are final 교환 및 환불은 불가하다 purchase ~을 구입하다

153 광고는 무엇에 관한 것인가?

(A) 개장식
(B) 제품 출시
(C) 정리 세일
(D) 매장 이전

해설 〈주제 및 목적〉
첫 단락에 해당 매장이 문을 닫는다고(~ closing its doors) 알리면서 정리 세일 행사라고(closeout event) 언급하고 있으므로 (C)가 정답이다.

어휘 launch 출시, 공개, 시작 relocation (위치) 이전, 이사

154 광고에서 암시된 것은 무엇인가?

(A) 행사장에서 다과가 제공될 것이다.
(B) 커튼이 맞춤 제작 사이즈로 주문될 수 있다.
(C) 아빌렌 가정용품은 여러 지점을 보유하고 있다.
(D) 고객들이 새로운 책임자와 만날 수 있다.

해설 〈진위 확인 (전체 진위 유형)〉
두 번째 단락에 23곳에 업체 매장이 있다는(~ all twenty-three of our stores) 내용을 통해 여러 지점을 보유하고 있다는 사실을 알 수 있으므로 이를 언급한 (C)가 정답이다.

어휘 refreshments 다과, 간식 serve (음식 등) ~을 제공하다, 내오다 custom 맞춤 제작의 multiple 여럿의, 다수의 location 지점, 지사, 위치

155 8월 1일과 7일 사이에 구입하는 제품에 관해 언급된 것은 무엇인가?

(A) 무료 배송이 된다.
(B) 모두 75퍼센트 할인된다.
(C) 반품될 수 없다.
(D) 연장된 품질 보증 서비스가 있다.

해설 〈세부 사항〉
8월 1일에서 7일까지에 해당되는 기간은 두 번째 단락에서 세일 행사 기간으로 제시되어 있는데, 마지막 단락에 사용된 'all sales are final'이란 표현은 교환 및 환불이 불가하다는 의미를 갖고 있으므로 (C)가 정답이다.

어휘 free 무료의 return ~을 반품하다, 반납하다 extended 연장된 warranty 품질 보증(서)

[156-157] 이메일

수신: hbaek@metairiellc.com
발신: thielev@sbmcon.org
날짜: 10월 10일
제목: 소기업 마케팅 컨퍼런스

백 씨에게.

작년에 개최된 소기업 마케팅 컨퍼런스에 참석해 주셔서 감사드립니다. **156** 저희 기록에 따르면 귀하께서는 아직 올해의 행사에 등록하지 않으신 것으로 나타나 있으며, 이는 10월 15일 혹은 이전까지 125달러의 사전 등록비로 여전히 등록하실 수 있습니다. 그날이 지나면, 요금은 온라인과 현장에서 모두 190달러가 될 것입니다.

이번 행사에 등록하시면 다음을 이용하실 수 있습니다.

- 모든 강연에 대한 일반 좌석
- 11월 3일에 열리는 인적 교류를 위한 칵테일 파티
- 11월 4일에 출시되는 기업가 조린 벤터 씨의 사인이 들어간 도서 한 권

다음은 등록비에 포함되지 않습니다.

- **157** 11월 5일에 진행되는 소규모 상담 시간 (셔틀 버스로 참가자들을 컨벤션 센터에서 해당 장소까지 모셔 드립니다. 추가 요금 수납 즉시, **157** 컨퍼런스 전용 출입증과 함께 특별 출입증을 보내 드립니다.)

또 한 번의 훌륭한 컨퍼런스에 저희와 함께 하시기를 바랍니다!

안녕히 계십시오.

빈스 틸레

어휘 appreciate ~에 대해 감사하다 attendance 참석 register for ~에 등록하다 advance-registration 사전 등록 fee 요금 give A access to B A에게 B를 이용할 수 있게 하다 general seating 일반 좌석 networking 인적 교류 signed 서명이 들어간, 사인이 된 entrepreneur 기업가 release ~을 출시하다, 공개하다, 발표하다 excluded from ~에 포함되지 않는, ~에서 제외되는 consultation 상담 session (특정 활동을 위한) 시간 participant 참가자 upon ~하는 즉시, ~하자마자 receipt 수납, 수령, 받음 extra 추가의, 별도의 payment 지불(액) admission badge 출입증 along with ~와 함께

156 틸레 씨는 왜 백 씨에게 이메일을 보냈는가?

(A) 정보 부족 문제에 대해 사과하기 위해
(B) 장소 변경에 관해 알리기 위해
(C) 다가오는 마감 기한에 관해 상기시키기 위해
(D) 기한이 지난 지불액을 요청하기 위해

해설 〈주제 및 목적〉
첫 단락을 보면, 아직 행사에 등록하지 않은 사실과 함께 아직 10월 15일까지 사전 등록할 수 있다는(Our records show that you have not yet registered ~ you can still do for the advance-registration price of $125 on or before October 15) 사실을 알리고 있다. 이는 등록 마감 기한과 관련된 정보를 알리는 것이므로 (C)가 정답이다.

어휘 apologize for ~에 대해 사과하다 lack 부족 inform A about B A에게 B에 관해 알리다 venue (행사 등의) 개최 장소 remind A about B A에게 B에 관해 상기시키다 approaching 다가오는 deadline 마감 기한 overdue 기한이 지난, 이미 했어야 하는 payment 지불(액)

157 11월 5일 행사에 관해 무엇이 언급되는가?

(A) 유명 기업가를 특징으로 할 것이다.
(B) 컨벤션 센터에서 개최될 것이다.
(C) 가장 인기 있는 시간이다.
(D) 다른 출입증으로 출입한다.

해설 〈진위 확인 (세부 진위 유형)〉
11월 5일이라는 날짜가 제시되는 세 번째 단락에, 소규모 상담 시간이 진행된다는(Small-group consultation session on November 5) 사실과 함께 컨퍼런스 출입증 외에 특별 출입증을 보내 준다고(~ a special admission badge will be sent along with your main conference badge) 알리고 있다. 이는 별도의 출입증을 이용해 해당 상담 시간에 참석하는 것을 나타내므로 (D)가 정답이다.

어휘 feature ~을 특징으로 하다 entrepreneur 기업가 take place (행사, 일 등) 개최되다, 발생되다 session (특정 활동을 위한) 시간 access ~에 출입하다, ~을 이용하다 pass 출입증

[158-160] 이메일

수신: 마티 포스터
발신: 필리스 카민스키
날짜: 5월 17일, 화요일
제목: 회신: 앰버 밸리 호텔 예약

포스터 씨께.

저희 기록에 따르면 귀하께서는 이번 주 금요일인 5월 20일에 저희 앰버 밸리 호텔에 체크인하셨다가 5월 24일 수요일에 체크아웃하시는 것으로 나옵니다. —[1]—. 저희와 함께 즐거운 숙박이 되시기를 바랍니다.

귀하의 계획에 도움을 드리기 위해, **158** 저희 도시에서 5월 21일 토요일에 연례 설립자 기념 퍼레이드가 개최된다는 점을 알려 드리고자 합니다. **159** 이 행사는 퀸시 공원에서 시작해 프레스턴 스트리트를 따라 이어지는 경로를 지난 뒤, 시청에서 종료됩니다. 이 퍼레이드는 모든 사람에게 무료이며, 즐거운 경험이 되겠지만, **160** 당일에, 프레스턴 스트리트를 따라 위치한 많은 업체가 문을 닫을 것이며, 여기에는 저희 도시의 유명한 유리 가공 예술품 박물관도 포함됩니다. —[2]—.

저희 호텔의 차량 출입구가 에버튼 로드에 있으므로, 퍼레이드로 인해 영향을 받지는 않습니다. —[3]—. 하지만, **159** 저희 호텔이 퍼레이드 출발점 바로 근처에 위치해 있기 때문에, 아침 일찍부터 준비 작업을 하는 사람들이 많을 것입니다. —[4]—.

안녕히 계십시오.

필리스 카민스키
고객 서비스 직원, 앰버 밸리 호텔

어휘 booking 예약 assist with ~을 돕다, ~에 도움이 되다 aware that ~임을 알고 있는, ~라는 점에 유의하는 hold ~을 개최하다, 열다 annual 연례적인, 해마다의 follow ~을 따라 지나가다 along (길 등) ~을 따라 free 무료인 including ~을 포함해 vehicle 차량 affect ~에 영향을 미치다 be located 위치해 있다 by ~ 옆에 set up 준비하다, 설치하다, 설정하다

158 이메일의 목적은 무엇인가?
(A) 한 박물관에 관해 알아 두도록 권하는 것
(B) 포스터 씨에게 지역 사회 행사를 알리는 것
(C) 체크인 정책과 관련된 문의 사항에 답변하는 것
(D) 입장권 구매에 대해 도움을 제공하는 것

해설 〈주제 및 목적〉
첫 단락에 숙박 예약 정보를 간단히 언급한 뒤, 두 번째 단락에서 5월 21일 토요일에 연례 설립자 기념 퍼레이드가 개최된다는 점을 알리며 (~ I want to make you aware that the city is holding its annual Founders Day Parade on Saturday, May 21) 관련 정보를 제공하고 있다. 이는 지역에서 개최되는 행사를 알리는 것이므로 (B)가 정답이다.

어휘 inform A about B A에게 B에 관해 알리다 community 지역 사회, 지역 공동체 respond to ~에 답변하다, 대응하다 inquiry 문의 policy 정책, 방침 offer ~을 제공하다 assistance 도움, 지원

159 앰버 밸리 호텔과 관련해 무엇이 암시되는가?
(A) 하나가 넘는 차량용 출입구가 있다.
(B) 5월 21일에 예약이 초과되어 있다.
(C) 프레스턴 스트리트에 신규 지점을 열었다.
(D) 퀸시 공원 근처에 위치해 있다.

해설 〈진위 확인 (세부 진위 유형)〉
세 번째 단락에서 글쓴이가 소속 호텔인 앰버 밸리 호텔을 we로 언급해 이 호텔이 퍼레이드 출발점 바로 근처에 위치해 있다는 사실을(~ because we are located right by the start of the parade ~) 알리고 있다. 이 출발점과 관련해, 두 번째 단락에 퍼레이드 행사가 퀸시 공원에서 시작된다는(It will begin at Quincy Park) 사실이 쓰여 있으므로 (D)가 정답이다.

어휘 more than ~가 넘는 vehicle 차량 overbook ~을 초과 예약하다 branch 지점, 지사 be located near ~ 근처에 위치해 있다

160 [1], [2], [3], [4]로 표기된 위치들 중에서 다음 문장이 들어가기에 가장 적절한 곳은 어디인가?

"하지만 귀하께서는 며칠 동안 도시에 계실 것이므로, 여전히 방문할 시간이 있을 것입니다."

(A) [1]
(B) [2]
(C) [3]
(D) [4]

해설 〈문장 넣기〉
제시된 문장은 대조 또는 반대를 나타낼 때 사용하는 though(하지만)와 함께 여전히 방문할 시간이 있을 것이라는 의미를 나타내므로 이와

반대되는 사실로서 방문할 수 없는 내용을 담은 문장 뒤에 위치해야 한다. 따라서 두 번째 단락에서 여러 업체 및 유명 박물관이 문을 닫는다는 사실을 말하는 문장 뒤에 표기된 [2]에 들어가 방문 기회가 여전히 있음을 알리는 흐름이 되어야 알맞으므로 (B)가 정답이다.

어휘 several 몇몇의, 여럿의 though (문장 중간이나 끝에서) 하지만

[161-163] 이메일

수신: 미공개 수신인
발신: 맥스트로닉스 엔터프라이즈 고객 관리부
날짜: 4월 18일
제목: 트랙스 2.0

소중한 고객 여러분,

161 저희 맥스트로닉스는 귀사에서 올해 초에 구입하신 예산 관리 스마트폰 앱 트랙스의 최신 버전에 대해 기쁘게 생각합니다. 귀사가 버전 2.0에서 기대하실 만한 몇 가지 사항들을 아래에서 확인해 보실 수 있습니다.

기업 할인 제도 (CDS)
고객들께서는 곧 저희 기업 할인 제도(CDS)를 통해 레스토랑과 호텔, 사무용품 매장을 비롯한 여러 곳에서 할인을 받으실 수 있게 됩니다. CDS는 5월 1일부터 시행되며, **162** 다음 주중으로 이 프로그램에 등록하기 위한 양식을 우편으로 받으시게 될 것입니다.

강화된 보안
5자리 비밀번호를 통한 접속뿐만 아니라, 지문 인식 기술을 활용한 별도의 보안 기능도 추가하실 수 있습니다. 이는 전화기를 분실하시는 경우에 귀사의 지출 데이터가 도난에 취약한 상태가 되지 않도록 보장해 드립니다.

24시간 지원 서비스
신입 직원들을 부서별 예산 업무에 **163** 관련시키거나 기록된 데이터를 이용하시는 데 어려움이 있으실 경우, 저희 채팅 서비스로 연락 주시기만 하면 됩니다. 친절하고 경험 많은 저희 직원들이 귀사에서 겪으실 수 있는 어떤 문제든 해결하도록 도와드릴 수 있습니다.

저희 맥스트로닉스는 고객 여러분께 항상 최고의 서비스를 제공해 드리기 위해 애쓰고 있으며, 저희 제품을 개선하는 데 지속적으로 전념할 것입니다.

안녕히 계십시오.

로랑 피쉐트

어휘 undisclosed 미공개의 recipient 수신인, 수령인 budget-tracking 예산 파악, 비용 추적 look forward to ~을 고대하다, 기대하다 scheme 제도, 계획 be able to do ~할 수 있다 go live 시행되다 form 양식, 서식 sign up for ~에 등록하다, ~을 신청하다 enhanced 강화된, 향상된 in addition to ~뿐만 아니라, ~ 외에도 PIN 비밀번호 access n. 접속, 접근, 이용 v. ~을 이용하다, ~에 접속하다 fingerprint recognition technology 지문 인식 기술 ensure that ~임을 보장하다 be susceptible to ~에 취약하다, ~의 대상이 되다 theft 도난, 절도 round-the-clock 24시간의 have trouble -ing ~하는 데 어려움을 겪다 associate A to B A를 B와 관련시키다 archived 기록으로 보관

된 contact ~에게 연락하다 experienced 경험 많은 agent 직원, 대리인 resolve ~을 해결하다 strive to do ~하기 위해 애쓰다 at all times 항상 continue ~을 지속하다 commitment 전념, 헌신 improve ~을 개선하다, 향상시키다

161 이메일은 왜 보내졌는가?
(A) 일부 작동 안내 사항을 정정하기 위해
(B) 단골 고객들에게 이용에 대해 감사하기 위해
(C) 휴대전화 어플리케이션에 관한 정보를 제공하기 위해
(D) 제품에 관한 의견을 요청하기 위해

해설 〈주제 및 목적〉
첫 단락에 스마트폰 앱의 최신 버전이 나온 사실과 함께 그 특징을 간략히 설명하고 있다(Here at Maxtronics, we're excited about the newest version of Trax, the budget-tracking smartphone app ~ Below you can find just a few of the things to look forward to in version 2.0.). 이는 어플리케이션에 관한 정보를 제공하기 위한 것이므로 (C)가 정답이다.

어휘 correct ~을 정정하다, 바로잡다 operating 작동의, 조작의 instructions 안내, 설명, 지시 loyal customer 단골 고객 patronage 애용, 후원 provide ~을 제공하다 feedback 의견

162 맥스트로닉스 고객들에게 무엇이 우송되는가?
(A) 할인 쿠폰
(B) 등록 양식
(C) 제품 카탈로그
(D) 보안 코드

해설 〈세부 사항〉
고객들에게 우송되는(being mailed) 것을 묻고 있으므로 고객들이 우편으로 받는 것과 관련된 정보를 찾아야 한다. 두 번째 단락에 다음 주 중으로 기업 할인 프로그램에 등록하기 위한 양식을 우편으로 받는다고(~ you will be sent a form by mail to sign up for this program sometime next week) 알리고 있으므로 (B)가 정답이다.

어휘 registration 등록 form 양식, 서식 catalog (제품 관련 설명을 담은) 카탈로그 security 보안, 경비

163 네 번째 단락, 두 번째 줄의 단어 "associating"과 의미가 가장 가까운 것은 무엇인가?
(A) 모집하는
(B) 연결시키는
(C) 포함하는
(D) 사람들과 어울리는

해설 〈동의어〉
해당 문장에서 associating 뒤에 신입 직원(new employees)과 부서별 예산(departmental budget)을 뜻하는 말들이 쓰여 있다. 이는 신입 직원들을 해당 업무에 관련 혹은 연관시키도록 한다는 의미이므로 '연결시키는'을 뜻하는 (B) connecting이 정답이다.

수신: 랜지트 달라비〈r_dalavi@loftis.net〉
발신: 네프탈렘 루웜〈luwam.n@worldhealthep.org〉
날짜: 2월 3일
제목: 분기 세미나

달라비 씨께,

저희 세계 보건 평등 재단(WHEF)에서는 2월 26일에 로스앤젤레스 컨벤션 센터에서 열리는 분기 세미나에 귀하를 초대합니다. 이 세미나는 두 파트로 나뉘어 제공될 것이며, **164** 그 명칭은 "개발도상국의 정수 처리 과정 개선을 위한 연합체 구성"입니다. —[1]—. **165** 귀하와 같이 불안전한 식수가 건강에 미치는 영향을 연구하고 계신 업계 전문가들께서 자선 단체들이 **164** 지방 정부 당국자들과의 협업을 통해 실행할 수 있는 가능한 해결책과 관련된 통찰을 공유하시게 될 것입니다. 공동의 목표에 초점을 맞추는 **164** 동반자 관계를 만들어냄으로써, 진척이 이뤄질 수 있습니다. —[2]—.

참석하시는 유명한 연사는 세계 보건 협회의 엘레나 렌츠 씨일 것입니다. —[3]—. 이 분께서는 분야 내에서 대단히 높은 평가를 받고 계시며, 그 업적에 대해 여러 국제적인 상을 수상하신 바 있습니다.

167 강연에 관심이 있으시다면, WHEF 웹 사이트를 통해 입장권을 구입하실 수 있습니다. —[4]—. **166** 이 강연을 보완하기 위한 정보를 담은 디지털 파일이 2월 20일에 저희 웹 사이트에 게시될 것입니다.

안녕히 계십시오.

네프탈렘 루웜
WHEF 교육 진행 책임자

어휘 quarterly 분기의 invite A to do A에게 ~하도록 초대하다 attend ~에 참석하다 present ~을 제공하다. 제시하다 be entitled A 명칭이 A이다. 제목이 A이다 form ~을 구성하다. 형성하다 alliance 연합(체) enhance ~을 개선하다, 강화하다 water purification 정수 process (처리) 과정 expert 전문가 effect of A on B A가 B에 미치는 영향 insight 통찰력 solution 해결책 implement ~을 실시하다, 시행하다 charity 자선 단체 in collaboration with ~와의 협업으로, 공동 작업으로 official 당국자, 관계자 focus on ~에 초점을 맞추다 make progress 진척시키다 distinguished 유명한, 뛰어난 highly respected 대단히 높은 평가를 받는, 크게 존경받는 field 분야 purchase ~을 구입하다 complement ~을 보완하다, 보충하다 post ~을 게시하다

164 세미나는 무엇과 관련될 것인가?
(A) 병입 장비의 새로운 발전
(B) 식수 기반 시설 수리를 위한 보조금 수령 기회
(C) 동반자 관계를 통한 수질 개선
(D) 물과 관련된 질병을 식별하는 방법

해설 〈주제 및 목적〉
세미나의 명칭 및 목표를 알리는 첫 단락에, 개발도상국의 정수 처리 과정 개선을 위한 연합체 구성(Forming Alliances to Enhance Water Purification Processes in Developing Countries)이라는 명칭과 함께 지방 정부와의 협업(~ in collaboration with local government officials)과 동반자 관계 형성(By creating partnerships ~)이라는 방식이 제시되어 있다. 따라서 이러한 관계 구축 및 목표를 언급한 (C)가 정답이다.

어휘 advance 발전, 진보 bottling 병입(병 안에 채워 넣는 작업) equipment 장비 grant 보조금 opportunity 기회 repair ~을 수리하다 infrastructure (사회) 기반 시설 improve ~을 개선하다, 향상시키다 through ~을 통해 partnership 동반자 관계, 제휴 관계 method 방법 identify ~을 식별하다, 확인하다 A-related A와 관련된 illness 질병

165 달라비 씨는 누구일 것 같은가?
(A) 업계 수상 경력자
(B) 의료 연구 전문가
(C) 자선 단체 기부자
(D) 정부 법률 전문가

해설 〈세부 사항〉
달라비 씨의 이름은 지문 상단에 수신인으로 언급되어 있으며, 첫 단락에 달라비 씨를 you로 지칭해 불안전한 식수가 건강에 미치는 영향을 연구하는 업계 전문가라고(Industry experts, who, like you, are studying the effects of unsafe drinking water on health ~) 지칭하고 있다. 이는 의료 연구 전문가가 하는 일로 볼 수 있으므로 (B)가 정답이다.

어휘 award winner 수상자, 수상 경력자 researcher 연구가 donor 기부자 charity 자선 단체

166 2월 20일에 무슨 일이 있을 예정인가?
(A) 한 연구 내용이 렌츠 씨에 의해 발표될 것이다.
(B) 입장권이 일부 고객에게 우송될 것이다.
(C) 보충 자료가 이용 가능하게 될 것이다.
(D) 등록 기간이 끝날 것이다.

해설 〈세부 사항〉
2월 20일이라는 날짜가 언급되는 마지막 문장에, 강연을 보완하기 위한 정보를 담은 디지털 파일이 2월 20일에 웹 사이트에 게시된다고 (Digital files with information to complement the lecture will be posted on our Web site on February 20) 알리고 있다. 이는 해당 보충 자료를 이용할 수 있는 날짜를 알리는 것이므로 (C)가 정답이다.

어휘 publish (출판물 등으로) ~을 발표하다, ~을 출간하다 mail ~을 우송하다 supplemental 보충하는 material 자료, 물품, 재료 available 이용 가능한 registration 등록

167 [1], [2], [3], [4]로 표기된 위치들 중에서 다음 문장이 들어가기에 가장 적절한 곳은 어디인가?
"또는, 컨벤션 센터로 곧장 연락하셔도 됩니다."
(A) [1]
(B) [2]
(C) [3]
(D) [4]

해설 〈문장 넣기〉
제시된 문장은 추가 방법을 알릴 때 사용하는 부사 Alternatively와 함께 컨벤션 센터로 곧장 연락해도 된다는 의미를 지니고 있다. 즉 특정 방법 한 가지를 제시하는 문장 뒤에 위치해 또 다른 방법을 알리는 흐름이 되어야 적절하다는 것을 나타낸다. 따라서 웹 사이트를 통한 입장권 구매 방법을 말하는 문장 뒤에 표기된 [4]에 들어가 입장권을 구할 수 있는 추가 방법을 말하는 흐름이 되어야 알맞으므로 (D)가 정답이다.

어휘 alternatively 또는, 그렇지 않으면 contact ~에게 연락하다 directly 곧장, 직접적으로

아키노부 이구치 [오후 2:11]	안녕하세요, 티지아노 그리고 코니 씨. **168** 두 분 중 한 분께서 다음 주 화요일에 은행 해외 송금 보고서를 작성해 주실 수 있으세요? 제가 신입 직원 오리엔테이션을 진행하고 있어서 제 모든 정규 업무를 처리할 수 없어요.
티지아노 샐타렐리 [오후 2:14]	저는 꽤 한참 동안 그 일을 하지 않았어요. 얼마나 오래 걸리는지 다시 한 번 알려 주시겠어요?
아키노 부이구치 [오후 2:15]	약 한 시간 정도인데, 그 서비스가 3시나 되어야 이용할 수 있어요.
코니 틸튼 [오후 2:16]	제 모든 일이 화요일 오후 중반까지 완료될 것이기 때문에 제가 처리할 수 있어요, 아키노부 씨.
티지아노 샐타렐리 [오후 2:18]	**170** 저는 그날 병원 예약 때문에 2시 30분에 나가 봐야 할 것 같아요.
아키노부 이구치 [오후 2:21]	괜찮아요, 알겠습니다. 코니 씨, 자원해 주셔서 감사합니다!
코니 틸튼 [오후 2:22]	도와드릴 수 있어서 기쁩니다. **171** 필요한 양식을 회사 웹 사이트에서 다운로드하기만 하면 되나요?
아키노부 이구치 [오후 2:23]	**171** 시도로프 씨께서 양식을 갖고 계시긴 하지만, 제가 한 부 받아 드릴게요. **169** 금요일 회의 시간에 봐요, 코니 씨. 그때 갖다 드리겠습니다.

어휘 either 둘 중 하나 fill out ~을 작성하다 international transfer 해외 송금 task 업무, 일 lead ~을 진행하다, 이끌다 in quite a while 꽤 한참 동안 remind ~에게 다시 한 번 알려 주다, 상기시키다 take ~의 시간이 걸리다 not A until B B나 되어야 A하다 available 이용 가능한 have A p.p. A가 ~되게 하다 by ~쯤, ~ 무렵에 handle ~을 처리하다, 다루다 appointment 예약, 약속 volunteer 자원하다, 자진해서 하다 form 양식, 서식 then 그때, 그렇다면, 그리고 나서

168 이구치 씨는 왜 동료 직원들에게 문자 메시지를 보냈는가?
(A) 조언을 좀 해 주기 위해
(B) 추가 직무 설명서를 요청하기 위해
(C) 자신의 직무에 대해 도움을 요청하기 위해
(D) 연락처를 교환하도록 요청하기 위해

해설 〈주제 및 목적〉
첫 메시지에서 이구치 씨가 나머지 두 사람 중 한 명이 은행 해외 송금 보고서를 작성할 수 있는지 물으면서 신입 직원 오리엔테이션 때문에 자신이 할 수 없는(Could either of you fill out the bank's international transfer report next Tuesday? I can't do all of my regular tasks ~) 상황임을 알리고 있다. 이는 업무에 대한 도움을 요청하는 것에 해당되므로 (C)가 정답이다.

어휘 coworker 동료 (직원) request ~을 요청하다, 요구하다 employee manual 직무 설명서 ask for ~을 요청하다 help with ~에 대한 도움 duty 직무, 임무 ask A to do A에게 ~하도록 요청하다 exchange ~을 교환하다 contact information 연락처

169 틸튼 씨와 관련해 무엇이 암시되는가?
(A) 병원 예약 때문에 일찍 퇴근할 것이다.
(B) 이번 주 후반에 이구치 씨와 만날 예정이다.
(C) 평소에 해외 은행 송금 업무를 처리한다.
(D) 직원 오리엔테이션 시간에 발표할 계획이다.

해설 〈진위 확인 (전체 진위 유형)〉
맨 마지막 메시지에서 이구치 씨가 코니 틸튼 씨에게 금요일 회의 시간에 보자고(See you at the meeting on Friday, Connie) 언급하는 말이 쓰여 있다. 이는 틸튼 씨가 이번 주 후반에 이구치 씨와 만난다는 뜻이므로 (B)가 정답이다.

어휘 appointment 예약, 약속 be scheduled to do ~할 예정이다 meet with (약속하여) ~와 만나다 ordinarily 평소에, 보통 handle ~을 처리하다, 다루다 plan to do ~할 계획이다 give a presentation 발표하다

170 오후 2시 21분에, 이구치 씨가 "I get it"이라고 쓸 때 무엇을 의미하는 것 같은가?
(A) 샐타렐리 씨의 상황을 이해하고 있다.
(B) 틸튼 씨가 경험이 더 많다고 생각하고 있다.
(C) 샐타렐리 씨의 컨디션을 우려하고 있다.
(D) 한 가지 물품의 배송을 기다리고 있다.

해설 〈의도 파악〉
앞선 메시지에서 샐타렐리 씨가 병원 예약 때문에 2시 30분에 나가야 한다고(I'm afraid I'm leaving for a doctor's appointment at 2:30 that day) 알리는 것에 대해 이구치 씨가 괜찮다는(No problem) 말과 함께 알겠다고(I get it) 대답하는 상황이다. 이는 샐타렐리 씨의 입장을 이해한다는 의미로 말하는 답변에 해당되므로 (A)가 정답이다.

어휘 situation 상황, 사정 be concerned about ~에 대해 우려하다, 걱정하다 expect ~을 기다리다, ~을 기대하다

171 시도로프 씨와 관련해 무엇이 암시되는가?
(A) 웹 사이트에 일부 정보를 업로드할 것이다.
(B) 회사의 신입 직원들 중 한 명이다.
(C) 마지막 순간에 몇몇 업무를 할당했다.
(D) 양식을 제공하는 일을 맡고 있다.

해설 〈진위 확인 (세부 진위 유형)〉
시도로프 씨의 이름이 언급되는 마지막 메시지에서, 시도로프 씨가 양식을 갖고 있다고(Mr. Sidorov has the forms ~) 알리고 있다. 이는 바로 앞선 메시지에서 웹 사이트를 통해 다운로드하면 되는지 묻는 것에 대해 양식을 배부하는 사람, 즉 시도로프 씨에게서 받아야 한다는 뜻을 나타내는 것이므로 (D)가 정답이다.

어휘 assign ~을 할당하다, 배정하다 task 업무, 일 at the last minute 마지막 순간에 be responsible for ~을 맡고 있다, ~에 대한 책임이 있다 provide ~을 제공하다 form 양식, 서식

[172-175] 공지

오그덴 엔터프라이즈 전 직원에게 전하는 공지

우리가 환경에 미치는 영향을 줄이기 위한 노력의 일환으로, **172** 오그덴 엔터프라이즈 경영팀은 전 직원에게 우리 회사의 새로운 환경 책임 계획을 준수하도록 요청드립니다.

172 우리는 회사의 재활용 프로그램을 확대해 단지 음료수 병뿐만 아니라 모든 종류의 플라스틱을 포함할 것입니다. 쓰레기통은 직원 라운지에 놓여 있습니다.

172 우리 구매 담당 부서는 재활용 용지, 보충 가능한 잉크 카트리지, 그리고 화학 성분이 없는 화이트보드용 마커로 교체할 것입니다.

직원들에게 양면 복사를 하도록 권장하는 것뿐만 아니라, 인쇄를 하는 대신 **173** 회사 인트라넷에 모든 일일 업무 요약 정보를 게시함으로써 용지 낭비도 줄여 나갈 것입니다.

사무실에서 근무하실 때 에너지 소비량을 줄여야 한다는 점을 기억하시기 바랍니다.

- 다이코-360 난방 시스템이 항상 화씨 65도로 설정되어 있도록 유지해야 하며, 절대적으로 필요할 경우에만 실내 난방기를 사용하십시오.

- 일정 시간 미사용 상태가 되면 대기 모드로 바뀌도록 개인 데스크탑 컴퓨터의 전원 관리 설정을 변경하십시오.

- **175** 회의실에서 나갈 때 반드시 전등, 천장 선풍기, 그리고 발표용 장비(프로젝터, 음향 시스템, 그리고 마이크)를 끄도록 하십시오.

- 효율성을 개선하기 위해, 다이코-360 장비는 매일 점검될 것입니다. **174** 기타 모든 사무용 장비는 분기마다 한 번씩 점검됩니다.

여러분의 협조에 감사드립니다.

어휘 in an effort to do ~하기 위한 노력의 일환으로 impact on ~에 미치는 영향 ask that ~하도록 요청하다 follow ~을 준수하다, 따르다 responsibility 책임(감) initiative 계획 expand ~을 확대하다, 확장하다 include ~을 포함하다 beverage 음료 bin 쓰레기통 be located in ~에 위치해 있다 purchasing department 구매 담당 부서 refillable 보

충 가능한 chemical-free 화학 성분이 없는 in addition to ~뿐만 아니라, ~ 외에도 encourage A to do A에게 ~하도록 권장하다, 장려하다 cut down on ~을 줄이다(= reduce) by (방법) ~함으로써, ~해서 post ~을 게시하다 briefing 요약(된 정보) rather than ~하는 대신, ~가 아니라 consumption 소비(량) keep A p.p. A를 계속 ~된 상태로 유지하다 at all times 항상 space heater 실내 난방기 if necessary 필요 시에 setting (기기 등의) 설정 so that (목적) ~하도록 go into (상태, 설정 등이) ~로 바뀌다, ~로 접어들다 inactivity 미사용, 비활성화 make sure to do 반드시 ~하도록 하다 ceiling 천장 equipment 장비 improve ~을 개선하다, 향상시키다 efficiency 효율성 quarter 분기 cooperation 협조, 협동

172 공지의 목적은 무엇인가?
(A) 일부 정부 규정을 간략히 설명하는 것
(B) 직원들에게 의견을 요청하는 것
(C) 한 계획의 세부 사항을 살펴보는 것
(D) 행사에 필요한 자원 봉사자를 모집하는 것

해설 〈주제 및 목적〉
첫 문장에서 전 직원에게 회사의 새로운 환경 책임 계획을 준수하도록 요청한다고(~ the Ogden Enterprises management team asks that all employees follow our new Environmental Responsibility Initiative) 알린 뒤로, 해당 정책을 상세히 설명하는 흐름이다. 따라서 이 계획의 세부 사항을 살펴보는 것이 목적임을 알 수 있으므로 (C)가 정답이다.

어휘 outline ~을 간략히 설명하다, 개괄적으로 말하다 regulation 규정, 규제 ask A for B A에게 B를 요청하다 opinion 의견 review ~을 살펴보다, 검토하다 details 세부 사항, 상세 정보 initiative n. 계획 recruit ~을 모집하다 volunteer 자원 봉사자

173 회사가 쓰레기를 줄이는 한 가지 방법으로 무엇이 언급되는가?
(A) 지역에서 용품을 구입하는 것
(B) 한 제품의 포장재를 변경하는 것
(C) 직원 라운지에서 그릇을 재사용하는 것
(D) 온라인으로 정보를 공유하는 것

해설 〈진위 확인 (세부 진위 유형)〉
네 번째 단락에 인쇄를 하는 대신 회사 인트라넷에 정보를 게시할 것이라는(~ we will also cut down on paper waste by posting all daily briefings on our company intranet) 내용이 쓰여 있는데, 이는 온라인으로 정보를 공유하는 일에 해당되므로 (D)가 정답이다.

어휘 reduce ~을 줄이다, 감소시키다 purchase ~을 구입하다 supplies 용품, 물품 locally 지역 내에서, 지역적으로 packaging 포장(재) reuse ~을 재사용하다 share ~을 공유하다

174 개인 컴퓨터가 얼마나 자주 점검될 것인가?
(A) 매일
(B) 일주일마다
(C) 격월로
(D) 분기마다

해설 〈세부 사항〉

장비 점검 주기가 언급되는 마지막 단락 네 번째 항목에, 다이코-360 장비 외의 모든 사무용 장비는 분기마다 한 번씩 점검된다고(~ the Dyco-360 equipment will be checked daily. All other office equipment will be checked once a quarter) 쓰여 있다. 따라서 개인 컴퓨터는 분기마다 한 번씩 점검되는 것으로 볼 수 있으므로 (D)가 정답이다.

어휘 inspect ~을 점검하다, 조사하다 every other month 격월로, 두 달에 한 번 quarterly 분기마다, 분기별로

175 회의실에 쓰이는 장비로 무엇이 언급되지 않는가?

(A) 노트북 컴퓨터
(B) 프로젝터
(C) 천장 선풍기
(D) 마이크

해설 〈세부 사항〉
회의실 장비가 제시되는 다섯 번째 단락 세 번째 항목에, (~ turn off the lights, ceiling fan, and presentation equipment (projector, sound system, and microphone) when leaving the meeting room) 천장 선풍기와 프로젝터, 그리고 마이크는 언급되고 있지만 노트북 컴퓨터는 제시되어 있지 않으므로 (A)가 정답이다.

어휘 equipment 장비 ceiling 천장

[176-180] 이메일과 티켓

수신: 카트린 게르슈타인〈k_gerstein@ackermanninc.de〉
발신: 조나스 드레셔〈jonasdrescher@besondere.de〉
날짜: 1월 3일
제목: 프랑크푸르트 여행

게르슈타인 씨께,

베손데르 철도는 1월 한 달 동안에 걸쳐 판촉 행사를 운영하고 있습니다. **176** 저희는 더 많은 분들께서 저희 1등석 구역을 한 번 이용해 보시기를 바라고 있기 때문에, 고객들께 단 30유로의 비용으로 일반 티켓을 1등석 티켓으로 변경하실 수 있는 기회를 제공해 드리고 있습니다. 추가로, 이 특가를 이용하시는 분들께서는 또한 **177** 베손데르 브랜드의 무료 토트백도 받으시게 됩니다. 이 가방은 가죽 끈이 달린 고품질의 캔버스로 만들어진 제품이며, 앞면에 저희 로고가 인쇄되어 있습니다. 가방이 비어 있을 경우, **177** 소형 사이즈로 접어 두실 수 있으며, 핸드백 또는 재킷 주머니에 쉽게 넣으실 수 있습니다.

178 현재 귀하의 여행에 대해 여전히 이용 가능한 1등석 좌석이 있습니다.

178 F561	출발, 함부르크	1월 5일, 오전 7:38	도착, 프랑크푸르트	오후 2:09	1회 환승

또한 열차 환승을 필요로 하지 않는 것으로 조금 늦게 출발하는 열차로 변경하실 수도 있습니다.

180 F563	출발, 함부르크	1월 5일, 오전 8:28	**180** 도착, 프랑크푸르트	**180** 오후 2:41	0회 환승

이 특가 제공 서비스는 온라인으로 이용하실 수 없다는 점에 유의하시기 바랍니다. **178** 귀하의 티켓을 변경하고자 하실 경우, 기차역에 일찍 도착하셔서 매표소에 들러 주시기 바랍니다. 수하물 제한과 관련된 질문이 있으시면, 0333-555-2121번으로 저희 전화 상담 서비스로 전화 주십시오.

저희 베손데르 철도의 고객이 되어 주신 것에 대해 감사드립니다.

안녕히 계십시오.

조나스 드레셔
고객 서비스 직원

178 고객 성명: 카트린 게르슈타인	확인 번호: 189765328
180 열차: F563 출발: 함부르크	**179** 구역: A (1등석)
날짜: 1월 5일 도착: 프랑크푸르트	좌석: 15C

보관 공간에 더 큰 가방을 위한 공간을 남겨 둘 수 있도록 작은 가방들은 머리 위쪽의 선반 또는 좌석 밑에 놓아 주시기 바랍니다. **179** 출발 승강장은 탑승하시기 약 15분 전에 공지될 것입니다. 탑승 정보를 보실 수 있도록 디지털 화면을 확인하시기 바랍니다.

어휘 journey 여행 run ~을 운영하다, 가동하다 promotion 판촉, 홍보 throughout ~ 동안에 걸쳐 want A to do A가 ~하기를 원하다 offer A B A에게 B를 제공하다 standard 일반의, 표준의 in addition 추가로, 게다가 take advantage of ~을 이용하다, 활용하다 receive ~을 받다 free 무료 high-quality 고품질의 leather 가죽 strap 끈, 줄 have A p.p. A가 ~되게 하다 on the front 앞면에 compress A into B A를 B한 상태로 꾹 누르다, 압축하다 make A 형용사 A를 ~한 상태로 만들다 fit in (크기 등이) ~에 꼭 들어맞다, 적합하다 available 이용 가능한 current 현재의 switch to ~로 변경하다, 바꾸다 slightly 조금, 약간 require ~을 필요로 하다 note that ~라는 점에 유의하다 would like to do ~하고자 하다, ~하고 싶다 arrive 도착하다 stop by ~에 들르다 restriction 제한 helpline 전화 상담 서비스 place ~을 놓다, 두다 overhead 머리 위쪽의 leave room 공간을 남겨놓다 storage 보관, 저장 departure 출발 announce ~을 공지하다, 알리다 approximately 약, 대략 prior to ~ 전에, ~에 앞서 boarding 탑승

176 드레셔 씨는 왜 게르슈타인 씨에게 이메일을 썼는가?
(A) 비용 지불을 마무리 짓는 것을 상기시키기 위해
(B) 철도 회사의 수하물 정책을 설명하기 위해
(C) 업그레이드를 받도록 권장하기 위해
(D) 일정 지연 문제를 알리기 위해

해설 〈주제 및 목적〉
첫 지문인 이메일의 첫 단락을 보면, 고객들에게 단 30유로의 비용으로 일반 티켓을 1등석 티켓으로 변경할 수 있는 기회를 제공하고 있다고 (~ we are offering customers the chance to change from a standard ticket to a first-class ticket for just €30) 알리는 것이 목적에 해당된다. 이는 좌석 업그레이드를 하도록 권하는 말이므로 (C)가 정답이다.

어휘 remind A to do A에게 ~하도록 상기시키다, 다시 알리다 finalize ~을 마무리 짓다, 최종 확정하다 payment 지불(액) explain ~을 설명하다 policy 정책, 방침 encourage A to do A에게 ~하도록 권장하다, 장려하다 inform A of B A에게 B를 알리다 delay 지연, 지체

177 토트백에 관해 언급된 것은 무엇인가?
(A) 완전히 가죽으로 만들어졌다.
(B) 고객 성명이 인쇄될 것이다.
(C) 여러 개의 내부 주머니가 있다.
(D) 작은 공간에 잘 들어갈 수 있다.

해설 〈진위 확인 (세부 진위 유형)〉
첫 지문 첫 단락의 후반부에, 그 가방을 it으로 지칭해 작게 접어서 핸드백이나 재킷 주머니에 쉽게 넣을 수 있다는(~ it can be compressed into a compact size, making it easy to fit in your handbag or jacket pocket) 내용이 있으므로 이와 같은 특징에 해당되는 (D)가 정답이다.

어휘 be made of ~로 만들어지다 entirely 완전히, 전부 leather 가죽 several 여럿의, 몇몇의 interior 내부의 fit into ~에 잘 들어맞다

178 게르슈타인 씨에 관해 무엇이 사실일 것 같은가?
(A) 전화 상담 서비스로 전화했다.
(B) 온라인으로 원래의 티켓을 구입했다.

(C) 매표소를 방문했다.

(D) 우수 고객 프로그램에 등록했다.

해설 〈지문 연계〉

첫 지문의 예약 정보에는 열차 번호 F561이라고 적혀 있는데, 두 번째 지문의 티켓을 보면 열차 번호 F563의 1등석으로 티켓을 변경했음을 알 수 있다. 첫 지문 하단에, 티켓을 변경하고자 할 경우 기차역에 일찍 도착해서 매표소에 들르라고(If you would like to change your ticket, please arrive early at the station and stop by the ticketing office) 알리고 있으므로 게르슈타인 씨가 매표소에 들렀다는 것을 알 수 있다. 따라서, (C)가 정답이다.

어휘 helpline 전화 상담 서비스 purchase ~을 구입하다 original 원래의, 애초의 sign up for ~에 등록하다, 가입하다 loyalty program 우수 고객 프로그램

179 티켓이 게르슈타인 씨의 열차 여행에 관해 나타내는 것은 무엇인가?

(A) 탑승객들이 여권을 필요로 할 것이다.

(B) 승강장이 아직 선택되지 않았다.

(C) 초과 수하물에 대한 공간이 없다.

(D) 이른 오후 시간에 출발할 것이다.

해설 〈진위 확인 (전체 진위 유형)〉

두 번째 지문에 출발 승강장이 탑승하기 약 15분 전에 공지된다는(The departure platform will be announced approximately fifteen minutes prior to boarding) 내용이 있는데, 이는 해당 승강장이 아직 정해지지 않았음을 의미하는 것이므로 (B)가 정답이다.

어휘 passenger 탑승객 select ~을 선택하다 room (관사 없이) 공간, 여지 excess 초과한 depart 출발하다, 떠나다

180 게르슈타인 씨는 언제 프랑크푸르트에 도착할 것인가?

(A) 오전 7:38에

(B) 오전 8:28에

(C) 오후 2:09에

(D) 오후 2:41에

해설 〈지문 연계〉

두 번째 지문 상단에 게르슈타인 씨의 열차 번호가 F563으로 표기되어 있는데, 첫 지문 중간 부분의 일정표에 F563 열차의 프랑크푸르트 도착 시간이 오후 2시 41분으로 쓰여 있으므로 (D)가 정답이다.

어휘 arrive 도착하다

[181-185] 이메일과 영수증

수신: orders@starcroftcl.com
발신: gallagherspence@regalantiques.net
날짜: 3월 16일
제목: 주문 번호 97823

관계자께,

제가 스타크로프트 클리닝 사에 최근 주문한 사항과 관련해 이메일을 씁니다. **181** 저는 3월 11일 오전에 주문했으며, 그것이 다음 날 도착한 것을 보고 기분 좋게 놀랐습니다. 이 서비스가 훌륭하긴 했지만, 제품 자체에 대해서도 동일하게 말씀 드리지는 못할 것 같습니다. 청소용 천은 처음 사용한 후 구멍이 생겼습니다. 웹 사이트에 쓰여진 것과는 달리 욕실용 거품 세척제 통에는 대리석에 사용할 수 없다고 쓰여 있어서 심지어 한 번도 사용을 해 보지 않았습니다. 게다가, 왁스 색상은 상자에 보여지는 것과 아주 많이 달랐습니다. 아쉽게도, **184** 러스틱 파인 색상 제품 상자는 버렸지만, 다크 오크 색상 제품 상자는 여전히 갖고 있습니다.

184 저는 A에서 D에 해당되는 제품들에 대해 환불받을 수 있도록 반품하고자 합니다. 이 제품들을 우편으로 돌려보내는 과정을 저에게 알려 주시기 바랍니다. **182** 제 친구가 귀사를 이용해 보도록 권해 주었을 때, 새로운 공급업체를 찾게 되어 기뻤습니다. 하지만, 앞으로 귀사의 서비스를 **183** 계속 이용할 것을 예상하지 않고 있습니다.

안녕히 계십시오.

스펜서 갤러거

스타크로프트 클리닝
www.starcroftcl.com
— 가정용 및 상업용 청소용품 —

고객 영수증		주문 날짜: 3월 11일		주문 번호: 97823
	제품 설명	수량 / 품목당 가격	항목별 총액	
A	30 온스 셀프 포밍 욕실 세척제	2 / 3.79달러	7.58달러	
B	15 온스 왁스 광택제(다크 오크)	1 / 12.99달러	12.99달러	
C	**184** 15 온스 왁스 광택제(러스틱 파인)	1 / 12.99달러	12.99달러	
D	22 온스 카펫 얼룩 제거제	2 / 5.79달러	11.58달러	
E	3개 들이 내구성이 뛰어난 청소용 천	1 / 4.99달러	4.99달러	
	185 저희 스타크로프트 클리닝은 현재 반복적으로 사용하시는 제품에 대해 매일 1일에 자동 배송 서비스를 제공해 드리고 있으므로 계속 재주문하실 필요가 없습니다. 이 서비스를 설정하는 방법을 알아보시려면, 저희 웹 사이트를 방문하시기 바랍니다.	소계	50.13달러	
		쿠폰 코드 왁스5	− 1.30달러	
		일반 배송	2.50달러	
		총계	51.33달러	

참고: **184** 반품은 반드시 30일 이내에 이뤄져야 하며, 원래의 포장에 넣어 반품되어야 합니다.

어휘 regarding ~와 관련해 recent 최근의 order 주문(품) place an order 주문하다 arrive 도착하다 foaming 거품 (생성) marble 대리석 even though ~이기는 하지만 in addition 게다가, 추가로 unfortunately 아쉽게도, 안타깝게도 throw away ~을 버리다 return ~을 반납하다, 반납하다 refund 환불 let A know B A에게 B를 알리다 process 과정 mail back ~을 우편으로 돌려보내다 supplier 공급업체 expect to do ~할 것으로 예상하다, 기대하다 carry on ~을 계속하다 supplies 용품, 물품 domestic 가정의 receipt 영수증 description 설명 quantity 수량 durable 내구성이 뛰어난 automated 자동의, 자동화된 on a recurring basis 반복적으로 keep -ing 계속 ~하다 find out ~을 알아내다, 파악하다 how to do ~하는 법 set up ~을 설정하다 original 원래의, 애초의 packaging 포장(재)

181 갤러거 씨의 제품과 관련해 무엇이 암시되는가?

(A) 유통 기한이 지난 제품이었다.

(B) 엉뚱한 브랜드를 포함하고 있었다.

(C) 3월 12일에 도착했다.

(D) 세 가지 종류의 왁스를 포함하고 있었다.

해설 〈진위 확인 (전체 진위 유형)〉

갤러거 씨가 작성한 이메일인 첫 지문 시작 부분에, 3월 11일 오전에 주문한 제품이 다음 날 도착했다는(I placed an order on the morning of March 11, and I was pleasantly surprised that it arrived the next day) 내용이 있다. 따라서 3월 12일에 주문 제품이 도착했다는 것을 알 수 있으므로 (C)가 정답이다.

어휘 expired 기한이 지난, 만료된 contain ~을 포함하다, 담고 있다 arrive 도착하다 include ~을 포함하다

182 갤러거 씨는 자신의 이메일에서 무엇을 언급하는가?

(A) 고객 콜 센터에 연락하는 데 어려움을 겪었다.

(B) 몇몇 제품을 직접 매장으로 가져갈 것이다.

(C) 해당 업체에 대해 추천을 받았다.

(D) 해당 회사의 웹 사이트에 후기를 작성할 계획이다.

해설 〈진위 확인 (전체 진위 유형)〉

갤러거 씨가 작성한 이메일인 첫 지문 두 번째 단락에, 친구가 해당 업체를 이용해 보도록 권해 주었을 때(When my friend suggested that I use your business ~) 새로운 공급업체를 찾게 되어 기뻤다는 내용이 있다. 이는 친구로부터 추천을 받았음을 나타내는 말이므로 (C)가 정답이다.

어휘 have trouble -ing ~하는 데 어려움을 겪다 contact ~에게 연락하다 in person 직접 가서 receive ~을 받다 recommendation 추천(서) plan to do ~할 계획이다 review 후기, 의견, 평가

183 이메일에서, 두 번째 단락, 세 번째 줄의 표현 "carry on"과 의미가 가장 가까운 것은 무엇인가?

(A) 지지하다

(B) 만들어내다

(C) 운송하다

(D) 지속하다

해설 〈동의어〉

해당 문장에서 carry on 앞뒤 부분을 읽어 보면, 앞으로 상대방 업

체를 이용할 것으로 예상하고 있지 않다는 의미를 나타낸다. 따라서 carry on이 이용하는 일을 계속하는 것을 나타내는 표현임을 알 수 있으므로 '지속하다'를 뜻하는 (D) continue가 정답이다.

184 갤러거 씨는 어느 제품을 갖고 있어야 할 것 같은가?
(A) 셀프 포밍 욕실 세척제
(B) 다크 오크 왁스 광택제
(C) 러스틱 파인 왁스 광택제
(D) 카펫 얼룩 제거제

해설 〈지문 연계〉
첫 지문 첫 번째 단락 후반부와 두 번째 단락 시작 부분에, 갤러거 씨는 러스틱 파인 색상 제품 상자를 버린(~ I threw away the box for the Rustic Pine color ~) 사실과 A에서 D에 해당되는 제품을 반품하고 환불받고 싶다는(I would like to return items A–D ~) 뜻을 나타내고 있다. 그리고 두 번째 지문 도표의 C 항목을 보면 러스틱 파인 색상 제품이 광택제로(15-oz. Wax Polish (Rustic Pine)) 표기되어 있고, 하단에는 원래의 포장 용기가 없는 제품은(~ without all of their original packaging) 반품할 수 없다고 적혀 있다. 따라서 반품이 불가한 러스틱 파인 왁스 광택제는 그대로 갖고 있어야 한다는 사실을 알 수 있으므로 (C)가 정답이다.

185 스타크로프트 클리닝 고객이 이용할 수 있는 것은 무엇인가?
(A) 무료 제품 샘플
(B) 정기적인 월간 배송
(C) 단골 고객 포인트 획득
(D) 익일 배송 보장 서비스

해설 〈세부 사항〉
두 번째 지문 도표 왼쪽 하단에, 정기적으로 사용하는 제품에 대해 매달 1일에 자동 배송 서비스를 제공하고 있다는 내용(Starcroft Cleaning now offers automated shipments on the first of every month ~)이 있으므로 (B)가 정답이다.

어휘 available to ~가 이용할 수 있는 free 무료의 regular 정기적인, 정규의 loyalty point 단골 고객 포인트 earning 획득, 소득 guaranteed 보장된 overnight delivery 익일 배송, 야간 배송

[186-190] 기사와 웹 페이지, 그리고 이메일

런던 (8월 1일) - **186** 불과 5년 만에 한 개에서 세 개의 지사로 컨설팅 회사를 확장해 온 리더십 전문가 크레이그 레넌 씨가 최근 연설 투어로 영국 전역의 청중들을 방문한다.

이번 투어는 8월 3일과 4일 이틀 연속으로 캔터베리 강당에서 런던을 기점으로 하는 강연과 함께 시작된다. **187** 그 후, 레넌 씨는 8월 5일에 브리스톨에 위치한 굿윈 플라자에서 연설할 것이다. 그 다음 날인 8월 6일에, 이 연설 투어는 에든버러에 위치한 애쉬포드 대학 강당에 들르게 된다. 그 이후, 레넌 씨는 8월 7일에 셰필드에 위치한 폭스 애비뉴 지역 문화 센터에서 강연할 예정이다. 이 투어의 종착지는 8월 8일 맨체스터의 빅토리아 오페라 하우스이다.

www.lennonleadership.co.uk/augustevents				
홈	크레이그 씨의 이야기	8월 행사	추천 후기	연락처

최종 확정된 크레이그 레넌 씨의 8월 일정표

행사 도시	날짜	강연 주제	시작 시간	입장권
런던	8월 3일	직장 내의 다양성 증진	오후 7:00	구매
런던	8월 4일	의사소통의 어려움과 마주하기	오후 7:30	구매
187 브리스톨	8월 5일	**187** 직원 동기 부여 및 유지 방법	오후 7:00	구매
에든버러	8월 6일	직원 업무 능력 평가	오후 7:00	구매
189 셰필드	**189** 8월 7일	스트레스 없는 과도기	오후 8:00	구매
맨체스터	8월 8일	의사소통의 어려움과 마주하기	오후 7:30	구매

"구매" 버튼을 클릭하시면 개별 행사장의 입장권 판매 페이지로 넘어 갑니다.

수신: 멀린 티보 〈mtebo@miracle-consulting.co.uk〉
발신: 사티야 애너갤 〈s.anagal@lennonleadership.co.uk〉
날짜: 8월 12일
제목: 크레이그 레넌

티보 씨께,

188 레넌 씨께 귀사의 연례 전문 능력 개발 워크숍에서 연설하시도록 요청해 주셔서 감사드립니다. 레넌 씨께서 이 기회에 대해 대단히 큰 관심을 지니고 계시기는 하지만, 이미 일정을 잡아 놓으신 다른 개인 행사와 겹치게 됩니다.

189 귀하께서 최근 셰필드에서 있었던 연설이 즐거우셨다는 점을 기쁘게 생각하며, 향후에 있을 여러 행사에도 참석하시기를 바랍니다. 귀사의 워크숍의 대체 날짜가 있으신 경우, **190** 주저하지 마시고 저에게 공유해 주시면, 그와 관련하여 레넌 씨께 확인해 보도록 하겠습니다.

안녕히 계십시오.

사티야 애너갤
레넌 리더십

어휘 expert 전문가 build up ~을 확장하다, 증강하다, 강화하다 branch 지사, 지점 audience 청중, 관객, 시청자 back-to-back 연속된 A-based A를 중심으로 하는, 기반으로 하는 following 다음의 give a lecture 강연하다 testimonial (이용 고객이 작성한) 추천 후기 finalize ~을 최종 확정하다 promote ~을 증진하다, 촉진하다 diversity 다양성 face v. ~와 마주하다 motivation 동기 부여 how to do ~하는 법 maintain ~을 유지하다 assess ~을 평가하다 performance 업무 능력, 성과, 실적 keep A 형용사 A를 ~한 상태로 유지하다 transition 과도기, 이행, 전환 free from ~가 없는 be redirected to ~로 넘어가다 individual 개별의 venue 행사장, 개최 장소 invite A to do A에게 ~하도록 요청하다 annual 연례적인, 해마다의 professional development 전문 능력 개발, 직무 능력 개발 be highly interested in ~에 대단히 관심이 크다 opportunity 기회 conflict with (일정 등이) ~와 겹치다 attend ~에 참석하다 alternative 대체의, 대안의 hesitate to do ~하기를 주저하다, 망설이다 share A with B A를 B와 공유하다 check with ~에게 문의하다, ~와 상담하다

186 레넌 씨와 관련해 무엇이 언급되는가?
(A) 사업체가 세 개의 지사를 보유한 곳으로 성장했다.
(B) 강연이 대학생들에게 무료이다.
(C) 일 년에 한 번씩 연설 투어를 한다.
(D) 런던에서 태어나고 자랐다.

해설 〈진위 확인 (세부 진위 유형)〉
레넌 씨의 이름이 처음 언급되는 첫 지문 첫 단락에, 불과 5년 만에 한 개에서 세 개의 지사로 회사를 확장한(~ has built up his consulting business from one to three branches ~) 사실이 쓰여 있으므로 (A)가 정답이다.

어휘 grow 성장하다, 자라다 location 지사, 지점, 위치 free 무료인 born 태어난 raise ~을 기르다, 키우다

187 청중들은 어디에서 직원에게 동기를 부여하는 것과 관련해 배울 수 있는가?

(A) 굿윈 플라자에서
(B) 애쉬포드 대학 강당에서
(C) 폭스 애비뉴 지역 문화 센터에서
(D) 빅토리아 오페라 하우스에서

해설 〈지문 연계〉
두 번째 지문의 도표 세 번째 항목에 직원에게 동기를 부여하는 일(Staff Motivation and How to Maintain It)이 주제로 언급되어 있고 장소는 브리스톨(Bristol)로 표기되어 있다. 이와 관련해, 첫 지문 두 번째 단락에 8월 5일에 브리스톨에 위치한 굿윈 플라자에서 연설하는(Then Lennon will speak at the Goodwin Plaza in Bristol on 5 August) 일정이 언급되어 있으므로 (A)가 정답이다.

어휘 audience members 청중, 관객, 시청자 motivate ~에게 동기를 부여하다

188 애너갤 씨는 왜 이메일을 보냈는가?

(A) 입장권 가격을 확인해 주기 위해
(B) 실수에 대해 사과하기 위해
(C) 제안을 거절하기 위해
(D) 신규 서비스를 홍보하기 위해

해설 〈주제 및 목적〉
세 번째 지문 첫 번째 단락을 보면, 레넌 씨에게 연설하도록 요청한 것에 대해 감사하다는 인사말과 함께 이미 일정을 잡아 놓은 다른 개인 행사와 겹치게 된다는(Thank you for inviting Mr. Lennon to speak ~ it conflicts with another private event that he already has scheduled) 사실을 알리고 있다. 이는 일정상의 문제로 거절할 수밖에 없다는 뜻을 나타내는 말이므로 (C)가 정답이다.

어휘 confirm ~을 확인해 주다 apologize for ~에 대해 사과하다 decline ~을 거절하다 offer 제안, 제공 promote ~을 홍보하다

189 티보 씨는 어느 날짜에 레넌 씨의 행사 중 하나에 참석했는가?

(A) 8월 5일
(B) 8월 6일
(C) 8월 7일
(D) 8월 8일

해설 〈지문 연계〉
티보 씨의 이름은 세 번째 지문 상단에 수신인으로 표기되어 있으며, 이 지문 두 번째 단락에 티보 씨를 you로 지칭해 셰필드에서 있었던 연설을 즐거워한 사실을(We're pleased that you enjoyed his recent talk in Sheffield ~) 언급하고 있다. 두 번째 지문 도표에서 장소가 셰필드(Sheffield)로 표기된 행사의 개최 날짜가 8월 7일(7 Aug.)로 쓰여 있으므로 (C)가 정답이다.

어휘 attend ~에 참석하다

190 애너갤 씨는 누구일 것 같은가?

(A) 회사 창립자
(B) 지역 기자

(C) 사무실 비서
(D) 행사장 소유주

해설 〈세부 사항〉
애너갤 씨가 작성한 이메일인 세 번째 지문 맨 마지막에, 워크숍 대체 날짜와 관련해 주저하지 말고 자신에게 공유해 주면 레넌 씨에게 확인해 보겠다고(~ please do not hesitate to share them with me, and I will check with Mr. Lennon about those) 알리고 있다. 이는 보통 비서 업무를 맡고 있는 사람이 하는 일로 유추할 수 있으므로 (C)가 정답이다.

어휘 founder 창립자, 설립자 local 지역의, 현지의 assistant 비서, 보조, 조수 venue (행사 등의) 개최 장소

[191-195] 구인 광고와 편지, 그리고 이메일

행정 업무 보조 구인

저희 업타운 부동산은 서머빌과 찰스타운, 그리고 **191** 에버렛에 새롭게 자리 잡은 사무실에서 고객들께 서비스를 제공해 드리는 것을 자랑스럽게 여겨 왔습니다. 거의 20년 동안, 저희는 주거용 건물을 매각 또는 매입하는 분들을 위해 전문 지식을 제공해 왔습니다. 저희는 현재 찰스타운에서 근무할 시간제 행정 업무 보조 직원을 찾고 있습니다. 직무에 포함되는 것으로는 전화 응대, 문서 정리 보관, **192** 오픈 하우스 행사용 안내 책자 페이지 구성 준비, 그리고 데이터베이스 업데이트가 있습니다. **193** 이 일자리는 일주일에 20시간 근무이며, 주중 오전과 오후뿐만 아니라 몇몇 주말 근무도 포함합니다. 관심 있는 분들은 늦어도 9월 30일까지 찰스타운, 굿윈 레인 3144번지, MA 02120으로 애슐리 미드 씨에게 이력서를 우편으로 제출해야 합니다. **194** 영업 및 고객 지원 부서장이 10월 7일부터 면접을 실시할 것입니다.

9월 23일

애슐리 미드 씨, 찰스타운, 굿윈 레인 3144번지, MA 02129

미드 씨께,

귀사의 찰스타운 지사 행정 업무 보조 직책에 대한 관심을 표하기 위해 편지를 씁니다.

193 저는 현재 에버렛에서 시간제로 오전 수업에 참석하고 있기는 하지만, 오후 또는 주말 업무를 위해 찰스타운까지 거뜬히 갈 수 있습니다. 동봉해 드린 이력서에서 확인해 보시겠지만, 제 컴퓨터 활용 능숙도는 높은 수준이며, 사무실 환경에서 근무한 경험도 있습니다. 게다가, 저는 그 지역 주민이기 때문에 여러 주거 지역을 꽤 잘 알고 있습니다.

요청 시에 과거의 고용주 또는 현재 학교의 교수님들로부터 추천서를 받아 제공해 드릴 수 있습니다.

귀하의 고려에 감사드립니다.

안녕히 계십시오.

헬렌 탤벗

수신: 헬렌 탤벗 〈htalbot@jolex5.com〉
발신: 애슐리 미드 〈ashley.mead@uptownrealty.net〉
날짜: 10월 14일
제목: 업타운 부동산 일자리

탤벗 씨께,

저희 업타운 부동산에서 근무하는 것에 대한 귀하의 관심에 감사드립니다. **194** 귀하께서 면접 중에 보여 주신 긍정적인 태도와 뛰어난 대인 관계 능력에 대해 호지 씨께서 매우 깊은 인상을 받으셨습니다. 귀하께서는 분명 가장 뛰어난 후보자이시므로, 수업 일정을 피해 근무하는 것으로 귀하께 이 직책을 제안해 드릴 의향이 있습니다.

저희 표준 고용 계약서를 첨부해 드렸으니 확인해 보시기 바랍니다. **195** 이번 주중으로 검토해 보시고 기꺼이 이 조건대로 진행하실 것인지의 여부를 저에게 알려 주시기 바랍니다. 그렇게 하실 경우, 서명하고 돌려 보내 주실 인쇄본을 한 부 우송해 드릴 예정이며, 첫 근무 시작일은 10월 23일이 될 것입니다.

답변 전해 주시기를 기다리고 있겠습니다.

안녕히 계십시오.

애슐리 미드

어휘 administrative 행정의 assistant 보조, 조수 be proud to do ~해서 자랑스러워하다 serve ~에게 서비스를 제공하다 newly 최근에, 새로이 established 자리 잡은, 인정받는 nearly 거의 provide ~을 제공하다 expertise 전문 지식 residential 주거의 property 건물, 부동산 currently 현재 seek ~을 찾다, 구하다 job responsibility 직무 include ~을 포함하다 file v. ~을 정리해 보관하다 paperwork 문서 (작업) prepare ~을 준비하다 brochure 안내 책자, 소책자 layout (지면 등의) 구성, 배치 open house 오픈 하우스(주택이나 아파트 등을 공개해 둘러보게 하는 행사) as well as ~뿐만 아니라 …도 party 사람, 당사자 submit ~을 제출하다 résumé 이력서 no later than 늦어도 ~까지 outreach 고객 지원 conduct ~을 실시하다, 수행하다 express (생각, 감정 등) ~을 표명하다, 표현하다 interest in ~에 대한 관심 currently 현재 get to ~로 가다, ~에 도착하다 enclosed 동봉된 proficiency 능숙(도) setting 환경, 배경 in addition 게다가, 추가로 local 지역의, 현지의 quite 꽤, 상당히 be familiar with ~을 잘 알고 있다, ~에 익숙하다 residential 주거의 neighborhood 지역, 인근 reference 추천서 employer 고용주 provide ~을 제공하다 upon request 요청 시에 consideration 고려, 숙고 appreciate ~에 대해 감사하다 be impressed with ~에 깊은 인상을 받다 positive 긍정적인 attitude 태도 people skills 대인 관계 능력 definitely 분명히, 확실히 candidate 후보자, 지원자 be willing to do ~할 의향이 있다, 기꺼이 ~하다 work around ~을 피해 일하다 offer A B A에게 B를 제공하다 Attached you will find A A를 첨부해 드렸으므로 확인해 보십시오 employment contract 고용 계약서 review ~을 검토하다, 살펴보다 let A know A에게 알리다 whether or not ~인지 아닌지의 여부 go forward 진행하다 under (조건, 영향 등) ~에 따라, ~ 하에서 term 조건, 조항 look forward to -ing ~하기를 기다리다, 고대하다

191 업타운 부동산과 관련해 무엇이 언급되는가?

(A) 곧 더 많은 공석이 있을 것으로 예상하고 있다.
(B) 20주년 기념 행사를 개최할 것이다.
(C) 최근에 또 다른 지사를 열었다.
(D) 오직 일주일에 20시간만 문을 연다.

해설 〈진위 확인 (세부 진위 유형)〉
첫 지문 초반부에 에버렛에 새롭게 자리 잡은 사무실이(~ our newly established office in Everett) 언급되는 것으로 볼 때, 최근에 새로운 지사를 열었다는 사실을 알 수 있으므로 (C)가 정답이다.

어휘 expect to do ~할 것으로 예상하다, 기대하다 open position 공석 hold ~을 개최하다 anniversary 기념일 recently 최근에 branch 지사, 지점

192 광고에 언급되는 직책의 한 가지 직무는 무엇인가?

(A) 홍보용 자료를 위한 디자인을 개발하는 일
(B) 서면으로 된 서신에 답변하는 일
(C) 웹 사이트를 변경하는 일
(D) 직원을 대신해 용품을 주문하는 일

해설 〈세부 사항〉
구인 광고인 첫 지문 중반부에 해당 직책의 직무들이 설명되어 있으며, 그중에서 오픈 하우스 행사용 안내 책자 페이지를 구성하는 일이 (preparing brochure layouts for open houses) 홍보 행사에 필요한 자료의 디자인과 관련된 것이므로 (A)가 정답이다.

어휘 duty 직무, 임무 develop ~을 개발하다 promotional 홍보의 material 자료, 재료, 물품 respond to ~에 답변하다, 대응하다 correspondence 서신, 편지 make a change to ~을 변경하다 supplies 용품, 물품 on behalf of ~을 대신해, 대표해

193 탈벗 씨와 관련해 언급되는 것은 무엇인가?

(A) 지원 마감 기한을 놓쳤다.
(B) 회사에서 요구하는 근무 가능 시간이 부족하다.
(C) 찰스타운으로 이사할 계획이다.
(D) 부동산 중개사 자격증을 따기 위해 노력하고 있다.

해설 〈지문 연계〉
첫 지문 중반부에 반드시 주중 오전과 오후뿐만 아니라 몇몇 주말 근무도 포함한다고(~ must include weekday mornings and afternoons as well as some weekends) 알리고 있다. 이와 관련해 탈벗 씨가 쓴 이메일인 두 번째 지문 두 번째 단락에 오전에는 수업에 참석하고 있지만 오후 또는 주말 업무를 위해 찰스타운까지 갈 수 있다고(~ attending morning classes part-time in Everett, but I can easily get to Charleston for afternoon or weekend work) 언급하고 있다. 이는 회사 측의 요구와 달리 오전 시간에 근무할 수 없는 상황에 해당되므로 (B)가 정답이다.

어휘 miss ~을 놓치다, 지나치다 application 지원(서), 신청(서) deadline 마감 기한 lack ~가 부족하다 availability 시간이 날 수 있음, 이용할 수 있음 request ~을 요구하다, 요청하다 plan to do ~할 계획이다 real estate license 부동산 중개사 자격증

194 호지 씨와 관련해 무엇이 암시되는가?

(A) 최근에 찰스타운 지사로 전근했다.
(B) 10월 23일에 탈벗 씨에게 전화할 것이다.
(C) 업타운 부동산에서 부서장으로 근무하고 있다.
(D) 미드 씨에 의해 고용되었다.

해설 〈진위 확인 (전체 진위 유형)〉
호지 씨의 이름이 제시되는 세 번째 지문 첫 단락에, 상대방이 면접 중에 보여준 태도와 능력에 대해 호지 씨가 매우 깊은 인상을 받았다는 내용(Mr. Hodge was very impressed ~ during your interview with him)이 있다. 이 면접과 관련해, 첫 지문 마지막 문장에 영업 및 고객 지원 부서장이 면접을 실시한다고(The manager of the Sales and Outreach Department will conduct interviews ~) 쓰여 있어 호지 씨가 해당 부서장임을 알 수 있으므로 (C)가 정답이다.

어휘 recently 최근에 transfer to ~로 전근하다 branch 지사, 지점 department head 부서장 hire ~을 고용하다

195 미드 씨는 탈벗 씨에게 무엇을 하도록 요청하는가?

(A) 사무실을 방문해 교육 시간에 참석하는 일
(B) 호지 씨에게 희망 연봉을 이메일로 보내는 일
(C) 학력 증명 자료를 제공하는 일
(D) 계약 조건에 만족하는지 확인해 주는 일

해설 〈세부 사항〉
미드 씨가 작성한 이메일인 세 번째 지문 두 번째 단락에 고용 계약서를 첨부한 사실과 함께 이번 주중으로 검토해 보고 그대로 진행할 것인지의 여부를 알려 달라고(Please review it sometime this week and let me know whether or not you are happy to go forward under these terms) 요청하고 있다. 이는 계약서상의 조건에 만족하는지 확인해 달라고 요청하는 것에 해당되므로 (D)가 정답이다.

어휘 ask A to do A에게 ~하도록 요청하다 attend ~에 참석하다 session (특정 활동을 위한) 시간 expectation 예상(치) provide ~을 제공하다 proof 증거(물) confirm that ~임을 확인해 주다 be satisfied with ~에 만족하다 contract 계약(서) terms (계약 등의) 조건, 조항

[196-200] 품질 보증 카드와 웹 페이지, 그리고 이메일

클랜튼 홈 굿즈

클랜튼 에스프레소 기계 품질 보증서 [모델명 K70, K71, K72, K73]

저희 클랜튼 홈 굿즈는 **199** 구매 시에 3년간의 품질 보증 서비스 연장에 대한 옵션과 함께 자사의 모든 상품에 대해 자동으로 1년간의 품질 보증 서비스를 제공해 드리고 있습니다. 결함이 있는 가전제품은 적격성 기준을 충족할 경우 수리 또는 교환해 드릴 것입니다.

품질 보증 서비스는 제조 또는 조립 과정의 결함에서 비롯된 모든 문제를 포함합니다. 고객들께서는 **196** 수리 작업이 반드시 공인된 클랜튼 브랜드의 수리점에서 이뤄져야 한다는 점에 유의하셔야 합니다. 다른 수리 서비스 업체를 이용하시면 그 시점 이후 향후의 모든 품질 보증 서비스 요청이 무효화될 것입니다. 일반 품질 보증 서비스를 요청하셔야 하는 경우, 저희 웹 사이트에서 요청 양식을 다운로드하여 출력해 작성하신 후, 해당 양식과 제품을 다음 주소로 보내 주시기 바랍니다: 포트 워스, 올리버 로드 9200번지, 클랜튼 홈 굿즈, TX 76102.

www.clantonhg.com/news

| 홈 | 제품 카탈로그 | 이용 후기 | **197** 클랜튼 소식 | 연락처 |

지난 2년 동안 클랜튼 K72 에스프레소 기계를 구입하신 고객들께서는 **197** 저희가 스팀 완드와 온도 조절용 다이얼에 결함을 발견했다는 점에 유의하셔야 합니다. 한 번 사용 후 다음 사용시까지 상당한 휴식 시간이 없는 경우, 이 두 부품 사이의 연결이 이뤄지지 않을 수 있으며, 이는 우유 거품을 일게 하기 위한 최대 온도가 낮아지는 결과를 낳게 됩니다.

197 저희 연구팀에서 이 두 가지 요소를 다시 설계했으므로, 더 새로운 버전의 K72는 영향을 받지 않습니다. 새로운 버전을 갖고 계신지 확인하시려면, **198** 고객 여러분께서는 완드에 작은 나선 표시가 있는지 찾아보시기 바랍니다.

필요한 부품들을 교체하시려면, 고객 여러분께서는 포장지에 제공되는 주소를 이용해 우편으로 기기를 제조사에 돌려보내실 수 있습니다. **200** 또는, 해당 기계를 클랜튼 서비스 센터로 가져가셔도 됩니다. 이 경우, 가장 가까운 곳으로 가는 방법과 관련된 정보를 얻으실 수 있도록 우편번호와 함께 저희에게 먼저 연락하셔야 합니다.

200 수신: clserv@clantonhg.com
발신: ammon.s@spring-post.com
날짜: 3월 9일
제목: 품질 보증 서비스

관계자께,

199 저는 2년 전에 품질 보증 연장 서비스와 함께 구입한 클랜튼 K72 에스프레소 기계를 갖고 있습니다. 최근에, 귀사에서 웹 사이트를 통해 설명한 온도 조절 문제를 계속 겪고 있습니다.

필요시에 원본 영수증과 상자를 제공해 드릴 수 있으며, **200** 제 우편번호는 68103입니다. 이것은 기계와 관련해 처음 겪는 문제이기 때문에 제대로 처리하고 싶습니다.

대단히 감사합니다.

쇼나 애먼

어휘 warranty 품질 보증(서) provide ~을 제공하다 goods 상품, 제품 extended 연장된 purchase 구매 defective 결함이 있는 appliances 가전제품 repair ~을 수리하다 replace ~을 교체하다, 대체하다 meet (조건 등)을 충족하다 eligibility 적격(성) criteria 기준 cover (범위 등)~을 포함하다. 아우르다 issue 문제, 사안 stem from ~에서 비롯되다 manufacturing 제조 assembly 조립 defect 결함, 흠 note that ~임에 유의하다. 주목하다 certified 공인된 invalidate ~을 무효화하다 claim 요청, 주장 after that point 그 시점 후로 form 양식, 서식 fill A out A를 작성하다 following 다음의, 아래의 review 후기, 평가, 의견 purchase ~을 구입하다 be aware that ~라는 점에 유의하다, ~임을 알고 있다 identify ~을 발견하다, 확인하다 steam wand 스팀 완드(커피 기계에서 뜨거운 증기가 나오는 금속 봉) temperature-control dial 온도 조절 다이얼 substantial 상당한, 많은 break 중단, 휴식, 단절 part 부품 fail 되지 않다, 하지 못하다, 실패하다 result in ~라는 결과를 낳다, ~을 초래하다 temperate 적당한, 알맞은 froth ~에 거품이 일게 하다 element 요소 affect ~에 영향을 미치다 whether ~인지 (아닌지) spiral 나선형의 marking 무늬, 표시 in order to do ~하기 위해 replace ~을 교체하다 device 기기, 장치 manufacturer 제조사 packaging 포장(지) alternatively 또는, 그렇지 않으면 how to do ~하는 법 get to ~로 가다, ~에 도착하다 along with ~와 함께 recently 최근에 experience ~을 겪다, 경험하다 describe ~을 설명하다 original 원본의, 원래의 receipt 영수증 if necessary 필요시에 handle ~을 처리하다, 다루다 properly 제대로, 적절히

196 품질 보증 카드에 무엇이 언급되는가?
(A) 공인되지 않은 수리 작업은 품질 보증을 무효로 만든다.
(B) 고객들은 우편으로 청구 양식을 요청할 수 있다.
(C) 품질 보증 연장 서비스가 더 이상 제공되지 않는다.
(D) 회사 측에서 반품 배송 비용을 충당해 줄 수 있다.

해설 〈진위 확인 (전체 진위 유형)〉
품질 보증 카드인 첫 지문 두 번째 단락을 보면, 수리 작업이 반드시 공인된 클랜튼 브랜드의 수리점에서 이뤄져야 한다는 점과 다른 수리 서비스 업체를 이용하면 모든 품질 보증 서비스 요청이 무효화된다

고(~ repairs must be performed by a certified Clanton-branded repair shop. The use of other repair services will invalidate all future warranty claims ~) 알리고 있다. 따라서 공인되지 않은 수리 작업에 따른 불이익을 언급한 (A)가 정답이다.

어휘 warranty 품질 보증(서) unauthorized 공인되지 않은 repair 수리 void ~을 무효화하다 ask for ~을 요청하다 claim form 청구 양식, 요청서 extended 연장된 no longer 더 이상 ~ 않다 offer ~을 제공하다 cover (비용 등)~을 충당하다. 포함하다 return 반품, 반납

197 클랜튼 홈 굿즈와 관련해 무엇이 사실인가?
(A) 오직 주방용 가전제품만 판매한다.
(B) 2년에 한 번씩 새 에스프레소 기계를 출시한다.
(C) 기계의 부품 문제를 바로잡았다.
(D) 안전에 대한 우려로 인해 제품을 회수했다.

해설 〈진위 확인 (전체 진위 유형)〉
두 번째 지문 첫 단락에는 스팀 완드와 온도 조절용 다이얼에 결함을 발견한 사실이(~ we have identified flaws in the steam wand and temperature-control dial), 두 번째 단락에는 연구팀에서 재설계하여 새로운 버전의 K72는 영향을 받지 않는다는 사실이(Our research team redesigned these two elements, so the newer version of K72 is not affected) 각각 쓰여 있다. 이는 기계 부품에 발생된 문제를 바로잡았음을 알리는 내용에 해당되므로 (C)가 정답이다.

어휘 appliances 가전제품 release ~을 출시하다, 공개하다 correct v. ~을 바로잡다, 고치다 component 부품 recall (결함 제품에 대해) ~을 회수하다, 리콜하다 due to ~로 인해 concern 우려, 걱정

198 클랜튼 K72 에스프레소 기계의 변경된 부품과 관련해 무엇이 언급되는가?
(A) 공간을 더 적게 차지한다.
(B) 기호로 표시되어 있다.
(C) 세척을 위해 분리될 수 있다.
(D) 재활용 재료로 만들어져 있다.

해설 〈진위 확인 (전체 진위 유형)〉
K72 에스프레소 기계의 부품에 대한 조치와 관련된 내용이 제시되는 두 번째 지문 두 번째 단락에, 새로운 버전인지 확인하는 방법으로 완드에 작은 나선 표시가 있는지 찾아보라고(~ customers should look for a small spiral marking on the wand) 알리고 있다. 이는 특정 기호로 표기한 사실을 말하는 것이므로 (B)가 정답이다.

어휘 part 부품 take up ~을 차지하다 less 더 적은, 덜한 mark ~을 표시하다, 표기하다 remove ~을 분리하다, 제거하다 be made from ~로 만들어지다 recycled 재활용된 material 재료, 자재

199 애먼 씨의 에스프레소 기계와 관련해 무엇이 암시되는가?
(A) 올바른 사용자 설명서가 들어 있지 않았다.
(B) 웹 사이트를 통해 구입되었다.
(C) 더 이상 생산되지 않고 있다.
(D) 여전히 품질 보증 서비스 요청 대상이다.

해설 〈지문 연계〉
애먼 씨가 작성한 이메일인 세 번째 지문 첫 단락에, 2년 전에 품질 보증 연장 서비스와 함께 구입한 클랜튼 K72 에스프레소 기계를 갖고 있다고 알리고 있다. 이 품질 보증 서비스와 관련해, 첫 지문 첫 번째 단락에 구매 시에 3년간의 품질 보증 서비스 연장에 대한 옵션이 있다고(~ an option for a three-year extended warranty at the time of purchase) 쓰여 있으므로 구매한지 2년 된 애먼 씨의 기계는 여전히 품질 보증 서비스를 받을 수 있는 상태임을 알 수 있다. 따라서 이를 언급한 (D)가 정답이다.

어휘 correct a. 올바른, 정확한, 맞는 user manual 사용자 설명서 purchase ~을 구입하다 no longer 더 이상 ~ 않다 be eligible for ~에 대한 대상이다, ~에 대한 자격이 있다 claim 요청, 신청

200 애먼 씨는 왜 클랜튼 홈 굿즈에 이메일을 보냈을 것 같은가?
(A) 새로운 상자를 받고 싶어 한다.
(B) 회사의 최신 카탈로그를 받고 싶어 한다.
(C) 배송 주소를 변경하고 싶어 한다.
(D) 서비스 센터로 가는 길을 알고 싶어 한다.

해설 〈지문 연계〉
애먼 씨가 작성한 이메일인 세 번째 지문 상단에 수신인 이메일 주소가 clserv@clantonhg.com으로 쓰여 있고(To: clserv@clantonhg.com), 두 번째 단락에는 우편번호가 68103이라고(my zip code is 68103) 알리고 있다. 이는 두 번째 지문 마지막 단락에서 가장 가까운 클랜튼 서비스 센터로 가는 방법과 관련된 정보를 얻을 수 있도록 우편번호와 함께 먼저 연락하라고(Alternatively, the machines can be taken to a Clanton Service Center. In this case, you should first contact us with your zip code for information about how to get to the nearest site) 알린 것과 관련된 내용이므로 (D)가 정답이다.

어휘 would like to do ~하고 싶다, ~하고자 하다 receive ~을 받다 latest 최신의 directions to ~로 가는 길, 길 안내

Actual Test 01   036 • 037

Actual Test

02

PART 1

1 (B)	2 (A)	3 (D)	4 (A)	5 (D)	6 (A)

PART 2

7 (C)	8 (A)	9 (C)	10 (C)	11 (C)	12 (C)	13 (B)	14 (C)	15 (B)	16 (B)
17 (A)	18 (B)	19 (C)	20 (C)	21 (C)	22 (C)	23 (C)	24 (A)	25 (C)	26 (B)
27 (C)	28 (B)	29 (B)	30 (B)	31 (C)					

PART 3

32 (B)	33 (D)	34 (C)	35 (A)	36 (C)	37 (A)	38 (D)	39 (B)	40 (A)	41 (A)
42 (B)	43 (C)	44 (B)	45 (C)	46 (D)	47 (D)	48 (A)	49 (B)	50 (A)	51 (D)
52 (C)	53 (D)	54 (C)	55 (A)	56 (D)	57 (B)	58 (B)	59 (D)	60 (B)	61 (D)
62 (D)	63 (C)	64 (C)	65 (D)	66 (B)	67 (A)	68 (A)	69 (C)	70 (D)	

PART 4

71 (C)	72 (B)	73 (A)	74 (D)	75 (D)	76 (B)	77 (B)	78 (D)	79 (B)	80 (C)
81 (A)	82 (C)	83 (B)	84 (C)	85 (B)	86 (D)	87 (A)	88 (A)	89 (B)	90 (D)
91 (D)	92 (B)	93 (A)	94 (A)	95 (B)	96 (C)	97 (C)	98 (B)	99 (B)	100 (A)

PART 5

101 (C)	102 (B)	103 (A)	104 (A)	105 (B)	106 (C)	107 (A)	108 (B)	109 (C)	110 (D)
111 (C)	112 (C)	113 (B)	114 (D)	115 (D)	116 (B)	117 (C)	118 (D)	119 (C)	120 (B)
121 (A)	122 (C)	123 (D)	124 (B)	125 (C)	126 (B)	127 (C)	128 (B)	129 (D)	130 (D)

PART 6

131 (B)	132 (D)	133 (B)	134 (C)	135 (C)	136 (D)	137 (B)	138 (B)	139 (D)	140 (C)
141 (B)	142 (C)	143 (C)	144 (B)	145 (A)	146 (B)				

PART 7

147 (D)	148 (C)	149 (C)	150 (A)	151 (C)	152 (A)	153 (D)	154 (C)	155 (B)	156 (D)
157 (C)	158 (B)	159 (A)	160 (B)	161 (B)	162 (C)	163 (D)	164 (C)	165 (C)	166 (D)
167 (B)	168 (D)	169 (A)	170 (D)	171 (D)	172 (D)	173 (C)	174 (B)	175 (B)	176 (B)
177 (C)	178 (D)	179 (D)	180 (C)	181 (C)	182 (A)	183 (D)	184 (A)	185 (C)	186 (B)
187 (D)	188 (C)	189 (B)	190 (A)	191 (D)	192 (B)	193 (C)	194 (D)	195 (C)	196 (C)
197 (D)	198 (B)	199 (C)	200 (B)						

1 (A) She is putting up a tent.
캐W (B) **She is checking her mobile phone.**
(C) She is tying her shoelaces.
(D) She is cutting down a tree.

(A) 여자가 텐트를 설치하고 있다.
(B) **여자가 휴대전화기를 확인하고 있다.**
(C) 여자가 신발끈을 매고 있다.
(D) 여자가 나무를 잘라 넘어뜨리고 있다.

해설 여자가 휴대전화기를 보는 모습에 초점을 맞춰 묘사한 (B)가 정답이다. 텐트를 설치하는 동작과 신발끈을 매는 동작, 그리고 나무를 자르는 동작은 사진에서 볼 수 없다.

어휘 put up ~을 세워 설치하다 tie one's shoelaces 신발끈을 매다 cut down ~을 잘라 넘어뜨리다

2 (A) One of the men is giving a talk.
호M (B) One of the men is setting up a screen.
(C) The men are leaving the meeting.
(D) The men are writing on a board.

(A) **남자들 중의 한 명이 발표를 하고 있다.**
(B) 남자들 중의 한 명이 스크린을 설치하고 있다.
(C) 남자들이 회의장에서 나가고 있다.
(D) 남자들이 보드에 뭔가 쓰고 있다.

해설 남자 한 명이 앞에 서서 뭔가를 설명하는 동작에 초점을 맞춰 묘사한 (A)가 정답이다. 스크린을 설치하는 동작과 회의실에서 나가는 동작, 그리고 보드에 뭔가를 쓰는 동작은 사진에서 볼 수 없다.

어휘 give a talk 발표하다, 연설하다 set up ~을 설치하다, 준비하다, 설정하다 leave ~에서 나가다, 떠나다

3 (A) The woman is pouring some cleaning products.
영W (B) The woman is wiping a mirror.
(C) The woman is washing silverware in a sink.
(D) **The woman is opening the cupboards.**

(A) 여자가 세척용품을 붓고 있다.
(B) 여자가 거울을 닦고 있다.
(C) 여자가 싱크대에서 은식기류를 씻고 있다.
(D) **여자가 수납장을 열고 있다.**

해설 세면대 하단의 수납장을 여는 여자의 동작에 초점을 맞춰 묘사한 (D)가 정답이다. 뭔가를 붓거나 닦는 동작, 설거지를 하는 동작은 사진에서 볼 수 없다.

어휘 pour ~을 붓다, 따르다 cleaning product 세척용품 wipe (행주, 걸레를 써서) 닦다 silverware (특히 나이프, 포크, 접시 등의) 은식기류 sink 싱크대, 개수대 cupboard 수납장, 찬장, 벽장

4 (A) **An office is unoccupied.**
미M (B) Chairs are facing the windows.
(C) There are papers piled on the floor.
(D) There are posters attached to the wall.

(A) **사무실이 비어 있는 상태이다.**
(B) 의자들이 창문을 향해 있다.
(C) 종이들이 바닥에 쌓여 있다.
(D) 포스터들이 벽에 부착되어 있다.

해설 사무실에 아무도 없는 상태에 초점을 맞춰 묘사한 (A)가 정답이다. 의자들은 창문을 향해 있지 않으며, 바닥에 쌓여 있는 종이와 벽에 부착된 포스터는 사진에서 볼 수 없다.

어휘 unoccupied (사람이 살거나 이용하지 않고) 비어 있는 face v. ~을 향하다, 마주보다 There is A p.p. A가 ~되어 있다 pile ~을 쌓다, 쌓아 올리다 attach A to B A를 B에 부착하다, 붙이다

5 (A) The chef is picking up a stack of plates.
캐W (B) The kitchen staff is changing into their uniforms.
(C) One of the men is slicing some vegetables.
(D) **The men are preparing food at the stove.**

(A) 요리사가 접시 더미를 집어 들고 있다.
(B) 주방 직원들이 유니폼으로 갈아입고 있다.
(C) 남자들 중의 한 명이 몇몇 채소를 얇게 썰고 있다.
(D) **남자들이 가스레인지 앞에서 음식을 준비하고 있다.**

해설 두 남자가 함께 가스레인지 앞에 서서 음식을 준비하는 모습에 초점을 맞춘 (D)가 정답이다. 접시를 집어 드는 동작과 유니폼으로 갈아입는 동작, 그리고 채소를 써는 동작은 사진에서 볼 수 없다.

어휘 pick up ~을 집어 들다 stack 더미, 묶음, 쌓아 놓은 무더기 plate 접시 change into ~로 갈아입다 slice v. ~을 얇게 썰다 prepare ~을 준비하다 stove 가스레인지, 난로, 화덕

6 (A) **The stairs lead to the doors.**
호M (B) Potted plants are hanging in a greenhouse.
(C) A fence runs along the sidewalk.
(D) Some windows have been left open.

(A) **계단들이 문으로 이어져 있다.**
(B) 온실 안에 화분식물들이 걸려 있다.
(C) 울타리가 보도를 따라 이어져 있다.
(D) 일부 창문들이 열린 채로 있다.

해설 두 곳의 계단이 모두 문으로 이어져 있는 상태에 초점을 맞춘 (A)가 정답이다. 온실과 울타리, 열린 창문은 사진에서 볼 수 없다.

어휘 stairs 계단 lead to ~로 이어지다, 연결되다 potted plant 화분에 심은 식물 hang 걸리다, 매달리다, ~을 걸다 greenhouse 온실 run 이어지다, 잇다 along (길 등) ~을 따라 sidewalk 보도 be left + 형용사 ~한 상태로 있다

7 When will the construction workers arrive?
미M (A) It's already open.
영W (B) The doors are to the left.
(C) At 9 A.M.

공사 인부들이 언제 도착하죠?
(A) 이미 열었어요.
(B) 문은 왼편에 있습니다.
(C) 오전 9시요.

해설 〈When 의문문〉
공사 인부들이 도착하는 시점을 묻는 When 의문문에 대해 정확한 시각을 알리는 (C)가 정답이다.
(A) 문이 열려 있는 상태임을 나타내는 말이므로 질문의 핵심에서 벗어난 오답
(B) 문의 위치를 알리는 말이므로 질문의 핵심에서 벗어난 오답

어휘 construction 공사, 건설 arrive 도착하다 to the left 왼편에, 왼쪽에

8 Where did Mr. Taylor go for his business trip?
호M **(A) He visited the headquarters in Chicago.**
캐W (B) Yes, he finalized the deal.
(C) For about a week.

테일러 씨가 어디로 출장 가신 거죠?
(A) 시카고에 있는 본사를 방문하셨어요.
(B) 네, 그가 거래 계약을 마무리 지었어요.
(C) 약 일주일 동안이요.

해설 〈Where 의문문〉
테일러 씨가 출장 간 곳을 묻는 Where 의문문에 대해 Mr. Taylor를 He로 지칭해 특정 장소를 말하는 (A)가 정답이다.
(B) 의문사 의문문에 맞지 않는 Yes로 답변하는 오답
(C) 기간 표현이므로 Where와 어울리지 않는 오답

어휘 headquarters 본사 finalize ~을 마무리 짓다, 최종 확정하다 deal 거래 (계약), 거래 조건 about 약, 대략

9 Would you like the oak or the pine bed frame?
영W (A) It's a framed photo.
미M (B) For my new apartment.
(C) I like the look of the oak.

오크 나무 침대 프레임으로 하시겠어요, 아니면 소나무로 된 것으로 하시겠어요?
(A) 액자에 담긴 사진이요.
(B) 제 새 아파트에서 쓸 거예요.
(C) 오크 나무 스타일이 마음에 들어요.

해설 〈선택 의문문〉
원하는 침대 프레임 재질의 종류를 묻는 선택 의문문에 대해 오크 나무가 마음에 든다는 뜻을 직접적으로 밝힌 (C)가 정답이다.
(A) 사진 보관 방법에 해당되는 말이므로 질문의 핵심에서 벗어난 오답

/ 질문의 frame이 지닌 다른 뜻을 활용해 반복한 오답
(B) 용도를 나타내는 말이므로 질문의 핵심에서 벗어난 오답 / 질문의 bed frame에서 연상되는 new apartment를 사용한 오답

어휘 Would you like ~? ~로 하시겠어요? framed 액자에 담긴 look n. 스타일, 모습, 외모, 표정

---

10 Where's the path that leads to the Tourist Center?
(캐W) (A) A range of souvenirs.
(호M) (B) Yes, there's a bathroom.
(C) Your guide can help you.
관광객 안내 센터로 이어지는 길이 어디 있나요?
(A) 다양한 기념품이요.
(B) 네, 화장실이 있습니다.
(C) 담당 가이드가 도와드릴 수 있습니다.

해설 〈Where 의문문〉
관광객 안내 센터로 이어지는 길이 어디 있는지 묻는 Where 의문문에 대해 그 정보를 제공해 줄 수 있는 사람을 언급하는 (C)가 정답이다.
(A) 기념품의 다양성과 관련된 말이므로 질문의 핵심에서 벗어난 오답 / 질문의 Tourist에서 연상되는 souvenirs를 사용한 오답
(B) 의문사 의문문에 맞지 않는 Yes로 답변하는 오답

어휘 path 길, 이동로, 경로 lead to ~로 이어지다, 연결되다 a range of 다양한 souvenir 기념품

---

11 Did you hear our agency's new commercial on this
(미M) morning's Breakfast Radio Show?
(영W) (A) I haven't discussed it with her.
(B) A new talk show host.
(C) Yes, and it sounds great.
오늘 아침에 브레이크퍼스트 라디오 쇼에 나온 우리 회사의 새 광고 들으셨어요?
(A) 그걸 그녀와 논의한 적 없습니다.
(B) 새 토크쇼 진행자요.
(C) 네, 그리고 아주 좋은 것 같아요.

해설 〈Do 일반 의문문〉
라디오 쇼에 나온 자사의 새 광고를 들었는지 확인하는 Do 일반 의문문에 대해 긍정을 뜻하는 Yes와 함께 그 광고에 대한 의견을 밝히는 (C)가 정답이다.
(A) 누군지 알 수 없는 her와 논의한 적이 없다는 사실을 나타낸 말이므로 질문의 핵심에서 벗어난 오답
(B) 토크쇼 진행자를 언급하는 말이므로 질문의 핵심에서 벗어난 오답 / 질문의 Radio Show에서 연상되는 show host를 사용한 오답

어휘 agency 회사, 대행사, 대리점 commercial n. (상업용) 광고 discuss ~을 논의하다, 이야기하다 host (방송) 진행자 sound + 형용사 ~한 것 같다, ~하게 들리다

---

12 Who's the choreographer of this musical?
(호M) (A) I'll carry it for you.
(캐W) (B) No, a professional photographer.
(C) Let's check the program.
누가 이 뮤지컬 안무 책임자인가요?
(A) 제가 대신 옮겨 드릴게요.
(B) 아니요, 전문 사진가요.
(C) 프로그램 책자를 확인해 봅시다.

해설 〈Who 의문문〉
뮤지컬 안무 책임자가 누군지 묻는 Who 의문문에 대해 그 정보를 확인할 수 있는 방법을 제안하는 (C)가 정답이다.
(A) 대신 옮겨 주겠다고 제안하는 말이므로 질문의 핵심에서 벗어난 오답 / 질문의 choreographer와 일부 발음이 유사한 carry를 사용한 오답
(B) 의문사 의문문에 맞지 않는 No로 답변하는 오답

어휘 choreographer 안무가 carry ~을 옮기다, 나르다, 휴대하다, (매장 등에서) ~을 취급하다 photographer 사진가 program (공연 등을 안내하는) 프로그램 책자, 일정표

---

13 Could you repair the bottom shelf for me?
(영W) (A) No, we didn't display that.
(미M) (B) Sure, I'll be with you in a minute.
(C) A pair of speakers.
제 대신 맨 아래쪽 선반 좀 수리해 주시겠어요?
(A) 아니요, 저희는 그걸 진열하지 않았어요.
(B) 그럼요, 잠시 후에 그쪽으로 가겠습니다.
(C) 스피커 한 쌍이요.

해설 〈Could 일반 의문문〉
맨 아래쪽 선반 좀 수리해 달라고 요청하는 Could 일반 의문문에 대해 수락을 나타내는 Sure와 함께 상대방이 있는 쪽으로 곧 가겠다는 뜻을 나타낸 (B)가 정답이다.
(A) 거절을 뜻하는 No 뒤에 이어지는 말이 수리 작업과 관련 없는 말이므로 오답
(C) 스피커 한 쌍을 언급하는 말이므로 질문의 핵심에서 벗어난 오답 / 질문의 repair와 일부 발음이 유사한 pair를 사용한 오답

어휘 repair ~을 수리하다 bottom 맨 아래의, 밑바닥의 shelf 선반 display ~을 진열하다, 전시하다 in a minute 잠시 후에

---

14 Why was the Henderson Bridge closed this morning?
(호M) (A) Yes, it's fairly close to us.
(캐W) (B) On Friday afternoons.
(C) There was an automobile accident.
왜 헨더슨 다리가 오늘 아침에 폐쇄된 거죠?
(A) 네, 우리와 꽤 가까워요.
(B) 매주 금요일 오후에요.
(C) 자동차 사고가 있었어요.

해설 〈Why 의문문〉
헨더슨 다리가 오늘 아침에 폐쇄된 이유를 묻는 Why 의문문에 대해 자동차 사고가 발생된 사실을 언급하는 (C)가 정답이다.
(A) 의문사 의문문에 맞지 않는 Yes로 답변하는 오답
(B) 반복 주기를 나타내는 말이므로 Why와 어울리지 않는 오답

어휘 fairly 꽤, 상당히 close to ~와 가까운 automobile 자동차 accident 사고

---

15 I hope customers are happy with the new clothing
(미M) collection.
(영W) (A) Did you vote in the election?
(B) It's already selling well.
(C) At the flagship store.
고객들이 의류 신상품에 만족했으면 좋겠어요.
(A) 선거에서 투표하셨어요?
(B) 이미 잘 판매되고 있습니다.
(C) 대표 매장에서요.

해설 〈평서문〉
고객들이 새 의류 제품에 만족했으면 좋겠다는 바람을 말하는 평서문에 대해 이미 잘 판매되고 있다는 말로 고객들의 만족도가 높다는 뜻을 나타낸 (B)가 정답이다.
(A) 선거 여부를 확인하는 말이므로 핵심에서 벗어난 오답 / 평서문에 제시된 collection과 일부 발음이 유사한 election을 사용한 오답
(C) 위치 표현이므로 상대방의 바람에 대한 반응으로 어울리지 않는 오답

어휘 new clothing collection 의류 신상품들 vote 투표하다 election 선거 flagship store 대표 매장, 주력 매장

---

16 When will the merger be announced?
(캐W) (A) No, we couldn't find it.
(호M) (B) Not until the end of the month.
(C) Sure, I'll ask them.
합병이 언제 발표되죠?
(A) 아니요, 우리는 그걸 찾을 수 없었어요.
(B) 이달 말이나 되어야 합니다.
(C) 네, 제가 그 사람들에게 물어볼게요.

해설 〈When 의문문〉
합병이 발표되는 시점을 묻는 When 의문문에 대해 대략적인 미래 시점으로 답변하는 (B)가 정답이다.
(A) 의문사 의문문에 맞지 않는 No로 답변하는 오답
(C) Yes와 마찬가지로 의문사 의문문에 맞지 않는 Sure로 답변하는 오답

어휘 merger 합병, 통합 announce ~을 발표하다, 공지하다 not until ~나 되어서야, 돼서야

17 You don't have last week's sales report, do you?

미M (A) No, but Ms. Presley does.
영W (B) Probably sometime this week.
(C) A big increase in profits.

지난주 영업 보고서를 갖고 계시지 않으시죠, 그런가요? (= 갖고 계신가요?)
(A) 제가 아니라, 프레슬리 씨가 갖고 있어요.
(B) 아마 이번 주 중으로요.
(C) 수익의 대폭 증가요.

해설 〈부가 의문문〉
지난주 영업 보고서를 갖고 있지 않은지 확인하는 부가 의문문에 대해 동일한 조동사 does와 함께 프레슬리 씨가 갖고 있다고 알리는 (A)가 정답이다.
(B) 대략적인 시점 표현이므로 보고서 보관 여부를 묻는 질문의 핵심에서 벗어난 오답 / 질문의 week를 반복한 오답
(C) 보고서 내용에 해당되는 말이므로 보고서 보관 여부를 묻는 질문의 핵심에서 벗어난 오답 / 질문의 sales에서 연상되는 increase in profits를 사용한 오답

어휘 sales 영업, 판매, 매출 increase in ~의 증가, 인상 profit 수익

18 Haven't you signed the lease agreement yet?

호M (A) A few pages long.
영W (B) It's under review.
(C) He completely agrees with me.

혹시 임대 계약서에 서명하시지 않았나요? (= 서명하셨나요?)
(A) 몇 페이지 정도 되는 길이입니다.
(B) 검토 중입니다.
(C) 그는 제 말에 완전히 동의하고 있어요.

해설 〈부정 의문문〉
임대 계약서에 서명하지 않았는지 확인하는 부정 의문문에 대해 lease agreement를 It으로 지칭해 검토 중이라는 말로 아직 서명하지 않았음을 나타내는 (B)가 정답이다.
(A) 문서의 길이를 나타내는 말이므로 질문의 핵심에서 벗어난 오답
(C) 누군지 알 수 없는 He의 동의 여부를 말하고 있으므로 질문의 핵심에서 벗어난 오답 / 질문의 agreement와 일부 발음이 같은 agrees를 사용한 오답

어휘 sign ~에 서명하다 lease 임대 agreement 계약(서), 합의(서) under (영향, 진행 등) ~ 하에 있는, ~ 중인 review 검토, 평가, 의견, 후기 completely 완전히, 전적으로 agree with ~에 동의하다

19 Should we confirm the menu with the caterer?

캐W (A) Was there enough food for everyone?
미M (B) In the kitchen.
(C) Yes, I'll give them a call now.

우리가 출장 요리 업체에 메뉴를 확인해 줘야 하나요?
(A) 모든 사람을 위한 음식이 충분히 있었나요?
(B) 주방에요.
(C) 네, 제가 지금 그쪽에 전화할게요.

해설 〈Should 일반 의문문〉
출장 요리 업체에 메뉴를 확인해 줘야 하는지 확인하는 Should 일반 의문문에 대해 긍정을 뜻하는 Yes와 함께 메뉴를 확인해 주기 위한 조치를 말하는 (C)가 정답이다.
(A) 과거에 있었던 일에 대해 확인하는 말이므로 앞으로 해야 할 일에 관해 묻는 질문과 시점이 맞지 않는 오답 / 질문의 menu에서 연상되는 food를 사용한 오답
(B) 장소 표현이므로 메뉴 확인 여부와 관련 없는 오답

어휘 confirm ~을 확인해 주다 caterer 출장 요리 업체 give A a call A에게 전화하다

20 How do I use my travel pass on the bus?

영W (A) I travel frequently.
호M (B) It goes to the city center.
(C) Hold the card on the reader.

버스에서 제 승차권을 어떻게 사용하죠?
(A) 저는 자주 여행해요.
(B) 도심 지역으로 갑니다.
(C) 리더기에 카드를 갖다 대세요.

해설 〈How 의문문〉
버스 승차권 사용 방법을 묻는 How 의문문에 대해 리더기에 카드를 갖다 대야 한다고 알리는 (C)가 정답이다.
(A) 여행 빈도를 나타내는 말로서 How often에 어울리는 답변이므로 오답 / 질문의 travel을 반복한 오답
(B) 버스 운행 경로에 해당되는 말이므로 질문의 핵심에서 벗어난 오답 / 질문의 bus에서 연상되는 goes to the city center를 사용한 오답

어휘 travel pass (버스, 기차 등의) 승차권 frequently 자주, 빈번히 hold (특정 위치로) ~을 유지하다 reader 리더기, 판독기

21 Why aren't the summer dresses displayed in the store window?

미M
캐W (A) Yes, it's a seasonal sale.
(B) In the new catalog.
(C) The shipment hasn't arrived.

왜 여름 드레스들이 매장 진열창에 진열되어 있지 않은 거죠?
(A) 네, 계절 세일 행사입니다.
(B) 새 카탈로그에요.
(C) 배송 물품이 아직 도착하지 않았어요.

해설 〈Why 의문문〉
여름 드레스들이 진열되어 있지 않은 이유를 묻는 Why 의문문에 대해 그 제품들이 아직 배송되지 않았다는 사실을 밝히는 (C)가 정답이다.
(A) 의문사 의문문에 맞지 않는 Yes로 답변하는 오답
(B) 제품 정보를 확인할 수 있는 방법을 나타내는 말이므로 질문의 핵심에서 벗어난 오답

어휘 display ~을 진열하다, 전시하다 seasonal 계절의, 계절에 따라 다른 catalog (제품을 소개하는) 카탈로그 shipment 배송(품) arrive 도착하다

22 How much printer paper should I pick up for our department?

영W
호M (A) When should I meet you?
(B) Unfortunately, the text is hard to read.
(C) Enough for two weeks.

우리 부서에 필요한 인쇄 용지를 얼마나 가져와야 하죠?
(A) 언제 당신을 만나야 하죠?
(B) 아쉽게도, 글이 읽기 어려워요.
(C) 2주 동안 충분할 만큼이요.

해설 〈How much 의문문〉
부서에 필요한 인쇄 용지를 얼마나 가져와야 하는지 묻는 How much 의문문에 대해 2주 동안 충분할 만큼이라는 말로 두 사람이 알고 있는 대략적인 수량을 언급하는 (C)가 정답이다.
(A) 상대방을 만나는 시점을 묻는 말이므로 질문의 핵심에서 벗어난 오답
(B) 읽기 어려운 상태임을 나타내는 말이므로 질문의 핵심에서 벗어난 오답

어휘 pick up ~을 가져오다, 가져가다, 구입하다 department 부서 unfortunately 아쉽게도, 안타깝게도 text 글, 글자, 문자 enough 충분한

23 Do you dry-clean the clothing yourself, or do you send it offsite?

미M
캐W (A) At a fashion show.
(B) The size is incorrect.
(C) We do it here.

옷을 직접 드라이클리닝하시나요, 아니면 다른 곳으로 보내시나요?
(A) 패션쇼에요.
(B) 사이즈가 부정확해요.
(C) 저희가 여기서 합니다.

해설 〈선택 의문문〉
옷을 직접 드라이클리닝하는지, 아니면 다른 곳에 맡기는지 확인하는 선택 의문문에 대해 dry-clean the clothing을 do it으로 바꿔 표현해 직접 한다고 밝히는 (C)가 정답이다.
(A) 장소 표현에 해당되므로 질문의 핵심에서 벗어난 오답 / 질문의 clothing에서 연상되는 fashion show를 사용한 오답
(B) 사이즈의 정확성을 말하는 답변이므로 질문의 핵심에서 벗어난 오답 / 질문의 clothing에서 연상되는 size를 사용한 오답

어휘 dry-clean 드라이클리닝하다 oneself (부사처럼 쓰여) 직접 offsite 다른 곳으로, 부지 밖에서 incorrect 부정확한

24 It looks like this parking lot is full.

영W (A) There's another one on Simpson Avenue.
호M (B) We had a picnic outdoors.
(C) It's a lovely park.

이 주차장이 꽉 차 있는 것 같아요.
(A) 심슨 애비뉴에 다른 곳이 하나 있어요.
(B) 저희는 야외로 피크닉 갔어요.

(C) 아주 멋진 공원입니다.

해설 〈평서문〉
주차장이 꽉 차 있다는 사실을 밝히는 평서문에 대해 주차 가능한 대체 장소를 언급하는 (A)가 정답이다.
(B) 과거에 피크닉을 한 사실을 말하는 답변이므로 핵심에서 벗어난 오답
(C) 공원에 대한 의견을 말하는 답변이므로 핵심에서 벗어난 오답 / 평서문에 제시된 parking과 일부 발음이 같은 park를 사용한 오답

어휘 It looks like ~인 것 같다 parking lot 주차장 outdoors 야외에서

25 Which software should I use to protect important
미M company files?
캐W (A) On top of the pile.
(B) To enhance network security.
(C) You're the IT technician.

중요한 회사 파일을 보호하려면 어느 소프트웨어를 사용해야 하나요?
(A) 그 더미 맨 위에요.
(B) 네트워크 보안을 강화하기 위해서요.
(C) 당신이 IT 기술자잖아요.

해설 〈Which 의문문〉
중요한 파일을 보호하기 위해 어느 소프트웨어를 사용해야 하는지 묻는 Which 의문문에 대해 상대방이 IT 기술자임을 언급해 더 잘 알고 있을 것이라는 뜻을 나타낸 (C)가 정답이다.
(A) 물리적인 위치 표현으로서 질문의 Which software에 대한 선택 조건으로 맞지 않으므로 오답 / 질문의 files와 발음이 유사한 pile을 사용한 오답
(B) 목적을 나타내는 말이므로 질문의 핵심에서 벗어난 오답 / 질문의 software에서 연상되는 network security를 사용한 오답

어휘 protect ~을 보호하다 on top of ~ 맨 위에, 꼭대기에 pile (쌓여 있는) 더미, 무더기 enhance ~을 강화하다 security 보안

26 I just heard I have to attend a teleconference after lunch.
호M (A) The new convention center.
영W **(B) OK, I can meet the clients for you.**
(C) Thanks, but I already ate.

제가 점심 식사 후에 화상 회의에 참석해야 한다는 얘기를 막 들었습니다.
(A) 새 컨벤션 센터요.
(B) 알겠어요, 그럼 제가 대신 고객들을 만나러 갈게요.
(C) 감사합니다만, 저는 이미 식사했습니다.

해설 〈평서문〉
점심 식사 후에 화상 회의에 참석해야 한다는 얘기를 막 들었다는 말로 갑작스러운 일정 변화를 알리는 평서문에 대해 그에 따른 조치로서 상대방 대신 고객들을 만나러 가겠다는 의사를 밝힌 (B)가 정답이다.
(A) 장소 표현이므로 핵심에서 벗어난 오답 / 평서문에 제시된 teleconference에서 연상되는 convention center를 사용한 오답
(C) 이미 식사한 사실을 밝히는 말이므로 핵심에서 벗어난 오답 / 평서문에 제시된 lunch에서 연상되는 ate을 사용한 오답

어휘 attend ~에 참석하다 teleconference 화상 회의

27 Can you collect my suit from the dry cleaner?
캐W (A) Clean it after every use.
미M (B) The formal attire is on the 2nd floor.
(C) I think they'll be closed for lunch now.

세탁소에서 제 양복 좀 찾아다 주실래요?
(A) 매번 사용 후에 닦으세요.
(B) 정장은 2층에 있습니다.
(C) 이제 점심 시간이라 그곳이 닫을 것 같아요.

해설 〈Can 일반 의문문〉
세탁소에서 양복을 찾아다 달라고 요청하는 Can 일반 의문문에 대해 점심 시간이라 문을 닫는다는 사실을 언급하는 것으로 지금 찾을 수 없다는 뜻을 나타낸 (C)가 정답이다.
(A) 세척 또는 세탁 방법에 해당되는 말이므로 요청하는 질문에 대한 반응으로 맞지 않는 오답 / 질문의 cleaner와 발음이 거의 같은 Clean을 사용한 오답
(B) 매장 위치를 알리는 말이므로 질문의 핵심에서 벗어난 오답 / 질문의 suit에서 연상되는 formal attire를 사용한 오답

어휘 collect ~을 가지러 가다, 수거하다, 모으다 suit 양복, 정장 dry cleaner 세탁소 formal attire 정장

28 Shouldn't we order more of these blenders?
호M (A) No, I have more space.
영W **(B) They have been discontinued.**
(C) A recipe for fruit smoothies.

이 믹서기를 더 주문해야 하지 않나요? (= 주문해야 하죠?)
(A) 아니요, 저에게 더 넓은 공간이 있어요.
(B) 그것들은 단종되었습니다.
(C) 과일 스무디를 만드는 조리법이요.

해설 〈부정 의문문〉
특정 믹서기를 더 주문해야 하지 않는지 확인하는 부정 의문문에 대해 질문의 these blenders를 They로 지칭해 단종되었다는 말로 주문할 수 없다는 뜻을 나타낸 (B)가 정답이다.
(A) 공간의 넓이와 관련된 말이므로 질문의 핵심에서 벗어난 오답 / 질문의 more를 반복한 오답
(C) 스무디 조리법을 언급하는 답변이므로 질문의 핵심에서 벗어난 오답 / 질문의 blenders에서 연상되는 recipe와 smoothies를 사용한 오답

어휘 order ~을 주문하다 blender 믹서기 discontinue ~을 단종시키다 recipe 조리법

29 Are you taking a direct flight to New York or having a
미M layover?
캐W (A) No, I'd rather not.
(B) It depends on the fares.
(C) Next month's journalism convention.

뉴욕으로 직항편으로 타고 가시나요, 아니면 경유지가 있나요?
(A) 아니요, 그러고 싶지 않습니다.
(B) 요금에 따라 다릅니다.
(C) 다음 달에 있을 저널리즘 컨벤션이요.

해설 〈선택 의문문〉
뉴욕으로 가는 항공편 종류를 묻는 선택 의문문에 대해 항공편 선택을 위한 조건으로 요금을 언급하면서 그에 따라 다를 수 있음을 나타낸 (B)가 정답이다.
(A) 요청이나 제안에 대한 거절을 뜻을 나타낼 때 사용하는 말이므로 질문의 핵심에서 벗어난 오답
(C) 행사 종류를 나타내는 답변이므로 항공편 선택과 관련해 묻는 질문의 핵심에서 벗어난 오답

어휘 direct flight 직항편 layover 경유지, 중간 기착지 would rather not do ~하고 싶지 않다 depend on ~에 따라 다르다, ~에 달려 있다 fare (교통) 요금

30 Please restart your computer to update the software.
영W (A) Let's begin on page 12.
호M **(B) I did that this morning.**
(C) A program for editing videos.

소프트웨어를 업데이트하시려면 컴퓨터를 다시 시작하세요.
(A) 12페이지부터 시작해 보겠습니다.
(B) 오늘 아침에 그렇게 했어요.
(C) 동영상 편집용 프로그램이요.

해설 〈평서문〉
소프트웨어를 업데이트하려면 컴퓨터를 다시 시작해야 한다는 사실을 말하는 평서문에 대해 다시 시작하는 일을 that으로 지칭해 오전에 이미 했음을 알리는 (B)가 정답이다.
(A) 시작 페이지를 알리는 말이므로 컴퓨터를 다시 시작하는 일과 관련 없는 오답 / 평서문에 제시된 restart에서 연상되는 begin을 사용한 오답
(C) 특정 프로그램 종류를 알리는 말이므로 컴퓨터를 다시 시작하는 일과 관련 없는 오답 / 평서문에 제시된 computer와 software에서 연상되는 program을 사용한 오답

어휘 restart ~을 다시 시작하다 edit ~을 편집하다

31 What's wrong with the main elevator?
미M (A) To the top floor.
캐W (B) Yes, that'll be faster.
(C) The building manager is having a look now.

중앙 엘리베이터에 무슨 문제라도 있나요?
(A) 맨 위층으로요.
(B) 네, 그게 더 빠를 겁니다.
(C) 건물 관리 책임자가 지금 살펴보고 있어요.

해설 〈What 의문문〉
중앙 엘리베이터에 무슨 문제가 생겼는지 묻는 What 의문문에 대해 책임자가 원인을 파악 중이라는 뜻을 나타낸 (C)가 정답이다.

PART 3
P63

Questions 32-34 refer to the following conversation. (캐W) (미M)

W ㉜ Thank you for calling Everton Appliance Repairs. How may I help you?

M Hello. I'm having ㉝ a problem with my air conditioner, and my friend recommended your business.

W All right. Can you please describe the problem?

M Yes. Whenever I turn it on, ㉝ water starts leaking from the bottom of the machine.

W All right, sir. ㉜ I can send someone to make the necessary repairs for you around 2 P.M. today. ㉞ What is your address?

M It's 578 Howard Avenue.

W OK. See you this afternoon.

여 에버튼 어플라이언스 리페어즈에 전화 주셔서 감사합니다. 무엇을 도와드릴까요?

남 안녕하세요. 제 에어컨에 문제가 있는데, 친구가 귀사를 추천해 주었습니다.

여 알겠습니다. 어떤 문제인지 설명해 주시겠습니까?

남 네. 작동시킬 때마다, 기계 하단에서 물이 새어 나오기 시작합니다.

여 알겠습니다, 고객님. 오늘 오후 2시쯤 누군가를 보내서 필요한 수리 작업을 해 드릴 수 있습니다. 주소가 어떻게 되죠?

남 하워드 애비뉴 578번지입니다.

여 좋습니다. 오늘 오후에 뵙겠습니다.

어휘 air conditioner 에어컨 recommend ~을 추천하다 business 회사, 업체 describe ~을 설명하다 whenever ~할 때마다 turn A on A를 켜다, 틀다 start -ing ~하기 시작하다 leak (물, 가스 등이) 새다, 누출되다 bottom 하단, 밑부분 make a repair 수리하다 necessary 필요한, 필수의 around ~쯤, 약, 대략

32 Where most likely does the woman work?
(A) At a real estate agency
(B) At a repair shop
(C) At an accounting office
(D) At a landscaping company

여자는 어디에서 일하고 있을 것 같은가?
(A) 부동산 중개업체에서
(B) 수리점에서
(C) 회계 사무소에서
(D) 조경 회사에서

해설 〈근무지를 묻는 문제〉
여자가 대화 시작 부분에는 Thank you for calling Everton Appliance Repairs라는 말로 수리와 관련된 말이 포함된 업체 이름을 언급하고 있고, 후반부에는 수리 작업을 하러 가는 일정을(I can send someone to make the necessary repairs for you) 밝히고 있으므로 (B)가 정답이다.

33 What problem does the man mention?
(A) A computer is not working.
(B) A delivery did not arrive.
(C) A component is missing.
(D) A machine is leaking.

남자는 어떤 문제를 언급하는가?
(A) 컴퓨터가 작동하지 않는다.
(B) 배송 물품이 도착하지 않았다.
(C) 부품이 빠져 있다.
(D) 기계에서 물이 샌다.

해설 〈문제점을 묻는 문제〉
대화 중반부에 남자가 앞서 언급한 air conditioner를 the machine으로 지칭해 그 기계에서 물이 샌다고(water starts leaking from the bottom of the machine) 알리고 있으므로 (D)가 정답이다.

어휘 work (기계 등이) 작동되다, 가동되다 arrive 도착하다 component 부품 missing 빠진, 없는, 사라진 leak (물, 가스 등이) 새다, 누출되다

34 What is the man asked to provide?
(A) The name of a customer
(B) A receipt code
(C) A street address
(D) A phone number

남자는 무엇을 제공하도록 요청받는가?
(A) 고객 성명
(B) 영수증 코드
(C) 거리 주소
(D) 전화번호

해설 〈요청 사항을 묻는 문제〉
대화 후반부에 여자가 What is your address?라는 말로 남자의 주소를 묻고 있으므로 (C)가 정답이다.

어휘 provide ~을 제공하다 receipt 영수증

Questions 35-37 refer to the following conversation. (영W) (호M)

W Hello. I'm a member ㉟ at this gym, but I forgot my membership card.

M That's all right. ㊱ What is your e-mail address?

W It's kelseymiller@fastmail.com.

M OK. I'll print you a temporary pass so that ㉟ you can still work out today. Do you need anything else?

W Well, ㊲ I'm wondering if the pool is open now or if a swimming class is going on.

M It's open for everyone until 7 P.M.

W That's perfect. ㊲ I'll head there right now.

여 안녕하세요. 제가 이 체육관 회원인데, 회원 카드를 깜빡 잊고 왔어요.

남 괜찮습니다. 이메일 주소가 어떻게 되죠?

여 kelseymiller@fastmail.com입니다.

남 알겠습니다. 오늘 여전히 운동하실 수 있도록 임시 출입증을 출력해 드리겠습니다. 필요하신 다른 게 또 있으신가요?

여 저, 수영장이 지금 열렸는지 또는 수영 강습이 진행되고 있는지 궁금해요.

남 모든 분을 대상으로 오후 7시까지 엽니다.

여 아주 잘됐네요. 지금 거기로 갈게요.

어휘 gym 체육관 forget ~을 잊다 temporary 임시의, 일시적인 so that ~할 수 있도록 work out 운동하다 wonder if ~인지 궁금하다 go on 진행되다 until (지속) ~까지 head 가다, 향하다

35 Where is the conversation most likely taking place?
(A) At a fitness facility
(B) At a bank
(C) At a post office
(D) At a theater

대화가 어디에서 이뤄지고 있는 것 같은가?
(A) 피트니스 시설에서
(B) 은행에서
(C) 우체국에서
(D) 영화관에서

해설 〈대화 장소를 묻는 문제〉
대화 시작 부분에 여자가 현재 있는 곳을 at this gym이라고 지칭하고 있고, 중반부에는 남자가 오늘 운동할 수 있다고(you can still work out today) 알리고 있다. 따라서 운동 시설에 배경임을 알 수 있으므로 (A)가 정답이다.

어휘 take place (일, 행사 등이) 발생되다, 개최되다

36 What information does the man ask for?
(A) The woman's name
(B) The woman's credit card number
(C) The woman's e-mail address
(D) The woman's phone number

남자는 어떤 정보를 요청하는가?
(A) 여자의 이름
(B) 여자의 신용카드 번호
(C) 여자의 이메일 주소
(D) 여자의 전화번호

해설 〈요청 사항을 묻는 문제〉
대화 초반부에 남자가 What is your e-mail address?라는 말로
여자의 이메일 주소를 묻고 있으므로 (C)가 정답이다.

어휘 ask for ~을 요청하다

37 What will the woman most likely do next?
(A) Take a swim
(B) Make a payment
(C) Order some food
(D) Attend a consultation
여자는 곧이어 무엇을 할 것 같은가?
(A) 수영을 하는 일
(B) 비용을 지불하는 일
(C) 음식을 주문하는 일
(D) 상담 시간에 참석하는 일

해설 〈곧이어 할 일을 묻는 문제〉
여자가 대화 후반부에 수영장 이용과 관련해 궁금해하자(I'm
wondering if the pool is open now) 남자가 7시까지 연다고 알
린 뒤로 지금 그곳으로 가겠다고(I'll head there right now) 언급하
고 있으므로 (A)가 정답이다.

어휘 order ~을 주문하다 attend ~에 참석하다 consultation 상담, 상의

Questions 38-40 refer to the following conversation. 미M 캐W

M Good morning. This is Viscount Camping Company.
How may I assist you?
W Hi, ㉓ I purchased a new tent from your store last night,
㉓ but when I put it up in the garden to try it, I noticed
some of the fabric on the outside was ripped.
M Oh, sorry to hear that.
W So, will you be able to send me a replacement?
M Yes, I'll arrange that immediately. ㊵ Could you please
tell me the name of the item you purchased?

남 안녕하세요. 비스카운트 캠핑 컴퍼니입니다. 무엇을 도와드릴까요?
여 안녕하세요. 제가 어젯밤에 그쪽 매장에서 새 텐트를 구입했는데, 한 번 확
인해 보려고 정원에 세웠을 때, 외피 직물 일부가 찢겨 있다는 걸 알았어요.
남 아, 그 말씀을 듣게 되어 유감입니다.
여 그래서, 교환 제품을 보내 주실 수 있으신가요?
남 네, 즉시 조치해 드리겠습니다. 구입하신 제품의 이름을 알려 주시겠습니까?

어휘 assist ~을 돕다 purchase ~을 구입하다 put A up A를 세워 놓다, 설
치하다 try ~을 한 번 확인해 보다 notice (that) ~임을 알게 되다, 알아
차리다 fabric 직물 ripped 찢긴, 뜯긴 be able to do ~할 수 있다
replacement 교체(품) arrange ~을 조치하다, 준비하다 immediately
즉시

38 What did the woman do yesterday?
(A) She went on a hiking trip.
(B) She requested repairs.
(C) She ordered some clothing.
(D) She bought an item.
여자는 어제 무엇을 했는가?
(A) 등산 여행을 떠났다.
(B) 수리를 요청했다.
(C) 일부 의류를 주문했다.
(D) 제품을 구입했다.

해설 〈과거에 일어난 일을 묻는 문제〉
대화 초반부에 여자가 어젯밤에 새 텐트를 구입하고(I purchased a
new tent from your store last night) 알리고 있으므로 (D)가 정
답이다.

어휘 go on a trip 여행을 떠나다 request ~을 요청하다 repair 수리
order ~을 주문하다 clothing 의류, 옷

39 Why is the woman calling?
(A) To complain about an employee
(B) To report a problem with a purchase
(C) To ask about store opening times
(D) To check the status of a payment
여자는 왜 전화를 하는가?
(A) 직원에 대해 불만을 제기하기 위해
(B) 구매 제품의 문제를 알리기 위해
(C) 매장 운영 시간에 대해 묻기 위해
(D) 비용 지불 상태를 확인하기 위해

해설 〈목적을 묻는 문제〉
여자가 대화 초반부에 텐트 구입 사실과 함께 일부 찢긴 부분이 있
다는(but when I put it up in the garden to try it, I noticed
some of the fabric on the outside was ripped) 사실을 알고
있으므로 (B)가 정답이다.

어휘 complain about ~에 대해 불만을 제기하다 purchase 구입(품)
status 상태

40 What information does the man ask for?
(A) A product name
(B) An order number
(C) A delivery address
(D) A credit card number

남자는 어떤 정보를 요청하는가?
(A) 제품 이름
(B) 주문 번호
(C) 배송 주소
(D) 신용카드 번호

해설 〈요청 사항을 묻는 문제〉
대화 맨 마지막에 남자가 문제 해결을 위해 구입 제품의 이름을 알려
달라고(Could you please tell me the name of the item you
purchased?) 요청하고 있으므로 (A)가 정답이다.

어휘 ask for ~을 요청하다

Questions 41-43 refer to the following conversation with three
speakers. 미M 호M 영W

M1 Dave, it was good to see you, and you're looking great!
㊶ I hope you're happy with your new haircut. Maggie,
please book a follow-up appointment for Dave so that I
can add the color he wants.
M2 I love my new look, Louis. Thanks! Hi, Maggie.
W Hi. So, would you be able to come in around 3 on
Tuesday?
M2 I'm afraid I have a hectic schedule all week. ㊷ Could I
get an appointment next Saturday or Sunday?
W No problem. Louis has some free time on Saturday
morning. Would 10:30 work for you?
M2 Sounds perfect.
W Great, I've put it in our schedule. ㊸ I'll send you a
text notification the day before your appointment as a
reminder.

남1 데이브 씨, 만나서 반가웠어요. 그리고 아주 멋져 보이시네요! 새로 자른 머
리가 마음에 드시길 바랍니다. 매기 씨, 데이브 씨가 원하시는 색을 제가
넣어 드릴 수 있게 다음 예약 일정을 잡아 주세요.
남2 새로운 스타일이 아주 마음에 듭니다. 루이스 씨. 고마워요! 안녕하세요, 매
기 씨.
여 안녕하세요. 그럼, 화요일 3시쯤 오실 수 있으신가요?
남2 제가 일주일 내내 일정이 정신없이 바쁠 것 같아요. 다음 주 토요일이나 일
요일로 예약을 잡을 수 있을까요?
여 좋습니다. 루이스 씨가 토요일 오전에 여유 시간이 좀 있습니다. 10시 30
분이면 될까요?
남2 아주 좋아요.
여 좋습니다. 저희 일정표에 포함해 두었습니다. 예약 하루 전날에 알림 메시
지로 문자를 보내 통지해 드리겠습니다.

어휘 look + 형용사 ~하게 보이다. ~한 것 같다 book an appointment 예약 일 정을 잡다 follow-up 후속의, 후속적인 so that ~할 수 있도록 add ~을 추가하다 look n. 스타일, 모습 be able to do ~할 수 있다 around ~ 쯤, 약, 대략 I'm afraid (that) (부정적인 말을 할 때) ~인 것 같다, 유감이지만 ~이다 hectic 정신없이 바쁜 work for (일정 등이) ~에게 괜찮다, 좋다 put A in B A를 B에 포함하다, 넣어 두다 send A text notification 문자를 보내 통지하다 reminder (상기시키기 위한) 알림 메시지

41 Where most likely are the speakers?
(A) In a hair salon
(B) In a hospital
(C) In a clothing store
(D) In a fitness center

화자들은 어디에 있는 것 같은가?
(A) 미용실에
(B) 병원에
(C) 의류 매장에
(D) 피트니스 센터에

해설 〈대화 장소를 묻는 문제〉
대화 초반부에 남자 한 명이 새로 자른 머리가 마음에 들기를 바란다 는 말과 함께 데이브 씨가 원하는 색을 넣는 것과 관련해 예약 시간 을 잡는 일을(I hope you're happy with your new haircut. Maggie, please book a follow-up appointment ~ I can add the color he wants) 언급하고 있다. 이는 미용실에서 발생될 수 있는 일이므로 (A)가 정답이다.

42 What does Dave ask for?
(A) A discount
(B) A weekend appointment
(C) A complimentary service
(D) An application form

데이브 씨는 무엇을 요청하는가?
(A) 할인
(B) 주말 예약
(C) 무료 서비스
(D) 신청서

해설 〈요청 사항을 묻는 문제〉
대화 중반부에 남자가 다음 주 토요일이나 일요일로 예약을 잡을 수 있는지(Could I get an appointment next Saturday or Sunday?) 묻고 있으므로 (B)가 정답이다.

어휘 ask for ~을 요청하다 appointment 예약, 약속 complimentary 무료의 application 신청(서), 지원(서) form 양식, 서식

43 What does the woman say she will do?
(A) Make a phone call
(B) Change a business policy
(C) Send a text message
(D) Schedule a delivery

여자는 무엇을 할 것이라고 말하는가?

(A) 전화를 거는 일
(B) 사업 정책을 변경하는 일
(C) 문자 메시지를 보내는 일
(D) 배송 일정을 잡는 일

해설 〈미래에 할 일을 묻는 문제〉
대화 마지막 부분에 여자가 문자 메시지를 보내 통지하겠다고(I'll send you a text notification) 알리고 있으므로 (C)가 정답이다.

어휘 policy 정책, 방침 text message 문자 메시지 schedule ~의 일정을 잡다

Questions 44-46 refer to the following conversation. 미M 캐W

M Louisa, **44** I'd like to hear more about the renovation of our technical support call center.
W Well, **44** the renovation work was well worth it. We have so much more space thanks to the new open design.
M That sounds good. I bet it's a much more organized and productive work environment now.
W Definitely. Also, **45** I'm planning to hire some extra part-time employees now that we have a larger workspace.
M Hmm, I have an idea for how we can find some new part-timers. **46** Why don't we go to the job fair next month and recruit people there?
W That's a great idea! I'll try to secure us a booth at the event.

남 루이자 씨, 우리 기술 지원 콜 센터의 개조 공사와 관련해 더 많은 얘기를 들어 보고 싶습니다.
여 음, 그 개조 공사는 그만한 가치가 충분히 있었습니다. 지금 훨씬 더 넓은 공간이 있어서 현대적이고 개방된 디자인을 갖추고 있습니다.
남 좋은 것 같네요. 지금이 훨씬 더 체계적이고 생산적인 업무 환경인 것이 분명해요.
여 바로 그렇습니다. 그리고, 이제 더 넓은 업무 공간이 있으니 몇몇 시간제 직원을 추가로 고용할 계획입니다.
남 흠, 우리가 어떻게 몇몇 새로운 시간제 근무자들을 찾을 수 있는지에 대한 아이디어가 있습니다. 다음 달에 있을 취업 박람회에 가서 거기서 사람들을 모집하는 건 어때요?
여 아주 좋은 아이디어입니다! 그 행사장에서 부스를 확보해 보도록 하겠습니다.

어휘 would like to do ~하고 싶다, ~하고자 하다 renovation 개조, 보수 technical support 기술 지원 well worth + 명사 ~할 만한 가치가 충분한 much (비교급 수식) 훨씬 bet (that) ~인 것이 분명하다 organized 체계적인, 조직적인 productive 생산적인 plan to do ~할 계획이다 hire ~을 고용하다 extra 추가의, 별도의 now that (이제) ~이므로 Why don't we ~? ~하는 게 어때요? job fair 취업 박람회 recruit ~을 모집하다 try to do ~하려 하다 secure A B A에게 B를 확보해 주다

---

44 What has the company recently done?
(A) Launched a new service
(B) Renovated a building
(C) Moved to a new location
(D) Implemented a work policy

회사에서 최근에 무엇을 했는가?
(A) 신규 서비스를 시작하는 일
(B) 건물을 개조하는 일
(C) 새로운 곳으로 이전하는 일
(D) 업무 방침을 시행하는 일

해설 〈과거에 일어난 일을 묻는 문제〉
대화 시작 부분에 남자가 기술 지원 콜 센터의 개조 공사와 관련된 얘기를 더 들어 보고 싶다고(I'd like to hear more about the renovation of our technical support call center) 언급하자, 여자가 과거 시제 동사 was와 함께 그만한 가치가 충분했다고(the renovation work was well worth it) 알리고 있다. 따라서 최근에 건물을 개조한 사실을 알 수 있으므로 (B)가 정답이다.

어휘 recently 최근에 launch ~을 시작하다, 출시하다 renovate ~을 개조하다, 보수하다 location 장소, 위치, 지점 implement ~을 시행하다 policy 정책, 방침

45 Why does the woman want to hire additional staff?
(A) Consumer demand has increased.
(B) A work deadline is approaching.
(C) More space is available.
(D) Some employees have left.

여자는 왜 추가 직원을 고용하고 싶어 하는가?
(A) 소비자 수요가 증가했다.
(B) 업무 마감기한이 다가오고 있다.
(C) 더 넓은 공간이 이용 가능하다.
(D) 일부 직원들이 그만두었다.

해설 〈기타 세부 사항을 묻는 문제〉
대화 중반부에 여자가 더 넓은 업무 공간이 있어서 시간제 직원을 추가로 고용할 계획이라고(I'm planning to hire some extra part-time employees now that we have a larger workspace) 밝히고 있으므로 (C)가 정답이다.

어휘 hire ~을 고용하다 additional 추가적인 consumer 소비자 demand 수요 increase 증가하다, 오르다 deadline 마감기한 approach 다가오다, 다가가다 available 이용 가능한 leave 그만두다, 떠나다

46 What does the man recommend doing?
(A) Posting an advertisement
(B) Updating a Web site
(C) Running a training seminar
(D) Attending a job fair

남자는 무엇을 하도록 권하는가?
(A) 광고를 게시하는 일

(B) 웹 사이트를 업데이트하는 일
(C) 교육 세미나를 운영하는 일
(D) 취업 박람회에 참석하는 일

해설 〈제안 사항을 묻는 문제〉
대화 후반부에 남자가 다음 달에 있을 취업 박람회에 가서 사람들을 모집하면 어떨지 묻는 것으로(Why don't we go to the job fair next month and recruit people there?) 권하고 있으므로 (D)가 정답이다.

어휘 post ~을 게시하다 advertisement 광고 run ~을 운영하다, 진행하다 attend ~에 참석하다 job fair 취업 박람회

Questions 47-49 refer to the following conversation. (영W) (호M)

W Good morning, David. I've been told you're team leader for our new advertising project.
M That's right. We've just completed our radio commercial and ㊼ I'm quite proud of the catchy song we've added to it.
W That sounds interesting. I hear we have produced some billboards, too. ㊽ Those will be placed around town today, right?
M Sheila said next week would be fine.
W I see. Actually, I think it's more urgent than that. I'd hate for us to fall behind. ㊾ I'll send the schedule to Sheila for her to have a look at.

여 안녕하세요, 데이비드 씨. 우리 새 광고 프로젝트 팀장이 되었다는 얘기를 들었습니다.
남 맞습니다. 라디오 광고를 막 완료했는데, 우리가 거기에 추가한 주제곡이 꽤 자랑스럽습니다.
여 흥미로운 것 같네요. 제가 듣기로는 우리가 몇몇 옥외 광고판도 만들었다고 하던데요. 그것들이 오늘 도시 곳곳에 놓일 거죠, 맞나요?
남 쉴라 씨는 다음 주가 좋을 거라고 말했어요.
여 알겠습니다. 사실, 저는 그보다 더 긴급하다고 생각해요. 우리가 일정에 뒤처지고 싶진 않거든요. 쉴라 씨에게 한 번 살펴보시라고 일정표를 보내 드리겠습니다.

어휘 be told (that) ~라는 얘기를 듣다 advertising 광고 (활동) complete ~을 완료하다 commercial 광고 방송 be proud of ~을 자랑스러워하다 quite 꽤, 상당히 catchy 기억하기 쉬운 add A to B A를 B에 추가하다 billboard 옥외 광고판 urgent 긴급한, 시급한 I'd hate for A to do A가 ~하는 게 싫을 거예요 fall behind (일정, 진도 등) ~에 뒤처지다 schedule 일정(표) have a look at ~을 한 번 보다

47 What part of the commercial does the man say he is proud of?
(A) The introduction
(B) The script
(C) The acting
(D) The song

남자는 광고 방송의 어떤 부분이 자랑스럽다고 말하는가?
(A) 도입부
(B) 대본
(C) 연기
(D) 노래

해설 〈기타 세부 사항을 묻는 문제〉
대화 초반부에 남자가 라디오 광고를 언급하면서 거기에 넣은 주제곡이 자랑스럽다고(I'm quite proud of the catchy song we've added to it) 알리고 있으므로 (D)가 정답이다.

48 Why does the man say, "Sheila said next week would be fine"?
(A) To correct a misunderstanding about a task
(B) To explain why a document has not been submitted
(C) To apologize for missing a meeting
(D) To complain about a colleague's performance

남자는 왜 "Sheila said next week would be fine"이라고 말하는가?
(A) 업무에 대한 오해를 바로잡기 위해
(B) 문서가 왜 제출되지 않았는지 설명하기 위해
(C) 회의에 빠진 것에 대해 사과하기 위해
(D) 동료 직원의 업무 능력에 대해 불평하기 위해

해설 〈의도 파악 문제〉
대화 중반부에 여자가 옥외 광고판을 언급하면서 오늘 도시 곳곳에 놓이는 것이 맞는지 확인하는 질문을 하자(Those will be placed around town today, right?), 남자가 '쉴라 씨가 다음 주가 좋을 것이라고 말했다'고 언급하는 흐름이다. 이는 광고판을 설치하는 업무가 진행되는 일정을 잘못 알고 있는 것에 대해 여자에게 정확한 정보를 제공함으로써 오해를 바로잡기 위해 한 말이므로 (A)가 정답이다.

어휘 correct ~을 바로잡다 misunderstanding 오해, 착오 task 업무, 일 explain ~을 설명하다 submit ~을 제출하다 apologize for ~에 대해 사과하다 miss ~에 빠지다, ~을 놓치다 complain about ~에 대해 불평하다 colleague 동료 (직원) performance 수행 능력, 성과, 실적

49 What does the woman plan to send to Sheila?
(A) A staff list
(B) A schedule
(C) An expense report
(D) A billboard design

여자는 쉴라 씨에게 무엇을 보낼 계획인가?
(A) 직원 명단
(B) 일정표
(C) 지출 비용 보고서
(D) 옥외 광고판 디자인

해설 〈기타 세부 사항을 묻는 문제〉
대화 마지막 부분에 여자가 쉴라 씨에게 일정표를 보내겠다고(I'll send the schedule to Sheila) 언급하고 있으므로 (B)가 정답이다.

어휘 plan to do ~할 계획이다 schedule 일정(표) expense 지출 비용, 경비

Questions 50-52 refer to the following conversation with three speakers. (미M) (캐W) (영W)

M I think ㊿ we can be proud to be part of the most innovative research lab in the country. We all deserve a break. (51) Have you had a chance to look at potential venues for the company retreat?
W1 I really like the look of Shady Acres. It has premium spa facilities and a five star golf course.
M And how about that other local venue?
W2 You must mean Forest Hills. Some of our colleagues rate it very highly.
M I see. I'm not really sure how to decide. (52) I feel a little bit concerned because I wouldn't want to choose a bad destination.

남 우리가 전국에서 가장 혁신적인 연구소의 일원이라는 걸 자랑스럽게 여겨도 될 것 같아요. 우리 모두 휴가를 받을 만해요. 회사 야유회로 가 볼 만한 장소를 살펴볼 기회가 있으셨나요?
여1 저는 쉐이디 에이커스의 스타일이 정말 마음에 들어요. 프리미엄 스파 시설과 5성급 골프 코스가 있거든요.
남 그럼 저 다른 지역의 장소는 어때요?
여2 포레스트 힐즈를 말씀하시는 게 틀림없는 것 같네요. 우리 동료들 중 몇몇이 그곳을 아주 높이 평가하고 있어요.
남 알겠습니다. 어떻게 결정해야 할지 정말 잘 모르겠네요. 좋지 않은 여행지를 선택하고 싶진 않아서 조금 우려스러운 기분입니다.

어휘 be proud to do ~해서 자랑스럽다 innovative 혁신적인 research 연구, 조사 lab 실험실 deserve ~에 대한 자격이 있다, ~을 받을 만하다 break 휴식, 휴가 have a chance to do ~할 기회가 있다 potential 잠재적인, 가능성 있는 venue 장소, 행사장 retreat 야유회 look 스타일, 모습, 외관 facility 시설(물) how about ~? ~는 어때요? local 지역의 must ~인 게 틀림없다 colleague 동료 (직원) rate ~을 평가하다, 등급을 매기다 how to do 어떻게 ~하는지, ~하는 법 decide 결정하다 a little bit 조금, 약간 concerned 우려하는, 걱정하는 choose ~을 선택하다 destination 여행지, 목적지

50 What kind of business do the speakers work for?
(A) A research laboratory
(B) A library
(C) A real estate agency
(D) A leisure park

화자들은 어떤 종류의 회사에서 근무하는가?
(A) 연구소
(B) 도서관
(C) 부동산 중개업체
(D) 여가 공원

해설 〈근무지를 묻는 문제〉
남자가 대화를 시작하면서 자신들이 전국에서 가장 혁신적인 연구소의 일원이라는 게 자랑스럽다고(we can be proud to be part of the most innovative research lab in the country) 언급하고 있으므로 (A)가 정답이다.

51 What is the main topic of the conversation?
(A) The results of a recent golf tournament
(B) The recruitment policy of a company
(C) The latest findings of a project
(D) The venue for an employee retreat

대화의 주제는 무엇인가?
(A) 최근에 있었던 골프 토너먼트의 결과
(B) 회사의 고용 방침
(C) 프로젝트의 최근 결과물
(D) 직원 야유회 장소

해설 〈주제를 묻는 문제〉
남자가 대화 초반부에 회사 야유회로 갈 만한 장소를 살펴봤는지(Have you had a chance to look at potential venues for the company retreat?) 물은 뒤로 특정 장소와 관련해 이야기하고 있으므로 (D)가 정답이다.

어휘 result 결과(물) recent 최근의 recruitment 인력 채용, 인력 모집 policy 방침, 정책 findings 결과물 venue (개최) 장소, 행사장 retreat 야유회

52 Why is the man feeling worried?
(A) He needs to hire more staff urgently.
(B) He must submit a project before a deadline.
(C) He wants to choose an ideal destination.
(D) He has been working long hours recently.

남자는 왜 걱정스러운 기분인가?
(A) 긴급하게 추가 직원을 고용해야 한다.
(B) 반드시 마감기한 전에 프로젝트를 제출해야 한다.
(C) 이상적인 여행지를 선택해야 한다.
(D) 최근에 계속 오랜 시간 근무해 오고 있다.

해설 〈기타 세부 사항을 묻는 문제〉
대화 맨 마지막에 남자가 좋지 않은 여행지를 선택하고 싶지 않아서 조금 우려된다고(I feel a little bit concerned because I wouldn't

want to choose a bad destination) 언급하고 있다. 이는 이상적인 여행지를 선택해야 한다는 걱정에서 비롯된 것이므로 (C)가 정답이다.

어휘 hire ~을 고용하다 urgently 긴급히 submit ~을 제출하다 deadline 마감기한 choose ~을 선택하다 ideal 이상적인 destination 여행지, 목적지 recently 최근에

Questions 53-55 refer to the following conversation. 호M 영W

M Hi, Amanda. Have you seen the quarterly report on our viewer numbers? It seems that ⑤ our comedy shows, especially *Family Matters*, are being watched by fewer people across all age groups.
W That's disappointing news.
M I know, and the report recommended that our network should focus on more serious programming, like documentaries and drama series.
W Well, I guess we could do that. ⑤ Perhaps we could move our 11 P.M. documentary series into our primetime slot at 7 P.M.
M That's our most important slot. ⑤ Umm how about putting it on at 9 instead?
W Okay, ⑤ I'll arrange a meeting with the show runners for that series to let them know the plan.

남 안녕하세요, 아만다 씨. 시청자 숫자에 관한 분기 보고서를 확인해 보셨나요? 우리 코미디 프로그램들, 특히 〈패밀리 매터스〉를 시청하는 사람들이 전 연령층에 걸쳐 더 줄어들고 있는 것 같아요.
여 실망스러운 소식이네요.
남 그러니까요. 그리고 보고서에서 우리 방송국이 다큐멘터리나 드라마 시리즈 같이 더 진지한 프로그램 편성에 초점을 맞추도록 권했어요.
여 음, 그렇게 할 수 있을 것 같아요. 아마 오후 11시 다큐멘터리 시리즈를 황금 시간대인 오후 7시로 옮길 수 있을 거예요.
남 그때가 우리에게 가장 중요한 시간대잖아요. 음 대신 9시에 방송하는 건 어떨까요?
여 좋아요, 계획을 알릴 수 있도록 그 시리즈 프로그램 진행 책임자들과 회의 자리를 마련할게요.

어휘 quarterly 분기의 viewer 시청자 It seems that ~인 것 같다 especially 특히 across ~에 걸쳐, ~ 전체적으로 disappointing 실망시키는 recommend that ~하도록 권하다, 추천하다 network 방송국 focus on ~에 초점을 맞추다 programming 프로그램 편성 primetime slot 황금 시간대 how about -ing? ~하는 건 어때요? put A on A를 방송하다, 상영하다 instead 대신 arrange ~을 마련하다, 조치하다 show runner 프로그램 진행 책임자 let A know B A에게 B를 알리다

53 What problem does the man mention?
(A) A show received poor reviews.

(B) A network is closing down.
(C) An employee is retiring.
(D) A show is losing viewers.

남자는 무슨 문제를 언급하는가?
(A) 한 가지 프로그램이 형편없는 평가를 받았다.
(B) 한 방송국이 문을 닫는다.
(C) 한 직원이 은퇴한다.
(D) 한 프로그램이 시청자를 놓치고 있다.

해설 〈문제점을 묻는 문제〉
대화 초반부에 여자가 〈패밀리 매터스〉를 시청하는 사람들이 전 연령층에 걸쳐 더 줄어들고 있는 것 같다는(our comedy shows, especially *Family Matters*, are being watched by fewer people across all age groups) 문제점을 언급하고 있으므로 시청자 감소 문제를 말한 (D)가 정답이다.

어휘 receive ~을 받다 review 평가, 후기, 의견 close down 문을 닫다 retire 은퇴하다 viewer 시청자, 보는 사람

54 What does the man imply when he says, "That's our most important slot"?
(A) He recommends a new TV show.
(B) He is pleased about a show's success.
(C) He is concerned about the woman's idea.
(D) He will give the woman an assignment.

남자가 'That's our most important slot'라고 말할 때 무엇을 의도하는가?
(A) 새로운 TV 프로그램을 추천하고 있다.
(B) 프로그램의 성공에 대해 기뻐하고 있다.
(C) 여자의 아이디어에 대해 우려하고 있다.
(D) 여자에게 업무를 할당해 줄 것이다.

해설 〈의도 파악 문제〉
대화 중반부에 여자가 11시 다큐멘터리 시리즈를 황금 시간대인 7시로 옮길 수 있다고(Perhaps we could move our 11 P.M. documentary series into our primetime slot at 7 P.M.) 언급하자, 남자가 '가장 중요한 시간대이다'라고 밝히면서 대신 9시로 옮기는 게 어떤지(Umm how about putting it on at 9 instead?) 되묻고 있다. 이는 여자의 생각이 좋지 않다는 뜻으로서 일종의 우려를 나타내는 것이므로 (C)가 정답이다.

어휘 success 성공 be concerned about ~에 대해 우려하다 assignment 할당(되는 일), 배정(되는 일)

55 What does the woman say she will do?
(A) Organize a meeting
(B) Cancel a TV show
(C) Hire a new director
(D) Stay late at work

여자는 무엇을 할 것이라고 말하는가?
(A) 회의 자리를 마련하는 일
(B) 한 TV 프로그램을 취소하는 일

(C) 신임 이사를 고용하는 일
(D) 늦게까지 회사에 머무르는 일

해설 〈미래에 할 일을 묻는 문제〉
대화 맨 마지막에 프로그램 진행 책임자들과 회의를 마련하겠다고(I'll arrange a meeting with the show runners) 알리고 있으므로 (A)가 정답이다.

어휘 organize ~을 마련하다, 조직하다 cancel ~을 취소하다 hire ~을 고용하다 director 이사, 부장, 책임자

Questions 56-58 refer to the following conversation. 캐W 미M

W William, 56 I've asked someone to come and repair the two broken shelves in our non-fiction section.
M Great! Actually, that whole non-fiction section of the store biographies, textbooks, encyclopedias could really use some improvement.
W Well, 57 we're planning to rearrange the store next month, so many of those non-fiction items will be put in a different spot. I want to take a lot of them and put them on some new shelves.
M I see. Will the store close while we are rearranging everything?
W No, we'll do it ourselves after business hours. 58 Would you be prepared to stay late one night?
M 58 Sure, I'd be happy to help.

여 윌리엄 씨, 제가 우리 비소설 구역에 망가진 선반 두 개를 수리하러 와 달라고 사람을 불렀어요.
남 잘됐네요! 실은, 우리 매장에서 위인전과 교재, 백과사전이 있는 그 비소설 구역 전체가 정말로 개선되어야 하거든요.
여 음, 우리가 다음 달에 매장 구역을 재편할 계획이기 때문에 그 비소설 도서들 중 많은 것들이 다른 자리에 놓이게 될 거예요. 저는 그 많은 도서들을 가져다가 몇몇 새로운 선반에 놓아 두고 싶어요.
남 알겠습니다. 우리가 모든 구역을 재편하는 동안 매장이 문을 닫나요?
여 아니요, 영업 시간 후에 우리가 직접 할 겁니다. 하루 저녁 늦게까지 남아 있을 준비를 해 주실 수 있으세요?
남 그럼요, 기꺼이 도와드리겠습니다.

어휘 ask A to do A에게 ~하도록 요청하다 repair ~을 수리하다 broken 망가진, 고장 난, 부서진 shelf 선반 non-fiction 비소설의, 논픽션의 actually 실은, 사실은 whole 전체의 biography 위인전, 전기 textbook 교재 encyclopedia 백과사전 could use improvement 개선되어야 하다, 향상되어야 하다 plan to do ~할 계획이다 rearrange ~을 재편하다, 재구성하다 put A in B A를 B에 놓다, 두다 spot 자리, 지점, 위치 while ~하는 동안 oneself (부사처럼 쓰여) 직접, 스스로 be prepared to do ~할 준비가 되다 stay late 늦게까지 남아 있다

---

56 Where do the speakers most likely work?
(A) At a movie theater
(B) At a furniture shop
(C) At a post office
(D) At a bookstore
화자들은 어디에서 일하고 있을 것 같은가?
(A) 영화관에서
(B) 가구 매장에서
(C) 우체국에서
(D) 서점에서

해설 〈근무지를 묻는 문제〉
대화 시작 부분에 여자가 비소설 구역에 망가진 선반 두 개를 수리하기 위해 사람을 부른 사실(I've asked someone to come and repair the two broken shelves in our non-fiction section) 언급하고 있는데, 그 구역은 서점에서 볼 수 있는 공간에 해당되므로 (D)가 정답이다.

57 What will happen at the business next month?
(A) Rooms will be painted.
(B) Products will be moved.
(C) Lighting will be replaced.
(D) Software will be updated.
업체에서 다음 달에 무슨 일이 있을 것인가?
(A) 방마다 페인트칠 작업을 할 것이다.
(B) 제품들이 옮겨질 것이다.
(C) 조명이 교체될 것이다.
(D) 소프트웨어가 업데이트될 것이다.

해설 〈특정 시점의 일을 묻는 문제〉
대화 중반부에 여자가 다음 달에 매장 구역을 재편하는 계획과 함께 비소설 도서들 중 많은 것들이 다른 자리에 놓인다고(we're planning to rearrange the store next month, so many of those non-fiction items will be put in a different spot) 알리고 있다. 이는 일부 제품이 다른 자리로 옮겨진다는 뜻이므로 (B)가 정답이다.

어휘 lighting 조명 replace ~을 교체하다

58 What does the man agree to do?
(A) Order products
(B) Work late
(C) Train staff
(D) Attend a meeting
남자는 무엇을 하는 데 동의하는가?
(A) 제품을 주문하는 것
(B) 늦게까지 일하는 것
(C) 직원을 교육하는 것
(D) 회의에 참석하는 것

해설 〈기타 세부 사항을 묻는 문제〉
대화 후반부에 여자가 늦게까지 남아 있을 준비를 해 줄 수 있는지(Would you be prepared to stay late one night?) 묻는 것에 대해 남자가 Sure, I'd be happy to help라는 말로 동의하고 있으므로 (B)가 정답이다.

어휘 agree to do ~하는 데 동의하다 train ~을 교육하다 attend ~에 참석하다

Questions 59-61 refer to the following conversation. 미M 영W

M Hi, Jenny. 59 Thanks for agreeing to this interview with Art & Animation Magazine. Last month, after years of planning you finally opened the American Comic Book Museum. 60 What was the main problem you faced?
W 60 Undoubtedly attracting interested investors. It took me a long time to secure the financing I needed.
M Well, I'm glad you managed to find some investors eventually. Have you had many visitors since opening?
W Yes. It seems like the museum will be rather popular, so 61 we're discussing holding a comic convention in the main exhibition room. That should take place sometime before the end of the year.

남 안녕하세요, 제니 씨. 아트 앤 애니메이션 매거진과 함께 하는 이번 인터뷰에 동의해 주셔서 감사합니다. 지난달에 수년간의 기획 끝에, 마침내 아메리칸 코믹북 박물관을 개장하셨습니다. 직면하셨던 주된 문제가 무엇이었습니까?
여 의심의 여지없이, 관심 있는 투자자들을 끌어들이는 일이었죠. 제가 필요로 했던 자금을 확보하는 데 시간이 오래 걸렸어요.
남 음, 결국 몇몇 투자자들을 찾아내셨다니 다행입니다. 개장 후에 방문객들이 많았나요?
여 네. 박물관이 좀 인기 있을 것 같아서, 주 전시실에서 만화책 컨벤션을 개최하는 것을 논의하고 있습니다. 이 행사는 올 연말이 되기 전에 개최될 겁니다.

어휘 planning 기획 finally 마침내, 결국(= eventually) face v. ~에 직면하다 undoubtedly 의심의 여지없이 attract ~을 끌어들이다 interested 관심 있는 investor 투자자 take A B A에게 B의 시간이 걸리다 secure ~을 확보하다 financing 자금 (제공) manage to do ~해내다 since ~ 이후에 It seems like ~인 것 같다 rather 좀, 약간, 다소 popular 인기 있는 discuss ~을 논의하다 hold ~을 개최하다 exhibition 전시(회) take place (행사, 일 등이) 개최되다, 발생되다

59 Who most likely is the man?
(A) A comic collector
(B) An exhibition organizer
(C) A building designer
(D) A magazine writer

남자는 누구일 것 같은가?
(A) 만화책 수집가
(B) 전시 주최자
(C) 건물 디자이너
(D) 잡지사 기자

해설 〈직업을 묻는 문제〉
대화 시작 부분에 남자가 아트 앤 애니메이션 매거진과 함께 하는 인
터뷰에 동의한 것에 대해 감사의 인사를(Thanks for agreeing to
this interview with Art & Animation Magazine) 전하고 있는데,
이는 해당 잡지사의 기자가 할 수 있는 말이므로 (D)가 정답이다.

60 According to the woman, what was the woman's main
problem?
(A) Finding a location
(B) Attracting investors
(C) Creating exhibits
(D) Hiring qualified staff

여자의 말에 따르면, 여자의 주된 문제는 무엇이었는가?
(A) 장소를 찾는 일
(B) 투자자들을 끌어들이는 일
(C) 전시물을 만드는 일
(D) 자격 있는 직원을 고용하는 일

해설 〈문제점을 묻는 문제〉
대화 초반부에 남자가 여자에게 직면했던 주된 문제가 무엇이었는지
(What was the main problem you faced?) 묻자, 여자가 의
심의 여지없이 투자자들을 끌어들이는 일이라고(Undoubtedly
attracting interested investors) 답변하고 있으므로 (B)가 정답이
다.

어휘 according to ~에 따르면 location 장소, 위치, 지점 attract ~을
끌어들이다 investor 투자자 create ~을 만들어내다 hire ~을 고용
하다 qualified 자격 있는, 적격인

61 What will the museum do by the end of the year?
(A) Open a second branch
(B) Enlarge a building
(C) Unveil a new collection
(D) Host a convention

박물관이 연말까지 무엇을 할 것인가?
(A) 두 번째 지점을 개장하는 일
(B) 건물을 확장하는 일
(C) 새로운 소장품을 공개하는 일
(D) 컨벤션을 주최하는 일

해설 〈특정 시점의 일을 묻는 문제〉
대화 맨 마지막에 여자가 만화책 컨벤션을 개최하는 것을 논의하고
있다는 말과 함께 그 행사가 올 연말이 되기 전에 개최된다고(we're
discussing holding a comic convention ~ That should
take place sometime before the end of the year) 알리고 있
으므로 (D)가 정답이다.

어휘 branch 지점, 지사 enlarge ~을 확장하다 unveil ~을 공개하다
collection 소장(품), 수집(품) host ~을 주최하다

Questions 62-64 refer to the following conversation and flyer. 〈호M〉
〈캐W〉

M Welcome to our shop. I see that you have a flyer there.
   ㉚ Would you like us to make some copies?
W Yes, please. I need 500 printed in A5 size. Is that
   possible?
M Absolutely. Let me have the document. **㉛ Wow, you
   really sell 25 of these? That's a lot!**
W Yes, we like to give customers a wide choice. I really
   want these flyers to stand out. **㉜ Are you able to print
   them in full color?**
M **㉜ It's a little more expensive,** but sure, that's no
   problem.

┌─────────────────────────────────┐
│   **Sherpa Indian Restaurant**   │
│   │
│   75 varieties of curry   │
│   50 types of side dish   │
│   ㉛ 25 traditional beverages   │
│   10 delicious desserts   │
└─────────────────────────────────┘

남 저희 매장에 오신 것을 환영합니다. 거기 전단을 갖고 오신 게 보이네요. 사
   본을 좀 만들어 드릴까요?
여 네, 해 주세요. A5 사이즈로 500장 인쇄해야 합니다. 가능한가요?
남 물론입니다. 저에게 그 문서를 주세요. 와우, 정말로 이것들을 25가지나 판
   매하시나요? 종류가 많네요!
여 네, 저희가 고객들에게 넓은 선택의 폭을 제공해 드리고 싶어요. 이 전단
   이 정말로 눈에 잘 띄었으면 좋겠습니다. 완전히 컬러로 인쇄해 주실 수 있
   으세요?
남 약간 더 비싸긴 하지만, 네, 문제없습니다.

┌─────────────────────────────────┐
│   **셰르파 인도 레스토랑**   │
│   │
│   75가지 다른 종류의 카레   │
│   50가지의 곁들임 요리   │
│   25가지 전통 음료   │
│   10가지 맛있는 디저트   │
└─────────────────────────────────┘

어휘 flyer 전단 Would you like us to do? 저희가 ~해 드릴까요? make
a copy 사본을 만들다, 복사하다 need A p.p. A가 ~되어야 하다 wide
choice 넓은 선택의 폭 want A to do A가 ~하기를 원하다 stand out
눈에 띄다, 두드러지다 be able to do ~할 수 있다 in full color 완전
히 컬러로 a little 약간, 조금 variety 종류, 다양성 traditional 전통적인
beverage 음료

62 Where does the man most likely work?
(A) In a restaurant
(B) At city hall
(C) In a museum
(D) In a copy shop

남자는 어디에서 일하고 있을 것 같은가?
(A) 레스토랑에서
(B) 시청에서
(C) 박물관에서
(D) 인쇄소에서

해설 〈근무지를 묻는 문제 〉
대화 초반부에 남자가 소속 업체를 us로 지칭하면서 여자에게 사본을
만들어 줄지(Would you like us to make some copies?) 묻고
있으므로 (D)가 정답이다.

63 Look at the graphic. What aspect of the restaurant is the
man impressed by?
(A) The number of curries
(B) The number of side dishes
(C) The number of traditional beverages
(D) The number of desserts

시각 자료를 보시오. 남자는 레스토랑의 어떤 점에 대해 깊은 인상을 받는가?
(A) 카레 숫자
(B) 곁들임 요리 숫자
(C) 전통 음료 숫자
(D) 디저트 숫자

해설 〈2열 도표 문제 〉
대화 중반부에 남자가 감탄사와 함께 25가지나 판매하는지(Wow,
you really sell 25 of these? That's a lot!) 묻는 것으로 인상적이
라는 뜻을 나타내고 있다. 시각 자료에서 25가지로 표기된 것이 세 번
째 줄에 있는 25 traditional beverages이므로 (C)가 정답이다.

어휘 be impressed by ~에 깊은 인상을 받다

64 What will the woman have to pay more for?
(A) A larger size
(B) An express service
(C) A colored option
(D) An electronic copy

여자는 무엇에 대해 비용을 더 지불해야 할 것인가?
(A) 더 큰 사이즈
(B) 빠른 서비스
(C) 컬러 적용 선택권
(D) 전자 복사

해설 〈기타 세부 사항을 묻는 문제 〉
대화 후반부에 완전히 컬러로 해 줄 수 있는지(Are you able to
print them in full color?) 물은 것에 대해 남자가 비용이 조금 더
비싸다는(It's a little more expensive) 말로 더 지불해야 한다는 뜻
을 나타내고 (C)가 정답이다.

Questions 65-67 refer to the following conversation and graph.
영W 미M

W Tom, I guess **65 you must be getting ready for our monthly meeting. Would you like me to present the data about customer complaints to our fellow board members?**

M Thanks, Lisa, but I don't think we need to discuss those figures this time. We aren't receiving as many complaints as we did **66 when you first joined the company.**

W So I've heard. As I recall, **66 there were over 150 calls from unhappy customers that month.** Well, just let me know if you want me to make any sort of presentation.

M Actually, **67 I haven't had a chance to create meeting handouts for participants yet. Would you mind handling that for me?**

Customer Complaints

200	
150	
100	
50	
0	

September **68 October** November December

여 톰 씨, 월간 회의를 준비하고 계시는 게 틀림없을 거 같은데요. 제가 회사의 이사진을 대상으로 고객 불만 사항에 관한 데이터를 발표할까요?

남 고마워요, 리사 씨. 그런데 이번엔 그 수치에 대해 이야기할 필요가 없을 것 같아요. 당신이 처음 입사하셨을 때만큼 많은 불만 사항을 접수하는 않고 있거든요.

여 저도 그렇게 들었어요. 제가 기억하는 바로는, 그 달에 불만이 있는 고객들로부터 걸려온 전화가 150통 넘게 있었어요. 음, 제가 어떤 종류의 발표든 하기를 원하시면 말씀만 해 주세요.

남 실은, 아직 회의 참가자들에게 나눠줄 유인물을 만들 기회가 없었어요. 이 일을 대신 좀 처리해 주시겠어요?

고객 불만 사항

200	
150	
100	
50	
0	

9월 10월 11월 12월

어휘 must ~하는 게 틀림없다 get ready for ~을 준비하다 Would you like me to do? 제가 ~해 드릴까요? present ~을 발표하다, 제시하다, 제공하다 complaint 불만, 불평 fellow 동료의, 같은 입장에 있는 board members 이사진, 이사회 discuss ~을 이야기하다, 논의하다 figure 수치, 숫자 receive ~을 받다 as many A as B B만큼 많은 A join ~에 입사하다, 합류하다 recall 기억하다, 회상하다 over ~가 넘는 let A know A에게 알리다 want A to do A에게 ~하기를 원하다 sort 종류 presentation 발표 have a chance to do ~할 기회가 있다 create ~을 만들어내다 handout 유인물 participant 참가자 Would you mind -ing? ~해 주시겠어요? handle ~을 처리하다, 다루다

65 What is the man preparing for?
(A) A product launch
(B) A client visit
(C) A career fair
(D) A board meeting

남자는 무엇을 준비하고 있는가?
(A) 제품 출시
(B) 고객 방문
(C) 취업 박람회
(D) 이사회 회의

해설 〈주제를 묻는 문제〉
대화 초반부에 여자가 남자에게 월간 회의를 준비하고 있는 게 틀림없다고 말하면서 이사진을 대상으로 특정 데이터를 발표하는 일을 (you must be getting ready for our monthly meeting. ~ to present the data about customer complaints to our fellow board members?) 묻고 있다. 따라서 이사회와 함께 하는 월간 회의를 준비하고 있음을 알 수 있으므로 (D)가 정답이다.

어휘 prepare for ~을 준비하다 launch 출시, 공개, 시작 board 이사회, 이사진

66 Look at the graphic. When did the woman begin her employment at the company?
(A) In September
(B) In October
(C) In November
(D) In December

시각 자료를 보시오. 여자는 언제 이 회사에서 일을 시작했는가?
(A) 9월에
(B) 10월에
(C) 11월에
(D) 12월에

해설 〈그래프 문제〉
남자가 대화 중반부에 여자가 처음 입사했을 때의 불만 사항 접수 수준을 언급하자(when you first joined the company), 여자가 그 달에 불만이 있는 고객들이 건 전화가 150통 넘게 있었다고(there were over 150 calls from unhappy customers that month) 알리고 있다. 그래프에서 150통을 초과한 달이 10월이므로 (B)가 정답이다.

어휘 employment 일자리, 고용

67 What task does the man ask for assistance with?
(A) Preparing handouts
(B) Contacting customers
(C) Organizing a room
(D) Printing schedules

남자는 어떤 업무에 대해 도움을 요청하는가?
(A) 유인물을 준비하는 일
(B) 고객들에게 연락하는 일
(C) 방 하나를 준비하는 일
(D) 일정표를 출력하는 일

해설 〈요청 사항을 묻는 문제〉
대화 맨 마지막에 남자가 회의 참가자들에게 나눠줄 유인물을 만들 기회가 없었다는 말과 함께 여자에게 대신 처리해 달라고(I haven't had a chance to create meeting handouts for participants yet. Would you mind handling that for me?) 요청하고 있으므로 (A)가 정답이다.

어휘 task 업무, 일 ask for ~을 요청하다 assistance with ~에 대한 도움 prepare ~을 준비하다 handout 유인물 contact ~에게 연락하다 organize ~을 준비하다, 조직하다

W Curtis, I've sent the invitations for the grand opening of the modern art exhibit next week. ⑥⑧ Remember, you're in charge of ordering the coffee and snacks for the reception.

M I'll take care of that this afternoon. Also, ⑥⑨ I recommend putting out more seats in the main hall, as one of the artists will give a brief talk.

W Okay. Did you see that I finished putting up the labels?

M Yes, but I noticed an error regarding the painting next to the entrance. ⑦⓪ According to the artist's wishes, the eight-by-ten sized canvas shouldn't be $250. It's supposed to be twice that much.

W I'll print a new label right away.

Title:	*Spring Tulips*
Artist:	Lydia Sandoval
Medium:	Oil Paints
Size:	8"x10"
⑦⓪ Price:	$250

여 커티스 씨, 제가 다음 주에 열리는 현대 미술 전시회의 개막식 초청장을 발송했습니다. 기억하셔야 할 점은, 당신이 축하 연회에 필요한 커피와 간식을 주문하는 일을 책임지고 있다는 것입니다.

남 오늘 오후에 그 일을 처리하겠습니다. 그리고, 본관 홀에 더 많은 의자를 내놓도록 권해 드리고 싶은데, 미술가들 중의 한 분이 간단한 강연을 할 예정이기 때문입니다.

여 알겠습니다. 제가 라벨 부착하는 일을 완료한 것을 보셨나요?

남 네, 하지만 입구 옆에 있는 그림과 관련해 한 가지 오류를 발견했어요. 그 작가의 의사에 따라, 폭 8인치에 길이가 10인치 크기의 캔버스로 된 그림이 250달러가 되면 안 됩니다. 그 두 배가 되어야 해요.

여 즉시 새 라벨을 출력하겠습니다.

제목:	봄의 튤립
작가:	리디아 산도발
재료:	유화 물감
크기:	8"x10"
가격:	250달러

어휘 invitation 초청(장) in charge of ~을 책임지고 있는 reception 축하 연회 take care of ~을 처리하다 put out ~을 내놓다 give a talk 강연하다 brief 간단한 put up ~을 붙이다, 내걸다 notice ~을 알아차리다 wish 의사, 바람, 소망 A by B 폭이 A에 길이가 B인 be supposed to do ~하기로 되어 있다 twice that much (앞서 언급된 것에 대해) 그것보다 두 배 많은 oil paint 유화 물감 medium 재료, 표현 수단, 도구

68 What does the woman remind the man to do?
(A) Order some refreshments
(B) Place an advertisement
(C) Design an invitation
(D) Pick up an artist

여자는 남자에게 무엇을 하도록 상기시키는가?
(A) 몇몇 다과를 주문하는 일
(B) 광고를 내는 일
(C) 초대장을 디자인하는 일
(D) 한 미술가를 차로 데려오기

해설 〈상기시키는 것을 묻는 문제〉
대화 시작 부분에 여자가 Remember라는 말로 상기시키려는 정보가 있음을 알리면서 커피와 간식을 주문하는 일을 책임지고 있음을 (you're in charge of ordering the coffee and snacks) 언급하고 있으므로 (A)가 정답이다.

어휘 remind A to do A에게 ~하도록 상기시키다 refreshments 다과, 간식 place an advertisement 광고를 내다 pick up ~을 차로 데려오다, 데리러 가다

69 What does the man recommend?
(A) Contacting a colleague
(B) Decorating a room
(C) Preparing more seating
(D) Rescheduling a delivery

남자는 무엇을 권하는가?
(A) 동료 직원에게 연락하는 일
(B) 방을 장식하는 일
(C) 추가 좌석을 준비하는 일
(D) 배송 일정을 재조정하는 일

해설 〈제안 사항을 묻는 문제〉
남자가 권하는 일이 언급되는 중반부에, I recommend putting out more seats라는 말로 의자를 더 갖다 놔야 한다고 권하고 있으므로 (C)가 정답이다.

어휘 contact ~에게 연락하다 colleague 동료 (직원) decorate ~을 장식하다 prepare ~을 준비하다 reschedule ~의 일정을 재조정하다

70 Look at the graphic. Which part of the label should be changed?
(A) Title
(B) Medium
(C) Size
(D) Price

시각 자료를 보시오. 라벨의 어느 부분이 변경되어야 하는가?
(A) 제목
(B) 재료
(C) 크기
(D) 가격

해설 〈기타 시각 자료 문제〉
대화 후반부에 남자가 오류가 있는 부분을 지적하면서 250달러가 아니라 그 두 배가 되어야 한다고(~ shouldn't be $250. It's supposed to be twice that much) 알리고 있다. 시각 자료에 $250으로 표기된 항목이 Price이므로 (D)가 정답이다.

Questions 71-73 refer to the following excerpt from a meeting.
호M

To wrap up our weekly meeting, I'd just like to remind you all about ⑦⓵ a special event this weekend. The city will hold its annual outdoor music festival this Saturday and Sunday. During the event, ⑦⓶ a lot of people will stop by our business to buy snacks and drinks before heading to the festival. So we'll have two more cashiers working to keep up with the demand. Also, according to the newspaper, event planners are expecting record attendance this year. That means a lot more traffic in the area, so ⑦⓷ I suggest that you leave for work earlier than usual so you're not late for your shift.

주간 회의를 마무리하면서, 여러분 모두에게 이번 주말에 있을 특별 행사에 관해 상기시켜 드리고자 합니다. 시에서 이번 주 토요일과 일요일에 연례 야외 음악 축제를 개최합니다. 이 행사 기간에, 많은 사람들이 축제 장소로 향하기 전에 우리 업체에 들러 간식과 음료를 구입할 것입니다. 따라서 그 수요에 뒤처지지 않도록 하기 위해 두 명의 추가 계산 담당 직원을 근무하게 할 것입니다. 또한, 신문 기사에 따르면, 행사 주최 측에서 올해 기록적인 참가자 수를 예상하고 있습니다. 이는 우리 지역에 교통량이 훨씬 더 많아질 것이라는 뜻이기 때문에 교대 근무에 늦지 않도록 평소보다 더 일찍 출근하시길 권해 드립니다.

어휘 wrap up ~을 마무리하다 remind ~에게 상기시키다 hold ~을 개최하다 annual 연례적인, 해마다의 stop by ~에 들르다 business 업체, 회사, 매장 head to ~로 향하다, 가다 have A -ing A에게 ~하게 하다 cashier 계산 담당 직원 keep up with (속도, 진도 등) ~에 뒤처지지 않다, ~에 발맞춰 가다 demand 수요 according to ~에 따르면 event planners 행사 주최 측 expect ~을 예상하다, 기대하다 attendance 참가, 참가자의 수 a lot (비교급 수식) 훨씬 더 traffic 교통(량), 차량들 suggest that ~하도록 권하다 leave 출발하다, 떠나다 than usual 평소보다 shift 교대 근무(조)

71 What is scheduled to take place this weekend?
(A) A local election
(B) A community parade
(C) A music festival
(D) A sports tournament

이번 주말에 무슨 일이 있을 예정인가?

(A) 지역 선거
(B) 지역 사회 퍼레이드 행사
(C) 음악 축제
(D) 스포츠 토너먼트

해설 〈특정 시점의 일을 묻는 문제〉
담화 시작 부분에 화자가 주말에 열릴 특별 행사를 언급하면서 연례 음악 축제가 개최된다고(a special event this weekend. The city will hold its annual outdoor music festival) 알리고 있으므로 (C)가 정답이다.

어휘 be scheduled to do ~할 예정이다 take place (일, 행사 등이) 발생되다, 개최되다 local 지역의, 현지의 election 선거 community 지역 사회, 지역 공동체

72 Where most likely does the speaker work?
(A) At a newspaper agency
(B) At a supermarket
(C) At a car rental company
(D) At a jewelry store

화자는 어디에서 일하고 있을 것 같은가?
(A) 신문사에서
(B) 슈퍼마켓에서
(C) 렌터카 회사에서
(D) 장신구 매장에서

해설 〈근무지를 묻는 문제〉
담화 중반부에 화자가 소속 업체를 our business로 지칭해 사람들이 간식과 음료를 구입하기 위해 자신이 속한 업체에 들를 것이라고(a lot of people will stop by our business to buy snacks and drinks) 알리고 있다. 이러한 종류의 제품을 구입할 수 있는 곳이 슈퍼마켓이므로 (B)가 정답이다.

어휘 agency 회사, 대행사

73 What does the speaker recommend doing?
(A) Leaving for work early
(B) Wearing warm clothing
(C) Using public transportation
(D) Bringing a packed lunch

화자는 무엇을 하도록 권하는가?
(A) 일찍 출근하는 일
(B) 따뜻한 옷을 착용하는 일
(C) 대중교통을 이용하는 일
(D) 도시락을 챙겨 오는 일

해설 〈제안 사항을 묻는 문제〉
담화 맨 마지막에 교통 문제가 있을 것이라는 말과 함께 평소보다 일찍 출근하도록(I suggest that you leave for work earlier than usual) 제안하고 있으므로 (A)가 정답이다.

어휘 leave for work 출근하다 clothing 옷, 의류 public transportation 대중교통 packed lunch 점심 도시락

Questions 74-76 refer to the following broadcast. 캐W

Good morning, listeners! The mayor has confirmed that our annual outdoor summer concert, ⑦4 which was canceled last year due to low ticket sales, will be going ahead this year! The two-day concert will be held in High Park on August 12th and 13th. The concert organizers say that ⑦5 this year's festival will be the best they've ever hosted, because many popular singers and bands will be there playing their biggest hits. A variety of movies will also be shown on a large outdoor screen, including the latest work from ⑦6 Andrew Carlson, a successful local film director.

안녕하세요, 청취자 여러분! 시장님께서 작년에 저조한 입장권 판매량으로 인해 취소되었던 연례 야회 여름 콘서트가 올해 진행될 예정이라고 확인해 주셨습니다 대 이 이틀간의 콘서트는 8월 12일과 13일에 하이 파크에서 개최될 것입니다. 콘서트 주최 측에서는 올해의 축제가 그 어느 때보다 가장 뛰어난 행사가 될 것이라고 말하고 있는데, 많은 인기 가수와 밴드들이 최고의 히트곡을 그곳에서 연주할 것이기 때문입니다. 다양한 영화들 또한 대형 야외 스크린에서 상영될 것이며, 여기에는 성공한 지역 영화 감독 앤드류 칼슨의 최신작도 포함됩니다.

어휘 confirm that ~라고 확인해 주다 annual 연례적인, 해마다의 cancel ~을 취소하다 sales 판매(량), 매출 go ahead 진행되다 hold ~을 개최하다, 주최하다 organizer 주최자, 조직자 ever (최상급과 함께) 그 어느 때보다 a variety of 다양한 show ~을 상영하다 including ~을 포함해 latest 최신의 work 작품 local 지역의, 현지의

74 According to the broadcast, why was last year's concert canceled?
(A) Due to a permit problem
(B) Due to inclement weather
(C) Due to a schedule conflict
(D) Due to a lack of interest

방송에 따르면, 작년 콘서트가 왜 취소되었는가?
(A) 허가 문제로 인해
(B) 악천후로 인해
(C) 일정 충돌로 인해
(D) 관심 부족으로 인해

해설 〈기타 세부 사항을 묻는 문제〉
화자는 담화 초반부에 작년 콘서트를 언급하면서 저조한 입장권 판매량으로 인해 취소되었다고(which was canceled last year due to low ticket sales) 알리고 있다. 이는 사람들의 관심이 부족했음을 나타내는 것이므로 (D)가 정답이다.

어휘 due to ~로 인해 permit 허가(증) inclement weather 악천후 conflict 충돌, 겹침 lack 부족 interest 관심(사)

---

75 Why do organizers say the concert will be the best ever?
(A) Ticket prices will be reduced.
(B) It will be broadcast live on the radio.
(C) It will include a wider variety of food.
(D) Famous musicians will be performing.

주최 측에서 왜 해당 콘서트가 그 어느 때보다 가장 뛰어날 것이라고 말하는가?
(A) 입장권 가격이 할인될 것이다.
(B) 라디오에서 라이브로 방송될 것이다.
(C) 훨씬 더 다양한 음식을 포함할 것이다.
(D) 유명한 음악가들이 공연할 것이다.

해설 〈기타 세부 사항을 묻는 문제〉
담화 중반부에 가장 뛰어난 행사가 될 것임을 말하면서 많은 인기 가수와 밴드들이 최고의 히트곡을 연주할 것이기 때문에 그렇다고(this year's festival will be the best they've ever hosted, because many popular singers and bands will be there playing their biggest hits) 알리고 있으므로 (D)가 정답이다.

어휘 reduce ~을 할인해 주다, 감소시키다 include ~을 포함하다 a wider variety of 훨씬 더 다양한 famous 유명한

76 Who is Andrew Carlson?
(A) An event organizer
(B) A movie director
(C) A musician
(D) A city mayor

앤드류 칼슨은 누구인가?
(A) 행사 조직 담당자
(B) 영화 감독
(C) 음악가
(D) 시장

해설 〈직업을 묻는 문제〉
앤드류 칼슨의 이름이 언급되는 맨 마지막 부분에 성공한 지역 영화 감독이라고(Andrew Carlson, a successful local film director) 알리고 있으므로 (B)가 정답이다.

Good afternoon, Wendy. ⑦ This is Michael from the customer service call center. I'm calling because ⑦ I need your authorization to buy thirty office chairs for my team members. We've had a lot of complaints from staff recently about back pain and uncomfortable chairs. If I provide them with a more comfortable work environment, I think their productivity will increase. I'd like to get the chairs right away. ⑦ I'm confident you'll see it as a profitable investment in our staff. Employee comfort is a high priority, right? ⑦ Please let me know what you think. Thanks.

안녕하세요, 웬디 씨. 저는 고객 서비스 콜 센터에서 전화 드리는 마이클입니다. 제가 전화 드리는 이유는 저희 팀원들이 사용할 사무용 의자 30개를 구입할 수 있도록 승인받아야 하기 때문입니다. 최근에 직원들로부터 요통과 불편한 의자에 관련된 불만 사항이 많이 나왔습니다. 제가 더욱 편안한 업무 환경을 제공해 준다면, 직원들의 생산성이 증가할 것이라고 생각합니다. 저는 이 의자들을 즉시 구입하고자 합니다. 우리 직원들에 대한 수익성 있는 투자로 생각하시게 될 것이라고 확신합니다. 직원 편의가 최우선 사항이지 않은가요? 어떻게 생각하시는지 알려 주시기 바랍니다. 감사합니다.

어휘 authorization 승인 complaint 불만, 불평 recently 최근에 back pain 요통 uncomfortable 불편한(↔ comfortable) provide A with B A에게 B를 제공하다 work environment 업무 환경 productivity 생산성 increase 증가하다, 늘어나다 right away 즉시, 당장, 곧바로 be confident (that) ~임을 확신하다 see A as B A를 B로 여기다 profitable 수익성 있는 investment in ~에 대한 투자 priority 우선 사항 let A know A에게 알리다

77 Where does the speaker work?
(A) In a factory
(B) In a call center
(C) In a bank
(D) In a medical clinic

화자는 어디에서 근무하는가?
(A) 공장에서
(B) 콜 센터에서
(C) 은행에서
(D) 병원에서

해설 〈근무지를 묻는 문제〉
담화를 시작하면서 화자가 This is Michael from the customer service call center라는 말로 자신의 이름 및 소속 부서를 밝히고 있으므로 (B)가 정답이다.

78 What does the speaker want to purchase?
(A) Company vehicles
(B) Staff uniforms
(C) Electronic devices
(D) Office furniture

화자는 무엇을 구입하고 싶어 하는가?
(A) 회사 차량
(B) 직원 유니폼
(C) 전자 기기
(D) 사무용 가구

해설 〈기타 세부 사항을 묻는 문제〉
담화 초반부에 화자가 직원들을 위해 사무용 의자 30개를 구입할 수 있게 승인받아야 한다고(I need your authorization to buy thirty office chairs) 알리고 있다. 이는 사무용 가구의 하나이므로 (D)가 정답이다.

어휘 purchase ~을 구입하다 vehicle 차량 device 기기, 장치

79 Why does the speaker say, "Employee comfort is a high priority, right"?
(A) To praise the current work conditions
(B) To encourage the listener to approve a request
(C) To suggest providing a bonus to new workers
(D) To invite the listener to visit a workplace

화자는 왜 "Employee comfort is a high priority, right"라고 말하는가?
(A) 현재의 업무 환경을 칭찬하기 위해
(B) 청자에게 요청 사항을 승인하도록 부추기기 위해
(C) 신입 직원들에게 보너스를 제공하도록 제안하기 위해
(D) 청자에게 한 업무 장소를 방문하도록 요청하기 위해

해설 〈의도 파악 문제〉
담화 마지막 부분에 직원들에 대한 수익성 있는 투자로 여기게 될 것이라고(I'm confident you'll see it as a profitable investment in our staff) 말한 뒤로, '직원 편의가 최우선이지 않은가요?'라고 물으면서 어떻게 생각하는지 알려 달라고(Please let me know what you think) 요청하고 있다. 이는 앞서 언급한 의자 구입의 당위성을 밝히는 것으로 승인하도록 부추기는 말에 해당되므로 (B)가 정답이다.

어휘 praise ~을 칭찬하다 current 현재의 condition 환경, 상태, 조건 encourage A to do A에게 ~하도록 부추기다, 권하다 approve ~을 승인하다 suggest -ing ~하도록 권하다, 제안하다 provide ~을 제공하다 invite A to do A에게 ~하도록 요청하다

Since the workday is almost over, I'd like to make a quick announcement. Some of you may have heard that ⑧ we're changing the dress code policy for lab workers. From next Monday, you will have to change your clothes and shoes before entering the lab. This will help to reduce the contamination in the lab, ⑧ so the accuracy of our test results will improve. ⑧ Each of you will be given a uniform. This must be worn whenever you are in the lab. You can pick one up from your immediate supervisor anytime this week. Additional sets will also be available upon request. Thank you for your cooperation in this matter.

오늘 근무가 거의 끝났기 때문에 간단히 공지해 드리고자 합니다. 여러분 중 일부는 우리가 실험실 직원을 대상으로 하는 복장 규정 정책을 변경한다는 얘기를 들어 보셨을 수도 있습니다. 다음 주 월요일부터, 실험실에 들어가시기 전에 옷과 신발을 바꿔 착용하셔야 할 것입니다. 이는 실험실 내 오염을 줄이는 데 도움이 되어 우리 실험 결과물의 정확성이 향상될 것입니다. 여러분 각자에게 유니폼이 지급됩니다. 이는 실험실 내에 계실 때마다 반드시 착용하셔야 합니다. 이번 주 아무 때나 여러분의 직속 상관을 통해 한 벌 받을 수 있습니다. 추가 세트도 요청 시에 받으실 수 있습니다. 이 사안에 대한 여러분의 협조에 감사드립니다.

어휘 over 끝난, 종료된 would like to do ~하고자 하다, ~하고 싶다 make an announcement 공지하다, 발표하다 may have p.p. ~했을 수도 있다 dress code 복장 규정 policy 정책, 방침 lab 실험실 help to do ~하는 데 도움이 되다 reduce ~을 줄이다, 감소시키다 contamination 오염 accuracy 정확(성) result 결과(물) improve 향상되다, 개선되다 whenever ~할 때마다 pick A up A를 가져가다, 가져오다 immediate supervisor 직속 상관 anytime 아무 때나, 언제든지 additional 추가의 available 이용 가능한, 구매 가능한 upon request 요청 시에 cooperation 협조 matter 사안, 문제

80 What is the announcement mainly about?
(A) A security upgrade
(B) A piece of equipment
(C) A policy change
(D) A deadline extension

공지는 주로 무엇에 관한 것인가?
(A) 보안 업그레이드
(B) 한 가지 장비
(C) 정책 변경
(D) 마감시한 연장

해설 〈주제를 묻는 문제〉
담화 초반부에 복장 규정과 관련된 정책이 변경되는 것을(we're changing the dress code policy) 언급한 뒤로 해당 변경 사항을 설명하는 것으로 담화를 진행하고 있으므로 (C)가 정답이다.

어휘 equipment 장비 policy 정책, 방침 deadline 마감시한 extension 연장

81 What benefit does the speaker mention?
(A) Results will be more precise.
(B) Employees will be safer.
(C) Productivity will increase.
(D) Company sales will improve.

화자는 어떤 이점을 언급하는가?
(A) 결과물이 더 정확해질 것이다.
(B) 직원들이 더 안전해질 것이다.
(C) 생산성이 증대될 것이다.
(D) 회사 매출이 향상될 것이다.

해설 〈기타 세부 사항을 묻는 문제〉
담화 중반부에 실험실 내의 오염을 줄여 실험 결과물의 정확성이 향상될 것이라는(so the accuracy of our test results will improve) 이점을 언급하고 있으므로 (A)가 정답이다.

어휘 benefit 이점, 혜택 result 결과(물) precise 정확한 productivity 생산성 increase 증가되다, 늘어나다 sales 매출, 판매, 영업 improve 향상되다, 개선되다

82 According to the speaker, what are the listeners required to do?
(A) Read a report
(B) Exchange their IDs
(C) Wear a uniform
(D) Take a test

화자의 말에 따르면, 청자들은 무엇을 해야 하는가?
(A) 보고서를 읽는 일
(B) 각자의 사원증을 교환하는 일
(C) 유니폼을 착용하는 일
(D) 테스트를 받는 일

해설 〈요청 사항을 묻는 문제〉
담화 중반부에 유니폼이 지급된다는 사실과 함께 반드시 착용해야 한다는(Each of you will be given a uniform. This must be worn) 점을 알리고 있으므로 (C)가 정답이다.

어휘 exchange ~을 교환하다

Questions 83-85 refer to the following introduction. 캐W

Good evening, ladies and gentlemen. ⓫ Thank you for being here for the final session in the academic lectures hosted by the Bakersfield Community Center. It is my pleasure to introduce our guest speaker for tonight, Ms. Francisca Brown. ⓬ She will give a presentation on the best ways to learn how to speak a foreign language. These tips come directly from Ms. Brown's extensive research on the topic. At the end of the session, Ms. Brown will answer questions from the audience. Also, ⓭ on your way out, don't forget to sign up for our mailing list. This will help you to stay informed about upcoming activities at the community center.

안녕하세요, 신사 숙녀 여러분. 베이커스필드 지역 문화 센터에서 주최하는 학술 강연 마지막 시간을 위해 자리해 주셔서 감사합니다. 오늘 밤 초청 연사이신 프란치스카 브라운 씨를 소개해 드리게 되어 기쁩니다. 브라운 씨께서 외국어를 말하는 법을 배우는 가장 좋은 방법들에 관해 발표하실 것입니다. 이 팁은 같은 주제에 대한 브라운 씨의 폭넓은 연구를 통해 직접적으로 얻게 된 것입니다. 이 시간이 종료될 때, 브라운 씨께서 청중 여러분의 질문에 답변해 드리겠습니다. 또한, 퇴장하시는 도중에, 잊지 마시고 저희 우편물 발송 명단에 등록하시기 바랍니다. 이는 지역 문화 센터에서 곧 있을 여러 활동에 관해 지속적으로 정보를 얻으시는 데 도움이 될 것입니다.

어휘 session (특정 활동을 위한) 시간 academic lecture 학술 강연 host ~을 주최하다 introduce ~을 소개하다 give a presentation 발표하다 way to do ~하는 방법 how to do ~하는 법 come from ~에서 비롯되다, 나오다 directly 직접적으로, 곧바로 extensive 폭넓은, 광범위한 research 연구 audience 청중, 관객, 시청자 on one's way out 나가는 길에 forget to do ~하는 것을 잊다 sign up for ~에 등록하다, ~을 신청하다 mailing list 우편물 발송 명단 stay + 형용사 계속 ~한 상태로 있다. ~한 상태를 유지하다 informed 정보를 얻은, 잘 아는 upcoming 곧 있을, 다가오는

83 Where does the introduction take place?
(A) At a group interview
(B) At a lecture series
(C) At an orientation session
(D) At a press conference

소개가 어디에서 진행되고 있는가?
(A) 단체 인터뷰에서
(B) 강연 시리즈에서
(C) 오리엔테이션 시간에
(D) 기자 회견에서

해설 〈담화의 장소를 묻는 문제〉
담화를 시작하면서 학술 강연 시리즈 마지막 시간에 온 것에 대해 감사의 인사를(Thank you for being here for the final session in the academic lectures) 전하고 있으므로 (B)가 정답이다.

어휘 take place (일, 행사 등이) 발생되다, 개최되다 session (특정 활동을 위한) 시간

84 What topic will Ms. Brown discuss?
(A) Reducing energy consumption
(B) Improving working relationships
(C) Learning a foreign language
(D) Managing time wisely

브라운 씨는 어떤 주제를 이야기할 것인가?
(A) 에너지 소비를 줄이는 일
(B) 업무상의 관계를 개선하는 일
(C) 외국어를 배우는 일
(D) 현명하게 시간을 관리하는 일

해설 〈주제를 묻는 문제〉
담화 중반부에 브라운 씨를 She로 지칭해 외국어를 말하는 법을 배우는 가장 좋은 방법에 관해 발표한다고(She will give a presentation on the best ways to learn how to speak a foreign language) 알리고 있으므로 (C)가 정답이다.

어휘 reduce ~을 줄이다, 감소시키다 consumption 소비 improve ~을 개선하다, 향상시키다 relationship 관계 wisely 현명하게

85 What are the listeners reminded to do before they leave?
(A) Make a donation
(B) Join a mailing list
(C) Complete a survey form
(D) Leave a business card

청자들은 나가기 전에 무엇을 하도록 상기되는가?
(A) 기부를 하는 일
(B) 우편물 발송 명단에 포함되는 일
(C) 설문 조사 양식을 작성 완료하는 일
(D) 명함을 놓고 가는 일

해설 〈상기시키는 것을 묻는 문제〉
담화 후반부에 밖으로 나가는 길에 잊지 말고 우편물 발송 명단에 등록하도록(on your way out, don't forget to sign up for our mailing list) 요청하고 있으므로 (B)가 정답이다.

어휘 be reminded to do ~하도록 상기되다 leave 나가다, 떠나다, ~을 놓다, 두다 donation 기부(금) mailing list 우편물 발송 명단 complete ~을 완료하다 survey 설문 조사(지) form 양식, 서식

This is Sue calling from Dream Travel. 86 I just have some information regarding your scheduled flight. When I took your booking, you wanted a business class seat, but we only had economy class available. Since then, we have had a cancelation from another customer, so 87 I've moved your seat up to business class. I just need some details from you in order to finalize this. 88 Could you e-mail your account number to me as soon as possible?

저는 드림 여행사에서 전화 드리는 수입니다. 귀하의 예정 항공편과 관련해 전해 드릴 정보가 있습니다. 제가 예약을 받았을 때, 귀하께서는 비즈니스 클래스 좌석을 원하셨지만, 오직 이코노미 클래스 좌석만 이용 가능했습니다. 그 이후로, 다른 고객께서 취소하신 자리가 생기면서, 귀하의 좌석을 비즈니스 클래스로 올려 드렸습니다. 이를 최종 확정하려면 귀하의 일부 상세 정보가 필요합니다. 가능한 한 빨리 저에게 이메일로 계좌번호를 보내 주시겠습니까?

어휘 regarding ~와 관련해 scheduled 예정된 booking 예약 have A available 이용 가능한 A가 있다 since then 그때 이후로 cancelation 취소(한 것) move A up to B (등급 등) A를 B로 올리다 details 상세 정보, 세부 사항 in order to do ~하기 위해 finalize ~을 최종 확정하다 account 계좌, 계정 as soon as possible 가능한 한 빨리

86 What is the speaker calling about?
(A) A cruise
(B) A hotel suite
(C) A train ticket
(D) A flight

화자는 무엇과 관련해 전화하는가?
(A) 여객선
(B) 호텔 스위트룸
(C) 열차 탑승권
(D) 항공편

해설 〈주제를 묻는 문제〉
담화 시작 부분에 예정된 상대방 항공편과 관련된 정보가 있다고(I just have some information regarding your scheduled flight) 알리고 있으므로 (D)가 정답이다.

어휘 regarding ~에 관한, ~와 관련된

87 What does the speaker say she has done?
(A) She has upgraded a seat.
(B) She has refunded a payment.
(C) She has amended a contract.
(D) She has canceled a reservation.

여자는 무엇을 했다고 말하는가?
(A) 좌석을 업그레이드했다.
(B) 비용을 환불해 주었다.

(C) 계약서를 수정했다.
(D) 예약을 취소했다.

해설 〈과거에 일어난 일을 묻는 문제〉
담화 중반부에 상대방의 좌석을 비즈니스 클래스로 올려 놓았다고(I've moved your seat up to business class) 알리고 있는데, 이는 좌석을 업그레이드한 것을 의미하므로 (A)가 정답이다.

어휘 refund A B A에게 B를 환불해 주다 amend ~을 수정하다, 변경하다 contract 계약(서) cancel ~을 취소하다 reservation 예약

88 What does the speaker request the listener do as soon as possible?
(A) E-mail some information
(B) Sign a contract
(C) Transfer some funds
(D) Complete a form

화자는 청자에게 가능한 한 빨리 무엇을 하도록 요청하는가?
(A) 일부 정보를 이메일로 보내는 일
(B) 계약서에 서명하는 일
(C) 일부 자금을 이체하는 일
(D) 양식을 작성 완료하는 일

해설 〈요청 사항을 묻는 문제〉
담화 맨 마지막에 가능한 한 빨리 이메일로 계좌번호를 보내 달라고(Could you e-mail your account number to me as soon as possible?) 요청하고 있으므로 (A)가 정답이다.

어휘 as soon as possible 가능한 한 빨리 transfer funds 자금을 이체하다 complete ~을 완료하다 form 양식, 서식

Hi, Jacqueline. It's Albert. 89 Thanks for changing to the afternoon shift at the café so I could go to the doctor. I'm on the bus now, but I just heard a weather announcement saying that there will be strong winds tonight. I'm about halfway to the clinic. 90 Could you make sure the outdoor furniture in the patio area gets stacked up and secured? Also, I know you have the day off 91 tomorrow, but the new uniforms will be delivered. I'll be sure to set one aside for you. Thanks.

안녕하세요, 재클린 씨. 저는 알버트입니다. 제가 의사 선생님의 진료를 받으러 갈 수 있도록 카페의 오후 교대 근무로 변경해 주셔서 감사드립니다. 제가 지금 버스를 타고 가는 중인데, 오늘 밤에 강한 바람이 분다는 내용의 일기 예보를 막 들었습니다. 저는 진료소로 가는 길의 절반 정도에 와 있습니다. 테라스 구역의 옥외 가구를 반드시 차곡차곡 쌓아서 안전한 상태로 만들어 주시겠어요? 그리고, 내일 하루 쉬신다는 것을 알고 있지만, 새로운 유니폼이 배송될 겁니다. 당신을 위해 한 벌 꼭 챙겨 두겠습니다. 감사합니다.

어휘 change to ~로 변경하다 shift 교대 근무(조) announcement 공지, 알림 about 약, ~ 정도 halfway to ~로 가는 길의 절반, 중간 make sure (that) 반드시 ~하도록 하다 patio 테라스 get p.p. ~되게 하다 stack up ~을 차곡차곡 쌓다 secure ~을 안전하게 지키다 have a day off 하루 쉬다 be sure to do 꼭 ~하다 set A aside A를 따로 챙겨 두다

89 What is the purpose of the message?
(A) To make an appointment
(B) To thank a colleague
(C) To advertise a new product
(D) To describe a design plan

메시지의 목적은 무엇인가?
(A) 예약을 하는 것
(B) 동료 직원에게 감사하는 것
(C) 신제품을 광고하는 것
(D) 디자인 계획을 설명하는 것

해설 〈기타 세부 사항을 묻는 문제〉
화자가 담화 초반부에 오후 교대 근무로 변경해 준 것에 대해 감사하다는 말로(Thanks for changing to the afternoon shift at the café ~) 인사하고 있다. 교대 근무를 변경해 주는 것은 함께 근무하는 동료 관계에 있는 사람이 할 수 있는 일이므로 (B)가 정답이다.

어휘 make an appointment 예약하다, 약속을 잡다 colleague 동료 (직원) advertise ~을 광고하다 describe ~을 설명하다

90 What does the speaker most likely mean when he says, "I'm about halfway to the clinic"?
(A) He will meet Jacqueline soon.
(B) He may be late for a meeting.
(C) He got a ride from a coworker.
(D) He cannot do a task himself.

화자가 "I'm about halfway to the clinic"라고 말할 때 무엇을 의미할 것 같은가?
(A) 곧 재클린 씨를 만날 것이다.
(B) 회의에 늦을 수도 있다.
(C) 동료 직원에게서 차를 얻어 탔다.
(D) 일을 직접 할 수 없다.

해설 〈의도 파악 문제〉
중반부에 화자가 진료소로 가는 길의 절반 정도에 와 있다고 말한 뒤로 테라스 구역의 옥외 가구를 차곡차곡 쌓아서 안전한 상태로 만들어 달라고(Could you make sure the outdoor furniture in the patio area gets stacked up and secured?) 요청하는 상황이다. 이는 자신이 직접 할 수 없는 일을 부탁하는 것이므로 (D)가 정답이다.

어휘 get a rider from ~에게서 차를 얻어 타다 coworker 동료 (직원) task 일, 업무 oneself (부사처럼 쓰여) 직접, 스스로

91 What is scheduled to happen tomorrow?
(A) A business trip will begin.
(B) A new employee will join a team.
(C) Some equipment will be repaired.
(D) Some uniforms will be delivered.

내일 무슨 일이 있을 예정인가?
(A) 출장이 시작될 것이다.
(B) 신입 사원이 팀에 합류할 것이다.
(C) 일부 장비가 수리될 것이다.
(D) 일부 유니폼이 배송될 것이다.

해설 〈특정 시점의 일을 묻는 문제〉
후반부에 내일 새 유니폼이 배송된다는(~ tomorrow, but the new uniforms will be delivered) 사실을 알리고 있으므로 (D)가 정답이다.

어휘 be scheduled to do ~할 예정이다 join ~에 합류하다, ~와 함께 하다 equipment 장비 repair ~을 수리하다

Questions 92-94 refer to the following tour information. [미|M]

Welcome to Madison Baseball Stadium. During your tour today, **92 you'll see our senior baseball team play a training match against our youth team.** **93 We expected around forty people for this tour, but it seems like we're still waiting for a few people to arrive. Well, let's give them another five minutes.** Also, **94 I'd like to remind you that many areas inside the stadium are closed to the public, so please don't leave the group.** I wouldn't want any of you to get in trouble with security.

매디슨 야구 경기장에 오신 것을 환영합니다. 오늘 투어 시간 중에, 여러분께서는 저희 성인 야구팀이 저희 유소년 야구팀을 상대로 연습 경기를 치르는 것을 보시게 됩니다. 저희가 이번 투어에 약 40명의 인원을 예상했는데, 여전히 몇몇 분들께서 도착하시기를 기다리고 있는 것 같습니다. 자, 이분들께 5분 더 시간을 드려 보겠습니다. 또한, 경기장 내의 많은 구역이 일반인을 대상으로 폐쇄되어 있기 때문에 그룹을 떠나지 않도록 상기시켜 드리고자 합니다. 여러분 중 누구도 보안과 관련해 곤란에 처하지 않으셨으면 합니다.

어휘 training match 연습 경기 against ~을 상대로, ~에 맞서 expect ~을 예상하다, 기대하다 around 약, 대략, ~쯤 it seems like ~인 것 같다 wait for A to do A가 ~하기를 기다리다 arrive 도착하다 give A another five minutes A에게 5분 더 시간을 주다 remind A that A에게 ~임을 상기시키다, 다시 한 번 알리다 closed to ~에게 폐쇄된 the public 일반 대중 want A to do A에게 ~하기를 원하다 get in trouble 곤란에 처하다 security 보안

92 What type of sport will the listeners watch?
(A) Football
(B) Baseball
(C) Basketball
(D) Tennis

청자들은 어떤 종류의 스포츠를 볼 것인가?
(A) 축구
(B) 야구
(C) 농구
(D) 테니스

해설 〈주제를 묻는 문제〉
담화 시작 부분에 야구팀이 경기하는 것을 보게 된다고(you'll see our senior baseball team play a training match against our youth team) 알리고 있으므로 (B)가 정답이다.

93 What does the speaker imply when he says, "Let's give them another five minutes"?
(A) He will wait a little longer for group members.
(B) He will give a short presentation to the listeners.
(C) A building is opening later than expected.
(D) A special guest has been delayed.

화자가 "Let's give them another five minutes"라고 말할 때 무엇을 의도하는가?
(A) 그룹 인원들을 조금 더 기다릴 것이다.
(B) 청자들에게 간단한 발표를 할 것이다.
(C) 건물이 예상보다 더 늦게 개장한다.
(D) 특별 손님이 지체되었다.

해설 〈의도 파악 문제〉
담화 중반부에 약 40명의 인원을 예상했는데 여전히 몇몇 사람들이 도착하기를 기다리고 있다는(We expected around forty people for this tour, but it seems like we're still waiting for a few people to arrive) 언급한 뒤로 '그 사람들에게 5분 더 시간을 주겠다'고 말하는 상황이다. 이는 아직 오지 않은 나머지 인원을 조금 더 기다리겠다는 뜻이므로 (A)가 정답이다.

어휘 a little 조금, 약간 give a presentation 발표하다 than expected 예상보다 delay ~을 지체시키다, 지연시키다

94 What does the speaker ask the listeners to do?
(A) Stay in the group
(B) Keep their voices down
(C) Refrain from eating
(D) Obtain a security pass

화자는 청자들에게 무엇을 하도록 요청하는가?
(A) 그룹 내에 머물러 있는 일
(B) 목소리를 낮추는 일
(C) 음식물 섭취를 삼가는 일
(D) 보안 출입증을 받는 일

해설 〈요청 사항을 묻는 문제〉
담화 후반부에 많은 구역이 일반인을 대상으로 폐쇄되어 있기 때문에 그룹을 떠나지 말라고(~ many areas inside the stadium are closed to the public, so please don't leave the group) 주의를 주고 있다. 이는 그룹 내의 다른 사람들과 계속 함께 머물러 있으라는 뜻이므로 (A)가 정답이다.

어휘 keep A + 형용사 A를 ~한 상태로 유지하다 refrain from -ing ~하는 것을 삼가다 obtain ~을 받다, 얻다 pass 출입증, 입장권, 승차권

Questions 95-97 refer to the following excerpt from a meeting and menu. [호M]

I'd like to thank **95 all of our servers** for coming in a bit early for this meeting. Today is the start of a four-day weekend, so we're expecting **95 the restaurant** to be very busy. Unfortunately, one of our refrigerators malfunctioned overnight, so we had to throw out some of our food. **96 That means we can't make the special for Sunday.** The chef will replace it with something else and post a description at two o'clock. So, **97 please check the bulletin board for that information** sometime after two so you can explain to customers what's available over the weekend.

4-Day Weekend Special Menu
Friday: Grilled Salmon with Herbs
Saturday: Pan Roasted Pork
96 Sunday: Fresh Crab Salad
Monday: Cream and Mushroom Spaghetti

이 회의를 위해 조금 일찍 나와 주신 모든 종업원 여러분께 감사드리고자 합니다. 오늘은 4일간의 주말 연휴 첫날이기 때문에 레스토랑이 아주 바쁠 것으로 예상하고 있습니다. 유감스럽게도, 우리 냉장고 중의 한 대가 간밤에 오작동하여 일부 식품을 버려야 했습니다. 이는 일요일 특선 요리를 만들 수 없다는 뜻입니다. 주방장님께서 다른 것으로 대체해 2시에 안내 설명을 게시하실 예정입니다. 따라서, 주말 동안 이용 가능한 것을 고객께 설명해 드릴 수 있도록 2시 후에 아무 때나 게시판에서 그 정보를 확인하시기 바랍니다.

4일간의 주말 연휴 특선 메뉴
금요일: 허브를 곁들여 그릴에 구운 연어
토요일: 팬에 구운 돼지고기
일요일: 신선한 게살 샐러드
월요일: 크림 버섯 스파게티

어휘 server 종업원 a bit 조금, 약간 expect A to do A가 ~할 것으로 예상하다, 기대하다 unfortunately 유감스럽게도, 안타깝게도 refrigerator 냉장고 malfunction 오작동하다, 기능 고장을 일으키다 overnight 밤사이에, 야간에 throw out ~을 버리다 special 특선 요리 replace A with B A를 B로 대체하다, 교체하다 post ~을 게시하다 description 설명 bulletin board 게시판 explain ~을 설명하다 available 이용 가능한, 구입 가능한 grilled 그릴에 구운 pan roasted 팬에 구운

95 Who are the listeners?
(A) Health inspectors
(B) Restaurant servers
(C) Delivery drivers
(D) Repair technicians

청자는 누구인가?
(A) 위생 검사관들
(B) 레스토랑 종업원들
(C) 배송 기사들
(D) 수리 기사들

해설 〈직업을 묻는 문제〉
담화를 시작하면서 all of our servers라는 말로 청자들이 종업원임을 알리고 있고, 뒤이어 the restaurant을 언급하는 것으로 레스토랑이 배경임을 알리고 있으므로 (B)가 정답이다.

어휘 address v. ~에게 이야기하다, 연설하다 inspector 검사관들, 조사관 server 종업원 repair 수리

96 Look at the graphic. Which dish will not be available?
(A) Grilled Salmon with Herbs
(B) Pan Roasted Pork
(C) Fresh Crab Salad
(D) Cream and Mushroom Spaghetti

시각 자료를 보시오. 어느 요리가 이용할 수 없을 것인가?
(A) 허브를 곁들여 그릴에 구운 연어
(B) 팬에 구운 돼지고기
(C) 신선한 게살 샐러드
(D) 크림 버섯 스파게티

해설 〈2열 도표 문제〉
화자가 담화 중반부에 냉장고 문제를 알리면서 일요일 특선 요리를 만들 수 없게 된 상황임을(That means we can't make the special for Sunday) 밝히고 있다. 메뉴에서 세 번째 줄에 쓰여 있는 일요일에 해당되는 요리가 Fresh Crab Salad이므로 (C)가 정답이다.

어휘 available 이용할 수 있는

97 According to the speaker, what should the listeners do after two o'clock today?
(A) Unload some supplies
(B) Pick up a paycheck
(C) Check a notice board
(D) Print a new menu

화자의 말에 따르면, 청자들은 오늘 2시 이후에 무엇을 해야 하는가?
(A) 일부 물품을 차에서 내리는 일
(B) 급여 명세서를 받아 가는 일
(C) 알림판을 확인하는 일
(D) 새 메뉴를 인쇄하는 일

해설 〈특정 시점의 일을 묻는 문제〉
담화 후반부에 2시 이후에 게시판에서 정보를 확인하도록(please check the bulletin board for that information sometime after two) 알리고 있으므로 (C)가 정답이다.

어휘 unload ~을 차에서 내리다 supplies 용품, 물품 pick up ~을 가져가다, 가져오다 notice board 알림판, 게시판

Questions 98-100 refer to the following announcement and flight schedule. 캐W

Attention, all Eagle Air passengers. ㉘ Due to heavy snowstorms, some flights will be delayed today. Please see our information screen in order to see if you are affected. Also, we regret to inform you that the 9:30 flight to Chicago has been canceled. ㉙ If you need to travel to Chicago, you are advised to take the flight to Tallahassee and then catch a connecting flight. We are also pleased to announce that ㉚ our air miles program starts next week. Passengers will be rewarded with points for each flight, which you will be able to exchange for prizes.

Destination	Flight Number	Status
Los Angeles	L201	2 hour delay
㉙ Tallahassee	T304	45 minute delay
Chicago	C492	Canceled
San Antonio	S420	2 hour delay

모든 이글 에어 탑승객 여러분께 알립니다. 폭설로 인해 일부 항공편이 오늘 지연될 것입니다. 여러분께서 영향을 받으시는지 알아 보실 수 있도록 안내 전광판을 확인해 보시기 바랍니다. 또한, 시카고행 9시 30분 항공편이 취소되었다는 사실을 알려 드리게 되어 유감스럽게 생각합니다. 시카고로 여행하셔야 하는 경우, 탤로해시로 향하는 항공편을 타고 가신 다음, 연결 항공편을 이용하시도록 권해 드립니다. 또한 다음 주에 저희 항공 마일리지 프로그램이 시작된다는 사실도 알려 드리게 되어 기쁩니다. 탑승객들께서는 각 항공편에 대해 포인트로 보상받으시게 되며, 이는 상품으로 교환하실 수 있으실 것입니다.

목적지	항공편 번호	현황
로스앤젤레스	L201	2시간 지연
탤러해시	T304	45분 지연
시카고	C492	결항
샌안토니오	S420	2시간 지연

어휘 due to ~로 인해, ~ 때문에 delay v. ~을 지연시키다, 지체시키다 n. 지연, 지체 in order to do ~할 수 있도록, ~하기 위해 see if ~인지 알아 보다 affect ~에 영향을 미치다 regret to do ~해서 유감이다 inform A that A에게 ~라고 알리다 cancel ~을 취소하다 be advised to do ~하도록 권장되다 take (교통편) ~을 타다, 이용하다(= catch) connecting flight 연결 항공편 announce that ~임을 알리다, 발표하다 reward ~에게 보상하다 be able to do ~할 수 있다 exchange A for B A를 B로 교환하다 prize 상품, 경품 destination 목적지, 도착지 status 현황, 상태

98 What does the speaker say is responsible for flight delays?
(A) Technical problems
(B) Bad weather
(C) A security issue
(D) A computer system failure

화자는 무엇이 항공편 지연의 원인이라고 말하는가?
(A) 기술적인 문제
(B) 궂은 날씨
(C) 보안 문제
(D) 컴퓨터 시스템 오류

해설 〈문제 원인을 묻는 문제〉
담화 초반부에 폭설 때문에 일부 항공편이 오늘 지연될 것이라고(Due to heavy snowstorms, some flights will be delayed today) 알리고 있으므로 (B)가 정답이다.

어휘 be responsible for ~에 대한 원인하다 issue 문제, 사안 failure (기계 등의) 오류, 고장

99 Look at the graphic. Which flight should passengers board in order to travel to Chicago?
(A) L201
(B) T304
(C) C492
(D) S420

시각 자료를 보시오. 시카고로 여행하려면 승객들이 어느 항공편에 탑승해야 하는가?
(A) L201
(B) T304
(C) C492
(D) S420

해설 〈3열 이상 도표 문제〉
담화 중반부에 시카고로 여행하려면 탤러해시로 향하는 항공편을 타고 가서 연결 항공편을 이용하도록(If you need to travel to Chicago, you are advised to take the flight to Tallahassee and then catch a connecting flight) 권하고 있다. 도표에서 탤러해시가 표기된 두 번째 줄에 쓰여 있는 항공편 번호가 T304이므로 (B)가 정답이다.

어휘 in order to do ~하려면, ~하기 위해

100 What does the speaker say begins next week?
(A) A reward program
(B) A renovation project
(C) A staff training course
(D) A new flight route

화자는 다음 주에 무엇이 시작된다고 말하는가?
(A) 보상 프로그램
(B) 개조 공사 프로젝트
(C) 직원 교육 과정
(D) 새 항공 노선

해설 〈특정 시점의 일을 묻는 문제〉
담화 후반부에 다음 주에 항공 마일리지 프로그램이 시작된다는 점과 각 항공편에 대해 포인트로 보상받게 된다는 점을(our air miles program starts next week. Passengers will be rewarded with points for each flight) 알리고 있다. 이는 보상 프로그램이 시작된다는 뜻이므로 (A)가 정답이다.

어휘 reward 보상 renovation 개조, 보수 training 교육, 훈련

PART 5
P70

101 해설 저희 단체의 회원이 되시려면, 지원서를 작성하셔서 제출하시기만 하시면 됩니다.

해설 〈부사 자리(동사 앞)〉
to부정사구 뒤로 빈칸이 있고, 그 뒤에 동사원형으로 시작되는 명령문 구조가 이어져 있으므로 빈칸은 동사원형을 수식할 부사 자리이다. 따라서 부사인 (C) simply가 정답이다.

어휘 organization 단체, 기관 fill out ~을 작성하다 application form 지원서, 신청서 turn A in A를 제출하다 simply 단지, 그저 simplify ~을 간소화하다

102 해설 미술가 리차드 트루먼 씨는 관람객들이 쉽게 어느 것이 자신의 작품인지 알아볼 수 있도록 자신의 그림 각각에 서명을 한다.

해설 〈소유대명사〉
which ones의 보어로서 be동사 are 뒤에 위치해 동격에 해당되는 대명사가 빈칸에 쓰여야 한다. 여기서 ones는 앞서 언급된 paintings를 대신 가리키므로 동격에 해당되는 대명사가 쓰이려면 사물을 가리키는 것이어야 한다. 따라서 '그의 것'이라는 의미로 사물에 대해 사용하는 소유대명사 (B) his가 정답이다.

어휘 sign ~에 서명하다 painting 그림 so that (목적) ~할 수 있도록, (결과) 그래서, 그러므로 viewer 관람객, 시청자 recognize ~을 알아보다, 인정하다

103 해석 방문객들께서는 시설물 이용을 위해 정문에서 사진이 부착된 신분증을 제시해 주셔야 합니다.

해설 〈동사 어휘(부정사와 어울리는 어휘)〉
빈칸 앞뒤에 각각 위치한 be동사 are 및 to부정사와 어울리는 과거분사가 필요하므로 이 둘과 함께 '~해야 하다, ~할 필요가 있다'라는 의미를 나타낼 때 사용하는 (A) required가 정답이다.

어휘 be required to do ~해야 하다, ~할 필요가 있다 present ~을 제시하다 a form of picture ID 사진이 부착된 신분증 gain access to ~을 이용하다, ~에 접근하다 facility 시설(물) apply 지원하다, 신청하다, ~을 적용하다 expire 만료되다 respect ~을 존중하다, 존경하다

104 해석 레지날드 푸드 사는 유통 기한이 지난 것으로 표기된 음식을 섭취함으로써 발생되는 모든 문제에 대해 책임을 지지 않습니다.

해설 〈형용사 자리(be동사 뒤)〉
be동사 is 뒤에 위치한 빈칸은 보어 역할을 할 형용사 또는 명사가 쓰여야 하는 자리이다. 명사인 (D) responsibility는 보어로 쓰일 경우 주어와 동격이 되어야 하는데 주어와 동격 관계가 성립되지 않으므로 오답이 된다. 따라서 형용사인 (A) responsible이 정답이다.

어휘 be responsible for ~에 대한 책임이 있다 incur ~을 발생시키다 marked as ~한 것으로 표기된 beyond ~을 지나, ~ 이후에 date 유통 기한 responsibleness 책임을 짐 responsibly 책임감 있게 responsibility 책임, 책무

105 해석 그 회사의 웹 사이트에 따르면, 구입되는 모든 제품은 영업일로 2일 내에 배송될 것이다.

해설 〈전치사 어휘〉
빈칸 뒤에 위치한 명사구 two business days는 기간을 나타내므로 기간 명사구를 목적어로 취하는 전치사 (B) within이 정답이다.

어휘 according to ~에 따르면 purchase ~을 구입하다 ship ~을 배송하다 among ~ 사이에서, ~ 중에서 within ~ 이내에 behind (위치) ~ 뒤에, (진행 등) ~에 뒤처져, ~보다 늦어

106 해석 현지에서 생산된 식품에 대한 수요는 앞으로 3년 동안 최소 50퍼센트 증가할 것이다.

해설 〈시제(미래)〉
빈칸 앞에는 주어와 전치사구가, 빈칸 뒤에는 숫자 표현과 전치사구만 있으므로 빈칸은 문장의 동사 자리이다. 따라서 동사의 형태인 (B) will have grown, (C) will grow, (D) has grown 중에서 하나를 골라야 하는데, in the next three years는 단순 미래시제와 함께 쓰이는 부사이므로 단순 미래 시제인 (C) will grow가 정답이다.

어휘 demand for ~에 대한 수요 locally 지역에서, 지역적으로 grow 증가하다, 늘어나다, ~을 재배하다 at least 최소한, 적어도

107 해석 작업 현장에서 저희는 자원 봉사자들께 못과 망치, 안전 장비, 그리고 기타 용품을 제공해 드릴 것입니다.

해설 〈명사 어휘〉
other의 수식을 받는 빈칸은 앞에 and로 연결되는 명사들과 유사한 다른 것들을 하나로 아우를 수 있는 범주를 나타내는 명사가 쓰여야 한다. nails, hammers, safety gear는 모두 작업용 물품에 해당되므로 '용품, 물품'을 의미하는 (A) supplies가 정답이다.

어휘 site 현장, 장소, 부지 provide A with B A에게 B를 제공하다 volunteer 자원 봉사자 nail 못 safety gear 안전 장비 supplies 용품, 물품 quality (제품 등의) 질, 품질, (사람의) 자질, 특성 facility 시설(물) treatment 치료(법), 대우, 취급, 처리

108 해석 수석 엔지니어 직책 지원자인 조셉 해리슨 씨는 내일 인사부장과 이야기할 것이다.

해설 〈① 명사 자리 (관사 뒤) ② 사람 명사 VS. 사물 명사〉
빈칸은 주어 Joseph Harrison과 동사 사이에 삽입되어 주어를 보충 설명하는 명사구에 속해 있다. 따라서 빈칸은 사람 주어 Joseph Harrison을 가리킬 사람 명사가 필요한 자리이므로 '지원자'를 뜻하는 사람 명사 (B) applicant가 정답이다.

어휘 position 직책, 일자리 human resources director 인사부장 apply 지원하다, 신청하다, ~을 적용하다 applicant 지원자, 신청자 application 지원(서), 신청(서), 적용

109 해석 IT 팀에 의해 시행된 업그레이드로 인해, 인트라넷이 현재 가동되고 있다.

해설 〈부사 어휘〉
빈칸에 쓰일 부사는 바로 앞에 현재 시제로 쓰인 동사 is와 의미가 어울려야 하므로 '현재'라는 뜻으로 현재 시제 혹은 현재진행 시제와 함께 사용하는 부사 (C) currently가 정답이다.

어휘 thanks to ~로 인해, ~ 덕분에 implement ~을 시행하다 intranet 인트라넷(회사 등의 내부 전산망) operational 가동되는, 운영 중인 closely 면밀히, 밀접하게, 단단히, 꽉 shortly 곧, 머지않아 currently 현재 quickly 빠르게

110 해석 조립 과정의 변화에 대한 월시 씨의 제안이 점점 더 유용한 것으로 드러나고 있다.

해설 〈부사 자리(형용사 앞)〉
2형식 동사 prove와 뒤에 쓰인 주격 보어 형용사 helpful 앞에 위치한 빈칸은 형용사를 수식할 부사 자리이므로 부사인 (D) increasingly가 정답이다.

어휘 suggestion 의견, 제안 assembly 조립 process 과정 prove + 형용사 ~한 것으로 드러나다, 판명되다 helpful 유용한, 도움이 되는 increase 증가하다, ~을 증가시키다 increasingly 점점 더, 갈수록 더

111 해석 브로드웨이 호텔은 셔틀 버스를 활용해 공항을 오가는 믿을 만한 교통편을 제공한다.

해설 〈형용사 어휘〉
빈칸에 쓰일 형용사는 바로 뒤에 위치한 명사 transportation을 수식해 호텔에서 제공하는 교통편의 특성을 나타내야 하므로 '믿을 만한'이라는 의미로 쓰이는 (C) reliable이 정답이다. '전체의'라는 의미의 whole은 'a[the] whole + 단수 명사'와 같이 관사와 함께 사용해야 한다.

어휘 transportation 교통(편) to and from ~을 오가는 by means of ~을 활용해, ~의 도움으로 whole 전체의, 모든 skilled 숙련된, 능숙한 reliable 믿을 만한 vacant 비어 있는, 사람이 없는

112 해석 회사는 올해 신입 사원들에 대한 폭넓은 교육을 더욱 강조할 것이다.

해설 〈형용사 자리(관사와 명사 사이)〉
전치사 on과 명사 목적어 training 사이에 위치한 빈칸은 명사를 수식할 형용사 자리이므로 형용사인 (C) extensive가 정답이다. 부사인 (D) extensively는 동명사를 수식할 수 있지만 training은 동명사가 아닌 명사이므로 오답이다.

어휘 place emphasis on ~을 강조하다 training 교육 recruit 신입 사원 extend ~을 연장하다, 확장하다 extensive 폭넓은, 광범위한

113 해석 출장 이후에, 앳킨스 씨는 해외 구매자들과 무엇을 논의했는지에 관해 이야기할 것이다.

해설 〈전치사 VS. 접속사〉
빈칸은 바로 뒤에 위치한 명사구를 목적어로 취할 전치사 자리인데, '출장 후에 ~와 논의한 것에 관해 이야기할 것이다'와 같은 의미가 되어야 자연스러우므로 '~ 후에'라는 의미로 일의 전후 관계를 나타낼 때 사용하는 전치사 (B) After가 정답이다. (C) Since가 전치사로 쓰이면, '~이후로'라는 의미로 시작점을 나타내며, 현재완료 시제 동사와 함께 사용한다.

어휘 discuss ~을 논의하다 then 그렇다면, 그런 다음, 그때 since ~ 이후로

114 해석 공인 엔지니어가 되기 위해서는 반드시 기계와 관련된 많은 전문 지식을 보유하고 있어야 한다.

해설 〈명사 어휘〉
공인 엔지니어가 되기 위해 기계와 관련해 지니고 있어야 하는 것을 나타낼 명사가 빈칸에 쓰여야 하므로 '전문 지식'을 의미하는 (D) expertise가 정답이다.

어휘 in order to do ~하기 위해 certified 공인된, 인증된 possess ~을 보유하다, 소유하다 a large amount of 아주 많은 (양의) mechanical 기계와 관련된, 기계적인 impression 인상, 감명 approval 승인 importance 중요성 expertise 전문 지식

115 해석 오직 최대 80명에 달하는 사람들만 수용할 수 있는 아르모 홀은 대규모 행사에 적절한 곳으로 여겨지지 않는다.

해설 〈형용사 어휘〉
최대 80명밖에 수용할 수 없다는 점은 대규모 행사를 개최하기에 어

울리지 않는다는 의미가 되어야 알맞으므로 '적절한'을 뜻하는 (D) appropriate이 정답이다.

어휘 accommodate ~을 수용하다 up to 최대 ~에 달하는 be considered + 형용사 ~한 것으로 여겨지다 significant 상당한, 중요한 complete 완료된, 완전한 intentional 의도적인 appropriate 적절한

116 해석 기니비에브 텍스타일 사는 아시아 전역에 위치한 여러 곳에서 들여오는 외래 직물, 특히 비단을 다루는 것을 전문으로 한다.

해설 〈동사 어휘〉
빈칸 뒤에 위치한 전치사 in과 어울려 쓰이는 자동사가 빈칸에 필요하므로 in과 함께 '~을 전문으로 하다'라는 의미를 나타낼 때 사용하는 (B) specializes가 정답이다.

어휘 specialize in ~을 전문으로 하다 handle ~을 다루다, 처리하다 exotic 외래의, 이국적인 material 직물, 재료, 자재, 물품 especially 특히 location 위치, 지점 throughout ~ 전역에서 identify ~을 확인하다, 발견하다 measure ~을 측정하다 consider ~을 고려하다, 여기다

117 해석 그 회사는 보안 소프트웨어를 주기적으로 업데이트함으로써 자사의 기록에 대한 기밀을 유지할 계획이다.

해설 〈동명사 자리(전치사와 관사 사이)〉
전치사 by와 명사구 사이에 위치한 빈칸은 이 명사구를 목적어로 취함과 동시에 by의 목적어 역할을 할 동명사가 필요한 자리이므로 동명사의 형태인 (C) updating이 정답이다.

어휘 firm 회사 intend to do ~할 계획이다, 작정이다 maintain ~을 유지하다 confidentiality 기밀 (상태) by + -ing (방법) ~함으로써 regularly 주기적으로, 정기적으로

118 해석 보너스가 다음 달에 직원들에게 지급될 것인데, 회사가 이번 분기에 엄청난 수익을 기록했기 때문이다.

해설 〈접속사 VS. 부사〉
빈칸 앞뒤로 각각 주어와 동사(will be paid와 has recorded)가 하나씩 포함된 절이 위치해 있으므로 빈칸은 두 절을 연결할 접속사 자리이다. 접속사인 (B) whether와 (D) because 중에서, '엄청난 수익을 기록했기 때문에 보너스가 지급될 것이다'와 같은 의미가 되어야 하므로 이유를 나타낼 때 사용하는 부사절 접속사 (D) because가 정답이다. (A) therefore와 (C) as a result는 부사이므로 오답이다.

어휘 firm 회사 huge 엄청난, 막대한 profit 수익 quarter 분기 therefore 그러므로, 따라서 whether ~인지 (아닌지) as a result 결과적으로

119 해석 그 행사에 책을 기부하고자 하는 사람들은 이번 주 금요일까지 마시 웨인 씨에게 연락해야 한다.

해설 〈주격 관계대명사〉
사람 명사인 선행사 Individuals를 수식함과 동시에 동사 wish 앞에 위치해 주어 역할을 할 주격 관계대명사가 빈칸에 쓰여야 알맞으므로 (C) who가 정답이다. (A) whose 뒤에는 수식 받을 명사가 위치해야 하며, (D) whoever는 선행사를 수식할 수 없으므로 오답이다.

어휘 individual 사람, 개인 donate A to B A를 B에 기부하다 contact ~에게 연락하다 by (기한) ~까지 whoever ~하는 사람은 누구든

120 해석 운전자들이 모든 연료 경비를 지불해야 하지만, 환급 비용이 나중에 제공될 것입니다.

해설 〈대등 접속사〉
빈칸 앞뒤로 각각 주어와 동사(are expected와 will be provided)가 하나씩 포함된 절이 위치해 있으므로 빈칸은 두 절을 연결할 접속사 자리이다. 접속사인 (B) but과 (D) as soon as 중에서, '운전자들이 경비를 지불해야 하지만, 환급이 나중에 제공된다'와 같은 의미가 되어야 알맞으므로 '하지만, 그러나' 등의 의미로 쓰이는 (B) but이 정답이다. (A) likewise는 부사이며, (C) rather than은 병렬 구조를 이끌 수는 있으나 두 개의 완전한 절을 연결할 수는 없으므로 오답이다.

어휘 be expected to do (기대되는 일로서) ~해야 하다, ~할 것으로 예상되다 expense 경비, 지출 비용 reimbursement 환급 (비용) provide ~을 제공하다 likewise 마찬가지로 rather than ~가 아니라, ~ 대신 as soon as ~하자마자

121 해석 롱펠로우 씨가 결정을 내리는 대로, 회사의 향후 방침과 관련된 보도 자료가 배부될 것이다.

해설 〈전치사 VS. 접속사〉
빈칸 뒤로 각각 주어와 동사(makes와 will be distributed)가 하나씩 포함된 절이 위치해 있으므로 빈칸은 두 절을 연결할 접속사 자리이다. 따라서 보기 중에 유일하게 접속사인 (A) Once가 정답이다. (B) Still과 (D) Already는 부사이며, (C) Owing to는 전치사이다.

어휘 make a decision 결정을 내리다 press release 보도 자료 distribute ~을 배부하다, 나눠 주다 regarding ~와 관련된 course 방향, 진로, 방침 once ~하는 대로, ~하자마자 owing to ~로 인해, ~ 덕분에

122 해석 오늘 아침에 레이크 씨는 주로 본관 대회의실에서 열린 많은 회의에 참석해야 했다.

해설 〈부사 어휘〉
빈칸은 뒤에 있는 전치사구 in the main conference room(대회의실에서)을 수식하는 자리인데, 보기 중 의미상 이와 가장 잘 어울리는 부사인 '주로'라는 의미의 (C) primarily를 정답으로 선택한다. (B) relatively는 원급 형용사 혹은 부사만 수식하므로 오답이다.

어휘 attend ~에 참석하다 a number of 많은 (수의) roughly 대략 relatively 비교적, 상대적으로 primarily 주로 gradually 점차적으로

123 해석 부이사로서 킴버 씨는 회사의 부사장인 애니타 워커 씨에게 직접 진행 상황을 보고하도록 요청받는다.

해설 〈부사 자리(완전한 문장 구조 뒤)〉
빈칸 앞에 완전한 문장 구조가 갖춰져 있으므로 빈칸은 부사가 필요한 자리이다. 따라서 부사인 (D) directly를 정답으로 선택한다. directly는 여기서 뒤의 전치사구(to Anita Walker)를 수식하여 '애니타 워커 씨에게 직접'이란 의미로 사용되었다.

어휘 as (자격, 신분 등) ~로서 assistant 부~, 보조의 be asked to do ~하도록 요청받다 progress 진행, 진척 vice president 부사장, 부

대표 direct ~을 감독하다, 지휘하다, ~에게 안내하다 direction 감독, 방향, 지휘, 명령 directly 곧장, 직접

124 해석 참석자들은 신규 지점 개장 가능성을 제외한 안건의 모든 항목을 논의했다.

해설 〈전치사 어휘〉
빈칸 앞에 안건의 모든(every) 항목을 논의했다는 말이 쓰여 있는데, 빈칸 뒤에 특정한 한 가지 항목이 언급되어 있으므로 '이 항목을 제외한'이라는 의미가 되어야 알맞다. 따라서 '~을 제외하고'를 뜻하는 전치사 (B) except가 정답이다. 이와 같이 except는 all 혹은 every와 어울려 '~을 제외하고 모든'이란 의미로 자주 사용된다.

어휘 attendee 참석자 discuss ~을 논의하다 item 항목, 품목 agenda 안건, 의제 possibility 가능성 branch 지점, 지사 unlike ~와 달리 except ~을 제외하고 despite ~에도 불구하고 opposite ~ 맞은편에, 반대편에

125 해석 벤추라 씨가 수락하기 전까지 많은 지원자들이 프라임 은행의 지점장 직책에 관해 문의했다.

해설 〈시제(대과거)〉
접속사 before가 두 절을 연결하는 형태이므로 빈칸은 동사 자리이다. 동사의 형태가 아닌 (B) inquiring을 제외한 나머지 동사들은 모두 시제가 다른데, before절에 과거 시제 동사(accepted)가 쓰이면 주절은 과거보다 이전을 나타내는 과거완료 혹은 과거 시제를 쓰는 것이 원칙이므로 과거완료 시제 (C) had inquired가 정답이다. 이와 같이 과거보다 더 이전의 의미를 나타내는 had + p.p.를 '대과거'라고 부르기도 한다.

어휘 applicant 지원자, 신청자 inquire about ~에 관해 문의하다 position 직책, 일자리 branch 지점, 지사 accept ~을 수용하다, 받아들이다

126 해석 웨스턴에 있는 우리 소매 판매점을 방문하는 고객은 거의 없는데, 이곳이 인기 있는 명소가 없는 비교적 작은 마을이기 때문이다.

해설 〈부사 어휘〉
빈칸에 쓰일 부사는 바로 뒤에 위치한 원급 형용사 small을 수식해 마을의 규모가 작은 정도와 관련된 의미를 나타내야 하므로 '비교적, 상대적으로'라는 뜻으로 정도를 나타낼 때 사용하는 (B) relatively가 정답이다.

어휘 few 거의 없는 retail store 소매 판매점 as ~하기 때문에 without ~가 없는 popular 인기 있는 attraction 명소, 인기 장소 normally 보통, 일반적으로 relatively 비교적, 상대적으로 closely 면밀히, 밀접하여, 단단히, 꽉 exactly 정확히

127 해석 호바트 학원의 강좌에 등록할 때, 자리를 보장받으려면 비용 지불이 즉시 이뤄져야 한다.

해설 〈분사구문〉
접속사 When은 주어와 동사가 포함된 절을 이끌어야 하는데, When 뒤로 빈칸과 for 전치사구만 위치해 있다. 이러한 경우, '접속사 + 분사'로 구성된 분사구문이 되어야 알맞은 문장 구조가 되므로 현재 분사인 (C) registering이 정답이다. 빈칸에 명사 (D) registration이 쓰이면

주어의 역할을 하게 되는데 하나의 절이 구성되기 위해서는 동사가 있어야 한다.

어휘 register for ~에 등록하다 make a payment 비용을 지불하다 immediately 즉시 guarantee ~을 보장하다 registration 등록

128 해석 해밀턴 씨의 은퇴 기념 파티에서, 많은 동료 직원들이 그의 뛰어난 공헌에 대해 감사의 뜻을 표현했다.

해설 〈동사 어휘〉
빈칸에 쓰일 동사의 목적어인 명사 appreciation은 '감사, 감사의 뜻'을 의미한다. 따라서 '감사의 뜻을 표현했다'와 같은 의미가 되어야 알맞으므로 '~을 표현하다, 나타내다'라는 뜻으로 쓰이는 (B) expressed가 정답이다.

어휘 retirement 은퇴, 퇴직 colleague 동료 직원 appreciation 감사(의 뜻) outstanding 뛰어난, 우수한 contribution 공헌, 기여 express (감정 등) ~을 표현하다, 나타내다 appear 나타나다, 보이다 comment 의견을 말하다

129 해석 그 도서 사인회 행사에 대한 계획은 잠정적인 것인데, 행사 자금 액수가 아직 결정되지 않았기 때문이다.

해설 〈형용사 어휘〉
행사에 필요한 자금의 액수가 아직 결정되지 않았다는 말이 쓰여 있는 것으로 보아 행사 계획이 확정되지 않은 것으로 판단할 수 있다. 따라서 여전히 미정인 상태를 나타낼 형용사로 '잠정적인'을 뜻하는 (D) tentative가 정답이다.

어휘 signing event 사인회 since ~하기 때문에 amount 액수, 금액 funding 자금 determine ~을 결정하다 steady 꾸준한, 변함없는 immense 엄청난, 어마어마한 unwanted 원하지 않는, 필요하지 않는 tentative 잠정적인

130 해석 150달러가 넘는 모든 구매에 대한 승인을 받으려면 회계부에 근무하는 직원에게 연락하시기 바랍니다.

해설 〈명사 자리(준동사의 목적어)〉
to부정사로 쓰인 타동사 obtain과 전치사 for 사이에 위치한 빈칸은 부정사 obtain의 목적어 역할을 할 명사 자리이므로 명사인 (D) approval이 정답이다.

어휘 get in touch with ~에게 연락하다 Accounting 회계부 obtain ~을 받다, 얻다 purchase 구매(품) over ~가 넘는 approve ~을 승인하다 approval 승인

PART 6   P73

[131-134] 이메일

수신: 〈미공개_수신인〉
발신: tworthy@dentondiner.com
제목: 신규 정책
날짜: 8월 21일

전 직원들께,

우리는 손님들을 위한 커피 **131** 리필과 관련해 새로운 정책을 시행할 예정입니다. 지금부터, 종업원들은 더 이상 테이블마다 비어 있거나 절반 정도 비어 있는 컵들을 가득 채우지 않아도 됩니다. 고객께서 새로운 커피 한 잔을 따르도록 요청하실 때까지 기다려야 합니다. 이는 우리가 매일 끓여내는 커피의 양을 **132** 최소화해 줄 것입니다. **133** 결과적으로, 우리는 더 적은 커피 콩을 구입함으로써 상당한 액수의 금액을 절약하게 될 것입니다. 정문 옆에 우리 정책에 대한 공지를 게시할 것입니다. **134** 여러분은 또한 이 변경 사항을 손님들께 알려 드려야 합니다. 앞으로 며칠 동안 고객들께서 어떻게 반응하시는지 우리에게 알려 주시기 바랍니다.

티나 워시
매니저, 덴튼 다이너

어휘 policy 정책, 방침 implement ~을 시행하다 diner 식사(식당) 손님 as of + 시점 ~부터, ~부로 no longer 더 이상 ~ 않다 fill up ~을 가득 채우다 wait for A to do A가 ~할 때까지 기다리다 ask A to do A에게 ~하도록 요청하다 pour ~을 따르다, 붓다 amount 양, 수량, 액수 brew ~을 끓여내다 on a daily basis 하루 단위로, 매일 significant 상당한 by (방법) ~으로써 (위치) ~ 옆에 purchase ~을 구입하다 fewer 더 적은 (수의) post v. ~을 게시하다 notice 공지 let A know B A에게 B를 알리다 respond 반응하다, 응답하다

131 해설 〈전치사 자리(명사와 명사 사이)〉
빈칸 앞뒤에 각각 위치한 명사구 a new policy와 coffee refills를 연결할 수 있는 전치사가 빈칸에 쓰여야 알맞으므로 '~와 관련해'라는 뜻의 전치사 (B) regarding이 정답이다.

어휘 regard ~을 …으로 여기다, 간주하다 regarding ~와 관련해 regardless (of) (~에) 상관없이

132 해설 〈동사 어휘(문맥)〉
문장의 주어 this는 문맥상 앞선 내용인 '빈 컵들을 채우지 않고 고객이 요청할 때까지 기다린다'는 내용을 지칭하는 대명사인데, 이렇게 되면 매일 끓여내는 커피의 양이 줄어들게 될 것이므로 '~을 최소화하다'를 뜻하는 (D) minimize가 정답이다.

어휘 remove ~을 제거하다, 없애다 exchange ~을 교환하다 double ~을 두 배로 만들다 minimize ~을 최소화하다

133 해설 〈접속부사〉

빈칸 앞 문장에는 하루 단위로 끓여내는 커피 양이 줄어들 것이라는 내용이, 빈칸 뒤에는 비용을 절약하게 될 것이라는 내용이 쓰여 있는데, 이는 앞선 문장의 결과를 말하는 흐름에 해당된다. 따라서 '결과적으로, 그 결과' 등의 의미로 결과를 나타내는 문장 앞에 사용하는 (B) As a result가 정답이다.

어휘 on the other hand 반면, 다른 한편으로 as a result 결과적으로, 그 결과 however 하지만 despite ∼에도 불구하고

134 (A) 직원 회의가 일부 추가 상세 정보를 제공해 주었습니다.
(B) 이 기간 동안, 가격이 오를 것으로 예상됩니다.
(C) 여러분은 또한 이 변경 사항을 손님들께 알려 드려야 합니다.
(D) 여러분이 어느 교대 근무조로 근무하기를 선호하는지 저에게 알려 주십시오.

해설 〈빈칸에 알맞은 문장 넣기〉

빈칸 앞에 해당 정책 변경에 관한 공지를 게시한다는 내용이 있으므로, also와 함께 손님들에게 변경 사항을 알리는 또 다른 방법을 언급한 (C)가 정답이다. 나머지 문장들은 정책 변경과 관련된 흐름에 부합하지 않는다.

어휘 provide ∼을 제공하다 details 상세 정보, 세부 사항 during ∼ 중에, ∼ 동안 be expected to do ∼할 것으로 예상되다 rise 오르다, 상승하다 inform A of B A에게 B를 알리다 diner 식사 손님 let A know B A에게 B를 알리다 shift 교대 근무(조) prefer to do ∼하기를 선호하다

[135-138] 웹 페이지

http://www.hamptongamersclub.org

햄튼 게이머즈 클럽(HGC)은 지역 사회 내에서 게임에 대한 관심을 증대시키기 **135** 위해 특별 행사뿐만 아니라 월간 게임 활동 시간들을 마련하고 있습니다. 이 행사들은 흔히 현실적인 롤플레잉 게임들을 특징으로 합니다. **136** 이들 중 많은 것들은 어떻게 롤플레잉 게임들이 진행되는지 보고 싶어 하는 많은 사람들에 의해 관전됩니다. 추가로, HGC는 매년 5월에 게임 토너먼트를 개최합니다. 올해의 콘테스트에서는 게이머들이 '던전스'와 '위저즈'와 경기해야 합니다. **137** 전국 각지에서 게이머들이 그곳에 올 것입니다. 해럴드 모스 씨가 작년 **138** 우승자였습니다. 그분이 경기한 캐릭터가 7시간에 걸친 게임에서 다른 모든 캐릭터들을 물리쳐 낼 수 있었습니다.

어휘 organize ∼을 마련하다, 조직하다 monthly 월간의, 달마다의 session (특정 활동을 위한) 시간 as well as ∼뿐만 아니라 …도 interest in ∼에 대한 관심 local 지역의, 현지의 community 지역 사회, 지역 공동체 feature ∼을 특징으로 하다, 포함하다 realistic 현실적인 a large number of 아주 많은 (수의) in addition 추가로, 게다가 require A to do A에게 ∼하도록 요구하다, A가 ∼해야 하다 manage to do ∼해 내다 defeat ∼을 물리치다, 이기다

135 해설 〈부정사(부사적 용법)〉

빈칸 뒤 increase가 명사 interest를 목적어로 취하는 동사로 사용되고 있는데, 문장에 동사 organizes가 이미 존재하므로 increase를 준동사의 형태로 바꾸어 줄 수 있는 (C) in order to가 정답이다. 대등

접속사인 (C) so는 완전한 절과 절을 연결하는 것은 가능하지만 뒤에 주어를 생략한 채 동사만 사용하는 것은 불가능하다.

어휘 even if (만약) ∼라 할지라도 in order to do ∼하기 위해 so that ∼할 수 있도록

136 해설 〈지시 대명사〉

Many of의 수식을 받으려면 복수를 나타내는 대명사가 빈칸에 쓰여야 한다. 또한 이 대명사가 지칭하는 대상은 바로 앞에 위치한 realistic role-playing games이어야 하므로 바로 앞서 언급된 복수 명사를 대신할 때 사용하는 (D) these가 정답이다.

어휘 another 또 다른 하나의

137 (A) 관전자들을 위해 남겨진 좌석이 많지 않습니다.
(B) 전국 각지에서 게이머들이 그곳에 올 것입니다.
(C) 내년에는 이 토너먼트가 8월에 열릴 것입니다.
(D) 그것은 대대적인 성공으로 널리 여겨졌습니다.

해설 〈빈칸에 알맞은 문장 넣기〉

빈칸 앞에는 올해 있을 대회에 대한 정보가 언급되어 있는데, 이 대회를 그곳(there)으로 언급하며 전국 각지에서 게이머들이 올 것이라고 해당 대회에 대한 추가적인 정보를 언급하고 있는 (B)가 문맥상 가장 적합한 정답이다. (D)의 경우, It이 This year's contest를 지칭할 수 있는데, 앞 문장의 시제(will require)와 맞지 않는 과거의 일(was)을 언급하고 있어 시제가 맞지 않는다.

어휘 There be A A가 있다 viewer 관전자, 시청자, 보는 사람 from around the country 전국 각지에서 widely 널리, 폭넓게 consider A B A를 B로 여기다 major 대대적인, 아주 큰, 주요한 success 성공

138 해설 〈명사 어휘 (문맥)〉

Harold Moss라는 사람의 신분과 관련된 명사가 빈칸에 쓰여야 한다. 다음 문장에 다른 모든 캐릭터를 게임에서 물리친 사실이 언급되어 있는데, 이는 우승자임을 나타내는 말이므로 (B) winner가 정답이다.

어휘 judge 심사위원 winner 우승자, 승리자 expert 전문가 consultant 상담 전문가

[139-142] 이메일

날짜: 7월 24일
수신: 전 직원
발신: 에릭 머드
제목: 사직

안녕하세요, 여러분.

제가 다른 회사와 일하게 될 **139** 마이애미로 옮기기로 결정함에 따라 서머즈 대표이사님께 사직서를 막 제출했다는 사실을 여러분께 알려 드리고자 합니다. 제 **140** 마지막 날은 돌아오는 금요일인 7월 28일이 될 것입니다.

제가 이곳에서 근무를 시작한 이후로 줄곧, 업계에서 몇몇 가장 뛰어난 분들과 함께 근무하는 기쁨을 누려 왔습니다. 지난 5년 동안, 우리는 수많은 신규 고객들을 확보해 왔습니다. 그 과정에서, 우리는 섬유 업계에서 최고의 회사들 중 한 곳으로 입지를 **141** 구축했습니다. 이곳에서 모든 분과 함께 근무한 것이 영광이었습니다. **142** 제가 떠난 후에 여러분 모두가 정말로 그리울 것입니다.

모두 계속해서 열심히 근무해 주시기를 바라며, 앞으로도 지속적인 성공을 기원합니다.

안녕히 계십시오,

에릭 머드

어휘 resignation 사직, 사임 would like to do ∼하고자 하다, ∼하고 싶다 inform A that A에게 ∼라고 알리다 hand in ∼을 제출하다 decide to do ∼하기로 결정하다 ever since ∼한 이후로 줄곧 have the pleasure to do ∼하는 기쁨을 누리다 past 지난, 과거의 acquire ∼을 얻다, 획득하다 numerous 수많은, 다수의 in the process 그 과정에서 textile 섬유 honor 영광, 영예 continue to do 계속해서 ∼하다 success 성공

139 해설 〈관계부사〉

빈칸 앞의 절 마지막에 장소 명사(Miami)가 있으며, 빈칸 뒤에는 완전한 구조의 절이 있는데 해당 구조와 어울리는 것은 장소를 나타내는 관계부사이므로 (D) where이 정답이다. (B) that은 콤마 뒤에 사용할 수 없으며 (C) beside는 전치사이다.

어휘 beside ∼ 옆에

140 해설 〈형용사 어휘(문맥)〉

앞 문장에 다른 회사와 일하기 위해 마이애미로 가기로 결정했다는 말과 함께 사직서를 제출했다고 알리고 있다. 따라서 빈칸 뒤에 언급되는 날짜가 마지막 근무일을 뜻하는 것으로 판단할 수 있으므로 '마지막의'를 뜻하는 (C) last가 정답이다.

어휘 latest 최신의, 최근의 closest 가장 가까운

141 해설 〈시제(문맥)〉

각 보기가 모두 동사인데 시제만 다르므로 시제 관련 단서를 찾아야 한다. 빈칸 앞에 쓰여 있는 In the process는 앞 문장에서 언급한 지난 5년간의 과정 동안을 의미하므로 이와 어울릴 수 있는 과거 시제 (B) built가 정답이다.

어휘 build (입지, 관계 등) ∼을 구축하다

142 (A) 제 상사가 몇몇 서류에 서명해야 합니다.
(B) 저는 추가적인 직무를 맡는 것이 즐겁습니다.
(C) 제가 떠난 후에 여러분 모두가 정말로 그리울 것입니다.
(D) 그분의 후임자가 다음 주 월요일에 근무를 시작합니다.

해설 〈빈칸에 알맞은 문장 넣기〉
회사를 옮기는 것과 관련해 사직서를 제출한 사실과 회사에서 자신이 이룬 일 등을 언급하면서 바로 앞 문장에 함께 근무해서 영광이었다는 말이 쓰여 있다. 따라서 앞 문장과 흐름이 어울리려면 회사를 떠나는 사람의 마음가짐과 관련된 문장이 쓰여야 자연스러우므로 '모두가 그리울 것'이라는 의미를 나타내는 (C)가 정답이다.

어휘 supervisor 상사, 책임자, 부서장 sign ~에 서명하다 take on (책임, 직책 등) ~을 맡다 additional 추가적인 responsibility 책임, 책무 miss ~을 그리워하다 leave 떠나다, 나가다 replacement 후임(자), 대체(품)

[143-146] 편지

10월 13일
린다 마벗 씨
애플턴 스트리트 54번지
잭슨빌, FL

마벗 씨께,

이 편지는 귀하께서 10월 6일에 문의하신 내용에 대한 **143** 답변입니다. 귀하께서는 5년 넘게 라레도 의류회사의 고객이셨지만 2주 전에야 저희 회원제에 관해 알게 되었음을 언급하셨습니다. 귀하께서는 회원 자격이 있으신지 알고 싶어 하셨습니다. 저희를 통해 두 번의 제품 구매를 하신 사실을 증명하시기만 하면 되는데, 저희 기록에 따르면 저희 온라인 매장에서 여러 차례 쇼핑하신 것으로 나타납니다. **144** 따라서, 귀하께서는 해당 클럽에 가입하실 수 있는 자격이 있으십니다. 저희 웹 사이트 www.laredoclothes.com/members을 방문하셔서 **145** 신청하실 수 있습니다. **146** 그렇게 하시려면 "등록하기" 버튼을 클릭하신 다음, 안내 사항을 따르시면 됩니다. 신청서가 접수되는 대로, 해당 클럽의 회원이 되어 여러 가지 혜택을 받으시게 될 것입니다.

안녕히 계십시오.

쳇 로저스
고객 서비스 담당 직원
라레도 의류 회사

어휘 make an inquiry 문의하다 note that ~라고 (특별히) 언급하다 more than ~을 넘는 not A until B B나 되어서 A하다 know if ~인지 알다 qualify for ~에 대한 자격이 있다 All you need to do is do ~하시기만 하면 됩니다 prove ~을 증명하다 make a purchase 구매하다 show that ~임을 나타내다, 보여 주다 several 여럿의, 몇몇의 be eligible to do ~할 자격이 있다, ~할 수 있다 join ~에 가입하다, 합류하다 by (방법) ~함으로써 once ~하는 대로, ~하자마자 application 신청(서), 지원(서) accept ~을 수용하다, 받아들이다 gain ~을 얻다, 받다 benefit 혜택, 이득

---

143 **해설** 〈명사 자리(전치사 뒤)〉
전치사 in과 to 사이에 위치한 빈칸은 명사 자리이므로 보기 중 유일한 명사인 (C) response가 정답이다. in response to는 '~에 대한 답변으로, ~에 응하여'라는 의미의 표현이다.

어휘 respond 응답하다, 반응하다 response 응답, 반응

144 **해설** 〈접속 부사〉
앞 문장에는 회사의 기록에 여러 차례 쇼핑한 사실이 나타나 있음을 알리는 내용이, 빈칸 뒤에는 가입 자격이 있음을 언급하는 말이 쓰여 있다. 따라서 빈칸 앞 문장은 가입 자격의 근거를, 빈칸 다음 문장은 그 근거에 따라 자격이 있다는 결과를 알리는 흐름임을 알 수 있으므로 '따라서, 그러므로'라는 의미로 결과 앞에 사용하는 (B) Therefore가 정답이다.

어휘 meanwhile 그 사이에, 그러는 동안 therefore 따라서, 그러므로 nevertheless 그럼에도 불구하고 otherwise 그렇지 않으면, 그 외에는

145 **해설** 〈시제(문맥)〉
주어 You와 빈칸이 있고 그 뒤로 전치사구만 있으므로 빈칸은 문장의 동사 자리이다. 또한 신청하는 것은 과거의 행위가 아닌 일반적으로 웹 사이트를 방문해 신청할 수 있다는 가능성을 의미하는 것이므로, 가능성이나 허락을 나타낼 때 사용하는 조동사 may와 함께 사용된 (A) may apply가 정답이다.

어휘 apply 신청하다, 지원하다 would have p.p. ~했을 것이다

146 (A) 이 제품들에 대한 구매로 인해 할인 받으실 자격이 있습니다.
(B) 그렇게 하시려면 "등록하기" 버튼을 클릭하신 다음, 안내 사항을 따르시면 됩니다.
(C) 저희 기록에 따르면, 귀하의 카드가 이미 귀하께 발송되었습니다.
(D) 안타깝게도, 저희는 그 매장들을 닫아야 한다고 결정을 내렸습니다.

해설 〈빈칸에 알맞은 문장 넣기〉
앞 문장에 웹 사이트를 방문해 신청하라는 말이 쓰여 있는데, 그렇게 하는 일을 'do it'으로 지칭하며 웹 사이트에서 신청하기 위한 과정을 간략히 언급한 (B)가 정답이다. 나머지 문장들은 모두 웹 사이트에서 회원 자격을 신청하는 일과 관련 없는 의미를 나타낸다.

어휘 qualify A for B A에게 B에 대한 자격을 주다 register 등록하다 follow ~을 따르다, 따라 하다 directions 안내, 설명, 지시 according to ~에 따르면 mail ~을 우송하다 unfortunately 안타깝게도, 아쉽게도 decide that ~라고 결정하다

PART 7

[147-148] 초대장

147 시에라 체육관 개관식
유클리드 애비뉴 738번지
147 1월 8일, 토요일
여러분께 적합한지 알아보실 수 있도록 저희 시설을 확인해 보십시오.
향후 방문용 무료 1일권을 받아 가십시오.
견학 및 다과: 오전 10시 — 오후 5시
148 무료 요가 강좌 참가*: 오전 11시 또는 오후 3시

***148 메리 도킨스 씨에게 직접 연락해 운동 복장 및 레벨에 대한 추천 사항과 관련해 문의하시기 바랍니다.**

어휘 check out ~을 확인하다 facility 시설(물) see if ~인지 알아보다 pick up ~을 받아 가다, 가져가다 free 무료의 day pass 1일권 refreshments 다과, 간식 participate in ~에 참가하다 contact ~에게 연락하다 directly 직접, 곧장 inquire about ~에 관해 문의하다 recommendation 추천, 권장 workout 운동 gear 장비, 복장 ability 능력

147 1월 8일 행사의 목적은 무엇인가?
(A) 정부 보건 프로그램을 시작하는 것
(B) 업체의 새로운 개조 사항을 보여 주는 것
(C) 업체에 필요한 직원들을 모집하는 것
(D) 새로운 피트니스 센터를 소개하는 것

해설 〈주제 및 목적〉
지문 시작 부분에 시에라 체육관 개관식(Grand Opening of Sierra Gym)이 1월 8일에 열린다고 쓰여 있으며, 이 행사의 진행과 관련된 정보가 전체적으로 제시되어 있다. 따라서 새로 문을 여는 체육관을 소개하는 것이 목적임을 알 수 있으므로 (D)가 정답이다.

어휘 launch ~을 시작하다, ~에 착수하다 renovation 개조, 보수 recruit ~을 모집하다 introduce ~을 소개하다

148 메리 도킨스 씨는 누구일 것 같은가?
(A) 점검 담당자
(B) 영업사원
(C) 강사
(D) 부동산 중개업자

해설 〈세부 사항〉
메리 도킨스 씨의 이름은 마지막 문장에 제시되어 있으며, 요가 강좌와 관련하여 도킨스 씨에게 직접 연락해 복장 등에 대해 문의하라는 내용이 쓰여 있다. 해당 강좌 참가와 관련해 추천을 해 줄 수 있는 사람은 강사인 것으로 판단할 수 있으므로 (C)가 정답이다.

[149-150] 문자 메시지 대화

고든 보스	[오전 11:48]
컨퍼런스는 어때요?	
애나 로크	[오전 11:50]
아주 좋아요! 많은 흥미로운 분들을 만나고 있어요. 그리고 오늘 오후에 소셜 미디어에 관한 **149** 맥칼리스터 주식회사의 강연에 참석할 겁니다.	
고든 보스	[오전 11:51]
그곳에 일찍 가도록 하세요. **149** 아마 빠르게 만석이 될 거예요.	
애나 로크	[오전 11:52]
의심의 여지가 없죠.	
고든 보스	[오전 11:53]
그에 관련된 이야기를 들어 볼 수 있기를 고대하고 있습니다.	
애나 로크	[오전 11:54]
150 그 자리에 참석하실 수 없으시니, 따로 유인물을 챙겨 드릴까요?	
고든 보스	[오전 11:55]
그렇게 해 주시면 감사하겠습니다.	

어휘 attend ~에 참석하다 be sure to do 꼭 ~하다 get there 그곳에 가다 fill up 가득 차다, 꽉 차다 No doubt 의심의 여지가 없다 look forward to -ing ~하기를 고대하다 be able to do ~할 수 있다 grab ~을 가져오다 extra 별도의, 추가의 handout 유인물 appreciate ~에 대해 감사하다

149 오전 11시 52분에, 로크 씨가 "No doubt"이라고 썼을 때 의미한 것은 무엇이겠는가?
(A) 오후에 보스 씨를 만날 계획이다.
(B) 맥칼리스터 주식회사에 일자리를 얻고 싶어 한다.
(C) 한 행사 시간이 인기 있을 가능성이 있다는 데 동의한다.
(D) 다음 달에 컨퍼런스에 참석할 것으로 확신하고 있다.

해설 〈의도 파악〉
제시된 표현은 '의심의 여지가 없다'는 의미를 지니며, 앞서 보스 씨가 빠르게 만석이 될 것이라고(It will probably fill up quickly) 말한 것에 대한 동의를 나타낸다. 여기서 It은 그 앞에 로크 씨가 언급한 맥칼리스터 주식회사의 강연(~ the McAlister Inc. lecture ~)을 가리키므로 그 강연에 많은 사람이 온다는 점에 동의한다는 말이라는 것을 알 수 있다. 따라서 이와 같은 의미에 해당되는 (C)가 정답이다.

어휘 plan to do ~할 계획이다 agree that ~임에 동의하다 session (특정 활동을 위한) 시간 be likely to do ~할 가능성이 있다 be sure (that) ~임을 확신하다 attend ~에 참석하다

150 보스 씨에 관해 암시된 것은 무엇인가?
(A) 맥칼리스터 주식회사의 강연에 가지 못할 것이다.
(B) 소셜 미디어 분야의 전문가이다.

(C) 몇몇 중요한 컨퍼런스 관련 문서를 분실했다.
(D) 연설 준비를 하느라 바쁘다.

해설 〈진위 확인 (전체 진위 유형)〉
로크 씨가 11시 54분에 작성한 메시지를 보면, 앞서 이야기하고 있던 맥칼리스터 사의 강연과 관련해 상대방인 보스 씨가 참석할 수 없다는 (Since you won't be able to attend ~) 말이 쓰여 있다. 따라서 이와 같은 상황을 언급한 (A)가 정답이다.

어휘 miss ~을 놓치다, 지나치다 talk 강연, 연설 expert 전문가 be busy -ing ~하느라 바쁘다 prepare for ~을 준비하다, ~에 대비하다

[151-152] 이메일

수신: 조엘리 버넷
발신: 로렌스 홀컴
날짜: 8월 21일
제목: 할 일

안녕하세요, 조엘리 씨.

151 저와 렘센 엔터프라이즈 사와의 회의 세부 사항을 업데이트해 주셨으면 합니다. 원래, 그쪽 직원들 중 한 분이 우리 사무실을 방문하실 예정이었습니다. 하지만 그 일은 더 이상 가능하지 않기 때문에 대신 제가 그쪽 사무실을 방문하기 위해 뉴욕으로 출장을 갈 것입니다. 회의가 하루 연기되었기 때문에 이제 9월 6일에 열릴 것입니다.

152 늦어도 9월 6일 오전 10시에 뉴욕에 도착하는 항공편 티켓을 준비해 주시겠습니까? 돌아오는 항공편에 대해서는 9월 7일 아침에 출발하는 것이 좋겠습니다. 도와주셔서 감사합니다.

로렌스

어휘 would like A to do A에게 ~하기를 원하다 details 세부 정보, 상세 사항 originally 원래, 애초에 representative 직원 however 하지만, 그러나 no longer 더 이상 ~않다 instead 대신 postpone ~을 연기하다 by (차이) ~만큼, ~ 정도 take place (일, 행사 등이) 개최되다, 발생되다 arrange ~을 마련하다, 조치하다 arrive 도착하다 no later than 늦어도 ~까지는 prefer ~을 선호하다 departure 출발

151 이메일의 목적은 무엇인가?
(A) 마감 기한 연장을 요청하기 위해
(B) 한 회사를 소개하기 위해
(C) 회의 계획을 수정하기 위해
(D) 일부 계약서 조항을 확인해 주기 위해

해설 〈주제 및 목적〉
첫 단락 시작 부분에 회의 세부 정보를 업데이트하도록 상대방에게 요청하는(I would like you to update the details of my meeting ~) 내용이 목적에 해당된다. 세부 정보를 업데이트하는 것은 기존의 일정이나 계획 등을 수정하는 것이므로 이를 언급한 (C)가 정답이다.

어휘 ask for ~을 요청하다 deadline 마감 기한 extension 연장 introduce ~을 소개하다 revise ~을 수정하다, 개정하다 confirm ~을 확인해 주다 contract 계약(서) terms (계약 등의) 조항, 조건

152 버넷 씨는 무엇을 하도록 요청받는가?
(A) 일부 항공권 예약하기
(B) 렘센 엔터프라이즈에 연락하기
(C) 항공사에 환불 요청하기
(D) 뉴욕에 있는 호텔 추천하기

해설 〈세부 사항〉
버넷 씨의 이름은 상단의 수신인 항목에서 찾아볼 수 있으며, 두 번째 단락에서 뉴욕에 도착하는 항공편 티켓을 준비하도록(Could you please arrange tickets for a flight ~) 버넷 씨에게 요청하는 내용이 있으므로 (A)가 정답이다.

어휘 book v. ~을 예약하다 contact ~에게 연락하다 request ~을 요청하다, 요구하다 refund 환불

[153-154] 광고

오늘 패스트 패스를 구입하세요!

153 샘슨 카운티 전역에서 통행료를 지불하기 위해 긴 줄에서 대기하시는 동안 차량에 앉아 계시는 것이 지겨우신가요? 패스트 패스를 구입해 멈추지 않고 지정된 차로를 이용해 보세요. 저희 카메라가 위치를 녹화해 정확한 통행료를 청구해 드리며, 매달 말일에 청구서를 보내 드립니다. 시간을 절약하실 수 있을 뿐만 아니라, 비용도 절약하실 수 있습니다. 에이번데일에 있는 **154** 중앙 주차장(CPL)에서 입차 시에 패스트 패스를 제시하시고 주차 요금에 대해 10퍼센트 할인 받으십시오. **154** 이 주차장은 우리 시의 주 버스 터미널에서 걸어서 갈 수 있는 거리의 편리한 위치에 있습니다. 패스트 패스를 구입하시려면, www.sampsonfastpass.com을 방문하십시오. 이 통행권은 등록 후 영업일로 3일 내에 여러분께 우송됩니다.

어휘 be tired of ~가 싫으시다, 지긋지긋하다 vehicle 차량 while ~하는 동안 toll (도로의) 통행료 throughout ~ 전역에서 designated 지정된 without ~하지 않고, ~ 없이 location 위치, 지점 charge A B A에게 B를 청구하다 correct 정확한 bill 청구서, 고지서 in addition to ~뿐만 아니라, ~ 외에도 present ~을 제시하다 lot 주차장 be conveniently located 편리한 위치에 있는 within walking distance of ~에서 걸어서 갈 수 있는 거리에 있는 mail ~을 우송하다 within ~ 이내에 registration 등록

153 누가 이 광고에 관심이 있을 것 같은가?
(A) 투어 가이드 지원자들
(B) 과거 에이번데일 주민들
(C) 전문 사진가들
(D) 샘슨 카운티 운전자들

해설 〈글의 대상〉
첫 문장에 흥미를 끌기 위한 질문으로서 샘슨 카운티 전역에서 통행료를 지불하기 위해 오래 차량에 앉아 있는 것이 지겨운지(Are you tired of sitting in your vehicle ~ throughout Sampson County?) 묻는 말을 통해 그 지역 운전자들이 대상임을 알 수 있으므

로 (D)가 정답이다.

어휘 be interested in ~에 관심이 있다 applicant 지원자, 신청자 former 과거의, 이전의, 전직 ~의 resident 주민

154 CPL에 관해 암시된 것은 무엇인가?
(A) 월간 청구서를 발송한다.
(B) 여러 지점이 있다.
(C) 버스 터미널과 가깝다.
(D) 3일 동안 주차를 허용한다.

해설 〈진위 확인 (세부 진위 유형)〉
CPL이 언급된 중반부에, 중앙 주차장임을 언급하며 그 주차장이 버스 터미널에서 걸어서 갈 수 있는 거리에 있다고(The lot is conveniently located within walking distance of the city's main bus terminal) 알리고 있다. 이는 버스 터미널과 가깝다는 뜻이므로 (C)가 정답이다.

어휘 monthly 월간의, 달마다의 bill 청구서, 고지서, 계산서 several 여럿의, 몇몇의 location 지점, 지사, 위치 close to ~와 가까운 allow ~을 허용하다 parking 주차

[155-157] 안내 책자

> **패링턴 주식회사**
>
> 에코 블리바드 394번지, 롤리, NC 27616
> www.farringtonco.com · 984-555-6472
>
> 절대로 첫인상을 과소평가하지 마십시오! 옥외 공간은 손님께서 여러분의 부지를 방문하실 때 가장 먼저 주목하시게 되는 것들 중 하나입니다. 저희 패링턴 주식회사에서 전문적인 서비스를 통해 그 공간이 최고의 모습을 갖추도록 도와드립니다.
>
> - 말끔한 외관을 보장하기 위한 **155** 나무 및 가지 손질
> - 필요에 따라 연간으로 또는 계절적으로 진행되는 **155** 정기적인 잔디 유지 관리
> - **155** 화단 심기 및 유지 관리
> - **155** 큰 가지와 잔가지, 그리고 돌 제거
>
> 각 주택 부지는 특별합니다. **156** 여러분의 특정 건물에 대한 대략적인 서비스 요금을 알아보시려면, 저희 직원들 중 한 명과 상담 일정을 잡으시기 바랍니다. 저희는 여러분께서 필요로 하시는 것을 더 알아보기 위해 직접 주택 부지를 방문합니다. 이는 무료로 이용 가능하며, 이 서비스를 이용하셔야 할 의무는 없습니다.
>
> 저희 패링턴 주식회사와 함께 하시면, 저희 전문가들이 항상 여러분의 건물을 존중하는 마음과 신중함을 갖고 대할 것이라는 점을 믿으실 수 있습니다. 추가로, 저희는 지역 사회에 환원하는 일을 하고 있는데, **157** 롤리 취업 센터와의 제휴 관계를 통해, 기술적인 능력을 전하기 위해 이곳 롤리 지역에 거주하는 저소득층 사람들을 교육하고 있기 때문입니다. 이는 그분들이 가족을 재정적으로 부양하는 데 도움이 될 수 있습니다.
>
> 저희 이야기와 관련해 더 많은 것을 알아보시거나 고객 추천 후기를 읽어 보시려면, 저희 웹 사이트를 방문하시기 바랍니다.

어휘 underestimate ~을 과소평가하다 impression 인상 notice ~을 주목하다, 알아차리다 site 부지, 장소, 현장 let A do A에게 ~하게 하다 look one's best 최고의 모습을 보이다 expert a. 전문적인, n. 전문가 trim ~을 손질하다, 다듬다 branch (큰) 가지 ensure ~을 보장하다 tidy 말끔한 appearance 외관, 겉모습 maintenance 유지 관리(= upkeep) planting (식물) 심기 flowerbed 화단 removal 제거 twig 잔가지 unique 특별한, 독특한 find out ~을 알아보다, 확인하다 approximate 대략적인 particular 특별한, 특정한 property 건물, 부동산 consultation 상담 in person 직접 가서 available 이용 가능한 at no cost 무료로 obligation 의무 trust that ~임을 믿다 respect 존중 care 관심, 주의, 배려 in addition 추가로, 게다가 give back to ~에 환원하다, 되갚다 as ~하기 때문에 through ~을 통해 train ~을 교육하다 low-income 저소득층의 individual 사람, 개인 in order to do ~하기 위해 financially 재정적으로 support ~을 부양하다, 지원하다 testimonial 고객 추천 후기

155 패링턴 주식회사는 무슨 종류의 업체인가?
(A) 운송 서비스 회사
(B) 조경 회사
(C) 건축 업체
(D) 부동산 중개 업체

해설 〈주제 및 목적〉
첫 단락에 네 가지 세부 작업 사항이 언급된 부분을 보면, 나무 손질(Trimming trees ~), 잔디 관리(Regular lawn maintenance ~), 화단 심기(Planting ~), 가지와 돌 제거(Removal of branches)가 쓰여 있다. 이는 모두 조경 작업과 관련된 것이므로 (B)가 정답이다.

어휘 transportation 교통(편) landscaping 조경 architectural 건축의 firm 업체, 회사 real estate agency 부동산 중개 업체

156 고객들이 어떻게 서비스에 대한 견적을 받아 볼 수 있는가?
(A) 신청서를 발송함으로써
(B) 업체 소유주에게 이메일을 보냄으로써
(C) 온라인 양식을 작성 완료함으로써
(D) 무료 상담 서비스를 예약함으로써

해설 〈세부 사항〉
질문에 쓰인 estimate은 견적 또는 견적서를 의미한다. 두 번째 단락을 보면, 대략적인 서비스 요금을 알아보려면 상담 일정을 잡으라고(To find out the approximate cost of services ~, please schedule a consultation ~) 쓰여 있고, 무료로 진행된다고(This is available at no cost to you ~) 알리고 있으므로 (D)가 정답이다.

어휘 estimate 견적(서) application 신청(서), 지원(서) complete ~을 작성 완료하다 form 양식, 서식 book v. ~을 예약하다 free 무료의 consultation 상담

157 패링턴 주식회사에 관해 언급된 것은 무엇인가?
(A) 업계에서 최고의 안전 등급을 보유하고 있다.
(B) 환경 친화적인 제품을 활용한다.
(C) 지역 주민들에게 직업 교육을 제공한다.
(D) 가치 있는 자선 단체에 기부를 한다.

해설 〈진위 확인 (전체 진위 유형)〉
세 번째 단락에 롤리 취업 센터와의 제휴 관계를 통해 롤리 지역에 거주하는 저소득층 사람들을 교육하고 있다는(~ we train low-income individuals living here in Raleigh in order to give them technical skills) 내용이 쓰여 있다. 따라서 이와 같은 교육 기회를 제공하는 사실을 언급한 (C)가 정답이다.

어휘 industry 업계 rating 등급, 평점 environmentally friendly 환경 친화적인 provide ~을 제공하다 training 교육, 훈련 local 지역의, 현지의 resident 주민 make a donation to ~에 기부하다 worthwhile 가치 있는 charity 자선 단체

[158-160] 이메일

> 수신: 미쉘 에버트 〈m.ebert@blevins.net〉
> 발신: 제리 프레스콧 〈j.prescott@blevins.net〉
> 날짜: 7월 28일
> 제목: 업데이트
>
> 에버트 씨께,
>
> **158** 벨트리 제조사의 대니얼 서터 씨로부터 방금 전화를 받았는데, 그분께서 내일 당신 사무실을 방문하실 수 없습니다. 안타깝게도, 그분 회사의 제조 시설들 중 한 곳에 발생된 문제를 처리하기 위해 예기치 못하게 다른 지역으로 가셔야 했습니다. **158** **159** 대신, 8월 12일 오후 2시에 당신을 만나실 것입니다. **159** 당신이 하루 전날에 케임브리지 센터에서 강연을 한다는 사실을 알고 있기는 하지만, 그 이후에 평소와 마찬가지로 다시 출근하실 것이라고 저에게 말씀해 주셨습니다. **160** 내일로 예정된 서터 씨의 시간대는 제품 시연회로 대체될 것입니다.
>
> 7월 29일
>
> | 시간 | 활동 | 직원/게스트 |
> |---|---|---|
> | 오전 9:30 | 교육 | 평사원 |
> | **160** 오후 1:00 | 대면 회의 | 대니얼 서터, 벨트리 제조사 |
> | 오후 2:30 | 화상 회의 | 니나 셔먼, 셔먼 컨설팅 |
> | 오후 7:00 | 리오스에서의 식사 | 프리다 힐라드 |
>
> 위 일정을 업데이트해 출력본을 남겨 드리겠습니다. 질문이 있으실 경우, 저에게 알려만 주십시오.
>
> 안녕히 계십시오.
>
> 제리

어휘 receive ~을 받다 be unable to do ~할 수 없다 unfortunately 안타깝게도, 아쉽게도 go out of town 다른 지역으로 가다 unexpectedly 예기치 못하게 deal with ~을 처리하다, 다루다 manufacturing 제조 facility 시설(물) instead 대신 present a lecture 강연하다 as usual 평소와 마찬가지로, 늘 그렇듯이 time slot 시간대 replace A with B A를 B로 대체하다, 교체하다 demonstration 시연(회) personnel 직원들, 인사(부) training 교육 in-person 직접 만나는 video conference 화상 회의 above 위에 leave ~을 남기다, 놓다

158 이메일의 목적은 무엇인가?

(A) 에버트 씨에게 다가오는 마감 시한을 상기시키는 것
(B) 에버트 씨에게 일정 변경을 알리는 것
(C) 한 제조회사에 관한 조사 내용을 제공하는 것
(D) 일전에 있었던 실수에 대해 사과하는 것

해설 〈주제 및 목적〉
지문 첫 문장에 대니얼 서터 씨가 내일 상대방의 사무실을 방문할 수 없다고 알리면서 뒤이어 8월 12일에 대신 만날 것이라고(~ he is unable to visit you at your office tomorrow. ~ Instead, he'll meet you on August 12 at 2 P.M.) 언급하는 내용이 있다. 이는 예정된 일정이 변경되었음을 알리는 것이므로 (B)가 정답이다.

어휘 remind A of B A에게 B를 상기시키다 approaching 다가오는 deadline 마감 기한 inform A of B A에게 B를 알리다 provide ~을 제공하다 research 조사, 연구 manufacturing firm 제조 회사 apologize for ~에 대해 사과하다

159 에버트 씨는 8월 11일에 무엇을 할 것인가?

(A) 연설하기
(B) 해외 출장 가기
(C) 서터 씨의 사무실 방문하기
(D) 신제품 출시하기

해설 〈세부 사항〉
첫 단락 중반부에 8월 12일이라는 날짜를 말하며, 수신인인 에버트 씨가 하루 전날에 케임브리지 센터에서 강연을 한다는 사실을(~ August 12 at 2 P.M. I know you're presenting a lecture at the Cambridge Center the day before ~) 언급하는 내용이 있다. 따라서 8월 11일에 연설한다는 것을 알 수 있으므로 (A)가 정답이다.

어휘 give a talk 연설하다 overseas 해외로 launch ~을 출시하다, 공개하다

160 에버트 씨는 언제 시연회를 볼 것인가?

(A) 오전 9시 30분에
(B) 오후 1시에
(C) 오후 2시 30분에
(D) 오후 7시에

해설 〈세부 사항〉
제품 시연회가 언급되는 첫 단락 마지막 문장에 서터 씨의 시간대가 제품 시연회로 대체된다고(Mr. Sutter's time slot for tomorrow will be replaced with a product demonstration) 쓰여 있다. 그리고 그 밑에 위치한 표에는 오후 1시가 서터 씨와 만나기로 했던 시간으로(1:00 P.M. / Daniel Sutter, Veltri Manufacturing) 표기되어 있으므로 (B)가 정답이다.

어휘 demonstration 시연(회), 시범

[161-163] 기사

(바르셀로나, 8월 2일) — 독일 가전제품 제조사 홀츠먼이 자사의 신규 공장 설립을 위해 롱뷰를 선택했다고 어제 기자회견에서 발표했습니다. —[1]—.

161 "주요 도로들과 매우 가깝기 때문에 해당 부지가 저희 목적에 이상적인 곳입니다,"라고 회사 대변인 헤이크 베커 씨가 말했습니다. "저희는 환경에 깊은 관심을 갖고 있으며, 원자재 및 완제품 운송에 필요한 이동 거리를 단축하는 것은 대기 오염에 저희가 미치는 영향을 최소화하는 한 가지 방법입니다." —[2]—.

프랑크푸르트에 본사를 둔 이 제조사는 믿을 수 없을 정도의 성장을 경험하고 있으며, 작년에는 캐나다의 몬트리올에 네 번째 공장을 세웠습니다. **162** 회사 관계자들은 가까운 미래의 어느 시점에 아시아 지역에서 자사의 제품을 판매할 기회를 이미 찾고 있습니다. —[3]—. **163** 소매 대리점 위치로 고려되는 곳은 상하이와 우한입니다. —[4]—.

어휘 appliance 가전제품 manufacturer 제조사 announce that ~라고 발표하다 press conference 기자회견 select ~을 선택하다 plant 공장 close to ~와 가까운 site 부지, 장소 ideal 이상적인 spokesperson 대변인 care about ~에 관심이 있다, ~을 신경 쓰다 environment 환경 decrease ~을 감소시키다 travel distance 이동 거리 raw materials 원자재 finished goods 완성 제품 way to do ~하는 방법 minimize ~을 최소화하다 impact on ~에 미치는 영향 pollution 오염, 공해 based ~에 본사를 둔 experience ~을 경험하다 incredible 믿을 수 없을 정도의 growth 성장 officials 관계자들 look for ~을 찾다 opportunity to do ~할 기회 at some point 어느 시점에 consider ~을 고려하다 retail store 소매점

161 베커 씨는 새 부지의 어떤 이점을 언급하는가?

(A) 직원들에게 지급되는 저렴한 임금
(B) 제반 교통 시설과의 근접성
(C) 친환경적인 장비의 사용
(D) 세금 혜택 시스템

해설 〈세부 사항〉
베커 씨가 부지의 특징을 언급한 두 번째 단락에, 주요 도로들과 매우 가깝기 때문에(Because it is so close to major roadways ~) 이상적인 장소라고 말하고 있으므로 이와 같은 교통 편의성에 해당되는 (B)가 정답이다.

어휘 affordable (가격이) 저렴한, 적당한 proximity 근접성, 가까움 environmentally friendly 친환경적인

162 기사에 따르면, 홀츠먼은 곧 무엇을 하고 싶어 하는가?

(A) 신제품 출시하기
(B) 캐나다에서 고객층 확대하기
(C) 아시아 시장 진입하기
(D) 온라인 소매점 개설하기

해설 〈세부 사항〉
이 회사의 계획이 제시된 마지막 단락에 아시아 지역에서 제품을 판매할 기회를 찾고 있다고(~ are already looking for an opportunity to sell their goods in Asia ~) 알리고 있다. 이는 아시아 시장 진출 계획을 뜻하는 것이므로 (C)가 정답이다.

---

163 [1], [2], [3], [4]로 표시된 위치들 중에서, 다음 문장이 들어가기에 가장 적절한 곳은 어디인가?

"나머지 다른 곳은 청두와 톈진입니다."

(A) [1]
(B) [2]
(C) [3]
(D) [4]

해설 〈문장 넣기〉
제시된 문장은 특정 대상 중 일부를 제외한 나머지를 가리킬 때 사용하는 는 The others와 함께 두 곳의 장소가 제시되어 있다. 따라서 두 곳의 다른 장소인 상하이와 우한을 먼저 언급한 문장 뒤의 위치인 [4]에 들어가는 것이 적절하므로 (D)가 정답이다.

[164-167] 회람

수신: 전 바셀 직원들
발신: 킴벌리 포스터, 운영 부장
날짜: 3월 3일
제목: 앞두고 있는 변화

164 고객들은 우리 회사의 성능에 대한 높은 기준으로 인해 바셀 에어컨을 신뢰할 수 있다는 사실을 알고 있습니다. 하지만, **165** 우리의 훌륭한 명성에도 불구하고, 지속적인 매출 하락을 겪고 오고 있습니다. 이전의 여러 회의에서 논의한 바와 같이, 우리 지역에서 점점 더 많은 업체들이 에어컨을 판매하기 시작하고 있습니다. 우리는 가격을 인하하고 싶지 않은데, 그 이유는 그렇게 할 경우 제품에 드는 비용을 **166** 충당하기 어렵게 만들 것이기 때문입니다. 우리는 또한 광고를 늘리기 위해 노력했지만, 지금까지 큰 차이를 만들어 내지 못했습니다.

우리의 현 판매량 문제에 대처하기 위해, 우리가 고객들에게 제공하는 것과 관련된 전략을 조정할 계획입니다. **167** 다음 달부터, 우리 에어컨 중 하나를 구입하는 고객들은 첫 3년 동안 1년에 한 번씩 우리 기술자 중 한 명으로부터 무료 방문 서비스를 받을 자격을 얻게 될 것입니다. 해당 기술자가 주의를 필요로 하는 모든 성능 문제를 확인할 것입니다. 우리는 이것이 다른 업체들보다 우리를 돋보이게 하는 데 도움이 되기를 바랍니다.

어휘 depend on ~을 신뢰하다, ~에 의존하다 due to ~로 인해 performance 성능, 실적, 수행 능력 despite ~에도 불구하고 reputation 명성, 평판 steady 지속적인 drop in ~의 하락 as discussed 논의된 바와 같이 previous 이전의, 과거의 business 업체 be reluctant to do ~하기를 꺼려하다 lower v. ~을 낮추다, 내리다 make A 형용사 A를 ~하게 만들다 cover (비용 등) ~을 충당하다, 부담하다 increase ~을 늘리다, 증가시키다 advertising 광고 make much of a difference 큰 차이를 만들다 so far 지금까지 deal with ~에 대처하다, ~을 다루다, 처리하다 current 현재의 sales 판매(량), 매출 issue 문제, 사안 plan to do ~할 계획이다 adjust ~을 조정하다 strategy 전략 regarding ~와 관련해 be eligible for ~에 대한 자격이 있다 complimentary 무료의 check for ~가 있는지 확인하다 attention 주의, 관심 set A apart from B B보다 A를 돋보이게 만들다

164 바셀에 관해 언급된 것은 무엇인가?
(A) 여러 국가에서 운영되고 있다.
(B) 최근에 새 지점을 개장했다.
(C) 높은 품질로 알려져 있다.
(D) 추가 기술자들을 고용했다.

해설 〈진위 확인 (전체 진위 유형)〉
첫 단락 시작 부분에 성능에 대한 높은 기준으로 인해 고객들이 바셀 에어컨을 신뢰한다는(~ they can depend on Bassell air conditioners ~) 말이 쓰여 있는데, 이는 품질의 우수성을 뜻하므로 (C)가 정답이다.

어휘 operate 운영되다 several 여럿의, 몇몇의 recently 최근에 branch 지점, 지사 be known for ~로 알려져 있다 hire ~을 고용하다

165 바셀은 왜 사업 전략을 변경하는가?
(A) 원자재 가격이 올랐다.
(B) 공급 업체가 폐업했다.
(C) 치열한 경쟁에 직면해 있다.
(D) 고객들이 불만을 제기했다.

해설 〈세부 사항〉
첫 단락 시작 부분에 매출 하락 문제를 언급하면서 점점 더 많은 업체들이 에어컨을 판매하기 시작했다는(~ we have been experiencing a steady drop in sales. ~ more and more businesses in our area are starting to sell air conditioners) 언급을 통해 변화가 필요한 이유를 설명하고 있다. 이는 경쟁이 치열해지고 있다는 뜻이므로 (C)가 정답이다.

어휘 strategy 전략 raw material 원자재 increase 오르다, 증가되다 supplier 공급 업체 go out of business 폐업하다 face v. ~에 직면하다 heavy (수량, 정도 등이) 심한, 많은, 큰 competition 경쟁 make a complaint 불만을 제기하다, 불평하다

166 첫 번째 단락, 다섯 번째 줄의 단어 "cover"와 의미가 가장 가까운 것은 무엇인가?
(A) 달성하다
(B) 손을 떼다
(C) 가장하다
(D) 비용을 지불하다

해설 〈동의어〉
해당 문장에서 cover의 목적어로 제품에 드는 비용을 의미하는 products' costs가 쓰여 있다. 따라서 cover가 해당 비용을 지불하는 일을 나타내기 위해 쓰인 것으로 판단할 수 있으므로 '~에 대한 비용을 지불하다'라는 의미를 나타내는 (D) pay for가 정답이다.

167 앞으로 고객들은 무엇을 받을 것인가?
(A) 연간 카탈로그
(B) 무료 연례 점검
(C) 교체 부품
(D) 무료 배송

해설 〈세부 사항〉
고객들이 받는 것이 언급된 두 번째 단락에, 다음 달부터 에어컨을 구입하는 고객들은 첫 3년 동안 1년에 한 번씩 무료 방문 서비스를 받을 자격이 있다고(~ will be eligible for a complimentary visit from one of our technicians ~) 알리고 있으므로 이와 같은 서비스에 해당되는 (B)가 정답이다.

어휘 receive ~을 받다 yearly 연간의, 해마다의 free 무료의(= complimentary) annual 연례적인, 해마다의 inspection 점검 replacement 교체, 대체 component 부품

[168-171] 편지

4월 8일
키넌 콜
굿윈 애비뉴 438번지
샌포드, FL 32771

콜 씨께,

제12회 연례 샌포트 마라톤 행사에서 자원 봉사자가 되어 주시기를 요청드리고자 합니다. —[1]—. 이 경주 대회는 6월 13일 일요일에 개최되며, 퀸시 공원에서 시작되고 종료됩니다. 저희는 이번 행사의 성공을 위해 자원 봉사자들에게 의존하고 있는데, 다양한 업무에 대해 많은 분들이 필요하기 때문입니다. —[2]—.

저희는 **168** 선수들이 경주에 참가 수속을 할 수 있도록 돕는 등록 테이블을 운영하는 데 약 5명의 자원 봉사자가 필요합니다. 또한 경주 선수들에게 **168** 방향을 틀어야 하는 곳을 보여주기 위해 코스 전역에 걸쳐 배치되는 자원 봉사자들도 있습니다. 다른 자원 봉사자들은 **168** 코스 전역에 걸쳐 스탠드를 설치하고 물과 에너지 음료, 그리고 바나나를 나눠 드리게 될 것입니다. —[3]—.

저와 공동 행사 진행 책임자인 **171** 브랜든 멩겔 씨가 **169** 작년에 뵌 귀하를 기억하고 계시며, 그 행사 중에 정말로 열심히 일해 주셨다고 말씀하셨습니다. —[4]—. 마라톤 행사가 어떻게 운영되는지 잘 알고 계시는 분들이 자원 봉사자 팀에 있다는 것은 특히 도움이 됩니다. **170** 참가하실 수 있으시면, 늦어도 4월 25일까지 저희에게 알려 주시기 바랍니다. events@sanford.gov로 이메일 보내셔서 그렇게 하실 수 있습니다. 곧 귀하로부터 소식 들을 수 있기를 바랍니다.

감사합니다.

다이애나 홈즈

어휘 invite A to do A에게 ~하도록 요청하다 volunteer 자원 봉사자 take place (일, 행사 등이) 개최되다, 발생되다 depend on ~에 의존하다 success 성공 various 다양한 duty 업무, 일 operate ~을 운영하다, 운영되다 registration 등록 athlete 운동 선수 get p.p. ~ 되다 position ~을 배치하다, 위치시키다 throughout ~ 전역에 걸쳐 where to do ~하는 곳 make turns 방향을 틀다, 회전하다 necessary 필요한 set up ~을 설치하다 pass out ~을 나눠 주다 co-coordinator 공동 진행 책임자 particularly 특히 useful 도움이 되는, 유용한 be familiar with ~을 잘 알고 있다, ~에 익숙하다 be able to do ~할 수 있다 participate 참가하다 let A know A에게 알리다 no later than 늦어도 ~까지는

168 자원 봉사자들이 하는 업무로 언급되지 <u>않은</u> 것은 무엇인가?
(A) 선수들에게 코스 방향 알려 주기
(B) 간식용 스탠드 설치하기
(C) 등록 과정에서 선수들 돕기
(D) 수상자들에게 상품 제공하기

해설 〈진위 확인 (세부 진위 유형)〉
자원 봉사자들이 하는 일이 구체적으로 제시된 두 번째 단락에, 방향을 틀어야 하는 곳을 보여주는 일이(~ show runners where to make the necessary turns) 언급된 부분에서 (A)를, 물 등을 나눠 주는 스탠드를 설치하는 일을(~ set up stands throughout the course, passing out water ~) 말한 부분에서 (B)를 확인할 수 있다. 그리고 경주를 위해 선수들이 체크인하도록 돕는다는 내용에서(~ helping athletes to get checked in ~) (C)도 확인할 수 있다. 하지만 상품을 제공하는 일과 관련된 정보는 찾아볼 수 없으므로 (D)가 정답이다.

어휘 duty 업무, 직무 volunteer 자원 봉사자 direct ~에게 길을 안내하다 set up ~을 설치하다, 마련하다 refreshments 간식, 다과 assist A in -ing ~하는 데 있어 A를 돕다 sign in 등록하다, 가입하다 award ~을 주다, 수여하다 prize 상, 상품

169 콜 씨에 관해 언급된 것은 무엇인가?
(A) 이전의 행사에서 멩겔 씨와 일했다.
(B) 공동 진행 책임자로서의 직책에 지원했다.
(C) 마라톤에 대비해 훈련해 왔다.
(D) 최근에 샌포드 시로 이사했다.

해설 〈진위 확인 (세부 진위 유형)〉
콜 씨는 이 편지의 수신인이(Dear Mr. Cole)이며, 세 번째 단락에 콜 씨를 you로 지칭해 브랜든 멩겔 씨가 작년의 행사에서 콜 씨를 본 기억과 함께 정말로 열심히 일했다는(Brandon Mengel, remembers you from last year and said that you worked really hard ~) 내용이 쓰여 있다. 이는 두 사람이 함께 일한 적이 있다는 것을 의미하므로 (A)가 정답이다.

어휘 previous 이전의, 과거의 apply for ~에 지원하다, ~을 신청하다 co-coordinator 공동 진행 책임자 train 훈련하다, 교육받다 recently 최근에

170 콜 씨는 무엇을 하도록 요청받는가?
(A) 자원 봉사 업무에 대한 선호 사항을 이메일로 보내기
(B) 의견 설문 조사지 작성 완료하기
(C) 자신의 개인 연락 정보 업데이트하기
(D) 마감 기한까지 참석 여부 확인해 주기

해설 〈세부 사항〉
세 번째 단락을 보면, 참가할 수 있으면 콜 씨에게 4월 25일까지 알려 달라고(If you are able to participate, please let us know no later than April 25) 요청하는 말이 쓰여 있다. 이는 참석 여부를 확인해 달라는 뜻이므로 (D)가 정답이다.

어휘 preference 선호(하는 것) complete ~을 작성 완료하다 feedback 의견 questionnaire 설문 조사지 contact details 연락 정보 confirm ~을 확인해 주다 attendance 참석 deadline 마감 기한

171 [1], [2], [3], [4]로 표시된 위치들 중에서, 다음 문장이 들어가기에 가장 적절한 곳은 어디인가?

"귀하의 지원이 그분에게 큰 도움이 될 것입니다."

(A) [1]
(B) [2]
(C) [3]
(D) [4]

해설 〈문장 넣기〉
제시된 문장은 특정 인물을 지칭하는 him과 함께 상대방의 지원이 그 사람에게 큰 도움이 될 것이라는 의미를 나타낸다. 따라서 him으로 지칭할 수 있는 사람인 브랜든 멩겔 씨가 언급된 문장 뒤인 [4]에 들어가는 것이 알맞으므로 (D)가 정답이다.

어휘 assistance 지원, 도움

[172-175] 온라인 채팅

앤서니 바넷	[오전 9:03]

172 우리의 새 건설 프로젝트에 투자하시는 분들이 약 1시간 후에 이곳으로 오실 겁니다. **175** 제가 2번 회의실에서 모든 것을 준비하는 중입니다.

키스 세르반테스	[오전 9:04]

173 1번 회의실이 더 크기 때문에 그곳을 예약하셨다고 생각했는데요.

앤서니 바넷	[오전 9:05]

처음엔 그랬는데, **173** 천장에 있는 파이프가 어젯밤에 망가져서 물이 사방으로 새고 있었어요. 우리가 그것을 치우기는 했지만, **173** 천장에 얼룩이 져 있고, 회반죽이 곳곳에 금이 가 있어요. 2번 회의실도 우리 목적에 충분히 큽니다.

샤나 팔라지	[오전 9:06]

일정표에 따르면, 재무팀이 오늘 그곳을 예약해 두었어요.

앤서니 바넷	[오전 9:07]

걱정하지 마세요. 우리 회의 일정을 재조정할 수 없어서 그쪽 사람들에게 일정을 조정하도록 이미 요청했어요. 하지만 **174** 천장에서 비디오 화면을 내리는데 문제를 겪고 있습니다. 키스 씨, 당신이 항상 그걸 작동하게 만드는 요령을 알고 계신 것 같은데요.

키스 세르반테스	[오전 9:08]

지금 갑니다.

앤서니 바넷	[오전 9:09]

다과는 길 건너편의 제과점에 준비되어 있습니다. 제가 아직 회의실 준비 작업을 하고 있기 때문에 직접 제과점에 들를 시간이 없습니다.

샤나 팔라지	[오전 9:10]

제가 할 수 있습니다. **175** 제가 9시 45분쯤에 그곳으로 음식을 가져갈게요. 그 제과점에 우리 회사 이름을 말하기만 하면 되나요?

앤서니 바넷	[오전 9:12]

주문 확인 번호가 필요하실 텐데, RC7394입니다. 정말 감사합니다!

샤나 팔라지	[오전 9:13]

별 말씀을. 다른 어떤 것이든 필요하시면, 저에게 알려만 주세요.

어휘 invest in ~에 투자하다 in + 시간 ~ 후에 about 약, 대략 get A ready A를 준비하다 reserve ~을 예약하다 originally 처음에, 애초에 ceiling 천장 break 망가지다, 고장 나다 leak (물, 가스 등) 새다, 누출되다 have A p.p. A가 ~되게 하다 stained 얼룩진 plaster 회반죽 cracked 금이 간, 깨진 purpose 목적 according to ~에 따르면 finance 재무, 재정 ask A to do A에게 ~하도록 요청하다 reschedule ~의 일정을 재조정하다 since ~하기 때문에 have trouble -ing ~하는 데 문제를 겪다 lower v. ~을 낮추다, 내리다 seem to do ~하는 것 같다 trick 요령 make A do

---

A가 ~하게 만들다 on the way 가는 중인, 오는 중인 refreshments 다과, 간식 stop by ~에 들르다 oneself (부사적으로) 직접 set up ~을 준비하다, 설치하다 around ~쯤에 confirmation 확인(서) let A know A에게 알리다

172 바넷 씨는 오늘 무엇을 하고 있는가?

(A) 제품 테스트를 하는 사람들에게 샘플 소개하기
(B) 동료 직원들에게 교육 제공하기
(C) 몇몇 신입 사원들과 만나기
(D) 투자자들의 방문 준비하기

해설 〈세부 사항〉
바넷 씨의 첫 번째 메시지에, 새 건설 프로젝트에 투자하는 사람들이 곧 온다는 말과 함께 자신이 2번 회의실에서 모든 것을 준비하고 있다는(The people investing in our new building project will be here in about an hour. I'm getting everything ready ~) 내용이 있다. 이는 투자자들의 방문을 준비하는 일을 의미하므로 (D)가 정답이다.

어휘 introduce ~을 소개하다 provide ~을 제공하다 training 교육 coworker 동료 (직원) prepare for ~을 준비하다, ~에 대비하다 investor 투자자

173 1번 회의실의 무슨 문제점이 언급되는가?

(A) 알맞은 장비가 없다.
(B) 해당 그룹에 대해 충분히 넓지 않다.
(C) 일부 손상을 입었다.
(D) 다른 팀과 이중으로 예약되었다.

해설 〈세부 사항〉
9시 4분에 세르반테스 씨가 1번 회의실을 언급하자, 바로 뒤이어 바넷 씨가 천장에 있는 파이프가 망가진 사실과 함께 그로 인해 발생된 얼룩 및 금이 간 부분을(~ a pipe in the ceiling broke last night ~ the ceiling is stained and the plaster is cracked ~) 말하고 있다. 이는 그 회의실에 손상이 생겼음을 뜻하는 것이므로 (C)가 정답이다.

어휘 equipment 장비 sustain (손상, 피해 등) ~을 입다, 당하다 double-book ~을 이중 예약하다

174 오전 9시 8분에, 세르반테스 씨가 "I'm on the way"라고 말할 때 의미한 것은 무엇이겠는가?

(A) 몇몇 서류 작업을 끝마칠 것이다.
(B) 바넷 씨를 도울 의향이 있다.
(C) 일부 물품을 가지러 가기 위해 들를 수 있다.
(D) 고객의 본사를 방문할 것이다.

해설 〈의도 파악〉
제시된 문장은 어딘가로 가는 중일 때 흔히 사용하는 말이다. 바로 앞서 바넷 씨가 문제를 겪고 있다는 사실과 함께 상대방인 키스 씨가 해결 방법을 알고 있다고(I'm having trouble ~ you always seem to know the trick ~) 언급한 것에 대해 '지금 간다'고 답변하는 것은 도와주러 가겠다는 뜻이므로 (B)가 정답이다.

어휘 be willing to do ~할 의향이 있다, 기꺼이 ~하다 pick up ~을 가져 가다, 가져오다 headquarters 본사, 본부

175 대략 오전 9시 45분에 무슨 일이 있을 것인가?
(A) 바넷 씨가 제과점에 전화할 것이다.
(B) 팔라지 씨가 2번 회의실로 물품을 가져갈 것이다.
(C) 1번 회의실이 점검될 것이다.
(D) 팔라지 씨에게 확인 번호가 보내질 것이다.

해설 〈세부 사항〉
9시 45분이라는 시점은 9시 10분에 팔라지 씨가 작성한 메시지에 제시되어 있다. 이 메시지에서 팔라지 씨는 9시 45분쯤에 음식을 가져가겠다고(I'll bring the food there around 9:45) 알리고 있는데, 이는 바넷 씨가 첫 메시지에서 투자자 방문을 위해 예약했다고 말한 2번 회의실로 가져가는 것을 의미하므로 (B)가 정답이다.

어휘 approximately 약, 대략 inspect ~을 점검하다 confirmation 확인(서)

[176-180] 명함과 이메일

⑰⑧ 펜드렐 금융 서비스

리디아 갤러거
수석 금융 분석가

로빈슨 빌딩, 4호 사무실	이메일: lydiagal@pendrellfinancial.com
니콜라 애비뉴 876번지	사무실 전화번호: 604-555-8078, 내선번호 24
⑱⑩ 캐나다, 밴쿠버	휴대전화 번호: 778-555-6641
V5K 1A6	웹 사이트: www.pendrellfinancial.com

---

⑰⑦ 수신: 리디아 갤러거 〈lydiagal@pendrellfinancial.com〉
발신: 대니얼 램지 〈d_ramsey@lindaleco.com〉
날짜: 2월 16일
제목: 서류

갤러거 씨께,

⑰⑦ 오타와에서 열린 워크숍에서 만나 뵙게 되어 기뻤습니다. 저는 귀하의 가르침으로부터 아주 많은 것을 배웠습니다. ⑰⑧ 귀사의 공석에 관해 저에게 말씀해 주신 것에 대해 정말로 감사하게 생각합니다. 저는 그토록 평판이 좋은 회사에서 근무할 기회를 꼭 갖고 싶습니다. ⑰⑥ 요청하신 바와 같이, 참고하실 수 있도록 제 이력서와 자기소개서를 보내 드립니다. 또한 ⑰⑨ 공인 금융 설계사 자격증 사본도 첨부해 드렸으며, 이는 향후 4년 동안 유효합니다.

⑰⑨ 제가 토론토 대학교에서 경제학 학사 학위를 받고 이후 경영학 석사를 받고 졸업한 사실을 보실 수 있으실 겁니다. 저는 웨이크필드 은행에서 인턴으로 근무했습니다. 이는 금융 컨설팅 분야에 관해 아주 많은 것을 배울 수 있는 기회가 되었습니다. 그 후에, 저는 L.S. 컨설팅 사에서 5년 동안 재직했습니다. ⑰⑨ 그곳에서 저는 업계 전문가들과 폭넓은 인적 관계를 구축하는 데 도움이 되었던 수많은 분들을 만났습니다. ⑱⑩ 저는 다음 달 몬트리올에서 귀사가 있는 도시로 이사할 예정입니다. 따라서 그때 꼭 직접 만나 뵙고 이 문제를 더욱 논의해 보고 싶습니다.

안녕히 계십시오.

대니얼 램지

어휘 financial 금융의, 재정의 analyst 분석가 extension 내선전화(번호) appreciate one's -ing ~가 …한 것에 대해 감사하다 job opening 공석, 빈자리 firm 회사 would love 꼭 ~하고 싶다, 꼭 ~을 원하다 opportunity to do ~할 기회 work for ~에서 근무하다 highly respected 평판이 좋은, 크게 존경받는 as requested 요청한 대로 résumé 이력서 cover letter 자기소개서 reference 참고 attach ~을 첨부하다 certificate 자격증, 인증서 valid 유효한 graduate from ~에서 졸업하다 bachelor's degree 학사 학위 economics 경제학 master's degree 석사 학위 business management 경영학 serve as ~로 일하다, ~의 역할을 하다 learn a great deal 아주 많은 것을 배우다 field 분야 following ~ 후에 numerous 수많은, 다수의 build a network 인적 관계를 구축하다 professional 전문가 meet with (약속하여) ~와 만나다 then 그때 discuss ~을 논의하다 matter 문제, 사안 further 더욱, 한층 더

176 이메일의 목적은 무엇인가?
(A) 행사에 등록하는 것
(B) 요청 사항에 대해 후속 조치를 하는 것
(C) 테스트 결과에 관해 문의하는 것
(D) 구직 기회를 알리는 것

해설 〈주제 및 목적〉
두 번째 지문 첫 단락에서, 간단한 배경 설명 후 상대방이 요청한 대로 이력서와 자기소개서를 보낸다고(As requested, I'm sending my résumé and cover letter for your reference) 알리는 내용이 있는데, 이는 기존의 요청에 따른 후속 조치를 취하는 것임을 나타내는 말이므로 (B)가 정답이다.

어휘 register for ~에 등록하다 follow up on ~에 대한 후속 조치를 하다 request 요청, 요구 inquire about ~에 관해 문의하다 result 결과(물) opportunity 기회

177 갤러거 씨에 관해 사실인 것은 무엇인가?
(A) 과거에 한때 L.S. 컨설팅 사에서 일했다.
(B) 램지 씨를 4년 전부터 알고 지냈다.
(C) 오타와에서 워크숍을 통해 가르침을 전했다.
(D) 동료 직원을 통해 램지 씨를 만났다.

해설 〈진위 확인 (전체 진위 유형)〉
수신인이 갤러거 씨로 되어 있는 두 번째 지문에서, 상대방인 갤러거 씨를 you로 지칭해 오타와에서 열린 워크숍에서 상대방의 가르침으로부터 많은 것을 배운 사실을 언급하고(~ the workshop in Ottawa. I learned so much from your teaching) 있으므로 (C)가 정답이다.

어휘 used to do (과거) 한때 ~하다 through ~을 통해 colleague 동료 (직원)

178 램지 씨는 무엇을 하는 데 관심이 있는가?
(A) 인턴 프로그램에 관한 의견 제공하기
(B) 새로운 금융 컨퍼런스 시작하기
(C) 다가오는 행사에 등록하기
(D) 펜드렐 금융 서비스의 직원으로 입사하기

해설 〈세부 사항〉
램지 씨가 쓴 이메일인 두 번째 지문에서, 자신이 원하는 일이 상대방 회사, 즉 갤러거 씨의 회사에서 근무할 기회를 갖는 것이라고(~ the

job opening at your firm. I would love the opportunity to work for such a highly respected company) 알리고 있다. 또한, 첫 번째 지문 상단에 갤러거 씨의 회사 이름이 'Pendrell Financial Services'로 표기되어 있는 것을 통해 펜드럴 금융 서비스사에 입사하기를 원한다는 것을 알 수 있으므로 (D)가 정답이다.

어휘 be interested in ~에 관심이 있다 feedback 의견 launch ~을 시작하다, ~에 착수하다 financial 금융의, 재무의 register for ~에 등록하다 upcoming 다가오는, 곧 있을 join ~에 입사하다, 합류하다

179 램지 씨에 관해 언급되지 않은 것은 무엇인가?
(A) 사업적인 인맥이 많다.
(B) 현재 두 개의 학위를 소지하고 있다.
(C) 자신의 분야에서 공인받은 사람이다.
(D) 개인 사업체를 운영해 왔다.

해설 〈진위 확인 (전체 진위 유형)〉
램지 씨가 자신에 관한 이야기를 하는 두 번째 지문에서, 두 번째 단락의 폭넓은 인적 관계를 구축한 사실(~ build my extensive network of business professionals)을 통해 (A)를, 그리고 같은 단락 시작 부분에서 학사 학위와 석사 학위를 취득한 사실(~ a bachelor's degree in economics and later a master's degree in business management)을 통해 (B)를 확인할 수 있다. 또한 첫 단락에서 공인 금융 설계사 자격증 사본(a copy of my Certified Financial Planner certificate)을 첨부한 것을 통해 (C)도 확인 가능하다. 하지만 개인 사업체를 운영한 사실은 언급되어 있지 않으므로 (D)가 정답이다.

어휘 contacts n. 인맥, 연락 관계 있는 사람 currently 현재 hold ~을 보유하다, 소지하다 degree 학위 certified 공인된 field 분야 run ~을 운영하다

180 램지 씨는 다음 달에 어디에서 갤러거 씨를 만나고 싶어 하는가?
(A) 오타와에서
(B) 몬트리올에서
(C) 밴쿠버에서
(D) 토론토에서

해설 〈지문 연계〉
두 번째 지문 마지막 부분에, 램지 씨는 상대방인 갤러거 씨가 있는 도시로 이사할 계획임을 알리며 그때 직접 만나고 싶다는 뜻을 (I'll be moving from Montreal to your city next month. So, I would love to meet with you in person ~) 밝히고 있다. 갤러거 씨의 명함인 첫 지문에서 주소를 보면 갤러거 씨가 밴쿠버(Vancouver, Canada)에 있다는 것을 알 수 있으므로 (C)가 정답이다.

[181-185] 이메일과 문자 메시지

수신: **181** 케네스 러셀 〈russellk@billericamail.com〉
발신: 멘도자 호텔 〈bookings@mendozahotel.com〉
날짜: 6월 3일
제목: 예약 확인 번호 57823

저희 멘도자 호텔에 객실을 예약해 주셔서 감사드립니다. 아래에서 귀하의 예약 확인 상세 정보를 확인해 보시기 바랍니다.

성명: 케네스 러셀　　　**지점:** 보스턴　　　**객실 형태:** 싱글
체크인 날짜: 6월 27일　**체크아웃 날짜:** 6월 30일　**배정된 객실:** 306호

182 공항 셔틀버스
도착 셔틀버스: 오후 2시　　**출발 셔틀버스:** 이용 안 함(렌터카)

위에 표기된 선호하시는 셔틀버스 시간을 놓치실 경우, 다음 셔틀버스를 이용하시면 됩니다. **181** 멘도자 우수 고객 클럽의 회원이신, **182** 귀하께서는 무료 편도 셔틀버스 이용에 대한 자격이 있으십니다. 저희 셔틀버스 일반 요금은 아래에 기재되어 있습니다.

	일반 셔틀버스 (오전 9시 – 오후 9시)	이른 셔틀버스 (오전 9시 이전)	늦은 셔틀버스 (오후 9시 이후)	개별 이용 승합차 (상시)
편도	5.00달러	6.00달러	7.50달러	25.00달러
왕복	7.50달러	10.00달러	12.50달러	45.00달러

일부 저희 고객들께서 전망과 바닥재, 또는 공용 편의시설과의 거리를 이유로 특정 객실을 요청하신다는 사실을 알고 있습니다. **184** 저희가 이 예약 확인서에서 지정된 것과 동일한 객실을 제공해 드릴 수 없을 경우, 무료 아침 뷔페 식사 쿠폰을 발급해 드리겠습니다. 이는 체크인하실 때 프런트 데스크에서 받아 가실 수 있습니다.

수신 번호: 846-555-7023
발신 번호: 763-555-0112
수신 시간: 6월 18일, 오전 11:52

케네스 러셀 고객님께 전해 드리는 메시지입니다. **183** **184** 멘도자 호텔 예약 번호 57823에 대해 211호 객실로 재예약되었음을 알려 드리고자 메시지 보내 드립니다. 귀하의 객실 배정이 **185** 확정된 이후에 조정된 점에 대해 사과의 말씀 드립니다. 귀하의 양해에 감사드립니다.

어휘 reservation 예약 confirmation 확인(서) book ~을 예약하다 details 상세 정보, 세부 사항 below 아래에, 밑에 branch 지점, 지사 assign ~을 배정하다, 할당하다 incoming 도착하는, 들어오는 outgoing 출발하는, 나가는 ~을 놓치다, 지나치다 preferred 선호하는 above 위에 (표기된) be eligible for ~에 대한 자격이 있다 free 무료의 regular 일반의, 정규의 fee 요금 understand that ~하는 것을 알다, 이해하다 request ~을 요청하다 specific 특정한, 구체적인 due to ~로 인해 shared 공용의, 공유된 amenities 편의시설 be unable to do ~할 수 없다 provide A with B A에게 B를 제공하다 exact 정확한 designated 지정된 voucher 쿠폰, 상품권 pick up ~을 가져가다, 가져오다 upon ~할 시에,

---

~하자마자 inform A that A에게 ~라고 알리다 rebook ~을 재예약하다 make an adjustment 조정하다, 수정하다 assignment 배정(된 것), 할당(된 것) fix ~을 확정하다, 고정하다

181 러셀 씨에 관해 언급된 것은 무엇인가?
(A) 4일 밤을 머무를 것이다.
(B) 원래 보스턴 출신이다.
(C) 우수 고객 프로그램에 등록했다.
(D) 누군가와 방을 공유할 것이다.

해설 〈진위 확인 (전체 진위 유형)〉
러셀 씨에게 보내는 이메일의 도표 바로 위의 단락에서 러셀 씨의 자격과 관련하여 멘도자 우수 고객 클럽의 회원이라고(As a member of the Mendoza Loyalty Club ~) 설명하고 있으므로 이를 언급한 (C)가 정답이다.

어휘 originally 원래, 애초에 enroll in ~에 등록하다 loyalty program 우수 고객 프로그램 share A with B A와 B를 공유하다

182 러셀 씨는 셔틀버스 서비스에 대해 얼마를 청구받을 것인가?
(A) 0.00달러
(B) 5.00달러
(C) 6.00달러
(D) 7.50달러

해설 〈세부 사항〉
예약 확인 내역에서 러셀 씨는 셔틀의 편도 이용을 할 예정이라는 것을 알 수 있는데(Incoming Shuttle: 2 P.M. Outgoing Shuttle: none (renting car)) 도표 바로 위에 위치한 단락에서 무료 편도 셔틀버스 이용 자격이 있다고(~ you are eligible for a free one-way shuttle trip ~) 알리고 있으므로 (A)가 정답이다.

어휘 charge A B A에게 B를 청구하다

183 멘도자 호텔은 왜 러셀 씨에게 문자 메시지를 보냈는가?
(A) 최종 비용 지불을 요청하기 위해
(B) 새로운 서비스를 홍보하기 위해
(C) 객실 업그레이드를 제공하기 위해
(D) 객실 변경 사실을 알리기 위해

해설 〈주제 및 목적〉
문자 메시지인 두 번째 지문에 수신인인 러셀 씨의 객실이 211호실로 재예약된 사실을 알리기 위해 메시지를 보낸다고(We are writing to inform you that you have been rebooked into Room 211 ~) 쓰여 있으므로 (D)가 정답이다.

어휘 request ~을 요청하다, 요구하다 payment 지불(금) promote ~을 홍보하다 offer ~을 제공하다 inform A of B A에게 B를 알리다

184 프런트 데스크 직원에 의해 러셀 씨에게 무엇이 제공될 것인가?
(A) 식권
(B) 주차권
(C) 인근 지도
(D) 부분 환불

해설 〈지문 연계〉

첫 번째 지문 마지막 단락에 지정된 것과 동일한 객실을 제공하지 못할 경우 무료 아침 뷔페 식사용 쿠폰을 발급해준다고(If we are unable to provide you with the exact room designated ~ we will give you a voucher for a free breakfast buffet) 쓰여 있는데, 두 번째 지문에 객실이 다른 방으로 다시 예약되었다고(We are writing to inform you that you have been rebooked into Room 211 ~) 알리고 있으므로 해당 뷔페 식사 쿠폰을 받을 것임을 알 수 있다. 따라서 (A)가 정답이다.

어휘 voucher 쿠폰, 상품권 pass 입장권, 출입증 neighborhood 인근, 지역 partial 부분적인 refund 환불

185 문자 메시지에서, 첫 번째 단락 네 번째 줄의 단어 "fixed"와 의미가 가장 가까운 것은 무엇인가?
(A) 수리된
(B) 집중된
(C) 최종 확정된
(D) 고정된

해설 〈동의어〉

해당 문장은 '객실 배정이 ~된 이후에 조정된 것에 대해 사과한다'라는 의미를 나타낸다. 앞선 문장에서 객실이 재예약되었다고(rebooked) 알린 것으로 볼 때 이미 배정된 객실이 다른 객실로 옮겨진 상황임을 알 수 있다. 따라서 확정되었던 객실이 다시 예약된 것으로 판단할 수 있으므로 '최종 확정된'을 뜻하는 (C)가 정답이다.

[186-190] 기사와 이메일, 그리고 웹 페이지

186 르넥스 빌딩이 최근 댈러스 도심 지역에서 완공되었으며, 단기간에 이반 스트리트에서 쉽게 알아볼 수 있는 명소가 되었다. **186** 이 빌딩의 독특한 형태는 시내 지역에 현대적인 모습을 더해 주고 있으며, 결국에는 40개의 다른 사무실들이 들어서는 보금자리가 될 것이다. 이미 대부분의 공간들이 주로 금융 회사에 의해 임대된 상태이지만, 여전히 몇몇 남은 자리가 있다.

186 이 빌딩의 초대형 창문들은 단열 처리가 잘 되어 있는데, 이는 **187** 동일한 규모의 다른 건물들에 비해 냉난방에 더 적은 전기가 필요하다는 것을 의미한다. 이는 환경에 좋은 것이며, 이 빌딩의 건축가인 티모시 블레어 씨에게 있어 중요했던 특징이다. 내부로 들어서면, 방문객들은 **188** 인테리어 디자이너 가브리엘 할스테드 씨가 선택한 화사한 색상에 의해 놀라게 될 것이다. 개별 용도로 쓰이는 상층부 외에, 1층에 일반 대중을 위한 커피 매장 두 개와 해산물 레스토랑이 하나 있다.

수신: 애니 라부아 〈a.lavoie@floresdesigns.com〉
발신: 제시 오초아 〈j.ochoa@floresdesigns.com〉
날짜: 11월 16일
제목: 출장

애니 씨께,

댈러스로 떠나는 당신의 출장 동안, 시내에 있는 알링턴 호텔에서 머무르실 예정입니다. 공항에 도착하시면, **189** 모건 렌터카에서 차량 한 대가 당신을 기다리고 있을 것입니다. 비행기를 타고 돌아오시기 전에 동일한 장소에 해당 렌터카를 반납하실 수 있습니다. 우리는 티모시 블레어 씨와 가브리엘 할스테드 씨 **188** 두 분 모두 회의에 참석하실 수 있기를 바랐습니다. 하지만, 오직 할스테드 씨께서만 그곳에 오실 겁니다. 그분의 프로젝트를 통해 많은 것을 배우시기 바랍니다.

안녕히 계십시오.

제시

---

http://www.morganrentals.com/about

189 저희 모건 렌터카가 이제 영업을 시작했습니다! 저희는 댈러스에서의 멋진 렌트 사업 시작을 축하하기 위해 4월에 성공적인 개업식을 가졌습니다. 저희가 보유하고 있는 완전히 새로운 차량들이 편안하게 운전하실 수 있도록 도와드릴 것입니다. 각 차량에는 열선 시트와 백업용 카메라, GPS, 그리고 뛰어난 음향 시스템이 갖춰져 있습니다. 저희 앱 또는 웹 사이트를 통해 편리하게 예약 기간을 연장하실 수 있습니다. 또한, 저희를 통해 차량을 대여하는 각 날짜에 대해, **190** 저희 제휴 업체인 센터 에어와 펜사콜라 에어라인, 또는 스톨링즈 에어라인 중의 한 곳으로부터 항공사 마일리지를 받으실 수 있습니다.

어휘 recently 최근에 complete ~을 완료하다, 완수하다 recognizable 쉽게 알아볼 수 있는 landmark 명소, 인기 장소 unique 독특한, 특별한 bring A to B B에 A를 가져다주다, 불어 넣다 eventually 결국, 마침내 rent out ~을 임대하다, 대여하다 mainly 주로, 대체로 financial firm 금융 회사 spot 자리, 장소, 위치 insulated 단열 처리된 mean that ~임을 의미하다 electricity 전기 compared to ~에 비해, ~와 비교해 environment 환경 quality 특징, 특성 architect 건축가 be amazed by ~에 놀라다 cheerful 화사한, 쾌적한 select ~을 선택하다 in addition to ~ 외에, ~뿐만 아니라 private 개별적인, 사적인 upper 상부의, 위쪽의 ground floor 1층 the public 일반 대중 during ~ 동안에, ~ 중에 arrive 도착하다 return ~을 반납하다, 반환하다 fly 비행기를 타고 가다 both A and B A와 B 둘 모두 attend ~에 참석하다 however 하지만, 그러나 open for business 영업 중인 opening ceremony 개업식, 개장식 celebrate 축하하다 fleet (한 단체가 보유한 차량이나 선박 등의) 무리 brand-new 완전히 새로운 in comfort 편안하게 be equipped with ~을 갖추고 있다 extend ~을 연장하다 booking 예약 earn ~을 받다, 얻다

---

186 기사는 왜 쓰여졌는가?
(A) 재정 문제를 알리기 위해
(B) 사무용 건물을 간략히 소개하기 위해
(C) 도시 축제를 알리기 위해
(D) 시내 커피 매장들을 평가하기 위해

해설 〈주제 및 목적〉

첫 지문의 첫 단락과 두 번째 단락에 걸쳐, 건물 공사 완공 사실(The Rennex Building has recently been completed ~)과 독특한 형태(The building's unique shape ~), 창문이 지닌 특징(The building's giant windows are well insulated ~) 등을 설명하고 있다. 이 내용들을 통해 해당 건물을 간략히 소개하는 것이 목적임을 알 수 있으므로 (B)가 정답이다.

어휘 financial 재정의, 금융의 profile ~을 간략히 소개하다 review ~을 평가하다, 검토하다

187 기사에 따르면, 프로젝트가 어떻게 환경에 도움을 줄 것인가?
(A) 태양열 전지판을 설치함으로써
(B) 재활용 자재를 사용함으로써
(C) 빗물을 모아 둠으로써
(D) 전기를 덜 소비함으로써

해설 〈세부 사항〉

환경에 도움이 되는 일과 관련된 내용은 첫 지문 두 번째 단락에 나타나 있는데, 냉난방에 필요한 전기를 덜 사용하게 되어 환경에 좋다는(~ less electricity for heating and cooling will be needed compared to other buildings of its size. This is good for the environment ~) 내용이 쓰여 있으므로 (D)가 정답이다.

어휘 according to ~에 따르면 by (방법) ~함으로써, ~해서 install ~을 설치하다 solar panels 태양열 전지판 recycled 재활용된 material 자재, 재료 collect ~을 모으다, 수집하다 consume ~을 소비하다

188 누가 댈러스에서 라부아 씨와 함께 회의에 참석할 것인가?
(A) 건축가
(B) 시 관계자
(C) 인테리어 디자이너
(D) 호텔 지배인

해설 〈지문 연계〉

두 번째 지문을 보면, 티모시 블레어 씨와 가브리엘 할스테드 씨 모두 회의에 참석하기를 바랐지만 오직 가브리엘 할스테드 씨만 참석한다고(~ only Ms. Halstead will be there) 적혀 있다. 첫 지문 두 번째 단락에 가브리엘 할스테드 씨가 인테리어 디자이너로(interior designer Gabrielle Halstead) 소개되어 있으므로 (C)가 정답이다.

어휘 attend ~에 참석하다 official n. 관계자, 당국자

189 라부아 씨에 관해 사실인 것은 무엇인가?

(A) 회의 장소와 더 가까운 호텔을 요청했다.
(B) 새롭게 문을 연 업체를 통해 차량을 이용할 것이다.
(C) 차량에 GPS를 포함하기 위해 추가 요금을 지불해야 한다.
(D) 이반 스트리트에 있는 호텔에 머무를 것이다.

해설 〈지문 연계〉
애니 라부아 씨에게 쓰는 이메일인 두 번째 지문을 보면, 모건 렌터카의 차량을 이용할 것임을(~ there will be a car waiting for you at Morgan Rentals) 알 수 있다. 그리고 세 번째 지문 시작 부분에 모건 렌터카가 이제 막 영업을 시작한 사실이(Morgan Rentals is now open for business) 언급되어 있어 새 업체의 차량을 이용한 다는 것을 알 수 있으므로 (B)가 정답이다.

어휘 request ~을 요청하다, 요구하다 close to ~와 가까운 site 장소, 현장, 부지 extra 추가의, 별도의 fee 요금 vehicle 차량

190 웹 페이지상의 렌터카 회사에 관해 언급된 것은 무엇인가?

(A) 항공사들과 제휴 관계를 맺고 있다.
(B) 대규모 단체 고객에게 할인을 제공한다.
(C) 인상적인 안전 기록을 유지하고 있다.
(D) 댈러스 전역에 지점을 보유하고 있다.

해설 〈진위 확인 (전체 진위 유형)〉
세 번째 지문 마지막 문장에 모건 렌터카가 여러 항공사와 제휴 관계에 있다고(~ one of our partners — Center Air, Pensacola Airlines, or Stollings Airlines) 알리는 내용이 있으므로 이를 언급한 (A)가 정답이다.

어휘 partnership 제휴 관계, 동반자 관계 provide ~을 제공하다 maintain ~을 유지하다 impressive 인상적인 branch 지점, 지사 throughout (장소) ~ 전역에 걸쳐, (시간) ~ 동안 내내

[191-195] 광고와 이메일, 그리고 안내 정보

차맥스 – 스펜스 주식회사가 만드는 숯 방향제

대부분의 방향제는 혼합된 화학 물질로 만들어집니다. 차맥스는 100퍼센트 활성탄을 사용해 다음과 같은 특징과 함께 안전하고 효과적인 결과를 보장해 드립니다.

1. 효과성 - 차맥스는 여러분의 자택 내의 불쾌한 냄새를 감추는 것이 아니라, 숯이 흡수하게 해 공기 중에서 그 냄새를 제거합니다. 불과 며칠 만에 그 차이를 보시게 될 것입니다.

2. 무향 - 차맥스를 사용하시면, 대부분의 방향제에서 나는 것과 같은 독하고 인공적인 냄새를 견딜 필요가 없습니다. 대신 쾌적하고 깨끗한 공기를 즐길 수 있습니다.

193 3. 천연 성분 - 차맥스는 화학 물질이 들어 있지 않기 때문에, 시중에 나와 있는 다른 방향제들에 대한 무독성 대체 상품입니다.

4. 편리성 - 차맥스의 용기는 벽에 걸거나 수평으로 놓여 있을 수 있도록 디자인되어 있으므로, 자택 내의 어느 곳이든 놓아 두실 수 있습니다.

5. 장기 지속성 - 적절한 관리를 통해, 차맥스 한 팩이면 최대 1년까지 지속적으로 효과를 낼 수 있습니다.

191 대량으로 구매하시어 비용을 절약해 보세요! 10팩 이상 차맥스를 구입하시면 주문품에 대해 10퍼센트 할인을 받으실 수 있습니다.

수신: 스펜스 주식회사 고객 서비스팀
발신: 제시카 퍼타도
날짜: 7월 19일
제목: 차맥스

고객 서비스팀,

저는 최근에 차맥스 5팩을 구입했으며, 제가 구입한 것에 매우 만족하고 있습니다. 저희 집의 독소의 양을 줄이기 위해 노력 중이기 때문에, **193** 귀사의 제품이 자연에서 찾은 재료로 만들어져 있다는 사실에 매우 기뻤습니다.

비용을 절약하고 쓰레기를 줄이기 위해, 이 팩들이 효과를 내는 시간을 극대화하기를 원합니다. **192** 숯 조각들이 더 오래 지속되도록 만들 수 있는 방법에 관해 어떤 것이든 알고 계신 것이 있으신가요? **194** 제가 가장 큰 사이즈인 250그램짜리 팩을 구입했는데, 이것을 제대로 관리할 수 있기를 원합니다.

감사합니다.

제시카 퍼타도

스펜스 주식회사의 차맥스 사용 관련 팁

습기를 제거할 수 있도록 한 달에 한 번 햇볕에 팩을 놓아 두어 차맥스의 수명을 연장시키세요.

사이즈	매달 햇볕에 놓아 두어야 하는 시간
50그램	45분
75그램	1시간
150그램	2시간
194 250그램	3시간

차맥스가 냄새를 흡수하는 수명을 다 했을 때도, 아직 그 유용성이 끝난 것은 아닙니다. 팩을 개봉한 후, 덩어리들을 더 작은 조각으로 으깨어, **195** 숯 조각들을 옥외 화단의 흙과 섞으십시오.

어휘 charcoal 숯 air freshener 방향제 be made from ~로 만들어지다 a mixture of ~의 혼합 chemical 화학 물질 activated charcoal 활성탄 ensure ~을 보장하다, ~을 확실하게 하다 effective 효과적인 result 결과(물) following 다음의 feature 특징, 기능 cover up ~을 감추다, 덮어 버리다 unpleasant 불쾌한 odor 냄새, 악취 absorb ~을 흡수하다 eliminate ~을 제거하다, 없애다 notice ~을 인식하다, 알아차리다 fragrance 향, 향기 free (복합어로 쓰여) ~ 없는 deal with ~에 대처하다, ~을 처리하다 harsh (냄새 등이) 독한 artificial 인공적인 instead 대신 contain ~을 포함하다 non-toxic 무독성의 alternative 대안, 대체(품) on the market 시중에 나와 있는 convenient 편리한 container 용기, 그릇 hang up ~을 걸다 sit (사물이) 놓여 있다 horizontally 수평으로 place v. ~을 놓다, 두다 long-lasting 오래 지속되는 proper 적절한, 제대로 된 care 관리, 보살핌, 주의 work 효과가 있다 continuously 지속적으로 up to 최대 ~까지 stock up 대량으로 구매하다 order 주문(품) recently 최근에 be pleased with ~에 만족하다 purchase 구입(품) reduce ~을 줄이다, 감소시키다 amount 양, 수량 toxin 독소 be thrilled that ~해서 흥분하다, 기뻐하다 be made from ~로 만들어지다 ingredient 재료, 성분 in order to do ~하기 위해 maximize ~을 극대화하다 make A do A가 ~하게 만들다 last v. 지속되다 make sure (that) 반드시 ~하도록 하다 care for ~을 관리하다, 다루다, 보살피다 properly 적절히, 제대로 extend ~을 연장하다, 늘리다 by (방법) ~함으로써 remove ~을 제거하다, 없애다 moisture 습기 reach ~에 도달하다, 이르다 usefulness 유용함 crush ~을 으깨다 chunk 덩어리 soil 흙, 토양 flowerbed 화단

191 차맥스에 관해 사실인 것은 무엇인가?

(A) 다양한 향으로 나온다.
(B) 스펜스 주식회사의 베스트셀러 제품이다.
(C) 100퍼센트 환불 보장 서비스가 포함되어 있다.
(D) 대량 주문 할인을 받을 수 있다.

해설 〈진위 확인 (전체 진위 유형)〉
차맥스에 관해 상세히 설명하는 첫 지문의 마지막 문장에, 대량 구매에 따른 비용 절약 방법을 알리는(Stock up and save! Buy 10 or more Charmax bags and get 10% off your order) 내용이 쓰여 있으므로 이와 같은 할인 서비스를 언급한 (D)가 정답이다.

어휘 come in (제품 등이) ~로 나오다 **a variety of** 다양한 **scent** 향, 향기 **come with** ~을 포함하다, ~가 딸려 있다 **guarantee** 보장, 보증 **be eligible for** ~할 수 있다, ~에 대한 자격이 있다 **bulk** a. 대량의

192 이메일의 목적은 무엇인가?
(A) 변경을 추천하는 것
(B) 일부 의견을 요청하는 것
(C) 구입 제품의 문제점을 알리는 것
(D) 추가 제품을 주문하는 것

해설 〈주제 및 목적〉
이메일인 두 번째 지문의 첫 단락은 배경 설명에 해당되며, 두 번째 단락에서 숯 조각들이 오래 가도록 하는 방법을 묻는(Do you have any ideas about how I can make the charcoal pieces last longer?) 것이 목적에 해당된다. 이는 의견의 제공을 부탁하는 말이므로 (B)가 정답이다.

어휘 ask for ~을 요청하다 **suggestion** 의견, 제안 **purchase** 구입(품) **place an order for** ~을 주문하다

193 퍼타도 씨는 차맥스의 어느 특징에 대해 깊은 인상을 받았는가?
(A) 1번 특징
(B) 2번 특징
(C) 3번 특징
(D) 4번 특징

해설 〈지문 연계〉
퍼타도 씨가 쓴 이메일인 두 번째 지문 첫 단락에, 자연의 재료로 제품이 만들어진 사실이 마음에 든다(I was thrilled that your product is made from an ingredient found in nature) 언급이 있다. 이는 첫 지문에 제시된 특징들 중에서 3번 항목(3. Natural - Charmax contains no chemicals ~)에 해당되는 것이므로 (C)가 정답이다.

어휘 be impressed with ~에 깊은 인상을 받다

194 퍼타도 씨는 매일 얼마나 오랫동안 차맥스를 햇볕에 놓아 두어야 하는가?
(A) 45분 동안
(B) 1시간 동안
(C) 2시간 동안
(D) 3시간 동안

해설 〈지문 연계〉
두 번째 지문 두 번째 단락에, 퍼타도 씨는 250그램짜리 제품을 구입했다고(I purchased the largest size, the 250-gram bags) 알리고 있다. 세 번째 지문의 도표에서 250그램짜리 제품은 3시간 동안 햇볕에 놓아 두도록 표기되어 있으므로 (D)가 정답이다.

어휘 leave ~을 놓다, 두다

195 차맥스에 대한 어떤 처분 방법이 스펜스 주식회사에 의해 권장되는가?
(A) 회사로 반품하기
(B) 재활용 센터로 가져가기
(C) 정원에서 활용하기
(D) 가정 쓰레기에 추가하기

해설 〈세부 사항〉
세 번째 지문 마지막 부분에, 차맥스에 들어 있는 숯 조각을 작게 으깬 후 화단에 있는 흙과 섞으라는(~ mix the charcoal into the soil of your outdoor flowerbeds) 내용이 있다. 이는 정원에서 사용할 수 있다는 뜻이므로 (C)가 정답이다.

어휘 disposal 처분, 처리 **method** 방법 **return** ~을 반품하다, 반납하다 **add A to B** A를 B에 추가하다 **household** 가정의

[196-200] 두 이메일과 일정표

수신: 전 직원 〈parksstafflist@parks.najeracity.gov〉
발신: 리키 베어드 〈r.baird@najeracity.gov〉
날짜: 4월 13일
제목: 읽어 보시기 바랍니다

우리 도시의 인구 증가로 인해, 더 많은 사람들이 도시 내의 여러 공원을 이용하고 있으므로, 두루 상황을 파악해 두는 것이 그 어느 때보다 더 필수적입니다.

⓳⓺ 여러분에게 공원 관리부의 5월 직무와 관련된 일부 정보를 공유해 드리고자 합니다. ⓳⓻ 웨슬리 도노번 씨가 개인 조경 업체를 운영하기 위해 우리 팀을 떠나기로 결정하셨습니다. 우리는 이러한 노력에 대해 그분께 행운을 빌어 드리겠지만, 이는 우리가 바쁜 시기로 접어듦에 따라 분명 인력 부족 문제를 남기게 됩니다.

⓳⓼ 도노번 씨가 하시던 정원 식수 업무를 담당하기 위해 계절 근로자로 켄튼 페리 씨를 고용할 수 있었지만, ⓳⓺ 여전히 촉박하게 나머지 업무들을 넘겨받을 다른 누군가가 필요합니다. 관심이 있을 수 있는, 5월 1일에 일을 시작할 수 있는 누구든 알고 계시는 분이 있으시면, 제 연락처를 전달해 주시기 바랍니다.

감사합니다!

리키

공원 유지 관리 업무	직원	근무 요일
스포츠 시설 및 놀이터 장비	요나스 쿠자와	월요일, 화요일, 수요일, 목요일, 금요일
생울타리 및 나무 손질	린다 하빈	화요일, 수요일, 금요일
⓴⓪ 잔디 깎기 및 급수	미배정	화요일, 금요일, 토요일
정원 식수 및 제초	⓳⓼ 켄튼 페리	월요일, 목요일
전기 관련 수리 및 유지 관리	헥터 멘도자	목요일
주차장 유지 관리	아놀드 산타나	월요일, 목요일, 토요일

수신: 리키 베어드 〈r.baird@najeracity.gov〉
발신: 준 젱 〈gengjun@tatumpc.com〉
날짜: 4월 14일
제목: 공원 관리부 공석

베어드 씨께,

⓳⓽ 소속 직원들 중 한 분인 헥터 멘도자 씨를 통해 현재 팀에서 일할 새로운 직원을 찾고 계신다는 얘기를 들었습니다. ⓴⓪ 저는 그 공석에 지원하는 데 관심이 있습니다. 제 이전 고용주이신 LH 주식회사의 루 호우킨 씨께서 제 직무 능력 및 직업 의식과 관련된 추천서를 제공해 드릴 수 있습니다. 또한 제가 주말마다 자원 봉사를 하고 있는 지역 문화 센터의 운영 책임자이신 리타 파보네 씨와 이야기 나눠 보셔도 좋습니다. 원하시는 날짜인 5월 1일 또는 필요 시에 더 빨리 일을 시작할 수 있습니다.

곧 연락 주실 수 있기를 바랍니다.

안녕히 계십시오.

준 젱

어휘 population 인구 **expansion** 팽창, 확장, 확대 **essential** 필수적인 **than ever** 그 어느 때보다 **keep on top of things** 두루 상황을 파악해 두다, 매사를 훤히 알아 두다 **share A with B** A를 B와 공유하다 **regarding** ~와 관련해 **responsibility** 직무, 책임 **decide to do** ~하기로 결정하다 **pursue a career in** ~의 경력을 추구하다 **run** ~을 운영하다 **landscaping firm** 조경 회사 **endeavor** 노력, 시도 **leave A with B** A에게 B를 남기다 **labor** 인력, 노동력 **shortage** 부족 **be able to do** ~할 수 있다 **seasonal** 계절의, 계절적인 **handle** ~을 처리하다 다루다 **planting** 식수, 나무 심기 **on short notice** 촉박하게, 급한 공지에도 **take over** ~을 넘겨받다 **task** 업무, 일 **pass along** ~을 전달하다 **contact details** 연락처 **maintenance** 유지 관리, 시설 관리 **facility** 시설(물), 설비 **equipment** 장비 **hedge** 생울타리 **trimming** 손질, 다듬기 **mowing** 잔디 깎기 **watering** 급수, 살수 **weeding** 제초 **repair** 수리 **parking lot** 주차장 **opening** 공석, 빈자리 **currently** 현재 **seek** ~을 찾다, 구하다 **be interested in** ~에 관심이 있다 **apply for** ~에 지원하다, ~을 신청하다 **former** 이전의, 전직 **~의 provide A with B** A에게 B를 제공하다 **testimonial** 추천서, 추천 후기 **work ethic** 작업 의식 **volunteer** 자원 봉사하다 **available** (사람) 시간이 있는, (사물) 이용 가능한 **desired** 원하는, 바라는 **if needed** 필요시에

196 첫 번째 이메일의 목적은 무엇인가?
(A) 새로운 정원용 장비를 소개하는 것
(B) 한 공원의 확장을 발표하는 것
(C) 업무 배정상의 변동을 이야기하는 것
(D) 새로운 초과 근무 정책을 설명하는 것

해설 〈주제 및 목적〉
첫 번째 지문 두 번째 단락에 공원 관리부의 5월 직무와 관련된 일부 정보를 공유한다(I would like to share some information with you regarding the Parks Department responsibilities ~) 말이 쓰여 있고, 세 번째 단락에는 도노번 씨가 하던 업무를 처리하기 위해 계절 근로자를 고용했지만 여전히 나머지 업무를 처리할

사람이 필요하다고(I was able to hire a seasonal worker ~ still need someone else on short notice to take over the other tasks) 알리는 내용이 있다. 이는 해당 팀 구성원들의 업무 변화와 관련된 내용이므로 (C)가 정답이다.

어휘 introduce ~을 소개하다 equipment 장비 announce ~을 발표하다, 알리다 expansion 확장, 확대 discuss ~을 이야기하다, 논의하다 assignment 배정, 할당 explain ~을 설명하다 overtime 초과 근무 policy 정책, 방침

197 도노번 씨는 무엇을 할 계획인가?
(A) 동료 직원을 추천하는 일
(B) 신입 직원을 교육하는 일
(C) 다른 도시로 이사하는 일
(D) 사업을 시작하는 일

해설 〈세부 사항〉
도노번 씨의 이름이 언급되는 첫 지문 두 번째 단락에, 웨슬리 도노번 씨가 개인 조경 업체를 운영하기 위해 팀을 떠나기로 결정한(Wesley Donovan has decided to leave our team to pursue a career in running his own landscaping firm) 사실을 알리고 있다. 이는 개인 사업을 시작한다는 뜻이므로 (D)가 정답이다.

어휘 plan to do ~할 계획이다 colleague 동료 (직원) train ~을 교육하다

198 베어드 씨가 고용한 계절 근로자와 관련해 무엇이 암시되는가?
(A) 최근에 자격증을 받았다.
(B) 일주일에 이틀 일할 것이다.
(C) 몇몇 업무에 대해 쿠자와 씨를 도울 것이다.
(D) LH 주식회사에서 받은 추천서를 제출했다.

해설 〈지문 연계〉
리키 베어드 씨가 작성한 이메일인 첫 지문 세 번째 단락에 자신이 켄튼 페리라는 계절 근로자를 고용한(I was able to hire a seasonal worker, Kenton Perry ~) 내용이 언급되어 있다. 두 번째 지문 도표에 해당 인물의 이름이 표기된 네 번째 항목에 월요일과 목요일에 일하는 것으로 쓰여 있으므로 이러한 근무 특성을 말한 (B)가 정답이다.

어휘 recently 최근에 receive ~을 받다 certification 자격증, 수료증 assist A with B B에 대해 A를 돕다 duty 업무, 직무 submit ~을 제출하다 reference 추천(서)

199 누가 처음으로 공석과 관련된 정보를 젱 씨에게 제공했는가?
(A) 베어드 씨
(B) 호우킨 씨
(C) 멘도자 씨
(D) 파보네 씨

해설 〈세부 사항〉
젱 씨가 작성한 이메일인 세 번째 지문 시작 부분에, 소속 직원들 중 한 명인 헥터 멘도자 씨를 통해 새로운 직원을 찾고 있다는 얘기를 들었다는(I heard from one of your employees, Hector Mendoza, that you are currently seeking ~) 내용이 있다. 따라서 (C)가 정답이다.

어휘 open position 공석

200 젱 씨는 어떤 업무를 인계받고 싶어 하는가?
(A) 생울타리 및 나무 손질
(B) 잔디 깎기 및 급수
(C) 정원 식수 및 제초
(D) 주차장 유지 관리

해설 〈지문 연계〉
젱 씨가 작성한 이메일인 세 번째 지문 시작 부분에, 공석에 지원하는 데 관심이 있다고(I am interested in applying for the job opening) 알리는 말이 쓰여 있다. 이는 두 번째 지문 도표에서 직원 미배정(Not assigned) 상태로 표기된 업무, 즉 잔디 깎기 및 급수 업무(Mowing and watering)에 관심이 있다는 뜻이므로 (B)가 정답이다.

어휘 take over ~을 인계 받다, 이어받다

Actual Test

03

PART 1

1 (D)	2 (C)	3 (D)	4 (D)	5 (C)	6 (A)

PART 2

7 (C)	8 (B)	9 (C)	10 (B)	11 (C)	12 (B)	13 (B)	14 (C)	15 (A)	16 (B)
17 (B)	18 (C)	19 (A)	20 (A)	21 (C)	22 (C)	23 (C)	24 (A)	25 (A)	26 (C)
27 (C)	28 (B)	29 (B)	30 (C)	31 (B)					

PART 3

32 (D)	33 (A)	34 (B)	35 (C)	36 (D)	37 (B)	38 (C)	39 (B)	40 (D)	41 (B)
42 (A)	43 (D)	44 (D)	45 (C)	46 (A)	47 (B)	48 (D)	49 (C)	50 (B)	51 (D)
52 (A)	53 (C)	54 (A)	55 (D)	56 (D)	57 (B)	58 (C)	59 (C)	60 (A)	61 (B)
62 (B)	63 (D)	64 (B)	65 (D)	66 (C)	67 (B)	68 (B)	69 (B)	70 (C)	

PART 4

71 (A)	72 (B)	73 (D)	74 (B)	75 (A)	76 (D)	77 (C)	78 (A)	79 (B)	80 (D)
81 (B)	82 (C)	83 (D)	84 (C)	85 (A)	86 (D)	87 (C)	88 (B)	89 (D)	90 (A)
91 (B)	92 (D)	93 (B)	94 (C)	95 (D)	96 (C)	97 (B)	98 (B)	99 (A)	100 (C)

PART 5

101 (C)	102 (B)	103 (B)	104 (C)	105 (C)	106 (B)	107 (B)	108 (D)	109 (C)	110 (B)
111 (C)	112 (D)	113 (B)	114 (D)	115 (B)	116 (B)	117 (D)	118 (C)	119 (B)	120 (D)
121 (C)	122 (B)	123 (D)	124 (C)	125 (A)	126 (B)	127 (D)	128 (A)	129 (C)	130 (D)

PART 6

131 (C)	132 (D)	133 (C)	134 (D)	135 (A)	136 (C)	137 (D)	138 (B)	139 (D)	140 (D)
141 (B)	142 (C)	143 (B)	144 (A)	145 (C)	146 (B)				

PART 7

147 (B)	148 (C)	149 (C)	150 (D)	151 (C)	152 (B)	153 (D)	154 (B)	155 (C)	156 (C)
157 (D)	158 (A)	159 (D)	160 (B)	161 (C)	162 (A)	163 (B)	164 (C)	165 (B)	166 (B)
167 (A)	168 (C)	169 (B)	170 (D)	171 (D)	172 (A)	173 (D)	174 (B)	175 (D)	176 (C)
177 (D)	178 (B)	179 (B)	180 (A)	181 (B)	182 (A)	183 (D)	184 (C)	185 (B)	186 (B)
187 (B)	188 (D)	189 (A)	190 (D)	191 (A)	192 (D)	193 (C)	194 (B)	195 (C)	196 (C)
197 (A)	198 (B)	199 (C)	200 (D)						

1
(A) He's mowing the lawn.
개W (B) He's raking up some leaves.
(C) He's trimming the tree.
(D) He's doing some outdoor work.

(A) 남자가 잔디를 깎고 있다.
(B) 남자가 갈퀴로 낙엽을 모으고 있다.
(C) 남자가 나무를 다듬고 있다.
(D) 남자가 야외 작업을 하고 있다.

해설 옥외 공간에서 일을 하고 있는 남자의 동작에 초점을 맞춰 묘사한 (D)가 정답이다. 잔디를 깎는 동작, 갈퀴로 낙엽을 모으거나 나무를 다듬는 동작은 사진에서 볼 수 없다.

어휘 mow the grass 잔디를 깎다 rake ~을 갈퀴로 모으다 trim ~을 다듬다 outdoor 야외의, 옥외의

2
(A) Some people are climbing some rocks.
호M (B) Some people are sitting in a row.
(C) Some people are leaning over the railing.
(D) Some people are building a bridge.

(A) 몇몇 사람들이 바위를 기어오르고 있다.
(B) 몇몇 사람들이 한 줄로 앉아 있다.
(C) 몇몇 사람들이 몸을 숙여 난간에 기대고 있다.
(D) 몇몇 사람들이 다리를 만들고 있다.

해설 몇몇 사람들이 함께 몸을 숙여 난간에 기대어 있는 자세에 초점을 맞춘 (C)가 정답이다. 사람들이 바위를 기어오르는 동작, 앉아 있거나 다리를 만드는 동작도 사진에서 볼 수 없다.

어휘 climb (기어) 오르다, 등반하다 rock 바위, 돌 in a row 한 줄로 lean 기대다 over ~ 너머로, ~ 위로 가로질러 railing 난간 bridge 다리

3
(A) A woman is shoveling the snow.
영W (B) A woman is mopping the floor.
(C) A woman is putting away a broom.
(D) A woman is sweeping the steps.

(A) 여자가 눈을 삽으로 퍼내고 있다.
(B) 여자가 바닥을 대걸레로 닦고 있다.
(C) 여자가 빗자루를 치우고 있다.
(D) 여자가 계단을 쓸고 있다.

해설 여자 한 명이 계단에 쌓인 눈을 빗자루로 쓸고 있는 모습에 초점을 맞춘 (D)가 정답이다. 삽질하는 동작과 대걸레로 닦는 동작, 빗자루를 다른 곳으로 치우는 동작은 사진에서 볼 수 없다.

어휘 shovel ~을 삽으로 퍼내다 mop ~을 대걸레로 닦다 put away ~을 치우다 broom 빗자루 sweep (빗자루로) ~을 쓸다, 쓸어내다

4
(A) Awnings are being adjusted.
미M (B) Some people are browsing in a bookstore.
(C) A skyscraper is under construction.
(D) Some vendors are conducting a sale.

(A) 차양이 조절되고 있다.
(B) 몇몇 사람들이 서점에서 둘러보고 있다.
(C) 고층 건물 하나가 공사 중이다.
(D) 몇몇 판매상들이 판매를 진행하고 있다.

해설 천막이 설치된 공간과 여러 물품이 놓인 탁자들, 그리고 구경하는 사람들이 있는 것으로 볼 때 판매 행사가 진행 중인 것으로 볼 수 있으므로 이 모습에 초점을 맞춘 (D)가 정답이다. 차양이 조절되는 동작과 서점, 그리고 건물 공사 현장은 사진에서 볼 수 없다.

어휘 awning 차양, 햇빛 가리개 browse 둘러보다 skyscraper 고층 건물 under construction 공사 중인 vendor 판매상, 판매업자 conduct ~을 진행하다, 실시하다 sale 판매, 할인 행사

5
(A) A microscope is stored in a display case.
개W (B) She's putting on protective gloves.
(C) Some laboratory equipment is being used.
(D) She's examining safety glasses.

(A) 현미경이 진열창에 보관되어 있다.
(B) 여자가 보호 장갑을 착용하는 중이다.
(C) 실험실 장비가 사용되고 있다.
(D) 여자가 보호 안경을 점검하고 있다.

해설 여자가 실험 장비를 사용하는 모습에 초점을 맞춰 사물 주어 및 수동태 동사로 묘사한 (C)가 정답이다. 진열창, 보호 장갑을 착용하는 동작, 그리고 보호 안경을 점검하는 동작은 사진에서 볼 수 없다.

어휘 microscope 현미경 store v. ~을 보관하다, 저장하다 display case 진열창 put on (동작) ~을 착용하다 protective 보호용의 laboratory 실험실 equipment 장비 examine ~을 점검하다, 조사하다

6
(A) Dishes have been set on the tables.
호M (B) The sun umbrellas have been removed.
(C) Beach chairs are stacked on top of each other.
(D) The restaurant is full of diners.

(A) 접시가 탁자마다 놓여 있다.
(B) 파라솔이 치워져 있다.
(C) 해변용 의자가 차곡차곡 쌓여 있다.
(D) 레스토랑이 식사 손님들로 가득하다.

해설 여러 탁자에 접시들이 놓여 있는 상태에 초점을 맞춘 (A)가 정답이다. 파라솔이 설치된 상태이므로 치워진 것으로 볼 수 없으며, 차곡차곡 쌓여 있는 의자와 식사 손님들은 사진에서 볼 수 없다.

어휘 be set on ~에 놓여 있다, 설치되어 있다 sun umbrella 파라솔 remove ~을 치우다, 없애다 be stacked on top of each other 차곡차곡 쌓여 있다 be full of ~로 가득하다, 꽉 차 있다 diner 식사 손님

7
Who selected the logo design?
미M (A) Yes, unanimously elected.
영W (B) A green star shape.
(C) Ms. Guzman did.

누가 로고 디자인을 선정했나요?
(A) 네, 만장일치로 선택되었습니다.
(B) 녹색 별 모양이요.
(C) 구즈먼 씨가 하셨어요.

해설 〈Who 의문문〉
로고 디자인을 선정한 사람이 누군지 묻는 Who 의문문에 대해 특정 인물의 이름과 selected를 대신하는 did로 답변하는 (C)가 정답이다.
(A) 의문사 의문문에 맞지 않는 Yes로 답변하는 오답
(B) 로고에 포함된 모양을 나타낸 말이므로 Who와 어울리지 않는 오답 / 질문의 logo design에서 연상되는 green star shape를 사용한 오답

어휘 select ~을 선정하다, 선택하다 unanimously 만장일치로 elect ~을 선택하다, (선거로) ~을 선출하다

8
Do you think Ms. Green liked the presentation?
개W (A) No, I'm too busy.
호M (B) I believe so.
(C) I can set it up.

그린 씨가 발표를 마음에 들어 하신 것 같으세요?
(A) 아니요, 제가 너무 바쁩니다.
(B) 그런 것 같아요.
(C) 제가 그걸 설치할 수 있습니다.

해설 〈Do 일반 의문문〉
그린 씨가 발표를 마음에 들어 한 것 같은지 확인하는 Do 일반 의문문에 대해 마음에 들어 한 사실을 so로 지칭해 그런 것 같다는 긍정의 의미를 나타낸 (B)가 정답이다.
(A) 부정을 뜻하는 No 뒤에 이어지는 말이 그린 씨의 의견을 묻는 질문의 핵심에서 벗어난 오답
(C) 자신이 할 수 있음을 나타내는 말이므로 그린 씨의 의견을 묻는 질문의 핵심에서 벗어난 오답 / 질문의 presentation에서 연상되는 set up을 사용한 오답

어휘 presentation 발표(회) believe so (앞선 말에 대해) 그런 것 같다 set A up A를 설치하다, 설정하다, 준비하다

9
Who could I discuss my overtime rate with?
영W (A) On the weekends.
미M (B) Approximately $15.
(C) Ms. Jones in Accounting.

어느 분과 제 초과 근무 수당을 이야기할 수 있을까요?
(A) 주말마다요.
(B) 약 15달러입니다.

(C) 회계팀의 존스 씨요.

해설 〈Who 의문문〉
초과 근무 수당을 이야기할 수 있는 사람이 누군지 묻는 Who 의문문에 대해 특정 인물의 이름과 부서를 밝히는 (C)가 정답이다.
(A) 반복 주기를 나타내는 말이므로 Who와 어울리지 않는 오답
(B) 비용 표현이므로 Who와 어울리지 않는 오답

어휘 discuss ~을 이야기하다, 논의하다 overtime rate 초과 근무 수당 approximately 약, 대략 Accounting 회계부

10 Which file needs to be printed?
호M (A) This computer isn't working.
캐W **(B) The one with the guest list.**
(C) She had posters printed.

어느 파일이 인쇄되어야 하죠?
(A) 이 컴퓨터가 작동하지 않고 있어요.
(B) 초대 손님 명단이 있는 것이요.
(C) 그녀가 포스터를 인쇄해 두었어요.

해설 〈Which 의문문〉
인쇄되어야 하는 파일이 어느 것인지 묻는 Which 의문문에 대해 file을 one으로 대신해 초대 손님 명단이 있는 것이라고 알리는 (B)가 정답이다.
(A) 컴퓨터 작동 여부를 언급하는 말이므로 질문의 핵심에서 벗어난 오답 / 질문의 file에서 연상되는 computer를 사용한 오답
(C) 누군지 알 수 없는 She에 대해 말하고 있으므로 질문의 핵심에서 벗어난 오답 / 질문의 printed를 반복한 오답

어휘 work (기계 등이) 작동하다, 기능하다 have A p.p. A를 ~되게 하다

11 When are you choosing the award winner?
미M (A) Yes, I loved his speech, too.
영W (B) This winter has been cold.
(C) During the committee meeting.

언제 수상자를 선정하시나요?
(A) 네, 저도 그분 연설이 아주 마음에 들었어요.
(B) 올 겨울은 계속 추웠어요.
(C) 위원회 회의 중에요.

해설 〈When 의문문〉
수상자를 선정하는 시점을 묻는 When 의문문에 대해 회의 중에 한다는 말로 대략적인 시점을 밝히는 (C)가 정답이다.
(A) 의문사 의문문에 맞지 않는 Yes로 답변하는 오답
(B) 날씨 표현이므로 질문의 핵심에서 벗어난 오답 / 질문의 winner와 발음이 유사한 winter를 사용한 오답

어휘 choose ~을 선정하다, 선택하다 award winner 수상자 during ~ 중에, ~ 동안 committee 위원회

12 Why is Downton Bakery closed?
캐W (A) Mostly bagels and donuts.
호M **(B) Due to renovations.**
(C) Just two blocks from here.

다운턴 베이커리가 왜 문을 닫은 거죠?
(A) 대부분 베이글과 도넛이요.
(B) 개조 공사 때문에요.
(C) 여기서 두 블록밖에 되지 않습니다.

해설 〈Why 의문문〉
다운턴 베이커리가 문을 닫은 이유를 묻는 Why 의문문에 대해 Why와 짝을 이루는 Due to와 함께 개조 공사가 있음을 알리는 (B)가 정답이다.
(A) 제과제품 종류를 말하는 답변이므로 질문의 핵심에서 벗어난 오답 / 질문의 Bakery에서 연상되는 bagels and donuts를 사용한 오답
(C) 위치 표현이므로 Why와 어울리지 않는 오답

어휘 mostly 대부분, 대체로 due to ~ 때문에, ~로 인해 renovation 개조, 보수

13 Where did you leave this year's quality control report?
미M (A) He leaves in the afternoon.
영W **(B) On your desk.**
(C) She is a famous reporter.

올해의 품질 관리 보고서를 어디에 두셨죠?
(A) 그가 오후에 나갈 거예요.
(B) 당신 책상에요.
(C) 그녀는 유명 기자입니다.

해설 〈Where 의문문〉
품질 관리 보고서를 둔 곳을 묻는 Where 의문문에 대해 상대방 책상이라는 위치 표현으로 답변하는 (B)가 정답이다.
(A) 누군지 알 수 없는 He에 대해 말하고 있으므로 Where와 어울리지 않는 오답 / 질문의 leave가 지닌 다른 표현을 활용해 반복한 오답
(C) 누군지 알 수 없는 She에 대해 말하고 있으므로 Where와 어울리지 않는 오답 / 질문의 report와 발음이 거의 유사한 reporter를 사용한 오답

어휘 leave ~을 두다, 놓다, 나가다, 떠나다 quality control 품질 관리 famous 유명한

14 Would you prefer to have some food at home or out in the park?
캐W (A) I'd prefer a large portion.
호M (B) A lot of community events.
(C) I'd like to eat outdoors.

집에서 뭐 좀 드시겠어요, 아니면 공원으로 나가시겠어요?
(A) 저는 양이 많은 게 좋아요.
(B) 지역 사회의 많은 행사들이요.
(C) 야외에서 먹고 싶어요.

해설 〈선택 의문문〉
집에서 음식을 먹을지 아니면 공원으로 나갈 것인지 묻는 선택 의문문에 대해 야외에서 먹고 싶다는 말로 공원에 가자는 뜻을 나타낸 (C)가 정답이다.
(A) 선호하는 음식 분량을 나타낸 말이므로 질문의 핵심에서 벗어난 오답
(B) 지역 사회 행사를 언급하고 있으므로 질문의 핵심에서 벗어난 오답 / 질문의 park에서 연상되는 events를 사용한 오답

어휘 Would you prefer to do? ~하시겠어요?, ~하는 게 좋으세요? would prefer ~을 좋아하다, ~을 원하다 portion (음식의) 양, 1인분 community 지역 사회 would like to do ~하고 싶다, ~하고자 하다

15 Where will the trade conference be held this year?
미M **(A) At a hotel in New Delhi.**
영W (B) It holds 30 passengers.
(C) About two hours long.

올해는 어디서 무역 회의가 개최되나요?
(A) 뉴델리에 있는 호텔에서요.
(B) 30명의 승객을 수용합니다.
(C) 약 2시간 길이요.

해설 〈Where 의문문〉
올해 무역 회의가 개최되는 장소를 묻는 Where 의문문에 대해 특정 지역의 호텔이라는 장소 표현으로 말하는 (A)가 정답이다.
(B) 수용 가능한 인원 수를 나타낸 말이므로 Where와 어울리지 않는 오답
(C) 시간 길이를 나타낸 말이므로 Where와 어울리지 않는 오답 / 질문의 conference에서 연상되는 two hours long을 사용한 오답

어휘 trade conference 무역 회의, 통상 회의 hold ~을 개최하다, 수용하다, 보유하다 about 약, 대략

16 Shouldn't we increase the number of questions?
캐W (A) Yes, let's decrease production.
호M **(B) Let's ask a manager.**
(C) A higher salary.

질문 숫자를 늘려야 하지 않을까요? (= 늘려야 하죠?)
(A) 네, 생산량을 줄입시다.
(B) 책임자 한 분께 여쭤 봅시다.
(C) 더 높은 연봉이요.

해설 〈부정 의문문〉
질문 숫자를 늘려야 하지 않는지 확인하는 부정 의문문에 대해 이를 결정하기 위한 방법으로 책임자에게 물어 보자고 제안하는 (B)가 정답이다.
(A) 생산량과 관련된 말이므로 질문의 핵심에서 벗어난 오답 / 질문의 increase에서 연상되는 decrease를 사용한 오답
(C) 연봉 수준을 나타낸 말이므로 질문의 핵심에서 벗어난 오답 / 질문의 increase에서 연상되는 higher를 사용한 오답

어휘 increase ~을 늘리다, 증가시키다 decrease ~을 줄이다, 감소시키다 production 생산(량) salary 연봉, 급여

17 Is it possible to recruit another receptionist?

미M (A) She mainly answers phone calls.

영W **(B) We don't have room in the budget.**

(C) A talented group of recruits.

다른 안내 담당 직원을 모집하는 게 가능한가요?

(A) 그녀는 주로 전화 문의에 답변합니다.

(B) 우리가 예산에 여유가 없습니다.

(C) 재능 있는 사람들로 구성된 신입 사원들입니다.

해설 〈Be 일반 의문문〉

다른 안내 담당 직원을 모집하는 게 가능한지 확인하는 Be 일반 의문문에 대해 예산에 여유가 없다는 말로 불가능하다는 뜻을 나타낸 (B)가 정답이다.

(A) 누군지 알 수 없는 She의 직무를 알리는 말이므로 질문의 핵심에서 벗어난 오답 / 질문의 receptionist에서 연상되는 answers phone calls를 사용한 오답

(C) 신입 사원들의 능력과 관련된 말이므로 질문의 핵심에서 벗어난 오답 / 질문의 recruit가 지닌 다른 의미를 활용해 반복한 오답

어휘 recruit v. ~을 모집하다 n. 신입 사원 receptionist 안내 담당 직원, 접수 담당자 mainly 주로, 대부분 room (관사 없이) 여유, 여지 budget 예산 talented 재능 있는

18 When did they change our sick leave policy?

호M (A) To cut down on staff absences.

캐W (B) No, I'm feeling better now.

(C) Didn't you receive the memo?

언제 우리의 병가 정책을 변경한 거죠?

(A) 직원 결근 문제를 줄이기 위해서요.

(B) 아니요, 지금 몸 상태가 더 나아졌어요.

(C) 회람 못 받으셨어요?

해설 〈When 의문문〉

병가 정책을 변경한 과거 시점을 묻는 When 의문문에 대해 시점 표현 대신 그 정보를 확인할 수 있는 방법인 회람을 받지 못했는지 되묻는 (C)가 정답이다.

(A) 목적을 나타내는 말이므로 When과 어울리지 않는 오답

(B) 의문사 의문문에 맞지 않는 No로 답변하는 오답

어휘 sick leave 병가 policy 정책, 방침 cut down on ~을 줄이다 absence 결근, 결석, 부재 feel better (몸 상태, 기분이) 더 낫다 receive ~을 받다 memo 회람, 메모

19 We should distribute flyers at several locations, shouldn't we?

영W

미M **(A) Yes, that's the best method.**

(B) The store's annual summer sale.

(C) It's conveniently located.

우리가 여러 지점에서 전단을 배부해야 하죠, 그렇지 않나요? (= 배부해야 하죠?)

(A) 네, 그게 최고의 방법입니다.

(B) 매장의 연례 여름 세일 행사요.

(C) 그곳은 편리한 곳에 위치해 있습니다.

해설 〈부가 의문문〉

여러 지점에서 전단을 배부해야 하지 않는지 확인하는 부가 의문문에 대해 동의를 나타내는 Yes와 함께 그렇게 배부하는 것을 that으로 지칭해 가장 좋은 방법임을 언급한 (A)가 정답이다.

(B) 세일 행사 종류를 나타낸 말이므로 질문의 핵심에서 벗어난 오답 / 질문의 flyers 또는 locations에서 연상되는 summer sale을 사용한 오답

(C) 위치상의 특징을 나타낸 말이므로 질문의 핵심에서 벗어난 오답 / 질문의 locations와 발음이 거의 유사한 located를 사용한 오답

어휘 distribute ~을 배부하다, 나눠 주다 flyer 전단 several 여럿의, 몇몇의 location 지점, 위치, 장소 method 방법 annual 연례적인, 해마다의 be conveniently located 편리한 곳에 위치해 있다

20 We're working on upgrading our entire security system.

캐W **(A) The clients will be glad to hear that.**

호M (B) No, a team of technical specialists.

(C) The user manual is too old.

우리가 전체 보안 시스템을 업그레이드하는 작업을 하고 있습니다.

(A) 고객들이 그 얘기를 들으면 기뻐할 거예요.

(B) 아니요, 기술 전문가들로 구성된 팀이요.

(C) 사용 설명서가 너무 오래됐어요.

해설 〈평서문〉

전체 보안 시스템 업그레이드 작업 중인 사실을 밝히는 평서문에 대해 그에 따른 결과로 고객들의 생각을 추측하는 (A)가 정답이다.

(B) 한 팀의 구성 인원을 나타낸 말이므로 핵심에서 벗어난 오답 / 평서문에 제시된 upgrading과 security에서 연상되는 technical specialists를 사용한 오답

(C) 사용 설명서의 상태를 나타낸 말이므로 핵심에서 벗어난 오답 / 평서문에 제시된 upgrading에서 연상되는 too old를 사용한 오답

어휘 work on ~에 대한 작업을 하다 entire 전체의 security 보안 client 고객, 의뢰인 specialist 전문가 user manual 사용 설명서

21 What did you think of the changes to the manual?

미M (A) She should send it soon.

영W (B) For some new machines.

(C) It is now much easier to understand.

설명서 변경 사항들이 어떠셨어요?

(A) 그녀가 그걸 곧 보내야 합니다.

(B) 몇몇 새 기계들을 위해서요.

(C) 이제 훨씬 더 이해하기 쉽습니다.

해설 〈What 의문문〉

설명서 변경 사항들이 어땠는지 의견을 묻는 What 의문문에 대해 더 이해하기 쉽다는 말로 변경에 따른 긍정적인 결과를 밝히는 (C)가 정답이다.

(A) 누군지 알 수 없는 She에 대해 말하고 있으므로 의견을 묻는 What did you think와 어울리지 않는 오답

(B) 목적을 나타내는 말이므로 의견을 묻는 What did you think와

어울리지 않는 오답 / 질문의 manual에서 연상되는 machines를 사용한 오답

어휘 What did you think of ~? ~는 어떠셨어요?, ~를 어떻게 생각하셨어요? manual (제품 등의) 설명서 much (비교급 수식) 훨씬

22 How long does it take to get to the concert stage?

캐W (A) The singer is on tour.

호M (B) I get nervous performing on stage.

(C) It is just a short walk from here.

콘서트 무대로 가는 데 얼마나 걸리나요?

(A) 그 가수는 투어 중이에요.

(B) 저는 무대에서 공연하는 게 긴장돼요.

(C) 여기서 조금만 걸으면 됩니다.

해설 〈How long 의문문〉

콘서트 장소로 가는 데 얼마나 걸리는지 묻는 How long 의문문에 대해 조금만 걸으면 된다는 말로 가까운 거리임을 알리는 (C)가 정답이다.

(A) 특정 가수의 현재 일정을 나타낸 말이므로 How long과 어울리지 않는 오답 / 질문의 concert에서 연상되는 singer를 사용한 오답

(B) 답변자 자신이 긴장 상태를 겪는 상황을 나타낸 말이므로 How long과 어울리지 않는 오답 / 질문의 stage를 반복한 오답

어휘 take ~의 시간이 걸리다 get to ~로 가다 get + 형용사 ~한 상태가 되다 nervous 긴장한, 떨리는 just a short walk from ~에서 조금만 걸으면 되는 거리

23 Why don't you contact the Finance Department?

미M (A) That's the correct number.

영W (B) For financial advice.

(C) I already called them.

재무팀에 연락해 보시는 게 어때요?

(A) 그게 정확한 번호입니다.

(B) 재무와 관련된 조언을 위해서요.

(C) 이미 그쪽에 전화했습니다.

해설 〈Why don't you 의문문〉

재무팀에 연락해 보도록 제안하는 Why don't you 의문문에 대해 Finance Department를 them으로 지칭해 이미 전화했다는 말로 연락했음을 밝히는 (C)가 정답이다.

(A) 특정 번호의 정확성 여부를 나타낸 말이므로 Why don't you 제안 의문문에 어울리지 않는 오답 / 질문의 contact에서 연상되는 number를 사용한 오답

(B) 목적을 나타내는 말이므로 Why don't you 제안 의문문에 어울리지 않는 오답 / 질문의 Finance와 발음이 거의 같은 financial을 사용한 오답

어휘 contact ~에게 연락하다 finance 재무, 재정, 금융 correct 정확한, 맞은, 옳은 financial 재무의, 재정의, 금융의

24 Are we meeting at the theater at 7:30 or 8:30?
(캐W) (A) **The film starts at 8:00.**
(호M) (B) Try the new action movie.
(C) No, I've met her before.

우리가 영화관에서 7시 30분에 만나나요, 아니면 8시 30분에 만나나요?
(A) **영화가 8시에 시작합니다.**
(B) 새로 나온 액션 영화 한 번 보세요.
(C) 아니요, 전에 그녀를 만난 적이 있어요.

해설 〈선택 의문문〉
영화관에서 만날 시간을 묻는 선택 의문문에 대해 영화가 8시에 시작한다는 말로 7시 30분에 만나도록 제안하는 뜻을 나타낸 (A)가 정답이다.
(B) 특정 장르의 영화를 권하는 말이므로 질문의 핵심에서 벗어난 오답 / 질문의 theater에서 연상되는 movie를 사용한 오답
(C) 누군지 알 수 없는 her를 언급해 과거의 경험을 나타낸 말이므로 질문의 핵심에서 벗어난 오답 / 질문의 meet의 과거 시제 형태인 met을 사용한 오답

어휘 film 영화 try ~을 한 번 해 보다

25 I'd like to reserve three tickets for the afternoon performance.
(호M)
(미M) (A) **Sorry, that one is sold out.**
(B) The box office.
(C) I'm sitting in an aisle seat.

오후 공연으로 입장권 세 장을 예매하려고 합니다.
(A) **죄송하지만, 그 공연은 매진되었습니다.**
(B) 매표소요.
(C) 저는 복도 쪽 좌석에 앉아 있어요.

해설 〈평서문〉
오후 공연으로 입장권 세 장을 예매하겠다는 의사를 밝히는 평서문에 대해 매진되었다는 말로 예매할 수 없다는 뜻을 나타낸 (A)가 정답이다.
(B) 매표소를 언급하고 있어 입장권 예매 의사를 밝히는 말에 어울리지 않는 반응이므로 오답 / 평서문에 제시된 tickets에서 연상되는 box office를 사용한 오답
(C) 좌석 구역을 나타낸 말로서 입장권 예매 요청을 받은 사람이 보일 수 있는 반응으로 맞지 않는 오답 / 평서문에 제시된 tickets에서 연상되는 aisle seat을 사용한 오답

어휘 would like to do ~하고 싶다, ~하고자 하다 reserve ~을 예약하다 performance 공연, 연주(회) sold out 매진된, 품절된 aisle 복도, 통로

26 My vacation request for next month was approved, right?
(미M) (A) Yes, we selected one.
(캐W) (B) A vacation resort.
(C) **No, I'm still reviewing it.**

제 다음 달 휴가 요청서가 승인됐죠, 맞나요?
(A) 네, 우리가 하나 선택했습니다.
(B) 휴양지 리조트요.
(C) **아니요, 여전히 검토하고 있습니다.**

해설 〈부가 의문문〉
다음 달 휴가 요청서가 승인되었는지 확인하는 부가 의문문에 대해 부정을 뜻하는 No와 함께 vacation request를 it으로 지칭해 여전히 검토 중이라는 말로 승인되지 않았음을 나타낸 (C)가 정답이다.
(A) 긍정을 나타내는 Yes 뒤에 이어지는 말이 휴가 요청서 승인 여부와 관련 없는 오답
(B) 휴가 장소를 나타내는 말이므로 휴가 요청서 승인 여부와 관련 없는 오답 / 질문의 vacation을 반복한 오답

어휘 vacation 휴가 request 요청(서) approve ~을 승인하다 select ~을 선택하다, 선정하다 review ~을 검토하다, 살펴보다

27 How much did we spend on stationery?
(영W) (A) Thanks, here's my credit card.
(호M) (B) For 5 boxes of paper.
(C) **Gene has that information.**

우리가 문구류에 얼마나 많이 소비했죠?
(A) 감사합니다. 여기 제 신용카드입니다.
(B) 용지 5박스를 위해서요.
(C) **진 씨가 그 정보를 갖고 있어요.**

해설 〈How much 의문문〉
문구류에 얼마나 많이 소비했는지 묻는 How much 의문문에 대해 그 정보를 갖고 있는 사람을 통해 확인할 수 있다는 뜻을 나타낸 (C)가 정답이다.
(A) 신용카드를 제시할 때 할 수 있는 말이므로 질문의 핵심에서 벗어난 오답 / 질문의 spend에서 연상되는 credit card를 사용한 오답
(B) 목적을 나타낸 말이므로 How much와 어울리지 않는 오답 / 질문의 stationery에서 연상되는 paper를 사용한 오답

어휘 spend (돈, 시간 등) ~을 소비하다, 쓰다 stationery 문구류

28 Our library patrons requested more variety.
(캐W) (A) I enjoy reading as a hobby.
(영W) (B) **The collection is fairly small.**
(C) Searching for titles online.

우리 도서관 고객들이 더 많은 종류를 요청했어요.
(A) 저는 취미로 독서를 즐깁니다.
(B) **소장품 규모가 꽤 작긴 하죠.**
(C) 온라인으로 서적을 검색하는 일이요.

해설 〈평서문〉
도서관 고객들이 더 많은 다양성을 요청한 사실을 밝히는 평서문에 대해 소장품 규모가 작다는 말로 고객들의 요청에 수긍하는 뜻을 나타낸 (B)가 정답이다.
(A) 취미의 종류를 나타낸 말이므로 핵심에서 벗어난 오답 / 평서문에 제시된 library에서 연상되는 reading을 사용한 오답
(C) 특정 검색 방법을 나타낸 말이므로 핵심에서 벗어난 오답 / 평서문에 제시된 library에서 연상되는 titles를 사용한 오답

어휘 patron 고객, 후원자 request ~을 요청하다 variety 종류, 다양성 collection 소장(품), 수집(품) fairly 꽤, 상당히 search for ~을 검색하다, 찾다 title 서적, 출판물

29 Have you finished interviewing all the candidates?
(미M) (A) Please post the job opening soon.
(영W) (B) **No, the interviews are scheduled for tomorrow.**
(C) An application form and résumé.

모든 지원자들을 면접 보시는 일을 마치셨나요?
(A) 곧 그 공석 구인 공고를 게시해 주세요.
(B) **아니요, 그 면접은 내일로 예정되어 있습니다.**
(C) 지원서와 이력서요.

해설 〈Have 일반 의문문〉
지원자들을 면접 보는 일을 끝냈는지 확인하는 Have 일반 의문문에 대해 부정을 뜻하는 No와 함께 면접이 내일로 예정된 사실을 말하는 것으로 끝나지 않았음을 나타낸 (B)가 정답이다.
(A) 구인 공고를 게시하도록 요청하는 말이므로 면접 종료 여부와 관련 없는 오답 / 질문의 interviewing과 candidates에서 연상되는 job opening을 사용한 오답
(C) 제출 서류의 종류를 나타낸 말이므로 질문의 핵심에서 벗어난 오답 / 질문의 interviewing과 candidates에서 연상되는 application form and résumé를 사용한 오답

어휘 candidate 지원자, 후보자 post ~을 게시하다 job opening 공석, 빈자리 be scheduled for + 날짜/요일 ~로 예정되어 있다 application form 지원서, 신청서 résumé 이력서

30 The delivery truck isn't here yet, is it?
(호M) (A) An aisle seat, please.
(영W) (B) All deliveries require a signature.
(C) **It should come in the afternoon.**

배송 트럭이 아직 여기에 와 있지 않죠, 그런가요? (= 여기에 와 있나요?)
(A) 복도 쪽 좌석으로 부탁합니다.
(B) 모든 배송에 서명이 필요합니다.
(C) **오후에 올 겁니다.**

해설 〈부가 의문문〉
배송 트럭이 아직 오지 않았는지 확인하는 부가 의문문에 대해 오후에 올 예정임을 알리는 것으로 아직 오지 않았다는 뜻을 나타낸 (C)가 정답이다.
(A) 선호 좌석을 나타낸 말이므로 질문의 핵심에서 벗어난 오답
(B) 배송 물품을 받기 위한 조건을 나타낸 말이므로 질문의 핵심에서 벗어난 오답 / 질문의 delivery를 반복한 오답

어휘 delivery 배송(품) aisle 복도, 통로 require ~을 필요로 하다 signature 서명

31 Would you mind revising the media pack?

미M (A) A new television.

캐W (B) Actually, I have too many tasks.

(C) To promote our insurance services.

언론 홍보 자료 좀 수정해 주시겠어요?

(A) 새 텔레비전이요.

(B) 실은, 제 업무가 너무 많습니다.

(C) 우리 보험 서비스를 홍보하기 위해서요.

해설 〈Would 일반 의문문〉

언론 홍보 자료를 수정해 달라고 요청하는 would 일반 의문문에 대해 업무가 너무 많다는 말로 거절 의사를 밝힌 (B)가 정답이다.

(A) 텔레비전 상태를 나타낸 말이므로 질문의 핵심에서 벗어난 오답 / 질문의 revising과 일부 발음이 유사한 television을 사용한 오답

(C) 목적을 나타낸 말이므로 요청 사항에 대한 반응으로 어울리지 않는 오답

어휘 Would you mind -ing? ~해 주시겠어요? revise ~을 수정하다 media pack 언론 홍보 자료 actually 실은, 사실은 task 업무, 일 promote ~을 홍보하다, 촉진하다, 승진시키다 insurance 보험

Questions 32-34 refer to the following conversation. 캐W 미M

W I'd like to welcome everybody to our annual general meeting. We are going to hear from ㉜ Colin, who will tell us about the new research project his department has been working on. Over to you, Colin.

M Thank you. The sales of our kitchen appliances have declined quite dramatically. It seems ㉝ people just aren't buying these kinds of products in stores anymore. Our research indicates people commonly buy them online.

W I think ㉞ we should launch an aggressive online ad campaign to encourage people to visit our Web site.

M ㉞ My team has the same opinion. If we don't follow the online shopping trend, we may really struggle.

여 연례 총회에 오신 모든 분을 환영합니다. 우리는 콜린 씨의 말씀을 들을 예정인데, 이분의 부서에서 그동안 맡아 작업해 온 새 연구 프로젝트와 관련해 이야기해 주실 것입니다. 당신 순서입니다, 콜린 씨.

남 감사합니다. 우리 주방용품의 매출이 꽤 급격하게 감소해 왔습니다. 사람들이 더 이상 이런 종류의 제품을 매장에서 구입하지 않는 것 같습니다. 저희 조사에 따르면 사람들이 일반적으로 온라인상에서 구입하는 것으로 나타나 있습니다.

여 사람들에게 우리 웹 사이트를 방문하도록 권장할 수 있게 공격적인 온라인 광고 캠페인을 시작해야 할 것 같아요.

남 저희 팀도 같은 의견입니다. 우리가 온라인 쇼핑 추세를 따르지 않으면, 정말로 힘겨워질 수 있습니다.

어휘 annual 연례적인, 해마다의 general meeting 총회 research 연구, 조사 department 부서 work on ~에 대한 일을 하다 Over to A (행사 등에서) 다음 순서는 A입니다, A에게 마이크를 넘기겠습니다 sales 매출, 판매, 영업 kitchen appliances 주방용품 decline 감소하다, 하락하다 quite 꽤, 상당히 dramatically 급격하게 It seems (that) ~인 것 같다 not ~ anymore 더 이상 ~ 않다 indicate (that) ~임을 나타내다, 가리키다 commonly 일반적으로, 흔히 follow ~을 따르다 trend 추세, 경향 struggle 힘겨워하다, 발버둥 치다

32 Which department does the man most likely work in?

(A) Accounting

(B) Human resources

(C) Technical Support

(D) Research and Development

남자는 어느 부서에서 근무하고 있을 것 같은가?

(A) 회계

(B) 인사

(C) 기술 지원

(D) 연구 및 개발

해설 〈근무지를 묻는 문제〉

대화 시작 부분에 여자가 콜린 씨의 이름을 언급하면서 이 사람의 부서에서 작업한 새 연구 프로젝트에 관한 얘기를 들을 것이라고 (Colin, who will tell us about the new research project his department has been working on) 알리고 있으므로 (D)가 정답이다.

33 According to the man, what are customers doing differently?

(A) They are buying more items online.

(B) They are buying cheaper items.

(C) They are shopping at later times.

(D) They are taking out fewer payment plans.

남자의 말에 따르면, 고객들이 무엇을 다르게 하고 있는가?

(A) 온라인상에서 더 많은 제품을 구입하고 있다.

(B) 더 저렴한 제품을 구입하고 있다.

(C) 더 늦은 시간대에 쇼핑하고 있다.

(D) 지불 약정에 더 적게 가입하고 있다.

해설 〈기타 세부 사항을 묻는 문제〉

대화 중반부에 남자가 사람들이 실제 매장에서 제품을 구입하지 않고 온라인상에서 구입하는 것으로 나타났다는(people just aren't buying these kinds of products in stores anymore. Our research indicates people commonly buy them online) 조사 결과를 알리고 있으므로 (A)가 정답이다.

어휘 take out (보험, 대출 등) ~에 가입하다, ~ 서비스를 받다 payment plan 지불 약정

34 What action do the speakers agree to take?

(A) Developing a new range of products

(B) Starting an advertising campaign

(C) Opening several new stores

(D) Redesigning a Web site

화자들은 어떤 조치를 취하는 데 동의하는가?

(A) 새로운 제품군을 개발하는 것

(B) 광고 캠페인을 시작하는 것

(C) 여러 신규 매장을 개장하는 것

(D) 웹 사이트를 다시 디자인하는 것

해설 〈기타 세부 사항을 묻는 문제〉

대화 후반부에 여자가 공격적인 온라인 광고 캠페인을 시작해야 한다고(we should launch an aggressive online ad campaign) 제안하자, 남자가 자신의 팀도 같은 의견이라고(My team has the same opinion) 동의하고 있으므로 (B)가 정답이다.

어휘 take action 조치를 취하다 agree to do ~하는 데 동의하다 develop ~을 개발하다 range 제품군, 범위 advertising 광고 (활동) several 여럿의, 몇몇의

W Hi, I'm Caroline from Fresh Home Services. ㉟ I'm here to clean your house, as you requested.

M Hi, Caroline. As you can probably see, my home is a bit of a mess right now. ㊱ Sorry, but my water supply has been temporarily cut off due to a plumbing problem. Will that be a problem?

W It's not a big deal. ㊲ I'll start unloading all of my equipment out of my van and get set up inside. Let me know if you have any special requests.

여 안녕하세요, 저는 프레시 홈 서비스의 캐롤린입니다. 요청하신 대로 자택을 청소하러 왔습니다.

남 안녕하세요, 캐롤린 씨. 아마 보시겠지만, 저희 집이 지금 약간 엉망입니다. 죄송하지만, 배관 문제 때문에 수도 공급이 일시적으로 끊긴 상태입니다. 이게 문제가 될까요?

여 큰 문제는 아닙니다. 제 승합차에서 장비를 모두 내리기 시작해서 내부에 준비해 두겠습니다. 어떤 특별 요청 사항이든 있으면 알려 주세요.

어휘 request v. 요청하다 n. 요청 a bit 약간, 조금 mess 엉망(인 상태) supply 공급 temporarily 일시적으로, 임시로 cut off ~을 끊다, 중단하다 due to ~ 때문에, ~로 인해 plumbing 배관 big deal 큰 문제 unload A out of B (짐 등) A를 B에서 내리다, 꺼내다 equipment 장비 get set up 준비해 놓다, 설치해 놓다 let A know A에게 알리다

35 What service does the woman offer?
(A) Interior design
(B) Garden landscaping
(C) House cleaning
(D) Property sales

여자는 어떤 서비스를 제공하는가?
(A) 실내 디자인
(B) 정원 조경
(C) 주택 청소
(D) 부동산 판매

해설 〈기타 세부 사항을 묻는 문제〉
대화 시작 부분에 여자가 요청대로 집을 청소하러 왔다고(I'm here to clean your house, as you requested) 알리고 있으므로 (C)가 정답이다.

어휘 offer ~을 제공하다 landscaping 조경 (작업) property 부동산, 건물

36 Why does the man apologize?
(A) He has another appointment.
(B) His home has no electricity.
(C) He misplaced some materials.
(D) His water has been shut off.

남자는 왜 사과하는가?
(A) 다른 약속이 있다.
(B) 집에 전기가 들어오지 않는다.
(C) 몇몇 물품을 잃어버렸다.
(D) 수도가 끊긴 상태이다.

해설 〈기타 세부 사항을 묻는 문제〉
남자가 대화 중반부에 Sorry라는 사과의 말과 함께 배관 문제 때문에 수도 공급이 일시적으로 끊겼다고(but my water supply has been temporarily cut off due to a plumbing problem) 알리고 있으므로 (D)가 정답이다.

어휘 apologize 사과하다 appointment 약속, 예약 electricity 전기 misplace ~을 분실하다, ~을 둔 곳을 잊다 material 물품, 재료, 자료 shut off ~을 차단하다, 끊다

37 What does the woman say she will do?
(A) Inspect a building
(B) Unload a vehicle
(C) Put on special clothing
(D) Purchase supplies

여자는 무엇을 할 것이라고 말하는가?
(A) 건물을 점검하는 일
(B) 차량에서 짐을 내리는 일
(C) 특수 의복을 착용하는 일
(D) 용품을 구입하는 일

해설 〈미래에 할 일을 묻는 문제〉
여자가 대화 후반부에 승합차에서 장비를 내리기 시작해서 내부에 준비해 놓겠다고(I'll start unloading all of my equipment out of my van and get set up inside) 언급하고 있으므로 (B)가 정답이다.

어휘 inspect ~을 점검하다 unload ~에서 짐을 내리다 vehicle 차량 put on ~을 착용하다 clothing 의복, 의류 purchase ~을 구입하다 supplies 용품, 물품

M Oh, hello Susan! ㊳ I didn't expect to see you here at this restaurant. It's far from where you live.

W Hi, Richard. Well, I read a review that said not only that the food is excellent, but also that the view from the patio is amazing.

M It's wonderful, isn't it? ㊴ I always try to get a table out on the patio.

W Actually, I was just leaving, ㊴ if you want this one.

M Are you sure? I'd appreciate that, as I might have to wait a while for another one.

W My pleasure. By the way, ㊵ did you know they run a cooking class here? You should sign up. I'm planning to come on Friday after work.

남 아, 안녕하세요, 수잔 씨! 여기 이 레스토랑에서 만날 거라고 예상하지 못했어요. 당신이 사는 곳에서 멀잖아요.

여 안녕하세요, 리차드 씨. 음, 제가 후기 하나를 읽었는데 음식이 훌륭할 뿐만 아니라 테라스에서 보이는 경관이 놀랍다고 하더라고요.

남 아주 멋지지 않나요? 저는 항상 밖에 있는 테라스에 테이블을 잡으려 해요.

여 실은, 제가 막 나가려던 참이었는데, 이 테이블을 원하시면 이용하세요.

남 정말이에요? 그럼 감사해요, 왜냐하면 다른 자리를 좀 기다려야 할 수도 있거든요.

여 별 말씀요. 그건 그렇고, 이곳에서 요리 강좌를 진행한다는 거 아셨어요? 등록해 보세요. 저는 금요일 퇴근 후에 올 계획이에요.

어휘 expect to do ~할 것으로 예상하다, 기대하다 far from ~에서 멀리 있는 review 후기, 평가, 의견 not only A but also B A뿐만 아니라 B도 view 경관, 전망 amazing 놀라운 try to do ~하려 하다 actually 실은, 사실은 leave 나가다, 떠나다 appreciate ~에 대해 감사하다 might have to do ~해야 할 수도 있다 wait a while 잠시 기다리다 My pleasure (감사 인사에 대해) 별 말씀요 by the way (화제 전환을 위해) 그건 그렇고, 그런데 sign up 등록하다, 신청하다 plan to do ~할 계획이다

38 Where most likely is the man?
(A) In a supermarket
(B) In a library
(C) In a restaurant
(D) In a university

남자는 어디에 있는 것 같은가?
(A) 슈퍼마켓에서
(B) 도서관에서
(C) 레스토랑에서
(D) 대학교에서

대화 시작 부분에 남자가 현재 있는 장소를 here at this restaurant 라고 지칭하고 있으므로 (C)가 정답이다.

어휘 take place (일, 행사 등이) 발생되다, 개최되다

39 What does the woman imply when she says, "I was just leaving"?
(A) She does not have time to discuss an issue.
(B) She will give the man her table.
(C) She wants the man to accompany her.
(D) She is dissatisfied with a service.

여자가 "I was just leaving"이라고 말할 때 무엇을 의도하는가?
(A) 문제를 논의할 시간이 없다.
(B) 남자에게 자신의 테이블을 줄 것이다.
(C) 남자가 자신과 동행하기를 원한다.
(D) 서비스에 만족하지 못하고 있다.

해설 〈의도 파악 문제〉
대화 중반부에 남자가 항상 테라스에 있는 테이블을 잡으려 한다고(I always try to get a table out on the patio) 알리자, 여자가 '막 나가려던 참이었다'는 말과 함께 이 테이블을 원하면 이용하라고(if you want this one) 알리고 있다. 이는 자신이 앉아 있던 테이블을 남자에게 이용하게 하겠다는 뜻이므로 (B)가 정답이다.

어휘 discuss ~을 논의하다, 이야기하다 issue 문제, 사안 accompany ~와 동행하다, ~을 동반하다 be dissatisfied with ~에 만족하지 못하다

40 What does the woman recommend that the man do?
(A) Purchase a membership
(B) Take a day off work
(C) Buy tickets for an event
(D) Sign up for a class

여자는 남자에게 무엇을 하도록 권하는가?
(A) 회원권을 구입하는 일
(B) 회사에서 하루 쉬는 일
(C) 행사 입장권을 구입하는 일
(D) 강좌에 등록하는 일

해설 〈제안 사항을 묻는 문제〉
대화 후반부에 여자가 해당 레스토랑에서 요리 강좌를 진행한다는 사실을 알았는지 물으면서 등록해 보라고(did you know they run a cooking class here? You should sign up) 권하고 있으므로 (D)가 정답이다.

어휘 purchase ~을 구입하다 take A off A만큼 쉬다 sign up for ~에 등록하다, ~을 신청하다

Questions 41-43 refer to the following conversation. 호M 영W

M Good afternoon. **41 I hope you are enjoying your stay with us at Fairfields Resort.** I'm Toby. May I help you?
W Hi. **42 I was just wondering where the nearest shopping malls are.** I'd like to buy a new dress to wear to dinner tonight.
M The Calmwater Complex in Fairfields Heights is the closest. It contains a range of designer fashion outlets you can visit.
W Great, thanks! **43 Could you arrange a taxi for me?**
M Right away. It will pick you up from outside the main entrance.

남 안녕하세요. 저희 페어필즈 리조트와 함께 즐거운 숙박이 되시기를 바랍니다. 저는 토비입니다. 무엇을 도와드릴까요?
여 안녕하세요. 가장 가까운 쇼핑몰이 어디 있는지 궁금했어요. 오늘 밤 저녁 식사 자리에 입고 갈 새 드레스를 사려고 하거든요.
남 페어필즈 하이츠에 있는 캄워터 콤플렉스가 가장 가깝습니다. 그곳에 방문하실 수 있는 다양한 유명 패션 브랜드 전문 매장들이 있습니다.
여 잘됐네요, 감사합니다! 택시를 좀 준비시켜 주시겠어요?
남 곧바로 준비해 드리겠습니다. 택시가 중앙 출구 바깥쪽에서 모시고 갈 겁니다.

어휘 wonder ~을 궁금해하다 the nearest 가장 가까운(= the closest) contain ~을 포함하다, 담고 있다 outlet 전문 매장, 할인점 arrange ~을 준비하다, 조치하다 right away 곧바로, 당장 pick up ~을 태우고 가다, 데리러 가다

41 What is the man's job?
(A) A travel agent
(B) A resort employee
(C) A fashion designer
(D) A store clerk

남자의 직업은 무엇인가?
(A) 여행사 직원
(B) 리조트 직원
(C) 패션 디자이너
(D) 매장 점원

해설 〈직업을 묻는 문제〉
남자가 자신이 속한 페어필즈 리조트와 함께 즐거운 숙박이 되기를 바란다고(I hope you are enjoying your stay with us at Fairfields Resort) 인사하고 있으므로 (B)가 정답이다.

42 What are the speakers mainly discussing?
(A) Store locations
(B) Restaurant reviews
(C) Building plans
(D) Travel itineraries

화자들은 주로 무엇을 이야기하고 있는가?
(A) 매장 위치
(B) 레스토랑 후기
(C) 건물 설계도
(D) 여행 일정

해설 〈주제를 묻는 문제〉
대화 초반부에 여자가 가장 가까운 쇼핑몰이 어디 있는지 궁금했다고(I was just wondering where the nearest shopping malls are) 알린 뒤로 특정 쇼핑몰의 위치 및 매장 특성 등과 관련해 이야기하고 있으므로 (A)가 정답이다.

어휘 review 후기, 평가, 의견 plan 설계도 itinerary 일정(표)

43 What does the woman request?
(A) A discount coupon
(B) A flight schedule
(C) A city map
(D) A taxi

여자는 무엇을 요청하는가?
(A) 할인 쿠폰
(B) 항공편 일정표
(C) 도시 안내 지도
(D) 택시

해설 〈요청 사항을 묻는 문제〉
대화 후반부에 여자가 택시를 준비시켜 줄 수 있는지(Could you arrange a taxi for me?) 묻고 있으므로 (D)가 정답이다.

W Felix, ㉔ I wanted to congratulate you on getting your photos published in this month's issue of *Garden World Magazine*.

M Thanks! I think it will also help our site get more attention.

W That's great! Oh, and I had an idea to make those photos into a calendar to sell at the gift shop. ㊺ Would you be willing to donate the images?

M Of course. But I'd need to fill out a form to give official permission. ㊻ I'd like to put that off until after my vacation. I'm flying to Bali tomorrow.

여 펠릭스 씨, 〈가든 월드 매거진〉 이번 달 호에 당신 사진이 실리게 된 것에 대해 축하 인사를 드리고 싶었어요.

남 감사합니다! 그게 우리 웹 사이트가 더 많은 관심을 받는 데에도 도움이 될 것 같아요.

여 아주 잘됐네요! 아, 그리고 그 사진들을 달력에 넣어 선물 매장에서 판매하는 생각도 했었어요. 이미지들을 기부해 주실 의향이 있으신가요?

남 물론이죠. 하지만 정식으로 허용하는 양식을 한 부 작성해야 할 겁니다. 이 일은 제가 휴가를 다녀온 다음으로 미루고 싶어요. 내일 발리로 가는 비행기를 타거든요.

어휘 congratulate A on B B에 대해 A를 축하하다 get A p.p. A가 ~되게 하다 issue (출판물의) 호 help A do A가 ~하는 것을 돕다 attention 관심, 주의, 주목 have an idea to do ~할 생각을 갖고 있다 be willing to do ~할 의향이 있다, 기꺼이 ~하다 donate ~을 기부하다 fill out ~을 작성하다 form 양식, 서식 give permission 허용하다 official 정식의, 공식적인 would like to do ~하고 싶다 put A off A를 미루다 fly to ~로 비행기를 타고 가다

44 Why does the woman congratulate the man?
(A) He won an important contract.
(B) He was given a job promotion.
(C) He recently received an award.
(D) He had some images published.

여자는 왜 남자에게 축하 인사를 하는가?
(A) 중요한 계약을 따냈다.
(B) 회사에서 승진했다.
(C) 최근에 상을 하나 받았다.
(D) 몇몇 이미지를 출간했다.

해설 〈기타 세부 사항을 묻는 문제〉
대화를 시작하면서 여자가 특정 잡지에 남자의 사진이 실린 것에 대해 축하하고(I wanted to congratulate you on getting your photos published in this month's issue of *Garden World Magazine*) 있으므로 (D)가 정답이다.

어휘 congratulate ~을 축하하다 win a contract 계약을 따내다

---

promotion 승진 recently 최근에 receive ~을 받다 have A p.p. A가 ~되게 하다 publish ~을 출간하다

45 What does the woman want the man to do?
(A) Share a recommendation
(B) Work at the gift shop
(C) Make a donation
(D) Renew a subscription

여자는 남자에게 무엇을 하기를 원하는가?
(A) 추천 사항을 공유하는 일
(B) 선물 매장에서 근무하는 일
(C) 기부를 하는 일
(D) 구독 기간을 갱신하는 일

해설 〈요청 사항을 묻는 문제〉
대화 중반부에 여자가 이미지를 기부할 의향이 있는지(Would you be willing to donate the images?) 묻고 있는데, 이는 기부하도록 요청하는 것과 같으므로 (C)가 정답이다.

어휘 share ~을 공유하다 recommendation 추천, 권고 donation 기부(금) renew ~을 갱신하다 subscription 구독, 서비스 이용

46 What does the man plan to do tomorrow?
(A) Take a trip
(B) Sign a contract
(C) Send some information
(D) Update a Web site

남자는 내일 무엇을 할 계획인가?
(A) 여행을 떠나는 일
(B) 계약서에 서명하는 일
(C) 일부 정보를 보내는 일
(D) 한 웹 사이트를 업데이트하는 일

해설 〈특정 시점의 일을 묻는 문제〉
대화 맨 마지막에 남자가 휴가를 다녀 온 뒤로 미루는 것을 언급하면서 내일 비행기를 타고 발리로 간다고(I'd like to put that off until after my vacation. I'm flying to Bali tomorrow) 알리고 있으므로 (A)가 정답이다.

어휘 plan to do ~할 계획이다 contract 계약(서)

M1 Hi, Oliver. You're just in time ㊼ to meet Ms. Jennifer Rourke, a representative from a chain of home appliance stores in Canada. Ms. Rourke's firm is considering stocking our refrigerators.

M2 Oh, it's a pleasure to meet you, Ms. Rourke. Is this your first trip to the UK?

W Yes, and ㊽ I can't wait to attend your product launch event at the trade show tomorrow morning.

M2 Well, I hope to see you there. We're proud to be introducing our new range of Polar 300 refrigerators.

W Yes, those are the ones that my company is most interested in.

M1 Well, I hope you're impressed. ㊾ The fridges use 30 percent less energy than any other similarly-sized products on the market.

남1 안녕하세요. 올리버 씨. 캐나다의 가전기기 매장 체인회사의 직원이신 제니퍼 루크 씨를 만나 뵐 수 있게 마침 딱 맞춰서 오셨네요. 루크 씨 회사에서 우리 냉장고를 재고로 갖춰 놓는 것을 고려하고 있습니다.

남2 아, 만나서 반갑습니다 루크 씨. 영국 출장은 처음이신가요?

여 네, 그리고 내일 오전에 무역 박람회에서 있을 귀사의 제품 출시 행사에 빨리 참석하고 싶어요.

남2 음. 그곳에서 뵐 수 있기를 바랍니다. 저희가 새로운 폴라 300 냉장고 제품군을 소개하게 되어 자랑스럽게 생각합니다.

여 네. 그 제품들이 바로 저희 회사가 가장 관심 있어 하는 것들입니다.

남1 저, 좋은 인상을 받으시기를 바랍니다. 이 냉장고 제품들은 시중에 나와 있는 다른 어떤 유사한 크기의 제품들보다 30퍼센트나 전력을 덜 사용합니다.

어휘 just in time 마침 시간에 딱 맞춰 representative 직원 home appliance 가전기기 consider -ing ~하는 것을 고려하다 stock v. ~을 재고로 갖춰 놓다 refrigerator 냉장고(= fridge) can't wait to do 빨리 ~하고 싶다 attend ~에 참석하다 launch 출시, 공개 trade show 무역 박람회 be proud to do ~해서 자랑스럽다 introduce ~을 소개하다 range 제품군, 종류, 범위 be interested in ~에 관심이 있다 impressed 좋은 인상을 받은 similarly-sized 유사한 크기의 on the market 시중에 나와 있는

47 What industry do the speakers work in?
(A) Clothing
(B) Appliances
(C) Computers
(D) Furniture

화자들은 어떤 업계에서 일하고 있는가?
(A) 의류
(B) 가전기기

(C) 컴퓨터
(D) 가구

해설 〈근무 분야를 묻는 문제〉
대화 시작 부분에 남자 한 명이 가전기기 매장 체인회사의 직원인 제니퍼 루크 씨를 만나는 상황임을 언급하면서 루크 씨 회사가 남자의 회사에서 만드는 냉장고를 재고로 갖춰 놓는 것을 고려하고 있다고(a representative from a chain of home appliance stores in Canada. Ms. Rourke's firm is considering stocking our refrigerators) 알리고 있다. 따라서 화자들이 가전기기 업계 종사자임을 알 수 있으므로 (B)가 정답이다.

48 What will Ms. Rourke do tomorrow morning?
(A) Tour a production plant
(B) Return to her company
(C) Meet with shareholders
(D) Attend a product launch

루크 씨는 내일 오전에 무엇을 할 것인가?
(A) 제조 공장을 견학하는 일
(B) 소속 회사로 복귀하는 일
(C) 주주들과 만나는 일
(D) 제품 출시 행사에 참석하는 일

해설 〈특정 시점의 일을 묻는 문제〉
대화 중반부에 여자가 내일 오전에 무역 박람회에서 있을 상대방 회사의 제품 출시 행사에 빨리 참석하고 싶다고(I can't wait to attend your product launch event at the trade show tomorrow morning) 알리고 있으므로 (D)가 정답이다.

어휘 production 제조, 생산 plant 공장 meet with (약속하여) ~와 만나다 shareholder 주주 attend ~에 참석하다 launch 출시, 공개

49 What is mentioned about some products?
(A) They are affordably priced.
(B) They are very durable.
(C) They use less power.
(D) They have won awards.

일부 제품과 관련해 무엇이 언급되는가?
(A) 가격이 알맞게 책정되어 있다.
(B) 내구성이 매우 뛰어나다.
(C) 전력을 덜 사용한다.
(D) 여러 상을 받았다.

해설 〈기타 세부 사항을 묻는 문제〉
대화 맨 마지막에 남자 한 명이 자사의 냉장고 제품에 대해 시중에 나와 있는 다른 어떤 유사한 크기의 제품들보다 30퍼센트나 전력을 덜 사용한다는(The fridges use 30 percent less energy than any other similarly-sized products on the market) 특징을 설명하고 있으므로 (C)가 정답이다.

어휘 affordably priced 가격이 알맞게 책정된 durable 내구성이 좋은 less 덜 한, 더 적은 win an award 상을 받다

Questions 50-52 refer to the following conversation. (미M) (캐W)

M Connie, I just finished talking with the owner of 87 Smith Avenue about (50) our plans for the gardens there. She wants (50) our landscaping project to include a water fountain. She already chose the classic 3-tiered design she saw on our homepage.

W (51) The classic 3-tiered fountain is attractive, but I don't think the property is big enough to have the design. So, we need to look at the full layout and see if there's any way we can fit one in.

M Exactly. (52) I'll get in touch with Fred Wallace in our design team and see if he has any ideas. He visited the site with me yesterday and mentioned that there may be ways to use the space more efficiently.

남 코니 씨, 제가 방금 스미스 애비뉴 87번지의 소유주와 그곳 정원에 대한 우리 계획과 관련해 이야기하는 것을 마쳤습니다. 그분께서 우리 조경 프로젝트에 분수대를 포함하기를 원하세요. 우리 홈페이지에서 보신 클래식 3단 디자인을 이미 선택하셨습니다.

여 그 클래식 3단 분수대가 매력적이기는 하지만, 그 건물이 이 디자인을 넣을 만큼 충분히 크진 않은 것 같아요. 그래서, 전체적인 배치를 살펴보고 우리가 맞춰 넣을 수 있는 어떤 방법이든 있는지 알아 봐야 합니다.

남 맞아요. 제가 우리 디자인팀의 프레드 월러스 씨에게 연락해서 어떤 아이디어라도 있는지 알아 보겠습니다. 어제 저와 함께 그 장소를 방문했는데, 공간을 더 효율적으로 활용할 방법이 있을 수도 있다고 언급했거든요.

어휘 owner 소유주 plan 계획 landscaping 조경 include ~을 포함하다 water fountain 분수대 choose ~을 선택하다 3-tiered 3단으로 된 attractive 매력적인 property 건물, 부동산 enough to do ~하기에 충분히 layout 배치, 구획, 구성 fit A in A를 맞춰 넣다 get in touch with ~에게 연락하다 see if ~인지 알아 보다 site 장소, 부지, 현장 mention that ~라고 언급하다 way to do ~하는 방법 efficiently 효율적으로

50 What type of business is being discussed?
(A) A cleaning service
(B) A landscaping firm
(C) A Web design company
(D) A hardware store

어떤 종류의 업체가 이야기되고 있는가?
(A) 청소 서비스 업체
(B) 조경회사
(C) 웹 디자인 회사
(D) 철물점

해설 〈주제를 묻는 문제〉
대화 초반부에 남자가 자신과 여자를 our로 지칭해 정원에 대한 자신들의 계획(our plans for the gardens there)과 자신들이 맡은 조경 프로젝트를(our landscaping project) 언급하고 있다. 따라서 조경 업무를 진행하는 회사가 이야기되고 있다는 것을 알 수 있으므로 (B)가 정답이다.

51 Why does the woman say she is concerned?
(A) A project is behind schedule.
(B) A budget is limited.
(C) An item is sold out.
(D) An area is too small.

여자는 왜 우려된다고 말하는가?
(A) 프로젝트가 일정에 뒤처져 있다.
(B) 예산이 제한적이다.
(C) 제품이 품절되었다.
(D) 공간이 너무 작다.

해설 〈기타 세부 사항을 묻는 문제〉
대화 중반부에 여자가 클래식 3단 분수대를 언급하면서 그것이 매력적이기는 하지만 그 건물이 이 디자인을 넣을 만큼 충분히 크진 않은 것 같다고(The classic 3-tiered fountain is attractive, but I don't think the property is big enough to have the design) 언급하고 있다. 이는 작은 공간을 우려하는 말이므로 (D)가 정답이다.

어휘 concerned 우려되는, 걱정되는 behind schedule 일정에 뒤처진 budget 예산 limited 제한된, 한정된 sold out 품절된, 매진된

52 What does the man say he will do?
(A) Contact a coworker
(B) Prepare a cost estimate
(C) Visit a work site
(D) Change a schedule

남자는 무엇을 할 것이라고 말하는가?
(A) 동료 직원에게 연락하는 일
(B) 비용 견적서를 준비하는 일
(C) 작업 현장을 방문하는 일
(D) 일정을 변경하는 일

해설 〈미래에 할 일을 묻는 문제〉
대화 마지막 부분에 남자가 소속 회사 디자인팀의 프레드 월러스 씨에게 연락해서 어떤 아이디어라도 있는지 알아 보겠다고(I'll get in touch with Fred Wallace in our design team and see if he has any ideas) 말하고 있다. 이는 회사 동료 직원에게 연락하는 일을 말하는 것이므로 (A)가 정답이다.

어휘 contact ~에게 연락하다 coworker 동료 (직원) prepare ~을 준비하다 estimate n. 견적(서) site 현장, 장소, 부지

Questions 53-55 refer to the following conversation with three speakers. 캐W 호M 영W

W1 Good morning, Mr. Sherman. I'd like to ⑤⑥ introduce you to Carmen, who will be helping me prepare the food for your colleague's retirement party. We'll discuss the plan today to make sure we're all on the same page.

M That sounds great. ⑤④ I'd like to know how we should arrange the dining tables, chairs, and food tables.

W2 We'll need two long tables for our items, but other than that, you can do what you want.

W1 Carmen, ⑤⑤ why don't you show him some photos of past events so he can get some ideas?

여1 안녕하세요, 셔먼 씨. 동료 분의 은퇴 기념 파티에 필요한 음식을 준비하는 데 저를 도와주실 카르멘 씨를 소개해 드리고자 합니다. 우리 모두가 반드시 같은 내용을 공유하고 있도록 해 두기 위해 오늘 그 계획을 논의할 겁니다.

남 아주 좋은 것 같습니다. 우리가 어떻게 식탁과 의자, 그리고 음식용 탁자를 배치해야 하는지 알고 싶습니다.

여2 저희 음식 제품을 놓아 둘 긴 탁자가 2개 필요할 텐데, 그 외에는, 원하시는 대로 하셔도 됩니다.

여1 카르멘 씨, 아이디어를 좀 얻으실 수 있도록 과거의 행사 사진을 좀 보여 드리는 건 어떠세요?

어휘 would like to do ~하고자 하다, ~하고 싶다 introduce A to B A에게 B를 소개하다 help A do A가 ~하는 것을 돕다 prepare ~을 준비하다 colleague 동료 (직원) retirement 은퇴 discuss ~을 논의하다, 이야기하다 plan 계획 make sure (that) ~하는 것을 확실히 하다, 반드시 ~하도록 be on the same page 이해하고 있는 내용이 같다 arrange ~을 배치하다, 마련하다, 조정하다 other than ~ 외에는 why don't you ~? ~하는 게 어때요? show A B A에게 B를 보여 주다

53 Who most likely are the women?
(A) Designers
(B) Musicians
(C) Caterers
(D) Photographers
여자들은 누구일 것 같은가?
(A) 디자이너
(B) 음악가
(C) 출장 요리 공급업자
(D) 사진가

해설 〈직업을 묻는 문제〉
대화 시작 부분에 여자 한 명이 은퇴 파티에 필요한 음식을 준비하도록 자신에게 도움을 줄 카르멘 씨를 소개한다고(introduce you to Carmen, who will be helping me prepare the food for your colleague's retirement party) 알리고 있다. 따라서 여자들

은 요리와 관련된 서비스를 제공한다는 것을 알 수 있으므로 (C)가 정답이다.

54 What does the man want to know about?
(A) A furniture setup
(B) A delivery schedule
(C) A series of fees
(D) A cancellation period
남자는 무엇에 관해 알고 싶어 하는가?
(A) 가구 배치
(B) 배달 일정
(C) 일련의 요금
(D) 취소 기간

해설 〈기타 세부 사항을 묻는 문제〉
대화 중반부에 남자가 어떻게 식탁과 의자, 그리고 음식용 탁자를 배치해야 하는지 알고 싶다고(I'd like to know how we should arrange the dining tables, chairs, and food tables) 말하고 있는데, 이는 가구 배치를 뜻하므로 (A)가 정답이다.

어휘 setup 배치, 설치, 설정 a series of 일련의 cancellation 최소

55 What will the man most likely do next?
(A) Select some colors
(B) Wait for a manager
(C) Sign a contract
(D) Look at some photographs
남자는 곧이어 무엇을 할 것 같은가?
(A) 몇몇 색상을 선택하는 일
(B) 책임자를 기다리는 일
(C) 계약서에 서명하는 일
(D) 몇몇 사진을 살펴보는 일

해설 〈곧이어 할 일을 묻는 문제〉
대화 맨 마지막에 여자 한 명이 남자에게 과거의 행사 사진을 보여 주도록 카르멘 씨에게 권하고(why don't you show him some photos of past events) 있으므로 (D)가 정답이다.

어휘 select ~을 선택하다 contract 계약(서)

Questions 56-58 refer to the following conversation. 미M 영W

M Georgina, you're familiar with the Kruger account. ⑤⑥ I need the sales figures for the last quarter.

W ⑤⑦ Have you looked at the spreadsheets on our system?

M ⑤⑦ Yes, I did that an hour ago. The figures don't seem to be there for this period.

W ⑤⑧ Sue in Accounts must have forgotten to update them.

M I see. ⑤⑧ I need to e-mail her about a few other things anyway, so I will raise the issue with her. I'll do that right away.

남 조지나 씨, 당신이 크루거 거래처를 잘 아시잖아요. 지난 분기에 대한 판매 수치 자료가 필요합니다.

여 우리 시스템에 있는 스프레드시트는 확인해 보셨어요?

남 네, 한 시간 전에 그렇게 했어요. 이 기간에 대한 수치가 거기 있는 것 같지 않아요.

여 회계팀 수 씨가 업데이트하는 걸 깜빡 잊은 게 틀림없어요.

남 알겠습니다. 제가 어쨌든 몇 가지 다른 일로 그분께 이메일을 보내야 해서, 이 문제를 제기해 볼게요. 지금 바로 그렇게 하겠습니다.

어휘 be familiar with ~을 잘 알다, ~에 익숙하다 account 거래처, 고객사 sales 판매, 매출, 영업 figure 수치, 숫자 quarter 분기 spreadsheet 스프레드시트(표 계산 프로그램) seem to do ~하는 것 같다, ~하는 것처럼 보이다 Accounts 회계팀 must have p.p. ~한 게 틀림없다, 분명하다 forget to do ~하는 것을 잊다 anyway 어쨌든 raise an issue 문제를 제기하다 right away 지금 바로, 당장

56 Why does the man say, "Georgina, you're familiar with the Kruger account"?
(A) To make a complaint
(B) To place an order
(C) To thank the woman for her efforts
(D) To request some information
남자는 왜 "Georgina, you're familiar with the Kruger account"라고 말하는가?
(A) 불만을 제기하기 위해
(B) 주문을 하기 위해
(C) 여자의 노력에 대해 감사하기 위해
(D) 일부 정보를 요청하기 위해

해설 〈의도 파악 문제〉
남자가 대화를 시작하면서 '조지나 씨, 당신이 크루거 거래처를 잘 아시잖아요'라고 말한 뒤로 지난 분기에 대한 판매 수치 자료가 필요하다고(I need the sales figures for the last quarter) 알리고 있다. 이는 상대방인 여자에게 해당 수치 정보를 달라고 요청하는 것이므로 (D)가 정답이다.

어휘 make a complaint 불만을 제기하다, 불평하다 place an order 주문하다 effort 노력 request ~을 요청하다

57 What did the man do earlier?
(A) Proofread a proposal
(B) Checked a spreadsheet
(C) Made a phone call
(D) Visited a branch

남자는 이전에 무엇을 했는가?
(A) 제안서를 교정 보는 일
(B) 스프레드시트를 확인하는 일
(C) 전화를 거는 일
(D) 지점을 방문하는 일

해설 〈과거에 일어난 일을 묻는 문제〉
대화 초반부에 여자가 회사 시스템이 있는 스프레드시트를 확인해 봤는지(Have you looked at the spreadsheets on our system?) 물은 것에 대해 남자가 한 시간 전에 했다고(Yes, I did that an hour ago) 알리고 있으므로 (B)가 정답이다.

어휘 proofread ~을 교정 보다 proposal 제안(서) spreadsheet 스프레드시트(표 계산 프로그램) make a phone call 전화하다 branch 지점, 지사

58 What will the man most likely do next?
(A) Perform some calculations
(B) Read a document
(C) E-mail a colleague
(D) Produce a presentation

남자는 곧이어 무엇을 할 것 같은가?
(A) 몇 가지 계산을 해 보는 일
(B) 문서를 읽어 보는 일
(C) 동료에게 이메일을 보내는 일
(D) 발표 자료를 만드는 일

해설 〈곧이어 할 일을 묻는 문제〉
대화 후반부에 여자가 회계팀의 수 씨를 언급하자, 남자가 그 사람을 her로 지칭하면서 다른 일들로 이메일을 보내야 한다고(I need to e-mail her about a few other things anyway) 알리고 있으므로 (C)가 정답이다.

어휘 perform ~을 수행하다, 실시하다 calculation 계산 colleague 동료 (직원) produce ~을 만들어내다 presentation 발표

Questions 59-61 refer to the following conversation. 호M 캐W

M Can I ask for your help, Karina? I need to arrange the conference room for ⑤⑨ the job interview scheduled for ten o'clock.
W Are you having trouble with something?
M Yes. ⑥⓪ When I scan my ID card on the sensor, the door doesn't open.
W Have you updated your ID?
M No. It's the one I've always used.
W That's why you're locked out. The system has just been updated, so ⑥① you should get a replacement card from the security team. But I can let you in for now.
M OK, thanks. And I'll take care of that this afternoon.

남 도움을 요청해도 될까요, 카리나 씨? 제가 10시로 예정된 구직자 면접 때문에 회의실을 정리해야 해서요.
여 무슨 문제라도 겪고 계신가요?
남 네, 센서에 제 사원증을 스캔할 때 문이 열리지 않아요.
여 사원증은 업데이트해 보셨어요?
남 아니요. 항상 사용하던 것이에요.
여 그래서 들어가지 못하는 거예요. 시스템이 막 업데이트되었기 때문에 보안팀에서 대체 카드를 받으셔야 해요. 하지만 일단은 제가 들어가시도록 해드릴 수 있어요.
남 네, 감사합니다. 그리고 오늘 오후에 그 부분을 처리하겠습니다.

어휘 ask for ~을 요청하다 arrange ~을 정리하다, 마련하다, 조치하다 scheduled for + 날짜/시간 ~로 예정된 have trouble with ~에 문제가 있다, ~로 어려움을 겪다 be locked out 열고 들어가지 못하는 상태이다 replacement 대체(품) let A in A를 들여보내다 for now 일단은, 지금으로서는, 당분간은

59 What will happen at ten o'clock?
(A) An item will be delivered.
(B) A team meeting will be held.
(C) An interview will be conducted.
(D) A client will visit.

10시에 무슨 일이 있을 것인가?
(A) 물품이 배송될 것이다.
(B) 회의가 열릴 것이다.
(C) 면접이 실시될 것이다.
(D) 고객이 방문할 것이다.

해설 〈특정 시점의 일을 묻는 문제〉
대화 초반부에 남자가 10시로 예정된 구직자 면접(the job interview scheduled for ten o'clock)을 언급하고 있으므로 (C)가 정답이다.

어휘 hold ~을 개최하다, 열다 conduct ~을 실시하다, 수행하다

60 What problem does the man mention?
(A) He cannot access a room.
(B) He needs help setting up equipment.
(C) His schedule contained an error.
(D) His parking pass has expired.

남자는 어떤 문제를 언급하는가?
(A) 방에 출입할 수 없다.
(B) 장비를 설치하는 데 도움이 필요하다.
(C) 일정표에 오류가 있었다.
(D) 주차권이 만료되었다.

해설 〈문제점을 묻는 문제〉
남자가 대화 중반부에 사원증을 스캔해도 문이 열리지 않는다는 (When I scan my ID card on the sensor, the door doesn't open) 문제점을 말하고 있으므로 (A)가 정답이다.

어휘 access ~에 출입하다, ~을 이용하다 set up ~을 설치하다, 설정하다, 준비하다 equipment 장비 contain ~을 포함하다, 담고 있다 parking pass 주차권 expire 만료되다

61 What does the woman suggest doing?
(A) Hiring an assistant
(B) Replacing an ID card
(C) Postponing an event
(D) Reading a user manual

여자는 무엇을 하도록 권하는가?
(A) 보조 직원을 고용하는 일
(B) 사원증을 교체하는 일
(C) 행사를 연기하는 일
(D) 사용 설명서를 읽어 보는 일

해설 〈제안 사항을 묻는 문제〉
대화 후반부에 여자가 보안팀에서 대체 카드를 받아야 한다고(you should get a replacement card from the security team) 알리고 있으므로 (B)가 정답이다.

어휘 hire ~을 고용하다 assistant 보조, 조수, 비서 replace ~을 교체하다 postpone ~을 연기하다, 미루다 user manual 사용 설명서

W Welcome to the Park Valley Music Festival. Do you need some assistance?

M Yes, please. I just arrived here, and ⑫ I know the festival is finishing in a couple of hours. I want to use my time wisely, so can you tell me where to go to see some bands?

W Well, ⑬ there are still a few bands scheduled to perform on the Pop Music Stage, so I'd suggest heading over there. You can take this map of the festival site.

M Thanks a lot. Is the ground muddy there?

W Well, ⑭ you chose a perfect time to arrive because the rain has finally stopped and the sun is shining, but the ground might still be a bit muddy.

Red Stage: Rock Music	Restroom	Blue Stage: Dance Music
Information Center		
Green Stage: Jazz Music		⑬ Yellow Stage: Pop Music

Entrance

여 파크 밸리 음악 축제에 오신 것을 환영합니다. 도움이 필요하신가요?

남 네, 그렇습니다. 제가 이곳에 막 도착했는데, 축제가 두어 시간 후에 끝나는 것으로 알고 있습니다. 제 시간을 현명하게 쓰기를 원하기 때문에 어디로 가면 몇몇 밴드들을 볼 수 있는지 알려 주시겠어요?

여 음, 팝 뮤직 무대에서 공연할 예정인 몇몇 밴드들이 여전히 있기 때문에 그쪽으로 건너가 보시길 권해 드리고 싶습니다. 이 축제 장소 약도를 가져가시면 됩니다.

남 정말 감사합니다. 그쪽 땅바닥이 진흙투성이인가요?

여 음, 비가 드디어 그치고 해가 나고 있기 때문에 완벽한 시간을 선택해 도착하시긴 했지만, 땅바닥이 여전히 좀 진흙투성이일 수 있습니다.

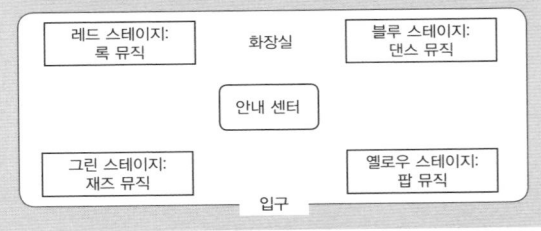

레드 스테이지: 록 뮤직	화장실	블루 스테이지: 댄스 뮤직
안내 센터		
그린 스테이지: 재즈 뮤직		옐로우 스테이지: 팝 뮤직

입구

어휘 assistance 도움, 지원 arrive 도착하다 in + 시간 ~ 후에 wisely 현명하게 where to do 도움, ~하는 곳 scheduled to do ~할 예정인 suggest -ing ~하도록 권하다, 제안하다 head over there 그쪽으로 건너가다 site 장소,

---

현장, 부지 muddy 진흙투성이인 choose ~을 선택하다 a bit 조금, 약간

62 What problem does the man mention?
(A) A performance was canceled.
(B) The festival will end soon.
(C) A festival ticket is missing.
(D) The information center is closed.

남자는 무슨 문제를 언급하는가?
(A) 공연이 취소되었다.
(B) 축제가 곧 끝날 것이다.
(C) 축제 입장권이 없는 상태이다.
(D) 안내 센터가 문을 닫았다.

해설 〈문제점을 묻는 문제〉
대화 초반부에 남자가 막 도착한 사실과 함께 축제가 두어 시간 후에 끝나는 것으로 알고 있다고(I know the festival is finishing in a couple of hours) 언급하고 있으므로 (B)가 정답이다.

어휘 cancel ~을 취소하다 missing 없는, 사라진, 빠진

63 Look at the graphic. Which stage of the music festival will the man go to?
(A) Red Stage
(B) Blue Stage
(C) Green Stage
(D) Yellow Stage

시각 자료를 보시오. 남자는 음악 축제의 어느 무대로 갈 것인가?
(A) 레드 스테이지
(B) 블루 스테이지
(C) 그린 스테이지
(D) 옐로우 스테이지

해설 〈배치도 문제〉
대화 중반부에 여자가 팝 뮤직 무대에서 공연할 예정인 몇몇 밴드들이 있다고 말하면서 그쪽으로 가 보기를 권하고 있다(there are still a few bands scheduled to perform on the Pop Music Stage, so I'd suggest heading there). 배치도에서 팝 뮤직이 쓰여 있는 곳이 옐로우 스테이지(Yesllow Stage: Pop Music)이므로 (D)가 정답이다.

64 Why does the woman say it is a perfect time to arrive at the festival?
(A) The site is less crowded now.
(B) The weather has improved.
(C) The tickets have been discounted.
(D) The main performance has just begun.

여자는 왜 지금이 축제 장소에 도착하기에 완벽한 시간이라고 말하는가?
(A) 장소가 지금 덜 붐비고 있다.
(B) 날씨가 나아졌다.
(C) 입장권이 할인되었다.
(D) 주요 공연이 막 시작되었다.

해설 〈기타 세부 사항을 묻는 문제〉
대화 후반부에 여자가 완벽한 시점에 도착했음을 언급하면서 그 이유로 비가 그치고 해가 나고 있기 때문이라고(you chose a perfect time to arrive because the rain has finally stopped and the sun is shining) 알리고 있으므로 (B)가 정답이다.

어휘 site 장소, 현장, 부지 crowded 붐비는 improve 나아지다, 개선되다

Questions 65-67 refer to the following conversation and schedule. 호M 캐W

M I was surprised that the afternoon sessions of the conference were canceled, but it gives us some time to go sightseeing. ⑮ It would be fun to visit Harper Studio. That's where they film a lot of popular TV shows.

W I would love to go there.

M ⑯ But we have to be back in time for this evening's keynote speech.

W We won't be very far from the conference hall, so that shouldn't be a problem. Now, let's check the ticket availability on my smartphone. Hmm, it looks like ⑰ this tour has four tickets still available. How about going at that time?

M That sounds great to me.

Guided Tour	Remaining Tickets
1:00 P.M.	Sold Out
⑰ 2:30 P.M.	4 tickets
4:00 P.M.	2 tickets
5:30 P.M.	8 tickets

남 컨퍼런스의 오후 시간들이 취소되어서 놀랍지만, 우리에게는 관광을 할 수 있는 시간이 좀 생기네요. 하퍼 스튜디오를 방문하면 재미있을 거예요. 그곳은 많은 인기 TV 프로그램을 촬영하는 곳이잖아요.

여 저도 꼭 그곳에 가 보고 싶어요.

남 하지만 오늘 저녁에 있을 기조 연설 시간에 맞춰 다시 돌아와야 합니다.

여 우리가 컨퍼런스 홀에서 그렇게 멀리 떨어져 있지는 않을 것이기 때문에 그건 문제가 되지 않을 겁니다. 자, 제 스마트폰으로 티켓 구매 가능 여부를 확인해 보겠습니다. 이 투어에 티켓 4장이 아직 구매 가능한 것 같아요. 이 시간에 가는 게 어떠세요?

남 저는 아주 좋습니다.

가이드 동반 투어	남은 티켓
오후 1:00	매진
오후 2:30	4장
오후 4:00	2장
오후 5:30	8장

be surprised that ∼해서 놀라다 session (특정 활동을 위한) 시간
cancel ∼을 취소하다 go sightseeing 관광하러 가다 film ∼을 촬영하다
popular 인기 있는 in time for ∼ 시간에 맞춰 keynote speech 기조 연
설 far from ∼에 멀리 떨어진 availability 이용 가능성 it looks like ∼인
것 같다 available 구매 가능한, 이용 가능한 How about -ing? ∼하는 게
어때요? guided 가이드가 동반된 remaining 남아 있는 sold out 매진된,
품절된

65 What are the speakers interested in visiting?
(A) A science museum
(B) A sports venue
(C) A historic home
(D) A television studio

화자들은 무엇을 방문하는 데 관심이 있는가?
(A) 과학 박물관
(B) 스포츠 행사장
(C) 역사적인 주택
(D) 텔레비전 스튜디오

해설 〈기타 세부 사항을 묻는 문제〉
대화 초반부에, 남자가 하퍼 스튜디오를 말하면서 인기 TV 프로그램
을 촬영하는 곳이라고(It would be fun to visit Harper Studio.
That's where they film a lot of popular TV shows) 알리고 있
으므로 (D)가 정답이다.

어휘 be interested in ∼하는 데 관심이 있다 venue 행사장, 개최 장소
historic 역사적인

66 What do the speakers have to do?
(A) Bring a room key
(B) Make a dinner reservation
(C) Attend a speech
(D) Check a shuttle time

화자들은 무엇을 해야 하는가?
(A) 객실 열쇠를 가져가는 일
(B) 저녁 식사를 예약하는 일
(C) 연설에 참석하는 일
(D) 셔틀버스 시간을 확인하는 일

해설 〈기타 세부 사항을 묻는 문제〉
대화 중반부에 남자가 저녁에 있을 기조 연설 시간에 맞춰 다시 돌아가
야 한다고(But we have to be back in time for this evening's
keynote speech) 알리고 있으므로 (C)가 정답이다.

어휘 make a reservation 예약하다 attend ∼에 참석하다

67 Look at the graphic. When do the speakers want to go on
a tour?
(A) 1:00 P.M.
(B) 2:30 P.M.
(C) 4:00 P.M.
(D) 5:30 P.M.

시각 자료를 보시오. 화자들은 언제 투어를 하고 싶어 하는가?
(A) 오후 1시
(B) 오후 2시 30분
(C) 오후 4시
(D) 오후 5시 30분

해설 〈2열 도표 문제〉
대화 후반부에 여자가 티켓 4장이 남아 있는 투어를(∼ this tour has
four tickets still available) 언급하고 있는데, 시각 자료에서 4장으
로 표기된 시간이 2:30 P.M.이므로 (B)가 정답이다.

Questions 68-70 refer to the following conversation and sign. (M)(W)

M 68 I think dumping the old household appliances
ourselves is a good idea. It will be less time-consuming
than having our client do it.
W Yes. But, it looks like this landfill is closed right now. 69
The sign says no dumping between 9 A.M. and 4 P.M.
Let's go to the Eastside Landfill instead.
M We'd better hurry over there then. 70 We still need to go
back and redo the client's kitchen floor.

NO DUMPING!
Monday-Thursday: 6 P.M. to 9 A.M.
69 Friday: 9 A.M. to 4 P.M.
Saturday: 5 P.M. to 8 A.M.
Sunday: 9 A.M. to 8 P.M.

남 우리가 직접 낡은 가전제품을 버리는 게 좋은 생각인 것 같아요. 이게 우리
고객에게 하도록 하는 것보다 시간이 덜 소모될 거예요.
여 네. 하지만. 이 매립지가 지금 문을 닫은 것 같아요. 표지판에 오전 9시에서
오후 4시 사이에는 쓰레기를 버리지 말라고 쓰여 있어요. 대신 이스트사이
드 매립지로 가 봐요.
남 그럼 서둘러 그쪽으로 가는 게 좋을 거예요. 여전히 다시 돌아가서 고객의
주방 바닥을 다시 깔아야 하잖아요.

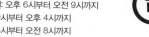

쓰레기를 버리지 마시오!
월요일—목요일: 오후 6시부터 오전 9시까지
금요일: 오전 9시부터 오후 4시까지
토요일: 오후 5시부터 오전 8시까지
일요일: 오전 9시부터 오후 8시까지

어휘 dump ∼을 버리다 household appliances 가전제품 oneself (부사처
럼 쓰여) 직접 time-consuming 시간이 소모되는 have A do A에게 ∼하
게 하다 it looks like ∼인 것 같다 landfill (쓰레기) 매립지 sign 표지(판)
between A and B A와 B 사이에 instead 대신 had better do ∼하는
게 좋다 hurry over there 서둘러 그쪽으로 가다 redo the floor 바닥을 다
시 깔다

68 Why did the man decide to dump the appliances himself?
(A) To avoid a fee
(B) To save time
(C) To help a colleague
(D) To thank a client

남자는 왜 직접 가전제품을 버리기로 결정하는가?
(A) 수수료를 피하기 위해
(B) 시간을 절약하기 위해
(C) 동료를 돕기 위해
(D) 고객에게 감사하기 위해

해설 〈기타 세부 사항을 묻는 문제〉
대화를 시작하면서 남자가 고객들에게 하도록 하는 것보다 자신들이
직접 낡은 가전제품을 버리는 게 좋은 생각이라고(I think dumping
the old household appliances ourselves is a good idea. It
will be less time-consuming than having our client do it)
언급하고 있다. 이는 시간 절약 문제를 말하는 것이므로 (B)가 정답이
다.

어휘 decide to do ∼하기로 결정하다 oneself (부사처럼 쓰여) 직접, 스스
로 avoid ∼을 피하다 fee 요금, 수수료 colleague 동료 (직원)

69 Look at the graphic. What day is it?
(A) Thursday
(B) Friday
(C) Saturday
(D) Sunday

시각 자료를 보시오. 오늘은 무슨 요일인가?
(A) 목요일
(B) 금요일
(C) 토요일
(D) 일요일

해설 〈2열 도표 문제〉
대화 중반부에 여자가 표지판에 오전 9시에서 오후 4시 사이에는 쓰
레기를 버리지 말라고 쓰여 있다고(The sign says no dumping
between 9 A.M. and 4 P.M.) 언급하고 있다. 표지판에서 오전 9시
에서 오후 4시 사이에 해당되는 요일이 금요일로(Friday: 9 A.M. to
4 P.M.) 표기되어 있으므로 (B)가 정답이다.

70 According to the man, what do the speakers still need to
do?
(A) Order materials
(B) Pick up tools
(C) Replace some flooring
(D) Install a device

남자의 말에 따르면, 화자들은 여전히 무엇을 해야 하는가?
(A) 자재를 주문하는 일
(B) 공구를 가져오는 일
(C) 바닥재를 교체하는 일
(D) 기기를 설치하는 일

해설 〈기타 세부 사항을 묻는 문제〉
대화 후반부에 남자가 다시 돌아가서 고객의 주방 바닥을 다시 깔아야 한다고(We still need to go back and redo the client's kitchen floor) 알리고 있으므로 (C)가 정답이다.

어휘 order ~을 주문하다 material 자재, 재료, 물품 pick up ~을 가져오다, 가져가다 tool 공구, 도구 replace ~을 교체하다 flooring 바닥재 install ~을 설치하다

PART 4
P109

Questions 71-73 refer to the following announcement. 호M

May I have your attention, please? ㉛ Passengers are advised that Flight 431 to Beijing has been delayed. Unfortunately, ㉜ the incoming flight on this route arrived late, and we need time for cleaning and refueling. The new departure time is 5:45 P.M. We'll make another announcement when we're ready to board. At that time, ㉝ please have your boarding pass ready to show it to the gate agents. Thank you.

잠시 주목해 주시겠습니까? 탑승객들께서는 베이징행 431 항공편이 지연되었다는 점에 유의하시기 바랍니다. 유감스럽게도, 이 노선의 입국 항공편이 늦게 도착했으며, 기내 청소 및 급유를 위한 시간이 필요합니다. 새로운 출발 시각은 오후 5시 45분입니다. 탑승 준비가 되면 다시 한 번 공지해 드리겠습니다. 그때, 탑승구 직원에게 보여 드릴 탑승권을 준비해 주시기 바랍니다. 감사합니다.

어휘 be advised that ~임에 유의하다, ~임을 명심하다 delay ~을 지연시키다 unfortunately 유감스럽게도, 안타깝게도 incoming 들어오는, 도착하는 route 노선, 경로 arrive 도착하다 refueling 급유 departure 출발, 떠남 make an announcement 공지하다, 발표하다 be ready to do ~할 준비가 되다 board 탑승하다 have A ready A를 준비하다 boarding pass 탑승권

71 Where most likely are the listeners?
(A) At an airport
(B) At a taxi stand
(C) At a bus stop
(D) At a train station
청자들은 어디에 있을 것 같은가?
(A) 공항에
(B) 택시 승강장에
(C) 버스 정류장에
(D) 기차역에

---

72 What has caused a delay?
(A) Severe weather
(B) A late arrival
(C) A computer error
(D) An employee absence
무엇이 지연을 초래했는가?
(A) 극심한 날씨
(B) 늦은 도착
(C) 컴퓨터 오류
(D) 직원 부재

해설 〈문제 원인을 묻는 문제〉
담화 중반부에 항공편 지연의 원인으로 해당 노선의 입국 항공편이 늦게 도착한(the incoming flight on this route arrived late) 사실을 알리고 있으므로 (B)가 정답이다.

어휘 cause ~을 초래하다, 야기하다 severe 극심한 arrival 도착 absence 부재, 결근

73 What are the listeners asked to prepare?
(A) A government ID
(B) A luggage tag
(C) A sales receipt
(D) A boarding pass
청자들은 무엇을 준비하도록 요청받는가?
(A) 정부 발급 신분증
(B) 수하물 꼬리표
(C) 판매 영수증
(D) 탑승권

해설 〈요청 사항을 묻는 문제〉
담화 맨 마지막에 탑승구 직원에게 보여 줄 탑승권을 준비하도록(please have your boarding pass ready) 요청하고 있으므로 (D)가 정답이다.

어휘 prepare ~을 준비하다 sales 판매, 영업, 매출 receipt 영수증

Questions 74-76 refer to the following broadcast. 캐W

You're listening to the local news update. At last night's city council meeting, the Henning Property Development firm outlined its ㉔ proposal to build an upscale shopping complex here in Highgate. City officials are overwhelmingly in favor of the idea. ㉕ They believe that the project will bring a lot more tax income to the city. However, some residents are concerned about increased traffic congestion. On the show with me today, I have city council member Glenda Rooney and local activist Dwayne Jennings, ㉖ who will debate this topic. That's all coming up right now.

여러분은 최신 지역 뉴스를 청취하고 계십니다. 어젯밤 시의회 회의 시간에 헤닝 부동산 개발 회사는 이곳 하이게이트에 고급 쇼핑몰을 건설하자는 내용의 제안서를 개괄적으로 설명했습니다. 시 관계자들은 압도적으로 이 제안에 찬성하고 있습니다. 관계자들은 이 프로젝트가 시에 훨씬 더 많은 세입을 안겨 줄 것으로 생각하고 있습니다. 하지만 일부 주민들은 교통 체증 증가를 우려하고 있습니다. 오늘 이 시간에 시의회의 글렌다 루니 의원과 지역 운동가 드웨인 제닝스 씨를 모시고 이 주제로 토론해 보겠습니다. 지금 바로 이어가겠습니다.

어휘 local 지역의, 현지의 council 의회 firm 회사, 업체 outline ~을 개괄적으로 말하다 proposal 제안(서) upscale 고급의 official 관계자, 당국자 overwhelmingly 압도적으로 in favor of ~에 찬성하여 tax income 세입 resident 주민 be concerned about ~에 대해 우려하다 increased 증가된, 늘어난 traffic congestion 교통 체증 activist 운동가, 활동가 debate ~을 토론하다 come up (다음 순서로) 이어지다, 다가오다

74 What is the topic of the broadcast?
(A) A highway project
(B) A shopping center
(C) A sport stadium
(D) A manufacturing facility
방송의 주제는 무엇인가?
(A) 고속도로 프로젝트
(B) 쇼핑 센터
(C) 스포츠 경기장
(D) 제조 시설

해설 〈주제를 묻는 문제〉
담화 초반부에 화자가 고급 쇼핑몰 건설 제안이 있었다고(proposal to build an upscale shopping complex) 언급한 뒤로 해당 제안과 관련된 정보를 전달하는 것으로 담화를 진행하고 있으므로 (B)가 정답이다.

어휘 manufacturing 제조 facility 시설(물)

75 According to the broadcast, what benefit do city officials expect?
(A) Tax revenues will increase.
(B) Pollution will be reduced.

(C) New jobs will be created.
(D) Residents will be healthier.

방송 내용에 따르면, 시 관계자들은 어떤 이점을 기대하고 있는가?
(A) 세수가 증가될 것이다.
(B) 오염이 감소될 것이다.
(C) 새로운 일자리가 창출될 것이다.
(D) 주민들이 더 건강해질 것이다.

해설 〈기타 세부 사항을 묻는 문제〉
시 관계자들이 언급되는 중반부에 더 많은 세입이 생길 것으로 생각한다는(They believe that the project will bring a lot more tax income) 점을 밝히고 있으므로 (A)가 정답이다.

어휘 revenue 수입, 수익 increase 증가되다, 늘어나다 pollution 오염 reduce 감소되다, 줄어들다 create ~을 만들어내다 resident 주민

76 What will be broadcast next?
(A) A traffic update
(B) A weather report
(C) An advertisement
(D) A debate

다음 순서로 무엇이 방송될 것인가?
(A) 교통 소식
(B) 일기 예보
(C) 광고
(D) 토론

해설 〈곧이어 할 일을 묻는 문제〉
담화 맨 마지막에 초대 손님과 함께 한 가지 주제로 토론한다고 언급하면서 그 토론이 바로 이어진다고(who will debate this topic. That's all coming up right now) 알리고 있으므로 (D)가 정답이다.

Questions 77-79 refer to the following announcement. 영W

Attention, members. I'd like to draw your attention to ⑰ our range of new treadmills and exercise bikes located at the back of the room. ⑱ We also have one case of the new sports drink, Reboot, to give away for free. You can collect one bottle from our reception desk, but be aware this is only while stocks last. Finally, make sure you have submitted your online application to enter ⑲ our competition to win a free set of weights. The draw will take place at 6 P.M. today and the winner will be notified by e-mail.

주목해 주십시오, 회원 여러분. 뒤쪽 공간에 위치해 있는 새로운 종류의 저희 러닝머신과 운동용 자전거에 주목해 주셨으면 합니다. 또한 무료로 증정해 드릴 새 스포츠 음료 리부트 한 상자도 있습니다. 저희 안내 데스크에서 한 병 받아 가실 수 있지만, 이는 오직 물품이 남아 있는 동안에만 해당된다는 점에 유의하시기 바랍니다. 마지막으로, 온라인 신청서를 제출하셔서 무료 웨이트 기구 한 세트를 받으실 수 있는 행사 대회에 꼭 참가하시기 바랍니다. 이 추첨 행사는 오늘 오후 6시에 있을 예정이며, 당첨자는 이메일로 통보됩니다.

79 What will happen at 6 P.M.?
(A) A discount sale

어휘 would like to do ~하고자 하다, ~하고 싶다 draw one's attention to ~에 주목하게 하다, ~에 관심을 갖게 만들다 range 종류, 범위, 제품군 treadmill 러닝머신 located at ~에 위치한 give away ~을 증정하다, 나눠 주다 for free 무료로 collect ~을 받아 가다, 가지러 가다 reception desk 안내 데스크 be aware (that) ~임에 유의하다 while ~하는 동안 last v. 지속되다 make sure (that) 꼭 ~하다, ~하는 것을 확실히 해 두다 submit ~을 제출하다 application 신청(서), 지원(서) enter ~에 참가하다 competition 행사, 대회, 경연대회 free 무료의 weight 웨이트 기구 draw 추첨 (행사) take place (일, 행사 등이) 발생되다, 개최되다 notify ~에게 통보하다

77 Where most likely does the speaker work?
(A) At a factory
(B) At a library
(C) At a health club
(D) At a supermarket

화자는 어디에서 일하고 있을 것 같은가?
(A) 공장에서
(B) 도서관에서
(C) 헬스 클럽에서
(D) 슈퍼마켓에서

해설 〈근무지를 묻는 문제〉
담화 시작 부분에 화자가 뒤쪽 공간에 위치해 있는 새로운 종류의 저희 러닝머신과 운동용 자전거에 주목해 달라고(our range of new treadmills and exercise bikes located at the back of the room) 요청하고 있는데, 이는 헬스 클럽에서 볼 수 있는 물품들이므로 (C)가 정답이다.

78 What can the listeners receive for a limited time?
(A) A drink
(B) A membership card
(C) A t-shirt
(D) A catalog

청자들은 제한된 시간에 무엇을 받을 수 있는가?
(A) 음료
(B) 회원 카드
(C) 티셔츠
(D) 카탈로그

해설 〈기타 세부 사항을 묻는 문제〉
담화 중반부에 화자가 무료로 증정하는 스포츠 음료가 한 상자 있다는 말과 함께 안내 데스크에서 받을 수 있고 물품이 남아 있는 동안에만 해당된다고(We also have one case of the new sports drink, ~ collect one bottle from our reception desk, but be aware this is only while stocks last) 알리고 있으므로 (A)가 정답이다.

어휘 receive ~을 받다 limited 제한된, 한정된

79 What will happen at 6 P.M.?
(A) A discount sale

(B) A prize draw
(C) Web site maintenance
(D) An orientation class

오후 6시에 무슨 일이 있을 것인가?
(A) 할인 판매 행사
(B) 경품 추첨
(C) 웹 사이트 유지 보수 작업
(D) 오리엔테이션 강좌

해설 〈특정 시점의 일을 묻는 문제〉
담화 후반부에 무료 웨이트 기구 한 세트를 받을 수 있는 행사가 있다는 점과 그 추첨 행사가 오후 6시에 있을 것이라고(our competition to win a free set of weights. The draw will take place at 6 P.M.) 알리고 있으므로 (B)가 정답이다.

어휘 prize 경품, 상품 maintenance 유지 보수, 시설 관리

Questions 80-82 refer to the following telephone message. 호M

Hi. My name is Simon Andrews, and ⑳ I'm calling from Palm Acres Resort. We have a number of vegetarian customers staying with us this weekend and ㉑ I'm looking to purchase some fresh vegetables to use when preparing their meals. I know you are able to provide a range of exotic fruit and vegetables that may be hard to find elsewhere. ㉒ I would need to receive everything by Friday. Could you please call my office to let me know whether this is possible? My number is 555-3092.

안녕하세요. 제 이름은 사이먼 앤드류스이며, 팜 에이커즈 리조트에서 전화 드립니다. 이번 주말에 저희 리조트에서 머무르시는 채식주의자 고객들이 많이 계셔서, 그분들 식사를 준비할 때 사용할 신선한 채소를 좀 구입할 예정입니다. 귀사에서 다른 곳에서는 찾기 힘들 수 있는 다양한 이국적인 과일과 채소를 제공해 주실 수 있는 것으로 알고 있습니다. 제가 금요일까지 모두 받아야 할 겁니다. 제 사무실로 전화 주셔서 이것이 가능한지 알려 주시겠습니까? 제 전화번호는 555-3092입니다.

어휘 a number of 많은 (수의) vegetarian 채식주의자 look to do ~할 예정이다 purchase ~을 구입하다 prepare ~을 준비하다 be able to do ~할 수 있다 provide ~을 제공하다 a range of 다양한 exotic 이국적인 elsewhere 다른 곳에서 receive ~을 받다 by (기한) ~까지 let A know A에게 알리다 whether ~인지 (아닌지)

80 What kind of business does the speaker work for?
(A) A delivery company
(B) A cell phone provider
(C) A supermarket
(D) A vacation resort

화자는 어떤 종류의 업체에서 일하는가?

(A) 배송 회사
(B) 휴대전화 제공 업체
(C) 슈퍼마켓
(D) 휴양지 리조트

해설 〈근무지를 묻는 문제〉
담화 시작 부분에 화자가 이름과 함께 I'm calling from Palm Acres Resort라는 말로 리조트가 소속 업체임을 밝히고 있으므로 (D)가 정답이다.

81 Why is the speaker calling?
(A) To hire some staff members
(B) To purchase some ingredients
(C) To confirm business hours
(D) To return an order

화자는 왜 전화하는가?
(A) 몇몇 직원을 고용하기 위해
(B) 몇몇 재료를 구입하기 위해
(C) 영업 시간을 확정하기 위해
(D) 주문품을 반품하기 위해

해설 〈목적을 묻는 문제〉
담화 중반부에 손님들 식사를 준비할 때 사용할 신선한 채소를 좀 구입할 예정이라고(I'm looking to purchase some fresh vegetables to use when preparing their meals) 밝히고 있는데, 이는 음식 재료를 구입하겠다는 뜻이므로 (B)가 정답이다.

어휘 hire ~을 고용하다 purchase ~을 구입하다 ingredient (음식) 재료, 성분 confirm ~을 확인해 주다, 확정하다 business hours 영업 시간 return ~을 반품하다, 반납하다 order 주문(품)

82 Why does the speaker request a phone call?
(A) To negotiate a price
(B) To reply to a complaint
(C) To confirm a delivery date
(D) To inquire about a business location

화자는 왜 전화 통화를 요청하는가?
(A) 가격을 협의하기 위해
(B) 불만 사항에 답변하기 위해
(C) 배달 날짜를 확인해 두기 위해
(D) 업체 위치에 관해 문의하기 위해

해설 〈기타 세부 사항을 묻는 문제〉
담화 후반부에 금요일까지 모두 받아야 한다고 알리면서 그것이 가능한지 전화해서 알려 달라고(I would need to receive everything by Friday. Could you please call my office to let me know whether this is possible?) 요청하고 있다. 이는 물품을 받을 날짜를 확인하려는 것이므로 (C)가 정답이다.

어휘 negotiate ~을 협의하다, 협상하다 reply to ~에 답변하다 complaint 불만, 불평 confirm ~을 확인해 주다 inquire about ~에 관해 문의하다 location 위치, 지점

Questions 83-85 refer to the following excerpt from a meeting.
영W

Good morning, everyone. Thank you for coming in before your usual shift. **83** I realize that you have some tasks to do after this meeting. You should have no problem starting work at nine. **84** Last week, we had an expert visit our bakery and evaluate our financial data. He determined that we could improve our profits by focusing on our custom-decorated cakes. We'd like all of you to help increase the sales of these cakes. Now, I understand that you may not feel comfortable **85** introducing our decorating options and encouraging customers to use this service. Therefore, **85** we're going to role-play a discussion with a customer now so that you can get some practice.

안녕하세요, 여러분. 여러분의 정규 교대 근무 시간에 앞서 와 주셔서 감사합니다. 여러분께서 이 회의 이후에 하셔야 할 업무들이 있다는 것을 알고 있습니다. 여러분께서 9시에 일을 시작하시는 데 아무런 문제도 없을 것입니다. 지난주에 우리 제과점에 전문가 한 분께서 방문하셔서 우리의 재무 자료를 평가해 주셨습니다. 그분께서는 우리가 맞춤 제작으로 장식되는 케이크에 초점을 맞추는 방법으로 수익을 개선할 수 있을 것이라고 결정을 내리셨습니다. 우리는 여러분 모두가 이 케이크 제품의 매출을 증대하는 데 도움을 주셨으면 합니다. 자, 저는 여러분이 우리의 장식 옵션을 소개하고 고객들에게 이 서비스를 이용하도록 권장하는 일이 편하게 느껴지지 않을 수 있다는 것을 알고 있습니다. 따라서, 여러분께서 연습을 좀 하실 수 있도록 고객 한 분과 함께 역할극 토론 시간을 갖도록 하겠습니다.

어휘 usual 보통의, 평상시의 shift 교대 근무(조) realize that ~임을 알게 되다, 깨닫다 task 업무, 일 have A do A에게 ~하게 하다 expert 전문가 evaluate ~을 평가하다 financial 재무의, 재정의 determine that ~라고 결정하다 improve ~을 개선하다 profit 수익 by (방법) ~함으로써 focus on ~에 초점을 맞추다 custom-decorated 맞춤 제작으로 장식되는, 주문 제작 방식으로 장식되는 would like A to do A에게 ~하기를 원하다 help do ~하는 것을 돕다 increase ~을 증대하다 sales 매출, 판매(량) comfortable 편한, 편안한 introduce ~을 소개하다 encourage A to do A에게 ~하도록 권하다, 장려하다 therefore 따라서, 그러므로 role-play ~을 역할극으로 하다 discussion 토론, 논의 get practice 연습하다

83 What does the speaker imply when she says, "You should have no problem starting work at nine"?
(A) A team is well-trained.
(B) A system has been installed.
(C) A manual has clear instructions.
(D) A meeting will be short.

화자가 "You should have no problem starting work at nine"라고 말할 때 암시하는 것은 무엇인가?
(A) 팀이 잘 교육되어 있다.
(B) 시스템이 설치되었다.

(C) 설명서에 명확한 설명이 들어 있다.
(D) 회의가 짧게 진행될 것이다.

해설 〈의도 파악 문제〉
화자가 담화 초반부에 회의 이후에 해야 할 업무들이 있다는 것을 안다고(I realize that you have some tasks to do after this meeting) 언급한 뒤로 9시에 일을 시작하는 데 문제가 없을 것이라고 말하는 상황이다. 이는 회의 시간이 길지 않을 것임을 나타내는 말이므로 (D)가 정답이다.

어휘 well-trained 잘 교육된 install ~을 설치하다 manual 설명서, 안내서 clear 명확한 instructions 설명, 안내, 지시

84 What happened at the business last week?
(A) Sales were much lower than usual.
(B) A new service for customers was launched.
(C) Financial information was analyzed.
(D) Some orders were not filled on time.

지난주에 해당 업체에 무슨 일이 있었는가?
(A) 매출이 평소보다 훨씬 더 낮았다.
(B) 고객을 위한 새로운 서비스가 출시되었다.
(C) 재무 정보가 분석되었다.
(D) 일부 주문이 제때 이행되지 않았다.

해설 〈특정 시점의 일을 묻는 문제〉
담화 중반부에, 전문가 한 명이 지난주에 방문해 재무 자료를 평가했다고(Last week, we had an expert visit our bakery and evaluate our financial data) 말하고 있다. 이는 재무 정보를 분석한 일에 해당되므로 (C)가 정답이다.

어휘 much (비교급 수식) 훨씬 than usual 평소보다 launch ~을 출시하다 analyze ~을 분석하다 fill ~을 이행하다 on time 제때

85 What will the listeners have an opportunity to practice?
(A) Discussing decorating options
(B) Reading a profit report
(C) Packaging baked goods
(D) Placing a rush order

청자들은 무엇을 연습할 기회를 가지게 될 것인가?
(A) 장식 옵션에 대해 이야기하기
(B) 수익 보고서 읽어보기
(C) 제과제품 포장하기
(D) 급한 물품 주문하기

해설 〈기타 세부 사항을 묻는 문제〉
담화 후반부에 장식 옵션을 소개하는 일(introducing our decorating options)을 언급하면서 역할극 토론을 통해 그것을 연습해 보겠다고(~ we're going to role-play a discussion ~ you can get some practice) 말하고 있으므로 (A)가 정답이다.

어휘 have an opportunity to do ~할 기회를 갖다 practice 연습하다 package ~을 포장하다 place an order 주문하다 rush 급한

I'm pleased to report that we've had steady sales of ⑧⑥ our line of makeup and skincare products. Because the products work so well, we're starting to build brand loyalty. I've been reviewing the comments on our Web site, and ⑧⑦ a lot of customers have asked us to make our product available in larger bottles for bulk savings and smaller ones for traveling. This is fairly easy to do, so we've already started working on that. ⑧⑧ Sometime this afternoon, I'll e-mail you an updated catalog that has all of these new options listed in it.

우리 메이크업 제품과 스킨케어 제품 라인이 지속적인 판매량을 기록해 오고 있다는 사실을 알려 드리게 되어 기쁩니다. 이 제품들이 아주 좋은 성과를 내고 있기 때문에 우리는 브랜드 충성도를 높여 나가기 시작할 것입니다. 제가 우리 웹 사이트에서 의견을 계속 살펴보고 있는데, 많은 고객들께서 우리 제품을 대량 구매 할인이 되는 대용량 용기 및 여행용 소형 용기로 구매 가능하게 만들어 달라고 요청하셨습니다. 이는 꽤 쉬운 일이기 때문에 이미 이에 대한 작업을 시작했습니다. 오늘 오후 중으로, 이 모든 선택 대상을 기재해 업데이트된 카탈로그를 여러분께 이메일로 보내 드리겠습니다.

어휘 steady 지속적인, 꾸준한 sales 판매(량), 매출 makeup 메이크업, 화장, 분장 work 성과를 내다, 결실을 맺다, 효과가 있다 brand loyalty 브랜드 충성도 review ~을 살펴보다, 검토하다 comment 의견, 발언 ask A to do A에게 ~하도록 요청하다 make A + 형용사 A를 ~하게 만들다 available 구매 가능한, 이용 가능한 bulk savings 대량 구매 할인 fairly 꽤, 상당히 work on ~에 대한 작업을 시작하다 listed in ~에 기재된, 목록으로 작성된

86 What kind of goods does the speaker's company sell?
(A) Clothing
(B) Vitamins
(C) Electronics
(D) Cosmetics

화자의 회사는 어떤 종류의 상품을 판매하는가?
(A) 의류
(B) 비타민
(C) 전자기기
(D) 화장품

해설 〈주제를 묻는 문제〉
담화 초반부에 화자가 자사의 제품을 our line of makeup and skincare products라고 언급하고 있으므로 (D)가 정답이다.

87 According to the speaker, what have customers requested?
(A) Faster delivery times
(B) Less expensive products
(C) A variety of sizes
(D) Environmentally friendly packaging

화자의 말에 따르면, 고객들이 무엇을 요청했는가?
(A) 더 빠른 배송 시간
(B) 덜 비싼 제품
(C) 다양한 크기
(D) 환경 친화적인 포장

해설 〈요청 사항을 묻는 문제〉
담화 중반부에 고객 의견을 언급하면서 대량 구매 할인이 되는 대용량 용기와 여행용 소형 용기로 제품을 만들어 달라고(a lot of customers have asked us to make our product available in larger bottles for bulk savings and smaller ones for traveling) 요청한 사실을 알리고 있다. 이는 크기의 다양성을 요청한 것이므로 (C)가 정답이다.

어휘 less ad. 덜, 더 적게 a variety of 다양한 environmentally friendly 환경 친화적인 packaging 포장(재)

88 What will be sent to the listeners later today?
(A) A sample contract
(B) An updated catalog
(C) A list of duties
(D) A logo design

오늘 늦게 청자들에게 무엇이 보내질 것인가?
(A) 견본 계약서
(B) 업데이트된 카탈로그
(C) 직무 목록
(D) 로고 디자인

해설 〈기타 세부 사항을 묻는 문제〉
담화 후반부에 오후 중으로 업데이트된 카탈로그를 이메일로 보내겠다고(Sometime this afternoon, I'll e-mail you an updated catalog) 알리고 있으므로 (B)가 정답이다.

어휘 contract 계약(서)

Hi, Maria. I just saw a copy of the managers' itinerary for ⑧⑨ the company hiking trip we organized for staff this Saturday. It says that Patrick was supposed to carry the equipment for the games we plan to play, but he can't join us due to a family matter. ⑨⓪ I know that you can't take the equipment either because you are bringing many other items, but I am not taking much with me. I'd like to know exactly what equipment I'll need to bring, though, so ⑨① please give me a call back. Talk to you soon.

안녕하세요, 마리아 씨. 우리가 직원들을 위해 이번 주 토요일로 준비한 사내 등산 여행의 부서장용 일정표 한 부를 방금 확인했습니다. 여기 보면 우리가 계획하고 있는 게임용 장비를 패트릭 씨가 나르기로 되어 있다고 나와 있는데, 이분은 집안 문제로 인해 함께 하실 수 없습니다. 당신이 다른 물품을 많이 가져가기 때문에 마찬가지로 그 장비를 챙겨 갈 수 없다는 것을 알고 있지만, 제가 짐을 많이 챙겨 가지 않을 겁니다. 하지만 제가 정확히 어떤 장비를 챙겨 가야 하는지 알면 좋을 것 같아서 저에게 다시 전화 주세요. 곧 다시 얘기해요.

어휘 itinerary 일정(표) organize ~을 준비하다, 조직하다 be supposed to do ~하기로 되어 있다, ~할 예정이다 equipment 장비 plan to do ~할 계획이다 join ~와 함께 하다, ~에 합류하다 due to ~로 인해 matter 문제, 일 either (부정문에서) ~도 (마찬가지로) would like to do ~하고 싶다, ~하고자 하다 exactly 정확히 though (문장 중간 또는 끝에 쓰여) 하지만, 그러나 give A a call back A에게 다시 전화하다

89 According to the speaker, what will take place on Saturday?
(A) A grand opening event
(B) A staff orientation
(C) A client presentation
(D) A company outing

화자의 말에 따르면, 토요일에 무슨 일이 있을 것인가?
(A) 개장 기념 행사
(B) 직원 오리엔테이션
(C) 고객 대상 발표
(D) 사내 야유회

해설 〈특정 시점의 일을 묻는 문제〉
담화를 시작하면서 화자가 토요일로 준비한 사내 등산 여행을(the company hiking trip we organized for staff this Saturday) 언급하고 있는데, 이는 야유회와 마찬가지이므로 (D)가 정답이다.

어휘 take place (일, 행사 등이) 발생되다, 개최되다 presentation 발표(회) outing 야유회

90 What does the speaker mean when he says, "I am not taking much with me"?
(A) He is happy to carry some items.
(B) He thinks a task will not take long.

(C) He would appreciate some assistance.
(D) He believes a price will be low.

화자가 "I am not taking much with me"라고 말할 때 무엇을 의미하는가?
(A) 기꺼이 몇몇 물품을 나를 것이다.
(B) 한 가지 일이 오래 걸리지 않을 것으로 생각한다.
(C) 약간의 도움에 대해 감사할 것이다.
(D) 한 가지 가격이 낮을 것으로 생각한다.

해설 〈의도 파악 문제〉
담화 중반부에 화자가 상대방이 다른 물품을 많이 가져가기 때문에 마찬가지로 그 장비를 챙겨 갈 수 없다는 것을 알고 있다고(I know that you can't take the equipment either because you are bringing many other items, but) 언급한 뒤로 '제가 짐을 많이 챙겨 가지 않습니다'라고 알리는 흐름이다. 이는 자신이 물품을 챙겨 가는 일을 돕겠다는 뜻이므로 (A)가 정답이다.

어휘 carry ~을 나르다, 옮기다 task 일, 업무 take long 오래 걸리다 appreciate ~에 대해 감사하다 assistance 도움, 지원

91 What does the speaker ask the listener to do?
(A) Send a document
(B) Return the call
(C) Make an announcement
(D) Update a schedule

화자는 청자에게 무엇을 하도록 요청하는가?
(A) 문서 하나를 보내는 일
(B) 답신 전화를 하는 일
(C) 공지를 하는 일
(D) 일정을 업데이트하는 일

해설 〈요청 사항을 묻는 문제〉
담화 맨 마지막에 please give me a call back이라는 말로 다시 전화해 달라고 요청하고 있으므로 (B)가 정답이다.

어휘 return a call 답신 전화를 하다 announcement 공지, 발표

Welcome to *Home is Where the Heart Is*, ㉜ your weekly broadcast that provides advice about decorating your home. Today's show will focus on room colors. ㉝ Who's heard that small rooms should never be painted in dark colors? Well, this might surprise you, but in actual fact, it's false. As long as a small room receives enough natural light, dark colors won't make it appear smaller or unattractive. But remember, if you choose a dark color, use gloss paint to create more ambience in the room. Speaking of which, ㉞ a lot of you have e-mailed asking for paint recommendations. We'll be discussing that next week.

매주 주택 장식에 관한 조언을 제공해 드리는 방송 프로그램 〈홈 이즈 웨어 더 하트 이즈〉를 찾아 주신 것을 환영합니다. 오늘 프로그램은 방 색상에 초점을 맞출 것입니다. 작은 방은 절대로 어두운 색으로 페인트칠하면 안 된다는 얘기를 들어 보신 분 계신가요? 자, 놀랄지 모르겠지만, 실제로는, 틀린 얘기입니다. 작은 방이더라도 자연광이 충분히 들어오는 한, 어두운 색으로 인해 방이 더 작아 보이거나 덜 매력적으로 보이지는 않습니다. 하지만 기억하셔야 하는 점은, 어두운 색상을 선택하시는 경우, 광택 페인트를 활용해 방에 분위기를 더해 주시기 바랍니다. 이 말씀을 드리고 보니, 여러분 중 많은 분들께서 페인트 추천을 요청하시는 이메일을 보내 주셨습니다. 저희가 다음 주에 이 부분을 이야기할 예정입니다.

어휘 broadcast 방송 (프로그램) provide ~을 제공하다 decorate ~을 장식하다, 꾸미다 focus on ~에 초점을 맞추다 in dark colors 어두운 색으로 surprise ~을 놀라게 하다 in actual fact 실제로는 false 틀린, 거짓된 as long as ~하는 한, ~하기만 하면 receive ~을 받다 natural light 자연광 make A do A를 ~하게 만들다 appear + 형용사 ~하게 보이다, ~한 것 같다 unattractive 매력적이지 않은 choose ~을 선택하다 gloss paint 광택 페인트 create ~을 만들어내다 ambience 분위기 Speaking of which (앞서 말한 것을 두고) 말이 나온 김에 ask for ~을 요청하다 recommendation 추천 discuss ~을 이야기하다, 논의하다

92 What is the broadcast mainly about?
(A) Financial management
(B) Party planning ideas
(C) Fashion
(D) Interior design tips

방송은 주로 무엇에 관한 것인가?
(A) 재무 관리
(B) 파티 기획 아이디어
(C) 패션
(D) 실내 디자인 팁

해설 〈주제를 묻는 문제〉
담화 시작 부분에 프로그램 이름과 함께 매주 주택 장식에 관한 조언을 제공해 주는 방송이라고(your weekly broadcast that provides advice about decorating your home) 알리고 있다. 이는 실내 디자인과 관련된 팁을 얻을 수 있다는 뜻이므로 (D)가 정답이다.

어휘 financial 재무의, 금융의

93 Why does the speaker say the listeners might be surprised?
(A) A new product has been launched.
(B) A common belief is wrong.
(C) A mistake was made on a previous show.
(D) A special guest will join the broadcast.

화자는 왜 청자들이 놀랄지도 모른다고 말하는가?
(A) 한 가지 신제품이 출시되었다.
(B) 한 가지 일반적인 생각이 잘못되었다.
(C) 한 가지 실수가 이전의 방송에서 발생되었다.
(D) 특별 초대 손님 한 명이 방송에 참여할 것이다.

해설 〈기타 세부 사항을 묻는 문제〉
담화 중반부에 작은 방은 어두운 색으로 칠하면 안 된다는 얘기를 들어 봤는지(Who's heard that small rooms should never be painted in dark colors?) 질문한 후, 놀랍게도 이것이 실제로는 틀렸다고(Well, this might surprise you, but in actual fact, it's false) 언급하고 있다. 이는 일반적인 생각이 틀렸다는 뜻이므로 (B)가 정답이다.

어휘 launch ~을 출시하다, 공개하다 make a mistake 실수하다 previous 이전의, 과거의 join ~에 참여하다, ~와 함께 하다

94 Why does the speaker say, "We'll be discussing that next week"?
(A) To invite listeners to call the station
(B) To signal the end of an interview
(C) To promote a future broadcast
(D) To demonstrate a specific product

화자는 왜 "We'll be discussing that next week"라고 말하는가?
(A) 청자들에게 방송국에 전화하도록 요청하기 위해
(B) 인터뷰 종료 신호를 보내기 위해
(C) 앞으로 있을 방송을 홍보하기 위해
(D) 특정 제품을 시연하기 위해

해설 〈의도 파악 문제〉
담화 후반부에 많은 사람들이 페인트 추천을 요청하는 이메일을 보냈다고(a lot of you have e-mailed asking for paint recommendations) 언급한 뒤로 '다음 주에 그 얘기를 할 것이다'라고 말하는 상황이다. 이는 다음 방송분에 대한 예고이자 일종의 홍보에 해당되므로 (C)가 정답이다.

어휘 invite A to do A에게 ~하도록 요청하다 signal v. ~을 신호로 알리다 promote ~을 홍보하다 demonstrate ~을 시연하다, 시범 보이다 specific 특정한, 구체적인

I'd like to begin today's meeting by discussing an issue related to ⑨⑤ the cooking show we aired on Channel 5 last week. We always pay close attention to feedback from our viewers, so I was really disappointed to hear that ⑨⑥ we've had a surprising number of complaints about the cheddar cheese sauce recipe. Many of our viewers e-mailed us to say that it's too thick. So, we're going to advise the program hosts ⑨⑦ to use less flour in the recipe in the future. We should also add the amended version to our Web site as soon as possible.

Cheddar Cheese Sauce
Preparation time: 15 minutes

Ingredients:
500 milliliters of milk
⑨⑦ 4 tablespoons of plain flour
50 grams of butter
100 grams of grated cheese

Directions:
1. Mix ingredients over medium heat
2. Allow to cool before serving

우리가 지난주에 5번 채널에서 방송한 요리 프로그램과 관련된 한 가지 사안을 이야기하는 것으로 오늘 회의를 시작할까 합니다. 우리는 항상 시청자들의 의견에 크게 주의를 기울이고 있기 때문에 체다 치즈 소스 조리법과 관련해 놀라울 정도로 많은 불만 사항을 접수했다는 얘기를 듣고 정말 실망스러웠습니다. 많은 우리 시청자들이 우리에게 이메일을 보내 너무 걸쭉하다고 말했습니다. 따라서, 우리는 해당 프로그램 진행자들에게 앞으로 그 조리법에 밀가루를 덜 사용하도록 조언할 것입니다. 우리는 또한 가능한 한 빨리 우리 웹 사이트에 수정된 버전도 추가해야 합니다.

체다 치즈 소스
조리 시간: 15분

재료:
우유 500밀리리터
일반 밀가루 4 테이블스푼
버터 50그램
갈은 치즈 100그램

설명:
1. 중간 불에 모든 재료를 섞습니다.
2. 식을 때까지 기다렸다가 제공합니다.

어휘 discuss ~을 이야기하다, 논의하다 issue 사안, 문제 related to ~와 관련된 air v. ~을 방송하다 pay close attention to ~에 크게 주의를 기울이다 feedback 의견 viewer 시청자, 보는 사람 be disappointed to

do ~해서 실망하다 a surprising number of 놀라울 정도로 많은 (수의) complaint 불만, 불평 recipe 조리법 thick 걸쭉한 advise A to do A에게 ~하도록 조언하다 host 방송 진행자 flour 밀가루 add A to B A를 B에 추가하다 amended 수정된, 개정된 as soon as possible 가능한 한 빨리 preparation 조리, 준비 ingredient (음식) 재료, 성분 directions 설명, 안내, 지시 allow to do ~하도록 두다 cool v. 식다 serve (음식 등) 제공하다, 내오다

95 Where is the talk most likely taking place?
(A) At a publishing firm
(B) At a restaurant
(C) At a culinary school
(D) At a television station

어디에서 담화가 진행되고 있을 것 같은가?
(A) 출판사에서
(B) 레스토랑에서
(C) 요리 학원에서
(D) 텔레비전 방송국에서

해설 〈담화의 장소를 묻는 문제〉
담화 초반부에 화자가 소속 단체를 we로 지칭해 '우리가 방송한 요리 프로그램(the cooking show we aired on Channel 5 last week)'을 언급하고 있다. 이는 텔레비전 방송국 직원이 할 수 있는 말이므로 (D)가 정답이다.

어휘 take place (일, 행사 등이) 발생되다, 개최되다 firm 회사, 업체 culinary 요리의

96 What problem does the speaker address?
(A) A business is becoming less profitable.
(B) A product will no longer be available.
(C) Several complaints have been received.
(D) Employees failed to follow a procedure correctly.

화자는 어떤 문제를 다루는가?
(A) 사업이 수익성이 떨어지고 있다.
(B) 제품을 더 이상 구매할 수 없을 것이다.
(C) 여러 불만 사항이 접수되었다.
(D) 직원들이 절차를 정확히 따르지 못했다.

해설 〈문제점을 묻는 문제〉
담화 중반부에 놀라울 정도로 많은 불만 사항을 접수한(we've had a surprising number of complaints) 사실을 언급하면서 이 문제와 관련된 조치 방법을 말하고 있으므로 (C)가 정답이다.

어휘 address v. (문제 등) ~을 다루다, 처리하다 profitable 수익성이 있는 no longer 더 이상 ~ 않다 available 구매 가능한, 이용 가능한 several 여럿의, 몇몇의 complaint 불만, 불평 receive ~을 받다 fail to do ~하지 못하다 follow ~을 따르다, 준수하다 procedure 절차 correctly 정확하게, 올바르게

97 Look at the graphic. Which information will most likely be changed?
(A) 15 minutes
(B) 4 tablespoons
(C) 50 grams
(D) 100 grams

시각 자료를 보시오. 어느 정보가 변경될 것 같은가?
(A) 15분
(B) 4 테이블스푼
(C) 50그램
(D) 100그램

해설 〈기타 시각 자료 문제〉
담화 후반부에 문제 해결을 위한 조치로 밀가루를 덜 사용하는 것을(to use less flour in the recipe in the future) 언급하고 있으며, 조리법에 밀가루를 넣는 양이 4 테이블스푼으로(4 table spoons of plain flour) 표기되어 있으므로 (B)가 정답이다.

Questions 98-100 refer to the following news report and weather forecast. (캐W)

In local news, tickets are selling well for a ⑨⑧ recital by the Mirage Dance Troupe taking place on Saturday at Stramler Park. The group members are known throughout the world for their amazing talent. This upcoming event marks the fourth time they have visited Brentwood. You can get tickets by calling the Kern Theater box office. ⑨⑨ Those planning to drive to the event are advised to print a parking pass in advance from the theater's Web site to save time and get a discounted rate. The venue is completely outdoors, so anyone going to the event should dress appropriately. ⑩⑩ Cloudy weather is expected for that day, but at least it won't be rainy.

July 25	July 26	⑨⑦ July 27	July 28
☀	☀	☁	☂
Sunny	Sunny	⑨⑦ Cloudy	Rain

지역 뉴스입니다. 토요일에 스트래머 공원에서 열리는 미라지 댄스 공연단 공연 입장권이 잘 판매되고 있습니다. 이 단체 구성원들은 놀라운 재능을 지닌 것으로 전 세계에 알려져 있습니다. 다가오는 이번 행사는 이 단체가 브렌트우드를 방문하는 네 번째 공연입니다. 케른 극장 매표소에 전화하시면 입장권을 구하실 수 있습니다. 행사장에 차를 운전해 방문하실 계획인 분들은 시간을 절약하고 요금 할인을 받으실 수 있도록 이 극장 웹 사이트에서 미리 주차권을 출력하시는 것이 좋습니다. 공연장이 완전히 야외 공간이므로 행사를 찾는 분들은 그에 알맞게 옷차림을 하시기 바랍니다. 당일에 흐린 날씨가 예상되지만, 최소한 비는 내리지 않을 것입니다.

7월 25일	7월 26일	7월 27일	7월 28일
☀	☀	☁	☂
맑음	맑음	흐림	비

어휘 local 지역의, 현지의 sell well 잘 판매되다 recital (음악회 등의) 공연 take place (일, 행사 등이) 일어나다, 발생되다 be known for ~로 알려져 있다 amazing 놀라운 talent 재능 upcoming 다가오는, 곧 있을 mark ~을 나타내다 by (방법) ~함으로써 those (수식어구와 함께) ~하는 사람들 plan to do ~할 계획이다 be advised to do ~하는 것이 좋다, ~하도록 권고되다 parking pass 주차권 in advance 미리, 사전에 rate 요금 venue 행사장 completely 완전히, 전적으로 appropriately 알맞게, 적절

98 What kind of event is the speaker discussing?
(A) A singing contest
(B) A dance performance
(C) An art exhibition
(D) A film festival

화자는 무슨 종류의 행사를 이야기하고 있는가?
(A) 노래 경연대회
(B) 댄스 공연
(C) 미술 전시회
(D) 영화제

해설 〈주제를 묻는 문제〉
담화를 시작하면서 미라지 댄스 공연단 공연(recital by the Mirage Dance Troupe)의 입장권 판매 상황을 언급하고 있으므로 (B)가 정답이다.

어휘 exhibition 전시(회)

99 What does the speaker say is available on a Web site?
(A) A parking pass
(B) A seating chart
(C) A list of venues
(D) An enrollment form

화자는 웹 사이트에 무엇이 이용 가능하다고 말하는가?
(A) 주차권
(B) 좌석 배치도
(C) 행사장 목록
(D) 등록 양식

해설 〈기타 세부 사항을 묻는 문제〉
담화 중반부에, 극장 웹 사이트에서 주차권을 출력할 수 있다고 (Those planning to drive to the event are advised to print a parking pass in advance from the theater's Web site ~) 알리고 있으므로 (A)가 정답이다.

어휘 available 이용 가능한 seating 좌석 enrollment 등록 form 양식, 서식

100 Look at the graphic. When is the event being held?
(A) July 25
(B) July 26
(C) July 27
(D) July 28

시각 자료를 보시오. 해당 행사는 언제 개최되는가?
(A) 7월 25일
(B) 7월 26일
(C) 7월 27일
(D) 7월 28일

해설 〈2열 도표 문제〉
화자는 담화 후반부에 공연 당일을 that day로 지칭해 그날 날씨가 흐리다고(Cloudy weather is expected for that day ~) 알리고 있다. 시각 자료에서 흐린 날씨로 표기된 날짜가 July 27이므로 (C)가 정답이다.

어휘 hold ~을 개최하다, 열다

101 해석 롱포드 해변의 비수기 중에 코벨로 씨는 혼자 자신의 작은 카페를 운영한다.

해설 〈재귀대명사〉
보기의 대명사는 주어인 Ms. Covello를 지칭하는데, 동사 또는 전치사의 목적어로 쓰이는 대명사가 주어와 동일인일 경우 재귀대명사를 사용해야 하므로 (C) herself가 정답이다. by oneself는 '혼자, 스스로'를 뜻하는 하나의 표현으로 기억해 두는 것이 좋다.

어휘 during ~ 중에, ~ 동안 off-season 비수기 run ~을 운영하다 by oneself 혼자, 스스로

102 해석 볼티모어에 위치한 포인츠먼 현대 미술 박물관은 해마다 50만 명이 넘는 방문객을 끌어들인다.

해설 〈동사 어휘〉
보기가 모두 동사이므로 의미가 알맞은 것을 찾아야 한다. 빈칸 뒤에 '방문객'을 뜻하는 명사구 more than 500,000 visitors가 쓰여 있으므로 박물관이 방문객을 대상으로 할 수 있는 일을 나타낼 동사가 필요하다. 따라서 '~을 끌어들이다'를 뜻하는 (B) attracts가 정답이다.

어휘 more than ~가 넘는 annually 해마다, 연간 observe ~을 관찰하다, 준수하다 attract ~을 끌어들이다 feature ~을 특징으로 하다 advance ~을 발전시키다, 승진시키다, 촉진하다

103 해석 연출자의 비서가 다음 달에 있을 리허설과 관련된 모든 일정 문의에 답변해 줄 것이다.

해설 〈① 복합명사 ② 사람 명사 VS. 사물 명사〉
동사 answer의 목적어로 '일정 관리'를 뜻하는 scheduling은 의미가 맞지 않는다. 따라서 빈칸에 또 다른 명사가 들어가 scheduling과 복합 명사를 구성해 답변 대상에 해당되는 의미를 나타내야 하므로 '문의'를 뜻하는 명사 (B) inquiries가 정답이다. (C) inquirer는 사람 명사이므로 의미상 어울리지 않는다.

어휘 assistant 비서, 보조, 조수 scheduling 일정 관리 regarding ~와 관련해 rehearsal 리허설, 예행 연습 inquire 문의하다 inquiry 문의 inquirer 문의자 inquiringly 호기심 많게, 물어보는 듯이

104 해석 롤랜드 일렉트로닉스는 테크 밸리 엑스포에서 차세대 냉장고 제품 라인에 관한 세부 정보를 공개할 것이다.

해설 〈형용사 어휘〉
보기가 모두 형용사이므로 의미가 알맞은 것을 찾아야 한다. 빈칸 바로 뒤에 위치한 명사 information을 수식해 그 특징을 나타낼 형용사가 필요하므로 '세부적인, 상세한'이라는 의미로 정보의 특징을 나타낼 수 있는 (C) detailed가 정답이다.

어휘 reveal ~을 공개하다, 드러내다 refrigerator 냉장고 loyal 단골의, 충성스러운 spacious 널찍한 detailed 세부적인, 상세한 experienced 경험 많은, 숙련된

105 해석 영업팀이 목표에 도달하지 못했기 때문에 내년 신입 사원 숫자를 줄일 예정이다.

해설 〈① 조동사 뒤 동사 원형 ② 능동태/수동태〉
조동사(will) 바로 뒤에 위치한 빈칸은 동사원형이 필요한 자리이며, 빈칸 뒤에 이어지는 명사구를 목적어로 취할 능동태 동사가 쓰여야 한다. 따라서 be동사의 동사원형과 -ing 형태가 결합되어 능동태 진행형을 구성하는 (C) be reducing이 정답이다.

어휘 fail to do ~하지 못하다 reach ~에 도달하다, 이르다 new hire 신입 사원, 신규 채용자 reduce ~을 줄이다, 감소시키다

106 해석 부정적인 후기에도 불구하고, 베스퍼 7 휴대전화기는 올해 베스트셀러 제품들 중 하나가 되었다.

해설 〈전치사 VS. 접속사〉
빈칸 뒤로 명사구 negative reviews와 콤마가 쓰여 있고, 그 뒤로 문장의 주어가 이어지는 구조이다. 따라서 명사구를 목적어로 취할 전치사가 빈칸에 쓰여야 알맞으므로 전치사인 (B) Despite이 정답이다. (A) Although와 (C) Unless, (D) Even if은 모두 접속사이므로 주어와 동사가 포함된 절을 이끌어야 한다.

어휘 negative 부정적인 review 후기, 의견, 평가 although 비록 ~이기는 하지만 despite ~에도 불구하고 unless ~하지 않는다면, ~가 아니라면 even if 설사 ~라 하더라도

107 해석 형편없는 캐릭터의 변화는 평론가들 사이에서 최신 영화 〈파블로의 비밀〉에 대한 큰 불만 사항이었다.

해설 〈명사 자리(관사와 형용사 뒤)〉
부정관사 a와 형용사 major 뒤에 위치한 빈칸은 형용사의 수식을 받을 단수 명사가 쓰여야 하는 자리이므로 (B) complaint가 정답이다.

어휘 character development 인물 변화, 캐릭터 변화 among ~ 사이의 critic 평론가 latest 최신의 complain 불만을 제기하다, 불평하다 complaint 불만, 불평

108 해석 회사의 웹 사이트에 따르면, 욕실 타일 제품들은 다양한 스타일로 구매 가능하다.

해설 〈명사 어휘〉
'a + 빈칸 + of + 복수 명사'의 구조이므로 부정 관사 a 및 전치사 of와 어울려 '다양한'이라는 의미로 복수 명사를 주로 수식하는 (D) variety가 정답이다.

어휘 according to ~에 따르면 available 구매 가능한, 이용 가능한 a variety of 다양한 phase 단계, 국면 distribution 배부, 유통 connection 연결, 접속, 관련(성)

109 해석 CPA 제조사와 홀스터 산업회사 사이의 합의서는 여러 차례의 수정 과정을 거쳤다.

해설 〈형용사 자리(명사 앞)〉
동사 has undergone과 복수 명사인 목적어 revisions 사이에 위치한 빈칸은 명사를 수식할 형용사 자리이므로 복수 명사를 수식하는 형용사인 (C) multiple이 정답이다.

어휘 agreement 합의(서), 계약(서) undergo ~을 거치다, 겪다 revision 수정, 변경 multiply 곱셈하다, ~을 증가시키다 multiple 여럿의, 많은, 다수의

110 해석 저희가 명부를 최신의 것으로 유지할 수 있도록 어떤 새로운 정보든 여러분의 프로필을 업데이트하시기 바랍니다.

해설 〈부사절 접속사〉
빈칸 뒤에 주어와 동사가 포함된 하나의 절이 쓰여 있으므로 이 절을 이끌 접속사가 빈칸에 필요하다. 또한 '명부를 현재의 것으로 유지할 수 있도록 프로필을 업데이트하십시오'와 같은 의미가 되어야 알맞으므로 조동사 can/may/will 등과 어울려 '~할 수 있도록'이라는 의미로 목적을 나타낼 때 사용하는 접속사 (B) so that이 정답이다.

어휘 keep A + 형용사 A를 ~한 상태로 유지하다 directory (주소, 전화번호 등의 정보를 담은) 명부 even if 설사 ~라 하더라도 so that (목적) ~할 수 있도록, (결과) 그래서, 그러므로 yet 아직, 이미, 벌써, (최상급과 함께) 지금까지 중에서 while ~인 반면, ~하는 동안

111 해석 점심 시간 중에 빠르게 사무실 건물에서 나가시려면, 엘리베이터 대신 계단을 이용하세요.

해설 〈명령문〉
목적을 나타내는 to부정사 뒤로 빈칸과 목적어, 그리고 instead of 전치사구가 이어지는 구조이다. 따라서 주어 없이 하나의 문장이 되려면 빈칸에 동사원형이 들어가 명령문 구조가 되어야 알맞으므로 동사원형인 (C) use가 정답이다.

어휘 leave ~에서 나가다, 떠나다 during ~ 중에, ~ 동안 instead of ~ 대신

112 해석 두 번째 터미널 공사가 거의 완공 상태이므로 헬싱키 공항의 인파는 곧 더 잘 관리될 수 있을 것이다.

해설 〈부사 어휘〉
빈칸에 쓰일 부사는 바로 뒤에 위치한 형용사 complete을 수식해 터미널 공사의 완료 정도와 관련된 의미를 나타내야 하므로 '거의'라는 뜻으로 쓰이는 (D) nearly가 정답이다.

어휘 crowd 인파, 군중, 사람들 manageable 관리할 수 있는 construction 공사, 건설 complete 완료된, 완성된, 완전한 highly 매우, 대단히 usually 일반적으로, 보통 recently 최근에 nearly 거의

113 해석 저희 웹 사이트를 통해 저장 유닛을 주문하실 때, 배송에 앞서 완전히 조립될 것입니다.

해설 〈전치사 VS. 접속사〉
빈칸 바로 앞에 수동태 동사 will be assembled가 쓰여 있으므로 빈칸 뒤에 위치한 명사 delivery는 동사의 목적어가 아니다. 따라서 빈칸은 이 명사를 목적어로 취할 전치사가 빈칸에 쓰여야 알맞으므로 (B) prior to가 정답이다. (A) wherever는 주어와 동사가 포함된 절을 이끄는 접속사이며, (C) previous는 형용사이다. (D) in addition은 부사의 역할을 하는 전치사구이다.

어휘 order ~을 주문하다 storage unit 저장 장치, (가구) 저장 유닛 fully 완전히, 전적으로, 모두, 최대로 assemble ~을 조립하다 delivery 배송(품) wherever ~하는 곳은 어디든, 어디서 ~하든 prior to ~에 앞서, ~ 전에 previous 이전의, 과거의 in addition 추가로, 게다가

114 해석 넬슨 테니스 클럽은 누구든 그 스포츠를 배우는 데 관심이 있는 사람을 위해 회비를 저렴한 수준으로 유지한다.

해설 〈형용사 어휘〉
보기가 모두 형용사이므로 의미가 알맞은 것을 찾아야 한다. 빈칸은 동사 keep의 목적어 뒤에 위치해 목적어의 상태나 특징 등을 나타내는 목적격 보어 자리이므로 목적어 membership fees(회비)의 비용 수준과 관련된 의미를 나타낼 형용사가 필요하다. 따라서 '(가격 등이) 저렴한'을 뜻하는 (D) affordable이 정답이다.

어휘 keep A + 형용사 A를 ~한 상태로 유지하다 fee 요금, 수수료 interested in ~에 관심이 있는 necessary 필요한, 필수의 adverse 불리한, 부정적인 potential 잠재적인 affordable (가격 등이) 저렴한, 감당할 수 있는

115 해석 포지 커피의 수많은 경쟁사들 중에, 그레이트 레이크스 카페보다 더 크게 도전장을 내민 곳은 거의 없다.

해설 〈수량 대명사〉
Among 전치사구 뒤로 빈칸과 동사 present가 이어지는 구조이므로 빈칸이 주어 자리임을 알 수 있다. 주어 자리에 사용 가능하며 동사 present와 수 일치가 맞는 대명사를 찾아야 하므로 few competitors를 줄여서 표현한 (B) few가 정답이다. few와 함께 쓰이는 복수 명사는 앞서 언급이 된 경우 이처럼 생략하여 few가 단독으로 대명사로서 사용이 가능하다. 셀 수 없는 개념에 사용하는 (A) little은 단수 취급하므로 동사와 수 일치가 맞지 않고, (C) both는 두 개의 대상이 있는 경우 사용한다. (D) other는 형용사이므로 주어 자리에 쓰일 수 없다.

어휘 numerous 수많은, 다수의 competitor 경쟁사, 경쟁자 present a challenge 도전장을 내밀다 significant 상당한, 아주 큰, 많은 little (셀 수 없는 명사에 대해) 거의 없는 few (셀 수 있는 명사에 대해) 거의 없음 both 둘 모두

116 해석 그 아파트는 시내 지역에서 불과 두 정거장 떨어져 있는 터너역에서 가까운 곳에 위치해 있다.

해설 〈전치사 어휘〉
빈칸 앞에 위치한 동사 is located는 전치사와 함께 '~에 위치해 있다'라는 의미를 나타낸다. 따라서 빈칸에는 아파트와 터너역 사이의 위치 관계를 나타낼 전치사가 필요한데, '터너역에서 가까운 곳에 위치해 있다'라는 뜻이 보기 중 가장 알맞으므로 '~에서 가까운'을 뜻하는 (B) near가 정답이다. (C) next는 형용사 또는 부사이며, next to와 같이 쓰여야 '~ 옆에'라는 의미로 위치 관계를 나타낼 수 있다.

어휘 be located 위치해 있다 stop 정거장, 정류장 away from ~에서 떨어져 있는 near ~ 근처에 between (A and B) (A와 B) 사이에

117 해석 Q-마트의 특급 배송 서비스로 배송되는 해외 주문품은 약 3~5일 후에 도착할 것입니다.

해설 〈부사 어휘〉
보기가 모두 부사이므로 의미가 알맞은 것을 찾아야 한다. 빈칸 뒤에 숫자 표현 three to five가 쓰여 있으므로 숫자 표현 앞에 쓰여 '약, 대략'이라는 뜻을 나타내는 부사 (D) approximately가 정답이다.

어휘 order 주문(품) express 급행의, 신속한 arrive 도착하다 finally 마침내, 결국 rapidly 신속히, 빠르게 briefly 간단히, 잠깐 approximately 약, 대략

118 해석 쇼핑몰의 평면도와 치수가 귀하의 참고용으로 제공되었습니다.

해설 〈명사 어휘〉
보기가 모두 명사이므로 의미가 알맞은 것을 찾아야 한다. 빈칸은 전치사 for의 목적어로서 평면도와 치수 정보가 제공된 목적을 나타내야 한다. 이 두 가지는 참고 또는 확인을 위한 정보에 해당되는 것으로 볼 수 있으므로 '참고'를 뜻하는 (C) reference가 정답이다.

어휘 floor plan 평면도 measurement 치수, 측정(치) be made available 제공되다 indication 지표, 표시, 징조 subject 주제, 대상, 과목 reference 참고, 추천(서), 언급 presence 존재(감)

119 해석 로마노프 씨는 호숫가 아파트에 대해 경쟁력 있는 수준의 제안을 했지만, 판매자들은 다른 구매자를 선택했다.

해설 〈형용사 자리(관사와 명사 사이)〉
부정관사 a와 명사 offer 사이에 위치한 빈칸은 명사를 수식할 형용사 자리이므로 (B) competitive가 정답이다. 복합명사를 구성하는 경우에 대해서도 생각해 볼 수 있지만, 명사 (C) competition은 offer와 복합명사를 구성하기에 의미상 적절하지 않다.

어휘 make an offer 제안하다 condominium 아파트 go with ~와 함께 하기로 하다, ~으로 결정하다 compete 경쟁하다 competitive 경쟁력 있는, 경쟁하는 competition 경쟁, (경기 등의) 대회 competitively 경쟁적으로

120 해석 날씨가 아주 좋은 상태가 지속된다면, 휴일 퍼레이드 행사는 토요일 오전 10시에 시작될 것이다.

해설 〈부사절 접속사〉
빈칸 앞뒤에 절이 하나씩 있으므로 두 절을 연결할 접속사가 빈칸에 필요하다. 또한 '날씨가 아주 좋은 상태가 지속된다면, 행사가 토요일 오전 10시에 시작될 것이다'와 같은 의미가 되어야 알맞으므로 '~하기만 하면, ~하는 한'을 뜻하는 접속사 (D) as long as가 정답이다. (A) unless와 (B) as if도 접속사이지만 의미가 맞지 않으며, (C) according to는 전치사이다.

어휘 remain + 형용사 계속 ~한 상태이다, ~한 상태로 유지되다 unless ~하지 않는다면, ~가 아니라면 as if 마치 ~인 것처럼 according to ~에 따라, ~에 따르면 as long as ~하기만 하면, ~하는 한

121 해석 트라이엄프 소프트웨어가 이번 주 후반에 완전히 새로운 운영 시스템을 공개한다는 소문이 있다.

해설 〈부사 자리(형용사 앞)〉
부정관사 a와 형용사 new 사이에 위치한 빈칸은 형용사를 수식하는 부사가 쓰이거나 또 다른 형용사가 추가될 수 있는 자리이다. 따라서 이러한 구조를 이룰 수 있는 부사 (C) completely가 정답이다.

어휘 be rumored to do ~한다는 소문이 있다 unveil ~을 공개하다, 발표하다 operating system 운영 시스템 complete a. 완료된, 완전한 v. ~을 완료하다 completely 완전히, 전적으로 completion 완료, 완성, 완수

122 해석 냉각 및 환풍 담당 부서에 배치된 공장 직원들은 회사의 새 에어컨 제품 라인을 조립하게 될 것이다.

해설 〈동사 어휘〉
빈칸에는 특정 부서에 배치된 직원이 새 에어컨 제품과 관련해 할 수 있는 일을 나타낼 동사가 쓰여야 알맞으므로 '~을 조립하다'를 뜻하는 (B) assemble이 정답이다.

어휘 assign A to B A를 B로 배치하다, 배정하다 cooling 냉각 ventilation 환풍 division (단체의) 부, 과, 국 line 제품 라인 air conditioner 에어컨 allow ~을 허용하다, 가능하게 하다 assemble ~을 조립하다 argue 언쟁하다, ~라고 주장하다 cooperate 협조하다

123 해석 엔지니어링 부서의 신임 부서장은 브라이언 에벤슨 박사님이시며, 이분의 인공 지능 시스템에 관한 연구가 다수의 상을 받았습니다.

해설 〈소유격 관계대명사〉
빈칸 앞뒤로 주어와 동사가 각각 포함된 절이 하나씩 위치한 구조이므로 빈칸에는 두 절을 연결할 접속사가 쓰여야 한다. 따라서 관계대명사 (C) who와 (D) whose 중에서 하나를 골라야 하는데, 바로 뒤의 명사를 수식하는 구조로 쓰일 수 있는 것은 소유격 관계대명사이므로 (D) whose가 정답이다. 주격관계대명사 (C) who 뒤에는 동사가 이어져야 한다.

어휘 director 부서장, 책임자, 이사 department 부서 research 연구 win an award 상을 받다 numerous 다수의, 수많은

124 해석 칸체 씨가 〈더 데일리 스테이트〉의 비즈니스 콘텐츠를 편집하는 일을 하는 반면, 듀프리 씨는 연예 주제를 다루는 기사를 총괄합니다.

해설 〈① 전치사 VS. 접속사 ② 부사절 접속사〉
빈칸 앞뒤로 주어와 동사가 각각 포함된 절이 하나씩 위치한 구조이므로 빈칸에는 두 절을 연결할 접속사가 쓰여야 한다. 또한 빈칸 앞뒤의 내용이 서로 다른 두 사람이 각각 맡고 있는 업무를 설명하고 있으므로 '~인 반면'이라는 의미로 대조적인 상황을 나타낼 때 사용하는 접속사 (C) while이 정답이다. (A) in spite of는 부사이며, (B) what도 접속사로 쓰일 수는 있지만 주어 혹은 목적어가 없는 불완전한 문장을 이끌어야 한다. (D) then은 부사이다.

어휘 edit ~을 편집하다 contents 콘텐츠, 내용(물) oversee ~을 총괄하다, 감독하다 article (잡지 등의) 기사 cover (주제 등) ~을 다루다, 포함하다 in spite of ~에도 불구하고 while ~인 반면, ~하는 동안 then 그 후, 그때

125 해석 한콕 회계 법인은 소득세를 신고하기에 너무 바쁜 고객들을 위해 막바지에 서비스를 제공하고 있다.

해설 〈원급 수식 부사〉
빈칸 앞뒤로 '~하기에 너무 …한'이라는 의미를 나타낼 'too + 형용사 + to do' 구조가 되어야 하는데, 이때 too 뒤에 원급 형용사를 사용하므로 (A) busy가 정답이다.

어휘 provide ~을 제공하다 last-minute 최종 순간의, 막바지의 too A to do ~하기에 너무 A한 file one's income tax 소득세를 신고하다 busyness 바쁨, 분주함

126 해석 응급 처치 자격증을 이미 취득한 직원들은 내일 있을 교육 시간에서 제외됩니다.

해설 〈형용사 어휘〉
보기가 모두 형용사이므로 의미가 알맞은 것을 찾아야 한다. 빈칸 뒤에는 전치사 from이 쓰여 있으므로 from과 어울리는 형용사로서 '~에서 제외된, 면제된'이라는 뜻을 나타낼 때 사용하는 (B) exempt가 정답이다.

어휘 earn ~을 획득하다, 얻다 certification 자격증, 수료증 first aid 응급 처치 training 교육, 훈련 session (특정 활동을 위한) 시간 be exempt from ~에서 제외되다 complimentary 무료의 apparent 분명한, 외견상의, 겉으로 보이는

127 해석 감자튀김 조리법을 변경하기로 한 래더 버거의 결정이 전반적인 매출의 급격한 하락을 초래했다.

해설 〈명사 어휘〉
보기가 모두 명사이므로 의미가 알맞은 것을 찾아야 한다. 또한 빈칸 앞뒤에 각각 위치한 전치사 in 및 '급격한'을 뜻하는 형용사 dramatic과 어울리려면 증가 또는 감소와 관련된 의미를 나타낼 명사가 필요하므로 '하락, 감소'를 뜻하는 (D) decline이 정답이다.

어휘 decision to do ~하려는 결정 recipe 조리법 cause ~을 초래하다, 야기하다 dramatic 급격한 a decline in ~의 하락, 감소 overall 전반적인 sales 매출, 영업, 판매(량) funding 자금 (제공) impact 영향, 충격

128 해석 사무실 쓰레기가 50퍼센트 감소된 것으로 볼 때, 우리의 새로운 환경 정책은 뚜렷하게 성공적이었다.

해설 〈부사 어휘〉
빈칸에 쓰일 부사는 바로 뒤에 위치한 형용사 successful을 수식해 성공의 정도를 나타내야 하므로 '뚜렷하게, 두드러지게, 현저히'라는 뜻으로 큰 폭으로의 변화를 나타낼 때 사용하는 (A) markedly가 정답이다.

어휘 environmental 환경의, 환경적인 policy 정책, 방침 successful 성공적인 reduce ~을 감소시키다, 줄이다 by (차이) ~만큼, ~ 정도 markedly 뚜렷하게, 두드러지게, 현저히 diligently 근면하게, 부지런히 jointly 공동으로 affordably (가격이) 저렴하게, 감당할 수 있게

129 해석 폭우가 발생되는 경우에, 모든 야외 공연이 별도의 공지가 있을 때까지 연기될 것입니다.

해설 〈능동태/수동태〉
빈칸 앞에는 전치사구와 주어, 그리고 뒤에는 until 전치사구만 쓰여 있으므로 빈칸은 문장의 동사 자리이며, 빈칸 뒤에 목적어 없이 until 전치사구만 있으므로 타동사 postpone은 수동태로 쓰여야 한다. 따라서 유일하게 수동태로 되어 있는 (C) will be postponed가 정답이다.

어휘 in the event of ~의 경우에 performance 공연, 연주(회) until further notice 별도의 공지가 있을 때까지 postpone ~을 연기하다, 미루다

130 해석 콜스태드 씨가 출판용 제출 원고를 선정하고 나면, 승인을 위해 편집장에게 전달됩니다.

해설 〈동사 어휘〉
보기가 모두 과거분사이므로 의미가 알맞은 것을 찾아야 한다. 빈칸 뒤에 전치사 to와 함께 사람 명사(lead editor)가 쓰여 있어 전달 대상자를 나타낸다는 것을 알 수 있으므로 전치사 to와 어울려 '~을 전달하다, 보내다'를 뜻하는 동사 forward의 과거분사인 (D) forwarded가 정답이다.

어휘 select ~을 선정하다 submission 제출(되는 것) publication 출판(물) lead editor 편집장 approval 승인 locate ~의 위치를 찾다 eliminate ~을 제거하다, 없애다 forward ~을 전달하다, 다시 보내다

PART 6   P115

[131-134] 이메일

수신: cmorrisey@westburypost.com
발신: service@movie-web1.com
날짜: 9월 6일
제목: 회신: 도와주시기 바랍니다

귀하가 동영상 재생 서비스에 로그인하는 데 발생된 문제를 **131** 알려 주셨기 때문에 이메일을 씁니다. 귀하께서 현재 이용 중이신 패키지는 오직 한 번에 하나의 기기상에서만 로그인을 허용하기 때문에 시스템은 제대로 작동하고 있는 중입니다. 또 다른 기기가 해당 계정을 이용하고 있다면 다른 로그인 시도를 **132** 거부할 것입니다. 이러한 문제를 겪으실 **133** 때마다, 반드시 다른 기기상의 계정에서 로그아웃하신 다음, 다시 시도해 보시기 바랍니다. **134** 이 조언이 해당 문제를 해결해 주지 못하는 경우, 저희에게 알려 주십시오.

안녕히 계십시오.

더 무비웹 팀

어휘 issue 문제, 사안 log on to ~에 로그인하다 streaming 재생 current 현재의 allow A to do A에게 ~하도록 허용하다, ~할 수 있게 해 주다 sign in 로그인하다, 서명하고 들어가다 device 기기, 장치 work (기기 등이) 작동하다 correctly 제대로, 올바르게, 정확히 attempt 시도 account 계정, 계좌 experience ~을 겪다, 경험하다 make sure (that) 반드시 ~하도록 하다

131 해설 〈시제(문맥)〉
빈칸이 속한 because절에 주어 you와 빈칸, 목적어와 전치사구가 이어져 있으므로 빈칸은 because절의 동사 자리이다. 또한 뒤에 이어지는 문장들을 보면, 특정 문제점에 대한 해결책을 설명하고 있는데, 이는 과거에 이미 해당 문제점을 알린 것에 대해 취하는 조치로 볼 수 있다. 따라서 과거 시제 동사의 형태인 (C) reported가 정답이다.

132 해설 〈동사 어휘(문맥)〉
빈칸 뒤에 '다른 로그인 시도들'을 의미하는 명사구가 있는데, 앞 문장에 한 번에 하나의 기기에서만 로그인하게 한다는 말이 있으므로 여러 기기에서 로그인을 못하게 한다는 의미가 구성되어야 알맞다. 따라서 '~을 거부하다, 거절하다'를 뜻하는 (D) reject가 정답이다.

어휘 share ~을 공유하다 depart 출발하다, 떠나다 guarantee ~을 보장하다 reject ~을 거부하다, 거절하다

133 해설 〈부사절 접속사〉
빈칸 뒤로 주어와 동사가 각각 포함된 절이 콤마 앞뒤로 하나씩 위치해 있으므로 빈칸에 두 절을 연결할 접속사가 쓰여야 한다. 또한 '이러한 문제를 겪을 때마다 반드시 ~하도록 하십시오'와 같은 의미가 되어야 알맞으므로 '~할 때마다'를 뜻하는 접속사 (C) Whenever가 정답이다. (A) Though는 접속사지만 의미가 맞지 않고, (B) What도 접속사이지만 주어 혹은 목적어가 없는 불완전한 절을 이끌며, (D) Already는 부사이다.

어휘 though 비록 ~이기는 하지만 already 이미

134 (A) 귀하의 비밀번호는 반드시 대문자 한 개와 기호 하나를 포함해야 합니다.
(B) 저희는 매일 저희 영화 라이브러리에 새 작품을 추가합니다.
(C) 귀하께서 초과 지불하신 액수는 며칠 내로 환불될 것입니다.
(D) 이 조언이 해당 문제를 해결해 주지 못하는 경우, 저희에게 알려 주십시오.

해설 〈빈칸에 알맞은 문장 넣기〉
빈칸 앞 문장의 '다른 계정에서 로그아웃 후 재시도해 보라는 내용'을 this advice(이러한 조언)로 지칭해 해당 방법대로 해도 해결되지 않을 경우 추가 조치로 회사에 연락하도록 알리는 (D)가 정답이다. 나머지 문장들은 지문에서 언급되는 특정 문제점과 관련 없는 내용을 담고 있다.

어휘 resolve ~을 해결하다 let A know A에게 알리다 add ~을 추가하다 title (영화, 책 등의) 작품 amount 액수, 금액 overpay ~을 초과 지불하다 refund ~을 환불하다 contain ~을 포함하다, 담고 있다 capital letter 대문자

[135-138]

여러분의 자택을 현대적이고 세련된 모습으로 꾸밀 방법을 찾고 계신가요? 저희 하트랜드 퍼니싱스가 그 해결책입니다. **135** 저희는 매우 다양한 스타일의 양탄자와 커튼, 그리고 기타 가정용 장식용품을 판매합니다. 이 제품들은 수많은 인기 색상으로 구매 가능합니다. 따라서, 어떤 색상의 배합이든 알맞은 **136** 제품을 찾으실 수 있습니다.

저희 하트랜드 **137** 퍼니싱스에서는 새로운 제품이 여러분의 전반적인 실내 장식에 어떻게 어울릴지 상상해 보는 것이 어려울 수 있다는 점을 알고 있습니다. 이것이 바로 저희가 고객들께 더 이상 제품을 원하시지 않을 경우 30일 이내에 반품하실 수 있도록 해 드리는 **138** 이유입니다. 반품하는 방법에 관한 명확한 안내 정보를 보시려면, www.heartland-furnishings.com을 방문하시기 바랍니다.

어휘 look for ~을 찾아보다 way to do ~하는 방법 classy 세련된, 고급스러운 solution 해결책 available 구매 가능한, 이용 가능한 numerous 수많은, 다수의 popular 인기 있는 color scheme 배색 fit into ~에 적합하다, 어울리다 overall 전반적인 décor 실내 장식 allow A to do A에게 ~할 수 있게 해 주다 return ~을 반품하다, 반납하다 within ~ 이내로 no longer 더 이상 ~ 않다 instructions 안내, 설명, 지시 make a return 반품하다, 반납하다

135 **(A)** 저희는 매우 다양한 스타일의 양탄자와 커튼, 그리고 기타 가정용 장식용품을 판매합니다.

(B) 각 직원이 실내 디자인 업계에서 폭넓은 경험을 지니고 있습니다.

(C) 저희 배송 직원이 주중 언제든 자택 또는 사무실로 주문품을 배송해 드릴 수 있습니다.

(D) 반드시 저희 회원 프로그램에 가입하셔서 단골 이용 고객 포인트를 받으시기 바랍니다.

해설 〈빈칸에 알맞은 문장 넣기〉
빈칸 앞에 집을 멋지게 꾸미는 일과 관련해 특정 업체가 해결책임을 알리는 광고 내용이 시작되고 있고, 빈칸 뒤에는 특정 물품들을 These로 지칭해 다양한 색상으로 구매 가능하다는 말이 쓰여 있다. 따라서 광고를 내는 업체인 하트랜드 퍼니싱스가 판매하는 물품과 관련된 정보를 담은 문장이 빈칸에 쓰여야 알맞으므로 장식용 제품의 종류를 소개하는 (A)가 정답이다.

어휘 household 가정의, 가정용의 accessories 장식용품, 부대용품 a wide range of 아주 다양한 extensive 폭넓은, 광범위한 drop off (사물) ~을 갖다 놓다, (사람) ~을 내려 주다 order 주문(품) be sure to do 반드시 ~하도록 하다, 꼭 ~하도록 하다 sign up for ~에 가입하다, 등록하다 earn ~을 받다, 얻다 loyalty points 단골 이용 고객 포인트

136 **해설** 〈명사 어휘 (문맥)〉
빈칸 앞 문장에서 여러 색상으로 구매 가능한 것으로 언급된 주어 These는 이전 문장의 제품(rugs, curtains, and other household accessories)을 지칭하고 있다. 따라서, 여러 색 조합으로 고객들이 찾을 수 있는 대상은 바로 이러한 제품들이므로 rugs, curtains 등의 제품을 바꾸어 표현한 명사인 (C) item이 정답이다.

어휘 place 장소 addition 추가, 추가된 것[사람] item 물품, 항목 parts 부품

137 **해설** 〈전치사 어휘〉
업체명 Heartland Furnishings가 빈칸 뒤에 쓰여 있고, 그 뒤에 다시 이 업체를 we를 주어로 사용한 문장 구조이다. 따라서, 회사/기관 명사 앞에 사용되어 '~에서'라는 의미를 갖는 (D) At이 정답이다.

어휘 as (자격, 신분 등) ~로서

138 **해설** 〈관계부사〉
빈칸 앞에 위치한 That이 앞 문장 전체를 가리키므로 앞 문장과 빈칸 다음 부분의 의미를 확인해 그 관계를 파악해야 한다. 앞 문장에 새로운 제품이 실내 장식에 적합할지 상상하는 것이 어려울 것이라는 내용이 쓰여 있는데, 이는 빈칸 뒤에서 제품을 원치 않을 경우 30일 이내로 반품이 가능하도록 한 이유로 볼 수 있다. 따라서 이유를 나타내는 명사절을 이끄는 (B) why가 정답이다.

[139-142] 기사

시 행정 담당자인 돈 레이놀즈 씨는 다음 주에 그로스맨 공원에 대한 작업이 시작될 것이라고 발표했다. 완료되어야 하는 첫 번째 일들 중 하나는 자전거 이용자들을 위한 새로운 도로를 만드는 것이다. 과거에는, 자전거 이용자들이 **139** 어쩔 수 없이 보행자들과 함께 길을 공유해야 했지만, 곧 자전거 전용 도로가 생기게 될 것이다. 또한, 세 곳의 새 화장실이 공원 내에 지어질 것이다. 이 화장실들은 공원 방문객의 통행이 많이 있는 구역 근처에 **140** 전략적으로 위치하게 될 것이다. 레이놀즈 씨는 "저희는 이 공원을 모든 주민들께 더욱 안전하고 깨끗하며 재미있는 곳으로 만들기를 원합니다. **141** 게다가, 저희는 훨씬 더 많은 분들께서 이곳을 찾아 주셨으면 합니다. 저희는 모든 분들께서 야외에서 많은 시간을 보내실 것을 권해 드립니다."라고 밝혔다. **142** 그는 이 작업이 늦어도 6월 1일에는 완료될 것으로 예상하고 있다.

어휘 city manager 시 행정 담당자 announce that ~라고 발표하다 commence 시작되다 establish ~을 설립하다, 확립하다 in the past 과거에는 share ~을 공유하다, 함께 이용하다 trail 길, 통행로(= path) one's own 자기 자신만의 be located near ~ 근처에 위치하다 receive ~을 받다 traffic (사람, 차 등의) 통행, 왕래 make A + 형용사 A를 ~한 상태로 만들다 resident 주민 would like A to do A에게 ~하기를 원하다 encourage A to do A에게 ~하도록 권하다, 장려하다 outdoors 야외에서

139 **해설** 〈능동태/수동태〉
동사 force는 'force + 목적어 + to do'의 구조로 쓰이는데, 빈칸 바로 뒤에 목적어 없이 to부정사구가 이어져 있으므로 force가 수동태로 쓰여야 한다는 것을 알 수 있다. 따라서 유일하게 수동태로 제시된 (D) were forced가 정답이다.

어휘 force A to do A에게 어쩔 수 없이 ~하게 하다, ~하도록 강요하다

140 **해설** 〈부사 자리(be + p.p. 뒤)〉
수동태 동사 will be located와 전치사 near 사이에 위치한 빈칸은 수동태 동사를 수식할 부사 자리이므로 부사인 (D) strategically가 정답이다.

어휘 strategy 전략 strategic 전략적인 strategize 전략을 짜다 strategically 전략적으로

141 **해설** 〈접속부사〉
빈칸 앞에는 더 나은 공원으로 만들기를 원한다는 말이, 빈칸 뒤에는 더 많은 사람들이 찾아 주기를 바란다는 말이 쓰여 있다. 이는 한 가지 희망 사항 뒤에 다른 희망 사항을 추가로 언급하는 흐름이므로 '게다가, 추가로' 등의 의미로 추가 정보를 언급할 때 사용하는 (B) In addition이 정답이다.

어휘 instead 대신 in addition 게다가, 추가로 in contrast 대조적으로 for instance 예를 들어

142 (A) 그곳은 시내 지역에서 가장 큰 공원이었다.
(B) 레이놀즈 씨는 유지 관리 문제에 대해 우려하고 있다.
(C) 그는 이 작업이 늦어도 6월 1일에는 완료될 것으로 예상하고 있다.
(D) 도시 전역에 10곳이 넘는 공원이 위치하고 있다.

해설 〈빈칸에 알맞은 문장 넣기〉
빈칸 앞 문장을 보면, 레이놀즈 씨가 공원에 예정된 공사 이후에 나타나길 바라는 긍정적인 일들을 말하고 있다. 따라서 레이놀즈 씨를 He로, 해당 공사를 the work로 지칭해 예상되는 공사 완료 시점을 언급하는 (C)가 정답이다. 나머지 문장들은 해당 공사의 진행과 거리가 먼 내용을 담고 있으므로 오답이다.

어휘 be concerned about ~에 대해 우려하다, 걱정하다 maintenance 유지 관리, 시설 관리 issue 문제, 사안 expect A to do A가 ~할 것으로 예상하다 no later than 늦어도 ~까지는 more than ~가 넘는 throughout ~ 전역에

[143-146] 이메일

수신: susan_logan@thehomeshop.com
발신: r_dexter@dgcookware.com
날짜: 3월 20일
제목: DG 쿡웨어

로건 씨께,

저희 DG 쿡웨어는 최고의 품질을 지닌 조리용 냄비를 **143** 제공해 드리는 데 전념하고 있으며, 저희 제품은 귀하 매장의 재고 목록에 훌륭한 보탬이 될 것입니다. 저희는 다양한 사이즈를 제공해 드리고 있으며, 모든 저희 조리 기구는 철로 만들어집니다. 이 **144** 재료는 매우 내구성이 뛰어나므로, 저희 냄비 제품은 오랜 시간 지속되며, 고온에도 견딜 수 있습니다. 귀하께서 현재 재고로 보유하고 계신 다른 제품들을 바탕으로 볼 때, 고객들께서 저희 제품 라인에 **145** 정말로 관심을 가지시게 될 것이라고 생각합니다. 시험 삼아 약 50개의 냄비로 시작해 보시기를 권해 드립니다. **146** 하지만 원하신다면 분명 더 많은 양의 초기 주문을 하셔도 됩니다. 언제 귀하께 전화 드리는 것이 이 기회에 관해 더 깊이 논의하기 좋을지 저에게 알려 주시기 바랍니다.

안녕히 계십시오.

라파엘 덱스터
수석 영업사원, DG 쿡웨어

어휘 cookware 조리 기구 be committed to -ing ~하는 전념하다, 헌신하다 top-quality 최고의 품질인 make an addition to ~에 보탬이 되다, ~에 추가되다 inventory 재고 (목록) offer ~을 제공하다 a variety of 다양한 be made of ~로 만들어지다 durable 내구성이 뛰어난 last v. 지속되다 withstand ~을 견디다 based on ~을 바탕으로, 기반으로 currently 현재 have A in stock A를 재고로 보유하다 be interested in ~에 관심이 있다 line 제품 라인 recommend -ing ~하도록 권하다, 추천하다 start out with ~로 시작하다 about 약, 대략 as a test run 시험 삼아, 시범적으로 let A know B A에게 B를 알리다 discuss ~을 논의하다, 이야기하다 opportunity 기회 further 더 깊이, 한층 더

143 **해설** 〈동명사 숙어〉
빈칸 앞에 위치한 be committed to에서 to는 전치사이므로 동명사 또는 명사와 결합해야 한다. 또한, 빈칸 뒤에 위치한 명사구 top-quality cooking pots를 목적어로 취하려면 동명사가 쓰여야 하므로 (B) providing이 정답이다.

어휘 provide ~을 제공하다 provision 제공, 공급(량), 준비, 식량

144 해설 〈명사 어휘(문맥)〉
빈칸에 쓰일 명사는 바로 앞에 위치한 this와 함께 앞서 언급된 특정 대상을 대신할 수 있는 것이어야 한다. 또한 빈칸 뒤에 내구성이 아주 뛰어나다는 말이 쓰여 있는데, 이는 바로 앞에 언급된 iron의 특징에 해당된다. 지문에서 iron은 제품을 만드는 재료임을 알 수 있으므로 '재료, 자재, 소재' 등을 뜻하는 (A) material이 정답이다.

어휘 material 재료, 자재, 소재 entry 참가(작), 입장, 출입 baggage 수하물 facility 시설(물)

145 해설 〈부사 어휘〉
문장의 의미상 '정말로, 참으로'라는 의미로 강조를 나타낼 때 사용하는 부사 (C) indeed가 보기 중 가장 적절한 정답이다. (B) once는 부사인 경우 '(과거) 한 때'라는 의미로 의미상 적절치 않으며, 나머지 부사들은 동사 앞에 위치할 수 없다.

어휘 quite 꽤, 상당히 once 한 번, 한때 indeed 정말로, 참으로 enough ad. 충분히 a. 충분한

146 (A) 그러실 경우, 환불 신청서를 빠짐없이 작성하기 바랍니다.
(B) 하지만 원하신다면 분명 더 많은 양의 초기 주문을 하셔도 됩니다.
(C) 분명히, 그 요리사의 능력이 고려되어야 합니다.
(D) 저희는 지난 30년 동안 영업을 해 왔습니다.

해설 〈빈칸에 알맞은 문장 넣기〉
빈칸 앞 문장에 시험 삼아 약 50개의 냄비를 먼저 주문하도록 권하는 말이 쓰여 있으므로 최초의 주문량과 관련된 추가 조언에 해당되는 (B)가 정답이다. 나머지 문장들은 빈칸 앞뒤에 각각 언급된 첫 주문 및 연락 가능한 시점 중 어느 것과도 관련 없는 내용을 담고 있으므로 오답이다.

어휘 fill out ~을 작성하다 refund 환불 request 요청, 요구 form 양식, 서식 in full 빠짐없이, 전부 certainly 분명히 place an order 주문하다 initial 초기의, 최초의 if you prefer 원한다면 clearly 분명히 take A into account A를 고려하다, 계산에 넣다 be in business 영업하다 decade 10년

[147-148] 정보

시사이드 커피점
켄우드 스트리트 739번지
438-555-8791
www.seasidecoffeeshop.com
"우리 도시 최고의 커피!"

영업 시간
월요일 – 금요일: 오전 7시 – 오후 9시
토요일: 오전 8시 – 오후 10시
일요일: 오전 10시 – 오후 8시

148 개별 회의 공간 이용 시간
월요일 – 금요일: 오전 9시 – 오후 8시
토요일: 오전 10시 – 오후 9시
일요일: 오전 10시 – 오후 6시

미리 전화 주셔서 주문품을 준비시키실 수 있습니다.

147 6잔 이상의 음료를 구입하시면 자동으로 15% 할인됩니다!

어휘 brew (재료를 끓는 물에 넣어 만드는) 커피, 차, 음료 private 개별의, 개인의, 사적인 availability 이용 가능성 in advance 미리, 사전에 have A ready A를 준비시키다 beverage 음료 automatic 자동의

147 정보에 따르면, 고객들은 어떻게 할인 자격을 얻을 수 있는가?
(A) 각자 가져갈 컵을 챙겨 옴으로써
(B) 5잔이 넘는 음료를 구입함으로써
(C) 웹 사이트에서 쿠폰을 다운로드함으로써
(D) 설문 조사지를 작성 완료함으로써

해설 〈세부 사항〉
할인 서비스가 언급된 맨 마지막 문장에, 6잔 혹은 그 이상의 음료를 구입하면 15% 할인을 받는다고(Buy six or more beverages to get an automatic 15% off!) 쓰여 있으므로 이와 같은 구입 조건에 해당되는 (B)가 정답이다.

어휘 bring in ~을 챙겨 오다 purchase ~을 구입하다 more than ~가 넘는 complete ~을 작성하다 questionnaire 설문 조사지

148 고객들은 언제 개별 회의 공간을 이용할 수 있는가?
(A) 화요일 오전 7시에
(B) 수요일 오전 8시에
(C) 금요일 오후 7시에
(D) 일요일 오후 7시에

해설 〈세부 사항〉
개별 회의 공간 이용 시간으로 제시된 시간대 중에서, 월요일에서 금요일, 오전 9시부터 오후 8시까지의(Private Meeting Room

Availability, Monday–Friday: 9 A.M.–8 P.M.) 시간대에 해당하는 금요일 오후 7시를 언급한 (C)가 정답이다.

[149-151] 편지

세다 골프 리조트
캘빈 스트리트 58번지
벨라 비스타, CA 96073

크레이그 워드
사우스 스트리트 2786
벨라 비스타, CA 96073

워드 씨께,

저희는 7월 15일에 발생된 사건과 관련해 귀하의 편지를 받았습니다. **150** 귀하의 차량이 저희 주차장에 주차되어 있는 동안 골프공에 맞아 전면 덮개에 움푹한 자국이 생겼다는 사실을 듣게 되어 매우 유감스러웠습니다.

저희 리조트는 그와 같은 문제를 피하기 위해 회원께서 오직 지정된 구역 내에서만 경기하시도록 최선을 다하고 있습니다. 하지만, 저희 회원 약정서에 명시되어 있고 주차장 전역에도 게시되어 있는 바와 같이, **149** 방문객께서는 각자의 책임하에 주차하고 계십니다. 따라서, 저희 세다 골프 리조트는 이 문제에 있어 어떠한 책임도 지지 않으며, 저희 내부 규정에 따라 수리 비용에 대한 지불 의무가 없습니다.

하지만, 귀하께서 저희 리조트에서 좋지 않은 경험을 하신 것에 대해 유감스럽게 생각하며, 호의의 표시를 해 드리고자 합니다. **151** 저희가 증정해 드리는 상품권을 동봉해 드렸으므로 확인해 보시기 바랍니다. 이는 식사 및 음료 구입용으로 클럽하우스에서 사용하실 수 있습니다. 계속해서 저희 세다 골프 리조트를 귀하의 주된 골프 장소로 이용해 주시기를 바랍니다. 다른 어떤 방법으로든 귀하께 도움을 드릴 수 있다면, 주저하지 마시고 저에게 다시 연락 주십시오.

안녕히 계십시오.

제이슨 커비

어휘 receive ~을 받다 regarding ~와 관련해 incident 사건 occur 발생되다, 일어나다 find out that ~임을 알게 되다 while ~하는 동안 park ~을 주차하다 parking lot 주차장 cause ~을 발생시키다, 초래하다 dent 움푹한 자국 hood 자동차 전면 덮개 ensure that 반드시 ~하도록 하다, ~하는 것을 보장하다 designated 지정된 in order to do ~하기 위해 avoid ~을 피하다 however 하지만, 그러나 as stated in ~에 명시된 바와 같이 agreement 약정(서), 계약(서) post ~을 게시하다 throughout ~ 전역에 at one's own risk 자신의 책임 하에 therefore 따라서, 그러므로 take no responsibility in ~에 있어 책임이 없다 be liable for ~에 대한 의무가 있다, 책임이 있다 repair 수리 according to ~에 따라 in-house 내부의 negative 좋지 못한, 부정적인 make a gesture of good will 호의의 표시를 하다 enclosed 동봉된 gift certificate 상품권 with one's compliments ~가 증정하는 beverage 음료 continue to do 계속 ~하다 primary 주된, 주요한 assist ~을 돕다 hesitate to do ~하기를 주저하다 contact ~에게 연락하다

149 커비 씨는 왜 편지를 보냈는가?
(A) 새로운 서비스를 홍보하기 위해
(B) 비용 지불을 요청하기 위해
(C) 정책을 분명히 말하기 위해
(D) 회원 자격 갱신을 촉구하기 위해

해설 〈주제 및 목적〉
첫 단락은 사건 발생의 배경을 간략히 언급하는 내용이며, 두 번째 단락에서 차량 주차가 방문객들의 책임이라는 점과 해당 골프 리조트가 상대방 차량의 문제와 관련해 책임 및 수리 비용 지불 의무가 없다고(~ visitors park in the lot at their own risk. Therefore, Cedar Golf Resort takes no responsibility in this matter and is not liable for repair costs ~) 알리는 것이 편지를 보낸 이유이다. 이는 해당 리조트의 정책을 분명히 해 두기 위한 것이므로 (C)가 정답이다.

어휘 promote ~을 홍보하다 request ~을 요청하다, 요구하다 payment 지불(금) clarify ~을 분명히 말하다, 명확히 해 두다 policy 정책, 방침 prompt ~을 촉구하다, 부추기다 renewal (계약 등의) 갱신

150 편지에 무슨 문제점이 언급되어 있는가?
(A) 워드 씨가 골프 레슨을 놓쳤다.
(B) 워드 씨가 금지 구역에 주차했다.
(C) 워드 씨의 회원권이 만료되었다.
(D) 워드 씨의 차량이 손상되었다.

해설 〈세부 사항〉
사건 배경을 설명하는 첫 단락에, 상대방의 차량이 주차장에서 골프공에 맞아 전면 덮개에 움푹한 자국이 생겼다고(~ your car was hit by a golf ball while it was parked in our parking lot, causing a dent ~) 언급하는 것이 문제점에 해당된다. 이는 차량 손상을 말하는 것이므로 (D)가 정답이다.

어휘 miss ~을 놓치다, 지나치다 park 주차하다 prohibit ~을 금지하다 expire 만료되다 damaged 손상된, 피해를 입은

151 커비 씨의 편지와 함께 무엇이 보내졌는가?
(A) 주차권
(B) 부분 환불액
(C) 상품권
(D) 회원 약정서

해설 〈세부 사항〉
편지에 동봉된 것이 언급되는 세 번째 단락에, 리조트 측에서 증정하는 상품권을 동봉했다고(Please accept the enclosed gift certificate ~) 알리는 부분이 있으므로 (C)가 정답이다.

어휘 pass 입장권, 출입증 partial 부분적인 refund 환불(액) contract 약정(서), 계약(서)

[152-153] 광고

에메랄드 스파 공석

(152) 저희 에메랄드 스파는 지난 15년 동안 지역 최고의 스파 중 하나였습니다. 저희는 매장 내의 채식 카페뿐만 아니라 다양한 신체 이완 및 미용 치료 서비스도 제공해 드리고 있습니다. 저희 서비스에 대한 늘어나는 수요로 인해, 현재 두 명의 정규직 마사지 치료사를 찾고 있습니다. 이 치료사의 직무에는 고객의 필요 사항 평가, 고객의 피부 연조직 및 근육 관리, 집에서 하는 스트레칭 방법에 대한 조언이 포함됩니다. 지원서는 9월 1일까지 접수를 받습니다. 면접은 총무부장님과 함께 9월 4일에서 8일 사이에 진행됩니다. **(153)** 전화 면접은 인정되지 않으므로 다른 지역 지원자들께서는 반드시 저희 스파의 방문 일정을 잡으셔야 합니다.

어휘 job opening 공석 offer ~을 제공하다 a variety of 다양한 relaxation 신체 이완, 긴장 완화, 휴식 treatment 치료, 처치 as well as ~뿐만 아니라 …도 on-site 구내의, 현장의 due to ~로 인해 growing 늘어나는, 증가하는 demand 수요 currently 현재 seek ~을 찾다, 구하다 therapist 치료사 responsibility 직무, 책무 include ~을 포함하다 evaluate ~을 평가하다 manipulate ~을 다루다, 처리하다 soft tissue (피부) 연조직 at-home 집에서 하는 application 지원(서), 신청(서) accept ~을 받아들이다, 수용하다 hold ~을 열다, 개최하다 out-of-town 다른 지역의 applicant 지원자 make an arrangement 준비하다, 조치하다

152 에메랄드 스파에 관해 사실인 것은 무엇인가?
(A) 지역 내 유일한 스파이다.
(B) 10년 넘게 운영되어 왔다.
(C) 최근에 식당 시설을 추가했다.
(D) 더 큰 시설로 이전한다.

해설 〈진위 확인 (세부 진위 유형)〉
지문 시작 부분에 15년 동안 최고의 업체였음을(Emerald Spa has been one of the area's top spas for the past 15 years) 알리는 내용이 있으므로 이와 같이 운영 기간과 관련된 사실을 말한 (B)가 정답이다.

어휘 operate 운영되다 more than ~가 넘게 decade 10년 recently 최근에 add ~을 추가하다 establishment (식당, 학교, 회사 등의) 시설, 건물 facility 시설(물)

153 면접에 관해 언급된 것은 무엇인가?
(A) 9월 1일까지 완료될 것이다.
(B) 약 2주 동안 진행될 것이다.
(C) 인사팀에 의해 진행될 것이다.
(D) 반드시 직접 만나 실시되어야 한다.

해설 〈진위 확인 (세부 진위 유형)〉
맨 마지막 문장에 전화 면접이 불가능하다는 말과 함께 다른 지역에 있는 지원자는 반드시 방문해야 한다는(Out-of-town applicants must make arrangements to visit the spa. ~) 내용이 있다. 이는 직접 만나는 방식으로 면접이 진행된다는 뜻이므로 (D)가 정답이다.

어휘 complete ~을 완료하다 by (기한) ~까지 run 진행되다, 운영되다 approximately 약, 대략 lead ~을 진행하다, 이끌다 conduct ~을 실시하다, 수행하다 in person 직접 만나서

[154-155] 온라인 채팅

조이스 (직원 번호 108)	[오전 10:42]
요컴 주식회사 고객 서비스 센터에 연락 주셔서 감사합니다. 무엇을 도와드릴까요?	

브라이언 로사도	[오전 10:43]
온라인으로 **(154)** 귀사의 소파들 중 하나를 주문하려는 중입니다. 웹 사이트에는 구매 가능하다고 나와 있지만, 결제 페이지로 넘어가면, 품절이라고 나옵니다.	

조이스 (직원 번호 108)	[오전 10:44]
불편을 드려 죄송합니다. 제품 번호와 귀하의 계정 번호를 말씀해 주시겠습니까?	

브라이언 로사도	[오전 10:45]
제품 번호는 TM4850이고, 제 계정 번호는 5814796입니다.	

조이스 (직원 번호 108)	[오전 10:46]
분명 그 제품을 재고로 보유하고 있습니다. **(155)** 제가 귀하 대신 주문해 귀하의 계정으로 비용을 청구해 드리겠습니다. 그렇게 해도 괜찮으시겠습니까?	

브라이언 로사도	[오전 10:47]
그렇게 해 주시면 감사하겠습니다.	

어휘 contact ~에게 연락하다 try to do ~하려 하다 order ~을 주문하다 available 구매 가능한, 이용 가능한 checkout (비용) 계산 out of stock 품절인, 재고가 없는 inconvenience 불편함 account 계정, 계좌 have A in stock A를 재고로 보유하다 on one's behalf ~을 대신해 charge ~에 대한 비용을 청구하다 work 도움이 되다, 작용하다, 효과가 있다 appreciate ~에 대해 감사하다

154 요컴 주식회사는 무슨 종류의 업체일 것 같은가?
(A) 화장품 회사
(B) 가구 매장
(C) 의류 회사
(D) 전자제품 매장

해설 〈주제 및 목적〉
로사도 씨가 10시 43분에 작성한 메시지에 주문하려는 제품으로 소파(your sofas)를 언급하고 있는데, 이는 가구 매장에서 판매하는 것이므로 (B)가 정답이다.

155 오전 10시 47분에, 로사도 씨가 "I would appreciate it"이라고 썼을 때 의미한 것은 무엇이겠는가?
(A) 자신의 컴퓨터를 다시 시작하는 데 도움이 필요하다.
(B) 제품이 반품될 수 있다는 점에 대해 고마워하고 있다.

(C) 문제에 대해 제안된 해결책을 받아들이고 있다.
(D) 해당 직원에게 주문품을 취소하기를 원하고 있다.

해설 〈의도 파악〉
제시된 문장은 감사의 인사를 할 때 사용하는 말인데, 이는 앞서 조이스 씨가 상대방 대신 주문하고 해당 계정으로 비용을 청구하는 것이 괜찮은지(I'd be happy to order it on your behalf and charge it ~) 묻는 것에 대한 답변이다. 따라서 조이스 씨가 권하는 문제 해결 방법대로 하겠다는 의미의 문장이므로 (C)가 정답이다.

어휘 assistance 도움, 지원 be grateful that ~라는 점에 대해 고마워하다 return ~을 반품하다, 반납하다 accept ~을 받아들이다, 수용하다 proposed 제안된 solution 해결책 issue 문제, 사안 would like A to do A에게 ~하기를 원하다 agent 직원, 대리인 cancel ~을 취소하다 order 주문(품)

[156-158] 광고

발견의 날!

컬링워스 역사 협회(CHS)는 우리 지역에 있는 (156) 역사적으로 중요한 장소에 관해 다른 분들께 교육해 드리는 데 전념하고 있는 비영리 단체입니다. 여름 기간(6월 - 8월) 중 첫 번째와 세 번째 토요일마다, (156) 컬링워스 성과 템프스포드 요새, 그리고 브램웰 틴 광산의 가이드 동반 견학을 제공해 드립니다.

이 견학 여행은 오전 9시에 시작되며, 약 오후 4시에 종료됩니다. 점심 식사는 참가비에 포함됩니다. 각 가이드는 여러 장소와 그 배경에 관련된 모든 것을 배우기 위한 3개월의 집중 과정을 수강하며, 대부분의 저희 가이드들은 관련 분야에 대한 학위도 소지하고 있습니다. 개별 그룹 일정을 잡으시거나 일반 그룹과 함께 등록하실 수도 있습니다. (157) 견학 중 일부 구역은 고르거나 평평하지 않은 계단 또는 돌로 된 통로가 포함되어 있다는 점에 유의하시기 바랍니다. 모든 분들께서 반드시 안전하게 이 구역들을 탐사할 수 있는 신체적 능력을 보유해야 합니다.

악천후로 인해 견학이 취소될 경우 전액 환불을 제공해 드립니다. (158) 등록은 하셨지만 견학이 취소되었는지 확실치 않으실 경우, 그러한 정보를 제공해 드리는 저희 웹 사이트 www.cullingworthhs.org를 확인해 보시기 바랍니다. 672-555-1306번으로 오늘 전화하셔서 예약하시기 바랍니다!

어휘 nonprofit 비영리의 organization 단체, 기관 dedicated to -ing ~하는 데 전념하는, 헌신하는 historically 역사적으로 significant 중요한 guided 가이드가 동반된 excursion (짧은) 여행 approximately 약, 대략 include ~을 포함하다 fee 요금, 수수료 take a course 강좌를 수강하다 intensive 집중적인 degree 학위 related 관련된 field 분야 as well ~도, 또한 arrange for ~에 대한 일정을 잡다, 조치하다 sign up 등록하다, 신청하다 Please note that ~임에 유의하세요 stony 돌로 된 walkway 통로, 보도 level (표면 등이) 고른, 평평한(= flat) physical capacity 신체적 능력 navigate ~을 탐사하다, 찾아다니다 full refund 전액 환불 cancel ~을 취소하다 due to ~로 인해, ~ 때문에 extreme weather 악천후 whether or not ~인지 아닌지 provide ~을 제공하다 make one's booking 예약하다

156 광고는 무엇에 관한 것인가?
(A) 일련의 역사 기반 강연
(B) 단체 회원 할인
(C) 유적지를 볼 수 있는 기회
(D) 지역 역사에 관한 강좌

해설 〈주제 및 목적〉
첫 단락에 역사적으로 중요한 장소(historically significant places)에 관해 교육한다는 말과 함께 컬링워스 성과 템프스포드 요새, 그리고 브램웰 틴 광산에 대한 가이드 동반 견학을 제공한다고(~ we offer a guided tour of Cullingworth Castle, Fort Tempsford, and the Bramwell Tin Mine) 알리고 있다. 이는 유적지를 둘러보는 일을 뜻하므로 (C)가 정답이다.

어휘 a series of 일련의 A-based A를 기반으로 하는, 바탕으로 하는 opportunity to do ~할 수 있는 기회 historical site 유적지 local 지역의, 현지의

157 그룹 구성원들은 무엇을 할 것으로 예상되는가?
(A) 안전 교육 시간에 참가하기
(B) 점심 도시락 지참하고 오기
(C) 미리 그룹 구성원들과 만나기
(D) 고르지 못한 지면에서 걷기

해설 〈세부 사항〉
그룹 구성원들이 할 일이 언급되는 두 번째 단락에, 고르거나 평평하지 않은 계단 또는 돌로 된 통로가 있다는 말과 함께 그곳을 안전하게 다닐 수 있는 신체적 능력이 필요하다는(~ include stairs or stony walkways that are not level or flat. Everyone must have the physical capacity to navigate ~) 내용이 있다. 따라서 이러한 특징의 장소에서 걷는 것을 언급한 (D)가 정답이다.

어휘 be expected to do ~할 것으로 예상되다 attend ~에 참석하다 training 교육, 훈련 session (특정 활동을 위한) 시간 bring along ~을 지참하다 in advance 미리, 사전에 uneven 고르지 못한 surface 지면, 표면

158 CHS에 관해 사실인 것은 무엇인가?
(A) 온라인으로 취소 상황을 알린다.
(B) 현재 추가 직원을 구하고 있다.
(C) 전국 각지에 지점이 있다.
(D) 약 3개월 전에 문을 열었다.

해설 〈진위 확인 (전체 진위 유형)〉
마지막 단락에 행사 취소 여부가 확실치 않을 경우에 관련 정보를 제공하는 웹 사이트를 확인해 보라는 언급이(~ but aren't sure whether or not your tour has been canceled, please check our Web site ~) 있으므로 (A)가 정답이다.

어휘 cancellation 취소 currently 현재 seek ~을 구하다, 찾다 branch 지점, 지사 across ~ 전역에 about 약, 대략

[159-160] 이메일

수신: 나탈리 로우
발신: 레이먼드 델가도
날짜: 8월 28일
제목: 정보 통신 워크숍

로우 씨께,

커크뷰 협회의 제4회 연례 정보 통신 무역 박람회 행사에 (159) 등록해 주셔서 감사합니다. 귀하를 위해 부스 한 곳이 정식으로 예약되었음을 확인해 드리고자 합니다. 이번 행사는 10월 11일에 오전 9시부터 오후 4시까지 포모나 호텔에서 개최됩니다. 이번 주 초에 우편으로 (160) 설문 조사 양식을 받으셨을 것입니다. (160) 해당 양식을 작성하신 다음, 제공해 드린 봉투에 돌려보내 주시기 바랍니다. 9월 5일까지 그렇게 해 주실 경우, 포모나 호텔의 구내 레스토랑에서 사용 가능한 50달러 상품권을 받으실 수 있는 경품 추첨 행사에 참가하시게 될 것입니다.

안녕히 계십시오.

레이먼드 델가도

어휘 register for ~에 등록하다 confirm that ~임을 확인해 주다 booth 부스, 칸막이 공간 officially 정식으로, 공식적으로 reserve ~을 예약하다 take place (일, 행사 등이) 개최되다, 발생되다 should have p.p. (과거에 대한 확신) ~했을 것이다 receive ~을 받다 survey 설문 조사 form 양식, 서식 complete ~을 작성 완료하다 envelop 봉투 by (기한) ~까지 enter A into B A를 B에 참가시키다 prize drawing 경품 추첨 행사 gift certificate 상품권 on-site 구내의, 부지 내의

159 델가도 씨는 왜 이메일을 보냈는가?
(A) 참가자에게 일정 변경을 알리기 위해
(B) 로우 씨에게 행사에서 연설하도록 요청하기 위해
(C) 다가오는 무역 박람회를 위한 출장 준비를 하기 위해
(D) 등록 과정의 성공을 알려 주기 위해

해설 〈주제 및 목적〉
지문 초반부에, 등록한 것에 대해 감사하다는 인사와 함께 정식으로 부스 한 곳이 예약된(Thank you for registering ~ a booth has been officially reserved for you) 사실을 알리고 있다. 이는 성공적으로 등록되었음을 알리는 내용에 해당되므로 (D)가 정답이다.

어휘 inform A of B A에게 B를 알리다 participant 참가자 invite A to do A에게 ~하도록 요청하다 give a talk 연설하다, 강연하다 make arrangements for ~을 위한 준비를 하다, 조치를 하다 upcoming 다가오는, 곧 있을 trade fair 무역 박람회 acknowledge ~을 알려 주다 success 성공 registration 등록 process 과정

160 델가도 씨는 로우 씨에게 무엇을 하도록 요청하는가?
(A) 호텔에 연락하기
(B) 문서 되돌려 보내기
(C) 지불 비용 보내기
(D) 주소 업데이트하기

해설 〈세부 사항〉
지문 중반부에, 상대방이 설문 조사 양식을 받은 사실과 함께 그것을

작성해 다시 보내 달라고(You should have received a survey form ~ Please complete it and send it back ~) 요청하는 내용이 있으므로 (B)가 정답이다.

어휘 contact ~에 연락하다 return ~을 되돌려 보내다, 반송하다 payment 지불(금)

[161-163] 광고

매리포사 아파트에서 여러분의 새 집을 찾아보세요!

분 애비뉴 2705번지, 볼티모어, MD 21212

매리포사 아파트는 콜드웰 공원 및 기타 인근 편의시설에서 걸어서 갈 수 있는 거리에 위치한 신축 아파트 단지입니다. —[1]—. **161** 각 세대에는 최신식 식기세척기와 냉장고, 그리고 전자레인지가 딸려 있습니다. 세입자들께서는 또한 **161** 저희 지하 주차장에 개별적으로 할당되는 주차 공간을 이용하실 수 있으며, 이곳은 하루 24시간 감시됩니다. **161** 지하에 배정되는 사물함이 있어 세입자들께서 자전거나 상자와 같이 부피가 큰 물품을 보관하실 수 있습니다.

매리포사 아파트는 가격 적정성을 염두에 두고 지어졌습니다. **163** 건물은 대체로 침실 1개짜리 아파트로 구성되어 있습니다. —[2]—. 모든 세입자들께서는 아름다운 조경 및 작은 피크닉 구역과 함께 평온한 환경을 즐기실 수 있습니다. 개별 세대뿐만 아니라 부지에 대한 사진도 www.mariposaapt.com/gallery에서 보실 수 있습니다. —[3]—.

모든 임대 업무는 저희 건물 관리팀의 질 램플리 씨에 의해 처리되고 있습니다. **162** 램플리 씨께서 언제든지 기꺼이 부지 곳곳을 보여 드릴 수 있으므로, 555-4817번으로 전화하셔서 견학 시간을 예약하시기 바랍니다. 인기 있는 지역의 아름다운 건물에서 생활하실 수 있는 기회를 놓치지 마시기 바랍니다. —[4]—. 매리포사 아파트로 이사해 보세요!

어휘 complex (건물) 단지, 복합건물 within walking distance to ~로 걸어서 갈 수 있는 거리에 있는 neighborhood 인근, 지역 amenities 편의시설 unit (아파트나 상가 등의) 세대, 점포 come with ~가 딸려 있다, ~을 포함하다 state-of-the-art 최신식의 tenant 세입자 assigned 배정된, 할당된 parking spot 주차 공간 monitor ~을 감시하다, 관찰하다 basement 지하(실) bulky 부피가 큰 create ~을 만들어 내다 with A in mind A를 염두에 두고, A를 감안해 affordability 가격 적정성 mostly 대체로 be made up of ~로 구성되다 landscaping 조경 grounds 부지, 구내 as well as ~뿐만 아니라 …도 available 이용 가능한 rental 임대, 대여 handle ~을 처리하다, 다루다 property 건물, 부동산 site 부지, 장소, 현장 book ~을 예약하다 viewing 견학, 둘러보기 miss ~을 놓치다, 지나치다 make the move to ~로 이사하다

161 매리포사 아파트의 편의 시설로 언급되지 않은 것은 무엇인가?
(A) 현대적인 가전기기
(B) 안전한 주차
(C) 피트니스 센터
(D) 추가 보관 공간

해설 〈진위 확인 (세부 진위 유형)〉
첫 단락에 최신식 식기세척기 등의 기기가(~ a state-of-the-art dishwasher ~) 있다고 언급하는 부분에서 (A)를, 바로 뒤이어 24시간 감시되는 개별 주차 공간이 있다고(~ their own assigned parking spot ~) 알리는 부분에서 (B)를, 그리고 지하실에 배정된 사물함이 있다는(There are assigned lockers ~) 내용을 통해 (D)를 각각 확인할 수 있다. 하지만 피트니스 센터와 관련된 정보는 제시되어 있지 않으므로 (C)가 정답이다.

어휘 amenity 편의 시설 appliance 가전기기 secure 안전한 additional 추가적인 storage 보관 (공간)

162 광고에 따르면, 관심 있는 사람들은 왜 램플리 씨에게 연락해야 하는가?
(A) 견학 일정을 잡기 위해
(B) 일부 사진을 요청하기 위해
(C) 신청서를 제출하기 위해
(D) 계약을 갱신하기 위해

해설 〈세부 사항〉
램플리 씨의 이름이 언급되는 마지막 단락에, 부지를 구경하려면 램플리 씨를 통해 견학 시간을 예약하라고(Ms. Lampley is happy to show you around the site anytime, so call 555-4817 to book a viewing) 알리고 있으므로 (A)가 정답이다.

어휘 interested 관심이 있는 party 사람, 당사자 contact ~에게 연락하다 arrange ~의 일정을 잡다, ~을 마련하다 request ~을 요청하다, 요구하다 submit ~을 제출하다 application 신청(서), 지원(서) renew ~을 갱신하다 contract 계약(서)

163 [1], [2], [3], [4]로 표시된 위치들 중에서, 다음 문장이 들어가기에 가장 적절한 곳은 어디인가?
"더 큰 세대들도 이용 가능하기는 하지만, 빠르게 임대될 것으로 예상됩니다."
(A) [1]
(B) [2]
(C) [3]
(D) [4]

해설 〈문장 넣기〉
제시된 문장은 더 큰 세대도 있지만 빠르게 임대될 것이라는 의미를 나타내므로, 세대 규모와 관련해 비교되는 대상이 언급되는 문장 뒤에 위치해야 흐름이 자연스러워진다. 따라서 대체로 침실 1개짜리 아파트로 구성되어 있다고 알리는 문장 뒤에 위치한 [2]에 들어가는 것이 흐름상 적절하므로 (B)가 정답이다.

어휘 available 이용 가능한, 구입 가능한 be expected to do ~할 것으로 예상되다 rent out ~을 임대하다

[164-167] 공지

글렌케언 재단의 후원을 받는 국립 접객업 협회(NHA)가 **167** 4월 10일 수요일부터 4월 13일 토요일까지 일련의 워크숍 행사를 주최합니다. **164** 이번 행사는 고급 숙박 시설을 관리하는 분들께서 자신의 업소로 더 많은 고객들을 유치하는 방법에 관해 배울 수 있는 훌륭한 방법입니다.

165 모든 워크숍은 몬트리올에 위치한 뷰마운트 컨퍼런스 센터에서 개최될 것입니다. 참가자들께서는 행사 기간 내내 소규모 그룹으로 배정되어 여러 가지 과제에 대해 함께 하시게 될 것입니다. **166** 마지막 날에는, 그룹들이 각자의 프로젝트에 관해 발표하고 청중으로부터 의견을 들어 보게 됩니다.

강사진에는 토론토 대학교의 제인 루이스 씨와 오타와에 본사를 둔 랜디스 트래블의 대표이신 베타나 랜디스 씨, 그리고 고향인 캘거리에서 인기 체인점 카바나인을 시작하신 레이날도 폰테인 씨가 포함되어 있습니다. **167** 폰테인 씨께서는 또한 베스트셀러인 〈체인 리액션〉을 저술하셨으며, 행사 첫 날에 책에 사인을 해 드릴 예정입니다.

이 흥미로운 행사에 등록하시려면, www.nationalhospitality.ca를 방문하시기 바랍니다.

어휘 with support from ~의 후원을 받는, 지원을 받는 host ~을 주최하다 a series of 일련의 way for A to do A가 ~할 수 있는 방법 oversee 관리하다, 감독하다 accommodation 숙박 시설 how to do ~하는 법 attract ~을 유치하다 site 장소, 부지, 현장 take place (일, 행사 등이) 개최되다, 발생되다 participant 참가자 assign A to B A를 B에 배정하다, 할당하다 several 여럿의, 몇몇의 task 과제, 일, 임무 throughout ~ 동안 내내 give a presentation 발표하다 receive ~을 받다 feedback 의견 audience 청중, 관객 instructor 강사 based (합쳐로 쓰여) ~에 본사를 둔 launch ~을 시작하다, 출시하다 sign ~에 사인하다, 서명하다 copy (출판물 등의) 권, 부, 사본 register for ~에 등록하다

164 공지는 누구를 대상으로 할 것 같은가?
(A) 경영학 교수들
(B) 여행사 직원들
(C) 호텔 지배인들
(D) 투자 은행가들

해설 〈글의 대상〉
행사 참여 대상은 보통 첫 번째 단락에서 유추 가능한데, 고급 숙박 시설을 운영하는 사람들이 더 많은 고객을 유치하는 방법에 관해 배울 수 있다고(This event is an excellent way for people operating luxury accommodations to learn about how to attract more guests to their site) 쓰여 있다. 따라서 (C)가 정답이다.

어휘 agent 직원, 대리인 investment 투자

165 워크숍이 어디에서 개최될 것인가?
(A) 캘거리에서
(B) 몬트리올에서
(C) 오타와에서
(D) 토론토에서

행사 개최 장소가 언급되는 두 번째 단락에 모든 워크숍이 몬트리올에 위치한 뷰마운트 컨퍼런스 센터에서 개최된다는 내용이(All workshops will take placeat Viewmount Conference Center in Montreal) 있으므로 (B)가 정답이다.

어휘 hold ~을 개최하다

166 참가자들은 행사 마지막 날에 무엇을 할 수 있는가?
(A) 시상식 관람하기
(B) 각자의 프로젝트 발표하기
(C) NHA 대표와 만나기
(D) 대학교 견학하기

해설 〈세부 사항〉
행사 마지막 날이 언급되는 두 번째 단락에 마지막 날에는, 그룹별 프로젝트에 관해 발표하고 청중으로부터 의견을 듣는다고(On the final day, groups will give a presentation on their project ~) 쓰여 있으므로 (B)가 정답이다.

어휘 participant 참가자 award ceremony 시상식 present ~을 발표하다, 제시하다, 제공하다 tour v. ~을 견학하다, 둘러보다

167 폰테인 씨는 언제 책에 사인할 것인가?
(A) 4월 10일
(B) 4월 11일
(C) 4월 12일
(D) 4월 13일

해설 〈세부 사항〉
마지막 문장에 폰테인 씨가 행사 첫 날에 책에 사인을 해 준다고(Mr. Fontaine ~, and he will be signing copies on the first day of the event) 쓰여 있는데, 첫 단락에 행사가 4월 10일부터 시작된다고(~ is hosting a series of workshops from Wednesday, April 10 ~) 알리고 있으므로 (A)가 정답이다.

[168-171] 온라인 채팅

> **스텔라 바 [오전 10:48]**
> 앨런 씨, 그리고 케네스 씨, 두 분 중에 사무실에 계신 분 있으신가요? **168** 제가 럽튼 파이낸셜 사의 새 본사 건물을 위해 만든 디자인을 함께 검토하기 위해 그 회사로 가는 중입니다. **169** 그런데 제 책상에 설계도를 놓고 왔어요.

> **앨런 타이슨 [오전 10:49]**
> **169** 제가 지금 스캔해 드릴 수 있어요.

> **스텔라 바 [오전 10:50]**
> 디지털 버전은 안 됩니다. 전체적인 배치와 함께 세부 사항을 확인하는 게 너무 어려울 거예요.

> **앨런 타이슨 [오전 10:51]**
> 돌아오셔서 가져가실 시간이 있으신가요?

> **케네스 오닐 [오전 10:52]**
> 사실, 그러실 필요는 없으실 거예요. 제가 어쨌든 밖에 나가 봐야 해요. 중간쯤에 있는 칼라일 지역에서 만날 수 있을 겁니다.

> **스텔라 바 [오전 10:53]**
> 잘됐네요! 그린 트리 커피 매장에서 뵙는 게 어떨까요?

> **케네스 오닐 [오전 10:54]**
> **170** 대신 렌리스 사무용품 매장에서 만나실 수 있을까요? **171** 오늘 오후에 있을 채용 면접을 보러 찾아오는 사람들 때문에 몇몇 폴더를 구입하기 위해 그곳에 들러야 해요.

> **앨런 타이슨 [오전 10:55]**
> 케네스 씨, 럽튼 파이낸셜 건물까지 쭉 가실 수는 없으세요? 자리를 비우신 동안 제가 대신 전화 받아 드릴 수 있어요.

> **케네스 오닐 [오전 10:56]**
> **171** 방문자들을 위해 준비해야 할 서류들이 여전히 좀 있어서 그렇게 오래 사무실에서 나가 있을 수 없어요.

> **스텔라 바 [오전 10:57]**
> **170** 그게 저는 좋아요. 얼마나 빨리 그곳에 오실 수 있으세요?

> **케네스 오닐 [오전 10:58]**
> 지금 나가면, 15분에서 20분 정도요.

어휘 either 둘 중 하나 be headed to ~로 가다, 향하다 go over ~을 검토하다, 살펴보다 create ~을 만들어 내다 headquarters 본사 leave ~을 놓고 오다, 나가다, 떠나다 blueprint 설계도, 도면 details 세부 사항, 상세 정보 along with ~와 함께 entire 전체의, 모든 layout 배치, 구획 pick A up A를 가져가다 actually 실은, 사실은 necessary 필요한 anyway 어쨌든 about halfway 중간쯤에서 neighborhood 지역, 인근 How about

---

어휘 ~? ~는 어때요? instead 대신에 all the way to ~까지 쭉 while ~하는 동안 away 자리를 비운 that ad. 그렇게, 그만큼 prepare ~을 준비하다 That works for me 저는 좋습니다 get there 그곳에 가다 about 약, 대략

168 바 씨는 누구일 것 같은가?
(A) 금융 컨설턴트
(B) 시 관계자
(C) 건축가
(D) 변호사

해설 〈세부 사항〉
첫 메시지에 바 씨가 자신의 일과 관련해 건물 디자인을 만든 사실(~ the design I created for their new headquarters building)이 언급되어 있는데, 이는 건축가가 하는 일에 해당되므로 (C)가 정답이다.

어휘 official n. 관계자, 당국자

169 오전 10시 50분에, 바 씨가 "A digital version won't do"라고 썼을 때 의미한 것은 무엇이겠는가?
(A) 자신의 컴퓨터가 작동하지 않을 것이라는 점을 우려하고 있다.
(B) 원본 설계도를 제시하고 싶어 한다.
(C) 일부 소프트웨어 사용법을 알지 못한다.
(D) 한 발표가 너무 지루하다고 생각한다.

해설 〈의도 파악〉
제시된 문장은 디지털 버전으로는 안 된다는 의미를 담고 있다. 이는 앞서 바 씨가 책상에 설계도를 놓고 왔다고(~ I've left the blueprints on my desk) 알리자 바로 뒤이어 타이슨 씨가 스캔해 줄 수 있다고(I could scan them ~) 말한 것에 대한 답변이다. 즉 스캔하지 않은 원래의 설계도가 필요하다는 뜻이므로 (B)가 정답이다.

어휘 be concerned that ~임을 우려하다 work (기계 등이) 작동하다, 기능하다 would like to do ~하고 싶다, ~하고자 하다 present ~을 제시하다, 제공하다 original 원본의, 원래의 how to do ~하는 법 presentation 발표(회)

170 바 씨와 오닐 씨는 어디에서 만나기로 합의하는가?
(A) 럽튼 파이낸셜 사의 사무실에서
(B) 한 커피 매장에서
(C) 바 씨의 사무실에서
(D) 한 사무용품 매장에서

해설 〈세부 사항〉
질문에 언급된 오닐 씨와 바 씨의 메시지를 보면, 오닐 씨가 10시 54분에 렌리스 사무용품 매장에서 만날 수 있는지(Could we meet at Renley's Office Supplies instead?) 묻자, 10시 57분에 바 씨가 That works for me라는 말로 동의하고 있다. 따라서 사무용품 매장에서 만날 것임을 알 수 있으므로 (D)가 정답이다.

어휘 agree to do ~하는 데 합의하다, 동의하다

171 오늘 씨는 무엇을 준비하고 있는가?
(A) 일부 고객들의 설문 조사
(B) 자문이 실시하는 점검
(C) 신규 고객과의 회의
(D) 일부 채용 후보자들의 방문

해설 〈세부 사항〉
오늘 씨가 10시 56분에 쓴 메시지에 방문자들을 위해 서류 준비를 해야 한다는(~ I still have some paperwork to prepare for the visitors) 말이 쓰여 있다. 이는 앞서 10시 54분에 오늘 씨가 언급한 채용 면접(~ coming for the job interviews this afternoon)을 준비하는 일을 가리킨다. 따라서 채용 후보자들이 방문한다는 것을 알 수 있으므로 (D)가 정답이다.

어휘 prepare for ~을 준비하다, ~에 대비하다 survey 설문 조사 inspection 점검, 조사 advisor 자문, 조언자 meet with (약속하여) ~와 만나다 candidate 후보자, 지원자

[172-175] 기사

소셜 미디어에 대한 이해

작성자, 글로리아 스펜서

(172) 여러분의 업체가 단지 몇몇 팀원들로만 되어 있든, 또는 여러 도시에서 근무하는 대규모 직원으로 되어 있든 상관없이, 명확하고 목적이 뚜렷한 소셜 미디어 정책이 필요합니다. **(173)** 소셜 미디어는 여러분의 업체가 제공하는 상품과 서비스에 대한 훌륭한 홍보 수단이 될 수 있습니다. —[1]—. **(173)** 사이트와 애플리케이션은 이용하기 편리하여, 심지어 초보자들조차도 그 특징을 쉽게 배울 수 있습니다. —[2]—. 하지만 소셜 미디어에는 단점도 있습니다. 직장 내에서의 개인적인 소셜 미디어 이용은 직원들을 산만하게 만들 수 있으며, **(173)** 소중한 업무 시간을 빈둥대며 날려 버릴 수 있습니다. 또한 회사에서 소셜 미디어 콘텐츠에 대해 주의하지 않는다면 해로울 수 있으며, 이는 불쾌감을 야기할 수 있습니다.

해결책은 무엇일까요? 직원들에게 여전히 스스로를 표현할 자유를 주면서 여러분의 회사를 보호할 정책을 만드십시오. —[3]—. 기업 소셜 미디어 계정을 운영하는 직원들에게 있어, 그 정책은 공유되어야 하는 것과 그렇지 않은 것을 분명히 해 두어야 합니다. **(175)** 이용자들은 특히 회사의 사적인 데이터가 노출되는 것에 대해 주의해야 합니다. —[4]—. **(174)** 정책이 수립되는 대로, 직원들이 그 가이드라인을 기억할 수 있도록 때때로 함께 살펴보시기 바랍니다.

어휘 get a handle on ~을 이해하다, 파악하다 whether A or B A이든 B이든 상관없이 multiple 여럿의, 다수의 purposeful 목적이 뚜렷한 policy 정책 promotional 홍보의 tool 수단, 도구 goods 상품 offer ~을 제공하다 even 심지어 (~도) novice 초보자 feature 특징, 기능 downside 단점 as well ~도, 또한 distract ~을 산만하게 하다 idle away (시간 등) 빈둥대며 날리다 precious 소중한 harmful 해로운 be careful about ~에 대해 주의하다 cause ~을 야기하다, 초래하다 offense 불쾌함, 위반 solution 해결책 create ~을 만들어 내다 protect ~을 보호하다 while ~하면서, ~하는 동안 express (생각, 감정 등) ~을 표현하다 operate ~을 운영하다, 작동하다 corporate 기업의 account 계정 make clear ~을 분명히 해 두다 particularly 특히 expose ~을 노출하다 private 사적

인, 개인의 once ~하는 대로, ~하자마자 establish ~을 수립하다, 확립하다 review ~을 살펴보다, 검토하다 once in a while 때때로 so that (목적) ~할 수 있도록

172 누가 이 기사의 대상이 되는 독자일 것 같은가?
(A) 업체 소유주들
(B) 웹 사이트 개발자들
(C) 금융 전문가들
(D) 채용 담당자들

해설 〈글의 대상〉
첫 문장에 'Whether your business ~'라는 말로 대상자를 가리키고 있으므로 업체를 소유한 사람들에게 필요한 정보를 전하는 기사인 것으로 판단할 수 있다. 따라서 (A)가 정답이다.

어휘 intended 대상이 되는, 의도된 developer 개발자, 개발 업체 expert 전문가

173 기사에서 소셜 미디어에 관해 언급되지 않은 것은 무엇인가?
(A) 시간을 낭비할 수 있다.
(B) 사용자 친화적이다.
(C) 서비스를 홍보할 수 있다.
(D) 사용자들에게 무료이다.

해설 〈진위 확인 (세부 진위 유형)〉
첫 단락에서 훌륭한 홍보 수단이라고(~ can be an excellent promotional tool ~) 말하는 부분에서 (C)를, 바로 뒤에 쉽게 이용할 수 있다고(The sites and applications are easy to use ~) 언급하는 부분에서 (B)를 확인할 수 있다. 또한 그 이후 문장에서 소중한 시간을 빈둥대며 날려 버릴 수 있다는(~ they may idle away precious work hours ~) 단점을 언급하는 부분에서 (A)도 확인 가능하다. 하지만 무료라는 특징을 말하는 내용은 본문에 없으므로 (D)가 정답이다.

어휘 user-friendly 사용자 친화적인 promote ~을 홍보하다 free 무료인

174 기사에 따르면, 주기적으로 무엇을 해야 하는가?
(A) 인기 있는 소셜 미디어 사이트 조사하기
(B) 직원들에게 정책에 관해 상기시키기
(C) 회사 소유의 컴퓨터 장비 업데이트하기
(D) 인터넷 이용 수준 확인하기

해설 〈세부 사항〉
문제의 키워드인 periodically(주기적으로)와 같은 의미의 표현인 once in a while(때때로)이 언급된 마지막 단락 마지막 문장에, 정책이 수립되는 대로 직원들이 기억할 수 있도록 때때로 함께 살펴보라는(Once the policy is established, review it with staff members once in a while ~) 내용이 쓰여 있다. 이는 직원들에게 해당 정책에 관해 상기시키는 일을 의미하므로 (B)가 정답이다.

어휘 periodically 주기적으로 remind A about B A에게 B에 관해 상기시키다 policy 정책, 방침 equipment 장비

175 [1], [2], [3], [4]로 표시된 위치들 중에서, 다음 문장이 들어가기에 가장 적절한 곳은 어디인가?

"예를 들어, 시제품 이미지와 같은 민감한 정보는 온라인으로 게시되지 말아야 합니다."
(A) [1]
(B) [2]
(C) [3]
(D) [4]

해설 〈문장 넣기〉
제시된 문장은 예를 들 때 사용하는 For example과 함께 시제품 이미지와 같은 민감한 정보가 온라인으로 게시되지 말아야 한다는 의미를 지니고 있다. 이는 특정 정보의 노출과 관련된 내용인데 사적인 데이터의 노출과 관련해 주의를 당부하는 문장 뒤에 위치한 [4]에 들어가는 것이 흐름상 자연스럽다. 따라서 (D)가 정답이다.

어휘 sensitive 민감한 prototype 시제품 post ~을 게시하다

[176-180] 광고와 이메일

신제품!   신제품!   신제품!

엘스워스 코즈메틱스

그린빌 몰 #A239 (JD 백화점 옆)

친구분들보다 먼저 엘스워스 코즈메틱스의 봄 신상품 라인을 사용해 보세요. 모든 저희 제품은 무독성 재료로 만들어지는데, 저희가 고객 여러분과 환경의 건강 상태를 **(176)** 소중히 여기고 있기 때문입니다.

쉬머 (제품 번호 624): 향기로운 이 오일은 여러분의 피부 톤을 개선해 드리고, 건강한 피부 빛을 드립니다.

(179) 리바이브 (제품 번호 625): 꽃 향기가 나는 이 얼굴 크림은 하루 종일 지속되는 보습 효과와 부드러운 마무리를 제공해 드립니다.

너리쉬 (제품 번호 626): 이 일일 세안제는 화장품과 때를 분해해, 피부에 깔끔하고 부드러운 느낌이 남도록 해 드립니다.

팸퍼 (제품 번호 627): 이 립 글로스는 색조를 제공해 드림과 동시에 입술에 보습 효과를 더하고 자외선 차단 효과를 제공해 드립니다.

훌륭한 제품들이 온라인상에서 그리고 저희 매장에서 여러분을 기다리고 있습니다. **(177)** 그리고 1회 구매 내역에 대해 50달러 넘게 소비하시는 경우, 샘플이 가득한 무료 엘스워스 화장용품 가방을 받으시게 됩니다.

수신: help@ellsworthcosm.com
발신: carlanavarre@wesley-media.com
178 날짜: 4월 2일
제목: 제품 문제

고객 서비스팀에 보냅니다.

3월 29일에, **179** 저는 귀사의 새 얼굴 크림을 온라인으로 주문했습니다(주문번호 24671). **178** 오늘 아침에 배송되었을 때, 튜브에 구멍이 하나 있었다는 점과 크림이 여기저기 새어 나오고 있었다는 점을 알게 되었습니다. 이 문제를 찍은 사진을 첨부해 드렸습니다. 이 제품은 사용할 수 없기 때문에 **180** 저에게 크림을 하나 더 보내 주시기 바랍니다. 제가 4월 6일 휴가를 떠날 계획이고, 이 제품을 가져가기를 원하기 때문에 4월 5일까지 받을 수 있다면 정말 감사하겠습니다.

감사합니다.

칼라 나바르

어휘 try ~을 한 번 사용해 보다 be made from ~로 만들어지다 non-toxic 무독성의 ingredient 재료, 성분 value ~을 소중히 여기다 scented 향기로운 enhance ~을 개선하다, 강화하다 glow (얼굴의) 홍조, 빛깔 floral-scented 꽃 향기가 나는 provide ~을 제공하다 moisture 수분, 습기 smooth 부드러운 finish n. 마무리, 끝손질 dissolve ~을 분해하다, 용해하다 grime 때 leave A -ing A가 ~하는 상태로 만들다 touch of color 색조 while ~하면서, ~하는 동안 moisturize ~을 촉촉하게 하다, ~에 수분을 제공하다 sun protection 자외선 차단 await ~을 기다리다 more than ~가 넘는 transaction 구매, 거래 free 무료의 packed with ~로 가득한 place an order 주문하다 leak (액체 등이) 새어 나오다, 누출되다 attach ~을 첨부하다 mail ~을 우송하다, 우편으로 보내다 since ~하기 때문에 usable 사용할 수 있는 I would really appreciate it if ~라면 정말 감사하겠습니다 receive ~을 받다 by (기한) ~까지 plan to do ~할 계획이다 take a vacation 휴가를 떠나다 take ~을 가져가다

176 광고에서 첫 번째 단락, 두 번째 줄의 단어 "value"와 의미가 가장 가까운 것은 무엇인가?
(A) ~을 준수하다
(B) ~에 대한 비용을 지불하다
(C) ~을 신경 쓰다
(D) ~에 참가하다

해설 〈동의어〉
해당 문장에서 value는 무독성 재료로 제품을 만드는 이유를 말하는 문장에 사용되었으며, 목적어로 고객과 환경의 건강함을 의미하는 명사구가 쓰여 있다. 따라서 고객과 환경의 건강함을 중요하게 생각한다는 의미를 나타내는 것으로 볼 수 있는데, 이는 크게 관심을 갖거나 신경을 쓴다는 의미로 볼 수 있으므로 '~을 신경 쓰다'를 뜻하는 (C) care about이 정답이다.

177 고객들은 어떻게 무료 선물을 받을 수 있는가?
(A) 소식지를 신청함으로써
(B) 제품 이용 후기를 작성함으로써
(C) 업체를 다른 사람들에게 추천함으로써

(D) 일정 금액을 소비함으로써

해설 〈세부 사항〉
무료 선물이 언급된 첫 지문 마지막 문장을 보면, 1회 구매 내역에 대해 50달러 넘게 소비하면 샘플로 가득한 무료 화장용품 가방을 받는다고 (~ if you spend more than $50 in any single transaction, you'll get a free Ellsworth makeup bag ~) 쓰여 있다. 이는 일정 금액을 소비하는 것을 의미하므로 (D)가 정답이다.

어휘 free 무료의 sign up for ~을 신청하다, ~에 등록하다 review 후기, 의견, 평가 certain 일정한, 특정한 amount 금액

178 나바르 씨는 언제 손상된 포장을 알아차렸는가?
(A) 3월 29일에
(B) 4월 2일에
(C) 4월 5일에
(D) 4월 6일에

해설 〈세부 사항〉
제품 손상 상태가 언급된 두 번째 지문 초반부에, '오늘 아침에 배송되었을 때 구멍이 난 것을 알게 되었다'고(When it was delivered this morning, I saw that the tube had a hole in it ~) 말하는 것으로 손상 상태를 알리고 있다. 그리고 지문 상단의 작성 날짜가 4월 2일로(Date: April 2) 쓰여 있으므로 '오늘 아침'은 4월 2일임을 알 수 있다. 따라서 (B)가 정답이다.

어휘 damaged 손상된, 피해를 입은 packaging 포장(재)

179 나바르 씨는 어느 제품을 구입했는가?
(A) 쉬머
(B) 리바이브
(C) 너리쉬
(D) 팸퍼

해설 〈지문 연계〉
나바르 씨가 쓴 이메일인 두 번째 지문 시작 부분에 얼굴 크림을 주문했다고(I placed an order for your new face cream ~) 밝히고 있는데, 첫 지문에서 얼굴 크림에 해당되는 것은 리바이브(Revive (Item 625): This floral-scented face cream ~)이므로 (B)가 정답이다.

어휘 purchase ~을 구입하다

180 나바르 씨는 고객 서비스팀에 무엇을 하도록 요청하는가?
(A) 교환 제품 보내기
(B) 전액 환불 지급하기
(C) 반품 과정 설명하기
(D) 사용 설명서 제공하기

해설 〈세부 사항〉
두 번째 지문 중반부에 크림을 하나 더 보내 달라고(Please mail another tube of the cream to me ~) 요청하는 말이 쓰여 있는데, 이는 바로 앞서 언급한 손상 제품에 대한 교환 제품을 보내 달라는 뜻이다. 따라서 (A)가 정답이다.

어휘 ask A to do A에게 ~하도록 요청하다 replacement 교체(품), 대체

(품) issue a refund 환불해 주다 explain ~을 설명하다 return 반품, 반납 process 과정 provide ~을 제공하다 instructions 설명, 안내, 지시

[181-185] 웹 페이지와 이메일

렘보 가전기기: 진공 청소기

렘보 가전기기는 여러 가지 필요성에 적합한 다양한 진공 청소기를 제공합니다. **181** 수상 경력이 있는 저희 업라이트 디자인과 스틱 디자인은 지속적으로 베스트셀러 제품이 되고 있습니다. 아래에서 모든 저희 모델을 확인해 보십시오.

14F 핸드헬드 진공 청소기

이 소형 진공 청소기는 크기가 작은 지저분한 것들을 신속히 청소하는 것뿐만 아니라 좁은 공간에 들어가기에도 완벽한 제품입니다. 주머니가 달려 있지 않은 제품인데, 이는 손쉽게 먼지 통을 분리해 비울 수 있음을 의미합니다.

185 360C 캐니스터 진공 청소기

저희 회사에서 가장 용도가 다양한 모델인, 이 진공 청소기는 손이 닿기 어려운 공간에 닿는 데 도움이 되는 긴 호스를 포함하고 있습니다. 10월 한 달 내내, 고객들께서는 이 모델에 대한 **185** 무료 판촉용 부가 용품 패키지(소매가: 19.99달러)를 받으실 수 있습니다. 성함과 우편 주소, 그리고 영수증 번호와 함께 promopack@lemboapp.com으로 이메일을 보내 주시기 바랍니다.

750R 스틱 진공 청소기

이 무선 진공 청소기를 완전히 충전된 상태로 유지하고 신속한 청소를 위해 쉽게 집어낼 수 있도록 접근이 용이한 곳에 **182** 벽걸이용 충전대를 설치하도록 권해 드립니다.

2000A 업라이트 진공 청소기

강력한 모터가 가장 힘든 청소 작업 해결도 도울 수 있도록 뛰어난 흡입 기능을 제공합니다. 일상적인 용도와 대청소에 모두 완벽한 제품입니다.

아래에 기재된 신뢰할 수 있는 저희 제휴 업체에서 렘보 진공 청소기를 찾아보실 수 있습니다.

일렉트로닉스 월드
오크웨이 스트리트 381번지
볼티모어, MD 21237

액세서리 익스프레스
에딩턴 애비뉴 6001번지
뉴욕, NY 10036

테크 타임
힐뷰 애비뉴 863번지
184 필라델피아, PA 19106

R-맥스
레인보우 블리바드 457번지
워싱턴, D.C. 20032

수신: promopack@lemboapp.com
발신: jwendel@karlata.com
날짜: 10월 14일
제목: 10월 제공 서비스

렘보 가전기기 사에 보냅니다.

저는 최근 제 아파트에서 길을 따라 가면 있는 매장에서 귀사의 진공 청소기 하나를 구입했습니다. **183** **185** 제가 무료 부가 용품을 받을 자격이 있다는 사실을 귀사의 웹 사이트를 통해 알게 되어 기뻤습니다. **183** 저는 다음 주소로 그 용품을 받아 보고 싶습니다: **184** 재니스 웬델, 필라델피아, 피어시 스트리트 865번지, 103호, PA 19106. 제 영수증 번호는 645801258입니다.

감사합니다.

재니스 웬델

어휘 vacuum cleaner 진공 청소기(= vacuum) offer v. ~을 제공하다 n. 제공(되는 것) a range of 다양한, 여러 가지의(= a variety of) suit ~에 적합하다, 알맞다 award-winning 수상 경력이 있는 upright 수직의, 곧은, 꼿꼿한 continue to do 지속적으로 ~하다 below 아래에, 밑에 compact 소형의 mess 지저분한 것, 엉망인 것 as well as ~뿐만 아니라 …도 get into ~로 들어가다 tight space 좁은 공간 bagless 주머니가 없는 remove ~을 제거하다, 없애다 collection chamber (진공 청소기의) 먼지 통 versatile 다목적의, 다용도의 get to ~에 도달하다, 이르다 hard-to-reach (손이) 닿기 어려운 throughout ~ 동안에 걸쳐 free 무료의 promotional 판촉의, 홍보의 retail value 소매가 receipt 영수증 install ~을 설치하다 wall-mounted 벽걸이의 docking station 충전대 accessible 접근 가능한, 이용 가능한 make it 형용사 to do ~하는 것을 ~하게 만들다 keep A p.p. A를 ~된 상태로 유지하다 fully charged 완전히 충전된 grab ~을 가져오다, 붙잡다 suction 흡입 (기능) help A do A가 ~하도록 돕다 tackle (문제 등) ~을 해결하다 deep cleaning 대청소 trusted 신뢰할 수 있는 recently 최근에 purchase ~을 구입하다 down (길 등) ~을 따라 discover that ~임을 알아내다, 발견하다 be eligible for ~에 대한 자격이 있다 receive ~을 받다 following 다음의, 아래의

181 렘보 가전기기 사에 관해 사실인 것은 무엇인가?
(A) 네 곳의 제조 시설을 보유하고 있다.
(B) 자사의 디자인으로 상을 받았다.
(C) 대량 구매에 대해 할인을 제공한다.
(D) 곧 새로운 진공 청소기를 출시할 것이다.

해설 〈진위 확인 (세부 진위 유형)〉
첫 지문 첫 단락에 제품 디자인으로 상을 받은 적이 있음을 나타내는(Our award-winning upright and stick designs) 내용이 있으므로 이러한 내용을 언급한 (B)가 정답이다. (B) 보기에 사용된 recognize는 '인정하다'는 뜻 외에도 '표창을 하다, 상을 주다'라는 의미도 있다.

어휘 manufacturing 제조 facility 시설(물) recognize ~에게 상을 주다, ~을 인정하다 provide ~을 제공하다 bulk a. 대량의 purchase 구매(품) launch ~을 출시하다, 공개하다

182 충전대에 관해 암시된 것은 무엇인가?
(A) 벽에 부착할 수 있다.
(B) 반드시 별도로 구매해야 한다.
(C) 모든 진공 청소기 모델에 작동한다.
(D) 다양한 크기로 나온다.

해설 〈진위 확인 (세부 진위 유형)〉
충전대가 언급된 첫 지문 네 번째 단락에 벽걸이형(wall-mounted docking station)이라고 언급되어 있으므로 이와 같은 특징을 언급한 (A)가 정답이다.

어휘 attach A to B A를 B에 부착하다 separately 별도로, 따로 work (기계 등) 작동하다, 기능하다 come in (제품 등) ~로 나오다. 출시되다 various 다양한

183 이메일의 목적은 무엇인가?
(A) 품질 보증에 관해 문의하는 것
(B) 기기의 일부 손상 문제를 알리는 것
(C) 추가 배터리를 주문하는 것
(D) 일부 진공 청소기 부품을 요청하는 것

해설 〈주제 및 목적〉
이메일인 두 번째 지문 초반부에 무료 부가 용품을 받을 자격이 있다는 사실을 알게 된 점과 함께 그 용품을 받아 보고 싶다는(~ I am eligible for some free accessories. I would like to receive them ~) 의사를 밝히고 있으므로 진공 청소기 부품 요청을 의미하는 (D)가 정답이다.

어휘 inquire about ~에 관해 문의하다 warranty 품질 보증(서) damage 손상, 피해 device 기기, 장치 additional 추가의 request ~을 요청하다, 요구하다 part 부품

184 웬델 씨는 어디에서 진공 청소기를 구입했을 것 같은가?
(A) 일렉트로닉스 월드
(B) 액세서리 익스프레스
(C) 테크 타임
(D) R-맥스

해설 〈지문 연계〉
두 번째 지문에서 웬델 씨가 자신의 주소를 알려 주는 부분을 보면 필라델피아에(Janice Wendel, 865 Pearcy Street, Unit 103, Philadelphia, PA 19106) 거주하는 것으로 나온다. 첫 지문에서 주소가 필라델피아로 되어 있는 매장이 Tech Time (863 Hillview Avenue, Philadelphia, PA 19106)이므로 (C)가 정답이다.

185 웬델 씨는 어떤 스타일의 진공 청소기를 구입했는가?
(A) 14F 핸드헬드
(B) 360 캐니스터
(C) 750R 스틱
(D) 2000A 업라이트

해설 〈지문 연계〉
두 번째 지문에 웬델 씨가 무료 부가 용품을 받을 자격이 있다는 사실을(~ I am eligible for some free accessories) 알리고 있는데, 첫 번째 지문에 이와 같은 서비스가(~ customers can get a free promotional pack of accessories ~) 제공되는 제품이 360C Canister Vacuum이므로 (B)가 정답이다.

[186-190] 두 이메일과 기록지

수신: itdesk@bernardoco.com
발신: vmayfield@bernardoco.com
날짜: 2월 9일

제목: 노트북 컴퓨터

IT 업무 지원 센터에 보냅니다.

188 회사에서 지급받은 제 노트북 컴퓨터(사번 02364)에 계속 문제를 겪고 있습니다. 갑자기 정지되고, 그 후에 재부팅하는 데 오랜 시간이 걸립니다. **186** 제가 전에 한 번도 IT 수리 작업을 요청한 적이 없었기 때문에, 제가 무슨 조치를 취해야 하는지에 관해 궁금합니다.

특별 소프트웨어가 설치되어 있기 때문에 제가 지금부터 **187** 3일 후에 떠나는 출장에 이 노트북 컴퓨터를 가져가고 싶습니다. 그때까지 수리되지 않는다면, 저희 팀에 있는 다른 누군가로부터 노트북 컴퓨터를 빌려야 하는데, 이는 바람직한 일이 아닙니다.

제가 예약을 해야 하는지, 또는 이후에 무엇을 해야 하는지 알려 주시기 바랍니다.

감사합니다.

빅터 메이필드

IT 업무 지원 센터 활동 일지: 2월 10일			
담당 기사: 제이슨 베어드			
사번	부서	작업 설명	예상 작업 시간
01258	인사부	노트북 스크린 교체	25분
01976	디자인부	데스크톱 컴퓨터에 소프트웨어 설치	20분
188 02364	마케팅부	오작동되는 노트북 컴퓨터 분석	35분
01807	회계부	프린터 설치	10분

수신: vmayfield@bernardoco.com
발신: jbaird@bernardoco.com
날짜: 2월 10일
제목: 업무 지원 센터 업데이트

메이필드 씨께,

귀하의 IT 관련 문제를 확인한 후에, 해당 문제점이 고장 난 팬으로 인한 것임을 알게 되었습니다. 이것이 기기가 과열되도록 하고 있습니다. **187** 제가 교체 부품에 대해 주문을 해 둔 상태이며, 4일 후에 도착할 것입니다. **189** 대략적인 예상으로, 제가 필요한 부품을 받는다면 수리 작업을 완료하는 데 약 1시간이 걸릴 것입니다. 해당 기기가 3년이 넘었기 때문에 **190** 모든 수리 비용이 귀하의 소속 부서 예산이 아닌 회사 총예산에 의해 부담된다는 점에 유의하시기 바랍니다. 이 수리 작업을 할 준비가 되는 대로 연락드리겠습니다.

제이슨

어휘 help desk 업무 지원 센터 have trouble with ~에 문제를 겪다, 어려움을 겪다 company-issued 회사에서 지급한, 회사에서 발급한 shut down (기계 등이) 정지하다, 멈추다 unexpectedly 예기치 못하게 then 그 후에, 그때 take a long time to do ~하는 데 오랜 시간이 걸리다 request ~을 요청하다 repair n. 수리 v. ~을 수리하다 take steps 조치를 취하다 install ~을 설치하다 by (기한) ~까지 borrow ~을 빌리다 ideal 이상적인 let A know whether A에게 ~인지 알리다 make an appointment 예약하다, 약속하다 log 기록 department 부서 description 설명 estimated 예상된, 추정된 replacement 교체(품) installation 설치 analysis 분석 malfunction 오작동하다, 제대로 작동하지 않다 setup 설치, 설정, 준비 issue 문제, 사안 find that ~임을 알게 되다 due to ~로 인해, ~ 때문에 broken 고장 난 cause A to do A가 ~하도록 초래하다, 유발하다 device 기기, 장치 overheat 과열되다 place an order 주문하다 replacement 교체(품) component 부품(= part) arrive 도착하다 in + 기간 ~ 후에 rough 대략적인 estimate 예상, 추정 take ~의 시간이 걸리다 about 약, 대략 complete ~을 완료하다 once ~하는 대로, ~하자마자 necessary 필요한 note that ~라는 점에 유의하다 cover (비용 등) ~을 부담하다, 충당하다 general budget 총예산 rather than ~가 아니라, ~ 대신 more than ~가 넘는 be in touch 연락하다 as soon as ~하자마자 be ready to do ~할 준비가 되다 make a repair 수리하다

186 메이필드 씨는 왜 첫 번째 이메일을 보냈는가?
(A) 약속 시간을 변경하기 위해
(B) 절차에 관해 문의하기 위해
(C) 청구 요금에 대해 불만을 제기하기 위해
(D) 새로운 장비를 주문하기 위해

해설 〈주제 및 목적〉
첫 지문 첫 단락에, 자신이 컴퓨터에 대해 겪고 있는 문제를 언급하며, 무슨 조치를 취해야 하는지 궁금하다고(~ so I'm wondering about what steps I need to take) 적고 있다. 이는 절차에 관해 문의하는 것이므로 (B)가 정답이다.

어휘 appointment 약속, 예약 inquire about ~에 관해 문의하다 process 절차, 과정 complain about ~에 대해 불만을 제기하다, 불평하다 charge 청구 요금 equipment 장비

187 메이필드 씨에 관해 암시된 것은 무엇인가?
(A) 컴퓨터를 재부팅하는 방법을 알지 못한다.
(B) 동료 직원으로부터 일부 장비를 빌릴 것이다.
(C) 한 부품에 대해 긴급 주문을 했다.
(D) 일부 소프트웨어의 구식 버전을 갖고 있다.

해설 〈진위 확인 (전체 진위 유형)〉
첫 지문 두 번째 단락을 보면, 메이필드 씨는 3일 후에 가는 출장에 노트북 컴퓨터가 필요하다는 말과 함께 그 전에 수리되지 않으면 다른 팀원에게 노트북 컴퓨터를 빌려야 한다고(~ bring this laptop with me on my business trip three days from now ~ I'll have to borrow a laptop from someone else ~) 알리고 있다. 그런데 세 번째 지문 초반부에 해당 수리 작업에 필요한 부품이 4일 후에 도착한다고(~ it will arrive in four days) 쓰여 있다. 따라서 메이필드 씨가 동료 직원으로부터 노트북 컴퓨터를 빌려야 하는 상황이므로 이와 같은 내용을 담은 (B)가 정답이다.

어휘 how to do ~하는 방법 reboot ~을 재부팅하다 borrow ~을 빌리다 coworker 동료 (직원) place an order 주문하다 rush a. 서두르는, 급한 part 부품 outdated 구식의, 낡은

188 베어드 씨는 메이필드 씨의 장비에 대해 대략 얼마나 오래 작업했는가?
(A) 10분
(B) 20분
(C) 25분
(D) 35분

해설 〈지문 연계〉
첫 지문 첫 단락에 메이필드 씨가 노트북 컴퓨터 문제를 알리면서 사번이 02364라고(employee #02364) 알리고 있으며, 두 번째 지문에서 이 번호에 해당되는 작업 시간이 35분으로 표기되어 있으므로 (D)가 정답이다.

어휘 about 약, 대략

189 두 번째 이메일에서 첫 번째 단락, 세 번째 줄의 단어 "rough"와 의미가 가장 가까운 것은 무엇인가?
(A) 대략적인
(B) 불쾌한
(C) 어려운
(D) 즉각적인

해설 〈동의어〉
해당 문장에서 rough가 수식하는 estimate은 '예상, 추정' 등을 의미하며, 그 뒤에 이어지는 내용을 보면 수리 작업을 완료하는 데 약 1시간이 걸릴 것이라고(~ it will take about an hour ~) 쓰여 있다. 따라서 rough estimate가 대략적인 예상이나 추정 등을 의미한다는 것을 알 수 있으므로 '대략적인'을 뜻하는 또 다른 형용사 (A)가 정답이다.

190 베어드 씨의 이메일에 언급된 것은 무엇인가?
(A) 베어드 씨가 회사에 3년 동안 근무해 왔다.
(B) 다른 IT 기술자가 몇몇 수리 작업을 처리할 것이다.
(C) 교체 부품이 단종된 상태이다.
(D) 메이필드 씨의 부서에 요금이 발생하지 않을 것이다.

해설 〈진위 확인 (전체 진위 유형)〉
세 번째 지문 후반부에 모든 수리 비용이 메이필드 씨의 소속 부서 예산이 아닌 총예산에 의해 부담된다는(~ all repair costs will be covered by the office's general budget, rather than your department budget) 내용이 있다. 즉 메이필드 씨의 부서에서 그 비용을 지불하지 않는다는 뜻이므로 이를 언급한 (D)가 정답이다.

어휘 work for ~에서 근무하다 handle ~을 처리하다. 다루다 repair 수리 replacement component 교체 부품 discontinue ~을 단종하다 department 부서 incur (비용) ~을 발생시키다 fee 요금, 수수료

[191-195] 광고와 청구서, 그리고 편지

로드리게즈 배수관 케어

— 주거용 및 상업용 배수관 청소 전문 —

193 3월 한 달 동안 전체 배수관 청소 서비스에 대해 25퍼센트 할인을 받아보세요! 저희 로드리게즈 배수관 케어는 거의 20년 동안 시리브포트 지역에 서비스를 제공해 오고 있습니다. **191** 저희는 현재 성수기가 아닌 관계로, 더 많은 고객들을 끌어들이기를 바라고 있습니다. 따라서, 배수관 청소에 대해 많은 비용을 절약하실 수 있는 아주 좋은 기회입니다. 이 중요한 일을 미루지 마시기 바랍니다. 막힌 배수관은 외부 벽에 손상을 초래하거나 물이 집 안으로 새어 나오게 만들 수 있습니다.

193 저희 표준 요금은 2층 주택에 대해 225달러, 단층 주택에 대해 180달러입니다. 업체는 저희 사무실로 연락 주셔서 가격 견적을 받아 보시기 바랍니다.

예약을 하시려면, **195** 555-7988번으로 저희 예약 담당 부서로 연락 주십시오.

로드리게즈 배수관 케어

거래 내역서 #8524

고객 성명: 가브리엘라 존스   주소: 월덱 애비뉴 263번지
193 건물 종류: 단층 주택   연락처: 555-0361
서비스: 배수관 청소   **192** 작업 완료일: 3월 12일
192 작업 팀장: 로버트 브랜   **193** 총 청구 비용: $180.00 + 6% 세금 = 190.80달러

지불 비용은 전화상에서 신용카드를 이용해 받습니다. 작업 완료 후 2주 내에 비용을 지불해 주시기 바랍니다.

로드리게즈 배수관 케어
캐리지 레인 974번지
시리브포트, LA 71106

3월 14일

가브리엘라 존스
월덕 애비뉴 263번지
시리브포트, LA 71106

존스 씨께,

(194) 귀하의 청구서에 발생된 문제점과 관련해 오늘 아침에 저희에게 연락 주셔서 감사합니다. 처음에 발급된 것은 무시하시고, 제가 동봉해 드린 새 것을 이용해 주시기 바랍니다. 이번이 저희 회사가 한 달 기간의 판촉 행사를 처음 진행하는 것이기 때문에, 저희가 바랐던 것만큼 순조롭게 진행되지 않았습니다. (194) 이로 인해 초래되었을 수 있는 모든 혼동이나 불편함에 대해 사과드립니다.

귀하께서 서비스에 만족하셨다는 사실과, 저희 팀이 그 과정 내내 공손했다는 사실에 기쁘게 생각합니다. 저희는 6개월에 한 번씩 배수관을 청소하시도록 권해 드리고 있기 때문에, 앞으로도 귀하로부터 연락받을 수 있기를 바랍니다.

안녕히 계십시오.

(195) 딘 렌델
(195) 예약 관리부장, 로드리게즈 배수관 케어

어휘 residential 주거의 commercial 상업의 drainpipe 배수관 serve ~에 서비스를 제공하다 community 지역 사회 nearly 거의 decade 10년 as ~이므로 between ~ 사이에, 중간에 between peak periods 성수기와 성수기 사이에 있는, 비수기에 look to do ~하기를 바라다 bring in ~을 끌어들이다 opportunity to do ~할 기회 save big 많은 비용을 절약하다 put off ~을 미루다 task 일, 업무 blocked 막힌 cause ~을 초래하다 damage 손상, 피해 exterior 외부의 allow A to do A가 ~하게 만들다 leak (물, 가스 등이) 새다, 누출되다 regular rate 표준 요금, 정상 요금 two-story 2층으로 된 contact ~에게 연락하다 quote 가격 견적(서) book an appointment 예약하다 invoice 거래 내역서 property 건물, 부동산 charge 청구 요금 payment (지불) 비용 accept ~을 받아들이다, 수용하다 settle ~을 지불하다, 정산하다 within ~ 이내에 completed 완료된 disregard ~을 무시하다 issue ~을 발급하다 enclose ~을 동봉하다 run ~을 진행하다, 운영하다 promotion 판촉 행사 go smoothly 순조롭게 진행되다 quite 꽤, 상당히 as A as B B만큼 A한 apologize for ~에 대해 사과하다 confusion 혼동, 혼란 inconvenience 불편함 may have p.p. ~했을 수도 있다 be satisfied with ~에 만족하다 respectful 공손한 throughout ~동안, ~ 내내 procedure 과정, 절차 get A p.p. A가 ~되게 하다

191 광고에 따르면, 로드리게즈 배수관 케어는 왜 할인을 제공하는가?
(A) 바쁘지 않은 기간에 더 많은 거래를 만들어 내기 위해
(B) 업적을 기념하기 위해
(C) 단골 고객들에게 감사의 뜻을 전하기 위해
(D) 새롭게 제공되는 서비스를 소개하기 위해

해설 〈세부 사항〉
광고인 첫 번째 지문 첫 단락에, 할인을 제공한다는 말과 함께 성수기

가 아닌 기간이기 때문에 더 많은 고객을 끌어들이기를 바라고 있다는 (As we're between peak periods, we are looking to bring in more customers) 말로 이유를 언급하고 있다. 즉 더 많은 거래가 필요하다는 뜻이므로 이와 같은 의미에 해당되는 (A)가 정답이다.

어휘 offer ~을 제공하다 generate ~을 만들어 내다, 발생시키다 slow 바쁘지 않은 celebrate ~을 기념하다, 축하하다 achievement 업적, 성취, 달성 appreciation 감사(의 뜻) loyal customer 단골 고객 introduce ~을 소개하다

192 브랜 씨는 3월 12일에 무엇을 했을 것 같은가?
(A) 일부 장비 주문하기
(B) 외부 벽 수리하기
(C) 지불 비용 처리하기
(D) 팀을 감독하기

해설 〈세부 사항〉
3월 12일이라는 날짜는 두 번째 지문 중간 부분의 작업 완료일(Work Completed: March 12)에 쓰여 있다. 그리고 바로 아랫줄에 브랜 씨가 작업팀장으로 표기되어 있어(Crew Leader: Robert Brann) 해당 작업팀을 감독하는 일을 한 것으로 판단할 수 있으므로 (D)가 정답이다.

어휘 equipment 장비 repair ~을 수리하다 exterior 외부의, 겉의 process v. ~을 처리하다 payment 지불(금) oversee ~을 감독하다, 총괄하다

193 청구서에 관해 언급된 것은 무엇인가?
(A) 지불 마감 기한이 변경되었다.
(B) 세금이 적용되지 말았어야 했다.
(C) 잘못된 가격이 청구되었다.
(D) 서비스에 더 큰 구역이 포함되었다.

해설 〈지문 연계〉
첫 지문 첫 단락에 25퍼센트 할인 서비스를 광고하면서(Get $25 off ~) 두 번째 단락에 단층 주택에 대한 표준 요금이 180달러라고(Our regular rates are ~ $180 for a one-story home) 쓰여 있다. 그런데 두 번째 지문을 보면 단층 주택에 대해(Property Type: one-story home) 180달러의 요금이 할인 적용이 되지 않은 채 청구되어 있으므로(Total Charge: $180.00) 잘못된 가격이 청구된 사실을 알 수 있다. 따라서 이와 같은 문제점을 말한 (C)가 정답이다.

어휘 deadline 마감 기한 tax 세금 apply ~을 적용하다 charge ~을 청구하다 include ~을 포함하다

194 렌델 씨는 왜 편지를 썼는가?
(A) 서비스를 추천하기 위해
(B) 실수를 인정하기 위해
(C) 피드백을 요청하기 위해
(D) 업무 일정을 잡기 위해

해설 〈주제 및 목적〉
렌델 씨가 쓴 편지인 세 번째 지문 첫 단락을 보면, 청구서에 발생된 문제점을(~ the problem with your bill) 언급하면서 그로 인해 초래되었을 수 있는 혼동과 불편함에 사과한다는(I apologize for any

confusion or inconvenience ~) 말이 쓰여 있다. 이는 잘못을 인정하는 말에 해당되므로 (B)가 정답이다.

어휘 acknowledge ~을 인정하다 request ~을 요청하다, 요구하다 feedback 의견 task 업무, 일

195 렌델 씨에 관해 암시된 것은 무엇인가?
(A) 직원들에게 더욱 전문적으로 일하도록 조언했다.
(B) 존스 씨에게 환불 금액을 보낼 것이다.
(C) 고객들이 555-7988번으로 그에게 연락할 수 있다.
(D) 로드리게즈 배수관 케어가 최근에 그를 고용했다.

해설 〈지문 연계〉
세 번째 지문 하단에 렌델 씨의 직책이 예약 관리부장(Bookings Manager)으로 쓰여 있고, 첫 지문 맨 마지막에 예약을 하려면 555-7988번으로 예약 담당 부서에 연락하라는(~ contact our Bookings Department at 555-7988) 말이 쓰여 있다. 따라서 555-7988번으로 렌델 씨에게 연락할 수 있다는 것을 알 수 있으므로 이를 언급한 (C)가 정답이다.

어휘 advise A to do A에게 ~하도록 조언하다 refund 환불(금) contact ~에게 연락하다 recently 최근에 hire ~을 고용하다

[196-200] 안내 책자와 이메일, 그리고 일정표

오델 비즈니스 인스티튜트
합리적인 해결책
온라인 전문 능력 개발 강좌
(198) 2월 24일, 오전 10시 – 정오

신규 고객에게 다가가는 것은 전적으로 연결하는 것과 관련된 것입니다. (196) 홍보 담당 직원께서는 특히 이 강좌를 통해 혜택을 얻게 될 것이며, 이 강좌는 소셜 미디어 플랫폼을 최대한 활용하는 방법을 설명해 드립니다. (198) 마테오 미디어 소속의 강사 엘리엇 오스본 씨에게 눈길을 끄는 페이지 개발과 소셜 미디어 존재감의 극대화, 그리고 더 많은 고객 참여를 만들어 내는 것에 대한 정보를 제공해 드릴 것입니다. 이미 기업 소셜 미디어 계정을 운영하고 계신다 하더라도, 여러분의 업체를 한 단계 더 끌어올리시는 데 도움이 되는 새로운 팁을 찾으시게 될 것입니다.

198 날짜: 2월 25일
제목: 오델 비즈니스 인스티튜트 강좌

오델 비즈니스 인스티튜트를 통해 몇몇 전문 능력 개발 강좌를 수강하고자 하는 제 요청을 승인해 주셔서 다시 한 번 감사드립니다. **198** 제 첫 번째 강좌는 소셜 미디어와 관련된 것이었으며, 어제 개최되었습니다. 안타깝게도, 저는 그 강좌가 제 시간을 들일 만한 가치가 있는 것이었는지 확실치 않습니다. 강사님께서 해당 분야의 전문가이기는 하지만, **197** 구체적인 것 없이 오직 전반적인 조언만 제공해 주었습니다. 그 대부분은 조금이라도 개인적으로 소셜 미디어를 이용해 오고 있는 사람이면 누구나 알 수 있는 일반 상식에 불과했습니다. 또한, **198** 그분이 이야기한 유일한 제품이 마테오 미디어에서 만든 것이었지만, 저는 다른 많은 선택 옵션이 시중에 존재한다는 것을 알고 있습니다.

199 저는 이 학원의 온라인 강좌들 중 하나를 더 수강해 볼 예정이며, 위기 관리 방법에 관해 곧 개최되는 것입니다. 만일 그것이 제 기준을 충족하지 못한다면, 비즈니스 강좌를 듣기 위해 다른 선택 옵션을 살펴봐야 할 수도 있다고 생각합니다. 곧 알려 드리도록 하겠습니다.

라홀

오델 비즈니스 인스티튜트: 3월 온라인 강좌			
날짜 및 시간	강좌명	강사	**200** 수강료
3월 2일, 오후 1시-4시	비즈니스 이메일 작성하기	도나 램지	£25
3월 9일, 오후 2시-5시	협상 전략	리오넬 뉴턴	£25
199 3월 16일, 오후 1시-4시	**199** 위기 관리	로버트 스테닉스	£25
3월 23일, 오전 9시-11시	올바른 팀 고용하기	도나 램지	£25

상기 강좌들 중 어느 것이든 신청하시려면, info@odellbusiness.com으로 이메일을 보내 주시기 바랍니다. 수강 신청은 강좌 날짜보다 3일 전에 마감됩니다.

어휘 savvy 합리적인, 요령 있는, 상식 있는 solution 해결책 professional development 전문 능력 개발, 직업 능력 개발 reach ~에게 다가가다, 도달하다 all about ~ 전적으로 ~에 관한, ~이 가장 중요한 connection 관계, 관련(성) public relations 홍보 particularly 특히 benefit from ~로부터 혜택을 얻다, 이득을 보다 explain ~을 설명하다 how to do ~하는 법 get the most out of ~을 최대한 활용하다 instructor 강사 provide A with B A에게 B를 제공하다 develop ~을 개발하다, 발전시키다 eye-catching 눈길을 끄는 maximize ~을 극대화하다 presence 존재감 create ~을 창출하다, 만들어 내다 customer engagement 고객 참여 even if ~라 하더라도 operate ~을 운영하다, 가동하다 account 계정 help A do A가 ~하는 것을 돕다 take A to the next level A를 한 단계 끌어올리다 approve ~을 승인하다 request 요청 through ~을 통해 hold ~을 개최하다, 열다 unfortunately 안타깝게도, 아쉽게도 worth ~의 가치가 있는 expert 전문가 field 분야 broad 전반적인, 개괄적인 specific 구체적인, 특정한 common sense 일반 상식 length (시간) 길이

---

although 비록 ~이기는 하지만 try ~을 한 번 해 보다 upcoming 곧 있을, 다가오는 how to do ~하는 법 risk 위기, 위험 (요소) meet ~을 충족하다 standard 기준, 표준 may have to do ~해야 할 수도 있다 look into ~을 살펴보다 let A know A에게 알리다 fee 요금, 수수료 negotiation 협상, 협의 strategy 전략 hire ~을 고용하다 sign up for ~을 신청하다, ~에 등록하다 above 상기의, 위의 registration 등록

196 안내 책자에 따르면, 누가 합리적인 해결책 강좌에 대한 이상적인 참가자일 수 있는가?
(A) 그래픽 디자이너
(B) 컴퓨터 기술자
(C) 홍보 책임자
(D) 재정 자문

해설 〈글의 대상〉
첫 지문 시작 부분에 홍보 담당 직원들이 특히 강좌를 통해 혜택을 얻을 수 있다는 내용이(Public relations employees will particularly benefit from this course ~) 있으므로 (C)가 정답이다.

어휘 ideal 이상적인 participant 참가자 public relations (대외) 홍보 financial 재정의, 금융의

197 다얄 씨가 강좌에 실망한 한 가지 이유는 무엇인가?
(A) 정보가 너무 일반적이었다.
(B) 질문할 시간이 충분하지 않았다.
(C) 강사가 아는 것이 많지 않았다.
(D) 개념이 이해하기 어려웠다.

해설 〈세부 사항〉
다얄 씨가 쓴 이메일인 두 번째 지문 첫 단락에, 아쉬웠던 부분을 언급하면서 강사가 구체적이지 않은 전반적인 조언만 제공해 주었다고(~ he only gave broad advice with nothing specific) 알리고 있다. 따라서 이와 같은 내용을 담은 (A)가 정답이다.

어휘 be disappointed with ~에 실망하다 general 일반적인 knowledgeable 아는 것이 많은, 박식한 follow (내용 등) ~을 이해하다, 따라잡다

198 다얄 씨가 오스본 씨에 관해 암시하는 것은 무엇인가?
(A) 학생을 가르치는 것을 불편해했다.
(B) 제품 추천을 마테오 미디어로 국한시켰다.
(C) 다얄 씨에게 다른 강좌를 추천했다.
(D) 개인 회사를 설립했다.

해설 〈지문 연계〉
두 번째 지문 이메일의 작성 날짜는 2월 25일이고, 지문 초반부에 소셜 미디어와 관련된 어제의 강의를 들었다는 내용이(My first class was ~ which was held yesterday) 있으므로 다얄 씨는 첫 번째 지문에서 언급된 2월 24일 강의를 들었음을 알 수 있다. 첫 번째 지문에서 해당 강좌의 강사 이름이 오스본 씨라는 것을 파악할 수 있는데, 두 번째 지문에서 해당 강사가 이야기한 유일한 제품이 마테오 미디어에서 만든 것이라고(~ the only products he talked about were those made by Mateo Media ~) 밝히고 있다. 이는 강좌

에서 소개한 제품을 마테오 미디어 제품으로만 한정했다는 뜻이므로 (B)가 정답이다.

어휘 be uncomfortable -ing ~하는 것을 불편해하다 limit ~을 국한시키다, 제한하다 suggestion 추천, 제안 found ~을 설립하다

199 다얄 씨는 언제 다른 강좌에 참석할 계획인가?
(A) 3월 2일
(B) 3월 9일
(C) 3월 16일
(D) 3월 23일

해설 〈지문 연계〉
두 번째 지문 두 번째 단락에 다얄 씨가 참석하려는 다른 강좌가 언급되어 있는데, 그것이 위기 관리 방법에 관한 것이라고(I'm going to try one more ~ the upcoming one on how to manage risk) 쓰여 있다. 세 번째 지문의 일정표에 강좌명이 위기 관리(Risk Management)인 것은 3월 16일로(March 16, 1-4 P.M.) 표기되어 있으므로 (C)가 정답이다.

어휘 plan to do ~할 계획이다 attend ~에 참석하다

200 모든 3월 온라인 강좌가 공통적으로 지니고 있는 점은 무엇인가?
(A) 일주일 전에 미리 등록할 필요가 있다.
(B) 오후 시간에 개최된다.
(C) 강사가 동일하다.
(D) 수강료가 동일하다.

해설 〈진위 확인 (전체 진위 유형)〉
세 번째 지문에 제시된 일정표에 수강료 항목이 모두 £25로 동일하게 기재되어 있으므로 이와 같은 공통점을 언급한 (D)가 정답이다.

어휘 have A in common A를 공통적으로 지니다 require ~을 필요로 하다 registration 등록 in advance 미리, 사전에 take place (행사, 일 등이) 개최되다, 발생되다

Actual Test 04

본책 P142

🎧 Listening Comprehension

PART 1

1 (C)	2 (D)	3 (A)	4 (A)	5 (D)	6 (B)

PART 2

7 (C)	8 (B)	9 (C)	10 (C)	11 (C)	12 (A)	13 (C)	14 (A)	15 (C)	16 (C)
17 (C)	18 (C)	19 (B)	20 (B)	21 (B)	22 (C)	23 (B)	24 (B)	25 (B)	26 (C)
27 (A)	28 (C)	29 (A)	30 (B)	31 (C)					

PART 3

32 (B)	33 (D)	34 (A)	35 (B)	36 (D)	37 (C)	38 (C)	39 (D)	40 (B)	41 (B)
42 (D)	43 (A)	44 (D)	45 (B)	46 (C)	47 (C)	48 (D)	49 (B)	50 (D)	51 (C)
52 (B)	53 (D)	54 (B)	55 (A)	56 (B)	57 (D)	58 (C)	59 (B)	60 (D)	61 (D)
62 (C)	63 (A)	64 (C)	65 (D)	66 (C)	67 (C)	68 (A)	69 (B)	70 (D)	

PART 4

71 (D)	72 (C)	73 (B)	74 (D)	75 (B)	76 (A)	77 (B)	78 (A)	79 (D)	80 (D)
81 (A)	82 (B)	83 (B)	84 (B)	85 (D)	86 (D)	87 (B)	88 (D)	89 (A)	90 (D)
91 (B)	92 (A)	93 (D)	94 (C)	95 (B)	96 (A)	97 (A)	98 (B)	99 (C)	100 (C)

📖 Reading Comprehension

본책 P154

PART 5

101 (D)	102 (B)	103 (C)	104 (D)	105 (C)	106 (B)	107 (D)	108 (B)	109 (B)	110 (C)
111 (A)	112 (D)	113 (B)	114 (C)	115 (D)	116 (C)	117 (C)	118 (C)	119 (B)	120 (D)
121 (B)	122 (D)	123 (A)	124 (B)	125 (A)	126 (B)	127 (A)	128 (D)	129 (C)	130 (A)

PART 6

131 (B)	132 (C)	133 (D)	134 (B)	135 (C)	136 (A)	137 (D)	138 (C)	139 (D)	140 (A)
141 (B)	142 (C)	143 (C)	144 (B)	145 (D)	146 (A)				

PART 7

147 (B)	148 (C)	149 (C)	150 (D)	151 (A)	152 (C)	153 (A)	154 (D)	155 (D)	156 (C)
157 (D)	158 (C)	159 (C)	160 (A)	161 (D)	162 (D)	163 (C)	164 (C)	165 (D)	166 (A)
167 (C)	168 (B)	169 (A)	170 (D)	171 (D)	172 (B)	173 (D)	174 (D)	175 (A)	176 (A)
177 (C)	178 (B)	179 (C)	180 (D)	181 (D)	182 (B)	183 (B)	184 (C)	185 (C)	186 (C)
187 (D)	188 (C)	189 (A)	190 (D)	191 (B)	192 (C)	193 (D)	194 (C)	195 (A)	196 (D)
197 (B)	198 (C)	199 (B)	200 (D)						

1
(A) A man is holding onto a handrail.
[캐W] (B) A man is locking a bike to a lamppost.
(C) A man is going up a stairway.
(D) A man is hiking in the woods.

(A) 남자가 난간을 붙잡고 있다.
(B) 남자가 가로등에 자전거를 묶어 잠그고 있다.
(C) 남자가 계단을 올라가고 있다.
(D) 남자가 숲에서 하이킹하고 있다.

해설   남자가 계단을 걸어서 올라가는 모습에 초점을 맞춘 (C)가 정답이다. 난간과 가로등, 숲은 사진에서 볼 수 없다.

어휘   hold onto ~을 붙잡다   handrail 난간   lock ~을 잠그다   lamppost 가로등   stairway 계단   hike 도보여행을 하다, 하이킹하다

2
(A) The woman is putting merchandise into a bag.
[호M] (B) A price tag is being cut off.
(C) A customer is trying on a scarf.
(D) Footwear is lined up on the shelves.

(A) 여자가 상품을 가방에 넣고 있다.
(B) 가격표가 절단되고 있다.
(C) 고객이 스카프를 착용해 보고 있다.
(D) 신발이 선반에 줄지어 놓여 있다.

해설   여러 신발이 선반에 나란히 놓여 있는 모습에 초점을 맞춘 (D)가 정답이다. 상품을 가방에 넣는 동작과 가격표가 절단되는 동작, 그리고 스카프를 착용하는 동작은 사진에서 볼 수 없다.

어휘   put A into B A를 B에 넣다   merchandise 상품   price tag 가격표   cut off ~을 절단하다, 잘라내다   try on ~을 (잘 맞는지 보기 위해) 착용해 보다   be lined up 줄지어 있다   shelf 선반, 진열대

3
(A) A vehicle has been raised for repairs.
[영W] (B) There's a car pulled up to the curb.
(C) Tools are being loaded into a car.
(D) The man is kneeling on the grass.

(A) 차량이 수리를 위해 들어 올려져 있다.
(B) 자동차가 연석 쪽으로 정차되어 있다.
(C) 도구들이 자동차에 실리고 있다.
(D) 남자가 잔디밭에 무릎을 꿇고 있다.

해설   정비소에서 자동차가 들어 올려져 있는 상태에 초점을 맞춘 (A)가 정답이다. 연석, 도구가 실리는 동작, 잔디밭은 사진에서 볼 수 없다.

어휘   vehicle 차량   raise ~을 들어 올리다, 끌어올리다   repair 수리   There is A p.p. A가 ~되어 있다   pull up ~을 정차하다, 멈춰 세우다   curb (도로와 인도의 경계를 이루는) 연석   tool 도구   load ~을 싣다   kneel 무릎을 꿇다

4
(A) They are on opposite sides of a counter.
[미M] (B) The woman is handing a briefcase to the man.
(C) They are shaking hands.
(D) The man is shopping for a business suit.

(A) 사람들이 서로 카운터의 맞은편에 있다.
(B) 여자가 서류 가방을 남자에게 건네고 있다.
(C) 사람들이 악수하고 있다.
(D) 남자가 정장을 구입하기 위해 쇼핑하고 있다.

해설   두 사람이 서로 카운터 맞은편에 서 있는 모습에 초점을 맞춘 (A)가 정답이다. 서류 가방을 건네는 동작과 악수하는 동작, 그리고 쇼핑하는 동작은 사진에서 볼 수 없다.

어휘   opposite 맞은편의, 반대편의   hand A to B A를 B에게 건네다   briefcase 서류 가방   shake hands 악수하다   shop for ~을 구입하려 쇼핑하다   business suit 정장, 양복

5
(A) Waiters are serving trays of food.
[캐W] (B) A magazine rack is positioned by the entrance.
(C) The server is fastening her apron.
(D) One of the women is studying the menu.

(A) 종업원들이 음식을 여러 쟁반에 담아 제공하고 있다.
(B) 잡지 거치대가 입구 옆에 자리 잡고 있다.
(C) 종업원이 앞치마를 매는 중이다.
(D) 여자들 중의 한 명이 메뉴를 살펴보고 있다.

해설   좌석에 앉은 여자 한 명이 메뉴를 확인하는 모습에 초점을 맞춘 (D)가 정답이다. 여러 종업원이 음식을 제공하는 동작, 입구, 그리고 앞치마를 매는 동작은 사진에서 볼 수 없다.

어휘   serve (음식 등) ~을 제공하다, 내오다   rack (얹거나 걸어 놓는) 거치대, 진열대   position v. ~을 위치시키다, 놓다   entrance 입구   fasten ~을 매다, 잠그다, 고정시키다   apron 앞치마   study ~을 살펴보다

6
(A) Motorbikes are blocking the intersection.
[호M] **(B) Some pedestrians are crossing the street.**
(C) Some cars are parked in a garage.
(D) Some trees are being planted on both sides of the street.

(A) 오토바이들이 교차로를 가로막고 있다.
(B) 몇몇 보행자들이 길을 건너고 있다.
(C) 몇몇 자동차들이 차고에 주차되어 있다.
(D) 몇몇 나무들이 거리 양측에 심어지고 있다.

해설   몇몇 사람들이 횡단보도를 이용해 길을 건너는 모습에 초점을 맞춘 (B)가 정답이다. 교차로를 막고 있는 오토바이, 차고, 그리고 나무를 심는 동작은 사진에서 볼 수 없다.

어휘   block ~을 가로막다   intersection 교차로   pedestrian 보행자   cross ~을 건너다, 가로지르다   park ~을 주차하다   garage 차고   plant ~을 심다   both 양쪽의, 둘 모두의

7
Where can I find a cheap clothing store?
[미M] (A) Even cheaper than I hoped.
[영W] (B) It looks fine on you.
(C) Try the one on 34th Street.

저렴한 의류 매장을 어디서 찾을 수 있나요?
(A) 제가 바랐던 것보다 훨씬 더 저렴해요.
(B) 당신에게 잘 어울리네요.
(C) 34번가에 있는 곳에 한 번 가 보세요.

해설   〈Where 의문문〉
저렴한 의류 매장을 찾을 수 있는 곳을 묻는 Where 의문문에 대해 특정 위치 표현과 함께 그곳에 한 번 가 보도록 권하는 (C)가 정답이다.
(A) 비용 수준을 나타낸 말이므로 Where와 어울리지 않는 오답 / 질문의 cheap을 반복한 오답
(B) 옷 등이 잘 어울린다는 의견을 나타낸 말이므로 Where와 어울리지 않는 오답 / 질문의 clothing에서 연상되는 looks fine on you를 사용한 오답

어휘   clothing 의류, 옷   even (비교급 수식) 훨씬   look fine on ~에게 잘 어울리다   try ~에 한 번 가 보다, ~을 한 번 해 보다

8
Does your restaurant serve soup?
[캐W] (A) I don't feel comfortable in a suit.
[호M] **(B) No, I'm afraid we don't.**
(C) The service was very impressive.

당신의 레스토랑에서 수프를 제공하나요?
(A) 저는 양복을 입으면 편하게 느껴지지 않아요.
(B) 아니요, 유감스럽게도 그렇지 않습니다.
(C) 서비스가 매우 인상적이었어요.

해설   〈Do 일반 의문문〉
레스토랑에서 수프를 제공하는지 확인하는 Do 일반 의문문에 대해 부정을 뜻하는 No와 함께 동일한 조동사 do를 부정형으로 사용해 제공하지 않는다는 뜻을 나타낸 (B)가 정답이다.
(A) 양복 착용 시의 불편함을 나타낸 말이므로 질문의 핵심에서 벗어난 오답 / 질문의 soup과 발음이 유사한 suit를 사용한 오답
(C) 서비스의 수준을 나타낸 말이므로 질문의 핵심에서 벗어난 오답 / 질문의 restaurant에서 연상되는 service를 사용한 오답

어휘   serve (음식 등) ~을 제공하다, 내오다   feel comfortable 편하게 느껴지다   suit 양복, 정장   I'm afraid (that) (부정적인 일을 말할 때) 유감이지만 ~이다, ~인 것 같다   impressive 인상적인

9
Who is heading the organizing committee for the event?
[미M] (A) This Saturday night.
[영W] (B) A charity auction.
(C) The managing director.

누가 행사 조직 위원회를 이끌고 있나요?
(A) 이번 주 토요일 밤이요.

(B) 자선 경매 행사요.
(C) 전무이사님입니다.

해설 〈Who 의문문〉
행사 조직 위원회를 이끌고 있는 사람을 묻는 Who 의문문에 대해 특정 직책을 말하는 (C)가 정답이다.
(A) 시점 표현이므로 Who와 어울리지 않는 오답 / 질문의 event에서 연상되는 Saturday night를 사용한 오답
(B) 행사 종류를 나타낸 말이므로 Who와 어울리지 않는 오답 / 질문의 event에서 연상되는 charity auction을 사용한 오답

어휘 head v. ~을 이끌다, 책임지다 organizing committee 조직 위원회 charity 자선 (단체) auction 경매 managing director 전무이사

10 When will Ms. Malik book the tour tickets?
캐W (A) A local sightseeing activity.
호M (B) Yes, they had a great time.
(C) Sometime next week.

말릭 씨가 언제 투어 입장권을 예매하나요?
(A) 현지 관광 활동이요.
(B) 네, 그분들이 즐거운 시간을 보내셨어요.
(C) 다음 주 중으로요.

해설 〈When 의문문〉
말릭 씨가 투어 입장권을 예매하는 시점을 묻는 When 의문문에 대해 다음 주라는 대략적인 시점을 말하는 (C)가 정답이다.
(A) 활동 종류를 나타낸 말이므로 When과 어울리지 않는 오답 / 질문의 tour에서 연상되는 sightseeing을 사용한 오답
(B) 의문사 의문문에 맞지 않는 Yes로 답변하는 오답

어휘 book v. ~을 예약하다 local 현지의, 지역의 sightseeing 관광

11 Didn't we pay this electricity bill already?
미M (A) Sure, I'll turn it off.
영W (B) I'll play the song again.
(C) Yes, it was by bank transfer.

우리가 이미 이 전기세를 내지 않았나요? (= 냈죠?)
(A) 네, 제가 끌게요.
(B) 제가 그 노래를 다시 틀게요.
(C) 네, 은행 계좌 이체로요.

해설 〈부정 의문문〉
이미 전기세를 내지 않았는지 확인하는 부정 의문문에 대해 긍정을 뜻하는 Yes와 함께 납부 방법을 언급하는 (C)가 정답이다.
(A) 긍정을 나타내는 Sure 뒤에 이어지는 말이 전기세 납부 여부와 관련 없는 오답 / 질문의 electricity에서 연상되는 turn off를 사용한 오답
(B) 자신이 노래를 틀겠다는 의사를 밝힌 말이므로 전기세 납부 여부와 관련 없는 오답 / 질문의 pay와 발음이 유사한 play를 사용한 오답

어휘 pay the electricity bill 전기세를 내다 turn A off A를 끄다 by (방법) ~로, ~해서 bank transfer 은행 계좌 이체

12 Which suitcase has a broken lock?
영W **(A) The black leather one.**
캐W (B) I certainly do.
(C) I have one just in case.

어느 여행 가방에 고장 난 잠금 장치가 있죠?
(A) 검은색 가죽으로 된 것이요.
(B) 저는 분명 그럴습니다.
(C) 저는 만일을 대비해서 하나 갖고 있어요.

해설 〈Which 의문문〉
잠금 장치가 고장 난 여행 가방이 어느 것인지 묻는 Which 의문문에 대해 suitcase를 대명사 one으로 대신해 가방의 특징을 말하는 (A)가 정답이다.
(B) 강한 긍정을 나타낼 때 사용하는 말이므로 가방의 특징 등을 묻는 질문의 핵심에서 벗어난 오답
(C) 답변자 자신의 상황을 나타낸 말이므로 가방의 특징 등을 묻는 질문의 핵심에서 벗어난 오답 / 질문의 suitcase와 일부 발음이 같은 case를 사용한 오답

어휘 suitcase 여행 가방 broken 고장 난, 망가진 lock 잠금 장치 certainly 분명히, 확실히 just in case 만일의 경우에 (대비해)

13 What time are we meeting with the inspector?
호M (A) Yes, he sometimes does that.
캐W (B) To check on the kitchen.
(C) First thing tomorrow morning.

우리가 몇 시에 조사관과 만나나요?
(A) 네, 그가 가끔 그 일을 합니다.
(B) 주방을 확인해 보기 위해서요.
(C) 내일 아침에 바로요.

해설 〈What time 의문문〉
조사관과 만나는 시점을 묻는 What time 의문문에 대해 대략적인 미래 시점으로 답변하는 (C)가 정답이다.
(A) 의문사 의문문에 맞지 않는 Yes로 답변하는 오답
(B) 목적을 나타낸 말이므로 What time과 어울리지 않는 오답

어휘 inspector 조사관, 검사관 check on ~을 확인하다 first thing tomorrow morning 내일 아침에 바로, 내일 아침에 가장 먼저

14 Who refills the water in the vases?
영W **(A) Stephanie is in charge of that.**
미M (B) No, I'm not thirsty.
(C) For the floral decorations.

누가 꽃병마다 물을 다시 채우죠?
(A) 스테파니 씨가 그 일을 맡고 있어요.
(B) 아니요, 저는 목이 마르지 않아요.
(C) 꽃 장식물을 위해서요.

해설 〈Who 의문문〉
꽃병에 물을 다시 채우는 사람이 누군지 묻는 Who 의문문에 대해 특정 인물의 이름과 함께 물을 주는 일을 that으로 지칭해 책임지고 있는 사람을 밝히는 (A)가 정답이다.

(B) 의문사 의문문에 맞지 않는 No로 답변하는 오답
(C) 목적을 나타낸 말이므로 Who와 어울리지 않는 오답

어휘 refill ~을 다시 채우다 in charge of ~을 맡고 있는, 책임지고 있는 thirsty 목이 마른 floral decorations 꽃 장식물

15 How far is it from here to the mall?
호M (A) Did you buy anything?
캐W (B) I like its clothing stores.
(C) About five kilometers.

여기서 쇼핑몰까지 얼마나 먼가요?
(A) 뭐 좀 구입했어요?
(B) 저는 그곳 의류 매장들이 마음에 들어요.
(C) 약 5킬로미터요.

해설 〈How far 의문문〉
쇼핑몰이 얼마나 멀리 떨어져 있는지 묻는 How far 의문문에 대해 대략적인 거리를 말하는 (C)가 정답이다.
(A) 제품 구입 여부를 확인하는 말이므로 How far와 어울리지 않는 답변 / 질문의 mall에서 연상되는 buy anything을 사용한 오답
(B) 마음에 들어 하는 대상을 나타낸 말이므로 How far와 어울리지 않는 답변 / 질문의 mall에서 연상되는 clothing stores를 사용한 오답

어휘 How far ~? 얼마나 멀리 ~? clothing 의류, 옷 about 약, 대략

16 Should I leave my luggage here or outside?
미M (A) Your table is ready now.
영W (B) An overseas client.
(C) You can put it here.

제 짐을 여기에 놓아도 되나요, 아니면 밖에 놓아야 하나요?
(A) 지금 손님 테이블이 준비되어 있습니다.
(B) 해외 고객이요.
(C) 여기에 놓으셔도 됩니다.

해설 〈선택 의문문〉
짐을 놓을 곳을 묻는 선택 의문문에 대해 here를 반복해 여기에 놓아도 된다고 허락하는 (C)가 정답이다.
(A) 테이블 준비 상태를 나타낸 말이므로 질문의 핵심에서 벗어난 오답
(B) 고객의 특징을 나타낸 말이므로 질문의 핵심에서 벗어난 오답

어휘 leave ~을 놓다, 두다(= put) luggage 짐, 수하물 overseas 해외의 client 고객, 의뢰인

17 Would you like to try on these shoes in a bigger size?
미M (A) No, I'd rather stay home.
호M (B) I have a bigger briefcase.
(C) What sizes do you have?

이 신발을 더 큰 사이즈로 한 번 신어 보시겠습니까?
(A) 아니요, 저는 집에 있고 싶어요.
(B) 저한테 더 큰 서류 가방이 있어요.
(C) 어떤 사이즈가 있나요?

해설 〈Would 일반 의문문〉

신발을 더 큰 사이즈로 한 번 신어 보도록 권유하는 Would 일반 의문문에 대해 신어 보기 위한 조건인 사이즈 확인을 위해 되묻는 (C)가 정답이다.
(A) 거절을 뜻하는 No 뒤에 이어지는 말이 신발을 신어 보는 것과 관련 없는 오답
(B) 가방의 특징을 나타낸 말이므로 신발을 신어 보는 것과 관련 없는 오답 / 질문의 bigger를 반복한 오답

어휘 Would you like to do? ~하시겠습니까? try on ~을 한 번 착용해 보다 in a bigger size 더 큰 사이즈로 would rather do ~하고 싶다 briefcase 서류 가방

18 Why don't you assign the task to your assistant?
[호M] (A) In alphabetical order, please.
[영W] (B) About three hours.
(C) I need to handle it myself.

보조 직원에게 그 일을 맡겨 보시는 건 어때요?
(A) 알파벳 순서로 부탁드립니다.
(B) 약 3시간이요.
(C) 제가 직접 처리해야 합니다.

해설 〈Why don't you 의문문〉
보조 직원에게 일을 맡겨 보도록 제안하는 Why don't you 의문문에 대해 직접 해야 한다는 말로 맡기지 않겠다는 뜻을 나타낸 (C)가 정답이다.
(A) 파일이나 물품 등의 정렬 방식을 나타낸 말이므로 Why don't you 의문문에 대한 반응으로 맞지 않는 오답
(B) 소요 시간을 나타낸 말이므로 Why don't you 의문문에 대한 반응으로 맞지 않는 오답

어휘 Why don't you ~? ~하는 게 어때요? assign (일, 책임 등) ~을 맡기다. 배정하다 task 일, 업무 assistant 보조, 조수, 비서 in alphabetical order 알파벳 순서로 about 약, 대략 handle ~을 처리하다, 다루다 oneself (부사처럼 쓰여) 직접

19 You can join our evening running group.
[미M] (A) He's been running the company for two years.
[캐W] **(B) That sounds like a good way to get fit.**
(C) Thanks, I had a lovely evening.

저희 저녁 달리기 모임에 함께하셔도 됩니다.
(A) 그분은 2년 동안 그 회사를 운영해 오고 있어요.
(B) 몸매를 유지하는 좋은 방법인 것 같아요.
(C) 감사합니다. 아주 즐거운 저녁 시간이었어요.

해설 〈평서문〉
달리기 모임에 함께해도 된다고 알리는 평서문에 대해 달리기 하는 것을 That으로 지칭해 달리기의 긍정적인 영향을 언급하는 (B)가 정답이다.
(A) 누군지 알 수 없는 He의 회사 운영 기간을 나타낸 말이므로 핵심에서 벗어난 오답 / 평서문에 제시된 running의 다른 의미를 활용해 반복한 오답
(C) 감사를 표하는 Thanks 뒤에 이어지는 말이 달리기 모임 참석 여부와 관련 없는 오답 / 평서문에 제시된 evening을 반복한 오답

어휘 join ~에 함께 하다, 합류하다 run ~을 운영하다 sound like ~인 것 같다, ~인 것처럼 들리다 way to do ~하는 방법 get fit 몸매를 유지하다, 건강을 유지하다

20 How often do the hotel pools get cleaned?
[영W] (A) No, I'm staying at home.
[호M] **(B) Every 12 hours.**
(C) Deluxe room, third floor.

호텔 수영장들이 얼마나 자주 청소되고 있나요?
(A) 아니요, 저는 집에 있을 겁니다.
(B) 12시간마다요.
(C) 3층에 있는 디럭스룸입니다.

해설 〈How often 의문문〉
호텔 수영장들이 얼마나 자주 청소되는지 묻는 How often 의문문에 대해 그 반복 주기를 나타낸 (B)가 정답이다.
(A) 의문사 의문문에 맞지 않는 No로 답변하는 오답
(C) 객실 종류 및 위치를 나타낸 말이므로 How often과 어울리지 않는 오답 / 질문의 hotel에서 연상되는 Deluxe room을 사용한 오답

어휘 How often ~? 얼마나 자주 ~? get p.p. ~ 되다 every 시간 ~마다 (한 번씩)

21 Could you tell me what happened at the meeting?
[미M] (A) May I see the agenda items?
[캐W] **(B) I missed it, too.**
(C) Around 5 P.M.

회의에서 무슨 일이 있었는지 말씀해 주시겠어요?
(A) 안건 사항들을 볼 수 있을까요?
(B) 저도 그 자리에 빠졌어요.
(C) 오후 5시쯤이요.

해설 〈Could 일반 의문문〉
회의 중에 있었던 일을 알려 달라고 요청하는 Could 일반 의문문에 대해 meeting을 it으로 지칭해 자신도 가지 않아 알 수 없다는 뜻을 나타낸 (B)가 정답이다.
(A) 안건을 보여 달라고 요청하는 말이므로 요청 질문의 핵심에서 벗어난 오답 / 질문의 meeting에서 연상되는 agenda를 사용한 오답
(C) 시점 표현이므로 요청 질문의 핵심에서 벗어난 오답 / 질문의 meeting에서 연상되는 5 P.M.을 사용한 오답

어휘 agenda 안건, 의제, 일정(표) item 사항, 항목 miss ~에 빠지다, ~을 놓치다 around ~쯤, 약, 대략

22 Do you think we should make the walls more colorful, or
[호M] keep them white?
[영W] (A) This key will open it.
(B) Thanks, it looks much better.
(C) I prefer a plain style.

우리가 벽들을 더욱 화려하게 만들어야 한다고 생각하세요, 아니면 흰색으로 유지할까요?
(A) 이 열쇠로 열릴 겁니다.

(B) 감사합니다, 훨씬 더 좋아 보이네요.
(C) 저는 무난한 스타일을 선호합니다.

해설 〈선택 의문문〉
벽 색상과 관련된 선택 의문문에 대해 무난한 스타일을 선호한다는 말로 흰색을 선택하겠다는 뜻을 나타낸 (C)가 정답이다.
(A) 열쇠를 사용해 열 수 있다는 뜻을 나타낸 말이므로 질문의 핵심에서 벗어난 오답
(B) 색상을 선택해 적용한 후에야 그에 대한 의견으로 할 수 있는 말이므로 질문의 핵심에서 벗어난 오답

어휘 make A + 형용사 A를 ~하게 만들다 colorful 화려한, 다채로운 keep A + 형용사 A를 ~하게 유지하다 look + 형용사 ~하게 보이다, ~한 것 같다 much (비교급 수식) 훨씬 더 prefer ~을 선호하다 plain 무난한, 평범한, 단조로운

23 I'm concerned that I won't meet the tight deadline.
[캐W] (A) A full department review.
[미M] **(B) Can't you work overtime?**
(C) Feel free to borrow mine.

제가 빡빡한 마감시한을 맞추지 못할까 우려됩니다.
(A) 부서 전체 평가서요.
(B) 초과 근무를 하실 수 없으세요?
(C) 얼마든지 제 것을 빌려 가셔도 됩니다.

해설 〈평서문〉
빡빡한 마감시한을 맞추지 못할까 우려된다는 뜻을 나타낸 평서문에 대해 마감시한을 맞추기 위한 방법으로 초과 근무를 제안하는 (B)가 정답이다.
(A) 특정 업무를 언급하는 말에 해당되므로 마감시한 맞추는 일과 관련 없는 오답
(C) 뭔가를 빌려 가도록 허락하는 말에 해당되므로 마감시한 맞추는 일과 관련 없는 오답 / 평서문에 제시된 deadline과 일부 발음이 유사한 mine을 사용한 오답

어휘 be concerned that ~할까 우려하다, 걱정하다 meet (조건 등)을 맞추다, 충족하다 tight (일정, 비용 등이) 빡빡한, 빠듯한 deadline 마감기한 department 부서 review 평가(서), 검토, 의견, 후기 work overtime 초과 근무를 하다 feel free to do 얼마든지 ~하세요, 언제든지 ~하세요 borrow ~을 빌리다

24 Don't you have a lunch meeting?
[호M] (A) I'll read that this afternoon.
[영W] **(B) That was rescheduled for Friday.**
(C) 30 people.

오찬 회의가 있지 않으신가요? (= 있으시죠?)
(A) 오늘 오후에 그걸 읽어 볼게요.
(B) 그게 금요일로 일정이 재조정되었어요.
(C) 30명이요.

해설 〈부정 의문문〉
오찬 회의가 있지 않은지 확인하는 부정 의문문에 대해 lunch meeting을 That으로 지칭해 일정이 재조정된 사실을 밝히는 (B)가

정답이다.

(A) 뭔가 읽어 보겠다는 뜻을 나타낸 말이므로 오찬 회의 일정과 관련해 묻는 질문의 핵심에서 벗어난 오답

(C) 인원수를 나타낸 말이므로 오찬 회의 일정과 관련해 묻는 질문의 핵심에서 벗어난 오답 / 질문의 meeting에서 연상되는 30 people을 사용한 오답

어휘 reschedule A for B A의 일정을 B로 재조정하다

25 Amanda's starting her own consulting business, right?
미M (A) To the office building.
캐W **(B) No, she's staying with our firm.**
(C) You can consult the manual.

아만다 씨가 개인 컨설팅 사업을 시작하시죠, 맞나요?
(A) 사무실 건물로요.
(B) 아니요, 그분은 우리 회사에 남을 거예요.
(C) 설명서를 참고하시면 됩니다.

해설 〈부가 의문문〉
아만다 씨가 개인 컨설팅 사업을 시작하는지 확인하는 부가 의문문에 대해 부정을 나타내는 No 및 Amanda를 대신하는 she와 함께 회사에 남는다는 말로 개인 사업을 하지 않는다는 뜻을 나타낸 (B)가 정답이다.
(A) 이동 위치를 나타낸 말이므로 아만다 씨의 개인 사업 시작 여부와 관련 없는 오답
(C) 설명서를 참고하도록 권하는 말이므로 아만다 씨의 개인 사업 시작 여부와 관련 없는 오답 / 질문의 consulting과 일부 발음이 같은 consult를 사용한 오답

어휘 consulting 컨설팅, 상담 firm 회사, 업체 consult (사물 목적어) ~을 참고하다, 찾아보다, (사람 목적어) ~와 상의하다, 상담하다

26 Should we purchase our tickets for the concert now?
영W (A) At the main train station.
호M (B) The guitar player was excellent.
(C) We'd better check the price first.

우리가 그 콘서트 입장권을 지금 구입해야 하나요?
(A) 중앙역에서요.
(B) 그 기타 연주자가 훌륭했어요.
(C) 가격을 먼저 확인하는 게 좋겠어요.

해설 〈Should 일반 의문문〉
콘서트 입장권을 지금 구입해야 하는지 확인하는 Should 일반 의문문에 대해 입장권 구입을 위한 조건으로서 가격을 확인하는 일을 먼저 제안하는 (C)가 정답이다.
(A) 위치 표현이므로 입장권 구입 여부를 묻는 질문의 핵심에서 벗어난 오답 / 질문의 tickets에서 연상되는 train station을 사용한 오답
(B) 특정 기타 연주자의 연주에 대한 의견을 나타낸 말이므로 질문의 핵심에서 벗어난 오답 / 질문의 concert에서 연상되는 guitar player를 사용한 오답

어휘 purchase ~을 구입하다 had better do ~하는 게 좋다

27 This medication doesn't look the same as before.
미M **(A) Ask the pharmacist to check it.**
캐W (B) One pill after every meal.
(C) I hope you get well soon.

이 약이 예전과 똑같은 것 같지 않아요.
(A) 약사에게 확인해 달라고 요청해 보세요.
(B) 매 식사 후에 한 알입니다.
(C) 곧 나아지시기를 바랍니다.

해설 〈평서문〉
약이 예전과 똑같은 것 같지 않다는 의견을 말하는 평서문에 대해 그에 대해 확인할 수 있는 방법을 제안하는 (A)가 정답이다.
(B) 약 복용 방법을 나타내는 말이므로 약 성분에 대한 의구심을 나타내는 평서문의 핵심에서 벗어난 오답 / 질문의 medication에서 연상되는 pill을 사용한 오답
(C) 곧 낫기를 바란다는 격려의 말에 해당되므로 약 성분에 대한 의구심을 나타내는 평서문의 핵심에서 벗어난 오답 / 질문의 medication에서 연상되는 get well을 사용한 오답

어휘 medication 약(물) look the same 똑같은 것 같다 as before 예전처럼 ask A to do A에게 ~하도록 요청하다 pharmacist 약사 pill 알약 get well 나아지다

28 When is your financial report due?
영W (A) I paid for it.
호M (B) A closed bank account.
(C) By the end of this month.

재정 보고서는 언제까지 제출해야 하나요?
(A) 제가 지불했어요.
(B) 폐쇄된 은행 계좌요.
(C) 이번 달 말까지요.

해설 〈When 의문문〉
"When is A due?"는 A의 기한이 언제까지인지를 묻는 질문 형태이므로, 재정 보고서 제출 기한을 묻는 When 의문문에 대해 기한을 나타내는 시점 표현으로 답변하는 (C)가 정답이다.
(A) 과거에 지불했다는 내용과 보고서 제출 기한은 관련 없으므로 오답 / 질문의 financial에서 연상되는 pay for를 사용한 오답
(B) 은행 계좌와 보고서 제출기한은 관련 없으므로 오답 / 질문의 financial에서 연상되는 bank account를 사용한 오답

어휘 financial 재정의 pay for ~을 지불하다 bank account 계좌 by the end of ~의 말까지

29 You've posted the job opening online, haven't you?
미M **(A) I'm typing it up now.**
캐W (B) The grand opening is July 1.
(C) A post office receipt.

온라인으로 구인 공고를 게시하셨죠, 그렇지 않나요? (= 게시하셨죠?)
(A) 지금 작성하고 있어요.
(B) 개장식이 7월 1일입니다.
(C) 우체국 영수증이요.

온라인으로 구인 공고를 게시하지 않았는지 확인하는 부가 의문문에 대해 지금 작성하고 있다는 말로 아직 게시하지 않았음을 알리는 (A)가 정답이다.
(B) 개장식 일정을 나타낸 말이므로 구인 공고 게시 여부와 관련 없는 오답 / 질문의 opening을 반복한 오답
(C) 우체국 영수증을 뜻하는 말이므로 구인 공고 게시 여부와 관련 없는 오답 / 질문의 post가 지닌 다른 의미를 활용해 반복한 오답

어휘 post ~을 게시하다 job opening 공석, 빈자리 online 온라인으로, 온라인에서 type A up A를 작성하다 receipt 영수증

30 Why is the warehouse so empty right now?
호M (A) She will check your payment.
영W **(B) Didn't you hear about the water leak?**
(C) Sure, I can fill it up for you.

지금 창고가 왜 그렇게 비어 있는 건가요?
(A) 그녀가 지불 금액을 확인해 드릴 겁니다.
(B) 누수 얘기를 못 들으셨어요?
(C) 네, 제가 대신 가득 채워 드릴 수 있어요.

해설 〈Why 의문문〉
창고가 왜 비어 있는지 묻는 Why 의문문에 대해 누수 문제가 발생된 사실을 알지 못했느냐고 되묻는 것으로 이유를 언급하는 (B)가 정답이다.
(A) 누군지 알 수 없는 She에 대해 얘기하고 있으므로 질문의 핵심에서 벗어난 오답
(C) Yes와 마찬가지로 의문사 의문문에 맞지 않는 Sure로 답변하는 오답

어휘 warehouse 창고 empty 비어 있는 payment 지불(금) leak (물, 가스 등의) 누출 fill A up A를 가득 채우다

31 Where can I hire temporary construction workers?
미M (A) Yes, the machinery is working fine.
캐W (B) The higher number is concerning.
(C) Do you want me to recommend a Web site?

어디서 임시 공사 인부들을 고용할 수 있나요?
(A) 네, 기계가 잘 작동하고 있습니다.
(B) 더 높은 숫자가 우려하게 만드네요.
(C) 웹 사이트를 하나 추천해 드릴까요?

해설 〈Where 의문문〉
임시 공사 인부들을 고용할 수 있는 곳을 묻는 Where 의문문에 대해 웹 사이트를 하나 추천해 주겠다고 제안하는 (C)가 정답이다.
(A) 의문사 의문문에 맞지 않는 Yes로 답변하는 오답
(B) 높은 수치에 대한 우려를 나타낸 말이므로 Where와 어울리지 않는 오답 / 질문의 hire와 발음은 같지만 의미가 다른 higher를 사용한 오답

어휘 hire ~을 고용하다 temporary 임시의, 일시적인 construction 공사, 건설 machinery 기계 work (기계 등이) 작동되다, 기능하다 concerning 우려하게 만드는, 걱정시키는 want A to do A에게 ~하기를 원하다 recommend ~을 추천하다, 권하다

Questions 32-34 refer to the following conversation. 미M 캐W

> M Thanks for meeting me, Sue. I've been reviewing the sales figures over the last week, and ㉜ you sold the most mobile phones out of anybody in the store over the last year. I've also seen how good you are at helping out new staff members.
>
> W Thank you. ㉝ I feel teamwork is important for any business.
>
> M ㉝ I agree. That's why I'd like to transfer you to our education center to help train new staff. Would you be happy to do this?
>
> W That's a great honor. I'm shocked. Can I tell you my decision later today?
>
> M Absolutely. ㉞ Here's some coupons for the restaurant downstairs. Go get some lunch and think things over.
>
> W I will. Thanks again.

남 만나러 와 주셔서 감사합니다. 수 씨, 제가 지난주 동안 매출 수치를 검토해 봤는데, 지난 한 해 동안에 걸쳐 매장 내 모든 사람들 중에서 수 씨가 가장 많은 휴대전화기를 판매하셨습니다. 그리고 그동안 우리 신입 사원들을 얼마나 잘 도와주고 계신지도 잘 알고 있습니다.

여 감사합니다. 어느 회사든 팀워크가 중요한 것 같습니다.

남 동의합니다. 그게 바로 신입 사원들을 교육하는 데 도움이 될 수 있도록 우리 교육 센터로 전근시켜 드리고자 하는 이유입니다. 이렇게 하시는 게 괜찮으시겠어요?

여 대단한 영광입니다. 얼떨떨하네요. 오늘 늦게 제 결정을 말씀 드려도 될까요?

남 물론입니다. 여기 아래층 레스토랑에서 사용하실 수 있는 쿠폰이 좀 있습니다. 가셔서 점심 식사하시면서 차분히 생각해 보세요.

여 그러겠습니다. 다시 한 번 감사합니다.

어휘 review ~을 검토하다, 살펴보다 sales 매출, 판매, 영업 figure 수치, 숫자 over ~ 동안에 걸쳐 out of anybody 모든 사람들 중에서, 그 누구보다 be good at -ing ~하는 것을 잘하다 help out ~을 돕다 agree 동의하다 would like to do ~하고 싶다, ~하고자 하다 transfer A to B A를 B로 전근시키다, 자리를 옮기다 help do ~하는 데 도움이 되다 honor 영광, 영예 shocked 얼떨떨한, 충격받은 decision 결정 downstairs 아래층에 think A over A를 차분히 생각하다, 곰곰이 생각하다

32 What kind of business do the speakers probably work at?
(A) A recruitment agency
(B) A mobile phone store
(C) An Internet provider
(D) A clothing manufacturer

화자들은 어떤 종류의 업체에서 일하고 있을 것 같은가?
(A) 인력 채용 대행사
(B) 휴대전화기 매장
(C) 인터넷 공급업체
(D) 의류 제조사

해설 〈근무지를 묻는 문제〉
대화를 시작하면서 남자가 여자에게 매장 내 모든 사람들 중에서 가장 많은 휴대전화기를 판매했다는(you sold the most mobile phones out of anybody in the store over the last year) 사실을 밝히고 있는데, 이는 휴대전화기 매장에서 함께 일하는 직원들끼리 나눌 수 있는 얘기이므로 (B)가 정답이다.

33 What do the speakers agree is an important skill?
(A) Being on time for work
(B) Creating attractive displays
(C) Being friendly to customers
(D) Working in a team

화자들은 무엇이 중요한 능력이라는 데 동의하는가?
(A) 회사에 제때 출근하는 것
(B) 매력적인 진열 상태를 만드는 것
(C) 고객들에게 친절하게 대하는 것
(D) 팀으로서 일하는 것

해설 〈기타 세부 사항을 묻는 문제〉
대화 중반부에 여자가 어떤 회사든 팀워크가 중요하다는(I feel teamwork is important for any business) 의견을 밝히는 것에 대해 남자가 I agree라는 말로 동의하고 있으므로 (D)가 정답이다.

어휘 agree 동의하다 on time 제때 create ~을 만들어내다 attractive 매력적인 display 진열(품), 전시(품)

34 What does the man provide to the woman?
(A) Some meal vouchers
(B) Some work assignments
(C) An e-mail address
(D) A job reference

남자는 여자에게 무엇을 제공하는가?
(A) 식사 상품권
(B) 할당 업무
(C) 이메일 주소
(D) 취업 추천서

해설 〈기타 세부 사항을 묻는 문제〉
대화 후반부에 남자가 아래층 레스토랑에서 사용할 수 있는 쿠폰이 있다고(Here's some coupons for the restaurant downstairs) 알리면서 전달하고 있으므로 (A)가 정답이다.

어휘 voucher 상품권, 쿠폰 assignment 할당(된 것), 배정(된 것) reference 추천서

Questions 35-37 refer to the following conversation. 영W 호M

> W Hi, Brad. Did you have a nice weekend?
>
> M Yes. ㉟ The city has just opened a new park in my neighborhood, so I spent most of Sunday there.
>
> W Oh, I heard about that. It's always great to spend some time outdoors.
>
> M Right, and ㊱ I really like it because they have an area with exercise equipment. That makes it really easy to work out in my free time.
>
> W I think there will be regular activities there as well. ㊲ You should visit the city's Web site to find out about the upcoming events. You might find something you're interested in.

여 안녕하세요, 브래드 씨, 즐거운 주말 보내셨나요?

남 네. 시에서 제가 사는 지역에 새 공원을 막 개장했기 때문에 그곳에서 일요일 대부분을 보냈어요.

여 아, 그 얘기 들었어요. 야외에서 시간을 좀 보내는 건 항상 기분 좋은 일이죠.

남 맞아요, 그리고 운동 장비가 있는 구역이 있어서 정말 마음에 들어요. 그것 때문에 제가 여유 시간에 운동하는 게 쉬워졌거든요.

여 그곳에서 주기적인 활동들도 있을 것 같아요. 곧 있을 행사들에 관해서 알아 보실 수 있게 시 웹 사이트를 방문해 보세요. 관심 있으신 것을 찾으실 수도 있잖아요.

어휘 neighborhood 지역, 인근 outdoors ad. 야외에서 exercise 운동 equipment 장비 A make it B to do A 때문에 ~하는 것을 B하게 되다, A가 ~하는 것을 B하게 만들다 regular 주기적인, 정기적인 activity 활동 as well ~도, 또한 find out about ~에 관해 알아내다, 파악하다 upcoming 곧 있을, 다가오는 be interested in ~에 관심이 있다

35 What has recently happened in the man's neighborhood?
(A) A competition was held.
(B) A park was opened.
(C) A road was repaired.
(D) A cleanup project was completed.

남자가 사는 지역에서 최근에 무슨 일이 있었는가?
(A) 경연대회가 개최되었다.
(B) 공원이 개장했다.
(C) 도로가 수리되었다.
(D) 정화 프로젝트가 완료되었다.

해설 〈과거에 일어난 일을 묻는 문제〉
대화 초반부에 남자가 시에서 새 공원을 막 개장한(The city has just opened a new park in my neighborhood) 사실을 언급하고 있으므로 (B)가 정답이다.

36 Why does the man say he likes the change?
(A) He can win a prize.
(B) He can meet new people.
(C) He can save money.
(D) He can get exercise easily.

남자는 왜 변화가 마음에 든다고 말하는가?
(A) 상품을 탈 수 있다.
(B) 새로운 사람들을 만날 수 있다.
(C) 돈을 절약할 수 있다.
(D) 쉽게 운동할 수 있다.

해설 〈기타 세부 사항을 묻는 문제〉
남자가 대화 중반부에 운동 장비가 있어서 마음에 든다는 말과 함께 여유 시간에 운동하는 게 쉬워졌다고(I really like it because they have an area with exercise equipment. That makes it really easy to work out in my free time) 이유를 밝히고 있으므로 (D)가 정답이다.

어휘 win a prize 상품을 타다 get exercise 운동하다

37 What does the woman suggest doing?
(A) Contacting a city official
(B) Printing out a map
(C) Checking a Web site
(D) Joining a mailing list

여자는 무엇을 하도록 권하는가?
(A) 시 관계자 한 명에게 연락하는 일
(B) 지도를 출력하는 일
(C) 웹 사이트를 확인해 보는 일
(D) 우편물 발송 대상자 명단에 가입하는 일

해설 〈제안 사항을 묻는 문제〉
대화 후반부에 여자가 시 웹 사이트를 방문해 보도록(You should visit the city's Web site) 권하고 있는데, 이는 웹 사이트를 확인해 보라는 뜻이므로 (C)가 정답이다.

어휘 contact ~에게 연락하다 official n. 관계자, 당국자 join ~에 가입하다, 합류하다, ~와 함께 하다 mailing list 우편물 발송 대상자 명단

Questions 38-40 refer to the following conversation. 미M 캐W

M Hello, ㊳ I'd like to reserve a ticket to travel to Manchester tonight. I'd prefer a bus that has reclining seats, if possible.
W Apologies, sir, but ㊴ there is no available space on any of our buses tonight. Lots of people must be heading to Manchester for the New Year's celebrations.
M I see. But, I really need to travel tonight. Do you know how I can get there?
W ㊵ The only other way is by taxi. Here's the phone number of a recommended firm.

남 안녕하세요, 오늘 밤에 맨체스터로 가는 승차권을 한 장 예매하려고 합니다. 가능하다면, 등받이를 젖힐 수 있는 좌석이 있는 버스를 원합니다.
여 고객님, 죄송하지만, 오늘 밤에 저희 버스들 중 어느 것도 이용 가능한 자리가 없습니다. 많은 사람들이 새해 기념 행사 때문에 맨체스터로 가고 있는 게 분명합니다.
남 알겠습니다. 하지만 제가 오늘 밤에 꼭 가야 합니다. 그곳에 어떻게 갈 수 있는지 아시나요?
여 유일한 다른 방법은 택시를 타는 것입니다. 여기 추천해 드리는 업체 전화번호가 있습니다.

어휘 would like to do ~하고 싶다, ~하고자 하다 reserve ~을 예매하다, 예약하다 travel 이동하다, 여행하다 would prefer ~을 원하다 reclining 등받이를 젖힐 수 있는 if possible 가능하다면 available 이용 가능한, 구입 가능한 must ~한 것이 틀림없다, 분명하다 head to ~로 향하다, 가다 celebration 기념 행사, 축하 행사 get there 그곳에 가다 recommend ~을 추천하다 firm 업체, 회사

38 Where does the conversation take place?
(A) At an airport
(B) At a hotel
(C) At a bus terminal
(D) At a cinema

대화가 어디에서 진행되는가?
(A) 공항에서
(B) 호텔에서
(C) 버스 터미널에서
(D) 극장에서

해설 〈대화 장소를 묻는 문제〉
남자가 대화를 시작하면서 승차권 예매 및 특정 버스 좌석을(I'd like to reserve a ticket to travel to Manchester tonight. I'd prefer a bus that has reclining seats, if possible) 언급하고 있으므로 (C)가 정답이다.

어휘 take place (일, 행사 등이) 발생되다, 개최되다

39 Why is the woman not able to help the man?
(A) A vehicle has broken down.
(B) A special offer has ended.
(C) Some products have sold out.
(D) Some tickets are unavailable.

여자는 왜 남자를 도울 수 없는가?
(A) 차량이 고장 났다.
(B) 특가 제공 서비스가 종료되었다.
(C) 일부 제품이 품절되었다.
(D) 승차권을 구입할 수 없다.

해설 〈기타 세부 사항을 묻는 문제〉
대화 중반부에 여자가 어느 버스도 이용 가능한 자리가 없다는(there is no available space on any of our buses tonight) 문제점을 알리고 있는데, 이는 승차권을 구입할 수 없다는 뜻이므로 (D)가 정답이다.

어휘 be able to do ~할 수 있다 vehicle 차량 break down 고장 나다 special offer 특가 제공 서비스 sold out 품절된, 매진된 unavailable 구입할 수 없는, 이용할 수 없는

40 What will the man probably do next?
(A) Reserve a room
(B) Call a taxi company
(C) Purchase a ticket
(D) Speak to the woman's manager

남자는 곧이어 무엇을 할 것 같은가?
(A) 방을 예약하는 일
(B) 택시 회사에 전화하는 일
(C) 승차권을 구입하는 일
(D) 여자의 상사와 이야기하는 일

해설 〈곧이어 할 일을 묻는 문제〉
대화 맨 마지막에 여자가 택시를 이용하도록 권하면서 추천 업체 전화번호를 알려 주고(The only other way is by taxi. Here's the phone number of a recommended firm) 있으므로 (B)가 정답이다.

어휘 reserve ~을 예약하다 purchase ~을 구입하다

M Hi, Katie. ㊶ We're running out of space here at the warehouse, so I think we're going to need to buy more shelving units. Do we have enough money in the budget for that?

W Yes, I think so. Should we just use the same company that supplies our crates?

M Well, ㊷ I'm not sure about that. They always take a long time to deliver their orders, and we need those shelves right away.

W All right. ㊸ I'll research a few different companies to find out our options.

남 안녕하세요. 케이티 씨. 이곳 창고에 공간이 부족해지고 있어서, 선반 제품을 추가로 구입해야 할 것 같아요. 예산에 그럴 만한 돈이 충분히 있나요?

여 네, 그런 것 같아요. 우리에게 상자를 공급하는 그 회사를 이용하면 되나요?

남 음, 그건 잘 모르겠어요. 그곳은 항상 주문품을 배송하는 데 시간이 오래 걸리는데, 우린 그 선반이 당장 필요하거든요.

여 알겠습니다. 선택 가능한 곳을 알아 볼 수 있도록 몇몇 다른 회사들을 조사해 볼게요.

어휘 run out of ~가 다 떨어지다, 바닥나다 warehouse 창고 shelving unit 선반 budget 예산 supply ~을 공급하다 crate (큰) 상자 take a long time to do ~하는 데 시간이 오래 걸리다 order 주문(품) right away 당장, 곧장 research ~을 조사하다 find out ~을 알아내다, 파악하다

41 Where most likely do the speakers work?
(A) At a financial institution
(B) At a warehouse
(C) At a bookstore
(D) At a factory

화자들은 어디에서 근무하고 있을 것 같은가?
(A) 금융 기관에서
(B) 창고에서
(C) 서점에서
(D) 공장에서

해설 〈근무지를 묻는 문제〉
대화 시작 부분에 남자가 현재 있는 곳을 here at the warehouse라고 지칭하면서 창고에 공간이 부족해지고 있다는 말로(We're running out of space here at the warehouse) 창고 운영과 관련된 정보를 언급하고 있다. 이는 창고에 근무하는 사람이 할 수 있는 말이므로 (b)가 정답이다.

42 What is the man concerned about?
(A) Lack of selection
(B) Poor quality
(C) A high price
(D) A slow delivery

남자는 무엇을 우려하고 있는가?
(A) 선택 대상의 부족
(B) 좋지 못한 품질
(C) 높은 가격
(D) 느린 배송

해설 〈기타 세부 사항을 묻는 문제〉
대화 중반부에 남자가 한 업체에 대해 주문품을 배송하는 데 항상 시간이 오래 걸린다는(I'm not sure about that. They always take a long time to deliver their orders) 문제점을 말하고 있으므로 (D)가 정답이다.

어휘 be concerned about ~에 대해 우려하다 lack 부족 selection 선택(할 수 있는 것들) quality 품질, 질

43 What does the woman plan to do?
(A) Conduct some research
(B) Write a report
(C) Adjust a budget
(D) Open a business

여자는 무엇을 할 계획인가?
(A) 약간의 조사를 하는 일
(B) 보고서를 작성하는 일
(C) 예산을 조정하는 일
(D) 업체를 개업하는 일

해설 〈미래에 할 일을 묻는 문제〉
대화 마지막 부분에 여자가 몇몇 다른 회사들을 조사해 보겠다고(I'll research a few different companies) 언급하고 있으므로 (A)가 정답이다.

어휘 plan to do ~할 계획이다 conduct ~을 실시하다, 수행하다 research 조사, 연구 adjust ~을 조정하다, 조절하다 budget 예산

M1 ㊹ Welcome to SuperSports Footwear. Can I help you?

W Yes, ㊹ I'm looking to buy some sturdy running shoes for a marathon I'm planning to run in.

M1 Let me just check with my supervisor. Paul, do we have any shoes suitable for long distance running?

M2 We sure do. Our most popular model is endorsed by ㊺ Thomas Valeny. He became famous after winning the marathon at last year's Olympics.

W I remember him. He was fantastic.

M2 We are running a special promotion at the moment. ㊻ If you buy this product this week, you can get 20 percent off the normal price.

남1 슈퍼스포츠 풋웨어에 오신 것을 환영합니다. 무엇을 도와드릴까요?

여 네, 제가 참가할 계획인 마라톤에서 신을 튼튼한 운동화를 구입하려고 합니다.

남1 제가 상사에게 잠시 확인해 보겠습니다. 폴 씨, 우리 매장에 장거리 달리기에 적합한 운동화가 있나요?

남2 분명 있습니다. 가장 인기 있는 모델이 토머스 발레니가 광고하는 제품입니다. 그는 작년 올림픽 마라톤에서 우승을 한 후에 유명해졌죠.

여 기억나요. 환상적이었죠.

남2 저희가 현재 특별 판촉 행사를 진행하고 있습니다. 이번 주에 이 제품을 구입하시면, 정상가에서 20퍼센트 할인받으실 수 있습니다.

어휘 look to do ~하기를 바라다, ~할 예정이다 sturdy 튼튼한, 건고한 plan to do ~할 계획이다 supervisor 상사, 책임자, 부서장 suitable for ~에 적합한, 어울리는 long distance running 장거리 달리기 popular 인기 있는 endorse (유명인이) ~을 광고하다, 홍보하다 run ~을 진행하다, 운영하다 promotion 판촉 (행사) at the moment 현재

44 Where most likely are the speakers?
(A) At a gym
(B) At an advertising agency
(C) At a sports stadium
(D) At a shoe store

화자들은 어디에 있을 것 같은가?
(A) 체육관에
(B) 광고 대행사에
(C) 스포츠 경기장에
(D) 신발 매장에

해설 〈대화 장소를 묻는 문제〉
대화 초반부에 남자 한 명이 Welcome to SuperSports Footwear라는 말로 신발 매장에 있다는 것을 밝히고 있고, 곧이어 여자도 튼튼한 운동화를 구입하려 한다고(I'm looking to buy some sturdy running shoes) 알리고 있으므로 (D)가 정답이다.

45 What is Thomas Valeny known for?
(A) Designing a product
(B) Winning a race
(C) Hosting a television show
(D) Founding a business

토머스 발레니는 무엇으로 유명한가?
(A) 제품을 디자인하는 것으로
(B) 경주에서 우승한 것으로
(C) 텔레비전 프로그램을 진행하는 것으로
(D) 사업체를 설립한 것으로

해설 〈기타 세부 사항을 묻는 문제〉
대화 중반부에 남자 한 명이 토머스 발레니를 언급하면서 올림픽 마라톤에서 우승한 후 유명해졌다고(Thomas Valeny. He became famous after winning the marathon at last year's Olympics) 알리고 있으므로 (B)가 정답이다.

어휘 be known for ~으로 유명하다 win an award 상을 받다 found ~을 설립하다

46 What extra benefit does a product come with?
(A) An extended warranty
(B) Express shipping
(C) A lower price
(D) Upgraded service

제품에 어떤 추가 혜택이 포함되어 있는가?
(A) 연장된 품질 보증
(B) 빠른 배송
(C) 더 저렴한 가격
(D) 업그레이드된 서비스

해설 〈기타 세부 사항을 묻는 문제〉
대화 맨 마지막에 남자 한 명이 이번 주에 구입하면 20퍼센트 할인받을 수 있다고(If you buy this product this week, you can get 20 percent off the normal price) 알리고 있으므로 (C)가 정답이다.

어휘 extra 추가의, 별도의 benefit 혜택, 이점 come with ~을 포함하다, ~가 딸려 있다 extended 연장된 warranty 품질 보증(서) express 빠른, 특급의

Questions 47-49 refer to the following conversation. 영W 호M

W Hi, Sam. ㊼ How are the arrangements going for this month's employee orientation session? The HR manager asked me to give you a hand.

M I still need to find a suitable space where we can hold the session. Our big conference rooms won't be available on that day.

W Hmm... ㊽ Let's just hold the session in the meeting room on the third floor, just like last month.

M Well, we have more participants this month.

W Oh, I see. ㊾ Let me speak with Patricia in General Affairs. She might be able to make a conference room available to us.

여 안녕하세요, 샘 씨. 이번 달 직원 오리엔테이션 시간 준비는 어떻게 되어 가고 있나요? 인사부장님께서 도와드리라고 요청하셨어요.
남 그 시간을 개최할 수 있는 적합한 장소를 여전히 찾아야 합니다. 우리 대회의실을 그날 이용할 수 없거든요.
여 흠... 그냥 3층에 있는 회의실에서 그 시간을 개최하죠, 지난달처럼요.
남 저, 이번 달엔 참가자가 더 많습니다.
여 아, 알겠어요. 제가 총무부의 패트리샤 씨에게 얘기해 볼게요. 대회의실을 우리가 이용할 수 있도록 만들어 주실지도 몰라요.

어휘 How is A going? A는 어떻게 되어 가고 있나요? arrangement 준비, 조치, 배치, 정리 session (특정 활동을 위한) 시간 HR manager 인사부장 ask A to do A에게 ~하도록 요청하다 hold ~을 개최하다, 열다 participant 참가자 General Affairs 총무부 be able to do ~할 수 있다 make A + 형용사 A를 ~하게 만들다 available 이용 가능한

47 What is the man responsible for?
(A) Recruiting new staff
(B) Remodeling a room
(C) Planning an orientation
(D) Responding to customers

남자는 무엇을 책임지고 있는가?
(A) 신입 사원을 모집하는 일
(B) 방을 리모델링하는 일
(C) 오리엔테이션을 계획하는 일
(D) 고객들에게 응대하는 일

해설 〈기타 세부 사항을 묻는 문제〉
대화를 시작하면서 여자가 남자에게 이번 달 직원 오리엔테이션 준비가 어떻게 되어 가고 있는지(How are the arrangements going for this month's employee orientation session?) 묻는 것을 통해 남자가 오리엔테이션을 준비 작업을 맡고 있음을 알 수 있으므로 (C)가 정답이다.

어휘 be responsible for ~을 책임지다, 맡고 있다 recruit ~을 모집하다 plan ~을 계획하다 respond to ~에 답변하다, 대응하다

48 Why does the man say, "we have more participants this month"?
(A) To thank the woman for her contribution
(B) To express satisfaction with a result
(C) To request assistance with a task
(D) To disapprove of a suggestion

남자는 왜 "we have more participants this month"라고 말하는가?
(A) 여자에게 공헌에 대해 감사하기 위해
(B) 결과물에 만족을 표현하기 위해
(C) 업무에 대해 도움을 요청하기 위해
(D) 제안에 반대하기 위해

해설 〈의도 파악 문제〉
대화 중반부에 여자가 3층에 있는 회의실에서 개최하자고(Let's just hold the session in the meeting room on the third floor, just like last month) 말하자, 남자가 '이번 달에 참가자가 더 많다'고 알리는 상황이다. 이는 인원이 더 많아서 3층 회의실을 이용할 수 없다는 뜻으로 반대 의견을 나타내는 말이므로 (D)가 정답이다.

어휘 contribution 공헌, 기여, 기부 express (감정 등) ~을 표현하다, 나타내다 satisfaction with ~에 대한 만족 result 결과(물) assistance 도움, 지원 task 업무, 일 disapprove of ~에 반대하다 suggestion 제안, 의견

49 What does the woman say she will do?
(A) Cancel an appointment
(B) Contact a colleague
(C) Make an announcement
(D) Have a room cleaned

여자는 무엇을 할 것이라고 말하는가?
(A) 약속을 취소하는 일
(B) 동료 직원에게 연락하는 일
(C) 공지를 하는 일
(D) 방을 청소해 놓는 일

해설 〈미래에 할 일을 묻는 문제〉
대화 맨 마지막에 여자가 총무부의 패트리샤 씨에게 얘기해 보겠다고(Let me speak with Patricia in General Affairs) 알리고 있는데, 이는 회사 내 동료 직원과 얘기하는 것을 의미하므로 (B)가 정답이다.

어휘 cancel ~을 취소하다 appointment 약속, 예약 contact ~에게 연락하다 colleague 동료 (직원) announcement 공지, 발표 have A p.p. A를 ~되게 하다

M Hello, ⑤ I'm calling about the catering service for our office party here at Dixon Corporation. Your team just arrived, but they brought chicken curry instead of vegetable curry.

W Oh, I could either offer you a refund or send the vegetable curry out to you. That might take around an hour.

M ⑤ One hour isn't too bad, so we will just wait until the vegetable curry arrives. Many of our employees are vegetarians.

W I see. I'm sorry for the inconvenience. ⑤ Would you mind confirming the address of your office again, please?

남 안녕하세요. 이곳 딕슨 주식회사에서 열리는 저희 사무실 파티에 필요한 출장 요리 서비스와 관련해서 전화 드렸습니다. 귀사의 팀이 막 도착했는데, 채소 카레가 아니라 치킨 카레를 가져오셨어요.

여 아, 환불을 제공해 드리거나 채소 카레를 보내 드릴 수 있습니다. 그렇게 하려면 한 시간쯤 걸릴 수 있습니다.

남 한 시간이면 그렇게 나쁘진 않기 때문에 그냥 채소 카레가 도착할 때까지 기다리겠습니다. 저희 직원들 중에서 많은 사람들이 채식주의자라서요.

여 알겠습니다. 불편함에 대해 사과 드립니다. 사무실 주소를 다시 한 번 확인해 주시겠습니까?

어휘 catering 출장 요리(업) arrive 도착하다 instead of ~가 아니라, ~ 대신 either A or B A 또는 B, 둘 중의 하나 send A out to B A를 B에게 보내다 take ~의 시간이 걸리다 around ~쯤, 약, 대략 until (지속) ~할 때까지 vegetarian 채식주의자 inconvenience 불편함 Would you mind -ing? ~해 주시겠습니까? confirm ~을 확인해 주다

50 Who most likely is the woman?
(A) A restaurant server
(B) An office supervisor
(C) A food critic
(D) A catering manager
여자는 누구일 것 같은가?
(A) 레스토랑 종업원
(B) 부서장
(C) 음식 평론가
(D) 출장 요리 관리 책임자

해설 〈직업을 묻는 문제〉
대화 시작 부분에 남자가 자신이 일하는 사무실의 파티에 필요한 출장 요리 서비스와 관련해 전화했다고(I'm calling about the catering service for our office party here at Dixon Corporation) 알리고 있다. 따라서 상대방인 여자는 출장 요리 서비스를 관리하는 사람으로 볼 수 있으므로 (D)가 정답이다.

어휘 supervisor 부서장, 책임자, 감독 critic 평론가, 비평가 catering 출장 요리 제공(업)

51 What does the man say he will do?
(A) Receive a refund
(B) Cancel an event
(C) Wait for an item
(D) Increase an order
남자는 무엇을 할 것이라고 말하는가?
(A) 환불을 받는 일
(B) 행사를 취소하는 일
(C) 제품을 기다리는 일
(D) 주문을 늘리는 일

해설 〈미래에 할 일을 묻는 문제〉
대화 중반부에 남자가 한 시간이면 그렇게 나쁘진 않기 때문에 채소 카레가 도착할 때까지 기다리겠다고(One hour isn't too bad, so we will just wait until the vegetable curry arrives) 알리고 있으므로 (C)가 정답이다.

어휘 receive ~을 받다 refund 환불 cancel ~을 취소하다 increase ~을 늘리다, 증가시키다 order 주문(품)

52 What will the man provide to the woman?
(A) An order number
(B) A business address
(C) A preferred delivery time
(D) A credit card number
남자는 여자에게 무엇을 제공할 것인가?
(A) 주문 번호
(B) 회사 주소
(C) 선호하는 배달 시간
(D) 신용카드 번호

해설 〈기타 세부 사항을 묻는 문제〉
대화 맨 마지막에 여자가 사무실 주소를 다시 한 번 확인해 달라고(Would you mind confirming the address of your office again, please?) 요청하고 있으므로 (B)가 정답이다.

어휘 provide ~을 제공하다 preferred 선호하는

M1 Nadine, this is Dennis, the contractor I told you about.

W ⑤ Hi, Dennis. ⑤ Let me show you the bathrooms that we would like renovated at our restaurant. The bathrooms haven't had any work done on them for a long time, so it's definitely time for an upgrade. I'm sure our customers will appreciate more modern facilities.

M2 Well, the main thing you need to decide is what kind of sinks and floor tiles you'd like. We have lots of samples in our showroom, and ⑤ it's best to see them for yourself.

W OK, I can come by tomorrow. But before you leave, ⑤ could you measure the floors and walls so I know the exact size we're dealing with?

남1 나딘 씨, 이 분은 제가 말씀 드렸던 계약업자이신 데니스 씨입니다.

여 안녕하세요, 데니스 씨. 저희 레스토랑에서 개조되기를 원하는 화장실을 보여 드릴게요. 이 화장실에 오랫동안 아무런 작업도 해 놓지를 않아서, 분명 업그레이드할 때가 되었어요. 분명 저희 고객들이 더욱 현대적인 시설에 감사하게 생각할 거예요.

남2 음, 결정하셔야 하는 중요한 부분이 원하시는 개수대와 바닥 타일의 종류입니다. 저희 진열실에 샘플이 많이 있기 때문에 직접 확인해 보시는 게 가장 좋습니다.

여 네, 내일 들를 수 있어요. 하지만 가시기 전에, 저희가 처리하게 되는 정확한 사이즈를 알 수 있도록 바닥과 벽들을 측정해 주시겠어요?

어휘 contractor 계약업자, 계약업체 show A B A에게 B를 보여 주다 would like A p.p. A가 ~되기를 원하다 renovate ~을 개조하다, 보수하다 have A p.p. A가 ~되게 하다 definitely 분명히, 확실히 appreciate ~에 대해 감사하다 facility 시설(물) decide ~을 결정하다 sink 개수대, 싱크대 showroom 진열실, 전시실 for oneself 직접, 스스로, 혼자 come by 들르다 leave 나가다, 떠나다 measure ~을 측정하다, 재다 so (that) ~할 수 있도록 exact 정확한 deal with ~을 처리하다, ~에 대처하다

53 What are the speakers discussing?
(A) The dates of a business trip
(B) Reservation procedures
(C) A software upgrade
(D) Bathroom renovations
화자들은 무엇을 이야기하고 있는가?
(A) 출장 날짜
(B) 예약 절차
(C) 소프트웨어 업그레이드
(D) 화장실 개조 공사

해설 〈주제를 묻는 문제〉
대화 초반부에 여자가 개조되기를 원하는 화장실을 보여 주겠다고

(Let me show you the bathrooms that we would like renovated ~) 알린 뒤로, 그 화장실의 상태 및 세부 작업 요소 등을 이야기하는 것으로 대화가 진행되고 있으므로 (D)가 정답이다.

54 What does Dennis recommend that the woman do?
(A) Place an online order
(B) View items in person
(C) Join a mailing list
(D) Read customer reviews

데니스 씨는 여자에게 무엇을 하도록 권하는가?
(A) 온라인으로 주문하는 일
(B) 직접 방문해 제품을 보는 일
(C) 우편물 발송 명단에 등록하는 일
(D) 고객 후기를 읽어 보는 일

해설 〈제안 사항을 묻는 문제〉
여자가 데니스 씨 이름을 부른(Hi, Dennis) 뒤로 말하는 남자 한 명이 진열실에 샘플이 많다는 말과 함께 직접 확인해 보는 게 가장 좋다는 말로(it's best to see them for yourself) 권하고 있으므로 (B)가 정답이다.

어휘 place an order 주문하다 view ~을 보다 in person 직접 방문해서, 직접 가서 mailing list 우편물 발송 명단 review 후기, 의견, 평가

55 What does the woman ask Dennis to do?
(A) Take some measurements
(B) Update an address
(C) Confirm a price
(D) Suggest a brand

여자는 데니스 씨에게 무엇을 하도록 요청하는가?
(A) 치수를 측정하는 일
(B) 주소를 업데이트하는 일
(C) 가격을 확인해 주는 일
(D) 브랜드를 권해 주는 일

해설 〈요청 사항을 묻는 문제〉
대화 맨 마지막에 여자가 바닥과 벽을 측정해 달라고(could you measure the floors and walls) 요청하고 있으므로 (A)가 정답이다.

어휘 take a measurement 치수를 측정하다 confirm ~을 확인해 주다 suggest ~을 제안하다, 권하다

Questions 56-58 refer to the following conversation. 캐W 호M

W Hello, ⑤ this is Eve calling from A-Plus Work Apparel. I'm currently preparing the work uniforms you ordered for your new staff. Did you receive the invoice I sent you by e-mail?

M Oh, hi, Eve. Thanks, ⑤ I did receive the invoice for the 20 uniforms. But, there has been a development. We actually have more new hires.

W OK, no problem. Can you tell me how many? That way I can be sure to get the right number of uniforms ready for you.

M Thirty in total. ⑤ Please update the invoice and send it to me again by the end of today.

여 안녕하세요, 저는 에이플러스 워크 어패럴에서 전화 드리는 이브입니다. 제가 현재 귀하께서 신입 사원들을 위해 주문하신 근무용 유니폼을 준비하고 있습니다. 제가 이메일로 보내 드린 거래 내역서를 받으셨나요?
남 아, 안녕하세요, 이브 씨. 감사합니다. 유니폼 20벌에 대한 거래 내역서를 분명히 받았습니다. 하지만 일이 좀 있었어요. 사실 신입 사원이 더 늘었습니다.
여 아, 괜찮습니다. 몇 분이나 되는지 알려 주시겠습니까? 그래야 정확한 수량으로 유니폼을 확실히 준비해 드릴 수 있거든요.
남 전부 합쳐서 30명입니다. 거래 내역서를 업데이트하셔서 오늘 일과가 끝날 때까지 다시 보내 주세요.

어휘 currently 현재 prepare ~을 준비하다 order ~을 주문하다 receive ~을 받다 invoice 거래 내역서, 송장 development (새롭게 생긴) 일, 사건 actually 사실, 실은 new hires 신입사원들 that way 그렇게 해야, 그런 방법으로 be sure to do 확실히 ~하다, 꼭 ~하다 get A ready A를 준비하다 in total 전부 합쳐서, 총 by (기한) ~까지

56 What type of business is the woman calling from?
(A) A catering company
(B) A clothing supplier
(C) A recruitment agency
(D) An electronics store

여자는 어떤 종류의 업체에서 전화를 거는가?
(A) 출장 요리 전문 회사
(B) 의류 공급업체
(C) 인력 채용 전문 업체
(D) 전자제품 매장

해설 〈근무지를 묻는 문제〉
대화 시작 부분에 여자가 this is Eve calling from A-Plus Work Apparel이라는 말로 의류 업체 소속 직원임을 밝히고 있고, 이어서 상대방이 주문한 근무용 유니폼을 준비하고 있다고(preparing the work uniforms you ordered) 알리고 있으므로 (B)가 정답이다.

---

57 What does the man imply when he says, "We actually have more new hires"?
(A) He is pleased with his company's efforts.
(B) He can meet an important deadline.
(C) He is confirming receipt of a job application.
(D) He would like to change an order.

남자가 "We actually have more new hires"라고 말할 때 무엇을 의도하는가?
(A) 소속 회사의 노력에 만족하고 있다.
(B) 중요한 마감기한을 맞출 수 있다.
(C) 구직 지원서의 접수를 확인해 주고 있다.
(D) 주문 사항을 변경하고자 한다.

해설 〈의도 파악 문제〉
대화 중반부에 남자가 유니폼 20벌에 대한 거래 내역서를 분명히 받았지만 일이 좀 있었다고(I did receive the invoice for the 20 uniforms. But, there has been a development) 언급한 뒤로 '신입 사원이 늘었다'고 알리는 흐름이다. 이는 20벌보다 더 많게 수량을 변경해야 한다는 뜻이므로 (D)가 정답이다.

어휘 be pleased with ~에 만족하다, 기뻐하다 effort 노력 meet (조건 등) ~을 맞추다, 충족하다 deadline 마감기한 confirm ~을 확인해 주다 receipt 접수, 수취, 영수증 application 지원(서), 신청(서) would like to do ~하고자 하다, ~하고 싶다 order 주문(품)

58 What does the man ask the woman to do?
(A) Attend an interview
(B) Compare some prices
(C) Send a revised invoice
(D) Speak to her colleagues

남자는 여자에게 무엇을 하도록 요청하는가?
(A) 면접 시간에 참석하는 일
(B) 몇몇 가격을 비교해 보는 일
(C) 수정된 거래 내역서를 보내는 일
(D) 여자의 동료와 이야기하는 일

해설 〈요청 사항을 묻는 문제〉
대화 맨 마지막 부분에 남자가 거래 내역서를 업데이트해서 다시 보내 달라고(Please update the invoice and send it to me again by the end of today) 요청하고 있으므로 (C)가 정답이다.

어휘 attend ~에 참석하다 compare ~을 비교하다 revised 수정된, 변경된 invoice 거래 내역서 colleague 동료 (직원)

W Hi, Peter. 59 <u>You're in charge of the design team making the advertisement</u> for our telecoms client, aren't you?

M That's right. The client requested a full-page ad to be run in newspapers, and a half-page ad for magazines.

W The half-page one shouldn't take you too long.

M Right. That one is already done. 60 <u>I'm going to the client's workplace this afternoon</u> to discuss some issues about the full-page ad. I think they want to include more product images.

W 61 <u>How long do you think you'll need to finish the ad?</u>

M Most of the design is already finished, so we'll just need a couple of days.

여 안녕하세요, 피터 씨. 당신이 우리 통신사 고객을 대상으로 하는 광고를 만드는 디자인팀을 맡고 계신 게 맞죠?

남 그렇습니다. 그 고객께서 신문에 낼 전면 광고와 잡지용 반 페이지 광고를 요청하셨어요.

여 반 페이지 광고 작업은 그렇게 오래 걸리지 않으시겠네요.

남 맞아요. 그건 이미 완료되었습니다. 제가 전면 광고와 관련된 몇몇 문제들을 논의하기 위해 오늘 오후에 그 고객의 회사로 갑니다. 그쪽에서 더 많은 제품 이미지를 포함하고 싶어 할 것 같아요.

여 그 광고 작업을 끝내는 데 얼마나 오래 걸릴 것 같으세요?

남 대부분의 디자인은 이미 끝났기 때문에 이틀 정도만 있으면 될 겁니다.

어휘 in charge of ~을 맡고 있는, 책임지고 있는 advertisement 광고(= ad) request ~을 요청하다 full-page 전면의 run (광고, 기사 등) ~을 내다, 싣다 take A B A에게 B의 시간이 걸리다 discuss ~을 논의하다, 이야기하다 issue 문제, 사안 include ~을 포함하다 most of 대부분의

59 What is the conversation mainly about?
(A) Designing a building
(B) Creating an advertisement
(C) Repairing a machine
(D) Recruiting new employees

대화는 주로 무엇에 관한 것인가?
(A) 건물을 디자인하는 일
(B) 광고를 만드는 일
(C) 기계를 수리하는 일
(D) 신입 사원을 모집하는 일

해설 〈주제를 묻는 문제〉
대화를 시작하면서 여자가 남자에게 고객 대상 광고를 만드는 일을 맡고 있는지(You're in charge of the design team making the advertisement ~) 물은 후, 해당 광고 제작과 관련해 이야기하고 있으므로 (B)가 정답이다.

어휘 create ~을 만들어내다 advertisement 광고 repair ~을 수리하다 recruit ~을 모집하다

---

60 What does the man say he will do this afternoon?
(A) Submit a file
(B) Give a speech
(C) Test a product
(D) Visit a client

남자는 오늘 오후에 무엇을 할 것이라고 말하는가?
(A) 파일을 제출하는 일
(B) 연설하는 일
(C) 제품을 시험하는 일
(D) 고객을 방문하는 일

해설 〈특정 시점의 일을 묻는 문제〉
남자가 대화 중반부에 오늘 오후라는 시점을 언급하면서 몇몇 문제들을 논의하기 위해 오늘 오후에 고객의 회사로 간다고(I'm going to the client's workplace this afternoon ~) 알리고 있으므로 (D)가 정답이다.

어휘 submit ~을 제출하다 give a speech 연설하다

61 What does the woman ask about?
(A) A product sample
(B) A cost estimate
(C) A phone number
(D) A work timeframe

여자는 무엇에 관해 묻는가?
(A) 제품 샘플
(B) 비용 견적서
(C) 전화 번호
(D) 작업 진행 시간

해설 〈문의 사항을 묻는 문제〉
대화 후반부에 여자가 광고 작업을 끝내는 데 얼마나 오래 걸릴 것 같은지(How long do you think you'll need to finish the ad?) 묻고 있으므로 작업 진행 시간을 뜻하는 (D)가 정답이다.

어휘 estimate 견적(서) timeframe 진행 시간, 진행 기간

W Thank you for calling Springway Flowers. How may I help you?

M Hi, Tina. It's Robert. 62 <u>I'm doing my last delivery,</u> but there's an issue. 63 <u>The delivery form only says Benison Convention Hall. The room number has been left blank.</u>

W Does it list the customer's name?

M Let's see, it's Bryant Manufacturing.

W I'll check our system. Hmm, it only listed the building, not the room number. Are there any signs around there for their event?

M Oh, yes. 64 <u>It looks like they're right across from the ballroom.</u>

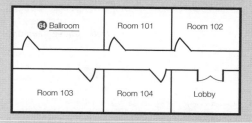

여 스프링웨이 플라워즈에 전화 주셔서 감사합니다. 무엇을 도와드릴까요?

남 안녕하세요, 티나 씨. 로버트입니다. 제가 마지막 배송을 하는 중인데, 문제가 하나 있습니다. 배송 주문서에는 베니슨 컨벤션 홀이라고만 쓰여 있고, 몇 호실인지는 비어 있는 상태입니다.

여 거기 고객 성명이 기재되어 있나요?

남 어디 보자, 브라이언트 제조사라고 되어 있어요.

여 제가 우리 시스템을 확인해 볼게요. 흠, 방 번호는 없고 건물만 기재되어 있네요. 그 주변에 그 업체 행사에 대한 표지판이라도 있나요?

남 아, 네. 연회장 바로 맞은편에 있는 것 같아요.

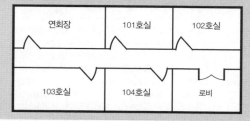

어휘 issue 문제, 사안 form 양식, 서식 say (문서 등에) ~라고 쓰여 있다, 나와 있다 be left + 형용사 ~한 채로 있다 blank 비어 있는 list ~을 기재하다 sign 표지(판) around ~ 주변에 It looks like ~인 것 같다 right across ~ 바로 맞은편에 ballroom 연회장

62 What is the man's profession?
(A) A florist
(B) A hotel clerk
(C) A delivery driver
(D) An interior designer

남자의 직업은 무엇인가?
(A) 꽃집 직원
(B) 호텔 직원
(C) 배송 기사
(D) 실내 디자이너

해설 〈직업을 묻는 문제〉
대화 초반부에 남자가 여자에게 마지막 배송을 하는 중이라고(I'm doing my last delivery) 알리고 있는데, 이는 배송 기사가 할 수 있는 말이므로 (C)가 정답이다.

63 According to the man, what has caused a problem?
(A) A form was incomplete.
(B) The customers have changed their minds.
(C) There is heavy traffic in the area.
(D) A payment has not been received yet.

남자의 말에 따르면, 무엇이 문제를 초래했는가?
(A) 양식이 완전하지 않다.
(B) 고객들이 마음을 바꿨다.
(C) 해당 지역에 교통량이 극심하다.
(D) 비용을 아직 받지 못했다.

해설 〈문제 원인을 묻는 문제〉
대화 초반부에 남자가 문제가 있음을 언급하면서 양식에 장소 이름만 있고 몇 호실인지는 비어 있다고(The delivery form only says Benison Convention Hall. The room number has been left blank) 알리고 있다. 이는 해당 양식이 완전히 작성된 상태가 아니라는 뜻이므로 (A)가 정답이다.

어휘 cause ~을 초래하다, 야기하다 form 양식, 서식 incomplete 완전하지 않은, 미완성의 traffic 교통(량), 차량들 payment 지불 (비용) receive ~을 받다

64 Look at the graphic. Where will the man most likely go next?
(A) Room 101
(B) Room 102
(C) Room 103
(D) Room 104

시각 자료를 보시오. 남자는 곧이어 어디로 갈 것 같은가?
(A) 101호실
(B) 102호실
(C) 103호실
(D) 104호실

해설 〈배치도 문제〉
대화 맨 마지막에 남자가 연회장 바로 맞은편에 있는 것 같다고(It looks like they're right across from the ballroom) 알리고 있으며, 배치도에서 Ballroom 맞은편에 위치한 방이 Room 103이므로 (C)가 정답이다.

Questions 65-67 refer to the following conversation and tent labels. (미M) (영W)

M Excuse me. Do you work here in the Camping Supplies Department?

W Yes. Can I help you with something?

M 65 I work for the local library, and I'm taking my staff on a camping trip next month. I'm wondering what kind of tent to purchase.

W How many people will be sleeping in the tent?

M I'd like to buy one for our whole group to sleep in; 66 there are five of us in total.

W Okay. This one comfortably sleeps five people. 66 But I'm afraid it only comes with a 1-year warranty.

M 66 That's fine. And can I sign up for a store membership now?

W Yes, and that's a great idea, because 67 I'll give you 5 percent off this purchase once you have a membership.

SUMMIT 250	TREK PRO
1-Year Warranty 👤	3-Year Warranty 👤👤👤👤👤
ALPINE MAX	RANGER 600
66 1-Year Warranty 👤👤👤👤👤	3-Year Warranty 👤👤👤

남 실례합니다. 이 캠핑용품 코너에서 일하시는 분이신가요?

여 네, 무엇을 도와드릴까요?

남 제가 지역 도서관에서 일하고 있는데, 다음 달에 직원들을 데리고 캠핑 여행을 떠납니다. 어떤 종류의 텐트를 구입해야 하는지 궁금해서요.

여 텐트에서 몇 분이나 잠을 자게 되나요?

남 전체 인원이 잘 수 있는 것을 구입하려고 하는데, 저희가 총 다섯 명입니다.

여 알겠습니다. 이 제품이 다섯 명이 편안하게 잘 수 있습니다. 하지만 유감스럽게도 오직 1년 품질 보증 서비스만 포함됩니다.

남 괜찮습니다. 지금 매장 회원으로 등록할 수 있나요?

여 네, 그리고 그게 아주 좋은 생각이신데, 회원 자격을 얻으시는 대로 이 구입품에 대해 5퍼센트 할인을 제공해 드릴 것이기 때문입니다.

써밋 250	트렉 프로
1년 보증 👤👤	3년 보증 👤👤👤👤👤
알파인 맥스	레이저 600
1년 보증 👤👤👤👤👤	3년 보증 👤👤👤

어휘 help A with B B에 대해 A를 돕다 work for ~에서 근무하다 local 지역의, 현지의 wonder ~을 궁금해 하다 purchase v. ~을 구입하다 n. 구입(품) whole 전체의 in total 총, 전부 합쳐서 comfortably 편안하게 sleep (사물 주어로) ~가 잘 수 있다 come with ~을 포함하다, ~가 딸려 있다 warranty 품질 보증(서) sign up for ~에 등록하다, ~을 신청하다 give A 5 percent off B B에 대해 5퍼센트 할인해 주다 once (일단) ~하는 대로, ~하자마자

65 Where does the man work?
(A) At a department store
(B) At a university
(C) At a city park
(D) At a library

남자는 어디에서 일하는가?
(A) 백화점에서
(B) 대학교에서
(C) 시립 공원에서
(D) 도서관에서

해설 〈근무지를 묻는 문제〉
대화 중반부로 넘어 가면서 남자가 I work for the local library라는 말로 일하는 곳을 언급하고 있으므로 (D)가 정답이다.

66 Look at the graphic. Which tent will the man most likely buy?
(A) Summit 250
(B) Trek Pro
(C) Alpine Max
(D) Ranger 600

시각 자료를 보시오. 남자는 어느 텐트를 구입할 것 같은가?
(A) 써밋 250
(B) 트렉 프로
(C) 알파인 맥스
(D) 레인저 600

해설 〈기타 시각 자료 문제〉
대화 중반부에 남자가 총 인원이 다섯 명이라고(there are five of us in total) 알리고 있고, 여자가 한 제품을 추천하면서 품질 보증 기간이 1년이라고(But I'm afraid it only comes with a 1-year warranty) 말하자 남자가 괜찮다고(That's fine) 대답하고 있다. 텐트 라벨 그림에서 다섯 명이 그려져 있고 기간이 1년인 제품이 왼쪽 아래에 있는 ALPINE MAX이므로 (C)가 정답이다.

67 What does the woman say she will do?
(A) Extend the length of a warranty
(B) Add the man to a mailing list
(C) Provide the man with a discount
(D) Demonstrate how to use a product

여자는 무엇을 할 것이라고 말하는가?
(A) 품질 보증 기간을 연장하는 일
(B) 남자를 우편물 발송 명단에 추가하는 일
(C) 남자에게 할인을 제공해 주는 일
(D) 제품 사용법을 시범 보이는 일

해설 〈미래에 할 일을 묻는 문제〉
대화 맨 마지막에 여자가 남자에게 회원 자격을 갖추게 되면 5퍼센트 할인을 제공해 준다고(I'll give you 5 percent off this purchase once you have a membership) 알리고 있으므로 (C)가 정답이다.

어휘 extend ~을 연장하다 length 기간, 길이 warranty 품질 보증(서) add A to B A를 B에 추가하다 mailing list 우편물 발송 명단 provide ~을 제공하다 demonstrate ~을 시범 보이다, 시연하다 how to do ~하는 법

Questions 68-70 refer to the following conversation and chart.
호M 캐W

M **68** Seneca Cosmetics. How may I help you?
W Good afternoon. **68** I tried placing an order through your Web site, but I kept getting an error message.
M I'm sorry about that, ma'am. We have contacted our IT team, and they are working on the issue. I would be happy to take your order over the phone.
W I'd like product number 4501. You offer two-day shipping to **69** the Midwest, don't you?
M Yes. **69** That's part of Region 2. Any order placed today will arrive by Thursday. But **70** you'll need to set up a customer account. I can help you with that.
W **70** Okay, thank you.

2-Day Domestic Shipping Rates		
Region 1	West	$5.50
69 Region 2	Midwest	$7.50
Region 3	South	$9.50
Region 4	Northeast	$11.50

남 세네카 코스메틱스입니다. 무엇을 도와드릴까요?
여 안녕하세요. 제가 귀사의 웹 사이트를 통해서 주문을 하려고 했는데, 계속 오류 메시지가 나타나요.
남 그 부분에 대해 사과 드립니다, 고객님. 저희가 내부 IT팀에 연락해 두었으며, 그 문제에 대해 작업 중입니다. 제가 전화상으로 고객님의 주문을 기꺼이 받을 수 있습니다.
여 저는 제품 번호 4501을 원합니다. 중서부 쪽으로 이틀간의 배송 서비스를 제공하는 것이 맞죠?
남 네. 그곳은 지역 2의 일부입니다. 오늘 주문하시는 모든 제품은 목요일까지 도착할 것입니다. 하지만 고객 계정을 설정해 주셔야 합니다. 제가 그 부분을 도와드릴 수 있습니다.
여 좋아요, 감사합니다.

국내 2일 배송 요금		
지역 1	서부	5.50달러
지역 2	중서부	7.50달러
지역 3	남부	9.50달러
지역 4	북동부	11.50달러

어휘 try -ing 한 번 ~해 보다 place an order 주문하다 through ~을 통해 keep -ing 계속 ~하다 contact ~에게 연락하다 work on ~에 대한 작업을 하다 issue 문제, 사안 take one's order 주문을 받다 over the phone 전화상으로 offer ~을 제공하다 shipping 배송, 선적 region 지역

---

arrive 도착하다 by (기한) ~까지 set up ~을 설정하다 account 계정, 계좌 help A with B B에 대해 A를 돕다 domestic 국내의 rate 요금

68 What most likely is the man's job?
(A) Customer service agent
(B) Delivery driver
(C) IT technician
(D) Product developer

남자의 직업은 무엇일 것 같은가?
(A) 고객 서비스 직원
(B) 배송 기사
(C) IT 기술자
(D) 제품 개발자

해설 〈직업을 묻는 문제〉
대화 시작 부분에 남자가 여자에게 회사명과 함께 무엇을 도와줄지 (Seneca Cosmetics. How may I help you?) 묻자, 여자가 웹 사이트에서 주문을 하려 한 사실과 오류 메시지가 나타난 사실(I tried placing an order ~ I kept getting an error message)을 밝히고 있다. 이는 고객인 여자가 서비스 담당 직원에게 도움을 요청하는 상황이므로 남자의 직업으로 (A)가 정답이다.

어휘 agent 직원, 대리인 developer 개발자, 개발업체

69 Look at the graphic. How much will the woman's shipping costs be?
(A) $5.50
(B) $7.50
(C) $9.50
(D) $11.50

시각 자료를 보시오. 여자의 배송 비용은 얼마가 될 것인가?
(A) 5.50달러
(B) 7.50달러
(C) 9.50달러
(D) 11.50달러

해설 〈3열 이상 도표 문제〉
대화 중반부에 여자가 the Midwest를, 남자가 That's part of Region 2를 각각 언급하고 있는데, 시각 자료에서 이 지역에 해당되는 곳의 요금이 $7.50로 표기되어 있으므로 (B)가 정답이다.

70 What will the woman probably do next?
(A) Review a product
(B) Select a size
(C) Request a catalog
(D) Set up an account

여자는 곧이어 무엇을 할 것 같은가?
(A) 제품을 검토하는 일
(B) 크기를 선택하는 일
(C) 카탈로그를 요청하는 일
(D) 계정을 설정하는 일

〈곧이어 할 일을 묻는 문제〉
대화 후반부에 남자가 고객 계정을 설정해야 한다고(~ you'll need to set up a customer account. I can help you with that) 알리자 여자가 동의하는(Okay, thank you) 상황이다. 따라서 계정을 설정할 것으로 생각할 수 있으므로 (D)가 정답이다.

어휘 review ~을 검토하다 select ~을 선택하다 request ~을 요청하다

PART 4
P151

Questions 71-73 refer to the following telephone message. 영W

Hi, Ronald. It's Cecelia. I got your e-mail about trying to attract more people to ⑪ our clothing store. ⑫ I agree that holding a prize drawing would help to get the attention of new customers. I think we should offer a high-end prize to make the drawing more exciting. For example, we could give away a flat-screen TV. We could include some other smaller prizes, too. Of course, some of them should be gift certificates for our store. ⑬ I'll need to officially ask for funds to buy the prizes. I'll do that tomorrow when I talk to the store's owner.

안녕하세요, 로널드 씨, 세실리아입니다. 우리 의류 매장으로 더 많은 사람들을 끌어들이려 하는 일과 관련해 보내 주신 이메일을 받았습니다. 경품 추첨 행사를 개최하면 새로운 고객들의 관심을 끄는 데 도움이 될 것이라는 말씀에 동의합니다. 이 추첨 행사를 더 흥미롭게 만들기 위해 고급 상품을 제공해야 할 것 같습니다. 예를 들어, 평면 TV를 증정할 수 있을 겁니다. 다른 몇몇 더 작은 상품도 포함할 수 있습니다. 당연히, 그 일부는 우리 매장에서 사용하는 상품권이 되어야 합니다. 상품을 구입할 수 있는 자금을 정식으로 요청해야 할 것입니다. 내일 사장님께 말씀 드릴 때 그렇게 하도록 하겠습니다.

어휘 try to do ~하려 하다 attract ~을 끌어들이다 clothing 의류 agree that ~라는 점에 동의하다 hold ~을 개최하다 prize drawing 경품 추첨 행사 help to do ~하는 데 도움이 되다 attention 관심, 주의, 주목 offer ~을 제공하다 high-end 고급의 make A + 형용사 A를 ~하게 만들다 give away ~을 증정하다, 나눠 주다 flat-screen TV 평면 TV include ~을 포함하다 gift certificate 상품권 officially 정식으로, 공식적으로 ask for ~을 요청하다 fund 자금

71 What type of business does the speaker work for?
(A) At a camping store
(B) At a bookshop
(C) At a hardware store
(D) At a clothing shop
화자는 어떤 종류의 업체에서 일하는가?
(A) 캠핑용품 매장에서

(B) 서점에서
(C) 철물점에서
(D) 의류 매장에서

해설 〈근무지를 묻는 문제〉
화자가 담화 초반부에 소속 업체를 our clothing store라고 지칭하고 있으므로 (D)가 정답이다.

72 What is the purpose of the message?
(A) To schedule a training session
(B) To explain a customer complaint
(C) To agree to a customer event
(D) To order some merchandise
메시지의 목적은 무엇인가?
(A) 교육 시간 일정을 정하는 것
(B) 고객 불만 사항을 설명하는 것
(C) 고객 관련 행사에 동의하는 것
(D) 일부 상품을 주문하는 것

해설 〈목적을 묻는 문제〉
담화 초반부에 화자가 경품 추첨 행사를 개최하는 일이(I agree that holding a prize drawing ~) 고객들의 관심을 끄는 데 도움이 될 수 있다는 점에 동의한다고 알리면서 해당 행사 진행 방식과 관련해 이야기하고 있으므로 (C)가 정답이다.

어휘 schedule ~의 일정을 정하다 training 교육, 훈련 session (특정 활동을 위한) 시간 explain ~을 설명하다 complaint 불만, 불평 agree to ~에 동의하다 order ~을 주문하다 merchandise 상품

73 What does the speaker plan to do tomorrow?
(A) Change a work schedule
(B) Request some funding
(C) Run an advertisement
(D) Order some supplies
화자는 내일 무엇을 할 계획인가?
(A) 업무 일정을 변경하는 일
(B) 일부 자금을 요청하는 일
(C) 광고를 내는 일
(D) 일부 용품을 주문하는 일

해설 〈특정 시점의 일을 묻는 문제〉
담화 후반부에 물품을 구입하는 데 필요한 자금을 요청해야 한다고 알리면서 그 일을 내일 하겠다고(I'll need to officially ask for funds to buy the prizes. I'll do that tomorrow) 언급하고 있으므로 (B)가 정답이다.

어휘 plan to do ~할 계획이다 request ~을 요청하다, 요구하다 funding 자금 (제공) run ~을 운영하다, 진행하다 advertisement 광고 order ~을 주문하다 supplies 용품, 물품

Questions 74-76 refer to the following news report. 호M

You're listening to ⑭ the traffic report on Radio 99.7 FM. Highway 15 is stopped in the northbound lanes due to an accident. And some of the side roads are also getting backed up because drivers are looking for alternative routes. Traffic is flowing freely in the southbound lanes. If you want to get the most up-to-date traffic information, ⑮ you should download our station's smartphone app, which is available for free on our Web site. Also, ⑯ Irvine Bridge will reopen on Saturday, which is great news for drivers in the area.

여러분은 지금 99.7 FM 라디오 교통 소식을 청취하고 계십니다. 15번 고속도로가 사고로 인해 북쪽 방면 차선들이 막혀 있습니다. 그리고 몇몇 갓길들도 운전자들이 대체 경로를 찾으면서 밀리고 있는 상황입니다. 남쪽 방면 차선의 차량들은 순조롭게 이동하고 있습니다. 최신 교통 정보를 얻고자 하시는 경우, 저희 방송국의 스마트폰 앱을 다운로드하시기 바라며, 저희 웹 사이트에서 무료로 이용 가능합니다. 또한, 어빈 대교가 토요일에 재개통될 것이며, 이는 지역 내 운전자들에게 아주 반가운 소식입니다.

어휘 traffic 교통, 차량들 northbound 북쪽으로 향하는(→ southbound) due to ~로 인해 accident 사고 side road 갓길 get backed up 밀려 있는 상태가 되다 look for ~을 찾다 alternative 대체의, 대안의 route 경로, 노선 flow (차량들이) 이동하다 most up-to-date 최신의 available 이용 가능한 for free 무료로

74 What is the report mainly about?
(A) A sports competition
(B) A local election
(C) Weather patterns
(D) Traffic conditions
보도는 주로 무엇에 관한 것인가?
(A) 스포츠 경기 대회
(B) 지역 선거
(C) 날씨 패턴
(D) 교통 상황

해설 〈주제를 묻는 문제〉
화자가 담화를 시작하면서 방송 종류를 the traffic report라고 알리고 있으므로 (D)가 정답이다.

어휘 competition 경기 대회, 경연 대회 local 지역의, 현지의 election 선거 traffic 교통, 차량들 condition 상태, 조건, 환경

75 What does the speaker encourage the listeners to do?
(A) Listen to an interview
(B) Download an application
(C) Take an alternative route
(D) Call the radio station

화자는 청자들에게 무엇을 하도록 권장하는가?
(A) 인터뷰를 듣는 일
(B) 애플리케이션을 다운로드하는 일
(C) 대체 경로를 이용하는 일
(D) 라디오 방송국에 전화하는 일

해설 〈제안 사항을 묻는 문제〉
담화 후반부에 최신 교통 정보를 얻을 수 있도록 방송국 스마트폰 앱을 다운로드하라고(you should download our station's smartphone app) 요청하고 있으므로 (B)가 정답이다.

어휘 alternative 대체하는, 대안의

76 According to the speaker, what will happen on Saturday?
(A) A bridge will reopen.
(B) A local law will change.
(C) A new radio show will be broadcast.
(D) An annual festival will be held.

화자의 말에 따르면, 토요일에 무슨 일이 있을 것인가?
(A) 다리가 재개통될 것이다.
(B) 지역 법이 변경될 것이다.
(C) 새 라디오 프로그램이 방송될 것이다.
(D) 연례 축제가 개최될 것이다.

해설 〈특정 시점의 일을 묻는 문제〉
담화 후반부에 어빈 대교가 토요일에 재개통될 것이라는(Irvine Bridge will reopen on Saturday) 소식을 전하고 있으므로 (A)가 정답이다.

어휘 local 지역의, 현지의 annual 연례적인, 해마다의 hold ~을 개최하다, 열다

Questions 77-79 refer to the following announcement. 영W

It's time to get creative and show your talents with **㉗** this year's Amateur Painting Contest. Starting from today, amateur artists can submit up to three paintings to be considered for a grand prize of five thousand dollars. **㉘** If you'd like to be a part of this fun activity, please visit www.clarkcity.gov to complete an entry form. You will need high-quality photos of your work. The finalists will be invited to display their original works in the Clark City Library. So, we are also **㉙** looking for volunteers to help set up the display area on July 10. Those who do so will receive a free lunch. To find out more about this or other city-sponsored events, contact Kelly Conner at 555-7713.

올해의 아마추어 그림 대회에서 창의성을 발휘하고 재능을 선보일 시간이 다가왔습니다. 오늘부터 아마추어 미술가들은 5천 달러의 상금이 걸린 대상을 위해 심사받을 수 있도록 최대 세 점까지 그림을 제출할 수 있습니다. 이 즐거운 활동의 일부가 되기를 원하실 경우, www.clarkcity.gov를 방문해 참가 양식을 작성 완료하시기 바랍니다. 제출 작품을 찍은 고화질 사진이 필요할 것입니다. 결선 진출자들은 클라크 시립 도서관에서 원본 작품을 전시하도록 요청받게 됩니다. 따라서, 저희는 7월 10일에 해당 전시 공간을 설치하는 데 도움을 줄 자원 봉사자를 찾고 있습니다. 이렇게 자원하는 분들은 무료 점심 식사를 제공받게 됩니다. 이 자원 봉사 또는 시에서 후원하는 기타 행사에 관해 더 많은 것을 알아 보시려면, 555-7713번으로 켈리 코너 씨에게 연락 주시기 바랍니다.

어휘 creative 창의적인 submit ~을 제출하다 up to 최대 ~의 consider ~을 고려하다 grand prize 대상 would like to do ~하고자 하다, ~하고 싶다 complete ~을 완료하다 entry 참가(작), 가입, 입장 form 양식, 서식 work 작품 finalist 결선 진출자 be invited to do ~하도록 요청받다 display v. ~을 전시하다, 진열하다 n. 전시, 진열 original 원본의, 원작의 look for ~을 찾다 volunteer 자원 봉사자 help do ~하는 것을 돕다 set up ~을 설치하다, 마련하다 those who ~하는 사람들 receive ~을 받다 free 무료의 find out more about ~에 관해 더 많은 것을 알아 보다 city-sponsored 시에서 후원하는 contact ~에게 연락하다

77 What kind of event is being announced?
(A) A music festival
(B) A painting competition
(C) A theater performance
(D) A book club meeting

어떤 종류의 행사가 공지되고 있는가?
(A) 음악 축제
(B) 그림 경연 대회
(C) 연극 공연
(D) 독서 동아리 모임

해설 〈주제를 묻는 문제〉
담화를 시작하면서 화자가 올해의 아마추어 그림 대회(this year's

Amateur Painting Contest)를 언급한 뒤로 이 행사의 참가와 관련된 정보를 제공하는 것으로 담화를 진행하고 있으므로 (B)가 정답이다.

어휘 competition 경연대회, 경기대회

78 According to the speaker, why should the listeners visit a Web site?
(A) To submit an entry
(B) To read some reviews
(C) To download a brochure
(D) To cast a vote

화자의 말에 따르면, 청자들은 왜 웹 사이트를 방문해야 하는가?
(A) 참가작을 제출하기 위해
(B) 몇몇 후기를 읽어 보기 위해
(C) 안내 책자를 다운로드하기 위해
(D) 투표를 하기 위해

해설 〈기타 세부 사항을 묻는 문제〉
담화 중반부에 행사의 일부가 되기를 원하는 사람은 www.clarkcity.gov를 방문해 참가 양식을 작성 완료하라고(If you'd like to be a part of this fun activity, please visit www.clarkcity.gov to complete an entry form) 알리고 있으므로 (A)가 정답이다.

어휘 submit ~을 제출하다 entry 참가(작) review 후기, 평가, 의견 brochure 안내 책자, 소책자 cast a vote 투표하다

79 What will be given to people who volunteer on July 10?
(A) An event T-shirt
(B) A front-row seat
(C) A complimentary ticket
(D) A free meal

7월 10일에 자원 봉사하는 사람들에게 무엇이 제공될 것인가?
(A) 행사 티셔츠
(B) 앞줄 좌석
(C) 무료 입장권
(D) 무료 식사

해설 〈기타 세부 사항을 묻는 문제〉
담화 후반부에 7월 10일에 자원 봉사자가 필요하다는 말과 함께 자원 봉사자에게 무료 점심을 제공한다고(looking for volunteers to help set up the display area on July 10. Those who do so will receive a free lunch) 알리고 있으므로 (D)가 정답이다.

어휘 front-row 앞줄의 complimentary 무료의(= free)

Questions 80-82 refer to the following talk. 미M

⑧⓪ Welcome to your first day at this new branch of Body Tech Fitness Center. First of all, some of you asked me about parking behind our building. ⑧⓪ A space is reserved for each gym employee, so ⑧① feel free to leave your vehicle there at no charge. Now, before I show you around, ⑧② you need uniforms. We have shorts and T-shirts in a wide selection of sizes. Please grab some and get changed in the changing rooms before we proceed. There are boxes at the front desk.

이곳 바디 테크 피트니스 센터의 새 지점 개장 첫날에 오신 것을 환영합니다. 가장 먼저, 여러분 중 몇몇 분께서 건물 뒤쪽의 주차와 관련해 저에게 물어보셨습니다. 공간 한 곳이 각 체육관 직원을 위해 지정되어 있으므로, 그곳에 얼마든지 무료로 여러분의 차량을 주차해도 됩니다. 자, 제가 곳곳을 보여 드리기 전에, 유니폼이 필요하실 겁니다. 아주 다양한 사이즈로 된 반바지와 티셔츠가 있습니다. 더 진행하기에 앞서 탈의실로 가져가셔서 갈아입으시기 바랍니다. 프런트 데스크에 상자들이 있습니다.

어휘 branch 지점, 지사 ask A about B A에게 B에 관해 묻다 parking 주차 behind ~ 뒤쪽에 reserved 지정된, 예약된 feel free to do 얼마든지 ~하세요, 마음껏 ~하세요 leave ~을 놓다, 두다 vehicle 차량 at no charge 무료로 show A around A에게 곳곳을 둘러보게 하다 shorts 반바지 a wide selection of 아주 다양한 grab ~을 가져가다, 가져오다 get changed 갈아입다 proceed 진행하다, 나아가다

80 Where does the speaker probably work?
(A) At an office
(B) At a clothing store
(C) At a city park
(D) At a gym

화자는 어디에서 일하고 있을 것 같은가?
(A) 사무실에서
(B) 의류 매장에서
(C) 시립 공원에서
(D) 체육관에서

해설 〈근무지를 묻는 문제〉
담화 시작 부분에 바디 테크 피트니스 센터의 새 지점에 온 것을 환영하고(Welcome to your first day at this new branch of Body Tech Fitness Center) 있고, 중반부에 체육관 직원들을 위한 주차 공간을(~ for each gym employee) 언급하고 있어 체육관이 근무 장소임을 알 수 있으므로 (D)가 정답이다.

81 According to the speaker, what will be offered to the listeners?
(A) Free parking
(B) Refreshments
(C) Corporate discounts
(D) Company cars

화자의 말에 따르면, 청자들에게 무엇이 제공될 것인가?
(A) 무료 주차
(B) 다과
(C) 기업 할인
(D) 회사 차량

해설 〈기타 세부 사항을 묻는 문제〉
담화 중반부에 특정 장소에 얼마든지 무료로 차량을 놓아 두어도 된다고(feel free to leave your vehicle there at no charge) 알리고 있으므로 무료 주차를 뜻하는 (A)가 정답이다.

어휘 offer ~을 제공하다, 제안하다 free 무료의 corporate 기업의, 회사의

82 Why does the speaker say, "There are boxes at the front desk"?
(A) To ask that the front desk be cleaned
(B) To give the location of clothing
(C) To announce that a business is being relocated
(D) To point out that a delivery has not been sent yet

화자는 왜 "There are boxes at the front desk"라고 말하는가?
(A) 프런트 데스크를 청소하도록 요청하기 위해
(B) 옷이 있는 곳을 알려 주기 위해
(C) 한 업체가 이전하고 있다고 알리기 위해
(D) 배송 물품이 아직 도착하지 않았음을 지적하기 위해

해설 〈의도 파악 문제〉
담화 후반부에 청자들에게 유니폼으로 사이즈가 다양한 반바지와 티셔츠가 있으며 갈아입어야 한다고(you need uniforms. We have shorts and T-shirts in a wide selection of sizes. Please grab some and get changed in the changing rooms ~) 알리면서 '프런트 데스크에 상자들이 있다'고 말하는 상황이다. 이는 그곳에서 가서 유니폼을 가져가라는 뜻으로서 유니폼이 있는 곳을 알리는 것이므로 (B)가 정답이다.

어휘 ask that ~하도록 요청하다 location 위치, 지점 relocate ~을 이전하다 point out that ~임을 지적하다

Questions 83-85 refer to the following advertisement. 영W

Are you interested in selling your goods overseas? Do you want to make sure you keep up with new regulations and trends? Then become a subscriber of International Trade Monthly. If you're thinking of starting your own business, ⑧③ the upcoming June issue is perfect for you. All of its articles feature the theme of start-up companies and tips to learn from them. We'll also interview ⑧④ Jessie Ewing, who specializes in advising companies about their finances. In addition, ⑧⑤ anyone who subscribes this month will receive a free wireless speaker for home or office use.

여러분의 상품을 해외에서 판매하는 일에 관심이 있으신가요? 새로운 규정과 유행에 발맞춰 나아가기를 원하시나요? 그러시다면 〈월간 인터내셔널 트레이드〉의 구독자가 되어 보십시오. 개인 사업체를 시작할 생각이시라면, 곧 출간될 6월호가 여러분께 완벽할 것입니다. 그 모든 기사가 신생 기업들과 그 기업들로부터 배우는 팁이라는 주제를 특징으로 합니다. 저희는 또한 회사에 재무와 관련해 조언하는 일을 전문으로 하는 제시 유잉 씨를 인터뷰할 것입니다. 추가로, 이번 달에 구독 신청하시는 모든 분께서 가정용 또는 사무용으로 사용하실 수 있는 무료 무선 스피커를 받으시게 됩니다.

어휘 be interested in ~에 관심이 있다 goods 상품 overseas 해외에서, 해외로 make sure (that) 반드시 ~하도록 하다, ~하는 것을 확실히 해 두다 keep up with (속도, 진도 등) ~에 발맞춰 나아가다, 뒤처지지 않다 regulation 규정, 규제 trend 유행, 경향, 추세 subscriber 구독자, 서비스 가입자 upcoming 곧 있을, 다가오는 issue (잡지 등의) 호 article (잡지 등의) 기사 feature ~을 특징으로 하다 theme 주제 star-up company 신생 기업 specialize in ~을 전문으로 하다 finance 재무, 재정 in addition 추가로, 게다가 subscribe ~을 구독 신청하다, ~에 가입하다 receive ~을 받다 free 무료의

83 According to the advertisement, what is unique about the June issue?
(A) It will announce the winner of an award.
(B) It will focus on start-up companies.
(C) It will provide coupons for services.
(D) It will review new technology.

광고에 따르면, 6월호와 관련해 무엇이 특별한가?
(A) 수상자를 발표할 것이다.
(B) 신생 기업들에 초점을 맞출 것이다.
(C) 여러 서비스에 대한 쿠폰을 제공할 것이다.
(D) 신기술을 살펴 볼 것이다.

해설 〈기타 세부 사항을 묻는 문제〉
6월호가 언급되는 중반부에, 6월호에 실리는 모든 기사가 신생 기업들 자체에 대한 내용뿐만 아니라 그 업체들을 통해 배우는 팁을 주제로 한다고(the upcoming June issue is perfect for you. All of its articles feature the theme of start-up companies and tips to learn) 알리고 있으므로 (B)가 정답이다.

어휘 unique 특별한, 독특한 announce ~을 발표하다, 공지하다 focus on ~에 초점을 맞추다, 집중하다 provide ~을 제공하다 review ~을 살펴보다, 검토하다

84 Who is Jessie Ewing?
(A) A computer programmer
(B) A financial expert
(C) A corporate CEO
(D) A magazine editor

제시 유잉은 누구인가?
(A) 컴퓨터 프로그래머
(B) 재무 전문가
(C) 기업 CEO
(D) 잡지 편집자

해설 〈직업을 묻는 문제〉
제시 유잉 씨의 이름이 언급되는 후반부에 재무와 관련해 조언하는 일을 전문으로 하는 사람이라고(Jessie Ewing, who specializes in advising companies about their finances) 설명하고 있으므로 (B)가 정답이다.

어휘 financial 재무의, 금융의 expert 전문가 corporate 기업의, 회사의 editor 편집자

85 What can customers get if they sign up for a subscription this month?
(A) A best-selling book
(B) A tote bag
(C) A desktop clock
(D) A wireless speaker

고객들이 이번 달에 구독 서비스에 가입하면 무엇을 받을 수 있는가?
(A) 베스트셀러 도서
(B) 토트백
(C) 탁상용 시계
(D) 무선 스피커

해설 〈기타 세부 사항을 묻는 문제〉
담화 후반부에 이번 달에 구독하게 되면 무료 무선 스피커를 받는다고(anyone who subscribes this month will receive a free wireless speaker) 알리고 있으므로 (D)가 정답이다.

어휘 sign up for ~에 가입하다, ~을 신청하다 subscription 구독, 서비스 이용

Questions 86-88 refer to following telephone message. 캐W

Hello, Ms. Martinez. I've been making arrangements for ⑧⑥ your trip to Los Angeles for the fashion show this weekend. I'm having difficulty finding a vegan restaurant for your lunch meeting. The part of the city you'll be staying in doesn't have diverse restaurant options, and ⑧⑦ the few vegan places I found are already fully booked. I know a place in northwest LA. ⑧⑦ It shouldn't take more than 45 minutes to reach from your hotel. Please let me know if that's fine. Also, please remember that ⑧⑧ the CEO needs to authorize your use of a company car in advance.

안녕하세요. 마르티네즈 씨. 이번 주말에 패션쇼를 위해 로스앤젤레스로 떠나시는 출장을 준비해 드리고 있었습니다. 오찬 모임을 위한 엄격한 채식주의 레스토랑을 찾는 데 어려움이 있습니다. 머무르실 예정인 도시의 지역엔 선택 가능한 레스토랑이 다양하지 않고, 제가 찾은 몇몇 엄격한 채식주의 식당들은 이미 예약이 꽉 차 있습니다. 제가 로스앤젤레스 북서부 지역에 아는 곳이 한 군데 있습니다. 호텔에서 출발해 도착할 때까지 45분이 넘게 걸리지 않을 겁니다. 이곳이 괜찮으신지 알려 주시기 바랍니다. 그리고, 회사 차량 이용 시 대표이사님의 사전 승인이 필요하다는 점 기억하시기 바랍니다.

어휘 make an arrangement 준비하다, 조치하다 have difficulty -ing ~하는 데 어려움을 겪다 vegan 엄격한 채식주의 diverse 다양한 be fully booked 예약이 꽉 차 있다 take ~의 시간이 걸리다 more than ~가 넘는 reach ~에 도착하다, 이르다 let A know if A에게 ~인지 알리다 remember that ~임을 기억하다 authorize ~을 승인하다 in advance 미리, 사전에

86 What event is the listener attending soon?
(A) A charity banquet
(B) An awards ceremony
(C) A grand opening
(D) A fashion show

청자는 곧 어떤 행사에 참석하는가?
(A) 자선 연회
(B) 시상식
(C) 개장식
(D) 패션쇼

해설 〈특정 시점의 일을 묻는 문제〉
담화 시작 부분에 화자가 청자를 your로 지칭하면서 패션쇼를 위해 로스앤젤레스로 떠나는 출장을(your trip to Los Angeles for the fashion show this weekend) 언급하고 있으므로 (D)가 정답이다.

어휘 attend ~에 참석하다 charity 자선 (연회) banquet 연회

87 Why does the speaker say, "I know a place in northwest LA"?
(A) To confirm that some details are correct

(B) To suggest an alternative restaurant
(C) To recommend a place to stay
(D) To show his knowledge of a city

화자는 왜 "I know a place in northwest LA"라고 말하는가?
(A) 일부 상세 정보가 정확하다는 것을 확인해 주기 위해
(B) 대체 식당을 제안하기 위해
(C) 머무를 곳을 추천하기 위해
(D) 한 도시에 대한 지식을 보여 주기 위해

해설 〈의도 파악 문제〉
담화 중반부에 화자가 자신이 찾은 몇몇 엄격한 채식주의 식당들은 예약이 꽉 차 있다고(the few vegan places I found are already fully booked) 알린 뒤로, '로스앤젤레스 북서부 지역에 아는 곳이 한 군데 있다'고 언급하면서 호텔에서 45분 내로 도착할 수 있다고(It shouldn't take more than 45 minutes to reach from your hotel) 말하는 흐름이다. 이는 예약이 꽉 차 있는 곳 대신 제안하는 방법이므로 (B)가 정답이다.

어휘 confirm that ~임을 확인해 주다 details 상세 정보, 세부 사항 correct 정확한, 올바른, 맞는 alternative 대체하는, 대안의

88 What requires the CEO's authorization?
(A) Discussing a company issue
(B) Reserving a hotel room
(C) Upgrading a flight ticket
(D) Using a company vehicle

무엇이 대표이사의 승인을 필요로 하는가?
(A) 회사의 문제를 논의하는 일
(B) 호텔 객실을 예약하는 일
(C) 항공권을 업그레이드하는 일
(D) 회사 차량을 이용하는 일

해설 〈기타 세부 사항을 묻는 문제〉
담화 맨 마지막에 회사 차량을 이용하는 데 대표이사가 승인해야 한다고(the CEO needs to authorize your use of a company car) 알리고 있으므로 (D)가 정답이다.

어휘 authorization 승인 discuss ~을 논의하다, 이야기하다 issue 문제, 사안 reserve ~을 예약하다 vehicle 차량

Questions 89-91 refer to the following excerpt from a meeting.
호M

As the courses held at our conference center were in high demand last summer, ⑧⑨ we need to decide whether we should hire more staff. If we hire the same staff numbers, each lecturer will have to teach four classes a day. One of our managers, ⑨⓪ Mr. Benson, feels this workload is acceptable. Well, I was a teacher for several years. I know how important it is for our staff to be fresh. Teaching four classes is a lot. ⑨① I have received several résumés for prospective staff members, and I'm planning to read through them over the weekend and determine whether we have any suitable candidates.

우리 컨퍼런스 센터에서 개최된 교육 과정들이 지난여름에 수요가 높았기 때문에 더 많은 직원을 고용할 것인지 결정해야 합니다. 우리가 동일한 직원을 고용하는 경우, 각 강사가 하루에 네 번의 수업을 가르쳐야 할 것입니다. 우리 책임자들 중 한 분인 벤슨 씨는 이러한 업무량이 받아들일 수 있는 수준이라고 생각하고 계십니다. 음, 저는 수년 동안 교사였습니다. 우리 직원들이 생기 넘치는 상태로 있는 것이 얼마나 중요한지 알고 있습니다. 네 번의 수업을 가르치는 건 많습니다. 제가 잠재 직원들의 이력서를 몇 장 받았기에, 주말 동안에 걸쳐 꼼꼼히 읽어 보고 어떤 적합한 지원자들 있는지 결정할 계획입니다.

어휘 hold ~을 개최하다 in high demand 수요가 높은 decide ~을 결정하다 whether ~인지 (아닌지) hire ~을 고용하다 lecturer 강사 will have to do ~해야 할 것이다 workload 업무량 acceptable 받아들일 수 있는 several 몇몇의, 여럿의 fresh 생기 넘치는, 기운찬 receive ~을 받다 resume 이력서 prospective 잠재적인, 장차 ~가 될 plan to do ~할 계획이다 read through ~을 꼼꼼히 읽다 over ~ 동안에 걸쳐 determine ~을 결정하다, 밝혀내다 suitable 적합한 candidate 지원자, 후보자

89 What is the topic of the meeting?
(A) Staffing needs
(B) Event locations
(C) Course fees
(D) Lesson plans
회의 주제는 무엇인가?
(A) 직원 채용 필요성
(B) 행사 장소
(C) 수강료
(D) 강의 계획
해설 〈주제를 묻는 문제〉
담화 시작 부분에 더 많은 직원을 고용할 것인지 결정해야 한다고(we need to decide whether we should hire more staff) 알리고 있다. 이는 직원 채용의 필요성을 언급하는 말에 해당되므로 (A)가 정답이다.

어휘 staffing 직원 채용, 직원 구성 location 장소, 위치

90 What does the speaker imply when he says, "Teaching four classes is a lot"?
(A) He would like to apply for a teaching role.
(B) He would like to take some time off from work.
(C) He is impressed with the teachers' efforts.
(D) He disagrees with a colleague's opinion.
화자가 "Teaching four classes is a lot"이라고 말할 때 무엇을 암시하는가?
(A) 교사 직책에 지원하고 싶어 한다.
(B) 일을 조금 쉬고 싶어 한다.
(C) 선생님들의 노력에 깊은 인상을 받았다.
(D) 동료 직원의 의견에 동의하지 않는다.
해설 〈의도 파악 문제〉
담화 중반부에 책임자들 중 한 명인 벤슨 씨가 특정 업무량이 적합하다고 생각한다는 점과 함께 직원들이 생기 넘치는 상태가 되어야 한다고(Mr. Benson, feels this workload is acceptable. ~ I know how important it is for our staff to be fresh) 언급하면서 '네 번의 수업을 가르치는 건 많다'고 말하는 흐름이다. 이는 동료 직원인 벤슨 씨의 생각이 잘못되었음을 강조하는 것이므로 (D)가 정답이다.

어휘 would like to do ~하고 싶다 apply for ~에 지원하다 take A off A만큼 쉬다 be impressed with ~에 깊은 인상을 받다 effort 노력 disagree with ~에 동의하지 않다 colleague 동료 (직원)

91 What will the speaker most likely do this weekend?
(A) Place an advertisement
(B) Review some résumés
(C) Sign a contract
(D) Print some handouts
화자는 이번 주에 무엇을 할 것 같은가?
(A) 광고를 내는 일
(B) 몇몇 이력서를 검토하는 일
(C) 계약서에 서명하는 일
(D) 몇몇 유인물을 출력하는 일
해설 〈특정 시점의 일을 묻는 문제〉
담화 후반부에 몇몇 이력서를 받은 사실과 함께 주말 동안 그것을 꼼꼼히 읽어 볼 계획이라고(I have received several resumes for perspective staff members, and I'm planning to read through them over the weekend) 알리고 있으므로 (B)가 정답이다.

어휘 place an advertisement 광고를 내다 review ~을 검토하다, 살펴보다 contract 계약(서) handout 유인물

Questions 92-94 refer to the following telephone message. 미M

Hi, Megumi. It's Alfonso. I know you're really busy this week, but I just found out that a new hospital opening in Osaka would like to purchase ⑨② some of the medical machines that we make. It would be a huge order of ⑨② X-ray machines, heart monitors, and more. I've scheduled a teleconference with one of their representatives ⑨③ on January 10 to negotiate the contract details. I'd like to send them our product description report in advance. However, we only have a copy in English, not Japanese. ⑨④ I'm wondering if you could do a translation of the report. Please let me know. Thanks a lot.

안녕하세요, 메구미 씨, 알폰소입니다. 이번 주에 정말 바쁘시다는 것을 알고 있지만, 오사카에서 개원하는 새 병원이 우리가 만드는 의료 기계 일부를 구입하고 싶어 한다는 사실을 막 알게 되었습니다. 엑스레이 기계와 심장 모니터를 비롯해 다른 여러 가지에 대해 엄청 규모가 큰 주문이 될 겁니다. 제가 그쪽 직원들 중 한 분과 계약 세부 사항을 협의하기 위해 1월 10일로 화상 회의 일정을 잡아 뒀습니다. 이분들께 미리 우리 제품 설명 보고서를 보내 드리고자 합니다. 하지만, 일본어가 아닌 영어 사본만 있습니다. 이 보고서의 번역 작업을 해 주실 수 있는지 궁금합니다. 저에게 알려 주시기 바랍니다. 대단히 감사합니다.

어휘 find out that ~임을 알게 되다, 파악하다 would like to do ~하고 싶다 purchase ~을 구입하다 huge 엄청난, 막대한 order 주문(품) schedule ~의 일정을 잡다 teleconference 화상 회의 representative 직원 negotiate ~을 협의하다, 협상하다 contract 계약(서) details 세부 사항, 상세 정보 description 설명 in advance 미리, 사전에 wonder if ~인지 궁금하다 translation 번역 let A know A에게 알리다

92 What does the speaker's company manufacture?
(A) Medical equipment
(B) Delivery containers
(C) Work uniforms
(D) Office supplies
화자의 회사는 무엇을 제조하는가?
(A) 의료 장비
(B) 배달용 용기
(C) 작업용 유니폼
(D) 사무용품
해설 〈주제를 묻는 문제〉
담화 초반부에 화자가 소속 회사를 we로 지칭해 의료 기계를 만든다고(some of the medical machines that we make) 언급함과 동시에, 엑스레이 기계와 심장 모니터를(X-ray machines, heart monitors) 말하고 있으므로 (A)가 정답이다.

어휘 manufacture ~을 제조하다 equipment 장비 container 용기, 그릇 supplies 용품, 물품

93 What does the speaker say will happen on January 10?
(A) A new CEO will take over.
(B) A business will expand overseas.
(C) A corporate merger will be finalized.
(D) A negotiation will take place.

화자는 1월 10일에 무슨 일이 있을 것이라고 말하는가?
(A) 신입 대표이사가 취임할 것이다.
(B) 업체가 해외로 사업을 확장할 것이다.
(C) 기업 합병이 최종 확정될 것이다.
(D) 협의가 진행될 것이다.

해설 〈특정 시점의 일을 묻는 문제〉
담화 중반부에 1월 10일이라는 날짜와 함께 계약 세부 사항을 협의한다고(on January 10 to negotiate the contract details) 밝히고 있으므로 (D)가 정답이다.

어휘 take over 인계받다, 이어받다 expand 확장하다, 확대하다 overseas 해외로 corporate 기업의, 회사의 merger 합병 finalize ~을 최종 확정하다 negotiation 협의, 협상 take place (일, 행사 등이) 발생되다, 개최되다

94 What is the listener asked to do?
(A) Train new employees
(B) Check some sales figures
(C) Translate a document
(D) Sign a contract

청자는 무엇을 하도록 요청 받는가?
(A) 신입 사원을 교육하는 일
(B) 일부 매출 수치를 확인하는 일
(C) 문서를 번역하는 일
(D) 계약서에 서명하는 일

해설 〈요청 사항을 묻는 문제〉
담화 맨 마지막에 고객들에게 보낼 보고서를 번역해 줄 수 있는지(I'm wondering if you could do a translation of the report) 확인하는 것으로 요청 사항을 말하고 있으므로 (C)가 정답이다.

어휘 train ~을 교육하다 sales 매출, 판매, 영업 figure 수치, 숫자 contract 계약(서)

Questions 95-97 refer to the following talk and schedule. 호M

⑨⑤ I'd like to welcome all guests to the retirement party of Chad Bitterman. Let's thank him for his amazing thirty years of service here at Royal Charter Bank. ⑨⑥ An envelope was passed around the office this morning for people to insert cash in order to contribute to Chad's gift. If you didn't get a chance to contribute, there is still time to do so. We are planning to send Chad and his wife on a two-week cruise. ⑨⑦ Now, that's the end of our welcome refreshments, so it's time for the next event.

7:00	⑨⑦ Welcome refreshments
7:30	⑨⑦ Comedy show
8:30	Banquet
9:15	After-dinner speeches
10:00	Musical entertainment

채드 비터먼 씨의 은퇴 파티에 오신 모든 손님을 환영해 드리고자 합니다. 이곳 로얄 차터 은행에서 30년이라는 놀라운 기간을 재직해 오신 비터먼 씨께 감사의 인사를 전합시다. 오늘 아침에 사람들이 현금을 넣어 채드 씨의 선물에 보탤 수 있도록 사무실 전체에 봉투를 돌렸습니다. 보태 드릴 기회가 없었던 분은, 여전히 그렇게 하실 수 있는 시간이 있습니다. 우리는 채드 씨와 아내 분께 2주 동안의 유람선 여행을 보내 드릴 계획입니다. 자, 이것으로 환영 다과 시간을 마치고, 다음 행사로 이어질 차례입니다.

7:00	환영 다과
7:30	코미디 쇼
8:30	연회
9:15	식후 연설
10:00	음악 공연

어휘 retirement 은퇴 amazing 놀라운 service 재직, 근무, 봉사 envelope 봉투 pass (사람들에게) ~을 돌리다, 전달하다 insert ~을 넣다, 삽입하다 in order to do ~하기 위해, ~할 수 있도록 contribute to ~에 보탬이 되다, 기여하다 get a chance to do ~할 기회가 있다 plan to do ~할 계획이다 cruise 유람선 여행 refreshments 다과, 간식 banquet 연회 after-dinner 식사 후의

95 Where is the speech taking place?
(A) At a training seminar
(B) At a retirement celebration
(C) At a charity fundraiser
(D) At a board meeting

연설이 어디에서 진행되고 있는가?
(A) 교육 세미나
(B) 은퇴 기념 행사
(C) 자선 모금 행사
(D) 이사회 회의

해설 〈담화의 장소를 묻는 문제〉
담화를 시작하면서 채드 비터먼 씨의 은퇴 파티에 온 모든 손님을 환영한다고(I'd like to welcome all guests to the retirement party of Chad Bitterman) 인사하고 있으므로 (B)가 정답이다.

어휘 take place (일, 행사 등이) 발생되다, 개최되다 celebration 기념 행사, 축하 행사 charity 자선 (단체) fundraiser 모금 행사 board 이사회, 이사진

96 What was given to the listeners this morning?
(A) A collection envelope
(B) A set of directions
(C) A product specification
(D) A cruise brochure

오늘 아침에 청자들에게 무엇이 전달되었는가?
(A) 모금 봉투
(B) 일련의 지시 사항
(C) 제품 사양
(D) 유람선 여행 안내 책자

해설 〈기타 세부 사항을 묻는 문제〉
담화 중반부에 현금을 넣어 채드 씨의 선물에 보태기 위해 오늘 아침에 봉투를 돌렸다고(An envelope was passed around the office this morning for people to insert cash in order to contribute to Chad's gift) 알리고 있는데, 이는 돈을 모으기 위해 활용한 방법을 말하는 것이므로 (A)가 정답이다.

어휘 collection 모금, 수금, 수집 a set of 일련의 directions 지시 specification (제품 등의) 사양 brochure 안내 책자, 소책자

97 Look at the graphic. What activity will the listeners enjoy next?
(A) Comedy show
(B) Banquet
(C) After-dinner speeches
(D) Musical entertainment

시각 자료를 보시오. 청자들은 곧이어 어떤 활동을 즐길 것인가?
(A) 코미디 쇼
(B) 연회
(C) 식후 연설
(D) 음악 공연

해설 〈2열 도표 문제〉
담화 맨 마지막에 환영 다과를 마치고 다음 순서로 넘어가겠다고(Now, that's the end of our welcome refreshments, so it's time for the next event) 알리고 있다. 일정표에서 맨 윗줄에 쓰여 있는 Welcome refreshments 다음 순서가 Comedy show이므로 (A)가 정답이다.

Questions 98-100 refer to the following telephone message and customer ratings. 미M

Hi, Jessica. It's Christopher from the finance department. (98) Next month, my team is relocating to the Tyson Building, across the street. (99) I'm supposed to order a printer from KL Electronics for our team, but I'm not sure which model to choose. (99) Since you've bought several printers from that company, I'm wondering if you could give me some advice. We do quite a bit of printing, so (100) I'm considering the one that prints twenty-six pages per minute. However, it's not the highest rated one. I'd love to hear what you think. Please call me back. Thanks!

KL Electronics		
Model	Pages per Minute	Customer Rating
Lexel	23	9.8
Supra	15	9.6
(100) Indicon	26	8.4
Bolt	18	7.7

안녕하세요, 제시카 씨. 재무팀에서 전화 드리는 크리스토퍼입니다. 다음 달에, 저희 팀이 길 건너편에 있는 타이슨 빌딩으로 이전합니다. 제가 우리 팀을 위해 KL 일렉트로닉스에서 프린터를 한 대 주문할 예정인데, 어느 모델을 선택해야 할지 잘 모르겠습니다. 이 회사에서 프린터를 여러 대 구입하신 적이 있으시기 때문에 저에게 조언을 좀 해 주실 수 있으신지 궁금합니다. 저희가 꽤 많이 인쇄를 하기 때문에 분당 26페이지를 인쇄하는 제품을 고려하고 있습니다. 하지만, 가장 높은 평점을 받은 제품은 아닙니다. 어떻게 생각하시는지 꼭 들어 보고 싶습니다. 저에게 다시 전화 주시기 바랍니다. 감사합니다!

KL 일렉트로닉스		
모델명	분당 페이지	고객 평점
렉셀	23	9.8
수프라	15	9.6
인디콘	26	8.4
볼트	18	7.7

어휘 finance department 재무팀 relocate to ~로 이전하다, 이사하다 across ~ 건너편의 be supposed to do ~할 예정이다, ~하기로 되어 있다 order ~을 주문하다 choose ~을 선택하다 several 여럿의, 몇몇의 wonder if ~인지 궁금하다 quite a bit of 꽤 많은 consider ~을 고려하다 however 하지만, 그러나 the highest rated 가장 높은 평점을 받은 would love to do 꼭 ~하고 싶다 call A back A에게 다시 전화하다 rating 평점, 등급

98 What will the speaker's team do next month?
(A) Attend an industry conference
(B) Move to a new building
(C) Oversee a product launch
(D) Undergo a performance evaluation

화자의 팀은 다음 달에 무엇을 할 것인가?
(A) 업계 컨퍼런스에 참석하는 일
(B) 새로운 건물로 이사하는 일
(C) 제품 출시를 총괄하는 일
(D) 업무 능력 평가를 거치는 일

해설 〈특정 시점의 일을 묻는 문제〉
담화 초반부에 화자가 다음 달에 자신의 팀이 길 건너편에 있는 타이슨 빌딩으로 이전한다고(Next month, my team is relocating to the Tyson Building) 알리고 있으므로 (B)가 정답이다.

어휘 attend ~에 참석하다 industry 업계 oversee ~을 총괄하다, 감독하다 launch 출시, 공개 undergo ~을 거치다, 겪다 performance 수행 능력, 성과, 실적 evaluation 평가(서)

99 Why does the speaker ask the listener about KL Electronics?
(A) She sent the speaker some reviews.
(B) She used to work there.
(C) She has purchased items from it.
(D) She shared a coupon for its goods.

화자는 왜 청자에게 KL 일렉트로닉스에 관해 묻는가?
(A) 화자에게 몇몇 후기 내용을 보냈다.
(B) 전에 그곳에서 근무했다.
(C) 그곳에서 제품을 구입한 적이 있다.
(D) 그곳의 상품에 대한 쿠폰을 한 장 공유해 주었다.

해설 〈기타 세부 사항을 묻는 문제〉
화자는 담화 중반부에 자신이 KL 일렉트로닉스에서 프린터를 주문하려 한다는 사실과(I'm supposed to order a printer from KL Electronics) 상대방이 이 회사에서 프린터를 여러 대 구입했던 사실을(Since you've bought several printers from that company) 함께 밝히고 있으므로 (C)가 정답이다.

어휘 review 후기, 평가, 의견 used to do 전에 ~하곤 했다 purchase ~을 구입하다 share ~을 공유하다 goods 상품

100 Look at the graphic. Which model is the speaker thinking about buying?
(A) Lexel
(B) Supra
(C) Indicon
(D) Bolt

시각 자료를 보시오. 화자는 어느 모델을 구입하는 것에 대해 생각하고 있는가?
(A) 렉셀
(B) 수프라
(C) 인디콘
(D) 볼트

해설 〈3열 이상 도표 문제〉
화자는 담화 후반부에 분당 26페이지를 인쇄하는 제품을 고려하고 있다고(I'm considering the one that prints twenty-six pages per minute) 알리고 있으며, 도표에서 분당 페이지(Pages per Minute)가 26으로 표기된 제품이 세 번째 줄에 쓰여 있는 Indicon이므로 (C)가 정답이다.

PART 5

101 **해석** 비록 시미아 씨가 레스토랑의 서비스에 대해 불만을 제기하기는 했지만, 그곳 웹 사이트에 긍정적인 후기를 남겼다.

해설 〈부사 어휘〉
보기가 모두 부사이므로 의미가 알맞은 것을 찾아야 한다. 빈칸이 속한 주절은 긍정적인 내용을, Although절은 부정적인 내용을 담고 있어 서로 대조적인 의미 관계를 나타내고 있다. 따라서 '그럼에도 불구하고'라는 의미로 대조 또는 반대되는 관계를 나타낼 때 사용하는 (D) still이 정답이다. 참고로, (B) same은 정관사 the와 함께 the same의 형태로 사용한다.

어휘 although 비록 ~이기는 하지만 complain about ~에 대해 불만을 제기하다, 불평하다 leave ~을 남기다 positive 긍정적인 review 후기, 의견, 평가 ever 언젠가, 언제나, 이제까지, 지금까지 중에서 still 그럼에도 불구하고, 그래도, 여전히

102 **해석** 리차드슨 씨는 자신이 내일 사무실 전체를 위해 용품을 주문할 예정이라고 알렸다.

해설 〈주격 대명사〉
동사 announced의 목적어 역할을 하는 that절에서, that과 동사 will be ordering 사이에 위치한 빈칸은 that절의 주어 자리이므로 주격 대명사인 (B) she가 정답이다.

어휘 announce that ~라고 알리다, 발표하다 order ~을 주문하다 supplies 용품, 물품 entire 전체의

103 **해석** 인사부의 호트 씨는 직원들이 출장 교통편을 준비하도록 도움을 준다.

해설 〈동사 어휘〉
보기가 모두 동사이므로 의미가 알맞은 것을 찾아야 한다. 직원들이 교통편과 관련해 할 수 있는 일을 나타낼 동사가 쓰여야 하므로 '~을 마련하다, 준비하다' 등을 뜻하는 (C) arrange가 정답이다.

어휘 Human Resources 인사(부) transportation 교통(편) conduct ~을 실시하다, 수행하다 arrive 도착하다 arrange ~을 마련하다, 준비하다 proceed 진행하다, 계속 진행하다

104 **해석** 리즈 라인하트의 첫 번째 소설이 평론가들에게 높이 평가받기는 했지만, 서점에서 잘 판매되지 않았다.

해설 〈부사 자리(be동사와 p.p. 사이)〉
수동태 동사를 구성하는 be동사 was와 과거분사 regarded 사이에 위치한 빈칸은 수동태 동사를 중간에서 수식할 부사 자리이므로 부사

(D) highly가 정답이다.

어휘 highly regarded 높이 평가받는 critic 평론가, 비평가

105 해석 연구 참가자들은 개인 맞춤 일정표 및 테스트 현장으로 가는 길 안내 정보를 제공받을 것이다.

해설 〈동사 어휘〉
보기가 모두 동사의 과거분사이므로 의미가 알맞은 것을 찾아야 한다. 빈칸 뒤의 전치사 with와 어울리며, 일정표와 길 안내 정보를 '제공 받는다'와 같이 의미상으로 적합한 (C) provided가 정답이다. be provided with(~을 제공받다)는 provide A with B(A에게 B를 제공하다)의 수동태 형태이다.

어휘 participant 참가자 study 연구 personalized 개인에 맞춰진 directions to ~로 가는 길 안내 site 현장, 장소, 부지 alert (위험 등) ~에게 알리다, 주의시키다 grant ~을 주다, 승인하다 provide (A with B) (A에게 B를) 제공하다 request ~을 요청하다, 요구하다

106 해석 브리즈번 트래블 서비스에서 일하는 자원 봉사자들은 그 도시가 익숙하지 않은 어떤 방문객이든 도움을 제공할 수 있다.

해설 〈명사 자리(목적어)〉
빈칸은 타동사 give의 목적어 역할을 할 명사 자리이다. 또한 give의 목적어로서 전달 대상에 해당되는 것은 사물 명사여야 하므로 '도움, 지원' 등을 뜻하는 사물 명사 (B) assistance가 정답이다. 사람을 뜻하는 명사 (D) assistant는 give의 목적어로 의미상 적합하지 않으며, 또한 가산 명사이므로 관사나 한정사 없이 단수형으로 사용할 수 없다.

어휘 volunteer 자원 봉사자 be unfamiliar with ~가 익숙하지 않다, ~을 잘 알지 못하다 assist ~을 돕다 assistance 도움, 지원 assistant 보조, 조수

107 해석 전무이사님께서 출장으로 자리를 비우신 상태이기 때문에 주간 부서 회의가 연기될 것이다.

해설 〈전치사 VS. 접속사〉
빈칸 뒤로 주어와 동사가 각각 포함된 절이 콤마 앞뒤에 하나씩 위치해 있으므로 빈칸은 두 절을 연결할 부사절 접속사가 쓰여야 알맞다. 또한 '전무이사가 자리를 비웠기 때문에 회의가 연기될 것이다'와 같은 의미가 되어야 알맞으므로 '~이기 때문에'를 뜻하는 부사절 접속사 (D) Since가 정답이다. (A) Also는 부사, (B) Regardless of는 전치사이다. (C) Why도 접속사로 쓰이지만 명사절 접속사이므로 오답이다.

어휘 managing director 전무이사 away 자리를 비운, 멀리 있는 departmental 부서의 postpone ~을 연기하다, 미루다 regardless of ~에 상관없이 since ~이기 때문에, ~한 이후로

108 해석 최근의 흐린 날씨는 옥상 태양열 전지판에서 전기를 만드는 것을 어렵게 만들고 있다.

해설 〈형용사 자리 (목적격 보어)〉
빈칸 앞뒤가 'make it ~ to do'의 구조이므로 가목적어 it과 진목적어 to부정사로 된 구조임을 알 수 있다. 따라서 가목적어와 진목적어 사이에 위치한 빈칸은 목적격 보어 역할을 할 형용사 자리이므로 형용사인 (B) difficult가 정답이다.

어휘 recent 최근의 make it A to do ~하는 것을 A한 상태로 만들다

---

create ~을 만들어 내다 electricity 전기 solar panel 태양열 전지판 difficulty 어려움, 문제, 곤란함

109 해석 갤럭시 피트니스의 트레이너들은 체육관 회원들께 체중을 감량하는 가장 효과적인 방법을 가르쳐 드릴 것입니다.

해설 〈형용사 어휘〉
보기가 모두 형용사이므로 의미가 알맞은 것을 찾아야 한다. 빈칸에 쓰일 형용사는 명사 ways를 수식해 체중을 감량하는 방법이 지니는 특성을 나타내야 하므로 '효과적인'을 뜻하는 (B) effective가 정답이다.

어휘 way to do ~하는 법 lose weight 체중을 감량하다, 살을 빼다 effective 효과적인 enclosed 동봉된 reluctant 주저하는, 꺼리는

110 해석 교육 분야에 대한 지원을 분명히 보여주기 위해, 올반 오피스 서플라이즈 사는 교사 및 학교 행정 직원들에게 할인을 제공한다.

해설 〈① 명사 자리 (목적어) ② 가산/불가산 명사〉
타동사 offers와 전치사 to 사이에 위치한 빈칸은 동사의 목적어 역할을 할 명사 자리이다. 보기 중에 명사는 (A) discount와 (C) discounts가 있는데 discount는 가산 명사이므로 관사 혹은 한정사가 없는 경우 복수형으로 쓰여야 알맞다. 따라서 (C) discounts가 정답이다.

어휘 demonstrate (실례를 통해) ~을 입증하다, 보여주다, ~을 시연하다 support 지원, 후원 offer ~을 제공하다 administrator 행정 직원 discountable 할인할 수 있는

111 해석 인사부에서 부서장들에게 이번 주말까지 모든 직원 평가서를 완료하도록 요청했다.

해설 〈전치사 어휘〉
보기가 모두 전치사이므로 의미가 알맞은 것을 찾아야 한다. 빈칸 뒤에 '이번 주말'이라는 시점 표현이 쓰여 있는데, 이는 평가서를 완료하는 기한으로 볼 수 있다. 따라서 '~까지'라는 의미로 완료 기한을 나타낼 때 사용하는 (A) by가 정답이다.

어휘 HR Department 인사부 request that ~하도록 요청하다, 요구하다 complete ~을 완료하다 evaluation 평가(서) by (기한) ~까지 as (자격, 신분 등) ~로서

112 해석 베벌리 카운티 내의 지역 단체들은 올해의 겨울 축제를 위해 성공적으로 5,000달러 이상을 모금했다.

해설 〈부사 자리(have와 p.p. 사이)〉
현재완료 시제 동사를 구성하는 have와 과거분사 raised 사이에 위치한 빈칸은 이 동사를 중간에서 수식할 부사 자리이므로 (D) successfully가 정답이다.

어휘 local 지역의, 현지의 organization 단체, 기관 raise ~을 모금하다 over ~을 넘는 succeed 성공하다, ~을 이어받다, ~의 뒤를 잇다 successful 성공적인 successfully 성공적으로

113 해석 허니컴 케이블 사는 친구에게 자사의 서비스를 소개해 주는 경우 해당 고객에게 200달러의 상품권을 제공한다.

해설 〈접속사 VS. 부사〉
빈칸 앞뒤로 주어와 동사가 각각 포함된 절이 하나씩 위치해 있으므로

빈칸은 두 절을 연결할 접속사가 쓰여야 알맞다. 또한 '친구에게 서비스를 소개해 주는 경우에 상품권을 제공한다'와 같은 의미로 알맞으므로 '~하는 경우에, ~하면'을 뜻하는 접속사 (B) if가 정답이다. (C) while도 접속사이지만 의미가 맞지 않으며, (A) seldom과 (D) afterward는 부사이다.

어휘 voucher 상품권, 쿠폰 refer A to B A에게 B를 소개하다 seldom 좀처럼 ~ 않다 while ~하는 동안, ~인 반면 afterward 그 후에

114 해석 프로젝트 책임자가 제안된 초안 버전에 동의하는 경우, 공사 비용이 25% 넘게 증가할 것이다.

해설 〈현재분사 VS. 과거분사〉
정관사 the와 명사 version 사이에 위치한 빈칸은 명사를 수식할 단어가 필요한 자리이다. 보기에 형용사가 없을 경우, 같은 역할을 할 수 있는 분사를 찾아야 하며, 이때 분사와 명사 사이의 관계를 확인해야 한다. 초안 버전은 사람에 의해 '제안되는' 대상이므로 수동의 의미를 나타내는 과거분사 (C) suggested가 정답이다.

어휘 agree to ~에 동의하다 draft 초안 construction 공사, 건설 increase 증가하다, 오르다 by (차이) ~만큼, ~ 정도 over ~을 넘는 suggest ~을 제안하다, 권하다

115 해석 자연 애호가들은 국립 공원 바로 바깥쪽에 편리한 위치에 있는 포레스트 크릭 베드에 자주 머문다.

해설 〈부사 어휘〉
빈칸에 쓰이는 부사는 바로 뒤에 위치한 현재 시제 동사 stay를 수식하고 있는데, 현재 시제는 반복적인 습관 및 사실의 의미를 나타내므로 '자주, 빈번히'라는 의미로 이러한 현재 시제와 어울리는 부사인 (D) frequently가 정답이다.

어휘 enthusiast 애호가, 열성적인 팬 be located 위치해 있다 conveniently 편리하게 right outside ~ 바로 바깥쪽에 nearly 거의 originally 원래, 애초에 moderately 적정하게, 적당히 frequently 자주, 빈번히

116 해석 다가오는 회사 야유회가 다음 분기 동안 직원들이 생산적으로 일할 수 있도록 격려하는 시간이 되기를 바랍니다.

해설 〈부사 자리(자동사 뒤)〉
빈칸 앞에 to부정사로 쓰인 동사 work는 목적어를 필요로 하지 않는 자동사이다. 따라서 자동사와 전치사 over 사이에 위치한 빈칸은 자동사를 뒤에서 수식할 부사 자리이므로 (C) productively가 정답이다.

어휘 upcoming 다가오는, 곧 있을 retreat 야유회 hopefully 희망하여, 바라건대 encourage A to do A에게 ~하도록 격려하다, 권하다 over ~ 동안에 걸쳐 quarter 분기 productive 생산적인 productivity 생산성 productively 생산적으로 productiveness 생산적임, 다산

117 해석 버트 이노베이션즈 사는 웨어러블 기술에 대한 낮은 수요로 인해 새 스마트 안경 개발을 중단했다.

해설 〈명사 어휘〉
보기가 모두 명사이므로 의미가 알맞은 것을 찾아야 한다. low의 수식을 받을 수 있는 것으로서 높고 낮은 수준으로 표현 가능한 명사가 필

요하며, 제품 개발을 중단한 이유에 해당되면서 전치사 for와 어울릴 수 있는 명사여야 한다. 따라서 '수요'라는 의미로 이 조건들을 모두 만족하는 (C) demand가 정답이다.

어휘 stop -ing ~하는 것을 중단하다, 멈추다 develop ~을 개발하다 due to ~로 인해, ~ 때문에 wearable technology 웨어러블 기술 (IT 기술을 시계나 안경, 옷, 헬멧 등에 적용해 활용하는 기술) access 이용, 접근 population 인구 demand (for) (~에 대한) 수요, 요구 payment 지불(금)

118 해석 다큐멘터리가 90분 동안 지속되며, 나머지 시간은 질의 응답 시간으로 활용될 것입니다.

해설 〈현재분사 VS. 과거분사〉
정관사 the와 명사 time 사이에 위치한 빈칸은 명사를 수식할 단어가 필요한 자리이다. 보기에 형용사가 없으므로 명사를 수식하는 역할이 가능한 분사를 찾아야 하는데, remain은 자동사이기 때문에 현재분사의 형태로만 명사를 수식할 수 있다. 따라서 현재분사의 형태인 (C) remaining이 정답이다.

어휘 last v. 지속되다 question-and-answer session 질의 응답 시간 remain 남아 있다, 계속 ~한 상태이다 remaining 나머지의, 남은 remainder 나머지, 남은 것

119 해석 매일 영업 종료 시에, 크래프트 베이커리는 판매되지 않은 빵을 여러 자선 단체들 사이에서 나눠 준다.

해설 〈전치사 어휘〉
보기가 모두 전치사이므로 의미가 알맞은 것을 찾아야 한다. 빈칸 뒤에 위치한 복수 명사구는 '여러 자선 단체들'이라는 의미로, 판매되지 않고 남은 빵을 나눠 주는 대상에 해당된다. 따라서 '~ 사이에서'라는 의미로 복수 명사(구)를 목적어로 취해 분배 대상 혹은 범위를 나타낼 때 사용하는 (B) among이 정답이다. 동사 distribute은 distribute A among[to] B (A를 B사이에서[에게] 나눠 주다)의 형태로 주로 사용된다.

어휘 distribute ~을 나눠 주다, 분배하다 unsold 판매되지 않은 several 여럿의, 몇몇의 charity organization 자선 단체 beside ~ 옆에, ~ 곁에 among ~ 사이에 across ~을 가로질러, ~ 맞은편에, ~ 전역에 concerning ~와 관련해

120 해석 아메리칸 토털 버거 사는 지역별 입맛에 맞게 메뉴를 변경함으로써 전략적으로 아시아에 진출해 오고 있다.

해설 〈부사 자리(자동사 뒤)〉
빈칸 앞에 현재완료진행 시제로 쓰인 동사 expand는 자동사와 타동사로 모두 쓰일 수 있다. 그런데 보기에 제시된 명사 (A) strategy와 (C) strategist는 각각 '전략'과 '전략가'를 뜻하므로 특정 지역으로 진출시키거나 확장하는 대상으로 맞지 않는다. 따라서 빈칸은 명사 목적어 자리가 아니며, expand가 자동사로 쓰였음을 알 수 있다. 자동사와 전치사(into) 사이는 동사를 수식할 부사 자리이므로 (D) strategically가 정답이다.

어휘 expand into ~로 진출하다, ~로 사업을 확장하다 alter ~을 변경하다, 수정하다 by (방법) ~함으로써, ~해서 match ~에 맞추다, ~와 조화시키다 regional 지역의, 지방의 strategy 전략 strategic 전략

적인 strategist 전략가 strategically 전략적으로

121 해석 우드크래커 퍼니싱스 사는 매우 다양한 수제 가구 및 부대용품을 합리적인 가격에 제공한다.

해설 〈명사 어휘〉
보기가 모두 명사이므로 의미가 알맞은 것을 찾아야 한다. 빈칸 앞뒤에 각각 위치한 a diverse 및 of와 어울리는 명사로서 '매우 다양한, 다양하게 갖춰진'이라는 하나의 표현 덩어리를 구성할 때 사용하는 (B) selection이 정답이다.

어휘 offer ~을 제공하다 a diverse selection of 아주 다양한 handcrafted 수작업으로 제작된 accessories 부대용품 at a reasonable price 합리적인 가격에 position 자리, 위치, 입장, 직책 preference 선호(하는 것) experience 경험, 경력

122 해석 캐스퍼 웹 시큐리티 사는 사이버 위협 및 바이러스로부터 귀사의 네트워크를 보호하는 데 전념하고 있습니다.

해설 〈능동태/수동태〉
빈칸 앞뒤에 be동사 is와 전치사 to, 그리고 동명사(protecting)가 쓰여 있으므로 이 요소들과 어울려 '~하는 데 전념하다, 헌신하다'라는 표현 덩어리를 구성할 때 사용하는 (D) dedicated가 정답이다. 여기서 to가 전치사라는 것과 뒤에 동명사 목적어가 자주 쓰인다는 점도 함께 기억해 두는 것이 좋다.

어휘 be dedicated to -ing ~하는 데 전념하다, 헌신하다 protect A from B B로부터 A를 보호하다 threat 위협 dedication 전념, 헌신 dedicate (시간, 노력 등) ~을 바치다, 전념하다 dedicatedly 전념하여, 헌신적으로

123 해석 하트 씨는 스틸워크 은행 프로젝트에 대한 기여 덕분에 승진했다.

해설 〈명사 어휘〉
전치사 of 뒤에 위치한 contributions가 '기여, 공헌' 등을 의미하므로 승진의 이유를 나타낸다는 것을 알 수 있다. 따라서 빈칸 앞뒤에 각각 위치한 on the 그리고 of와 함께 '~로 인해, ~에 기반하여'라는 의미로 쓰이는 표현을 구성할 때 사용하는 (A) strength가 정답이다.

어휘 receive ~을 받다, 얻다 promotion 승진 on the strength of ~ 덕분에, ~로 인해, ~에 기반하여 contribution 기여, 공헌, 기부, 기고

124 해석 BNC 파이낸셜이 지속적으로 성장하는 경우 추가 사무 공간을 필요로 할 것이 분명하다.

해설 〈형용사 어휘〉
빈칸 앞뒤를 보면, 가주어 It과 진주어 that절로 구성된 문장임을 알 수 있다. 해당 구조 'It is ------- that ~' 자리에 위치할 수 있는 형용사 보어가 빈칸에 쓰여야 하므로 이 역할이 가능한 (B) apparent가 정답이다. 나머지 형용사들은 It is ~ that ~의 가주어/진주어 문장에서 보어로 쓰이지 않는다.

어휘 require ~을 필요로 하다 additional 추가적인 continue to do 지속적으로 ~하다, 계속 ~하다 grow 성장하다 adequate 충분한, 적절한 apparent 분명한 exceptional 우수한, 예외적인, 이례적인 profitable 수익성이 있는

125 해석 신입 사원들은 일주일간의 교육 워크숍에 참석하는 것 외에도 15페이지 분량의 보고서를 작성해야 합니다.

해설 〈전치사 어휘〉
보기가 모두 전치사이므로 의미가 알맞은 것을 찾아야 한다. 빈칸 앞뒤에 각각 제시된 '보고서 작성'과 '교육 워크숍 참석'은 모두 신입 사원들이 해야 하는 일인 것으로 볼 수 있다. 따라서 한 가지 의무 사항 뒤에 또 다른 의무 사항이 추가된 문장이므로 '~뿐만 아니라, ~ 외에도'라는 의미로 정보를 추가할 때 사용하는 (A) in addition to가 정답이다.

어휘 new recruit 신입 사원 be required to do ~해야 하다, ~할 필요가 있다 attend ~에 참석하다 training 교육, 훈련 in addition to ~뿐만 아니라, ~ 외에도 on behalf of ~을 대신해, 대표해 in accordance with ~에 따라, ~대로 as a result of ~에 따른 결과로

126 해석 심지어 가장 능력이 뛰어난 대중 연설가들도 대규모 기업 컨벤션 행사에서 발표하는 것에 대해 걱정한다.

해설 〈부사 어휘〉
각 보기의 품사가 다르므로 문장 구조부터 파악해야 한다. 빈칸 뒤에 명사구 주어 the most talented public speakers와 자동사 worry, 그리고 about 전치사구로 이어지는 완전한 문장이 쓰여 있으므로 빈칸은 부가적인 요소인 부사 자리이다. 또한 '심지어 가장 능력이 뛰어난 대중 연설가들도'와 같은 강조의 의미가 되어야 알맞으므로 '심지어 (~도)'를 뜻하는 부사 (B) Even이 정답이다. (A) Alike도 부사이지만 의미가 맞지 않으며, (C) Such는 형용사, (D) as는 전치사 또는 접속사로 쓰인다.

어휘 talented 능력 있는, 재능 있는 public speaker 대중 연설가 worry about ~을 걱정하다 present 발표하다 corporate 기업의 alike 똑같이, 마찬가지로 even 심지어 (~도) such 그러한, 그만큼, 그 정도의 as ~처럼, (자격, 신분 등) ~로서

127 해석 이전의 프로젝트에서 솔선수범한 직원들이 승진 대상으로 가장 크게 고려될 것입니다.

해설 〈명사 어휘〉
보기가 모두 명사이므로 의미가 알맞은 것을 찾아야 한다. 빈칸이 속한 who절은 승진 대상으로 고려되는 조건으로서 이전의 프로젝트에 대해 직원들이 한 일과 관련되어야 하므로 동사 take와 어울려 '솔선수범하다'라는 의미를 구성할 때 사용하는 (A) initiative가 정답이다.

어휘 take the initiative 솔선수범하다 previous 이전의, 과거의 receive the consideration for ~에 대해 고려되다 promotion 승진, 진급 requirement 요건, 필요 조건 advice 조언 restriction 제한, 제약

128 해석 연중 대부분의 기간을 해외에서 거주하는 사람들은 납세 신고를 할 때 연장된 마감 기한에 대한 자격이 있다.

해설 〈① 형용사 자리(관사와 명사 사이) ② 의미 혼동 형용사〉
부정관사 an과 명사 deadline 사이에 위치한 빈칸은 명사를 수식할 단어가 필요한 자리이다. 이 역할이 가능한 것으로서 보기에 형용사 (C) extensive와 과거분사 (D) extended가 쓰여 있는데, '마감 기한'을 뜻하는 deadline과 의미가 어울려야 하므로 '연장된'을 뜻하는 과거분사 (D) extended가 정답이다.

어휘 those who ~하는 사람들 **abroad** 해외에서 **during** ~ 동안 the **majority of** 대부분의, 대다수의 **qualify for** ~에 대한 자격이 있다 **deadline** 마감 기한 **file one's taxes** 납세 신고를 하다 **extend** ~을 연장하다 **extensive** 폭넓은, 광범위한

129 해석 폭풍우로 인한 피해 정도를 고려해 볼 때, 롱 비치 리조트는 아마 시즌 나머지 기간에 문을 계속 닫고 있을 것이다.

해설 〈전치사 VS. 접속사〉
각 보기가 부사와 접속사, 전치사로 구성되어 있으므로 문장 구조부터 파악해야 한다. 빈칸 뒤에 명사구 the extent of the damage from the storm이 쓰여 있고, 콤마 뒤로 주어와 동사(will remain)가 포함된 절이 이어지는 구조이다. 따라서 이 명사구를 목적어로 취할 전치사가 빈칸에 필요하며, '피해 규모를 고려해 볼 때'와 같이 판단 기준을 나타내는 의미가 되어야 알맞으므로 '~을 고려할 때, 감안할 때'를 뜻하는 전치사 (C) Given이 정답이다. (A) Just는 부사, (B) Provided는 접속사이며, (D) Like는 전치사이지만 의미가 맞지 않는다.

어휘 extent (중요성, 심각성 등의) 규모, 정도 damage 피해, 손해, 손상 likely 아마도 remain ~한 상태로 유지되다, 계속 ~한 상태이다 rest 나머지 provided (만약) ~라면 given ~을 고려할 때, 감안할 때

130 해석 스테파니 크레인 씨가 다음 주에 편집자와 만날 때쯤이면 자신의 소설 초안을 마무리 짓게 될 것이다.

해설 〈시제(미래 완료)〉
시간부사절 접속사인 by the time이 이끄는 절에 현재시제 동사 (meets)가 쓰이면 미래의 의미를 갖게 되는데, 이때 주절은 이보다 한 시점 이전을 나타내는 미래완료시제의 동사를 함께 사용하므로 (A) will have finished가 정답이다. 참고로 by the time이 이끄는 절에 과거시제 동사가 쓰이면, 주절에 과거완료시제 동사를 함께 사용한다.

어휘 first draft 초안 novel 소설 by the time ~할 때쯤이면 meet with (약속하여) ~와 만나다 editor 편집자

PART 6

P157

[131-134] 기사

더블린 (9월 3일) — **131** 제조 업계에서 아일랜드 최고의 기업 중 하나인 맥대니얼스 사가 가격 인하를 발표했다. 이 결정은 자사의 가전제품을 만드는 데 필요한 자재 비용의 감소로 인해 **132** 촉발되었다. 회사는 방금 자사의 웹 사이트를 업데이트했으며, 가격뿐만 아니라 특징까지 **133** 주목해 자사의 모든 제품을 살펴보도록 쇼핑객들에게 권하고 있다. 회사는 또한 향후 몇 개월 동안 여러 세일 행사를 개최할 예정이라고 발표하기도 했다. **134** 온라인 일정표에는 이 행사들에 대한 정확한 날짜가 나타나 있다. 이는 분명 쇼핑객들이 언제 훨씬 더 많은 비용을 절약할 수 있는지에 대해 알고 있도록 해 줄 것이다.

어휘 industry 업계 announce that ~라고 발표하다 lower ~을 낮추다, 내리다 decision 결정 reduction 감소, 인하, 할인 material 자재, 재료, 물품 appliance 가전 기기 encourage A to do A에게 ~하도록 권하다, 장

려하다 take note of ~에 주목하다, 유의하다 not only A but also B A 뿐만 아니라 B도 feature 특징 hold ~을 개최하다 several 여럿의, 몇몇의 guarantee that ~임을 보장하다, 보증하다 be aware of ~을 인식하고 있다, 알고 있다 even (비교급 수식) 훨씬 saving 비용 절약, 저축(한 돈)

131 해설 〈명사 어휘(문맥)〉
빈칸은 바로 뒤에 위치한 명사 industry와 복합 명사를 구성해 McDaniel's라는 회사가 속한 업계를 나타낼 단어가 필요한 자리이다. 뒤에 이어지는 문장을 보면, 이 회사가 가전제품(appliances)을 만든다고 쓰여 있으므로 제조 업계에 속한 회사임을 알 수 있다. 따라서 '제조'를 뜻하는 (B) manufacturing이 정답이다.

어휘 clothing 의류 manufacturing 제조 finance 금융, 재정, 재무 publishing 출판

132 해설 〈시제(문맥)〉
각 보기가 모두 수동태 동사의 형태이고 시제만 다르므로 시제 관련 단서부터 찾아야 한다. 빈칸 앞에 위치한 This decision(결정)은 앞 문장에서 말한 발표 내용을 가리키는데 결정이 내려진 시점은 과거 시제 announced와 같은 과거 시점에 이뤄진 일이어야 하므로 동일한 과거 시제인 (C) was prompted가 정답이다.

어휘 prompt ~을 촉발하다, 촉구하다

133 해설 〈분사구문〉
해당 문장은 두 개의 동사 updated와 encourages가 등위 접속사인 and를 통해 연결된 구조이므로, 빈칸에는 동사가 아닌 다른 품사가 쓰여야 한다. 따라서, 유일하게 동사가 아닌 보기인 (D) taking이 정답이다. 문장에서 taking은 분사구문을 이끄는 현재분사의 형태로 쓰였다. (A) take와 (B) takes는 현재 시제 동사이며 (C) took은 과거 시제 동사이다.

134 (A) 맥대니얼스는 앞으로 몇 달 동안 추가 매장을 개장하기를 바라고 있다.
(B) 온라인 일정표에는 이 행사들에 대한 정확한 날짜가 나타나 있다.
(C) 고객들이 최근 맥대니얼스에 대해 긍정적으로 이야기해 오고 있다.
(D) 가장 최근의 캠페인이 회사에 기록적인 수익이라는 결과를 낳았다.

해설 〈빈칸에 알맞은 문장 넣기〉
바로 앞 문장에 여러 세일 행사(several sales)를 개최할 예정이라고 알리는 말이 쓰여 있으므로 이 행사들을 these events로 언급해 행사 개최 날짜를 확인하는 방법을 언급한 (B)가 정답이다. 또한 빈칸 뒤의 This should guarantee ~ 문장 역시 (B)에서 언급된 내용과 흐름상 연결이 자연스럽다. 나머지 문장들은 앞선 문장과 관련 없는 의미를 지니고 있어 흐름상 어울리지 않는다.

어휘 calendar 일정표 precise 정확한 positively 긍정적으로 lately 최근에 recent 최근의 result in ~의 결과를 낳다, ~을 야기하다 revenue 수익

[135-138] 이메일

수신: 웬디 로버트슨 〈w.robertson@newtonspring.com〉
발신: 울트 덴 짐 〈mark@wolfdengym.com〉
날짜: 4월 1일
제목: 체육관 회원 자격

로버트슨 씨께,

귀하께서는 회원 자격이 이달 말에 갱신될 때 등급 변경을 요청하셨습니다. 5월 1일부터, 귀하의 월간 회비는 프리미엄 등급에서 일반 등급으로의 변경을 반영해 19.99달러로 **135** 인하될 것입니다. 이달 **136** 말까지는 계속해서 무제한 현장 강습 시간에 참석하실 수 있습니다. 전문 트레이너의 도움을 받아 운동하실 수 있는 시간이 마지막으로 한 번 진행될 것입니다. 언제든 프리미엄으로 다시 등급을 **137** 변경하기를 원하시는 경우, 저희 울프 덴 직원에게 말씀하시거나 이 이메일에 답장하시기만 하면 됩니다. 각 회원 자격 단계에 대한 다양한 혜택을 설명해 드리는 안내 책자를 한 부 첨부해 드렸습니다. **138** 그것들과 관련해 어떤 질문이든 있으실 경우, 언제든지 저에게 연락 주시기 바랍니다.

안녕히 계십시오.

마크 윌리엄스

어휘 request ~을 요청하다, 요구하다 status 등급, 지위, 상태 renew ~을 갱신하다 fee 요금 reflect ~을 반영하다 continue to do 계속 ~하다 attend ~에 참석하다 unlimited 무제한의 onsite 현장의 (특정 활동을 위한) session 시간 work out 운동하다 assistance 도움, 지원 at any time 언제든지 reply to ~에 답장하다 attach ~을 첨부하다 brochure 안내 책자, 소책자 explain ~을 설명하다 benefit 혜택, 이득 tier 단계, 등급

135 해설 〈시제(문맥)〉
해당 문장에 동사가 없으므로 빈칸이 문장의 동사 자리임을 알 수 있다. 또한 회비 인하가 시작되는 시점을 나타내는 From May 1이 지문 상단의 이메일 작성 날짜인 April 1보다 미래 시점에 해당되므로 미래 시제 동사인 (C) will decrease가 정답이다.

어휘 must have p.p. ~한 것이 틀림없다 decrease 인하되다, 하락하다

136 해설 〈전치사 어휘〉
빈칸 뒤에 위치한 시점 명사구 the end of this month를 목적어로 취할 전치사가 필요한데, 해당 시점까지 계속 무제한 현장 강습을 이용할 수 있다는 의미가 적합하므로 '~까지'라는 의미로 지속의 개념을 나타내는 전치사 (A) until이 정답이다.

어휘 until (지속) ~까지 since ~ 이후로

137 해설 〈부정사〉
빈칸 앞에 위치한 would like는 to부정사와 결합해 '~하기를 원하다, ~하고자 하다'라는 의미를 나타내므로 (D) to change가 정답이다.

138 (A) 저희는 장비를 구입하거나 업그레이드하기 위해 모든 여유 자금을 사용합니다.
(B) 사물함은 소액의 비용을 내시면 한 달 단위로 대여될 수 있습니다.
(C) 그것들과 관련해 어떤 질문이든 있으실 경우, 언제든지 저에게 연락 주시

기 바랍니다.

(D) 대신, 주간 강습 일정표를 다운로드해 이용하실 수 있을 것입니다.

해설 〈빈칸에 알맞은 문장 넣기〉
빈칸 앞 문장에 다양한 혜택(various benefits)을 설명하는 안내 책자를 첨부했다고 알리는 말이 쓰여 있으므로 various benefits를 them으로 지칭해 그 혜택들과 관련된 질문이 있을 경우에 취할 수 있는 조치를 알리는 (C)가 정답이다. 나머지 문장들은 앞선 문장에 언급된 정보와 관련 없는 내용을 담고 있다.

어휘 surplus 잉여의, 여분의 fund 자금 equipment 장비 rent ~을 대여하다 on a monthly basis 한 달 단위로 please feel free to do 언제든 ~하시기 바랍니다 contact ~에게 연락하다 instead 대신 available 이용 가능한

[139-142] 기사

5월 3일 – 전국 각지에서 행사들이 개최되는 가운데, VC 푸즈 사가 어제 스포츠 음료 신제품 라인을 **139** 출시했습니다. '파워 플러스'라고 불리는 이 음료들은 운동 중에 손실되는 것을 대체해 주는 필수 무기질과 함께 카페인이 들어 있어 에너지 촉진 효과를 제공해 줍니다. 제품 개발의 **140** 일환으로, VC 푸즈 사는 대상 소비자인 젊은 운동 선수들로부터 의견을 제공받았습니다. **141** 이는 회사가 시장을 더 잘 이해하는 데 도움을 주었습니다. 이 회사는 해당 음료가 지닌 고유한 특징을 강조하기 위해 소셜 미디어와 텔레비전 **142** 그리고 여러 잡지에 광고를 운영하고 있습니다. 조직화된 이 캠페인은 분명 향후 몇 달 동안 '파워 플러스'의 매출을 증대할 것입니다.

어휘 with A p.p. A가 ~되면서, A가 ~된 채로 hold ~을 개최하다 throughout ~ 전역에 걸쳐 beverage 음료 provide ~을 제공하다 boost 촉진, 증진, 향상 along with ~와 함께 essential 필수적인 mineral 무기질 replace ~을 대체하다 lost 손실된, 잃어버린, 사라진 while ~하는 동안 exercise 운동하다 develop ~을 개발하다 feedback 의견 target consumer 대상 소비자 athlete 운동 선수 run ~을 운영하다, 진행하다 ad 광고 highlight ~을 강조하다, 집중 조명하다 unique 고유의, 특별한 feature 특징, 기능 coordinated 조직화된, 조정된 be sure to do 분명 ~하다 fuel v. ~을 증대하다, 촉진하다

139 해설 〈동사 어휘〉
빈칸 앞에는 회사 이름이 주어로, 빈칸 뒤에는 스포츠 음료 신제품 라인을 뜻하는 명사구가 목적어로 쓰여 있다. 따라서 회사가 자사의 제품과 관련해 할 수 있는 일을 나타낼 동사가 필요하므로 '출시하다'를 뜻하는 launch의 과거 시제인 (D) launched가 정답이다.

어휘 sample v. ~을 시음하다, 시식하다 follow ~을 따르다, 준수하다, 따라 가다 hire ~을 고용하다 launch ~을 출시하다, 공개하다

140 해설 〈전치사 어휘〉
빈칸 뒤에 이어지는 내용을 보면, 소비자들에게 의견을 구한 사실이 쓰여 있다. 이는 제품 개발의 한 과정에 해당되므로 빈칸 뒤에 위치한 part of와 결합해 '~의 일환으로, 일부로서'라는 의미를 구성할 때 사용하는 전치사 (A) As가 정답이다.

141 (A) 제품 맛에 대한 목록이 아직 공개되지 않았습니다.
(B) 이는 회사가 시장을 더 잘 이해하는 데 도움을 주었습니다.
(C) 더 많은 사람들이 체육관 대신 집에서 운동하고 있습니다.
(D) 그것이 해당 스포츠 경기 대회의 결승전이 될 것입니다.

해설 〈빈칸에 알맞은 문장 넣기〉
빈칸 앞 문장의 제품 개발의 일환으로 소비자들에게 의견을 구한 일이 쓰여 있으므로 이러한 사실을 This로 지칭해 그러한 일에 따른 긍정적인 결과를 언급한 (B)가 정답이다. 나머지 문장들은 앞 문장에서 말하는 제품 개발의 한 과정 또는 다음 문장에 제시되는 광고 전략과 관련 없는 내용을 담고 있다.

어휘 flavor 맛, 풍미 reveal ~을 공개하다, 드러내다 work out 운동하다 rather than ~ 대신, ~가 아니라 final round 결승전 competition 경기, 대회

142 해설 〈병렬 구조〉
빈칸 앞뒤 부분을 보면, 광고를 운영하는 방식과 관련된 세 가지 전치사구 on social media와 on television, 그리고 in magazines가 차례로 나열되는 구조이다. 따라서 빈칸에 동일 요소를 나열할 때 사용하는 등위 접속사가 필요하므로 (C) and가 정답이다. '또한, ~도' 등을 뜻하는 (A) also는 부사이므로 동일 요소를 연결하는 역할을 하지 못한다.

어휘 either (A or B) (A 또는 B) 둘 중의 하나

[143-146] 편지

알린 마데라
플로렌스 컨설팅, 314호 사무실
블랙웰 스트리트 441번지
마이애미, FL 33146

마데라 씨께,

귀사의 재정 자문 일자리에 지원하신 테런스 프리드먼 **143** 씨를 대신해 편지를 씁니다. 세롤로 투자회사의 한 부서장으로서, 저는 지난 3년간 프리드먼 씨의 직속 상관이었습니다. 이 기간 중에, 프리드먼 씨는 고객들의 특정 요구 사항과 관련된 전문적인 조언을 제공해 드리기 위해 열심히 노력했습니다. **144** 프리드먼 씨는 또한 지식을 향상시키기 위해 전문 능력 개발 시간에도 참가했습니다. 더욱이, 훌륭한 서비스에 대한 프리드먼 씨의 평판이 저희 고객층을 상당히 확대하는 데 있어 저희에게 도움이 되었습니다. 프리드먼 씨는 항상 자신의 **145** 책임을 수행하는 데 있어 전문가다웠고 신속했으며, 팀 내 모든 사람이 그와 함께 일하는 것을 즐거워했습니다. 프리드먼 씨가 어떤 팀이든 훌륭한 보탬이 될 것이라는 데 의심의 여지가 **146** 없습니다.

안녕히 계십시오.

제임스 리
세롤로 투자회사

어휘 apply for ~에 지원하다, ~을 신청하다 financial advisor 재정 자문 position 일자리, 직책 firm 회사 immediate supervisor 직속 상관 provide ~을 제공하다 expert a. 전문적인, 전문가의 related to ~와 관

련된 specific 특정한, 구체적인 moreover 더욱이, 게다가 reputation 평판, 명성 client base 고객층 significantly 상당히, 많이 prompt 신속한, 즉각적인, 지체 없는 carry out ~을 수행하다, 이행하다 doubt 의심, 의혹 make an addition to ~에 보탬이 되다

143 해설 〈전치사 어휘〉
빈칸 뒤에 이어지는 내용을 보면, 프리드먼 씨가 상대방 회사에 지원한 사실과 함께 글쓴이 자신이 프리드먼 씨의 직속 상관이었음을 알리는 말이 쓰여 있다. 따라서 다른 회사에 지원하는 테런스 프리드먼 씨를 대신해 보내는 편지임을 알 수 있으므로 '~을 위하여, ~을 대신해'를 뜻하는 (C) on behalf of가 정답이다.

어휘 in case of ~의 경우에 in exchange for ~에 대한 대가로, ~와 교환해 on behalf of ~을 대신해, 대표해 except for ~을 제외하고

144 (A) 프리드먼 씨는 귀하의 투자 포트폴리오를 20퍼센트 넘게 늘려 드릴 수 있었습니다.
(B) 프리드먼 씨는 또한 지식을 향상시키기 위해 전문 능력 개발 시간에도 참가했습니다.
(C) 프리드먼 씨는 재무 관련 학업 프로그램으로 알려져 있는 명문 대학을 졸업했습니다.
(D) 프리드먼 씨는 가족으로서의 의무로 인해 다음 달에 새로운 도시로 자리를 옮길 것입니다.

해설 〈빈칸에 알맞은 문장 넣기〉
빈칸 앞 문장에는 프리드먼 씨가 고객들에게 전문적인 조언을 제공하기 위해 노력한 사실이, 빈칸 뒤에는 프리드먼 씨의 좋은 평판이 회사에 큰 도움이 된 사실이 각각 제시되어 있다. 이는 프리드먼 씨의 뛰어난 능력을 말하는 흐름에 해당되므로 'also'와 함께 프리드먼 씨가 가진 직원으로서의 또 다른 장점을 언급하는 (B)가 정답이다. 앞 문장에 언급된 During that time(이 기간 중에)은 프리드먼 씨와 함께 일한 지난 3년을 뜻하는데, 빈칸 역시 해당 기간 동안에 있었던 일을 언급하는 흐름이므로 대학 졸업과 관련된 내용을 담은 (C)는 적절치 않다.

어휘 be able to do ~할 수 있다 increase ~을 늘리다, 증가시키다 investment portfolio 투자 포트폴리오(투자한 상품 등에 관해 정리해 보유하고 있는 것) by (차이) ~만큼, ~ 정도 over ~ 넘게 participate in ~에 참가하다 professional development 전문 능력 개발 improve ~을 향상시키다, 개선하다 graduate from ~을 졸업하다 prestigious 명문의, 명망 있는 known for ~로 알려져 있는 finance 재무, 재정 relocate to ~로 자리를 옮기다, 이전하다 due to ~로 인해 obligation 의무

145 해설 〈명사 어휘〉
보기가 모두 명사이므로 의미가 알맞은 것을 찾아야 한다. 빈칸에 쓰일 명사는 동명사구 carrying out의 목적어로서 수행 또는 이행하는 업무를 나타내야 하므로 '책임, 책무' 등을 뜻하는 (D) responsibilities가 정답이다.

어휘 perspective 관점, 시각 performance 수행 능력, 성과, 실적 responsibility 책임, 책무

146 해설 〈수량 형용사〉
지문 전체적으로 프리드먼 씨의 좋은 점을 설명하고 있으므로 빈칸이

속한 문장은 '프리드먼 씨가 훌륭한 보탬이 될 것이라는 데 의심의 여지가 없다'와 같은 뜻이 되어야 알맞으므로 (A) no가 정답이다. 참고로, few도 부정의 의미를 내포하고 있지만 셀 수 있는 명사의 복수형을 수식해야 하므로 오답이다.

어휘 few (셀 수 있는 명사의 복수형 수식) 거의 없는 a little 약간의, 조금 있는

PART 7

P161

[147-148] 영수증

> 영수증 번호: 83389-47893
>
> (이 영수증은 오직 참고용입니다. 행사 당일에 비용 지불 증명용으로 가져오실 필요가 없습니다.)
>
> 리젠트 서점에서 참가비로 10달러를 수납함
>
> xxxx-8865로 번호가 끝나는 신용카드로 청구됨
>
> ⑭ 신용카드 소지자 성명: 멜라니 아노트
>
> ⑭ 상세 설명: 클레어 펠 씨가 7월 5일 일요일 오후 2시에 자신의 소설 〈사이드웨이 글랜스〉의 발췌 내용을 낭독해 드립니다.
>
> 공지사항: ⑭ 이미 〈사이드웨이 글랜스〉를 구입하신 분이시라면, 지참하고 오셔서 행사 종료 시에 펠 씨로부터 사인을 받으실 수 있습니다. 이 도서는 매장에서 16.95달러에 구매하실 수도 있습니다.

어휘 receipt 영수증 reference 참고 proof 증명(서) payment 지불(금) attendance fee 참가비 receive ~을 받다 charge A to B A를 B에게 청구하다 ending in (번호 등이) ~로 끝나는 holder 소지자, 보유자 details 상세 설명, 세부 사항 excerpt 발췌(본) purchase ~을 구매하다 along with ~와 함께 have A p.p. A가 ~되게 하다

147 아노트 씨는 7월 5일에 무엇을 할 계획인가?
(A) 신용카드 회사에 비용 지불하기
(B) 특별 낭독 행사에 참석하기
(C) 신간 소설 구매하기
(D) 서점에 전화하기

해설 〈세부 사항〉
7월 5일이라는 날짜가 제시되는 문장을 살펴보면 클레어 펠 씨가 7월 5일 오후 2시에 자신이 쓴 소설의 일부를 낭독하는(~ will read excerpts from her novel Sideways Glances on Sunday, July 5 ~) 행사를 한다고 쓰여 있다. 따라서 신용카드 소지자(Credit Card Holder), 즉 이 영수증의 소지자로 제시된 아노트 씨는 이 행사에 참석할 것으로 판단할 수 있으므로 (B)가 정답이다.

148 아노트 씨는 무엇을 지참하도록 권고 받는가?
(A) 은행 카드
(B) 유효한 신분증
(C) 책 한 권

(D) 지불 영수증

해설 〈세부 사항〉
요청사항이 언급되는 마지막 단락에, 소설책 〈사이드웨이 글랜스〉를 구입한 경우 지참하도록 오도록(If you have already purchased Sideways Glances, you may bring it ~) 알리고 있으므로 책 한 권을 의미하는 (C)가 정답이다.

어휘 receipt 수령, 영수증

[149-150] 광고

> **캠핑 익스프레스**
>
> ⑭ 8월 1일부터, 저희는 캠핑 익스프레스 웹 사이트를 통해 주문하시는 제품에 대해 무료 매장 픽업 서비스를 허용해 드립니다. 이 옵션을 이용하시려면, 온라인 주문 사항에 대한 배송 페이지에서 "매장 내 픽업" 항목을 선택하신 다음, 선호하시는 지점을 선정하시기만 하면 됩니다. 제품이 준비되면 이메일을 받으시게 됩니다. ⑮ 매장 내 고객 서비스 데스크로 가셔서 그곳에 있는 직원들 중 한 명에게 ⑮ 확인용 코드를 제공하시기만 하면 됩니다. 또한 해당 제품을 가져가셨다는 것을 보여주는 ⑮ 제품 양도 서식에도 서명해 주셔야 할 것입니다.

어휘 allow ~을 허용하다, 가능하게 하다 free 무료의 in-store 매장 내의 pickup 가져가기, 가져오기 take advantage of ~을 이용하다 choose ~을 선택하다 select ~을 선정하다 preferred 선호하는 location 지점, 위치 receive ~을 받다 provide ~을 제공하다 confirmation 확인(서) put one's signature on ~에 서명하다 release form 양도 서식

149 8월 1일에 무슨 일이 있을 것인가?
(A) 매장이 기념일을 축하할 것이다.
(B) 매장 정리 세일 행사가 시작될 것이다.
(C) 서비스 변동 사항이 효력을 발생할 것이다.
(D) 새로운 캠핑용품 브랜드가 이용 가능할 것이다.

해설 〈세부 사항〉
8월 1일이라는 날짜가 언급되는 첫 문장에, 8월 1일부터 웹 사이트를 통해 주문하는 제품에 대해 무료 매장 픽업 서비스를 실시한다고(Starting August 1, we will allow free in-store pickup for items ~) 알리고 있다. 이는 이전과 다른 새 정책, 즉 서비스 변동 사항을 알리는 말에 해당되므로 (C)가 정답이다.

어휘 occur 발생되다, 일어나다 celebrate ~을 축하하다, 기념하다 anniversary 기념일 clearance sale 정리 세일 행사 go into effect 효력을 발생하다, 발효되다 available 이용 가능한

150 제품을 가져가는 것의 단계로 언급되지 않은 것은 무엇인가?
(A) 매장에서 서식에 서명하기
(B) 고객 서비스 데스크 방문하기
(C) 확인 코드 제시하기
(D) 캠핑 익스프레스에 이메일 발송하기

해설 〈진위 확인 (세부 진위 유형)〉
지문 후반부의 '~ put your signature on a release form ~' 부분에서 서식에 서명하는 것을 뜻하는 (A)를, '~ go to the store's

---

customer service counter ~' 부분에서 고객 서비스 데스크 방문을 뜻하는 (B)를 확인할 수 있다. 또한 '~ provide the confirmation code ~' 부분에서 확인 코드를 제시하는 것을 말하는 (C)도 확인 가능하다. 하지만 이메일을 발송하는 일은 언급되어 있지 않으므로 (D)가 정답이다.

어휘 pick up ~을 가져가다, 가져오다 form 서식, 양식 present ~을 제시하다 confirmation 확인(서)

[151-152] 이메일

> 수신: 마르셀라 에스코바르 〈marcella_e@nuzompost.com〉
> 발신: 랜스 아얄라 〈l_ayala@brentwoodbi.com〉
> 날짜: 3월 8일
> 제목: 브렌트우드 비즈니스 협회 워크숍
>
> 에스코바르 씨께
>
> ⑮ 다가오는 비즈니스 워크숍을 준비하는 브렌트우드 비즈니스 협회의 기획팀을 대표해, 귀하의 등록에 대해 감사드리고자 합니다. 저희는 귀하께서 워크숍 기간 중에 아주 많은 것을 배우실 수 있기를 바랍니다. 귀하께서는 우편으로 환영 책자 묶음을 받으시게 됩니다. 오실 때 유마 컨퍼런스 센터로 해당 책자 묶음의 모든 자료를 지참하고 오시기 바랍니다. 워크숍은 오전 9시에 시작되며, 건물 내 주차 서비스를 이용하실 수 있습니다. ⑮ 워크숍에 참석하시는 동안 문서 복사나 스캔 작업, 또는 무언가 인쇄하셔야 하는 경우, 직원들에게 워크숍 참석자 신분증을 보여주시면, 직원들이 1층에 위치한 비즈니스 센터를 이용하도록 해 드릴 것입니다. 곧 뵐 수 있기를 고대합니다.
>
> 랜스 아얄라

어휘 on behalf of ~을 대표해, 대신해 planning 기획 upcoming 다가오는, 곧 있을 registration 등록 learn a great deal 아주 많은 것을 배우다 receive ~을 받다 packet 책자 묶음 material 자료, 재료, 물품 parking 주차 available 이용 가능한 on-site 건물 내에, 구내에 while ~하는 동안 attend ~에 참석하다 allow A to do A가 ~할 수 있게 해 주다 look forward to -ing ~하기를 고대하다

151 누가 이메일을 보냈을 것 같은가?
(A) 행사 기획 책임자
(B) 건물 소유주
(C) 채용 담당자
(D) 택배 회사

해설 〈주제 및 목적〉
지문 첫 문장에 워크숍을 준비하는 기획팀을 대표해 행사 등록에 대해 감사한다는(On behalf of Brentwood Business Institute's planning team for the upcoming business workshop ~) 말이 쓰여 있다. 따라서, 발신인은 행사 기획을 맡고 있는 주최 측 중 한 사람인 것으로 판단할 수 있으므로 (A)가 정답이다.

152 왜 신분증이 제시되어야 하는가?
(A) 주차에 대해 환불을 받기 위해
(B) 예약된 자리를 요청하기 위해

(C) 일부 사무용 장비를 이용하기 위해
(D) 무대 공간에 출입하기 위해

해설 〈세부 사항〉
신분증 제시와 관련된 정보가 언급된 후반부에, 문서 복사 등의 작업이 필요할 때 직원에게 워크숍 참석자 신분증을 보여주면 비즈니스 센터를 이용할 수 있다고(If you need to make copies or scans of documents, ~ you can show your workshop ID to the staff, and they will allow you to use the business center ~) 알리고 있다. 이는 해당 사무용 장비를 이용하는 방법을 말해 주는 것이므로 (C)가 정답이다.

어휘 present ~을 제시하다, 제공하다 refund 환불 parking 주차 claim ~을 요청하다, 신청하다 reserved 예약된 access ~을 이용하다, ~에 접근하다 equipment 장비

[153-155] 초대장

153 허벨 테크 사에 투자해 주신 것에 대한 감사의 뜻으로, 저희 연례 감사 연회 행사에 정중히 초대합니다.

12월 8일, 금요일

155 세르반테스 홀

제네바 스트리트 163번지

솔트레이크시티, UT 84116

오후 6:00 출입문 개방, 칵테일 제공
오후 7:00 베일리 켄델 대표의 연설
오후 7:30 뷔페 저녁 식사, 라이브 음악

154 배우자 또는 친구분을 동반하고 오셔도 좋습니다.

참석 여부 회답을 위해, 555-9762번으로 행사 기획자 말라 소우자 씨에게 전화 주십시오. 주차 및 행사장으로 찾아오시는 길 등과 관련된 정보를 원하시면, **155** 555-1133번으로 테오 던컨 씨에게 전화하셔서 행사장으로 직접 연락하시기 바랍니다.

어휘 invest in ~에 투자하다 you are cordially invited to ~에 정중히 초대합니다 annual 연례적인, 해마다의 appreciation 감사(의 뜻) banquet 연회 serve (음식 등) ~을 제공하다, 내오다 Please feel free to do ~하셔도 좋습니다, 마음껏 ~하세요 have A do A를 ~하게 하다 spouse 배우자 accompany ~와 동반하다, 동행하다 RSVP (행사 등의) 참석 여부 회답 parking 주차 directions to ~로 찾아 가는 길, 방법 etc. ~ 등등 contact ~에게 연락하다 venue 행사장, 개최지 directly 직접, 곧장 by (방법) ~함으로써, ~하는 것으로

153 12월 8일에 왜 행사가 개최될 것인가?
(A) 투자자들에게 감사의 뜻을 표현하기 위해
(B) 회사의 창립 기념일을 축하하기 위해
(C) 몇몇 직원 상을 수여하기 위해
(D) 새로운 서비스를 발표하기 위해

해설 〈세부 사항〉

초대장 상단에 투자한 것에 대한 감사의 뜻으로 연례 감사 연회 행사에 초대한다고(As a thank-you for investing in Hubbell Tech, you are cordially invited ~) 알리고 있으므로 (A)가 정답이다.

어휘 hold ~을 개최하다 express (생각, 감정 등) ~을 표현하다 gratitude 감사(의 마음) investor 투자자 celebrate ~을 축하하다, 기념하다 anniversary 기념일 present ~을 주다, 제공하다

154 초대장은 초청객에게 무엇을 하도록 권하는가?
(A) 기부금 내기
(B) 행사 기획자 만나기
(C) 후보 지명자 이름 제출하기
(D) 손님 모시고 오기

해설 〈세부 사항〉
초대장 하단에 배우자나 친구를 동반하고 와도 좋다고(Please feel free to have your spouse or a friend accompany you) 권하는 내용이 있으므로 (D)가 정답이다.

어휘 encourage A to do A에게 ~하도록 권하다, 장려하다 make a donation 기부하다 organizer 기획자, 주최자 submit ~을 제출하다 nomination 후보 지명

155 던컨 씨에 관해 암시된 것은 무엇인가?
(A) 켄델 씨 다음으로 연설할 것이다.
(B) 행사에서 음악을 연주할 것이다.
(C) 행사용 음식을 선정했다.
(D) 세르반테스 홀 직원이다.

해설 〈진위 확인 (세부 진위 유형)〉
던컨 씨의 이름이 언급되는 마지막 문장을 보면, 555-1133번으로 테오 던컨 씨에게 전화해서 행사장으로 직접 연락하라고 알리는 말이 있는데, 상단에 행사장 명칭이 세르반테스 홀이라고(at Cervantes Hall) 표기되어 있으므로 던컨 씨는 그곳 직원인 것으로 판단할 수 있다. 따라서 이를 언급한 (D)가 정답이다.

어휘 give a speech 연설하다

[156-158] 정보

캔들라이트 리조트
브리스톨, 잉글랜드
객실 정보

156 저희 캔들라이트 리조트에서, 고객 여러분은 각 객실에서 최상의 편의시설과 최고 수준의 청결함을 기대하실 수 있습니다. 저희는 추가 비용 없이 뛰어난 와이파이 서비스를 제공해 드립니다. 각 객실에는 대형 평면 텔레비전과 뛰어난 경관이 보이는 발코니, 그리고 월풀 욕조가 갖춰져 있습니다. 게다가, 룸서비스 식사는 저희 에버그린 레스토랑에서 주문하실 수 있습니다.

157 저희 시설 관리 직원들은 매일 철저하게 객실을 청소해 드릴 것입니다. **157** 이 직원들은 또한 추가 서비스를 제공해 드리기 위해 24시간 대기하고 있습니다. 엎질러진 것이 치워져야 하거나, 비누나 샴푸, 또는 별도의 타월과 같이 객실에 추가 물품이 필요하신 경우 객실 전화로 8번을 누르기만 하시면 됩니다. 저희 직원들은 편안함 및 서비스와 관련해 여러분의 필요 사항을 **158** 충족시켜 드릴 수 있도록 많은 교육을 받습니다.

객실과 관련된 질문 또는 불만 사항이 있으실 경우, 주저하지 마시고 프런트 데스크에 연락하시기 바라며, 이는 객실 전화로 0번을 눌러 하실 수 있습니다. 즐거운 숙박이 되시기 바라며, 그렇게 하기 위해 저희는 할 수 있는 모든 것을 다 할 것입니다. 저희 캔들라이트 리조트를 선택해 주셔서 감사합니다.

어휘 expect ~을 기대하다, 예상하다 amenities 편의시설 the highest standard of 최고 수준의 cleanliness 청결함 at no additional cost 추가 비용 없이 be equipped with ~을 갖추고 있다 stunning 눈부시게 아름다운 whirlpool bathtub (물이 소용돌이 모양으로 움직이는) 월풀 욕조 in addition 게다가 thoroughly 철저히 around the clock 24시간 provide A with B A에게 B를 제공하다 have A p.p. A가 ~되게 하다 spill 엎지른 것 require ~을 필요로 하다 extra 별도의, 추가의 highly 크게, 대단히, 매우 train ~을 교육하다 regarding ~와 관련해 comfort 편안함 complaint 불만 hesitate to do ~하기를 주저하다 contact ~에게 연락하다 pleasant 즐거운, 기분 좋은 make A do A가 ~하게 만들다 choose ~을 선택하다

156 이 정보는 누구를 위해 쓰여졌을 것 같은가?
(A) 에버그린 레스토랑 직원들
(B) 브리스톨 시 관계자들
(C) 캔들라이트 리조트 고객들
(D) 신입 시설 관리 직원들

해설 〈글의 대상〉
첫 단락 시작 부분에 고객들이 이 리조트에서 기대할 수 있는(At Candlelight Resort, guests can expect ~) 것을 언급한 뒤로 여러 서비스를 이용하는 방법 등과 관련된 정보가 제시되고 있으므로 (C)가 정답이다.

어휘 official n. 관계자, 당국자

157 시설 관리부에 관해 언급된 것은 무엇인가?
(A) 제한된 숫자의 타월을 갖고 있다.
(B) 추가 직원을 모집할 것이다.

(C) 최근에 정책을 변경했다.

(D) 언제든지 연락받을 수 있다.

해설 〈진위 확인 (세부 진위 유형)〉
시설 관리부 직원이 언급된 두 번째 단락에, 24시간 대기하고 있다는 (Our housekeeping staff ~ They are also ready around the clock ~) 말이 쓰여 있는데, 이는 언제든지 연락 가능하다는 뜻이므로 (D)가 정답이다.

어휘 limited 제한된 recruit ~을 모집하다 recently 최근에 policy 정책, 방침 contact ~에게 연락하다 anytime 언제든지

158 두 번째 단락 네 번째 줄의 단어 "meet"과 의미가 가장 가까운 것은 무엇인가?
(A) 조립하다
(B) 마주치다
(C) 완수하다
(D) 소개하다

해설 〈동의어〉
해당 문장에서 meet의 목적어로 your needs가 쓰여 있는 것으로 볼 때, '필요한 것을 충족시키다'와 같은 의미가 되어야 한다는 것을 알 수 있다. 즉 고객들이 필요로 하는 일을 완전히 처리해 준다는 뜻으로 볼 수 있으므로 이와 유사한 의미를 지닌 동사로 '완수하다'를 뜻하는 (C) fulfill이 정답이다.

[159-160] 문자 메시지 대화

> **[오후 3:32] 노라 볼드윈**
> 로자리오 씨, 회의에서 나오시면 저에게 문자 메시지 좀 보내 주시겠어요?
>
> **[오후 3:33] 로자리오 트렌티니**
> 이미 끝났어요. 무슨 일이시죠?
>
> **[오후 3:34] 159 노라 볼드윈**
> 우리의 신규 고객이신 앤젤라 한 씨에게 몇몇 샘플을 보내 드리기 위해 우체국에 와 있습니다. 159 그런데 제가 전체 주소를 적어 놓지 않았다는 사실을 알게 되었어요.
>
> **[오후 3:35] 로자리오 트렌티니**
> 어딘가에서 찾아봐 드릴까요?
>
> **[오후 3:36] 노라 볼드윈**
> 네. 160 제 사무실 파일 캐비닛에 있을 거예요.
>
> **[오후 3:41] 로자리오 트렌티니**
> 여기 파일 캐비닛이 다섯 개 있어요.
>
> **[오후 3:42] 노라 볼드윈**
> 160 죄송해요. 제가 말씀드린 건 구석에 있는 것인데, 맨 위쪽 서랍이요. 그분의 부서 번호만 있으면 됩니다.
>
> **[오후 3:43] 로자리오 트렌티니**
> 부서 번호가 503인 것 같아요.
>
> **[오후 3:44] 노라 볼드윈**
> 정말 감사합니다!

어휘 text ~에게 문자 메시지를 보내다 get out of ~에서 나오다 What's up? 무슨 일이시죠?, 왜 그러시죠? try to do ~하려 하다 realize that ~임을 알게 되다, 깨닫다 write down 적어 놓다, 받아 적다 look A up A를 찾아보다, 검색하다 drawer 서랍 department 부서 It looks like ~인 것 같다

159 볼드윈 씨는 무슨 문제점을 언급하는가?
(A) 우체국을 찾을 수 없다.
(B) 일부 중요한 샘플을 잊었다.
(C) 일부 주소 정보가 빠져 있다.
(D) 고객 회의에 늦을 것이다.

해설 〈세부 사항〉
볼드윈 씨가 3시 34분에 작성한 메시지를 보면, 전체 주소를 적어 놓지 않았다는(I realized that I didn't write down the full address) 문제점을 말하고 있으므로 이를 언급한 (C)가 정답이다.

어휘 forget ~을 잊다 miss ~을 빠트리다, 놓치다, 지나치다

160 오후 3시 41분에, 트렌티니 씨가 "There are five file cabinets in here"라고 썼을 때 의미한 것은 무엇이겠는가?
(A) 더 상세한 안내가 필요하다.
(B) 프로젝트 마감 기한을 변경하고 싶어 한다.
(C) 혼자 일부 물품을 들어 올릴 수 없다.
(D) 제품 주문을 할 필요가 없다.

해설 〈의도 파악〉
해당 문장 앞뒤에 제시된 메시지를 보면, 볼드윈 씨가 자신의 사무실에 있는 파일 캐비닛에 있다고(It'll be in the file cabinet in my office) 말하자 트렌티니 씨가 캐비닛이 5개라고 답변하는 상황이다. 이에 대해 볼드윈 씨가 바로 뒤이어 특정한 것을 가리키고 있으므로 (Sorry. I mean the one in the corner ~) 트렌티니 씨는 정확한 캐비닛을 찾기 위해 좀 더 상세한 설명이 필요했다는 것을 알 수 있다. 따라서 (A)가 정답이다.

어휘 detailed 상세한 deadline 마감 기한 lift ~을 들어 올리다 by oneself 혼자, 스스로 place an order 주문하다

[161-163] 이메일

> 수신: 벤자민 카스티요
> 발신: 블랙웰 풋웨어
> 날짜: 9월 29일
> 제목: 헤이븐 등산화
>
> 카스티요 씨께,
>
> 블랙웰 풋웨어에서 구입하신 귀하의 헤이븐 등산화와 관련해 연락 주셔서 감사드립니다. —[1]—. 161 귀하의 질문에 답변 드리자면, 해당 등산화는 세탁기에 넣으시면 안 됩니다. —[2]—. 만일 세척되어야 한다면, 먼저, 솔이나 부드러운 천으로 표면의 먼지를 제거해 주십시오. 그런 다음, 안창을 꺼내시고, 따뜻한 비눗물을 이용해 손으로 등산화를 세척하세요.
>
> 세척 후에는, 등산화에서 부분적으로 방수 코팅 처리가 사라질 수 있습니다. 163 블랙웰 풋웨어에는 이와 같은 상황에 완벽히 사용할 있는 방수 스프레이 제품이 있습니다. —[3]—. 이는 가죽과 캔버스에 모두 사용하실 수 있습니다. 추가로, 저희는 모든 고객들께서 편안하고 안전한 등산을 즐기시기를 원합니다. 따라서, 162 저희 블랙웰 풋웨어는 모든 고객들께 서로 다른 등산화 두 켤레를 번갈아 착용하시기를 요청 드립니다. —[4]—. 이렇게 하시면 각 등산화가 착용되지 않는 시간 동안 환기가 될 충분한 시간을 보장해 줍니다.
>
> 테레사 커
> 고객 서비스 직원, 블랙웰 풋웨어

어휘 contact ~에게 연락하다 in answer to ~에 대한 답변으로 place ~에 넣다, 두다 remove ~을 제거하다 surface 표면 cloth 천, 직물 then 그런 다음, 그 후에 take out ~을 꺼내다 insole 안창 soapy water 비눗물 partially 부분적으로 waterproof 방수의 both A and B A와 B 둘 모두 in addition 추가로, 게다가 want A to do A가 ~하기를 원하다 comfortable 편안한 therefore 따라서, 그러므로 invite A to do A에게

~하도록 요청하다 alternate ~을 번갈아 하다 between + 복수 명사 ~ 사이에서, ~ 중에서 ensure (that) ~임을 분명히 하다, 반드시 ~하도록 하다 sufficient 충분한 air out (냄새나 습기 등이 빠지도록) 환기하다

161 커 씨는 왜 이메일을 보냈는가?
(A) 실수에 대해 사과하기 위해
(B) 카스티요 씨를 면접에 초대하기 위해
(C) 매장 개장을 알리기 위해
(D) 문의 사항에 답변하기 위해

해설 〈주제 및 목적〉
첫 단락 시작 부분의 '상대방의 질문에 답변하기 위해(In answer to your question ~)'라는 내용으로 미루어 앞서 문의했던 내용에 대한 답변으로 보내는 이메일이라는 것을 알 수 있으므로 (D)가 정답이다.

어휘 apologize for ~에 대해 사과하다 respond to ~에 답변하다, 대응하다 inquiry 문의

162 카스티요 씨는 무엇을 하도록 요청받는가?
(A) 부츠를 착용하기 전에 몇몇 팁 읽어 보기
(B) 업체의 등산화에 대한 이용 후기 작성하기
(C) 등산화가 젖는 것을 피하기
(D) 한 켤레가 넘는 등산화 착용하기

해설 〈세부 사항〉
두 번째 단락 하단에 서로 다른 등산화 두 켤레를 번갈아 가면서 착용하도록 부탁하는(Blackwell Footwear invites all customers to alternate between two different pairs of boots) 말이 쓰여 있으므로 이를 언급한 (D)가 정답이다.

어휘 review 후기, 의견, 평가 avoid -ing ~하는 것을 피하다 get A + 형용사 A를 ~한 상태로 만들다 more than ~가 넘는

163 [1], [2], [3], [4]로 표시된 위치들 중에서, 다음 문장이 들어가기에 가장 적절한 곳은 어디인가?
"샘플을 받아 보실 수 있도록 선호하시는 우편물 발송 주소를 저에게 보내 주십시오."
(A) [1]
(B) [2]
(C) [3]
(D) [4]

해설 〈문장 넣기〉
제시된 문장은 샘플을 하나 받을 수 있도록 주소를 알려 달라고 요청하는 의미를 지니고 있다. 이는 특정 제품이 언급되는 문장 뒤에 위치하는 것이 바람직하므로 방수 스프레이 제품을 소개하는 문장인 [3]의 위치가 적합하다.

어휘 preferred 선호하는 receive ~을 받다

[164-167] 기사

플린 시티 (4월 25일) ─ 지난 25년 동안, ⑯165 세서미 베이커리(윌밍턴 지역의 다이슨 빌딩 1층에 위치)는 매장에서 수제로 만들어 갓 구운 제품을 제공해 왔습니다. 주인 캐롤린 풀리도 씨는 맛있는 음식뿐만 아니라 사람들을 따뜻하게 맞이하는 분위기로도 명성을 쌓아 왔습니다. 하지만, 풀리도 씨는 모든 고객들이 무료 샘플을 받거나 수다를 떨기 위해 매장에 들를 시간이 있는 것은 아니라는 사실을 알고 있습니다. ⑯164 그것이 바로 풀리도 씨가 고객들을 위해 새로운 배달 옵션을 도입하는 것을 기뻐하는 이유입니다. 5월 21일부터, 고객들은 전화로 주문해 자택이나 회사로 배송받을 수 있게 됩니다. 배달 요금은 주문상의 제품 수량을 바탕으로 하며, 대량 주문은 배달 요금을 전혀 발생시키지 않습니다.

풀리도 씨는 자신의 상품에 대해 늘어나는 인기로 인해 이와 같은 변화를 주기로 결정했습니다. 풀리도 씨는 종종 고객들로부터 ⑯165 근처에 버스 정류장이나 지하철역이 없어 그 제과점으로 가는 것이 얼마나 어려운지에 대한 의견을 받았습니다. ⑯166 "저는 윌밍턴으로 그렇게 자주 가지는 않는데, 약간 멀리 있기 때문입니다. 하지만 제가 이곳에 살았을 때는, 세서미 베이커리를 거의 매일 방문했습니다. 저는 이제 다시 캐롤린 씨의 맛있는 제과 제품을 쉽게 구입할 수 있게 되어 흥분됩니다."라고 ⑯166 라파엘 캘러웨이 씨(46세)가 밝혔습니다.

"저는 더 많은 사람들과 업체에 다가가는 것에 대해 들떠 있습니다."라고 풀리도 씨가 말했습니다. ⑯167 "처음에는, 충분한 경험을 지닌 신뢰할 수 있는 배송 기사들을 찾을 수 있을지 걱정했지만, 아주 뛰어난 팀을 채용했으며, 저희 모두는 새로운 장을 맞이하기를 고대하고 있습니다."

어휘 located on ~에 위치한 neighborhood 지역, 인근 serve up (음식) ~을 제공하다, 내오다 freshly baked 갓 구운 goods 제품, 상품 on site 현장에서, 구내에서 build a reputation for ~로 명성을 쌓다 not only A but also B A뿐만 아니라 B도 welcoming 사람들을 따뜻하게 맞이하는 atmosphere 분위기 stop into ~에 들르다 free 무료의 introduce ~을 도입하다 place an order 주문하다 over the phone 전화로 have A p.p. A가 ~되게 하다 be based on ~을 바탕으로 incur (비용) ~을 발생시키다 no ~ at all 전혀 ~가 아닌 decide to do ~하기로 결정하다 make a change 변화를 주다, 변경하다 growing 늘어나는, 증가하는 popularity 인기 get to ~로 가다 due to ~로 인해 the lack of ~의 부족 nearby 근처에 make it to ~로 가다 somewhat 약간, 다소 remote 멀리 떨어진 be able to do ~할 수 있다 individual 사람, 개인 be concerned that ~라는 점을 걱정하다, 우려하다 reliable 신뢰할 수 있는 recruit ~을 채용하다, 모집하다 look forward to ~을 고대하다 chapter (인생, 역사 등의) 장, 시기

164 기사의 주제는 무엇인가?
(A) 한 지역의 인기
(B) 건물 확장
(C) 업체의 새로운 서비스
(D) 제과점의 위치 이전

해설 〈주제 및 목적〉
첫 단락 초반부에 약간의 배경 설명을 제공한 후, 중반부에서 고객들을 위해 새로운 배달 옵션을 도입한다고(That's why she is pleased to be introducing a new delivery option for customers) 알리면서 해당 서비스 관련 정보를 전하고 있다. 따라서 업체의 새로운 서

비스가 주제이므로 (C)가 정답이다.

어휘 neighborhood 지역, 인근 popularity 인기 expansion 확장, 확대 relocation (위치) 이전, 이사

165 다이슨 빌딩에 관해 암시된 것은 무엇인가?
(A) 임대료가 인상되었다.
(B) 세입자가 주로 소기업들이다.
(C) 뛰어난 경관으로 알려져 있다.
(D) 대중교통에서 멀리 떨어져 있다.

해설 〈진위 확인 (전체 진위 유형)〉
다이슨 빌딩은 첫 단락 시작 부분에 세서미 베이커리가 위치한 건물로 언급되어 있다(~ Sesame Bakery─located on the ground floor of the Dyson Building ~). 그리고 이 업체와 관련된 설명 중, 세 번째 단락에 근처에 버스 정류장이나 지하철역이 없다는 내용이(~ due to the lack of a bus stop or subway station nearby) 있는데, 이는 대중교통이 멀리 있다는 뜻이므로 (D)가 정답이다.

어휘 rental 임대, 대여 increase 인상되다, 증가하다 tenant 세입자 mainly 주로 be known for ~로 알려져 있다 view 경관, 조망 far from ~에서 멀리 떨어진 public transportation 대중교통

166 라파엘 캘러웨이 씨는 누구일 것 같은가?
(A) 전 윌밍턴 주민
(B) 풀리도 씨의 사업 파트너
(C) 다이슨 빌딩 소유주
(D) 지역 음식 평론가

해설 〈세부 사항〉
캘러웨이 씨의 이름이 언급된 세 번째 단락에, 윌밍턴에 자주 가지 않는다는 말과 함께 과거 시제 동사(lived)와 함께 전에 그곳에 살았음을(I don't make it to Wilmington very often ~ But when I lived here, ~) 언급하고 있다. 이는 그가 과거 윌밍턴 주민이었음을 뜻하는 것이므로 (A)가 정답이다.

어휘 former 전 ~의, 이전의 resident 주민 owner 소유주 local 지역의, 현지의 critic 평론가, 비평가

167 기사에 따르면, 풀리도 씨는 무엇에 대해 걱정했는가?
(A) 가격을 낮게 유지하기
(B) 치열한 경쟁에 직면하기
(C) 자격 있는 직원 찾기
(D) 독특한 조리법 만들기

해설 〈세부 사항〉
풀리도 씨의 인터뷰 내용이 쓰여 있는 마지막 단락에 충분한 경험을 지닌 배송 기사들을 찾을 수 있을지 걱정했다는(I wouldn't be able to find reliable drivers with enough experience ~) 말이 쓰여 있다. 이는 자격이 있는 직원들을 찾는 것에 대해 걱정했음을 뜻하는 것이므로 (C)가 정답이다.

어휘 be worried about ~에 대해 걱정하다 keep A 형용사 A를 ~한 상태로 유지하다 face v. ~에 직면하다 heavy (수량, 정도 등이) 심한, 많은, 큰 competition 경쟁 qualified 자격 있는, 적격인 create ~을 만들어 내다 unique 독특한, 특별한 recipe 조리법

169 수신: 알바레즈 주식회사 직원들

발신: 토니 칼슨

날짜: 3월 5일

제목: 도체스터 공공 도서관

직원 여러분께,

도체스터 공공 도서관이 테일러스빌에 있는 유사한 프로그램을 본떠서 이곳 도체스터에서 강연 시리즈를 계획 중입니다. 이는 과학과 비즈니스에 초점이 맞춰질 것이며, 6월에 시작됩니다. —[1]—. 168 행사 진행 책임자인 폴린 피에로 씨가 단체 강연 시간을 진행할 의향이 있는 업계 전문가들을 찾고 있습니다. 우리 실험실 직원들은 169 우리가 어떻게 의약품을 개발하고 실험을 진행하는지에 관해 사람들을 가르칠 수 있을 것입니다. —[2]—.

이상적인 것은, 우리가 세 가지 강연을 다루는 것입니다. 이는 170 지역 주민들을 알바레즈 브랜드에 더욱 친숙해지게 할 뿐만 아니라 해당 프로그램을 지원할 수 있는 아주 좋은 방법일 것입니다. 저는 서로 다른 팀들이 각 강연을 다루는 게 최선일 것이라고 생각합니다. 발표 슬라이드 및 기타 자료를 준비하는 것뿐만 아니라 기획을 해야 할 필요성도 있기 때문에, 모든 역할에 공개 연설이 포함되는 것은 아닙니다. —[3]—.

3월 15일까지 저에게 이메일을 보내서 관심을 표현해 주시기 바랍니다. 171 다른 그룹 구성원들과 만남을 갖기에 가장 좋은 시간을 꼭 저에게 알려 주십시오. —[4]—. 추가 질문이 있으실 경우, 주저하지 마시고 물어보시기 바랍니다.

안녕히 계십시오.

토니

어휘 model A after B B를 본떠 A를 만들다 similar 유사한 be focused on ~에 초점이 맞춰지다 event coordinator 행사 진행 책임자 look for ~을 찾다 expert 전문가 field 분야 be willing to do ~할 의향이 있다. 기꺼이 ~하다 conduct ~을 진행하다, 수행하다 session (특정 활동을 위한) 시간 laboratory 실험실 develop ~을 개발하다 medication 의약품 run ~을 진행하다, 운영하다 trial 실험, 시험 ideally 이상적으로 cover (주제 등) ~을 다루다. 포함하다 way to do ~하는 방법 support ~을 지원하다 후원하다 as well as ~뿐만 아니라 ~도 local 지역의, 현지의 resident 주민 familiar with ~에 익숙한, ~을 잘 아는 handle ~을 다루다, 처리하다 include ~을 포함하다 planning 기획 prepare ~을 준비하다 material 자료, 재료, 물품 by (기한) ~까지 express (생각, 감정 등) ~을 표현하다, 나타내다 interest 관심(사) be sure to do 꼭 ~하십시오 let A know B A에게 B를 알리다 meet with (약속하여) ~와 만나다 further 추가의, 한층 더한 hesitate to do ~하기를 주저하다, 망설이다

168 칼슨 씨는 왜 이메일을 보냈는가?

(A) 직원들에게 도서관 카드를 받도록 권하기 위해

(B) 직원들에게 일부 시간들을 진행하도록 요청하기 위해

(C) 기금 마련 행사를 위한 기부금을 모으기 위해

(D) 산업 컨퍼런스 행사 초대장을 보내기 위해

해설 〈주제 및 목적〉

첫 단락에 한 행사 진행 책임자가 단체 강연 시간을 진행할 의향이 있

는 업계 전문가들을 찾는다고(~ looking for experts in the field who would be willing to conduct a group session) 언급한 뒤로, 자사의 직원들이 그 일을 하는 것과 관련해 설명하고 있다. 이는 직원들에게 일부 강연을 진행하도록 요청하는 것과 같으므로 (B)가 정답이다.

어휘 encourage A to do A에게 ~하도록 권하다, 장려하다 invite A to do A에게 ~하도록 요청하다 lead ~을 진행하다. 이끌다 session (특정 활동을 위한) 시간 gather ~을 모으다 donation 기부(금) fundraiser 기금 마련 행사 extend an invitation 초대장을 보내다

169 알바레즈 주식회사에 관해 암시된 것은 무엇인가?

(A) 제약 회사이다.

(B) 일부 직원들을 교육할 필요가 있다.

(C) 회사 규모 확대에 투자할 계획이다.

(D) 테일러스빌에 위치해 있다.

해설 〈진위 확인 (전체 진위 유형)〉

지문 시작 부분의 수신인 항목에 To: Alvarez Inc. Staff라고 되어 있는 부분을 통해 알바레즈 사의 직원들에게 보내는 이메일임을 알 수 있고, 첫 지문 끝부분에 we라는 대명사를 통해 자신들이 의약품을 개발하고 실험을 하는 일(~ how we develop our medications and run trials)을 한다고 밝히고 있으므로 (A)가 정답이다.

어휘 pharmaceutical 제약의 train ~을 교육하다 plan to do ~할 계획이다 invest in ~에 투자하다 expansion 확대, 확장 be located in ~에 위치해 있다

170 칼슨 씨는 행사의 무슨 이점을 언급하는가?

(A) 연간 수익 증대하기

(B) 신기술 습득하기

(C) 운영 비용 감축하기

(D) 브랜드 인지도 개선하기

해설 〈세부 사항〉

행사에 따른 이점은 두 번째 단락에서 확인할 수 있는데, 그 중 하나로 언급된 것이 지역 주민들이 알바레즈 브랜드와 친숙해지게 되는 것(~ make local residents more familiar with the Alvarez brand)이다. 이는 브랜드 인지도를 높이는 것에 해당되므로 (D)가 정답이다.

어휘 increase ~을 증가시키다, 늘리다 annual 연간의, 해마다의 revenue 수익 cut ~을 감축하다, 줄이다 operating costs 운영 비용 improve ~을 개선하다, 향상시키다 brand recognition 브랜드 인지도

171 [1], [2], [3], [4]로 표시된 위치들 중에서, 다음 문장이 들어가기에 가장 적절한 곳은 어디인가?

"이는 제가 사람들을 그룹으로 배정하는 일을 더욱 쉽게 만들어 줄 것입니다."

(A) [1]

(B) [2]

(C) [3]

(D) [4]

해설 〈문장 넣기〉

제시된 문장은 앞서 언급된 것을 지칭하는 This와 함께 그것이 그룹으로 배정하는 일을 더 쉽게 만들어 준다는 의미이다. 따라서, This에 해당되는 것으로서 다른 그룹 구성원들을 만나기에 좋은 시간을 알려 달라고 요청하는 문장(Be sure to let me know the best time for you to meet with other group members) 뒤에 위치한 [4]에 들어가 그에 따른 결과를 말하는 흐름이 되어야 자연스러우므로 (D)가 정답이다.

어휘 make it 형용사 for A to do A가 ~하는 것을 …하게 만들다 assign ~을 배정하다, 할당하다

샌드라 모리슨 [오전 10:46]	로체스터 여름 마라톤을 후원하는 일과 관련해 방금 그 경주대회 행사 기획자와 이야기 나눴습니다. 172 각 경주 참가자에게 원가에 셔츠를 하나 제공하는 일과 관련된 것인데, 이것은 많은 사람들이 우리 스포츠 의류를 한 번 착용해 보게 된다는 뜻이 될 것입니다.
폴 본 [오전 10:48]	좋은 아이디어인 것 같아요.
에디 자비스 [오전 10:50]	저도 동의해요. 173 우리의 이상적인 구매자는 운동 선수들이기 때문에, 이렇게 하는 게 그들이 우리 브랜드와 교류하는 완벽한 방법이 될 거예요.
폴 본 [오전 10:51]	바로 그렇습니다.
샌드라 모리슨 [오전 10:52]	작년에, 174 데슬러 주식회사가 이 경주대회에서 에너지 음료를 제공했는데, 직후에 근소한 매출 증가를 경험했어요.
에디 자비스 [오전 10:55]	그렇게 해 봐요.
샌드라 모리슨 [오전 10:56]	아주 좋습니다! 주최 측에서 올해 약 5천 명의 경주 참가자를 예상하고 있기 때문에, 그에 맞게 준비해야 할 겁니다.
폴 본 [오전 10:57]	주문 사항에 어떤 특별 요청이라도 있나요?
샌드라 모리슨 [오전 10:58]	네. 우리의 로고뿐만 아니라, 경주대회 명칭과 날짜 표기가 있을 거예요. 175 그쪽 그래픽 디자이너가 추가되어야 하는 이미지 파일들을 저에게 보내 주었습니다.
폴 본 [오전 10:59]	175 그걸 저에게 전달해 주시면, 제가 인쇄소와 이야기 나눠 보겠습니다.

어휘 event planner 행사 기획자 sponsor ~을 후원하다 involve ~와 관련

되다, ~을 포함하다 at cost 원가에 try ~을 한 번 해 보다 agree 동의하다 athlete 운동 선수 way for A to do A가 ~하는 방법 interact with ~와 교류하다, 상호 작용하다 see ~을 경험하다, 겪다 slight 약간의, 조금의 increase in ~의 증가 immediately afterwards 직후에 expect ~을 예상하다, 기대하다 request 요청, 요구 in addition to ~뿐만 아니라, ~ 외에도 lettering (글자 표기) add ~을 추가하다 forward ~을 전달하다 discuss ~을 이야기하다, 논의하다

172 모리슨 씨는 다른 메시지 작성자들에게 무엇에 관해 이야기하는가?
(A) 지역 사회 퍼레이드
(B) 홍보 기회
(C) 몇몇 설문 조사 결과
(D) 몇몇 조사 요건

해설 〈주제 및 목적〉
첫 번째 메시지에 모리슨 씨는 마라톤 행사 참가자들에게 셔츠를 제공하는 일을 언급하며 많은 사람들이 자사의 스포츠 의류를 착용해 볼 기회가 생긴다고(It involves providing a shirt to each runner at cost, but it would mean a lot of people would be trying our sportswear) 알리고 있다. 이는 회사 제품을 홍보할 수 있는 기회를 말하는 것이므로 (B)가 정답이다.

어휘 community 지역 사회, 지역 공동체 promotion 홍보의 opportunity 기회 survey 설문 조사 result 결과(물) inspection 조사, 점검 requirement 요건, 필요 조건

173 오전 10시 51분에, 본 씨가 "You're exactly right"이라고 쓸 때 무엇을 의미하는가?
(A) 프로젝트가 단시간에 완료될 수 있다.
(B) 행사의 참가자 수가 높을 것으로 예상된다.
(C) 한 브랜드가 최근에 더 많은 인기를 얻었다.
(D) 일부 대상 고객들에게 다가갈 수 있다.

해설 〈의도 파악〉
앞선 메시지에서 자비스 씨는 모리슨 씨의 방법대로 하는 것이 구매자들이 자사의 브랜드와 교류하는 완벽한 방법이 될 것이라고 한 것에 대해 '바로 그렇다(You're exactly right)'라고 대답하는 상황이다. 이는 고객들과의 교류 기회, 즉 고객들에게 다가갈 수 있는 기회에 대해 긍정적인 의견을 말하는 것이므로 (D)가 정답이다.

어휘 complete ~을 완료하다 attendance 참가, 참가자 수 be expected to do ~할 것으로 예상되다 recently 최근에 target customers 대상 고객들, 목표 고객들 reach ~에게 다가가다

174 데슐러 주식회사는 무엇일 것 같은가?
(A) 의류 디자인 업체
(B) 피트니스 센터
(C) 마케팅 회사
(D) 음료 제조사

해설 〈세부 사항〉
데슐러 주식회사가 언급되는 10시 52분 메시지에, 그 회사가 작년에 에너지 음료를 제공한(Deshler Inc. provided its energy drinks ~) 사실이 언급되어 있으므로 (D)가 정답이다.

어휘 firm 회사, 업체 beverage 음료 manufacturer 제조사

175 모리슨 씨는 무엇을 하도록 요청받는가?
(A) 몇몇 파일을 보내는 일
(B) 디자이너에게 전화하는 일
(C) 인쇄소를 방문하는 일
(D) 예산을 승인하는 일

해설 〈세부 사항〉
10시 58분에 모리슨 씨가, 그래픽 디자이너로부터 이미지 파일들을 받은 사실을(Their graphic designer has sent me the image files ~) 언급하자, 바로 다음 메시지에서 본 씨가 그 파일들을 자신에게 전달해 주면 인쇄소와 얘기하겠다고(If you forward those to me ~) 알리고 있다. 이는 해당 파일들을 전달해 달라고 요청하는 것이므로 (A)가 정답이다.

어휘 approve ~을 승인하다 budget 예산

[176-180] 웹 페이지와 이메일

http://www.rinehartappliances.com/homeservice

| 카탈로그 | 매장 위치 찾기 | 홈 서비스 | 연락 정보 | 구인 |

라인하트 가전기기 홈 서비스

구매 후 48시간 이내에 정상 작동되도록 보장해 드립니다!

라인하트 가전기기를 통해 기기를 구입하시면, 저희 배송 담당 직원이 즉시 자택으로 배송되도록 해 드립니다. 모든 저희 제품이 고품질이며 내구성이 뛰어나지만, 저희 직원들은 마치 깨지기 쉬운 제품인 것처럼 각 기기를 **⑰** 다루도록 지시받습니다. 이는 운송 중에 발생되는 손상을 방지해 줍니다.

아래에서 **⑲** 저희 홈 서비스 요금을 확인해 보시기 바랍니다.

제품 수량	배송 서비스만 제공되는 경우	**⑲** 배송 및 설치 작업	배송과 설치, **⑰⑥** 기존 기기의 제거 작업
1	15.00달러	**⑲** 35.00달러	60.00달러
2	20.00달러	50.00달러	90.00달러
3	25.00달러	55.00달러	100.00달러

수신: customerhelp@rinehartappliances.com
발신: avaikar@quickmail1.com
날짜: 5월 14일
제목: 주문 번호 08378

관계자께:

⑲ 제가 귀사의 오클랜드 지점에서 주문한 가스 오븐이 어제 배송되었습니다. 하지만, **⑱** 제품을 배송해 주신 분들께서는 그 제품을 연결하도록 공인된 분들이 아니라고 말씀해 주셨습니다. **⑲** 제가 배송 및 설치 작업 옵션을 선택했기 때문에, 이 서비스가 포함되었어야 했습니다. 금요일 오전까지 사람을 보내 주실 수 있기를 바랍니다. 그때까지 반드시 완료되어야 합니다. **⑱⓪** 금요일에 저희 집을 찾아오시는 방문객들이 있는데, 그분들을 위해 요리를 좀 할 계획입니다. 제 요청을 수용해 주시지 못할 경우, 가스 문제를 처리하는 지역 배관 전문 업체에 전화해야 하며, 이 청구 요금을 귀사 측에서 부담해 주셔야 할 것으로 예상합니다.

안녕히 계십시오.

앰리트 바이카르

어휘 employment 고용, 취업 up and running 정상 가동되는 guaranteed 보장된 appliance 가전기기 personnel 직원들, 인사(부) make sure (that) 반드시 ~하도록 하다, ~하는 것을 확실히 하다 get to ~로 가다, ~에 도달하다 promptly 즉시 of high quality 고품질인 extremely 대단히, 매우 durable 내구성이 뛰어난 be instructed to do ~하도록 지시받다, 안내받다 treat ~을 다루다, 처리하다 as if 마치 ~한 것처럼 fragile 깨지기 쉬운, 취약한 prevent ~을 방지하다 while ~하는 동안 in transit 운송 중인 rate 요금 below 아래에, 밑에 installation 설치 removal 제거, 없앰 order ~을 주문하다 branch 지점, 지사 however 하지만, 그런데 make a delivery 배송하다, 배달하다 be certified to do ~하도록 인증 받다, 공인되다 hook A up A를 연결하다 select ~을 선택하다 should have p.p. ~했어야 했다 include ~을 포함하다 be able to do ~할 수 있다 by (기한) ~까지 absolutely 반드시, 절대적으로 then 그때 plan to do ~할 계획이다 accommodate ~을 수용하다, 받아들이다 request 요청 local 지역의, 현지의 plumbing 배관 deal with ~을 처리하다, 다루다 expect A to do A가 ~할 것으로 예상하다, 기대하다 cover (비용 등) ~을 부담하다, 충당하다 charge 청구 요금, 부과 요금

176 웹 페이지에서 라인하트 가전기기에 대해 암시된 것은 무엇인가?
(A) 고객들의 기존 제품을 처분할 수 있다.
(B) 깨지기 쉬운 많은 제품을 제조한다.
(C) 대량 구매에 대해 무료 배송 서비스를 제공한다.
(D) 최근에 자사의 제품 라인에 새 기기를 추가했다.

해설 〈진위 확인 (전체 진위 유형)〉
라인하트 가전기기에서 제공하는 서비스 항목을 찾아볼 수 있는 첫 지문 도표를 보면, 기존 기기의 제거 작업(Removal of Old Appliance(s))이 언급되어 있는데, 이는 고객들이 기존에 보유하고 있던 제품에 대한 처분을 의미하므로 (A)가 정답이다.

어휘 dispose of ~을 처분하다, 처리하다 manufacture ~을 제조하다 a number of 많은 (수의) fragile 깨지기 쉬운, 취약한 provide ~을

제공하다 **free** 무료의 **bulk** a. 대량의 **purchase** 구매(품) **recently**
최근에 **add** ~을 추가하다 **line** 제품 라인

177 웹 페이지에서, 첫 번째 단락 세 번째 줄의 단어 "treat"와 의미가 가장 가까운 것은 무엇인가?
(A) 치료하다
(B) 행동하다
(C) 다루다
(D) 판단하다

해설 〈동의어〉
해당 문장에서 treat은 직원들이 기기 제품과 관련해 어떻게 하도록 지시받는지를 나타낸다. 문장 끝부분에 '마치 깨지기 쉬운 제품인 것처럼(as if it were fragile)'이라는 말이 있는 것으로 볼 때 제품을 아주 조심스럽게 다루도록 지시를 받는 것으로 판단할 수 있으므로 같은 의미의 '다루다'를 뜻하는 동사인 (C)가 정답이다.

178 바이카르 씨는 왜 이메일을 보냈는가?
(A) 교체 설명서를 요청하기 위해
(B) 설치 문제를 알리기 위해
(C) 배송 날짜에 대한 일정을 잡기 위해
(D) 새로운 주문을 하기 위해

해설 〈주제 및 목적〉
바이카르 씨가 쓴 이메일인 두 번째 지문 시작 부분에, 제품을 배송한 사람들이 그것을 연결할 자격을 갖추지 않았다고(~ the people making the delivery said they were not certified to hook it up) 말한 사실을 언급하며 설치 작업의 필요성을 말하고 있으므로 (B)가 정답이다.

어휘 **ask for** ~을 요청하다 **replacement** 교체(품) **manual** 설명서 **installation** 설치 **issue** 문제, 사안 **place an order** 주문하다

179 바이카르 씨는 홈 서비스에 대해 얼마를 지불했는가?
(A) 15달러
(B) 25달러
(C) 35달러
(D) 50달러

해설 〈지문 연계〉
바이카르 씨가 쓴 이메일인 두 번째 지문을 보면, 가스 오븐을 주문한 사실과(The gas oven I ordered ~) 함께 배송 및 설치 옵션을 선택했음을 알리고 있다(As I selected the option for delivery and installation. ~). 첫 지문의 도표에서 제품 1개에 대한 배송 및 설치(Delivery and Installation) 서비스 요금이 $35.00로 표기되어 있으므로 (C)가 정답이다.

180 이메일에 따르면, 바이카르 씨는 왜 지역 업체에 연락할 수도 있는가?
(A) 제품에 대해 더 나은 품질 보증을 받기를 바라고 있다.
(B) 새로운 모델을 구입할 수 있을 것으로 생각하고 있다.
(C) 특가 제품을 이용할 계획이다.
(D) 몇몇 손님들을 위해 기기를 사용하고 싶어 한다.

해설 〈세부 사항〉

두 번째 지문 하단에 방문객들을 위해 요리를 할 계획임을 알리며 자신의 요청을 수용해 주지 못할 경우 지역 배관 전문 업체에 전화할 것이라는(I have visitors coming to my home on Friday, and I plan to do some cooking for them. If you cannot accommodate my request, I'll have to call a local plumbing business that deals with gas ~) 내용이 있다. 이는 오븐, 즉 기기(appliance)를 사용하기 위해 배관 업체에 연락할 수도 있다는 의미이므로 (D)가 정답이다.

어휘 **contact** ~에게 연락하다 **local** 지역의, 현지의 **warranty** 품질 보증(서) **plan to do** ~할 계획이다 **take advantage of** ~을 이용하다 **special offer** 특가 (제품)

[181-185] 두 이메일

수신: 바스케즈 이동 통신 〈contact@vasqueztelecom.com〉
발신: 헤더 소더버그 〈h.soderberg@aaragoninc.com〉
날짜: 10월 5일
제목: 인터넷

관계자께,

제 9월 인터넷 요금 청구서에 청구된 액수를 보고 놀랐습니다. 저는 약 4개월 전 새집으로 이사했을 때, 프리미엄 패키지로 업그레이드했습니다. 처음 몇 번의 청구서 요금은 모두 각각 60달러였습니다. 하지만, 가장 최근의 청구서 요금은 90달러였습니다. **183** 이는 제가 예상하고 있던 것보다 30달러나 더 많은 금액입니다. 프리미엄 패키지를 통해, **182** 저는 무제한 다운로드 서비스를 이용하고 있으므로 사용량이 많을지라도 청구서 요금은 동일해야 합니다. 무엇이 이 문제를 초래했는지 알아볼 수 있도록 **181** 제 계정을 확인해 주신다면 감사하겠습니다.

감사합니다.

헤더 소더버그
계정 번호 01489833

수신: 헤더 소더버그 〈h.soderberg@aaragoninc.com〉
발신: 바스케즈 고객 서비스팀 〈brucep@vasqueztelecom.com〉
183 날짜: 10월 5일
제목: 회신: 인터넷
첨부: 바스케즈_이용권.pdf

소더버그 씨께,

귀하의 청구서에 문제가 발생된 것에 대해 사과 드립니다. 저희 팀이 귀하의 계정 상세 정보를 살펴보았으며, 귀하께서 실제로 9월 청구서에 대해 과다 청구되었음을 확인해 드릴 수 있습니다. **183** 과다 청구된 액수에 대해 환불 금액을 막지급해 드렸습니다. 이는 귀하의 직불 카드 지불이 출금되는 계좌로 환불되었습니다. 사과의 뜻으로, **184** 무료 1개월 바스케즈 이용권도 제공해 드리고자 합니다. 첨부된 문서에 있는 코드를 이용해 아주 다양한 인기 영화를 재생해 보실 수 있습니다. 이 서비스는 일반적으로 한 달에 12.99달러의 비용이 드는 것입니다.

저희 바스케즈 이동 통신은 항상 저희 서비스를 개선할 여러 방법을 찾고 있습니다. **185** 잠시 시간 내시어 저희 웹 사이트를 방문해 간단한 설문지를 작성해 주시겠습니까? 이는 저희 홈페이지의 "연락하기" 탭에서 찾아보실 수 있습니다. 이 문제와 관련해 귀하의 양해에 감사드리며, 앞으로도 계속 저희 바스케즈 이동 통신의 고객이 되어 주시기를 바랍니다.

안녕히 계십시오.

브루스 파월
고객 서비스팀 직원
바스케즈 이동 통신

어휘 **be surprised by** ~에 놀라다 **amount** 금액, 액수 **be charged for** ~에 대해 비용 청구되다 **bill** 청구서, 고지서 **about** 약, 대략 **recent** 최근의 **expect** ~을 예상하다 **through** ~을 통해 **unlimited** 무제한의 **even** 심지어 (~도) **would appreciate it if** ~한다면 감사하겠습니다 **account** 계정, 계좌 **find out** ~을 알아 보다, 확인하다 **cause** ~을 초래하다. 야기하다 **issue** n. 문제, 사안(= matter) v. ~을 지급하다, 발급하다 **look into** ~을 살펴보다. 조사하다 **details** 상세 정보, 세부 사항 **confirm that** ~임을 확인해 주다 **indeed** 사실, 정말로, 참으로 **overcharge** ~에게 과다 청구하다 **refund** 환불(금) **return** ~을 환불하다, 돌려보내다 **direct debit payment** 직불 카드 지불(액) **by way of apology** 사과의 뜻으로 **would like to do** ~하고자 하다, ~하고 싶다 **free** 무료의 **attached** 첨부된 **stream** (동영상 등) ~을 재생하다 **a wide variety of** 매우 다양한 **usually** 일반적으로, 보통 **cost** ~의 비용이 들다 **look for** ~을 찾다 **way to do** ~하는 방법 **improve** ~을 개선하다. 향상시키다 **take a moment to do** 잠시 시간 내어 ~하다 **complete** ~을 작성하다 **brief** 간단한, 잠시 동안의 **survey** 설문 조사(지) **get in touch** 연락하다 **appreciate** ~에 대해 감사하다 **continue to do** 계속 ~하다

181 첫 번째 이메일은 왜 쓰여졌는가?
(A) 고장 난 인터넷 연결 서비스를 알리기 위해
(B) 계정 업그레이드를 확인해 주기 위해
(C) 주소 변경 사실을 알리기 위해
(D) 계정 검토를 요청하기 위해

해설 〈주제 및 목적〉

첫 번째 이메일에서 문제가 발생된 사실을 먼저 설명한 후, 마지막 부분에 가서 그 원인을 파악하기 위해 계정을 확인하도록 요청하는 부분이(I would appreciate it if you would check my account ~) 목적에 해당된다. 따라서 계정 검토 요청을 의미하는 (D)가 정답이다.

어휘 broken 고장 난, 망가진, 깨진 confirm ~을 확인해 주다 request ~을 요청하다, 요구하다 review 검토

182 소더버그 씨에 관해 언급된 것은 무엇인가?
(A) 컴퓨터가 계속 느리게 작동되고 있다.
(B) 청구서가 사용량에 영향받지 말아야 한다.
(C) 인터넷 선을 수리받기 위해 비용을 지불했다.
(D) 과거에 한때 바스케즈 이동 통신에서 일했다.

해설 〈진위 확인 (전체 진위 유형)〉
소더버그 씨가 자신의 상황을 설명하는 첫 번째 이메일 후반부에, 무제한 서비스이므로 사용량과 상관없이 요금이 동일해야 한다는(~ even with heavy usage, the bill should be the same) 내용이 있다. 따라서, 이를 언급한 (B)가 정답이다.

어휘 run 작동되다, 운영되다 bill 청구서, 계산서, 고지서 affect ~에 영향을 미치다 have A p.p. A가 ~되게 하다 repair ~을 수리하다 used to do 과거에 한때 ~했다

183 소더버그 씨의 계좌로 10월 5일에 얼마나 송금되었는가?
(A) 10달러
(B) 30달러
(C) 60달러
(D) 90달러

해설 〈지문 연계〉
10월 5일이라는 날짜와 송금 처리 관련 내용이 제시된 두 번째 지문을 보면, 과다 청구된 액수를 환불했다고(I have just issued you a refund in the amount overcharged) 알리고 있다. 이는 첫 지문에서 소더버그 씨가 언급한 초과 청구 금액인 30달러(That's $30 more than I was expecting)에 대한 후속 조치이므로 (B)가 정답이다.

184 소더버그 씨는 파월 씨가 제공한 코드로 무엇을 할 수 있는가?
(A) 교체품 요청하기
(B) 청구서상의 금액 입금받기
(C) 일부 영화 감상하기
(D) 뉴스 사이트에 로그인하기

해설 〈세부 사항〉
파월 씨가 제공하는 코드가 언급되는 두 번째 지문 두 번째 단락을 보면, 해당 코드를 이용해 다양한 인기 영화를 볼 수 있다는(You can use the code on the attached document to stream a wide variety of popular films) 내용이 있으므로 (C)가 정답이다.

어휘 provide ~을 제공하다 replacement 교체(품) credit 입금 sign into ~에 로그인하다

185 소더버그 씨는 무엇을 하도록 요청받는가?
(A) 비용 지불 증명서 보내기

(B) 앞으로 직불 카드 사용하기
(C) 온라인에서 설문지 작성 완료하기
(D) 계정에 관해 추가 상세 정보 제공하기

해설 〈세부 사항〉
소더버그 씨에게 보내는 이메일인 두 번째 지문 두 번째 단락에, 회사 웹 사이트를 방문해 간단한 설문지 작성을 부탁하는(Would you please take a moment to visit our Web site and complete a brief survey?) 내용이 있으므로 이를 언급한 (C)가 정답이다.

어휘 proof 증거(물) debit card 직불 카드 complete ~을 작성 완료하다 questionnaire 설문지 details 상세 정보, 세부 사항

[186-190] 기사와 이메일, 그리고 온라인 후기

> **해티스버그 트리뷴**
>
> 4월 18일 — 휘트웰 공원 부지가 곧 더욱 다채로워집니다. **186** 시에서 공원의 외관을 개선하기 위해 이 공원의 야외 무대 근처에 있는 북서쪽 구역을 초대형 화원으로 변모시키는 계획을 발표했습니다. 이 작업은 5월 초에 시작되며, **189** 휘트웰 공원에서 개최되는 우리 도시의 연례 해티스버그 음악 축제 직전인 6월 초까지 완료될 것입니다.
>
> 시 관계자들은 땅을 파는 작업과 프레임 추가 작업, 그리고 식수 작업에 도움을 줄 자원 봉사자들을 찾고 있습니다. 약 50명의 자원 봉사자들이 공원 휴양 시설 관리부 직원들과 함께 작업하게 될 것입니다. 등록을 원하시면, 공원 휴양 시설 관리부장인 도리안 픽킨 씨에게 555-8471번으로 연락하시기 바랍니다. **188** 이 프로젝트에 충분한 자원 봉사자들이 구해지지 않을 경우, 지역 조경 업체가 해당 작업을 완료하기 위해 고용될 것입니다.
>
> 휘트웰 공원의 변화는 앤 맬리 시장이 직책을 **187** 맡은 이후로 제안된 많은 프로젝트 계획들 중의 하나에 불과합니다. 맬리 시장은 주민들이 더 많은 야외 활동에 참여하도록 권장하는 것을 원하고 있기 때문에, 지역 내 여러 야외 부지에 투자하고 있습니다.

> 수신: 웨이드 앳우드 〈wade@toplandscaping.com〉
> 발신: 도리안 픽킨 〈d.pipkin@hattiesburg.gov〉
> 날짜: 6월 16일
> 제목: 비용 지불
>
> 앳우드 씨께,
>
> **188** 귀하의 팀이 휘트웰 공원에 실시한 작업에 대해 톱 랜드스케이핑 사에서 발급한 거래 내역서를 받았습니다. 새로운 화원은 아주 멋져 보이며, 지역 주민과 외부 지역 방문객들에게 모두 특별한 명소가 될 것이라고 생각합니다. 저희 재무 팀이 은행 계좌 이체로 해당 지불 비용을 지급해 드렸으므로 곧 받으시게 될 것입니다.
>
> 안녕히 계십시오.
>
> 도리안 픽킨

---

http://www.communityreviews.org

미시시피 〉 해티스버그 〉 지역 행사

해티스버그 음악 축제

> **189** 저는 가장 최근에 열린 행사뿐만 아니라 작년에 열린 해티스버그 음악 축제에도 참석했었습니다. 두 번의 행사 모두 정말 즐거운 시간이었습니다. 밴드들은 관람하기에 훌륭했으며, 공원 내 대부분의 구역에서 좋은 음악 감상 경험이 될 수 있도록 음향 시스템이 준비되었습니다. **190** 저는 특히 푸드 코트가 놀라웠는데, 올해는 음악 축제 주최 측에서 판매업체들에게 일회용 접시 대신 진짜 접시를 사용하도록 요구했기 때문입니다. 훨씬 더 적은 쓰레기가 만들어지도록 확실히 한 아주 좋은 방법이었습니다. 저는 앞으로도 계속 이 정책을 유지하기를 바랍니다. — **190** D. 시글러, 엘스빌, 미시시피
>
> 게시 날짜, 7월 2일

어휘 grounds (건물이나 특정 구역의) 부지, 구내 be about to do 막 ~하려 하다 colorful 다채로운, 화려한 announce ~을 발표하다 turn A into B A를 B로 탈바꿈시키다, 변모시키다 enhance ~을 개선하다, 강화하다 appearance 외관, 모습 complete ~을 완료하다 by (기한) ~까지 annual 연례적인, 해마다의 hold ~을 개최하다 annually 연례적으로, 해마다 official 관계자, 당국자 look for ~을 찾다 volunteer 자원 봉사자 assist with ~을 돕다 digging 땅 파는 일 add ~을 추가하다 planting 식수, 식물 심기 about 약, 대략 alongside ~와 함께 sign up 등록하다, 신청하다 contact ~에게 연락하다 local 지역의, 현지의 landscaping 조경 firm 업체, 회사 hire ~을 고용하다 propose ~을 제안하다 assume (직책 등) ~을 맡다 mayor 시장 encourage A to do A에게 ~하도록 권장하다, 장려하다 resident 주민 get involved in ~에 참여하다, 관여하다 invest in ~에 투자하다 site 장소, 부지, 현장 receive ~을 받다 invoice 거래 내역서, 송장 attraction 명소, 인기 장소 both A and B A와 B 둘 모두 out-of-town 다른 지역의 finance 재무, 재정 issue ~을 지급하다, 발급하다 bank transfer 은행 계좌 이체 shortly 곧, 머지않아 attend ~에 참석하다 as well as ~뿐만 아니라 …도 recent 최근의 arrange ~을 마련하다, 준비하다 so that ~할 수 있도록 particularly 특히 be amazed by ~에 놀라다 organizer 주최자, 조직자 require A to do A에게 ~하도록 요구하다, 요청하다 vendor 판매업체, 판매업자 instead of ~ 대신에 disposable 일회용의 way to do ~하는 방법 make sure (that) 반드시 ~하도록 하다, ~하는 것을 확실히 하다 create ~을 만들어내다 continue ~을 계속하다, 지속하다 policy 정책 post ~을 게시하다

186 기사는 왜 쓰여졌는가?
(A) 축제 진행 책임자를 소개하기 위해
(B) 음악 콘테스트 우승자를 칭찬하기 위해
(C) 공원 업그레이드를 알리기 위해
(D) 원예에 관한 조언을 제공하기 위해

해설 〈주제 및 목적〉
첫 지문 첫 단락에, 시에서 공원의 외관을 개선하기 위해 일부 구역을 화원으로 바꿀 계획을 발표했다고(The city has announced plans to turn the northwest section of the park, ~ into a giant flower garden to enhance the park's appearance) 알리며 그 작업과 관련된 정보를 제공하고 있다. 이는 해당 공원에 대한

업그레이드 작업을 의미하므로 (C)가 정답이다.

어휘 introduce ~을 소개하다 coordinator 진행 책임자 praise ~을 칭찬하다 gardening 원예

187 기사에서 세 번째 단락, 첫 번째 줄의 단어 "assumed"와 의미가 가장 가까운 것은 무엇인가?
(A) 예측했다
(B) 제기했다
(C) 제안했다
(D) 맡았다

해설 〈동의어〉
해당 문장에서 사람 이름이 주어로, 그리고 '시장의 역할'을 뜻하는 명사구가 목적어로 쓰여 있다. 따라서 '시장 직책을 맡았다'와 같은 의미인 것으로 판단할 수 있으므로 '맡다, 넘겨받다'를 뜻하는 (D) took over가 정답이다.

188 핍킨 씨의 이메일에서 암시된 것은 무엇인가?
(A) 계약이 연장될 것이다.
(B) 거래 내역서가 정정되었다.
(C) 프로젝트에 자원 봉사자가 충분하지 않았다.
(D) 비용 지불이 아직 승인되지 않았다.

해설 〈지문 연계〉
첫 지문 두 번째 단락에, 충분한 자원 봉사자들이 구해지지 않을 경우 지역 조경업체가 고용될(If the project does not get enough volunteers, a local landscaping firm will be hired ~) 것이라고 쓰여 있다. 이와 관련해 두 번째 지문 시작 부분에 톱 랜드스케이핑 사가 휘트웰 공원에 작업했다는(~ Top Landscaping for the work your team did at Whitwell Park) 내용이 있으므로 자원 봉사자들을 충분히 구하지 못했음을 알 수 있다. 따라서 이를 언급한 (C)가 정답이다.

어휘 contract 계약(서) extend ~을 연장하다 invoice 거래 내역서 correct v. ~정정하다, 바로잡다 volunteer 자원 봉사자 payment 지불(금) approve ~을 승인하다

189 시글러 씨에 관해 무엇이 사실일 것 같은가?
(A) 6월에 휘트웰 공원을 방문했다.
(B) 일부 공연을 듣는 데 어려움을 겪었다.
(C) 한 프로젝트를 위해 자원 봉사하기를 원한다.
(D) 전문 음악가이다.

해설 〈지문 연계〉
시글러 씨가 작성한 세 번째 지문 첫 문장에, 작년과 최근에 열린 해티스버그 음악 축제에 참석했다고(I attended ~ as well as the most recent one) 알리는 말이 있다. 이 행사와 관련해 첫 지문 첫 단락에, 연례 해티스버그 음악 축제 직전인 6월 초까지 공사가 완료된다는(~ will be completed by early June, just before the city's annual Hattiesburg Music Festival, ~) 말이 있으므로 6월 중에 개최되는 이 행사에 참석한 것으로 판단할 수 있다. 따라서 이를 언급한 (A)가 정답이다.

어휘 have trouble -ing ~하는 데 어려움을 겪다

190 축제와 관련해 무엇이 시글러 씨에게 깊은 인상을 남겼는가?
(A) 다양한 음식 옵션
(B) 편리한 위치
(C) 전 세계에서 온 공연자들
(D) 환경 친화적인 정책

해설 〈세부 사항〉
세 번째 지문 중반부에, 시글러 씨는 일회용 접시 대신 진짜 접시가 사용된 사실이 놀라웠다고 밝히면서 쓰레기가 덜 생기도록 한 좋은 방법이라고(~ to use real dishes instead of disposable ones. It was a great way to make sure much less waste was created) 언급하고 있다. 이는 환경 친화적인 행사 정책에 대해 깊은 인상을 받았다는 뜻이므로 (D)가 정답이다.

어휘 impress ~에게 깊은 인상을 남기다 a variety of 다양한 convenient 편리한 location 위치, 지점 outstanding 뛰어난, 훌륭한 environmentally friendly 환경 친화적인 policy 정책, 방침

[191-195] 두 이메일과 가격 견적서

수신: 션 라미레즈 〈sramirez@mercerrealtyco.com〉
발신: 콘스턴스 애쉬비 〈constance@elitepartyplanning.net〉
날짜: 9월 16일
제목: 회신: 문의

라미레즈 씨께,

191 귀하의 동료 직원을 위해 계획 중이신 다가오는 은퇴 기념 파티와 관련해 연락 주셔서 감사합니다. 저에게 말씀해 주신 것을 바탕으로, **191** 행사장에 대한 몇몇 추천 사항이 있습니다. 가격 견적서를 첨부해 드렸으며, 이 가격들은 엘리트 파티 플래닝의 서비스를 이용함으로써 받으시게 되는 할인 혜택을 반영한 것입니다. **192** 귀하께서 해변 경관이 보이는 옵션을 원하신다고 언급해 주셨기 때문에, 목록에 그곳도 포함해 두었습니다.

결정하시는 대로 선호하시는 날짜에 기꺼이 예약해 드리도록 하겠습니다.

안녕히 계십시오.

콘스턴스

행사장 요약

머서 부동산 중개회사의 션 라미레즈 씨를 위해 콘스턴스 애쉬비 작성

행사 종류: 은퇴 기념 파티		손님 명단: 추후 결정	
선호하는 날짜: 10월 20일		시작 시간: 오후 7시	

행사장	수용 인원	대여료	특징
194 더 코너웨이	100	**194** 1,000달러	**194** 모든 손님들에게 대리 주차 무료
릿지 플라자	50	500달러	별도 요금으로 건물 내 야간 숙박 시설 이용 가능
192 도브테일 호텔	150	2,400달러	**192** 바닥에서 천장에 이르는 창문을 통해 보이는 해변 경관
GL 컨퍼런스 센터	250	1,200달러	업타운 기차역에서 걸어서 2분 거리
193 벨 호텔	200	850달러	**193** 최근에 설치된 현대적인 음향 시스템

대여료에는 테이블과 의자 등의 설치 서비스가 포함되어 있습니다. 각 장소에서 표준 테이블보가 이용 가능합니다. 추가 장식물품은 구매하시거나 별도로 대여하셔야 합니다.

수신: 콘스턴스 애쉬비 〈constance@elitepartyplanning.net〉
발신: 션 라미레즈 〈sramirez@mercerrealtyco.com〉
날짜: 9월 17일
제목: 행사장

애쉬비 씨께,

이렇게 빨리 저에게 다시 연락 주셔서 감사합니다. 저희 손님들 중 누구도 야간 숙박 시설이 필요하지는 않을 것입니다. 하지만, 거의 모든 분들께서 행사장에 차를 운전해 오실 계획이므로 **194** 대리 주차 서비스를 제공하는 행사장으로 결정하고자 합니다.

또한, **195** 행사를 담당할 수 있는 출장 요리 전문 업체를 추천해 주실 수 있는지 궁금합니다. 메뉴를 계획할 시간이 충분히 있도록 하기 위해 즉시 한 곳을 찾고자 합니다. 저희 예산으로는, 뷔페 식사가 가장 적합한 선택이 될 것이라고 생각하지만, 귀하의 의견을 듣는 데 귀 기울이겠습니다.

안녕히 계십시오.

션

어휘 inquiry 문의 contact ~에게 연락하다 upcoming 다가오는, 곧 있을 retirement 은퇴, 퇴직 coworker 동료 (직원) based on ~을 바탕으로, 기반으로 recommendation 추천 venue 행사장 quote 가격 견적(서) attach ~을 첨부하다 reflect ~을 반영하다 receive ~을 받다 by (방법) ~함으로써, ~해서 mention that ~라고 언급하다 include ~을 포함하다 as well ~도, 또한 make a booking 예약하다 preferred 선호하는 once ~하는 대로, ~하자마자 make a selection 선택하

다 summary 요약 prepare ~을 준비하다 to be determined 추후 결정되는 capacity 수용 인원 rental 대여, 임대 fee 요금, 수수료 feature 특징 valet parking 대리 주차 on-site 건물 내의, 구내의, 현장의 accommodation 숙박 시설 available 이용 가능한 separately 별도로, 따로 floor-to-ceiling 바닥에서 천장에 이르는 recently 최근에 install ~을 설치하다 setup 설치, 설정, 준비 additional 추가의 decoration 장식(품) purchase ~을 구입하다 rent ~을 대여하다 get back to ~에게 다시 연락하다 plan to do ~할 계획이다 drive to ~로 차를 운전해 가다 go with ~으로 결정하다 offer ~을 제공하다 wonder if ~인지 궁금하다 catering 출장 요리 제공(업) handle ~을 다루다, 처리하다 right away 즉시 ensure that ~임을 보장하다, ~하는 것을 확실히 하다 plenty of 많은 budget 예산 suitable 적합한, 어울리는 open (의견 등에 대해) 귀 기울이는, 마음이 열려 있는

191 애쉬비 씨는 왜 라미레즈 씨에게 연락했는가?
(A) 새로운 날짜를 선택하도록 요청하기 위해
(B) 행사를 위한 몇몇 옵션을 추천하기 위해
(C) 은퇴를 축하해 주기 위해
(D) 업데이트된 손님 명단을 보내기 위해

해설 〈주제 및 목적〉
애쉬비 씨가 발신인으로 되어 있는 첫 지문 시작 부분에, 은퇴 기념 파티를 위해 연락한 것과 관련해, 자신이 행사 장소로 몇 가지 추천해 줄 곳이 있다고(Thank you for contacting me about the upcoming retirement party ~ I have some recommendations for venues) 알리고 있으므로 (B)가 정답이다.

어휘 contact ~에게 연락하다 ask A to do A에게 ~하도록 요청하다 select ~을 선택하다 congratulate A on B B에 대해 A를 축하하다 retirement 은퇴

192 어느 행사장이 라미레즈 씨가 애초에 요청한 특징을 지니고 있는가?
(A) 더 코너웨이
(B) 릿지 플라자
(C) 도브테일 호텔
(D) GL 컨퍼런스 센터

해설 〈지문 연계〉
라미레즈 씨가 요청한 것이 언급되는 첫 지문 첫 단락 마지막에, 해변 경관이 보이는 옵션을 원한다고(~ you wanted the option of seaside views ~) 언급한 사실이 쓰여 있다. 두 번째 지문의 표를 보면, 도브테일 호텔에 바닥에서 천장에 이르는 창문을 통해 해변 경관이 보인다고(Floor-to-ceiling windows with view of coast) 쓰여 있으므로 (C)가 정답이다.

어휘 venue (행사 등의) 개최 장소 feature 특징 originally 애초에, 원래 request ~을 요청하다, 요구하다

193 벨 호텔에 관해 언급된 것은 무엇인가?
(A) 대중교통과 가까이 있다.
(B) 요금이 가장 낮다.
(C) 가장 많은 사람을 수용할 수 있다.
(D) 일부 장비를 업그레이드했다.

해설 〈진위 확인 (세부 진위 유형)〉

벨 호텔이라는 명칭이 제시된 두 번째 지문의 표에, 최근에 설치된 현대적인 음향 시스템이(Modern sound system recently installed) 특징으로 쓰여 있다. 이는 기존의 장비를 업그레이드한 것으로 볼 수 있으므로 (D)가 정답이다.

어휘 near ~와 가까운 public transportation 대중교통 fee 요금, 수수료 hold ~을 수용하다. 보유하다 equipment 장비

194 라미레즈 씨는 대여료로 얼마를 지불할 것 같은가?
(A) 500달러
(B) 850달러
(C) 1,000달러
(D) 1,200달러

해설 〈지문 연계〉
라미레즈 씨가 쓴 이메일인 세 번째 지문 첫 단락에, 대리 주차 서비스를 제공하는 행사장으로 결정하겠다고(~ I'd like to go with the venue that offers valet parking) 알리고 있다. 두 번째 지문의 표에서 이와 같은 특징이 제시된 더 코너웨이의 대여료가 $1,000로 표기되어 있으므로 (C)가 정답이다.

어휘 pay for ~에 대한 비용을 지불하다 rental 대여, 임대

195 라미레즈 씨는 다음으로 무엇을 할 계획인가?
(A) 출장 요리 업체 선정하기
(B) 일부 장식품 구입하기
(C) 일부 초대장 인쇄하기
(D) 음악 연주 그룹 고용하기

해설 〈세부 사항〉
세 번째 지문 두 번째 단락에, 라미레즈 씨는 행사를 담당할 수 있는 출장 요리 전문 업체를 추천해 줄 수 있는지 언급하면서 즉시 한 곳을 찾고 싶다고(I'm wondering if you can recommend a catering business ~ I would like to find one right away ~) 알리고 있다. 따라서 행사 준비를 위한 다음 순서로 출장 요리 업체를 선정하려는 것으로 생각할 수 있으므로 (A)가 정답이다.

어휘 plan to do ~할 계획이다 select ~을 선정하다, 선택하다 purchase ~을 구입하다 decoration 장식(품) invitation 초대(장) hire ~을 고용하다

[196-200] 안내 책자와 두 이메일

로즈 플라자

고급스러움과 현대적임, 그리고 프리미엄 고객 서비스를 원하시면, 로즈 플라자 외에 다른 곳을 찾아보실 필요가 없습니다. 인기 있는 뷰몬트 지역에 위치해 있는. 로즈 플라자는 여러분의 다음 번 행사에 완벽한 장소입니다. 이곳에서 열리는 비즈니스 컨퍼런스가 특히 인기 있는데, 참석자들이 휴식 시간에 도시 내에서 가장 잘 알려진 장소들을(버스로 불과 10분 거리에 있는 윌로우 해변과 같은) 편리하게 방문할 수 있기 때문입니다.

저희는 선택 가능한 다양한 공간을 보유하고 있습니다. 베스타 룸은 최대 40명까지 앉을 수 있으며, 헬릭스 룸은 50명에서 80명까지 앉을 수 있습니다. 세미나와 컨퍼런스, 결혼식, 그리고 기타 대규모 모임 행사를 위해, 저희는 두 곳의 연회실 중 하나를 추천해 드립니다. **198** 타이탄 룸은 80명에서 150명까지 수용할 수 있으며, 리갈 룸은 150명에서 300명까지 수용 가능합니다. 모든 행사 공간은 발표 장비와 현대적인 음향 시스템을 포함하고 있으며, 와이파이도 건물 전역에서 이용 가능합니다.

저희 직원들은 설치 및 장식에 대해 여러분을 도와드릴 준비가 되어 있습니다. **196** 저희는 마지막 순간의 예약도 기꺼이 받습니다. 예약을 원하시거나 더 많은 정보를 알아보시려면, 861-555-3640번으로 저희에게 전화 주십시오.

197 수신: 헬렌 깁슨 〈h.gibson@larkinconsulting.com〉
발신: 아르투로 케이힐 〈a.cahill@larkinconsulting.com〉
날짜: 10월 28일
제목: 연말 연회

안녕하세요, 헬렌 씨.

제가 오늘 아침에 로즈 플라자를 확인했습니다. **197** 이곳이 우리 라킨 컨설팅 사의 연말 연회에 완벽한 장소일 것이라는 당신의 말씀이 맞았습니다. 우리가 필요로 하는 사이즈의 공간이 12월 1일과 12월 6일, 12월 14일, 그리고 **200** 12월 17일 저녁 시간대에 이용 가능합니다. 이 마지막 이용 가능 날짜는 평일이기 때문에 무료 커피와 차 서비스가 포함됩니다. **199** 행사장이 12월 중으로 주차장 노면 재포장 공사를 할 예정이기 때문에, 행사장 자체에는 차량을 위한 공간이 있을 수도 있고 없을 수도 있다는 점에 유의해야 합니다.

엘리스 씨께서 로즈 플라자를 이용하는 것에 대해 찬성하시는지 알아볼 수 있도록 이야기 나눠 보겠습니다. 이 문제가 해결되는 대로, 초대장 작업을 시작할 수 있습니다.

아르투로

수신: 헬렌 깁슨 〈h.gibson@larkinconsulting.com〉
발신: 아르투로 케이힐 〈a.cahill@larkinconsulting.com〉
날짜: 10월 29일
제목: 행사장 승인

안녕하세요, 헬렌 씨.

엘리스 씨께서 로즈 플라자 이용을 승인해 주셨으며, ⑳ 우리가 무료 음료를 받을 수 있는 날짜에 하기로 결정했습니다. 계획할 것이 하나 줄어들게 되었습니다. 이번 주말으로 만나서 초대장에 관해 이야기하실 수 있으신가요? ⑲ 100명의 우리 손님 모두에게 발송해야 할 것입니다. 그러는 동안, 저는 손님 명단을 준비하기 시작하겠습니다.

아르투로

어휘 elegance 고급스러움, 우아함 modernity 현대적임 look no further than ~외에 다른 곳을 찾아볼 필요가 없다 located in ~에 위치한 neighborhood 지역, 인근 particularly 특히 attendee 참석자 best-known 가장 잘 알려진 site 장소, 현지, 부지 break 휴식 시간 a variety of 다양한 choose from ~에서 선택하다 up to 최대 ~까지 gathering 모임 ballroom 연회실 accommodate ~을 수용하다 feature ~을 포함하다, 특징으로 하다 presentation 발표 equipment 장비 available 이용 가능한 throughout ~ 전역에 걸쳐 be ready to do ~할 준비가 되다 assist A with B B에 대해 A를 돕다 setup 설치, 설정, 준비 decoration 장식(품) last-minute 마지막 순간의 reservation 예약 whenever possible 가능할 때마다, 가급적 늘 make a reservation 예약하다 find out more 더 많은 것을 알아 보다 year-end 연말의 banquet 연회 come with ~을 포함하다, ~가 딸려 있다 complimentary 무료의 note that ~을에 유의하다, 주목하다 venue 행사장 have A p.p. A가 ~되게 하다 parking lot 주차장 repave (도로 등) ~을 재포장하다 see if ~인지 확인해 보다 approve of ~을 찬성하다 once ~하는 대로, ~하자마자 settle ~을 해결하다 invitation 초대(장) approve ~을 승인하다 decide to do ~하기로 결정하다 go with (결정 대상 등에 대해) ~로 하다 free 무료의 beverage 음료 one less thing to do ~할 것이 하나 줄어든 send A out A를 발송하다 in the meantime 그러는 동안, 그 사이에 prepare ~을 준비하다

196 로즈 플라자에 관해 언급된 것은 무엇인가?
(A) 예약에 대해 선금을 필요로 한다.
(B) 윌로우 해변을 내려다보고 있다.
(C) 뷰몬트에서 가장 큰 모임 개최 장소이다.
(D) 갑작스러운 통보에도 예약을 받을 수 있다.

해설 〈진위 확인 (전체 진위 유형)〉
로즈 플라자에 관해 설명하는 첫 지문 마지막 단락에, 마지막 순간의 예약도 받는다는 말이 쓰여 있는데(We accommodate last-minute reservations whenever possible), 이는 날짜가 얼마 안 남은 상태에서도 예약을 받는다는 뜻이므로 (D)가 정답이다.

어휘 require ~을 필요로 하다 deposit 선금 reservation 예약 overlook (건물 등이) ~을 내려다보다 venue (행사 등의) 개최 장소 accept ~을 받아들이다, 수용하다 booking 예약 on short notice 갑작스러운 통보에도, 촉박하게

197 깁슨 씨에 관해 암시된 것은 무엇인가?
(A) 예산을 승인해야 한다.
(B) 로즈 플라자 이용을 권장했다.
(C) 연회에서 상을 받을 것이다.
(D) 반드시 최종 결정을 내려야 한다.

해설 〈진위 확인 (전체 진위 유형)〉
수신인이 헬렌 깁슨 씨로 되어 있는 두 번째 지문 첫 단락에, 로즈 플라자가 행사 개최에 완벽할 장소일 수 있다고 말해 준 것이 맞았다고 (You were right that this would be the perfect place ~) 알리는 말이 쓰여 있다. 이는 상대방인 깁슨 씨가 이전에 로즈 플라자를 이용하도록 권한 것을 의미하므로 (B)가 정답이다.

어휘 approve ~을 승인하다 budget 예산 receive ~을 받다 banquet 연회 make a decision 결정을 내리다

198 라킨 컨설팅 사의 행사는 어디에서 개최될 것 같은가?
(A) 베스타 룸에서
(B) 헬릭스 룸에서
(C) 타이탄 룸에서
(D) 리갈 룸에서

해설 〈지문 연계〉
세 번째 지문을 보면 초대 손님 규모가 100명인 것을 알 수 있다(We'll need to send them out to all one hundred of our guests). 첫 지문 두 번째 단락에, 100명의 인원을 수용할 수 있는 공간으로 제시된 곳은 80~150명을 수용할 수 있는 타이탄 룸이므로(The Titan Room can accommodate 80-150 people) (C)가 정답이다.

어휘 take place (행사, 일 등이) 개최되다, 발생되다

199 케이힐 씨는 무슨 잠재적 문제점을 언급하는가?
(A) 메뉴를 선정하는 문제
(B) 건물 내 주차에 대한 어려움
(C) 행사 초대장의 오류
(D) 넓은 방을 예약하는 문제

해설 〈세부 사항〉
두 번째 지문 첫 단락에, 주차장 노면 공사로 인해 행사장에 차량을 위한 공간이 없을 수도 있다는 점에 유의해야 한다는(~ there may or may not be space for cars at the venue itself) 내용이 있다. 이는 주차 문제를 언급하는 것이므로 (B)가 정답이다.

어휘 potential 잠재적인 issue 문제, 사안 select ~을 선정하다, 선택하다 on-site 구내의, 현장의 parking 주차 trouble -ing ~하는 문제 reserve ~을 예약하다

200 라킨 컨설팅 사는 언제 행사를 개최할 것 같은가?
(A) 12월 1일
(B) 12월 6일
(C) 12월 14일
(D) 12월 17일

해설 〈지문 연계〉
세 번째 지문을 보면, 무료 음료를 이용할 수 있는 날짜로 결정했다고(~ we've decided to go with the day on which we can get free beverages) 알리고 있다. 이 서비스와 관련해, 두 번째 지문 첫 단락에 언급된 날짜들 중에서 마지막 날짜인 12월 17일에 무료 커피와 차가 포함되어 있다고(~ December 17. This last open date comes with complimentary coffee and tea ~) 쓰여 있으므로 (D)가 정답이다.

어휘 hold ~을 개최하다, 열다

Actual Test

05

PART 1

1 (C)	2 (C)	3 (B)	4 (B)	5 (D)	6 (C)

PART 2

7 (A)	8 (B)	9 (B)	10 (C)	11 (A)	12 (A)	13 (A)	14 (A)	15 (A)	16 (C)
17 (A)	18 (A)	19 (B)	20 (C)	21 (B)	22 (A)	23 (A)	24 (C)	25 (B)	26 (A)
27 (B)	28 (B)	29 (A)	30 (B)	31 (C)					

PART 3

32 (C)	33 (A)	34 (D)	35 (D)	36 (C)	37 (B)	38 (A)	39 (D)	40 (D)	41 (B)
42 (D)	43 (C)	44 (B)	45 (D)	46 (C)	47 (C)	48 (B)	49 (D)	50 (C)	51 (D)
52 (B)	53 (C)	54 (C)	55 (D)	56 (D)	57 (B)	58 (A)	59 (C)	60 (D)	61 (A)
62 (C)	63 (D)	64 (A)	65 (B)	66 (C)	67 (A)	68 (A)	69 (B)	70 (D)	

PART 4

71 (B)	72 (D)	73 (B)	74 (B)	75 (D)	76 (A)	77 (D)	78 (C)	79 (D)	80 (D)
81 (B)	82 (A)	83 (A)	84 (D)	85 (B)	86 (B)	87 (B)	88 (C)	89 (B)	90 (C)
91 (D)	92 (B)	93 (A)	94 (C)	95 (B)	96 (A)	97 (D)	98 (C)	99 (D)	100 (B)

PART 5

101 (C)	102 (C)	103 (B)	104 (D)	105 (C)	106 (A)	107 (C)	108 (B)	109 (D)	110 (C)
111 (B)	112 (A)	113 (D)	114 (D)	115 (B)	116 (C)	117 (B)	118 (D)	119 (C)	120 (B)
121 (C)	122 (D)	123 (C)	124 (D)	125 (A)	126 (D)	127 (C)	128 (D)	129 (C)	130 (D)

PART 6

131 (C)	132 (B)	133 (D)	134 (B)	135 (D)	136 (C)	137 (C)	138 (C)	139 (B)	140 (C)
141 (D)	142 (D)	143 (B)	144 (D)	145 (B)	146 (C)				

PART 7

147 (B)	148 (C)	149 (A)	150 (B)	151 (C)	152 (B)	153 (B)	154 (C)	155 (D)	156 (D)
157 (A)	158 (C)	159 (A)	160 (D)	161 (B)	162 (A)	163 (D)	164 (D)	165 (C)	166 (B)
167 (C)	168 (D)	169 (B)	170 (A)	171 (C)	172 (C)	173 (A)	174 (B)	175 (B)	176 (B)
177 (C)	178 (D)	179 (B)	180 (B)	181 (C)	182 (A)	183 (D)	184 (C)	185 (A)	186 (B)
187 (C)	188 (C)	189 (C)	190 (C)	191 (B)	192 (C)	193 (D)	194 (B)	195 (A)	196 (B)
197 (C)	198 (D)	199 (C)	200 (A)						

1
(캐W) (A) She is pushing a shopping cart.
(B) She is paying for her groceries.
(C) She is carrying a basket.
(D) She is reaching for some food.

(A) 여자가 쇼핑 카트를 밀고 있다.
(B) 여자가 자신의 식료품 값을 지불하고 있다.
(C) 여자가 바구니를 들고 있다.
(D) 여자가 식품을 꺼내기 위해 팔을 뻗고 있다.

해설 바구니를 팔에 걸고 다니고 있는 여자의 모습에 초점을 맞춰 묘사한 (C)가 정답이다. 카트를 미는 동작과 돈을 지불하는 동작, 그리고 팔을 뻗는 동작은 사진에서 볼 수 없다.

어휘 pay for ~의 값을 지불하다 groceries 식료품 carry ~을 들고 다니다, 휴대하다 reach for ~을 잡기 위해 팔을 뻗다

2
(호M) (A) They're unpacking suitcases.
(B) They're getting into an automobile.
(C) They're handling their luggage.
(D) They're walking toward an archway.

(A) 사람들이 여행 가방을 풀고 있다.
(B) 사람들이 자동차에 타는 중이다.
(C) 사람들이 짐을 다루고 있다.
(D) 사람들이 아치형 통로 쪽으로 걸어가고 있다.

해설 두 사람이 모두 가방을 다루는 모습에 초점을 맞춘 (C)가 정답이다. 여행 가방을 푸는 동작과 자동차에 타는 동작, 아치형 통로 쪽으로 걸어가는 동작은 사진에서 볼 수 없다.

어휘 unpack (짐 등) ~을 풀다, 꺼내다 suitcase 여행 가방 get into ~ 안으로 들어가다 automobile 자동차 handle ~을 다루다, 처리하다 luggage 짐, 수하물 toward ~ 쪽으로 archway 아치형 통로, 아치형 입구

3
(영W) (A) A woman is drinking from a bottle.
(B) Some people are listening to a speaker.
(C) One of the men is taking off his glasses.
(D) The men are arranging mugs in a circle.

(A) 여자가 병에 들어 있는 것을 마시고 있다.
(B) 몇몇 사람들이 한 화자의 말을 듣고 있다.
(C) 남자들 중의 한 명이 안경을 벗는 중이다.
(D) 남자들이 머그잔을 원형으로 정리하고 있다.

해설 세 사람의 시선이 한 남자를 향해 있는 것을 볼 때 한 사람의 말을 듣는 것으로 볼 수 있으므로 이러한 모습에 초점을 맞춘 (B)가 정답이다. 뭔가 마시는 동작, 안경을 벗는 동작, 그리고 머그잔을 정리하는 동작은 사진에서 볼 수 없다.

어휘 drink from ~에 든 것을 마시다 listen to ~의 말을 듣다 take off ~을 벗다, 떼어내다 arrange ~을 정리하다, 정렬하다 in a circle 원형으로, 둥글게

4
(A) The woman is sewing some shirts.
(미M) **(B) Some clothes have been put on hangers.**
(C) Some artwork is propped against the wall.
(D) The woman is folding some laundry.

(A) 여자가 셔츠에 바느질을 하고 있다.
(B) 의류가 옷걸이에 걸려 있는 상태이다.
(C) 예술품이 벽에 기대어 있다.
(D) 여자가 빨래를 개고 있다.

해설 옷들이 옷걸이에 걸려 있는 상태에 초점을 맞춰 묘사한 (B)가 정답이다. 바느질을 하는 동작과 벽에 기대어 있는 예술품, 그리고 빨래를 개는 동작은 사진에서 볼 수 없다.

어휘 sew ~에 바느질을 하다 be put on ~에 놓여 있다 hanger 옷걸이 artwork 예술작품 be propped against (벽 등) ~에 기대어 있다 fold ~을 접다 laundry 빨래

5
(캐W) (A) The man is greeting the woman.
(B) The people are rearranging some furniture.
(C) A ladder is lying next to a column.
(D) The people are seated in a waiting area.

(A) 남자가 여자를 맞이하고 있다.
(B) 사람들이 가구를 재배치하고 있다.
(C) 사다리가 기둥 옆에 놓여 있다.
(D) 사람들이 대기 구역에 앉아 있다.

해설 대기 구역 소파에 나란히 앉아 있는 남녀의 모습에 초점을 맞춘 (D)가 정답이다. 남자가 여자에게 인사하는 동작과 가구를 재배치하는 동작, 그리고 사다리는 사진에서 볼 수 없다.

어휘 greet ~을 맞이하다, 인사하다 rearrange ~을 재배치하다 furniture 가구 ladder 사다리 lie (lying은 현재분사) 놓여 있다, 누워 있다 next to ~ 옆에 column 기둥 be seated in ~에 앉아 있다 waiting area 대기 공간, 대합실, 대기실

6
(A) Cyclists are riding through a park.
(호M) (B) Bicycle tires are being changed.
(C) Buildings overlook a waterway.
(D) Boats are sailing under the bridge.

(A) 자전거를 탄 사람들이 공원 사이로 달리고 있다.
(B) 자전거 타이어들이 교체되고 있다.
(C) 건물들이 수로를 내려다보고 있다.
(D) 보트들이 다리 밑을 지나고 있다.

해설 수로 양쪽에 줄지어 있는 건물들이 수로를 내려다보는 모습에 초점을 맞춘 (C)가 정답이다. 자전거를 타는 사람들과 타이어가 교체되는 동작, 그리고 다리 밑을 지나는 보트는 사진에서 볼 수 없다.

어휘 cyclist 자전거 타는 사람 ride (자동차, 자전거, 말 등을) 타고 달리다, 타고 가다 through ~ 사이로, ~을 통과해 overlook (건물, 나무 등이) ~을 내려다보다 waterway 수로 sail (배가) 지나가다, 항해하다

7
(미M) **(A) It was quite entertaining.**
(영W) (B) Alcala Concert Hall.
(C) Yes, in the evening.

지난주말에 있었던 댄스 공연이 어땠나요?
(A) 꽤 즐거웠어요.
(B) 알칼라 콘서트 홀이요.
(C) 네, 저녁에요.

해설 〈How 의문문〉
지난주말에 있었던 댄스 공연에 대한 의견을 묻는 How 의문문에 대해 dance performance를 It으로 지칭해 꽤 즐거웠다고 답변하는 (A)가 정답이다.
(B) 장소 표현이므로 How와 어울리지 않는 오답
(C) 의문사 의문에 맞지 않는 Yes로 답변하는 오답

어휘 How is A? A는 어떤가요? performance 공연, 연주(회) quite 꽤, 상당히 entertaining 즐거움을 주는

8
(캐W) (A) He has a university degree.
(호M) **(B) A few weeks ago.**
(C) On market trends.

가르자 씨가 언제 연구를 시작했죠?
(A) 그는 대학 학위가 있어요.
(B) 몇 주 전에요.
(C) 시장 동향에 관해서요.

해설 〈When 의문문〉
가르자 씨가 연구를 시작한 시점을 묻는 When 의문문에 대해 대략적인 과거 시점으로 답변하는 (B)가 정답이다.
(A) 대학 학위 소지 사실을 밝히는 말이므로 연구를 시작한 시점을 묻는 When 의문문에 어울리지 않는 오답
(C) 연구 주제를 나타낸 말이므로 연구를 시작한 시점을 묻는 When 의문문에 어울리지 않는 오답

어휘 research 연구, 조사 degree 학위 trend 동향, 추세, 유행

9
(미M) Don't you need a copy of the questionnaire?
(A) My apartment is nearby.
(영W) **(B) No, I've already downloaded one.**
(C) He asked me a few questions.

설문지가 한 부 필요하지 않으세요? (= 필요하시죠?)
(A) 제 아파트가 근처에 있습니다.
(B) 아니요, 이미 한 부 다운로드했어요.
(C) 그가 저에게 몇 가지 질문을 했어요.

해설 〈부정 의문문〉
설문지가 필요하지 않은지 확인하는 부정 의문문에 대해 부정을 뜻하는 No와 함께 questionnaire를 대명사 one으로 지칭해 이미 다운

로드 받았기 때문에 필요치 않다는 뜻을 나타낸 (B)가 정답이다.
(A) 아파트 위치를 나타낸 말이므로 설문지에 대한 필요성을 묻는 질문의 핵심에서 벗어난 오답
(C) 누군지 알 수 없는 He에 대해 말하는 답변으로 설문지에 대한 필요성을 묻는 질문의 핵심에서 벗어난 오답 / 질문의 questionnaire와 일부 발음이 같은 question을 사용한 오답

어휘 questionnaire 설문지 nearby 근처에 있는 ask A a question A에게 질문하다

10 Where is the film festival taking place?
⟨캐W⟩ (A) Before Friday evening.
⟨호M⟩ (B) A movie about space travel.
(C) In the south of France.
어디서 영화제가 개최되나요?
(A) 금요일 저녁 전에요.
(B) 우주 여행에 관한 영화요.
(C) 프랑스 남부 지역에서요.

해설 〈Where 의문문〉
영화제 개최 장소를 묻는 Where 의문문에 대해 특정 지역을 언급하는 (C)가 정답이다.
(A) 시점 표현이므로 Where와 어울리지 않는 오답
(B) 영화 주제를 나타낸 말이므로 Where와 어울리지 않는 오답 / 질문의 film에서 연상되는 movie를 사용한 오답

어휘 take place (행사, 일 등이) 개최되다, 발생되다 space travel 우주 여행

11 Why is the staff room refrigerator unplugged?
⟨미M⟩ (A) Because of the cleaning process.
⟨영W⟩ (B) Cold food and drink.
(C) At the main power outlet.
왜 직원 휴게실 냉장고 전기코드가 빠져 있는 거죠?
(A) 청소 과정 때문에요.
(B) 차가운 식품과 음료요.
(C) 주 전기 콘센트에서요.

해설 〈Why 의문문〉
왜 직원 휴게실 냉장고 전기코드가 빠져 있는지 묻는 Why 의문문에 대해 Why와 짝을 이루는 Because of와 함께 청소 작업을 이유로 언급한 (A)가 정답이다.
(B) 음식의 상태에 해당되는 말이므로 질문의 핵심에서 벗어난 오답 / 질문의 refrigerator에서 연상되는 food and drink를 사용한 오답
(C) 위치 표현에 해당되므로 Why와 어울리지 않는 오답 / 질문의 unplugged에서 연상되는 power outlet을 사용한 오답

어휘 refrigerator 냉장고 unplugged 전기코드가 빠진 process 과정 power outlet 전기 콘센트

12 I need to schedule a checkup.
⟨캐W⟩ (A) I can help you with that.
⟨호M⟩ (B) Can you ask him to check again?
(C) Walk down 8th Street.
제가 건강 검진 일정을 잡아야 합니다.
(A) 제가 도와드릴 수 있습니다.
(B) 그에게 다시 확인해 달라고 요청해 주시겠어요?
(C) 8번가를 따라 걸어가세요.

해설 〈평서문〉
건강 검진 일정을 잡아야 한다는 사실을 밝히는 평서문에 대해 일정을 잡는 일을 that으로 지칭해 자신이 도와주겠다는 의사를 밝힌 (A)가 정답이다.
(B) 누군지 알 수 없는 him에 대한 요청 사항을 나타낸 말이므로 핵심에서 벗어난 오답 / 질문의 checkup과 일부 발음이 같은 check를 사용한 오답
(C) 이동 방향에 해당되는 말이므로 핵심에서 벗어난 오답

어휘 schedule ~의 일정을 잡다 help A with B B에 대해 A를 돕다 ask A to do A에게 ~하도록 요청하다 down (길 등) ~을 따라

13 Who's in charge of making appointments?
⟨영W⟩ (A) I'm not sure.
⟨미M⟩ (B) That's a good point.
(C) Anytime next week.
누가 예약하는 일을 책임지고 있나요?
(A) 잘 모르겠습니다.
(B) 좋은 지적입니다.
(C) 다음 주에 언제든지요.

해설 〈Who 의문문〉
예약하는 일을 책임지고 있는 사람이 누군지 묻는 Who 의문문에 대해 잘 모르겠다는 말로 답변을 회피하는 (A)가 정답이다.
(B) 좋은 지적이라는 뜻으로 동의를 나타내는 말에 해당되므로 Who와 어울리지 않는 오답
(C) 대략적인 미래 시점을 나타내는 말이므로 Who와 어울리지 않는 오답 / 질문의 appointments에서 연상되는 next week을 사용한 오답

어휘 in charge of ~을 책임지고 있는, 맡고 있는 make an appointment 예약하다 That's a good point 좋은 지적입니다 anytime 언제든지, 아무 때나

14 Will the new internship program begin this Friday?
⟨호M⟩ (A) The schedule's online.
⟨캐W⟩ (B) Over a hundred applications.
(C) From the beginning, if you like.
이번 주 금요일에 새 인턴 프로그램이 시작되나요?
(A) 일정표가 온라인상에 있습니다.
(B) 100장이 넘는 지원서요.
(C) 괜찮으시면, 처음부터요.

해설 〈Will 일반 의문문〉
이번 주 금요일에 새 인턴 프로그램이 시작되는지 확인하는 Will 일반 의문문에 대해 그 시작 여부를 알 수 있는 방법을 알려 주는 (A)가 정답이다.
(B) 지원서 수량을 알리는 말이므로 인턴 프로그램 시작 여부를 묻는 질문의 핵심에서 벗어난 오답 / 질문의 internship에서 연상되는 applications를 사용한 오답
(C) 진행 단계를 나타낸 말이므로 인턴 프로그램 시작 여부를 묻는 질문의 핵심에서 벗어난 오답 / 질문의 begin과 일부 발음이 같은 beginning을 사용한 오답

어휘 online 온라인상에 over ~가 넘는 application 지원(서), 신청(서) if you like 괜찮으시면

15 When is the receptionist going on vacation?
⟨영W⟩ (A) The office manager will know.
⟨미M⟩ (B) Yes, you can keep them.
(C) I left it at the reception desk.
안내 담당 직원이 언제 휴가 가나요?
(A) 부장님께서 아실 거예요.
(B) 네, 그것들을 갖고 계셔도 됩니다.
(C) 제가 그걸 안내 데스크에 놓아 두었어요.

해설 〈When 의문문〉
안내 담당 직원이 휴가 가는 시점을 묻는 When 의문문에 대해 부장님께 묻는 것으로 확인 방법을 제시하는 (A)가 정답이다.
(B) 의문사 의문문에 맞지 않는 Yes로 답변하는 오답
(C) 무엇인지 알 수 없는 it을 언급해 그 위치를 알리는 말이므로 When과 어울리지 않는 오답 / 질문의 receptionist와 일부 발음이 같은 reception을 사용한 오답

어휘 receptionist 안내 담당 직원, 접수 담당자 go on vacation 휴가 가다 keep ~을 갖고 있다. 보관하다 leave ~을 놓다, 두다

16 Who's leading the presentation tomorrow?
⟨호M⟩ (A) Please present a valid ID.
⟨캐W⟩ (B) On a phone call.
(C) It hasn't been decided.
누가 내일 있을 발표를 진행하나요?
(A) 유효 신분증을 제시해 주십시오.
(B) 전화상에서요.
(C) 결정되지 않았습니다.

해설 〈Who 의문문〉
내일 있을 발표를 진행할 사람을 묻는 Who 의문문에 대해 결정되지 않았다는 말로 알 수 없다는 뜻을 나타낸 (C)가 정답이다.
(A) 신분증을 제시하도록 요청하는 말에 해당되므로 Who와 어울리지 않는 오답 / 질문의 presentation와 일부 발음이 같은 present를 사용한 오답
(B) 연락 수단에 해당되는 말이므로 Who와 어울리지 않는 오답

어휘 lead ~을 진행하다, 이끌다 presentation 발표(회) present v. ~을 제시하다, 보여 주다 valid 유효한 decide ~을 결정하다

17 Would you mind completing the forms for the building
영W permit?
캐W (A) Of course, I'll start right away.
(B) Photos are permitted.
(C) To make more space.

건축 허가서에 필요한 양식들을 작성 완료해 주시겠습니까?
(A) **물론이죠, 곧바로 시작하겠습니다.**
(B) 사진이 허용됩니다.
(C) 더 넓은 공간을 만들기 위해서요.

해설 〈Would 일반 의문문〉
건축 허가서에 필요한 양식들을 작성하도록 요청하는 Would 일반 의문문에 대해 수락을 뜻하는 Of course와 함께 바로 하겠다고 알리는 (A)가 정답이다.
(B) 사진이 허용된다는 방침을 나타낸 말이므로 양식 작성을 요청하는 질문의 핵심에서 벗어난 오답 / 질문의 permit이 지닌 다른 의미를 활용해 반복한 오답
(C) 목적을 나타낸 말이므로 양식 작성을 요청하는 질문의 핵심에서 벗어난 오답 / 질문의 building에서 연상되는 make more space를 사용한 오답

어휘 Would you mind ing? ~해 주시겠어요? complete ~을 완료하다 form 양식, 서식 permit v. 허가하다, 허가증 v. ~을 허용하다 right away 곧바로, 당장

18 What was the invoice number for the latest bill?
미M (A) Five-four-zero-seven.
호M (B) At the bank.
(C) Yes, for Bolman Accounting.

최근 청구서의 거래 내역서 번호가 뭐였죠?
(A) **5-4-0-7입니다.**
(B) 은행에서요.
(C) 네, 볼만 회계 법인입니다.

해설 〈What 의문문〉
최근 청구서의 거래 내역서 번호를 묻는 What 의문문에 대해 네 자리 특정 숫자를 말하는 (A)가 정답이다.
(B) 장소 표현이므로 번호를 묻는 What 의문문과 어울리지 않는 오답 / 질문의 bill에서 연상되는 bank를 사용한 오답
(C) 의문사 의문문에 맞지 않는 Yes로 답변하는 오답

어휘 invoice 거래 내역서, 송장 latest 최근의, 최신의 bill 청구서, 고지서, 계산서

19 Where do you recommend purchasing a winter coat?
미M (A) That's not available for purchase.
캐W (B) I know a place on Clearwater Avenue.
(C) It looks really good on you.

어디서 겨울 코트를 구입하도록 추천해 주시겠어요?

(A) 그건 구매 가능한 것이 아닙니다.
(B) **클리어워터 애비뉴에 아는 곳이 하나 있어요.**
(C) 정말 잘 어울리시네요.

해설 〈Where 의문문〉
겨울 코트를 구입할 곳을 추천해 달라는 Where 의문문에 대해 자신이 아는 특정 장소를 언급하는 (B)가 정답이다.
(A) 구매 가능성을 나타낸 말이므로 Where와 어울리지 않는 오답 / 질문에 제시된 purchasing의 원형 purchase를 사용한 오답
(C) 상대방이 착용한 의류 등에 대한 칭찬을 나타낸 말이므로 Where와 어울리지 않는 오답 / 질문의 winter coat에서 연상되는 looks really good을 사용한 오답

어휘 recommend -ing ~하도록 추천하다, 권하다 purchase v. ~을 구입하다 n. 구입(품) available 이용 가능한, 구입 가능한 look good on ~에 잘 어울리다

20 Why don't you emphasize the new features in your
영W presentation?
호M (A) Yes, it's a size small.
(B) It went pretty well.
(C) Which ones are most important?

발표에서 새로운 특징들을 강조해 보시는 건 어떠세요?
(A) 네, 스몰 사이즈입니다.
(B) 아주 잘 진행되었습니다.
(C) **어느 것들이 가장 중요한가요?**

해설 〈Why don't you 의문문〉
발표에서 새로운 특징들을 강조해 보도록 제안하는 Why don't you 의문문에 대해 feature를 대명사 one으로 대신해 어느 것을 강조해야 하는지 되묻는 (C)가 정답이다.
(A) 수락을 뜻하는 Yes 뒤에 이어지는 말이 발표에서 해야 하는 일과 관련 없는 오답 / 질문의 emphasize와 일부 발음이 같은 size를 사용한 오답
(B) 과거에 있었던 일의 진행 상황을 나타낸 말이므로 앞으로 발표에서 하도록 제안하는 질문과 관련 없는 오답

어휘 emphasize ~을 강조하다 feature 특징, 기능 presentation 발표(회) go well 잘 진행되다

21 Can you send me copies of Mr. Brown's travel receipts?
미M (A) At the checkout counter.
캐W (B) Sure, I'll do it after lunch.
(C) He works overseas.

브라운 씨의 출장 영수증 사본들을 저에게 보내 주시겠어요?
(A) 계산대에서요.
(B) **네, 점심 식사 후에 해 드릴게요.**
(C) 그분은 해외에서 근무합니다.

해설 〈Can 일반 의문문〉
브라운 씨의 출장 영수증 사본들을 보내 달라고 요청하는 Can 일반 의문문에 대해 수락을 뜻하는 Sure와 함께 send me copies를 do it으로 지칭해 조금 나중에 하겠다고 알리는 (B)가 정답이다.

(A) 위치 표현이므로 영수증 사본들을 보내 달라고 요청하는 질문의 핵심에서 벗어난 오답 / 질문의 receipts에서 연상되는 checkout counter를 사용한 오답
(C) 근무 장소를 나타낸 말이므로 영수증 사본들을 보내 달라고 요청하는 질문의 핵심에서 벗어난 오답 / 질문의 travel에서 연상되는 overseas를 사용한 오답

어휘 receipt 영수증 checkout counter 계산대 overseas 해외에서, 해외로

22 He submitted the paperwork for his visa, right?
영W (A) That's what I heard.
호M (B) We have more paper.
(C) This is the last copy.

그분께서 비자 신청 서류를 제출하셨죠, 맞나요?
(A) **그렇게 들었습니다.**
(B) 우리에게 추가 용지가 있어요.
(C) 이게 마지막 복사본입니다.

해설 〈부가 의문문〉
어떤 남성이 비자 신청 서류를 제출한 게 맞는지 확인하는 부가 의문문에 대해 그 사실을 That으로 지칭해 그렇게 들어서 알고 있다고 긍정의 뜻을 나타낸 (A)가 정답이다.
(B) 용지 보유 사실을 밝히는 말이므로 질문의 핵심에서 벗어난 오답 / 질문의 paperwork와 일부 발음이 같은 paper를 사용한 오답
(C) 복사본의 존재와 관련된 말이므로 질문의 핵심에서 벗어난 오답 / 질문의 paperwork에서 연상 가능한 copy를 사용한 오답

어휘 submit ~을 제출하다 paperwork 서류 (작업)

23 Your suitcase is positioned under your seat, right?
미M (A) No, I put it in the overhead compartment.
캐W (B) Yes, along the zipper.
(C) Is the manager position open?

당신 여행 가방이 좌석 밑에 놓여 있죠, 맞나요?
(A) **아니요, 머리 위쪽 수납 공간에 넣었어요.**
(B) 네, 지퍼를 따라서요.
(C) 그 관리자 직책이 공석인가요?

해설 〈부가 의문문〉
상대방 여행 가방이 좌석 밑에 놓여 있는지 확인하는 부가 의문문에 대해 부정을 뜻하는 No와 함께 suitcase를 it으로 지칭해 다른 위치를 언급하는 (A)가 정답이다.
(B) 긍정을 뜻하는 Yes 뒤에 이어지는 말이 여행 가방의 위치와 관련 없는 오답
(C) 특정 직책의 공석 여부를 확인하는 말이므로 여행 가방의 위치와 관련 없는 오답 / 질문의 positioned가 지닌 다른 의미를 활용해 반복한 오답

어휘 suitcase 여행 가방 position v. ~을 놓다, 두다, 위치시키다 n. 직책, 일자리 overhead 머리 위의 compartment 수납 공간 along (이동) ~을 따라

24
영W (A) I told him to expect you.
호M (B) Not as far as I know.
(C) Which one is faster?

Should we order room service or eat out?
룸서비스를 주문할까요, 아니면 나가서 먹을까요?
(A) 제가 그에게 당신을 기다리라고 말했어요.
(B) 제가 아는 한 그렇지 않습니다.
(C) 어느 것이 더 빠를까요?

해설 〈선택 의문문〉
룸서비스를 주문할지, 아니면 나가서 먹을지 묻는 선택 의문문에 대해 이를 결정하기 위한 조건으로서 그 선택 사항을 대명사 one으로 지칭해 더 빨리 먹을 수 있는 것을 되묻는 (C)가 정답이다.
(A) 누군지 알 수 없는 him에 대해 말하고 있으므로 질문의 핵심에서 벗어난 오답
(B) 경험 또는 지식을 토대로 자신이 아는 바를 밝힐 때 사용하는 말이 므로 질문의 핵심에서 벗어난 오답

어휘 order ~을 주문하다 tell A to do A에게 ~하라고 말하다 expect (오기로 되어 있는 대상에 대해) ~을 기다리다 as far as I know 내가 아는 한

25
미M (A) The bus to New York.
캐W **(B) No, I'll do that in the morning.**
(C) She was surprised, too.

Did you remember to contact the supplier?
잊지 않고 공급업체에 연락하셨죠?
(A) 뉴욕행 버스요.
(B) 아니요, 아침에 할 겁니다.
(C) 그녀도 놀라워했어요.

해설 〈Do 일반 의문문〉
잊지 않고 공급업체에 연락했는지 확인하는 Do 일반 의문문에 대해 부정을 뜻하는 No와 함께 아침에 하겠다는 말로 아직 연락하지 않았 다는 뜻을 나타낸 (B)가 정답이다.
(A) 교통 수단을 나타낸 말이므로 질문의 핵심에서 벗어난 오답
(C) 누군지 알 수 없는 She에 대해 말하고 있으므로 질문의 핵심에서 벗어난 오답 / 질문의 supplier와 발음이 유사한 surprised를 사용 한 오답

어휘 remember to do ~하는 것을 기억하다, 잊지 않고 ~하다 contact ~에게 연락하다 surprised 놀라워하는

26
영W The air conditioner in the break room is still malfunctioning, isn't it?
호M **(A) The maintenance team is on their way now.**
(B) No, I already took my lunch break.
(C) The working conditions have improved.

휴게실에 있는 에어컨이 여전히 오작동하고 있죠, 그렇지 않나요? (= 오작동 되고 있죠?)
(A) 시설 관리팀이 지금 가고 있어요.
(B) 아니요, 저는 이미 점심 식사했어요.
(C) 근무 조건이 개선되었어요.

해설 〈부가 의문문〉
휴게실 에어컨이 여전히 오작동하고 있지 않은지 확인하는 부가 의문 문에 대해 조치를 위해 시설 관리팀이 가고 있다는 뜻을 나타낸 (A)가 정답이다.
(B) 부정을 뜻하는 No 뒤에 이어지는 말이 에어컨 오작동 여부와 관련 없는 오답 / 질문의 break를 반복한 오답
(C) 근무 조건의 개선 사실을 나타낸 말이므로 에어컨 오작동 여부와 관련 없는 오답 / 질문의 conditioner와 거의 발음이 같은 conditions를 사용한 오답

어휘 break room 휴게실 malfunction 오작동되다, 제대로 작동되지 않 다 maintenance 시설 관리, 유지 보수 on one's way 가고 있는, 오고 있는 lunch break 점심 시간 working conditions 근무 조건 improve 개선되다, 향상되다

27
미M Can I start the presentation now, or should I wait for the accountant?
캐W (A) I'll go back to the start.
(B) Did she say she would be attending?
(C) You should count them again.

발표를 지금 시작해도 되나요, 아니면 회계 담당 직원을 기다려야 하나요?
(A) 처음으로 되돌아가겠습니다.
(B) 그분이 참석할 거라고 하던가요?
(C) 그것들을 다시 세어 보세요.

해설 〈선택 의문문〉
발표를 지금 시작할지, 아니면 회계 담당 직원을 기다려야 하는지 묻는 선택 의문문에 대해 the accountant를 she로 지칭해 그 사람이 참 석하는 건지 되묻는 (B)가 정답이다.
(A) 진행 단계에 해당되는 말이므로 질문의 핵심에서 벗어난 오답 / 질 문의 start를 반복한 오답
(C) 무엇인지 알 수 없는 them에 대해 말하고 있으므로 질문의 핵 심에서 벗어난 오답 / 질문의 accountant와 일부 발음이 유사한 count를 사용한 오답

어휘 presentation 발표(회) accountant 회계 담당자 go back to ~로 되돌아가다 attend 참석하다

28
영W How can I transfer some funds to an account overseas?
호M (A) It's a popular travel destination.
(B) Just follow the online instructions.
(C) A substantial amount more.

해외에 있는 계좌로 어떻게 일부 자금을 이체할 수 있나요?
(A) 인기 있는 여행지입니다.
(B) 온라인상의 안내를 따르기만 하면 됩니다.
(C) 상당한 액수 추가요.

해설 〈How 의문문〉
해외에 있는 계좌로 돈을 이체하는 방법을 묻는 How 의문문에 대해 그 정보를 확인할 수 있는 방법을 알려 주는 (B)가 정답이다.
(A) 여행지의 특성을 나타낸 말이므로 질문의 핵심에서 벗어난 오답 / 질문의 overseas에서 연상되는 travel destination을 사용한 오답
(C) 비용 규모에 해당되는 말이므로 질문의 핵심에서 벗어난 오답 / 질 문의 funds에서 연상되는 amount를 사용한 오답

어휘 transfer ~을 이체하다, 송금하다 fund 자금, 돈 account 계좌, 계 정 overseas 해외에, 해외로 popular 인기 있는 destination 목적 지, 도착지 follow ~을 따르다, 준수하다 instructions 안내, 설명, 지 시 substantial 상당한 amount 액수, 금액

29
미M Aren't we having a marketing meeting with Mr. Boyle at 4?
캐W **(A) It was postponed until 5.**
(B) I have an extra copy here.
(C) The presentation was interesting.

4시에 보일 씨와 마케팅 회의를 하지 않나요? (= 하는 거죠?)
(A) 5시로 연기되었습니다.
(B) 여기 여분으로 한 부 있습니다.
(C) 그 발표가 흥미로웠어요.

해설 〈부정 의문문〉
4시에 보일 씨와 마케팅 회의를 하지 않는지 묻는 부정 의문문에 대해 marketing meeting을 It으로 지칭해 연기된 사실과 바뀐 시각을 알 리는 (A)가 정답이다.
(B) 여분의 사본을 갖고 있다는 사실을 나타낸 말이므로 회의 개최 여 부를 묻는 질문의 핵심에서 벗어난 오답
(C) 과거에 있었던 발표에 대한 의견을 나타낸 말이므로 미래 시점의 회의 개최 여부를 묻는 질문과 시점이 맞지 않는 오답

어휘 postpone ~을 연기하다, 미루다 extra 여분의, 별도의 presentation 발표(회)

30
미M Which fabrics are currently in stock?
캐W (A) That's a good choice.
(B) Our entire selection is available now.
(C) Yes, the suits and dresses.

어느 직물이 현재 재고가 있나요?
(A) 좋은 선택입니다.
(B) 저희 모든 제품 종류가 지금 구매 가능합니다.
(C) 네, 양복과 드레스들이요.

해설 〈Which 의문문〉
현재 재고가 있는 직물이 어느 것인지 묻는 Which 의문문에 대해 모 든 제품이 구매 가능하다는 사실을 밝히는 (B)가 정답이다.
(A) 무엇인지 알 수 없는 That에 대해 말하고 있으므로 재고품 존재 여부와 관련해 묻는 질문의 핵심에서 벗어난 오답
(C) 의문사 의문문에 맞지 않는 Yes로 답변하는 오답

어휘 fabric 직물, 섬유　currently 현재　in stock 재고가 있는　choice 선택　entire 모든, 전체의　selection (선택 대상이 되는 제품 등의) 종류　available 구매 가능한, 이용 가능한　suit 양복, 정장

31 I'm thinking of getting an apartment in Stratford.
호M (A) Which moving company did you use?
영W (B) Only if my loan is approved.
(C) How long would your commute be from there?

제가 스트랫포드에 아파트를 구할 생각이에요.
(A) 어느 이사 전문 업체를 이용하셨어요?
(B) 제 대출이 승인되는 경우에만요.
(C) 거기서 통근하면 얼마나 오래 걸릴 것 같으세요?

해설 〈평서문〉
스트랫포드에 아파트를 구할 생각임을 밝히는 평서문에 대해 Stratford를 there로 지칭해 통근 시간을 확인하기 위해 되묻는 (C)가 정답이다.
(A) 과거 시점에 이용한 이사 전문 업체를 묻는 질문으로서 이미 이사한 후에 물을 수 있는 말이므로 핵심에서 벗어난 오답 / 질문의 getting an apartment에서 연상되는 moving company를 사용한 오답
(B) 자신의 대출 승인 여부를 조건으로 언급한 말인데, 이는 이사할 사람이 할 수 있는 말에 해당되므로 주체가 뒤바뀐 오답

어휘 only if 오직 ~하는 경우에만　loan 대출　approve ~을 승인하다　commute 통근

Questions 32-34 refer to the following conversation. 캐W 미M

W Hello, this is Kerry Lewis. **㉜ I am making a documentary,** and I'm hoping to arrange a tour of your manufacturing facility. **㉜ My next film** is about green energy, and I know your company uses solar power.

M That's right. **㉝ Our company recently won an environmental award for the solar panels we utilize,** and I'd love to show you around the factory. How about next Thursday at 9 A.M.?

W That would be perfect. I really appreciate it.

M Great. When you arrive, **㉞ the security guard will give you a safety helmet and glasses. You'll need to put those on** before entering the factory.

여 안녕하세요, 저는 케리 루이스입니다. 제가 다큐멘터리를 제작하고 있는데, 귀사의 제조 시설을 견학하는 일정을 잡고자 합니다. 제 다음 영화가 친환경 에너지에 관한 것인데, 귀사에서 태양열 발전 시스템을 활용하고 있는 것으로 알고 있어요.
남 맞습니다. 저희 회사가 최근에 저희가 활용하고 있는 태양열 전지판에 대해 환경 관련 상을 받았으며, 공장을 꼭 둘러보시게 해 드리고 싶습니다. 다음 주 목요일 오전 9시가 어떠세요?
여 아주 좋을 것 같아요. 정말 감사드립니다.
남 좋습니다. 도착하시면, 보안 직원이 안전모와 보호 안경을 제공해 드릴 겁니다. 공장에 들어오시기 전에 착용하셔야 합니다.

어휘 hope to do ~하기를 바라다　arrange ~의 일정을 잡다, ~을 마련하다　manufacturing 제조　facility 시설(물)　green 친환경의　solar power 태양열 발전 (시스템)　recently 최근에　win an award 상을 받다　utilize ~을 활용하다　would love to do 꼭 ~하고 싶다　show A around B A에게 B를 둘러보게 해 주다　How about ~? ~는 어떠세요?　appreciate ~에 대해 감사하다　arrive 도착하다　put A on A를 착용하다

32 Who most likely is the woman?
(A) A scientist
(B) An author
(C) A filmmaker
(D) A factory manager

여자는 누구일 것 같은가?
(A) 과학자
(B) 작가
(C) 영화감독
(D) 공장 관리 책임자

해설 〈직업을 묻는 문제〉
여자가 대화를 시작하면서 다큐멘터리를 제작한다는(I am making a documentary) 말과 함께 자신이 만드는 다음 영화의(My next film) 주제를 언급하고 있으므로 (C)가 정답이다.

33 What did the company receive an environmental award for?
(A) Using solar power
(B) Reducing waste
(C) Designing a product
(D) Recycling materials

회사에서 무엇 때문에 환경 관련 상을 받았는가?
(A) 태양열 발전 시스템을 이용하는 것
(B) 쓰레기를 줄인 것
(C) 제품을 디자인한 것
(D) 재료를 재활용한 것

해설 〈기타 세부 사항을 묻는 문제〉
대화 중반부에 남자가 회사에서 활용하는 태양열 전지판에 대해 환경 관련 상을 받았다고(Our company recently won an environmental award for the solar panels we utilize) 알리고 있으므로 (A)가 정답이다.

어휘 receive ~을 받다　reduce ~을 줄이다, 감소시키다　recycle ~을 재활용하다　material 재료, 자재, 물품

34 What does the man say the woman will have to do?
(A) Sign a document
(B) Attend a training class
(C) Obtain a security pass
(D) Wear safety gear

남자는 여자가 무엇을 해야 한다고 말하는가?
(A) 서류에 서명하는 일
(B) 교육 강좌에 참석하는 일
(C) 보안 출입증을 받는 일
(D) 안전 장비를 착용하는 일

해설 〈미래에 할 일을 묻는 문제〉
대화 맨 마지막에 남자가 보안 직원이 안전모와 보호 안경을 제공한다는 사실과 이를 착용해야 한다는 사실을(the security guard will give you a safety helmet and glasses. You'll need to put those on) 함께 언급하고 있으므로 (D)가 정답이다.

어휘 sign ~에 서명하다　attend ~에 참석하다　training 교육, 훈련　obtain ~을 받다, 얻다　security pass 보안 출입증　safety gear 안전 장비

W Samuel, are you still working on the business cards for Mortimer Enterprises? ㉟ We need to print them today.

M I'm almost finished. I wanted to make sure they were perfect.

W I'm glad to hear that. We need to get a good review from the company.

M Exactly. ㊱ Since we're hoping to bring in more customers to ㉟ our print shop ㊱ through this new design service, it needs to be done right. Here, you can see what I've done so far.

W Hmm that looks great. But ㊲ let me check if the contact information on the card is correct.

여 사무엘 씨, 여전히 모티머 엔터프라이즈 사의 명함 작업을 하고 계신가요? 우리가 오늘 그 명함들을 출력해야 해요.

남 거의 끝났어요. 완벽한 상태인지 확실히 해 두고 싶었습니다.

여 그 말씀을 들으니 다행이네요. 우리는 그 회사로부터 좋은 평가를 받아야 합니다.

남 맞아요. 이 새로운 디자인 서비스를 통해 우리 인쇄소로 더 많은 고객들을 끌어들이기를 바라고 있기 때문에, 제대로 완료되어야 해요. 여기, 제가 지금까지 완료한 것을 확인해 보실 수 있습니다.

여 흠 아주 좋아 보이네요. 하지만 명함에 연락처가 정확한지 확인해 볼게요.

어휘 work on ~에 대한 작업을 하다 business card 명함 make sure (that) ~임을 확실히 해 두다, 반드시 ~하도록 하다 review 평가, 의견, 후기 since ~이므로 bring in ~을 끌어들이다 through ~을 통해 right ad. 제대로, 정확히 so far 지금까지 look + 형용사 ~하게 보이다, ~한 것 같다 contact information 연락처 correct 정확한, 올바른, 알맞은

35 Where most likely do the speakers work?
(A) At a construction firm
(B) At a recruitment firm
(C) At a finance company
(D) At a printing company

화자들은 어디에서 일하고 있을 것 같은가?
(A) 건설 업체에서
(B) 인력 채용 전문 회사에서
(C) 금융회사에서
(D) 인쇄 업체에서

해설 〈근무지를 묻는 문제〉
대화 초반부에 여자가 한 회사에서 쓸 명함을 언급하면서 그것을 오늘 인쇄해야 한다고(We need to print them today) 말하고 있으며, 중반부에는 남자가 our print shop으로 소속 업체를 가리키고 있으므로 (D)가 정답이다.

---

36 How is the business trying to attract more customers?
(A) By adding a delivery option
(B) By reducing its prices
(C) By offering a new service
(D) By extending its business hours

해당 업체에서 어떻게 더 많은 고객을 끌어들이려 하고 있는가?
(A) 배송 선택 사항을 추가함으로써
(B) 가격을 인하함으로써
(C) 신규 서비스를 제공함으로써
(D) 영업 시간을 연장함으로써

해설 〈기타 세부 사항을 묻는 문제〉
대화 중반부에 남자가 새로운 디자인 서비스를 통해 인쇄소로 더 많은 고객들을 끌어들이기를 바란다고(Since we're hoping to bring in more customers to our print shop through this new design service) 언급하는 내용이 있으므로 신규 서비스 제공을 뜻하는 (C)가 정답이다.

어휘 try to do ~하려 하다 attract ~을 끌어들이다 by (방법) ~함으로써, ~해서 add ~을 추가하다 reduce ~을 줄이다, 감소시키다 offer ~을 제공하다 extend ~을 연장하다

37 What does the woman say she will do?
(A) Hire more employees
(B) Check some details
(C) Meet with a client
(D) Order more supplies

여자는 무엇을 할 것이라고 말하는가?
(A) 추가 직원을 모집하는 일
(B) 몇몇 세부 사항을 확인하는 일
(C) 한 고객과 만나는 일
(D) 추가 용품을 주문하는 일

해설 〈미래에 할 일을 묻는 문제〉
대화 맨 마지막에 여자가 명함에 연락처가 정확한지 확인해 보겠다고(let me check if the contact information on the card is correct) 알리고 있는데, 이는 명함에 표기되는 세부 사항을 확인하는 것을 뜻하므로 (B)가 정답이다.

어휘 hire ~을 고용하다 details 세부 사항, 상세 정보 meet with (약속하여) ~와 만나다 order ~을 주문하다 supplies 용품, 물품

W ㊳ Hi, I'm here for the marketing seminar. Are you the instructor?

M Yes, I'll be talking to you all about trends in how businesses market their products and services. What do you hope to learn from my seminar?

W ㊴ I'd like to receive a promotion at work, and I think the things I learn in this seminar might help me with that.

M Some of the knowledge I'll share with you today might give you an edge over the other promotion seekers. Now, before you take your seat, ㊵ could you please sign the attendance list I have here? Thanks.

여 안녕하세요. 마케팅 세미나 때문에 이곳에 왔습니다. 강사이신가요?

남 네, 저는 기업들이 어떻게 제품과 서비스를 마케팅하는지 전반적인 경향에 대해 말씀 드릴 겁니다. 제 세미나에서 어떤 것을 배우기를 바라시나요?

여 제가 회사에서 승진하기를 원하고 있어서, 이 세미나를 통해 배우는 것들이 도움이 될 수도 있을 거라고 생각합니다.

남 제가 오늘 공유해 드릴 지식의 일부가 다른 승진 희망자들보다 우위를 점하게 해 드릴 수 있을 것입니다. 자, 착석하시기 전에, 제가 여기 갖고 있는 참석자 명단에 서명해 주시겠습니까? 감사합니다.

어휘 instructor 강사 trend 경향, 추세 market v. ~을 마케팅하다 would like to do ~하고 싶다, ~하고자 하다 receive a promotion 승진하다 at work 직장에서 help A with B B에 대해 A를 돕다 share A with B A를 B와 공유하다 give A an edge over B B보다 A에게 우위를 점하게 해 주다 seeker 구하는 사람, 찾는 사람 take one's seat 착석하다 attendance 참석, 참석자 수

38 What is the topic of the seminar?
(A) Marketing
(B) Customer service
(C) Accounting
(D) Online sales

세미나 주제는 무엇인가?
(A) 마케팅
(B) 고객 서비스
(C) 회계
(D) 온라인 영업

해설 〈주제를 묻는 문제〉
여자가 대화를 시작하면서 마케팅 세미나 때문에 왔다고(Hi, I'm here for the marketing seminar) 언급하는 통해 세미나 주제를 파악할 수 있으므로 (A)가 정답이다.

39 What does the woman say she wants to do?
(A) Enroll at a university
(B) Move to a different company
(C) Attract new employees
(D) Gain a promotion

여자는 무엇을 하고 싶다고 말하는가?
(A) 대학교에 등록하는 일
(B) 다른 회사로 이직하는 일
(C) 신입 사원을 모집하는 일
(D) 승진하는 일

해설 〈기타 세부 사항을 묻는 문제〉
대화 중반부에 여자가 회사에서 승진하고 싶다는 말로(I'd like to receive a promotion at work) 원하는 바를 알리고 있으므로 (D)가 정답이다.

어휘 enroll 등록하다 attract ~을 끌어들이다 gain a promotion 승진되다

40 What will the woman most likely do next?
(A) Check a seating chart
(B) Show her ID card
(C) Read a pamphlet
(D) Add a signature

여자는 곧이어 무엇을 할 것 같은가?
(A) 좌석 배치도를 확인하는 일
(B) 신분증을 보여 주는 일
(C) 소책자를 읽어 보는 일
(D) 서명을 추가하는 일

해설 〈곧이어 할 일을 묻는 문제〉
대화 맨 마지막에 남자가 여자에게 자리에 앉기 전에 참석자 명단에 서명하도록(could you please sign the attendance list I have here?) 요청하고 있으므로 (D)가 정답이다.

어휘 seating chart 좌석 배치도 pamphlet 소책자 add ~을 추가하다 signature 서명

Questions 41-43 refer to the following conversation with three speakers. 영W 호M 캐W

W1 Good morning, Mr. Flynn? **㊶ This is Kristi Wheeler from Ashmore Technology. ㊷ We would like to offer you the senior programmer position.**
M That's wonderful. Thank you!
W1 The next step is to finalize the contract, so let me transfer you to one of the HR managers, Ms. Vincent.
M All right.
W2 Hi, Mr. Flynn. It's Melissa Vincent. We'd like you to come to the office on July 19 to go over the contract. Are you free at two o'clock?
M Yes. Last time I visited, I couldn't park on-site because **㊸ I didn't have a parking pass. Could I get one?**
W2 Sure, **㊸ I'll mail you one today.**

여1 안녕하세요, 플린 씨? 저는 애쉬모어 테크놀로지의 크리스티 휠러입니다. 저희가 수석 프로그래머 직책을 제안해 드리고자 합니다.
남 아주 잘됐네요. 감사합니다!
여1 다음 단계는 계약을 최종 완료하는 것이기 때문에, 저희 인사부장님들 중의 한 분이신 빈센트 씨께 연결해 드리겠습니다.
남 알겠습니다.
여2 안녕하세요, 플린 씨. 저는 멜리사 빈센트입니다. 7월 19일에 사무실로 오셔서 계약서를 검토해 보셨으면 합니다. 2시에 시간 괜찮으신가요?
남 네. 지난번에 방문했을 때, 주차권이 없어서 구내에 주차할 수 없었어요. 한 장 받을 수 있을까요?
여2 물론이죠. 오늘 우편으로 발송해 드리겠습니다.

어휘 would like to do ~하고자 하다, ~하고 싶다 offer A B A에게 B를 제안하다, 제공하다 position 직책, 일자리 finalize ~을 최종 완료하다 contract 계약(서) transfer A to B (전화상에서) A를 B에게 연결해 주다 HR manager 인사부장 go over ~을 검토하다, 살펴보다 park v. 주차하다 on-site 구내에, 현장에 parking pass 주차권 mail A B A를 B에게 우편으로 보내다

41 In what field do the women most likely work?
(A) Law
(B) Technology
(C) Medicine
(D) Education

두 여자는 어떤 분야에서 일하고 있을 것 같은가?
(A) 법률
(B) 기술
(C) 의학
(D) 교육

해설 〈근무 분야를 묻는 문제〉
대화를 시작하면서 여자 한 명이 소속 업체를 from Ashmore Technology라고 알리고 있으므로 (B)가 정답이다.

어휘 field 분야, 업계

42 Why did Ms. Wheeler call the man?
(A) To thank him for his help
(B) To conduct a job interview
(C) To ask for a résumé
(D) To make a job offer

휠러 씨는 왜 남자에게 전화했는가?
(A) 도움에 대해 감사하기 위해
(B) 구인 면접을 실시하기 위해
(C) 이력서를 요청하기 위해
(D) 일자리를 제안하기 위해

해설 〈목적을 묻는 문제〉
대화 초반부에 여자 한 명이 수석 프로그래머 직책을 제안하고자 한다고(We would like to offer you the senior programmer position) 말한 뒤로 고용 계약서 작성과 관련해 이야기하고 있으므로 (D)가 정답이다.

어휘 conduct ~을 실시하다, 수행하다 ask for ~을 요청하다 résumé 이력서 make a job offer 일자리를 제안하다

43 What will the man receive in the mail?
(A) A business card
(B) A signed contract
(C) A parking pass
(D) A work schedule

남자는 우편으로 무엇을 받을 것인가?
(A) 명함
(B) 서명된 계약서
(C) 주차권
(D) 업무 일정표

해설 〈기타 세부 사항을 묻는 문제〉
대화 후반부에 남자가 과거에 주차권을 받지 못했던 일을 언급하면서 한 장 받을 수 있는지 묻자(I didn't have a parking pass. Could I get one?), 여자 한 명이 오늘 우편으로 보내 주겠다고(I'll mail you one today) 알리고 있으므로 (C)가 정답이다.

어휘 receive ~을 받다 sign ~에 서명하다 contract 계약(서)

W ④④ I'm really looking forward to meeting our new investors from the financial firm in Japan.

M ④④ Same here. They'll be arriving at 9 A.M. tomorrow and coming straight here for our CEO's presentation at 10.

W ④⑤ Oh, the presentation is at 10? I'm interviewing job candidates all morning.

M Can you join us for the factory tour in the afternoon?

W Yeah, that shouldn't be a problem.

M Great. ④⑥ Please bring your business cards, too. I'm sure they will want to exchange them.

여 일본의 금융 회사에서 오는 새 투자자들을 만나기를 정말로 고대하고 있습니다.

남 저도 그렇습니다. 그분들이 내일 오전 9시에 도착해서 이곳에서 10시에 있을 우리 대표이사님 발표회장으로 곧장 오실 겁니다.

여 아, 그 발표가 10시인가요? 제가 오전 내내 구직 지원자들을 면접 보거든요.

남 오후에 있을 공장 견학은 함께 하실 수 있으세요?

여 네, 그건 문제없을 겁니다.

남 잘됐네요. 명함도 가져오세요. 분명 그분들이 교환하고 싶어 할 거예요.

어휘 look forward to -ing ~하기를 고대하다 investor 투자자 financial firm 금융 회사 arrive 도착하다 straight 곧장, 곧바로 presentation 발표(회) candidate 지원자, 후보자 join ~와 함께 하다 bring ~을 가져오다 business card 명함 exchange ~을 교환하다

44 What are the speakers mainly talking about?
(A) A monthly department meeting
(B) A visit from investors
(C) An overseas job opportunity
(D) A successful business merger

화자들은 주로 무엇에 대해 이야기하고 있는가?
(A) 월간 부서 회의
(B) 투자자들의 방문
(C) 해외 취업 기회
(D) 성공적인 회사 합병

해설 〈주제를 묻는 문제〉
대화 시작 부분에 여자가 일본에서 오는 새 투자자를 만나기를 고대하고 있다고(I'm really looking forward to meeting our new investors from the financial firm in Japan) 밝힌 것에 대해 남자도 Same here라는 말로 동의하고 있으므로 (B)가 정답이다.

어휘 monthly 월간의, 달마다의 department 부서 investor 투자자 overseas 해외의 opportunity 기회 successful 성공적인 merger 합병

45 What does the woman imply when she says, "I'm interviewing job candidates all morning"?
(A) She is confident a position will be filled.
(B) She is surprised by the number of applications.
(C) She would like the man to assist her.
(D) She is unable to attend a presentation.

여자가 "I'm interviewing job candidates all morning"라고 말할 때 무엇을 암시하는가?
(A) 직책이 충원될 것으로 확신하고 있다.
(B) 지원서 숫자에 놀라워하고 있다.
(C) 남자에게 자신을 도와주기를 원하고 있다.
(D) 발표에 참석할 수 없다.

해설 〈의도 파악 문제〉
대화 중반부에 여자가 발표가 10시인지 물으면서(Oh, the presentation is at 10?) '오전 내내 구직 지원자들을 면접 본다'고 언급하는 흐름이다. 이는 발표에 참석할 수 없는 이유를 밝히는 것이므로 (D)가 정답이다.

어휘 be confident (that) ~임을 확신하다 position 직책, 일자리 fill ~을 충원하다, 채우다 application 지원(서), 신청(서) would like A to do A에게 ~하기를 원하다 assist ~을 돕다 be unable to do ~할 수 없다 attend ~에 참석하다 presentation 발표(회)

46 What does the man remind the woman to do?
(A) Join a business lunch
(B) Contact a supervisor
(C) Bring business cards
(D) Make a reservation

남자는 여자에게 무엇을 하도록 상기시키는가?
(A) 업무상의 오찬에 함께 하는 일
(B) 부서장에게 연락하는 일
(C) 명함을 지참해 오는 일
(D) 예약을 하는 일

해설 〈상기시키는 것을 묻는 문제〉
담화 후반부에 남자가 여자에게 명함을 챙겨 오라고(Please bring your business cards, too) 당부하고 있으므로 (C)가 정답이다.

어휘 join ~에 함께 하다, 합류하다 contact ~에게 연락하다 supervisor 부서장, 책임자, 감독 make a reservation 예약하다

W Good morning, and ④⑦ welcome to Bluebird Bakery. How may I help you?

M Hello. ④⑧ I would like to order a custom decorated cake for my friend's birthday.

W Sure. We'll need to know exactly what you have in mind, such as the colors and the writing.

M That's no problem. I brought a picture of what I want. ④⑨ It is saved as a file on this flash drive.

W All right. ④⑨ Let me save that on our computer so we can use it as a reference.

여 안녕하세요, 그리고 블루버드 베이커리에 오신 것을 환영합니다. 무엇을 도와드릴까요?

남 안녕하세요. 제 친구 생일을 위해 맞춤 제작으로 장식된 케이크를 주문하려고 합니다.

여 네. 어떤 것을 생각해 두고 계신지 정확히 알아야 합니다. 색상이나 문구 같은 것을요.

남 좋습니다. 제가 원하는 것의 사진을 가져 왔습니다. 이 플래시 드라이브에 파일로 저장되어 있습니다.

여 알겠습니다. 저희가 참고용으로 사용할 수 있도록 저희 컴퓨터에 저장해 두겠습니다.

어휘 would like to do ~하고 싶다, ~하고자 하다 order ~을 주문하다 custom 맞춤 제작의, 주문 제작의 decorate ~을 장식하다 exactly 정확히 have A in mind A를 생각해 두다, A를 염두에 두다 writing 문구, 글 save A as B A를 B로 저장하다 so (that) ~할 수 있도록 reference 참고 (자료)

47 Where is the conversation taking place?
(A) At a bookstore
(B) At a clothing store
(C) At a bakery
(D) At a computer shop

대화가 어디에서 진행되고 있는가?
(A) 서점에서
(B) 의류 매장에서
(C) 제과점에서
(D) 컴퓨터 매장에서

해설 〈대화 장소를 묻는 문제〉
대화 시작 부분에 여자가 welcome to Bluebird Bakery라는 말로 제과점에 온 것을 환영하는 인사를 하고 있으므로 (C)가 정답이다.

어휘 take place (일, 행사 등이) 발생되다, 개최되다

48 What does the man want to do?
(A) Return an item
(B) Place a custom order
(C) Watch a demonstration
(D) Apply for a job

남자는 무엇을 하고 싶어 하는가?
(A) 제품을 반품하는 일
(B) 맞춤 주문을 하는 일
(C) 시연회를 보는 일
(D) 일자리에 지원하는 일

해설 〈기타 세부 사항을 묻는 문제〉
남자가 대화 초반부에 친구 생일을 위해 맞춤 제작으로 장식된 케이크를 주문하고 싶다고(I would like to order a custom decorated cake) 알리고 있으므로 (B)가 정답이다.

어휘 return ~을 반품하다, 반납하다 place an order 주문하다 custom 맞춤 제작의, 주문 제작한 demonstration 시연(회) apply for ~에 지원하다, ~을 신청하다

49 What will the woman most likely do next?
(A) Speak to a manager
(B) Write down an address
(C) Print out a form
(D) Save a file

여자는 곧이어 무엇을 할 것 같은가?
(A) 책임자와 이야기하는 일
(B) 주소를 적어 두는 일
(C) 양식을 출력하는 일
(D) 파일을 저장하는 일

해설 〈곧이어 할 일을 묻는 문제〉
남자가 대화 후반부에 자신이 원하는 것이 플래시 드라이브에 파일로 저장되어 있다고(It is saved as a file on this flash drive) 말한 것에 대해 여자가 그것을 컴퓨터에 저장하겠다고(Let me save that on our computer) 알리고 있으므로 (D)가 정답이다.

어휘 print out ~을 출력하다, 인쇄하다 form 양식, 서식

Questions 50-52 refer to the following conversation. 캐W 미M

W Hello, and (50) thank you for calling Riverside Bistro. How may I help you?
M Hi, my name is Ben Akers, and (50) I handed in my résumé to your restaurant last month. I'd just like to follow up on that. Can you tell me whether you are currently hiring?
W Unfortunately, we have all the staff we need for the moment. But, (51) if someone leaves and a job opens up, I could contact you.
M Thanks, I'd appreciate it.
W By the way, I should let you know that our business will be moving to March Street on the outskirts of town next week.
M Oh, really? (52) That's quite far. I doubt I could take a bus there.
W Well, there's a subway station opposite our new location.

여 안녕하세요, 그리고 리버사이드 비스트로에 전화 주셔서 감사합니다. 무엇을 도와드릴까요?
남 안녕하세요, 제 이름은 벤 에이커스이며, 지난달에 귀하의 레스토랑에 이력서를 제출했습니다. 이에 대해 어떻게 됐는지 알아 보려고 합니다. 현재 직원을 채용하고 계신지 알려 주실 수 있으신가요?
여 안타깝게도, 저희가 지금은 필요한 모든 직원이 있습니다. 하지만, 누군가 그만두게 되어 자리가 생기면, 연락드릴 수 있을 겁니다.
남 감사합니다, 그렇게 해 주시면 감사하겠습니다.
여 그건 그렇고, 저희 업체가 다음 주에 시 교외 지역에 위치한 마치 스트리트로 이전할 예정이라는 사실을 알려 드려야겠네요.
남 아, 그러세요? 거긴 꽤 먼 곳인데요. 제가 그곳으로 버스를 타고 갈 수 있을 것 같진 않습니다.
여 음, 저희 새 지점 맞은편에 지하철역이 있습니다.

어휘 hand in ~을 제출하다 résumé 이력서 follow up on ~에 대해 후속적으로 알아 보다, 후속 조치를 취하다 whether ~인지 (아닌지) currently 현재 hire 채용하다, 고용하다 unfortunately 안타깝게도, 아쉽게도 for the moment 지금은, 당분간은 open up (자리, 기회 등이) 생기다, 가능하게 되다 contact ~에게 연락하다 appreciate ~에 대해 감사하다 let A know that A에게 ~라고 알리다 outskirts 교외 doubt (that) ~라고 생각하지 않다, ~라는 데 의구심이 들다 opposite ~ 맞은편에 location 지점, 위치

50 Where does the woman work?
(A) At a travel agency
(B) At a grocery store
(C) At a restaurant
(D) At a bus company

여자는 어디에서 일하는가?
(A) 여행사에서
(B) 식료품점에서
(C) 레스토랑에서
(D) 버스 회사에서

해설 〈근무지를 묻는 문제〉
대화 시작 부분에 여자가 thank you for calling Riverside Bistro라는 말로 업체명을 밝히고 있고, 이어서 남자가 your restaurant이라는 말로 여자가 일하는 곳이 레스토랑임을 언급하고 있으므로 (C)가 정답이다.

51 What does the woman offer to contact the man about?
(A) Changes to business hours
(B) Promotional offers
(C) Investment opportunities
(D) Available jobs

여자는 남자에게 무엇과 관련해 연락하겠다고 제안하는가?
(A) 영업 시간의 변경
(B) 판촉용 특가 행사
(C) 투자 기회
(D) 지원 가능한 일자리

해설 〈기타 세부 사항을 묻는 문제〉
대화 중반부에 여자가 누군가 그만두면서 일자리가 생기면 연락해 줄 수 있다고(if someone leaves and a job opens up, I could contact you) 알리고 있다. 이는 지원 가능한 일자리가 생기는 경우를 말하는 것이므로 (D)가 정답이다.

어휘 offer to do ~하겠다고 제안하다 contact ~에게 연락하다 promotional offer 판촉용 특가 행사 investment 투자(금) opportunity 기회 available 지원 가능한, 이용 가능한

52 Why does the woman say, "There's a subway station opposite our new location"?
(A) To complain about local transportation
(B) To suggest that the man take a subway
(C) To correct the directions given to the man
(D) To recommend meeting at the station

여자는 왜 "There's a subway station opposite our new location"이라고 말하는가?
(A) 지역 교통에 대해 불만을 표현하기 위해
(B) 남자에게 지하철을 이용하도록 권하기 위해
(C) 남자에게 전달된 길 안내 정보를 바로잡기 위해
(D) 역에서 만나도록 권하기 위해

해설 〈의도 파악 문제〉
남자가 대화 후반부에 버스를 타고 갈 수 있을 것 같지 않다고(That's quite far. I doubt I could take a bus there) 말한 것에 대해 여자가 '새 지점 맞은편에 지하철역이 있다'고 알리는 상황이다. 이는 버스 대신 지하철을 이용하도록 권하는 말이므로 (B)가 정답이다.

어휘 complain about ~에 대한 불만을 제기하다 local 지역의, 현지의 transportation 교통(편) correct ~을 바로잡다, 고치다 directions 길 안내 (정보)

Questions 53-55 refer to the following conversation. 영W 호M

W Good morning, Juan. ⑤ I'm just calling to talk about the recent flight you booked to Chicago. We have to make some last-minute changes to your itinerary. We can offer you an alternative flight, but you would arrive in the city six hours later.
M That's not good enough. ⑤ I have a food critic visiting my restaurant tomorrow and I would have to postpone it.
W I understand. Well, if you are unable to take the later flight, I would be happy to offer you a full refund.
M I suppose that's fair. ⑤ Can I call you back tonight after I've had time to think about it?
W ⑤ Absolutely. Just ask for Rachel.

여 안녕하세요, 후안 씨. 최근에 예약하신 시카고행 항공편과 관련해서 말씀 드리기 위해 전화 드렸습니다. 저희가 마지막 순간에 귀하의 일정을 좀 변경해야 했습니다. 저희가 대체 항공편을 제공해 드릴 수는 있지만, 그 도시에 6시간 늦게 도착하실 겁니다.
남 그 정도로는 충분하지 않습니다. 내일 음식 평론가 한 분께서 제 레스토랑을 방문하시는데, 그걸 미뤄야 할 겁니다.
여 알겠습니다. 음, 더 나중의 항공편을 이용하실 수 없다면, 기꺼이 전액 환불을 제공해 드리겠습니다.
남 그게 공정한 것 같아요. 제가 생각해 볼 시간을 좀 가진 후에 오늘 밤에 다시 전화 드려도 될까요?
여 물론입니다. 레이첼을 찾아 주시면 됩니다.

어휘 recent 최근의 book ~을 예약하다 make a change to ~을 변경하다 last-minute 마지막 순간의 itinerary 일정(표) offer A B A에게 B를 제공하다 alternative 대체의, 대안의 arrive 도착하다 have A -ing ~하는 A가 있다 critic 평론가, 비평가 postpone ~을 미루다, 연기하다 be unable to do ~할 수 없다 would be happy to do 기꺼이 ~하겠습니다 refund 환불 suppose (that) ~라고 생각하다 fair 공정한, 공평한 ask for (전화 통화 시 방문 시) ~을 찾다

53 What type of business does the woman most likely work for?
(A) A restaurant
(B) A newspaper company
(C) A travel agency
(D) A vacation resort
여자는 어떤 종류의 업체에서 일하고 있을 것 같은가?
(A) 레스토랑
(B) 신문사

(C) 여행사
(D) 휴양지 리조트
해설 〈근무지를 묻는 문제〉
여자가 대화 초반부에 남자가 항공편을 예약한 점과 남자의 일정을 변경한 점, 그리고 대체 항공편을 제공해 줄 수 있다고 알리는 점으로(I'm just calling to talk about the recent flight you booked to Chicago. We have to make some last-minute changes to your itinerary. We can offer you an alternative flight) 볼 때, 여행사 직원임을 알 수 있으므로 (C)가 정답이다.

54 Why is the man disappointed?
(A) Some prices have been increased.
(B) He wanted to travel in first class.
(C) He might need to reschedule an appointment.
(D) He needs to travel to a different destination.
남자는 왜 실망하는가?
(A) 일부 가격이 인상되었다.
(B) 일등석으로 여행하기를 원했다.
(C) 약속 일정을 재조정해야 할 수도 있다.
(D) 다른 목적지로 여행해야 한다.
해설 〈기타 세부 사항을 묻는 문제〉
대화 중반부에 남자가 충분치 않다는 말로 실망감을 나타내면서 내일 음식 평론가가 자신의 레스토랑을 방문하는 일정을 미뤄야 할 것이라고(I have a food critic visiting my restaurant tomorrow and I would have to postpone it) 알리고 있으므로 일정 재조정을 뜻하는 (C)가 정답이다.
어휘 disappointed 실망한 increase ~을 인상하다, 증가시키다 reschedule ~의 일정을 재조정하다 appointment 약속, 예약 destination 목적지, 도착지

55 What will the speakers do tonight?
(A) Meet for dinner
(B) Cancel a reservation
(C) E-mail each other
(D) Speak on the phone
화자들은 오늘 밤에 무엇을 할 것인가?
(A) 저녁 식사를 위해 만나는 일
(B) 예약을 취소하는 일
(C) 서로에게 이메일을 보내는 일
(D) 전화 통화를 하는 일
해설 〈특정 시점의 일을 묻는 문제〉
대화 후반부에 남자가 생각해 본 후에 오늘 밤에 다시 전화해도 되는지(Can I call you back tonight after I've had time to think about it?) 묻자, 여자가 Absolutely라는 말로 동의하고 있으므로 (D)가 정답이다.
어휘 cancel ~을 취소하다 reservation 예약

Questions 56-58 refer to the following conversation. 캐W 미M

W Hello. ⑤ I purchased a Tryco brand washing machine at your store about three months ago, but ⑤ it's making a loud noise and keeps stopping for no reason.
M All right, ma'am. I can send a technician to your home. How long ago did you buy the machine?
W Just three months ago.
M Oh, in that case, ⑤ the product is still under warranty, so it can be fixed for free. I can look up your warranty number ⑤ through your e-mail address. Could you give that to me?
W Sure. It's janesanders@LTmail.com.

여 안녕하세요. 제가 약 3개월 전에 귀하의 매장에서 트라이코 브랜드의 세탁기를 구입했는데, 큰 소음을 발생시키는데다 아무런 이유도 없이 계속 멈춰요.
남 알겠습니다, 고객님. 자택으로 기술자를 한 명 보내 드릴 수 있습니다. 얼마나 오래 전에 그 기계를 구입하셨죠?
여 3개월밖에 안됐어요.
남 아, 그러시면, 그 제품은 여전히 품질 보증 기간에 해당되기 때문에, 무료로 수리될 수 있습니다. 제가 고객님 이메일 주소를 통해 품질 보증 번호를 찾아보겠습니다. 저에게 말씀해 주시겠어요?
여 네. janesanders@LTmail.com입니다.

어휘 purchase ~을 구입하다 about 약, 대략 make a noise 소음을 내다 keep -ing 계속 ~하다 for no reason 아무런 이유도 없이 technician 기술자 in that case 그렇다면, 그런 경우라면 under (영향, 감독, 조건 등) ~에 해당되는, ~하에 있는 warranty 품질 보증(서) fix ~을 고치다, 바로잡다 for free 무료로 look up (컴퓨터, 자료 등을 통해) ~을 찾아보다 through ~을 통해

56 What problem does the woman mention?
(A) She is missing some parts from an order.
(B) She was overcharged for an item.
(C) A delivery did not arrive on time.
(D) A machine is not working properly.
여자는 어떤 문제점을 언급하는가?
(A) 주문품에서 몇몇 부품이 빠져 있다.
(B) 제품에 대해 비용을 과도하게 청구받았다.
(C) 배송 물품이 제때 도착하지 않았다.
(D) 기계가 제대로 작동하지 않고 있다.
해설 〈문제점을 묻는 문제〉
대화 초반부에 여자가 세탁기를 구입한 사실과(I purchased a Tryco brand washing machine) 소음 발생 및 작동 중단이라는 문제를 일으키고 있다는 사실을(it's making a loud noise and keeps stopping for no reason) 함께 언급하고 있다. 이는 기계가 정상적으로 작동하지 않는다는 뜻이므로 (D)가 정답이다.

어휘 miss ~가 빠져 있다, 없다 part 부품 order 주문(품) overcharge
~에게 비용을 과도하게 청구하다 arrive 도착하다 on time 제때
work (기계 등이) 작동되다, 가동되다 properly 제대로, 적절하게

57 According to the man, what is the woman eligible to
receive?
(A) A refund
(B) Free repairs
(C) A catalog
(D) Some coupons

남자의 말에 따르면, 여자는 무엇을 받을 자격이 있는가?
(A) 환불
(B) 무료 수리
(C) 카탈로그
(D) 몇몇 쿠폰

해설 〈기타 세부 사항을 묻는 문제〉
대화 후반부에 남자가 여전히 품질 보증 기간에 해당되기 때문에 무료
로 수리받을 수 있다고(the product is still under warranty, so
it can be fixed for free) 알리고 있으므로 (B)가 정답이다.

어휘 be eligible to do ~할 자격이 있다 receive ~을 받다

58 What does the man ask the woman for?
(A) An e-mail address
(B) A purchase date
(C) A credit card number
(D) Driving directions

남자는 여자에게 무엇을 요청하는가?
(A) 이메일 주소
(B) 구매 날짜
(C) 신용카드 번호
(D) 운전 경로 정보

해설 〈요청 사항을 묻는 문제〉
대화 마지막 부분에 남자가 이메일 주소를 통한 정보 확인 방법을 언
급하면서 그것을 알려 달라고(through your e-mail address.
Could you give that to me?) 요청하고 있으므로 (A)가 정답이다.

어휘 purchase 구매(품) directions 길 안내 (정보)

Questions 59-61 refer to the following conversation with three
speakers. 영W 호M 미M

W   Hi, Richard and John. I asked you both to stop by so
that ㊾ we can discuss the head office designs we're
working on for Atlas Corporation. Richard, how are
things going?
M1 I've designed the layout and ordered furniture, but the
Atlas representative still hasn't chosen a color for the
walls.
W   I see. ㊿ I'll ask them to tell us their preferred color.
John, how about the lighting in the main office area?
M2 We've chosen the type of lighting, but I need to pick a
brand. I have quite a tight budget.
W   Okay. ㊽ Send me the prices for the lighting options.
I'll review them after lunch and let you know my
recommendation.

여   안녕하세요, 리차드 씨 그리고 존 씨. 우리가 아틀라스 주식회사를 위해 작
업하고 있는 본사 디자인을 논의할 수 있도록 두 분께 잠시 들러 달라고
요청 드렸습니다. 리차드 씨, 어떻게 진행되고 있죠?
남1 제가 공간 배치를 디자인하고 가구는 주문했는데, 그 아틀라스 직원이 여
전히 벽 색상을 선택하지 않으셨어요.
여   알겠습니다. 제가 선호하는 색상을 말해 달라고 그쪽에 요청할게요. 존 씨,
주 업무 공간의 조명은 어떤가요?
남2 조명 종류는 선택했는데, 브랜드를 골라야 합니다. 예산이 꽤 빠듯합니다.
여   좋아요, 선택 가능한 조명의 가격을 저에게 보내 주세요. 제가 점심 시간
후에 검토해서 추천 대상을 알려 드리겠습니다.

어휘 ask A to do A에게 ~하도록 요청하다 stop by 잠시 들르다 so that
(목적) ~할 수 있도록, (결과) 그래야, 그래서 discuss ~을 논의하다, 이야
기하다 head office 본사 work on ~에 대한 작업을 하다 how is A
going? A가 어떻게 되어 가고 있나요? layout 배치, 구획, 구성 order ~
을 주문하다 representative 직원 choose ~을 선택하다 preferred 선
호하는 how about ~? ~는 어떤가요? lighting 조명 pick ~을 고르다
quite (셀 수 있는 명사 앞에서) 꽤, 상당히 tight (일정, 비용 등이) 빠듯한, 빡빡
한 budget 예산 review ~을 검토하다 let A know B A에게 B를 알리다
recommendation 추천(하는 것)

59 Who most likely are the speakers?
(A) Event organizers
(B) Landscape gardeners
(C) Interior designers
(D) Software developers

화자들은 누구일 것 같은가?
(A) 행사 주최자
(B) 조경 전문가
(C) 실내 디자이너

(D) 소프트웨어 개발자

해설 〈직업을 묻는 문제〉
대화 초반부에 여자가 자신들을 we로 지칭해 아틀라스 주식회사
의 본사 디자인을 이야기하는(we can discuss the head office
designs we're working on for Atlas Corporation) 상황임을
언급하고 있다. 이는 실내 디자이너들이 할 수 있는 일에 해당되므로
(C)가 정답이다.

어휘 organizer 주최자, 조직자 landscape 조경 developer 개발자, 개
발업체

60 What will the woman request from Atlas Corporation?
(A) A project budget
(B) A deadline extension
(C) A business location
(D) A color preference

여자는 아틀라스 주식회사에 무엇을 요청할 것인가?
(A) 프로젝트 예산
(B) 마감기한 연장
(C) 업체 위치
(D) 선호 색상

해설 〈요청 사항을 묻는 문제〉
대화 중반부에 여자가 아틀라스 주식회사 사람들을 them으로 지칭해
선호하는 색상을 말하도록 요청할 것이라고(I'll ask them to tell us
their preferred color) 언급하고 있으므로 (D)가 정답이다.

어휘 budget 예산 deadline 마감기한 extension 연장 location 위치,
장소, 지점 preference 선호(하는 것)

61 What does the woman say she will do later?
(A) Compare some prices
(B) Contact a client
(C) Submit a report
(D) Purchase materials

여자는 이따가 무엇을 할 것이라고 말하는가?
(A) 몇몇 가격을 비교해 보는 일
(B) 고객에게 연락하는 일
(C) 보고서를 제출하는 일
(D) 자재를 구입하는 일

해설 〈특정 시점의 일을 묻는 문제〉
대화 맨 마지막에 여자가 선택 가능한 조명의 가격을 보내 달라는 말과
함께 점심 시간 후에 검토하겠다고(Send me the prices for the
lighting options. I'll review them after lunch) 알리고 있다. 이
는 조명 제품을 결정하기 위해 가격을 비교해 보겠다는 뜻이므로 (A)가
정답이다.

어휘 compare ~을 비교하다 contact ~에게 연락하다 submit ~을 제
출하다 purchase ~을 구입하다 material 자재, 재료, 물품

Questions 62-64 refer to the following conversation and sign. 미M 영W

M Hi, Monica. I really appreciate your hard work. ⑥ The decorations you put up in the theater's lobby look fantastic. Did you have any problems?

W Only at the end. ⑥ It was difficult to find the building manager to give him back his drill and hammer, but I finally tracked him down.

M That's good. It was nice of Ms. Burling to give the staff tickets to tonight's symphony show. Are you headed there now?

W Yes, I'm in seat F27.

M I'm also in row F, a few seats down. Oh, but ⑥ just a reminder, you can't bring that soda in there.

W Oh, you're right. I almost forgot about that rule.

Wisteria Theater Rules
⑥ 1. No outside food or beverages.
2. Cameras are not allowed.
3. Turn cell phones off.
4. Keep your ticket stub.

남 안녕하세요, 모니카 씨. 당신의 노고에 정말 감사드립니다. 극장 로비에 놓아 주신 장식물들이 아주 멋져 보이네요. 무슨 문제라도 있으셨나요?

여 마지막 순간에만요. 건물 관리자에게 드릴과 망치를 되돌려 주기 위해 그분을 찾는 것이 어려웠지만, 결국 찾아냈습니다.

남 잘됐네요. 벌링 씨가 오늘 밤에 열리는 교향악단 공연 입장권을 직원들에게 주신 것은 고마운 일이었어요. 지금 그곳으로 가시나요?

여 네, 제 좌석은 F27입니다.

남 저도 F열인데, 몇 좌석 아래쪽입니다. 아, 하지만 한 가지 말씀 드리자면, 그 탄산 음료를 그곳 내부로 가져가지실 수 없어요.

여 아, 맞아요. 그 규정을 거의 잊을 뻔했네요.

위스테리아 극장 규정
1. 외부 음식 또는 음료 반입 금지.
2. 카메라 촬영은 허용되지 않습니다.
3. 휴대전화기를 꺼 주세요.
4. 절취된 입장권을 소지하십시오.

어휘 appreciate ~에 대해 감사하다 decoration 장식(품) put up ~을 놓다. 게시하다 look + 형용사 ~하게 보이다 give A back B A에게 B를 돌려주다 track A down A를 찾아내다 symphony 교향곡 be headed there 그 곳으로 가다 row 열, 줄 reminder (상기시키기 위한) 말, 메시지 beverage 음료 allow ~을 허용하다 turn A off A를 끄다 stub (입장권 등의) 절취된 부분

---

62 What does the man thank the woman for?
(A) Hiring a performer
(B) Designing an advertisement
(C) Decorating an area
(D) Inspecting a building

남자는 무엇에 대해 여자에게 감사하는가?
(A) 공연자 고용하기
(B) 광고 디자인하기
(C) 구역 한 곳 장식하기
(D) 건물 점검하기

해설 〈기타 세부 사항을 묻는 문제〉
대화 시작 부분에 남자가 감사의 인사를 하면서 여자가 한 일과 관련해 극장 로비에 장식물을 놓은 사실을(The decorations you put up ~) 언급하고 있으므로 (C)가 정답이다.

어휘 hire ~을 고용하다 advertisement 광고 decorate ~을 장식하다 inspect ~을 점검하다

---

63 What did the woman have trouble doing?
(A) Finding a print shop
(B) Balancing a budget
(C) Tracking sales records
(D) Returning some tools

여자는 무엇을 하는 데 어려움을 겪었는가?
(A) 인쇄소 찾기
(B) 예산 균형 유지하기
(C) 매출 기록 파악하기
(D) 일부 공구 되돌려 주기

해설 〈문제점을 찾는 문제〉
대화 중반부에, 여자가 드릴과 망치를 되돌려 주기 위해 관리자를 찾는 일이 어려웠다고(It was difficult to find the building manager to give him back his drill and hammer ~) 알리고 있으므로 (D)가 정답이다.

어휘 have trouble -ing ~하는 데 어려움을 겪다 balance v. ~의 균형을 유지하다 budget 예산 tool 공구, 도구

---

64 Look at the graphic. Which rule does the man remind the woman about?
(A) Rule 1
(B) Rule 2
(C) Rule 3
(D) Rule 4

시각 자료를 보시오. 남자는 여자에게 어느 규정에 관해 상기시켜 주는가?
(A) 규정 1
(B) 규정 2
(C) 규정 3
(D) 규정 4

해설 〈기타 시각 자료 문제〉
대화 마지막에 남자가 탄산 음료를 갖고 들어갈 수 없다고(~ just a reminder, you can't bring that soda in there) 알리고 있다. 시각 자료에서 음료 반입과 관련된 규정이 1번에(1. No outside food or beverages) 쓰여 있으므로 (A)가 정답이다.

어휘 remind A about B A에게 B에 관해 상기시키다

Questions 65-67 refer to the following conversation and chart. 호M 캐W

M My cable subscription payment has been taken from my bank account but ⑥ I didn't receive an invoice this month. Could you send me one for my records?

W Absolutely.

M Thanks. I think your service is excellent value for money. ⑥ I get so many viewing options and it only costs me $27.95 each month.

W Great! ⑥ Could you please fill in our online feedback form so that I can pass this on to my manager?

Plan	Price
Silver	$19.95
Gold	$24.95
⑥ Gold Plus	$27.95
Platinum	$32.95

남 제 케이블 방송 서비스 이용료가 은행 계좌에서 빠져 나갔는데, 이번 달에 이용내역서를 받지 못했습니다. 제 기록 보관용으로 하나 보내 주시겠어요?

여 물론입니다.

남 감사합니다. 귀사의 서비스는 가성비가 훌륭한 것 같아요. 선택 가능한 시청 프로그램이 정말 많은데, 매달 겨우 27.95달러밖에 들지 않거든요.

여 잘됐네요! 말씀하신 것을 저희 부서장님께 전달해 드릴 수 있도록 온라인 의견 양식을 작성해 주시겠습니까?

서비스 약정	가격
실버	19.95달러
골드	24.95달러
골드 플러스	27.95달러
플래티넘	32.95달러

어휘 subscription (서비스 등의) 이용, 가입, 구독 payment 지불(금) account 계좌, 계정 receive ~을 받다 invoice 이용내역서, 거래 내역서 value for money 가성비, 비용 대비 가치 viewing 시청, 관람 cost A B A에게 B의 돈이 들다 fill in ~을 작성하다 feedback 의견 form 양식, 서식 so that (결과) ~할 수 있도록 pass A on to B A를 B에게 전달하다

65 What does the man ask the woman for?
(A) A repair service
(B) An invoice
(C) A refund
(D) A brochure

남자는 여자에게 무엇을 요청하는가?
(A) 수리 서비스
(B) 이용내역서
(C) 환불
(D) 안내 책자

해설 〈요청 사항을 묻는 문제〉
대화를 시작하면서 남자가 이용내역서를 받지 못했다는 사실과 함께 하나 보내 달라고(I didn't receive an invoice this month. Could you send me one for my records?) 요청하고 있으므로 (B)가 정답이다.

66 Look at the graphic. Which cable subscription does the man currently have?
(A) Silver
(B) Gold
(C) Gold Plus
(D) Platinum

시각 자료를 보시오. 남자는 현재 어느 케이블 서비스를 이용하고 있는가?
(A) 실버
(B) 골드
(C) 골드 플러스
(D) 플래티넘

해설 〈2열 도표 문제〉
대화 중반부에 남자가 시청할 수 있는 게 많다는 말과 함께 매달 27.95달러밖에 들지 않는다고(I get so many viewing options and it only costs me $27.95 each month) 알리고 있다. 도표에서 $27.95로 표기된 것이 세 번째 줄에 쓰여 있는 Gold Plus이므로 (C)가 정답이다.

67 What does the woman encourage the man to do?
(A) Complete a form
(B) Transfer some funds
(C) Speak to a manager
(D) Provide an account number

여자는 남자에게 무엇을 하도록 권하는가?
(A) 양식을 작성 완료하는 일
(B) 일부 자금을 이체하는 일
(C) 책임자와 이야기하는 일
(D) 계좌번호를 제공하는 일

해설 〈제안 사항을 묻는 문제〉
대화 맨 마지막에 여자가 부서장에게 전달할 수 있도록 온라인 의견 양식을 작성해 달라고(Could you please fill in our online feedback form) 요청하고 있으므로 (A)가 정답이다.

어휘 encourage A to do A에게 ~하도록 권하다, 장려하다 complete ~을 완료하다 form 양식, 서식 transfer ~을 이체하다 fund 자금 provide ~을 제공하다 account 계좌, 계정

Questions 68-70 refer to the following conversation and map. 미M 영W

M Oh! Hi, Kelsey! I didn't expect to see you ⑱ **here at this station**, but maybe you can help me. I'm trying to get to Morgan Concert Hall, but I can't figure out the best route. I've used Line A before, but it's currently closed.
W Let me search for the train map on my phone. Hmm, if I were you, ⑲ **I would take this route here. It'll be a bit crowded until Bower Pass, but it should be fine after that.**
M Thanks a lot.
W Are you catching a show at the concert hall?
M Actually, ⑳ **I'm presenting a lecture on economics this afternoon.**
W Good for you! I hope it goes well.

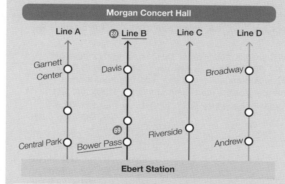

Morgan Concert Hall

Line A ⑲ Line B Line C Line D

Garnett Center — Davis — Broadway

⑲ Central Park — Bower Pass — Riverside — Andrew

Ebert Station

남 아! 안녕하세요, 켈시 씨. 이 역에서 뵐 거라고 예상하지 못했는데, 아마 저를 도와주실 수 있을 거예요. 제가 모건 콘서트 홀에 가려고 하는 중인데, 가장 좋은 노선을 찾을 수가 없어요. 제가 전에 A 노선을 이용했었는데, 현재 폐쇄되어 있어요.
여 제 전화기에서 기차 노선도를 검색해 볼게요. 흠, 제가 당신이라면, 여기 이 노선을 이용할 거예요. 바워 패스까지는 조금 붐비겠지만, 그 이후로는 괜찮을 겁니다.
남 정말 감사합니다.
여 그 콘서트 홀에서 공연을 보러 가시는 건가요?
남 실은, 오늘 오후에 경제학에 관한 강연을 합니다.
여 잘됐네요! 잘 진행되기를 바랍니다.

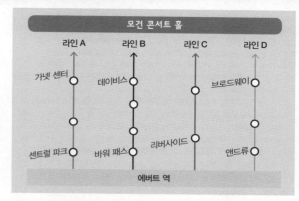

모건 콘서트 홀

라인 A 라인 B 라인 C 라인 D

가넷 센터 데이비스 브로드웨이

센트럴 파크 바워 패스 리버사이드 앤드류

에버트 역

어휘 expect to do ~할 것으로 예상하다 try to do ~하려 하다 get to ~로 가다 figure out ~을 찾아내다, 알아내다 currently 현재 search for ~을 검색하다, 찾다 if I were you 제가 당신이라면 take (교통편) ~을 이용하다, 타다 a bit 조금, 약간 crowded 붐비는 catch ~을 보다, 관람하다 actually 실은, 사실은 present a lecture 강연을 하다 economics 경제학 Good for you (칭찬) 잘됐네요, 잘하셨어요 go well 잘 진행되다

68 Where most likely are the speakers?
(A) At a train station
(B) At a hotel
(C) At a concert hall
(D) At a travel agency

화자들은 어디에 있을 것 같은가?
(A) 기차역에
(B) 호텔에
(C) 콘서트 홀에
(D) 여행사에

해설 〈대화 장소를 묻는 문제〉
대화 초반부에 남자가 화자들이 있는 장소를 here at this station와 같이 언급하고 있으므로 (A)가 정답이다.

69 Look at the graphic. Which line does the woman suggest taking?
(A) Line A
(B) Line B
(C) Line C
(D) Line D

시각 자료를 보시오. 여자는 어느 노선을 이용하도록 권하는가?
(A) 노선 A
(B) 노선 B
(C) 노선 C
(D) 노선 D

대화 중반부에 여자가 한 노선을 권하면서 바위 패스까지 붐빈다고 (I would take this route here. It'll be a bit crowded until Bower Pass ~) 알리고 있는데 시각 자료에서 바위 패스가 포함된 노선이 B이므로 (B)가 정답이다.

어휘 suggest -ing ~하도록 권하다

70 What will the man do today?
(A) Have a job interview
(B) Watch a performance
(C) Meet a new client
(D) Give a presentation
남자는 오늘 무엇을 할 것인가?
(A) 구직 면접 보기
(B) 공연 관람하기
(C) 새 고객과 만나기
(D) 발표하기

해설 〈특정 시점의 일을 묻는 문제〉
대화 후반부에 남자가 오늘에 해당되는 시점 표현 this afternoon 과 함께 오후에 강연을 한다고(I'm presenting a lecture on economics ~) 알리고 있으므로 이와 유사한 의미를 지니는 (D)가 정답이다.

어휘 performance 공연 give a presentation 발표하다

PART 4

Questions 71-73 refer to the following telephone message. 영W

Hi, Mr. Peterson. **71** This is Julia from Harrow Antique Furniture returning your call about restoring your old dining table. First, **72** we'll need to visit your home and take a look at the item to figure out what work needs to be done. **72** We also need to evaluate whether it is in suitable condition for restoration. Then we'll be able to provide a quote to you. I'd like to send one of our experts over to your home for an initial meeting, but **73** we'll be closed tomorrow for staff training. So, I hope you will be available on Wednesday.

안녕하세요, 피터스 씨. 저는 귀하의 낡은 식탁을 복원하는 일과 관련해 답신 전화 드리는 해로우 앤티크 퍼니처의 줄리아입니다. 우선, 귀하의 자택을 방문해 어떤 작업이 실시되어야 하는지 파악할 수 있도록 해당 물품을 한 번 확인해 봐야 합니다. 또한 복원 작업에 적합한 상태인지도 평가해야 합니다. 그런 다음, 비용 견적을 제공해 드릴 수 있을 것입니다. 첫 회의를 위해 귀하의 자택으로 저희 전문가들 중 한 명을 보내 드리고 싶지만, 저희가 내일 직원 교육으로 인해 문을 닫습니다. 따라서, 수요일에 시간이 되시기를 바랍니다.

어휘 return one's call ~에게 답신 전화를 하다 restore ~을 복원하다, 복구하다 take a look at ~을 한 번 보다 figure out ~을 파악하다, 알아내다 evaluate ~을 평가하다 whether ~인지 (아닌지) suitable 적합한 condition 상태, 조건 restoration 복원, 복구 be able to do ~할 수 있다 provide ~을 제공하다 quote 비용 견적(서) send A over to B A를 B로 보내다 expert 전문가 initial 처음의, 초기의 training 교육 available (사람이) 시간이 나는, (사물이) 이용 가능한, 구입 가능한

71 What kind of work is being discussed?
(A) Event catering
(B) Furniture restoration
(C) Electronics installation
(D) Overseas shipping
어떤 종류의 작업이 이야기되고 있는가?
(A) 행사 출장 요리 제공
(B) 가구 복원
(C) 전자제품 설치
(D) 해외 배송

해설 〈주제를 묻는 문제〉
담화를 시작하면서 화자가 상대방의 낡은 식탁을 복원하는 일과 관련해 답신 전화한다고(This is Julia from Harrow Antique Furniture returning your call about restoring your old dining table) 알린 뒤로, 그 식탁 복원 작업에 필요한 과정을 간략히 설명하고 있다. 이는 일종의 가구를 복원하는 것이므로 (B)가 정답이다.

어휘 catering 출장 요리 제공(업) restoration 복원, 복구 installation 설치 (작업) overseas 해외의

72 According to the speaker, what task should be carried out first?
(A) A tour of a building
(B) Product assembly
(C) Staff recruitment
(D) An item evaluation
화자의 말에 따르면, 어떤 일이 먼저 실시되어야 하는가?
(A) 건물 견학
(B) 제품 조립
(C) 직원 모집
(D) 제품 평가

해설 〈기타 세부 사항을 묻는 문제〉
화자는 담화 중반부에 상대방의 집을 방문해 제품을 확인해야 한다고(we'll need to visit your home and take a look at the item) 언급하면서, 그것이 제품 상태가 적합한지 평가하는 일에 해당된다고(We also need to evaluate whether it is in suitable condition for restoration) 알리고 있다. 따라서 (D)가 정답이다.

어휘 carry out ~을 실시하다, 수행하다 assembly 조립 recruitment 모집 evaluation 평가(서)

73 Why does the speaker say a meeting will be postponed?
(A) A renovation project will start.
(B) A training session will be held.
(C) A public holiday will be observed.
(D) A product delivery will be received.
화자는 왜 회의가 연기될 것이라고 말하는가?
(A) 개조 프로젝트가 시작될 것이다.
(B) 교육 시간이 개최될 것이다.
(C) 공휴일이 지켜질 것이다.
(D) 배송 제품을 받을 것이다.

해설 〈문제 원인을 묻는 문제〉
담화 마지막 부분에 내일 직원 교육 때문에 문을 닫기 때문에 수요일에 시간이 나기를 바란다는 말로(~ we'll be closed tomorrow for staff training. So, I hope you will be available on Wednesday) 회의가 연기되어야 하는 이유를 말하고 있다. 따라서 직원 교육 개최를 언급한 (B)가 정답이다.

어휘 postpone ~을 연기하다 renovation 개조, 보수 session (특정 활동을 위한) 시간 hold ~을 개최하다, 열다 public holiday 공휴일 observe ~을 지키다, 준수하다 receive ~을 받다

Questions 74-76 refer to the following announcement. 미M

Hi, everyone. I'd like to talk about **74** our bakery's upcoming contest. I'll be looking for five chefs to help judge who has made the best product. **75** I've also decided to provide all attendees with complimentary snacks and drinks as we wait to announce the winner. Please let me know as soon as possible if you would like to be one of the five judges. Don't forget, we would also like to collect the contact details of our guests. **76** Make sure you give a survey form to everyone who enters our bakery and ask them to complete it.

안녕하세요, 여러분. 우리 제과점에서 곧 있을 콘테스트에 관해 말씀 드리고자 합니다. 누가 최고의 제품을 만들었는지 심사하는 데 도움을 주실 다섯 명의 요리사를 찾을 예정입니다. 또한 우리가 우승자를 발표하기를 기다리면서 무료 간식과 음료를 모든 참석자들께 제공해 드리기로 결정했습니다. 여러분께서 다섯 명의 심사위원 중 한 사람이 되기를 원하시는 경우에 가능한 한 빨리 저에게 알려 주시기 바랍니다. 잊지 마셔야 하는 부분은, 우리가 초대 손님들의 연락처 정보도 수집하고자 한다는 점입니다. 반드시 우리 제과점에 들어오시는 모든 분께 설문지 양식을 드리고 작성 완료하시도록 요청해 주시기 바랍니다.

어휘 would like to do ~하고자 하다, ~하고 싶다 upcoming 곧 있을, 다가오는 look for ~을 찾다 help do ~하는 것을 돕다 judge v. ~을 심사하다 n. 심사위원 decide to do ~하기로 결정하다 provide A with B A에게 B를 제공하다 complimentary 무료의 announce ~을 발표하다, 공지하다 let A know A에게 알리다 as soon as possible 가능한 한 빨리 collect ~을 수집하다, 모으다 contact details 연락처 make sure (that) 반드시

~하도록 하다 survey 설문 조사(지) form 양식, 서식 ask A to do A에게 ~하도록 요청하다 complete ~을 완료하다

74 What is the speaker mainly discussing?
(A) An advertising campaign
(B) Contest judges
(C) A product recipe
(D) An IT system

화자는 주로 무엇을 이야기하고 있는가?
(A) 광고 캠페인
(B) 콘테스트 심사위원
(C) 제품 조리법
(D) IT 시스템

해설 〈주제를 묻는 문제〉
담화 초반부에 제과점 콘테스트를 언급하면서 누가 최고의 제품을 만들었는지 심사하는 데 도움을 줄 다섯 명의 요리사를 찾을 것이라고(our bakery's upcoming contest. I'll be looking for five chefs to help judge who has made the best product) 알리고 있다. 이는 콘테스트 심사위원을 찾는다는 뜻이므로 (B)가 정답이다.

어휘 advertising 광고 (활동) judge 심사위원 recipe 조리법

75 What will the bakery offer all attendees?
(A) Cookery lessons
(B) Branded T-shirts
(C) Free parking permits
(D) Refreshments

제과점에서 모든 참석자에게 무엇을 제공할 것인가?
(A) 요리 강습
(B) 유명 상표 티셔츠
(C) 무료 주차 허가증
(D) 다과

해설 〈기타 세부 사항을 묻는 문제〉
담화 중반부에 모든 참석자에게 무료 간식과 음료를 제공하기로 결정했다고(I've also decided to provide all attendees with complimentary snacks and drinks) 알리고 있다. 이는 무료 다과를 제공한다는 뜻이므로 (D)가 정답이다.

어휘 offer ~을 제공하다 cookery 요리 branded 유명 상표의 free 무료의 permit 허가증 refreshments 다과, 간식

76 What does the speaker remind the listeners to do?
(A) Distribute some forms
(B) Present a valid ticket
(C) Enter a contest
(D) Arrive on time

화자는 청자들에게 무엇을 하도록 상기시키는가?
(A) 일부 양식을 배부하는 것
(B) 유효 입장권을 제시하는 것

(C) 콘테스트에 참가하는 것
(D) 제때 도착하는 것

해설 〈상기시키는 것을 묻는 문제〉
담화 마지막 부분에 제과점에 들어오는 모든 사람에게 설문지 양식을 전달해 주고 그것을 작성 완료하도록 하라고(make sure you give a survey form to everyone who enters our bakery) 알리고 있는데, 이는 양식을 배부하라는 말이므로 (A)가 정답이다.

어휘 complete ~을 완료하다 form 양식, 서식 present ~을 제시하다 valid 유효한 enter ~에 참가하다 arrive 도착하다 on time 제때

Questions 77-79 refer to the following instructions. 호M

Good morning, everyone. We're glad to have you on board as new employees. Now, **㉗** before you begin working on the factory floor, you will need to complete our mandatory training. Our first trainer will be **㉘** Sam Pearson, who will go over the regulations regarding safety. That is a very important session. Then, **㉙** at eleven o'clock, I'll put you into small groups so that you can learn more about your specific duties. Each one will be led by a current employee. They can answer any questions you may have.

안녕하세요, 여러분. 신입 사원인 여러분과 한 배를 타게 되어 기쁘게 생각합니다. 자, 공장 작업장에서 근무를 시작하시기 전에, 우리 회사의 의무 교육을 완료하셔야 합니다. 첫 번째 교육 진행자는 샘 피어슨 씨로, 안전과 관련된 규정 사항들을 함께 살펴 볼 것입니다. 이는 매우 중요한 시간입니다. 그 다음으로, 11시에는, 여러분의 특정 직무에 관해 더 많은 것을 배우실 수 있도록 소규모 그룹으로 나누겠습니다. 각 그룹은 현재 재직 중인 직원 한 분께서 이끄실 것입니다. 이분들께서 여러분이 궁금해 하실 수 있는 어떤 질문이든 답변해 드릴 수 있습니다.

어휘 have A on board A와 한 배를 타다, A를 합류시키다 factory floor 공장 작업장 complete ~을 완료하다 mandatory 의무적인 training 교육 go over ~을 살펴보다, 검토하다 regulation 규정, 규제 regarding ~와 관련된 session (특정 활동을 위한) 시간 then 그런 다음, 그러고 나서 put A into small groups A를 소규모 그룹으로 나누다 so that ~할 수 있도록 specific 특정한, 구체적인 duty 직무, 업무 lead ~을 이끌다, 진행하다

77 Who most likely are the listeners?
(A) Tour guides
(B) Product testers
(C) Software developers
(D) Factory workers

청자는 누구일 것 같은가?
(A) 투어 가이드들
(B) 제품 테스트 담당자들
(C) 소프트웨어 개발자들
(D) 공장 직원들

해설 〈직업을 묻는 문제〉
담화 초반부에 화자가 청자들을 you로 지칭해 공장 작업장에서 근무를 시작하기 전에(before you begin working on the factory floor) 해야 하는 일을 언급하고 있으므로 (D)가 정답이다.

어휘 developer 개발자, 개발회사

78 What will Sam Pearson do?
(A) Write down suggestions
(B) Review the employment contracts
(C) Explain some safety rules
(D) Distribute some uniforms

샘 피어슨 씨는 무엇을 할 것인가?
(A) 의견을 적어 두는 일
(B) 고용 계약서를 검토하는 일
(C) 몇몇 안전 규칙을 설명하는 일
(D) 몇몇 유니폼을 지급하는 일

해설 〈미래에 할 일을 묻는 문제〉
담화 중반부에 샘 피어슨 씨의 이름을 언급하면서 안전과 관련된 규정 사항들을 살펴 볼 것이라고(Sam Pearson, who will go over the regulations regarding safety) 알리고 있다. 이는 안전 규칙을 설명한다는 뜻이므로 (C)가 정답이다.

어휘 suggestion 의견, 제안 review ~을 검토하다, 살펴보다 contract 계약(서) explain ~을 설명하다 distribute ~을 나눠 주다, 배부하다

79 What will happen at eleven o'clock?
(A) The speaker will collect some surveys.
(B) The speaker will respond to questions.
(C) The listeners will watch a video.
(D) The listeners will be assigned to groups.

11시에 무슨 일이 있을 것인가?
(A) 화자가 몇몇 설문지를 걷을 것이다.
(B) 화자가 질문에 답변할 것이다.
(C) 청자들이 동영상을 시청할 것이다.
(D) 청자들이 그룹에 배정될 것이다.

해설 〈특정 시점의 일을 묻는 문제〉
담화 후반부에 화자가 11시에 청자들을 소규모 그룹으로 나눌 것이라고(at eleven o'clock, I'll put you into small groups) 언급하고 있으므로 (D)가 정답이다.

어휘 collect ~을 모으다, 수집하다 survey 설문 조사(지) respond to ~에 답변하다, 대응하다 assign ~을 배정하다, 할당하다

Questions 80-82 refer to the following excerpt from a meeting.
[캐W]

I'm happy to begin this meeting with some exciting news. As of last month, ⑧⑩ we achieved our goal of hitting half a million subscribers. This gives ⑧① our magazine a third-place ranking for distribution in our category. It wouldn't have been possible without you, so keep up the good work, everyone. Now, I know that ⑧② many of you have reported difficulties with your computers since the software update, and that you have to keep restarting your computers to temporarily fix those issues. I understand that this really slows down your work. So, we'll have a technician visit today.

흥분되는 소식과 함께 이 회의를 시작하게 되어 기쁩니다. 지난달을 기준으로, 우리는 50만 구독자 도달 목표를 달성했습니다. 이로 인해 우리 잡지가 해당 부문에서 유통 순위 3위에 올라 있습니다. 여러분이 아니었다면 불가능했을 것이기 때문에, 모두 계속 수고해 주시기 바랍니다. 자, 여러분 중 많은 분들이 소프트웨어 업데이트 이후로 컴퓨터와 관련된 어려움을 호소해 오고 있다는 점과, 이러한 문제를 바로잡기 위해 일시적으로 계속 컴퓨터를 다시 시작해야 한다는 점을 알고 있습니다. 이것이 정말로 여러분의 업무를 더디게 하는 것으로 알고 있습니다. 따라서, 오늘 기술자가 방문할 것입니다.

어휘 as of 시점 ~을 기준으로, ~부로 achieve ~을 달성하다, 이루다 hit ~에 도달하다 half a million 50만 subscriber 구독자, 서비스 가입자 third-place ranking 3위 distribution 유통, 배부, 나눠 줌 category 부문, 범주 would have p.p. ~했을 것이다 keep up ~을 계속하다, 지속하다 difficulty 어려움, 문제 since ~ 이후로 keep -ing 계속 ~하다 temporarily 일시적으로, 임시로 fix ~을 바로잡다, 고치다 issue 문제, 사안 slow down ~을 느리게 만들다, 둔화시키다 have A do A에게 ~하게 하다

80 What news does the speaker share with the listeners?
(A) The company will hire more workers.
(B) The company can pay some bonuses.
(C) The company will receive an award.
(D) The company has reached a goal.

화자는 어떤 소식을 청자들과 공유하는가?
(A) 회사가 추가 직원을 고용할 것이다.
(B) 회사가 약간의 보너스를 지급할 수 있다.
(C) 회사가 상을 받을 것이다.
(D) 회사가 목표에 도달했다.

해설 〈기타 세부 사항을 묻는 문제〉
담화 초반부에 좋은 소식이 있음을 언급하면서 50만 명의 구독자에 도달하는 목표를 이뤘다고(we achieved our goal of hitting half a million subscribers) 알리고 있으므로 (D)가 정답이다.

어휘 share A with B B와 A를 공유하다 hire ~을 고용하다 receive ~을 받다 reach ~에 도달하다, 이르다

81 Where most likely do the listeners work?
(A) At a clothing shop
(B) At a magazine publisher
(C) At a financial institution
(D) At a shipping company

청자들은 어디에서 근무하고 있을 것 같은가?
(A) 의류 매장에서
(B) 잡지 출판사에서
(C) 금융 기관에서
(D) 배송 회사에서

해설 〈근무지를 묻는 문제〉
담화 초반부에 화자가 구독자(subscribers)를 언급하면서 소속 회사를 our magazine이라고 밝히는 것을 통해 잡지 출판사에서 일한다는 것을 알 수 있으므로 (B)가 정답이다.

어휘 institution 기관, 단체, 협회

82 What does the speaker mean when she says, "we'll have a technician visit today"?
(A) She is trying to resolve a problem.
(B) She needs to end the meeting early.
(C) She found an error in the schedule.
(D) She needs help from the listeners.

화자가 "we'll have a technician visit today"라고 말할 때 무엇을 의미하는가?
(A) 문제를 해결하려 하는 중이다.
(B) 회의를 일찍 끝내야 한다.
(C) 일정표에서 문제를 발견했다.
(D) 청자들의 도움이 필요하다.

해설 〈의도 파악 문제〉
담화 후반부로 넘어가면서 많은 사람들이 컴퓨터와 관련된 어려움을 알린 사실과 컴퓨터 사용을 위해 계속 다시 시작하는 것으로 대처하고 있다는 사실을(many of you have reported difficulties with your computers ~ that you have to keep restarting your computers to temporarily fix those issues) 언급한 뒤로 '오늘 기술자가 방문한다'고 알리는 상황이다. 이는 컴퓨터 문제를 해결하겠다는 뜻이므로 (A)가 정답이다.

어휘 try to do ~하려 하다 resolve ~을 해결하다

Questions 83-85 refer to the following news report. [호M]

You're listening to Radio 107's local news update. Our top story tonight is the start of the construction of Darcyville Stadium. ⑧③ This building project is one-of-a-kind, as it will be the only stadium in the country with a system that collects rainwater. The water will be reused for cleaning and watering landscaping. Darcyville will have its own local baseball team, but the team name has not been selected yet. ⑧④ The city is holding a contest next week for the naming of the team. ⑧⑤ If you're interested in participating, simply fill out the form on the city's Web site with your idea and your contact details.

여러분은 지금 라디오 107의 최신 지역 뉴스를 청취하고 계십니다. 오늘 밤 주요 뉴스는 다시빌 경기장의 착공 소식입니다. 이 건물 공사 프로젝트는 유례를 찾기 힘든 것으로서, 이곳이 빗물을 모으는 시스템을 갖춘 전국 유일의 경기장이 될 것이기 때문입니다. 이 물은 청소 및 조경용 급수를 위해 재사용될 것입니다. 다시빌에 자체 지역 야구팀도 생기게 되는데, 팀명은 아직 선정되지 않았습니다. 시에서 팀 명칭 결정을 위해 다음 주에 콘테스트를 개최합니다. 참가하는 데 관심 있으신 분은, 시 웹 사이트에서 아이디어와 상세 연락처를 포함해 해당 양식을 작성하시기만 하면 됩니다.

어휘 top story 주요 뉴스 construction 공사, 건설 one-of-a-kind 유례를 찾기 힘든, 아주 독특한 collect ~을 모으다, 수집하다 reuse ~을 재사용하다 water v. ~에 물을 주다 landscaping 조경 local 지역의, 현지의 select ~을 선정하다, 선택하다 hold ~을 개최하다 naming 이름 짓기, 작명 be interested in ~에 관심이 있다 participate 참가하다 fill out ~을 작성하다 form 양식, 서식 contact details 상세 연락처

83 What does the speaker say is unique about the stadium?
(A) It will have a water collection system.
(B) It will include a roof that can open up.
(C) It will have underground parking spaces.
(D) It will include solar panels.

화자는 해당 경기장과 관련해 무엇이 독특하다고 말하는가?
(A) 집수 시스템을 갖추게 될 것이다.
(B) 개방될 수 있는 지붕을 포함할 것이다.
(C) 지하 주차 공간을 갖추게 될 것이다.
(D) 태양열 전지판을 포함할 것이다.

해설 〈기타 세부 사항을 묻는 문제〉
담화 초반부에 새로운 경기장 건설 소식을 전하면서 경기장의 특징적인 요소로 빗물을 모으는 시스템을 갖춘 유일한 경기장이 될 것이라고(This building project is one-of-a-kind, as it will be the only stadium in the country with a system that collects rainwater) 말하고 있다. 따라서 이러한 집수 시스템을 언급한 (A)가 정답이다.

어휘 unique 독특한, 특별한 collection 모음, 수집 include ~을 포함하

다 parking 주차 solar panels 태양열 전지판

84 What will happen next week?
(A) A new coach will be hired.
(B) A baseball game will be played.
(C) A celebrity will visit the site.
(D) A contest will be held.

다음 주에 무슨 일이 있을 것인가?
(A) 신임 코치가 고용될 것이다.
(B) 야구 경기가 진행될 것이다.
(C) 유명인사가 현장을 방문할 것이다.
(D) 콘테스트가 개최될 것이다.

해설 〈특정 시점의 일을 묻는 문제〉
담화 후반부에 시에서 다음 주에 콘테스트를 개최한다고(The city is holding a contest next week) 알리고 있으므로 (D)가 정답이다.

어휘 hire ~을 고용하다 celebrity 유명인사 site 현장, 부지, 장소 hold ~을 개최하다, 열다

85 According to the speaker, how can listeners participate in an activity?
(A) By contacting a city council member
(B) By completing an online form
(C) By visiting the stadium in person
(D) By sending an e-mail

화자의 말에 따르면, 청자들은 어떻게 한 가지 활동에 참가할 수 있는가?
(A) 시의회 의원에게 연락함으로써
(B) 온라인 양식을 작성 완료함으로써
(C) 직접 해당 경기장을 방문함으로써
(D) 이메일을 발송함으로써

해설 〈기타 세부 사항을 묻는 문제〉
담화 마지막 부분에 콘테스트 참가 방법으로 시 웹 사이트에서 양식을 작성하면 된다고(If you're interested in participating, simply fill out the form on the city's Web site) 설명하고 있으므로 (B)가 정답이다.

어휘 by (방법) ~함으로써 contact ~에게 연락하다 council 의회 complete ~을 완료하다 in person 직접 (가서)

Questions 86-88 refer to the following excerpt from a meeting.
캐W

⑧⑥ Our town has seen a sharp decrease in tourism this year. As the members of the town council's tourism division, we need to come up with new strategies for bringing more visitors to our town. The nearby town, ⑧⑦ Abbotsford, has recently attracted many tourists by building a new hotel specifically designed for young people. They report that it has been fully booked ever since it opened. As a result, I propose that we do the same thing. ⑧⑧ Here's a blueprint I had an architect create for us. The building would be located on Main Street. ⑧⑧ Let's have a look at it together.

우리 도시는 올해 급격한 관광 산업 침체를 겪어 왔습니다. 우리는 시의회 관광 분과의 일원으로서, 우리 도시로 더 많은 방문객을 끌어들이기 위한 새로운 전략을 제시해야 합니다. 근처의 도시, 애버츠포드는 특히 젊은 사람들을 대상으로 디자인한 새로운 호텔을 지어 최근 많은 관광객들을 끌어들였습니다. 이곳은 개장한 이후로 줄곧 예약이 꽉 차 있는 것으로 전해지고 있습니다. 따라서, 저는 우리 시도 똑같이 해 보도록 제안합니다. 여기 제가 한 건축가에게 우리를 위해 만들도록 부탁한 설계도가 있습니다. 이 건물은 메인 스트리트에 위치하게 될 것입니다. 함께 한 번 살펴보시죠.

어휘 sharp (변화 등이) 급격한 decrease in ~의 감소 tourism 관광 산업 council 의회 division (단체 등의) 과, 부 come up with (아이디어 등) ~을 제시하다, 내놓다 strategy 전략 bring ~을 끌어들이다 nearby 근처의 recently 최근에 attract ~을 끌어들이다 specifically 특히, 특별히 designed for ~을 대상으로 디자인한, ~을 위해 고안한 be fully booked 예약이 꽉 차다 ever since ~한 이후로 줄곧 as a result 따라서, 그 결과 propose that ~하도록 제안하다 blueprint 설계도 have A do A에게 ~하게 하다 architect 건축가 create ~을 만들어내다 be located on ~에 위치해 있다 have a look at ~을 한 번 보다

86 What problem is the speaker discussing?
(A) An increase in unemployment
(B) A decline in tourism
(C) A failed business merger
(D) A budget reduction

화자는 어떤 문제를 이야기하고 있는가?
(A) 실업률의 증가
(B) 관광 산업의 쇠퇴
(C) 실패한 기업 합병
(D) 예산 감소

해설 〈문제점을 묻는 문제〉
화자가 대화를 시작하면서 도시의 급격한 관광 산업 침체(Our town has seen a sharp decrease in tourism this year)를 언급한 뒤로, 그 해결 방안과 관련된 내용을 이야기하고 있으므로 (B)가 정답이다.

어휘 increase in ~의 증가 unemployment 실업률 decline in ~의 감소 failed 실패한 merger 합병, 통합 budget 예산 reduction 감소

87 What recently happened in Abbotsford?
(A) A marketing campaign began.
(B) A hotel was opened.
(C) A concert was held.
(D) A building was demolished.

애버츠포드에서 최근에 무슨 일이 있었는가?
(A) 한 마케팅 캠페인이 시작되었다.
(B) 한 호텔이 개장했다.
(C) 한 콘서트가 개최되었다.
(D) 한 건물이 철거되었다.

해설 〈과거에 일어난 일을 묻는 문제〉
담화 중반부에 화자가 애버츠포드를 언급하면서 그곳에서 최근에 개장한 호텔과 관련된(Abbotsford, has recently attracted many tourists by building a new hotel) 정보를 전달하고 있으므로 (B)가 정답이다.

어휘 recently 최근에 hold ~을 개최하다, 열다 demolish ~을 철거하다

88 What are the listeners asked to look at?
(A) A guest list
(B) A cost analysis
(C) A blueprint
(D) A street map

청자들은 무엇을 보도록 요청받는가?
(A) 초대 손님 명단
(B) 비용 분석 자료
(C) 설계도
(D) 거리 안내도

해설 〈요청 사항을 묻는 문제〉
담화 후반부에 화자가 한 건축가가 만들어 준 설계도를 언급한 뒤로(Here's a blueprint I had an architect create for us), a blueprint를 it으로 지칭해 함께 한 번 살펴보자고(Let's have a look at it together) 요청하고 있으므로 (C)가 정답이다.

어휘 analysis 분석 (자료) blueprint 설계도, 청사진

Questions 89-91 refer to the following broadcast. 영W

Welcome to *Digital Digest*, the weekly podcast where we take a look at new technology. ⑧⑨ Today we'll be discussing advances in home appliances. We'll hear about how artificial intelligence is being integrated into washing machines and refrigerators. ⑨⓪ Edward Lee, the chief executive officer of Apex Electronics, will be here to discuss some advanced products his company is planning to launch. But before we welcome Mr. Lee to the show, please remember this show is always looking for talented people. ⑨① Visit our Web site for information on our openings.

매주 신기술을 살펴보는 팟캐스트 〈디지털 다이제스트〉를 찾아 주신 것을 환영합니다. 오늘, 우리는 가전 기기의 진화를 이야기할 예정입니다. 우리는 어떻게 인공 지능이 세탁기와 냉장고에 접목되는지에 관한 얘기를 들을 것입니다. 에이펙스 일렉트로닉스의 대표이사이신 에드워드 리 씨께서 이 자리에 나오셔서 본인의 회사가 출시할 계획인 몇몇 고급 제품을 이야기해 주시겠습니다. 하지만 리 대표이사님을 우리 프로그램으로 맞이하기에 앞서, 저희 프로그램이 항상 재능 있는 분들을 찾고 있다는 사실을 기억해 주시기 바랍니다. 공석에 관한 정보를 보실 수 있도록 저희 웹 사이트를 방문하시기 바랍니다.

어휘 take a look at ~을 한 번 살펴보다 discuss ~을 이야기하다, 논의하다 advances 진보, 발전(상) home appliances 가전 기기 artificial intelligence 인공 지능 integrate A into B A를 B로 통합하다, 결합시키다 refrigerator 냉장고 chief executive officer 대표이사 advanced 고급의, 발전된, 진보한 plan to do ~할 계획이다 launch ~을 출시하다, 공개하다 look for ~을 찾다 talented 재능 있는 opening 공석, 빈자리

89 What is the topic of this week's podcast?
(A) Electric vehicles
(B) Home appliances
(C) Business software
(D) Online advertising

이번 주 팟캐스트의 주제는 무엇인가?
(A) 전기 자동차
(B) 가전 기기
(C) 비즈니스 소프트웨어
(D) 온라인 광고

해설 〈주제를 묻는 문제〉
담화 초반부에 프로그램 소개와 함께 오늘은 가전 기기의 진화를 이야기할 것이라고(Today we'll be discussing advances in home appliances) 알리고 있으므로 (B)가 정답이다.

어휘 vehicle 차량 advertising 광고 (활동)

90 Who is the guest on this week's podcast?
(A) A Web designer
(B) A scientist

(C) A CEO
(D) A sales representative

이번 주 팟캐스트의 초대 손님은 누구인가?
(A) 웹 디자이너
(B) 과학자
(C) CEO
(D) 영업 사원

해설 〈직업을 묻는 문제〉
담화 중반부에 에이펙스 일렉트로닉스의 대표이사인 에드워드 리 씨가 함께 자리한다고(Edward Lee, the chief executive officer of Apex Electronics, will be here) 알리고 있으므로 (C)가 정답이다.

어휘 representative 사원, 직원

91 Why does the speaker say, "This show is always looking for talented people"?
(A) To give information about an upcoming episode
(B) To introduce today's special guest
(C) To thank listeners for their contributions
(D) To encourage listeners to apply for a job

화자는 왜 "This show is always looking for talented people"라고 말하는가?
(A) 곧 있을 방송분에 관한 정보를 제공하기 위해
(B) 오늘의 특별 초대 손님을 소개하기 위해
(C) 청자들의 기부금에 감사하기 위해
(D) 청자들에게 일자리에 지원하도록 권하기 위해

해설 〈의도 파악 문제〉
담화 후반부에 화자가 '항상 재능 있는 사람들을 찾고 있다'고 말한 뒤로 공석과 관련된 정보를 얻을 수 있도록 웹 사이트를 방문하라고(Visit our Web site for information on our openings) 알리고 있다. 이는 직원을 모집한다는 뜻으로서 지원하도록 권하는 말에 해당되므로 (D)가 정답이다.

어휘 upcoming 곧 있을, 다가오는 episode 1회 방송분 introduce ~을 소개하다 contribution 기부(금), 기여, 공헌 encourage A to do A에게 ~하도록 권하다 apply for ~에 지원하다, ~을 신청하다

Questions 92-94 refer to the following introduction. 캐W

Good morning. My name is Diane, and I'm the visitor coordinator ⑨② here at Hickory Botanical Garden. Our mission is to share beautiful and rare flowers with the public. We also educate people about connecting with nature in their daily lives. Today I'll be teaching you how to make a butterfly feeder using basic materials. This is our first ever craft workshop, so ⑨③ we were worried that it might not appeal to visitors. However, just take a look around the room. All of our tables are full. Now, I should warn you that we'll be working with a sticky sugar solution. So, ⑨④ please put your phones, cameras, and other electronics away in your bags so they don't get messy.

안녕하세요. 제 이름은 다이앤이며, 저는 이곳 히코리 식물원의 방문객 프로그램 진행 책임자입니다. 저희 사명은 일반 대중과 아름답고 희귀한 꽃을 공유하는 것입니다. 또한 일상 생활 속에서 자연과 가까워지는 일에 관해 사람들을 교육하기도 합니다. 오늘, 제가 기초적인 재료를 활용해 나비 먹이통을 만드는 방법을 가르쳐 드릴 예정입니다. 이번이 저희가 최초로 진행하는 공예 워크숍이기 때문에, 방문객들의 관심을 끌지 못할까 걱정스러웠습니다. 하지만, 방을 한 번 둘러보시기 바랍니다. 모든 탁자가 가득 차 있습니다. 자, 우리가 끈적한 설탕 용액으로 작업하는 점에 주의하셔야 한다는 말씀을 드립니다. 그럼, 전화기와 카메라, 그리고 기타 전자 기기를 가방에 넣어 엉망이 되지 않도록 하시기 바랍니다.

어휘 coordinator 진행 책임자 mission 사명, 임무 share ~을 공유하다 rare 희귀한, 드문 the public 일반 대중 educate ~을 교육하다 connect with ~와 연결되다, 관련되다 how to do ~하는 법 feeder 먹이통 material 재료, 소재, 물품 first ever 최초의, 사상 처음의 craft 공예(품) be worried that ~할까 걱정하다 appeal to ~의 관심을 끌다 take a look around 한 번 둘러보다 warn A that A에게 ~라고 주의를 주다, 경고하다 sticky 끈적한 solution 용액 put A in B A를 B에 넣다, 두다 electronics 전자 기기 so (that) (목적) ~하도록, (결과) 그래야, 그래서 get + 형용사 ~한 상태가 되다 messy 엉망인

92 Where are the listeners?
(A) At a beach resort
(B) At a botanical garden
(C) At a business institute
(D) At a historical home

청자들은 어디에 있는가?
(A) 해변 리조트에
(B) 식물원에
(C) 비즈니스 협회에
(D) 역사적인 저택에

해설 〈담화의 장소를 묻는 문제〉
담화 초반부에 화자가 현재 있는 곳을 here at Hickory Botanical Garden이라고 말하고 있으므로 (B)가 정답이다.

93 What does the speaker suggest when she says, "All of our tables are full"?
(A) People were interested in a workshop.
(B) Some more furniture will be brought in.
(C) The listeners can join a waiting list.
(D) An event will start later than expected.

화자가 "All of our tables are full"이라고 말할 때 무엇을 의도하는가?
(A) 사람들이 워크숍에 관심이 있었다.
(B) 몇몇 추가 가구를 들여놓을 것이다.
(C) 청자들이 대기 명단에 이름을 올릴 수 있다.
(D) 행사가 예상보다 더 늦게 시작될 것이다.

해설 〈의도 파악 문제〉
화자가 담화 중반부에 방문객들의 관심을 끌지 못할까 걱정했다는(we were worried that it might not appeal to visitors) 말과 함께 주변을 둘러보도록 요청하면서 '모든 탁자가 꽉 차 있다'고 말하는 상황이다. 이는 사람들로 꽉 차 있는 상태를 확인시킴으로써 많은 관심을 이끌어 냈음을 알리는 것이므로 (A)가 정답이다.

어휘 be interested in ~에 관심이 있다 bring in ~을 들여오다, 불러들이다 join ~에 가입하다, 합류하다, 참여하다 than expected 예상보다

94 What does the speaker request that the listeners do?
(A) Leave food and drinks outside
(B) Write down their questions
(C) Put away their electronic devices
(D) Pay close attention to a video

화자는 청자들에게 무엇을 하도록 요청하는가?
(A) 음식과 음료를 밖에 놓아 두는 일
(B) 질문 내용을 적어 두는 일
(C) 전자 기기를 치워 놓는 일
(D) 동영상에 크게 주의를 기울이는 일

해설 〈요청 사항을 묻는 문제〉
담화 맨 마지막에 전화기와 카메라, 그리고 기타 전자 기기를 가방에 넣어 두도록(please put your phones, cameras, and other electronics away in your bags) 요청하고 있으므로 (C)가 정답이다.

어휘 leave ~을 놓다, 두다 put away ~을 치우다 device 기기, 장치 pay close attention to ~에 크게 주의를 기울이다

Questions 95-97 refer to the following excerpt from a meeting and chart. 호M

Next on the agenda for ⑨⑤ this sales department meeting is the growth report. We've experienced an increase for all appliances compared to last year, so that's great news. Now, as we all know, our microwaves didn't perform very well, as there has been increased competition in this category. However, ⑨⑥ the management team has decided to redesign the product with the second-highest growth rate to make it more appealing to customers. I'm not sure when that will happen. But to help boost brand awareness, ⑨⑦ we'll start spending more on advertising from next month.

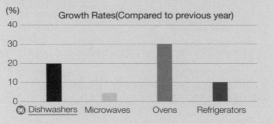

이 영업부 회의의 다음 안건은 성장 보고서입니다. 우리가 작년에 비해 모든 가전기기에 대해 증가를 경험했기 때문에 이는 아주 좋은 소식입니다. 자, 우리 모두가 알고 있다시피, 우리 전자레인지 제품이 아주 좋은 성과를 내지 못했다는 점은 놀랍지 않은데, 이 부문에서 경쟁이 치열해졌기 때문입니다. 하지만 경영팀은 두 번째로 높은 성장률을 기록한 제품을 고객들이 더 매력적으로 느끼도록 만들기 위해 다시 디자인하기로 결정했습니다. 언제 그렇게 될지는 확실하지 않습니다. 하지만 브랜드 인지도를 높이는 데 도움이 되기 위해, 우리는 다음 달부터 광고에 더 많은 비용을 지출하기 시작할 것입니다.

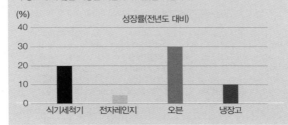

어휘 agenda 안건, 의제 sales 영업, 판매(량), 매출 growth 성장, 발전 experience ~을 겪다, 경험하다 increase 증가 appliance 가전기기 compared to ~와 비교해 microwave 전자레인지 perform well 좋은 성과를 내다 as ~이므로 competition 경쟁 category 부문, 범주 decide to do ~하기로 결정하다 redesign ~을 다시 디자인하다

---

second-highest 두 번째로 높은 growth rate 성장률 make A + 형용사 A를 ~한 상태로 만들다 appealing 매력적인 help do ~하는 것을 돕다 boost ~을 촉진하다, 증대하다 brand awareness 브랜드 인지도 spend A on B B에 대해 A를 소비하다, 지출하다 advertising 광고 (활동)

95 Who is the talk most likely intended for?
(A) Market researchers
(B) Sales personnel
(C) Store managers
(D) Product testers

담화는 누구를 대상으로 할 것 같은가?
(A) 시장 조사 담당자들
(B) 영업부 직원들
(C) 매장 관리자들
(D) 제품 테스트 담당자들

해설 〈직업을 묻는 문제〉
담화 시작 부분에 화자가 this sales department meeting이라는 말로 회의 참석자들의 소속 부서를 언급하고 있으므로 (B)가 정답이다.

어휘 be intended for ~을 대상으로 하다 personnel 직원들

96 Look at the graphic. What kind of appliances will be redesigned?
(A) Dishwashers
(B) Microwaves
(C) Ovens
(D) Refrigerators

시각 자료를 보시오. 무슨 종류의 가전기기가 다시 디자인될 것인가?
(A) 식기세척기
(B) 전자레인지
(C) 오븐
(D) 냉장고

해설 〈그래프 문제〉
담화 중반부에 화자는 두 번째로 높은 성장률을 기록한 제품을 언급하면서 그것을 다시 디자인하기로 결정했다고(~ the management team has decided to redesign the product with the second-highest growth rate ~) 알리고 있다. 시각 자료에 성장률이 두 번째로 높은 제품이 맨 왼쪽에 있는 Dishwashers이므로 (A)가 정답이다.

97 What does the company plan to do next month?
(A) Upgrade an online store
(B) Hire more experienced workers
(C) Open a new retail branch
(D) Increase an advertising budget

해당 회사는 다음 달에 무엇을 할 계획인가?
(A) 온라인 매장 업그레이드하기
(B) 경험 많은 추가 직원 고용하기
(C) 새로운 소매 지점 개장하기
(D) 광고 예산 늘리기

해설 〈특정 시점의 일을 묻는 문제〉
담화 후반부에, 다음 달부터 광고에 더 많은 비용을 지출할 것이라고
(~ we'll start spending more on advertising from next
month) 알리고 있다. 이는 광고 예산이 늘어난다는 뜻이므로 (D)가 정
답이다.

어휘 plan to do ~할 계획이다 hire ~을 고용하다 experienced 경험
많은, 숙련된 retail 소매 branch 지점, 지사 advertising 광고 (활동)
budget 예산

**Questions 98-100 refer to the following telephone message and
conference schedule. 캐W**

⑨ Hello, Ms. Hendry. I'm calling to confirm your participation
in the ⑨ Arcturus Graphic Design Seminar Series. You'll
be pleased to hear that several university professors have
already enrolled their graphic design students in the seminar
series as a result of your participation. I e-mailed a copy of
the seminar schedule to you this morning. ⑨ Your seminar
is scheduled to be the last one of the day. Also, don't forget
that all seminar speakers are encouraged to attend a meal
at 6 P.M. once the day's events have ended. ⑩ If you join
us for the dinner, you'll be given a gift certificate worth $100
for Sparks Office Supplies.

9:00 A.M.	Ms. Mary Kelley
10:45 A.M.	Mr. Brian Steltzer
12:30 P.M.	Break for lunch
1:30 P.M.	Mr. Fred Arnott
⑨ 3:15 P.M.	Ms. Anna Hendry

안녕하세요, 헨드리 씨. 저는 아르크투르스 그래픽 디자인 세미나 시리즈에 대한
귀하의 참가를 확인하고자 전화 드렸습니다. 귀하의 참가로 인해, 여러 대학 교
수님들께서 그래픽 디자인 전공 학생들을 이 세미나 시리즈에 등록하게 하셨다
는 사실을 들으시면 기쁘실 것입니다. 제가 오늘 아침에 이메일로 세미나 일정표
를 한 부 보내드렸습니다. 귀하의 세미나는 당일 마지막 순서가 될 예정입니다.
또한, 모든 세미나 연설자들께서는 당일 행사가 종료되는 대로 오후 6시에 있을
식사 자리에 참석하시기를 권해 드린다는 점도 잊지 마시기 바랍니다. 저희와 함
께 저녁 식사 자리에 참석하시는 경우, 100달러 상당의 스파크스 사무용품 상
품권을 받으시게 됩니다.

오전 9:00	메리 켈리 씨
오전 10:45	브라이언 셀처 씨
오후 12:30	점심 시간
오후 1:30	프레드 아노트 씨
오후 3:15	애나 헨드리 씨

어휘 confirm ~을 확인하다 participation 참가 be pleased to do ~해
서 기쁘다 several 여럿의, 몇몇의 enroll A in B A를 B에 등록하다 as a
result of ~에 따른 결과로 be scheduled to do ~할 예정이다 forget
that ~임을 잊다 be encouraged to do ~하도록 권장되다 attend
~에 참석하다 once ~하는 대로, ~하자마자 join ~와 함께하다, ~에 합류하
다 gift certificate 상품권 worth ~ 상당의, ~의 가치가 있는

98 What is the main topic of the seminar series?
(A) Architecture
(B) Human resources
(C) Graphic design
(D) Market research

세미나 시리즈의 주제는 무엇인가?
(A) 건축
(B) 인적 자원
(C) 그래픽 디자인
(D) 시장 조사

해설 〈주제를 묻는 문제〉
담화 초반부에 화자가 Arcturus Graphic Design Seminar
Series라는 말로 세미나 시리즈의 주제를 언급하고 있으므로 (C)가
정답이다.

99 Look at the graphic. When will the listener's seminar
begin?
(A) 9:00 A.M.
(B) 10:45 A.M.
(C) 1:30 P.M.
(D) 3:15 P.M.

시각 자료를 보시오. 청자는 언제 세미나를 시작할 것인가?
(A) 오전 9:00
(B) 오전 10:45
(C) 오후 1:30
(D) 오후 3:15

해설 〈2열 도표 문제〉
담화 초반부에는 청자, 즉 상대방인 헨드리 씨의 이름을 부르고 있고
(Hello, Ms. Hendry), 중반부에는 청자를 Your로 지칭해 청자의 세
미나가 당일 마지막 순서라고(Your seminar is scheduled to be
the last one of the day) 알리고 있다. 일정표에서 헨드리 씨의 이
름이 쓰여 있는 마지막 순서가 3시 15분으로 표기되어 있으므로 (D)
가 정답이다.

100 How can seminar speakers receive a gift certificate?
(A) By submitting a form
(B) By attending a meal
(C) By giving another talk
(D) By joining a discussion session

세미나 연설자들은 어떻게 상품권을 받을 수 있는가?
(A) 양식을 제출함으로써
(B) 식사 자리에 참석함으로써
(C) 한 번 더 연설함으로써
(D) 토론 시간에 함께 함으로써

해설 〈기타 세부 사항을 묻는 문제〉
담화 맨 마지막 부분에 저녁 식사 자리에 참석하면 100달러 상당의 스
파크스 사무용품 상품권을 받는다고(If you join us for the dinner,
you'll be given a gift certificate worth $100 for Sparks
Office Supplies) 알리고 있으므로 (B)가 정답이다.

어휘 receive ~을 받다 by (방법) ~함으로써 submit ~을 제출하
다 form 양식, 서식 give a talk 연설하다 discussion 토론, 논의
session (특정 활동을 위한) 시간

101 해석 기조 연설자 대니얼 오웬 씨께서 아시아 전역의 여러 국가에서 도착한 참석자들에게 연설하실 것입니다.

해설 〈전치사 어휘〉
보기가 모두 전치사이므로 의미가 알맞은 것을 찾아야 한다. 빈칸 앞에 '도착했다'를 뜻하는 동사 arrived가 쓰여 있는 것으로 볼 때, 빈칸 뒤에 위치한 장소 명사 countries가 출발 지역이 되어야 자연스럽다. 따라서 '~에서, ~로부터' 등의 의미로 출발점을 나타낼 때 사용하는 (C) from이 정답이다.

어휘 keynote speaker 기조 연설자　address v. ~에게 연설하다　attendee 참석자　arrive 도착하다　throughout ~ 전역에서, ~ 전체에 걸쳐　as to ~에 관해서는

102 해석 아파트 단지 내에서 발견되는 대부분의 꽃들은 심지어 비가 많이 내리는 날씨에도 잘 자란다.

해설 〈동사 어휘〉
빈칸 뒤에 명사 목적어가 아닌 부사 well이 쓰여 있으므로 자동사가 필요하며, 아파트 단지 내에서 발견되는 꽃들의 상태나 특성 등과 관련된 동사가 쓰여야 알맞으므로 '자라다, 성장하다'를 뜻하는 자동사 (C) grow가 정답이다.

어휘 apartment complex 아파트 단지　even 심지어 (~도)　operate 작동되다, 가동되다, 운영되다　choose ~을 선택하다　grow 자라다, 성장하다　explore ~을 탐구하다, 탐험하다

103 해석 조사 결과에 따르면 그 회사가 연간 수익 목표를 초과할 것이라는 점은 이미 보장되어 있다.

해설 〈부사 어휘〉
현재완료 시제 동사를 구성하는 have와 과거분사(guaranteed) 사이에 위치한 빈칸에 쓰일 수 있는 부사가 필요하므로 '이미'라는 의미로 현재완료 시제와 자주 어울려 사용하는 부사인 (B) already가 정답이다. (A) yet은 주로 부정문 또는 의문문에서 사용한다.

어휘 result 결과(물)　study 조사, 연구　guarantee that ~임을 보장하다　exceed ~을 초과하다　annual 연간의, 해마다의　revenue 수익, 수입　yet (부정문) 아직, (의문문) 이미, 벌써, (최상급과 함께) 지금까지 중에서　soon 곧, 머지않아

104 해석 그레이엄 씨가 센트럴 스트리트에 위치한 지역 문화 센터의 개장을 책임지게 되었다.

해설 〈① 명사 자리 (관사 뒤) ② 의미 혼동 명사〉
정관사 the와 전치사 of 사이에 위치한 빈칸은 the의 수식을 받을 명사 자리이다. 또한, in charge of의 목적어로서 지역 문화 센터라는 시설과 관련해 책임지는 일을 나타내야 하므로 '개장, 개업, 개통' 등을 뜻하는 명사 (C) opening이 정답이다.

어휘 be placed in charge of ~을 책임지게 되다, 맡게 되다　community center 지역 문화 센터　openness 솔직함, 마음이 열려 있음　opener 여는 도구, 여는 것　opening 개장, 개업, 개통

105 해석 커랜 씨는 다음 이사회 회의 전에 추가 정보에 대한 주주들의 요청을 처리할 것이다.

해설 〈동사 어휘〉
빈칸 뒤에 '주주들의 요청'을 의미하는 복합명사 shareholder requests가 쓰여 있어 이러한 요청에 대해 취할 수 있는 조치 등과 관련된 동사가 필요하므로 '(문제 등) ~을 처리하다, 다루다'를 뜻하는 (C) address가 정답이다. (B) inform은 주로 사람 명사를 목적어로 취하므로 오답이다.

어휘 shareholder 주주　request for ~에 대한 요청　board 이사회　advise ~에게 조언하다　inform ~에게 알리다　address v. (문제 등) ~을 처리하다, 다루다　install ~을 설치하다

106 해석 테일러 씨는 자신의 엔지니어링 팀에 생긴 세 공석에 대해 오직 자격 있는 지원자들만 모집할 것이다.

해설 〈형용사 자리 (명사 앞)〉
동사 recruit와 명사 목적어 applicants 사이에 위치한 빈칸은 명사를 수식할 형용사 자리이므로 보기에서 유일하게 형용사인 (A) qualified가 정답이다. 복합 명사가 구성되는 경우에 대해 생각해 볼 수도 있지만, (B) qualification은 applicants와 복합 명사를 구성하기에 의미상 적합하지 않으므로 오답이다.

어휘 recruit ~을 모집하다　applicant 지원자, 신청자　open position 공석　qualified 자격 있는, 적격인　qualification 자격 요건　qualify 자격이 있다, ~에게 자격을 주다

107 해석 대부분의 구독자들은 그 잡지 6월호의 도착을 간절히 기다리고 있다.

해설 〈명사 어휘〉
빈칸 앞뒤의 단어들로 볼 때 6월에 출간되는 잡지를 가리킬 명사가 필요하다는 것을 알 수 있으므로 '(출판물 등의) 호'를 뜻하는 (C) issue가 정답이다.

어휘 subscriber 구독자, 서비스 가입자　eagerly 간절히, 열망하여　await ~을 기다리다　arrival 도착　purchase 구매(품)　charge 청구 요금, 책임, 담당　issue (출판물 등의) 호　admission 입장, 입학, 입회

108 해석 베를린 다이나믹에서 오는 사람이 30분 후에 도착할 예정이라고 안내 담당자에게 알려 주시기 바랍니다.

해설 〈동사 어휘〉
빈칸 뒤에 이어지는 '사람 목적어 + that절'의 구조와 어울리는 동사가 필요하므로 이 구조와 함께 '~에게 …라고 알리다'라는 의미를 나타낼 때 사용하는 (B) notify가 정답이다.

어휘 receptionist 안내 담당자, 접수 담당자　arrive 도착하다　in 시간 ~ 후에　notify A that A에게 ~라고 알리다, 통지하다　accept ~을 받아들이다, 수락하다　deliver ~을 배송하다, 전달하다

109 해석 골든 메도우즈 지역은 지난 몇 년 동안 인구 증가와 함께 급격히 변화되었다.

해설 〈부사 자리 (자동사 뒤)〉
빈칸 앞에 현재완료 시제로 제시된 동사 change는 타동사와 자동사로 모두 쓰인다. 그런데 보기에 쓰여 있는 명사 (A) drama와 (B)

110 해석 그 강연은 젊은이들을 설득하여 제품을 구입하게 만드는 것에 중점을 둔 마케팅에 관한 것일 것이다.

해설 〈명사 자리 (전치사 뒤)〉
전치사 with와 on 사이에 위치한 빈칸은 with의 목적어 역할을 할 명사 자리이므로 명사인 (C) emphasis가 정답이다.

어휘 with emphasis on ~에 중점을 두어　convince A to do A를 확신시켜 ~하게 만들다, A를 설득해 ~하게 만들다　purchase ~을 구입하다　emphasize ~을 강조하다　emphatic (말 등이) 강한, (분명히) 강조하는

111 해석 마리노 씨의 발표가 너무 유익해서 저희는 내년 컨퍼런스에서 연설하시도록 요청 드렸습니다.

해설 〈형용사 어휘〉
보기가 모두 형용사이므로 의미가 알맞은 것을 찾아야 한다. be동사 was 뒤에 위치한 빈칸은 주어 Ms. Marino's presentation의 보어로서 마리노 씨의 발표가 지닌 특성을 나타내야 하므로 '유익한, 유용한 정보를 주는'을 뜻하는 (B) informative가 정답이다. (D) helping의 경우 올바른 형용사의 형태인 helpful(도움이 되는)로 수정해야 빈칸에 사용 가능하다.

어휘 presentation 발표(회)　so A that B 너무 A해서 B하다　invite A to do A에게 ~하도록 요청하다　pleased 기쁜, 만족한　informative 유익한, 유용한 정보를 주는　unable 할 수 없는

112 해석 접수 데스크에서 체크인하시는 모든 분은 일종의 사진이 부착된 신분증을 제시하셔야 합니다.

해설 〈동사 어휘〉
보기가 모두 동사이므로 의미가 알맞은 것을 찾아야 한다. 빈칸 뒤에 이어지는 명사구로 볼 때, 체크인할 때 사진이 부착된 신분증으로 해야 하는 행위를 나타낼 동사가 필요하다는 것을 알 수 있으므로 '~을 제시하다, 제공하다'를 뜻하는 (A) present가 정답이다.

어휘 reception desk 접수 데스크, 프런트　form 종류, 형태, 유형　photo identification 사진이 부착된 신분증　present ~을 제시하다, 제공하다　inspect ~을 점검하다　assign ~을 배정하다, 할당하다　place ~을 놓다, 두다

113 해석 부서장들은 각 직원과 직접 만나 이야기하고 모든 문제에 대해서 직접 해결책을 찾도록 해야 합니다.

해설 〈재귀대명사〉
빈칸이 속한 and절을 보면, 동사 try와 to부정사구, 그리고 전치사 to와 명사 목적어까지 구성이 완전한 상태이다. 따라서 그 뒤에 위치한 빈칸은 부사처럼 부가적인 요소가 필요한 자리이므로 '직접 스스로'라는 의미로 부사처럼 사용할 수 있는 재귀대명사 (D) themselves가 정답이다.

어휘 manager 부서장, 책임자, 관리자　in person 직접 만나서　try to

---

dramas는 모두 이 문장의 목적어로 의미상 맞지 않는다. 반면, '자동사 + 부사'의 구조로 (D) dramatically가 동사 has changed를 수식할 경우 '급격히 변화되었다'와 같이 의미상 적합하므로 (D) dramatically가 정답이다.

do ~하려 하다 solution 해결책 one's own 자신만의 oneself
(부사처럼 쓰여) 직접, 스스로

114 해석 우리는 모든 문서가 안전한 상태로 유지되도록 하기 위해 지속적으로 사무실들을 감시하고 있다.

해설 〈형용사 자리(5형식 동사의 수동태 뒤)〉
빈칸이 속한 that절은 '모든 문서가 유지되다'라는 의미를 나타낸다. 따라서 빈칸에 문서 보관 상태나 방법 등과 관련된 단어가 쓰여야 하는데, 수동태 동사 be kept는 형용사와 결합해 '~한 상태로 유지되다'라는 뜻을 나타내므로 형용사 (D) secure가 정답이다. 참고로, 이 표현은 'keep + 목적어 + 목적격 보어'에서 목적어가 주어 자리로 이동하고 keep이 수동태로 바뀌면서 그 뒤에 목적격 보어인 형용사가 남은 구조에 해당된다.

어휘 constantly 지속적으로, 끊임없이 monitor v. ~을 감시하다, 관찰하다 make sure that 반드시 ~하도록 하다, ~하는 것을 확실히 해 두다 be kept + 형용사 ~한 상태로 유지되다 secure a. 안전한 v. ~을 확보하다, 안전하게 하다

115 해석 직원 모두가 일주일간의 휴가를 떠나기 때문에 웰본 아카데미는 일시적으로 문을 닫는다.

해설 〈부사 어휘〉
보기가 모두 부사이므로 의미가 알맞은 것을 찾아야 한다. 빈칸에 쓰일 부사는 형용사 closed를 앞에서 수식해 한 단체가 문을 닫는 방식과 관련된 의미를 나타내야 하므로 '일시적으로, 임시로'를 뜻하는 (B) temporarily가 정답이다.

어휘 on the staff 직원으로 있는 take a vacation 휴가를 떠나다 promptly 정확히 제 시간에, 지체 없이, 즉각 temporarily 일시적으로, 임시로 extremely 대단히, 매우, 극도로 especially 특히

116 해석 록웰 극장은 곧 있을 공연 입장권에 관심이 있는 주민들로부터 수많은 문의를 받아왔다.

해설 〈감정동사의 현재분사 VS. 과거분사〉
빈칸 앞 부분을 보면, 주어와 동사(has received), 목적어, 그리고 from 전치사구까지 구성이 완전한 상태이므로 빈칸 이하 부분은 명사 residents를 뒤에서 수식하는 수식어구가 되어야 한다. 따라서 명사를 뒤에서 수식할 수 있는 형용사 (B) interesting과 (C) interested 중에서 하나를 골라야 하는데, 입장권에 '관심이 있는 주민들'이란 의미가 적합하므로 전치사 in과 어울려 '~에 관심이 있는'을 의미할 때 사용하는 (C) interested가 정답이다.

어휘 receive ~을 받다 numerous 수많은, 다수의 inquiry 문의 resident 주민 upcoming 곧 있을, 다가오는 interest n. 관심(사), 흥미, 이익, 이자 v. ~의 관심을 끌다 interesting 흥미롭게 만드는 interested in (사람이) ~에 관심이 있는

117 해석 분기 회의 시간에 참석하는 사람들을 위한 다과가 컴튼 씨의 연설 후에 제공될 것이다.

해설 〈전치사 VS. 접속사〉
빈칸 뒤에 위치한 Mr. Compton's talk가 명사구이므로 이 명사구를 목적어로 취할 수 있는 전치사 (B) following이 정답이다. (A)

somewhat은 부사, (C) whenever는 접속사이며, (D) depending은 동사 depend의 현재분사이다.

어휘 refreshments 다과, 간식 those who ~하는 사람들 quarterly 분기의 provide ~을 제공하다 somewhat 다소, 약간, 어느 정도 following ~ 후에 whenever 언제든 ~할 때, ~할 때마다 depending (on) (~에) 따라, 달려 있는

118 해석 쇼핑객들은 합리적으로 가격이 책정된 가전기기 및 훌륭한 고객 서비스로 인해 아먼드 일렉트로닉스를 방문한다.

해설 〈부사 자리(분사 앞)〉
명사 appliances를 수식하는 과거분사 priced와 정관사 the 사이에 빈칸이 위치해 있으므로 빈칸은 과거분사를 수식하는 부사의 자리이다. 따라서 부사인 (D) reasonably가 정답이다.

어휘 priced 가격이 책정된 appliances 가전기기 reason n. 이유, 근거 v. 추론하다, 논리적으로 생각하다 reasonable 합리적인 reasonably 합리적으로

119 해석 카파 텍스타일즈는 지난 10년 동안 고품질 양모 및 실크 제품을 제공한 것으로 명성을 쌓아 왔다.

해설 〈명사 어휘〉
보기가 모두 명사이므로 의미가 알맞은 것을 찾아야 한다. 한 업체가 오랫동안 품질이 좋은 제품을 제공하면서 발전시킬 수 있었던 것을 나타낼 명사가 필요하므로 빈칸 뒤 전치사 for와 어울려 '~에 대한 명성, 평판'을 뜻하는 (C) reputation이 정답이다.

어휘 develop ~을 발전시키다, 발달시키다, 개발하다 provide ~을 제공하다 quality a. 고급의, 양질의 n. 질, 품질 decade 10년 courtesy 공손함, 정중한 destination 목적지, 도착지 reputation 명성, 평판 consequence 결과

120 해석 직원들이 생산 시설의 제한 구역에 출입하려 시도하는 경우 경보가 울릴 것입니다.

해설 〈시제(시간부사절과 시제)〉
우선, 빈칸이 속한 when절에 동사가 없으므로 빈칸이 동사 자리임을 알 수 있다. 또한 주절에 미래 시제 동사(will sound)가 쓰일 때 시간부사절인 when절의 동사는 현재 시제여야 하므로 현재 시제 동사의 형태인 (B) attempt가 정답이다.

어휘 alarm 경보, 경고(음) sound 울리다, 소리가 나다 attempt to do ~하려 시도하다 restricted 제한된 facility 시설(물)

121 해석 고객과의 예약 일정을 잡으실 때, 충분한 시간을 할당하셔야 한다는 점에 유의하시기 바랍니다.

해설 〈명사 어휘〉
빈칸은 바로 앞에 위치한 또 다른 명사 client와 복합 명사를 구성해 분사 scheduling의 목적어로서 일정을 정하는 일의 대상이 되어야 하므로 '예약, 약속'을 뜻하는 (C) appointments가 정답이다.

어휘 be aware that ~임에 유의하다, ~임을 알고 있다 allocate ~을 할당하다, 배정하다 sufficient 충분한 location 장소, 위치, 지점 circumstance 상황, 사정, 환경 appointment 예약, 약속 achievement 성취, 달성, 업적

122 해석 만약 점검 담당자들이 촉박하게 방문한다 하더라도 그들에게 실험실에 대한 전면적인 출입 권한이 주어지는 것이 중요합니다.

해설 〈형용사 어휘〉
문장의 가주어 It과 진주어 that절의 구문에서 that절의 동사인 be가 동사원형의 형태인데, 이러한 구조를 이끌 수 있는 것은 '의무/필수'의 의미를 갖는 형용사이므로 (D) critical이 정답이다. 이러한 '의무/필수'의 의미를 갖는 형용사는 'It is critical that 주어 + (should) + 동사원형 ~'과 같이 that절에 should를 생략한 후 동사원형을 사용하는 것이 원칙이다.

어휘 inspector 점검 담당자, 조사관 give A full access to B A에게 B에 대한 전면적인 출입 권한을 주다 laboratory 실험실 on short notice 촉박하게, 급한 공지에도 particular 특정한, 특별한 immediate 즉각적인, 직속의 substantial 상당한 critical 중요한, 중대한

123 해석 최신 소설을 출간한 후에, 사만다 부스 씨는 전국 각지로 도서 사인회 투어를 떠날 계획이다.

해설 〈전치사 어휘〉
보기가 모두 전치사이므로 의미가 알맞은 것을 찾아야 한다. 빈칸 뒤에 위치한 명사 country는 넓은 장소를 나타내는 명사이므로 '~ 전역에서, ~ 전체에 걸쳐'라는 의미로 장소 명사를 목적어로 취하는 전치사 (C) throughout이 정답이다.

어휘 publish ~을 출간하다 newest 최신의 plan to do ~할 계획이다 go on a tour 투어를 떠나다 book-signing 도서 사인회 aboard prep. (배, 버스, 비행기 등)에 탑승해 ad. 탑승하여 ahead of ~보다 앞서, ~보다 빨리 throughout ~ 전역에서, ~ 전체에 걸쳐 besides prep. ~ 외에(도), ~뿐만 아니라 ad. 게다가, 뿐만 아니라

124 해석 계약 조항에 따르면 양측이 합의하는 경우에 언제든 계약이 취소될 수 있는 것으로 나타나 있다.

해설 〈명사절 접속사〉
타동사 indicate 바로 뒤에 빈칸이 있고, 그 뒤로 주어와 동사가 포함된 절이 이어지는 구조이므로 이 절은 indicate의 목적어 역할을 하는 명사절이 되어야 한다. 보기 중에 명사절 접속사는 (A) what과 (D) that이 있는데 what은 주어 혹은 목적어가 없는 불완전한 절을 이끌고, that은 완전한 구조의 절과 함께 쓰이므로 빈칸 뒤의 완전한 문장 구조와 어울리는 (D) that이 정답이다.

어휘 term 조항, 조건 contract 계약(서) indicate that ~임을 나타내다, 가리키다 cancel ~을 취소하다 at any time 언제든지, 아무나 both parties 양측, 쌍방 agree 합의하다 unless ~가 아니라면, ~하지 않는다면

125 해석 테일러 씨는 회의 시간을 엄수하는 것뿐만 아니라 세부 요소에 대한 면밀한 주의력으로 잘 알려져 있다.

해설 〈병렬 구조〉
빈칸 앞뒤에 테일러 씨가 무엇으로 잘 알려져 있는지를 나타내는 것으로서 for의 목적어에 해당되는 동일한 명사구가 각각 쓰여 있으므로 이러한 병렬 구조를 이끌 수 있는 (A) as well as가 정답이다. (B) moreover와 (C) accordingly는 부사이며, (D) in order that 뒤에

는 주어와 동사가 포함된 절이 이어져야 한다.

어휘 be well-known for ~로 잘 알려져 있다 punctuality 시간 엄수 close 면밀한, 정밀한, 철저한 attention to ~에 대한 주의(력), 주목, 관심 detail 세부 요소 as well as ~뿐만 아니라 …도 moreover 더욱이, 게다가 accordingly 그에 따라, 그러므로, 그런 이유로 in order that ~하기 위해

126 해석 랩터 컴퍼니는 호주에서 손꼽히는 화학 제품 제조사로 널리 인정받고 있다.

해설 〈현재분사 VS. 과거분사〉
정관사 the와 명사 manufacturer 사이에 위치한 빈칸은 명사를 수식할 형용사 자리이다. 보기 중 형용사로서 '선도적인, 일류의'라는 뜻으로 빈칸 뒤의 명사를 수식하기에 의미상으로도 적합한 (D) leading이 정답이다. 과거분사 (A) led는 의미상 적당하지 않으며, 명사 (C) leader 역시 또 다른 명사 manufacturer와 복합 명사를 구성하기에 의미상 적합하지 않다.

어휘 widely 널리, 폭넓게 recognize ~을 인정하다 manufacturer 제조사 chemical 화학의, 화학 물질의 lead ~을 이끌다, 진행하다 leading 손꼽히는, 선도적인, 앞서 가는

127 해석 이사회는 국내 경쟁사와의 합병 제안에 대해 만장일치로 찬성 투표를 했다.

해설 〈부사 어휘〉
보기가 모두 부사이므로 의미가 알맞은 것을 찾아야 한다. 빈칸에 쓰일 부사는 이사회가 투표를 한 방식과 관련된 의미를 나타내야 하므로 '만장일치로'를 뜻하는 (C) unanimously가 정답이다.

어휘 board members 이사회 vote 투표하다 in favor of ~에 찬성하여 proposed 제안된 merger 합병 domestic 국내의 competitor 경쟁사, 경쟁자 typically 일반적으로, 전형적으로 extremely 대단히, 매우, 극도로 unanimously 만장일치로 fondly 좋아하여, 애정을 담아

128 해석 덤바튼 씨가 컨퍼런스 센터에 도착하자마자, 대표이사님의 연례 연설이 시작되었다.

해설 〈시제(시간부사절과 시제)〉
동사 begin의 여러 형태가 보기에 제시되어 있으므로 능/수동, 주어와의 수 일치, 시제 등을 확인해 알맞은 것을 골라야 한다. '~하자마자, ~하는 대로'를 뜻하는 접속사 as soon as가 이끄는 절의 동사와 주절의 동사는 시제가 일치해야 하므로 arrived와 동일한 과거 시제 동사가 빈칸에 쓰여야 한다. 따라서 과거 시제인 (A) were begun과 (D) began 중에서 하나를 골라야 하는데, 주어 the CEO's annual speech가 3인칭 단수이므로 수 일치에 상관없이 사용할 수 있는 (D) began이 정답이다.

어휘 as soon as ~하자마자, ~하는 대로 arrive 도착하다 annual 연례적인, 해마다의

129 해석 각각의 연구원들은 적절한 방법으로 실험을 실시하기 위해 극도로 주의한다.

해설 〈부정 대명사〉
빈칸 바로 뒤에 'of + 복수 명사'로 구성된 전치사구가 있으므로 이 전

치사구의 수식을 받을 수 있는 대명사 (B) All와 (C) Each 중에서 하나를 골라야 한다. 또한 문장의 동사 takes에 어울리는 것은 3인칭 단수 주어이므로 단수 취급하는 대명사인 (C) Each가 정답이다. (B) All은 가산 명사와 함께 쓰이는 경우 복수 취급을 하므로 오답이다.

어휘 researcher 연구가, 연구원 take utmost care 극도로 주의하다 conduct ~을 실시하다, 수행하다 experiment 실험 in a proper manner 적절한 방법으로

130 해석 오직 회사의 특정한 사람들만 회사 창고에 보관되어 있는 기밀 문서에 대한 접근 권한이 승인된다.

해설 〈형용사 어휘〉
보기가 모두 형용사이므로 의미가 알맞은 것을 찾아야 한다. 빈칸에 쓰일 형용사는 바로 뒤에 위치한 명사 documents를 수식해 창고에 보관되어 있는 문서의 특성을 나타내야 하므로 '기밀의'를 뜻하는 (D) confidential이 정답이다.

어휘 certain 특정한, 일정한 individual n. 사람, 개인 firm 회사 grant A B A에게 B를 승인하다 access to ~에 대한 접근 권한, 이용 권한 store v. ~을 보관하다, 저장하다 warehouse 창고 considerate 사려 깊은, 배려하는 perishable (음식 등이) 잘 상하는, 부패성의 surrounding 인근의, 주위의 confidential 기밀의

PART 6
P199

[131-134] 기사

로즈메드 (4월 11일) – 〈더 로즈메드 트리뷴〉의 편집자는 전임 기고가로 신디아 엑슬리 씨가 고용되었음을 확인해 주었습니다. 엑슬리 씨는 새롭게 추가되어 이 신문에 정기적으로 실리게 될 '맛있는 식당' 섹션을 맡아 작업하게 됩니다. 이 섹션은 지역 레스토랑에 관한 **131** 평가 및 요리사 인터뷰를 포함할 것입니다. 엑슬리 씨는 수년 **132** 동안에 걸쳐 여러 인기 있는 음식 전문 잡지를 위해 기사를 작성해 왔습니다. 매우 많은 경험을 지닌, 엑슬리 씨는 이 역할에 완벽합니다. "저는 지역 비즈니스 업계에 적극적으로 관여하고 있기 때문에, 독자 여러분의 관심을 끌 수 있는 덜 알려진 레스토랑에 관해 알려 드릴 수 있습니다."라고 엑슬리 씨는 밝혔습니다. "저는 또한 음식과 관련된 **133** 다른 관심사도 추구하고 있습니다." **134** 실제로, 엑슬리 씨는 다음 달에 요리 워크숍에서 사람들을 가르칠 것이라고 설명했습니다. 로즈메드 지역 문화 센터에서 5월 20일로 예정된, 이 시간은 참가자들에게 건강에 좋은 음식을 준비하는 법을 가르쳐 드릴 것입니다.

어휘 editor 편집자 confirm that ~임을 확인해 주다 hire ~을 고용하다 full-time 전임의, 정규직의 contributor 기고자, 기고가 add ~을 추가하다 appear 보이다, 나타나다 regularly 정기적으로 include ~을 포함하다 local 지역의, 현지의 several 여럿의, 몇몇의 popular 인기 있는 be involved in ~에 관여하다 actively 적극적으로 community 업계, 분야, ~계 inform A about B A에게 B에 관해 알리다 lesser-known 덜 알려진 interest v. ~의 관심을 끌다 n. 관심(사), 흥미 pursue ~을 추구하다 A-related A와 관련된 scheduled for ~로 예정된 session (특정 활동을 위한) 시간 participant 참가자 how to do ~하는 법 prepare ~을 준비

하다

131 해설 〈명사 어휘(문맥)〉
보기가 모두 명사이므로 의미가 알맞은 것을 찾아야 한다. 주어 It이 가리키는 것은 기고 작가인 엑슬리 씨가 작업을 맡게 될 신문의 Fine Dining section인데 여기에 포함될 내용으로는 지역 레스토랑의 '평가, 후기, 의견'이 적합하므로 (C) reviews가 정답이다.

어휘 receipt 영수증, 수취, 받음 review 평가, 후기, 의견 renovation 개조, 보수

132 해설 〈전치사 어휘〉
빈칸 뒤에 기간을 나타내는 명사구 the years가 쓰여 있으므로 '~ 동안에 걸쳐'라는 의미로 기간 명사(구)를 목적어로 취하는 전치사 (B) over가 정답이다. (C) between도 기간을 나타낼 수는 있지만, 'A and B'의 구조로 두 가지 기준 시점이 제시되어야 한다.

어휘 over ~ 동안에 걸쳐 between (A and B) (A와 B) 사이에 toward (방향 등) ~ 쪽으로, ~을 향해, (목적) ~을 위해

133 해설 〈수량 형용사〉
빈칸이 동사 am pursuing과 명사구 목적어 food-related interests 사이에 위치해 있으므로 빈칸은 명사구를 수식하는 형용사 자리이다. 또한, food-related interests가 복수이므로 복수 명사구를 수식할 수 있는 (D) other가 정답이다. (A) another와 (C) one은 단수 명사를 수식하며, (B) each other는 목적어 자리에만 쓰인다.

어휘 another 또 다른 하나의 each other 서로

134 (A) 그 결과, 엑슬리 씨는 본인이 지니고 있는 몇몇 음식 알레르기에 관해 알렸습니다.
(B) 실제로, 엑슬리 씨는 다음 달에 요리 워크숍에서 사람들을 가르칠 것이라고 설명했습니다.
(C) 그렇지 않으면, 엑슬리 씨는 일주일 내로 여러 식당 시설을 방문할 것입니다.
(D) 더욱이, 엑슬리 씨는 개인 레스토랑을 여는 것에 대해 생각하고 있습니다.

해설 〈빈칸에 알맞은 문장 넣기〉
빈칸 앞 문장에 엑슬리 씨가 '음식과 관련된 다른 관심사도 추구하고 있다'고 말한 내용이 쓰여 있다. 따라서, Indeed(실제로)와 함께 다른 관심사 추구의 예로 워크숍 강의를 언급하고 있는 (B)가 정답이다. 또한 다음 문장의 명사 the session(강좌나 세미나와 같은 교육 시간)은 요리 워크숍(a cooking workshop)을 바꾸어 표현한 것이므로 (B)는 앞뒤 문장과의 연결이 모두 자연스럽다.

어휘 consequently 그 결과, 그래서 report on ~에 관해 알리다 indeed 실제로, 정말로 explain (that) ~라고 설명하다 otherwise 그렇지 않으면, 그 외에는 establishment (식당, 병원, 학교 등의) 시설 within ~ 이내로 furthermore 더욱이, 게다가 one's own 자신만의

[135-138] 공지

랭커스터 주민들께 알리는 공지

랭커스터의 로우 밸리 지역에 있는 여러 거리가 6월 2일부터 시작되어 약 2개월 동안 지속되는 일정으로 도로 공사 과정을 거칠 예정입니다. 이 프로젝트 기간 중에, 교통부 직원들이 도로를 **135** 업그레이드할 것입니다. **136** 구체적으로, 해당 작업 팀이 갈라진 틈들을 메우고, 배수 시스템을 정비하며, 몇몇 구역을 재포장할 계획입니다.

로우 밸리 지역 내에서 이동하시기 **137** 전에, 시 웹 사이트를 확인해 어느 거리가 현재 폐쇄되어 있는지 알아보시기 바랍니다. 운전자들께서는 또한 주차가 일시적으로 중단된 상태를 나타내는 표지판이 있는지 잘 살펴보셔야 한다는 점도 명심하시기 바랍니다. **138** 주차 금지 구역 내에 세워진 차량은 견인될 것입니다. 추가 정보를 원하시는 분은 www.lancaster.gov/rowevalleyroadwork 를 방문하시기 바랍니다.

어휘 notice 공지, 공고 resident 주민 neighborhood 지역, 인근 be scheduled to do ~할 예정이다 undergo ~을 거치다, 겪다 roadwork 도로 공사 last v. 지속되다 approximately 약, 대략 roadway 도로 crew (함께 작업하는) 팀, 조 plan to do ~할 계획이다 seal (특정 물질을 발라) ~을 메우다, 밀봉하다 crack 갈라진 틈, 금 fix ~을 수리하다, 바로잡다 drainage 배수 resurface (도로, 바닥 등) ~을 재포장하다 currently 현재 be reminded to do ~하는 것을 명심하다, 염두에 두다 watch for ~가 있는지 잘 살펴보다 sign 표지(판) indicate that ~임을 나타내다, 가리키다 parking 주차 temporarily 일시적으로, 임시로 suspend ~을 중단하다, 보류하다

135 해설 〈시제(문맥)〉
동사 upgrade의 여러 형태가 보기에 제시되어 있으므로 능/수동, 주어와의 수 일치, 시제 등을 확인해 알맞은 것을 골라야 한다. 앞 문장에 are scheduled to undergo라는 말을 통해 앞으로 예정된 작업이 있음을 알리고 있으므로 빈칸이 속한 문장에서 말하는 도로 업그레이드 작업은 미래에 발생될 일임을 알 수 있다. 따라서 미래시제 동사인 (D) will upgrade가 정답이다.

136 해설 〈접속부사〉
빈칸 앞에는 도로 공사가 예정되어 있다는 사실을 알리는 내용이, 빈칸 뒤에는 해당 공사와 관련해 진행될 특정 작업들을 구체적으로 언급하는 내용이 쓰여 있다. 따라서 '특히, 구체적으로'라는 의미로 세부적인 정보를 제공할 때 사용하는 접속부사 (C) Specifically가 정답이다.

어휘 even so 그렇다 하더라도 nonetheless 그럼에도 불구하고 specifically 특히, 구체적으로 otherwise 그렇지 않으면, 그 외에는, 달리

137 해설 〈분사구문〉
빈칸이 속한 문장의 주절에서 어느 거리가 폐쇄되어 있는지 웹 사이트를 확인해 알아 보는 일은 해당 지역 내에서 이동하기 전에 먼저 해야 하는 일이어야 한다. 따라서 '~하기 전에'라는 의미로 쓰이는 (C) Before가 정답이다. (B) During은 동명사 혹은 -ing 분사구문과 함께 쓰이지 않으므로 오답이다.

어휘 since ~ 이래로 during ~ 중에, ~ 동안 around ~ 주위에, ~ 곳곳에, ~ 전역에

138 (A) 주행로는 황색 선으로 분리되어 있습니다.
(B) 제한 속도가 내년에 낮아질 수도 있습니다.
(C) 주차 금지 구역 내에 세워진 차량은 견인될 것입니다.
(D) 시민들께서는 가장 좋아하시는 것에 투표하실 수 있습니다.

해설 〈빈칸에 알맞은 문장 넣기〉
빈칸 앞 문장에 주차가 일시적으로 중단된 상태를 알리는 표지판이 있는지 잘 살펴보도록 알리는 말이 쓰여 있다. 따라서 이 주차 문제와 관련해 주차 금지 구역에 세워진 차량에 대한 조치를 알리는 (C)가 정답이다. 나머지 문장들은 앞 문장에 언급된 주차 문제 또는 다음 문장에 제시된 정보 확인 방법 중 어느 것과도 어울리지 않는 내용을 담고 있으므로 오답이다.

어휘 separate ~을 분리하다 reduce ~을 낮추다, 줄이다 tow ~을 견인하다 vote for ~에 투표하다 favorite 가장 좋아하는

[139-142] 공지

고객 여러분께 알리는 공지

4월 2일부터, 저희 베니스 레스토랑이 계획된 건물 **139** 확장 공사 작업을 시작합니다. 이 프로젝트는 식사 공간에 부가적으로 1,200평방피트를 추가하는 것이 목적입니다. 이는 좌석 규모를 135석으로 변경해, **140** 현재의 70석을 거의 두 배로 늘리게 될 것입니다. 이 새로운 구역은 레스토랑 나머지 부분과 동일한 스타일 및 자재로 공사할 것입니다. 이번 프로젝트를 책임지고 있는 계약업체는 9월 초에 프로젝트가 **141** 마무리될 것으로 예상하고 있습니다. **142** 그동안, 저희 업소는 거의 매일 식당 손님들을 대상으로 계속 문을 열 것입니다. 휴무일 계획 일정을 알아보시려면, 저희 레스토랑 소셜 미디어를 확인해 보시거나 웹 사이트 www.venicerestaurant.net를 방문하시기 바랍니다.

어휘 notice 공지, 공고 planned 계획된 aim to do ~하는 것이 목적이다 add ~을 추가하다 additional 부가적인, 추가적인 dining area 식사 공간 seating capacity 좌석 규모 nearly 거의 double v. ~을 두 배로 늘리다 material 자재, 재료, 물품 rest 나머지 contractor 계약업체 in charge of ~을 책임지고 있는, 맡고 있는 expect A to do A가 ~할 것으로 예상하다, 기대하다 closure 휴무, 폐장, 닫음 follow (상황, 진행 등) ~을 계속 지켜보다, 주시하다

139 해설 〈명사 자리(관사와 형용사 뒤)〉
빈칸 앞뒤로 정관사 the와 과거분사 planned, 그리고 전치사 of가 각각 위치해 있으므로 빈칸은 분사 planned의 수식을 받을 명사 자리임을 알 수 있다. 따라서 명사인 (B) expansion이 정답이다.

어휘 expand ~을 확장하다, 확대하다 expansion 확장, 확대 expansive 포괄적인, 광범위한

140 해설 〈형용사 어휘 (문맥)〉
정관사 the와 명사구 70 seats 사이에 위치한 빈칸은 이 명사구를 수식할 형용사 자리이다. 또한 빈칸 앞에 좌석 규모가 135석으로 변경될 것이라고 알리는 내용으로 볼 때, 70 seats는 현재의 좌석 규모인 것

으로 판단할 수 있다. 따라서 '현재의'를 뜻하는 형용사 (C) current가 정답이다. (D) now는 부사로 사용되므로 오답이다.

어휘 following 다음의 current 현재의

141 해설 〈동사 어휘(문맥)〉
보기가 모두 동사이므로 의미가 알맞은 것을 찾아야 한다. 빈칸 뒤에 시점 표현이 제시되어 있는데, 이는 문맥상 앞서 언급된 프로젝트가 끝나는 것으로 예상하는 시점으로 볼 수 있으므로 '마무리되다, 끝나다'를 뜻하는 (D) conclude가 정답이다.

어휘 release ~을 출시하다, 발간하다 perform ~을 수행하다, 실시하다, 공연하다, 연주하다 maintain ~을 유지하다, 유지 관리하다 conclude 마무리되다, 끝나다

142 (A) 여름 기간 중에는, 저희 메뉴가 매주 생선 특선 요리를 특징으로 합니다.
(B) 한편, 종업원들에게는 새 유니폼을 받을 수 있는 선택권이 있습니다.
(C) 더 많은 사람들이 외식을 하는 대신 집에서 요리하고 있습니다.
(D) 그동안 저희 업소는 거의 매일 식당 손님들을 대상으로 계속 문을 열 것입니다.

해설 〈빈칸에 알맞은 문장 넣기〉
첫 문장에서 공사의 시작일이 4월 2일로 나와 있고, 빈칸 바로 앞 문장에는 공사가 마무리되는 시점으로 9월초가 언급되어 있다. 따라서, 공사가 진행되는 4월 2일부터 9월초까지의 기간을 In the interim(그동안)으로 지칭하여, 해당 기간 동안의 업소의 계획을 밝힌 (D)가 흐름상 가장 적합한 정답이다.

어휘 feature ~을 특징으로 하다 meanwhile 한편, 그러는 동안 server 종업원 have the option of -ing ~할 수 있는 선택권이 있다 rather than ~하는 대신, ~가 아니라 in the interim 그동안, 그 사이에 remain + 형용사 계속 ~한 상태이다, ~한 상태로 유지되다 diner 식사 손님

[143-146] 이메일

수신: 윌리엄 팔리 〈w.farley@meadowinc.com〉
발신: 글렌다 오닐 〈g.oneal@meadowinc.com〉
날짜: 10월 25일
제목: 사무실 이전

팔리 씨께,

우리 사무실 이전 준비로, 에이스 이사 전문 업체에 연락했습니다. 그쪽 접수 담당자에게 우리가 11월 18일에 이전하기를 원한다고 얘기했는데, **143** 보아하니, 그쪽 팀이 이 날짜에 시간이 되지 않는 것 같습니다. 이곳이 우리 가격 범위 내에 해당되었던 유일한 업체였습니다.

하지만, 예산을 늘려 주시면, 이용 가능여부를 확인해 볼 수 있도록 다른 여러 업체에 **144** 연락할 수 있습니다. 제가 최선을 다해 그 업체들의 다양한 현장 포장 서비스에 관해서도 알아보겠습니다. **145** 그런 다음, 우리의 요구를 충족하는 회사를 선택하도록 설명해 드리겠습니다.

필요하다고 생각하시는 경우, 제가 그 업체들의 **146** 보장 서비스를 확인해 보도록 하겠습니다. 이렇게 하면, 뭔가 분실되거나 고장 나는 경우 어떻게 될지 우리가 알게 될 것입니다.

어떻게 하고 싶으신지 알려 주시기 바랍니다.

글렌다

어휘 relocation (위치) 이전, 이사 in preparation for ~에 대한 준비로 contact ~에 연락하다 receptionist 접수 담당자 would like to do ~하고 싶다, ~하고자 하다 available 이용할 수 있는 within ~ 이내에 range 범위 increase ~을 늘리다, 증가시키다 budget 예산 availability 이용 가능성, 시간이 나는지의 여부 do one's best 최선을 다하다 various 다양한 on-site 현장의 packing (물품의) 포장 as well ~도, 또한 necessary 필요한, 필수의 don't mind -ing ~해도 상관없다, 괜찮다 this way 이렇게 하면, 이런 방법으로 lost 분실된, 사라진 broken 고장 난, 망가진, 깨진 let A know B A에게 B를 알리다

143 해설 〈부사 어휘〉
빈칸 뒤에 이어지는 내용을 보면, 바로 앞에서 언급한 11월 18일이라는 날짜에 이사 전문 업체가 시간이 나지 않는다는 말이 쓰여 있다. 이는 빈칸 앞에 언급된 것과 같이 접수 담당자와 이야기를 나누면서 파악한 사실이므로 '보아 하니, 듣자 하니' 등의 의미로 들어가 알게 된 정보를 말할 때 사용하는 (B) apparently가 정답이다.

어휘 apparently 보아 하니, 듣자 하니, 분명히 solely 오로지, 단지 considerably 상당히, 많이

144 해설 〈시제(부사절과 시제)〉
보기에 동사 contact의 여러 형태가 쓰여 있는데, 모두 능동태이고 시제만 다르므로 시제 관련 단서를 파악해야 한다. if가 이끄는 조건절에 미래를 대신하여 현재 시제 동사(increase)가 쓰이는 경우, 주절의 동사는 미래 시제 혹은 미래 시제를 대체할 수 있는 조동사인 may, can, should 등이 쓰일 수 있으므로 (D) can contact가 정답이다.

145 (A) 이 물품이 제가 혼자 옮기기엔 너무 무겁다는 점이 우려됩니다.
(B) **그런 다음, 우리의 요구를 충족하는 회사를 선택하도록 설명해 드리겠습니다.**
(C) 라벨들이 쉽게 읽을 수 있도록 큰 사이즈로 인쇄되어야 합니다.
(D) 예를 들어, 직원들이 새로운 곳에 더 넓은 공간이 생기는 것을 즐거워할 것입니다.

해설 〈빈칸에 알맞은 문장 넣기〉
빈칸 앞 문장에 다른 업체에 연락해 확인해 보겠다는 말과 포장 서비스에 관해서도 알아보겠다는 말이 쓰여 있다. 따라서 사무실 이전 준비 과정에서 업체에 연락하고 서비스에 관해 알아본 후 해야 하는 일로 업체를 선정하는 단계에 해당되는 내용을 담은 (B)가 정답이다. 나머지 문장들은 이러한 준비 과정상의 단계로 볼 수 없으므로 흐름상 맞지 않는 오답이다.

어휘 be concerned that ~라는 점을 우려하다 too A to do ~하기엔 너무 A한 on one's own 혼자 then 그런 다음, 그 후에, 그때, 그렇다면 guide A in -ing ~할 때[하는 데 있어] A에게 설명하다, 안내하다 choose ~을 선택하다 meet (조건 등) ~을 충족하다 in a large size 큰 사이즈로 for instance 예를 들어 site 곳, 장소, 부지

146 해설 〈명사 어휘(문맥)〉
빈칸은 동명사 checking의 목적어로서 확인 대상에 해당되는 것인데, 빈칸 뒤에 이것을 확인하는 일을 This way로 지칭하며 물품이 분실되거나 망가질 경우의 상황을 적고 있다. 이를 통해, 피해 보상 서비스를 확인해 본다는 것임을 알 수 있으므로 '(손해, 위험 등과 관련된) 보장, 보증(서)' 등을 뜻하는 (C) guarantees가 정답이다.

어휘 nomination 후보 지명 guarantee n. (손해, 위험 등과 관련된) 보장, 보증(서) estimate 견적(서)

PART 7

P203

[147-148] 공지

파라다이스 원예용품점
원예 작업 필요 사항에 대한 최고의 용품!

아래의 팁은 정원에 새로운 장미를 심으신 후 잘 자라도록 하는 데 도움을 줄 것입니다.

1 **148** 매일 6~8시간 동안 햇빛이 드는 장소를 선택하십시오.

2 뿌리가 흙에 의해 최소 2~3인치 두께로 덮일 수 있도록 충분히 깊게 구멍을 파십시오. **147** 식물이 담겨 있는 화분은 비료처럼 사용될 수 있는 것이므로, 식물을 꺼내지 않고 파 놓은 구멍 안에 곧바로 넣으실 수 있습니다.

3 **148** 흙이 마르지 않도록 꼼꼼히 그리고 주기적으로 물을 주십시오.

4 **148** 가위 또는 원예용 전지 가위를 이용해, 죽거나 부러진 줄기와 가지들을 다듬어 주십시오. 이는 성장을 촉진하는 데 도움이 됩니다.

어휘 supplies 용품, 물품 gardening 원예 below 아래에, 밑에 make sure (that) 반드시 ~하도록 하다, ~하는 것을 확실히 하다 thrive 잘 자라다, 번성하다 plant ~을 심다 choose ~을 선택하다 spot 장소, 지점, 위치 dig ~을 파다 so that ~할 수 있도록 cover ~을 덮다 by (차이 등) ~ 정도, ~만큼 at least 최소한, 적어도 soil 흙, 토양 pot 화분, 통, 단지 compostable 비료로 사용할 수 있는 set ~을 놓다, 두다 directly 곧바로, 직접 without ~하지 않고 water v. ~에 물을 주다 thoroughly 꼼꼼히, 철저히 regularly 주기적으로 dry out 마르다 shears 전지 가위 trim off ~을 다듬다 stem 줄기 branch 가지 promote ~을 촉진하다 growth 성장

147 식물을 담는 통에 관해 언급된 것은 무엇인가?
(A) 재활용 쓰레기통에 버릴 수 있다.
(B) **제거할 필요가 없다.**
(C) 업체로 반납되어야 한다.
(D) 보통 폭이 2~3인치로 되어 있다.

해설 〈진위 확인 (세부 진위 유형)〉
화분, 즉 식물이 담겨 있는 용기가 언급되는 2번 항목을 보면, 비료처럼 사용될 수 있어서 식물을 꺼내지 않고 그대로 땅에 심을 수 있다고(~ they can be set directly into the hole without taking the plant out first) 쓰여 있다. 이는 제거할 필요가 없다는 말과 같으므로 (B)가 정답이다.

어휘 container 용기, 그릇 put A into B A를 B에 넣다 recycling bin 재활용 쓰레기통 remove ~을 제거하다, 없애다 return ~을 반납하다, 반품하다 usually 보통, 일반적으로

148 장미를 심는 일에 대한 조언으로 언급되지 않은 것은 무엇인가?
(A) 부러진 부분 잘라내기
(B) 햇빛이 잘 드는 장소 이용하기
(C) **주기적으로 흙 교체해 주기**
(D) 흙을 촉촉하게 유지하기

해설 〈진위 확인 (세부 진위 유형)〉
4번 항목의 부러진 줄기 등을 다듬으라고(~ trim off dead or broken stems ~) 적힌 부분에서 (A)를, 1번 항목에서 매일 6~8시간 동안 햇빛이 드는 곳을 선택하라고(Choose a spot that will get 6-8 hours of sunlight daily) 알리는 부분에서 (B)를 확인할 수 있다. 또한 3번 항목에서 흙이 마르지 않도록 주기적으로 물을 주라고(~ soil does not dry out) 언급하는 부분에서 (D)도 확인할 수 있다. 하지만 주기적으로 흙을 교체하도록 권하는 말은 없으므로 (C)가 정답이다.

어휘 cut off ~을 잘라내다 broken 부러진 location 장소, 위치, 지점 replace ~을 교체하다 regularly 주기적으로 keep A 형용사 A를 ~한 상태로 유지하다 moist 촉촉한

149 휘태커 배스 앤 타일

149 파인 밸리에서 30년 넘게 신뢰를 얻어 온 타일 전문 업체

여러분의 집은 주요 투자 대상이며, 업그레이드를 하기에 절대 늦지 않습니다. 욕실 개조는 당신의 집을 더욱 편안하고 세련되도록 만드는 것뿐만 아니라 가치를 더 하는 데 도움이 될 수 있습니다.

2월의 한 달 동안에 걸쳐, 저희는 욕실 개조 공사에 대해 모든 자재는 15퍼센트, 모든 인건비에 대해서는 10퍼센트의 할인을 제공해 드립니다. 555-8463번으로 전화하셔서 이 서비스를 예약하고 이 환상적인 할인을 이용해 보시기 바랍니다. **150 이 판촉 행사에 포함된 것으로는 여러분께 어울리는 타일 색상과 배치, 그리고 욕실 설비를 선택하도록 도움을 드릴 욕실 디자이너와의 무료 상담 서비스가 있습니다.**

저희에게 수백 가지 타일 소장 제품이 있으므로, 필요로 하시는 것을 분명히 찾으실 수 있을 것입니다. 저희 웹 사이트 www.whitakerbath.com을 방문하셔서 저희 과거 프로젝트의 사진 갤러리를 확인해 보시기 바랍니다. 여러분께 서비스를 제공해 드리기를 고대합니다!

어휘 reliable 신뢰할 수 있는 investment 투자 (대상) make an upgrade 업그레이드하다 renovation 개조, 보수 add ~을 더하다, 추가하다 value 가치, 값어치 as well as …뿐만 아니라 …도 make A 형용사 A를 ~하게 만들다 comfortable 편안한 throughout ~ 동안에 걸쳐 offer ~을 제공하다 material 자재, 재료, 물품 labor costs 인건비 book ~을 예약하다 take advantage of ~을 이용하다 deal 거래 (조건), 거래 제품 include ~을 포함하다 promotion 판촉 행사 free 무료의 consultation 상담 help A do A가 ~하도록 돕다 choose ~을 선택하다 layout 배치, 구획 fixture 기구 work 효과가 있다, 작용하다, 잘 되다 collection 소장(품), 수집(품) be sure to do 분명 ~하다, 꼭 ~하다 view ~을 보다 previous 이전의, 과거의 look forward to -ing ~하기를 고대하다 serve ~에게 서비스를 제공하다

149 휘태커 배스 앤 타일에 관해 암시된 것은 무엇인가?
(A) 인정받는 회사이다.
(B) 더 많은 서비스를 추가하고 있다.
(C) 새로운 경영진 하에 있다.
(D) 가격이 가장 저렴하다.

해설 〈진위 확인 (세부 진위 유형)〉
해당 업체 이름이 제시된 상단에 30년 넘게 신뢰할 수 있는 업체였다고(Pine Valley's reliable tile specialist for over 30 years) 알리는 말이 쓰여 있는데, 이는 사람들로부터 인정받는 업체임을 강조하는 것이므로 (A)가 정답이다.

어휘 established 인정받는, 자리 잡은 add ~을 추가하다 under (영향 등) ~ 하에 있는 management 경영(진)

150 고객들은 특별 할인과 함께 무엇을 받을 수 있는가?
(A) 일부 방수 처리 작업
(B) 무료 디자인 서비스
(C) 타일 세척제 한 통

(D) 연장된 품질 보증 기간

해설 〈세부 사항〉
특별 할인이 언급되는 두 번째 단락을 보면, 판촉 행사에 타일 색상과 배치 및 선택 등에 도움을 줄 디자이너와의 상담 서비스가 있다는(Included in the promotion is a free consultation from a bathroom designer, who will help you choose the tile colors, ~) 내용이 있다. 이는 무료 디자인 서비스를 제공한다는 뜻이므로 (B)가 정답이다.

어휘 receive ~을 받다 special offer 특별 할인 서비스 waterproofing 방수의 treatment (약품 등의) 처리 free 무료의 extended 연장된 warranty 품질 보증(서)

[151-152] 정보

알메이다 주식회사는 가정용 및 사무용의 유용한 소프트웨어를 만드는 것에 대해 자랑스럽게 생각하며, 모든 저희 고객께서 가능한 한 빠르게 이 소프트웨어의 사용을 시작할 수 있도록 해 드리고자 합니다.

151 각 프로그램에는 소프트웨어를 설치하도록 돕기 위한 상세 설명서가 딸려 있습니다. 하지만, 저희는 일부 고객께서 추가 도움이 필요하시다는 사실을 알고 있습니다. 이것이 여러분께 해당된다면, 저희 웹 사이트 www.almeidainc. com을 방문하신 다음, 구입하신 소프트웨어 및 여러분의 컴퓨터 기종과 부합하는 안내 동영상을 찾아보시도록 권해 드립니다. 또는, 저희 **152 고객 상담 서비스 전화번호 1-800-555-0688번을 통해 하루 24시간, 일주일 내내 기술자와 이야기해 보실 수도 있습니다.** 어떠한 의견이나 불만 사항이 있으실 경우, service@almeidainc.com으로 저희에게 이메일을 보내실 수 있으며, 영업일로 3일 내에 답변을 받으시게 될 것입니다.

어휘 be proud to do ~해서 자랑스럽다 create ~을 만들어 내다 useful 유용한 make sure (that) 반드시 ~하도록 하다, ~하는 것을 확실히 하다 get started with ~을 시작하다 as A as possible 가능한 한 A하게 come with ~가 딸려 있다, ~을 포함하다 detailed 상세한 instructions 설명, 안내, 지시 install ~을 설치하다 additional 추가적인 case 경우, 사례 recommend -ing ~하도록 권하다, 추천하다 look up ~을 찾아보다 instructional 안내의, 교육용의 correspond to ~에 부합하다 alternatively 또는, 그렇지 않으면 helpline 고객 상담 전화 comment 의견 complaint 불만 receive ~을 받다 response 답변, 응답 within ~ 이내에

151 정보가 쓰여진 주된 이유는 무엇인가?
(A) 프로그램들 사이의 차이점을 간략히 설명하기 위해
(B) 소프트웨어 업데이트를 다운로드하도록 권하기 위해
(C) 설치 작업에 대해 도움을 받는 방법을 설명하기 위해
(D) 과거의 구매 제품에 대한 의견을 요청하기 위해

해설 〈주제 및 목적〉
첫 단락은 간단한 배경 설명에 해당되며, 두 번째 단락 시작 부분에 소프트웨어 설치를 위한 설명서가 있다는 말과 함께, 도움을 필요로 하는 일부 고객들을(~ some customers may need additional help) 언급하면서 도움을 받을 수 있는 방법들을 설명하고 있다. 따라서 이를 언급한 (C)가 정답이다.

어휘 outline ~을 간략히 설명하다, 개괄적으로 말하다 explain ~을 설명하다 how to do ~하는 방법 help with ~에 대한 도움 installation 설치 request ~을 요청하다, 요구하다 feedback 의견 past 과거의 purchase 구매(품)

152 알메이다 주식회사에 관해 언급된 것은 무엇인가?
(A) 그곳의 제품이 특정 컴퓨터에 대해서는 추천되지 않는다.
(B) 고객 지원 서비스가 항상 이용 가능하다.
(C) 더 많은 소매 판매 지점을 개장할 계획이다.
(D) 동영상 채팅을 통해 고객들을 도울 수 있다.

해설 〈진위 확인 (전체 진위 유형)〉
두 번째 단락 중반부에, 고객 상담 서비스 전화번호 1-800-555-0688번을 통해 하루 24시간 일주일 내내 기술자와 이야기할 수 있다고(~ you can also speak to a technician twenty-four hours a day, seven days a week ~) 알리는 부분이 있다. 이는 고객 지원 서비스가 항상 이용 가능하다는 뜻이므로 (B)가 정답이다.

어휘 certain 특정한, 일정한 at all times 항상 plan to do ~할 계획이다 retail 소매 branch 지점, 지사 assist ~을 돕다, 지원하다 through ~을 통해

[153-155] 광고

미드베일 배관
공인 업체 · 숙련된 작업 · 종합적인 서비스

- **154 파이프 누수 및 균열 수리**
- **154 식기 세척기, 세탁기, 온수기 설치 작업**
- 막힌 배수구 처리
- 샤워기, 싱크대, 변기 설치 작업
- **154 안전 규정 준수 여부 확인을 위한 가스관 점검**

153 합리적인 비용에 우수한 작업을 찾고 계신다면, 저희 미드베일 배관이 올바른 선택입니다. 555-7113번으로 저희에게 전화 주셔서 견적을 받아 보시거나 예약하시기 바랍니다. **155 요청하시는 모든 고객들께 기꺼이 고객 추천 글들을 제공해 드립니다.**

어휘 certified 공인된, 인증된 experienced 숙련된, 경험 많은 comprehensive 종합적인, 포괄적인 repair ~을 수리하다 leak (물, 가스 등의) 누출, 누설 crack 균열, 깨짐 install ~을 설치하다 clear ~을 깨끗하게 하다, 치우다 clogged 막힌 drains 배수구 compliance (규정 등의) 준수 look for ~을 찾다 exceptional 우수한, 아주 뛰어난 reasonable 합리적인, 저렴한 quote 견적(서) book an appointment 예약하다 provide ~을 제공하다 testimonial 추천(서), 추천의 글 ask for ~을 요청하다

153 미드베일 배관에 관해 암시된 것은 무엇인가?
(A) 매일 서비스를 제공한다.
(B) 가격이 저렴하다.
(C) 공인된 배관공을 찾고 있다.
(D) 이메일로 견적서를 제공한다.

해설 〈진위 확인 (전체 진위 유형)〉

두 번째 단락 시작 부분에 합리적인 비용으로(~ at a reasonable cost ~) 작업한다는 말이 있으므로 이와 같은 가격상의 장점을 말한 (B)가 정답이다.

어휘 offer ~을 제공하다(= provide) affordable (가격이) 저렴한, 알맞은 seek ~을 찾다, 구하다 certified 공인된 plumber 배관공 quote 견적서

154 미드베일 배관에 의해 실시되는 작업으로 언급되지 않은 것은 무엇인가?
(A) 가전기기 설치
(B) 가스관 안전 상태 확인
(C) 균열된 싱크대 교체
(D) 손상된 파이프 수리

해설 〈진위 확인 (세부 진위 유형)〉
첫 단락의 두 번째 항목 'Installing dishwashers ~'에서 가전기기 설치를 뜻하는 (A)를, 마지막 항목 'Testing gas lines ~'에서 가스관 안전 상태 확인을 의미하는 (B)를 확인할 수 있다. 또한 같은 단락 첫 번째 항목 'Repairing leaks and cracks in pipes'에서 손상된 파이프 수리를 뜻하는 (D)도 확인 가능하다. 하지만 균열된 싱크대 교체 작업은 언급되어 있지 않으므로 (C)가 정답이다.

어휘 task 일, 업무 perform ~을 실시하다, 수행하다 set up ~을 설치하다, 준비하다 appliance 가전기기 replace ~을 교체하다 cracked 균열된, 금이 간 fix ~을 고치다 damaged 손상된, 피해를 입은

155 광고에 따르면, 요청 시에 무엇이 제공될 수 있는가?
(A) 제안된 작업에 대한 도면
(B) 자격 증명서 사본
(C) 필요한 필수 자재 목록
(D) 이전 고객들의 추천

해설 〈세부 사항〉
요청 시에 무언가를 제공한다는 내용이 있는 맨 마지막 문장에 We are happy to provide professional references ~라는 내용이 있는데, 여기서 testimonial은 '추천서, 추천의 글'이란 의미이므로 이와 같은 의미의 recommendation으로 같은 내용을 표현한 (D)가 정답이다.

어휘 upon request 요청 시에 drawing 도면, 그림 proposed 제안된 certification 자격증, 수료증 necessary 필수의, 필요한 material 자재, 재료 former 이전의, 전 ~의

[156-158] 웹 페이지

http://www.roxburytheater.com

록스버리 극장 투어
지역 내에서 운영되는 가장 규모가 큰 극장의 무대 뒤 모습!

1900년대 초반까지 그 역사가 거슬러 올라가는 록스버리 극장은 연중 투어를 제공합니다. 투어 참가 비용은 1인당 11.50달러이며, 약 90분 동안 진행됩니다. 여러분의 투어 가이드가 어떻게 이 극장이 시간이 지남에 따라 어떻게 변화되어 왔는지에 관해 알려 드릴 것이며, 의상실과 무대 뒤 구역, 그리고 개별 좌석 공간과 같이 극장에서 몇몇 가장 흥미로운 곳들을 보실 수 있게 됩니다. **156** 투어는 영어로 진행되지만, 스페인어와, 독일어, 그리고 중국어로 된 안내 자료도 이용하실 수 있습니다. 록스버리 극장에는 항상 흥미로운 것이 있으므로, 투어 시작 시간은 공연 일정표에 따라 다릅니다. 일부 투어 참가자들께서는 심지어 곧 있을 공연 리허설을 보시게 될 수도 있습니다.

저희는 지역 연극계에 대한 기여에 자부심을 느끼고 있습니다. **157** 에델 색스턴 씨께서 공연 예술을 부활시키기 위한 노력의 일환으로 이 극장을 매입하신 이후 지난 5년 동안 특히 그러했습니다. 투어가 끝날 때, 참가자들께서는 얼마든지 극장 내 기념품 매장을 방문하셔도 좋습니다. 또한 **158** 극장 전문가의 강연에 참석하실 수 있는 옵션도 있습니다. 이 활동은 투어 참가비에 더해 8달러의 비용이 듭니다.

어휘 behind-the-scenes 무대 뒤의, 막후의 working 운영 중인, 가동 중인 date back to (기원, 유래 등이) ~까지 거슬러 올라가다 offer ~을 제공하다 last v. 지속되다 approximately 약, 대략 over time 시간이 지남에 따라 private 개별적인, 사적인 conduct ~을 수행하다, 실시하다 fact sheet 안내 자료 available 이용 가능한 vary 다르다, 다양하다 depending on ~에 따라, ~에 달려 있는 participant 참가자 even 심지어 (~도) get to do ~하게 되다 rehearsal 리허설, 예행 연습 upcoming 곧 있을, 다가오는 be proud of ~에 자부심을 갖다, ~을 자랑스러워하다 contribution 기여, 공헌 local 지역의, 현지의 community ~계, ~ 사회 especially 특히 since ~ 이후로 in an effort to do ~하기 위한 노력의 일환으로 revive ~을 부활시키다, 되살리다 performing arts 공연 예술 be welcome to do 얼마든지 ~해도 좋다 attend ~에 참석하다 expert 전문가 on top of ~에 더해, ~ 외에도

156 록스버리 극장 투어에 관해 사실인 것은 무엇인가?
(A) 참가자들에게 공연자들을 직접 만나게 해 준다.
(B) 2시간 넘게 진행된다.
(C) 그룹 규모가 너무 작으면 취소된다.
(D) 다양한 언어로 정보를 제공한다.

해설 〈진위 확인 (전체 진위 유형)〉
첫 지문 중반부에, 투어가 영어로 진행되는 것 외에 스페인어와, 독일어, 그리고 중국어로 된 안내 자료를 이용할 수 있다는(Tours are conducted in English, but fact sheets are available in Spanish, German, and Chinese) 내용이 있으므로 (D)가 정답이다.

어휘 allow A to do A에게 ~하게 해 주다, ~하도록 허용하다 participant 참가자 in person 직접 last v. 지속되다 cancel ~을 취소하다 provide ~을 제공하다 a variety of 다양한

157 색스턴 씨는 누구일 것 같은가?
(A) 극장 소유주
(B) 투어 가이드
(C) 유명 여배우
(D) 연예 평론가

해설 〈세부 사항〉
색스턴 씨의 이름이 언급되는 두 번째 단락 초반부에, 에델 색스턴 씨가 극장을 매입한 사실이(~ Ethel Saxton bought the theater ~) 언급되어 있는데, 이는 색스턴 씨가 극장 소유주라는 의미이므로 (A)가 정답이다.

어휘 owner 소유주 critic 평론가, 비평가

158 웹 페이지에 따르면, 극장 방문객들은 추가 요금으로 무엇을 할 수 있는가?
(A) 회원 프로그램에 가입하기
(B) 공연자들이 연습하는 모습 보기
(C) 강연 보기
(D) 무대 뒤 공간 방문하기

해설 〈세부 사항〉
추가 비용과 관련된 정보는 지문 마지막 부분에, 극장 전문가의 강연에 참석하려면 투어 참가비 외에 8달러의 비용이 든다는(There is also an option to attend a lecture ~ This activity costs $8 on top of the tour fee) 내용이 있으므로 (C)가 정답이다.

어휘 extra 추가의, 별도의 charge 청구 요금 join ~에 가입하다, 합류하다 practice 연습하다

[오전 10:05] 아디티 카얄
혹시 오늘 연구실에 오시나요?

[오전 10:06] 핀 홉킨스
아니요. 이번 주말에 초과 근무를 해야 할 수도 있다고 생각했는데, 다행히도 제 일을 전부 완료했어요. 왜 그러시죠?

[오전 10:07] 아디티 카얄
지금 여기 와 있는데, 159 출입문 코드가 작동되지 않아서요. 변경되었나요?

[오전 10:08] 핀 홉킨스
네, 금요일에요.

[오전 10:08] 아디티 카얄
그게 뭔지 알고 계세요?

[오전 10:09] 핀 홉킨스
죄송해요. 159 기억할 거라고 생각했어요. 적어 놓았다면 좋았을 텐데요.

[오전 10:10] 아디티 카얄
160 이곳에 제 사원증을 근거로 저를 들여보내 주실 수 있는 경비 직원이 있으신지 확인해 봐야겠어요. 정말로 내일 다시 오고 싶지 않거든요.

[오전 10:11] 핀 홉킨스
행운을 빌어요!

어휘 lab 연구실, 실험실 at all (의문문에서) 혹시, 조금이라도 might have to do ~해야 할지도 모른다 work overtime 초과 근무하다 fortunately 다행히도 get A p.p. A가 ~되게 하다 task 일, 업무 work 작동하다, 효과가 있다 I wish 주어 had p.p. ~했다면 좋았을 걸 see if ~인지 확인하다 let A in A를 들여보내다 based on ~을 바탕으로, ~을 기반으로

159 오전 10시 09분에, 홉킨스 씨가 "I wish I had written it down"이라고 썼을 때 암시하는 것은 무엇이겠는가?
(A) 코드를 기억하지 못한다.
(B) 정책에 대해서 잊었다.
(C) 전화번호를 찾을 수 없다.
(D) 오류에 대한 증거가 필요하다.

해설 〈의도 파악〉
제시된 문장에서 'I wish 주어 had p.p.'는 '~했더라면 좋았을텐데'라는 과거에 대한 후회의 의미를 담은 표현으로 바로 앞 문장에서 기억할 것이라고 생각했고(I thought I'd remember it) 말한 것과 관련해 실제로는 기억하지 못하는 아쉬움을 나타내고 있다. 여기서 it은 앞서 카얄 씨가 말한 출입문 코드(the door code)를 지칭하므로 그 코드를 기억하지 못한다는 의미로 쓰인 (A)가 정답이다.

어휘 forget ~을 잊다 policy 정책, 방침 proof 증거(물)

160 카얄 씨는 무엇을 하기로 결정하는가?
(A) 자신의 사원증 업데이트하기
(B) 홉킨스 씨가 도착하기를 기다리기
(C) 다음 날 다시 오기
(D) 다른 사람에게 도움 요청하기

해설 〈세부 사항〉
카얄 씨가 10시 10분에 작성한 메시지를 보면, 자신을 들여보내 줄 수 있는 경비원을 찾아보겠다는 (I'll see if there's a security guard here who can let me in ~) 내용이 있다. 이는 다른 직원에게 도움을 요청하는 것을 뜻하므로 (D)가 정답이다.

어휘 decide to do ~하기로 결정하다 arrive 도착하다 following 다음의 ask A for B A에게 B를 요청하다

〈밀워키 트리뷴〉 비즈니스 코너

9월 8일 — 161 밀워키 시내에 위치한 탄력적인 업무 공간인 스플릿웍스는 설립자 사이먼 랜드리 씨에 의해 기업가 샤나 듀란트 씨에게 매각되었습니다. —[1]—. 과거 자영업자로 일하고 있던 랜드리 씨는 시끄러운 커피 매장에서 일하는 것이 지겨워 이 사업을 시작했습니다. 조용한 사무실 환경을 이용하는 것뿐만 아니라, 회원들은 복사기나 프린터 같은 사무 장비도 이용할 수 있으며, 비즈니스 관련 우편물을 스플릿웍스 주소로 발송되도록 할 수도 있습니다. 듀란트 씨는 이 업체를 넘겨받는 것에 대해 기뻐하고 있습니다. —[2]—. "우리 지역 경제의 역학 관계가 변화됨에 따라, 점점 더 많은 사람들이 전업 혹은 파트 타임으로 자영업자가 되고 있습니다. 저는 이 뛰어난 사업 아이디어를 한 단계 더 끌어올릴 준비가 되어 있습니다." —[3]—." 162 스플릿웍스는 로건 빌딩 3층과 4층에 자리 잡고 있지만, 듀란트 씨는 2층도 추가하기 위해 건물주와 협의하고 있는데, 현재 세입자가 곧 나갈 예정이기 때문입니다. 스플릿웍스 회비는 합리적인 수준입니다. —[4]—. 163 그 후, 회원들은 해당 장소를 이용할 때마다 시간당 4달러 또는 하루에 15달러를 지불하기만 하면 됩니다.

어휘 flexible 탄력적인, 유동적인 founder 설립자, 창립자 entrepreneur 기업가 self-employed 자영업을 하는, 독자적으로 일하는 be tired of ~을 지겨워하다 in addition to ~뿐만 아니라, ~ 외에도 have access to ~을 이용할 수 있다 equipment 장비 have A p.p. A가 ~되게 하다 dynamics 역학 관계 local 지역의, 현지의 economy 경제 shift v. 변화되다 either A or B A 또는 B 둘 중의 하나 take A to the next level A를 한 단계 더 끌어올리다 occupy ~에 자리 잡고 있다, ~을 차지하다 negotiate 협의하다, 협상하다 add ~을 추가하다 as well ~도, 또한 current 현재의 tenant 세입자 be reasonably priced 합리적으로 가격이 책정되다

161 기사는 왜 쓰여졌는가?
(A) 시내에 있는 업체들의 동향을 설명하기 위해
(B) 한 회사의 경영권 변화를 알리기 위해
(C) 새로운 커피 매장의 개장을 알리기 위해
(D) 자영업의 이점을 설명하기 위해

해설 〈주제 및 목적〉
첫 문장에 스플릿웍스라는 업체가 설립자에 의해 기업가 샤나 듀란트 씨에게 매각되었다고(~ has been sold by founder Simon Landry to entrepreneur Shana Durant) 알리고 있는데, 이는 업체 경영권의 변화를 나타내는 것이므로 (B)가 정답이다.

어휘 explain ~을 설명하다 trend 동향, 추세 ownership 경영권 describe ~을 설명하다 benefit 이점, 혜택

162 기사 내용에 따르면, 듀란트 씨는 무엇을 하기를 희망하는가?
(A) 사무실 공간을 확장하는 일
(B) 일부 장비를 업그레이드하는 일
(C) 새로운 장소로 이전하는 일
(D) 더 많은 투자자를 끌어 들이는 일

해설 〈세부 사항〉
지문 후반부에 회사가 현재 로건 빌딩 3층과 4층에 자리 잡고 있지만 듀란트 씨가 2층도 추가하기 위해 협의 중에 있다는(Splitworks occupies the third and fourth floor of the Logan Building, but Ms. Durant is negotiating with the building owner to add the second floor as well ~) 내용이 있다. 이는 업체의 공간을 확장하는 일에 해당되므로 (A)가 정답이다.

어휘 expand ~을 확장하다, 확대하다 equipment 장비 location 장소, 위치, 지점 attract ~을 끌어 들이다 investor 투자자

163 [1], [2], [3], [4]로 표기된 위치들 중에서 다음 문장이 들어가기에 가장 적절한 곳은 어디인가?
"이 회사는 100달러의 초기 가입비를 부과합니다."
(A) [1]
(B) [2]
(C) [3]
(D) [4]

해설 〈문장 넣기〉
제시된 문장은 100달러의 초기 가입비를 부과한다는 의미를 나타내고, [4]번의 뒤 문장은 Then(그 후)이라는 시점 부사와 함께 초기 가입비를 낸 후의 이용 방법 및 요금에 관해 설명하고 있으므로 [4]번의 위치가 흐름상 가장 자연스럽다. 따라서, (D)가 정답이다.

어휘 charge ~을 부과하다, 청구하다 initial 초기의, 처음의 sign-up fee 가입비

[164-167] 회람

수산: 모든 Q-밸리 푸드 직원들
발산: 조슈아 디아즈
제목: 새 시리얼에 대한 계획

Q-밸리 푸드 직원 여러분,

아시다시피, 우리 회사는 아이들을 위한 새로운 초콜릿 튀밥 시리얼을 출시할 계획이며, **164** 해당 제품에 대한 마스코트가 필요합니다. 저희 부서에서는 직원들에게 다가가 많은 환상적인 아이디어를 받았습니다. 마케팅팀에서는 창의적인 아이디어를 공유해 주신 여러분께 감사하게 생각하고 있습니다. 저희는 총 50가지가 넘는 **165** 참가작을 받았습니다. 이 중에서, 아래에 있는 세 가지 옵션으로 그 범위를 좁혔습니다.

제안된 이름	설명	제출자
초코	재미있는 원숭이	캐서린 로제티
찰스 초콜릿	귀여운 테디 베어	재닛 도셋
맥스 브렉퍼스트	멋진 강아지	레이먼드 프래지어

이 세 가지 중에서, **164** 최종적으로 하나를 선택하는 데 있어 여러분의 도움이 필요합니다. Q-밸리 직원 웹 사이트를 방문하셔서 '콘테스트' 탭을 클릭하시기 바랍니다. 그곳에서 각 마스코트가 어떤 모습일지 보여주는 일부 샘플 그림들을 확인해 보실 수 있으며, 가장 마음에 드는 것에 대해 투표하실 수 있습니다. 투표는 이번 주 금요일인 9월 9일까지 가능합니다.

166 9월 15일 다음 월간 직원 회의에서, 당첨자를 발표할 것이며, 당첨된 아이디어를 제출한 직원에게 현금으로 상금이 제공됩니다. 이 시리얼이 10월 20일에 시중에 출시될 것이기 때문에, **167** 우리는 10월 13일부터 새 마스코트가 나오는 광고를 방송하기 시작할 것입니다. 10월 회의 시간에 직원 여러분께 보여드리겠습니다.

웹 사이트에서 해당 탭을 이용하시는 데 문제가 있으실 경우, IT 부서로 곧장 연락하시기 바랍니다.

감사합니다!

조슈아 디아즈

어휘 plan to do ~할 계획이다 launch ~을 출시하다 department 부서 reach out to ~에게 다가가다, 연락을 취하다 receive ~을 받다 thankful to ~에게 감사하는 those of you who 여러분 중 ~하는 사람들 creative 창의적인 over ~가 넘는 entry 참가작, 출품작 in total 총, 모두 합쳐 among ~ 중에서 narrow down to ~ 범위를 ~로 좁히다 suggest ~을 제안하다 description 설명 submit ~을 제출하다 choose ~을 선택하다 drawing 그림 what A look like A가 어떤 모습인지, A가 어떻게 생겼는지 vote for ~에 투표하다 announce ~을 발표하다 prize 상, 상금 since ~하기 때문에 hit the market 시중에 출시되다 air ~을 방송하다 commercial n. 광고 방송 contact ~에게 연락하다 directly 곧장, 직접

---

164 직원들은 디아즈 씨의 부서가 무엇을 하는 데 도움을 줄 것인가?
(A) 설문 조사 완료하기
(B) 광고 촬영하기
(C) 캐릭터 그리기
(D) 당첨자 선정하기

해설 〈세부 사항〉
첫 단락에서 언급한 제품 마스코트와(~ we need a mascot ~) 관련해, 도표를 통해 최종 후보작을 제시하면서 다음 단락에 최종적으로 하나를 선택하는 데 있어 도움이 필요하다고(~ we'd like your help in choosing the final one ~) 알리고 있다. 이는 당첨자 선정에 있어 도움을 청하는 것이므로 (D)가 정답이다.

어휘 assist A in -ing ~하는 데 있어 A를 돕다 department 부서 complete ~을 완료하다 survey 설문 조사 commercial 광고 방송 draw ~을 그리다 select ~을 선정하다, 선택하다

165 첫 번째 단락 네 번째 줄의 단어 "entries"와 의미가 가장 가까운 것은 무엇인가?
(A) 힘든 노력
(B) 경향
(C) 제출물
(D) 입구

해설 〈동의어〉
앞선 문장들을 보면, 제품 마스코트와 관련해 직원들에게 많은 아이디어를 받았다는 말이 쓰여 있으므로 entries가 아이디어의 '응모'를 가리키는 것으로 판단할 수 있다. 아이디어의 '응모'는 아이디어를 제출했다는 말과 같으므로 '제출(물)'을 의미하는 (C) submissions가 정답이다.

166 다음 월간 직원 회의 시간에 무슨 일이 있을 것인가?
(A) 투표가 실시될 것이다.
(B) 상이 주어질 것이다.
(C) 신입 직원이 소개될 것이다.
(D) 일부 샘플을 나눠줄 것이다.

해설 〈세부 사항〉
네 번째 단락에, 다음 번 월간 직원 회의가 열리는 9월 15일에 당첨자를 발표한다는 사실과 함께 그 사람에게 현금으로 상금이 제공된다고(At our next monthly staff meeting, ~ the person who submitted the winning idea will be given a cash prize) 쓰여 있다. 따라서 (B)가 정답이다.

어휘 take a vote 투표를 실시하다 prize 상, 상품 award ~을 주다, 수여하다 introduce ~을 소개하다 distribute ~을 나눠주다, 배포하다

167 Q-밸리는 언제 새 광고를 운영하기 시작할 계획인가?
(A) 9월 9일에
(B) 9월 15일에
(C) 10월 13일에
(D) 10월 20일에

해설 〈세부 사항〉
네 번째 단락을 보면, 10월 13일부터 새 마스코트가 나오는 광고를 방송하기 시작할 것이라는(~ we'll begin airing commercials with the new mascot from October 13) 내용이 있으므로 (C)가 정답이다.

어휘 plan to do ~할 계획이다 run ~을 운영하다, 진행하다

[168-171] 기사

사업을 시작하는 데는 많은 용기가 필요합니다. 아마 성공적인 사업의 방향을 바꾸는 일은 심지어 더 큰 도전일 수도 있습니다. **168** 그것이 바로 요리사 수 로딩 씨가 자신의 성공적인 고급 식당 '골든 오이스터'를 아시아의 거리 음식을 제공하는 '스트리트 잇츠'라는 이름의 편안한 작은 식당으로 탈바꿈시켰을 때 한 일입니다. "그 지역으로 갔던 여행 경험과 애정에 의해 크게 영감을 얻었어요. 제가 했어야 했던 일이었다는 걸 바로 알았죠."라고 수 씨는 말합니다. —[1]—.

업계 전문가 피터 랜돈 씨는 그와 같은 급격한 변화를 만들어내는 것이 본질적으로 위험하다고 생각합니다. "기본적으로 처음부터 다시 시작하는 일이죠. 과거의 명성은 별로 중요하지 않고, 밑바닥부터 다시 새로운 브랜드를 구축해야 합니다."라고 랜돈 씨는 말합니다. **169** "단골 고객들이 그런 변화를 마음에 들어 하지 않아서 식당에 발길을 끊을 수도 있어요." 그럼에도 불구하고, 로딩 씨는 보조 요리사 트레이 바넷 씨와 함께 과감하고 새로운 풍미가 조화를 이뤄 맛이 뛰어난 메뉴 제품을 고안하겠다는 자신의 비전에 완전히 전념하고 있습니다. —[2]—. 수 씨는 심지어 업계에서 **170** 뛰어난 작업물로 인해 최근에 알브라이튼 상을 받은 인테리어 디자이너 피터 베어스토우 씨를 고용하기까지 했습니다. **171** 레스토랑 손님들은 피터 씨의 생동감 있는 디자인적 특징들이 어떻게 북적대는 아시아의 도시에 와 있는 듯한 느낌을 만들어냈는지에 관해 의견을 말해 왔습니다. —[3]—.

이렇게 개장 후 2개월이 지나, 로딩 씨는 그와 같은 변화에 만족하고 있을까요? 로딩 씨는 "당연하죠"라고 말합니다. "사업이 번창하고 있고, '골든 오이스터'의 격식 있는 환경에서 밀려났던 훨씬 더 젊은 손님들을 끌어들이는 일도 해냈습니다." 미래에 대해, 수 씨는 현재로서는 멈출 계획을 갖고 있지 않으며, 시카고와 뉴욕 지역에 새로운 '스트리트 잇츠' 지점을 개장하기를 바라고 있습니다. —[4]—. 수 씨가 분명히 지니고 있는 열정 및 추진력으로, 그녀의 비전이 전국적인 성공이 되지 못할 이유가 없습니다.

어휘 It takes A to do ~하는 데 A가 필요하다 courage 용기 even 심지어 (~도) challenge 도전, 어려운 일 direction 방향 exactly 바로, 정확히 convert A into B A를 B로 탈바꿈시키다, 변모시키다 fining establishment 식당 diner 작은 식당 be inspired by ~로부터 영감을 받다 industry 업계 expert 전문가 make a change 변경하다 drastic 급격한 basically 기본적으로 start over 처음부터 다시 시작하다

Actual Test 05 **174 • 175**

previous 이전의, 과거의 reputation 명성, 평판 count for much 크게 중요하다 build up ~을 구축하다 premises 건물, 부지, 구내 nevertheless 그럼에도 불구하고 fully 완전히, 전적으로 be committed to ~에 전념하다, 헌신하다 devise ~을 고안하다 succulent 맛이 좋은, 육즙이 많은 bold 과감한, 대담한 flavor 풍미, 맛 combination 조화, 조합 alongside ~와 함께 go as far as to do ~하기까지 하다 hire ~을 고용하다 recently 최근에 receive ~을 받다 prize 상 outstanding 뛰어난, 우수한 field 분야 comment on ~에 관해 말하다, 의견을 내다 vibrant 생동감 있는 feature 특징 create ~을 만들어내다 bustling 북적대는 thrive 번창하다 manage to do ~해내다 attract ~을 끌어들이다 much (비교급 수식) 훨씬 crowd 사람들, 군중 be put off by ~에 의해 밀려나다 formal 격식 있는 setting (주변) 환경, 분위기 branch 지점, 분점 passion 열정 drive 추진력 possess ~을 소유하다 nationwide 전국적인 success 성공

168 이 기사의 목적은 무엇인가?
(A) 공석인 일자리를 광고하는 것
(B) 특별 개장 행사를 홍보하는 것
(C) 할인된 투어 패키지를 제공하는 것
(D) 한 사업체의 재창조에 관해 조명하는 것

해설 〈주제 및 목적〉
첫 단락에 요리사 수 로딩 씨가 자신의 고급 식당 골든 오이스터를 아시아의 거리 음식을 제공하는 스트리트 잇츠라는 이름의 작은 식당으로 탈바꿈시킨 일을(That's exactly what chef Sue Rodding did when she converted her successful fine dining establishment *The Golden Oyster* into a casual diner ~) 언급한 뒤로, 그 배경 및 사업 운영과 관련된 내용을 전달하고 있다. 따라서 이와 같은 사업체 변화에 해당되는 의미로 쓰인 (D)가 정답이다.

어휘 publicize 홍보하다, 알리다 highlight 강조하다, 집중 조명하다

169 피터 랜돈 씨는 무슨 경고를 하는가?
(A) 건물 임대 비용이 급격히 인상될 수 있다.
(B) 기존의 고객들이 만족하지 못할 수 있다.
(C) 다수의 지점에 사업체를 여는 것은 어렵다.
(D) 음식 재료를 공수하기 어려울 수 있다.

해설 〈세부 사항〉
랜돈 씨의 이름이 언급된 두 번째 단락 중반부에 단골 고객들이 변화를 마음에 들어 하지 않아서 식당에 발길을 끊을 수도 있다고(Loyal customers may dislike the changes and stop visiting your premises) 말한 것이 쓰여 있다. 이는 기존 고객들이 만족하지 못하는 상황에 해당되므로 (B)가 정답이다.

어휘 rental cost 임대료 existing 기존의, 존재하는 multiple 여러 개의, 다수의 location 지점 ingredient (음식의) 재료

170 베어스토우 씨에 관해 언급된 것은 무엇인가?
(A) 자신의 일에 대해 상을 받았다.
(B) 해당 레스토랑을 오래 이용해 온 고객이다.
(C) 뉴욕에 부동산을 소유하고 있다.
(D) 새로운 메뉴 제품을 만드는 데 도움을 주었다.

해설 〈진위 확인 (세부 진위 유형)〉
베어스토우 씨의 이름이 언급된 두 번째 단락 중반부에 뛰어난 작업물로 인해 최근에 알브라이튼 상을 받은 인테리어 디자이너라고(~ interior designer Peter Bairstow, who recently received the Albrighton prize for outstanding work in his field) 소개하고 있으므로 (A)가 정답이다.

어휘 long-term 장기적인 property 부동산

171 [1], [2], [3], [4]로 표시된 위치들 중에서, 다음 문장이 들어가기에 가장 적절한 곳은 어디인가?
"네온 조명의 활용이 정통적인 도시 분위기를 만들어내는 데 일조하고 있는 것으로 여겨지고 있습니다."
(A) [1]
(B) [2]
(C) [3]
(D) [4]

해설 〈문장 넣기〉
제시된 문장에 네온 조명의 활용과 도시 분위기의 조성이 언급되어 있다. 따라서 레스토랑 내의 생동감 있는 디자인적 특징으로서 북적대는 아시아의 도시에 와 있는 듯한 느낌이 언급된 문장 뒤에 위치한 [3]에 들어가 그 이유를 말하는 흐름이 되는 것이 알맞으므로 (C)가 정답이다.

[172-175] 온라인 채팅

데니스 파월 (오전 9:08) 안녕하세요, 리슈 씨 그리고 카우아 씨. 윌리 플라자가 9월 15일에 예약이 되어 있어서 우리가 그곳에서 은퇴 기념 만찬을 개최할 수 없다는 사실을 알려 드리고 싶었어요. **172** 제가 일을 처리해서 크루즈 홀에 대신 예약을 해 두었습니다.
리슈 파레크 (오전 9:09) 해결되었다니 기쁘네요.
카우아 소우사 (오전 9:10) 윌리 플라자가 분명 더 편리한 위치에 있는 곳이기는 하지만, **173** 크루즈 홀도 그만큼 좋은 곳이고 훨씬 더 저렴합니다.
리슈 파레크 (오전 9:11) 맞아요! 우리에게 훨씬 더 낫죠.
데니스 파월 (오전 9:12) 우리는 이제 출장 요리 선택권에 대해 생각해야 해요. **174** 잠깐 들러서 보러 오실 수 있으면 저에게 몇몇 안내 책자들이 있어요. 하지만 제가 점심 식사 후에 고객을 방문해야 하기 때문에 12시 전에 그렇게 하셔야 한다는 점을 알아두세요.
카우아 소우사 (오전 9:13) 꼭 한 번 보러 갈게요. 제가 생각해 둔 아이디어가 좀 있어요.
데니스 파월 (오전 9:13) 장식물과 관련된 계획도 최종 확정해야 해요. 무슨 색상을 주제로 활용할 예정이죠?
리슈 파레크 (오전 9:14) 녹색과 검정색으로 결정했어요. **175** 조명과 색 테이프, 그리고 풍선을 사용할 거예요. 제가 온라인에서 그것들을 구입할 수 있어요.
데니스 파월 (오전 9:15) 고맙습니다. 리슈 씨.
카우아 소우사 (오전 9:15) 리슈 씨, 며칠만 기다렸다가 해 주시겠어요? 제가 물품보관실에 무엇이 있는지 먼저 확인하러 가 봤으면 해서요. 우리가 재사용할 수 있는 것들이 있을 수 있어요.
리슈 파레크 (오전 9:16) 좋습니다.

어휘 let A know that A에게 ~라고 알리다 book ~을 예약하다 hold ~을 개최하다, 열다 retirement 은퇴, 퇴직 go ahead 처리하다, 추진하다 make a reservation 예약하다 settle ~을 해결하다 definitely 분명 convenient 편리한 location 위치, 지점 just as A 그만큼 A한 substantially (비교급 수식) 훨씬, 상당히 be better off 더 낫다 catering

출장 요리 제공(업) brochure 안내 책자 stop by 들르다 note that ~임에 유의하다. 주목하다 give A a look A를 한 번 보다 have A in mind A를 생각해 두다. A를 염두에 두다 finalize ~을 최종 확정하다 regarding ~와 관련된 decoration 장식(물) theme 주제, 테마 decide on ~으로 결정하다 streamer 색 테이프 purchase ~을 구입하다 would like to do ~하고 싶다 storage room 보관실, 저장실

172 파월 씨는 왜 다른 메시지 작성자들과 온라인 채팅을 시작했는가?
(A) 시설 견학 행사에 초대하기 위해
(B) 기획을 끝낼 시간을 제안하기 위해
(C) 장소 선정 문제에 대해 알리기 위해
(D) 행사 손님 숫자를 확인해 주기 위해

해설 〈주제 및 목적〉
첫 메시지에서 파월 씨는 월리 플라자가 아닌 크루즈 홀에 대신 행사 예약을 한 사실을 언급한(I've gone ahead and made a reservation at Cruz Hall instead) 뒤로 해당 행사의 개최와 관련해 이야기하고 있다. 따라서 장소 선정 문제를 언급한 (C)가 정답이다.

어휘 facility 시설 planning 기획 venue (행사 등의) 장소

173 오전 9시 11분에, 파레크 씨가 "We're much better off"라고 썼을 때 의미한 것은 무엇이겠는가?
(A) 최종 결정 사항에 대해 만족하고 있다.
(B) 행사 참석자 수가 높을 것으로 기대하고 있다.
(C) 자신이 직접 방문해 보고 싶어 한다.
(D) 출장 요리 업체가 일을 잘해 줄 것으로 생각하고 있다.

해설 〈주제 및 목적〉
앞서 파월 씨가 크루즈 홀로 예약한 것에 대해 9시 10분에 소우사 씨가 크루즈 홀도 좋은 곳이고 훨씬 더 저렴하다고 말한 것에 대해 파레크 씨가 Exactly라는 말로 강한 동의를 나타낸 뒤에 "We're much better off"라고 말하는 상황이다. 따라서 그와 같은 결정에 대한 기쁨을 나타내는 말임을 알 수 있으므로 (A)가 정답이다.

어휘 attendance 참석, 참석자 수 in-person 직접의 caterer 출장연회 업체

174 파월 씨는 점심 식사 전에 무엇을 할 계획인 것 같은가?
(A) 일부 메뉴 항목 시식하기
(B) 자신의 사무실에서 일하기
(C) 고객과의 회의에 참석하기
(D) 일부 상세 정보를 이메일로 보내기

해설 〈주제 및 목적〉
9시 12분 메시지에서 파월 씨는 브로셔가 있으니 필요하다면 자신의 사무실에 잠깐 들르라고(I've got some brochures if you want to stop by ~) 하며, 고객을 방문해야 하므로 점심 시간에 이전에 시간이 된다고(~ you'll want to do that before noon) 알리고 있다. 이는 점심 식사 전에는 자신의 사무실에서 업무를 보고 있는 것으로 판단할 수 있으므로 (B)가 정답이다.

어휘 sample 시식하다, 맛보다

175 소우사 씨는 파레크 씨가 무엇을 하기를 원하는가?
(A) 보관 구역에 있는 일부 물품에 라벨 부착하기
(B) 일부 장식물을 구입하는 일을 미루기
(C) 몇몇 다른 색상 선택권을 고려해 보기
(D) 동료 직원들에게 주제를 공지하기

해설 〈주제 및 목적〉
파월 씨가 9시 13분 메시지에 장식물 계획(~ our plans regarding decorations ~)을 언급한 뒤로 파레크 씨가 주제 색상과 구체적인 장식물을 구입하는(I can purchase those online) 일을 말하자, 소우사 씨가 며칠 기다려 달라고(Rishu, could you wait a few days to do that?) 요청하고 있다. 이는 장식물 구입을 미루는 것에 해당되므로 (B)가 정답이다.

어휘 label 라벨을 부착하다 theme 주제

[176-180] 기사와 이메일

숨은 보석

작성자, 멜라니 하이드

6월 18일 — 캐나다 전역을 돌아보는 제 여행의 다음 순서로, 노바 스코샤 주를 방문했습니다. 저는 수많은 해산물 레스토랑을 포함해 어업과 관련된 업체들만 마주칠 것으로 예상하고 있었습니다. 하지만, 다트머스에서 맛볼 수 있는 다양한 요리 옵션들로 인해 기분 좋은 놀라움을 경험했습니다. **179** 그 마을 자체는 노바 스코샤 주의 수도인 핼리팩스에서 10킬로미터도 채 되지 않는 곳에 있어서, 대중교통을 통해 연결되어 있으며, 이곳에서 윈드밀 로드에 위치한 **177** '파라디소'라는 이름의 근사한 이탈리안 식당을 한 곳 발견했습니다. 모든 식당 손님들은 **177** 이 지역에서 자란 단풍나무를 이용해 수작업으로 제작한 목재 테이블과 의자로 한층 끌어올린 이 레스토랑의 매력적인 분위기를 아주 마음에 들어 할 것입니다. 게다가, 메뉴는 세계적으로 유명한 요리사 레이몬도 세이게즈 씨에 의해 만들어졌습니다. 음식량도 아주 많고, 제가 주문한 모든 것이 맛있었습니다. **176** 다트머스에 가시게 되는 경우, 이곳을 꼭 목록에 포함해 두시기 바랍니다.

제 웹 갤러리 전용 사진들과 함께 제 여름 모험의 순간들을 함께 따라가 보시려면, www.melaniestravels.ca를 방문하시기 바랍니다.

178 수신: 가브리엘 데일 <g.dale@hammond-inc.com>
발신: 에바 허버트 <e.herbert@hammond-inc.com>
날짜: 6월 29일
제목: 연례 무역 박람회

데일 씨께.

178 무역 박람회 참석을 위한 제 출장과 관련해 회사의 비용 환급 절차를 설명해 주셔서 감사드립니다. 또한 언급해 주신 일일 최대 예산 금액을 초과하는 모든 식사에 대해서는 자비로 지불해야 한다는 점도 이해했습니다. 이런 일이 출장 중에 대부분 일어나지 않을 것으로 생각하고 있지만, **179** 파라디소에 가서 근사한 식사를 즐길지도 모르겠습니다. 이곳은 그 주의 수도에서 열리는 무역 박람회 장소로부터 불과 10킬로미터밖에 되지 않는 곳에 위치한 마을에 있습니다. 저는 또한 이번 출장을 위해 제가 선호하는 차량 대여 업체를 선택할 수 있는지도 궁금합니다. 회사에서 보통 에이스 카즈를 이용하고 있는 이유가 가장 저렴한 가격을 제공하는 곳으로 알려져 있기 때문이라는 것을 알고 있습니다. 하지만, **180** 로드웨이즈에 훨씬 더 최신 차량들이 있으며, 현재 모든 렌터카에 대해 15퍼센트 할인을 제공하고 있는데, 이는 에이스 카즈와 비슷한 가격대에 해당됩니다. 저에게 알려 주시기 바랍니다.

에바

어휘 segment 부분, 일부 province (행정 구역) 주 expect to do ~할 것으로 예상하다. 기대하다 encounter ~와 마주치다 related to ~와 관련된 including ~을 포함해 numerous 수많은, 다수의 diverse 다양한 culinary 요리의 available 이용 가능한 less than ~가 채 되지 않는, ~미만의 capital 수도 connect ~을 연결하다 via ~을 통해 public transportation 대중교통 bistro 식당 charming 매력적인 atmosphere 분위기 enhance ~을 강화하다, 향상시키다 in addition 게다가, 추가로 create ~을 만들어 내다 world-renowned 세계적으로 유명한 portion (음식의) 1인분 be sure to do 꼭 ~하다 put A on one's list A를 목록에 포함하다 follow ~을 따라가다, 지켜보다, 주시하다 exclusive 전용의, 독점적인 annual 연례적인, 해마다의 trade show 무역 박람회 explain ~을 설명하다 reimbursement 비용 환급 procedure 절차 regarding ~와 관련해 pay out of pocket 자비로 지불하다 exceed ~을 초과하다 budget 예산 maximum (비용, 속도, 규모 등의) 최대, 최고 treat A to B A에게 B를 대접하다, 한턱 내다 take place (일, 행사 등이) 개최되다, 발생되다 wonder if ~인지 궁금하다 choose ~을 선택하다 preferred 선호하는 car rental agency 차량 대여 업체 be known for ~로 알려져 있다 vehicle 차량 currently 현재 offer ~을 제공하다 similar 유사한 price point 가격대

176 기사의 목적은 무엇인가?
(A) 교통 서비스를 홍보하는 것
(B) 레스토랑을 추천하는 것
(C) 호텔을 설명하는 것
(D) 여행사 후기를 제공하는 것

해설 〈주제 및 목적〉
첫 지문 초반부에 약간의 배경 설명을 한 뒤로, 중반부터 '파라디소'라는 이름의 이탈리안 식당을 발견한(~ I found a delightful Italian bistro there called Paradiso ~) 사실과 그곳의 특징을,

그리고 후반부에 다트머스에 가면 그곳을 꼭 목록에 포함해 두도록 권하고(If you find yourself in Dartmouth, be sure to put this place on your list) 있다. 따라서 레스토랑을 추천하는 것이 기사의 목적임을 알 수 있으므로 (B)가 정답이다.

어휘 promote ~을 홍보하다 transportation 교통(편) give a recommendation 추천하다 describe ~을 설명하다 provide ~을 제공하다 travel agency 여행사 review 후기, 의견, 평가

177 가구와 관련해 무엇이 언급되는가?
(A) 사용하기 매우 편하다.
(B) 해외에서 수입되었다.
(C) 지역에서 공급되는 재료로 만들어진다.
(D) 독특한 지역적 양식을 특징으로 한다.

해설 〈진위 확인 (세부 진위 유형)〉
가구 제품에 해당되는 테이블과 의자가 언급되는 첫 지문 중반부에, 그 지역에서 자란 단풍나무를 이용해 수작업으로 제작한 목재 테이블과 의자(~ the wooden tables and chairs that were handmade using the maple trees grown in the area)에 관한 설명이 있으므로 (C)가 정답이다.

어휘 comfortable 편한, 편안한 import ~을 수입하다 from overseas 해외에서, 해외로부터 be made from ~로 만들어지다 locally 지역적으로 source ~을 공급받다 material 재료, 자재, 물품 feature ~을 특징으로 하다 unique 독특한, 특별한 regional 지역의, 지방의

178 데일 씨는 누구일 것 같은가?
(A) 무역 박람회 발표자
(B) 여행 가이드
(C) 유명 요리사
(D) 회계 담당 직원

해설 〈세부 사항〉
데일 씨의 이름은 두 번째 지문 상단에 수신인으로 표기되어 있으며, 이 지문 시작 부분에 데일 씨를 you로 지칭해 이 사람이 비용 환급 절차를 설명하고 일일 최대 예산 금액을 언급해 준 사실이(Thank you for explaining our company's reimbursement procedures regarding my business trip ~ the daily budget maximum that you mentioned) 제시되어 있다. 따라서 회사의 회계 관련 업무를 맡고 있다는 것을 알 수 있으므로 (D)가 정답이다.

179 무역 박람회와 관련해 무엇이 암시되는가?
(A) 참석자들에게 식사를 제공한다.
(B) 핼리팩스에서 개최될 것이다.
(C) 처음으로 개최된다.
(D) 단체에게 무료 입장 혜택을 제공한다.

해설 〈지문 연계〉
무역 박람회가 언급되는 두 번째 지문 중반부에, 파라디소에서 식사를 하는 일과 함께 이 식당이 그 주의 수도에서 열리는 무역 박람회장으로부터 불과 10킬로미터 밖에 되지 않는 곳에 위치한 마을에 있다고(~ at Paradiso. It's in a town only 10 kilometers from the trade show, which takes place in the province's capital)

알리고 있다. 이와 관련해, 첫 번째 지문 중반부에 파라디소를 발견한 마을을 설명하며 그 주의 수도가 핼리팩스라고(~ from Halifax, the capital of the province) 언급하고 있으므로 무역 박람회가 핼리팩스에서 개최된다는 사실을 알 수 있다. 따라서 (B)가 정답이다.

어휘 offer ~을 제공하다(= provide) attendee 참석자 take place (행사, 일 등이) 개최되다, 발생되다 hold ~을 개최하다, 열다 for the first time (사상) 처음으로 free 무료의 entry 입장, 출입

180 허버트 씨는 로드웨이즈와 관련해 무엇을 언급하는가?
(A) 보유 차량들을 업그레이드해야 한다.
(B) 현재 할인 행사 중이다.
(C) 직원들에 의해 자주 이용된다.
(D) 안전 평점이 높다.

해설 〈세부 사항〉
로드웨이즈가 언급되는 두 번째 지문 마지막 부분에, 로드웨이즈에 훨씬 더 새로운 차량들이 있다는 사실과 함께 현재 모든 렌터카에 대해 15퍼센트 할인을 제공하고 있다고(~ Roadwaze has much newer vehicles, and it is currently offering fifteen percent off all rentals) 알리고 있으므로 (B)가 정답이다.

어휘 vehicle 차량 currently 현재 have a sale 할인 행사를 하다, 세일하다 frequently 자주, 빈번히 rating 평점, 등급

[181-185] 광고와 양식

테트릭 기업 개발 센터 (TCDC)
www.tetrickcdc.com

경쟁적인 비즈니스 세계에서 교육은 우위를 점하는 데 필요한 올바른 수단입니다. 지난 10년 동안, **181** 저희 TCDC는 비즈니스 전략 및 기업 활동에 관한 재미있고 유익한 강좌를 통해 수천 명의 전문 능력 개발을 도와 왔습니다. 저희는 수강생 중심의 방식으로 이 행사에 **182** 접근하며, 이는 저희 전문 강사님이 여러분께서 필요로 하시는 지원을 꼭 받으실 수 있도록 해 드린다는 점을 의미합니다. 아래에서 저희 6월 교육 행사를 확인해 보시기 바랍니다.

행사 ID	제목	강사	날짜	시간
J082	증거 기반의 관리	린 양	6월 8일	오후 2시 – 오후 5시
J146	사회적 변화 촉진	제임스 울리히	6월 14일	오전 9시 – 오후 12시
184 J158	디지털 시대에 필요한 도구들	린 양	**184** 6월 20일	오전 10시 – 오후 1시
J273	전문 네트워크 구축	비닛 팬데이	6월 29일	오후 3시 – 오후 6시

모든 강좌는 TCDC 센터에서 개최되며, 이 센터는 록포드, 그랜드뷰 드라이브 943번지, IL 61101에 위치해 있습니다. 이 건물에 무료 구내 주차 공간이 있습니다. 각 강좌의 수강료는 85달러이며, 안전한 저희 온라인 포털을 통해, 또는 저희 사무실로 수표를 보내 지불하실 수 있습니다.

테트릭 기업 개발 센터 (TCDC)
수강생 등록 양식: **183** 6월 강좌
문의 또는 건의 사항: 779-555-6681

184 성명: 클레오 로시

이메일 주소: rossicleo@irvine-mail.com   전화번호: 779-555-0489

선호하는 연락 방식: [✔] 이메일   [ ] 전화

185 소속 회사: 반스 파이낸셜 컨설팅

184 참가 희망 행사: J158

TCDC에 대해 어떻게 알게 되셨나요? 동료 직원의 추천

지불 방식: [✔] 신용 카드 ("제출하기" 클릭 후 비용 지불 페이지로 안내됩니다.)
[ ] 수표 ("제출하기" 클릭 후 우편 주소가 나타납니다.)

다가오는 행사에 관해 더 많은 것을 알아보실 수 있도록 저희 우편물 발송 대상자 명단에 등록하시겠습니까? [ ] 네   [✔] 아니요

주의 사항: 등록은 선착순으로 가능합니다. 요청하시는 강좌가 마감일 경우, 대기자 명단에 추가될 것입니다. **183** 최소 20명의 인원이 강좌에 등록하지 않은 경우에는, 취소될 것입니다.

제출하기

어휘 corporate 기업의 development 개발 competitive 경쟁적인 tool 수단, 도구 edge 우위, 유리함 decade 10년 help A with B B에 대해 A를 돕다 professional development 전문 능력 개발 informative 유익한, 유용한 정보를 주는 strategy 전략 approach ~에 접근하다 student-centered 수강생 중심의 way 방식 expert a. 전문적인 instructor 강사 make sure (that) 반드시 ~하도록 하다 based (결합어로 쓰여) ~ 기반의, ~을 바탕으로 한 drive ~을 촉진하다, 추진하다 hold ~을 개최하다 be located at ~에 위치해 있다 free 무료의 on-site 구내의, 현장의 session (특정 활동을 위한) 시간 through ~을 통해 secure 안전한 by (방법)~해서, ~함으로써 check n. 수표 registration 등록 form 양식, 서식, 방식, 유형 inquiry 문의 preferred 선호하는 desired 희망하는 find out about ~에 대해 알게 되다, 확인하다 colleague 동료 직원 submit 제출하다 appear 나타나다 join ~에 합류하다, ~와 함께 하다 upcoming 다가오는, 곧 있을 available 이용 가능한 on a first-come, first-served basis 선착순으로 requested 요청된 add A to B A를 B에 추가하다 at least 최소한, 적어도 enroll in ~에 등록하다 cancel ~을 취소하다

181 TCDC는 무엇을 하는가?
(A) 마케팅 서비스 제공하기
(B) 일자리에 필요한 직원 모집하기
(C) 비즈니스 주제로 사람들을 교육하기
(D) 기업 야유회 주최하기

해설 〈진위 확인 (주제 및 목적)〉
첫 지문 시작 부분에, TCDC가 비즈니스 전략 및 기업 활동에 관한 강좌를 통해 사람들에게 도움을 제공해 왔다고(~ their professional development through our fun and informative classes on business strategies and corporate activities) 알리는 부분이

TCDC의 특징을 나타내는 말이다. 이는 비즈니스와 관련해 사람들을 교육하는 일에 해당되므로 (C)가 정답이다.

어휘 provide ~을 제공하다 recruit ~을 모집하다 train ~을 교육하다 host ~을 주최하다 corporate 기업의 retreat 야유회

182 광고에서 첫 번째 단락, 세 번째 줄의 단어 "approach"와 의미가 가장 가까운 것은 무엇인가?
(A) 다루다
(B) 접근하다
(C) 요청하다
(D) 도착하다

해설 〈동의어〉
해당 문장의 내용을 보면, 앞 문장에서 언급한 교육 행사들을 가리키는 these events와 수강생 중심의 방식을 뜻하는 in a student-centered way가 쓰여 있다. 따라서 강좌를 수강생 중심으로 진행한다는 의미인 것으로 판단할 수 있다. 이는 수강생 중심으로 강좌를 다룬다는 말과 같으므로 '다루다, 처리하다'를 뜻하는 (A) deal with가 정답이다.

183 6월 행사에 관해 언급된 것은 무엇인가?
(A) 일부는 이전 경험을 필요로 할 수 있다.
(B) 모두 오후 시간에 개최된다.
(C) 두 가지는 제임스 울리히 씨가 가르친다.
(D) **최소 숫자의 등록 인원을 필요로 한다.**

해설 〈진위 확인 (세부 진위 유형)〉
상단에 6월 강좌(June Sessions) 등록 양식이라고 쓰여 있는 두 번째 지문에, 최소 20명의 인원이 강좌에 등록하지 않으면 취소된다는(If at least twenty people do not enroll in a session, it will be canceled) 내용이 쓰여 있다. 즉 최소로 등록해야 하는 인원 기준이 있다는 것이므로 이를 언급한 (D)가 정답이다.

어휘 require ~을 필요로 하다 previous 이전의, 과거의 take place (행사, 일 등이) 개최되다, 발생하다 a minimum number of 최소 숫자의 register 등록하다

184 로시 씨는 언제 행사에 참석할 계획인가?
(A) 6월 8일에
(B) 6월 14일에
(C) **6월 20일에**
(D) 6월 29일에

해설 〈지문 연계〉
로시 씨의 이름이 쓰여 있는 등록 양식인 두 번째 지문에, 참가 희망 강좌로 J158이 기재되어 있다(Desired Event(s): J158). 그리고 첫 지문의 도표에서 J158에 해당되는 강좌인 Tools for the Digital Age의 날짜가 6월 20일로 쓰여 있으므로 (C)가 정답이다.

어휘 plan to do ~할 계획이다 attend ~에 참석하다

185 로시 씨에 관해 암시된 것은 무엇인가?
(A) **금융 업계에서 일하고 있다.**
(B) 관리자 직책에 있다.

(C) 더 많은 시간에 참석할 계획이다.
(D) 광고를 통해 TCDC에 대해 알게 되었다.

해설 〈진위 확인 (전체 진위 유형)〉
로시 씨가 작성한 등록 양식인 두 번째 지문에, 소속 회사 이름이 반스 파이낸셜 컨설팅(Company: Barnes Financial Consulting)이라고 쓰여 있는 것을 통해 금융 업계에서 일하는 사람임을 알 수 있으므로 (A)가 정답이다.

어휘 finance 금융, 재무 managerial position 관리자 직책, 책임자 자리 session (특정 활동을 위한) 시간 through ~을 통해 ad 광고

[186-190] 이메일과 광고, 그리고 짧은 편지

수신: 헥터 맥고완 〈h.mcgowan@leoindustries.com〉
186 발신: 나탈리아 파누치〈n.fanucci@leoindustries.com〉
날짜: 9월 2일
제목: 준비 작업

헥터 씨,

189 새로나 제조회사의 운영 이사님께서 9월 23일 우리 지사를 방문하실 때 당신이 그에 대한 준비의 책임을 맡게 되신다고 들었습니다. **186** 그분께서 지난 분기에 방문하셨을 때 제가 같은 일을 했기 때문에, 제가 알게 된 부분을 공유해 드리고 싶었습니다. 그분은 항공편 여행에 대해 매우 민감하신 분입니다. 따라서, 대부분의 고객들은 도착하는 당일에 업무를 위한 저녁 식사 자리를 갖는 것에 대해 기뻐하지만(디아즈 인터내셔널 사의 직원들을 위해 이렇게 하셨던 것을 알고 있습니다), **187** 그분께서는 본인의 객실에서 여유로운 시간을 갖고 저녁 식사하시는 것을 더 편안해 하실 것이라 생각됩니다. 호텔을 예약하실 때 이 점을 명심하시면 좋을 것입니다.

도움이 되기를 바라며,

나탈리아

바네타 호텔
애틀랜타

188 하츠필드 잭슨 애틀랜타 국제공항에서 차로 불과 5분 거리에 위치한 바네타 호텔에서 고급스러움과 편안함을 즐기십시오. 숙박 중에 다음 편의시설을 이용하실 수 있습니다.

- 각 객실에 설치된 킹 사이즈 침대 및 평면 TV
- **188** 호텔 내 모든 구역에서 이용 가능한 뛰어난 와이파이 연결 서비스
- **187** 4성급 레스토랑에서 제공하는 24시간 룸서비스
- 타이탄 체육관 무료 일일 이용권 **188** (호텔에서 길 아래쪽에 위치)
- **188** 10인 이상으로 예약되는 파티에 대한 10퍼센트 할인 서비스

555-6053번으로 전화하셔서 예약하시거나 더 많은 정보를 알아보시기 바랍니다.

바네타 호텔
— 여러분의 편안함이 저희의 사명입니다! —

189 190 9월 23일

189 에어즈 씨께,

189 레오 인더스트리 사를 대표해, 애틀랜타 오신 것을 환영합니다. 즐거운 비행이 되셨기를 바랍니다. 편안하게 저녁 시간을 즐기신 다음, **190** 내일 아침에 여유롭게 식사하시고 저희 사무실로 오시기 바랍니다. 귀하를 차로 모실 수 있도록 HM 트랜스포테이션 사에 조치해 두었습니다. 따라서, 출발하실 준비가 되기 약 15분 전에 그 업체에 전화하시기만 하면 됩니다. 그 업체의 명함이 이 편지에 첨부되어 있습니다. 어떤 것이든 필요하실 경우, 제 휴대 전화 번호 678-555-0622번으로 전화 주십시오.

내일 뵙기를 고대합니다!

190 헥터 맥고완

어휘 in charge of ~을 책임지는, 맡고 있는 make an arrangement 준비하다, 조치하다 branch 지사, 지점 quarter 분기 share ~을 공유하다 be sensitive to ~에 민감하다 air travel 항공편 여행 arrive 도착하다 representative 직원, 대표자 comfortable 편안한 have A free A를 여유롭게 보내다 keep A in mind A를 명심하다, 염두에 두다 book ~을 예약하다 comfort 편안함 located 위치한 following 다음의, 아래의 amenities 편의 시설 available 이용 가능한 connection 연결, 접속 round-the-clock 24시간 제공되는 free 무료의 pass 이용권 down (길 등) ~ 아래쪽에, 아래쪽으로 make one's booking 예약하다 on behalf of ~을 대표해, 대신해 leisurely 여유로운, 한가한 head to ~로 가다, 향하다 arrange for ~을 조치하다, 마련하다 pick A up A를 차로 데리러 가다, 데려 오다 about 약, 대략 be ready to do ~할 준비가 되다 leave 출발하다, 떠나다 attach ~을 첨부하다 look forward to -ing ~하기를 고대하다

186 파누치 씨는 왜 이메일을 보냈는가?
(A) 배정 업무에 대한 마감 기한을 변경하기 위해
(B) **방문 일정을 준비하는 일에 관해 조언하기 위해**
(C) 한 업무에 대해 동료 직원을 추천하기 위해
(D) 출장 계획에 대한 변경 사항을 알려 주기 위해

해설 〈주제 및 목적〉
파누치 씨의 이름이 발신인 항목에 제시된 첫 지문 초반부에, 상대방이 특정 인물의 방문을 준비한다고 언급하며 자신이 이전에 같은 일을 하면서 알게 된 부분을 공유해 주겠다고(I had that same job when he visited last quarter, so I wanted to share what I learned) 알리고 있다. 이는 방문 일정 준비에 대해 조언해 주겠다는 뜻이므로 (B)가 정답이다.

어휘 deadline 마감 기한 assignment 배정(되는 일), 할당(되는 일) prepare for ~을 준비하다, ~에 대비하다 colleague 동료 (직원)

187 파누치 씨는 왜 바네타 호텔이 좋은 선택이라고 생각할 것 같은가?
(A) 구내 비즈니스 센터가 있다.
(B) 각 객실에 큰 침대가 있다.
(C) **객실 내에서 먹을 음식을 준비할 수 있다.**

(D) 맥고완 씨에 의해 추천되었다.

해설 〈지문 연계〉
첫 지문 후반부에, 방문하는 사람이 객실에서 여유롭게 저녁 식사하는 것을(~ eating in his room) 좋아한다고 알리고 있고, 두 번째 지문 중반부에 레스토랑에서 24시간 룸서비스를 제공한다는 사실이(Round-the-clock room service from our four-star restaurant) 쓰여 있다. 따라서 객실에서 편하게 식사할 수 있다는 점이 바네타 호텔을 선택할 만한 이유일 것으로 볼 수 있으므로 이를 언급한 (C)가 정답이다.

어휘 choice 선택 on-site 구내의, 현장의 in-room 객실 내의 consumption 먹기, 마시기, 소비

188 광고 내용에 따르면, 바네타 호텔에 관해 사실이 아닌 것은 무엇인가?
(A) 건물 전역에서 인터넷을 이용할 수 있다.
(B) 공항과 가까운 곳에 있다.
(C) 구내에 운동 구역이 있다.
(D) 단체 고객들에게 할인을 제공한다.

해설 〈진위 확인 (전체 진위 유형)〉
두 번째 지문 중반부에, 모든 구역에서 이용 가능한 와이파이를(Wi-Fi connection in all parts of the hotel) 언급한 부분에서 (A)를, 하츠필드 잭슨 애틀랜타 국제공항에서 차로 5분 거리에 위치해 있다는(located just a five-minute drive from Hartsfield-Jackson Atlanta International Airport) 내용에서 (B)를 확인할 수 있다. 또한 10인 이상으로 예약되는 파티에 대해 10퍼센트 할인이(Ten percent off parties booking for ten or more people) 제시된 부분에서 (D)도 확인 가능하다. 하지만 운동 공간으로 언급된 곳은 호텔 밖에(down the street from our hotel) 위치해 있으므로 (C)가 정답이다.

어휘 based on ~에 따르면, ~을 바탕으로 throughout ad. 전역에, 전체에 near ~와 가까운 exercise 운동 offer ~을 제공하다

189 에어즈 씨는 무슨 업체에서 근무하는가?
(A) 디아즈 인터내셔널
(B) HM 트랜스포테이션
(C) 새로나 제조회사
(D) 바네타 호텔

해설 〈진위 확인 (지문 연계)〉
맥고완 씨가 작성한 세 번째 지문 상단에, 9월 23일이라는 날짜와 함께 에어즈 씨에게 애틀랜타에 온 것을 환영한다는 인사를 전하고 있다. 이 날짜와 관련해, 첫 지문 시작 부분에 새로나 제조회사의 운영 이사가 9월 23일에 방문한다는(~ the operations director from Sarona Manufacturing when he visits our branch on September 23) 내용이 있으므로 에어즈 씨가 새로나 제조회사의 운영 이사인 것으로 판단할 수 있다. 따라서 (C)가 정답이다.

---

190 에어즈 씨는 언제 맥고완 씨의 사무실로 갈 것 같은가?
(A) 9월 23일 점심 식사 후에
(B) 9월 23일 저녁 식사 후에
(C) 9월 24일 아침 식사 후에
(D) 9월 24일 저녁 식사 후에

해설 〈세부 사항〉
맥고완 씨가 보내는 메시지인 세 번째 지문 초반부에, 다음날 아침에 여유롭게 식사한 후 자신이 있는 사무실로 오도록(~ have a leisurely morning meal tomorrow before heading to our office) 권하고 있다. 이 메시지 상단에 작성 날짜가 9월 23일로 되어 있으므로 9월 24일 아침 식사 후 사무실을 방문하도록 부탁하고 있음을 알 수 있다. 따라서 (C)가 정답이다.

[191-195] 공지와 이메일, 그리고 후기

아티스트 마켓
5주년 기념 행사

191 5월 16일 토요일, 오전 9시부터 오후 6시

무료 다과도 즐기시고 재능 있는 저희 미술가들도 만나 보세요.

191 세 가지 독창적인 그림 중 하나를 받을 기회를 얻을 수 있는 추첨 행사에 참가하세요.

매장 안내:

클라우드 매니아: 공상 과학을 주제로 한 금속 조각품

지니스 월드: 수채화 물감으로 그린 풍경화

192 어스 투 어스: 점토 화병과 그릇, 컵

선샤인 팰리스: 수제 장신구 및 선물

수신: 앨런 벡 〈a_beck@eugeneproperties.com〉
발신: 린다 리 〈linda@lindaleecreations.com〉
192 날짜: 6월 4일
제목: 아티스트 마켓

벡 씨께,

192 아티스트 마켓의 도자기 매장이 다음 달에 문을 닫을 예정인 것으로 알고 있으며, **193** 해당 공간이 다른 판매업체에게 이용 가능한지 알고 싶습니다. 저는 월간 임대료와 어떤 종류의 보관 시설이 이용 가능한지, 그리고 정확한 크기가 궁금합니다. 저는 지난 3년 동안 작은 도자기 스튜디오에서 영업을 해 왔지만, 유동 인구가 더 많은 곳을 찾고 있습니다. **195** 저는 또한 사업 파트너로 또 다른 예술가를 추가했는데, 이분의 작품은 바로 지난달 퐁텐 갤러리에서 열린 전시회에 포함되었습니다. 이 문제를 더 깊이 논의해 볼 수 있도록 555-9643번으로 가급적 빨리 저에게 연락 주시기 바랍니다.

안녕히 계십시오.

린다 리

위치 이전 후 주목받고 있는 예술가들

8월 28일

194 작성자, 애드리안 해밀턴

195 린다 리 씨와 새로운 파트너인 노라 콜먼 씨는 최근 업체를 아티스트 마켓으로 이전했습니다. 해당 매장인 린다 리 크리에이션즈는 전문 기술과 애정으로 공들여 제작한 수제 도자기 제품을 특징으로 합니다. 저는 **194** 프로비던스 지역 중심부에 있던 기존의 스튜디오를 방문하면서 제 수집품을 서서히 늘려 왔습니다. 저는 더 많은 사람들이 더 편리한 장소에서 리 씨의 작품을, 그리고 이제는 콜먼 씨의 작품도 이용할 수 있게 될 것이라는 사실이 기쁩니다. 비록 **194** 이 스튜디오가 더 이상 저희 집에서 도보로 2분 거리에 있지는 않지만, 저는 여전히 단골 구매자입니다. 모든 분께서 이 매장을 확인해 보셔야 합니다.

어휘 anniversary (해마다 돌아오는) 기념일 celebration 기념 행사, 축하 행사 free 무료의 refreshments 다과 talented 재능 있는 enter ~에 참가하다 drawing 추첨 original 독창적인, 원본의, 기존의 sculpture 조각품 sci-fi 공상 과학의 landscape 풍경 It is my understanding that ~라고 알고 있습니다 pottery 도자기 would like to do ~하고 싶다 find out if ~인지 알아 보다, 확인하다 available 이용 가능한 monthly fee 월간 요금 storage 보관(소), 저장 (공간) exact 정확한 operate 영업하다, 가동하다, 작동하다 look for ~을 찾다 site 장소, 현장, 부지 foot traffic 유동 인구 piece (글, 그림, 음악 등의) 작품 feature ~을 포함하다, ~을 특징으로 하다 exhibition 전시회 contact ~에게 연락하다 at your earliest convenience 가급적 빨리 discuss ~을 논의하다 further 더 깊이, 한층 더 gain ~을 얻다, 획득하다 attention 주목, 관심 relocation 위치 이전 recently 최근에 business 회사, 업체, 매장 craft ~을 공들여 만들다 expertise 전문 기술, 전문 지식 add to ~을 늘리다, 증가시키다 collection 소장품, 수집품 neighborhood 지역, 인근 be able to do ~할 수 있다 access ~을 이용하다, ~에 접근하다 convenient 편리한 though 비록 ~이기는 하지만 no longer 더 이상 ~ 않다 regular shopper 단골 구매자 check A out A를 확인해 보다

191 5월 16일 행사에 관해 사실인 것은 무엇인가?
(A) 입장료가 있다.
(B) 일부 참가자들이 상품을 받을 것이다.
(C) 지역 자선 단체를 위해 모금할 것이다.
(D) 일부 음악가들이 공연할 것이다.

해설 〈진위 확인 (전체 진위 유형)〉
5월 16일 행사 정보가 제시되어 있는 첫 지문에, 세 가지 독창적인 그림 중 하나를 받을 수 있는 추첨 행사에 참가하도록(Enter our drawing for a chance to win ~) 권하는 말이 쓰여 있다. 이는 당첨된 참가자들이 상품을 받는다는 뜻이므로 (B)가 정답이다.

어휘 fee 요금, 수수료 admission 입장 (허가), 입학, 입회 participant 참가자 win a prize 상(품)을 받다 raise money 모금하다 local 지역의, 현지의 charity 자선 단체 give a performance 공연하다, 연주하다

192 어느 업체가 7월에 아티스트 마켓을 떠날 예정인가?
(A) 클라우드 매니아
(B) 지나스 월드
(C) 어스 투 어스
(D) 선샤인 팰리스

해설 〈지문 연계〉
작성 날짜가 6월 4일인 두 번째 지문 첫 문장에 아티스트 마켓의 도자기 매장이 다음 달에 문을 닫는다는(~ the pottery shop at The Artist Market will be closing next month ~) 내용이 쓰여 있다. 따라서 7월에 도자기 매장이 문을 닫는다는 것을 알 수 있으며, 첫 지문에서 '어스 투 어스: 점토 화병과 그릇, 컵(Earth to Earth: clay vases, bowls, and cups)'이라고 설명된 곳이 도자기 매장이므로 (C)가 정답이다.

어휘 leave ~을 떠나다, ~에서 나가다

193 이메일의 목적은 무엇인가?
(A) 제품 라인 홍보하기
(B) 매장으로 찾아 가는 방법 요청하기
(C) 자선 단체에 내는 기부금 요청하기
(D) 임대 공간에 관한 상세 정보 얻기

해설 〈주제 및 목적〉
이메일 초반부에, 문을 닫는 업체가 있던 공간을 다른 판매업체가 쓸 수 있는지, 그리고 월간 임대료, 보관 시설의 종류 등이 궁금하다고(~ find out if the space is available for another vendor. I'm wondering about the monthly fee, what kind of storage is available, and the exact size) 묻고 있다. 이는 임대하려는 공간에 관한 상세 정보를 얻고자 하는 것이므로 (D)가 정답이다.

어휘 promote ~을 홍보하다 ask for ~을 요청하다 directions to ~로 찾아 가는 방법, ~로 가는 길 안내 request ~을 요청하다, 요구하다 donation 기부(금) charity 자선 단체 details 상세 정보, 세부 사항 rental 임대, 대여

194 해밀턴 씨에 관해 암시된 것은 무엇인가?
(A) 예술가로서 정식으로 교육받았다.
(B) 프로비던스 지역에 살고 있다.
(C) 리 씨와의 인터뷰를 실시했다.
(D) 리 씨의 스튜디오를 매입하고자 한다.

해설 〈진위 확인 (전체 진위 유형)〉
해밀턴 씨의 이름이 작성자로 제시된 세 번째 지문에, 프로비던스 지역 중심부에 있던 기존의 스튜디오를 방문한(~ visits to the original studio in the center of the Providence neighborhood) 사실과 함께 그 스튜디오가 더 이상 집에서 도보로 2분 거리에 있지는 않다고(~ the studio is no longer a two-minute walk from my home ~) 언급하고 있다. 이는 해밀턴 씨가 현재 프로비던스 지역에 살고 있다는 것을 나타내는 말이므로 (B)가 정답이다.

어휘 train ~을 교육하다 formally 정식으로, 공식적으로 neighborhood 지역, 인근 conduct ~을 실시하다, 수행하다 purchase ~을 매입하다, 구입하다

195 콜먼 씨에 관해 언급된 것은 무엇인가?
(A) 최근 자신의 작품을 대중에게 전시했다.
(B) 몇몇 미술 강좌를 가르칠 계획이다.
(C) 리 씨와 함께 미술 학교에 다녔다.
(D) 자신의 창작품에 대해 상을 받았다.

해설 〈지문 연계〉
콜먼 씨의 이름은 세 번째 단락 시작 부분에 린다 리 씨의 파트너로 (new partner, Nora Coleman) 언급되어 있다. 그리고 린다 리 씨가 쓴 이메일인 두 번째 지문 중반부에 새 파트너의 작품이 지난달에 퐁텐 갤러리에서 열린 전시회에 포함된 사실을(I've also added another artist as a business partner, whose pieces were featured in an exhibition at the Fontaine Gallery just last month) 말하고 있다. 따라서 콜먼 씨의 작품이 최근에 전시되었다는 것을 알 수 있으므로 이를 언급한 (A)가 정답이다.

어휘 recently 최근에 display ~을 전시하다, 진열하다 publicly 대중적으로, 공개적으로 plan to do ~할 계획이다 attend ~에 참석하다 win an award 상을 받다, 수상하다 creation 창작(품)

[196-200] 기사와 초대장, 그리고 이메일

건강을 중요시하는 소비자들에게 특별함을 제공하는 프리스코

켄우드 (4월 4일) – 취미로 자신만의 제과 제품 조리법을 개발해 온 끝에, 앨리스 네빈 씨의 새 카페인 **(196)** 프리스코가 4월 6일에 영업을 위해 문을 엽니다. 이 커피 매장은 전형적인 커피 음료와 케이크, 그리고 꽈배기 모양의 패스트리를 특징으로 하며, 모든 제품에 설탕이 들어 있지 않습니다. 네빈 씨는 자신의 제품을 만들기 위해 과일 및 꿀과 같은 천연 감미료를 사용합니다.

네빈 씨가 항상 제과 업계에 속해 있었던 것은 아니었습니다. **(200)** 네빈 씨는 밸리 대학교에서 경제학을 공부한 다음, 졸업 직후에 레오나 파이낸셜 사에 일자리를 얻었습니다. 네빈 씨는 취미로 빵을 굽는 것을 항상 아주 좋아했습니다. 하지만, **(197)** 남동생의 담당 의사가 남동생에게 건강 문제로 설탕을 덜 섭취하도록 이야기했을 때, 네빈 씨는 남동생을 위해 맛이 좋으면서 설탕이 들어 있지 않은 대안을 만들기 시작했습니다. 네빈 씨는 많은 사람들이 유사한 질병을 갖고 있을지도 모른다고 생각했기 때문에, **(197)** 자신의 특별 음식을 일반적으로 이용 가능하도록 만들어야겠다는 영감을 얻었습니다. "많은 사람들이 요즘 설탕 소비를 줄이고 있어요."라고 네빈 씨는 말했습니다. "저는 자연의 맛이 맛있을 수 있다는 것을 알 수 있도록 모든 분들이 저희에게 기회를 주길 바라고 있습니다."

프리스코는 내시 스트리트 103번지에 위치해 있습니다. 이 매장은 **(198)** 매일 오전 7시 30분부터 오후 8시 30분까지 영업합니다.

— 프리스코가 여러분을 초대합니다 —

매우 다양한 무설탕 패스트리도 드셔 보시고
저희 새 커피 매장도 둘러보세요!

(198) 4월 13일 금요일, 오후 9시 - 오후 11시

또한 방문객들께 드리는 경품과 함께 카페인이 들어 있는 음료와
카페인 무첨가 음료도 이용 가능합니다.

이 초대장은 입장하시는 데 필수이므로 지참하고 오시기 바랍니다.

수신: 앨리스 네빈 〈a.nevin@friscocshop.com〉
발신: **(199) (200)** 피터 오튼 〈peterorton@hoffmaninc.com〉
날짜: 4월 5일
제목: 4월 13일 행사

앨리스에게,

너의 커피 매장에서 곧 열리는 행사에 대한 초대장을 우편으로 받게 되어 기뻤어. 내 생각을 해 줘서 고마워! **(199)** 난 이 행사를 정말로 고대하고 있어. 그동안 있었던 일도 얘기하고, 매장도 둘러본다면 정말 좋을 것 같아. 그리고 물론 네가 만든 맛있는 제품을 맛보는 것도. **(200)** 우리가 졸업 직후에 함께 일했을 때 네가 이미 건강에 좋은 음식에 관해 열정이 대단했다는 것을 기억해. 네가 요즘 어떻게 지내는지 빨리 더 얘기 들어 보고 싶어.

안녕,

피터

어휘 offer up ~을 제공하다 treat 특별한 것, 특별한 음식 health-conscious 건강을 중요시하는, 건강에 신경 쓰는 consumer 소비자 develop ~을 개발하다 recipe 조리법 baked goods 제과 제품 feature ~을 특징으로 하다 sugar-free 설탕이 없는 natural sweetener 천연 감미료 creation 만들어 낸 것, 창작(물) economics 경제학 right after ~ 직후에 tell A to do A에게 ~하도록 말하다 due to ~로 인해 create ~을 만들어 내다 alternative 대안, 대체(품) similar 유사한 condition 질병 be inspired to do ~할 영감을 얻다 publicly 일반적으로, 공공연하게 available 이용 가능한 cut down on ~을 줄이다, 감축하다 consumption 소비 so (that) ~할 수 있도록 flavor 맛, 풍미 be located at ~에 위치해 있다 operate 영업하다, 운영되다 a wide range of 매우 다양한 tour ~을 둘러보다, 견학하다 caffeinated 카페인이 들어 있는 along with ~와 함께 prize 경품, 상품 required 필요한, 필수의 entry 입장 receive ~을 받다 invitation 초대(장) upcoming 곧 있을, 다가오는 look forward to ~을 고대하다 catch up with ~와 그동안 못한 이야기를 하다 site 장소, 현장, 부지 graduate 졸업하다 be passionate about ~에 대한 열정이 대단하다 can't wait to do 빨리 ~하고 싶다 how A is doing A가 어떻게 지내는지

196 기사는 왜 쓰여졌는가?
(A) 지역 내에 있는 커피 매장들을 평가하기 위해
(B) 한 업체의 개장을 홍보하기 위해
(C) 메뉴상의 변화를 알리기 위해
(D) 설탕을 끊는 방법에 관한 팁을 제공하기 위해

해설 〈주제 및 목적〉

첫 번째 지문 첫 단락에, 프리스코라는 매장이 문을 연다고(Frisco, will be open for business ~) 알리며 그 배경과 특징에 관해 설명하고 있으므로 (B)가 정답이다.

어휘 review ~을 평가하다, ~에 대한 후기를 쓰다, ~을 검토하다 promote ~을 홍보하다 announce ~을 알리다, 발표하다 how to do ~하는 방법 cut out ~을 끊다, 그만두다

197 무엇이 네빈 씨에게 커피 매장에 대한 아이디어를 주었는가?

(A) 지역 사회 제과 제품 콘테스트

(B) 자신의 대학 교수들 중 한 명과의 대화

(C) 인척의 건강 관련 문제

(D) 해외에서 보낸 휴가

해설 〈세부 사항〉

첫 지문 두 번째 단락에, 남동생이 건강 문제로 인해 설탕을 줄여야 하는 상황이었음을 알리면서 네빈 씨가 그로 인해 자신의 음식을 일반 대중들도 이용할 수 있도록 만들 것을 결심했다는(~ her brother's doctor told him to eat less sugar due to health issues, ~ she was inspired to make her treats publicly available) 내용이 쓰여 있다. 따라서 (C)가 정답이다.

어휘 community 지역 사회, 지역 공동체 relative n. 인척, 친척

198 4월 13일 행사에 관해 언급된 것은 무엇인가?

(A) 음악 공연이 제공될 것이다.

(B) 입장 요금이 있을 것이다.

(C) 초대받은 사람이 손님을 데려올 수 있다.

(D) 영업 시간 이후에 개최된다.

해설 〈지문 연계〉

4월 13일이라는 행사 날짜와 시간이 언급된 두 번째 지문에, 오후 9시부터 11시까지(Friday, April 13, 9 P.M.–11 P.M.) 행사가 진행되는 것으로 쓰여 있다. 그런데 첫 번째 지문 마지막 문장에, 매장 개장 시간이 오전 7시 30분부터 오후 8시 30분까지라고(~ operate daily from 7:30 A.M. to 8:30 P.M.) 쓰여 있으므로 영업을 마치고 열리는 행사임을 알 수 있다. 따라서 이를 언급한 (D)가 정답이다.

어휘 provide ~을 제공하다 fee 요금, 수수료 invitee 초대받은 사람 take place (행사, 일 등이) 개최되다, 발생되다

199 오튼 씨는 왜 이메일을 보냈는가?

(A) 네빈 씨에게 조리법을 요청하기 위해

(B) 기사 내용을 바로잡기 위해

(C) 초대를 수락하기 위해

(D) 자신이 선호하는 음식을 확인해 주기 위해

해설 〈주제 및 목적〉

오튼 씨가 쓴 이메일인 세 번째 지문 초반부에, 행사 초대장을 받은 사실과 함께 그 행사를 고대하고 있다고(I'm really looking forward to the event) 언급하고 있다. 이는 초대에 응하겠다는 말에 해당되므로 (C)가 정답이다.

어휘 ask A for B A에게 B를 요청하다 recipe 조리법 correct ~을 바로잡다, 정정하다 accept ~을 수용하다, 받아들이다 confirm ~을 확인

해 주다 dietary 음식물의, 식사의 preference 선호(하는 것)

200 오튼 씨에 관해 암시된 것은 무엇인가?

(A) 과거에 한때 레오나 파이낸셜에서 근무했다.

(B) 네빈 씨에게 제품을 공급할 수 있다.

(C) 설탕을 먹을 수 없다.

(D) 개인 사업을 시작하고 싶어 한다.

해설 〈지문 연계〉

세 번째 이메일 중반부에, 오튼 씨가 네빈 씨와 졸업 직후에 함께 일한 사실을(~ when we worked together right after we graduated ~) 언급하는 내용이 있다. 그리고 첫 지문 두 번째 단락에 네빈 씨가 졸업 직후에 레오나 파이낸셜에 일자리를 얻었다는 말이 쓰여 있으므로(~ then got a job at Leona Financial right after graduating) 두 사람이 레오나 파이낸셜에서 함께 근무한 것으로 판단할 수 있다. 따라서 (A)가 정답이다.

어휘 used to do 과거에 한때 ~했다 supply ~을 공급하다 goods 제품, 상품 be unable to do ~할 수 없다 one's own 자신만의, 자기 자신의

MEMO

단 한 권으로 실전까지 완벽 대비

실제 시험에 나올 만한 적중률 높은 문제만 담았다!

✚ 최신 기출 유형을 완벽 반영한 실전 모의고사 5회분 수록

✚ 문제집과 해설집이 한 권으로 구성된 LC+RC 합본 실전서

✚ 문제의 키워드를 단숨에 파악하는 핵심 강의 해설집 수록

✚ 전문 성우의 발음을 통한 미국, 영국, 캐나다, 호주 발음 완벽 대비

✚ 실전용·복습용·고사장 버전의 3종 MP3 무료 다운로드

✚ 청취력 향상 및 핵심 구문을 복습하는 받아쓰기 테스트 제공

✚ 정답만 입력하면 점수를 바로 확인할 수 있는 자동 채점 시스템 제공

✚ 기출 어휘 추가 문제집 제공 ▶www.nexusbook.com

✚ 토익 빈출 어휘 리스트 & 테스트지 제공 ▶www.nexusbook.com

✚ 영국, 호주 발음 대비 추가 MP3 제공 ▶www.nexusbook.com

스마트폰으로
MP3 파일 다운로드
콜롬북스 APP

저자 동영상 강의 제공
(영단기 어학원, 유료)
eng.conects.com